GW01607013

Manoucher Yektai

Manoucher Yektai

Karma

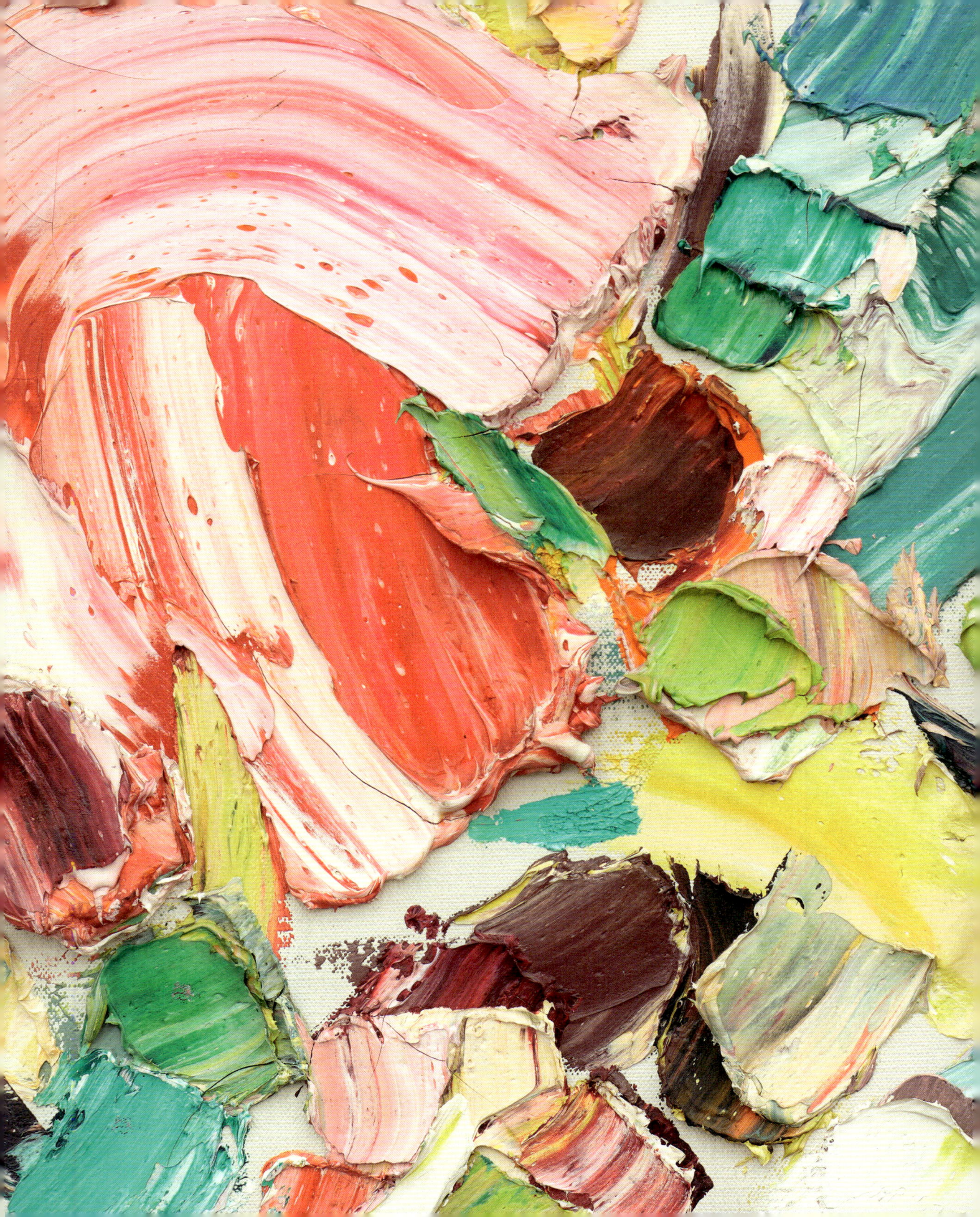

Yektai: A Search for Modernism

Fereshteh Daftari

In the mid-1940s, few Iranian artists could act on their desire to leave Iran to study in Europe. Manoucher Yektai and Monir Shahroudy (later Farmanfarmaian, Yektai's wife from 1948 to 1953) were among the first who did.[1] Their goal was France, not the American Dream, but facing restrictions on passage to war-torn France, they set sail in 1944 on a ship that took them to California by way of Bombay and immediately after that to New York, where they arrived in 1945.

It was not until the 1960s that a handful of other Iranian artists immigrated to the United States. Among them were Siah Armajani, in 1960; Maryam Javaheri, who arrived in New York in 1961 and found a mentor in Ad Reinhardt; and, later that decade, Nahid Haghighat and Nicky Nodjoumi. In the 1950s, despite New York's new status as the center of the art world, Iranian artists were aiming for Italy—the mecca that drew Marcos Grigorian, Bahman Mohassess, Behjat Sadr, and Parviz Tanavoli.

In reference to Iranians who had left their native land, Karim Emami, the prominent critic for the English version of the Tehran-based newspaper *Kayhan International*, wrote, in 1965:

Untitled, 1952 (detail)

> Most of them ("ambulant artists") will tell you they are enjoying their stay, along with the bigger artistic freedom of their new milieu and the presence of a larger and more sophisticated art-loving public there. And they will be quick in expressing their relief for having left behind (temporarily at least) the petty jealousies of Tehran's artistic circles, its dearth of proper critical evaluation and the close-fistedness of its would-be buyers.[2]

Among the "ambulant" artists living in the United States in the 1960s, Emami named Yektai, Grigorian (who had studied in Italy in the 1950s), and the Assyrian Iranian Hannibal Alkhas (who divided his time between Tehran and the United States), while three other prominent artists (Nasser Assar, Hossein Zenderoudi, and Abolhassan Saidi), he wrote, had chosen Paris.[3]

Yektai belonged to the generation of artists born in the 1920s.[4] After emigrating—with the exception of a few years in Paris (from 1946 to 1947 and again from 1959 to 1962), the summer of 1958 in Positano with his partner Ilse Getz, and sporadic visits to Iran (including a yearlong visit in 1969)—he lived and worked in New York City and its vicinity until he passed away in Sagaponack, New York, in 2019. He did not settle in New York, however, until he had exorcised his yearning for Paris. There he enrolled at the École des Beaux-Arts and took classes at the atelier of the Cubist painter André Lhote. He even encouraged Jalil Ziapour—a college mate from Tehran and the future champion of Cubism in Iran—to attend Lhote's atelier.[5]

The seed of Yektai's attraction to France had been sown in Tehran, at the Faculty of Fine Arts, a pseudo-Beaux-Arts institution founded by the French architect and archaeologist André Godard in 1940. It was originally located in the theological school, known as the Marvi Madresseh, and eventually moved to the campus of Tehran University. At the Faculty of Fine Arts, students discovered modern European art through the teachings of Madame Aminfar, also known as Madame Ashub, a French national married to an Iranian. The reproductions of works by Van Gogh and Cézanne she showed her students must have dazzled Yektai.[6] He was among the first students to enroll, but he left at the end of 1944, before graduating. It should be noted that it was the portrait painter Mehdi Vishkai (1920–2006), Yektai's lifelong friend in Tehran, who inspired him at eighteen with the love of painting. Once Yektai had gratified his thirst for a firsthand knowledge of art in Paris—which left him disappointed—he returned to New York in 1947. In Woodstock, he met Milton Avery, an influential personality who introduced him to the Grace Borgenicht Gallery in Manhattan. In 1951, 1952, and 1957, Borgenicht—who, incidentally, had herself studied painting in Paris with Lhote—gave Yektai solo exhibitions. He was the first Iranian artist to exhibit his works in New York and the first to experience Abstract Expressionism at close range.

His work was received positively and his exhibitions were widely reviewed by some of the most illustrious critics of the time: John Ashbery, Dore Ashton, Hilton Kramer, Annette Michelson, Robert Pincus-Witten, Fairfield Porter, Harold Rosenberg, Irving Sandler, Pierre Schneider, and Sidney Tillim, to name a few. The artists also embraced him. He recounted a comment Mark Rothko made when visiting his exhibition at New York's Poindexter Gallery (1957 or 1958): "He is either an animal who has turned into a human or a human who has become God."[7] A different (probably more accurate) version attributes the statement to Landès Lewitin, an American painter with whom Rothko visited the exhibition; whoever initiated it, Rothko made sure Yektai heard the remark.[8] Yektai was accepted as one of the many international artists then active in New York—from Surrealist refugees from Europe to American artists born elsewhere.

Some of the critical commentary on Yektai's work is retrospectively noteworthy for the assumptions it makes about the artist. For example, in 1952, on the occasion of his second solo exhibition, Dorothy Adlow wrote:

> Early in this century Henri Matisse was inspired by Persian forebears of Yektai, who painted miniatures with the subtlest skills and inordinate refinements of technique. How curious that this modern Persian should respond to Matisse though not to the Iranian elements in his design."[9]

Adlow's perspective still resonates today in critical expectations of Middle Eastern artists having fixed and prescribed identities and in their continuing the aesthetic legacy of their cultural heritage as expressed in calligraphy, in miniature painting, or, more recently, in addressing the relation of women to the symbolism of the veil. Why did Adlow not consider rupture as audacity, as a deliberate break with the past and a choice to communicate in a transnational language? Is transcending the local a betrayal of one's heritage, a repudiation of one's ethnicity, a transgression into a territory reserved for those who are, in Barack Obama's terms, "born into imperial cultures"?[10] Iranian historiography having been inaccessible to Western critics, they were, and often are, unaware that ties with local traditions had been severed way back in the late nineteenth century, when academic painting, imported from the West, infiltrated the pedagogy of art schools in Iran and paradoxically became a cipher for modernity.[11] Yektai's choice of themes (still life, landscape, portrait) may reflect his hybrid cultural origin; it may also be a manifestation of what came to be termed in Iran as "Westoxication," or the unhealthy lure of things Western—in other words, an alienation from one's own culture. Regarding this discourse, it is instructive to learn that Yektai saw his first miniature painting in New York, at the Metropolitan Museum of Art, and not in Iran.[12]

In curatorial predilections to this day, the "exotic" and the display of cultural provenance still prevail. Those artists dwelling on their ethnicity are favored. Thus, among the Iranian modernists, Farmanfarmaian (1922–2019)—with her dazzling mosaic painting-sculptures anchored in the traditional medium of mirror works, with ties to sacral and palatial decoration—acquired outside recognition, but those painters engaged in global abstraction have not. Among the contemporary artists, Shirin Neshat, staging an Islamic identity, has attained an iconic position far more visible than that of highly accomplished artists with other issues in mind or with less brazenly ethnic approaches to identity.

Yektai, on the other hand, shunned inherited, expected, mandated, and constructed boundaries and expedient identities. He underscored that he was Iranian in his poetry, which is dependent on the Persian language, but was "stateless" (my word) in his visual art.[13] Yet in sifting through myriad reviews of his work by the most prominent critics of the time (who considered him a member of the New York Abstract Expressionists),[14] it becomes evident that some detected an Iranian accent. "One might anticipate an ethnic novelty and it is brilliantly here, in the idiomatic arabesques of grand strokes, taut and arbitrary, and in Yektai's taste," wrote one critic.[15] "Calligraphy becomes descriptive," wrote another.[16] Thomas B. Hess insinuated a cultural link when declaring that Yektai employs "most of the conventional Western subjects—the landscape, still-life, the nude, portraits—but treats them in odd, perhaps Middle Eastern ways."[17] In fact, such inflections not only are absent in Yektai's oeuvre but were equally missing in the works of his contemporaries working inside Iran. Only their subject matter (in *Public Bath* of 1949, by the Cubist painter Ziapour, for instance) was of local derivation.[18] It was not until a younger generation arrived on the Tehran scene in the early 1960s that the valorization of the local was embraced in the short-lived, culturally specific modernist movement that came to be known as the Saqqakhaneh (ca. 1961–65). Its exponents, to counter ill-digested Western influences, rummaged through the local popular culture and unearthed an iconography, never before depicted in the "fine arts," that resonated with what critics called the "national conscience."[19] Subsequently, around 1965, another type of modernist movement, building on the calligraphic tradition and today referred to by Iftikhar Dadi as "calligraphic modernism," or textual abstraction, was developed by Zenderoudi and Faramarz Pilaram, who were formerly engaged with the Saqqakhaneh.[20] In Minneapolis, Armajani (cut off from both movements) was by the early 1960s creating his own allover textual abstractions.

Yektai was never swayed by "Middle Eastern ways" in his paintings, and they give no evidence of his Iranian roots. New York provided him with a permissive space, a fertile ground in which to grow and become the artist we know today. Unconcerned with a national language but passionate about a tradition that includes the plunging views of Cézanne and Pollock's action painting (Yektai also placed his canvases on the ground), he did acknowledge his admiration for Kamal al-Din Behzad (1450–1535), possibly his aerial perspectives.[21] Does this mere oral acknowledgment permit us to postulate an influence and conflate it with the range of other influences? Is it plausible to link Yektai to cultural traditions of his homeland, going back to the fifteenth and sixteenth centuries? It seems more relevant to frame him as a modernist, if modernism may be articulated not simplistically as a triumphalist American phenomenon of pure abstraction, but rather as a generous aesthetic harboring a diversity of visions derived from any tradition an artist is inspired by: Pollock by Mexican art and Native American sand painting, or Yektai following in the footsteps of Cézanne. Yektai tilts up the picture plane, but he goes further than Cézanne in allowing a still life to morph into a landscape and a landscape to glide into abstraction. A landscape crushed under heavy impasto or flattened into abstract gestures has an affinity with the New York vision, one that was alien to the traditional Iranian manuscript painters (who were attentive to a clear articulation of "edges and things," even from an aerial perspective) and the "modern" academicism, or Old Master Modernism, that dominated the art of the first half of the twentieth century in Iran.[22] Yektai inserted himself into a tradition that began with Cézanne and evolved via Pollock and de Kooning, but not necessarily in a Greenbergian sense. His attachment to representation—perhaps the only feature his work shares with Cubism, despite his studies with Lhote and Amédée Ozenfant—is essential to the dialectic he tackled from every direction throughout his career. Resenting all labels, Abstract Expressionist included, he claimed, "I try to be a contemporary painter."[23] These words should clearly answer both chauvinist and Orientalizing critics who demand or detect ethnic qualities. They should block ghettoizing impulses.

Yektai's preoccupation is best described in formalist and not nationalist terms, as a rejection of the abstraction–figuration binary. To Franz Kline, he retorted, "Ingres is abstraction."[24] Among his contemporaries, there were others who were also tethered to the two "oppositional" modes, a synthesis found in the works of artists represented by the Grace Borgenicht Gallery (Avery, Jimmy Ernst, Wolf Kahn) and even outside that roster. In the catalogue of an exhibition organized by Dorothy Miller at the Museum of Modern Art in 1956, Grace Hartigan is quoted as stating, "I want an art that is not 'abstract' and not 'realistic.'"[25] Of the major Abstract Expressionists to whom Yektai gravitated, his work was closest to that of de Kooning, who did not banish the figure, however violently disfigured it may appear. Yektai's commitment to an abstraction pregnant with figuration bears the stamp of the Paris and New York schools, of early French modernism, and of the raging Abstract Expressionist environment in which he was deeply embedded. (That he was an Iranian, something mentioned time and again by the reviewing critics, but an Iranian accepted as a member of the club and not a derivative or scorned outsider, is further proof that New York modernism was more open and pluralistic and less parochial than the triumphalist narrative would have it.)

To fulfill his vision, Yektai went through various stages and methods of painting. He deliberately limited his subjects in a self-imposed system that opened a myriad of formal possibilities, and he flirted promiscuously with both abstraction and figuration. He piled paint on the surface, but he also reversed course, leaving the canvas empty, allowing unambiguously decipherable subjects—a flowerpot, some fruit, a road to nowhere—to float in the void. His early works, with their regular vertical marks, are reminiscent of Hans Hofmann's abstractions. *Tactile* and *edible* are two adjectives used frequently to describe his thick application of paint, which he squeezed onto the canvas straight out of the tube. Soutine has been mentioned, as has Van Gogh. Like Bonnard, Yektai painted from memory. Like him and Matisse, he juxtaposed interiors with outdoor window views. The brush was only one item in his toolbox: he used a palette knife, spatulas, a whip, and trowels of different shapes—bricklayers' instruments—which he slid in one direction and then another, creating a rushed fluidity and the illusion of motion and, in the process, animating static images of conventional Beaux-Arts derivation, such as still lifes, landscapes, and portraits. Sometimes, obliterating the identity of his subject matter, he seemed to be painting his palette board. This device was best explained by Annette Michelson, who saw Yektai as "being involved in a brilliant attempt to reconcile the aesthetic of the 'oeuvre' with that of the 'action,' to make the paint speak for the figure, for itself, and for the 'act' or 'gesture.'"[26] Finally, his fingers may be added to the arsenal. Wearing a glove, he combed the surface of his paintings—notably his portrait paintings, in which the figure, the antithesis of abstraction, must be defaced, assassinated, if abstraction is to peek through. (Robert Pincus-Witten described this imperative as "Kill the sitter.")[27] An example of such a work, Yektai told me, is his *Portrait of Romain Gary* (1962), who he described as a "dark character."[28] It is no surprise that one of his portraits, *Concierge* (1960), was included in *Recent Painting USA: The Figure*, a circulating exhibition that opened in 1960 at the Museum of Modern Art, where, after ten or fifteen years of immersion in abstraction, the role of the figure was being reexamined.

Yektai came from Tehran to New York, then he traveled to Paris and back to New York. Modernism, however, was his route and his final destination. Thomas McEvilley was wrong when he asserted that in "Iran ... under Islamic strictures about imagery, free artistic expression was not available" but right when he defined Yektai's pursuit as "a search for Modernism, and for a participation in Modernism, indeed, for a home in it."[29]

NOTES

1 I am deeply grateful to Nico (Niki) Yektai (the artist's son with his second wife, Helene Kulukundis) for his gracious help regarding the timeline of Yektai's biography and for many bibliographical facts difficult to verify when, due to COVID-19, libraries were not accessible. I owe special thanks to the late artist, who granted me interviews and a studio visit when I was working on *Persia Reframed: Iranian Visions of Modern and Contemporary Art* (London: I.B. Tauris, 2019), hereafter referred to as *Persia Reframed*, and on the 2013–14 exhibition *Iran Modern* for the Asia Society, New York.

2 Karim Emami, "Ambulant Artists," in *Karim Emani on Modern Iranian Culture, Literature and Art*," ed. Houra Yavari (New York: Persian Heritage Foundation, 2014), 204.

3 Ibid.

4 The artist confirmed that he was born in 1920 and not in 1921, as is widely reported and even stated in his passport. Manoucher Yektai, communication with author, April 2014.

5 Yektai, communication with author, April 2014.

6 Monir Shahroudy Farmanfarmaian and Zara Houshmand, *A Mirror Garden: A Memoir* (New York: Anchor, 2007), 73; Yektai, communication with author, April 2014.

7 Yektai, communication with author, August 2013.

8 Biographical timeline of the artist prepared by Nico Yektai in consultation with the artist.

9 Dorothy Adlow, "Summer in New York Galleries," *Christian Science Monitor*, May 31, 1952, 16A.

10 Barack Obama, *Dreams from My Father: A Story of Race and Inheritance* (New York: Broadway, 2004), 312.

11 See chapter 1 in Daftari, *Persia Reframed*. This chapter also includes a section on Yektai.

12 Biographical timeline of the artist prepared by Nico Yektai in consultation with the artist.
13 Yektai, communication with author, April 2014.
14 In 1957 Sidney Geist wrote, "Yektai is in the Abstract Expressionist School, not as an undergraduate, but as a member of the faculty." See "Month in Review," *Arts* 32, no. 3 (December 1957): 49.
15 J[ames] S[chuyler], "Reviews and Previews: Yektai," *Art News* 56, no. 8 (December 1957): 12.
16 E.C.M., "Four Landscape Painters," *Art News* 59, no. 3 (May 1960): 15.
17 T[homas] B. H[ess], "Yektai," *Art News* 63, no. 7 (November 1964): 10.
18 For an image of *Public Bath*, see Daftari, *Persia Reframed*, 15.
19 Cyrus Zoka, quoted in Daftari, *Persia Reframed*, 22, 22n4.
20 Calligraphic modernism is sometimes erroneously conflated with the Saqqakhaneh stage, where letters were introduced into the composition but stayed secondary to the depicted imagery. It was not until the mid-1960s that, in the case of these artists, letters replaced all other imagery in their allover compositions. It is noteworthy that Siah Armajani's allover compositions, created in Minneapolis, with nothing else but letters, precede the calligraphic modernism of the Saqqakhaneh artists. On calligraphic modernism, see Iftikhar Dadi, *Rethinking Calligraphic Modernism* (London and Cambridge, MA: Institute of International Visual Arts and MIT Press, 2006), 95.
21 Yektai, communication with author, April 2014.
22 A critic noted of Yektai that "his style ... barely respects the shapes and edges of things." See S[idney] T[illim], "In the Galleries: Yektai," *Arts Magazine* 34 (February 1960): 56. On Old Master Modernism, see Daftari, *Persia Reframed*, 10.
23 Yektai, quoted in Lawrence Van Gelder, "A Studio in My Pocket," *New York Times*, January 9, 1983, LI2.
24 Yektai, communication with author, April 2014.
25 Grace Hartigan, quoted in Dorothy C. Miller, ed., *12 American Artists* (New York: Museum of Modern Art, 1956), 53.
26 Annette Michelson, "Paris," *Arts Magazine* 35, nos. 8–9 (May–June 1961): 19.
27 Robert Pincus-Witten, "Yektai and Boldini: Formal and Symbolic Interchange," *Ring* (Autumn 1961): 40.
28 Yektai, communication with author, August 2013.
29 McEvilley was imposing on art made before the 1979 revolution a reading that belongs to the postrevolutionary era. But even if he was referring to earlier strictures, painting in Iran, as attested by manuscripts and wall paintings, is replete with figures. Nudity, the only area of contention, is not a salient aspect of Yektai's expression. See Thomas McEvilley, *Manoucher Yektai: Paintings, 1951–1997* (East Hampton, NY: Guild Hall Museum, 1998), 5.

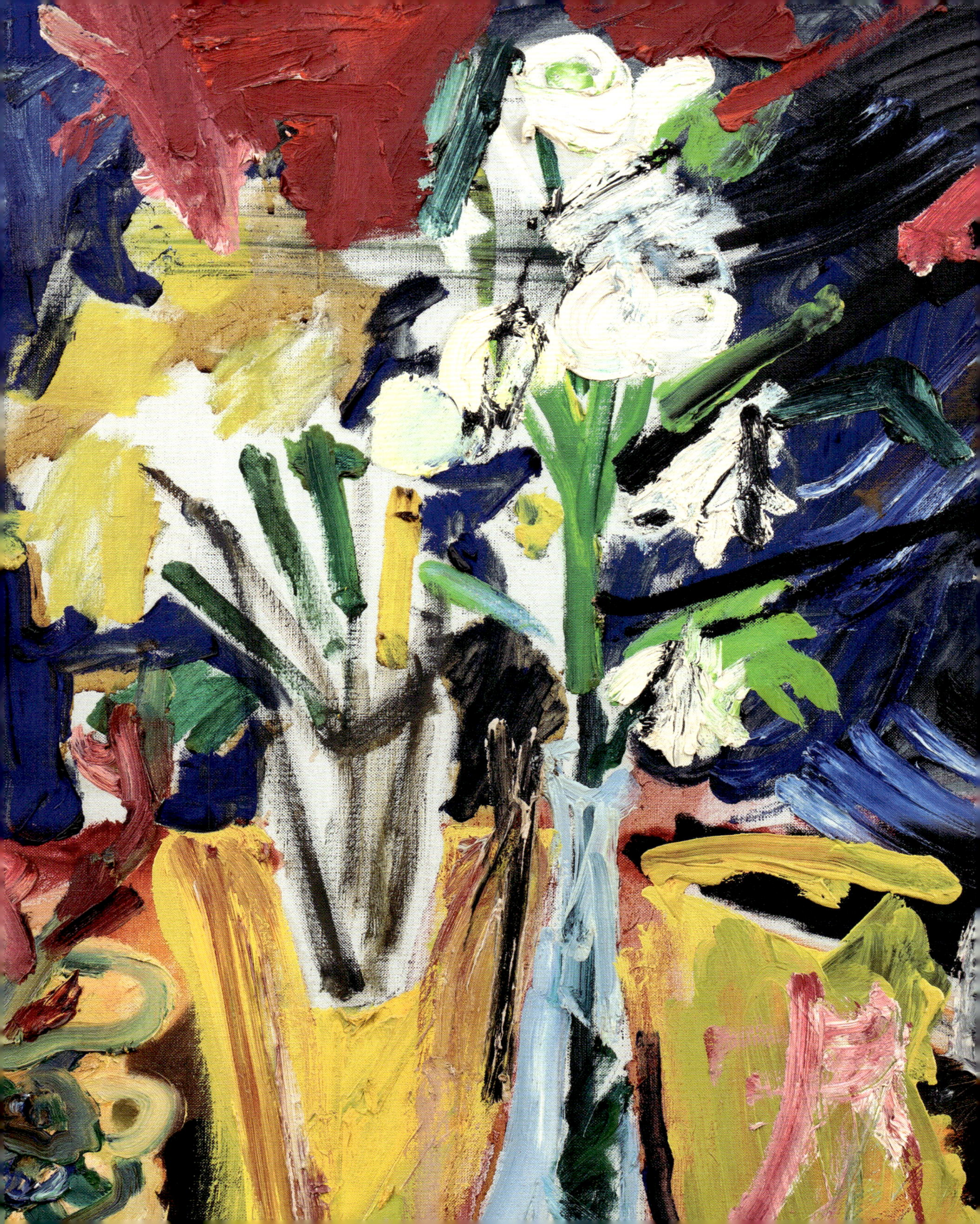

Manoucher Yektai: Tehran to New York

Media Farzin

When Manoucher Yektai entered the Fine Arts Academy at Tehran University in the early 1940s, he joined a cohort that would form Iran's first visual avant-garde. It was a transitional moment for painting, and the professors fell into two distinct camps. On one side were the academic realists, who had been trained by the renowned painter Kamal-ol-Molk—the forefather of modern Iranian painting, known for his breathtakingly detailed portraits of kings and courtiers—and who urged meticulous charcoal copies of classical busts. Then there were the handful of Europeans and Iranians returned from abroad, who passed around books with black-and-white reproductions of works by the French Impressionists, and spoke thrillingly of color, light, and (gasp!) imagination.

The school itself was brand new, located on the grand, as yet unpaved, Shah Reza Avenue, across from what quickly became a cluster of cafés and bookstores. The painters, relegated to the basement of the engineering department, formed an eclectic community: Shokouh Riazi, the abstract painter just back from Paris, had joined as a teaching assistant; Sadegh Hedayat, then beginning to publish his surreal, resolutely modern short stories, worked as an administrator. Yektai's classmates included Hossein Kazemi, who would rise to an important career as an abstract painter and educator, and Jalil Ziapour, who would

Still Life, 1956 (detail)

establish the *Fighting Rooster* society and journal, one of the most visible bastions of the intellectual youthquake. Yektai himself would credit his earliest encounters with modern European painting to his teenage friendship with Mehdi Vishkai (they would enter the Academy together), who would go on to a prolific career as a society portraitist known for his expressive brushwork. And of course, two of Yektai's friendships followed him abroad: Monir Shahroudy, one of the few members of this cohort, besides Yektai, to find international success (they were married between 1948 and 1953), and the multitalented Asad Behrouzan, known in Iran as a researcher, documentary photographer, and educator.

The Fine Art Academy's first students were an extraordinary—and extraordinarily ambitious—group, especially given the dearth of resources, knowledge, and opportunities in Iran in the immediate aftermath of World War II. Many, like Yektai, would continue their studies abroad: Ziapour to Paris (where, upon Yektai's recommendation, he joined the atelier of Cubist painter André Lhote), painters Behjat Sadr and Mohsen Vaziri to Italy, where they would forge deeply original approaches to abstraction, and the poet-painter Sohrab Sepehri to Japan, which would leave a lasting mark on his austere landscapes. But few found the degree of critical and financial success, or the sense of community, that Yektai would find so quickly in New York. And so the others returned, for short stints or permanently: to work, teach, and exhibit; to found journals, schools, galleries, biennials, and museums—taking cautious advantage of the Pahlavi monarchy's mercurial but growing embrace of art as a tool of soft power. Many even stayed through the Islamic Revolution of 1979; others still were persuaded to return for museum retrospectives in the 2000s.

Yektai, however—despite several long visits to Iran, solo exhibitions there, and multiple volumes of published Persian poetry—would never really return. The next six decades would carry him far from that formative context and its discourse, even as he came to be known in Iranian circles, to quote the title of a major survey book of 1998, as one of the core "pioneers of contemporary Persian painting, first generation."

•

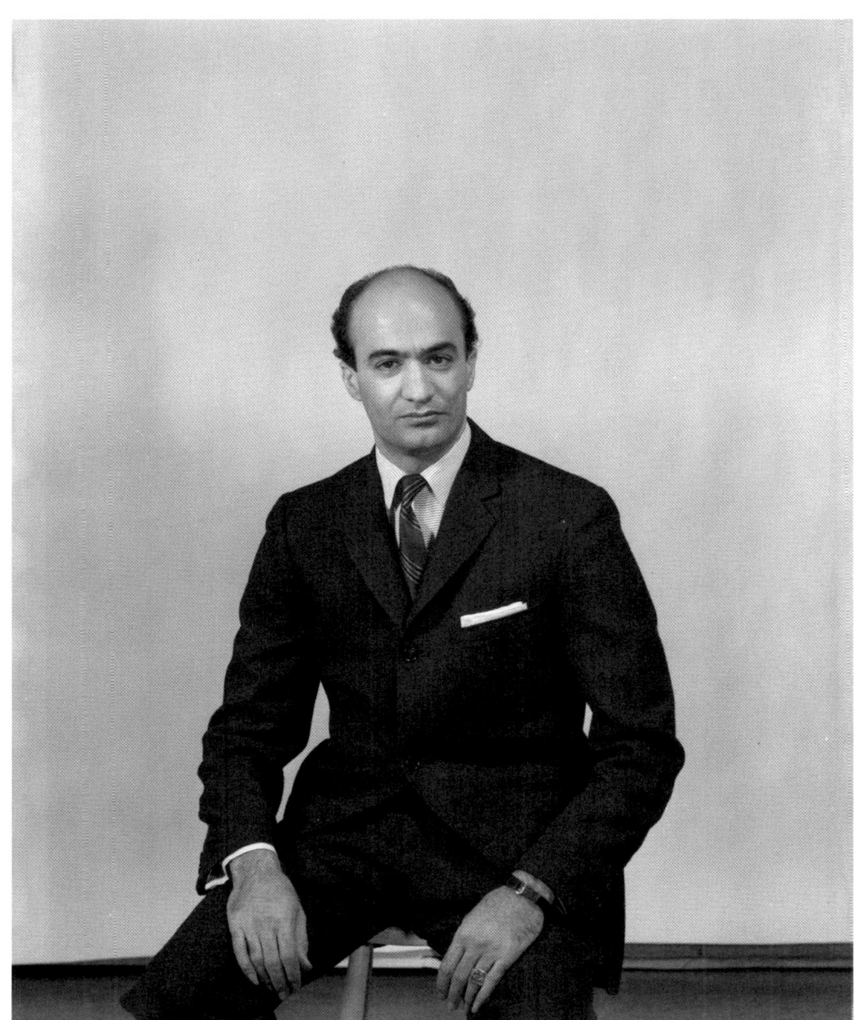

Manoucher Yektai passport photo

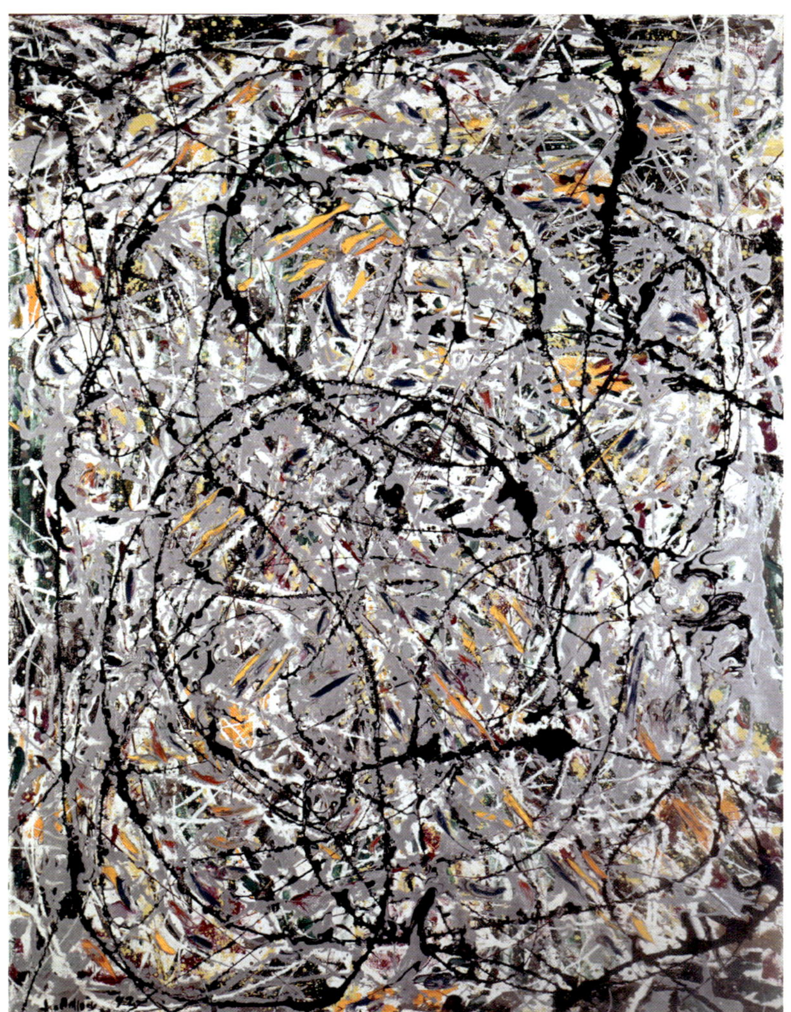

Jackson Pollock, *Watery Paths*, 1947
Oil on canvas, 44⅞ × 33⅞ inches (114 × 86 cm)

"Styles are meaningless," Yektai told an interviewer in 2005.[1] He was often dismissive of group affiliations and characterized his own approach in resolutely individual terms. "I'm searching for a firm truth, one that fulfills my own expectations," he said in a 1976 interview; "what I want is for the things I create to have a truth within them that is hard to shake."[2] But the decades-long steadfastness of his search generated a distinctly personal style nonetheless, one defied by his choice of intimate, familiar subjects (still lifes, landscapes, portraits); paint laid in thick impasto, often with a trowel; and vivid hues, whose brilliance feels all the more masterful given the rapid smearing and layering of wet pigment that has created them. Yellows are so sunny they feel as if they must be warm to the touch, and whites take on an endless range of nuanced hues, some borrowed from the bare ground of the canvas itself.

It wasn't always so. There is a marked Surrealism to Yektai's pre-1950 paintings, a reflection perhaps of the continued importance of the movement in postwar Paris during Yektai's long-awaited first visit in 1946–47. A 1948 painting shows biomorphic forms in a variety of blues against a deeper ground of beiges and browns; a darker rectangle floats in the center, a flag of depth that emphasizes the flatness of everything else. The composition is lively but careful, spreading across the entire canvas but stopping short of the edges. The squiggly forms recall Miró's dancing playfulness, Masson's feel for texture, and Arp's self-contained amoebas, but the short, repetitive brushstrokes look further back to Van Gogh.

What happens to Yektai's work between 1948 and 1950 is a classic epiphany of those years—an encounter with Jackson Pollock, in full color, in the pages of *Life* magazine in 1949. "I'd seen two of Pollock's works in a magazine," Yektai recalled in 2005. "As soon as I saw them, I knew it was an authentic approach, that it worked." His praise is double-edged: "When I saw the work itself though, it didn't add anything [to the experience]. ... Because with Pollock, it can make no difference. The *conception* is what lands the work. It was the ultimate path."[3] Yektai recognized the spontaneity Pollock had absorbed from Surrealist automatism and chance, and immediately realized how generative such a freedom could be. But in his own work, he was always more interested in what paint could *depict* on a picture plane.

From Pollock's gesture and speed, Yektai would build a body of work that never lost sight of the subject as both anchor and catapult of abstraction.

I think, for example, of two paintings he created thirty years apart: *Untitled (Yellow Tablecloth)* of 1952, and an untitled still life from 1982. The 1952 work has all the impact of his most complex work. Thick daubs of gold and lemon yellow form a vibrant pattern on a surface that tilts up vertically to meet the eye, even as swirls of sky blue suggest a receding background, and grass green laid at the lower edge gives the table a cool, shadowy depth. The composition is held in place by neutral bars of color running down each side; like much of Yektai's early work, the underlying structure is a sturdy grid of verticals and horizontals. But the work is all about the surface, as emphasized in the "tablecloth" of the title: it is the site of his observations and impressions, of speed and spontaneity, and a skillful experiment in what paint can convey in two (and three) dimensions.

The 1982 painting feels quieter, ruled by swathes of creamy white, and the subject easier to read: a table, a window, pots of blooming flowers, a bowl of fruit. The canvas is smaller, and the composition more confidently asymmetrical. The table slopes gently down, the bowl tapers to an upward point, and a flowerpot, rising above the lightly demarcated edge of the table, connects with a wide streak that forms the edge of the window and takes the eye up to the top of the painting. Everything rests comfortably within the four edges of the canvas; while Yektai always commands his surfaces, he will always keep well within the frame, as if to emphasize primacy of representational space. The colors are muted—thick pastel pigments form the flowers, thinner brushwork fills out trees and fruit—but no less commanding than the saturated hues he uses elsewhere. The composition flows in easy arcs, but still speaks of Yektai's attentiveness to horizontal and vertical, figure and ground, and the visual play that material accidents can stage between them. It's a classic Yektai, in that it feels simultaneously ordinary and timeless, at once impulsive and deliberate.

There were, naturally, a variety of approaches in between, especially in the first two decades: phases of thinned pigment (the interiors with snapdragons of the late fifties), works that pulled closer to abstraction

(I think of *Still Life D*, 1959), and periods devoted to a single subject (the tomato plants, the lemons), not to mention the portraits he painted throughout, heralded by New York critics of the 1960s as a serious riposte to the pure abstraction of earlier decades. Most prominent among these voices was a young Hilton Kramer, not quite yet the conservative gatekeeper he would become, who lauded Yektai as "one of the few serious practitioners of figure painting on the current scene."[4] But the US critics were also fond of bringing up Belle Époque society painter Giovanni Boldini—not an entirely flattering reference, and hardly as apt or helpful a comparison as Vishkai's work of the same period.

Yektai's poetry, which he wrote throughout his life—always in Persian, in a free verse uniquely his own—lends more nuance, I think, to his creative and social sensibilities. Most moving is the epic *Falgoosh*, published in Iran in 1970 and never translated. The title, which means "eavesdropping," refers to one of the many popular fortune-telling traditions of Iran, in which the fortune-seeker sets an intention, then takes the first words they hear (usually on the street, at night) as an omen. Yektai's *Falgoosh* tells the story of a group of men who have gathered for a quixotic, collective *falgoosh*. Identified only by where they're from ("A man from Salmas / one from Sistan / one from Birjand and Larestan"), they take to the streets of Tehran ("they made the *fal* and stood listening") but hear nothing acceptable ("a woman doesn't count / so they did not count her"). Night after night it continues, as winter turns into spring and then summer, as distinct characters emerge (the Yazdi is a troublemaker, the Shirazi a tyrant), and the answer to their unnamed problem perpetually eludes them.[5]

"Poetry was an everyday human need for him," Yektai's friend, poet Ahmad-Reza Ahmadi, has written.[6] *Falgoosh* reveals a different Yektai, a thinker interested in the possibilities of everyday speech, absurdist humor, and political parable. Its unusual combination of idiomatic Persian and medieval poetic syntax yields a surprisingly accessible story, one that is equally familiar and surreal. It is also unusual within his larger body of poetry, given its highly narrative, almost theatrical space: the baffling impasse at its heart rivals Beckett's *Waiting for Godot* and Buñuel's *Exterminating Angel*, while hinting at the endgame of Iranian democracy. The poem was in fact adapted as a stage play by renowned actor and director Parviz Sayyad for the Shiraz Arts Festival in 1970, and has been restaged several times by Sayyad since.

Falgoosh also prompts a closer look at Yektai's response to the cultural questions unfolding in Iran. In the 1976 interview, he moves between Europe and Asia, modern and medieval, with cosmopolitan ease: "The lines used by Ingres or Seurat or Picasso, you also see them in Soltan Mohammad or Kamal-ed-Din Behzad or Reza Abbasi; on the surface of their colors, in the distances, in the way they hold the masses on the page. I don't want to lose these in my own work ... I consider myself as an inheritor of the legacy of miniature painting."[7] The reference is to the overall composition and saturated colors of traditional Persian painting, and its curvilinear abstractions of flora and fauna—key influences for artists like Matisse, and central to histories of European abstraction, as Yektai intuitively understood.

"What I take from miniatures," Yektai continues, "is ... their truth. ... I work with the truth and technique that is possible for me today, which is the technique that we have imported from America and Europe."[8] Yektai is making an important distinction, between visual imagery and visual logic. His acknowledged reliance on a Euro-American matrix (which he characterizes as "oil paints from England, brushes from Holland, a perspective and sensibility that the West has given us") may feel obvious, but it is precisely what set him apart, especially in the mid-seventies, from many of his Iranian peers—from Shahroudy, who had begun working with craftsmen trained in traditional mirrorwork, or from Ziapour, whose youthful admiration of Cubism had translated into folk-inspired portraits of villagers in traditional costume. Most palpably, it set him apart from younger Iranian artists who had inaugurated, in the early 1960s, what became known as the Saqqakhaneh movement, an approach that brought a Nouveau réaliste interest in everyday objects to traditional Iranian artforms, themes, and subjects. Supported by the Iranian state from its inception, the Saqqakhaneh would go on to become one of the most recognizable, and collectible, movements in twentieth-century Iranian art.

The urgency of these issues was already clear in 1976. Yektai's interviewer asks him how he feels about the new trend toward "national, local markers" and "traditional principles of painting." ("You might prefer not to answer," he adds diplomatically, "but I must ask, because for us at least it's important.") Yektai's response is unequivocal. "This is a local issue, not a global one, and it's not a healthy subject either," he begins. "It is absolutely not possible to keep something on a canvas by force or will, to bring it into a canvas and make it true. The truth must [be allowed to] create its own demands. I can't make a painting from a superficially Iranian form. If I paint a *qalyan* [water pipe], I'm only following my feelings; if I bring it in deliberately, because it's Iranian, I've taken away from the force and authenticity of the painting. I see no point in this kind of local imagery." Then, as if realizing the scope of the critique implied in his words, and the friends and acquaintances it reflects on: "Naturally, if a *roobandeh* [a traditional face covering] is in keeping with how someone feels, that's of course not a problem."[9]

•

"The core of [Yektai's] aesthetics," Fereshteh Daftari writes in her definitive history of contemporary Iranian art, "is anchored in formal terms, in the context of New York Abstract Expressionism, and in the discourse of the time around abstraction versus figuration and materiality."[10] This was a discourse, she demonstrates throughout her book, as important in Tehran as in New York, but with unique contours in each setting. Yektai's career, by his own account, was dedicated to the pursuit of contemporaneity in painting, to visual experiences reflective of their historic moment. But his understanding of history was ultimately rooted in the postwar milieus of Tehran and New York. At the Academy, he sided with imagination and freedom; in New York, he figured out how that search might be brought to life on the picture plane, and spent the rest of his career exploring its permutations.

It feels difficult, at a time when the coordinates of an artist's identity—their representation on behalf of cultures and experiences and communities—pose such urgent questions, to understand Yektai's dismissal of "local forms." His pursuit of universal, timeless truths is especially contradictory given the degree to which US critics considered him an exemplary ambassador (rare is the review that fails to mention his background) and Iranian historians a "contemporary pioneer" of a national tradition. But contradictory reception is also what makes him a complicated figure, and his work and life worth investigating from a contemporary standpoint.

Yektai stands at the beginning of a lineage that almost any Iranian painter imagines inhabiting, at least once: a line that runs from the late nineteenth century into the twenty-first, that centers the eye while privileging the subjective, that holds out for visual beauty and sensory surprise. But more importantly, his pursuit of the truths in painting embodies the belief—unpopular perhaps, but still urgent for many of today's young artists, regardless of their identifications—that formal experimentation should be allowed the privilege to play. The long arc of Yektai's career demonstrates, with steadfast commitment, the joys of being allowed to shrug off the burdens of the messy, politicized world that any painting is born into. That such a pursuit may feel precarious, if not downright impossible today, may well be Yektai's most valuable lesson for us. "The truth is, Yektai has always been *yekta*," an Iranian critic has written: meaning, *unique*.[11]

NOTES

1 *Yektai*, directed by Shirin Saghaie, VOA Portraits, 2011, https://www.youtube.com/watch?v=TcH0fNqMHM4, my translation.
2 "That Lyricism Called Painting: Aydin Aghdashloo interviews Manoucher Yektai," *Rastakhiz*, 1976; reprinted in *Herfe-Honarmand* 15 (Spring 2006): 131–37, my translation.
4 Hilton Kramer, "The Figures of Yektai," *Arts Magazine* (September 1962): 34.
5 Manoucher Yektai, *Falgoosh* (Tehran: Rowzan Publications, 1970), 8, my translation.
6 Ahmad-Reza Ahmadi, "Manoucher Yektai: Poet and Painter," *Kelk: Art & Architecture* 41 (July–August 1993): 98, my translation.
7 "That Lyricism Called Painting," 133.
8 Ibid.
9 Ibid., 136.
10 Fereshteh Daftari, "Modernism(s): Contextualizing the Terms of Discussion," in *Persia Reframed: Iranian Visions of Modern and Contemporary Art* (London: I.B. Tauris, 2019), 18.
11 Dariush Kiaras, "Profile: Manoucher Yektai," *Tandis* 16, no. 134 (September–October 2008): 4–5, my translation.

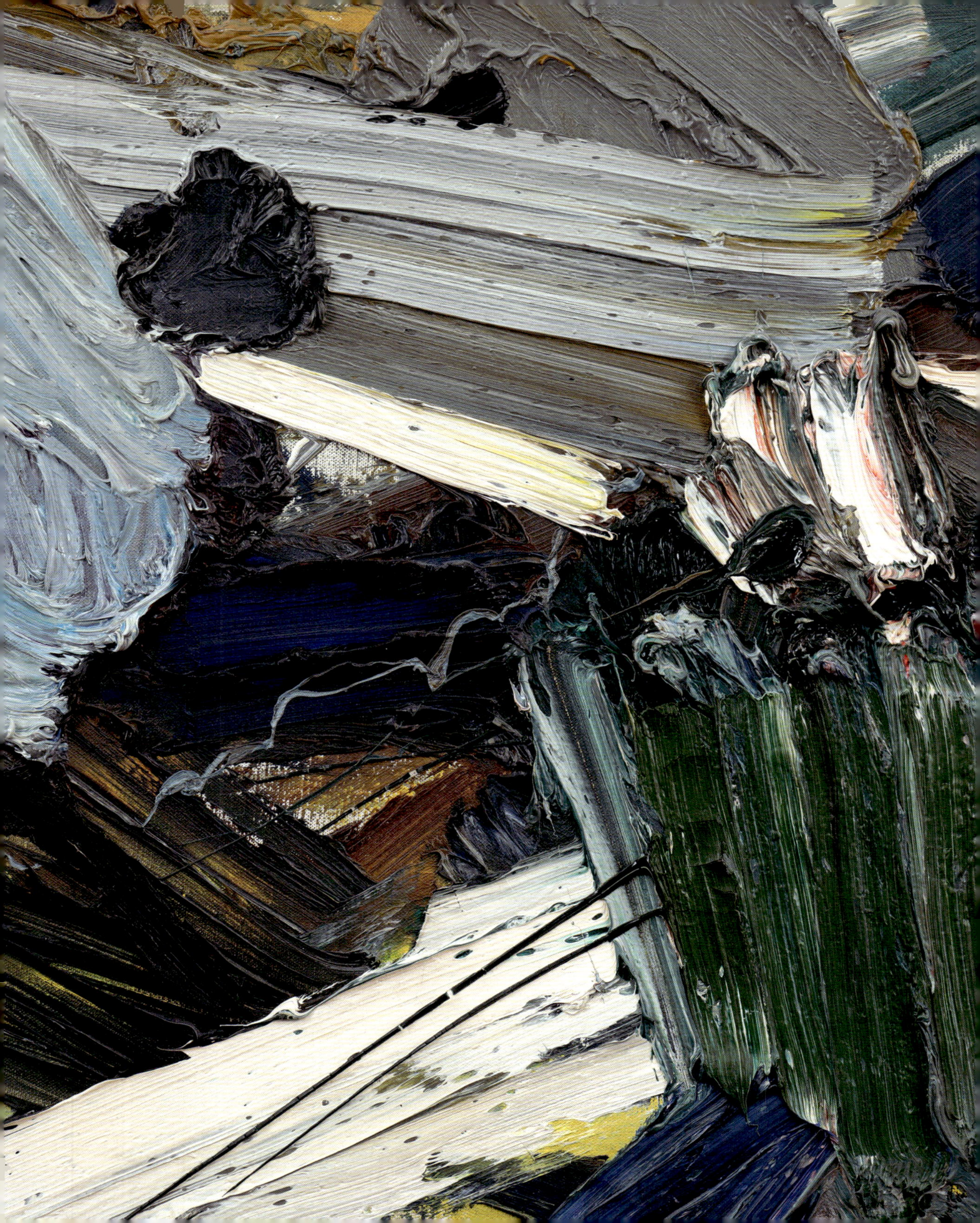

Transitive Abstraction and Homeless Representation

Robert Slifkin

Like many artists associated with Abstract Expressionism, Manoucher Yektai was never truly an abstract painter. His paintings, like the paintings of his better-known peers Jackson Pollock and Willem de Kooning, contain visual cues that integrally connect them to the world beyond the canvas. With their characteristically thick and vigorously applied paint, which often conveys a discernible sense of volumetric space, and their delicately hued palette summoning the effects of light as it falls upon physical entities in space, Yektai's works suggest intimations of phenomena that exceed their purely formal and material properties. In this regard, one could say that abstraction for Yektai—and, for that matter, for many of his contemporaries—was a decidedly *transitive* operation: the painter abstracts some*thing*, taking a subject, whether it is a human figure, an object, or even an emotional state or affective memory, and through an array of distilling and distorting processes renders it indeterminate, enigmatic, and in a constant state of becoming. In this way the painted image appears ambiguous while still maintaining a compelling allusiveness, which would ideally engender a response and a degree of recognition from an empathetic viewer.

Yektai's particularly transitive approach to abstraction—and painting more generally—is evident in an untitled work from 1960 in which a cluster of pink and white rosettes of thick paint surrounded by an array

Untitled, ca. 1950 (detail)

of diagonal dark-green brushstrokes in the upper right-hand corner summons a still life or perhaps the bough of a flowering tree, thus setting the scene of the picture as some sort of landscape. The painting's oscillation between two possible genres to a large extent pivots on how a viewer interprets a more angular armature of grayish-white passages in the center of the image, whose geometric contours can be construed as possibly a flower box as seen from above, or, perceived within a landscape matrix, as an architectural element, perhaps the eaves of a clapboard house, although the six long dark diagonal bands underneath this form and the large dark mass of painting in the upper left corner complicate either reading. Likewise, the presence of what appears to be writing across this area further disorients the painting's possible subject, simultaneously compromising the picture's illusory depth by emphasizing the canvas's materially flat and two-dimensional surface while the presence of language underlines the work's communicative aims.

On one level these calligraphic elements were a function of Yektai's practice of creating his paintings on the horizontal axis of the floor or on a table instead of on the more conventional vertical axis of an easel or wall. This rather eccentric mode of applying paint, which he shared with other artists of the period such as Pollock, Ad Reinhardt, and Helen Frankenthaler, can be understood as part of this generation's desire to reconceive the medium of painting, seeing it not as an illusionistic window onto the world but rather as a surface for gestural impression and inscription. If, according to certain scholars, this reorientation of painting onto the horizontal axis would emphasize the immediacy and embodied materiality of the work of art, it could be argued that for an artist like Yektai, who also wrote poetry in his native Farsi, a language whose calligraphic alphabet blurred the distinction between gesture and symbol, this act of aligning painting with writing could emphasize its capacity to serve as a means of communication, reference, and even self-expression, all of which is to say, its transitivity.[1]

This affinity between transitive painting and poetic missive is elaborated upon in another untitled work Yektai produced the following year, in 1961, in which a tabletop still life featuring two envelopes, each bearing marks of handwriting, can be discerned. (The words "I love you" can be read on the one closest to the top of the picture.) A striking green band culminating in one of the impasto globules of

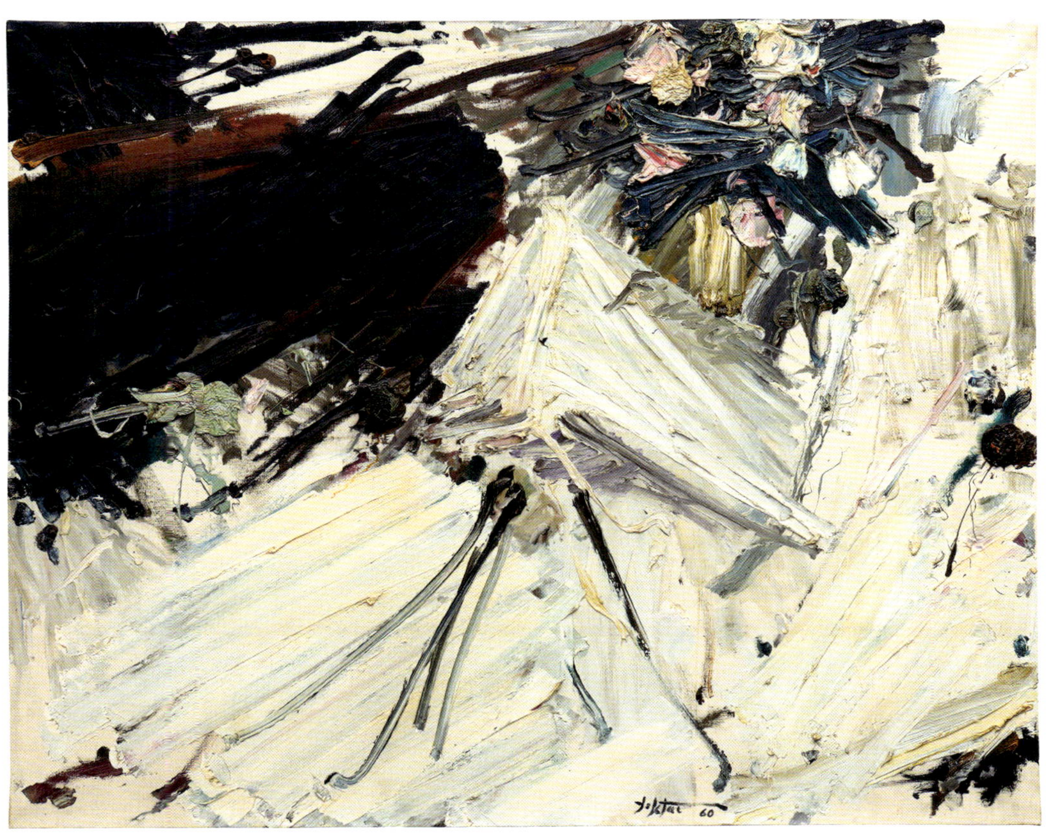

Manoucher Yektai, *Untitled*, 1960
Oil on canvas, 51 × 63 inches (130 × 160 cm)

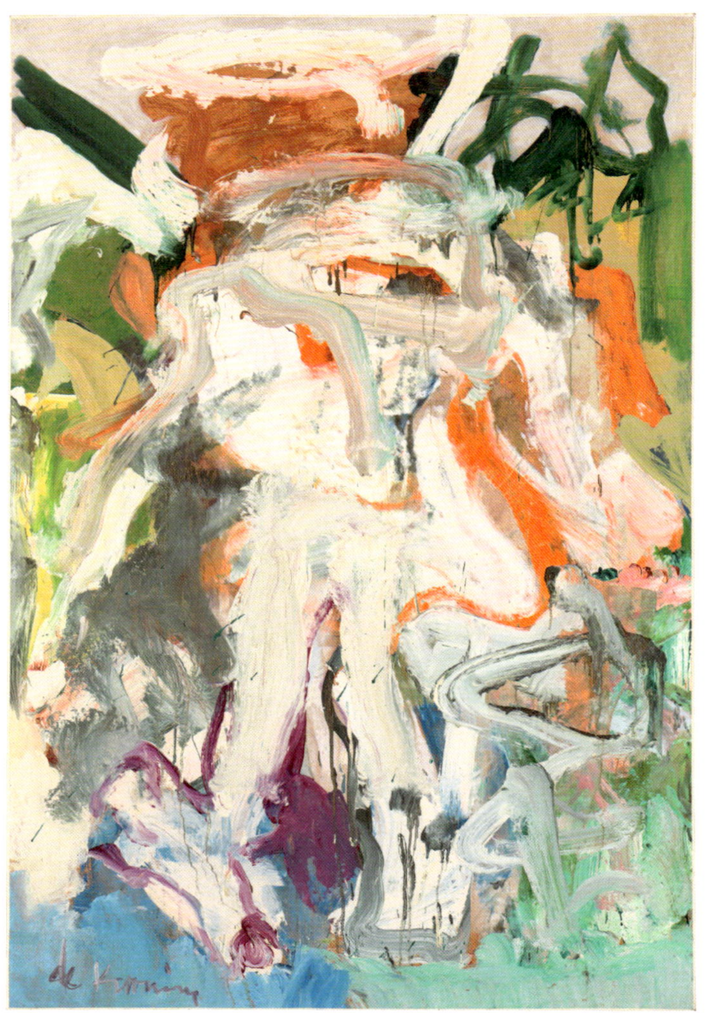

Willem de Kooning, *Woman in Landscape III*, 1968
Oil on paper, 63½ × 42½ inches (161.3 × 108 cm)

paint that would frequently appear in Yektai's work from this period respectively denote the painting's overhead perspective and mode of production; its tapered tail appears to recede like a flagpole seen from above while the congealed skin of its circular head signals its creation on the horizontal axis. Like Pollock's dripped paint, which makes gravity a creative element in its appearance, Yektai's thick pools of pigment with their almost primeval swirls marshal the physical laws of nature to invest subjective expression with a degree of materiality and arguably even metaphysical transcendence. By orienting viewers to experience the imagery as if looking down upon it, such works also crucially invite beholders to share the artist's own view of the canvas during its moment of creation, so that, as the critic Harold Rosenberg would memorably propose in his 1952 article "The American Action Painters," the physical gestures and creative decisions of the artist could become the meaning of the painting itself.[2] In this way Yektai's work, again like that of many of his New York School peers, drew upon a romantic ideal which postulated a vision of the work of art as a message from an individual artist to an audience who might be able to understand and emotionally empathize with its content, despite any distance of time and space separating sender and recipient.

Rosenberg would in fact cite Yektai's work in another essay from 1962 in which he reiterated his conception of such an active—and, arguably, transitive—dynamic of artistic creation and reception. This essay was written as a riposte to his critical rival Clement Greenberg, who had recently railed against artists like de Kooning (and by extension Yektai) who practiced what the critic called "homeless representation" in which the techniques of illusionistic painting, such as chiaroscuro and allusive figuration, are adopted for ostensibly abstract ends.[3] One can perceive such techniques at work in some of Yektai's more categorically abstract works, such as an untitled painting form 1960 in which an assemblage of thickly painted bands invests the picture with a discernible sense of spatial arrangement so that certain passages appear in front of others, while the modulated pigment, with its traces of lighter and darker hues, suggests volumetric recession and projection.

According to Greenberg, such vestiges of illusionism compromised the work of art's avowed "purity," associating it with other creative—and notably narrative—practices like theater and literature and, more damagingly, making it vulnerable (so he asserted, although this thesis has never been proven by research) to ideological and commercial manipulation. Viewed from a twenty-first-century perspective, these paradigms of modernist aesthetics which extol the ethical and even political superiority of a professed pure and nonobjective abstraction appear exceedingly academic, and their dogmatic policing of boundaries with terms like *purity* seems tainted by their possible complicity with the politics of white supremacy. (In this regard it is notable, if unfortunately all too predictable, that Yektai's "Persian" heritage was frequently mentioned by critics as a possible explanation for the bold colors and Orientalist sense of decoration in his painting, suggesting, as one writer put it, his "ethnic novelty.")[4]

And while Greenberg's dismissive dig of "homelessness" has its own problematic political implications, both in terms of class and nationalism, it is in fact possible to imagine how certain artists, especially those who were themselves immigrants—or, one might say, who were transient—would have found such homelessness not simply just an inevitable aspect of the process of painting but, moreover, something of a virtue. Yektai himself understood how his transitive conception of painting entailed a certain transience, circumventing the dominant categories for defining visual art in the second half of the twentieth century. In an interview published in the *New York Times* in 1983 the artist claimed that, if a beholder described his paintings as abstractions, he would reply, "I'll call them figures. If they call them figures, I'll say they're abstractions."[5] As early as 1952 one critic would revealingly describe his works as "near abstract."[6] Yektai's avoidance of such labels was no doubt in part motivated by a general reluctance among members of the New York School to be pigeonholed into a specific movement or style. Yet it could be argued that Yektai's identity as an immigrant and something of an "ethnic novelty" within the American art scene allowed him to recognize the limitations, if not the oppressiveness, that often accompanied the rhetoric of purity associated with nonobjective (i.e., abstract) painting in modernist art criticism. It is not surprising in this regard that some of the most remarkable practitioners of such allusive, transitive, "homeless" abstraction, such as Helen Frankenthaler, Norman Lewis, and Joan Mitchell, were women or people of color. For them, the question of representation (and its apparent antithesis, abstraction) was not simply a matter of aesthetic doxa but a vital

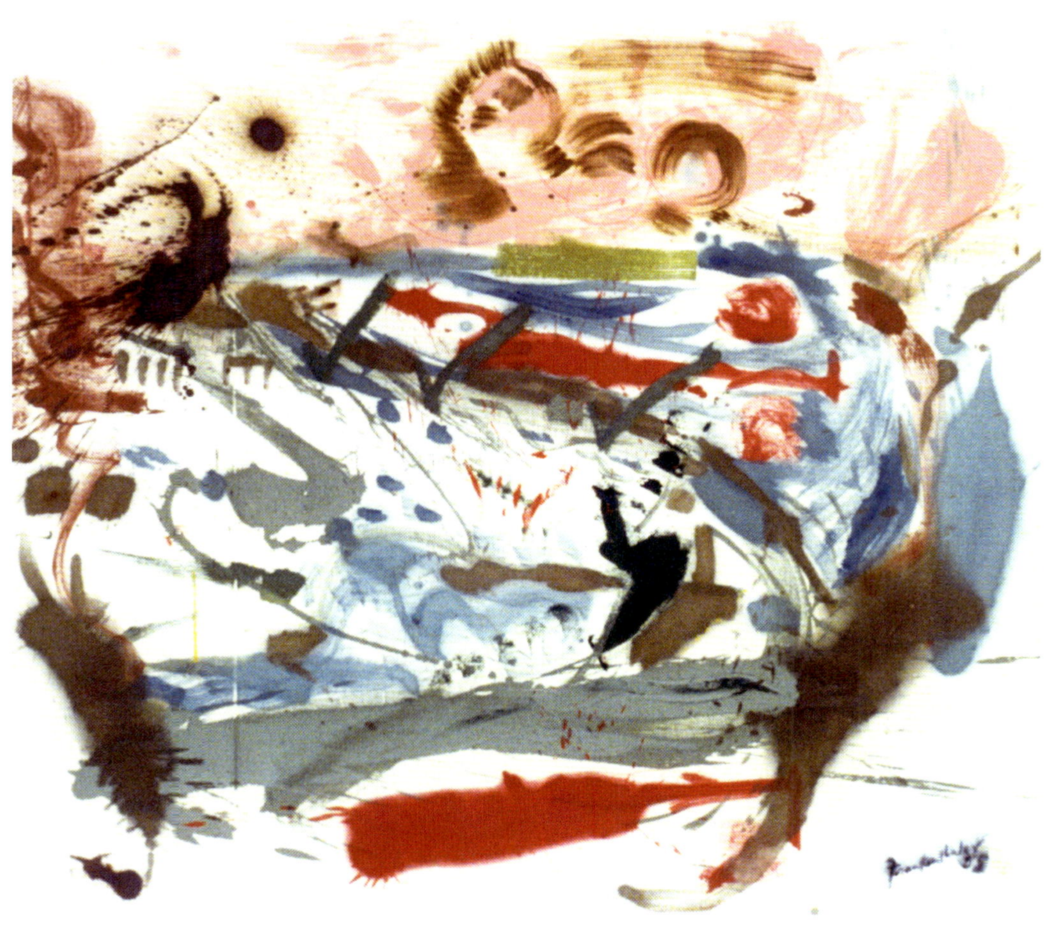

Helen Frankenthaler, *Hudson Valley*, 1958
Oil on unsized, unprimed canvas, 45½ × 49½ inches (115.6 × 22.9 cm)

political issue. That is to say, for artists who did not experience the full benefits of political representation, the possibilities of pictorial representation were far from played out.

Abstract Expressionism was in many ways a style born of outsiders and immigrants, and a number of the most celebrated members of the New York School, such as de Kooning, Arshile Gorky, Hans Hoffman, and Mark Rothko, were, like Yektai, émigrés. For these artists, the promise of intersubjective and intercultural communication was likely a hard-earned value and the idea of the creative act as a form of both self-invention and self-discovery was a virtue. In fact, one could argue that Rosenberg's conception of action painting as "the artist's re-creation of himself and as an evidence to the spectator of the kind of activities involved in this adventure" was ideally suited for artists like Yektai, who, despite being regularly consigned to an identity that positioned him outside of the dominant contours of modern subjectivity, sought to establish his place within the history of modernism. As Rosenberg's normalized use of "himself" in the above passage indicates, and as numerous scholars have since shown, such acts of self-realization were typically gendered and racialized, thus leaving many artists marginalized and underrepresented. And yet it is equally possible to see how Rosenberg's vision of "the use of art to recognize the self through visual experience" would have been especially appealing precisely to those who did not enjoy the full benefits of representation in the public sphere.[7] Yektai's transitive, homeless abstractions of still lifes, landscapes, and portraits sought to destabilize the expectations that these traditional genres offer. By inviting spectators to reexperience the work's creation and, as a corollary, possibly empathize with a vision different than their own, they express the hope for new and surprising encounters between artist and audience. In this way, one might see such transitive displacement as something to be embraced so that we might, as Stefano Harvey and Fred Moten have argued, come to recognize our shared condition of "being together in homelessness."[8] Such an awareness would in turn entail a mode of living that precludes a search for essences (whether in terms of identity or artistic media) and see transitive practices like Yektai's, not in terms of the dictates of aesthetic doctrine based on medium specificity, but as a specific means of self-determination through artistic discovery.

NOTES

1 On the significance of the horizontal axis in postwar art, see Leo Steinberg, "Other Criteria," in *Other Criteria: Confrontations with Twentieth-Century Art* (New York: Oxford University Press, 1972), 55–92, and Rosalind Krauss, *The Optical Unconscious* (Cambridge, MA: MIT Press, 1993), 243–320.
2 Harold Rosenberg, "The American Action Painters," *Art News* 51, no. 8 (December 1952): 22–33, 48–50; reprinted in *The Tradition of the New* (New York: Horizon Press, 1959), 23–39.
3 Harold Rosenberg, "After Next What?," in *The Anxious Object* (New York: Horizon Press, 1964), 257–63; Clement Greenberg, "After Abstract Expressionism," in John O'Brian, ed., *The Collected Essays and Criticism*, vol. 4, *Modernism with a Vengeance, 1959–1969* (Chicago: University of Chicago Press, 1993), 124.
4 J[ames] S[chuyler], "Reviews and Previews," *Art News* 56, no. 8 (December 1957): 12.
5 Lawrence Van Gelder, "'A Studio in My Pocket,'" *New York Times*, January 9, 1983, LI2.
6 Stuart Preston, "Gallery Roundup," *New York Times*, May 25, 1952, X9.
7 Rosenberg, "After Next, What?," in *The Anxious Object*, 259.
8 Stefano Harvey and Fred Moten, *The Undercommons: Fugitive Planning & Black Study* (New York: Minor Compositions, 2013), 96.

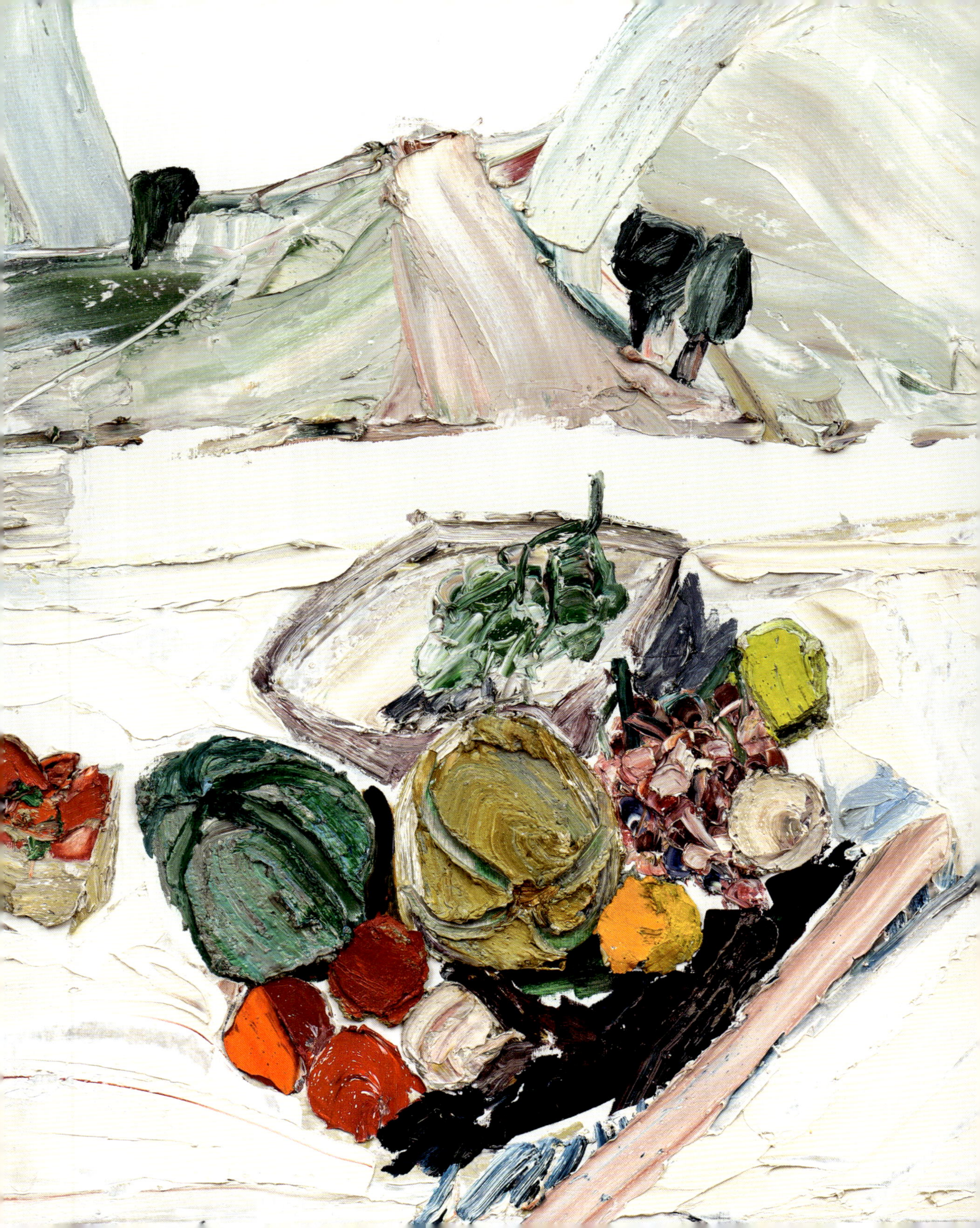

Hadi Fallahpisheh and Tahereh Fallahzadeh in Conversation

I spoke with my mother, Tahereh Fallahzadeh, about the work of Manoucher Yektai for the occasion of this publication on his work. We decided to hold our conversation in our photography darkrooms; I went to my darkroom in Brooklyn and spoke with Tahereh in her darkroom in Tehran. In the dark we talked about Yektai's paintings and poetry, how they have influenced our own work, and how his foresight and decisions changed our ideas about art. Over the course of three weeks, we met several times in our respective darkrooms, imagining and remembering Manoucher's work. Our conversation was in Farsi, and has been transcribed and translated here.

Hadi Fallahpisheh: I thought it would be good to go back and start from the first time we talked about Manoucher Yektai, which, for me, is the first memory I have of Manoucher, when I found his book in our library so many years ago. Maybe you can tell me again how you ended up with that book, because I know it wasn't readily available in bookstores or at all easy to find.

Tahereh Fallahzadeh: Well, you know, we have a large collection of poetry books, and the book you are talking about I have had forever, the one called *Falgoosh*. It was a very important book for me. It's a very

Untitled, 1976 (detail)

special book and unlike other poetry from that time. And yes, you're right, it wasn't an easy book to find; I remember I bought it on Enghelab Street from a bookstore that was famous for having special, rare books. It's a fascinating book; if I'm right, it's one of the earliest poems from the modernist school of poetry in Iran.

HF: Yes, I remember reading that it took him ten years to finish it. The way the text is, is also so unique; it doesn't have any style—in some ways, it's a narrative filled with inner conversations that take the form of a poem, which, at that time, was so radical. I think it wasn't even considered a poem, because it didn't look like any other poetry book published at the time.

TF: Yes, the book is all one long poem, that gets rid of the idea of rhyme and meter, and really works with the length of each line being determined by the idea and thought that is being expressed. Yet it's still a narrative, and it keeps a bridge of connection with very historical and traditional Persian poetry, and, in so many subtle ways, also manages to criticize the structure of Iranian society at the time. And in this specific work, *Falgoosh*, it's so powerful because of the legend and tradition it's pointing to.

HF: Yes, that's why I thought we should have this conversation in the dark. I remember the first time I read the book, I really wasn't understanding it but I remember talking to you, and how much time you took to explain the title of the work, *Falgoosh*, which describes the whole book and what the poem is about. Can you tell me again?

TF: Well, *Falgoosh,* literally, means "listening in the dark for one's fortune," and it's a very old and almost forgotten Persian tradition where, on a specific night, people wanting to know their future would go and stand in a dark corner at a busy intersection in order to listen and catch words from the conversations of passersby, which they would then try to interpret as hints for what awaited them in the future.

HF: I love that so much, and that's why I thought it would be interesting if we talked about Manoucher's work from our darkrooms. It's a very beautiful idea, that on a dark night, in an unlit corner, people would go and search for their fortunes among the drifting words of others just passing by in the night—that it depends so much on chance, what life has in store for you. And that also reminds me so much of how a photographer works in the darkroom, and how much photography is based on chance. To be honest, I don't think it would be untruthful to say that these two things, subconsciously, have formed what I do in my art—also, the idea of trusting that you can find your answers in the darkness.

TF: According to this tradition, the idea is that a person goes on this particular night with an intention in their heart, and they interpret whatever they hear as something related to that intention. It makes me think of the negatives I use in the darkroom, as if the negative is my intention and what happens in the darkness is an answer to it. Also, this idea of having an intention and allowing life to bring answers for it reminds me of Manoucher's paintings; there's always a subject but it's always defined by the other things that determine it—the brushstroke, the palette knife, a spatula or piece of wood, and the whole process as the painting comes into being.

HF: That's a very beautiful metaphor. I think you must remember, even before I went to college, how, one day, after I had seen a group show, I came back home asking if the painter who made the work was the same Manoucher who had written that book. It was this large white painting of fruit and bowls and plates with a background that was something like an open window to a landscape or maybe a painting, and I guess there was also a bouquet of flowers there.

TF: Yes, I remember—I knew the style of Manoucher's painting, especially those still life works with the window landscapes and flowers. In fact, I'm fairly sure I had told you about those works, but I think that must have been the first time you saw them in person.

HF: Yes, that was the first time, and it affected me so much. You can imagine how, based on what one would usually see in the galleries in Tehran, seeing a painting like that—how surprising it was. It had the feeling of a scene I had always seen in my life because it was almost like a *Haft-sin* that we make for the New Year, but, at the same time, it looked nothing like any painting I had seen before from an Iranian painter. It was so abstract and expressive, had so much action and gesture in it, that, to be honest, I was confused. It was like smelling perfume for the first time and loving it but also feeling confused, not knowing why it smells so good.

TF: It's as if Manoucher's paintings and poems are from two different worlds. His paintings have a very strong sense of universality in technique and imagery, while his poems are filled with local signifiers and references. And to me it's one of the qualities of his work to have two different worlds in balance. He wrote most of his poems abroad, with a nostalgic view to his past in Iran, and he was writing in Farsi, with so much remembrance, but, at the same time, the paintings he is known for are so far from any sense of nostalgia or even any references to Iran.

HF: The way I see it is that when he was in Iran he was already a modernist poet, and when he left he held that close to his heart and kept writing in Farsi from the same source; but, with his paintings, he established another kind of modernism that was shaped by European and American artists. And, as you say, I think his paintings achieved a kind of universality and communicated with a broader audience.

TF: Also, sitting here in the darkness and talking about *Falgoosh* and Manoucher's paintings, it's interesting that most of the poem happens in darkness, in the dark nights, while his paintings are mostly white, and have so much imagery of light.

HF: It's also interesting sitting here in the dark and thinking about the light reflecting back on us as viewers, and about how maybe these paintings full of light are the answers he found when he was searching in the dark. It's just so easy to remember those paintings—it only takes a moment to envision the table and fruit, the window, the landscape, the green trees. Do you have anything of the poems in your memory?

TF: There's one that I remember, it goes something like: "In the room of my memories, how many times you have loved someone, when was the last time you gave a wild flower on your path to your hand, are you walking with a lantern, or by the moonlight, I have to open my wings, it's time to get up, I have to finish things, I should bring the light."

HF: That's beautiful; it's so free. He's not the most famous Iranian poet, but it's very special to think of his words in relation to his paintings.

Here, they say that what makes his paintings so memorable and special is that he always kept a sense of poetry going on under the layers of thick paint, although the brushstrokes are very rough. I think something like this is in your photographs too: under the surface of your rough black-and-white photographs there's a poetic spirit running through.

TF: Well, a lot of Iranian artists were and are so influenced by his work and what he achieved. He opened a lot of doors, and he himself had an open mind about being contemporary, with, at the same time, such a deep admiration for the history of painting. I also really appreciated that, in his paintings, there's always a subject, but it's been nearly obliterated, and pushed to the limit of representation. In a lot of my photographs from the nineties, and even today, I have always tried to keep some sort of image recognizable, despite how hard it might be for the viewer to recognize it.

HF: I'm not sure I ever told you this story, because I was so disappointed, but when I first arrived in New York I asked a lot of people if they knew where Manoucher Yektai lived. I was told that he didn't want to be disturbed, and that, in recent years, he had really cut himself off from others. But I really wanted to meet him and talk with him. So eventually I found his address and I went to his apartment on the Upper West Side, but with little chance of meeting him, because he was already spending most of his time out of the city. I still wish I could have met him and told him how important his work and his poetry are to me.

TF: Oh, you never told me that. I wish you could have met him, but so much of him lives in his work.

HF: Yes, it's something like a shared experience, that I have and you also have with what he was thinking. I think it's a shared experience in our love of images, even though the final work is never about that image. Maybe it's also a semi-belief that we don't want to go fully abstract: there's always something represented, but the final work is beyond that very thing; it's something within this framework that keeps our approach poetic. I would also like to think that, although our works come from a place and are not ahistorical, they manage to be about now, and the present moment, which I think is one aspect of what makes Manoucher's paintings and poems so extraordinary.

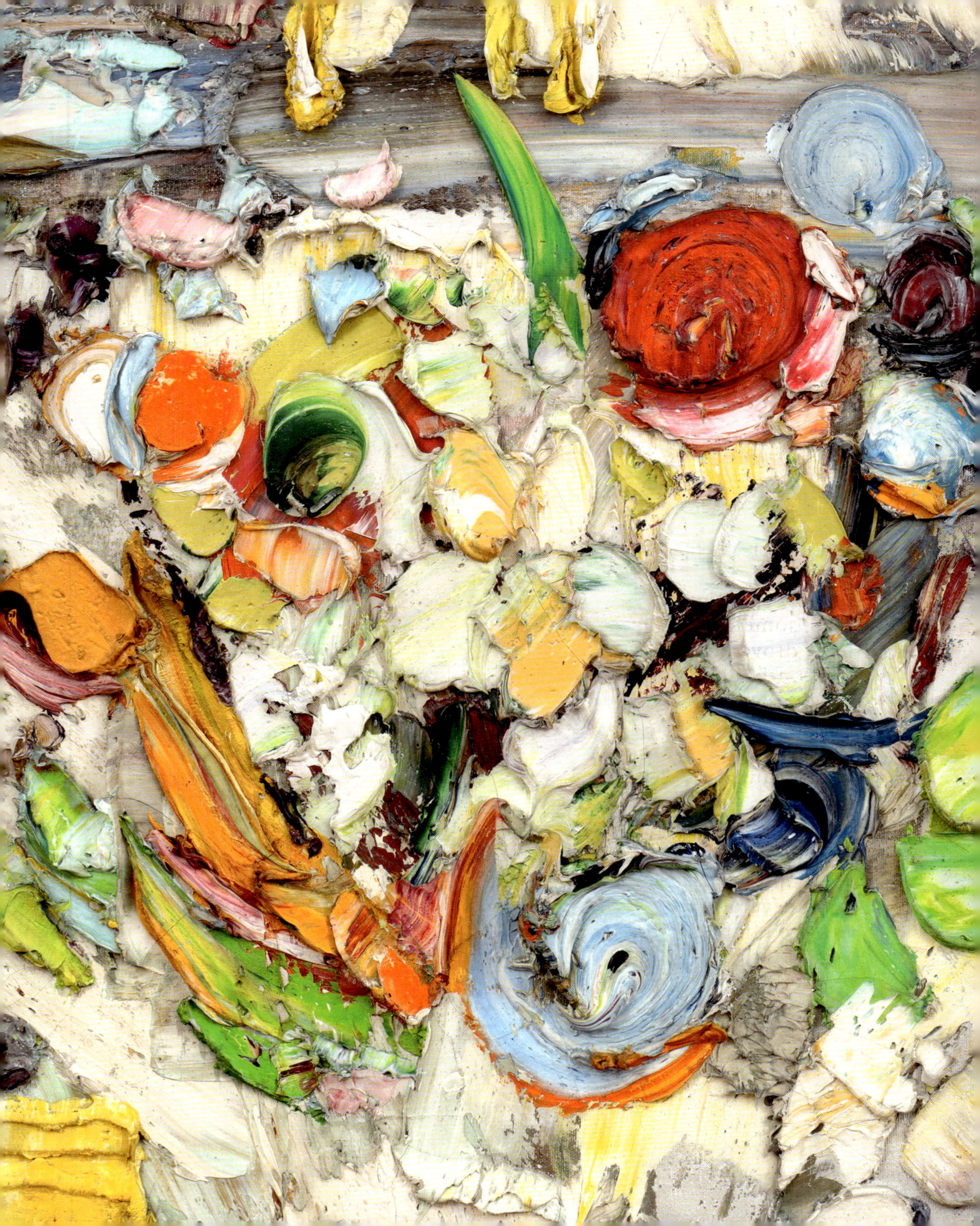

The Six-Hundred-Year Plan: The Eternal Confidence of Manoucher Yektai

Biddle Duke

Manoucher Yektai was stubborn about his aspirations.

From an early age he believed he possessed something of significance, something the world needed. He spoke of that belief all his life. It drove him as a youthful poet and inexperienced painter from tradition-bound Iran in the 1940s, and continued to animate him and provide powerful direction as he navigated the art worlds of Paris and New York. His whole life was an endeavor to meet his colossal self-imposed expectations, and he presented no shortage of hubris when it came to his ability to do so.

"I am a great artist," he frequently told those closest to him throughout his life. Boastful though the words may sound, usually delivered flatly, as a simple fact, his audiences in these moments didn't necessarily see it as exaggeration. It was unquestionable and long established: Yektai possessed immense talent.

To reach such heights, Yektai was purposeful, sometimes to the point of obsession, enabling him to devote himself fully to his work in a way that many people are unable to do.

Untitled, 1953–54 (detail)

When Yektai died on November 19, 2019, at his home in Sagaponack, New York, his life had been rewarded with recognition, wealth, and, for a little more than a decade, fame. To any outside observer he had been a success in most of the conventional ways, and in the intangible ones, too: he had met the world's beauty with his own.

Yektai left this life peacefully, in his living room, surrounded by his family—and yet, at ninety-eight, he still burned with a certainty that his work on Earth was not finished. His recognition had not been commensurate to his talent, his painting not risen to the heights he'd envisioned. He died believing an ineffable higher level of acclaim would come.

What that meant, precisely, is hard to know, as he spoke of it in generally abstract terms, a kind of great legacy that would only be achieved in time. Yet his conviction was unequivocal: the world would one day, long after he had taken his last breath, fully embrace what he had offered.

"Manouche certainly was arrogant, it was all about him," Niki, his widowed wife of fifty-two years, said. This description could be seen as unkind, but Niki offers it with tender admiration, adding, "He never complained about his lack of recognition. He just absolutely never did anything about it. He just worked. He painted. He wrote poems."

Yektai's drive and directness could come across as dark. He was a tough critic, his judgment often delivered with withering directness. Many characterized him as distant and unapproachable. Yet he sought the opposite in his art. His paintings were about finding the light, whether in people or in the simplest of everyday scenes.

"Manouche was an atheist," his friend, the Iranian writer Alimorad Fadaienia, said. "But he found the hand of god in everything. He saw the good in everything. An apple was as important as a human being. That is how he painted."

"When he was painting my portrait—as he did many times—he would say, 'you are no more or less important than this apple,'" Niki said. "That's the way he saw the world."

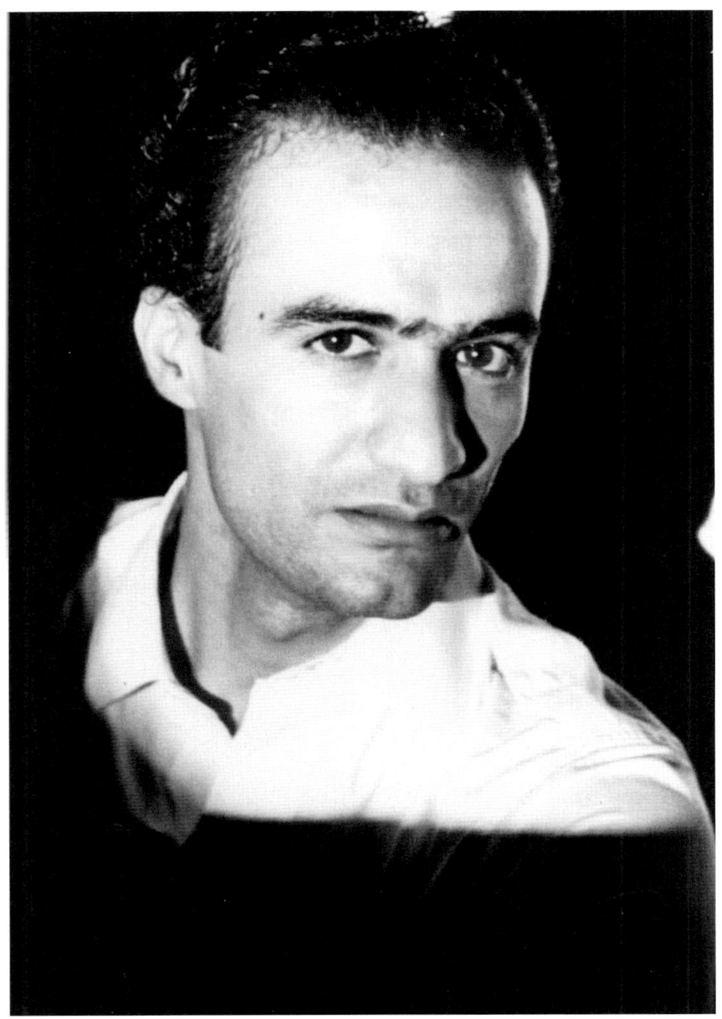

Manoucher Yektai, taken likely in Iran in the 1940s

Not long after his arrival in New York in 1945 Yektai was embraced as an emerging Abstract Expressionist. He gently dismissed the designation, but in many respects the art-world spotlight turned onto him thanks to his inclusion in the movement. Extraordinary praise from critics and fellow artists, including from his more celebrated contemporaries, followed. He was lauded as an "artist's artist."

"Either this is an animal becoming a man or a man becoming a god," Landès Lewitin reportedly commented to Mark Rothko cryptically after seeing Yektai's early works at a solo exhibition in the 1950s at the Poindexter Gallery in New York City, where many of the great Abstract Expressionists were represented.

"Yektai," the renowned poet John Ashbery wrote in 1961 in the French magazine *Aujourd'hui: Art et Architecture*, "wants to render us conscious of our existence from second to second, of the joy of breathing, of the rapid changes of things."

Yektai's arrival in the United States couldn't have come at a better moment. The West had defeated the Nazis and the Japanese thanks to America, which had been newly designated as a global superpower. Untethered from the war effort, he found a nation surging with energy and optimism, its art world exploding with exhilarating, wild abstraction. And his own work was, for almost two decades, powerfully in sync with the new American ideal, even as it was rooted in rich European sensibilities and Persian traditions.

"You could say his success was almost accidental: his timing was perfect," his son Nico said of his father's quick rise and success on the American art scene.

But in 1981, after more than a decade of declining sales, Yektai deliberately stepped away from the commercial art world. That isolation continued—with a few notable exceptions—until his death in 2019. Yet that period of more than four decades was also joyful and productive. His warm and easy relationship with Niki, who was his constant companion, would be his most enduring. The couple raised a family together. And, forever disciplined about making art, Yektai produced an immense volume of work, marking a stunning and largely unrecognized peak in his creative life. Which is why those decades only strengthened a powerful belief—a belief that Yektai himself expressed and fostered—that his painting would achieve the world's highest recognition.

That Yektai's name and work have not commanded the prices or achieved the recognition of, say, Jackson Pollock or Willem de Kooning is not a simple question of his originality or his excellence as an artist—it's more complicated and nuanced than that. Yektai believed his painting should speak for itself, and in his opinion—and many others—his work belongs in the pantheon of greats. His life and experience prove what many in the art world know to be true: achieving major museum exhibitions and widespread, sustained fame requires more than just making stunning paintings. Talent gets you some of the way there, but one must play the game to get all the way. He anticipated greatness but refused to do what was expected of him to achieve it while he was alive; he was stubbornly unwilling to swim in the art-world slipstream.

"He was a great painter," said gallerist Alex Rosenberg, who represented Yektai in the 1980s, "who did everything he could not to be one."

Rosenberg, whose century-long lifespan in the art world mirrored Yektai's, empathized with the artist's angst.

"He deserved every accolade. His talent was huge. But he was a very rebellious person in a very quiet fashion."

The person who knew him best, Niki Yektai, said, "He simply did not reach out to collectors or galleries. It was pride, shyness. He wasn't interested in any of that. He just would not promote himself. And, if it wasn't for me, he wouldn't have socialized."

TEHRAN

Manoucher Yektai's passport says he was born in Tehran on December 22, 1921, but in some of his early catalogue biographies he'd write his birth year as 1922. Confusion about Gregorian calendar dates is not uncommon among Persians of his era. In 2012, when asked his age by a Persian documentary filmmaker, he replied as only

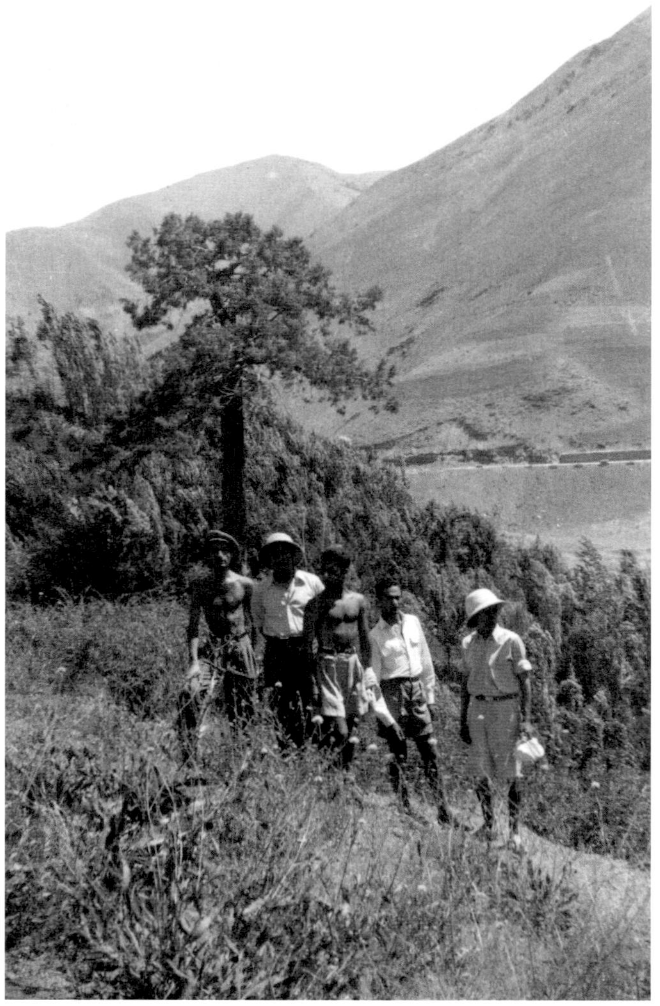

Yektai visited the villages and countryside of Iran, which inspired his poetry and paintings throughout his life.
Here he is (second from right) with friends in the mountains of Iran, in the early 1940s.

a Persian would: he was born in the Persian year 1300, which lines up with the late 1921 date.

Yektai grew up in a family of public servants and merchants, members of the emerging, educated Iranian elite. They owned six buildings on a busy commercial street, with shops on the first floors and apartments above.

The Tehran of his youth would be unrecognizable today. With over half a million people, the ancient city was a bustling high-desert capital at a historic cultural crossroads. Reza Shah, and subsequently his son Mohammed Shah, thrust Tehran into the twentieth century, modernizing the city and Iranian culture to the objection of the conservative mullahs and the many tribes. Women in veils were banned from public spaces, along with camels, while sections of the town were razed and rebuilt in the image of a European city. Late-model European and American cars—Fiats, Austins, Morrises, Packards—driven by a new urban elite shared the streets with visiting tribespeople and donkeys and horse carts delivering goods. The shahs tore up many of Tehran's original narrow tangled alleys and streets, and crisscrossed the city with tree-lined boulevards and avenues defined by new, imposing government buildings, monuments, parks, and squares.

Yelktai's mother was a child bride at the age of fourteen in an arranged marriage to a politically prominent family who worked for the shah. At some point in her twenties, displeased with her first husband for taking a second wife, Yektai's mother did the unthinkable at the time: she left him, becoming one of the first women to divorce in conservative Iran. At the age of twenty-seven, already with two children, she married Yektai's father, a member of a well-to-do family from southern Iran who was almost twice her age. He had recently returned to Iran to attend to family businesses after having been abroad for much of his life. When Yektai was born, his father was in his late sixties.

Yektai's memories of Iran, captured in various filmed interviews, are expressed with affection and detail. He would learn French and English but his language would forever be the Farsi of 1930s and '40s Iran. For his entire life he spoke with a dignified formality that has mostly vanished—modernity and the Iranian revolution have coarsened the language with Englishisms and rhetorical shortcuts.

Yektai was an observant child, recognizing early the importance of remembering life's moments. A first memory was of his father's death in 1926 at the age of seventy-two. The young Yektai came upon the elderly man's body ceremonially placed on the floor in a parlor in their house.

"I pulled back the curtain to enter the room," he recalled much later in one of many taped interviews with his son, Nico. "Then I jumped over his body three times."

He was just a kid playing.

"I don't know why I did it."

In an instant he realized this was no game. His father was dead, and he was flooded with sadness. "I began to cry."

Yektai's contemplative, observant nature soon yielded poems. They came to him starting at the age of eight. By the time he was in high school his poetry was being published in Tehran-based magazines and newspapers.

In many ways Yektai's renown in Iran as a poet would come to exceed his reputation as a painter: his books of poetry—two epic poems and four collections—are easily accessible and available, unlike his paintings, which are in museums and private collections. "He is known both as a painter and a poet in Iran, but it is his poetry that people can find, that the people know," the writer and former Brown University Persian language instructor Iraj Anvar said.

Painting wasn't a thought until Yektai was in his last year in high school and a friend introduced him to Mehdi Vishkai. A year or two older, Vishkai would go on to become one of Iran's most important portrait artists. They met in Vishkai's studio, amid the young artist's few works in progress. Yektai was captivated. Beautiful craft and stunning architecture were everywhere in Tehran in the 1940s, but modern works of art on canvas and on paper, particularly by working contemporary artists, were few. Galleries didn't exist and the rare art book could only be found in museums or libraries.

"It would have been easier to conquer Tehran than to go to one of the libraries to see those books," Yektai said.

Yektai would later recall the first moment he saw an original contemporary work of art: a self-portrait by Vishkai. The two men spent the afternoon and the rest of the night talking, and looking at Vishkai's work and postcards—the only images that could be found—of paintings by Matisse, Cézanne, Van Gogh, and other European artists.

"From then on all I could think about was painting," he recalled.

Until that afternoon he had resolved to be a poet. But the experience with Vishkai "gave me a sense of what was possible with painting, and of the limits of poetry."

Poetry, he decided, is constrained by the singular meaning of words and the limits of translation, while painting transcends language. The power and beauty of images is art's universality, understandable to any culture.

The following day he skipped a high school exam. He had been a diligent student, never one to miss an assignment. When his brother inquired if something was wrong, Yektai beamed, "I am a painter!"

It was a rebellious notion at the time for a well-to-do Persian boy with Yektai's prospects. His guardian, who had been appointed in his father's will, was unimpressed and even annoyed. He was unwilling to support the young man's reckless new obsession, so Yektai sold his winter overcoat to pay for the art supplies he needed to complete the university art-school entrance exam.

"Do you want to throw your life out the window for this?" Yektai remembered his guardian, an official in the Tehran mayor's office, telling him. "You were my hope! I wanted you to be the head of this country!"

By deciding to become a painter, Yektai was defying all the conventions and expectations his family had for him. He was turning his back on financial security and social standing. None of that mattered. An innate sense of not belonging, the inherent rebelliousness that drove that early decision, would define his life.

"My family went into politics, I didn't want to be a member of this club," he recalled. "I was alien, an outsider. I was always [an] outsider."

Yektai soon resolved to leave the country altogether to study art in Paris. The Iranian elite at the time revered Paris as the center of modern culture. Much of Iranian secondary and university education was populated by French professors and it had been molded in the image of the French lycée system. The shah opened Tehran University in 1934; it had been designed by French and Swiss architects, among them a Frenchman, André Godard, who served as dean at the Fine Arts College where Yektai became one of the first students.

Paris was also, at that moment, at the raging center of World War II. Although Tehran itself was not removed from the war—Iran would be invaded by the Soviets from the north and by the British, Americans, and Australians from the south—Yektai's memories of those years don't dwell on the soldiers in the streets and the political upheavals at the time. Mostly he remembers thinking Tehran and the arts education he was receiving were stultifying.

An anecdote from a much later exhibition catalogue tells of him walking out of a classroom, frustrated, after locking horns with a teacher who objected to his painting a cucumber the color red. He took his skills and his disregard for suffocating convention and left for Paris.

TO AMERICA

Yektai's exodus was joined by a clever, striking fellow art student who had caught his eye at the university. Like Yektai, Monir Shahroudy was driven to study art in the West. She came from an influential family and her father was a member of the Iranian parliament. Both their family connections would prove helpful as they sought visas and difficult-to-get passages on ships in wartime, and friends and a social life once they landed abroad.

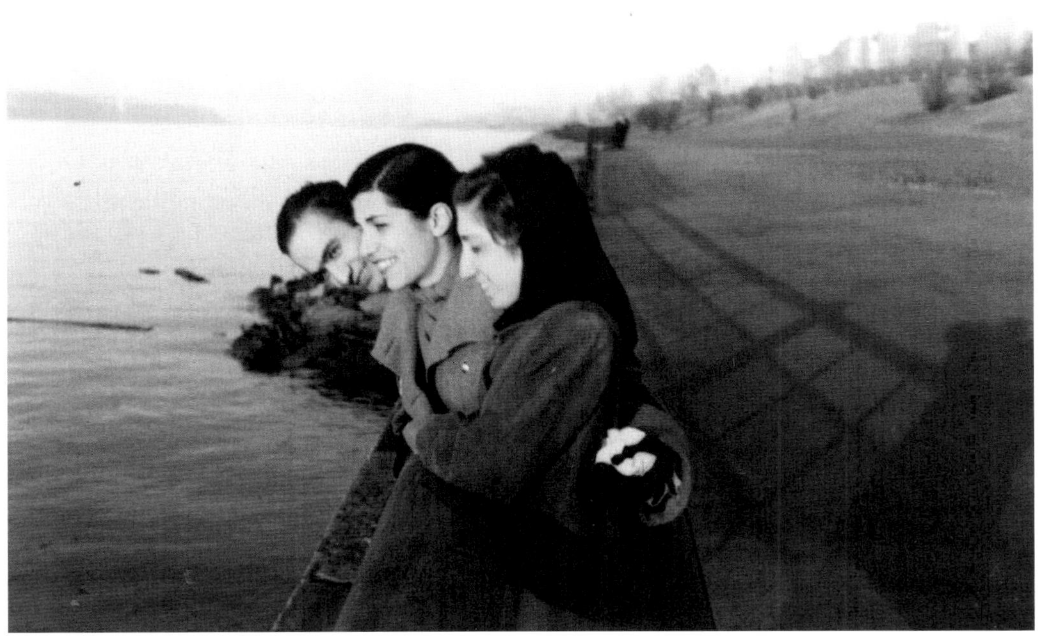

Yektai traveled to America in 1944 with Monir Shahroudy, who would become a well-known artist in her own right. They would marry in 1948. This photograph of the two of them with a friend (at right) is believed to be on a riverfront in New York.

The two could not have been more different. Shahroudy was outgoing, assertive, some say verging on aggressive, both socially and professionally, and comfortable asking for everything she wanted in life. Yektai, meanwhile, was reserved, unassuming, and, by most accounts, almost antisocial. If their natures had anything in common, it was stubbornness and ambition.

The courtship eventually became an engagement, which had less to do with personal warmth or affection than it did to serve Shahroudy's interests. After all, she would soon be a young Persian woman traveling the world in the 1940s. She explained it succinctly in her 2008 memoir, *A Mirror Garden*: "The convenience of a fiancé became especially clear when I decided to go to America."

The United States became the default choice after French officials in Tehran laughed them out of the embassy, scoffing at them for even considering traveling to Paris during the war. So the plan changed: they would travel to New York and then find passage to France as soon as they could.

Yektai, Shahroudy, her brother acting as chaperone, and a fourth friend made the long and complicated journey together to the United States. With much string-pulling they negotiated their way onto a small British military transport ship and set off from the Iranian port of Khorramshahr, through the straits of Hormuz, across the Indian Ocean to Bombay. Shahroudy managed to get one of two first-class cabins, while her male companions were sent to the ship's bowels. Being Shahroudy's fiancé gave Yektai at least one distinct advantage: spending days above deck with her.

In Bombay, Yektai and Shahroudy parlayed family contacts into evenings with diplomats and aristocrats. Through some American friends made in Iran, the traveling Iranians found passage on the *George Randall* US troop transport ship to Australia. The ship was loaded with thousands of Japanese prisoners of war from the fighting in Southeast Asia. Yektai and the other Iranian men joined US and Australian servicemen below deck, while Shahroudy bunked with refugees from China who had escaped the invading Japanese. The ship unloaded the Japanese prisoners in Sydney, then zigzagged across the Pacific to Los Angeles, dodging German and Japanese submarines.

From the West Coast the group traveled across the United States by train to New York. The layover there turned into a year. Yektai was dazzled by the museums and by the emerging New York School and the buzzing art scene. He studied with French purist painter Amédée Ozenfant in his Greenwich Village studio and took classes at the Art Students League. But the idea of Paris and its École des Beaux-Arts continued to burn for him. So, after many French visa delays, he went. Shahroudy, meanwhile, had settled in to New York. She had polished up her English in a Cornell University language course, made friends, was studying at the Parsons School of Design, and had landed a graphic design job. She decided to stay behind. Their relationship was, by all accounts, rocky, but they agreed to try again upon Yektai's return. Yektai had finished paintings in New York during his stay there, and he left them with her for safekeeping, a decision that would turn out badly.

PARIS

Paris, as it turned out, was a disappointment.

"The École des Beaux-Arts for me was truly dead," Yektai later recalled.

He revered the European masters, Paul Cézanne above all others, and would forever turn to them for insight and inspiration. But no sooner had he landed in Paris than he was consumed with a yearning to return to the excitement and fraternity of New York. Yektai was stunned to find that few in France knew the names of painters in America who were turning the art world on its head: Pollock, Barnett Newman, Milton Avery, de Kooning.

Yektai arrived in France less than a year after the end of the war and Paris was still reeling—and rebuilding—from four years of Nazi occupation. He searched the city for the vibrant art life of his imagination but, disillusioned, he realized it did not exist.

"At the museums I found dead paintings, on dead walls, on dead buildings," he said. "There was no life."

For visa reasons he had to remain in France for a year. He won a place at the École in a juried painting competition, one of forty students admitted out of more than 240 in the contest. Uninspired by the teachers and students at the school, he took lessons with noted French School painter Jean Souverbie. Yektai also sought out the Cubist painter and teacher André Lhote, who he found awkward and churlish, but whose eye he admired. Instead of drawing and painting in his atelier classroom, Yektai got Lhote's permission to simply observe him teaching, recognizing that approach as the most effective method to learn technique.

But he longed for New York.

"I just wanted to return to America, to that dynamic," he would later say, adding, "I wanted to get back to the MoMA, that corner of activity that belonged to the people, where there was a life of daily artistic communication."

As was characteristic, Yektai nevertheless didn't waste a minute in France. Relentless in his quest for technique, ideas, and insight, he visited every Parisian art space, every museum and opening, and sought out every living artist of note. One of the final shows he attended was an exhibition of paintings by Pierre Bonnard, one of his favorites. It was Bonnard's last show before his death months later. And finally, before returning to New York, Yektai spent several weeks in London, methodically visiting every museum and gallery in the city.

By the time he returned to the United States in 1947 he was finding the beginnings of his signature painting style. Paris had been brief and had not met his high expectations but the time in Paris would direct a classic style in his work that remained always, particularly his adherence to certain subject matter: nudes, still lifes, landscapes, portraits.

THE POLLOCK EFFECT

The late 1940s in New York marked a turning point for Yektai. He was growing into himself as a painter, and soon was recognized as an up-and-coming artist of note. He got his first American shows in the emerging arts community of Woodstock, New York, where he and Shahroudy, with whom he had reconnected, had begun to spend time in the summer. His paintings began to sell, both through galleries and out of his studio.

But the year 1949 belonged to Jackson Pollock. The now-famous *Life* magazine story published that August, illustrated with Pollock's iconoclastic drip paintings, asked: "Is he the greatest living painter in the United States?"

The article rocked the art world. No one had ever seen paintings like Pollock's. With that *Life* article, he suddenly and very publicly exploded all the conventional notions of art and art-making. Yektai, like almost every artist alive at the time, was blown away.

"It changed everything," Yektai would recall. "For me, it was the beginning of something new ... Pollock introduced to me overnight a language of painting, an immense freedom."

Yektai threw away his brush and tried using every possible tool—pieces of wood, a whip—to apply paint. It was a period of exploration and frustration that nevertheless eventually led to his return to traditional implements, the paintbrush and palette knife.

Pollock and Yektai were soon seeing one another at social and art gatherings. They became friends. Ever the Persian gentleman, dignified, cosmopolitan, polite, Yektai remembers Pollock as the opposite: rough and raw, speckling his speech with invective, and shattering social conventions. Yektai recalled a party at which Pollock pulled up to a table and barked at a female artist seated nearby, "Who're you fucking these days?"

The younger, reserved Persian painter was unfazed. All that mattered about Pollock was his brilliance, which was why Yektai cherished—and frequently recounted—the memory of Pollock attending his exhibitions and on several occasions commenting, "I'm an admirer of your work."

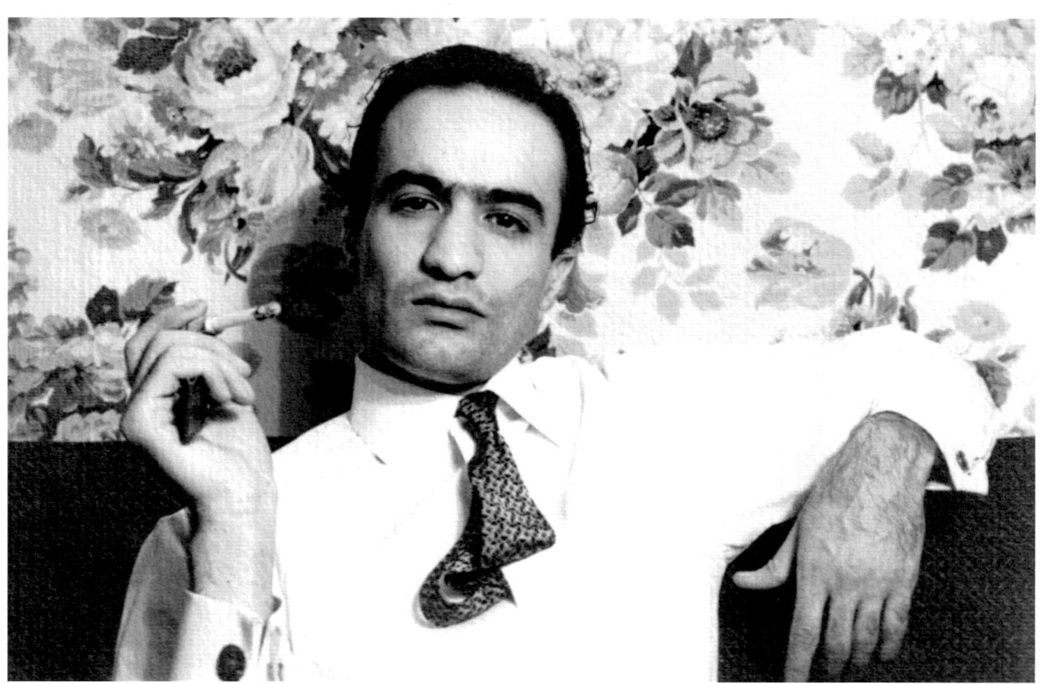

In the late 1940s Yektai was included among the founders of the Abstract Expressionist movement, but he resisted the label. "I don't like to be considered part of any group," he said. Portrait of Yektai, New York, early 1950s.

THE ABSTRACT EXPRESSIONIST TRAP

By 1950 Yektai was working in a style that would be familiar throughout his life: bright, broad, lush brushstrokes, vivid colors, the beginnings of a juicy and emotional impasto which he would build over the years, and an abstraction rooted in the classic themes of landscape, still life, and the figure. He was realizing his mission to evoke poetic beauty in simple, everyday life.

He had begun to move among the famous artists and the arts underknowns of the era. Influential art dealer Leo Castelli had the power to make careers, and when he brought some friends, including early Abstract Expressionist painters, to see Yektai's shows, his work entered at once, "almost too easily and smoothly, into the emerging profile of Abstract Expressionism," the art critic Thomas McEvilley wrote.

Castelli took a liking to Yektai and his work, and he brought him to the 10th Street Club gatherings. He became a regular alongside de Kooning, Newman, Rothko, Larry Rivers, Franz Kline, Lewitin, Philip Johnson, Paul Jenkins, the collector and gallerist Sidney Janis, the critic Clement Greenberg, and many others. The evenings often ended at the Cedar Tavern, drinking and debating art, ideas, styles, techniques, who was in, and who was out.

Abstract Expressionism was then in its infancy, blazing with energy but still searching for its audience. This was before it went big time, before it was fully embraced by the museums. The painters and the art world all around them were riding the first waves of recognition and enjoying meaningful sales. But where the movement would lead and what it would represent was still taking shape.

Yektai embraced the conversations, the artists and their work, and the fierce tilt into abstraction, but true to form, he resisted belonging. The Abstract Expressionist label had been pinned on him unsolicited. Clement Greenberg went so far as to call him a "founding member" of the movement. Yektai demurred.

It's hard to imagine any artist pushing back from that embrace. Abstract Expressionism would go on to be celebrated as one of the core movements of modern art; to be called a founding member was to be associated with the very thrust of one of the great turning points in art history.

Yet Yektai's nature as a man and an artist was iconoclasm, independence, freedom from any specific rules or ideas. He had returned to New York for the inspiration of being at the forefront of the art world, but not to be labeled as one kind of artist or another. He was finding his own artistic language, a language that had earned him—thanks to his talent and perfect timing—acceptance into the Abstract Expressionist club. But if he became a card-carrying member, he might never be able to leave. He gently shunned the classification whenever the opportunity presented itself.

He was careful not to overstate any of this. He enjoyed the limelight, he enjoyed the other artists, many of whom—de Kooning and Rivers, in particular—became lifelong friends, but his place in the Abstract Expressionist movement would remain forever murky.

"I try to be a contemporary painter," Yektai told the *New York Times* for an article in 1983. "By that I mean a new painter, a painter of the time, the kind of painting that you have not seen or experienced before … I don't like to be considered part of any group."

When Iranian filmmakers Shirin Saghaei and Parvin Ghassemi, who produced a short in 2012 entitled *Yektai*, asked him if he considered himself an Abstract Expressionist, he replied, unsurprisingly, somewhat cryptically: "When I was young I got rid of styles and I refused to accept any style. When I saw that this group felt the same, I joined them. With some of the members I became very close friends. And I thought this would last forever and with these painters we would grow old together. But it wasn't like that."

MONIR

When Yektai had returned from France he found to his astonishment that Shahroudy had sold some of the paintings he had left with her. She explained that she needed the money. Among them were a few

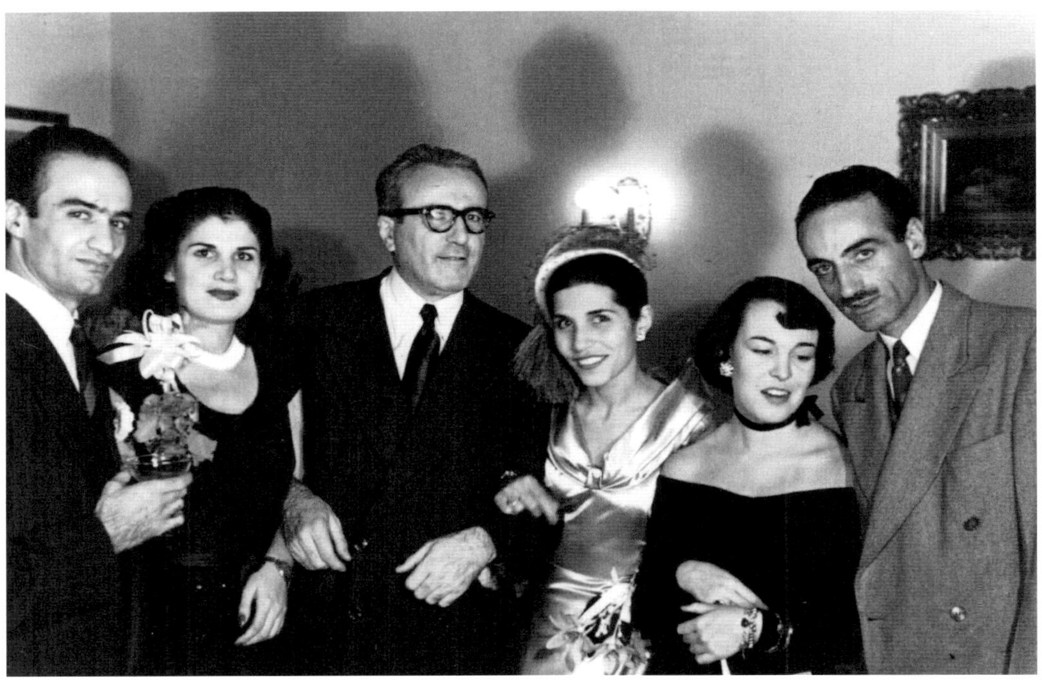

Soon after their arrival in New York, Yektai and Shahroudy began to move in expatriate Iranian and artist circles. Here they are posing on the day of their wedding, in 1948, Shahroudy (third from right), Yektai (left), and friends.

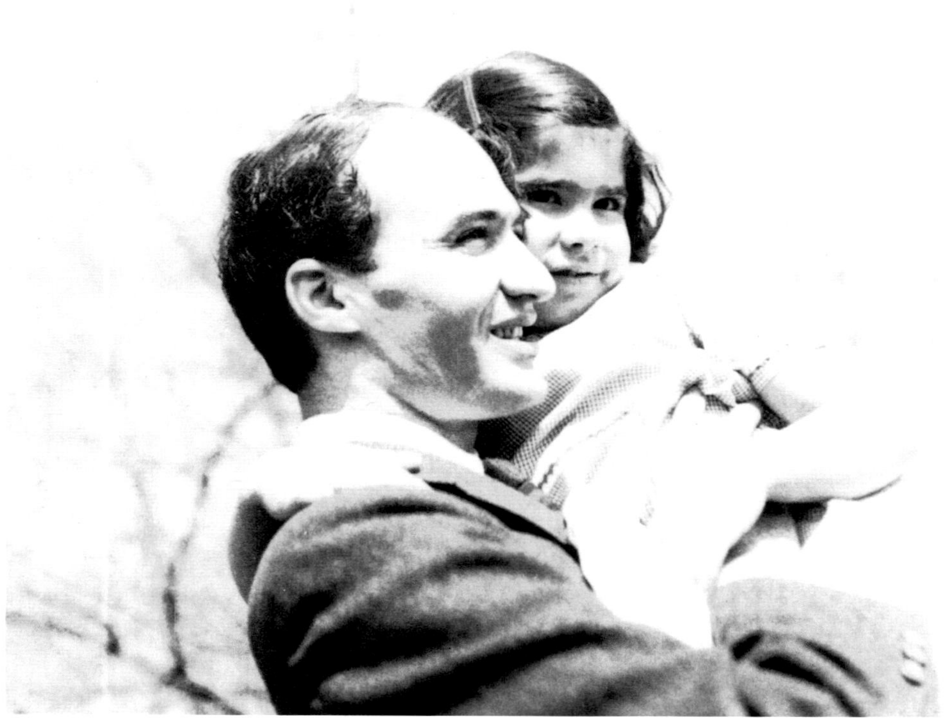

Yektai with his and Shahroudy's first child, Nima, 1950s

transitional, unfinished works that he had no intention of selling as he hadn't yet finished learning from them. Stunned by her thoughtlessness and furious at losing his work, he had no choice but to let it go. There was nothing to be done.

The relationship with Shahroudy was turbulent for other reasons: the two ambitious, headstrong, powerful egos clashed. Shahroudy bristled at the intensity and discipline with which Yektai approached his work and the confidence he had in his future as an artist. Yektai chose mostly to ignore her and keep working.

Despite their obvious differences, after their long engagement they both knew it was time to marry. They wed in October of 1948, both in their late twenties. Their only child, Nima, was born the following year.

Yektai remembered the day of Nima's birth as the making of two significant works—his reference point for many life events and special occasions. One was made after he was sent home by the doctor while Shahroudy was in labor, and a second after visiting his wife and newborn daughter at the hospital. Soon afterward, the paintings went to a show in Florida where they were exhibited alongside work by Henry Moore and Graham Sutherland. They garnered a reviewer's accolades, the first for him in a show with other, more established painters.

Yektai—with his stories of his ancient and mystical homeland and his exodus during the war, told in his intriguingly accented English—was an exotic touch on the New York art scene and at parties. At home, Shahroudy cooked classic Persian meals—aromatic stews, crispy *tahdig*—for dinner parties at their apartment with Castelli, Sidney Janis, Robert Hill, Samuel Kootz, Frederick Kiesler, and others in attendance.

The summers in Woodstock were spent in a mountainside cottage in the bohemian artist colony of Byrdcliffe, where Yektai and Shahroudy lived and worked alongside Milton and Sally Avery, Philip Guston, and the conductor of the National Orchestra, Léon Barzin. It was as magical a time as it was helpful to Yektai's career. The Averys and the Yektais became friends, and it was through them that Yektai was invited to begin showing at Milton's gallery in New York City, the Grace Borgenicht Gallery, where many of the leading Abstract Expressionists were represented.

The marriage lasted just a few years. As the relationship unraveled, Shahroudy began to spend time with a close childhood mutual friend, a Columbia University law student and the scion of a wealthy and powerful Iranian family, Abolbashar Farmanfarmaian. They married in 1957, and with Nima in tow, returned to live in Iran, where they had a daughter, Zahra.

The move to Iran catalyzed Monir Farmanfarmaian's own substantial artistic ambitions. Although she made paintings, drawings, and textile designs, her most well-known works would become elaborate mosaic mirror assemblages evocative of traditional Persian mirror artwork. Her fame with that work in particular would soar later in life, with major museum shows, including at the Guggenheim, and a Tehran museum in her name, the Monir Museum.

The Iranian revolution in the late 1970s drove the Farmanfarmaians back to New York where they would live until Abolbashar's death in 1991. Monir and Yektai were never close again. But Abol, as her husband Abolbashar Farmanfarmaian was called, was an ardent admirer of Yektai's poetry and painting, and the two maintained a warm friendship.

"They were good friends, they had huge respect for each other," Nima said of her two fathers. "It was Abol who mentored the [family] relationships."

Abol Farmanfarmaian is buried in the Oakland Cemetery in Sag Harbor, not far from Yektai. Eventually, after Abol's death and many roundtrips to Iran, Monir Farmanfarmaian moved back to Tehran, where she died in 2019, at the age of ninety-six.

THE HEYDAYS

The pinnacle of Yektai's art celebrity would come in the 1950s and early 1960s at the height of the Abstract Expressionist movement. His relationships with galleries in the United States and Europe flourished. At the Grace Borgenicht Gallery he appeared alongside such luminaries as Milton Avery, Wolf Kahn, Jimmy Ernst, Edward Corbett, and James

Brooks. He later moved to the Poindexter Gallery, owned by the influential, well-connected, upper-crust husband-and-wife team of Ellie and George Poindexter, who represented de Kooning, Richard Diebenkorn, Jules Olitski, Nell Blaine, Giorgio Spaventa, Franz Kline, Earl Kerkam, Milton Resnick, Eleanor Dickinson, Paul Harris, and Robert De Niro Sr.

The Poindexters nurtured Yektai's career, maintaining a lively (and well documented in the Smithsonian archives) correspondence with him into the mid-1960s. His paintings began appearing and selling around the world, in solo exhibitions in Los Angeles, London, Paris, and Chicago, smaller venues in the United States, and in traveling shows of leading modern artists.

In 1959, the Museum of Modern Art acquired a Yektai work, followed by the San Francisco Museum of Modern Art, the Hirshhorn Museum in Washington, DC, which would buy three for its collection, and several university museums.

Yektai was a well-known figure in New York artist circles by the mid-1950s, where he became friends with an accomplished German-born artist, Ilse Getz. A gifted woman with wide-ranging interests and a hunger to travel and learn about art, architecture, philosophy, and language, Getz loved Yektai's work. The admiration was mutual. Although Getz had fled Nazi Germany to America, she always longed for Europe, whose art and culture had also captivated Yektai since his youth in Iran. "The architecture, the landscape, a way of life, the people," she wrote of Europe for an exhibition catalogue in the 1970s.

The two began a relationship. Although the precise dates are unknown, memory and written records indicate they became a couple around 1958. Beginning in 1960 they traveled widely: they lived and worked together in Positano, Italy, for a summer, and for two years in Paris. Yektai's daughter, Nima, visited twice during the Paris years, and she recalled a trip to Venice with the sculptor Niki de Saint Phalle and her children Laura and Philip, and Getz's daughter Pat from her first marriage.

Getz and Yektai would themselves claim to be married—news accounts and obituaries called them husband and wife—but Yektai later privately conceded that the union was never made official.

Thanks in large part to Getz's keen curiosity and social ease, they counted among their friends Peggy Guggenheim, George and Ellie Poindexter, and Castelli (whom Yektai already knew well but with whom he grew closer with Getz, who had been Castelli's assistant for two years when he opened his gallery in a townhouse on 77th Street in 1957).

Getz championed Yektai's work. When they moved abroad to Paris, she acted as Yektai's letter writer and personal assistant, sorting out art transport issues, money transfers, and advocating for him when his financial situation turned precarious. During those years, Yektai made important connections in the European art world, securing solo exhibitions at prominent galleries in London, Paris, and Zurich, where in time he would find some of his most enduring collectors.

In 1960, Yektai spent several days at the Venice Biennale with artist friends, recalling fondly his friendship and several meals that went late into the night with Franz Kline, whose work was included in the Biennale that year. The ailing Kline would die of heart disease two years later.

Diverging ambitions drove Getz and Yektai apart in 1963, after a little more than four years together. She wanted to remain in Europe and travel, and Yektai returned to New York to settle into his work. "We were on different paths," he later remarked. Yektai would forever speak warmly of Getz and their time together. Her admiration of him was such that she continued to champion his work to the end of her life in 1992.

PORTRAITIST TO THE SHAH

Visa and legal residency issues and delays had dogged Yektai from the moment he had left Iran: in New York to get to Paris, then in Paris to get back to New York. So upon his first return from Paris in 1947, by a stroke of good timing and persistence, he got his name on a prospective roster of US citizenship candidates—scientists, writers, and artists. And after an interview on Ellis Island that same year he was sworn in as a full-fledged American, with President Harry Truman signing the document.

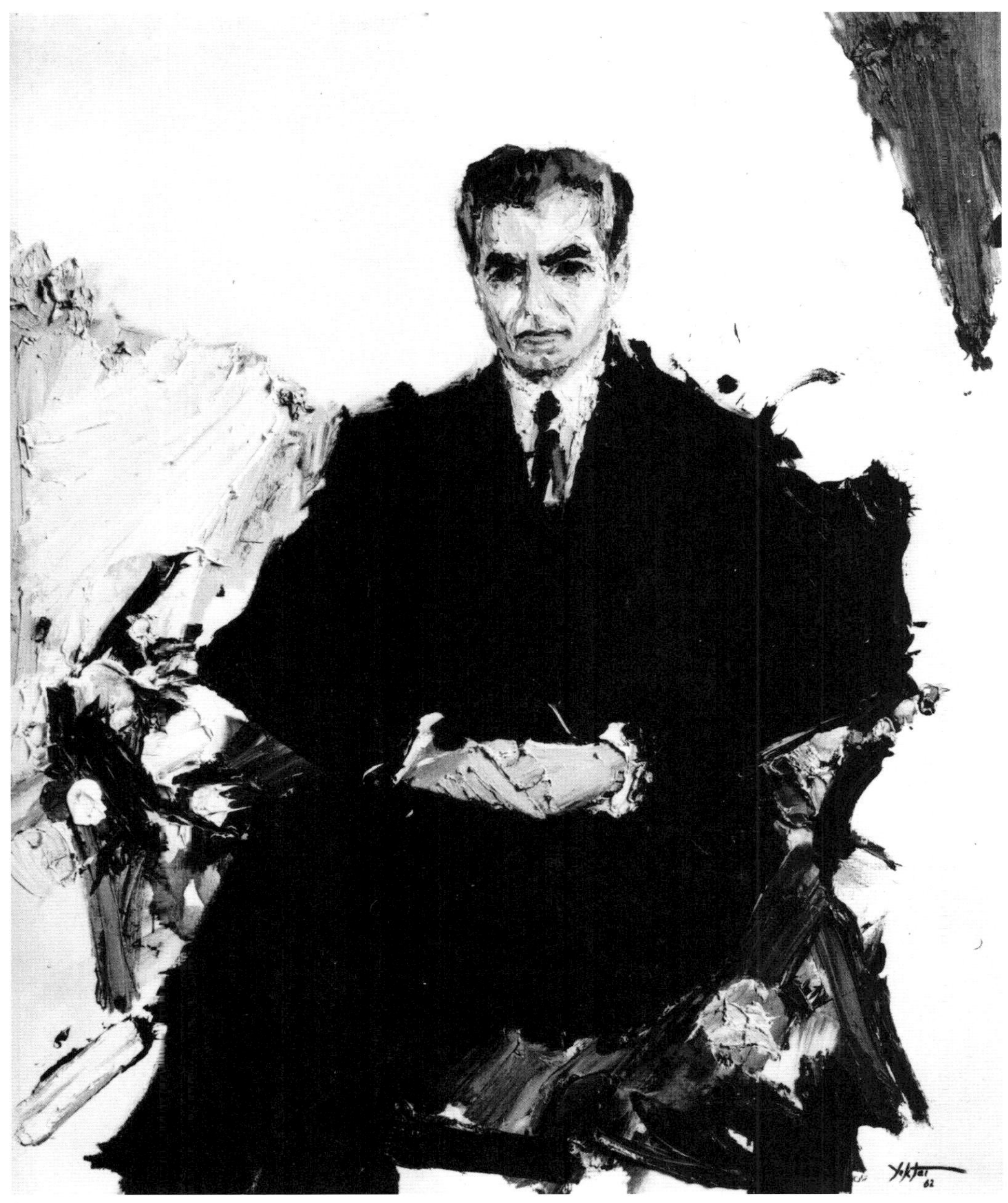

Portraiture was a major subject for Yektai. In 1961 a request came from Iran: the Shah would like Yektai to make his portrait. It took months for the Shah to show up for the sitting. The whereabouts of the portrait are unknown.

Citizenship gave Yektai peace of mind, and eliminated a huge element of aggravation and uncertainty from his life in America. But it hardly made him American—at least, not in the cultural sense. Yektai would remain Persian to the core forever. Yet, by the early 1960s, he was being embraced as an "American artist" of renown, and as an artist who not only understood the huge significance of the Abstract Expressionist movement but was a core contributor to it.

In 1959, the Museum of Modern Art included one of his paintings in an exhibition exploring "recent directions ... by American artists." Yektai's *Still Life D*, a large canvas of a recumbent figure, was one of seventy-four paintings selected for the show, out of some 10,000 entries from across the country. The museum would acquire the work for its collection. The exhibition, entitled *Recent Painting USA: The Figure*, with Yektai's painting and work by Larry Rivers, Elaine de Kooning, Leon Golub, and others, would travel over the course of several years to six major American museums.

In 1963, he was included in the 28th Biennial Exhibition of Contemporary American Painting at the Corcoran Gallery of Art in Washington, DC, followed by a series of solo exhibitions in Paris, Chicago, Cannes, Los Angeles, Detroit, San Francisco, and Scottsdale, Arizona.

Iran, meanwhile, was also claiming its native son. Amid Tehran's flourishing modern art scene in the early 1960s Yektai was regarded with pride as a somewhat mythic figure who had boldly ventured west to triumph as an artist. His reputation was such that a request arrived in 1961 from the second shah, Mohammad Reza: he wanted Yektai to make his portrait. Yektai agreed, flew to Iran, and began a long wait for his royal subject to pose.

After three months, the shah finally showed up, surprisingly alone, without any guards. Yektai was initially nervous, unsure how to behave around the powerful king who had rudely kept him waiting for so long. But the two men were the same age and an easy conversation began. The mood in the room lightened until Yektai, keenly aware of being alone with this targeted man, caught himself waving his palette knife aloft. Seized by the thought that the gesture and the tool might be threatening, he gingerly placed it on the ground and kicked it across the room. If the shah noticed, he didn't let on.

The portrait was largely completed in four days. The shah must have liked what he saw, as he asked the artist if he would paint his wife, the empress. Flattering as the request was, Yektai wasn't interested. He had waited long enough for the first sitting with the shah; who knows how long he would have to wait for the empress? And, he was ready to leave Iran. He declined politely and departed, taking the painting with him to finish in Paris.

Eventually Yektai sent the finished portrait to the shah, but its whereabouts remain a mystery.

Whether the shah and his empress took umbrage at Yektai's refusal to paint her portrait, he never knew. But their opinion of his place in the constellation of modern artists at the time was confirmed in New York in 1975. This time the Iranian court came to him.

Empress Farah Pahlavi had made it one of her missions to build a major Iranian modern art collection. As part of that effort she dispatched a team to Yektai's New York studio to select a painting. The group was led by her cabinet secretary and the Iranian diplomat Mehdi Vakil, with whom Yektai had a warm and long friendship. Also in attendance was a young American, Donna Stein, who had been hired by the Iranian court to assist in building the collection. Stein, who spent two years living in Tehran working on the project, would go on to become an art historian and curator. As fate would have it, decades later, she worked for a time at East Hampton's Guild Hall near Yektai's Sagaponack home, where she curated one of his few major late-in-life shows.

The Yektai still life they picked out that day in 1975 joined works by Picasso, Warhol, Lichtenstein, Braque, Hopper, and Rivera, among hundreds of others that comprise what is believed to be the most valuable modern art collection outside the United States and Western Europe. Assembled mostly over the course of a few years, its value is estimated to be somewhere in the realm of $3 billion. It resides in the Tehran Museum of Contemporary Art, whose design and construction Empress Farah also masterminded.

Despite Yektai's self-confidence, his success, and his disciplined work ethic, he had begun to struggle to sell work in the latter half of the 1960s. Even worse for his sales, if calls came in from gallerists for more of the kind of work that was selling, Yektai recoiled. He would never paint on demand; it went against everything he believed as an artist.

The struggle to make work that met his own expectations—and that he was willing to release for sale and exhibitions—was constant. During one earlier stretch of more than a year in the 1950s he pulled all his paintings from Grace Borgenicht's gallery and ceased communicating with Borgenicht altogether. During that period, he would paint and, unhappy with what he had made, he would destroy the work.

"It is like climbing a ladder," he would later explain to his son Nico. "Sometimes you must destroy each step so you can only keep climbing."

But if his work was not selling as well as he might have liked in the '60s, he had another new and important distraction. He found love.

NIKI

Yektai met Helene Kulukundis, known as Niki, at a party in New York City in 1963. Striking, bohemian-looking, with a tumble of dark, curly hair, Niki "felt a presence," she recalled. "I turned around and there he was. I wasn't sure what to say, so I asked: 'Do you have a light?'"

A lifelong cigar smoker, Yektai produced a flame. But the spark between them took a little longer. He was smitten, but Niki, some fourteen years his junior, took more time to warm. Yektai, always well dressed, was handsome, slender, with a slight scar on his cheek from a childhood accident. His manner was often serious; his smile, a gift.

"He grew on me," she said. "He was always a very dignified man ... There was an age difference. But he didn't look his age. He could have said he was any age."

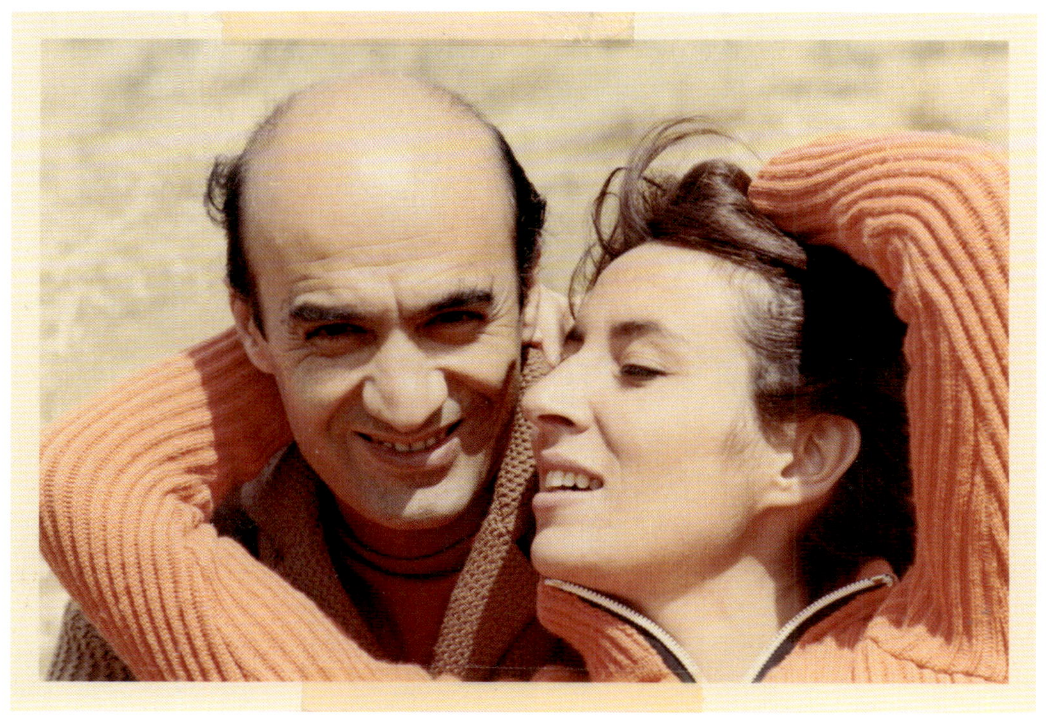

Yektai and Niki Kalukundis on an outing in the Iranian countryside in 1970. Their relationship and marriage endured for more than five decades, until Yektai's death. On the the couple's trip back to Iran in 1969–70 their first child, Nico, was born and Yektai completed his epic poem *Falgoosh*.

When she met Yektai she was twenty-eight, several years out of Smith College, living with a friend in New York and teaching.

"I didn't like Smith," she said. It had a clubby feel to it, and "I was unconventional—I didn't want to get married."

At their first meeting, Yektai asked if he could paint her portrait, which he did within a few days, the first of many portraits of Niki, who became his muse.

"I am a great artist and poet," Yektai told his young girlfriend. There was that line again. She found the remark amusing, even charming, for its astonishing conceit. "But soon," she said, "by living with his work, I completely agreed with him. I knew it was true, of course."

When the two met, Yektai was making plans for big changes in his life: a lengthy trip to Europe, perhaps a permanent move there. Instead, he decided to remain in New York to spend more time with Niki.

"From that day forward they were never apart again," their son Darius said.

Born in London and raised in Greenwich, Connecticut, by two Greek immigrants, Niki's father ran the family's immensely successful shipping business. Her mother was a force in Greenwich community affairs. Unlike their daughter, they were conventional, wanting to fit in to their new American home. When she presented Yektai to them, they instantly approved, taken by his dignified bearing and his success as an artist.

"My mother recognized what a gentleman Manouche was," she said. "They were just relieved to see me marry someone normal."

They married in 1969. The relationship was warm and easy. It yielded stability in Yektai's life in almost every respect. Although that very comfort also diminished his drive—and his need—to ply the commercial art world, it yielded other joys, children and a charmed life both in the city and the country.

In 1966, the still-unmarried couple purchased a property with a barn in Sagaponack, which would become Yektai's primary studio away from the city. It was the first of many property acquisitions in the place where they would live and he would work for the remainder of his life. Niki had spent summers in nearby Southampton and loved the South Fork of Long Island. Yektai also had visited artist friends there over the years, several of whom had settled in the area.

The potato fields, ponds, woods, sandy lanes, and beaches of Sagaponack became the family's haven. Every day when he was painting in Sagaponack, Niki would bring her husband lunch, and they would eat together, taking it outside his studio in the sunshine when the weather cooperated.

"We had a very simple life," Niki recalled. "Manouche would go every day to his studio, and we always had a walk and a picnic lunch. It was a life very focused on Manouche and his work."

The Yektais were friendly and socialized with art-world and intellectual heavyweights of the time who lived nearby, particularly Elaine and Bill de Kooning and Larry Rivers, Helen Frankenthaler, and Mark Rothko. Niki taught herself to cook traditional Persian food, and the pair often had dinner parties for their friends on Long Island. Known as a rare and light drinker in a heavy-drinking crowd, Yektai was often the designated end-of-evening driver for friends, his son Nico remembered, among them Betty Friedan, who lived in Sag Harbor.

Yektai's virtual sobriety, careful eating habits—little to no dairy, no fatty foods, and fruit every day—and his quiet, somewhat reclusive life could well have been the source of his longevity. He outlived almost all his contemporaries as, one by one, they slipped away, Rothko in 1970, de Kooning in 1997, Rivers in 2002, Frankenthaler in 2011, among many others.

Niki and Manoucher Yektai's life became to a great extent about family. It was something that had been absent up to this point in the artist's life—his first child, Nima, had been raised by her mother and stepfather. On a long visit to Iran with Niki in 1969 that extended into 1970, Niki gave birth to the couple's first child, Nico. Two more, fraternal

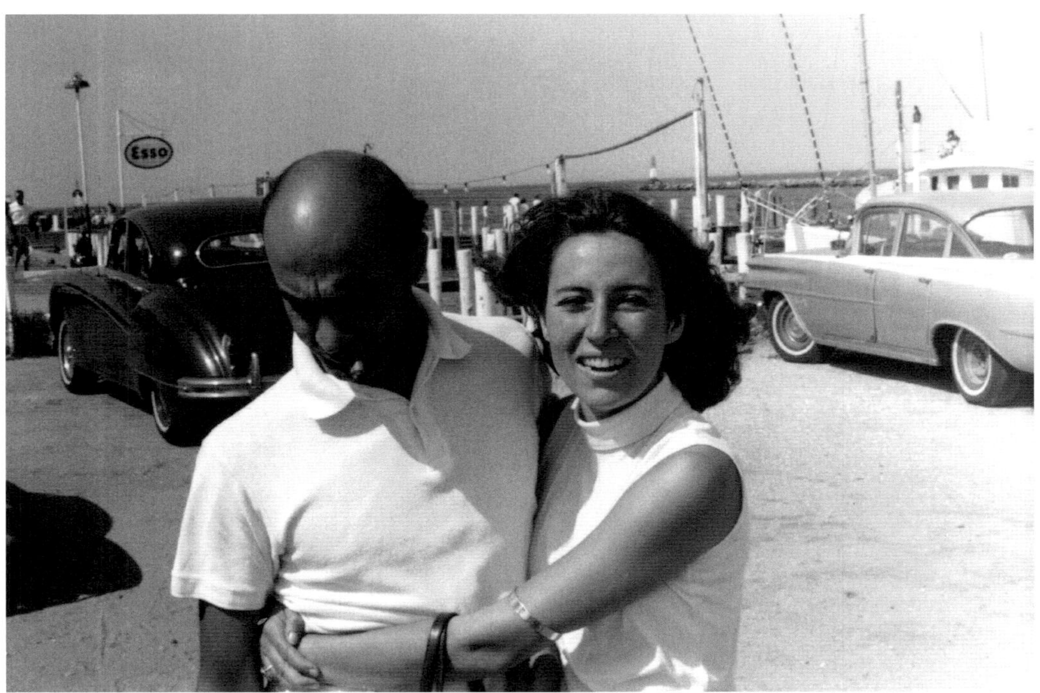

Niki and Yektai adored the South Fork of Long Island, their adopted home.
Montauk fishing harbor, 1970s.

twins (twins run in the Kulukundis family; Niki herself is an identical twin), Darius and Mahan, born in New York, would follow in 1973.

Although Yektai had a circle of mostly artist and writer friends, he wasn't particularly interested in having an active social life. He didn't have any hobbies or, despite being a gifted athlete as a young man, athletic pastimes. After an outing with a friend to play competitive croquet at a fancy club nearby, he was invited to join the club by some of the members who were impressed by his skills. He declined. It would take away time from making art, he explained.

"He never wanted to socialize," Niki said. "We would not have gone out if it wasn't for me."

His children were raised immersed in their father's passion and devotion to art. Through his disciplined, intense way of working and observing the world he entrusted to them the tools to witness life more deeply, and to share it. In his studio in the city after school, in Sagaponack, around the dinner table, conversations were about art and art history, and poetry, and the natural world. Vacations were spent not lolling on beaches or on ski mountains but visiting the great museums of Europe. "It was an education, always," said Darius, who became a painter, and his brother Nico a sculptural furniture maker. "He was always searching, in his painting, in his poetry, for his language, his voice. He shared that personal conversation with us."

Yektai would remind his children, "I am forever a student," and his message was obvious. One of the gifts from his father, Nico said, was that "I understood the pursuit, which is to always look for something more and different and original in yourself, and then to present that to the world through your work."

POETRY AND THE UNKNOWN

Yektai's creative impulses see-sawed between painting and poetry. He would spend weeks and months, sometimes years, doing one or the other, never the two at the same time.

"When I write, I cannot paint," he told the *New York Times* in 1983. "When I paint, I cannot write, and I miss poetry. I wish ... I had two different lives to spend on both of them."

No one who knew Yektai can explain precisely how each medium satisfied his artistic impulses, and what kind of divine timing drew him to one or the other. But there were clues: his paintings, as critics and artists would repeat over the course of his life, were to a great extent all about the intangible, about beauty, "finding the hand of god in everything," as his friend Fadaienia said.

Great paintings, he would tell his family and friends, should capture and evoke the indescribable "unknown." His poetry, meanwhile, enabled him to be more direct, to lament, to rage, to question, to pine—with the kind of precision only available with words.

"Three fourths of the guests are bored," he would write in a poem in 1959, translated into English by Iraj Anvar and Darius Yektai, "The Demon Over the Gates of the Bathhouse," which protests changes in Iran at the time.

> The conversations don't take root,
> The fame of one person agitates the moods of the others,
> Man feeds three quarters of the day to loneliness,
> He gives two thirds of the night to sleeplessness.

Yektai's late-'60s return to Iran was intended as a visit to his mother. Once there, however, he went to work finishing an epic poem, *Falgoosh*, a complex commentary on Iranian society.

The visit to Iran was a painful time for the artist. He found himself disenchanted with his homeland, an outsider in his own land, uneasy with the corruption and corrosion of the traditional Persian culture and what he saw as a civil society in turmoil. The ancient Iran he longed for, and that he had once belonged to, was vanishing.

"He loved the old villages and the countryside," Niki later reflected. "But he was not happy in Tehran."

An experience from his youth haunted him. He lived in fear that the course of his life could be swiftly and heedlessly undercut by authorities with indiscriminate and limitless power. As a teenager Yektai had been ordered to be transferred from his school and sent to another. He was separated brusquely from friends and familiar teachers from one day to the next. The move had come in the middle of the school year with no explanation from administrators and staff.

Later he learned that his transfer was ordered by the family of an Iranian prince. The prince's volleyball team had been trounced in a recent match by the high-jumping Yektai and his school's team. Yektai's crime was to have been the best player on the winning side. Humiliated, the prince's family broke Yektai's team apart to ensure the end of its winning prowess.

"He was always nervous in Iran; that's the story he would tell me," Niki said.

Falgoosh, however, was a hit in Iran the moment it was published, as a poem can only be in poetry-loving Iran. (All Yektai's poems were originally written in Farsi; thirty-eight were translated in two collections by Anvar, with assistance with the English from Darius Yektai; *Falgoosh* was never translated.) It is told in the voice of a storyteller who is listening to the conversations of passersby in the street and, from their words, conjuring their lives. The ritual of Falgoosh is a mostly extinct tradition in which young women eavesdrop to understand the lives of others, and interpret their own fortunes.

"*Falgoosh* is an excuse to criticize the shortcomings and injustices of Iranian society and is mostly a commentary on the negative aspects of Iranian thinking: prejudices, racism, classism, and the attitude toward the other and otherness," explained Anvar.

Almost the moment the poem was published it was swept up by celebrated Iranian film and theatrical star Parviz Sayyad and made into a play.

"*Falgoosh* was the beginning of my long journey and the turning point in my career," Sayyad said.

The first performance of *Falgoosh*, the theatrical version, was at the Shiraz Festival of the Arts in 1970. It would later have runs for Persian audiences in Tehran, Los Angeles, and New York.

OUT OF FAVOR

Precisely when Yektai began to pull away from the work of selling paintings isn't entirely clear. The softening of sales of his work that had begun in the 1960s deepened in the 1970s.

The first major turning point came with George and Ellie Poindexter. Their relationship with Yektai was warm and intimate, judging from a huge trove of archived correspondence. But at the end of 1964 the artist and the gallery parted ways. The most obvious explanation for the split, and one Niki and others advance, is that his work was simply falling out of favor. Letters at the time from the Poindexters to the artist reflect that reality, apologizing for lackluster sales.

The art market by the mid-1960s had begun a dynamic shift toward Pop Art and Minimalism, whose aesthetics and spirit were worlds away from Yektai's. He was no fan, but more to the point, he didn't understand the new currents.

"Don't you ever just want to paint an airplane?" Larry Rivers once asked him.

Yektai replied, "I want to paint an apple until it flies."

Ellie Poindexter explained what she saw happening in the art world this way in a 1970 interview for the Smithsonian Institition's Archives of American Art: "I felt it changed very much since I first went into it. It's become much more immediate and commercial ... It seems to me that the fashions have more impact now ... I think some [painters] are making more of a success financially because they are doing what the museums want at the moment, you know, the new things."

Yektai's final exhibition at Poindexter, in October 1964, consisted mostly of portraits and paintings of figures done in his inimitable

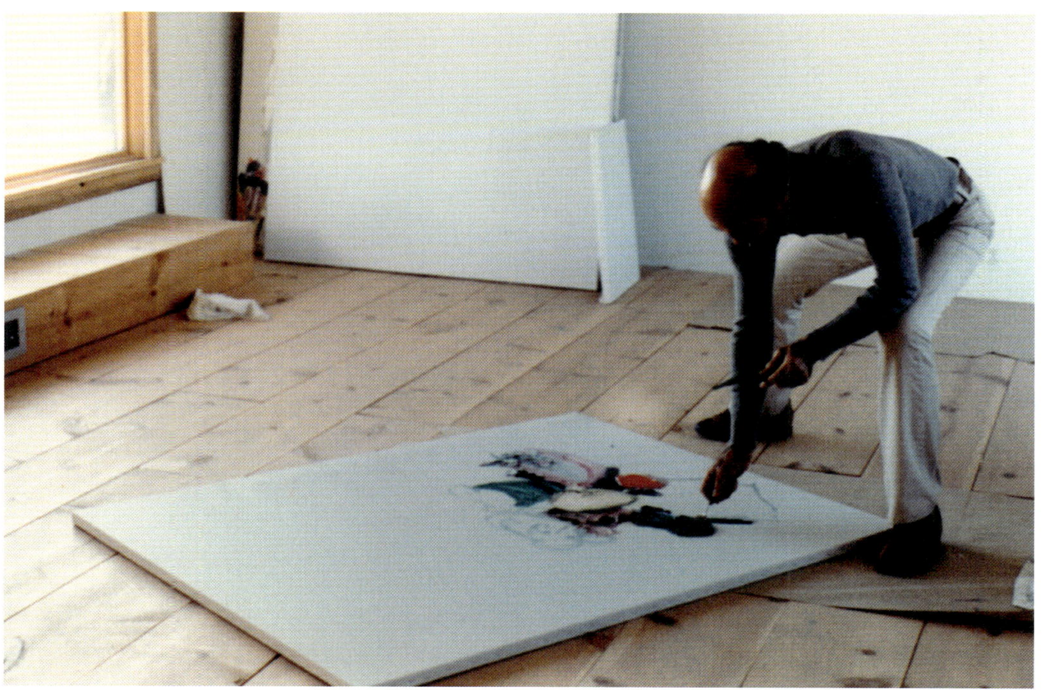

After his marriage to Niki, Bridgehampton and later Sagaponack became Yektai's home.
Yektai painting in his Sagaponack studio, ca. 1979.

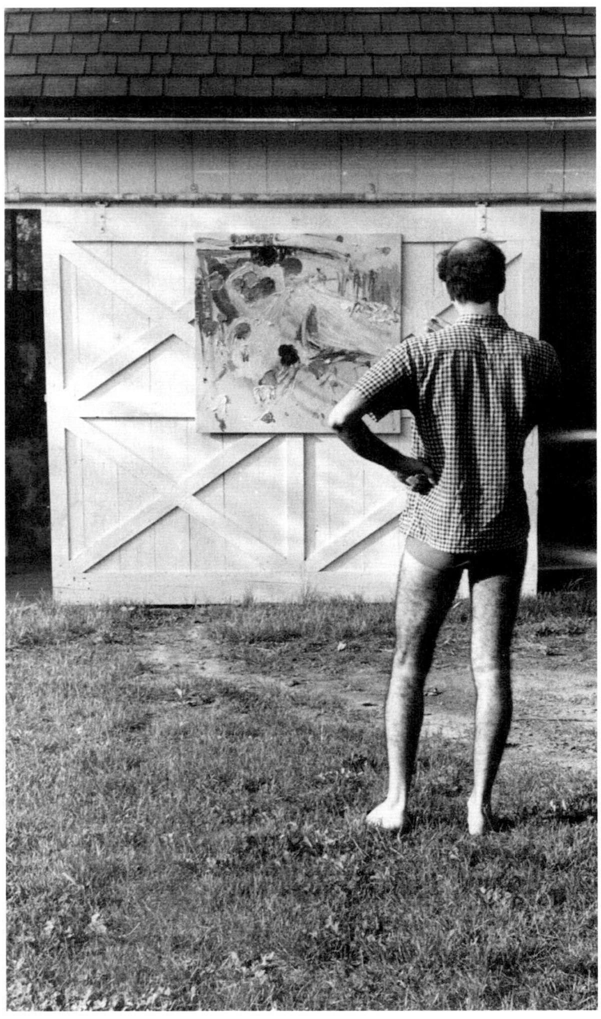

Examining a painting outside his Ocean Road studio barn, Bridgehampton, ca. 1978

abstract-infused style of broad, creamy brushstrokes. The beauty in the gallery was undeniable even as outside, in America, huge cultural and social changes were unfolding, changes that other artists of his generation were seeking to capture.

The historic March on Washington, led by Martin Luther King Jr., had taken place in 1963, leading to the passage of the groundbreaking 1964 Civil Rights Act. The women's rights movement was by then in a full roar: Betty Friedan had just published *The Feminine Mystique*. Some 23,000 US troops were fighting in the distant and terrible war in Vietnam. Man had begun to travel beyond the earth's atmosphere for the first time and we were getting our first, captivating look at our planet in photographs from outer space. And a new sound, rock 'n' roll, seized the nation. Thousands of screaming fans greeted the Beatles at JFK airport in 1964 and more than seventy million tuned in to watch them on the *Ed Sullivan Show* as the group launched the British Invasion music revolution and dominated the airwaves and the charts.

Meanwhile, the art world was witnessing the meteoric rise of Andy Warhol, Robert Rauschenberg, Roy Lichtenstein, Frank Stella, David Hockney, Jasper Johns, and James Rosenquist, among others. Suddenly, work was as simple as two shapes or a target on a canvas, or as garish as gigantic comic-strip-style images. Artists were using photography and modern cultural references in their paintings. In 1964, Warhol had just finished his *Death and Disaster* series of paintings inspired in part by photos of automobile accidents, the *Shot Marilyns*, consisting of four canvases of Marilyn Monroe shot through the head, and *Race Riot*, inspired by photographs of civil rights demonstrations. Lichtenstein by then was equally on a tear, churning out his huge parody paintings such as his now-famous *Whaam!*, *Varoom!*, and *Sleeping Girl*. Rauschenberg's 1963 *Retroactive II* silkscreen featured JFK and an astronaut.

"We felt the moral crisis of a world in shambles, a world devastated by a great depression and a fierce world war," Barnett Newman said in 1967. "And it was impossible at that time to paint the kind of painting that we were doing—flowers, reclining nudes, and people playing the cello ... So we actually began ... as if painting were not only dead but had never existed."

Reviewers had already begun to struggle to place Yektai's work. Commenting on a 1962 portrait show, the *New York Herald Tribune* more than hinted that he was out of step, comparing him to two dead, lesser-known, turn-of-the-century European painters: "The largeness and swashbuckling are still there," the newspaper said of Yektai's technique, "but the results look more like Boldini or Vertès than de Kooning or Kline."

Yektai's 1964 portraits at Poindexter were nevertheless warmly received by reviewers. And his fame in the mid-1960s—in some ways a kind of fame he likely did not welcome—was undeniable.

"Shipping heiress Helene Kulukundis and painter Manoucher Yektai are the picture of togetherness," wrote columnist Joseph X. Dexter for the lead in the *New York World-Telegram and the Sun*'s gossip-page coverage of the October 1964 opening. "His portrait of the dark-eyed post-deb is a standout in his recent show at the Poindexter Gallery."

After parting ways with Poindexter, Yektai only showed on three more occasions in New York City. He remained modestly popular in Europe, until at some point in the 1970s when his two galleries there dropped him. Just as it was to belong to Poindexter's stable of artists in New York, to be represented in Europe by Semiha Huber's gallery in Zurich and Godfrey Pilkington's Piccadilly Gallery in London meant you were among the most respected artists of the moment. But in succession Huber and Pilkington informed Yektai that it was over.

He greeted the grim news with disappointment but also with a kind of resignation, almost as if he knew it was coming, as if it had been foretold.

The news from Europe wasn't the final domino. Almost a decade of isolation followed—with the exception of shows at the Elaine Benson Gallery in Bridgehampton—before he returned to the New York City art scene in 1981 for a run at Alex Rosenberg's gallery. Rosenberg remembered it partly as an arrangement instigated by Ilse Getz, who had remained one of Yektai's ardent advocates.

The exhibition—Yektai's final solo show in Manhattan—produced what Rosenberg reported were "modest sales" and, far worse from Yektai's

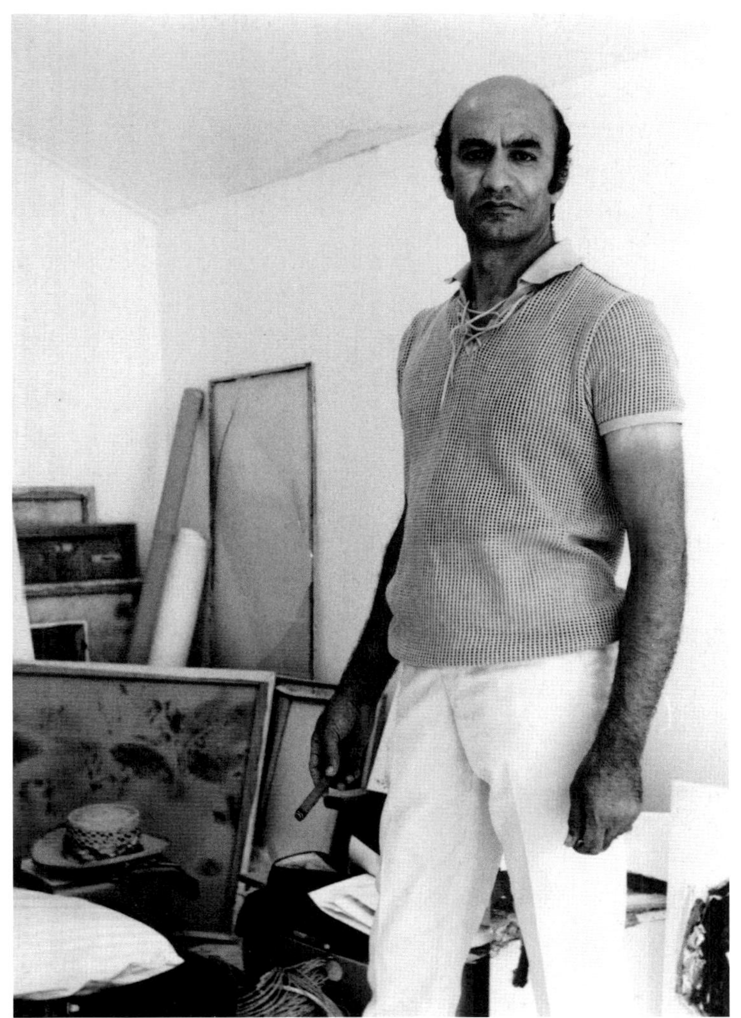

Yektai, in his Ocean Road studio, Bridgehampton, NY, ca. 1978

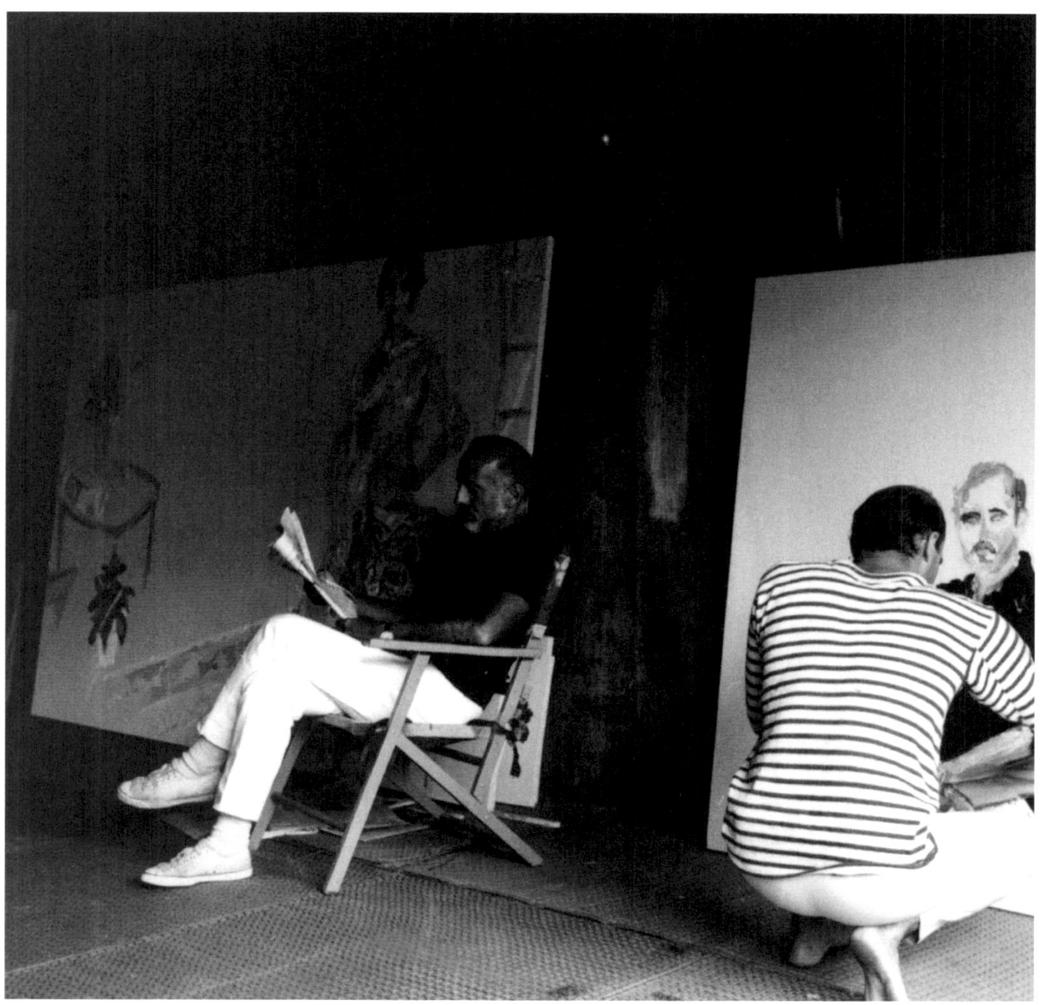

Yektai painting a portrait of Jerome Robbins, the theater and film producer and director, Bridgehampton, NY, ca. 1972

viewpoint, no reviews. Even more demoralizing than a takedown by the art world, his return to a major Manhattan gallery had been ignored altogether.

"That's what he cared about most, the reviews," Niki recalled of her husband after the Rosenberg show. "He was heartbroken. I'd never seen him so heartbroken."

After that, he stopped showing and selling altogether. The pride that drove him became the thing that pulled him away.

And, with Niki as his spouse and partner, retreating from the commercial art world was a viable choice. She had the financial resources to free her artist husband from the need to kowtow to buyers and gallerists—from the need to sell.

What's more, Niki was not in the art world. She adored her painter husband and his creations, and relished his artist life. She also pushed her husband to show his work. But she wasn't confident in taking the lead to navigate the galleries and collectors or to promote his art, so she left the driving of his career to him—"which he didn't do," she was quick to say.

"He never cultivated the galleries," she said. "He didn't charm them or anything like that. He wasn't like that. He wasn't a diplomat. He didn't want to promote himself. He was shy and very proud, too proud to ask for anything. He just wanted to paint and write his poems."

One wonders how things might have turned out differently if financial need had remained a factor.

"If you don't like me, what can I do?" Yektai wrote in "Unmatched," a poem penned on a trip to the Adirondacks in September 1998, when he was in his late seventies. It's not clear that the poem is directed at his disappointment as a painter, but the words and their timing are striking:

> The universe has tied me to seeking,
> I am the branded slave of moving on.

Yektai almost never expressed regrets about the course of his career. One of these few moments emerged in a conversation with his daughter, Nima, in his final years. They were discussing the significant number of paintings he had amassed during his long, late-in-life absence from galleries and the art world, when Yektai noted wryly, "Maybe I went too far." Nima took it to mean that he had stubbornly isolated himself from the art world for too long.

AMERICAN BUT PERSIAN

For three-quarters of a century, Yektai lived, worked, and raised a family in the United States, but he was never American.

"He was inspired by America, and he came here for that inspiration, but his soul was completely Persian," Niki said.

That abiding Persian soul emerged powerfully in his work in the final third of his life. Bright pots of flowers, moody landscapes, portraits of people he loved, bowls of fruit so common in traditional Persian households, his use of color and patterns, the paintings he produced during his last decades are brusque and masculine even as they are tender and reflective. They burst with color: bright, complex celebrations of rural and everyday scenes and the people in his life. Some might think it a stretch to see anything distinctly Persian in any of this, but those who knew him see his ancestral roots there.

"Inherent in his painting he retained his Persian heritage," Donna Stein, the curator and art historian, said. "He depicted ideas with a different scale and intensity as if he were blowing up little units of Persian miniatures ..."

"The way he did his paintings is the way he did his poetry," his friend Alimorad Fadaienia observed. "The roots of it are Iran: the reds are the reds of Isfahan, the blues of the tiles we see everywhere in Iran." Yektai's spoken English was rich with the immense vocabulary of someone who studied and loved language. But it was forever strongly accented. He regularly dropped articles in his speech, common among Iranian speakers of English. His Persian, by contrast, remained full and melodic, an ancient tongue that might still be found in the Iranian countryside but is otherwise gone.

"For me, to hear him speak, to hear him read his poems was like a bridge to another Iran, an Iran before decadence. He was the embodiment of Persian culture ... he had kept the cultural integrity of seventy and eighty years ago," the Persian linguist and writer Iraj Anvar said.

Yektai, however, didn't pass on his mastery of Farsi to his children. None of them speak Persian, nor does his wife of fifty-two years.

"He wanted us to have one language," Nico said of himself and his two siblings. "He didn't want us divided between two. I think that had to do with his relationship to his mother tongue. He wanted us to have the same intense relationship (with one language) in case any of us chose to be writers. Since we were raised here, it must be English."

Stein, the curator and art historian who had met Yektai in 1975, circled back into Yektai's life in 1998, for an event—his only retrospective, which took place in his adopted hometown—whose significance is undeniable. With the artist then in his late seventies, she curated an exhibition of his work—fifty years of paintings—at Guild Hall in East Hampton. The exhibition was a critical success, praised in a lengthy piece by the art critic Phyllis Braff in the *New York Times*. The *East Hampton Star*'s respected and longtime art critic, Rose Slivka, was so taken by the show, she dropped all pretense.

"*Open Window*, true to its title," she wrote of one of the paintings, "is riveting in its energy and sheer—sorry, folks, but there's no other word for it—beauty."

The Guild Hall show marked the first of several notable late-in-life highs for Yektai. Interest in his work had persisted in the Middle East and Europe where collectors had been early and, despite the loss of his two European galleries, remained consistent. A twenty-first-century surge came from those markets. Paintings from various stages of Yektai's career began to appear at auction in London and Tehran in the 2000s, drawing renewed tributes in the art world and record sales prices.

When one of his pictures was brought out at Tehran Auction, an independent Iranian auction house, and the name Manoucher Yektai was announced, the auctioneer had to pause his introduction as the Iranian audience rose to its feet and broke into long, warm, spontaneous applause. *Untitled*, a big splash of red flowers with green stems in a vase against a white canvas, set yet another record for a Yektai at the time. In 2017, Guild Hall again invited him back for a show entitled *Yektai*, in which he shared the spotlight with his two sons, Nico, who exhibited his sculptural furniture, and Darius, his paintings. The exhibition was a family celebration and, for any father, a triumph: the walls of the museum hung with Manoucher's portraits of his family. But, true to form, Yektai, ninety-six at the time, kept his distance, leaving the spotlight to his children.

A few years later, in 2019, Sotheby's London gallery held a survey exhibition of Yektai's work, including recent paintings that had never been seen outside the family. One of the organizers, the writer and art historian Roxane Zand, a Persian woman who had known Yektai since the 1970s, characterized him as "underrepresented in art historical terms," and "one of the enduring stars of the Iranian art market."

By then Yektai was unwilling to travel, rarely leaving his home on Long Island, and he didn't attend the show. Faithful to his manner, he only quietly welcomed these various moments of recognition. His heart was set on much more significant recognition to come.

IN SIX HUNDRED YEARS

In 2016, Yektai put his brush and palette down and never finished another painting—except one. A physical artist, he would often paint squatting, or on his hands and knees, his canvases on the ground. Even on upright canvases, the work of applying paint thickly and sculpturally required strength and precision.

"He just decided he couldn't execute as he wanted to anymore," his son Nico said.

One painting remained in the works almost to his final breath, a still life in the foreground set against a more distant landscape. He had placed it on a wall in his home within easy reach, with paints, brushes, and palette knife nearby. In his house filled with finished works, every day he would go to that one painting, and dab at it, adding just a little more of his signature sculptural paint one touch at a time.

The end came quietly. One day Niki, sitting next to him in their living room, noticed Yektai resting motionless. He was smiling even as he had stopped breathing. To that final moment, Niki Yektai was lovingly and happily at her husband's side.

In contrast to the tall and reserved Yektai, Niki is a vivacious, diminutive woman, whose sparkle is undiminished in her eighties. She is nothing but admiring of and still girlishly smitten by the man who was the center of her life for almost sixty years. The affection was mutual. Every wall in the house they shared is decorated with Yektai's work—with a few of their two sons' pieces here and there. The view from the living room, across a lawn and landscape that Yektai himself designed, is smattered with Pepperidge trees. Beyond that, a shimmering tongue of Sagaponack Pond, and, out of sight, the Atlantic Ocean.

If Yektai worried about his legacy, he spoke of it only in vague but optimistic terms. He left behind a significant collection of paintings, many completed after 1975. They combine all his experience, instincts, and skill: the use of materials, the sublime combination and interplay of abstraction and figuration. Most of it has only been seen by a few people.

"It's his best work," Darius declared. "He'd come fully into his own. He was a poet, and the paintings he created in the last part of his life are his most poetic."

What will become of Yektai's legacy? He made no plan, left no instructions for what to do, or how to reach the heights that he believed from the start of his life he would rightly reach.

Yektai often spoke of Paul Cézanne. He revered the French painter above all others and doubtless took comfort in Cézanne's story, which has certain parallels to his own. Cézanne had a tumultuous relationship with the official arbiters of contemporary art in his time. He was a rebel and not particularly sociable. And, for the last stretch of his life, Cézanne withdrew and painted in relative isolation. More to the point, Cézanne's fame and the desirability of his work soared after his death.

Will Yektai's work ultimately achieve a similar degree of recognition? If we are to take him on faith, yes. But, by his own count, such an ascent could take hundreds of years, which might seem like an eternity although, for Yektai, great art transcended the figment, the construct, of time. He would often remind his children that his favorite poet, the hugely popular Persian mystic Rumi, was for centuries known to relatively few. Rumi became a household name only when his poems appeared in English translations in the early 1900s—six centuries after his death. Yektai would say of his own legacy: "I am on the six-hundred-year plan."

"You can't destroy great work," his sons remember him telling them. "It will be here until the world gets it."

Author's note: This account of Manoucher Yektai's life is the result of interviews conducted in fall 2020 and winter 2021, many hours of videotaped interviews with the artist in his lifetime, oral histories, documents, books, and newspaper and magazine articles. All quotes attributed to Yektai are taken from taped interviews recorded by his family.

Sources:

Anvar, Iraj, and Biddle Duke. "Iraj Anvar, Writer, Theatrical Producer, Translator, Persian Language Teacher, Yektai Friend." Interview, February 16, 2021.

Ashbery, John. "Manoucher Yektai." *Aujourd'hui: Art et Architecture*, no. 31 (May 1961): 24–25.

Braff, Phyllis. "Affirming Vibrant Freedom of Method." *New York Times*, May 31, 1998, 14.

Cummings, Paul. "Oral History Interview with Elinor F. Poindexter, 1970 Sept. 9." Archives of American Art, Smithsonian Institution.

Fadaienia, Alimorad, and Biddle Duke. "Alimorad Fadaienia, Writer, Yektai Friend." Interview, February 28, 2021.

Farmanfarmaian, Monir Shahroudy, and Zara Houshmand. *A Mirror Garden: A Memoir*. New York: Anchor Books, 2008.

Guild Hall. *Manoucher Yektai, Paintings 1951–1977*. East Hampton, NY: Guild Hall, 1998.

Isham, Nima Farmanfarmaian, and Biddle Duke. "Nima Isham, Daughter." Interview, February 6, 2020.

Jahan Bakhsh, Zahra. "5th Tehran Auction, Manoucher Yektai." June 16, 2016. YouTube video, 3:15. www.youtube.com/watch?v=BJGvWrTDQvw.

Manoucher Yektai at the Request of His Family. Directed by Nico Yektai. April 23, 2019. YouTube video, 53:03. www.youtube.com/watch?v=D-G9eJNmDWo. (The series includes six video interviews available upon request from Manoucher Yektai's family.)

McEvilley, Thomas. "Manoucher Yektai – Abstract Expressionist Painter 1950s – Present." Yektai.com. Accessed January–February 2021. https://yektai.com/.

"Poindexter Gallery Records, 1931–1985, bulk 1955–1978." Archives of American Art, Smithsonian Institution.

Preston, Stuart. "Art: Action Paintings of Manoucher Yektai Show." *New York Times*, April 13, 1962, 27.

Rosenberg, Alex, and Biddle Duke. "Alex Rosenberg, Gallerist, Art Consultant." Interview, December 26, 2020.

Sampson, Christine. "Father-Son Legacy Exhibit and Poetry Reading Coming to Guild Hall." *Sag Harbor Express*, October 11, 2017.

Sayyad, Parviz. "Parviz Sayyad, Film and Theatrical Producer, Actor, Filmmaker." Email exchange, February 20, 2021.

Slivka, Rose C. S. "From the Studio." *East Hampton Star*, May 21, 1998.

Sotheby's. *Manoucher Yektai, The Night Is Your Day, April 25–30, 2019*. London: Sotheby's, 2019.

Stein, Donna, and Biddle Duke. "Donna Stein, Writer, Middle Eastern and Contemporary Art Consultant and Expert, Curator and Author: The Empress and I: How an Ancient Empire Collected, Rejected and Rediscovered Modern Art." Interview, December 28, 2020.

Van Gelder, Lawrence. "A Studio in My Pocket." *New York Times*, January 9, 1983, LI2.

Yektai. Directed by Shirin Saghaie. VOA Portraits, June 4, 2012. YouTube video, 30:00. www.youtube.com/watch?v=TcH0fNqMHM4.

Yektai, Darius, and Biddle Duke. "Darius Yektai, Son." Interviews, October 2020–April 2021.

Yektai, Manoucher. "Crooked and Uncomfortable Witness, Poems 1956–1963." Translation by Iraj Anvar and Darius Yektai, 1996.

———. "Paint Box, Poems 1997–2006." Translation by Iraj Anvar and Darius Yektai, 2006.

Yektai, Nico, and Biddle Duke. "Nico Yektai, Son." Interviews, October 2020–April 2021.

Yektai, Niki, and Biddle Duke. "Niki Yektai, Wife." Interviews, October 2020–April 2021.

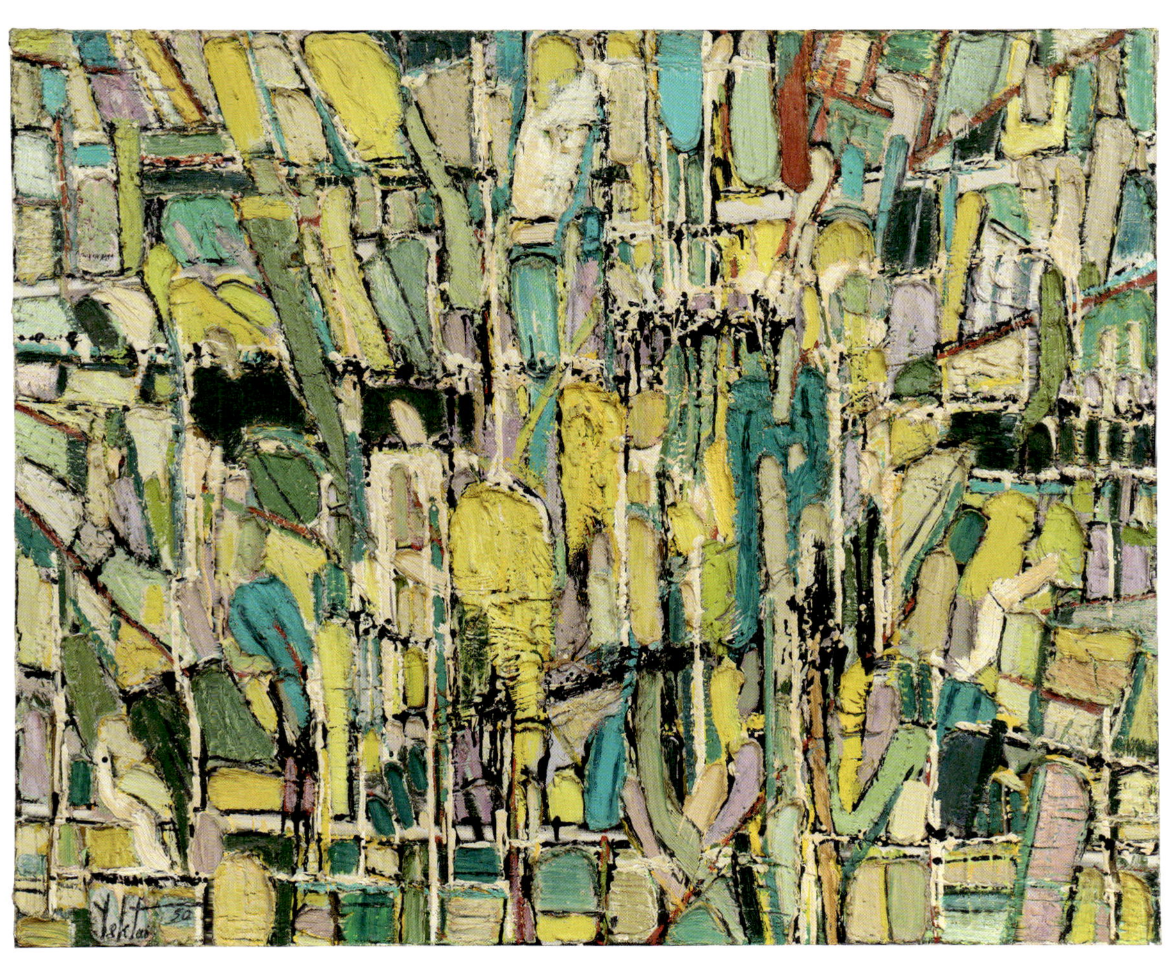

Untitled, 1950, oil on canvas, 49 × 59½ inches (124.5 × 151.1 cm)

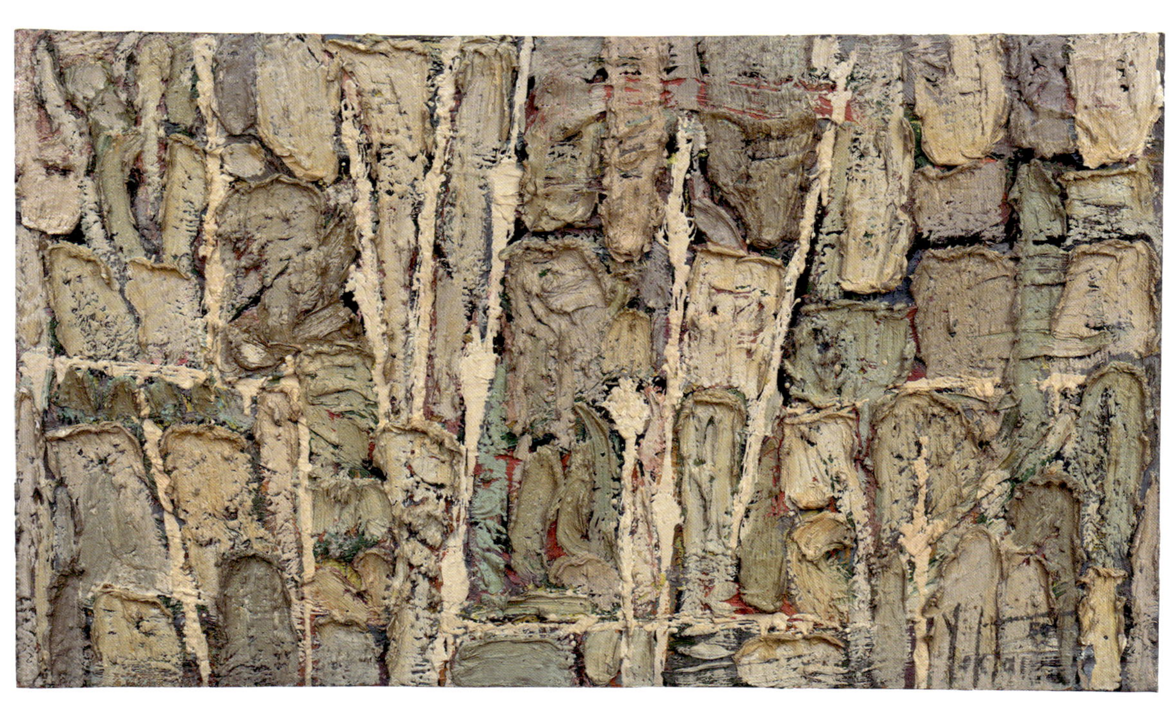

 Untitled, 1950, oil on canvas, 29¾ × 50 inches (75.6 × 127 cm)

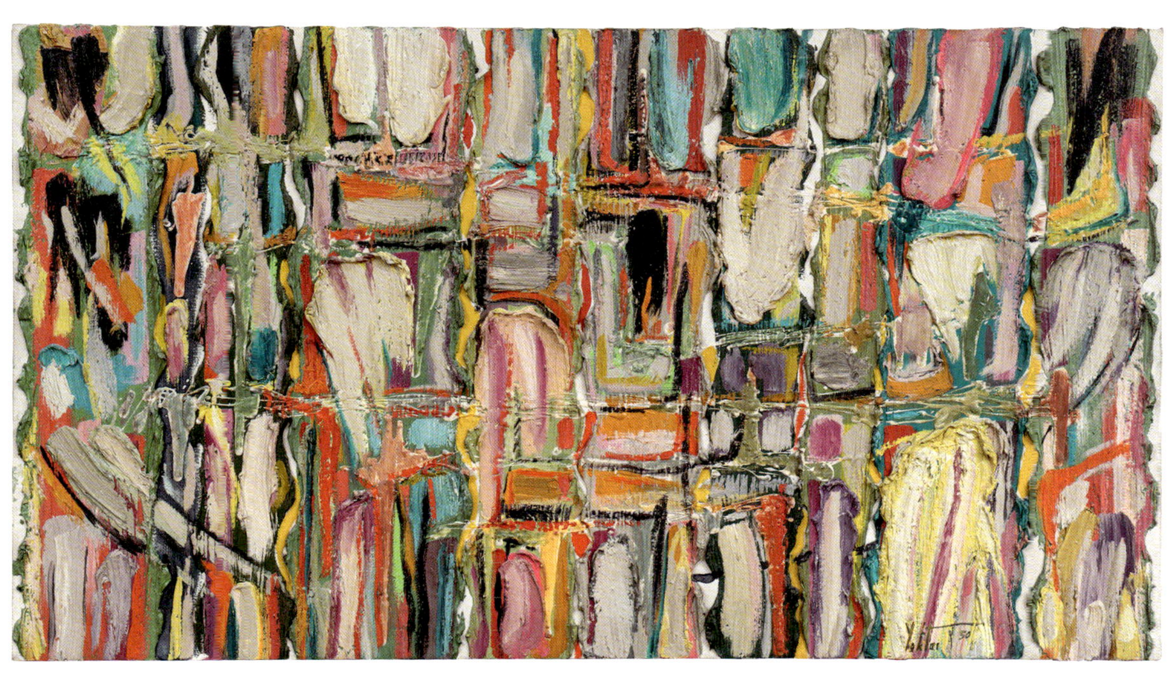

Untitled, 1950, oil on canvas, 23 × 40 inches (58.4 × 101.6 cm)

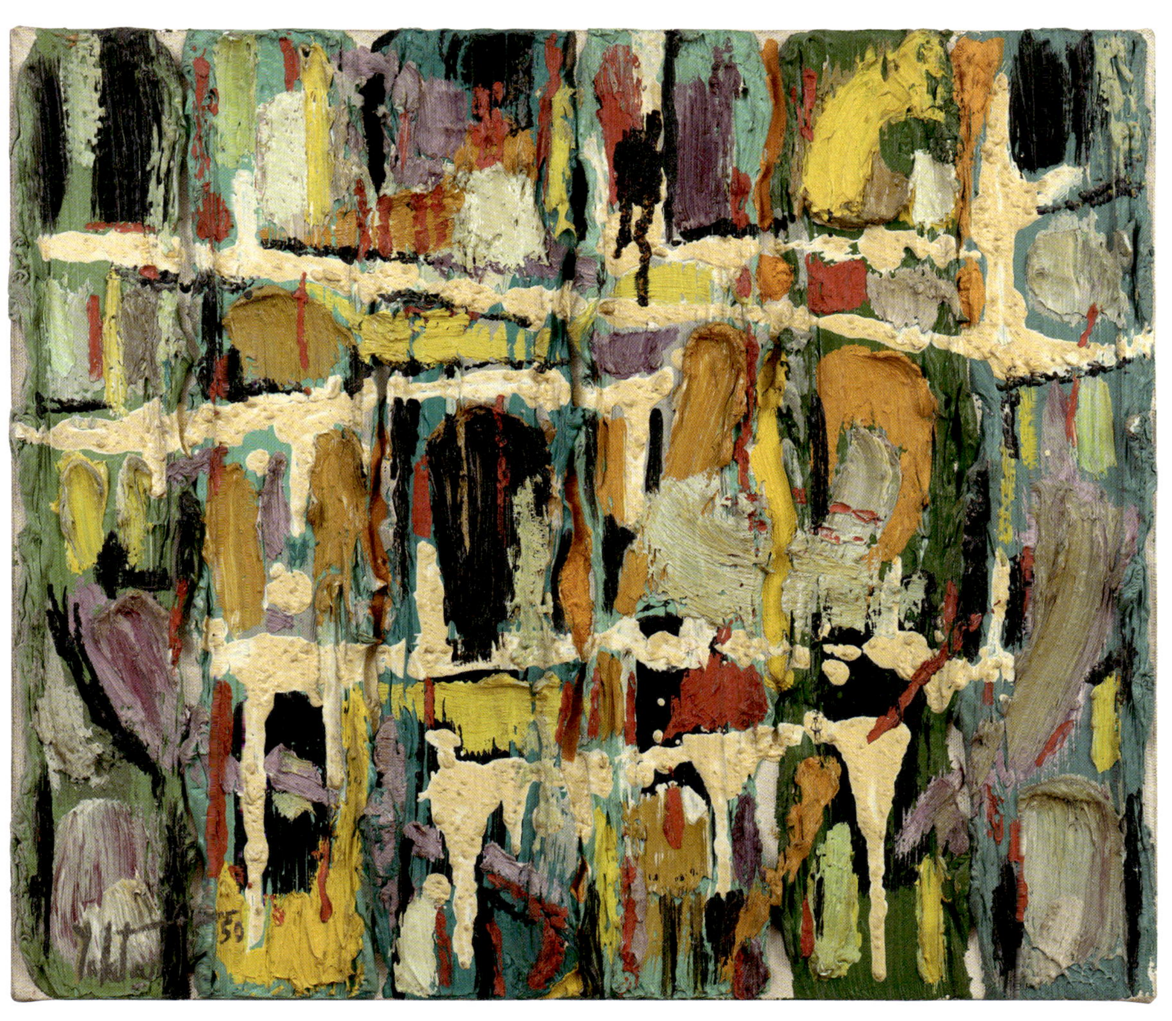

Untitled, 1950, oil on canvas, 14 × 16 inches (36 × 41 cm)

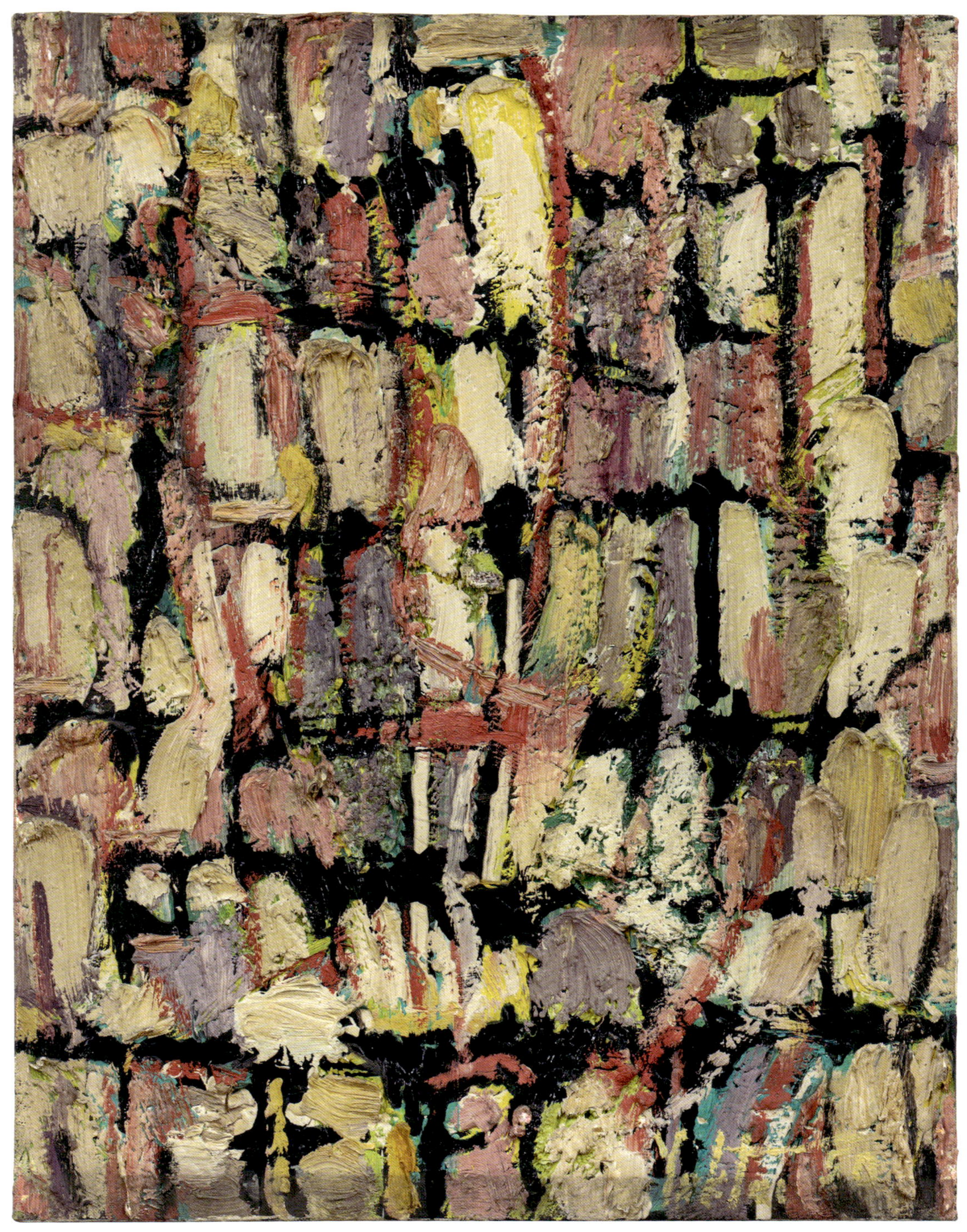

The City II, 1950, oil on canvas, 20 × 15¼ inches (50.8 × 38.7 cm)

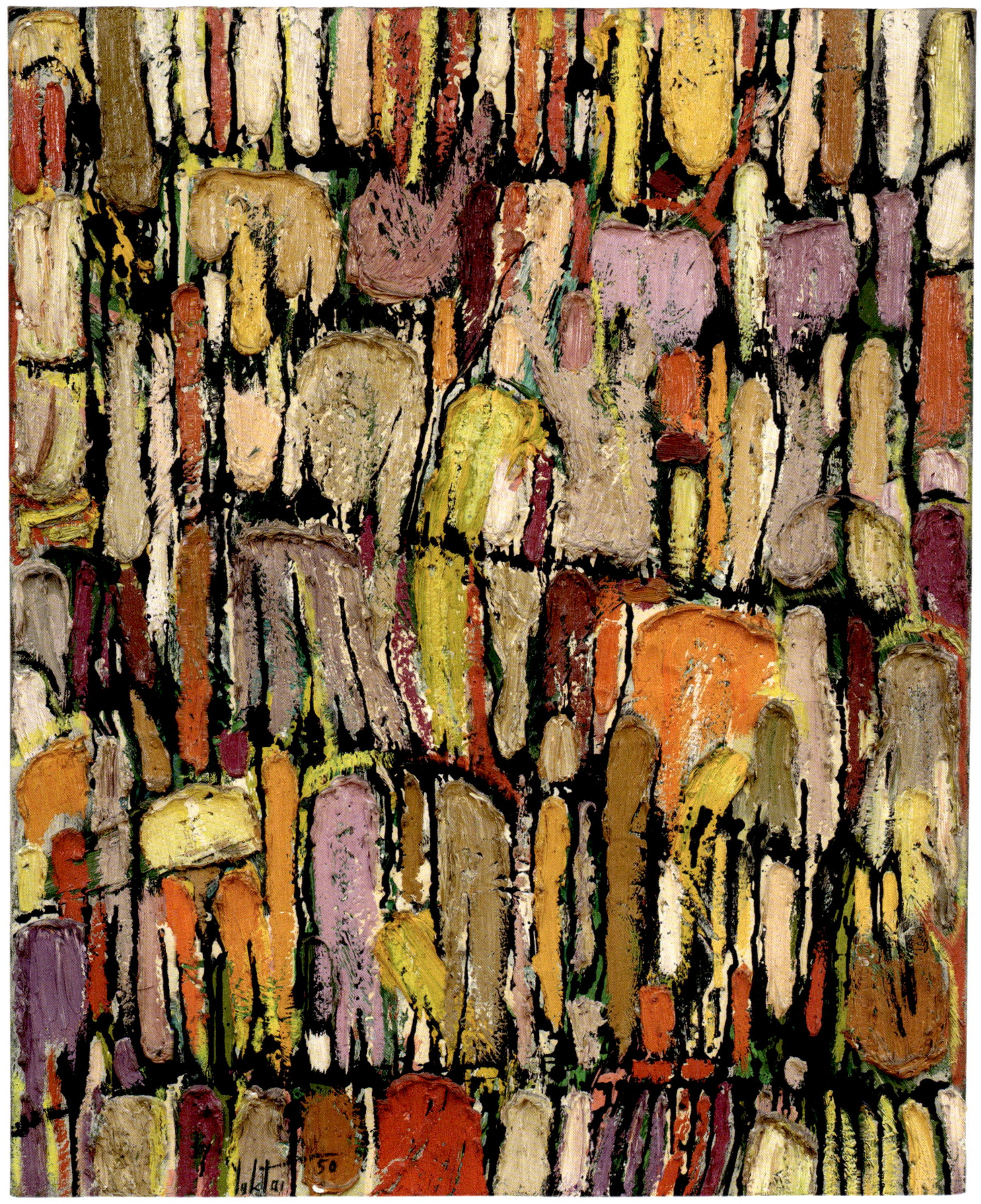

Untitled, 1950, oil on canvas, 33 × 26 inches (83.8 × 66 cm)

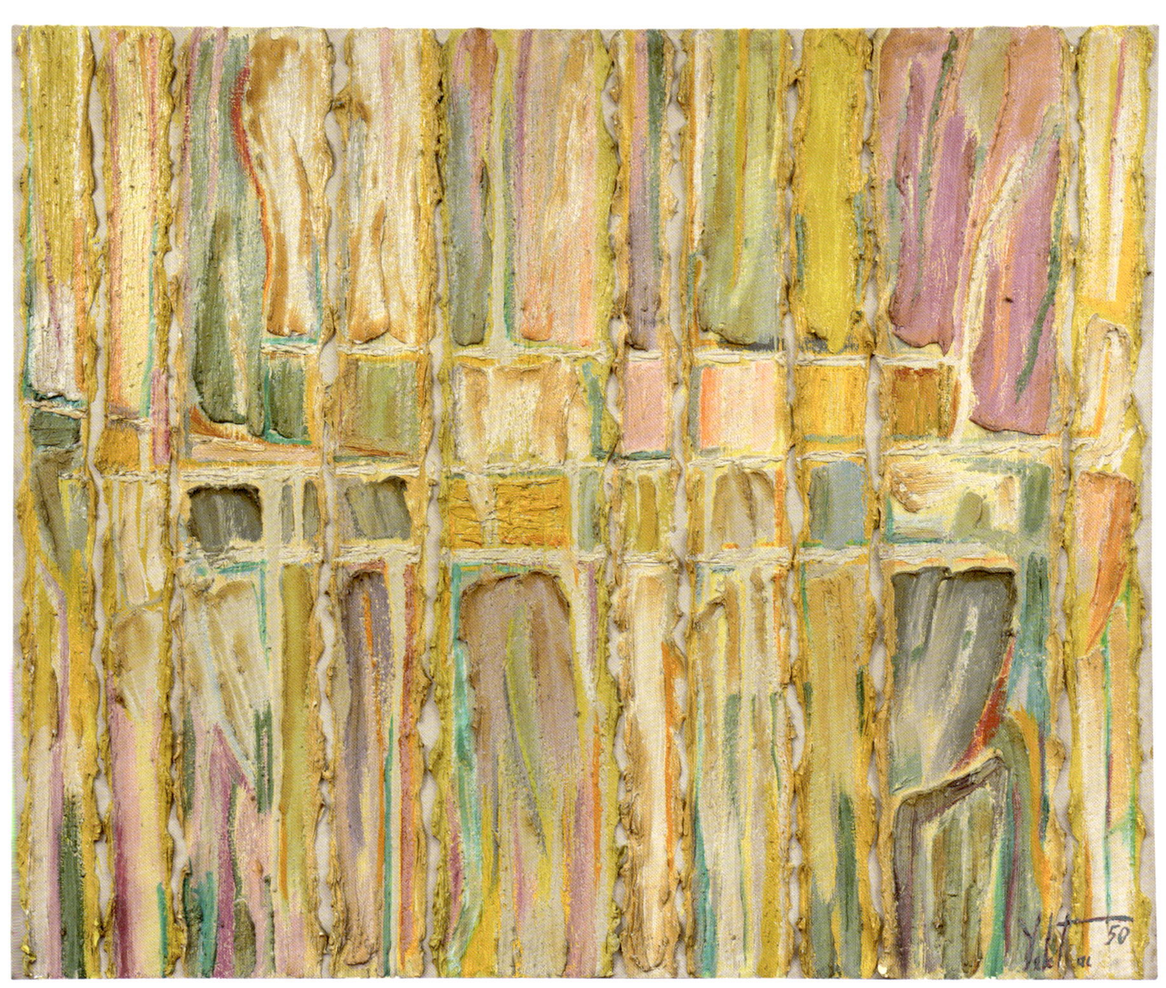

Untitled, 1950, oil on canvas, 42 × 48½ inches (106.7 × 123.2 cm)

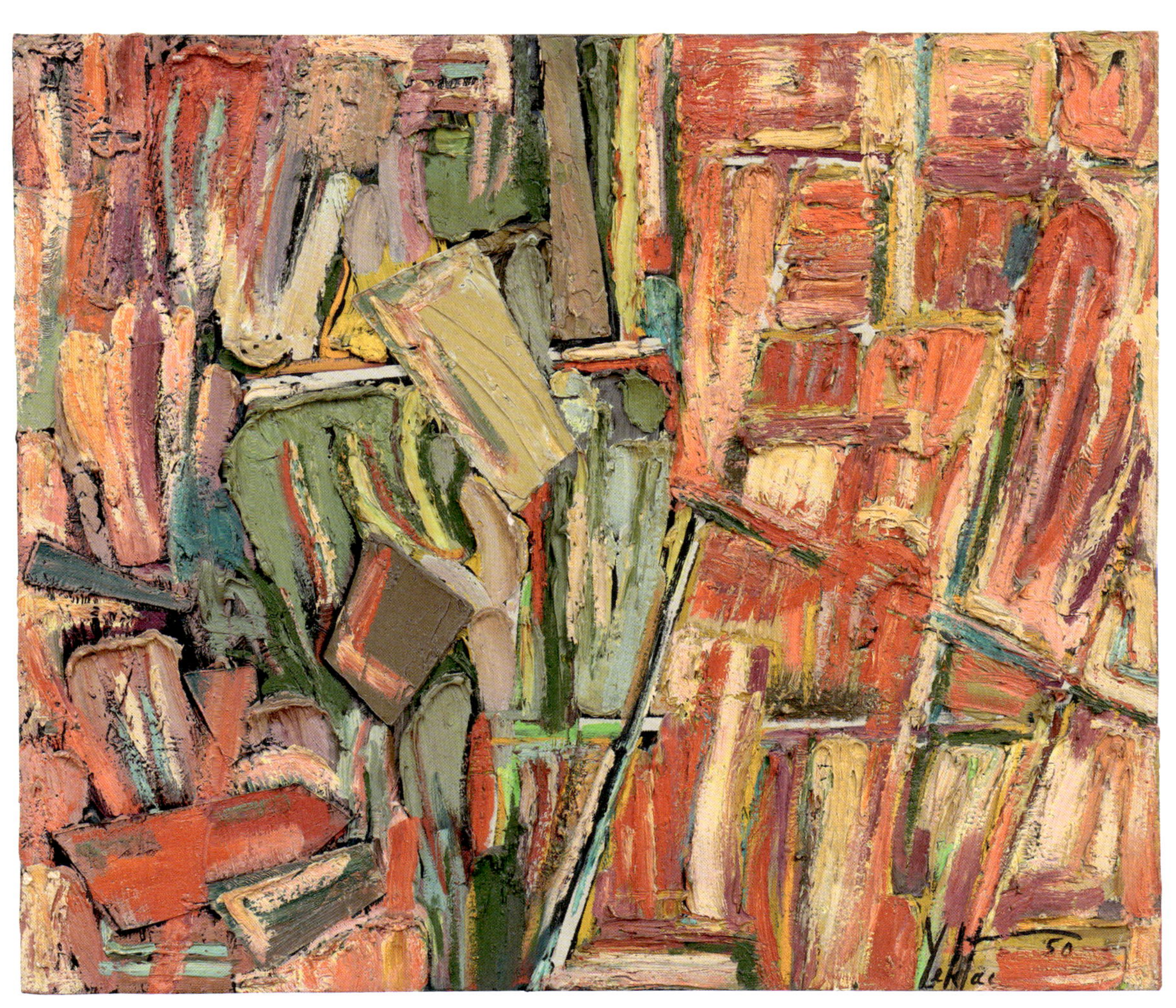

Untitled, 1950, oil on canvas, 35 × 40 inches (88.9 × 101.6 cm)

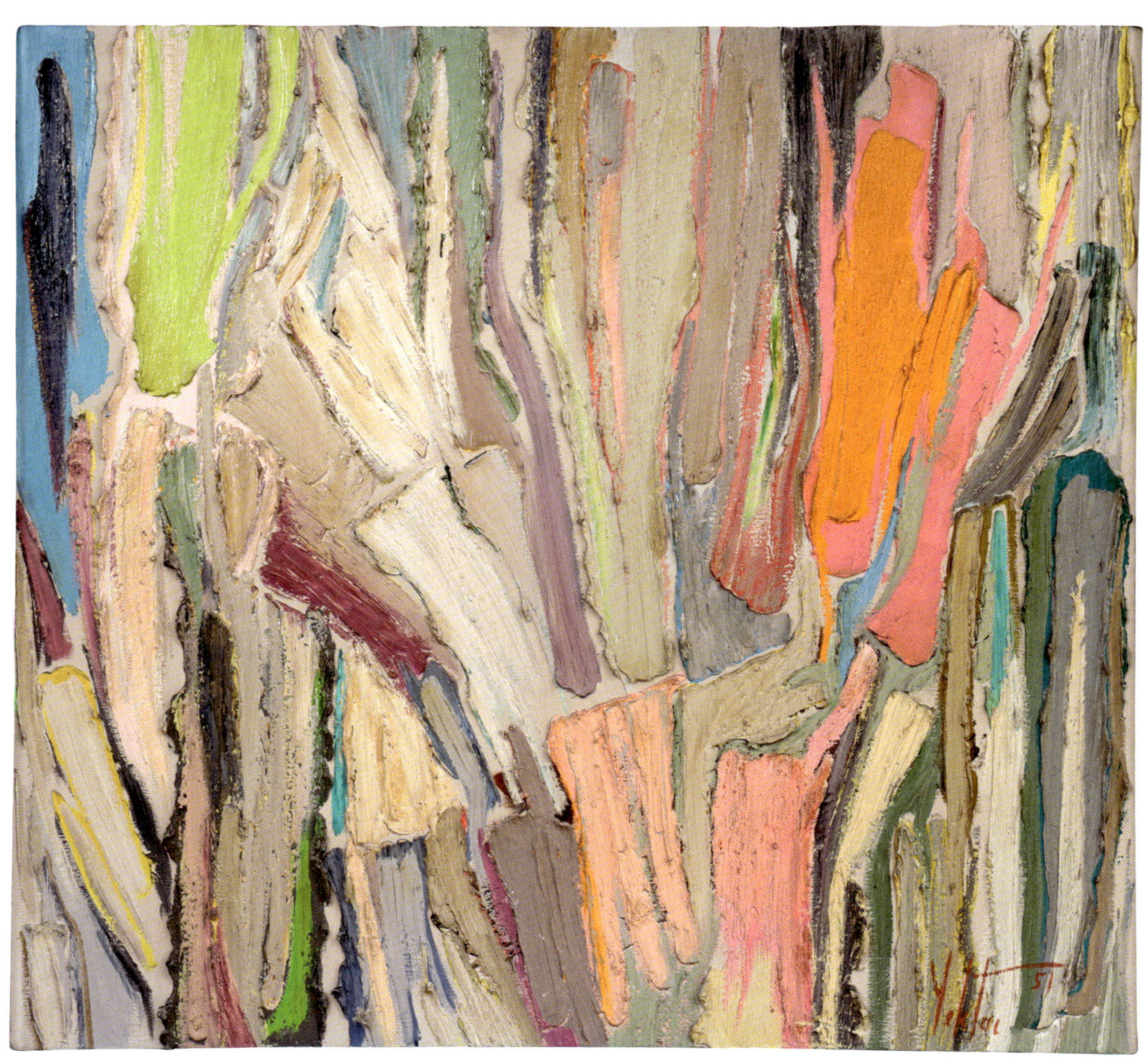

 Untitled, 1951, oil on canvas, 41¾ × 44¾ inches (106.1 × 113.7 cm)

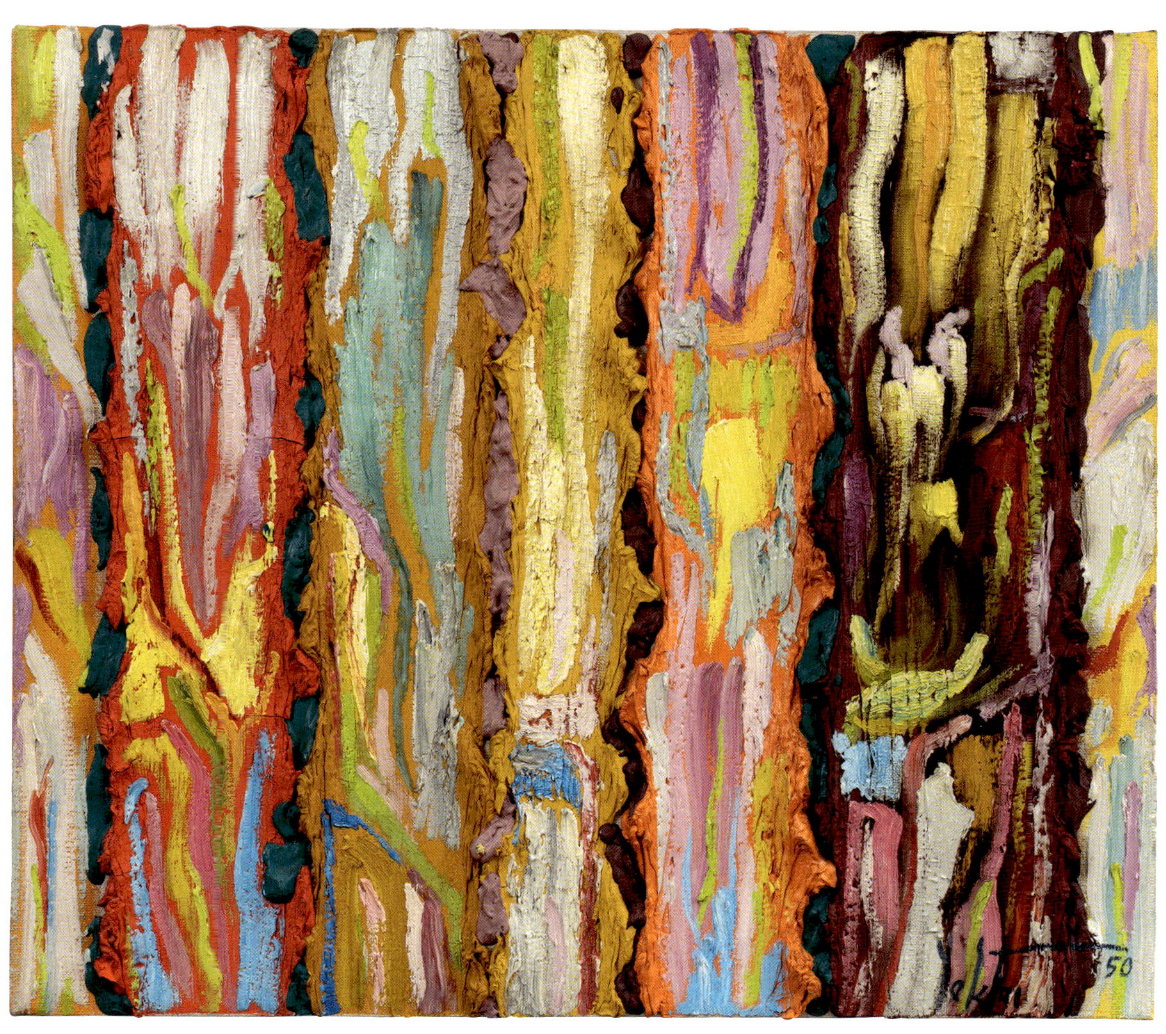

Untitled, 1950, oil on canvas, 16 × 18 inches (40.6 × 45.7 cm)

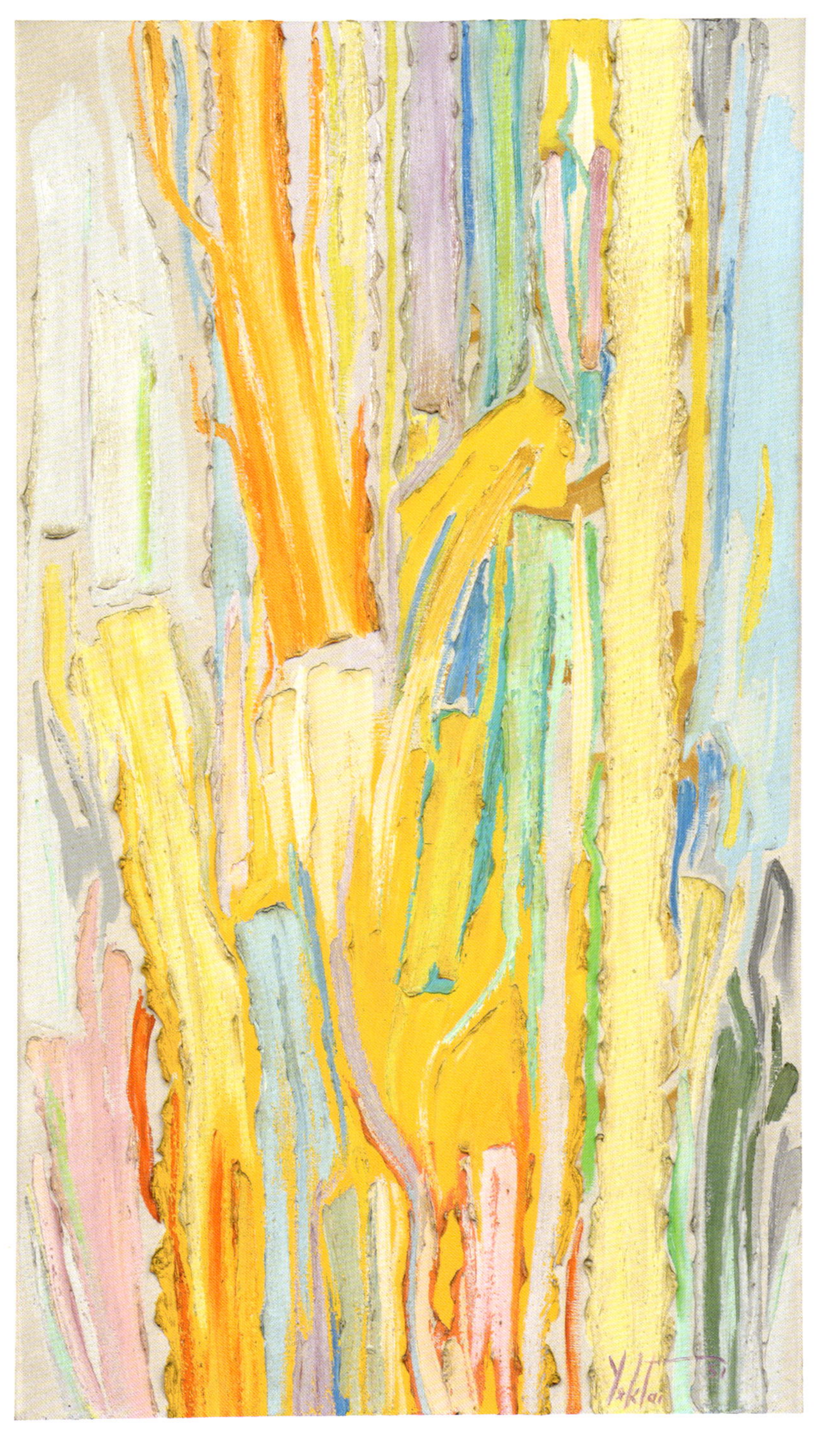

 Untitled, 1951, oil on canvas, 72 × 39½ inches (182.9 × 100.3 cm)

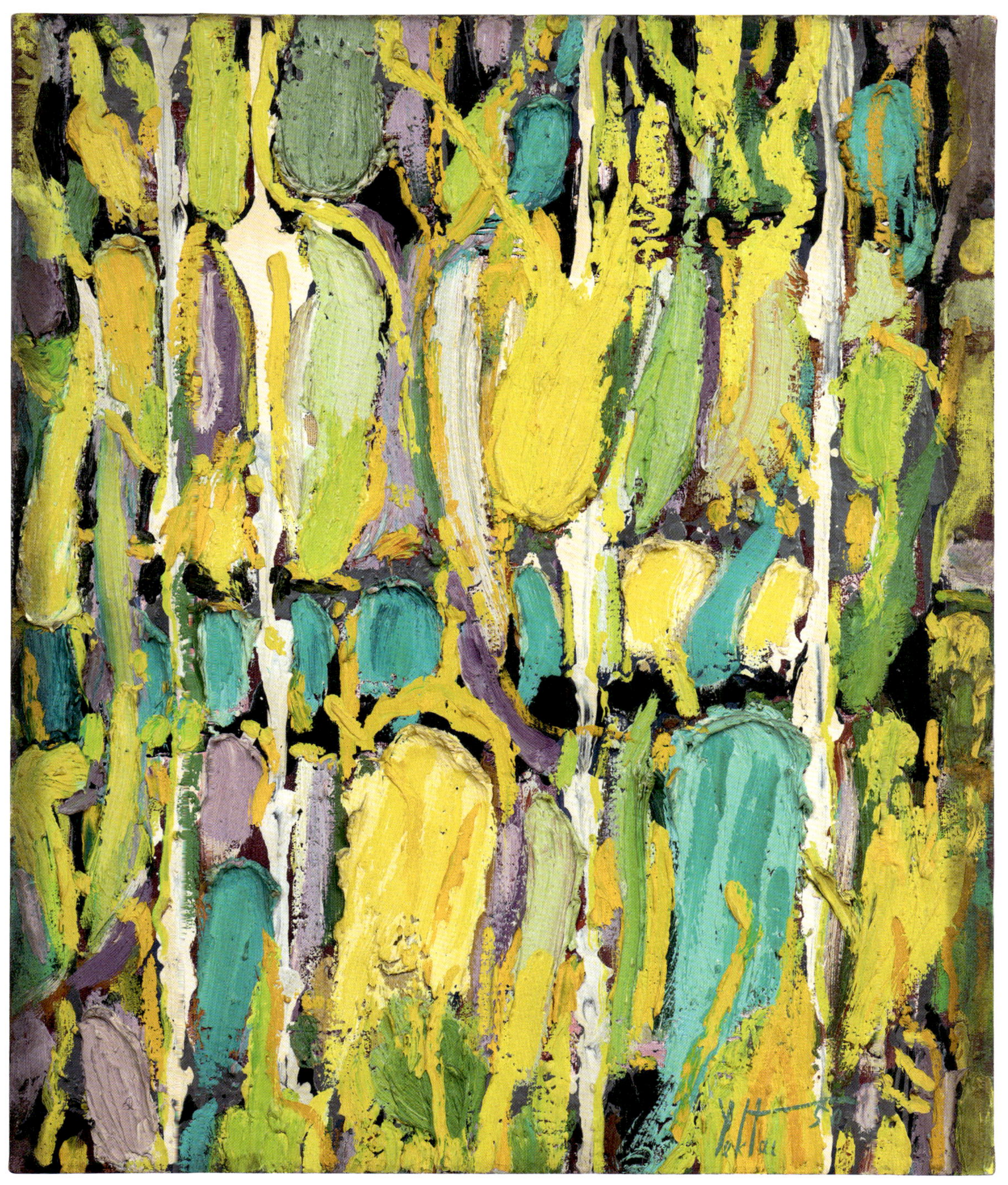

Untitled, 1951, oil on canvas, 24 × 20 inches (61 × 50.8 cm)

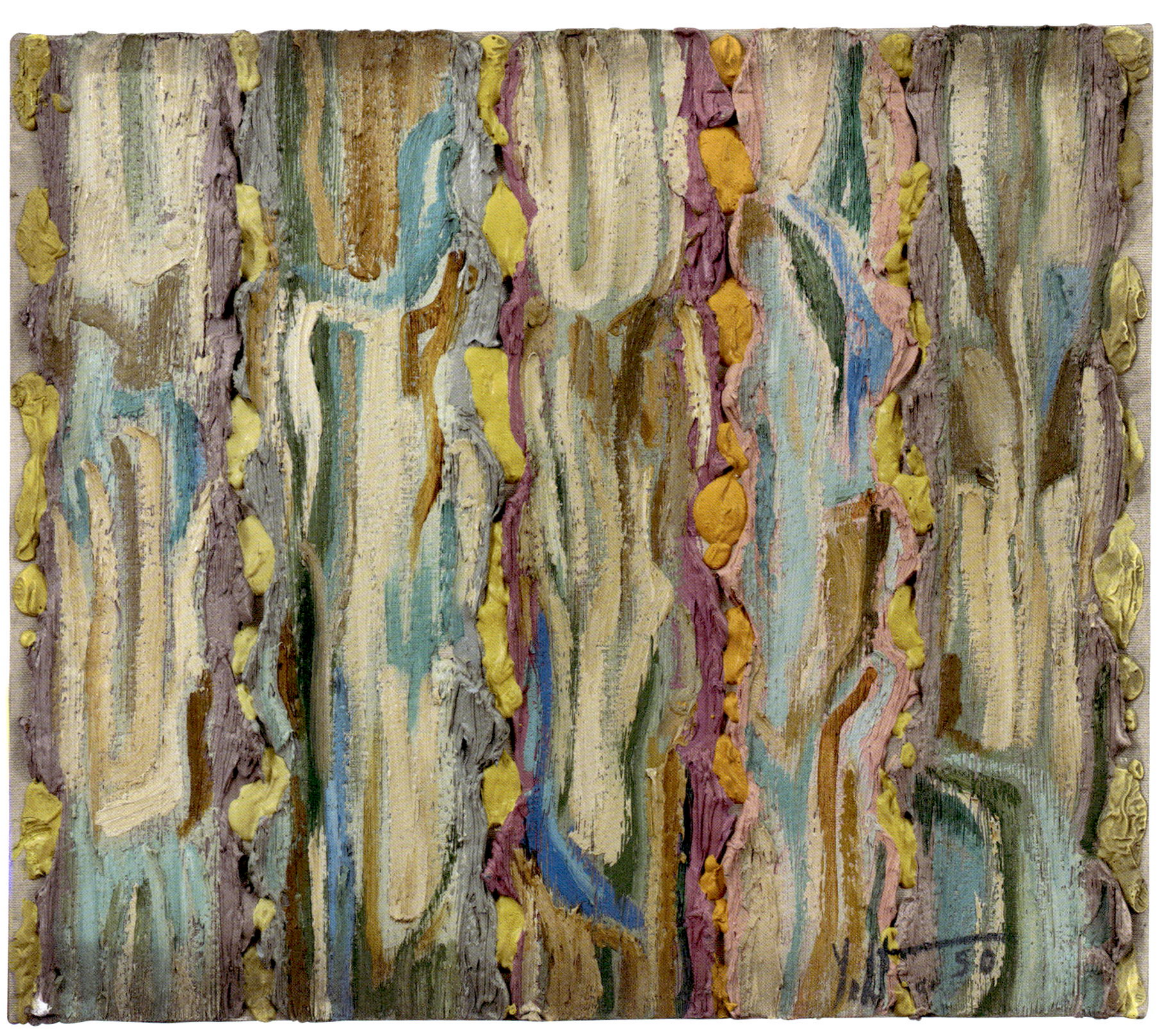

 Untitled, 1950, oil on canvas, 14 × 18 inches (35.6 × 45.7 cm)

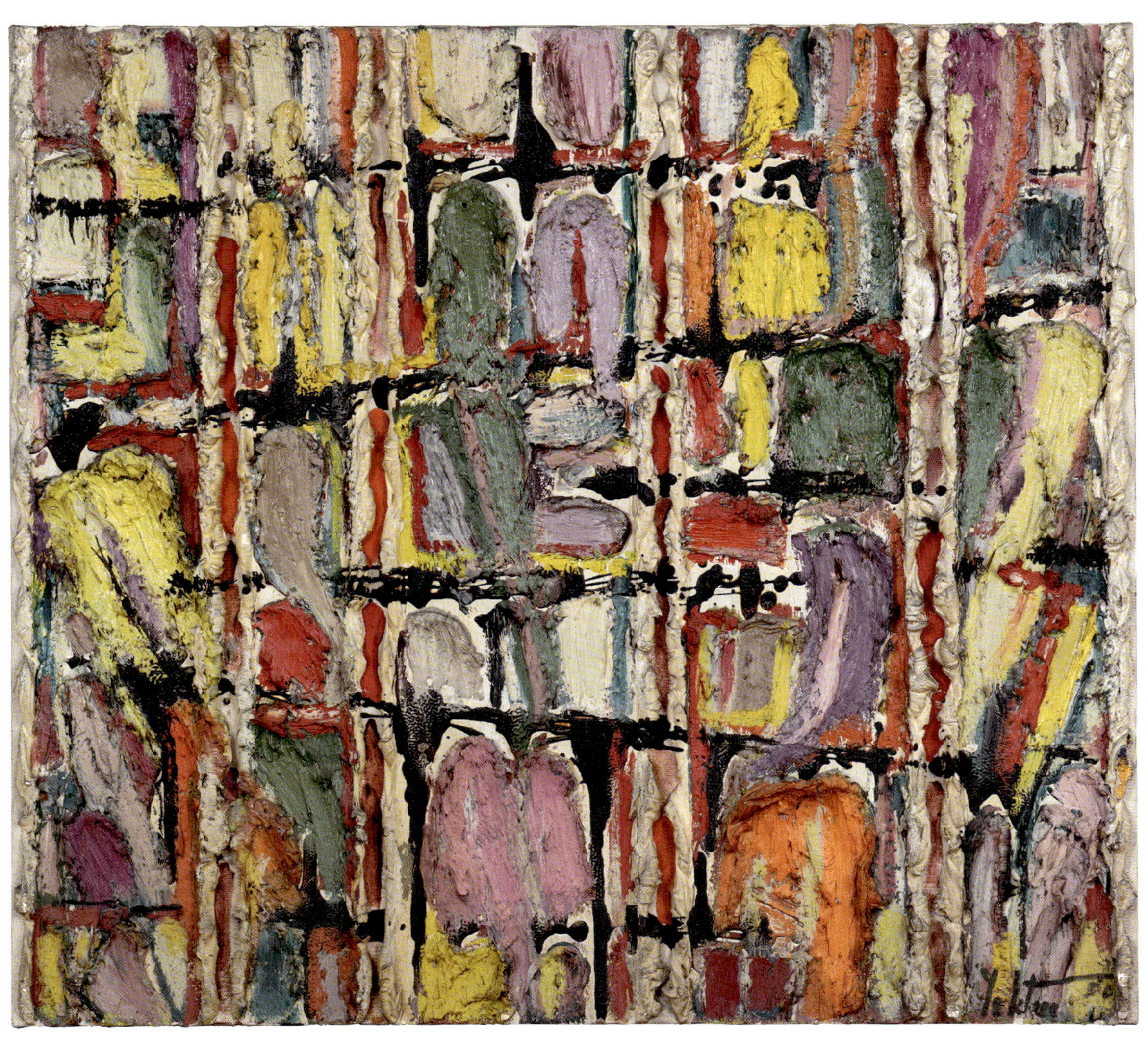

Untitled, 1950, oil on canvas, 19¾ × 21¾ inches (50.2 × 55.3 cm)

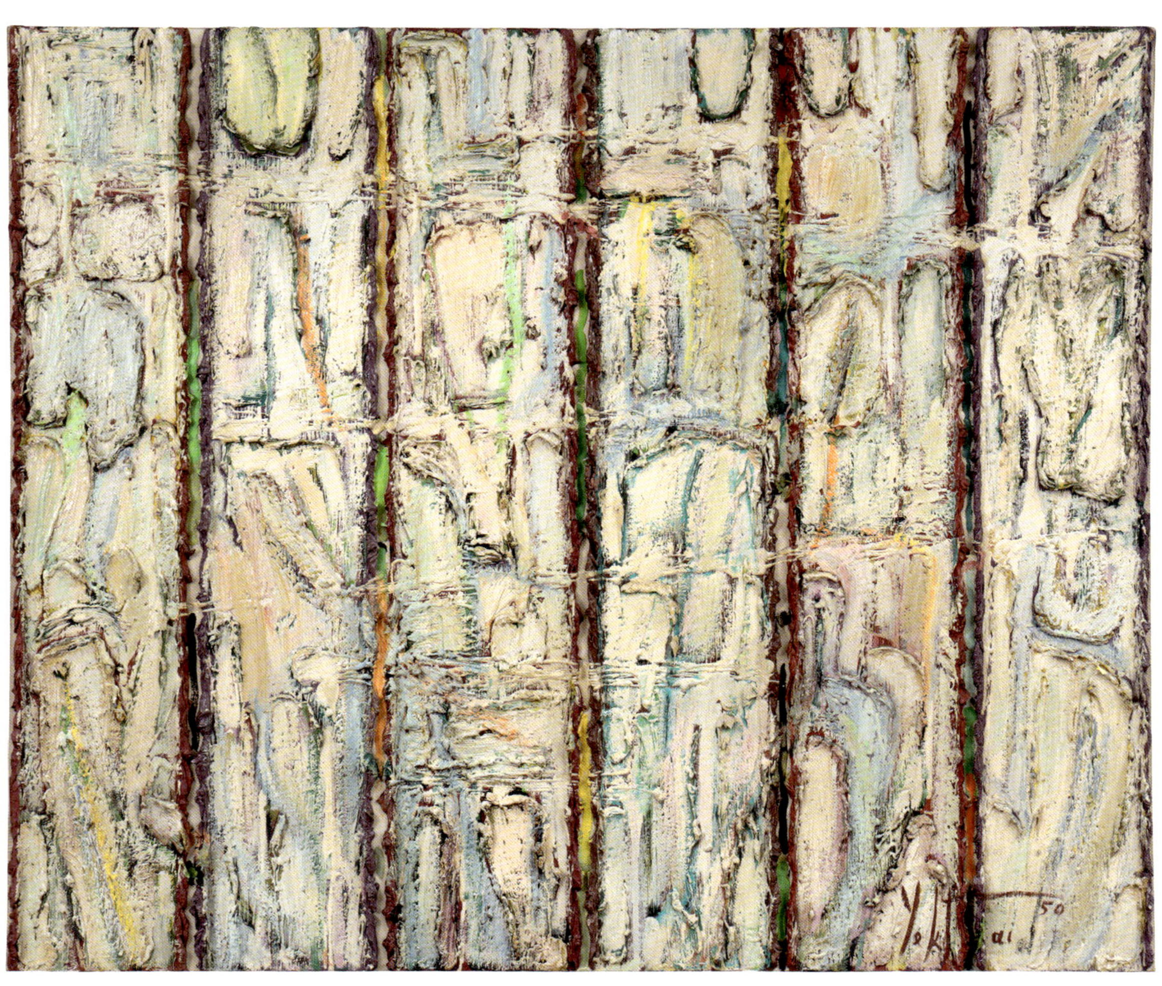

Untitled, 1950, oil on canvas, 38 × 44 inches (96.5 × 111.8 cm)

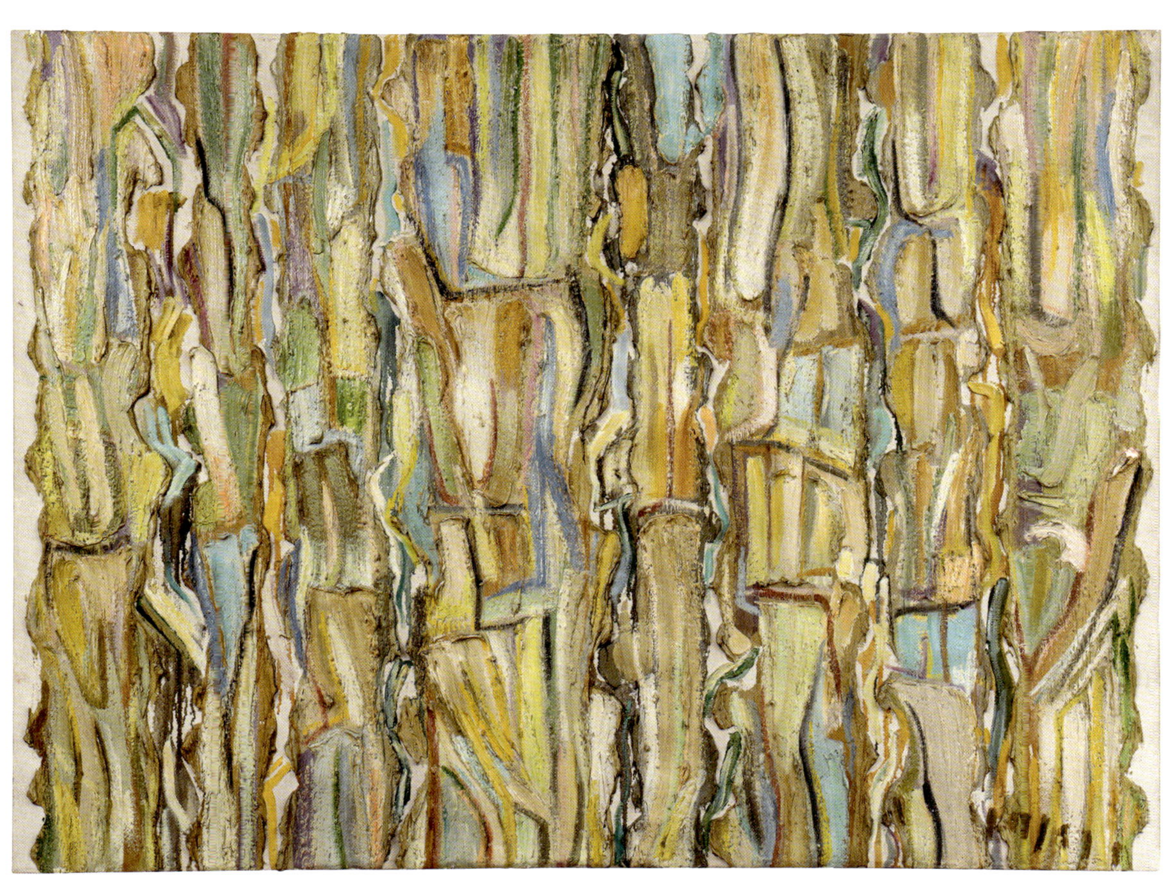

Untitled, 1951, oil on canvas, 39¾ × 52¾ inches (101 × 134 cm)

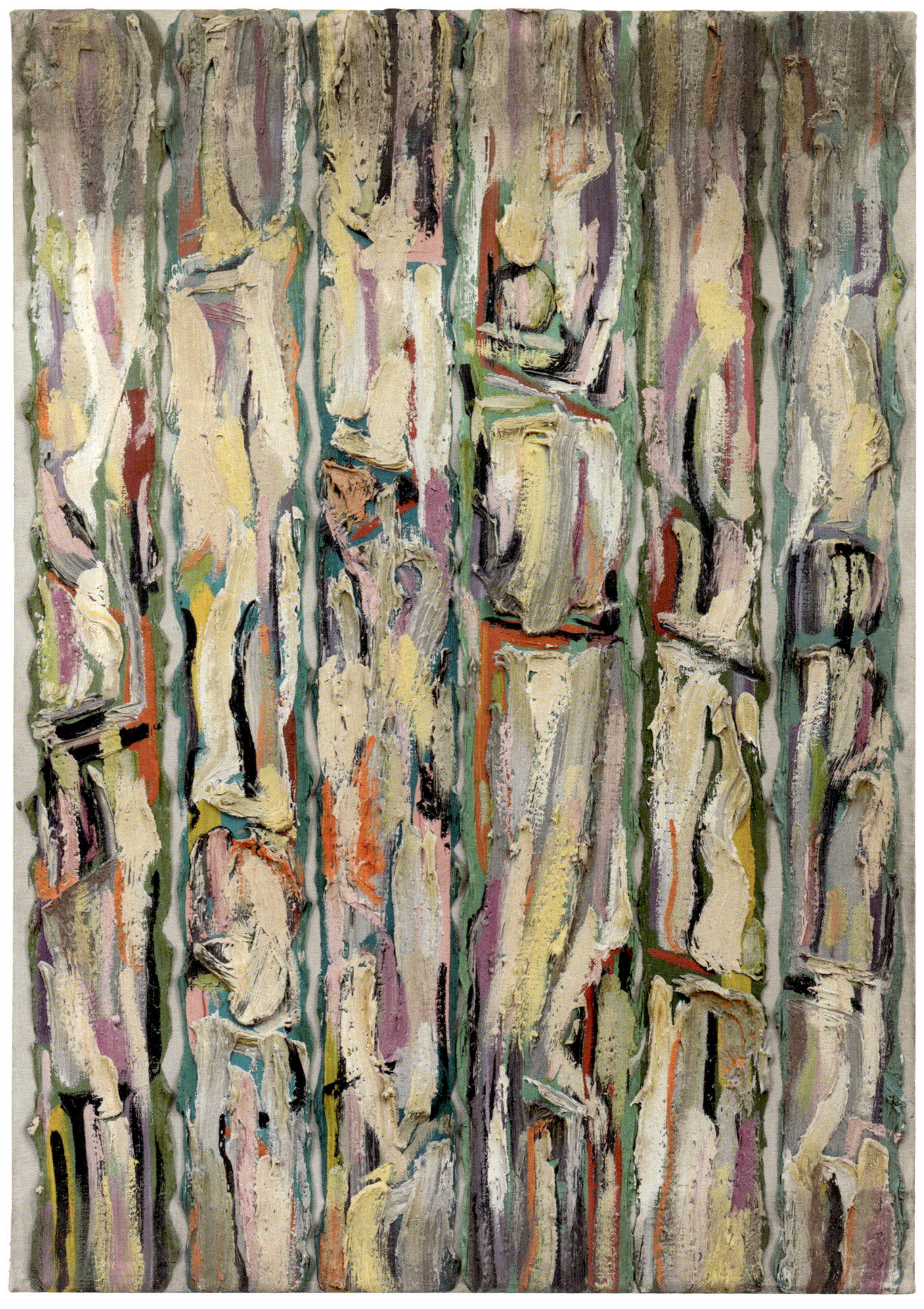

Untitled, 1951, oil on canvas, 29 × 20 inches (73.7 × 50.8 cm)

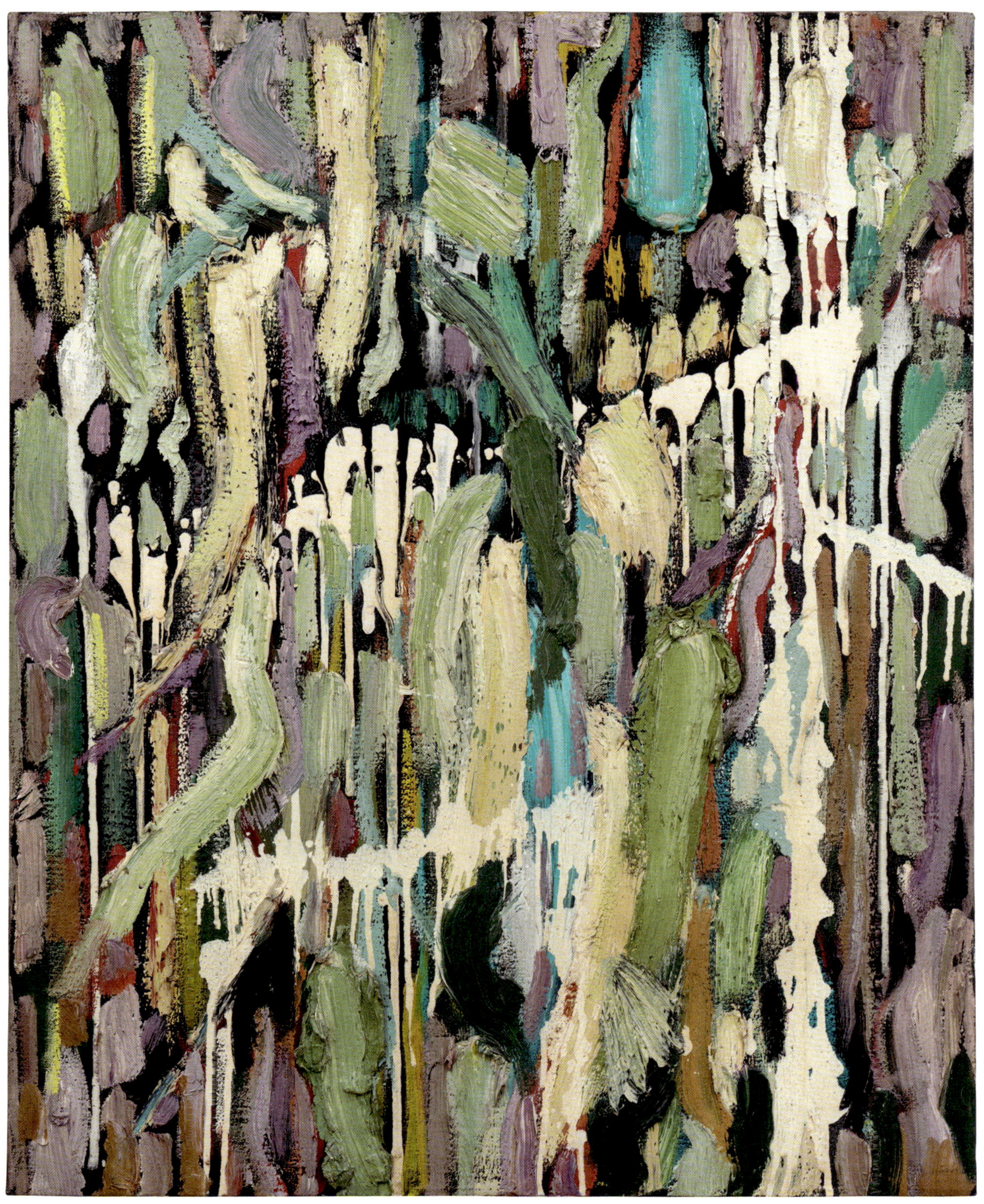

Untitled, 1951, oil on canvas, 30 × 24 inches (76.2 × 61 cm)

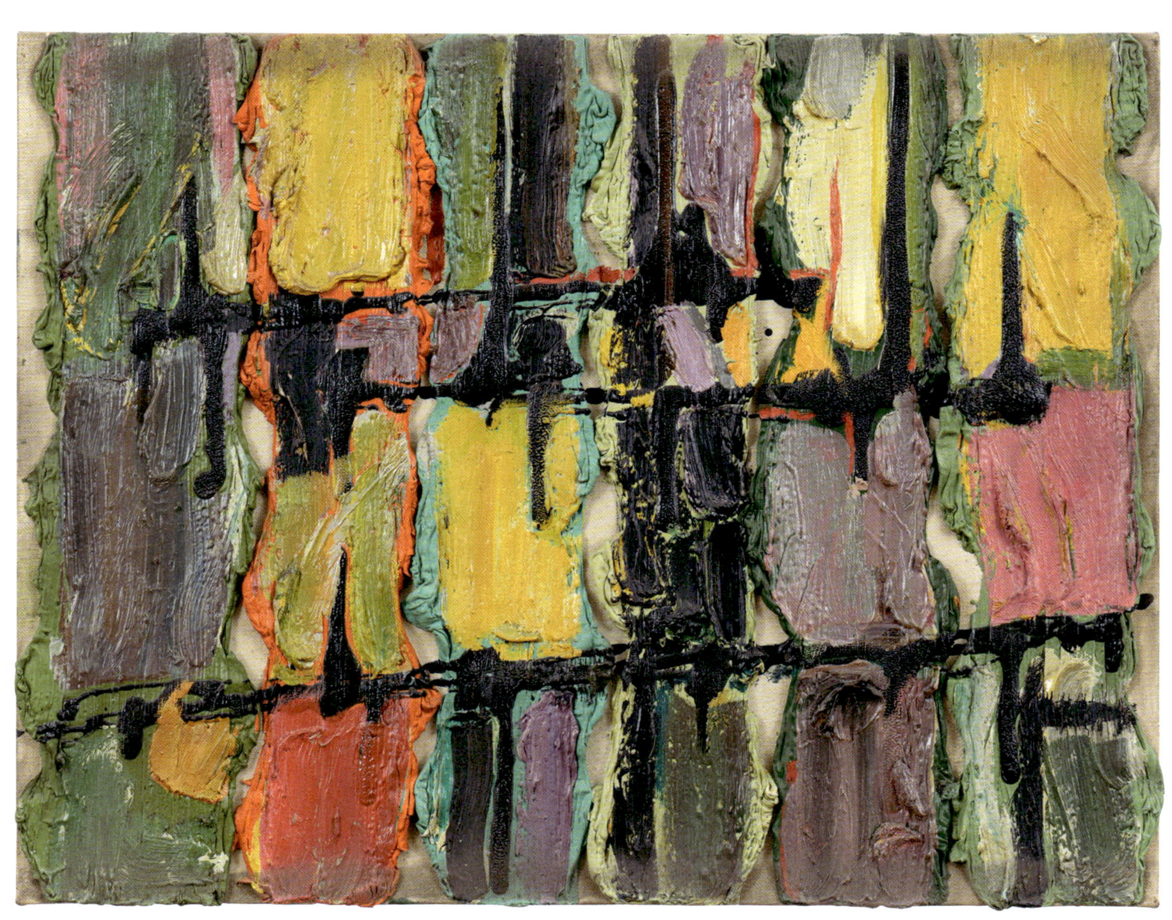

Untitled, 1951, oil on canvas, 14 × 18 inches (35.6 × 45.7 cm)

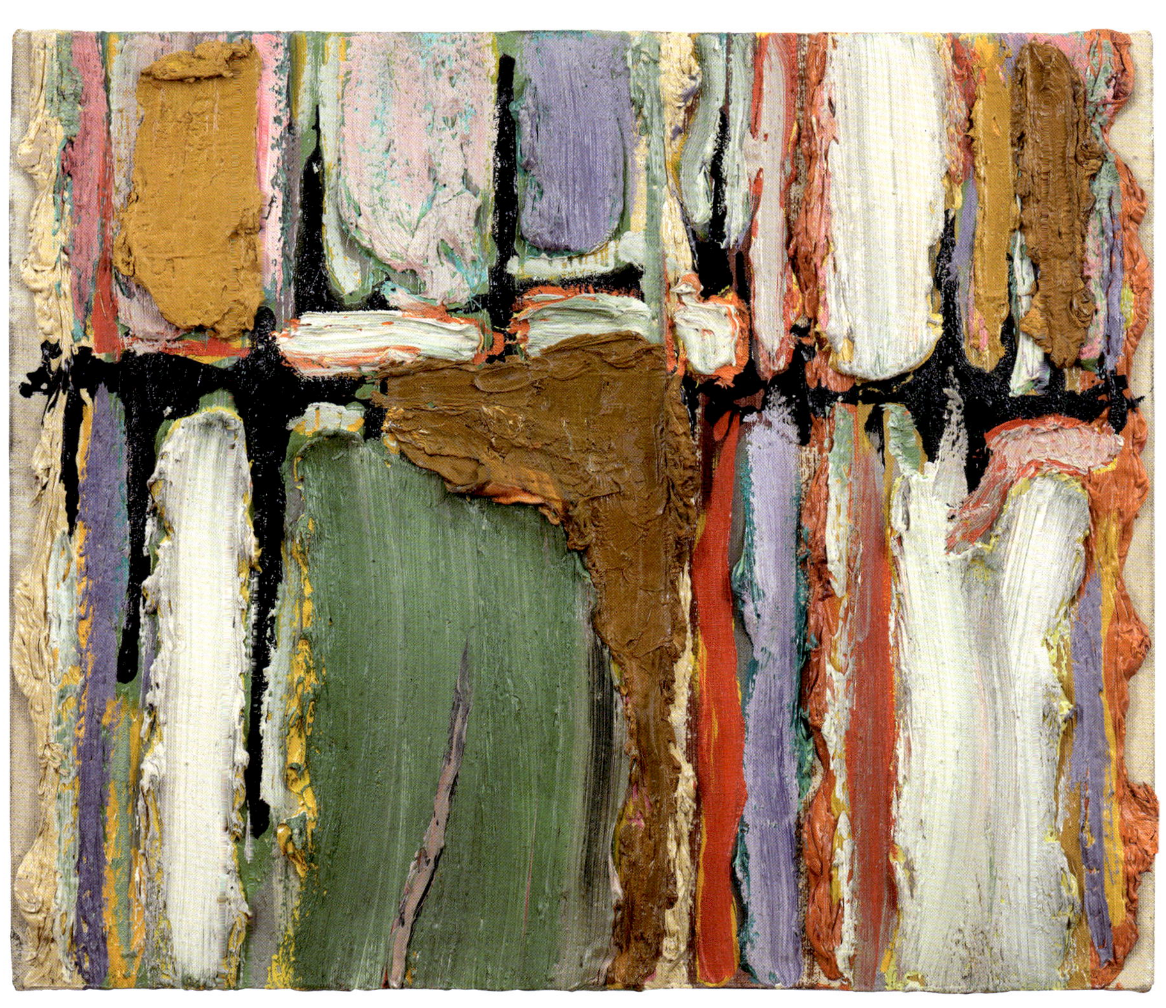

Untitled, 1951, oil on canvas, 12 × 14 inches (30.5 × 35.6 cm)

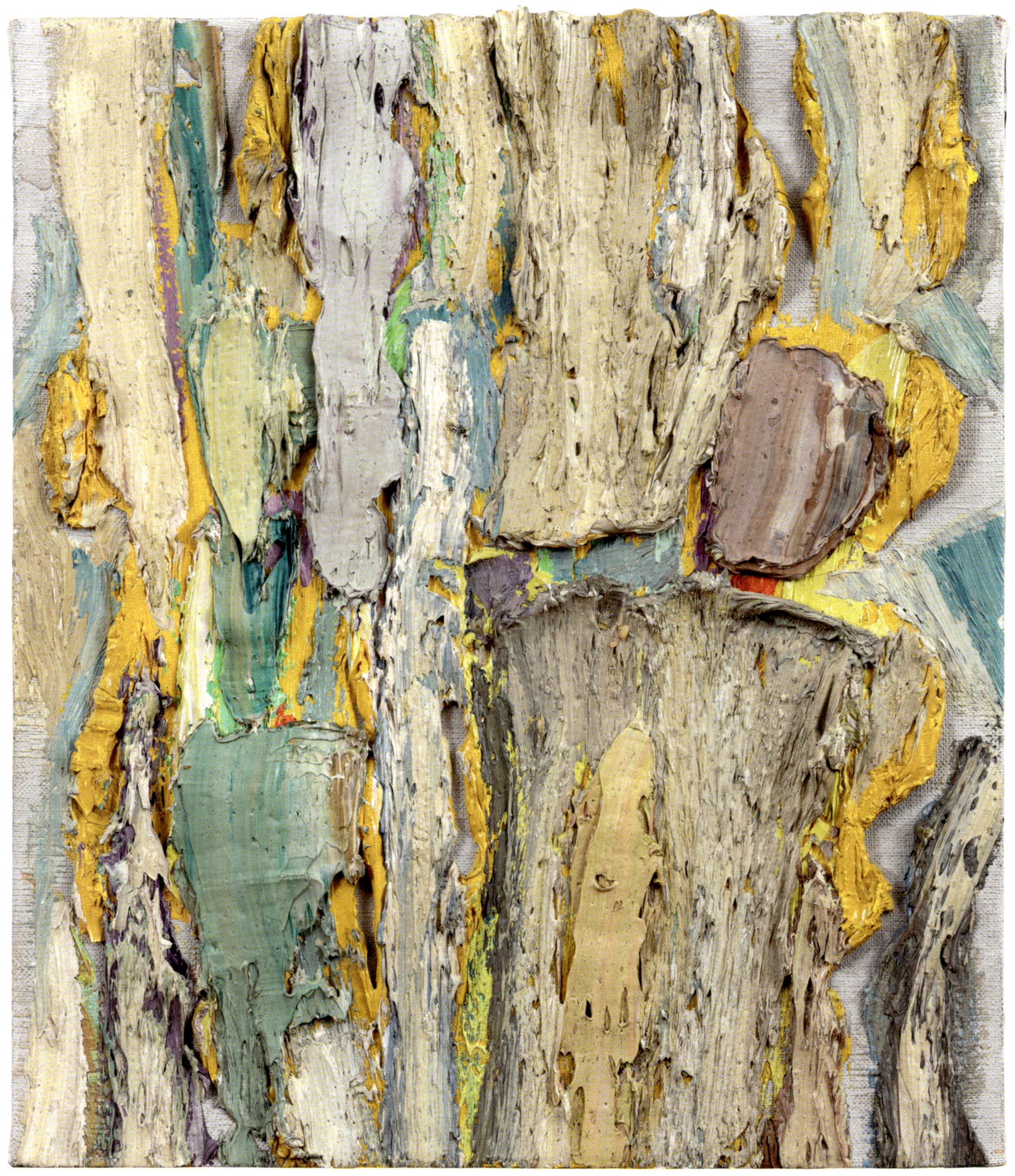

Untitled, 1951, oil on canvas, 12 × 10 inches (30.5 × 25.4 cm)

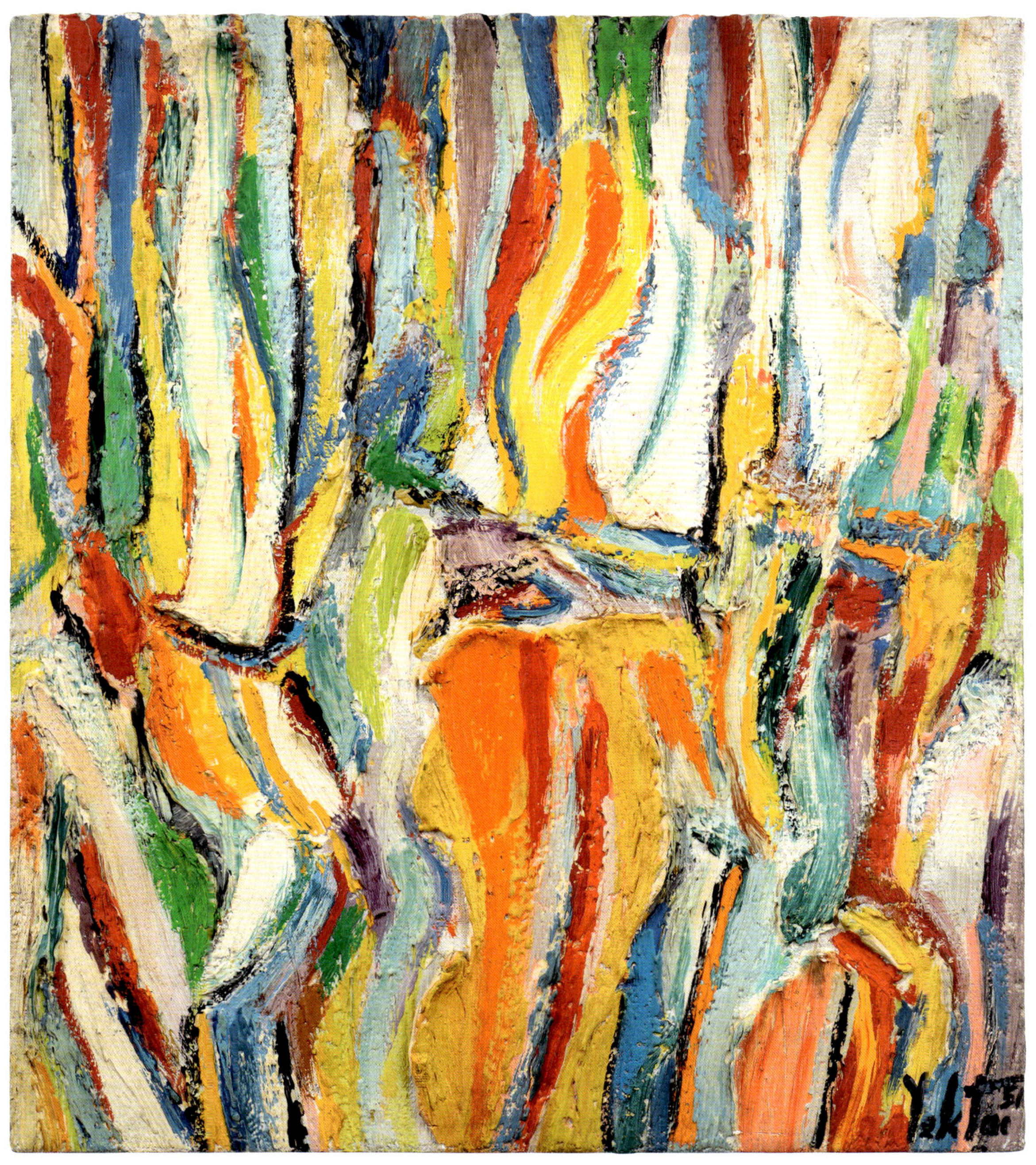

Untitled, 1951, oil on canvas, 16 × 14 inches (40.6 × 35.6 cm)

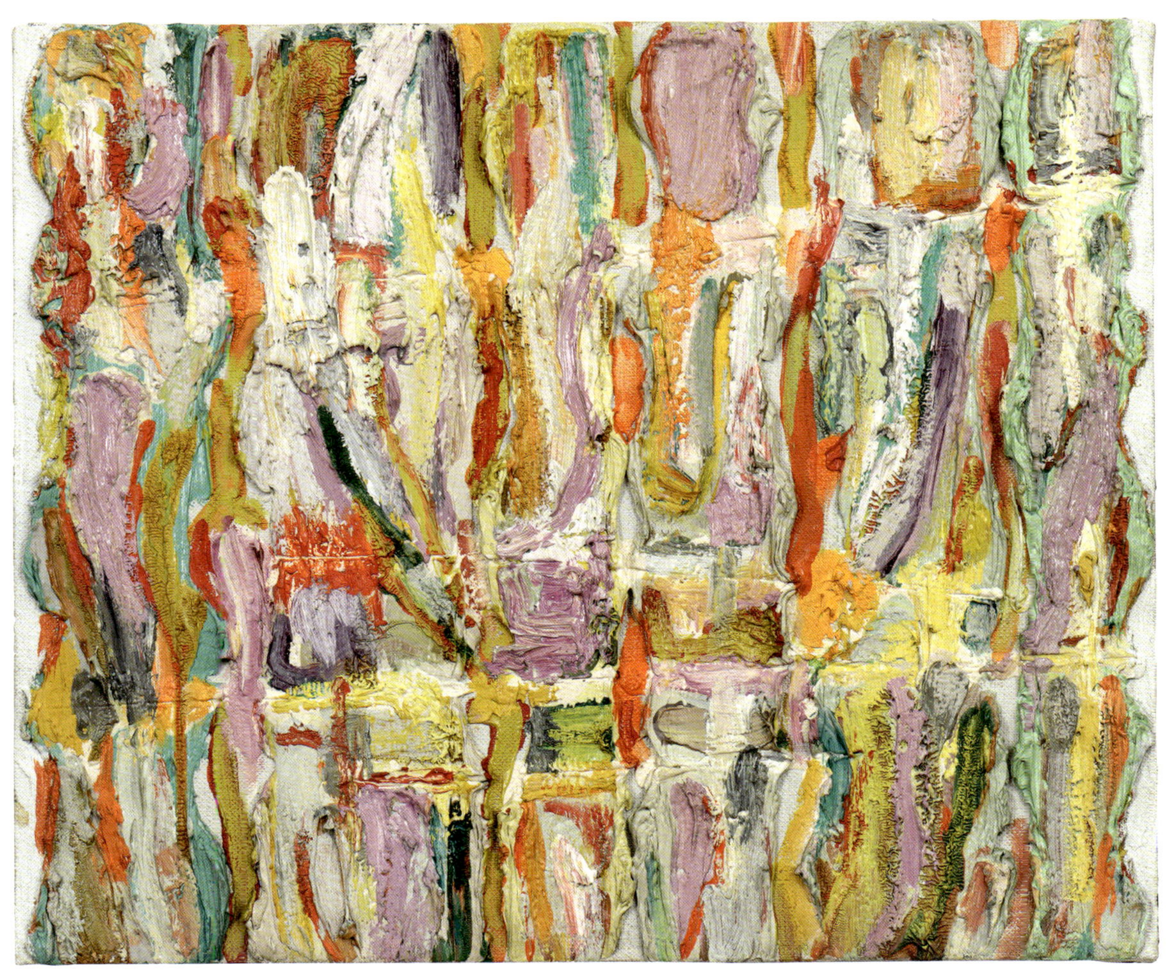

Untitled, 1952, oil on canvas, 10 × 12 inches (25.4 × 30.5 cm)

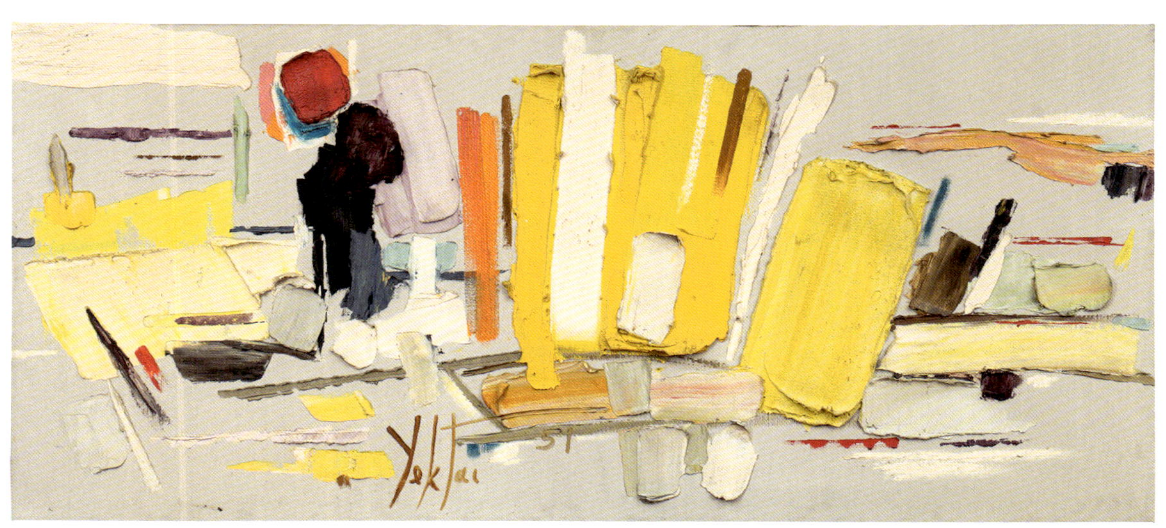

Untitled, 1951, oil on canvas, 21¾ × 49 inches (55.3 × 124.5 cm)

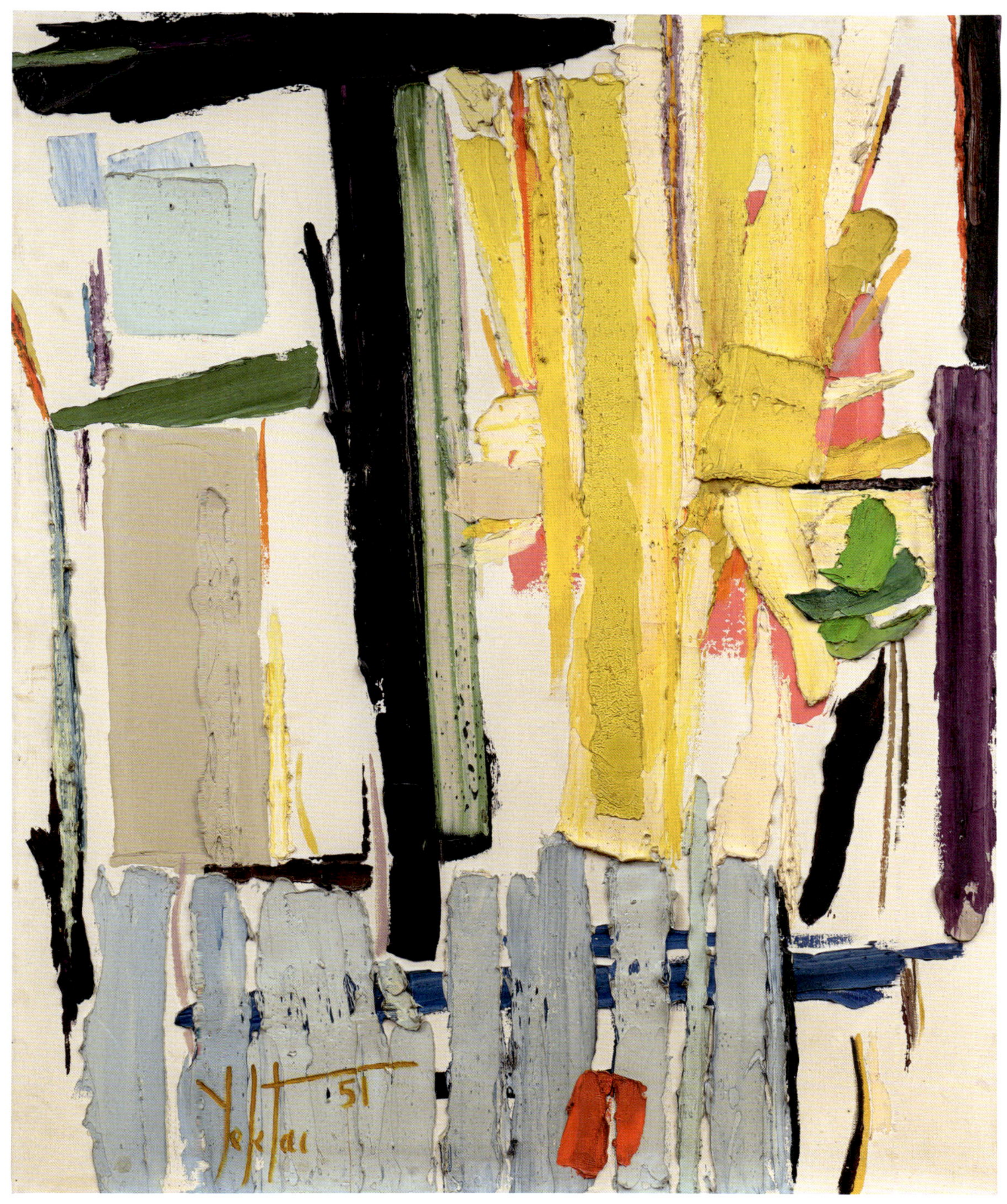

Open Window, 1951, oil on canvas, 49 × 40 inches (124.5 × 101.6 cm)

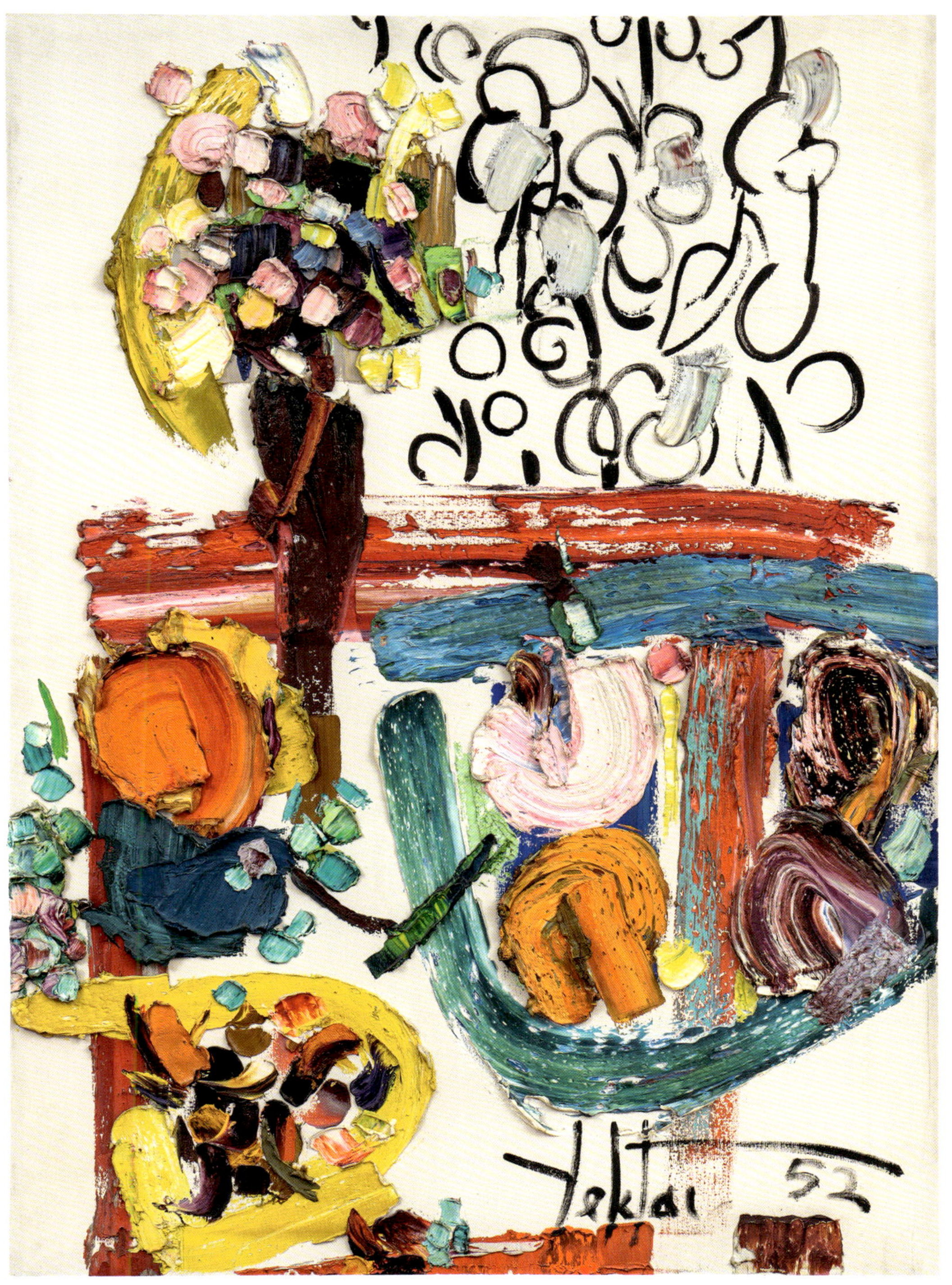

Curtain and Still Life, 1952, oil on canvas, 50 × 36 inches (127 × 91.4 cm)

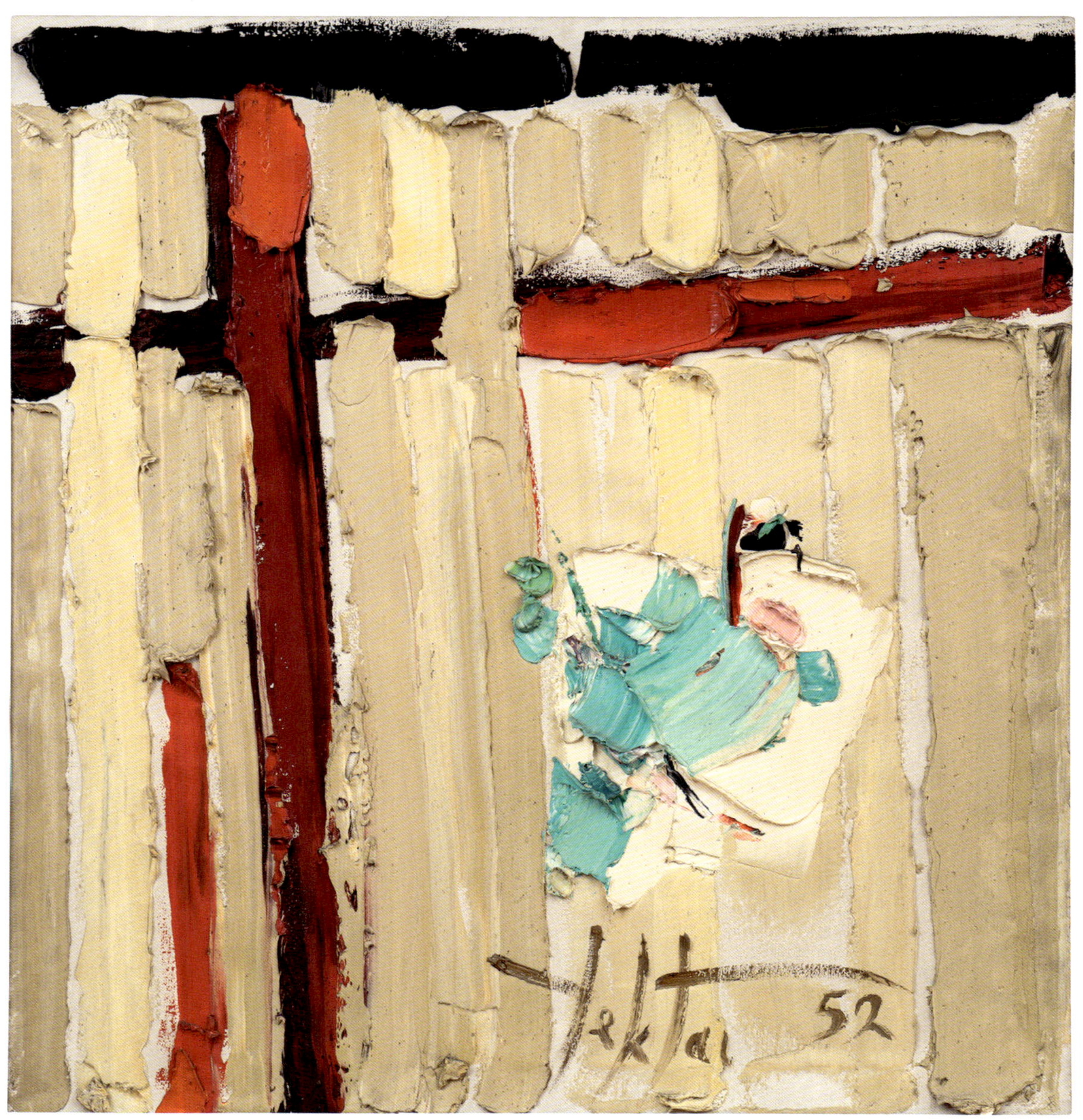

Untitled, 1952, oil on canvas, 36 × 34 inches (91.4 × 86.4 cm)

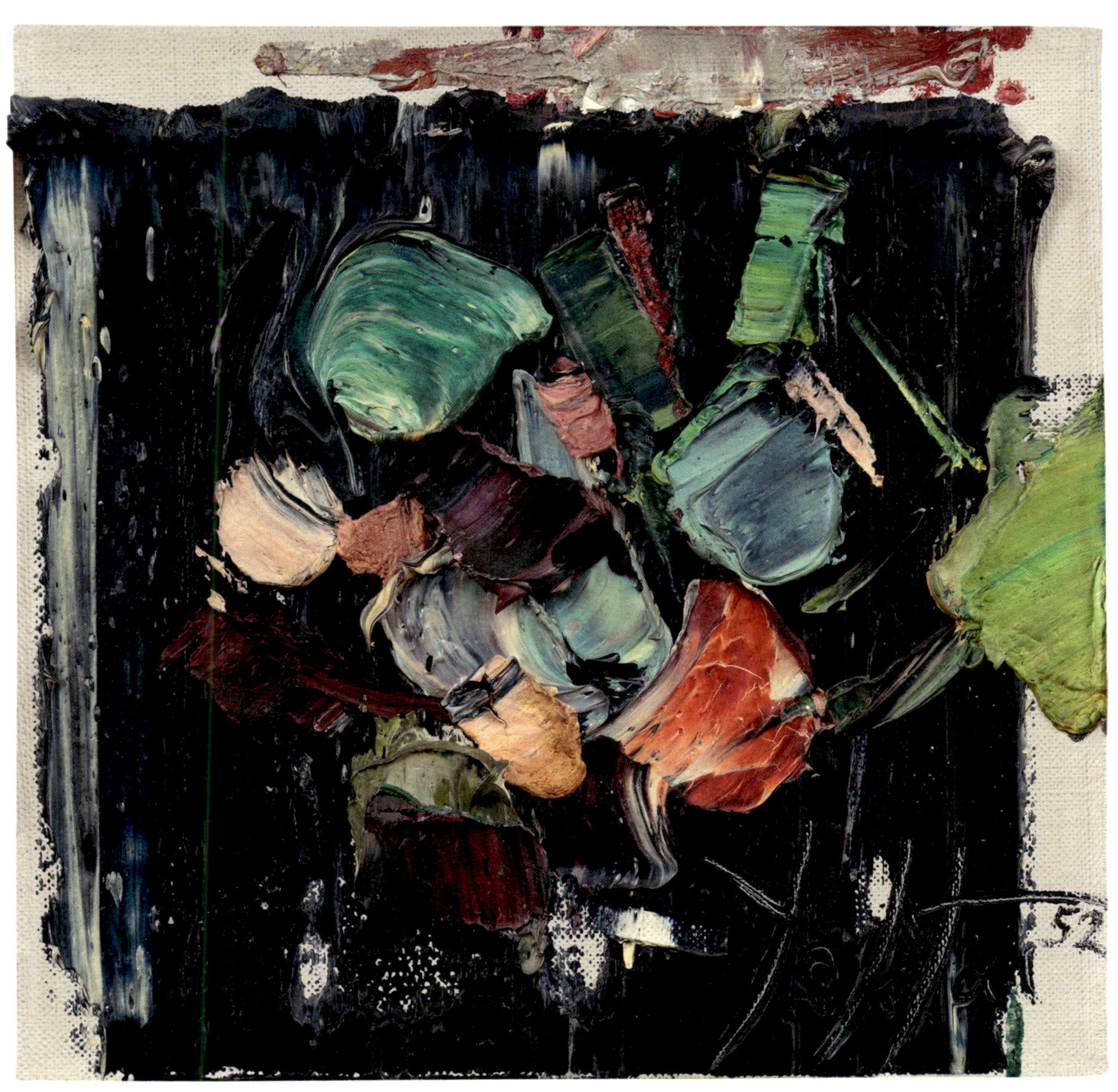

Untitled, 1952, oil on canvas, 8 × 8 inches (20.3 × 20.3 cm)

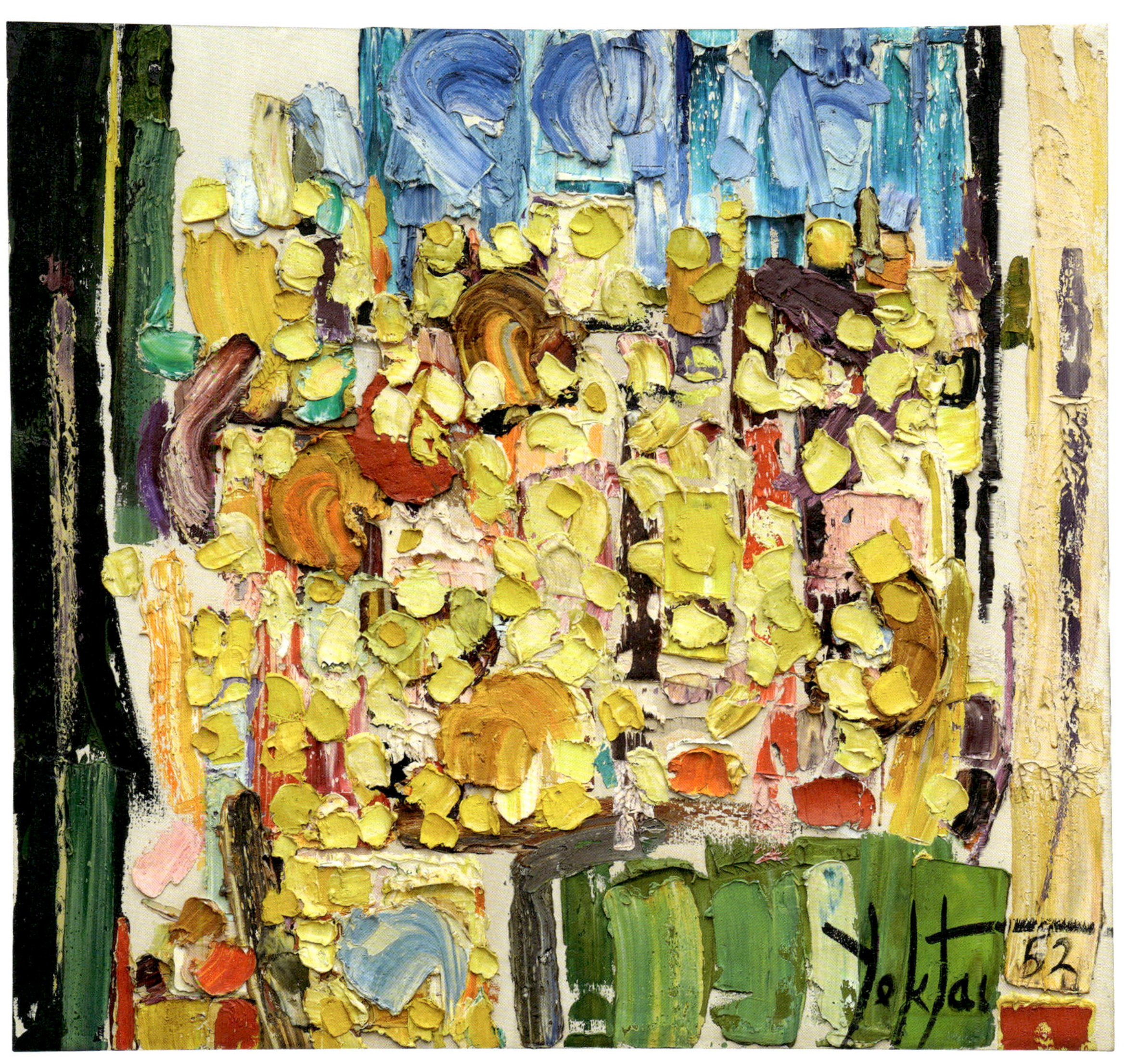

Yellow Table, 1952, oil on canvas, 48 × 50 inches (121.9 × 127 cm)

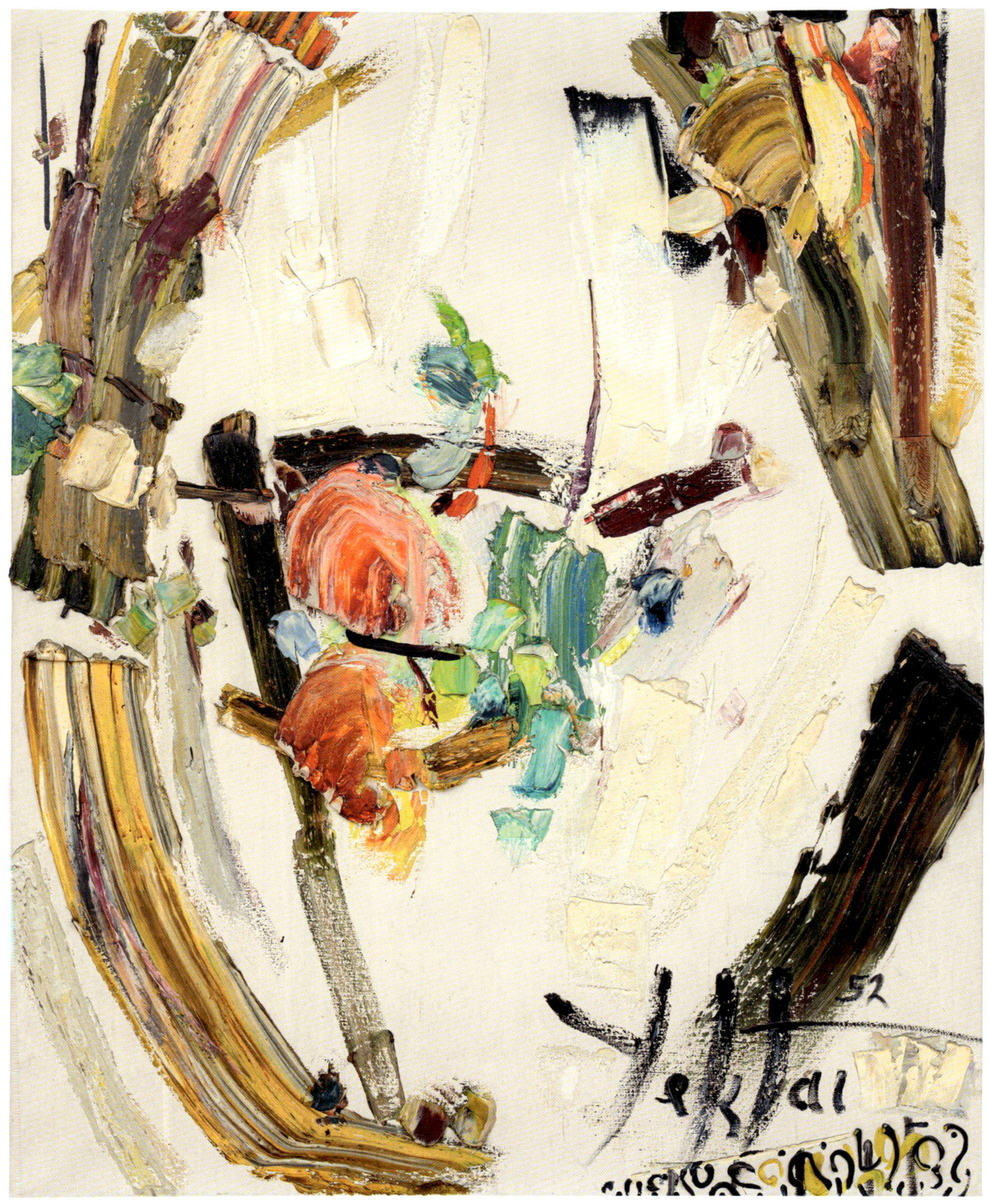

 Untitled, 1952, oil on canvas, 59¾ × 48 inches (151.8 × 121.9 cm)

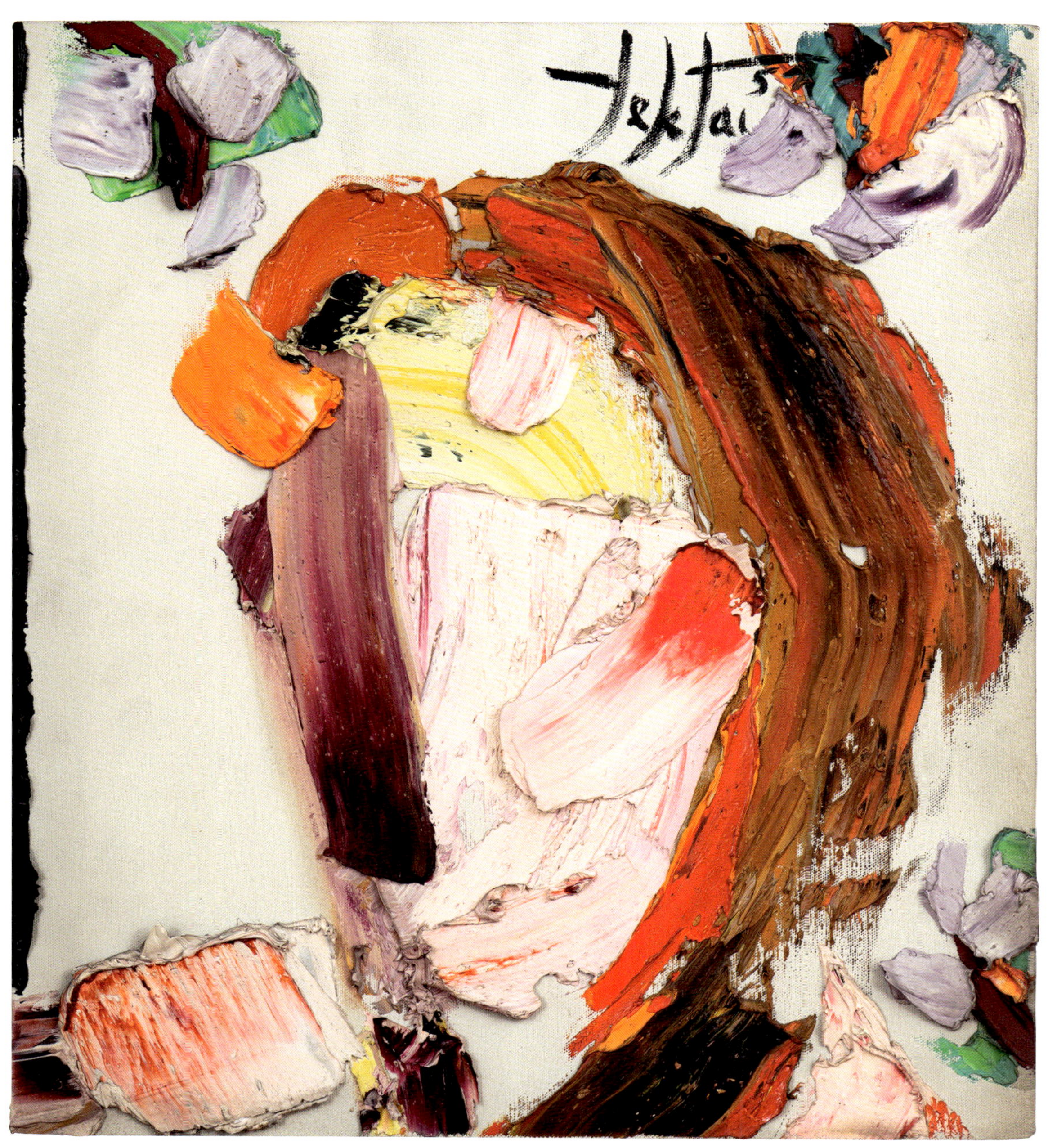

Untitled, 1952, oil on canvas, 20 × 18 inches (50.8 × 45.7 cm)

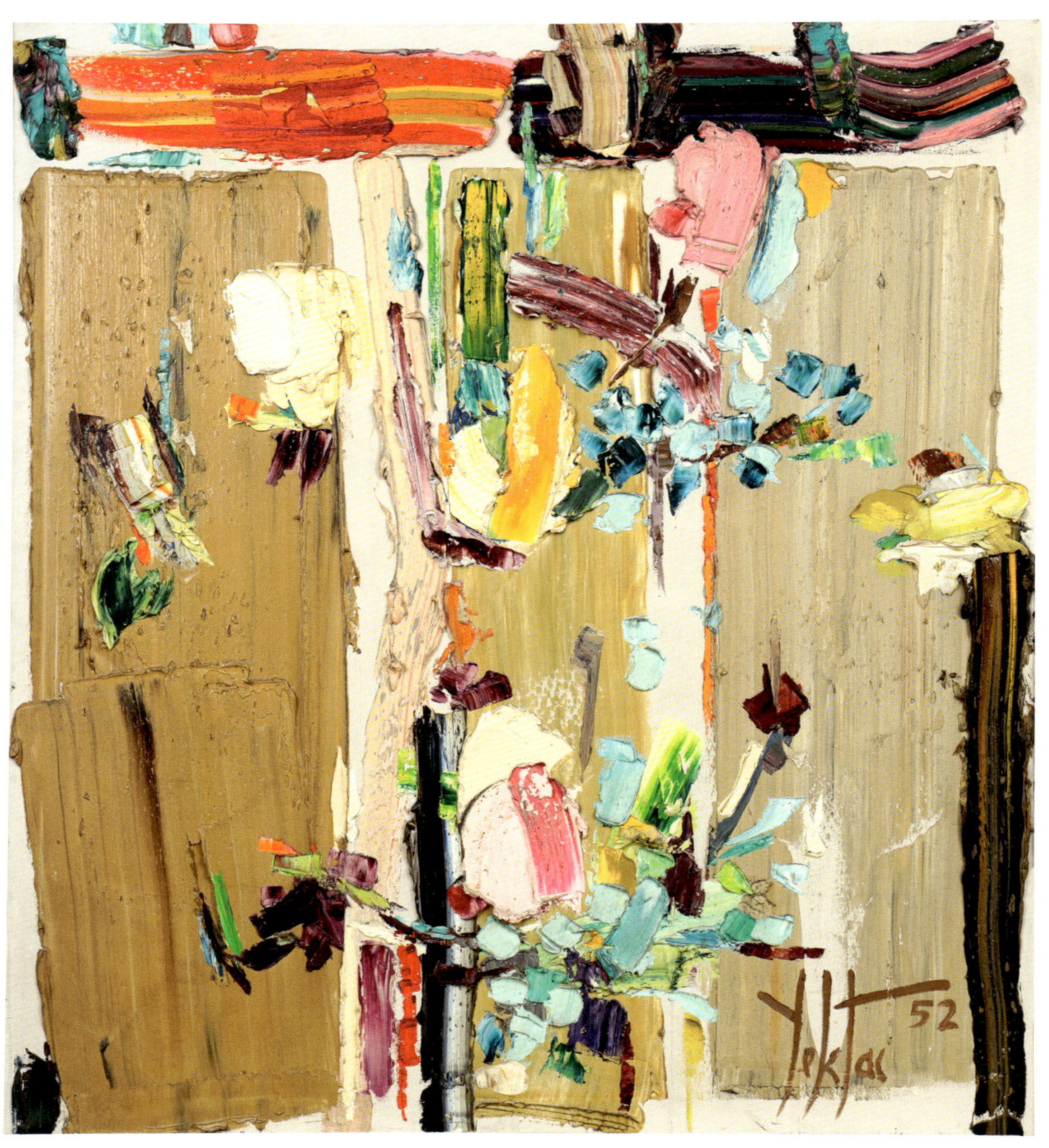

 Untitled, 1952, oil on canvas, 49¾ × 44¾ inches (126.4 × 113.7 cm)

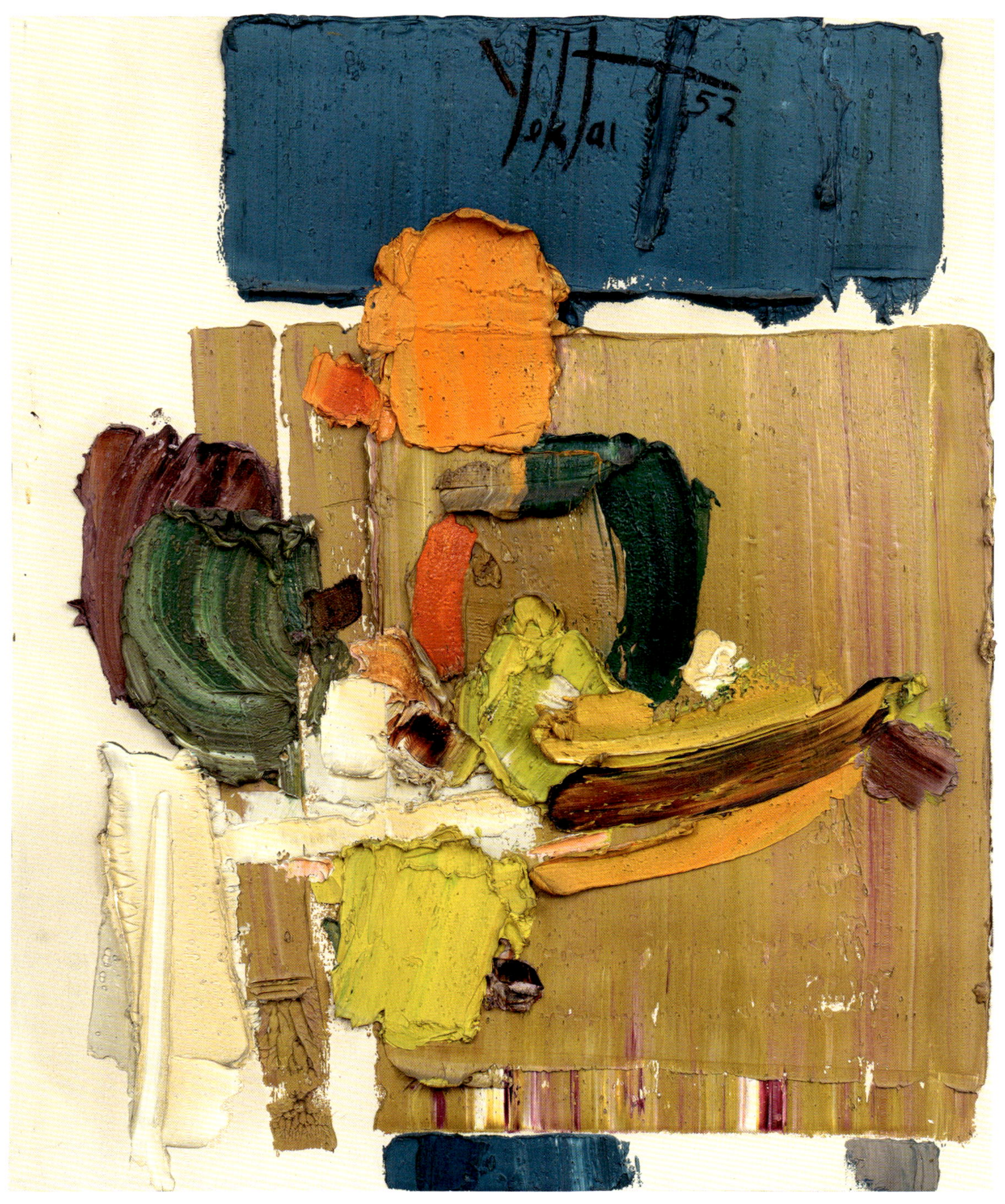

Untitled, 1952, oil on canvas, 32 × 26 inches (81.3 × 66 cm)

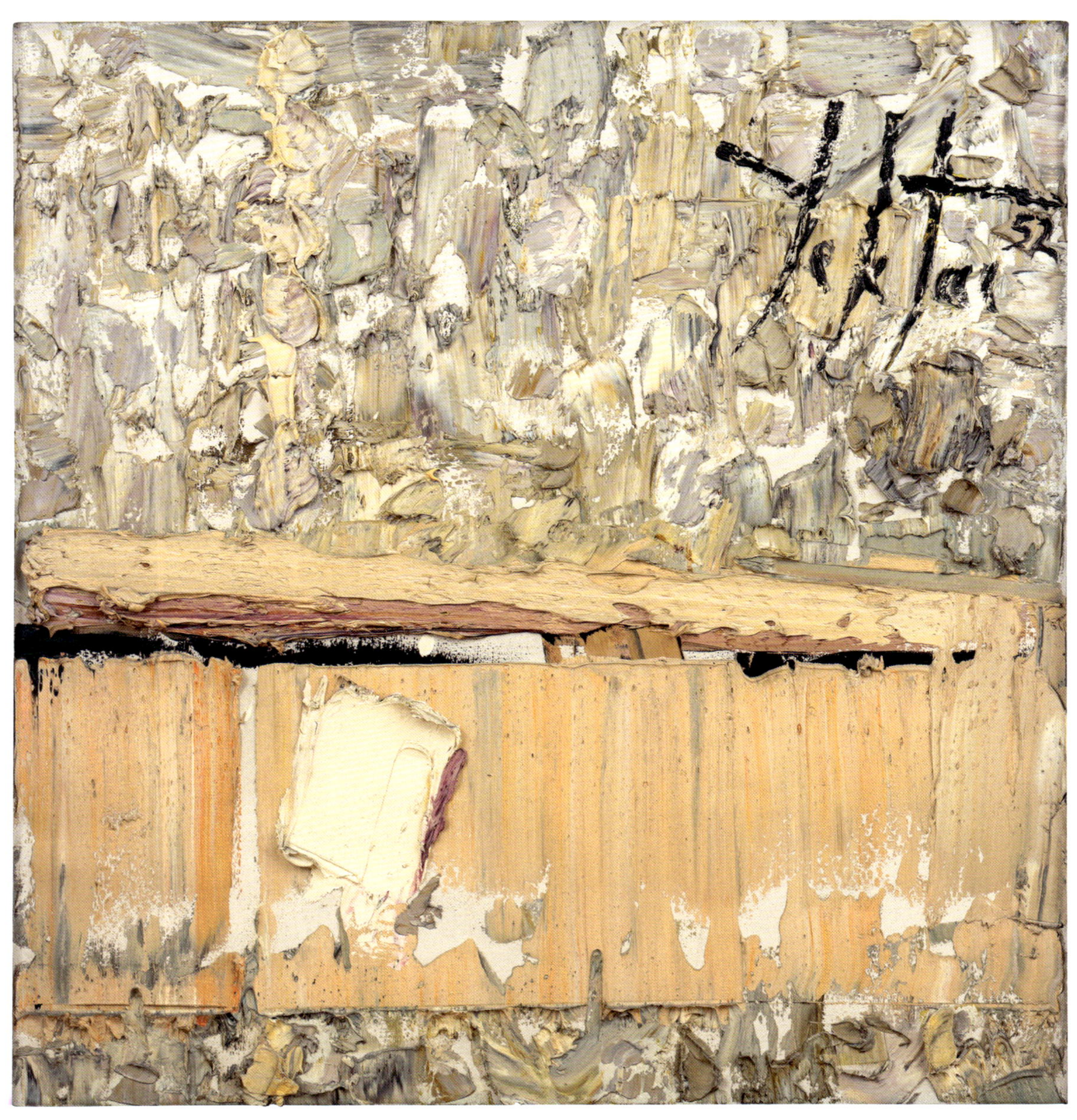

 Still Life with Playing Card, 1952, oil on canvas, 36 × 34 inches (91.4 × 86.4 cm)

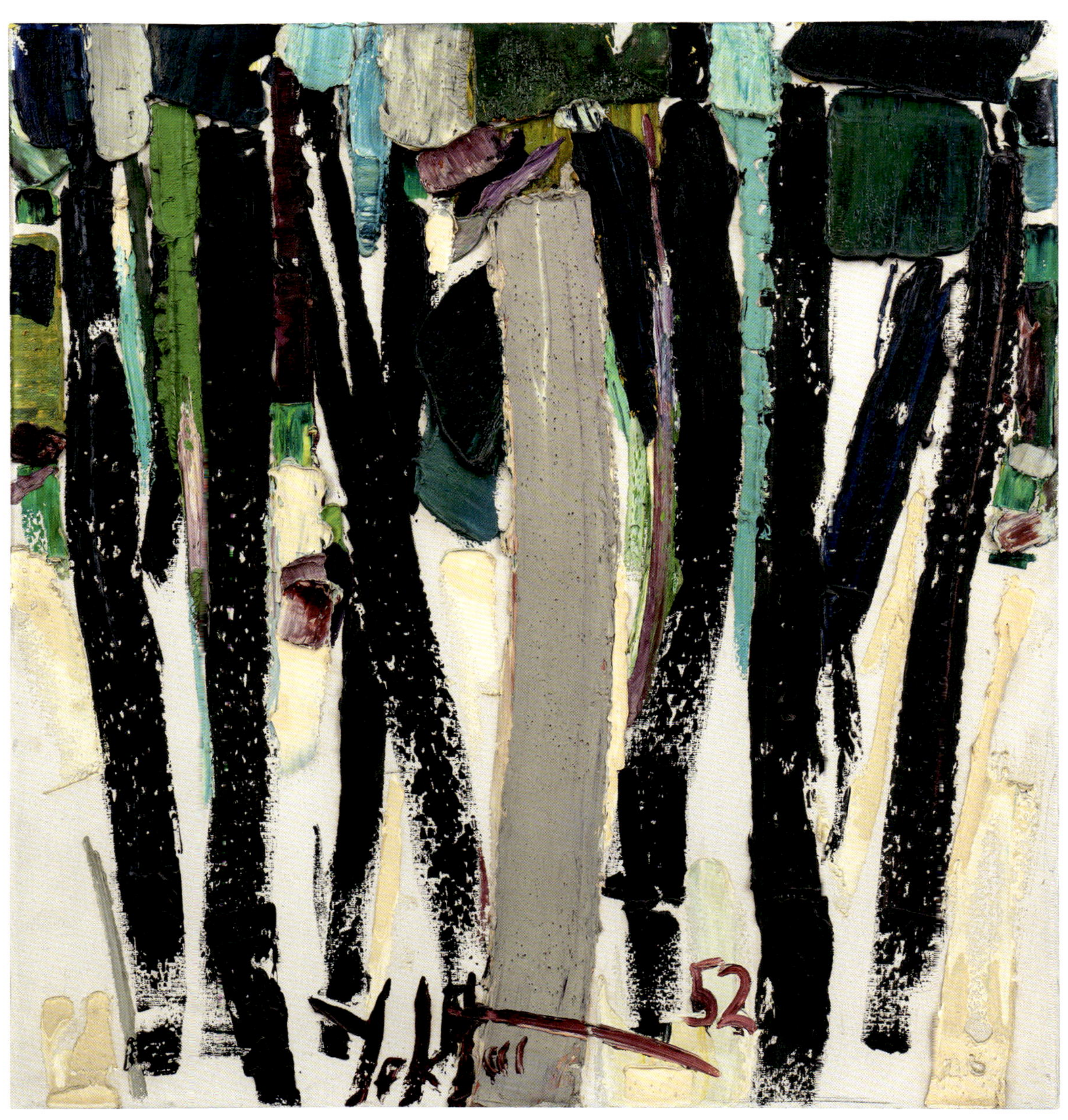

Trees, 1952, oil on canvas, 34 × 32 inches (86.4 × 81.3 cm)

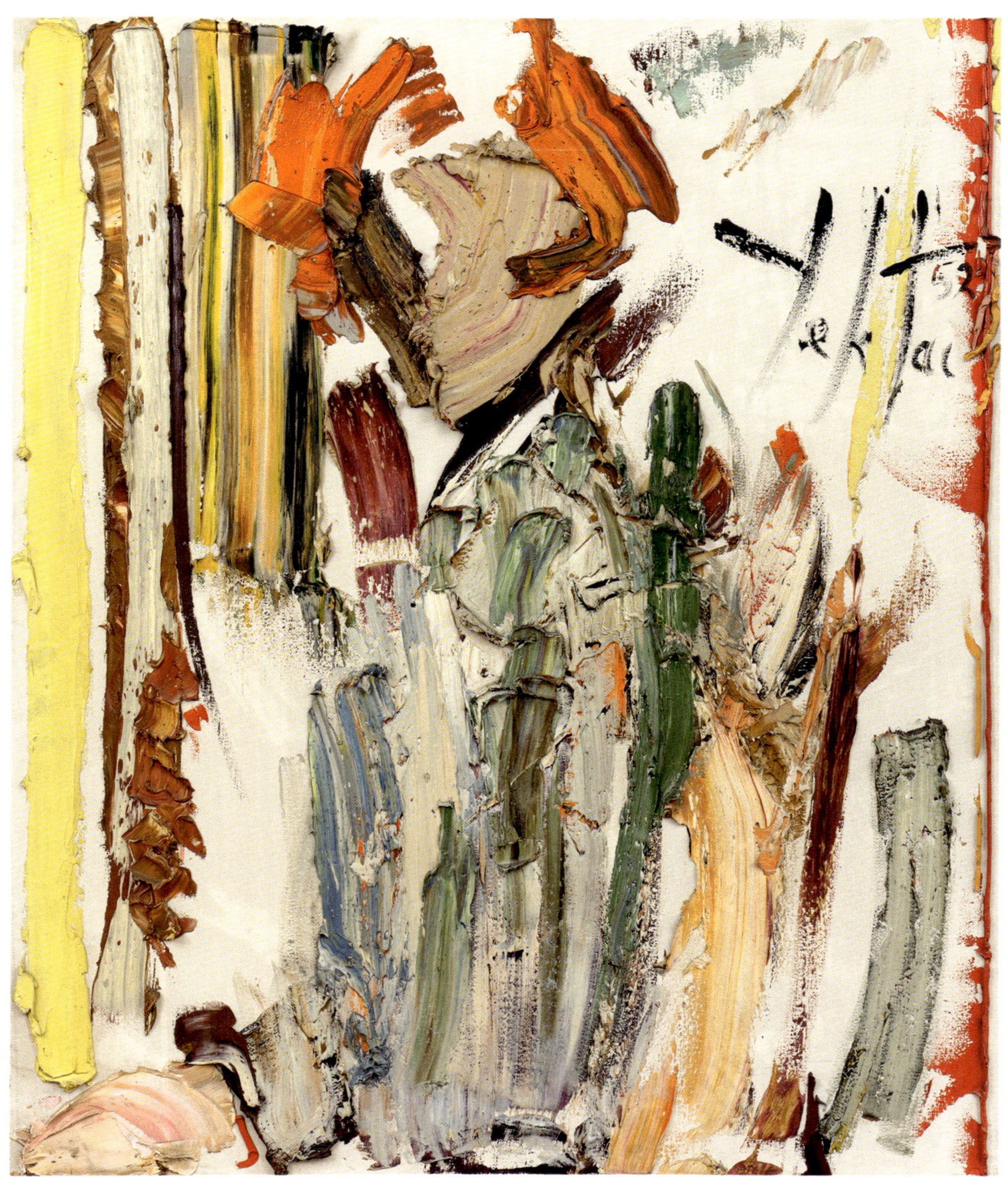

 Sitting Figure, 1952, oil on canvas, 48 × 40 inches (121.9 × 101.6 cm)

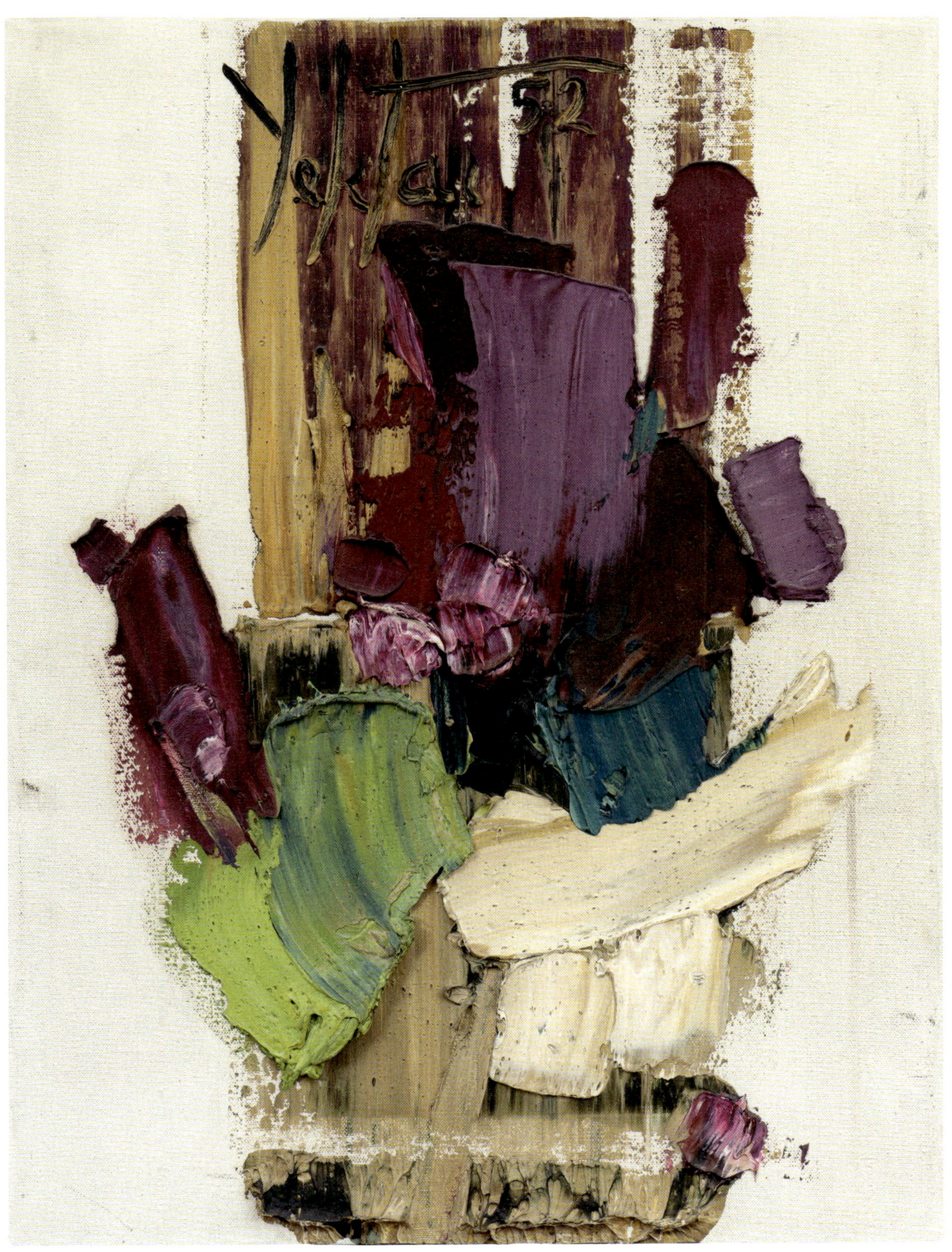

Untitled, 1952, oil on canvas, 16 × 12 inches (40.6 × 30.5 cm)

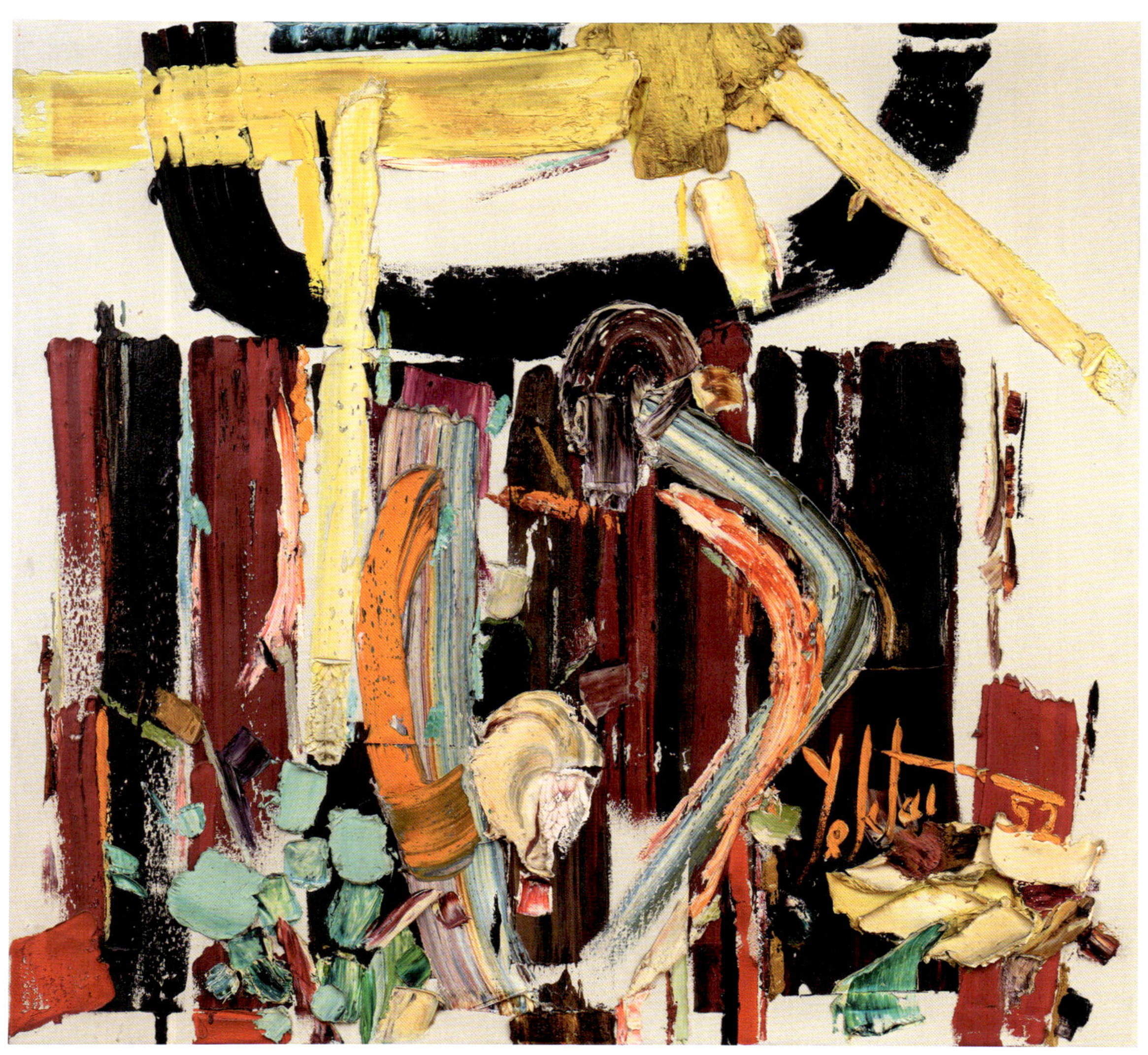

Untitled, 1952, oil on canvas, 46½ × 50 inches (118.1 × 127 cm)

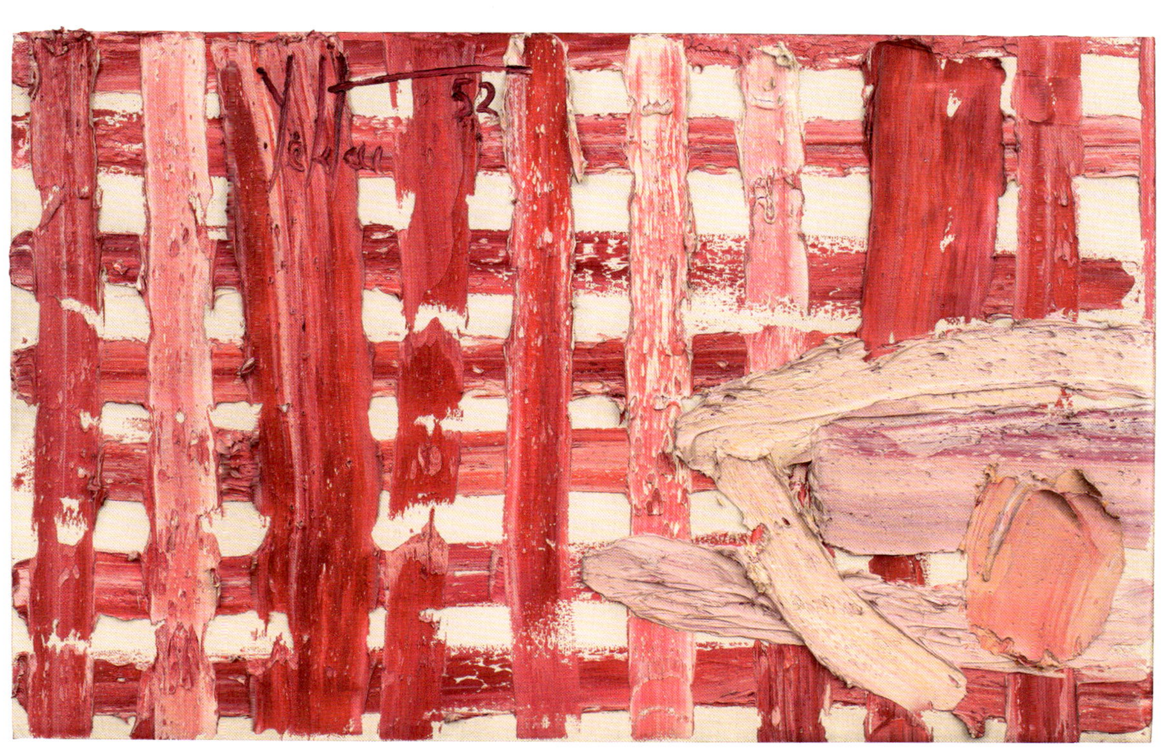

Composition, 1952, oil on canvas, 24 × 38 inches (61 × 96.5 cm)

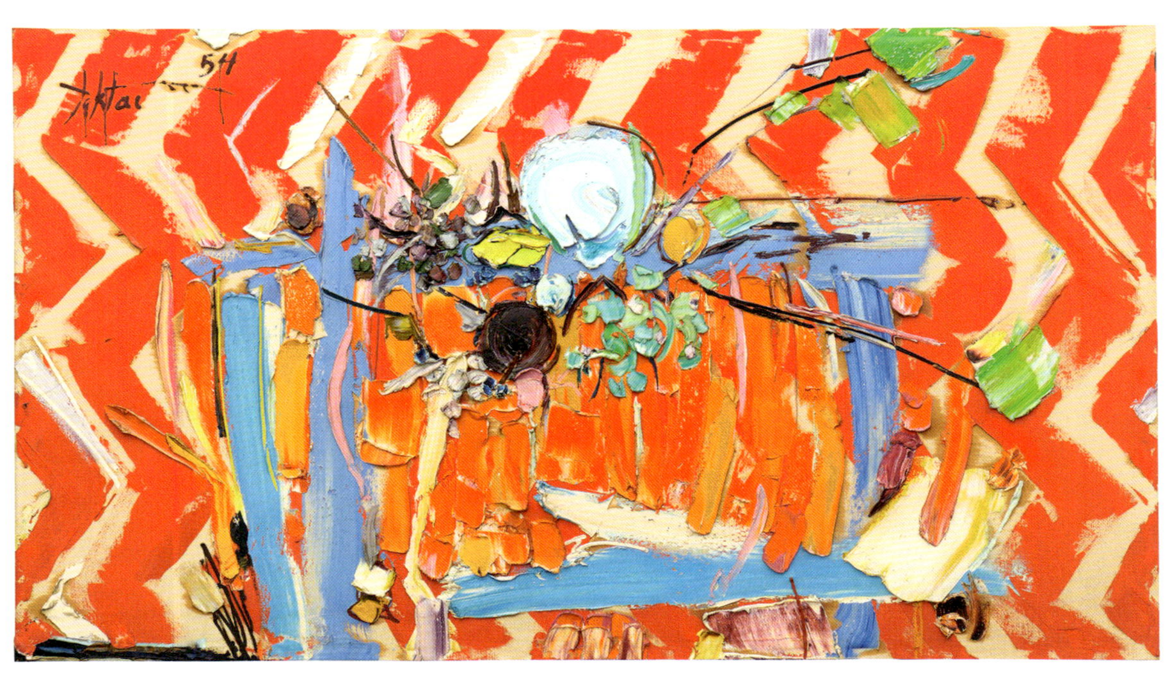

Untitled, 1954, oil on canvas, 48 × 85 inches (121.9 × 215.9 cm)

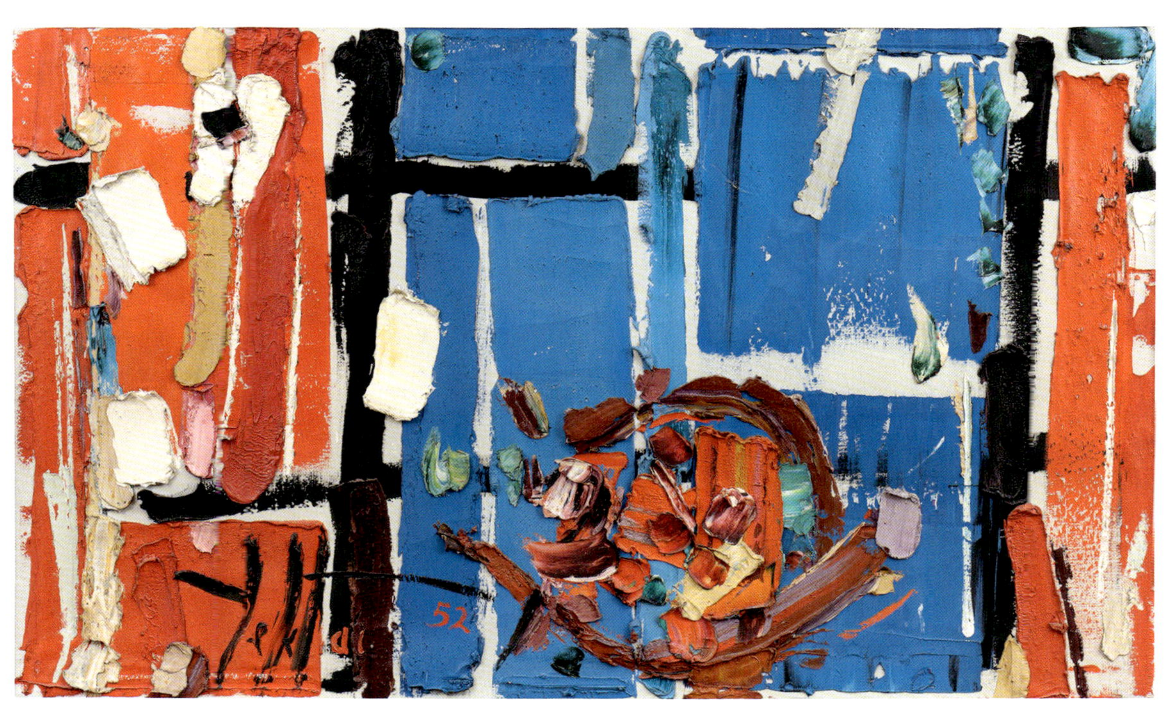

Untitled, 1952, oil on canvas, 36 × 60 inches (91.4 × 152.4 cm)

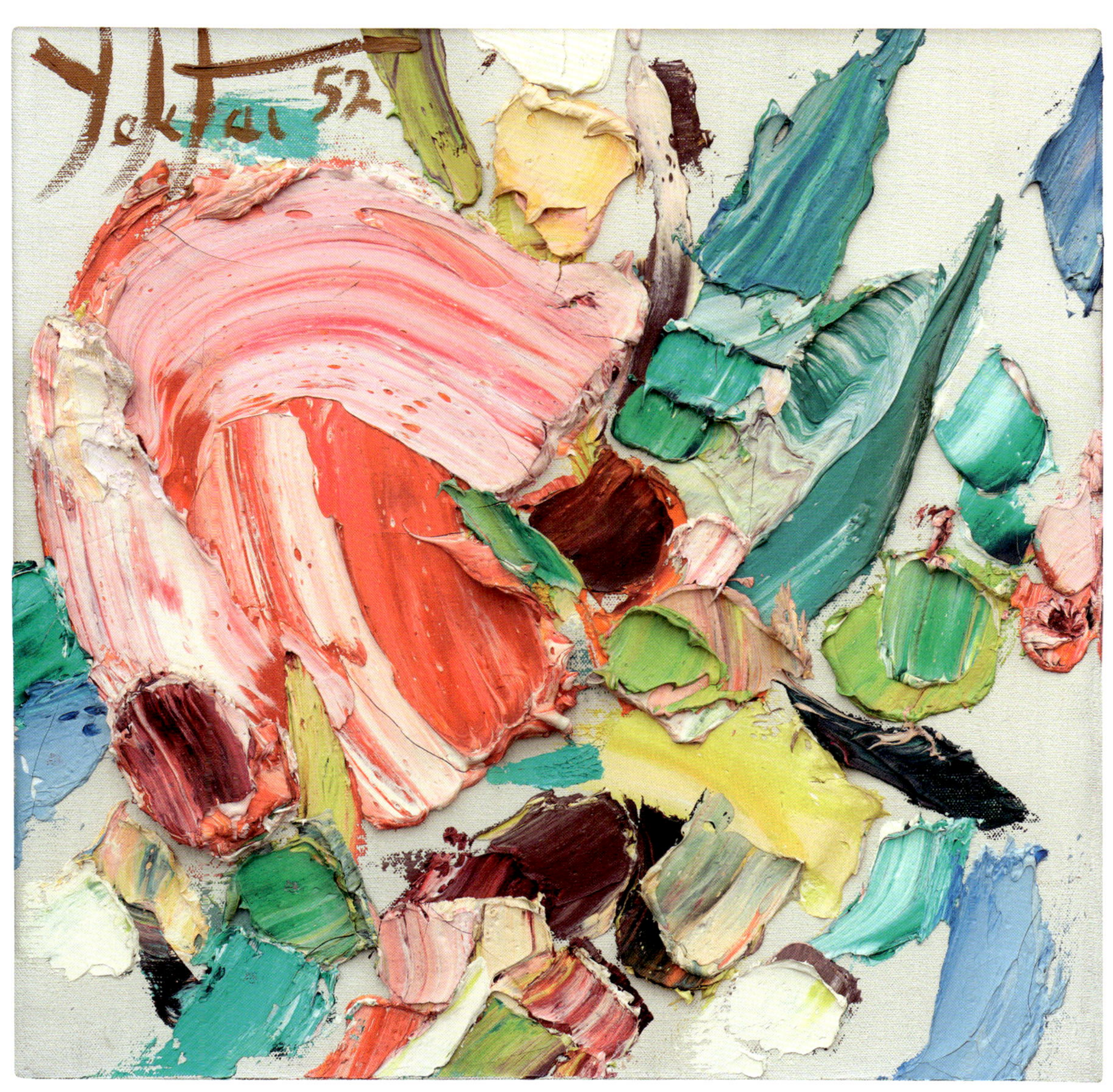

Untitled, 1952, oil on canvas, 12 × 12 inches (30.5 × 30.5 cm)

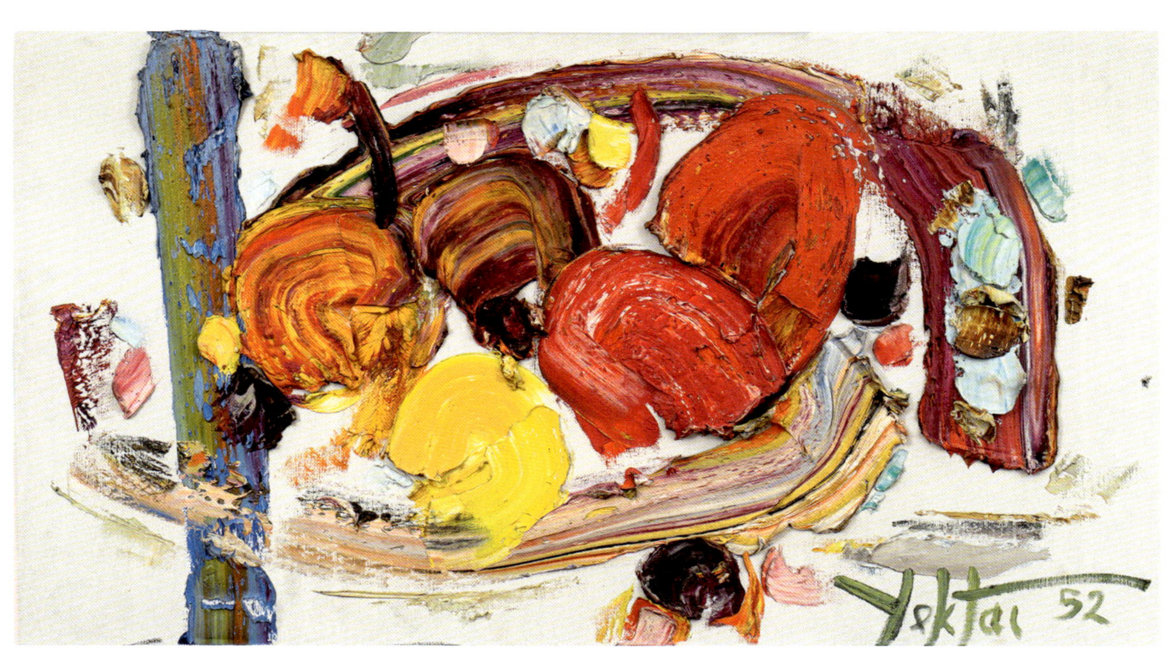

 Untitled, 1952, oil on canvas, 20 × 36 inches (50.8 × 91.4 cm)

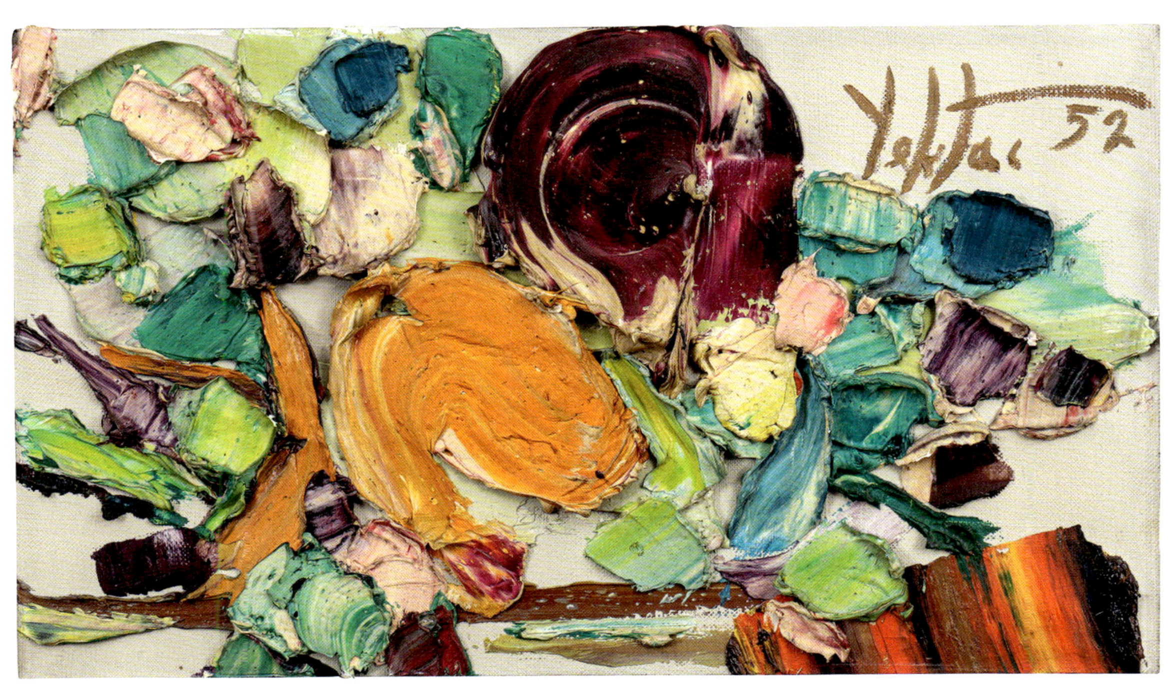

Untitled, 1952, oil on canvas, 8 × 13⅞ inches (20.3 × 35.3 cm)

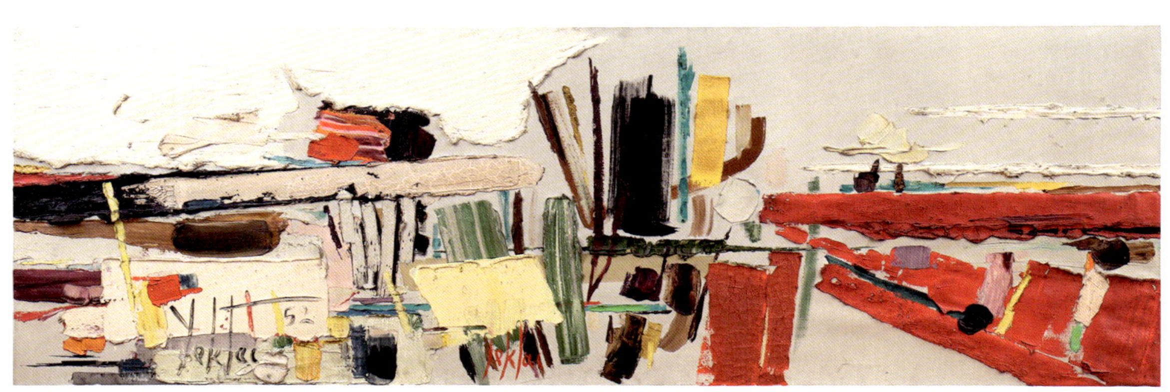

Untitled, 1952, oil on canvas, 26 × 80 inches (66 × 203.2 cm)

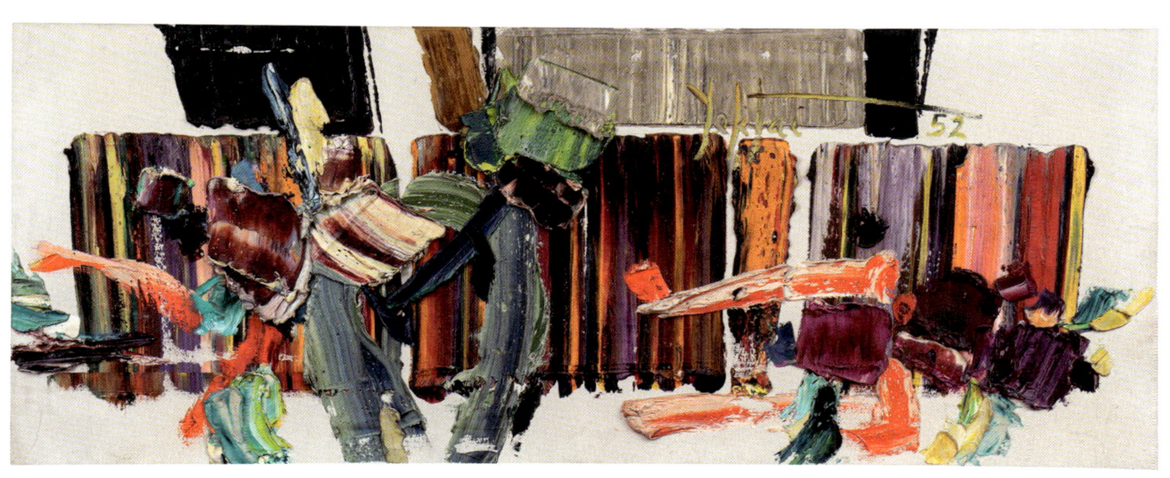

Untitled, 1952, oil on canvas, 19½ × 50 inches (49.5 × 127 cm)

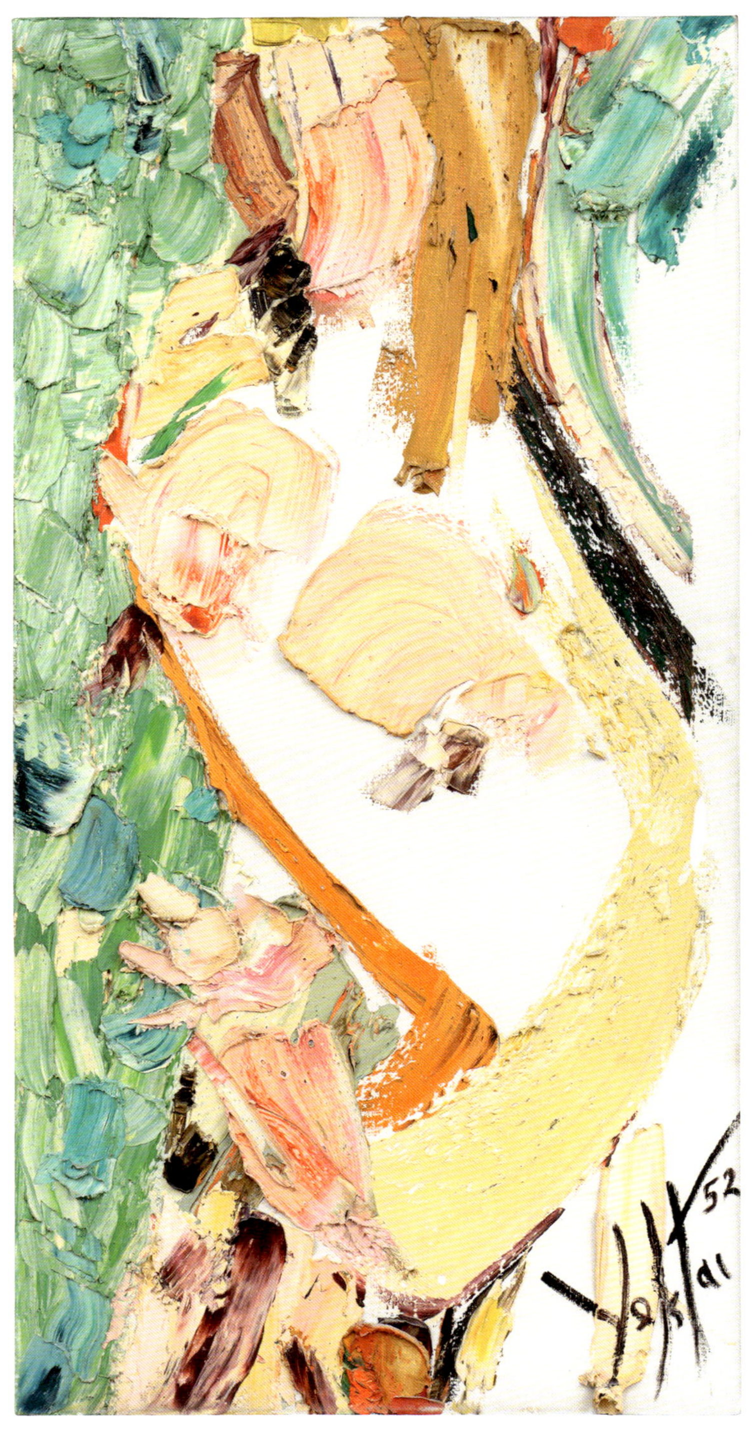

Untitled, 1952, oil on canvas, 47 × 28 inches (119.4 × 71.1 cm)

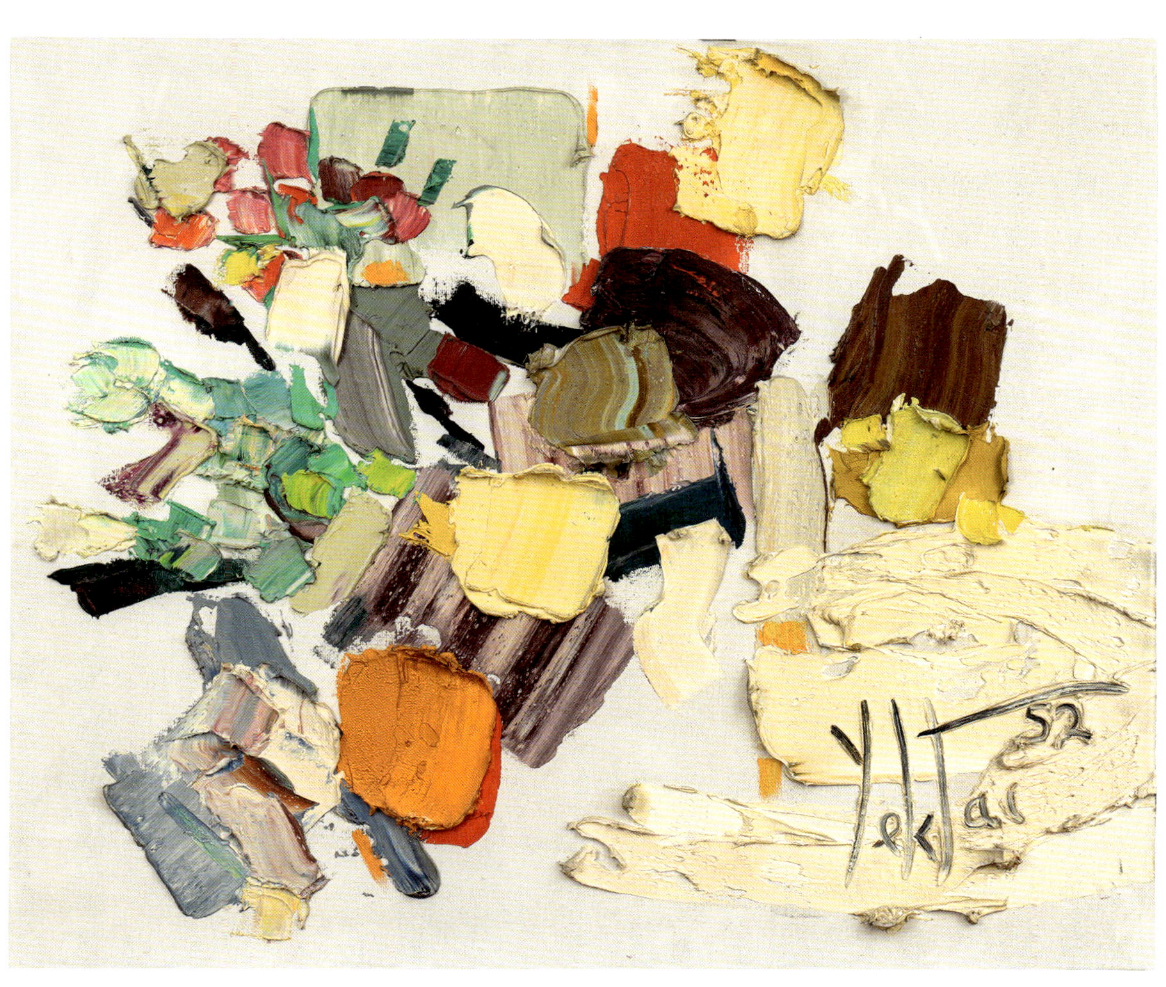

Still Life with Flowers, 1952, oil on canvas, 30 × 36 inches (76.2 × 91.4 cm)

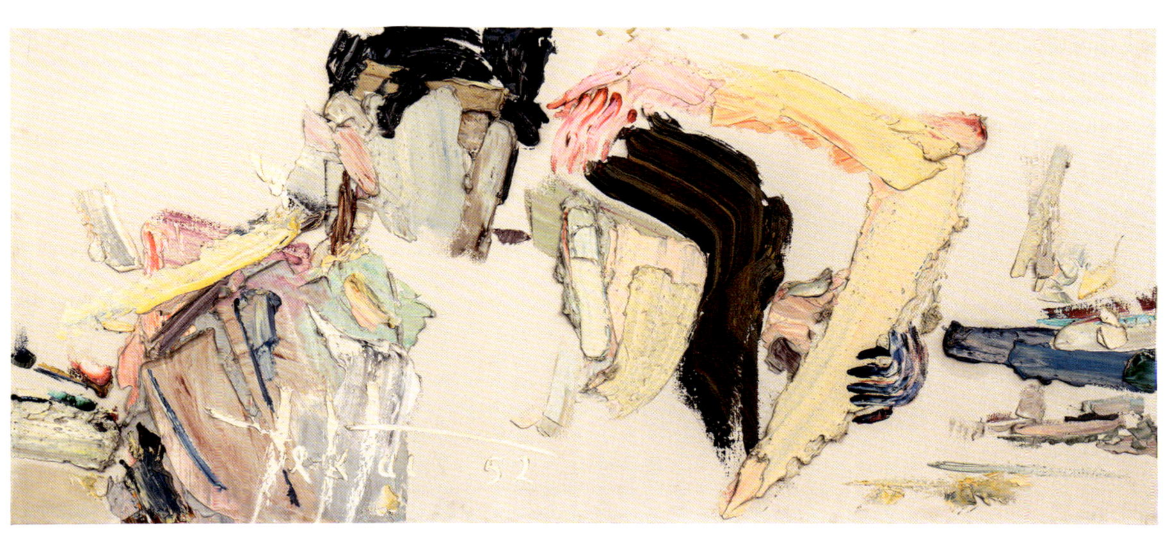

Untitled, 1952, oil on canvas, 32 × 72 inches (81.3 × 182.9 cm)

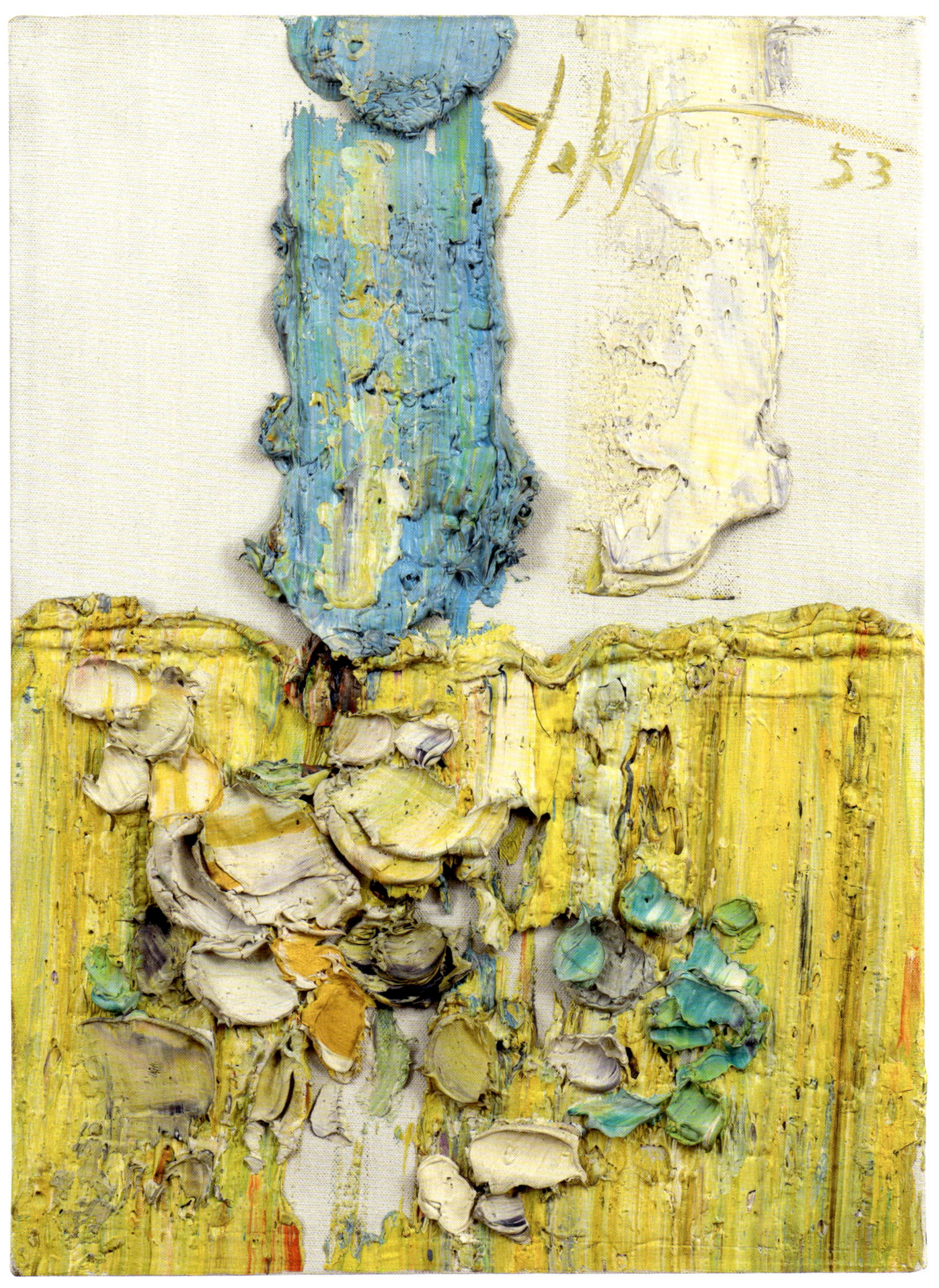

Untitled, 1953, oil on canvas, 14¼ × 10 inches (36.2 × 25.4 cm)

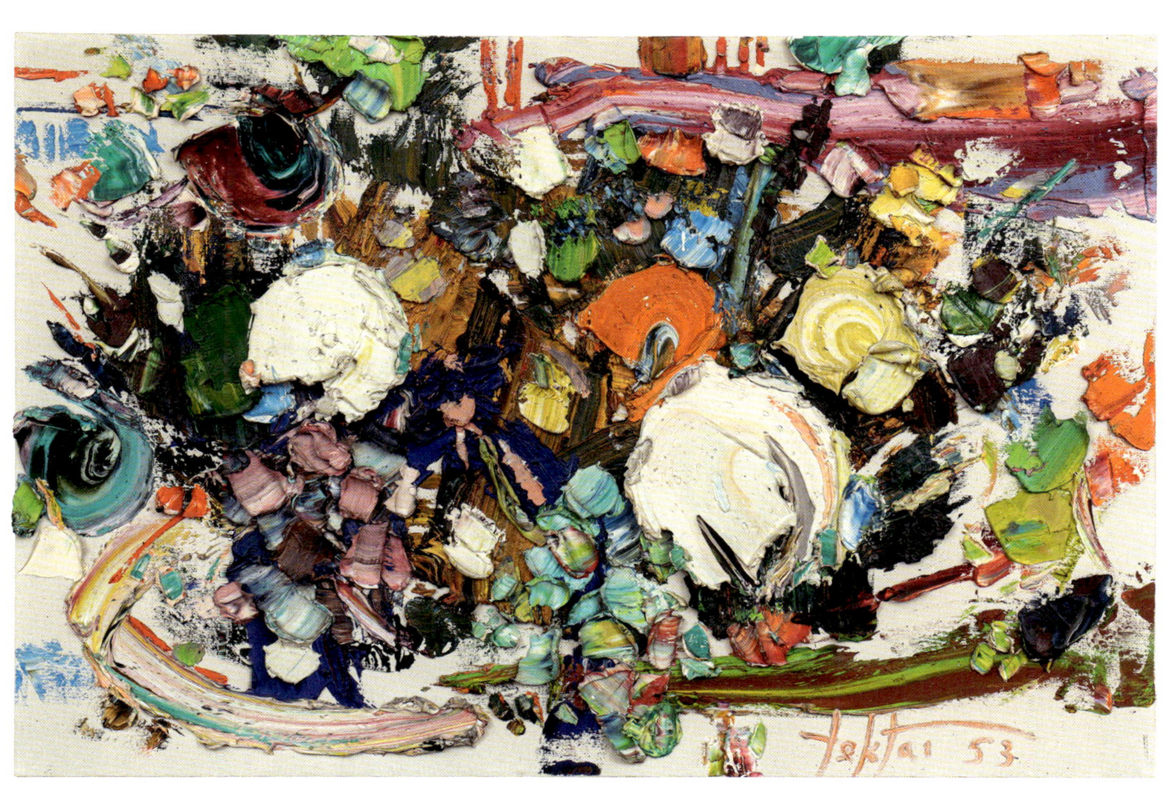

Fruit on Table, 1953, oil on canvas, 24 × 36 inches (61 × 91.4 cm)

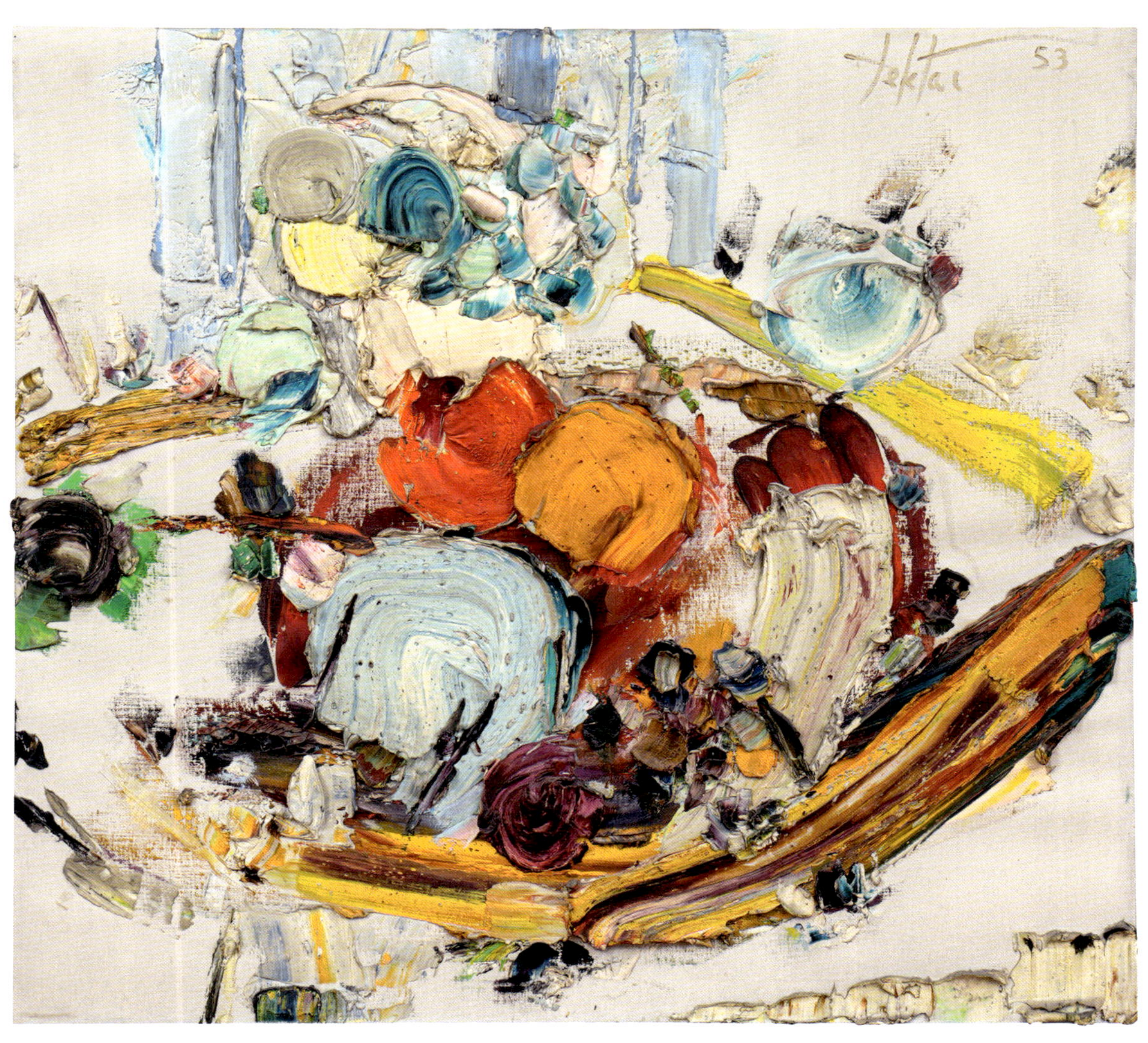

Untitled, 1953, oil on canvas, 36 × 40 inches (91.4 × 101.6 cm)

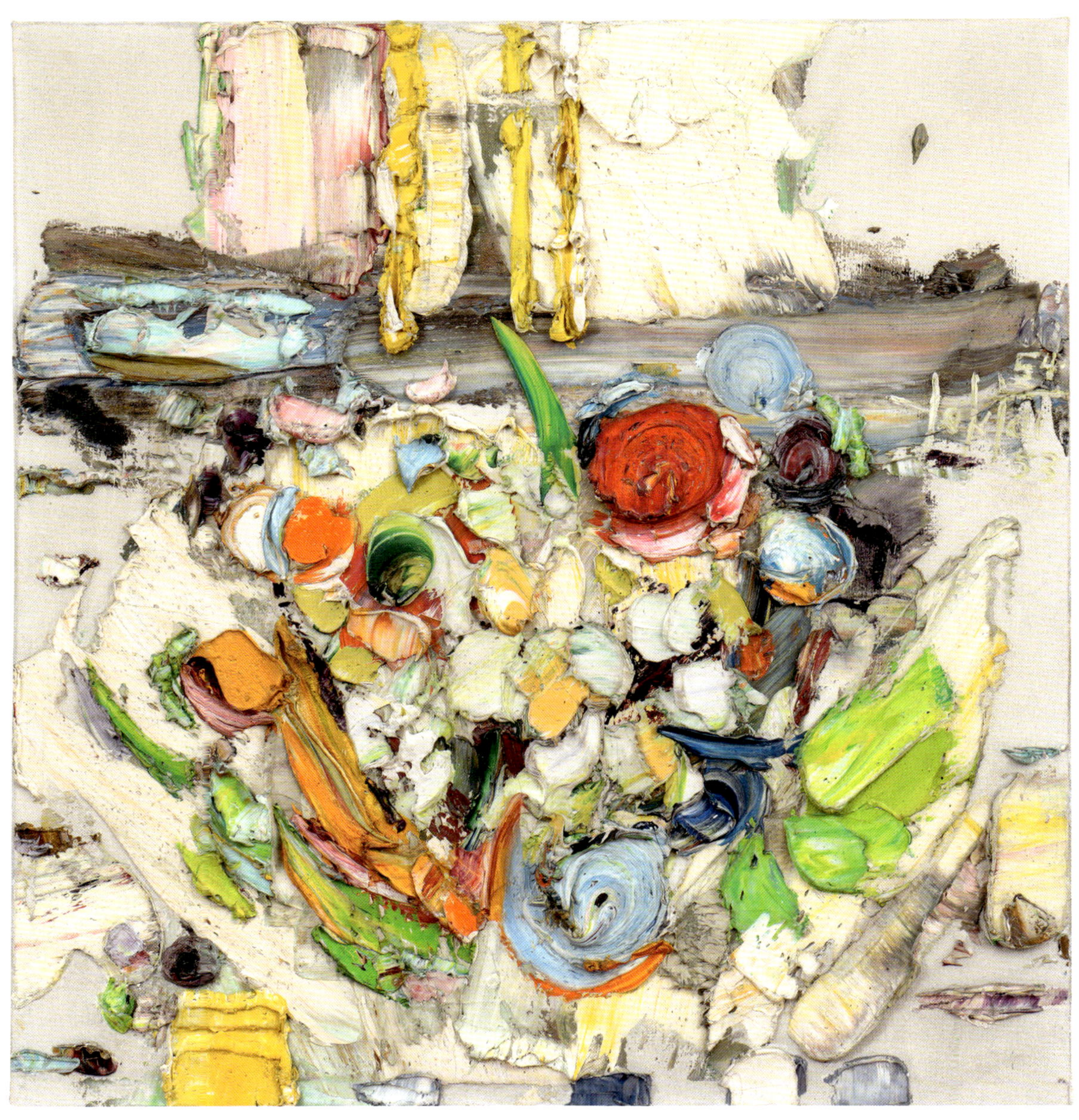

Untitled, 1953–54, oil on canvas, 29 × 27½ inches (73.7 × 69.9 cm)

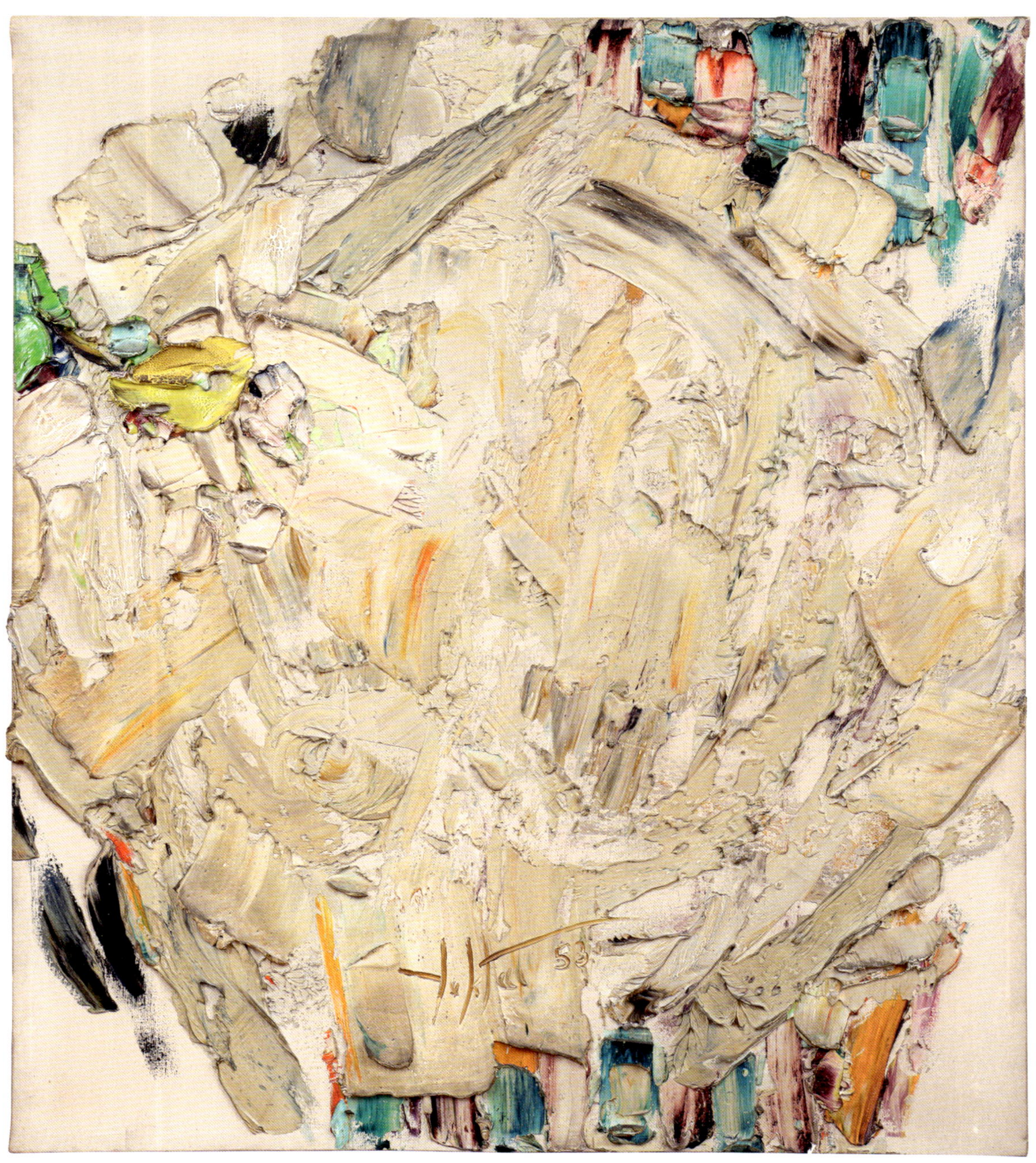

Untitled, 1953, oil on canvas, 44 × 39 inches (111.8 × 99.1 cm)

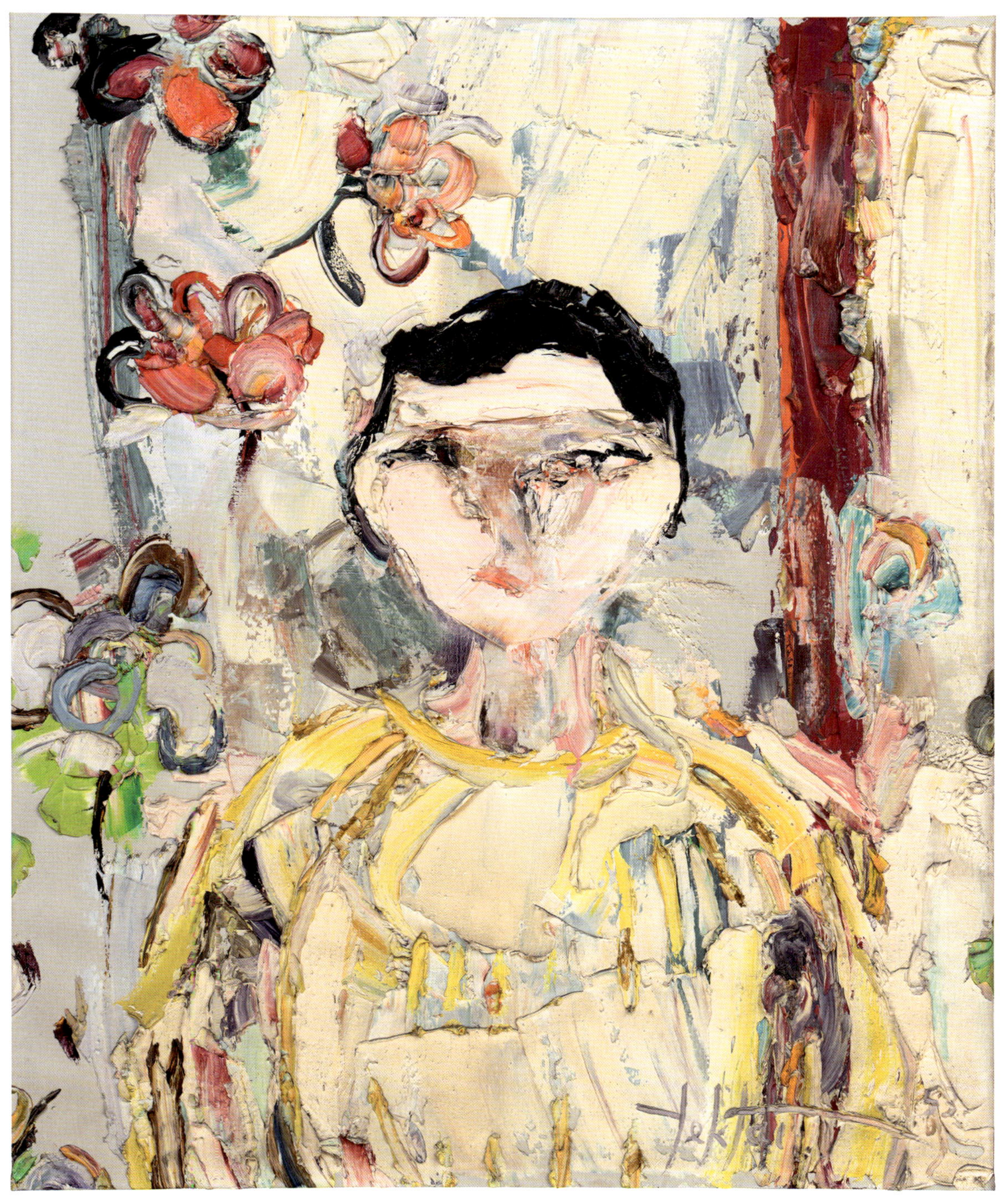

Untitled, 1953, oil on canvas, 51½ × 42 inches (130.8 × 106.7 cm)

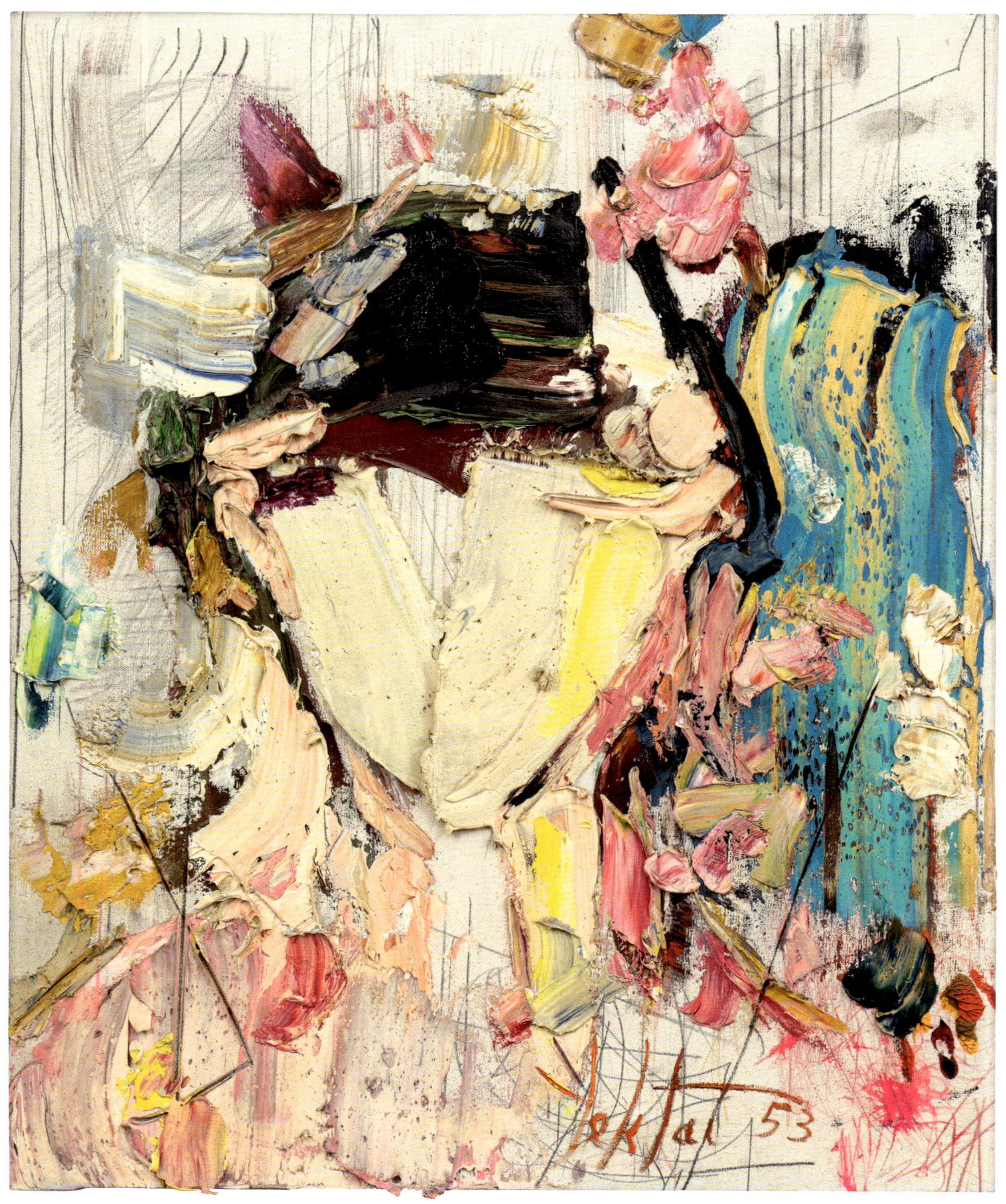

Untitled, 1953, oil on canvas, 30¼ × 24¾ inches (76.8 × 62.9 cm)

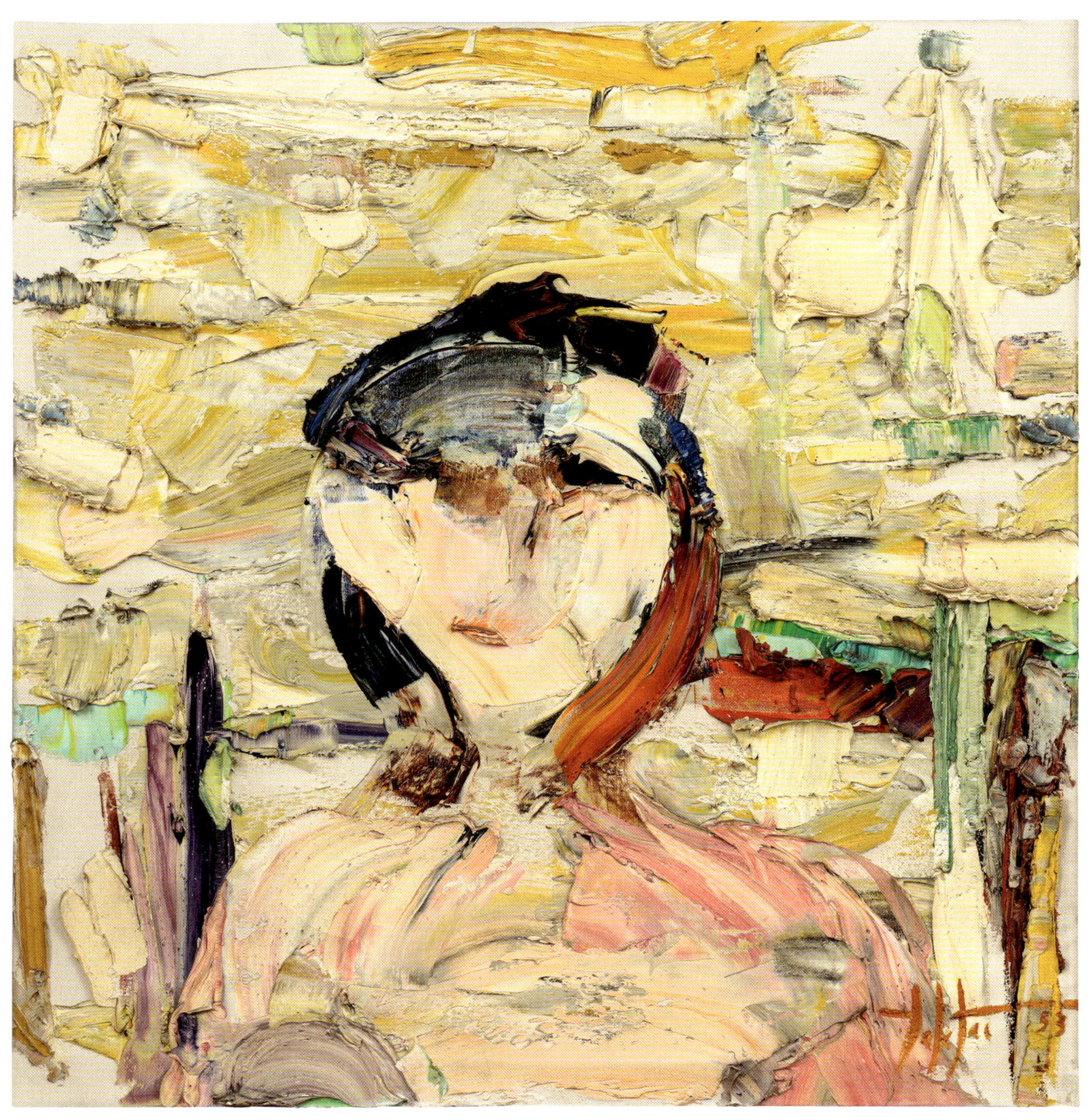

Untitled, 1953, oil on canvas, 36 × 34 inches (91.4 × 86.4 cm)

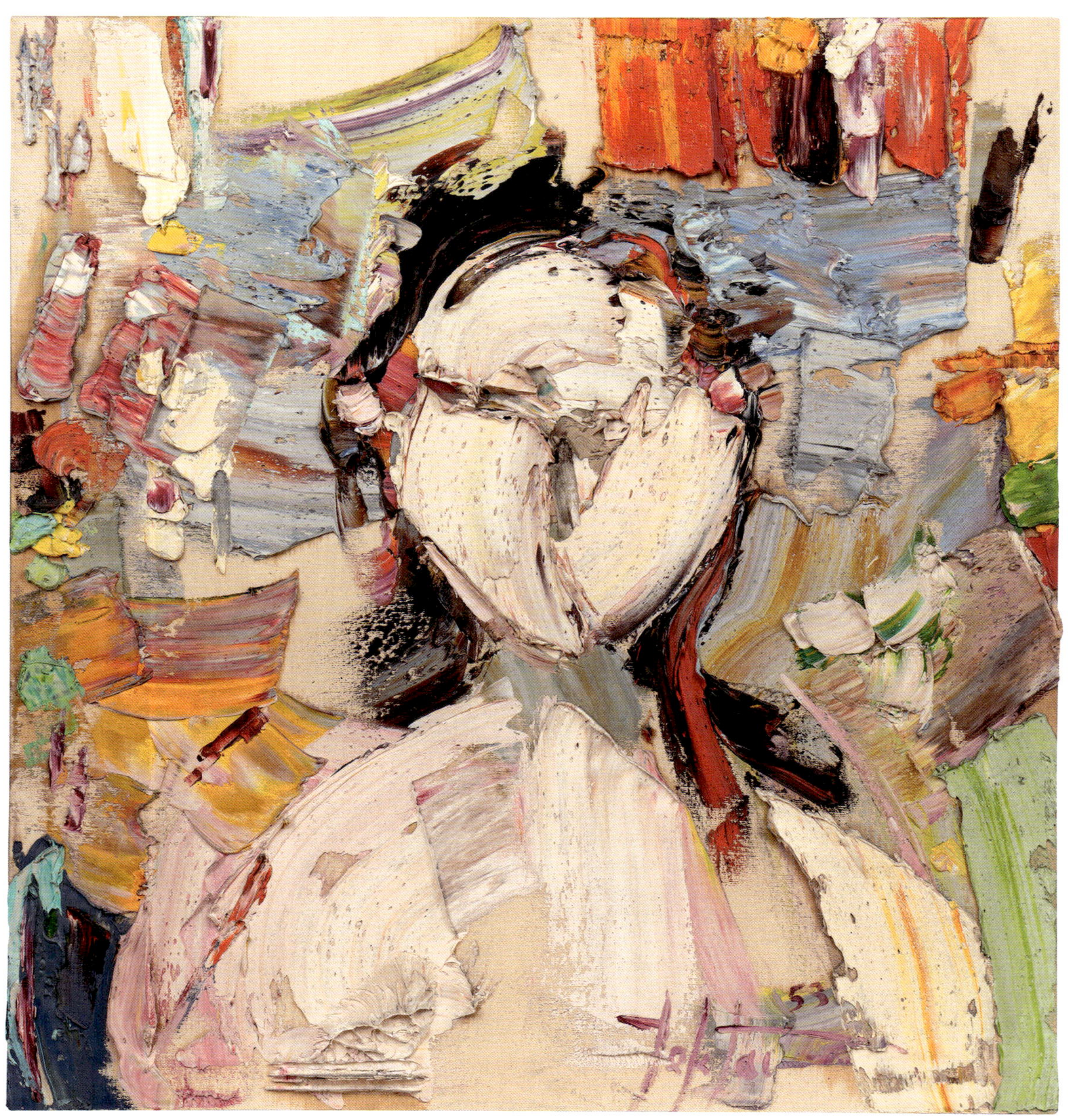

Portrait, 1953, oil on canvas, 36 × 34 inches (91.4 × 86.4 cm)

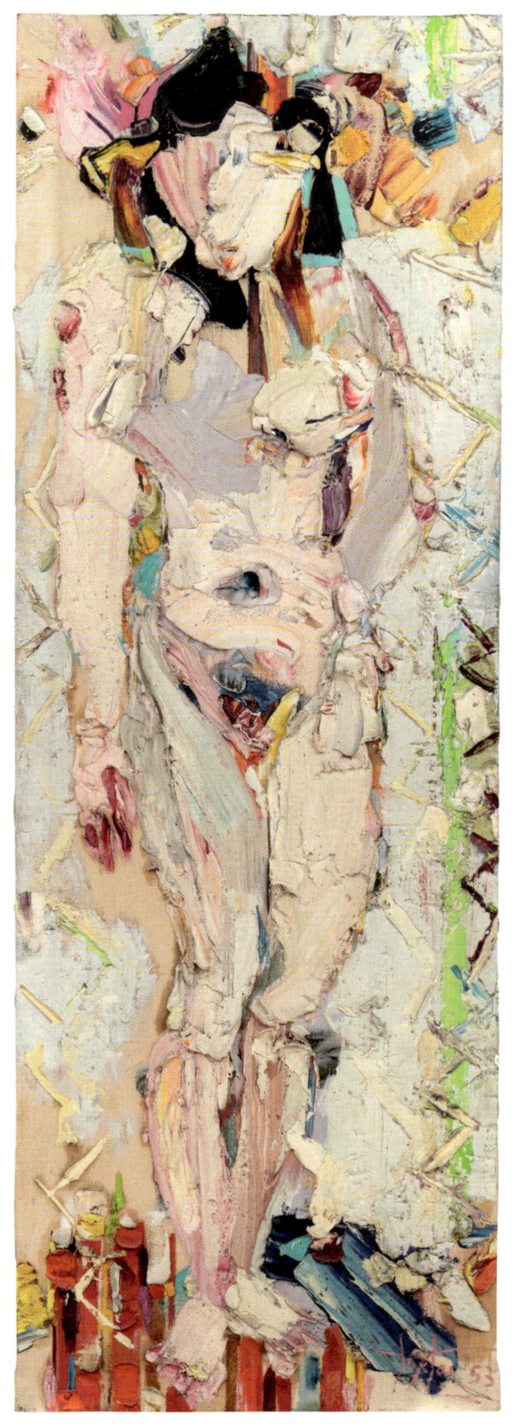

Untitled, 1953, oil on canvas, 87 × 29½ inches (221 × 74.9 cm)

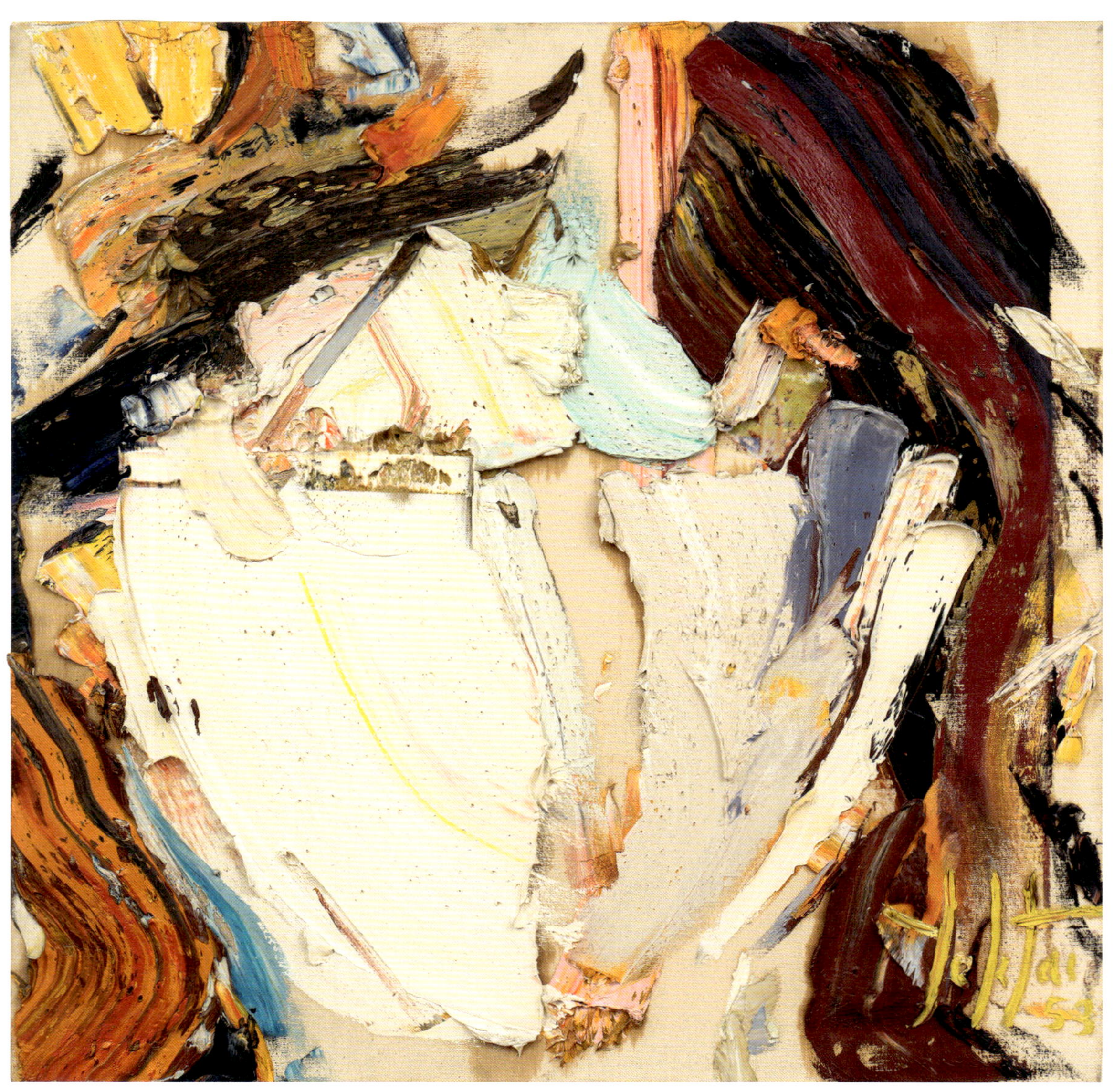

 Head of a Woman, 1953, oil on canvas, 34 × 34 inches (86.4 × 86.4 cm)

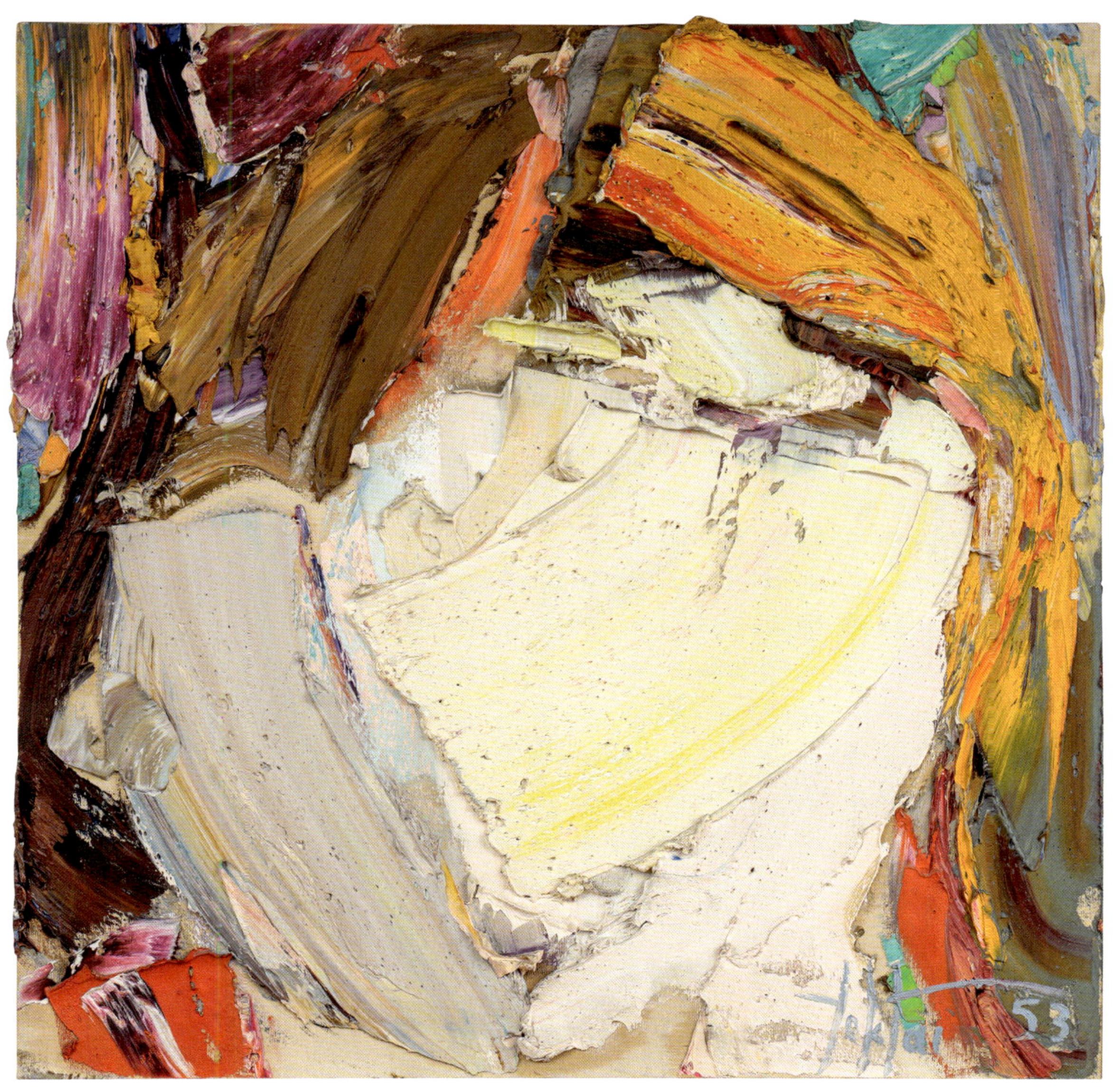

Untitled, 1953, oil on canvas, 34 × 34 inches (86.4 × 86.4 cm)

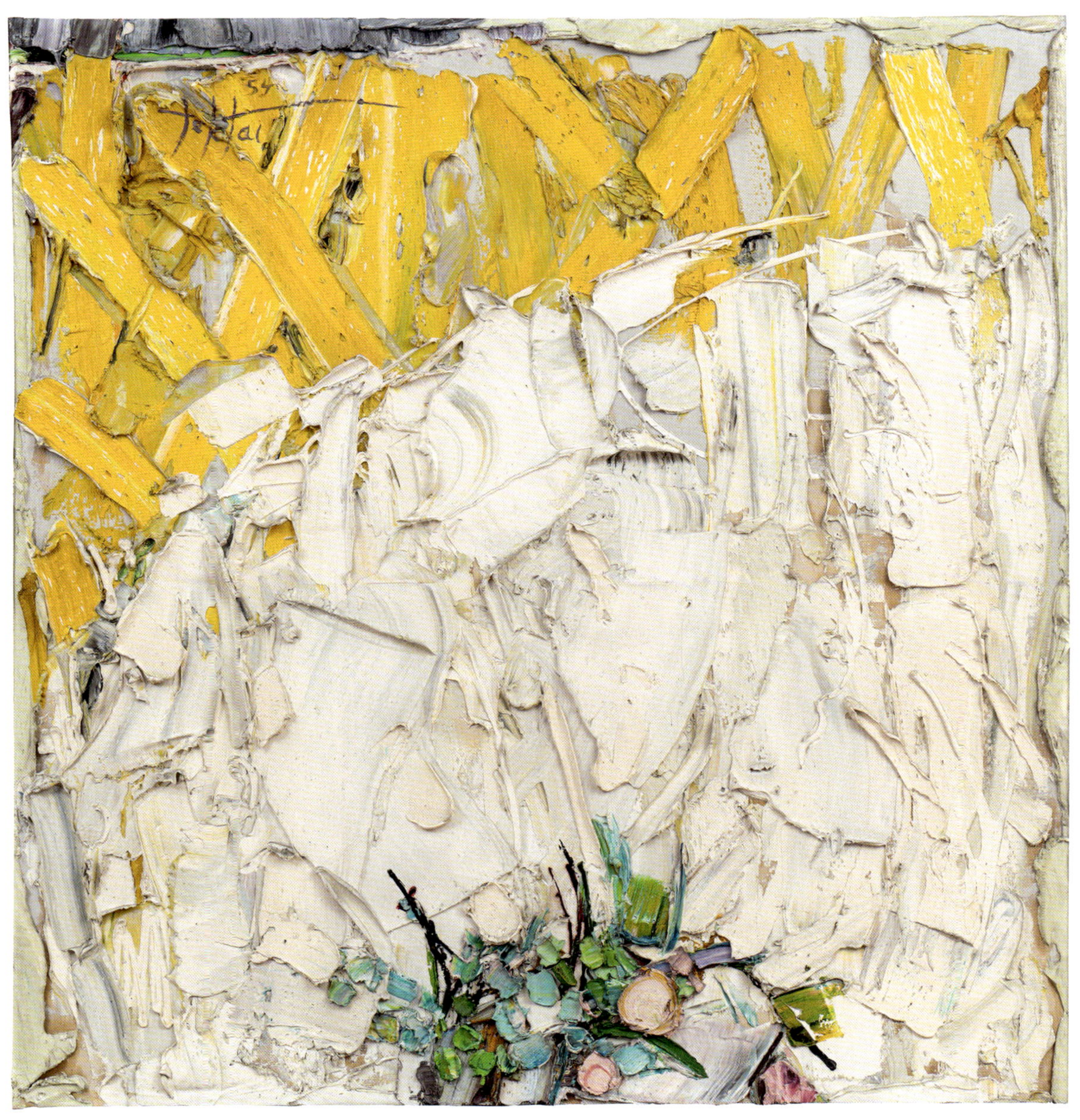

Yellow Curtain, 1954, oil on canvas, 55 × 52 inches (139.7 × 132.1 cm)

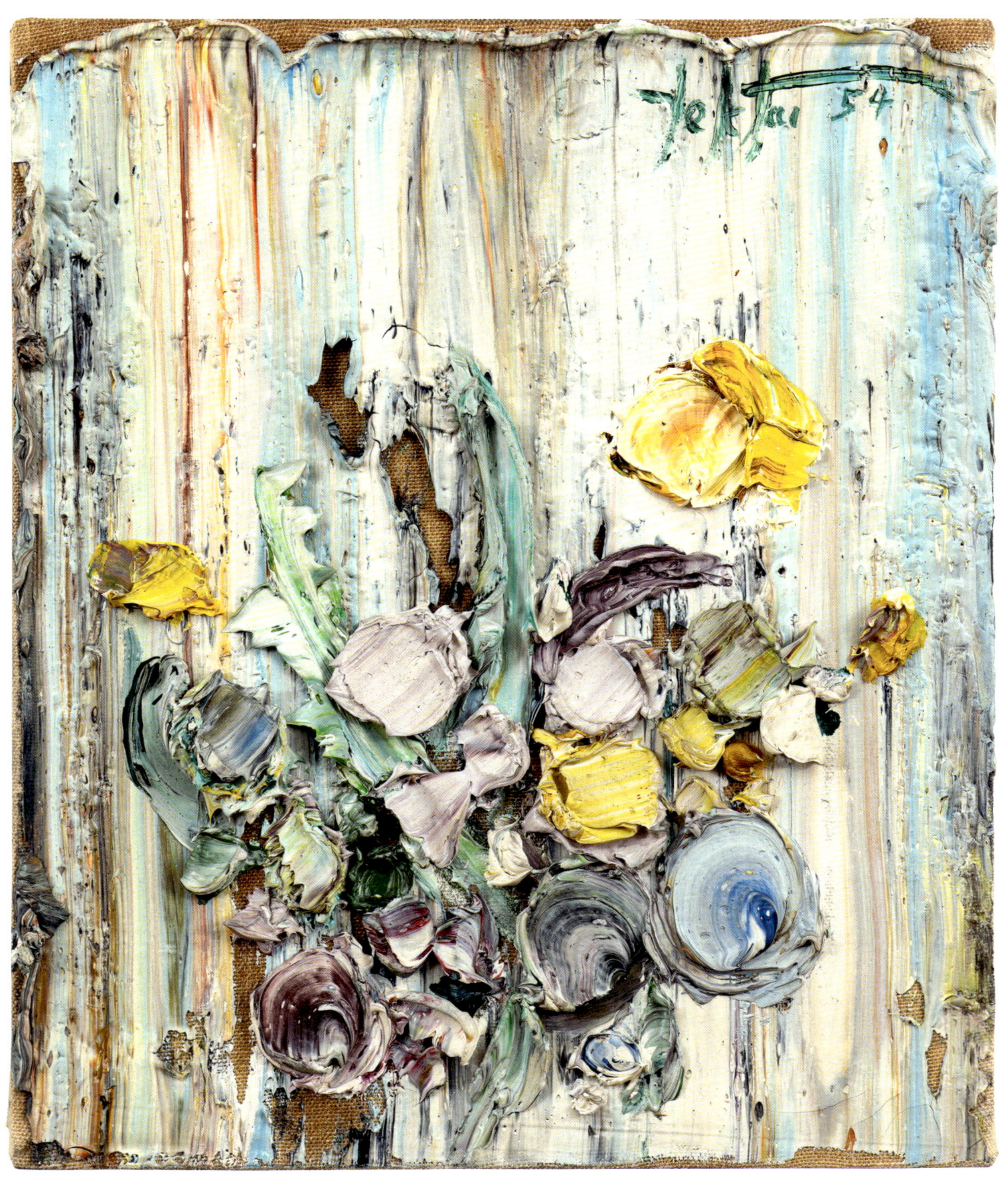

Untitled, 1954, oil on canvas, 12 × 10 inches (30.5 × 25.4 cm)

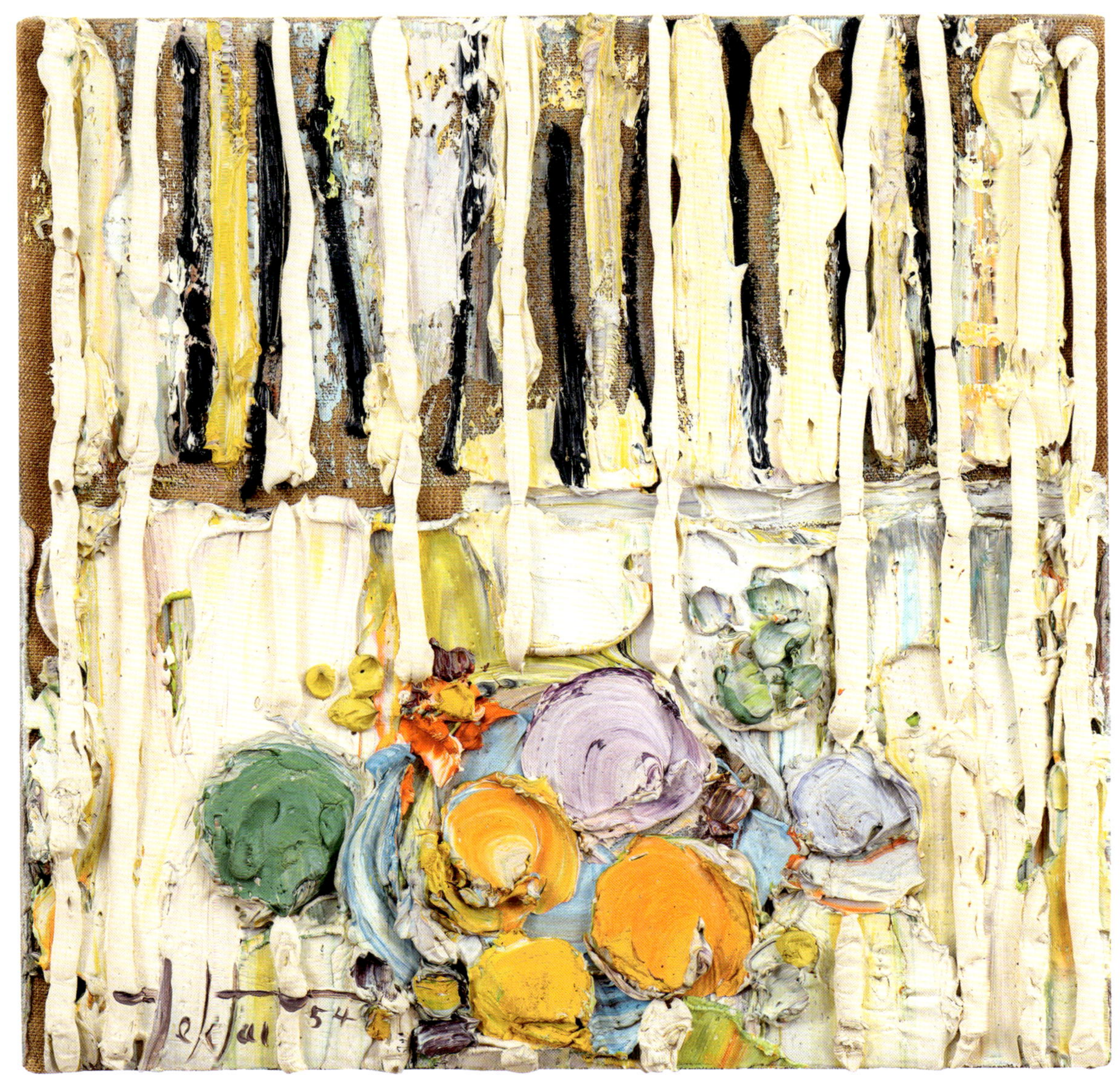

White Curtain, 1954, oil on canvas, 12 × 12 inches (30.5 × 30.5 cm)

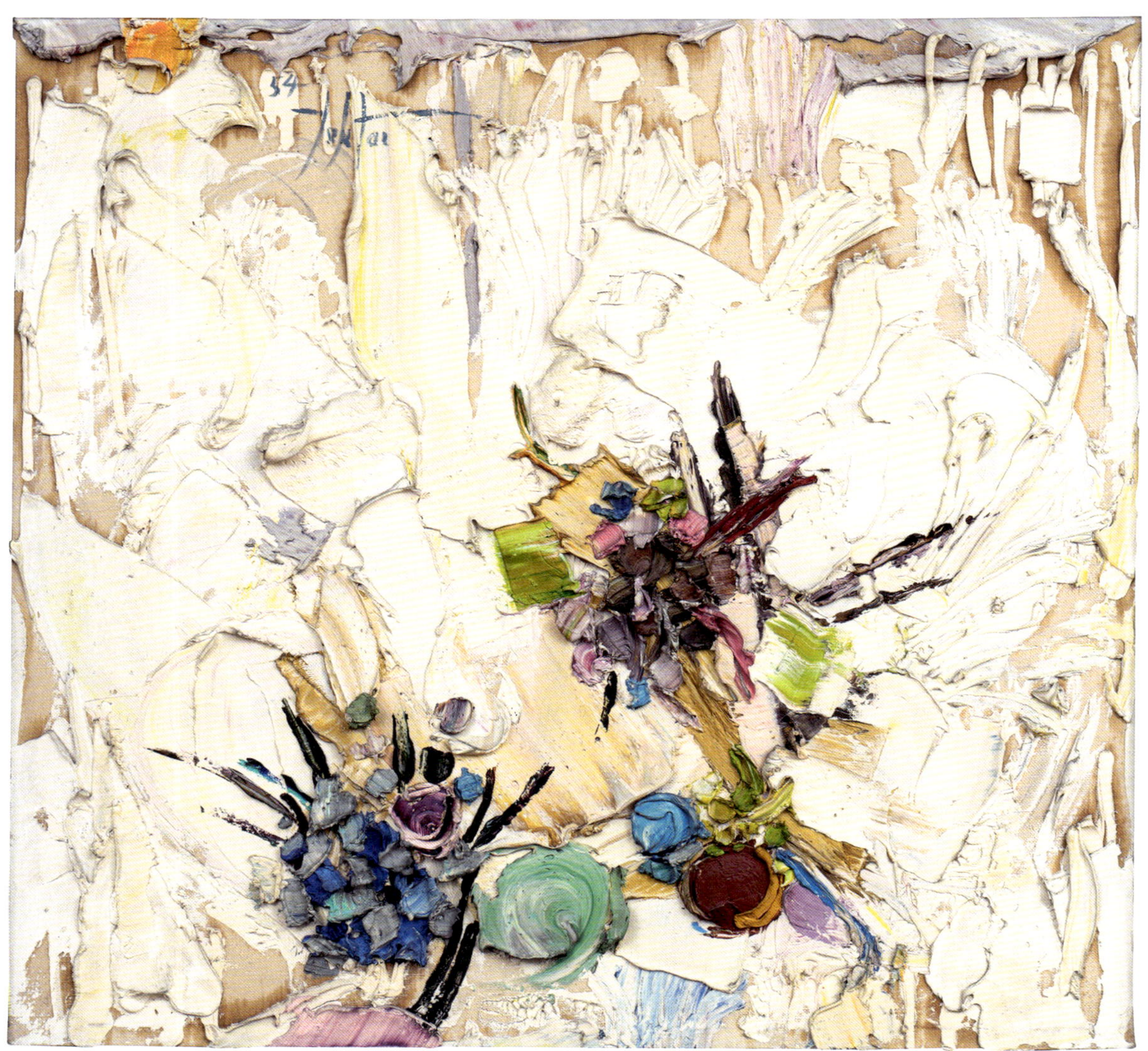

Untitled, 1954, oil on canvas, 34½ × 36½ inches (87.6 × 92.7 cm)

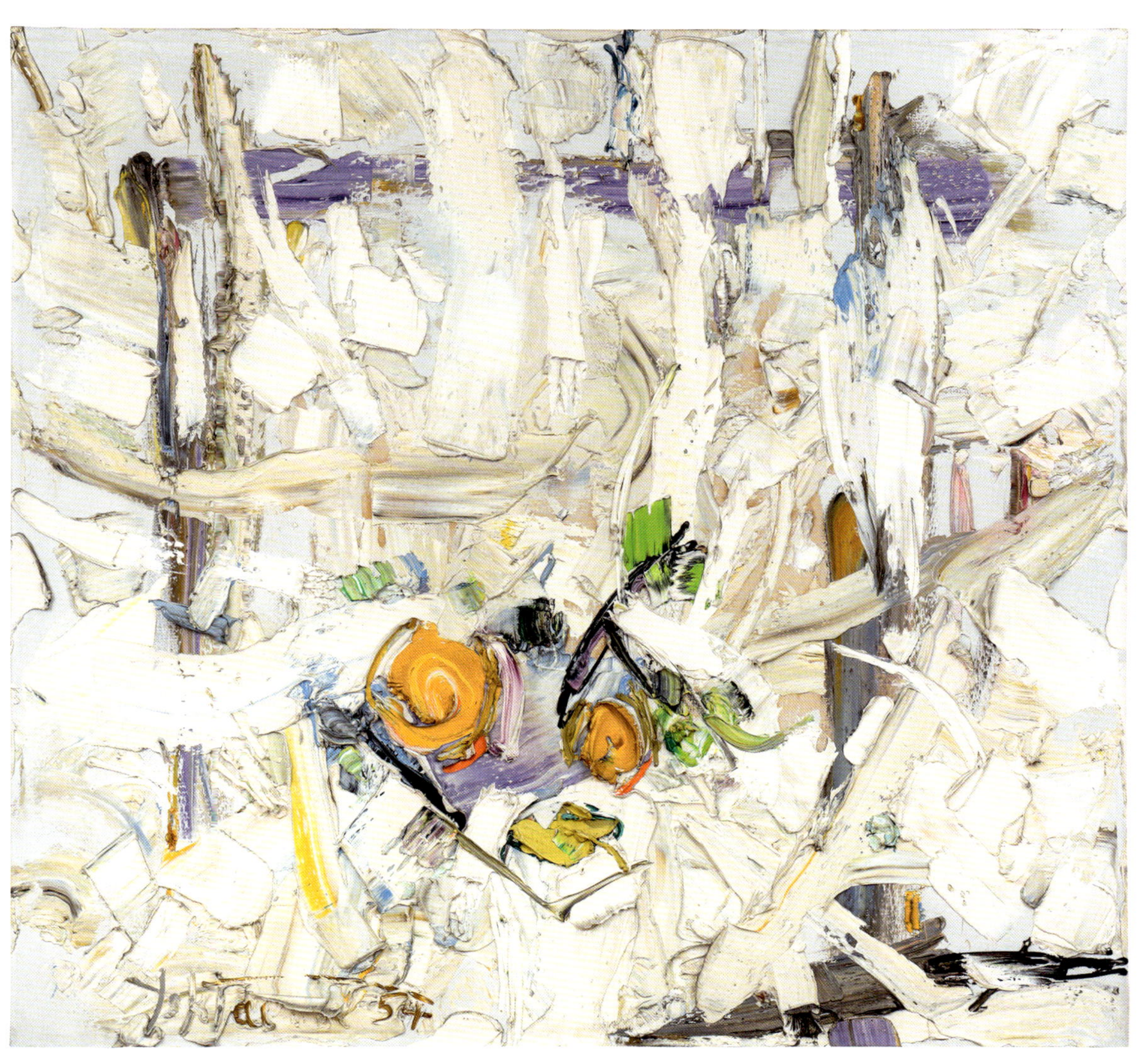

Untitled, 1954, oil on canvas, 59¾ × 64¾ inches (151.8 × 164.5 cm)

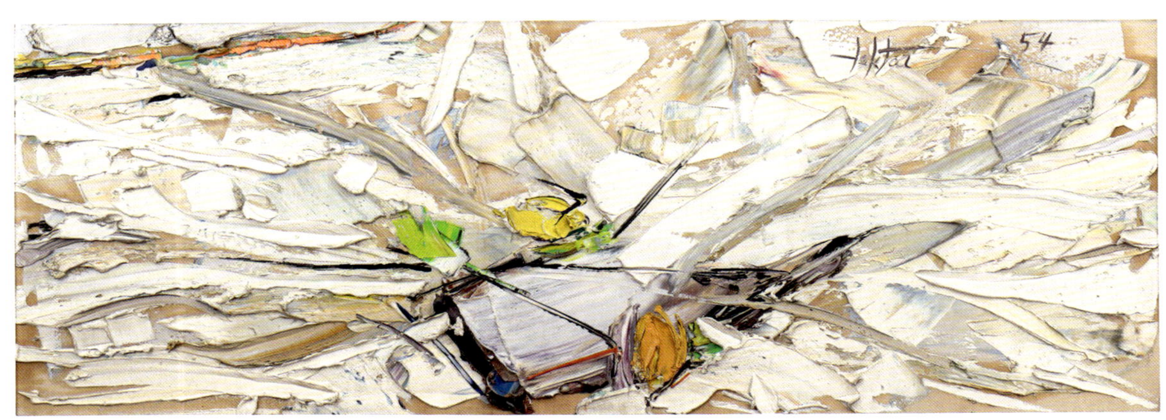

 Still Life with Tulip, 1954, oil on canvas, 28 × 80 inches (71.1 × 203.2 cm)

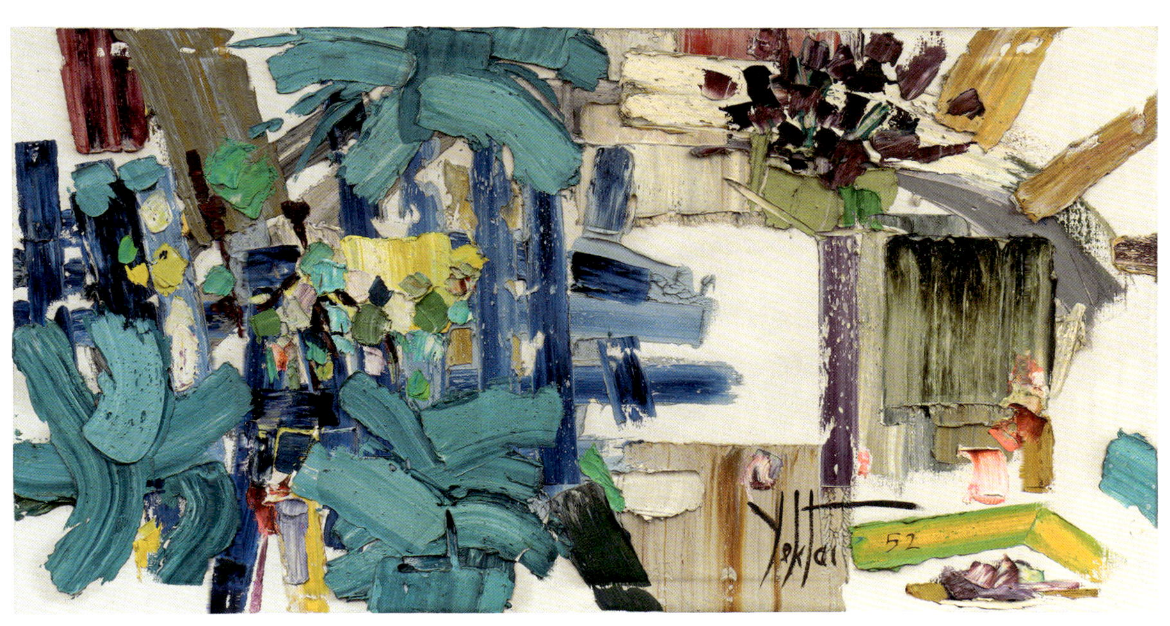

Untitled, 1952, oil on canvas, 32 × 60 inches (81.3 × 152.4 cm)

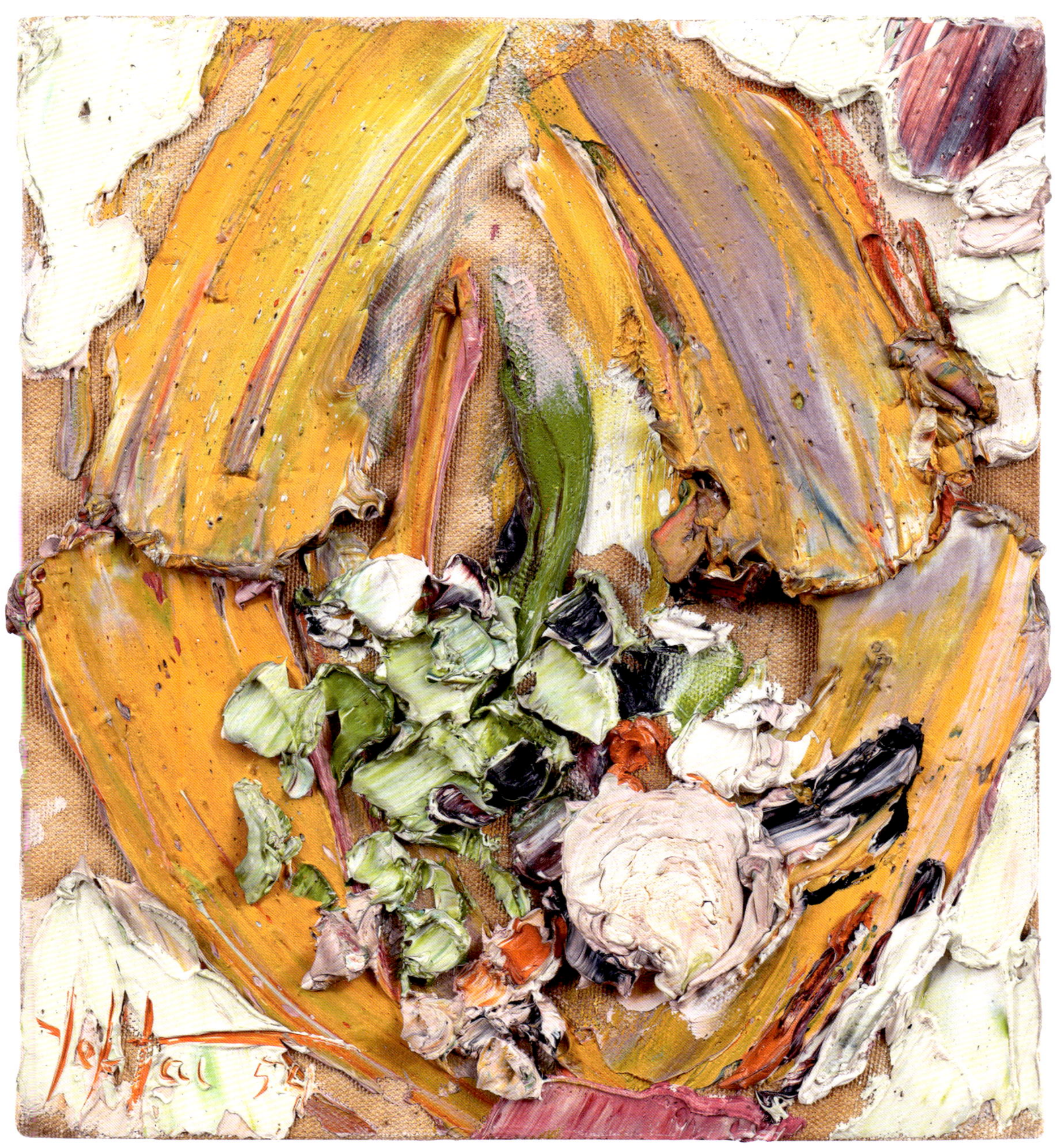

Untitled, 1954, oil on canvas, 10 × 9 inches (25.4 × 22.9 cm)

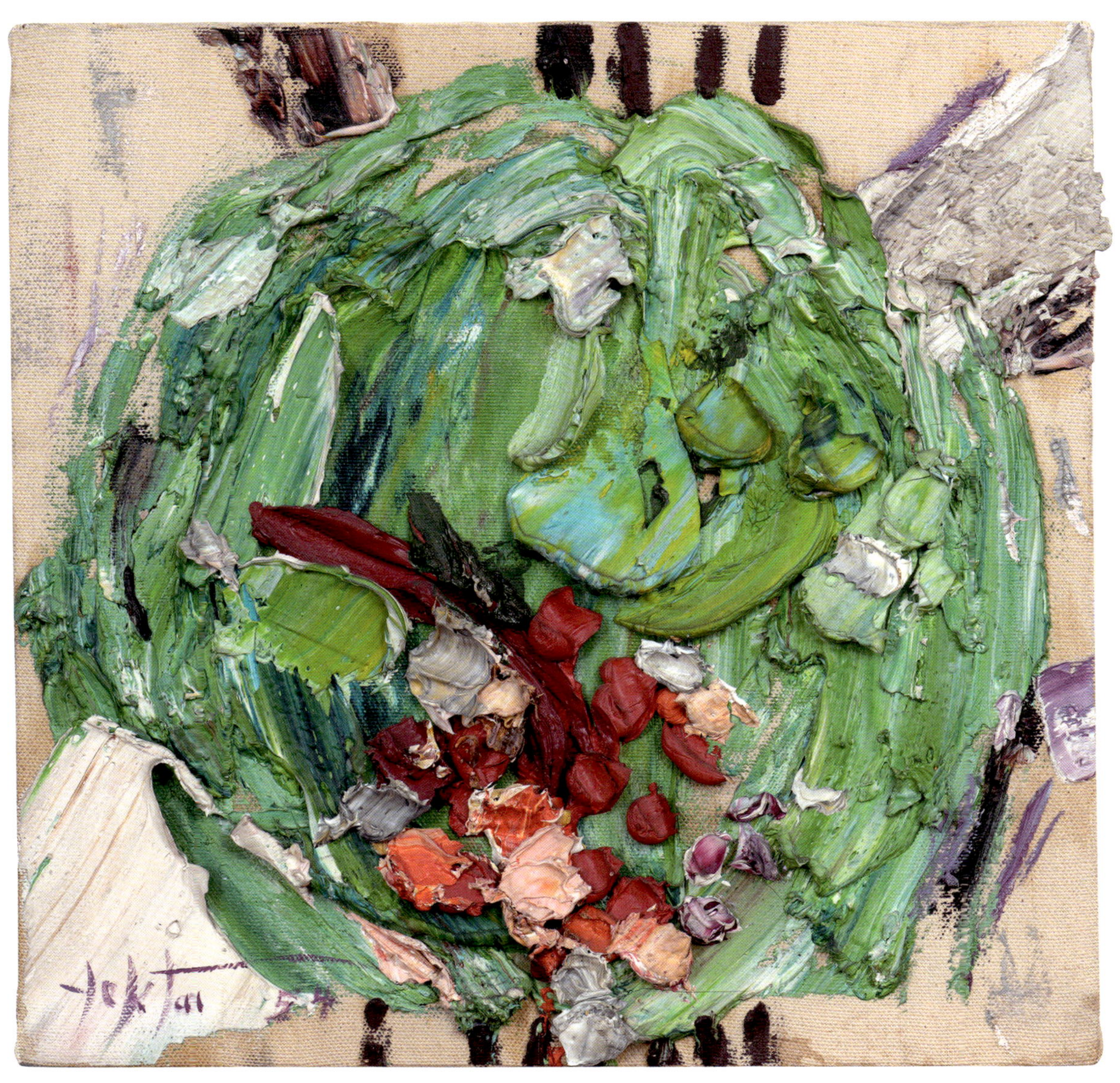

Untitled, 1954, oil on canvas, 11½ × 11½ inches (29.2 × 29.2 cm)

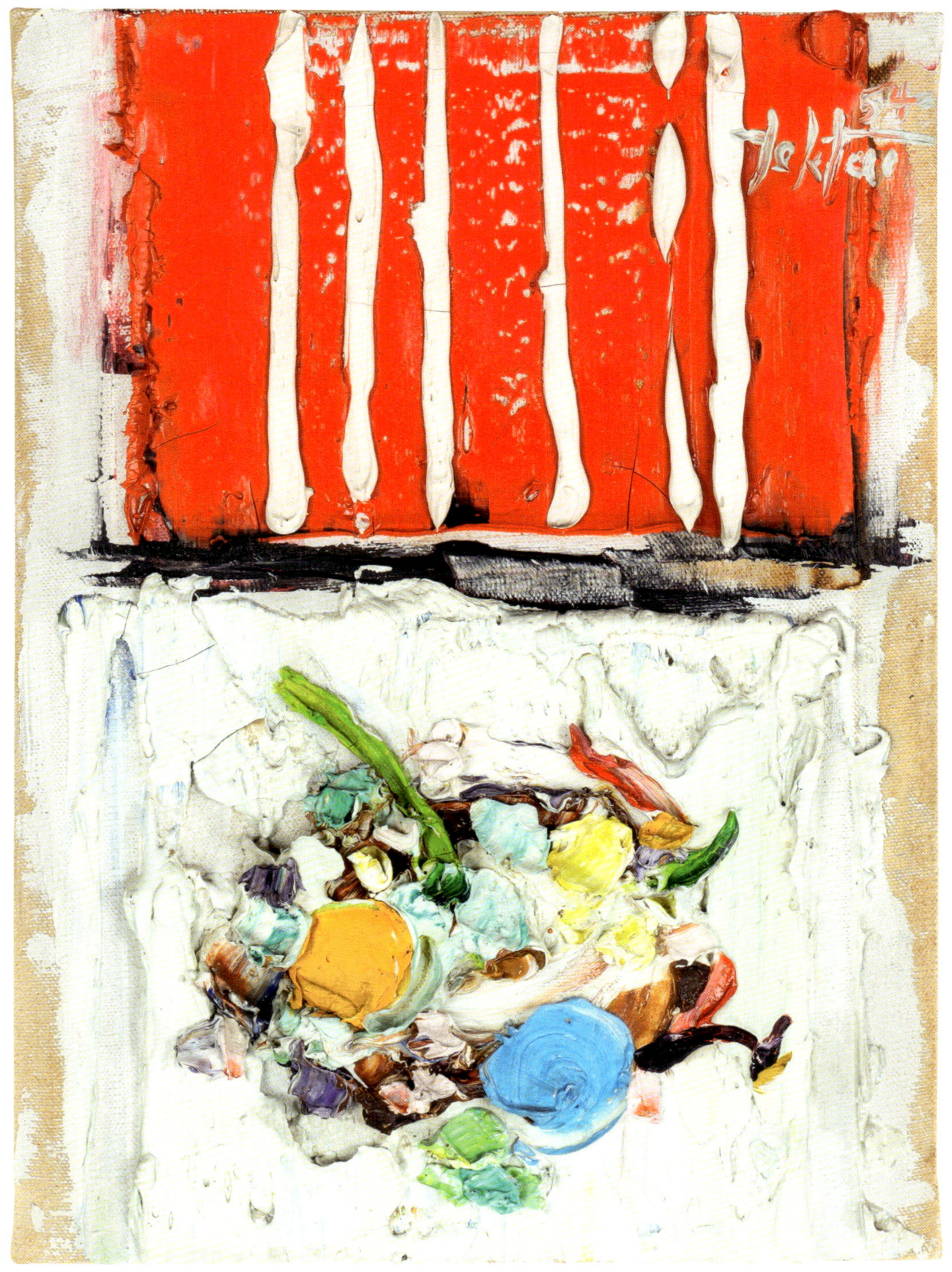

Untitled, 1954, oil on canvas, 12¼ × 9 inches (31.1 × 22.9 cm)

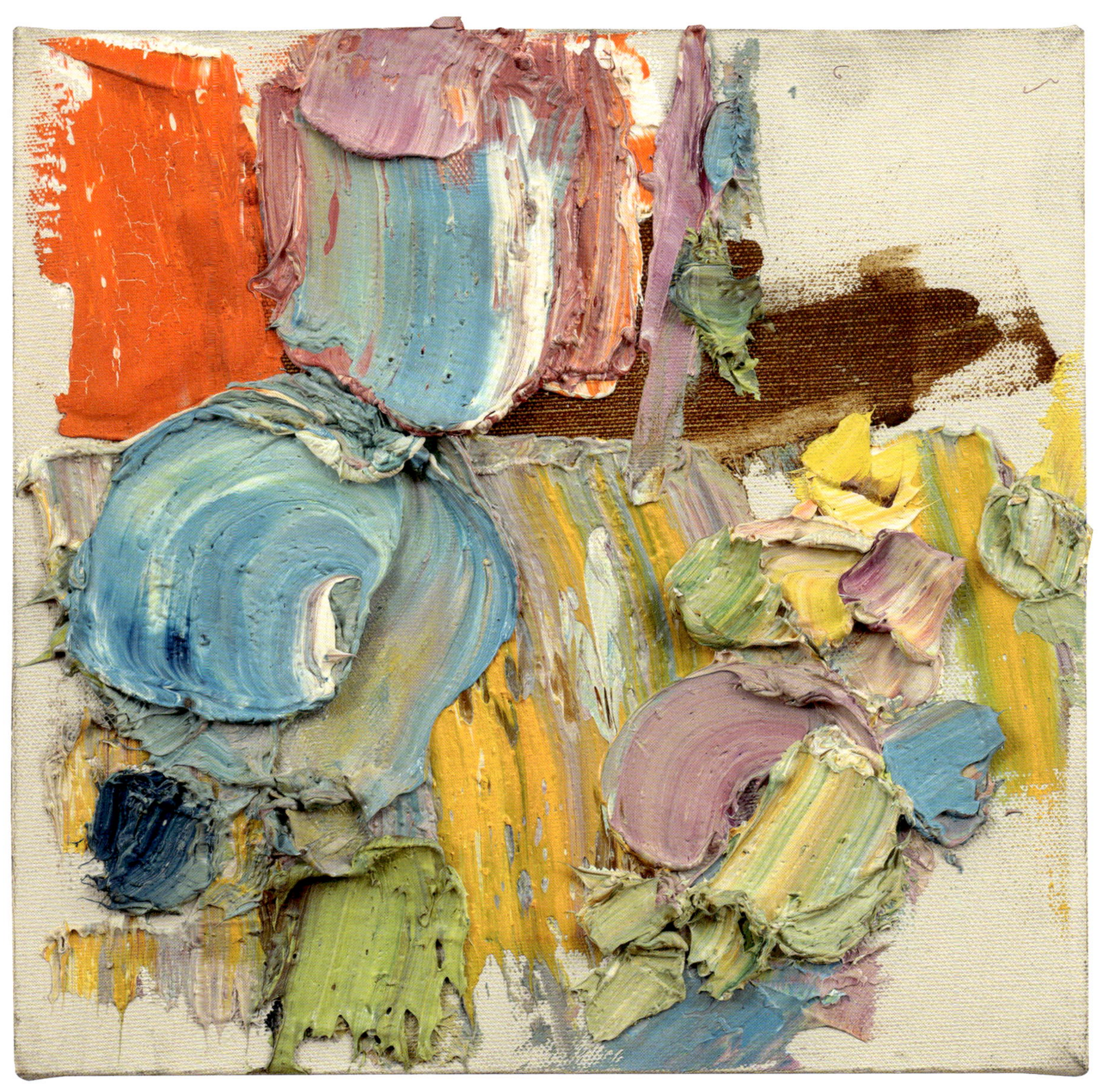

Untitled, ca. 1955, oil on canvas, 10 × 10 inches (25.4 × 25.4 cm)

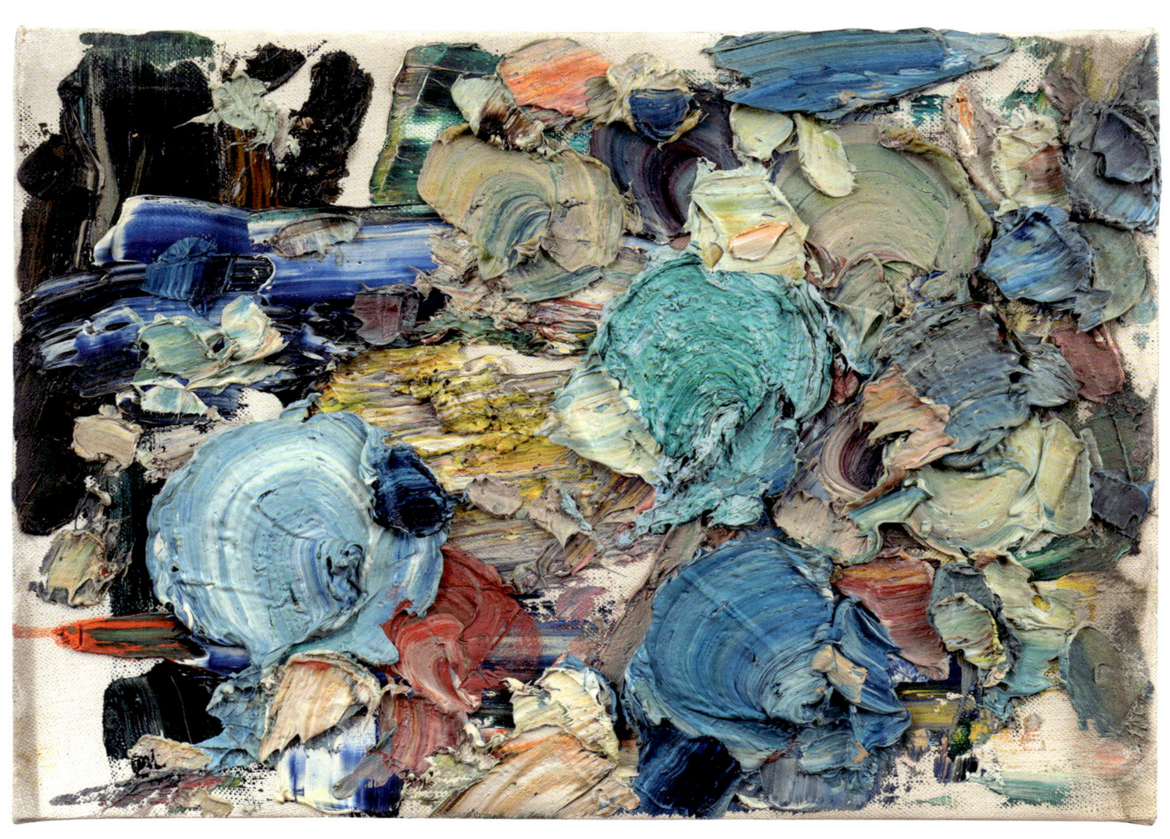

 Untitled, 1954, oil on canvas, 12¼ × 17¼ inches (31.1 × 43.8 cm)

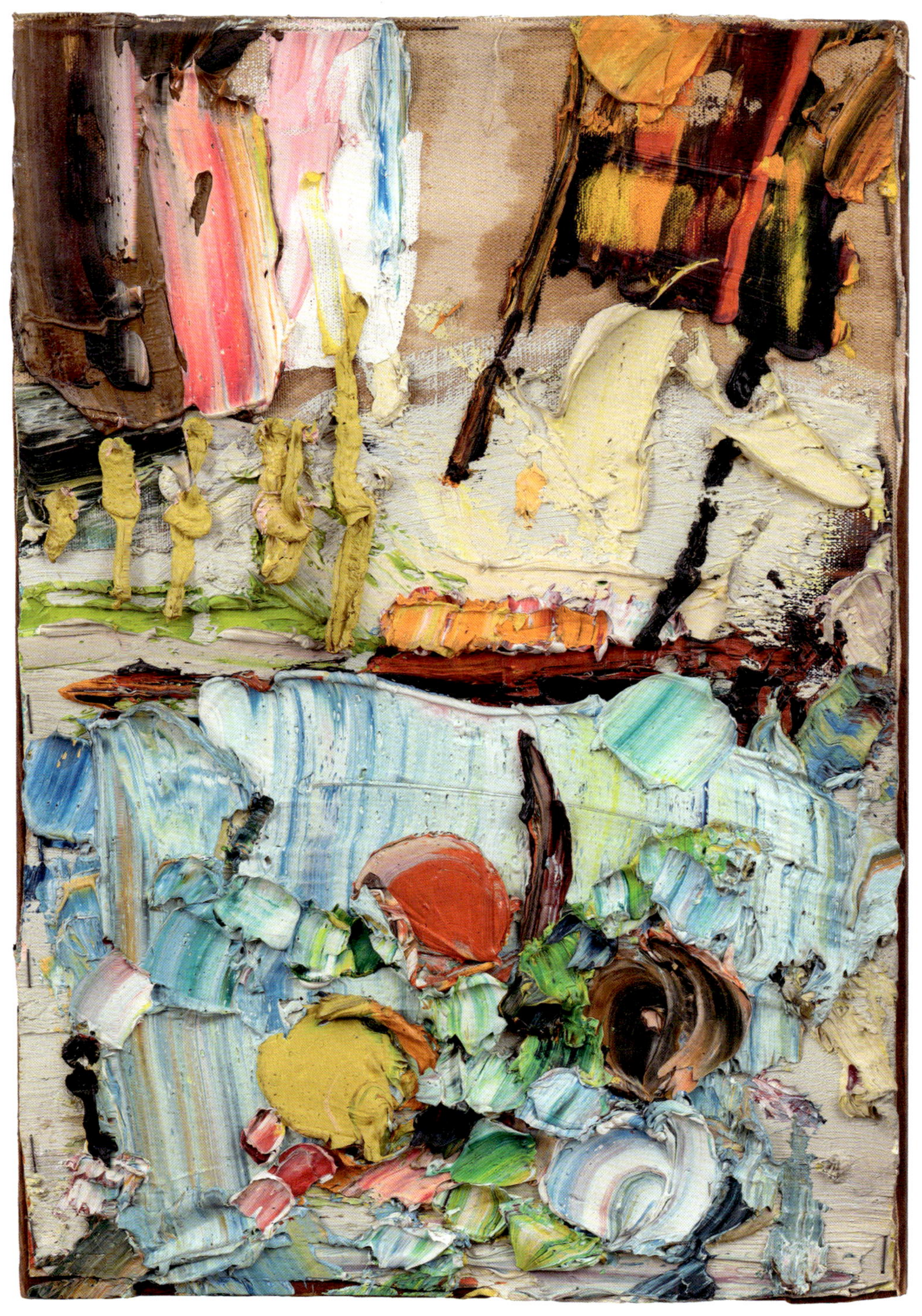

Untitled, 1954, oil on canvas, 17 × 11¾ inches (43.2 × 29.9 cm)

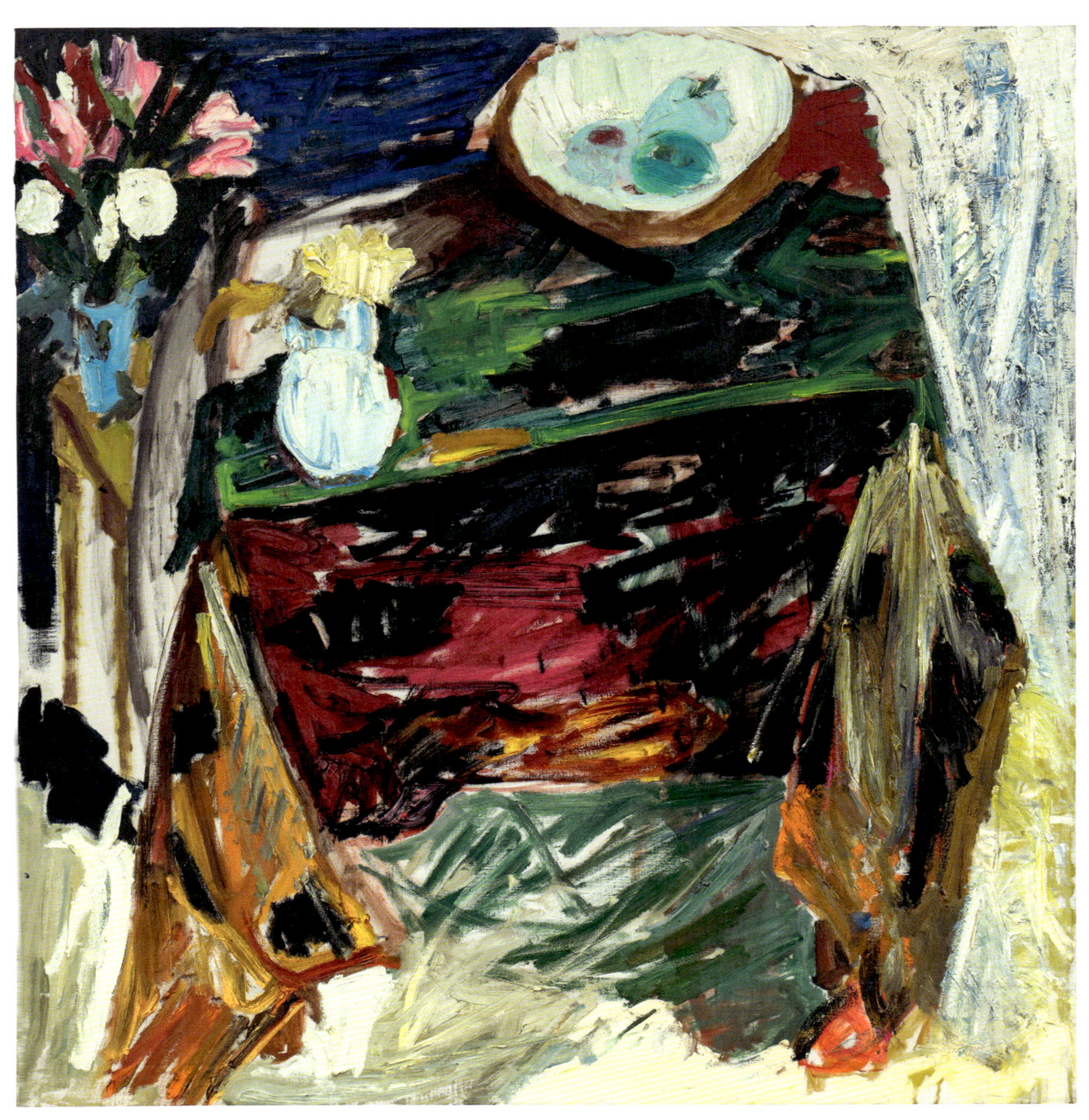

Untitled, 1955, oil on canvas, 53 × 50 inches (134.6 × 127 cm)

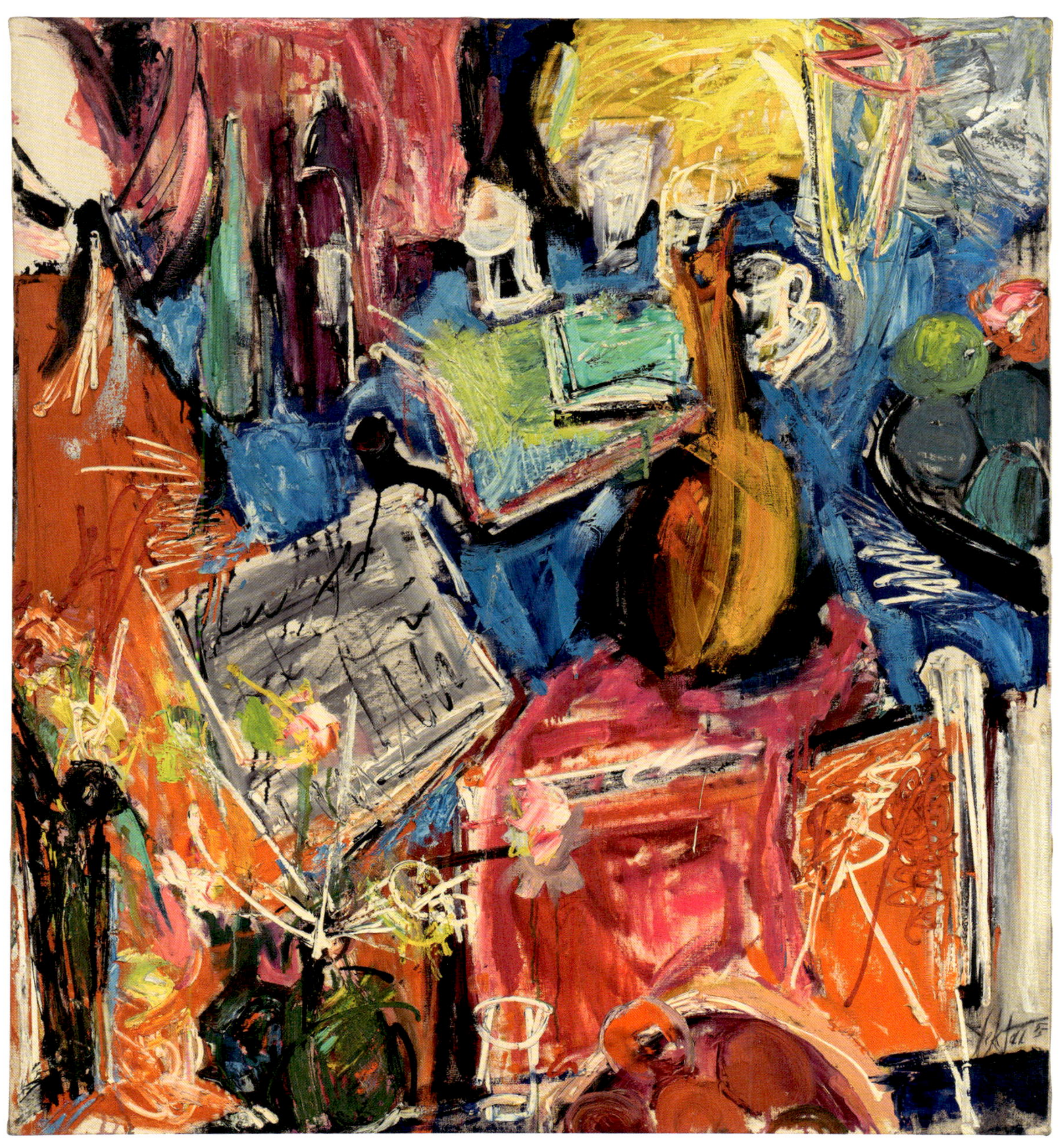

Untitled, 1955, oil on canvas, 60 × 54¼ inches (152.4 × 137.8 cm)

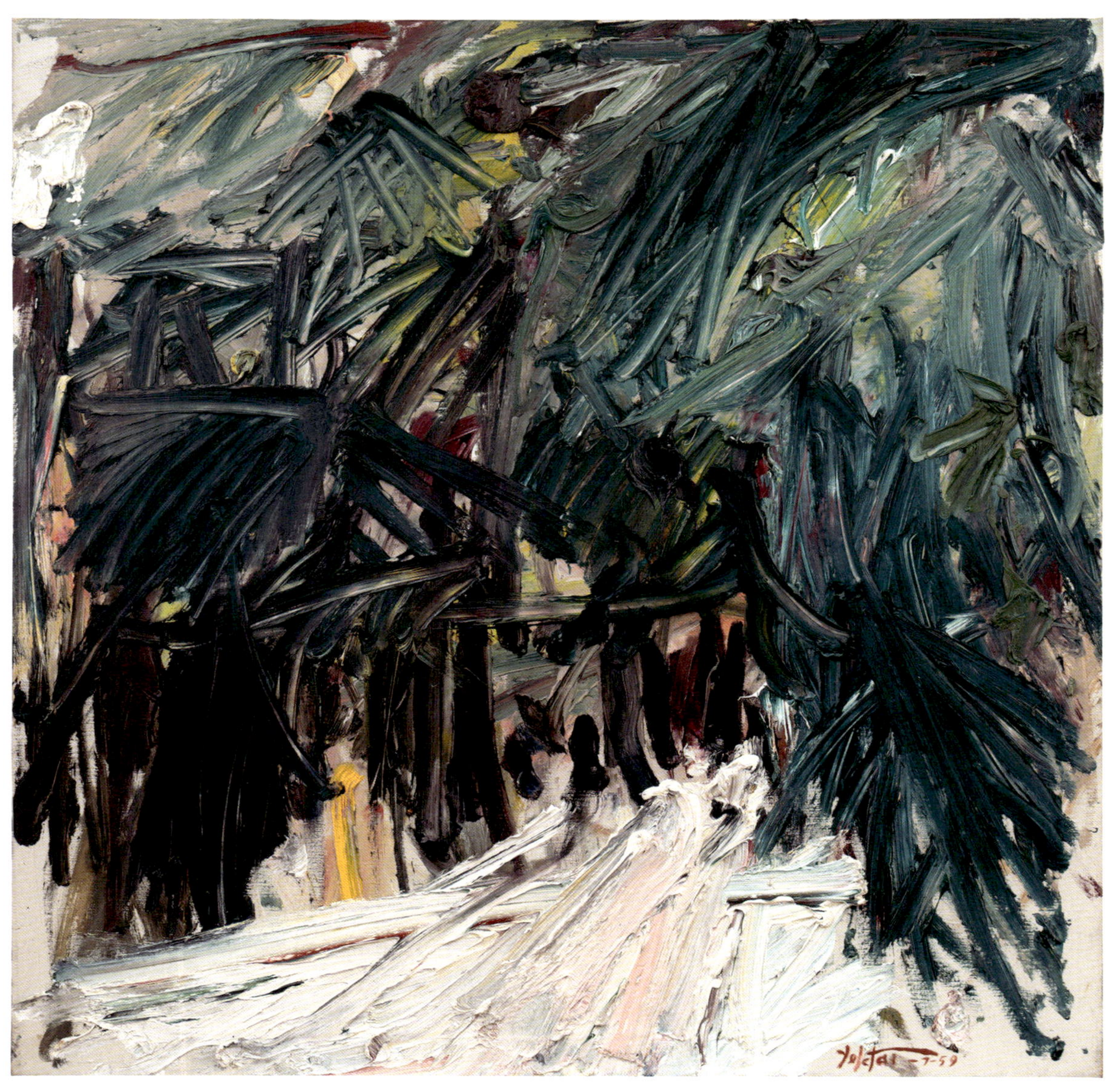

Forest 2, 1954, oil on canvas, 42 × 42 inches (106.7 × 106.7 cm)

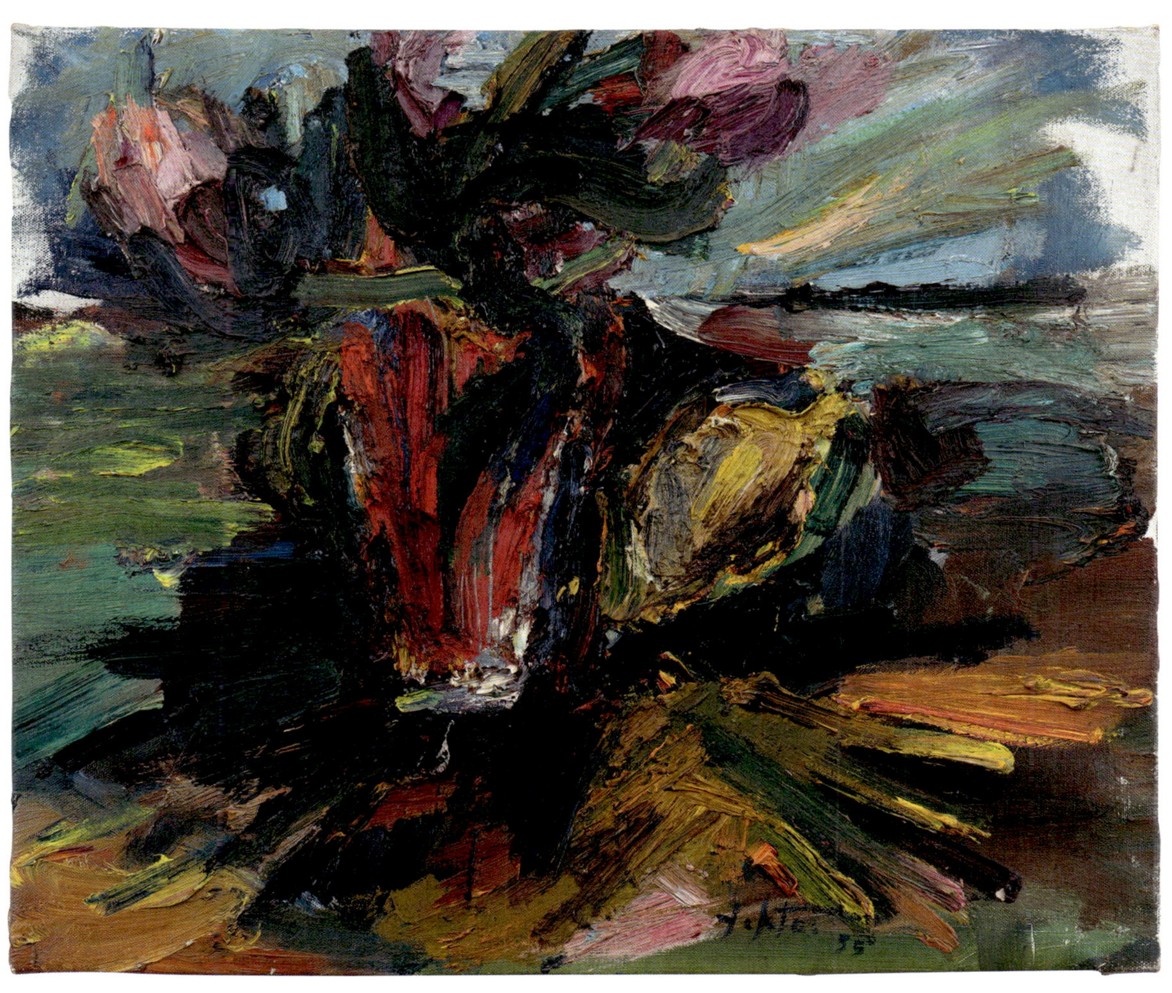

Untitled, 1955, oil on canvas, 13 × 15 inches (33 × 38.1 cm)

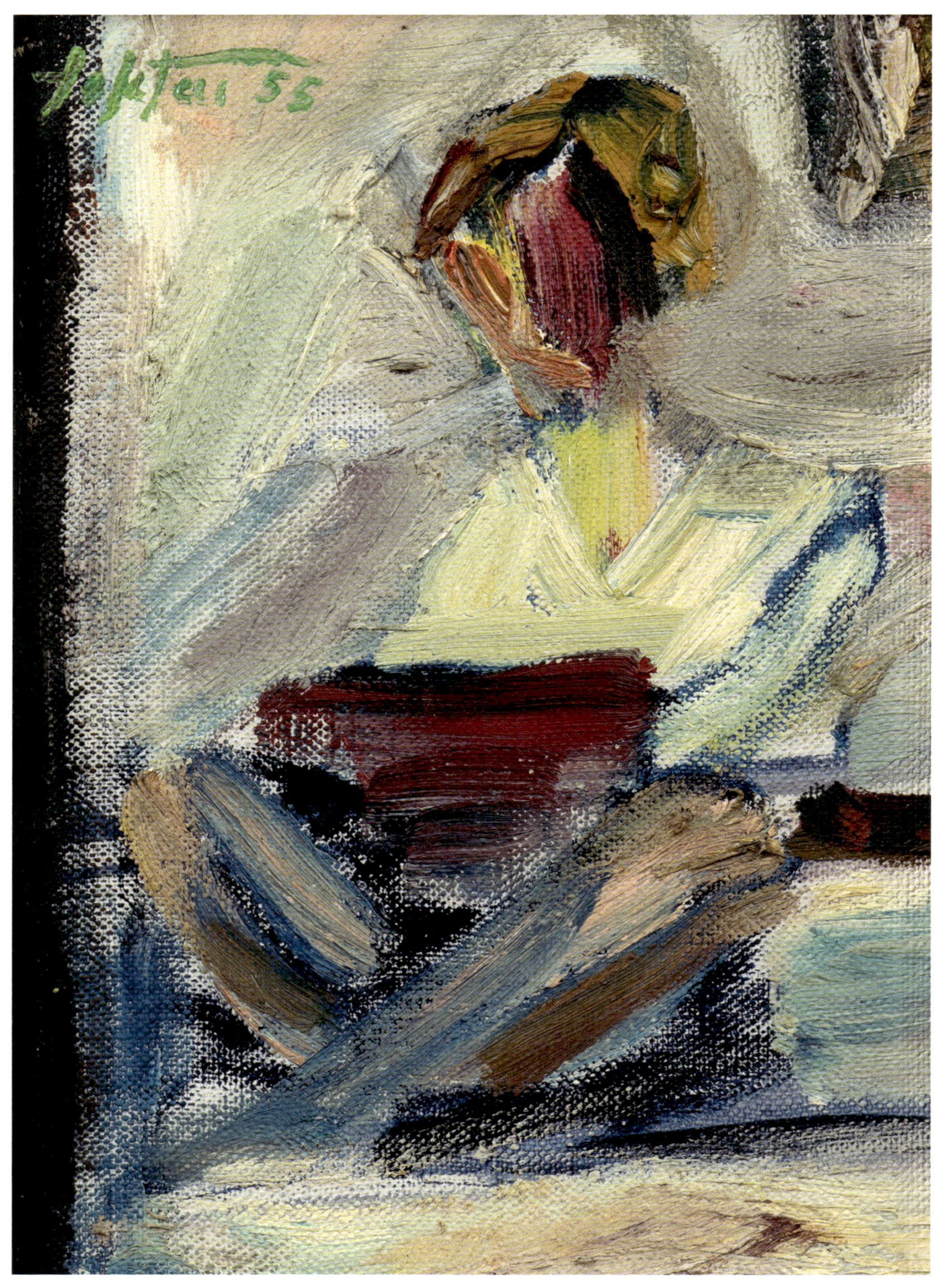

Untitled, 1955, oil on canvas, 8¾ × 6½ inches (22.2 × 16.5 cm)

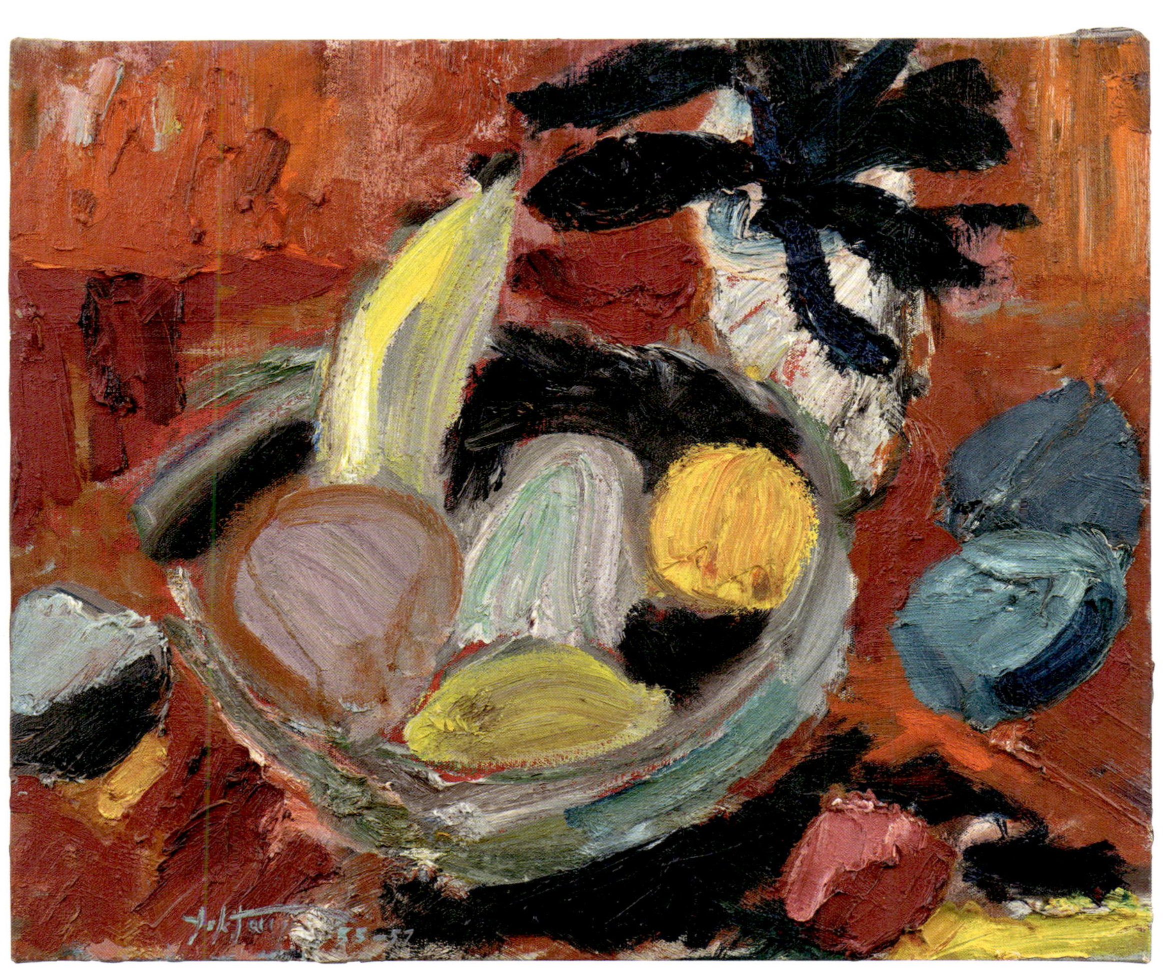

Untitled, 1955, oil on canvas, 19 × 23 inches (48.3 × 58.4 cm)

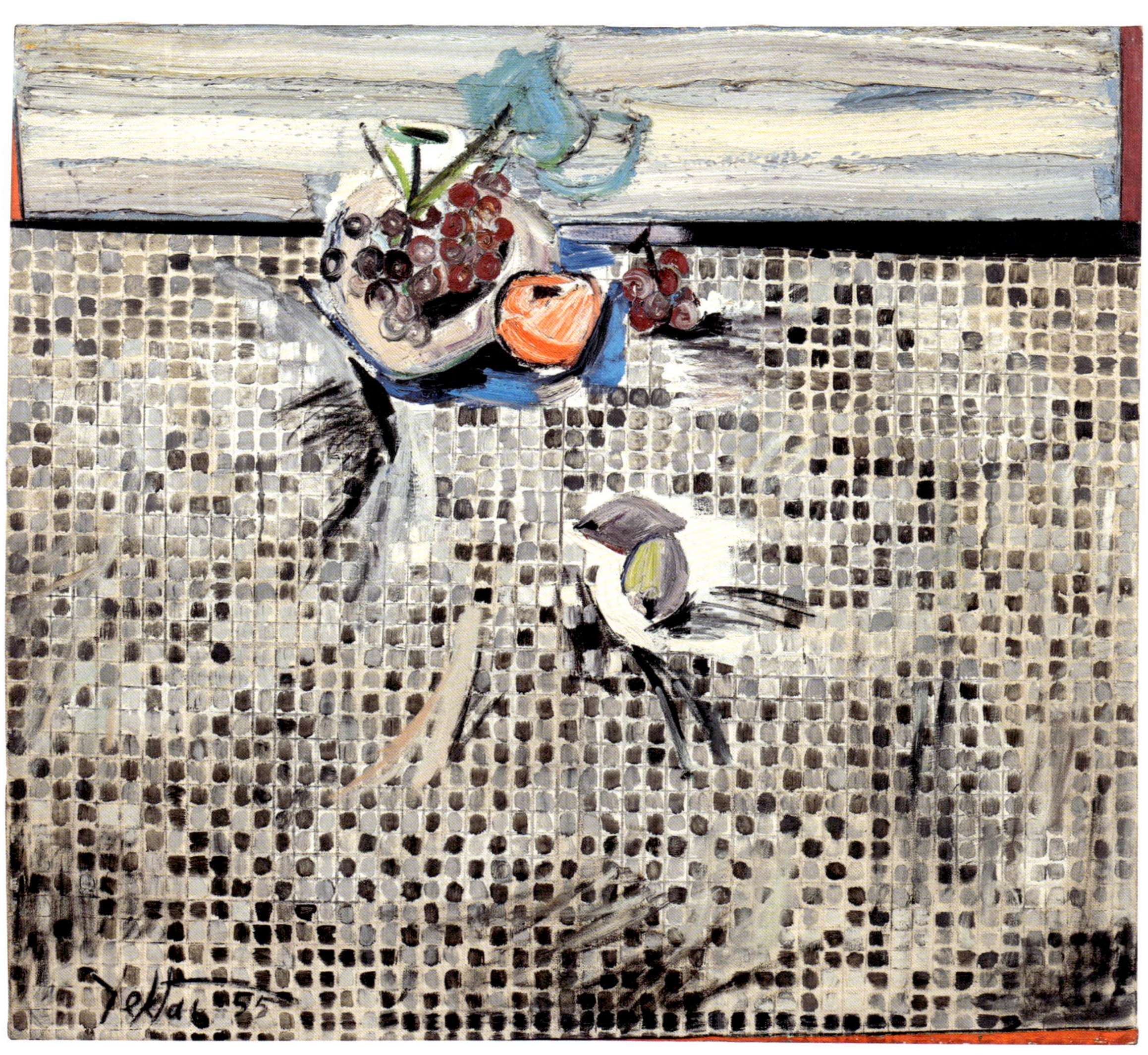

 Untitled, 1955, oil on canvas, 43¼ × 47¼ inches (109.9 × 120 cm)

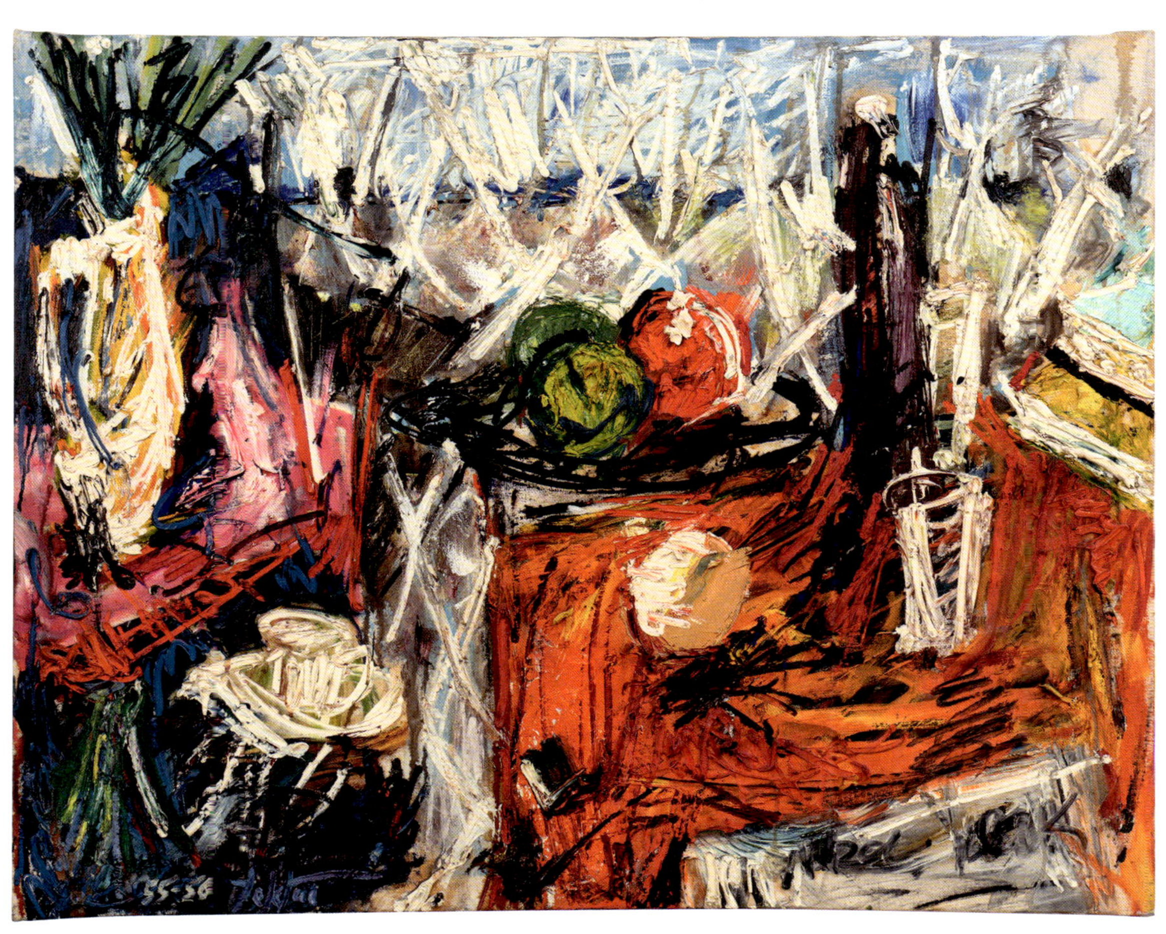

Untitled, 1955, oil on canvas, 37½ × 48 inches (95.3 × 121.9 cm)

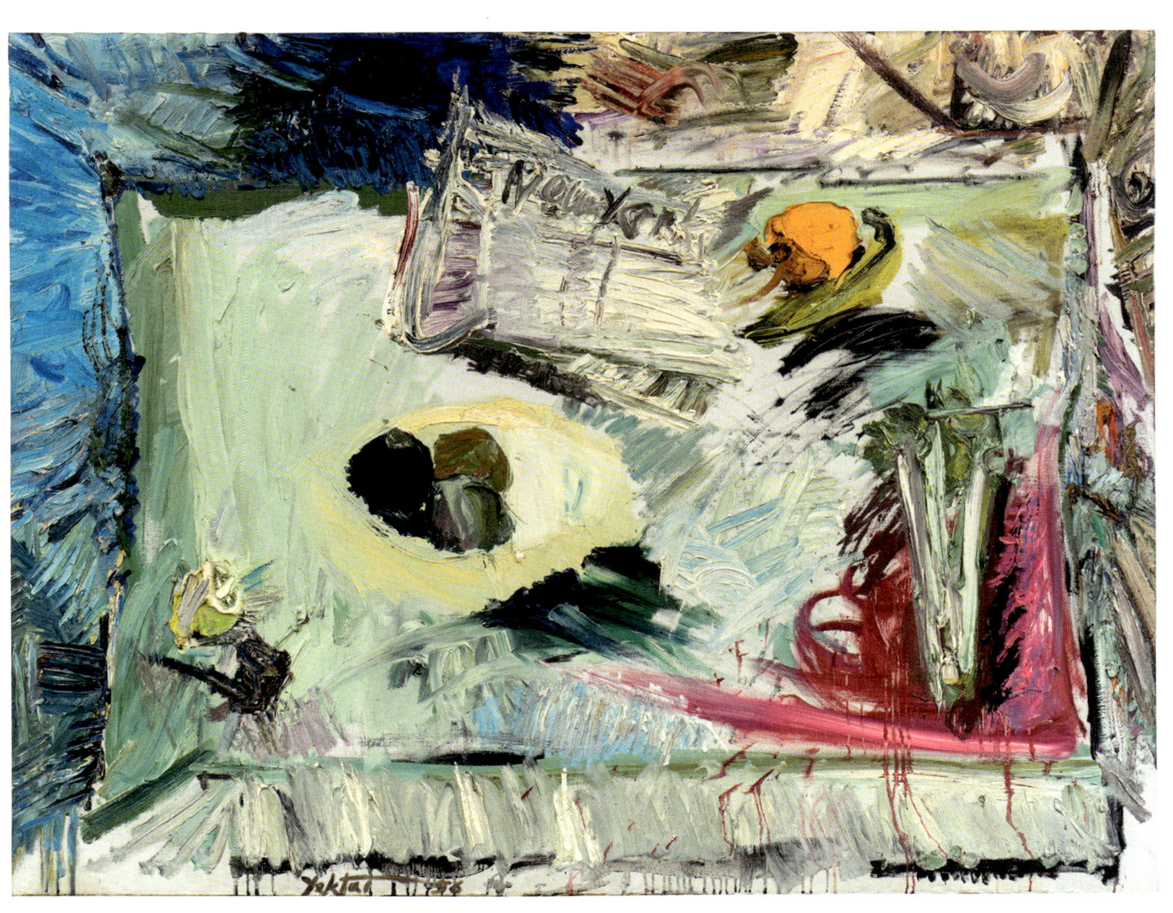

Newspaper, 1956, oil on canvas, 51 × 65½ inches (129.5 × 166.4 cm)

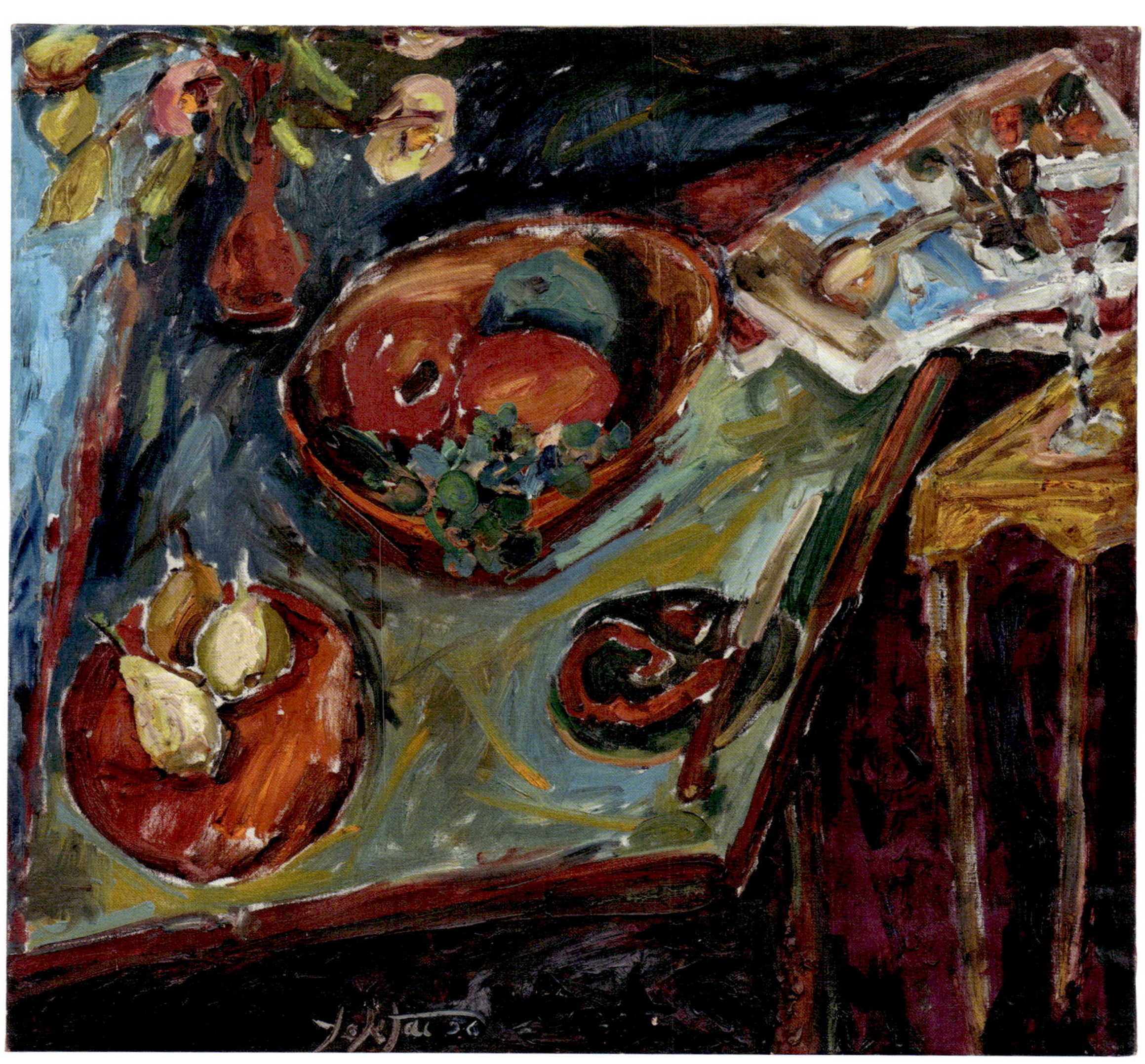

 Untitled, 1956, oil on canvas, 13⅜ × 14⅛ inches (34 × 36 cm)

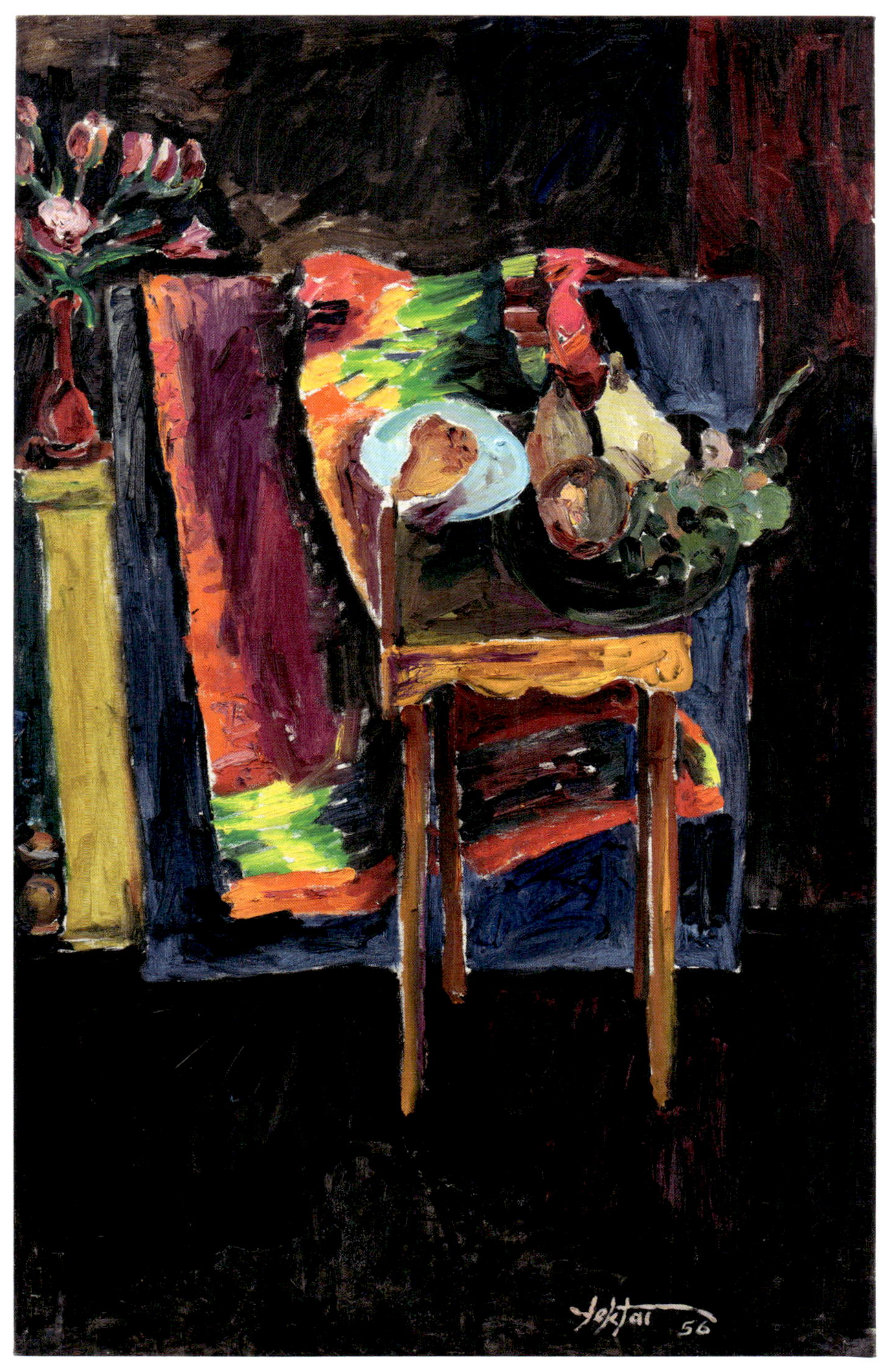

Untitled, 1956, oil on canvas, 48 × 30 inches (121.9 × 76.2 cm)

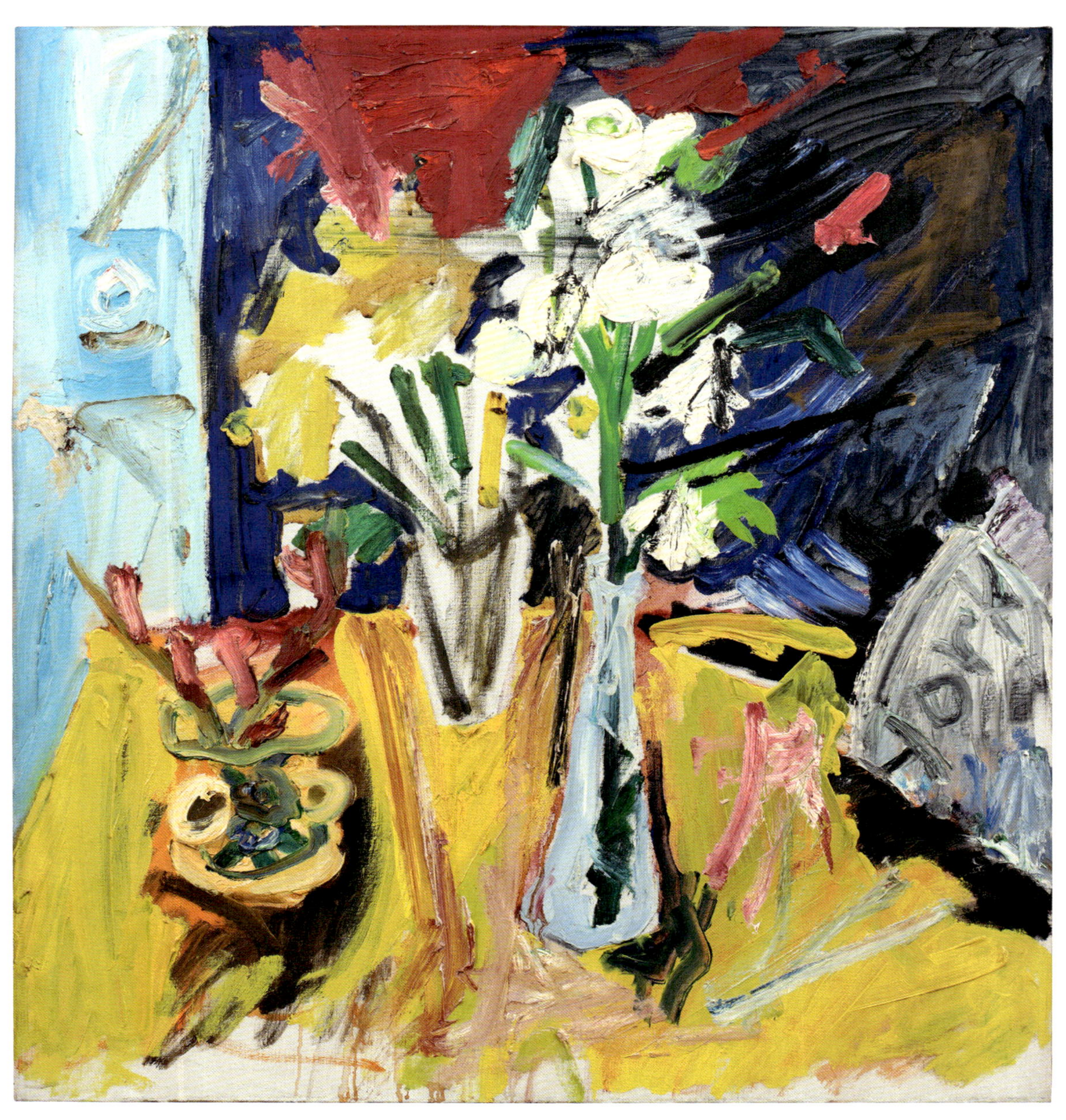

Still Life, 1956, oil on canvas, 36 × 34 inches (91.4 × 86.4 cm)

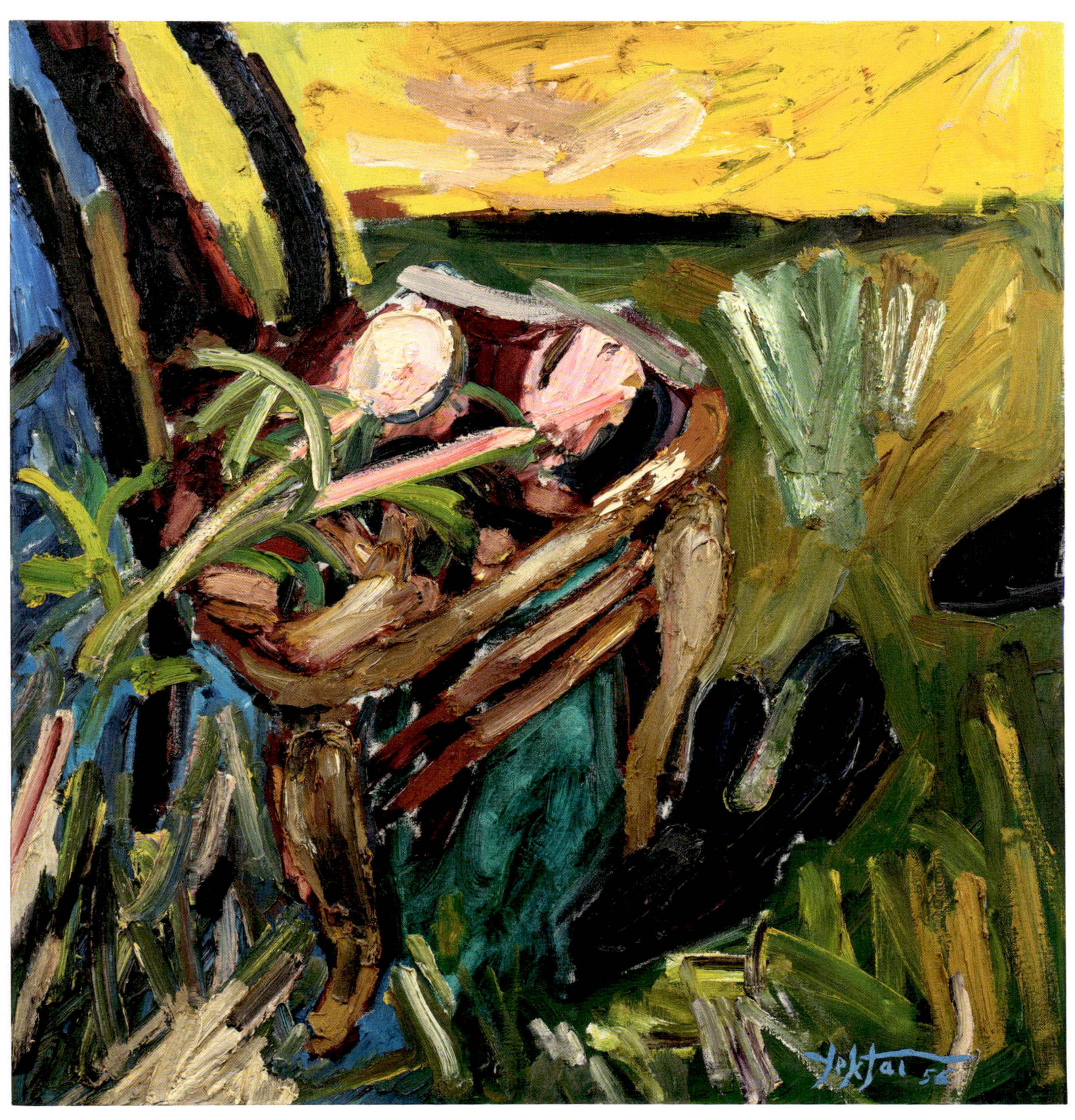

Untitled, 1956, oil on canvas, 36 × 34 inches (91.4 × 86.4 cm)

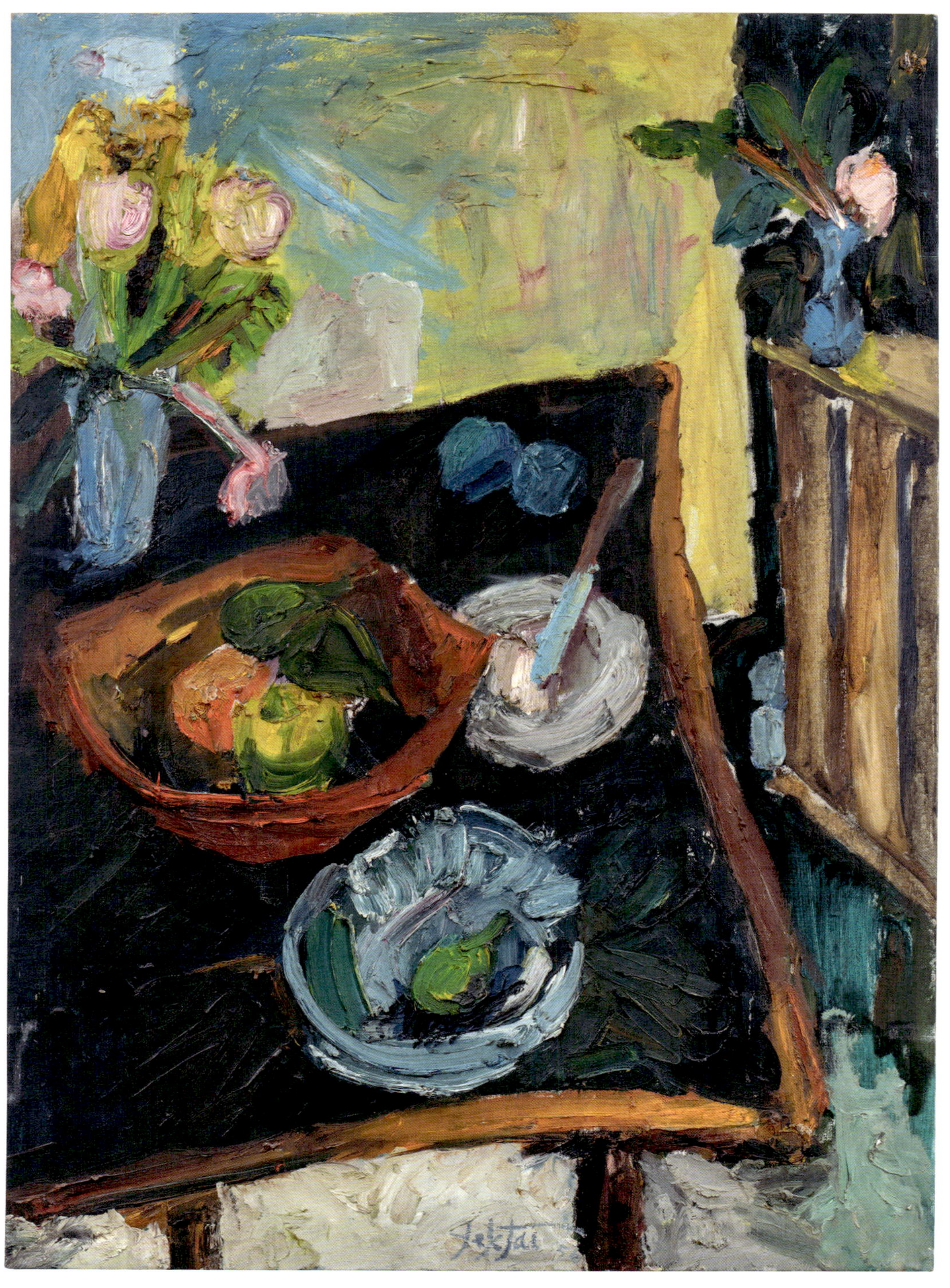

 Corner of Room, 1956, oil on canvas, 48½ × 35¼ inches (123.2 × 89.5 cm)

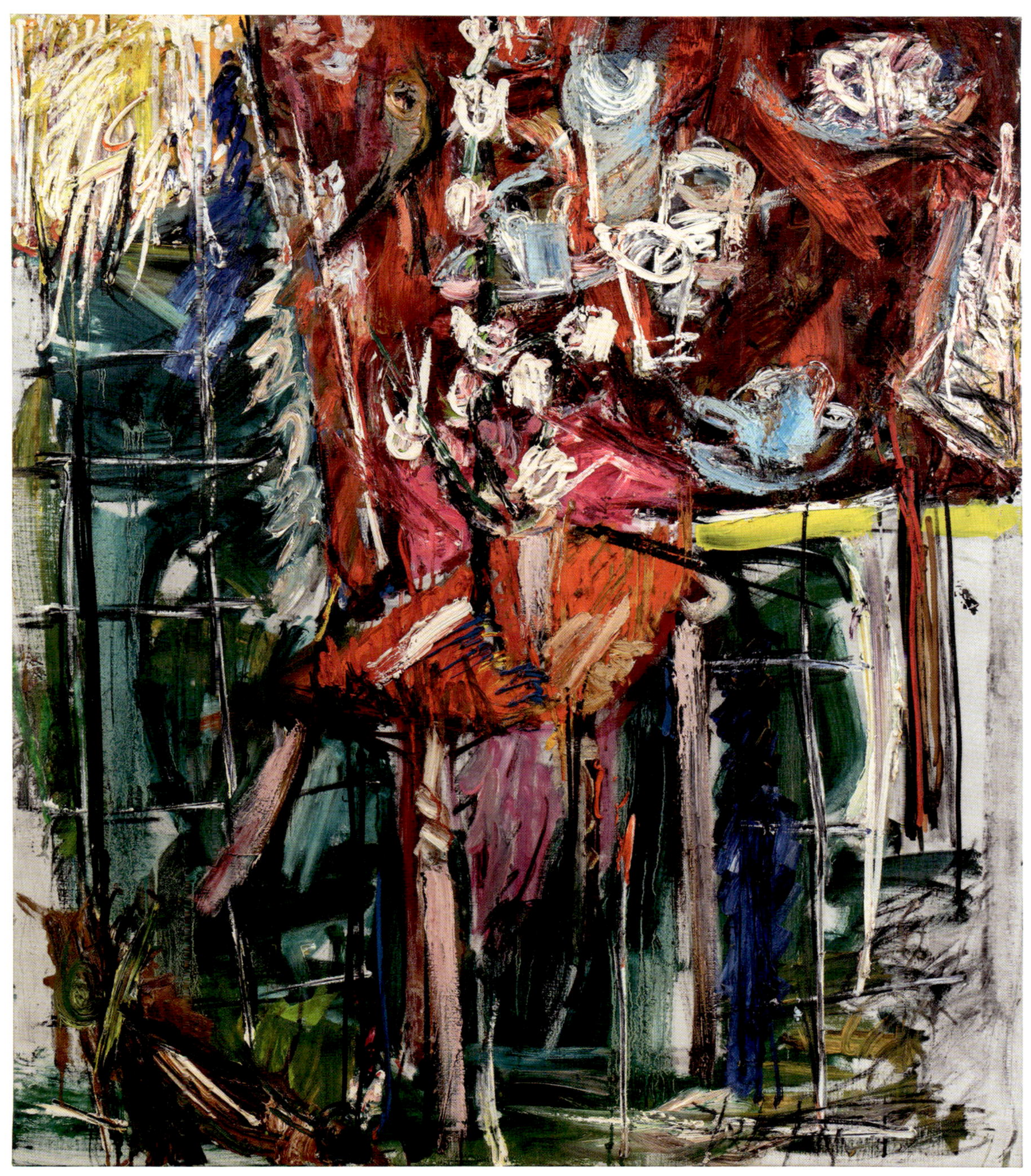

Still Life with Blossoms, 1956, oil on canvas, 57 × 49 inches (144.8 × 124.5 cm)

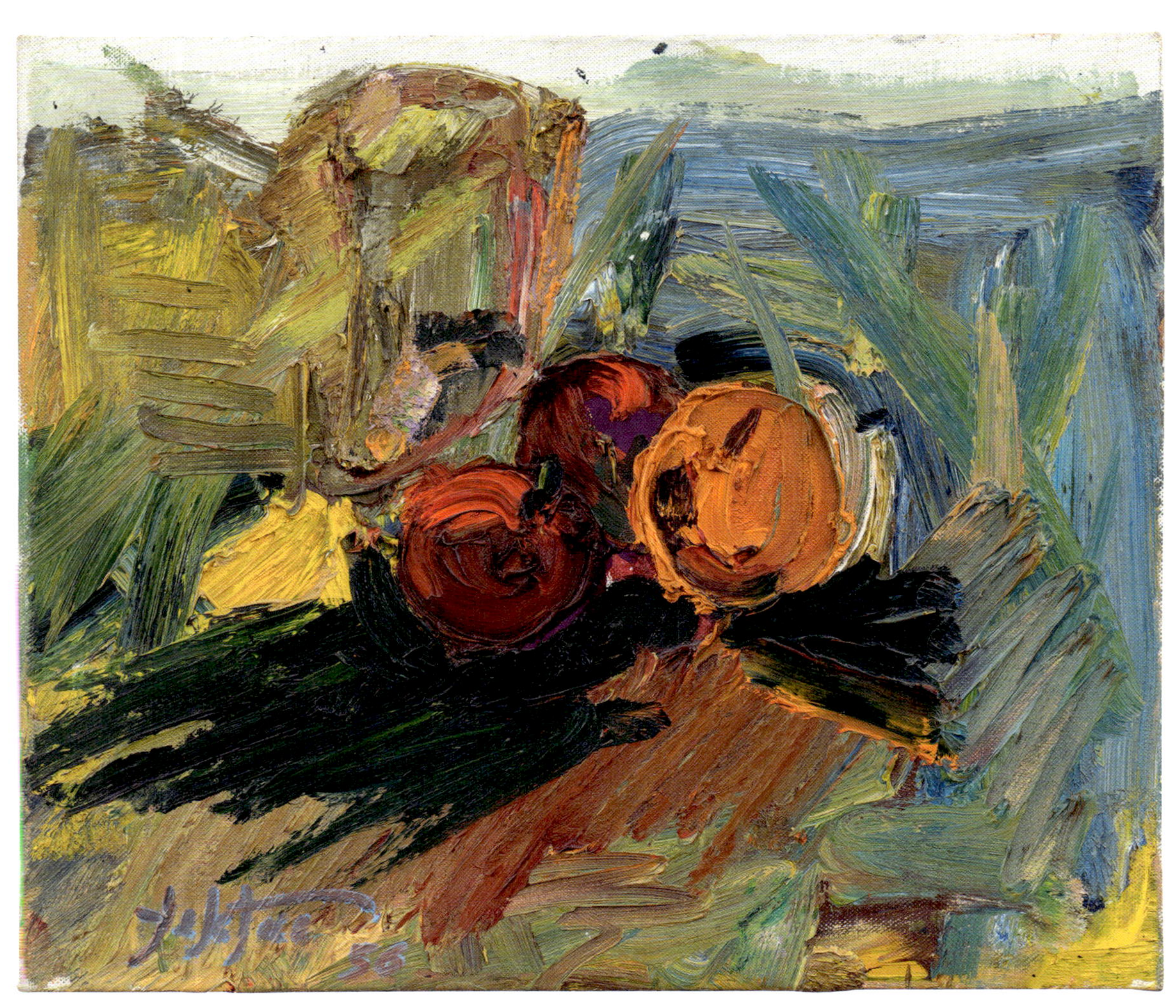

Untitled, 1956, oil on canvas, 13 × 15¼ inches (33 × 38.7 cm)

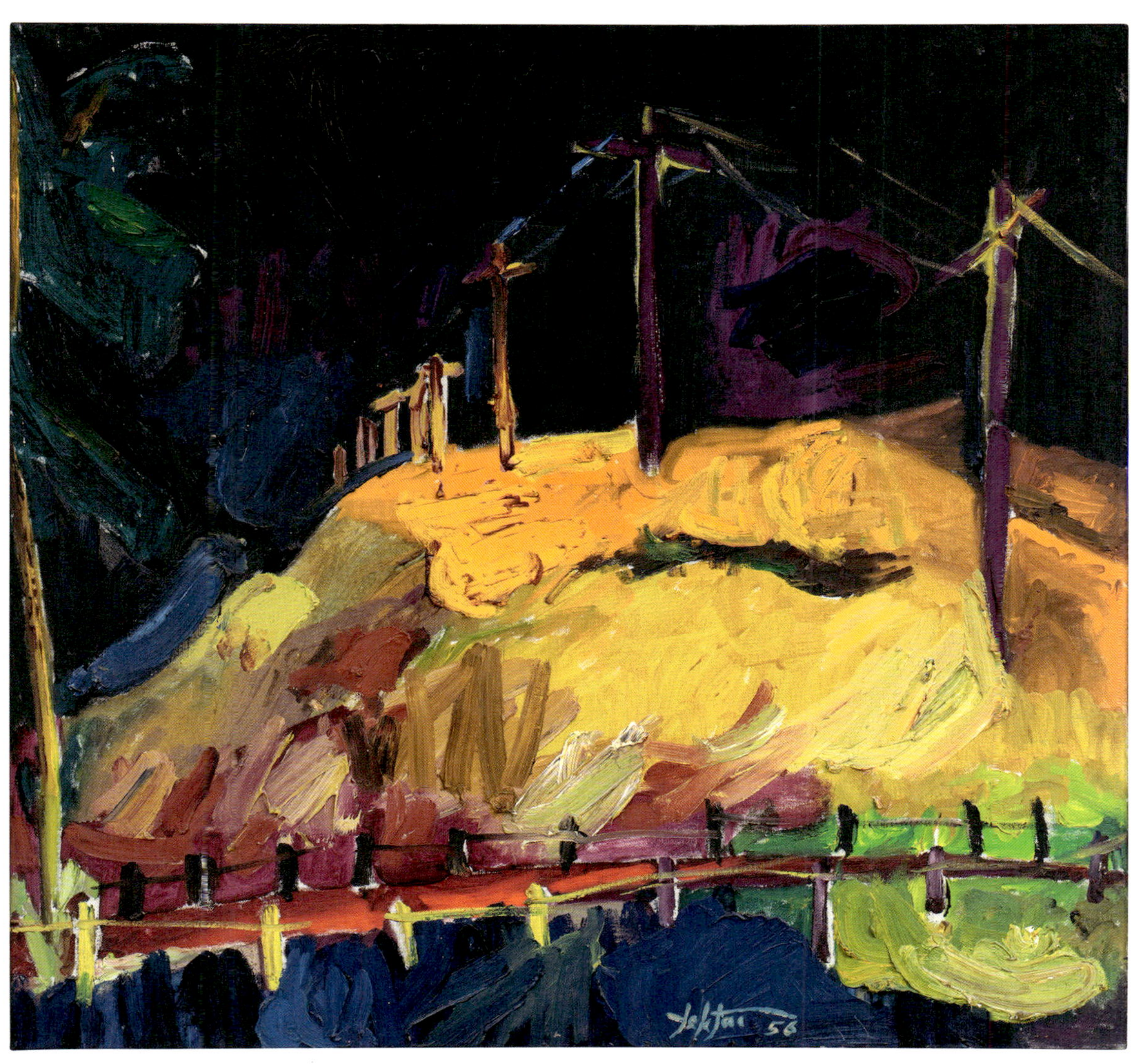

Vermont Landscape, 1956, oil on canvas, 34 × 36 inches (86.4 × 91.4 cm)

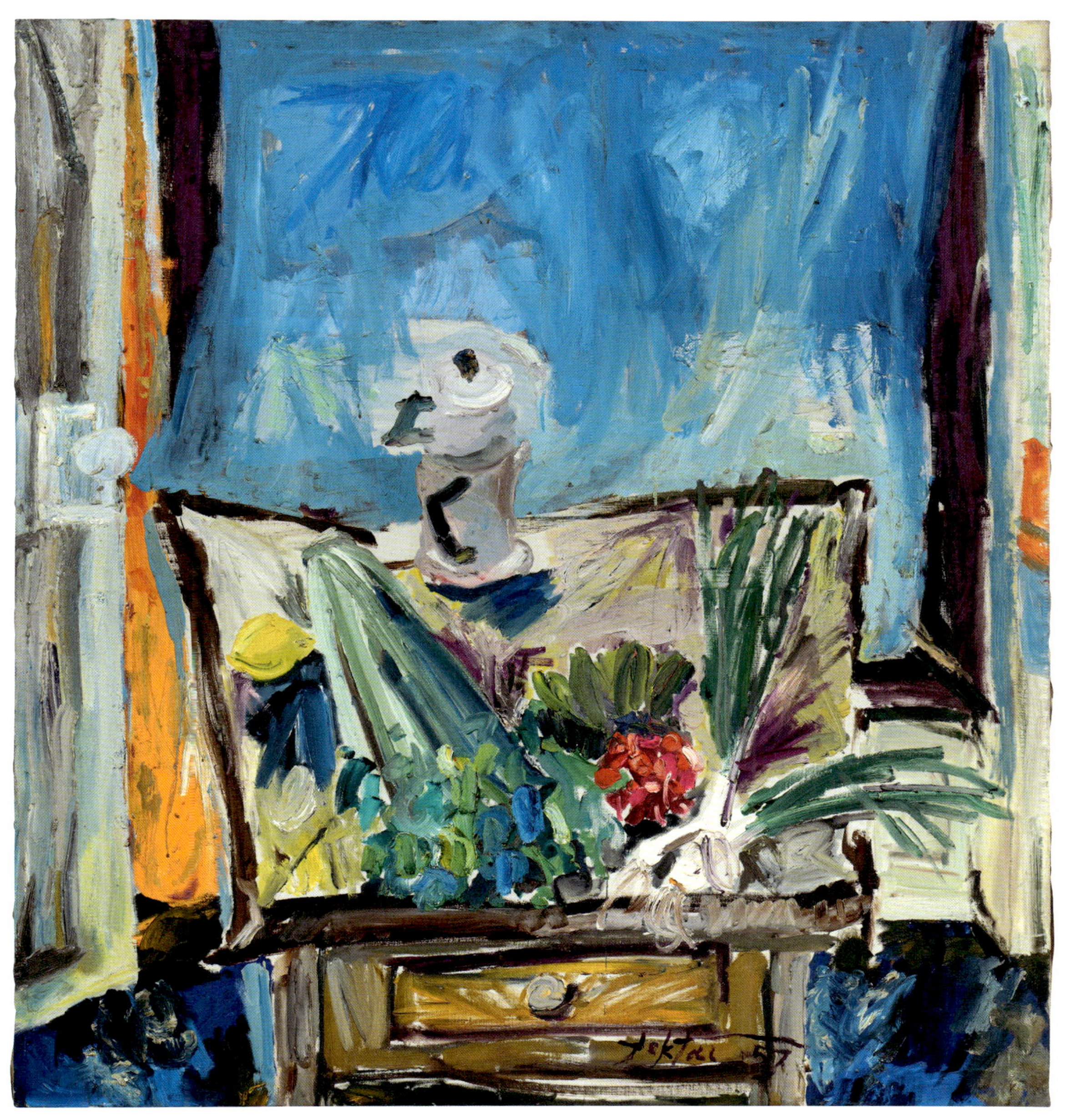

Vegetables and Coffee Pot, 1957, oil on canvas, 55 × 51 inches (139.7 × 129.5 cm)

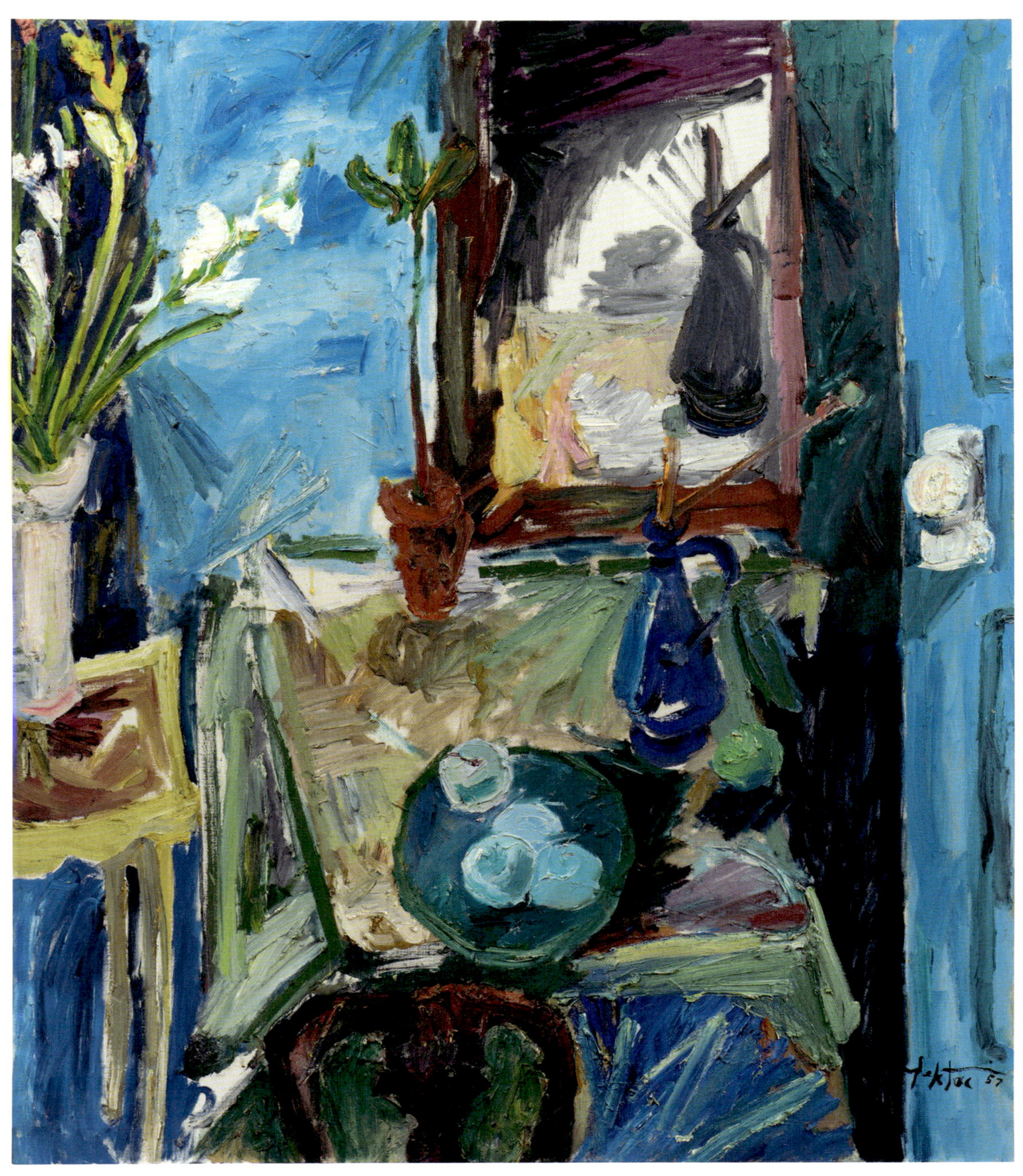

 Untitled, 1957, oil on canvas, 58¾ × 50¾ inches (149.2 × 128.9 cm)

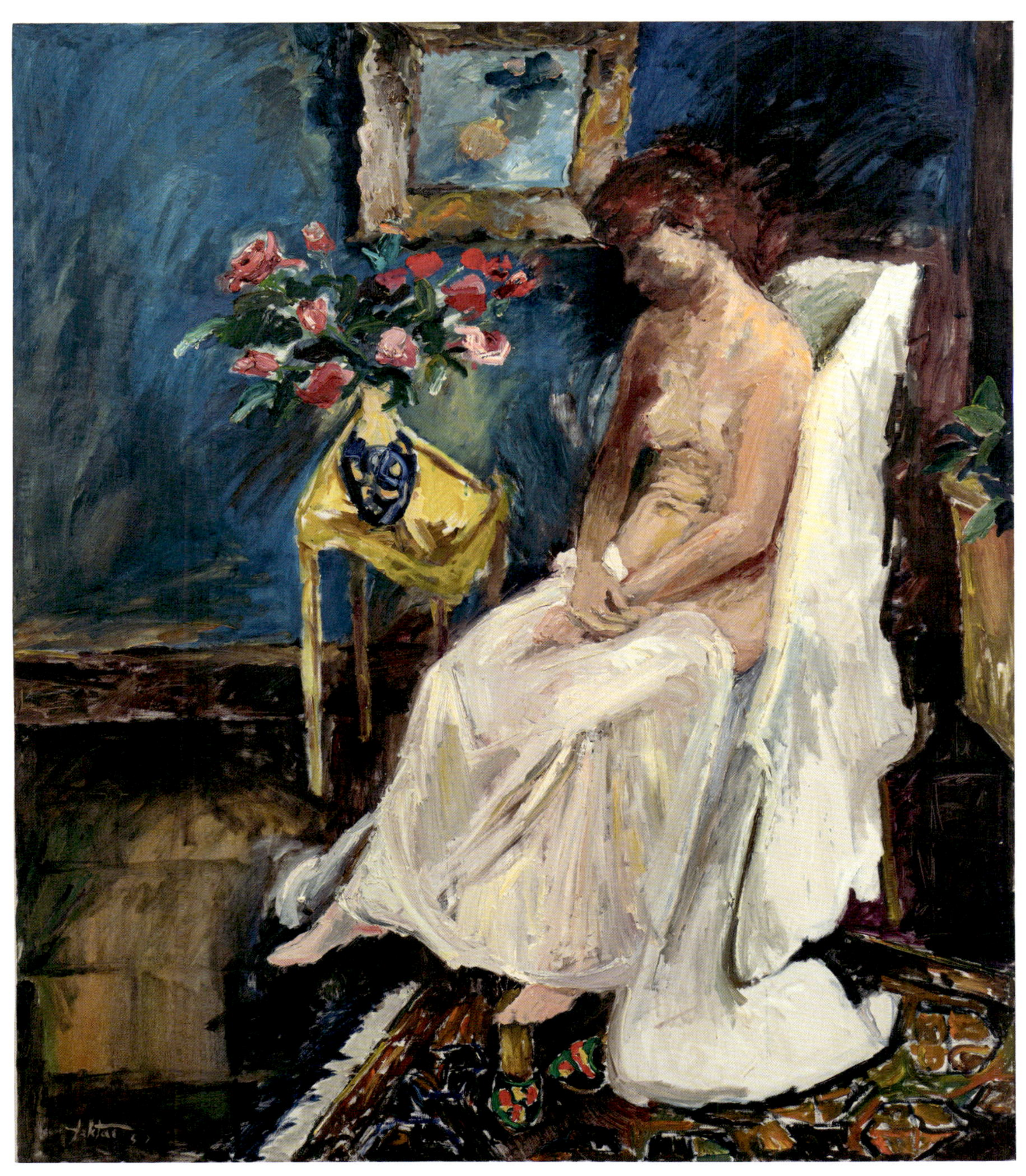

Untitled, 1957, oil on canvas, 84 × 72 inches (213 × 183 cm)

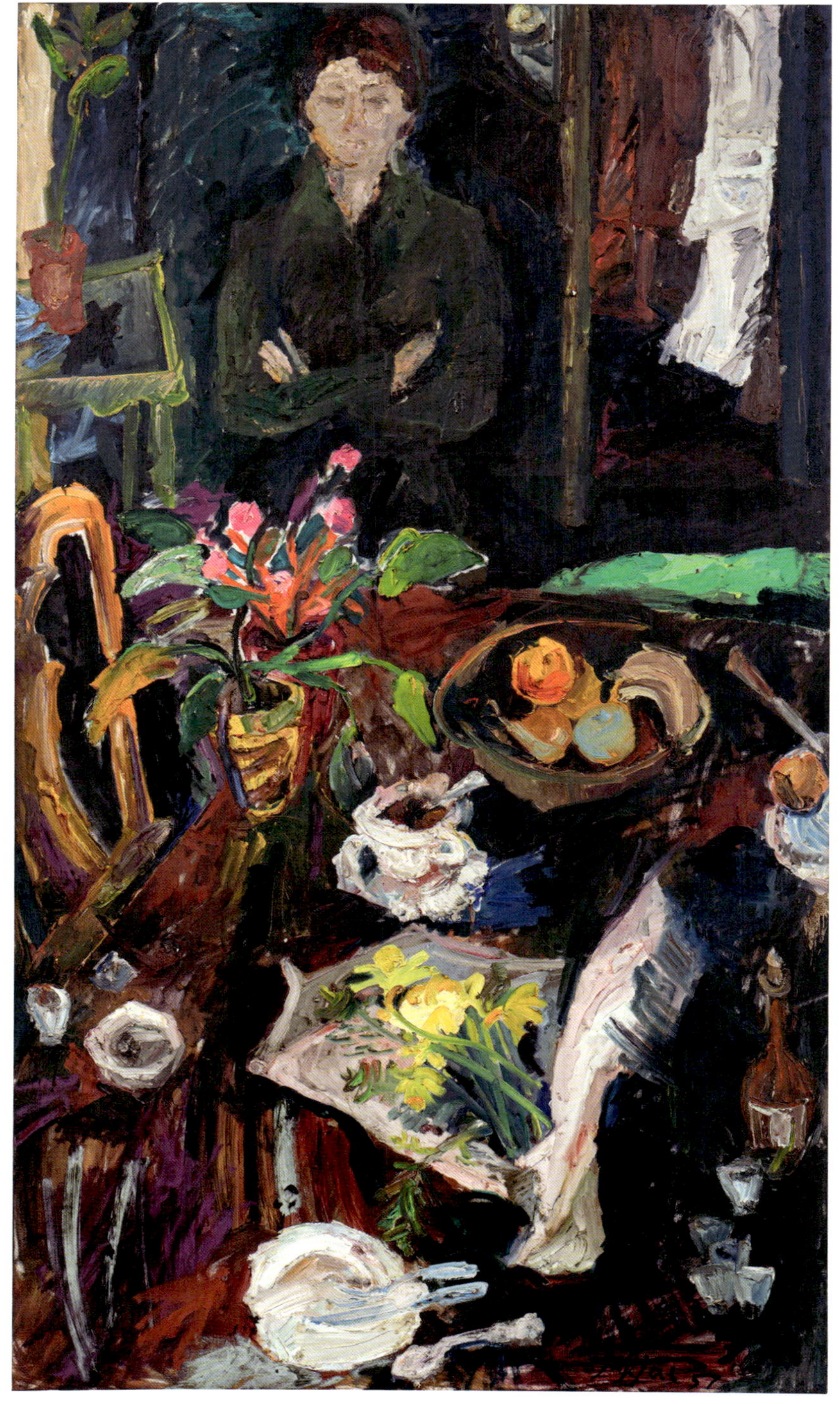

Untitled, 1957, oil on canvas, 88 × 50¾ inches (223.5 × 128.9 cm)

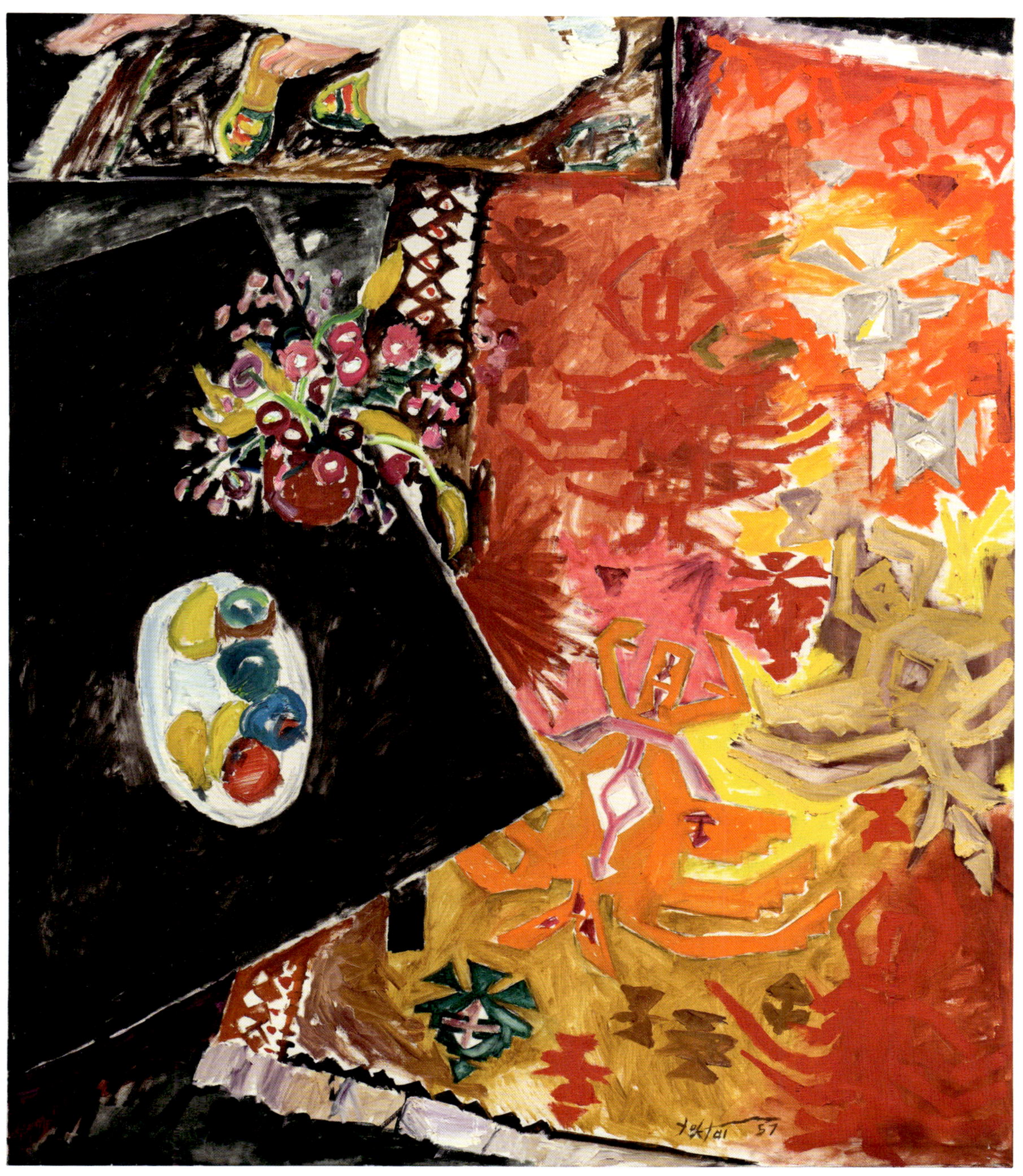

Untitled, 1957, oil on canvas, 84 × 72 inches (213 × 183 cm)

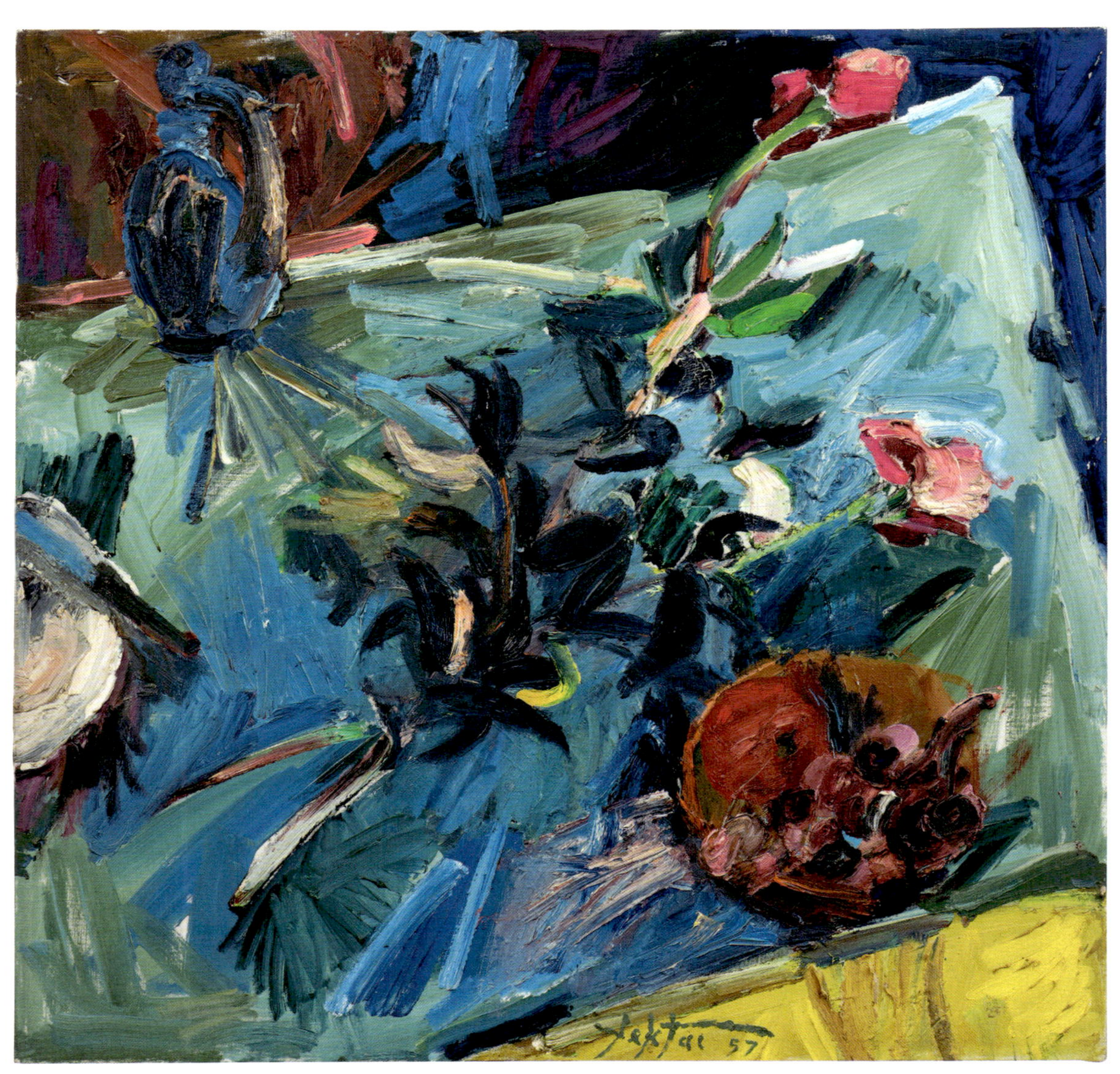

 Untitled, 1957, oil on canvas, 35½ × 37 inches (90.2 × 94 cm)

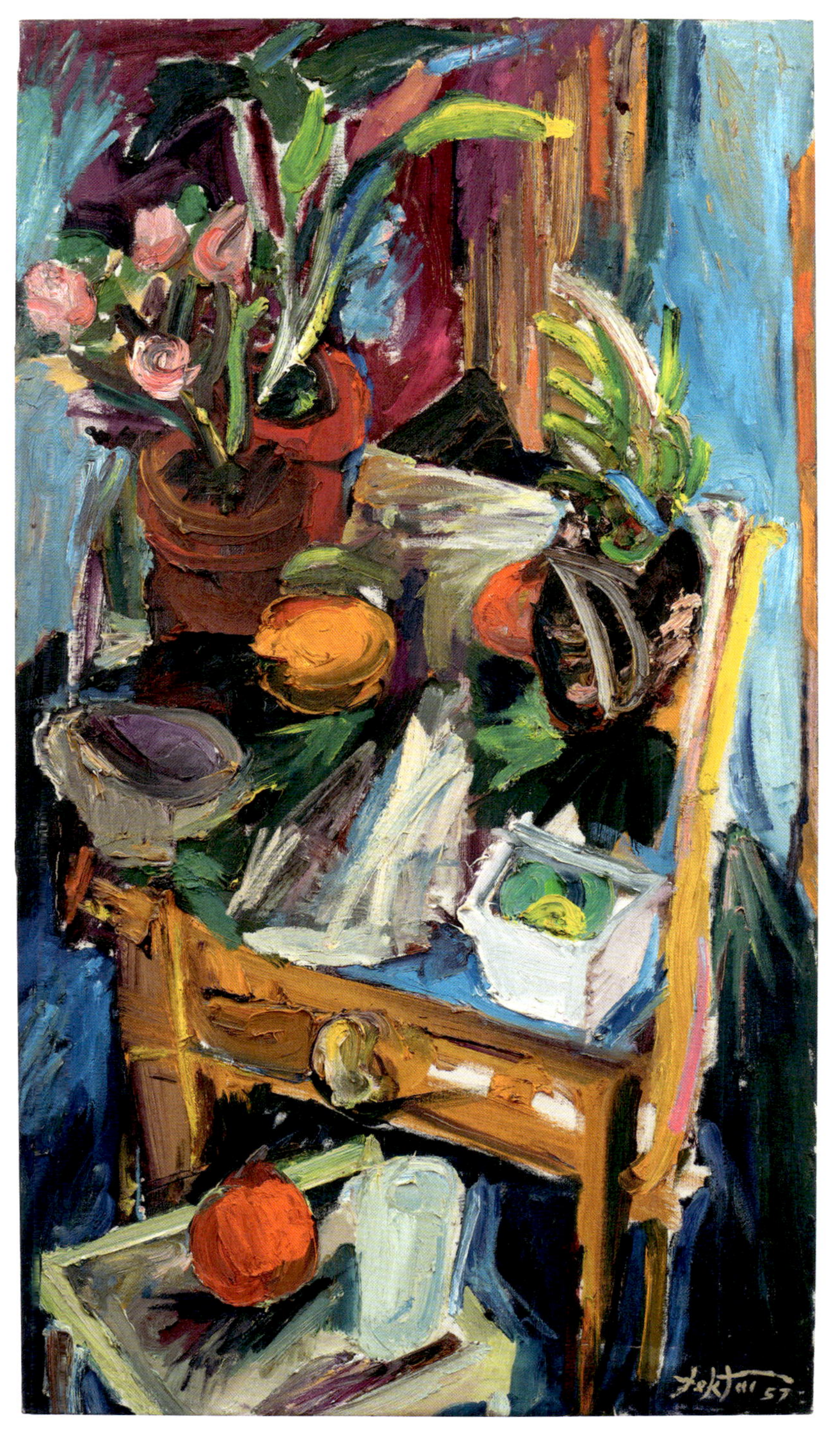

Untitled, 1957, oil on canvas, 50 × 27¼ inches (127 × 69.2 cm)

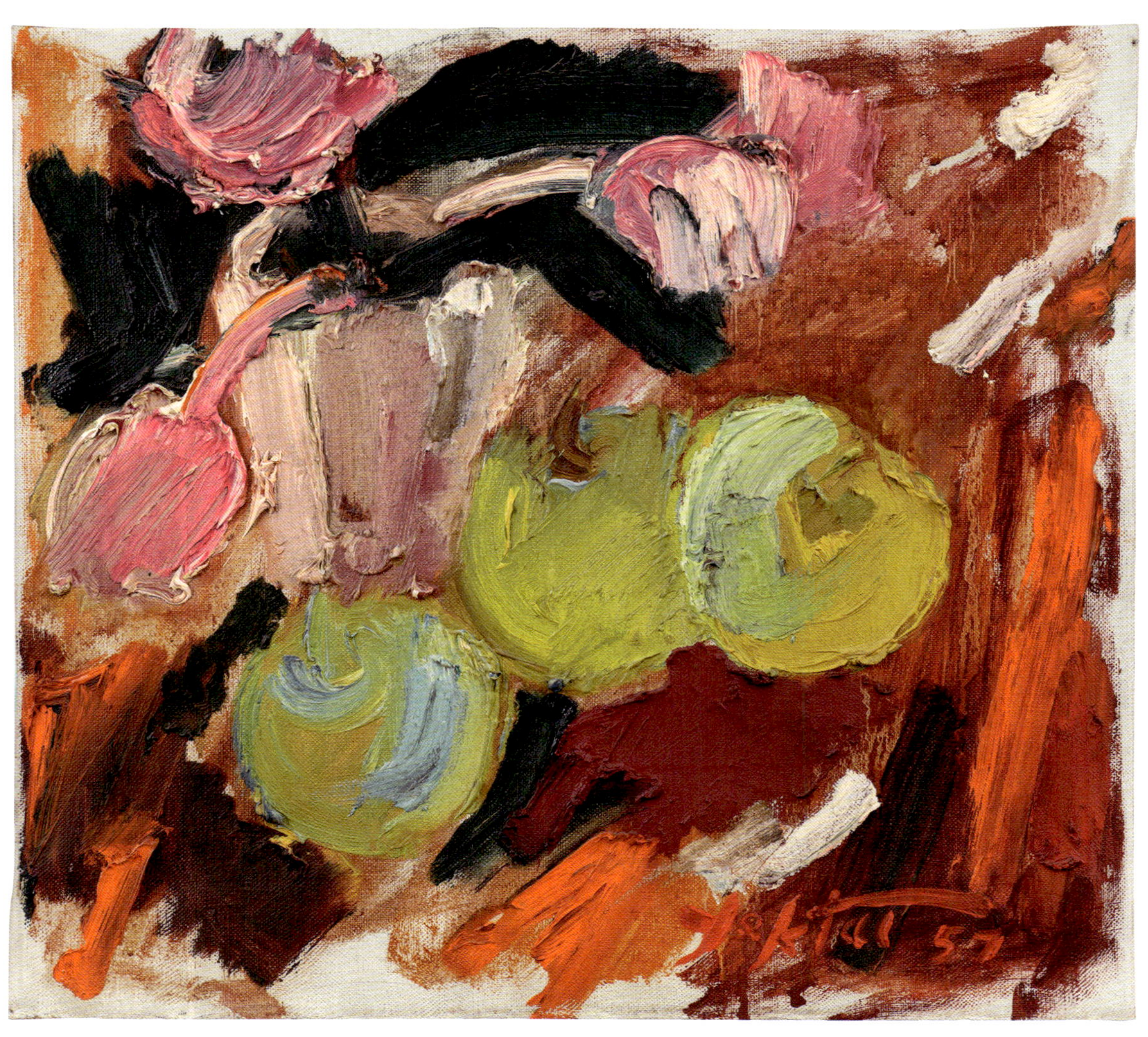

 Pink Flowers, 1957, oil on canvas, 14¼ × 14½ inches (36.2 × 36.8 cm)

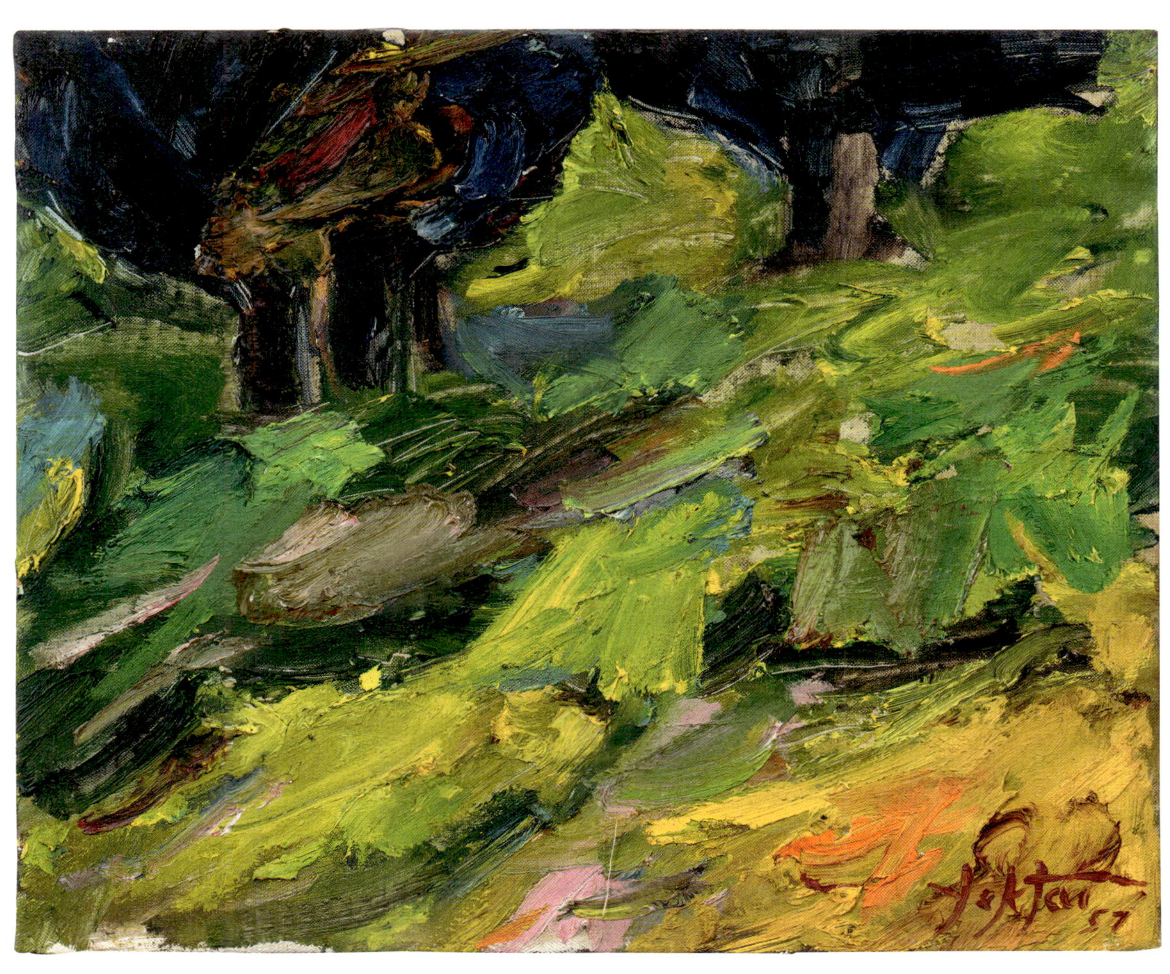

Untitled, 1957, oil on canvas, 14 × 17 inches (35.6 × 43.2 cm)

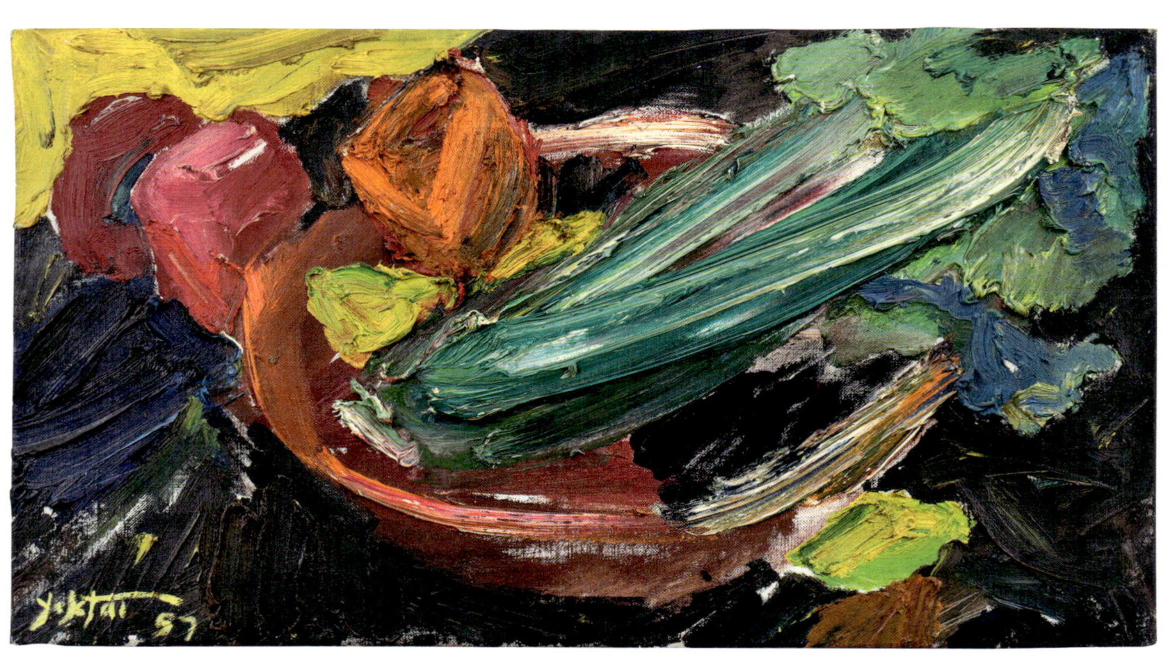

Still Life, 1957, oil on canvas, 14 × 25 inches (35.6 × 63.5 cm)

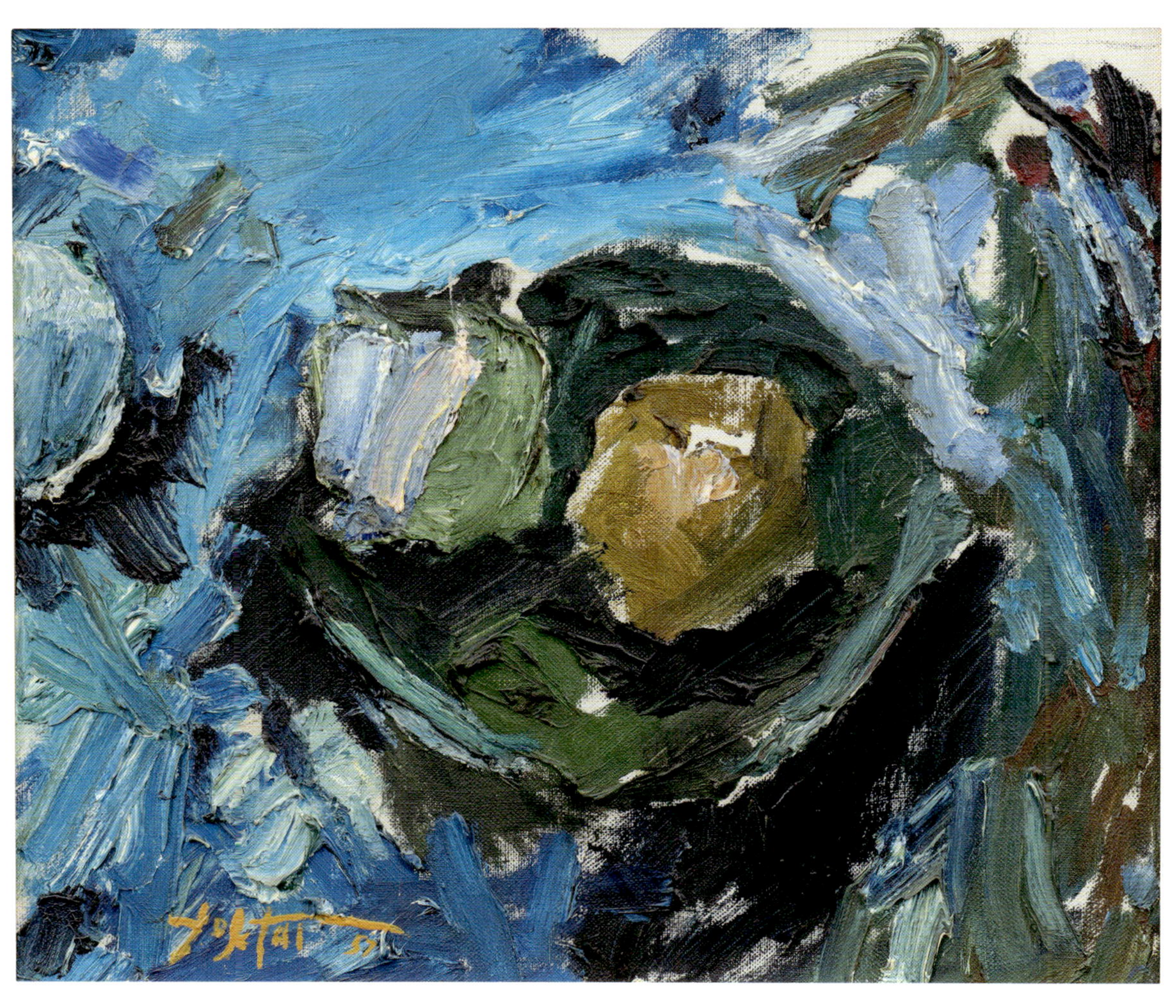

Blue Blossoms, 1957, oil on canvas, 13¾ × 15¾ inches (34.9 × 40 cm)

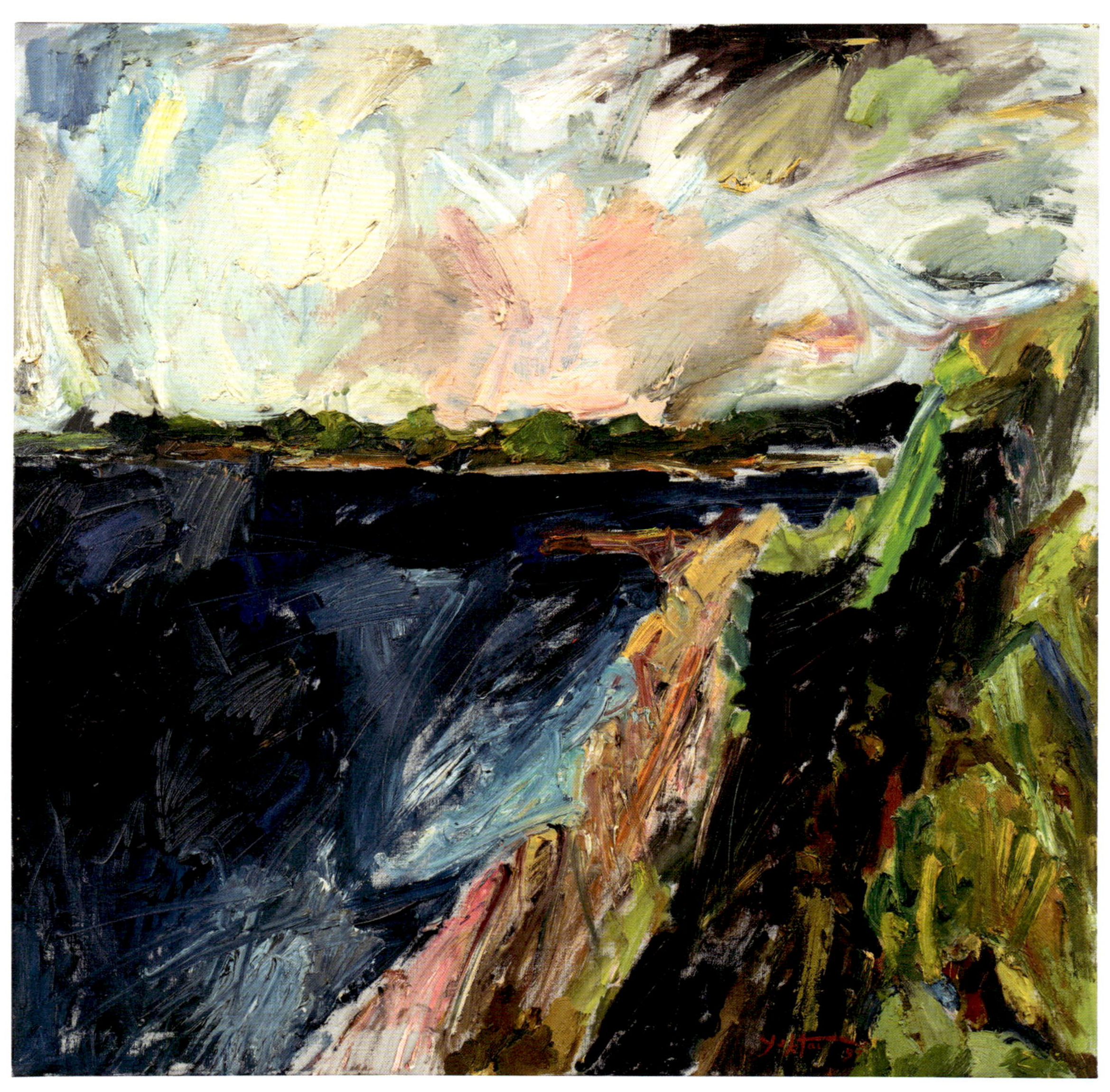

 Untitled, 1957, oil on canvas, 36 × 36 inches (91.4 × 91.4 cm)

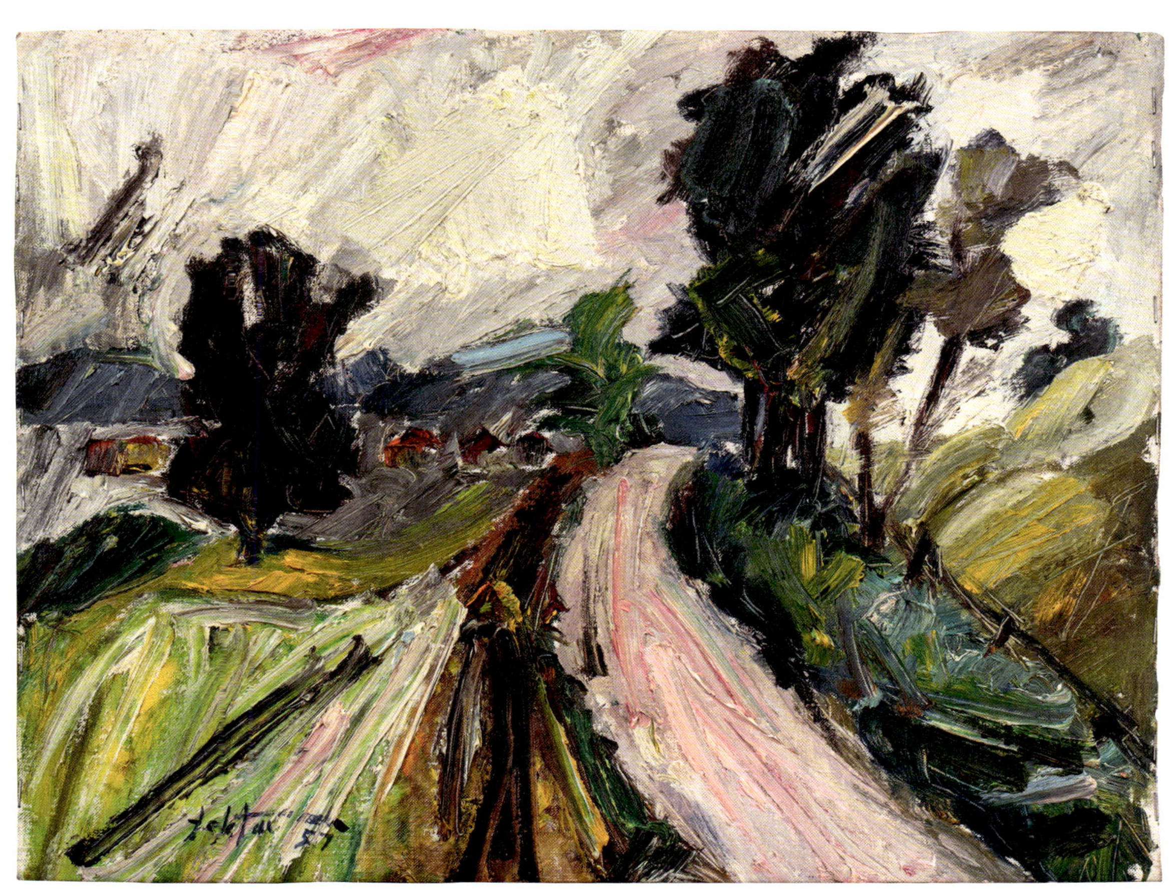

Untitled, 1957, oil on canvas, 15½ × 20⅜ inches (39.4 × 51.8 cm)

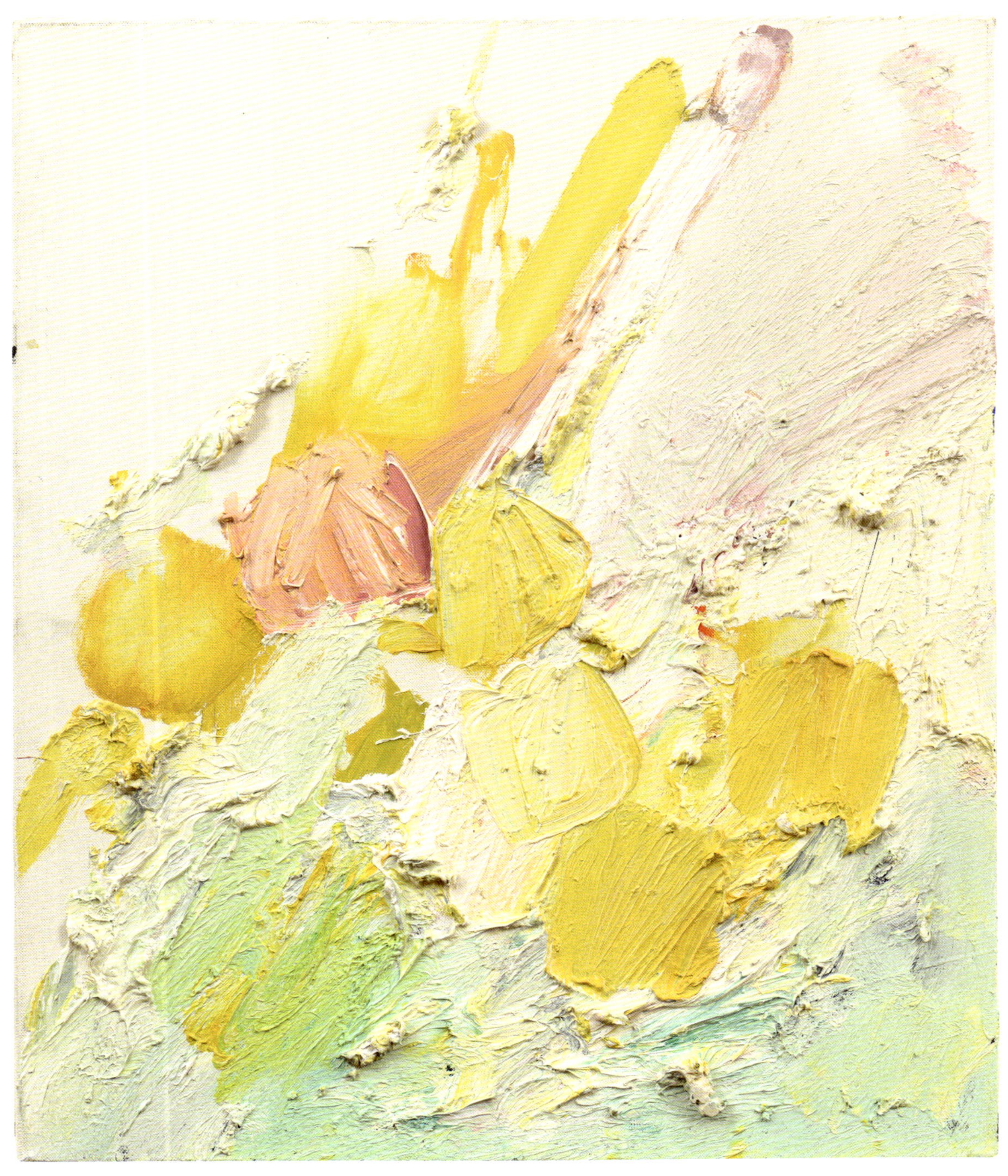

Untitled, ca. 1957, oil on canvas, 21¾ × 18 inches (55.3 × 45.7 cm)

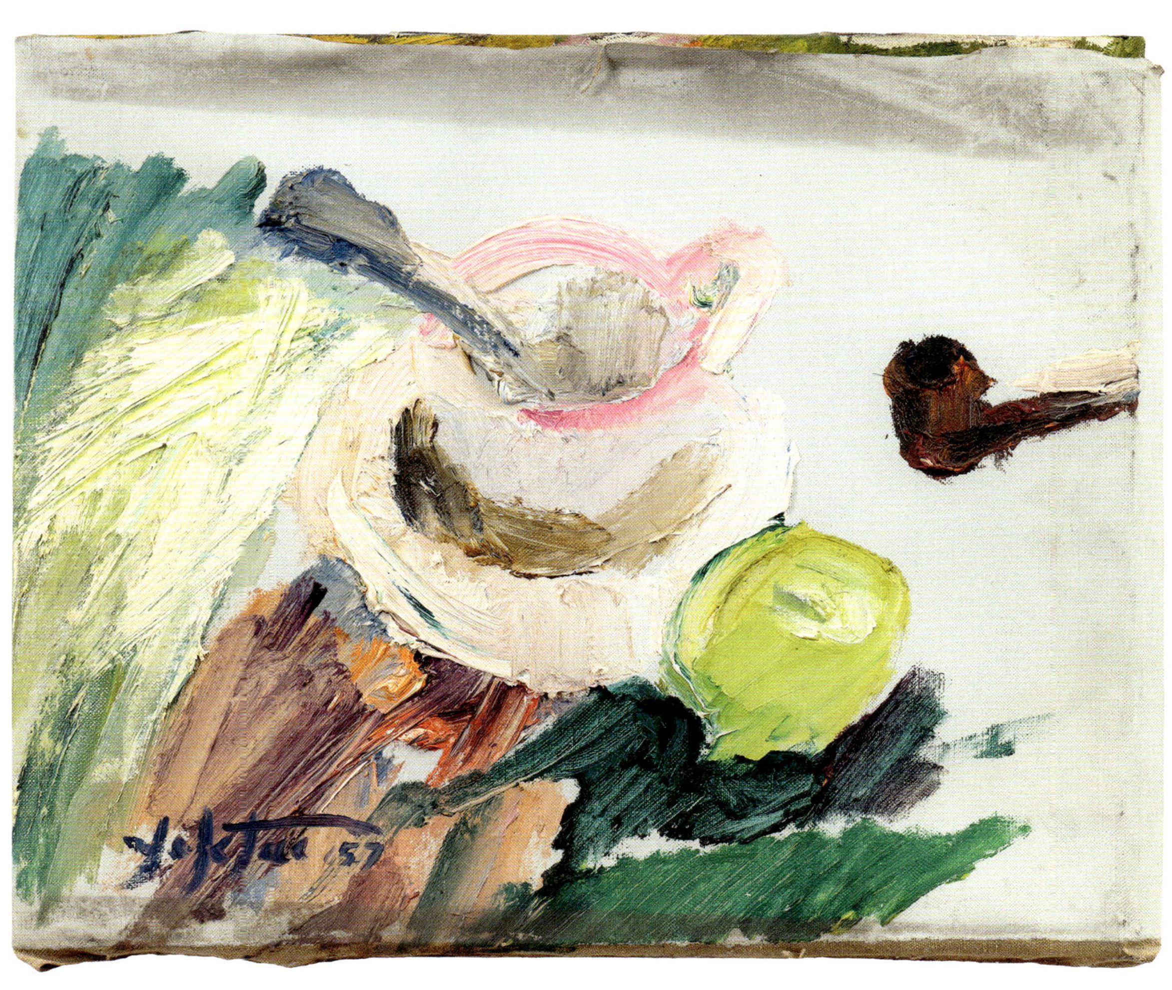

Untitled, 1957, oil on canvas, 14½ × 17 inches (36.8 × 43.2 cm)

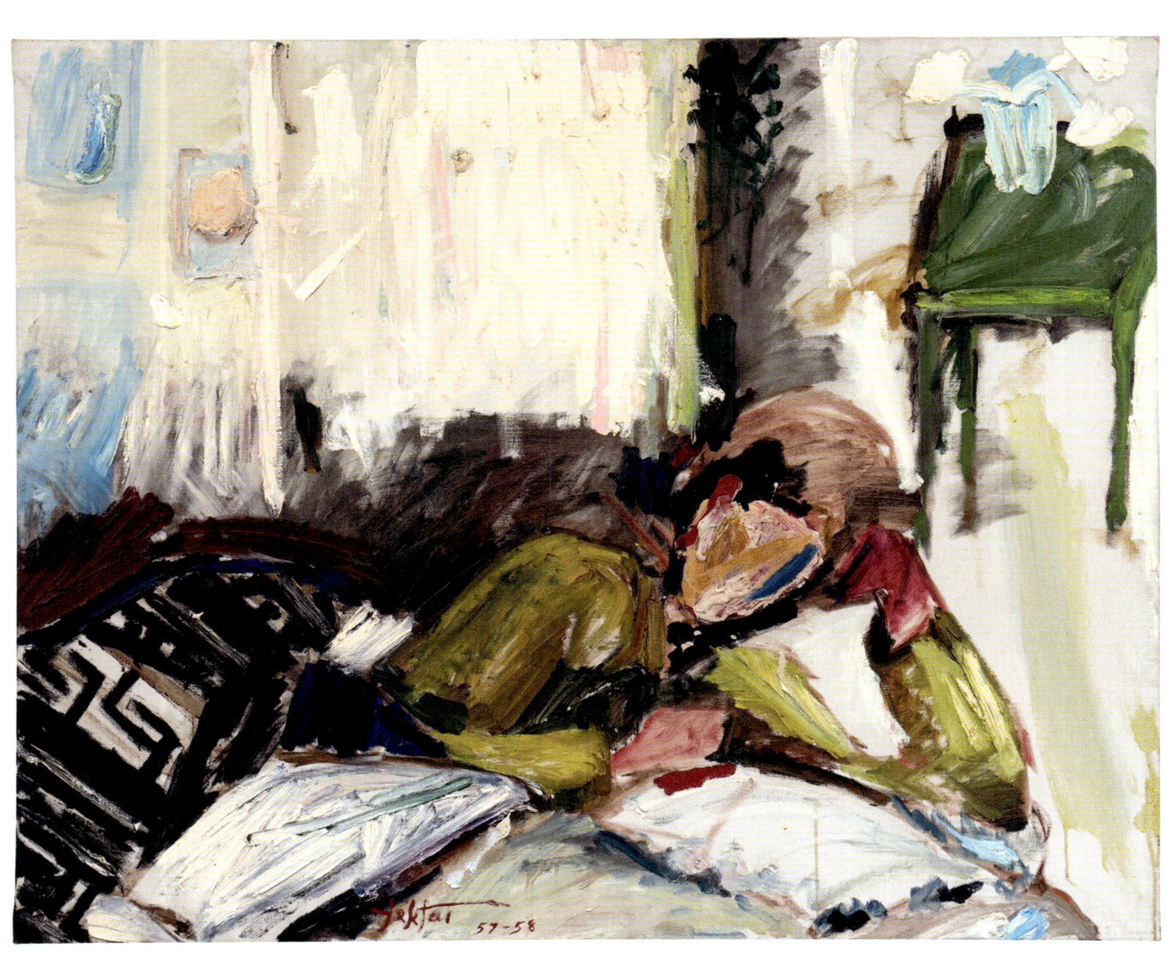

 Figure (7), 1957, oil on canvas, 43¾ × 53¾ inches (111.1 × 136.5 cm)

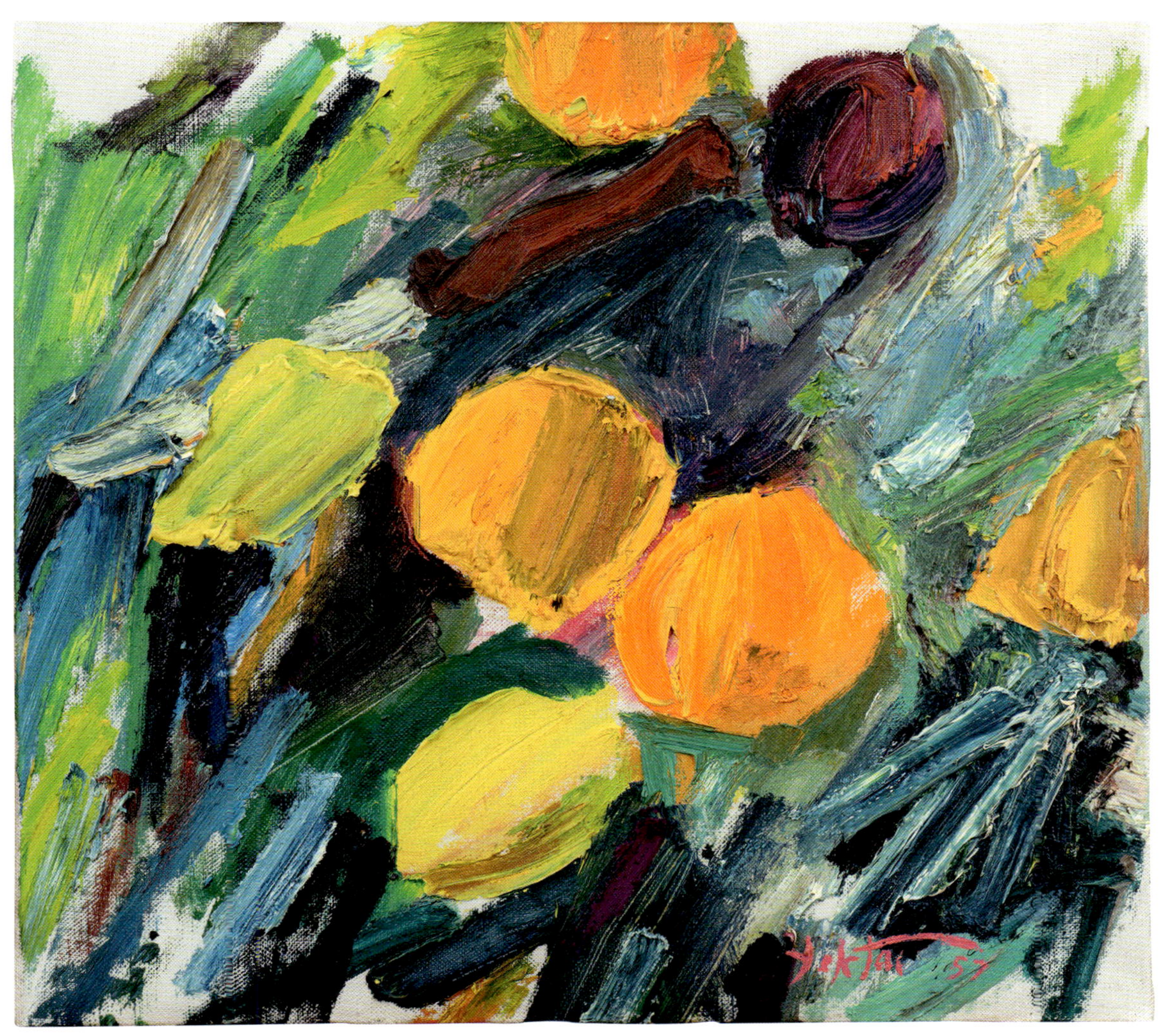

Oranges and Lemons, 1957, oil on canvas, 14 × 15⅜ inches (35.6 × 39.1 cm)

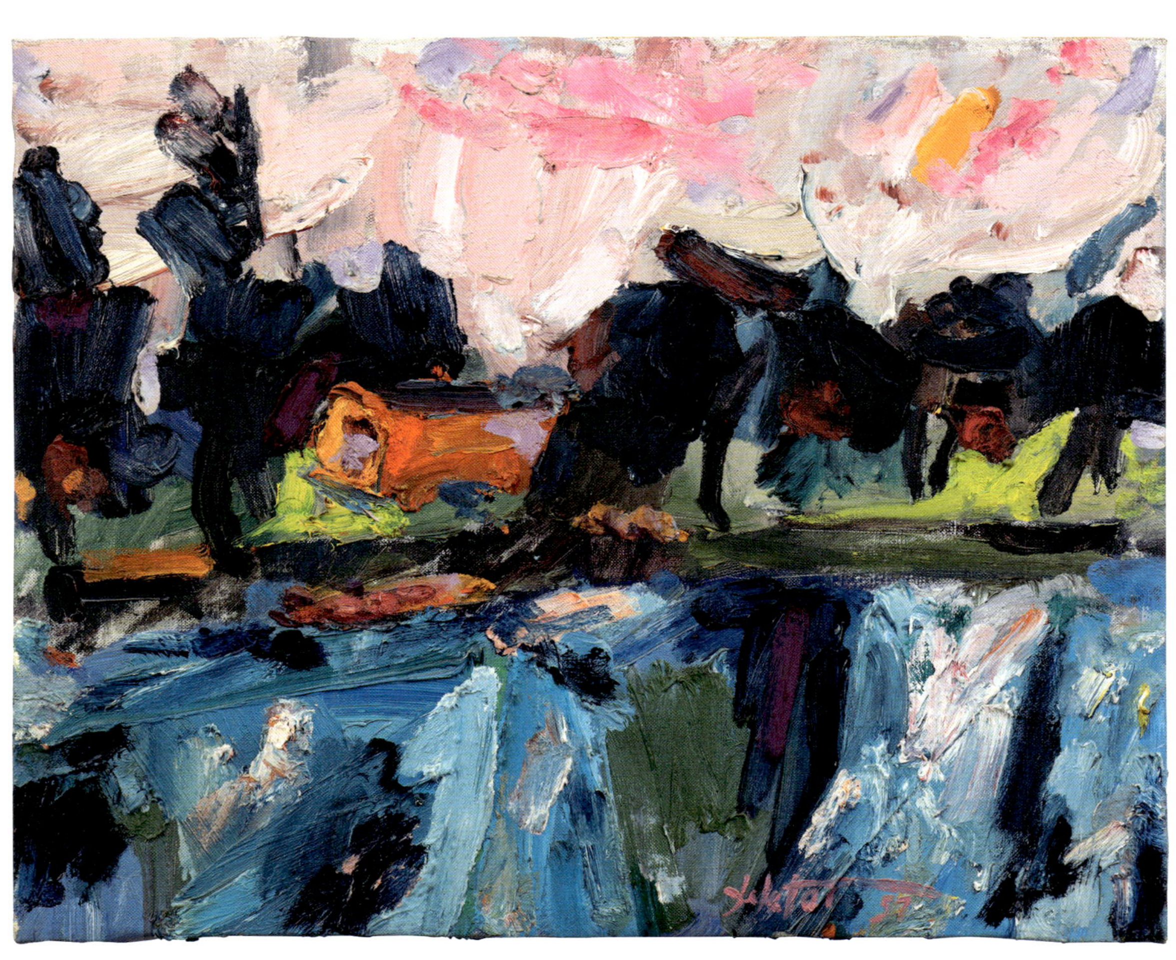

Untitled, 1957, oil on canvas, 17½ × 21½ inches (44.5 × 54.6 cm)

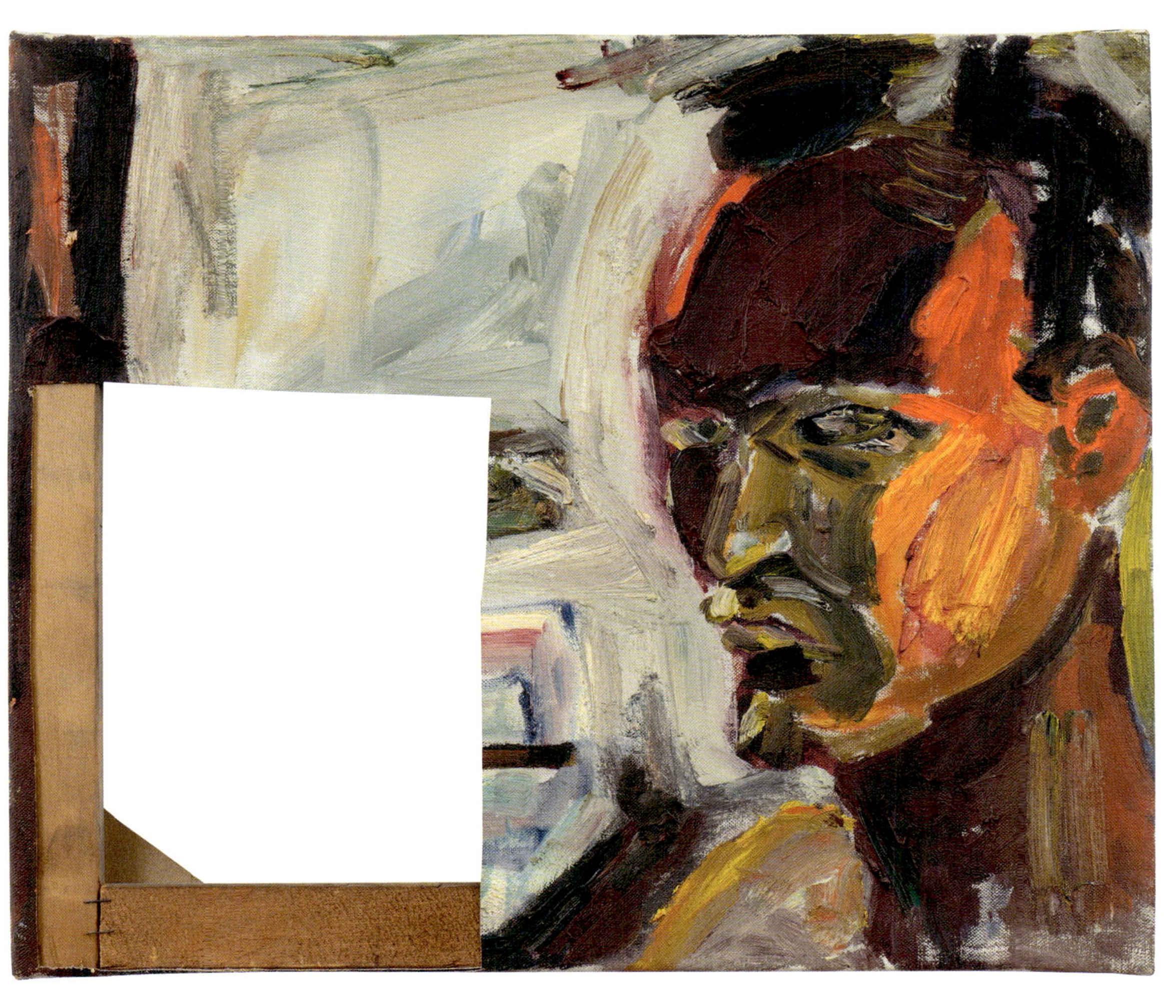

Self-Portrait, 1957, oil on canvas, 17¼ × 20¾ inches (43.8 × 52.7 cm)

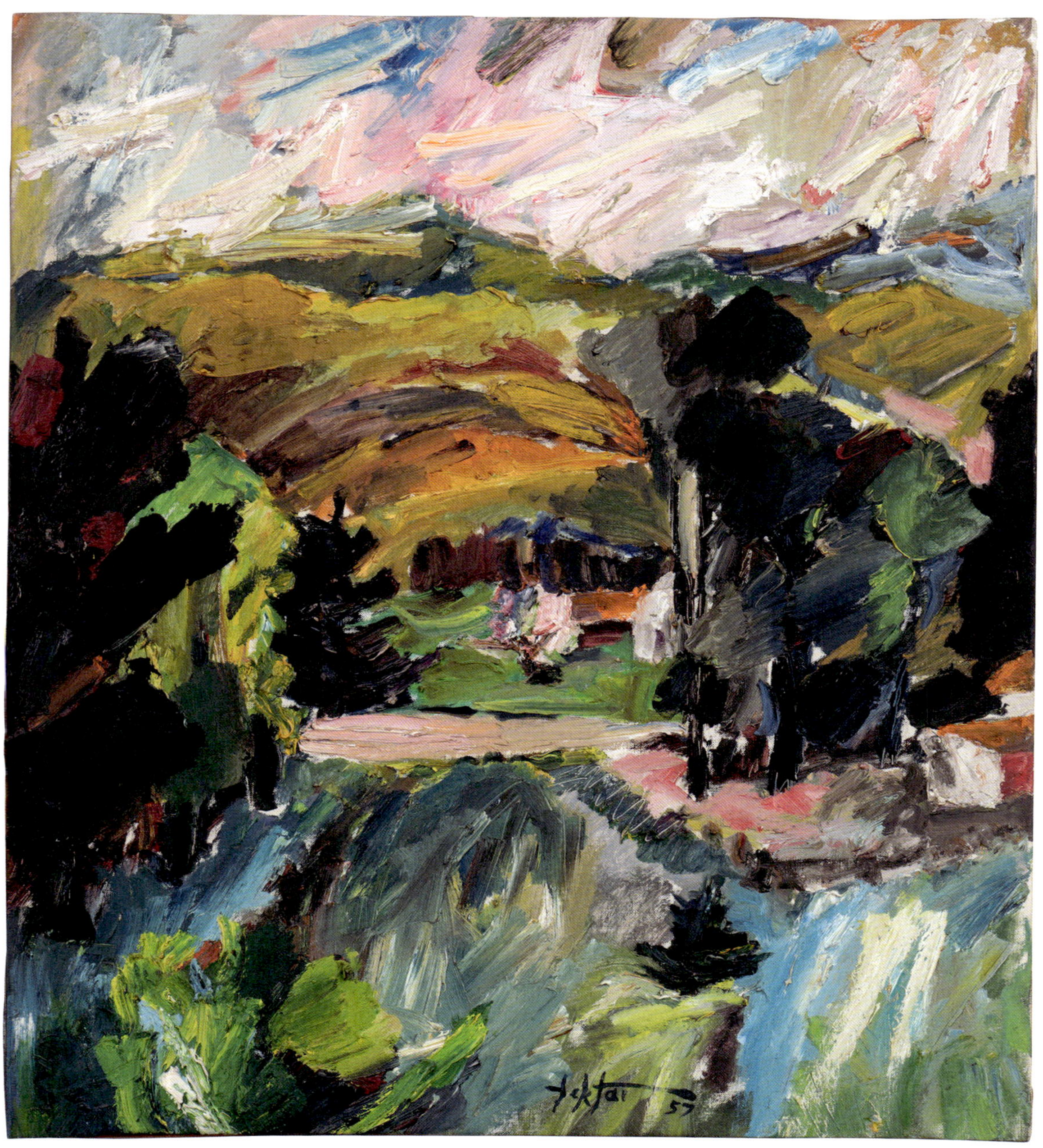

 Untitled, 1957, oil on canvas, 25½ × 23 inches (64.8 × 58.4 cm)

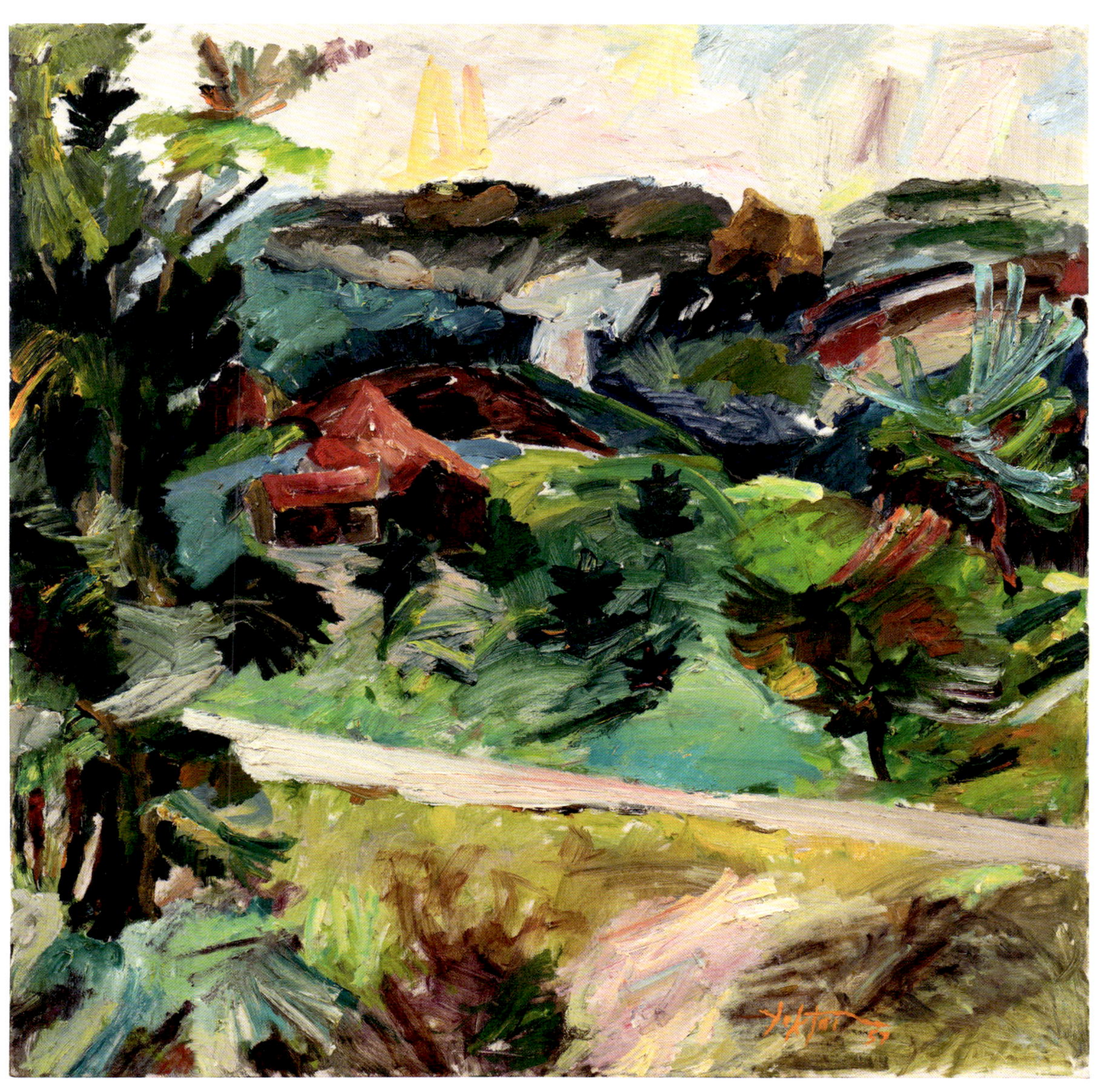

Vermont Landscape #4, 1957, oil on canvas, 48 × 48 inches (121.9 × 121.9 cm)

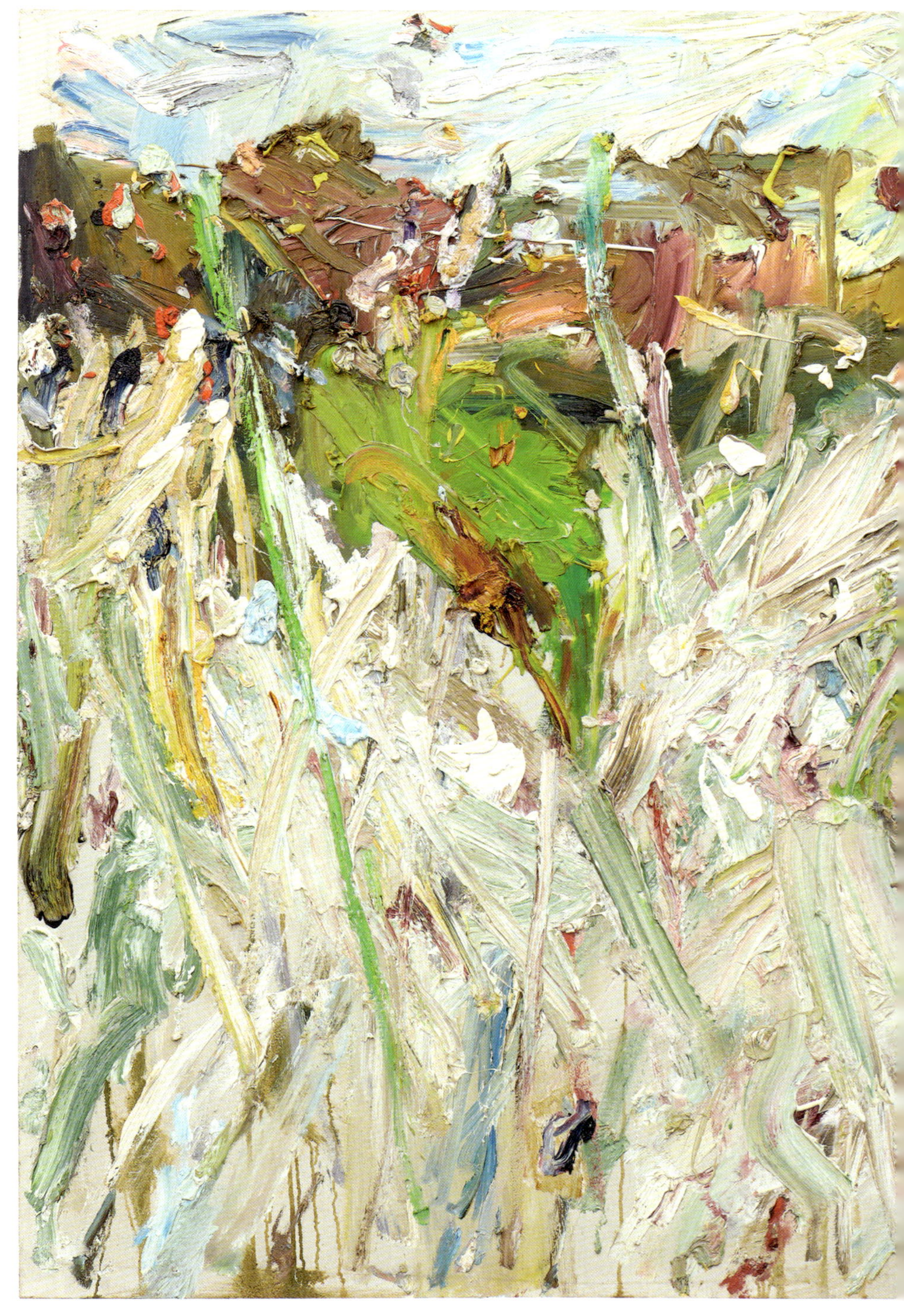

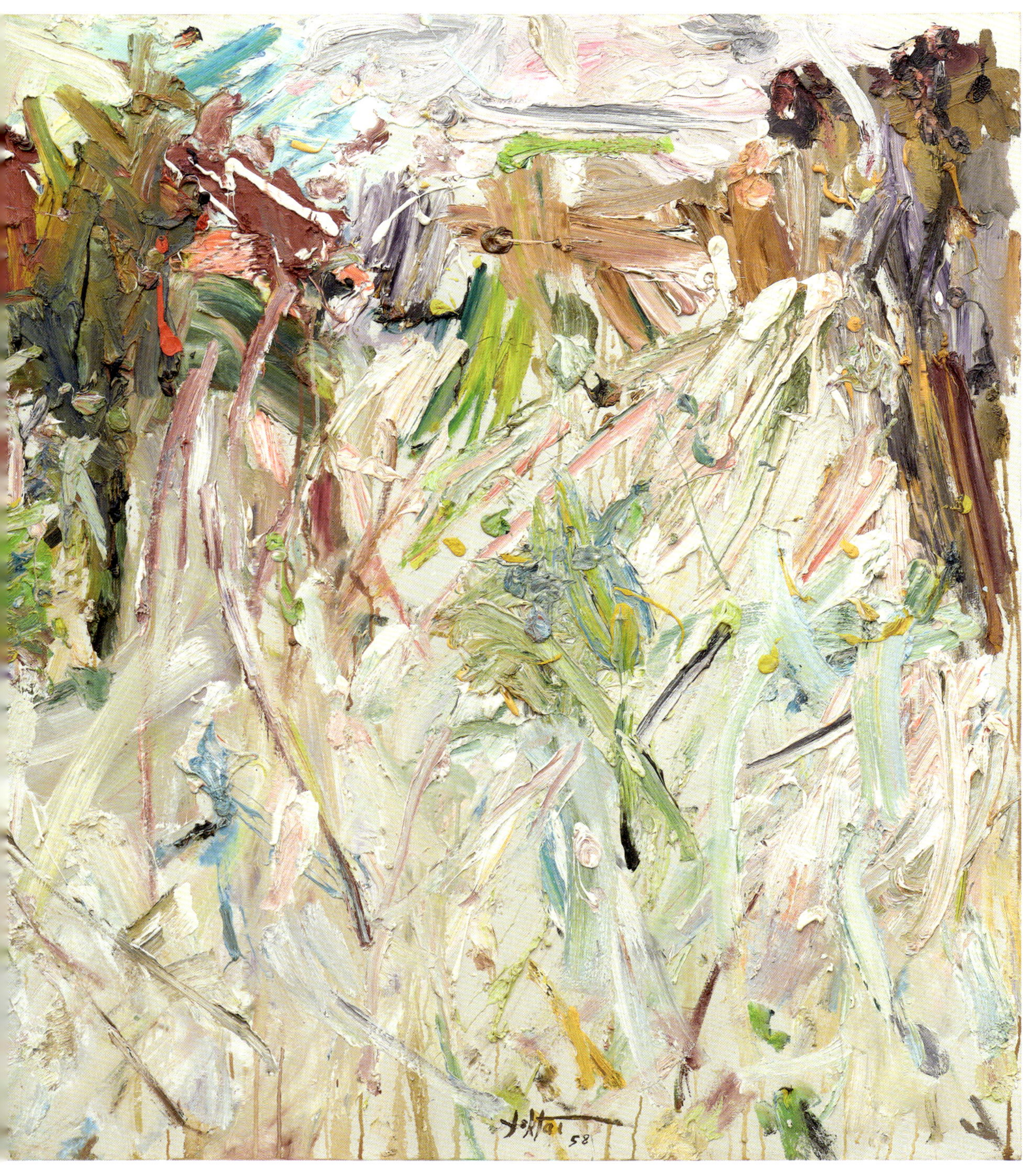

95th St, 1958, oil on canvas, 60 × 96 inches (152.4 × 243.8 cm)

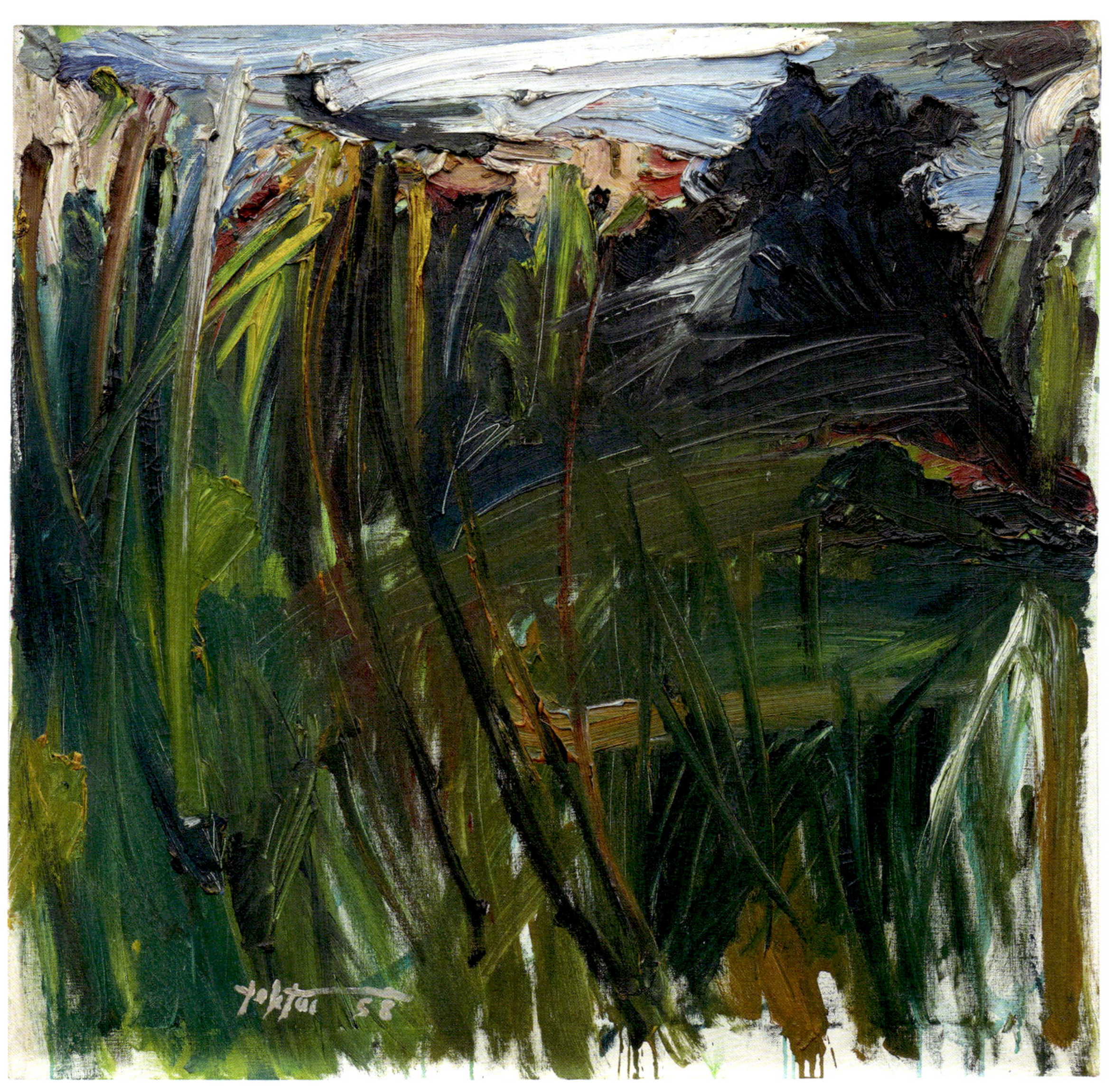

220 *Untitled (Abstract)*, 1958, oil on canvas, 33½ × 33½ inches (85.1 × 85.1 cm)

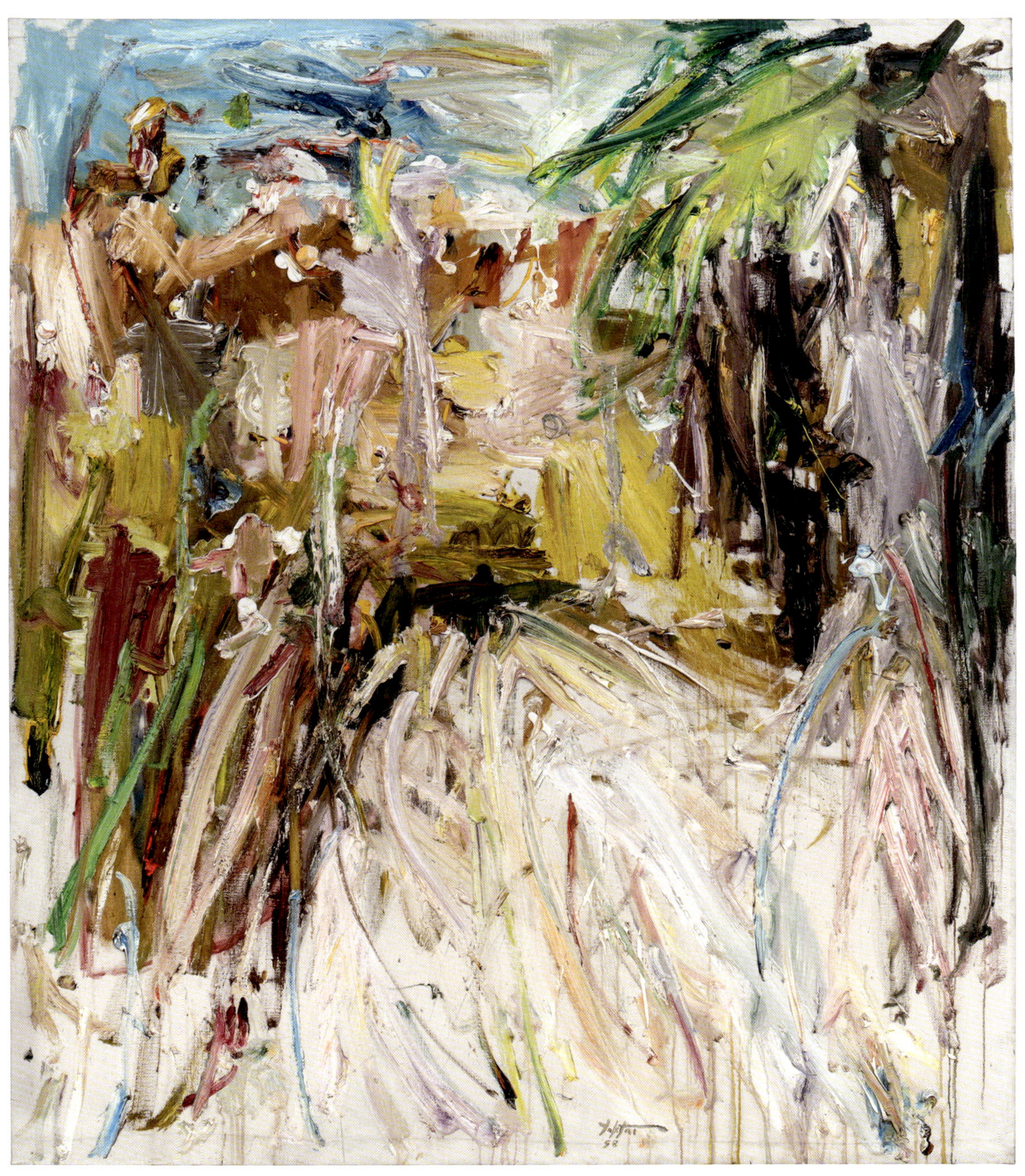

95th Street Landscape (#5), 1958, oil on canvas, 84 × 72 inches (213.4 × 182.9 cm)

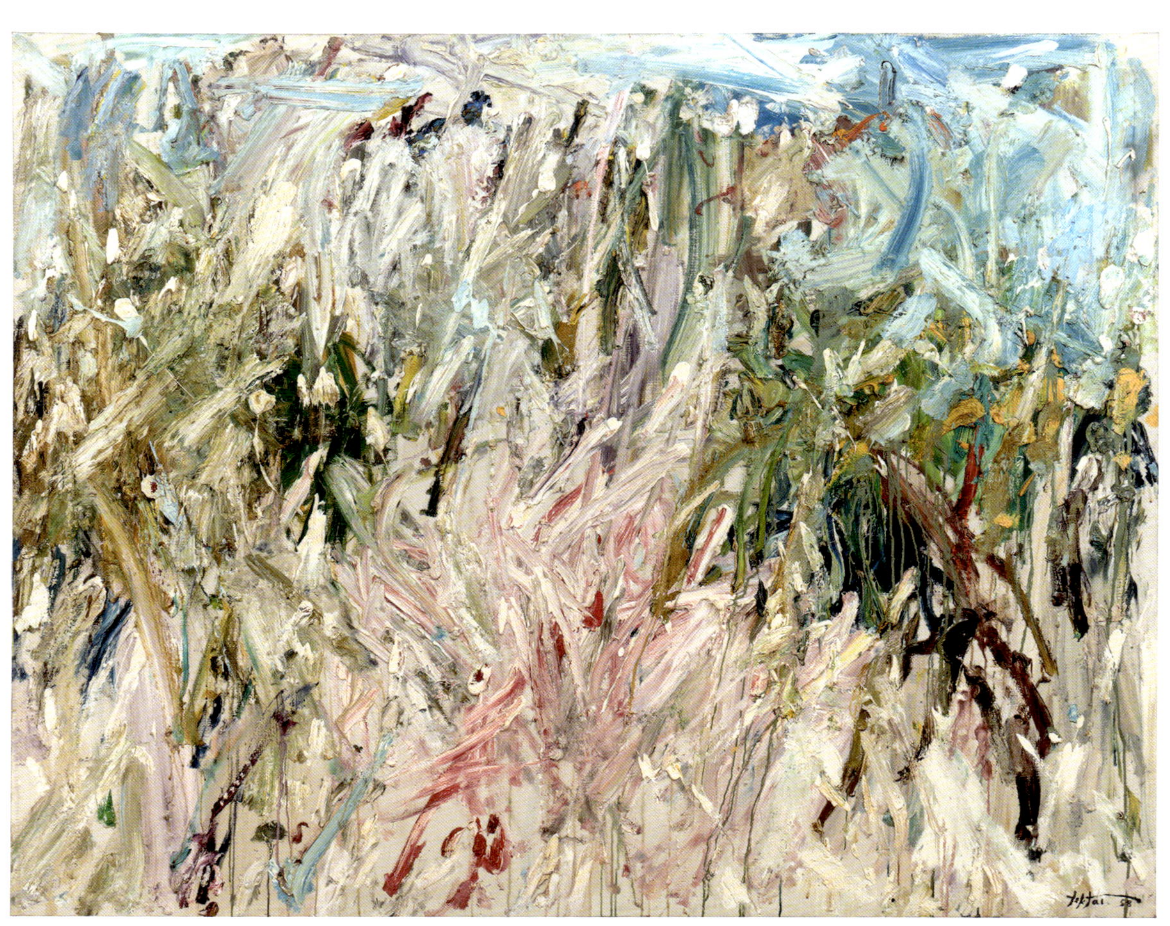

222 *#12 95th Street Landscape*, 1958, oil on canvas, 70 × 88 inches (177.8 × 223.5 cm)

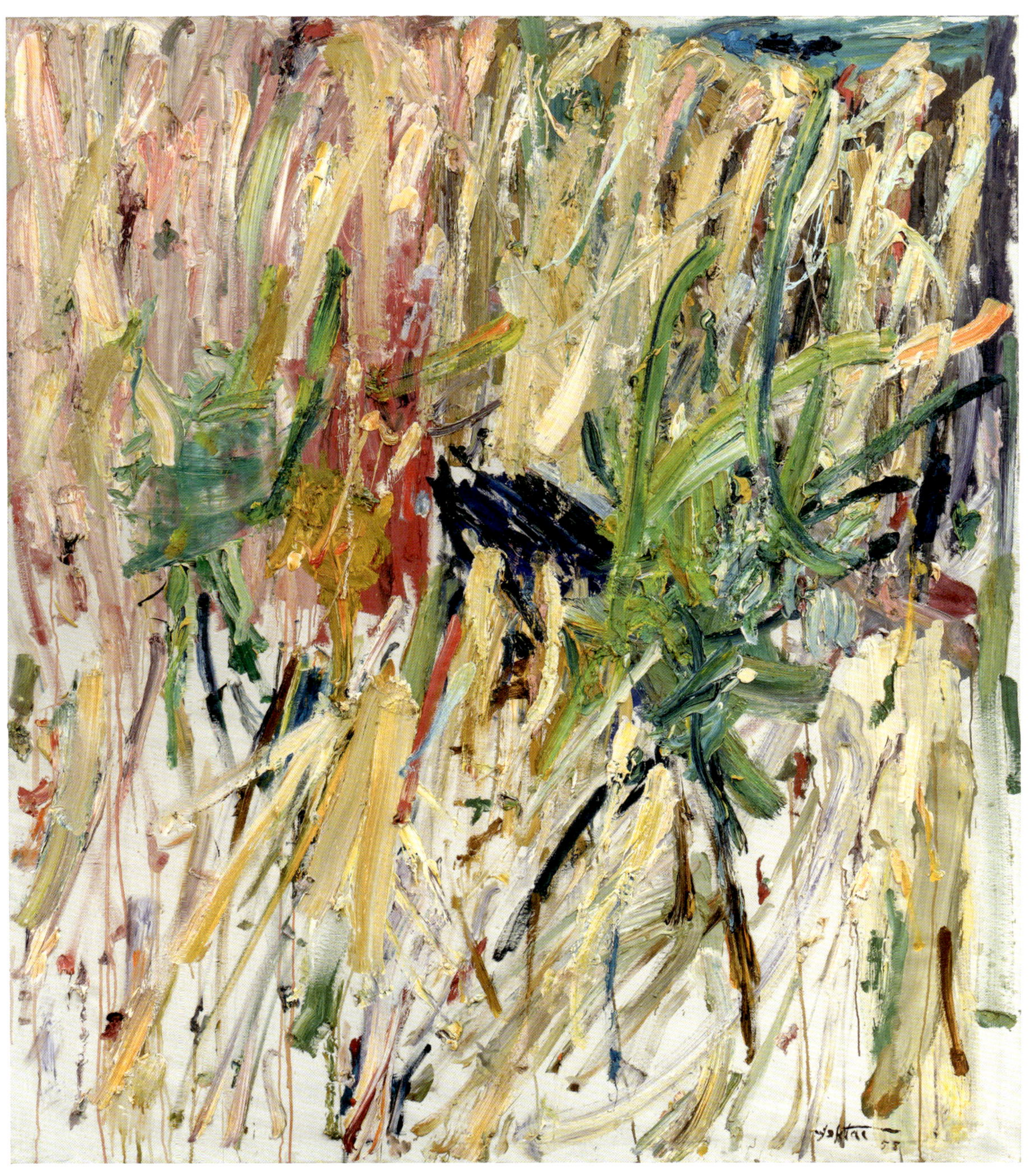

Landscape of 95th Street #15, 1958, oil on canvas, 84 × 72 inches (213.4 × 182.9 cm)

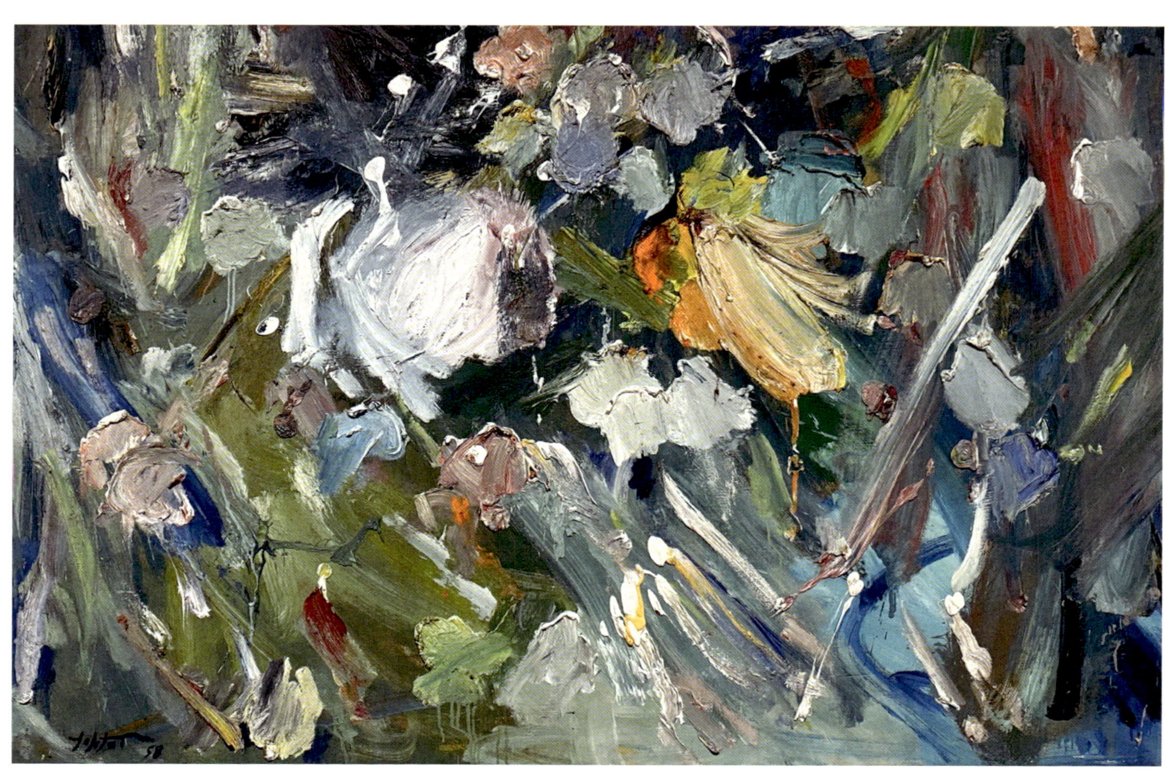

Untitled, 1958, oil on canvas, 42½ × 62 inches (108 × 157.5 cm)

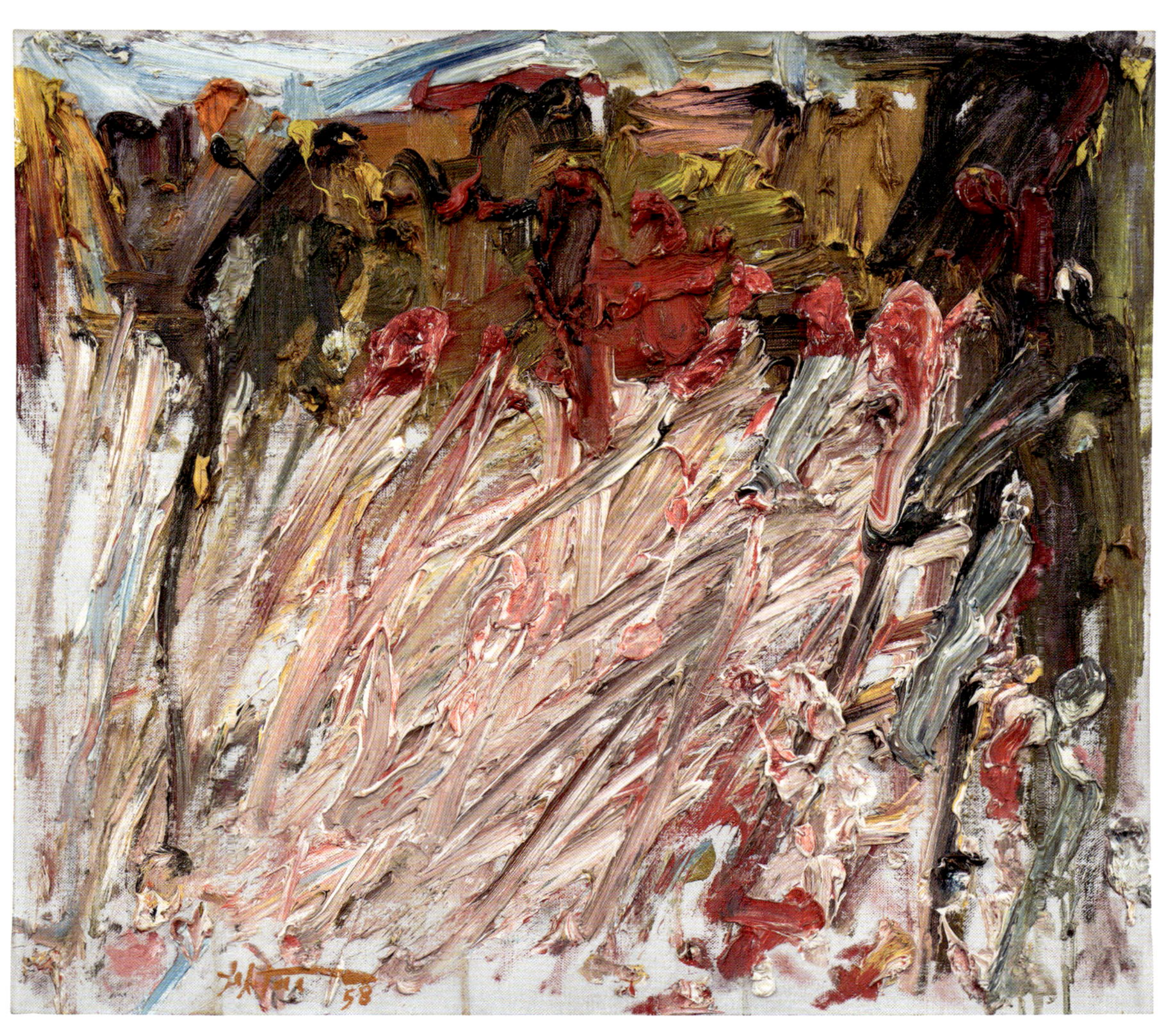

Untitled, 1958, oil on canvas, 21 × 23½ inches (53.3 × 59.7 cm)

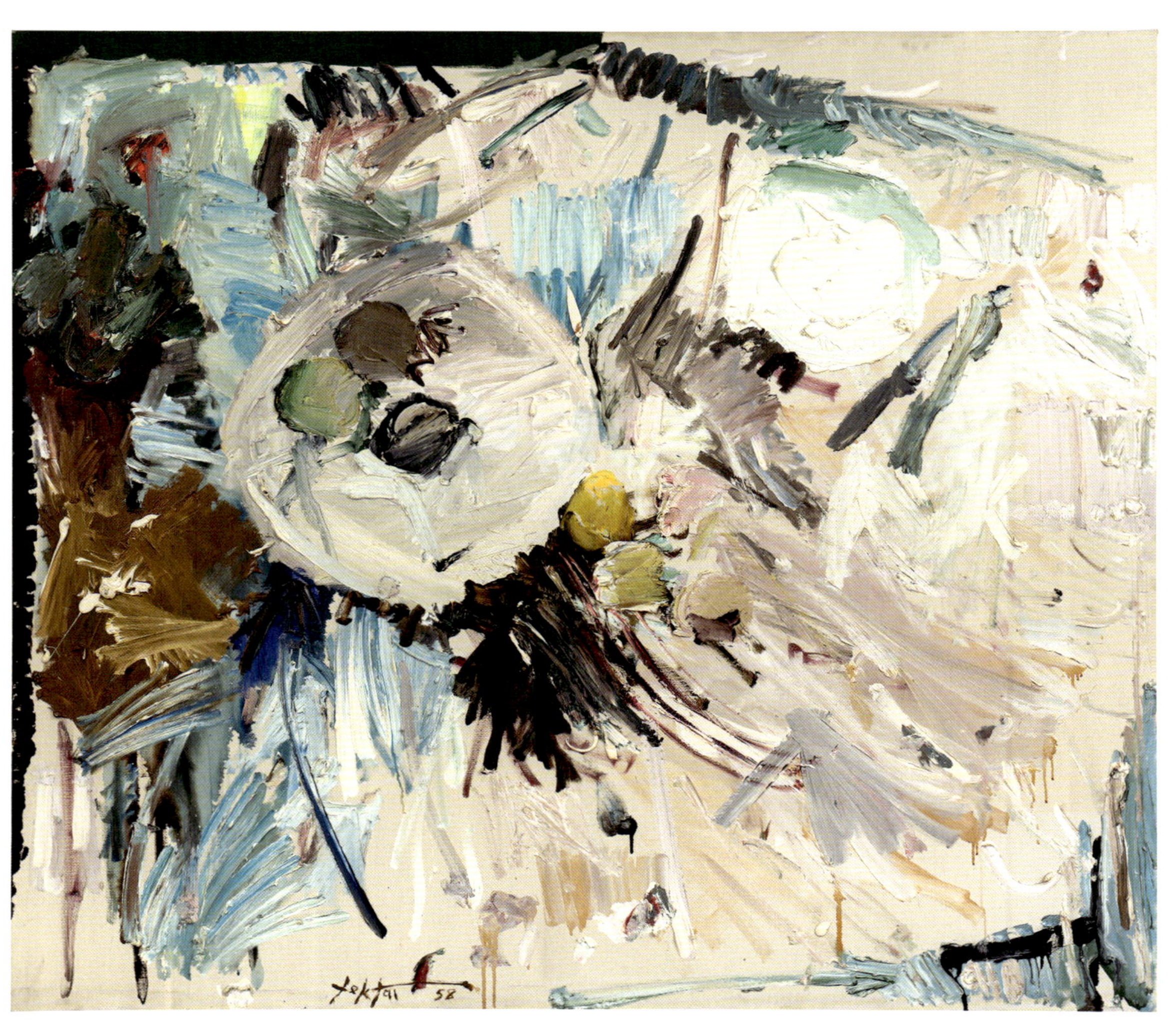

 Still Life, 1958, oil on canvas, 60 × 68 inches (152.4 × 172.7 cm)

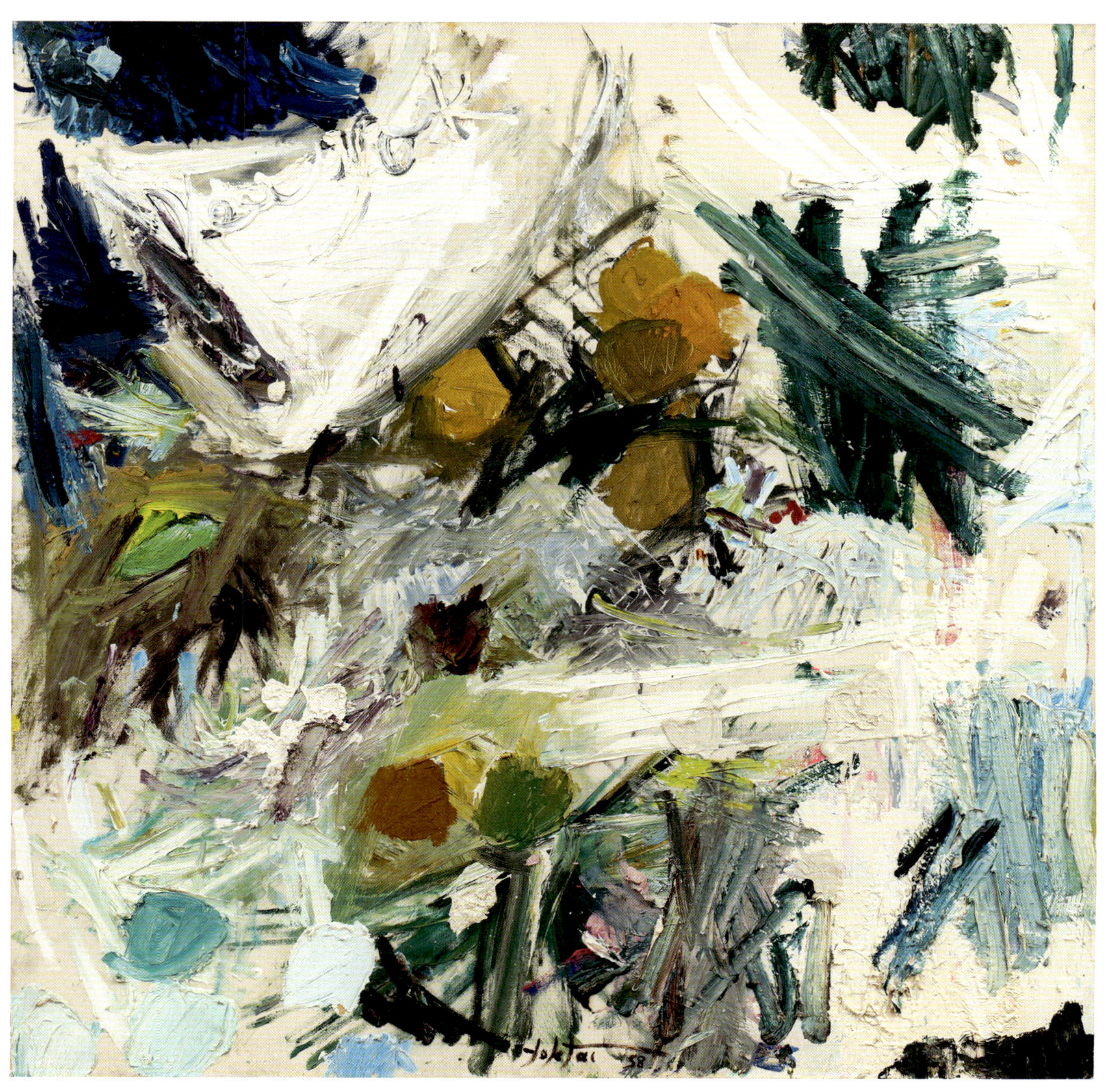

Still Life "A," 1958, oil on canvas, 48 × 48 inches (122 × 122 cm)

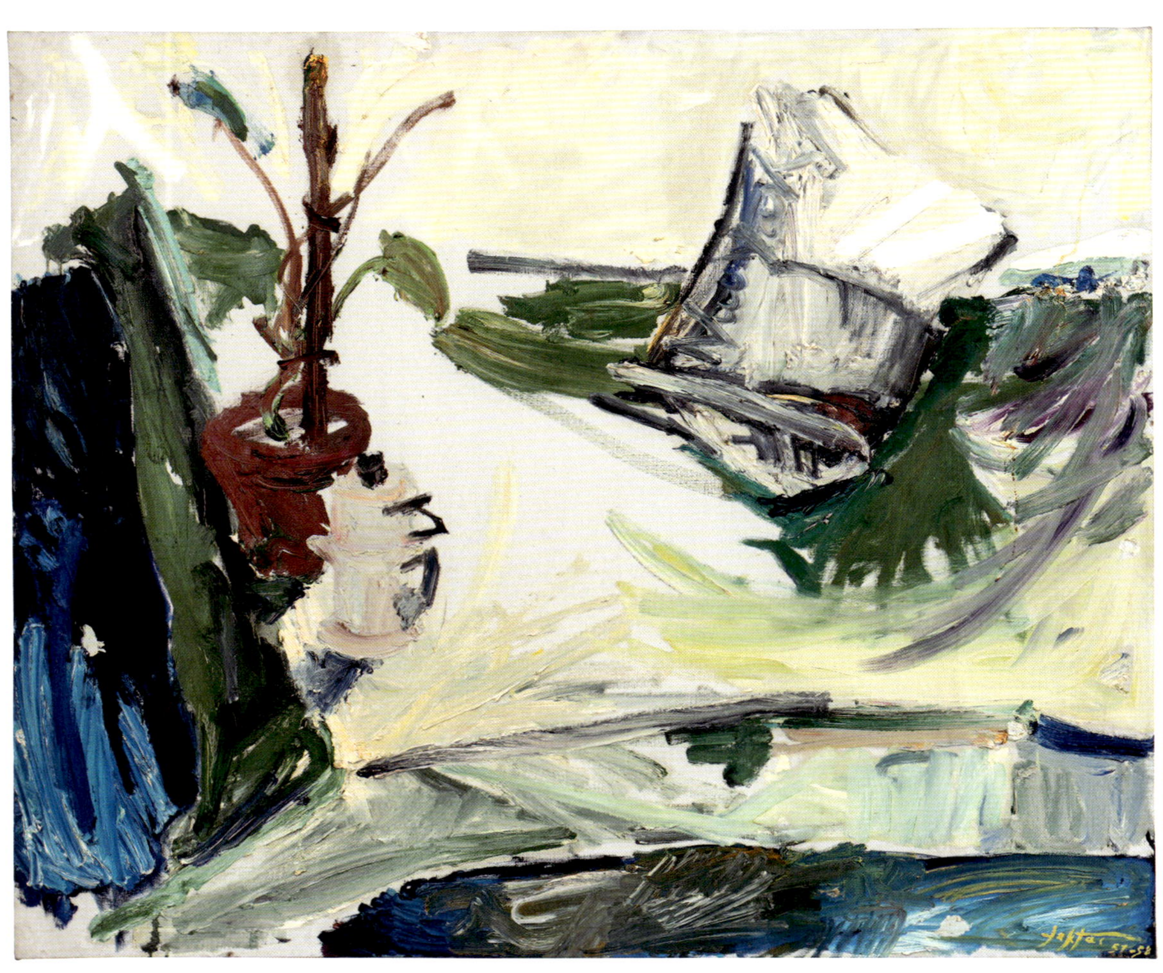

Untitled, 1957–58, oil on canvas, 50¾ × 60½ inches (128.9 × 153.7 cm)

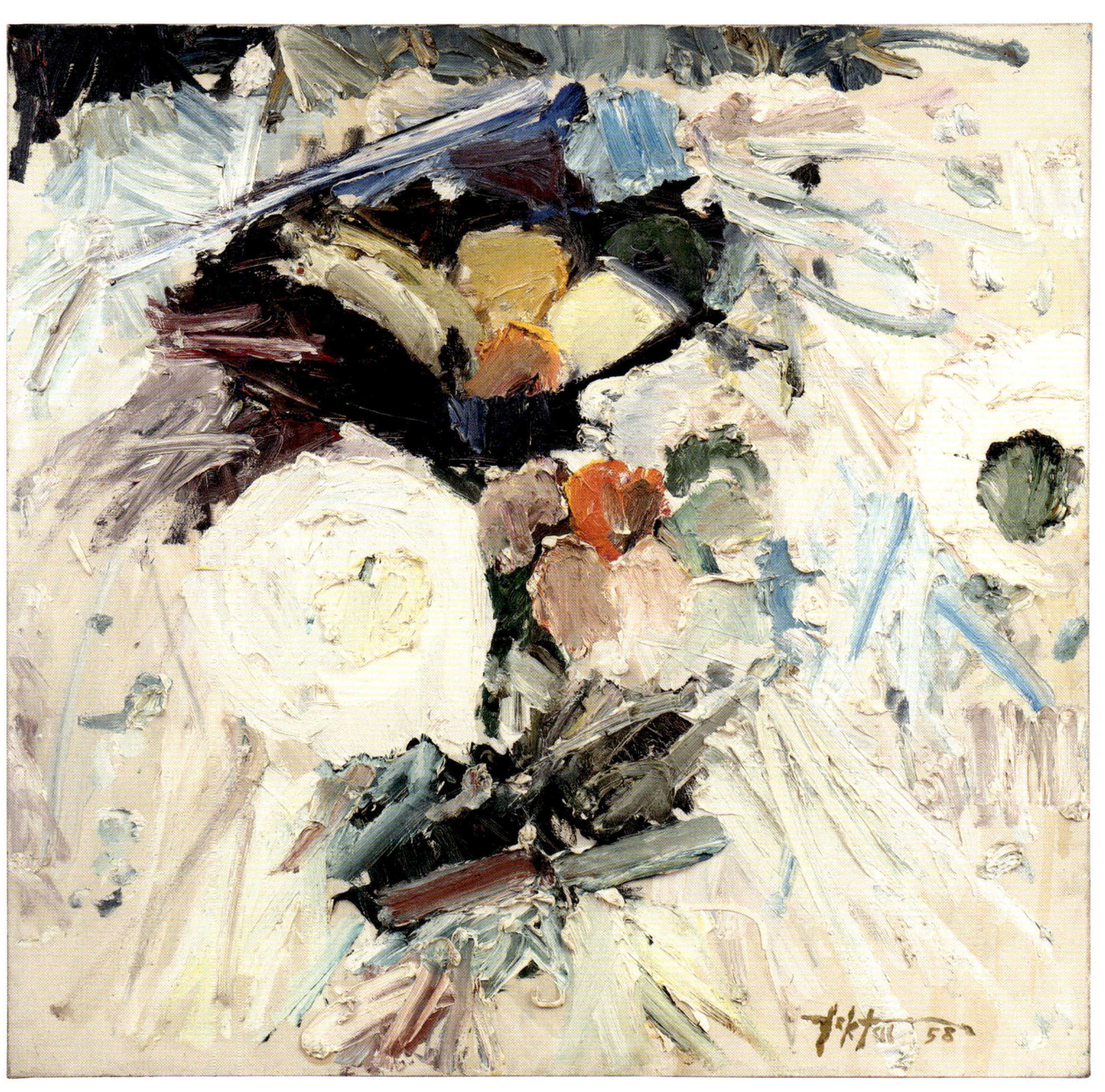

Still Life, 1958, oil on canvas, 48 × 48 inches (121.9 × 121.9 cm)

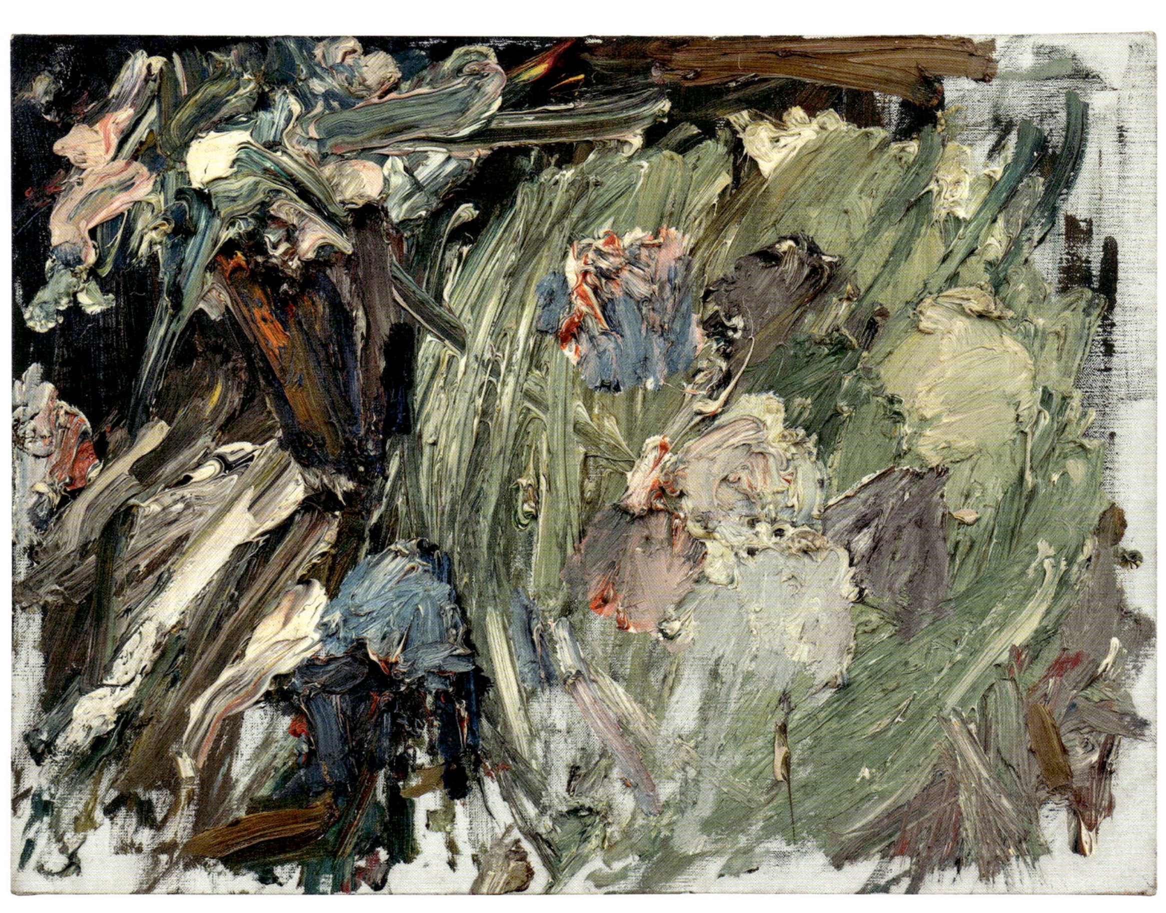

Untitled, 1958, oil on canvas, 20 × 26 inches (50.8 × 66 cm)

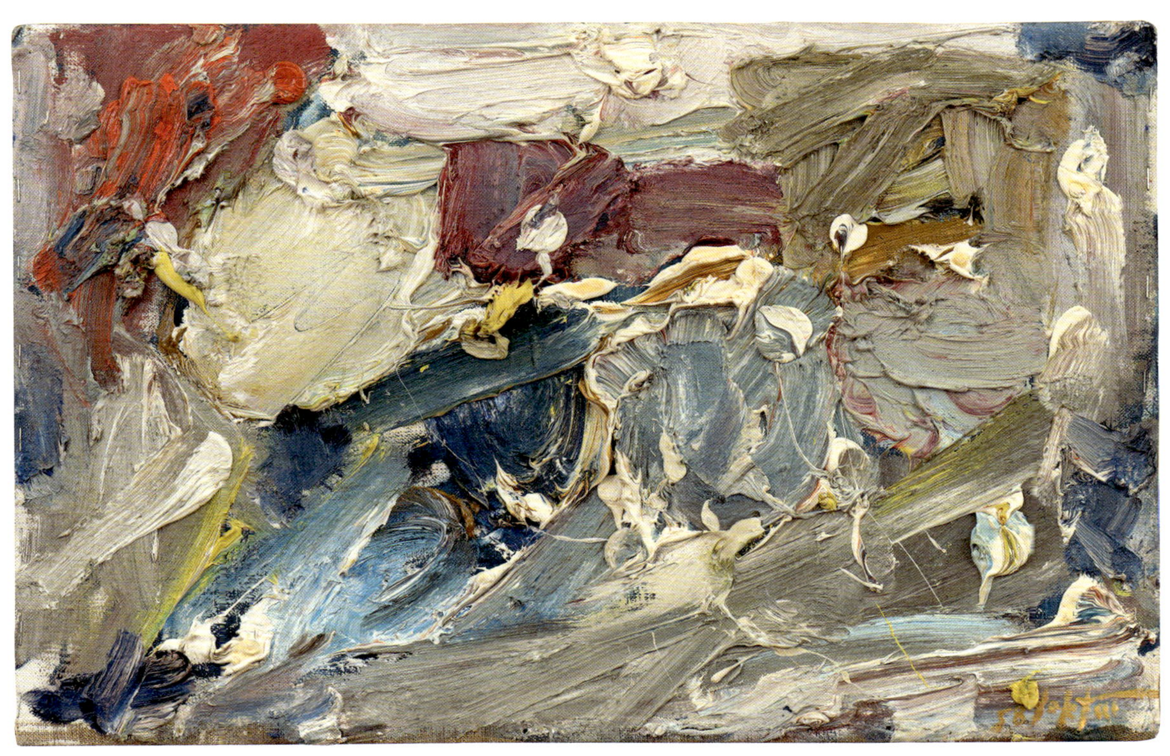

Still Life, 1958, oil on canvas, 14½ × 22¾ inches (36.8 × 57.8 cm)

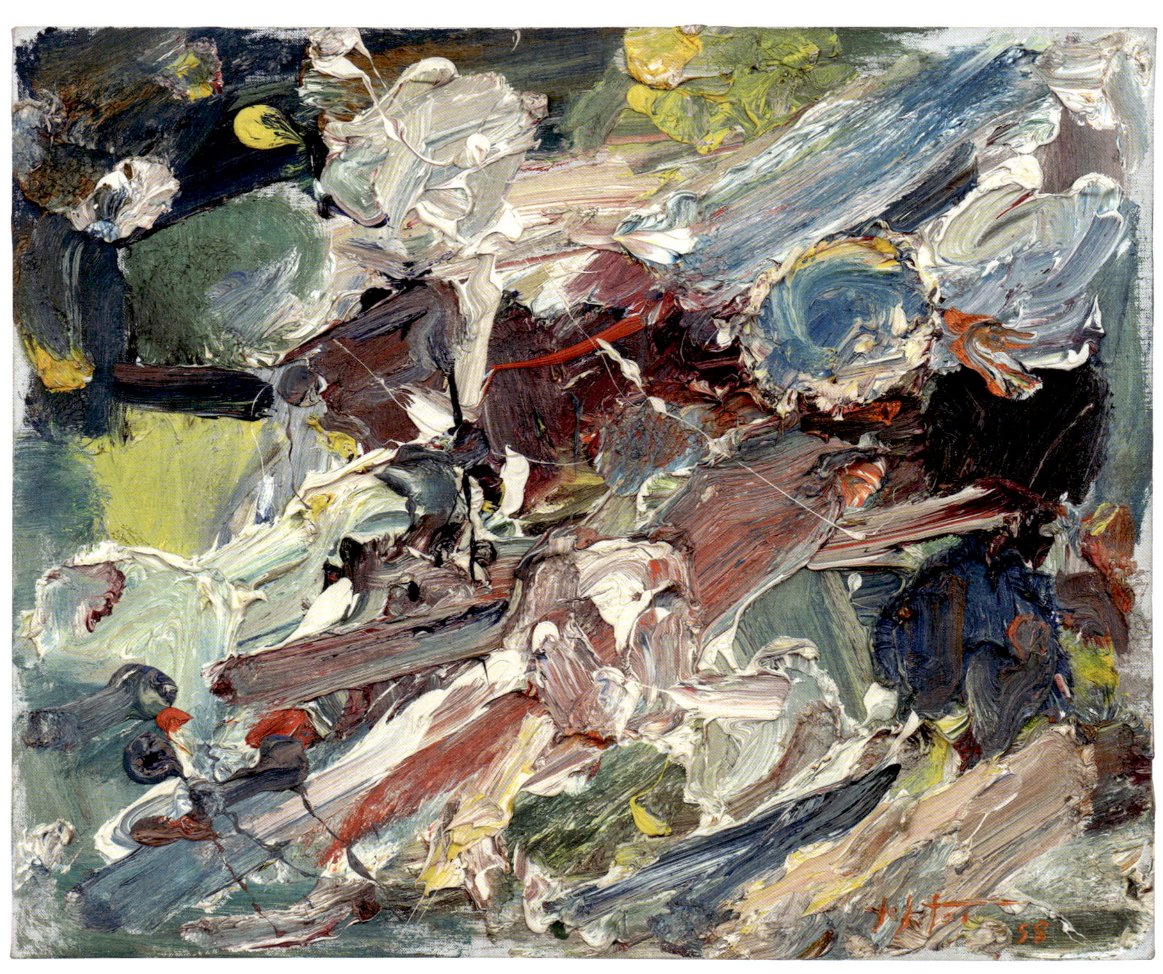

Untitled, 1958, oil on canvas, 23 × 27¼ inches (58.4 × 69.2 cm)

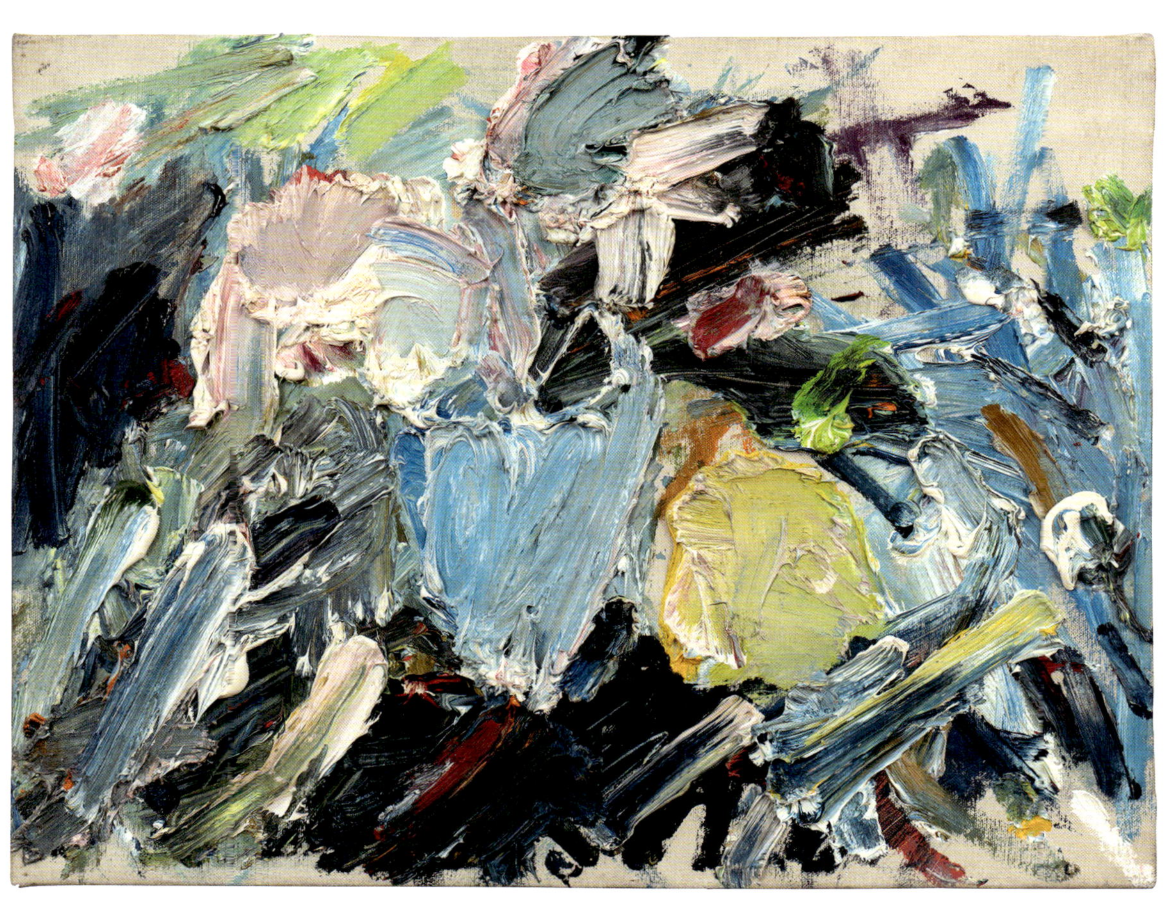

Still Life, 1958, oil on canvas, 15¼ × 20 inches (38.7 × 50.8 cm)

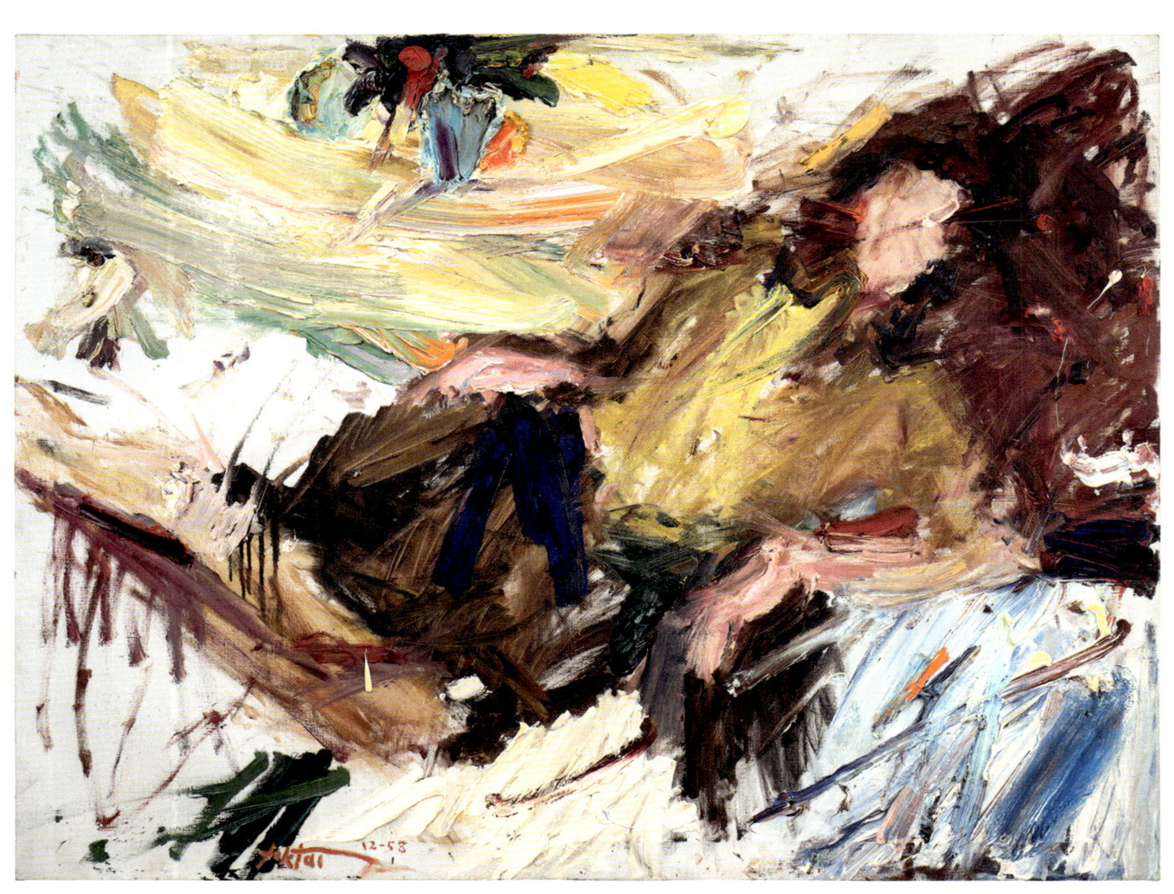

 #16 Figure, 1958, oil on canvas, 36½ × 48½ inches (92.7 × 123.2 cm)

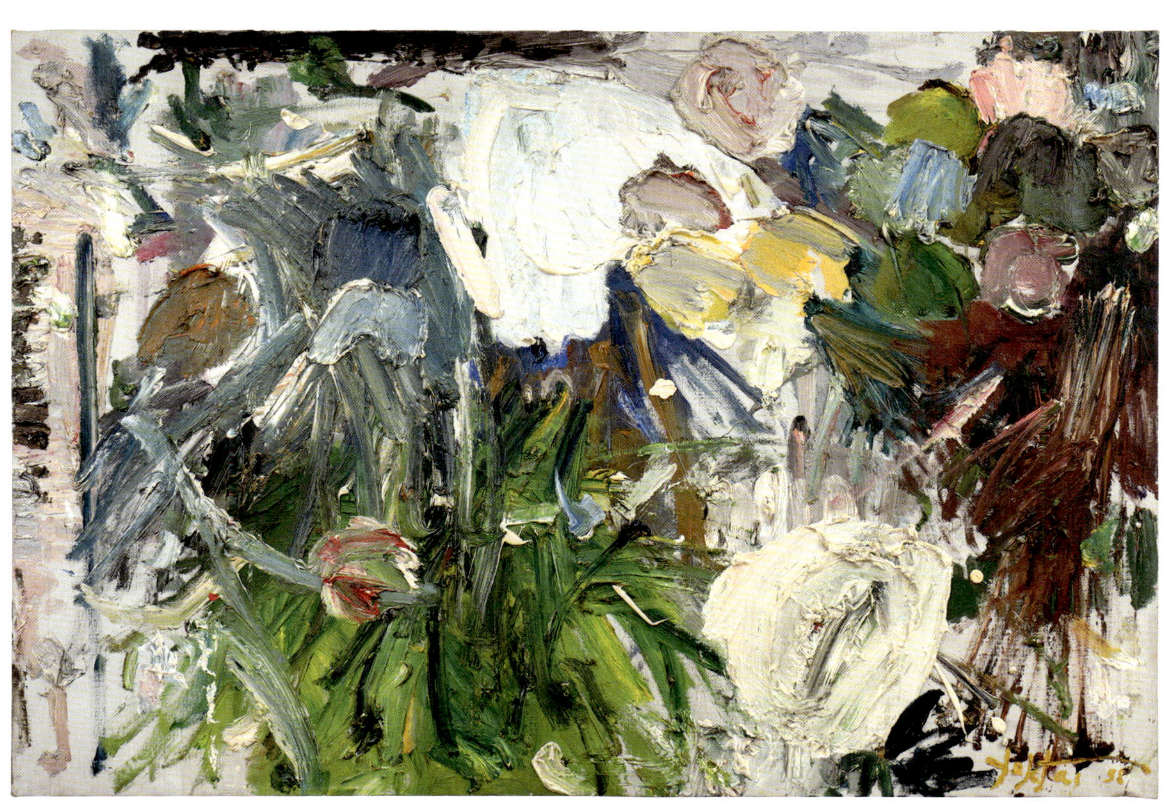

Untitled, 1958, oil on canvas, 35 × 51½ inches (88.9 × 130.8 cm)

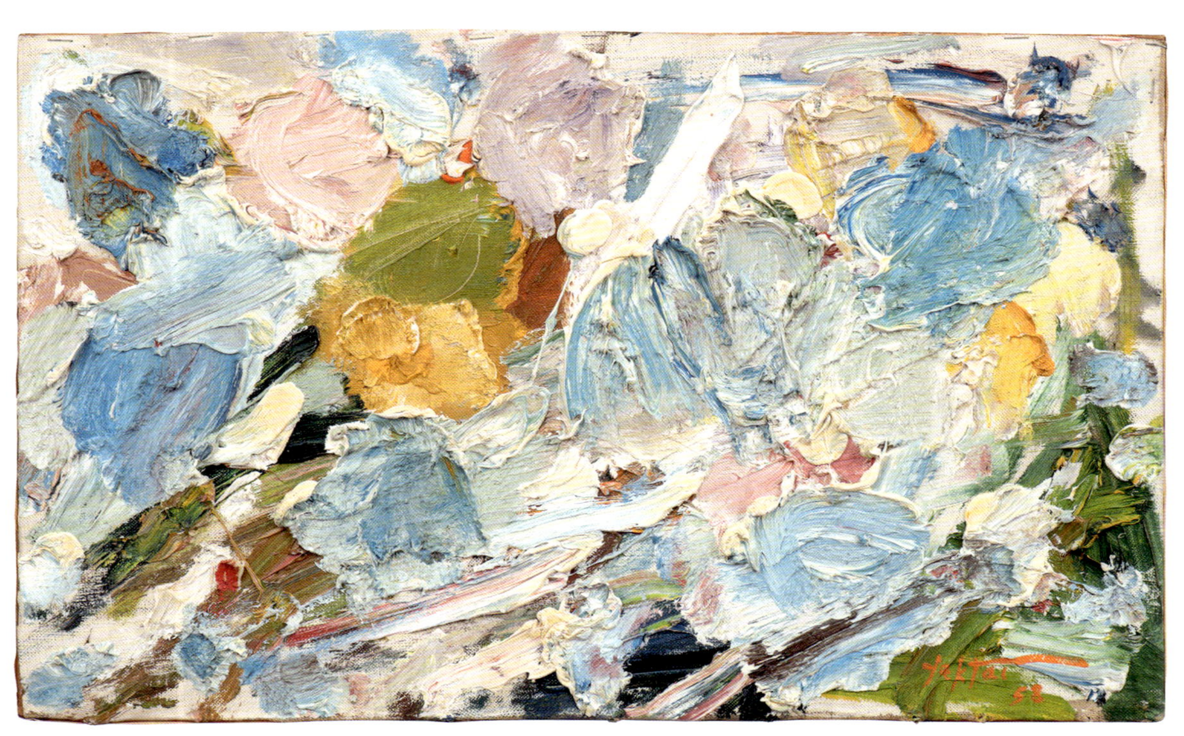

 Untitled, 1958, oil on canvas, 15 × 24 inches (38.1 × 61 cm)

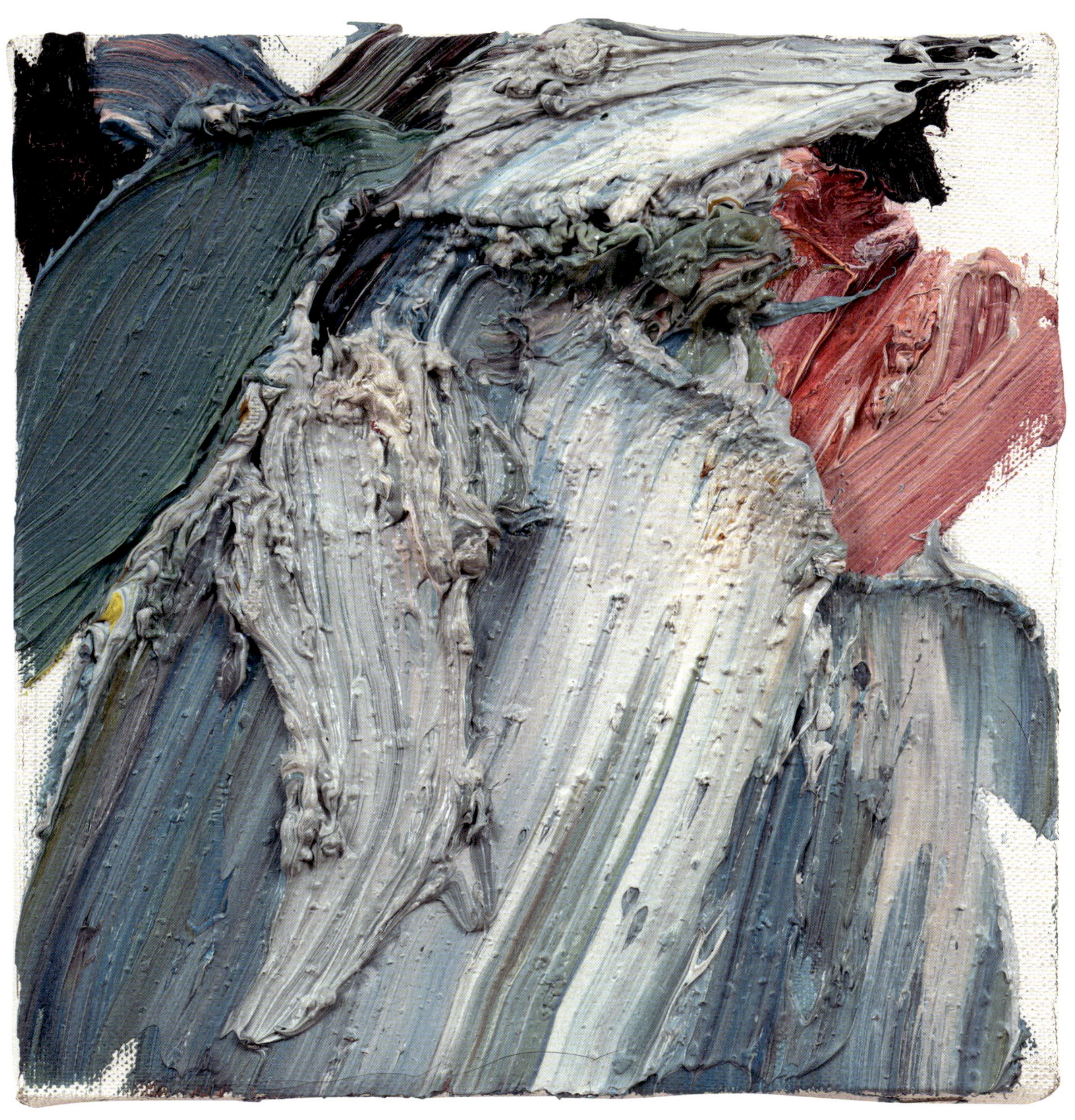

Untitled, 1958, oil on canvas, 8 × 8 inches (20.3 × 20.3 cm)

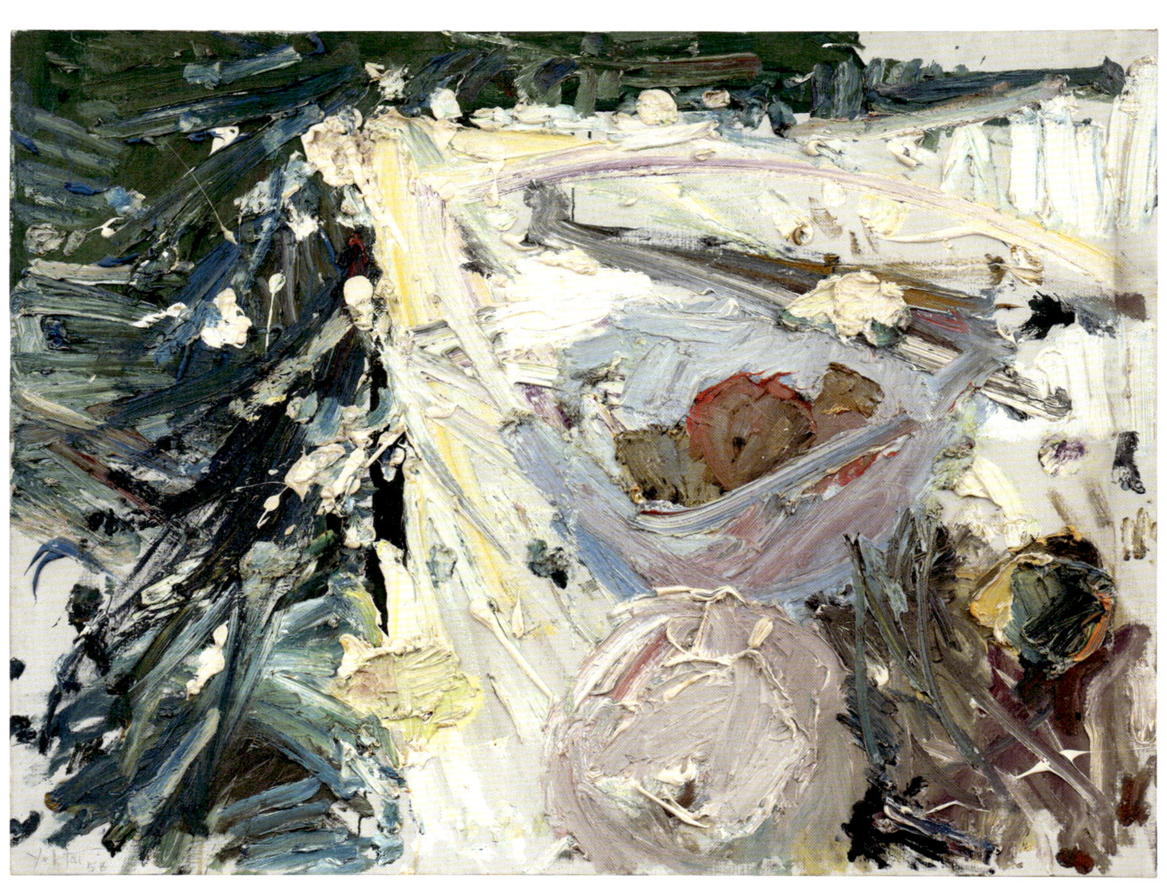

 Untitled, 1958, oil on canvas, 34¾ × 45¾ inches (88.3 × 116.2 cm)

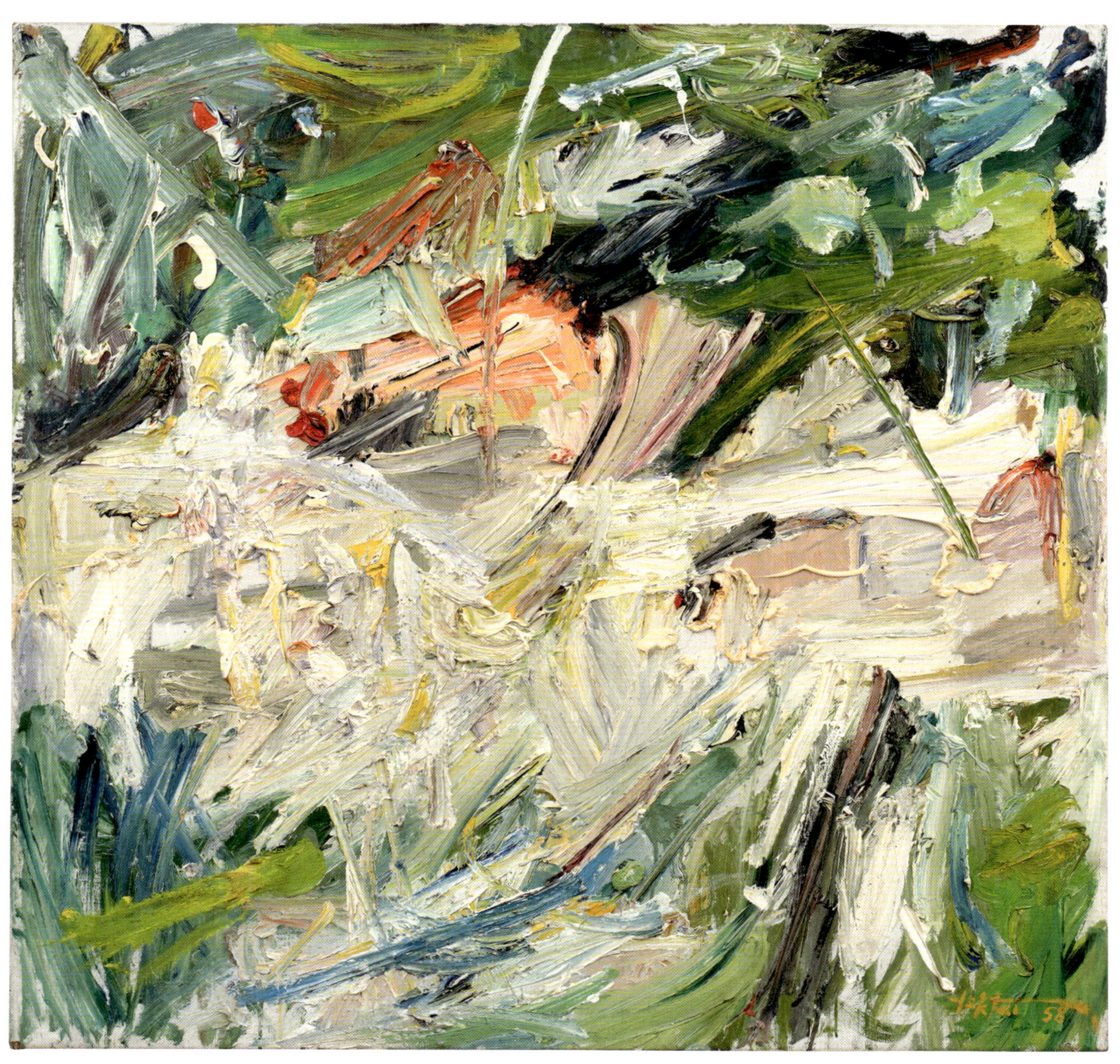

Landscape of Italy, 1958, oil on canvas, 39 × 41 inches (99.1 × 104.1 cm)

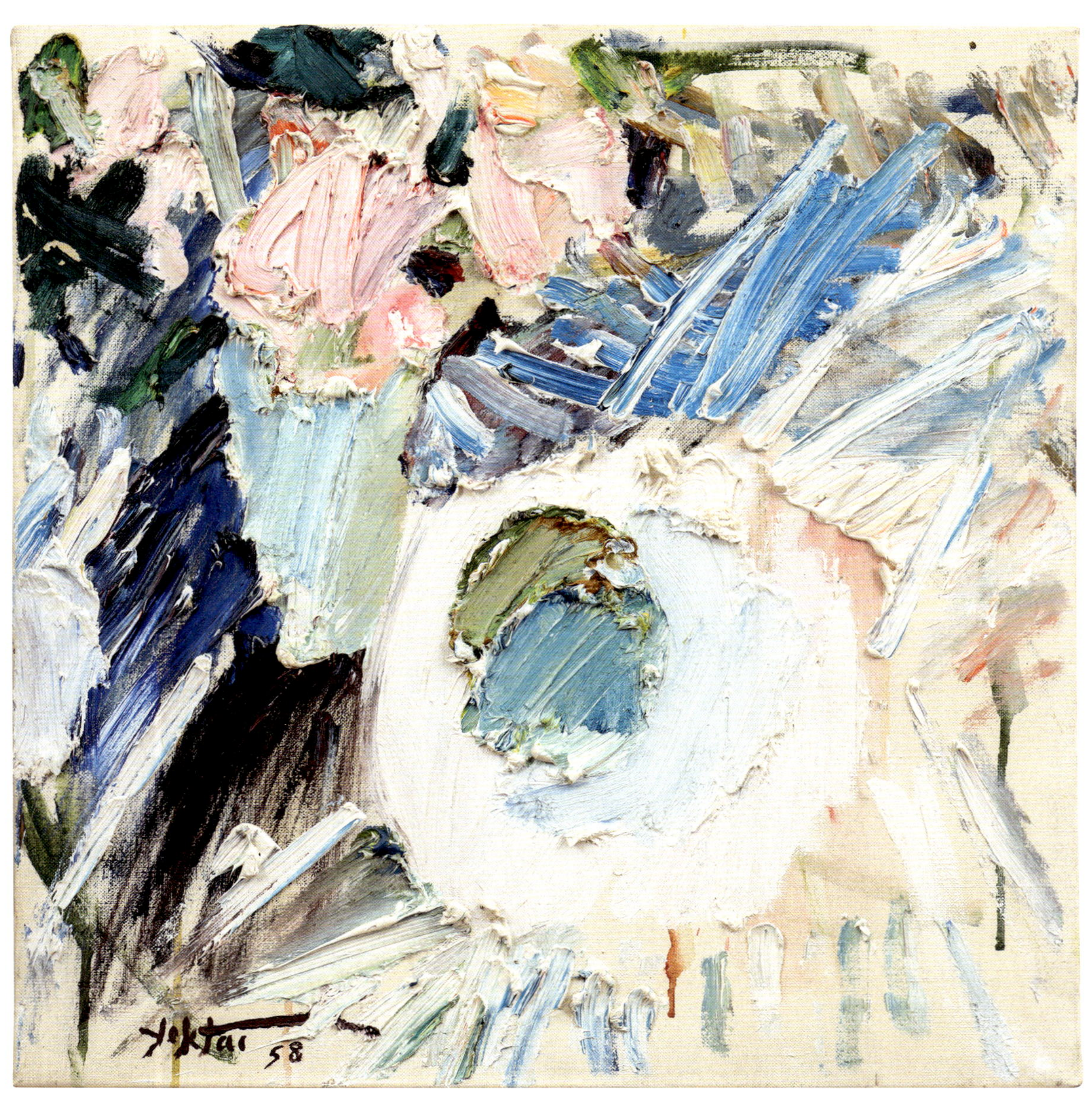

 Untitled, 1958, oil on canvas, 19½ × 19½ inches (49.5 × 49.5 cm)

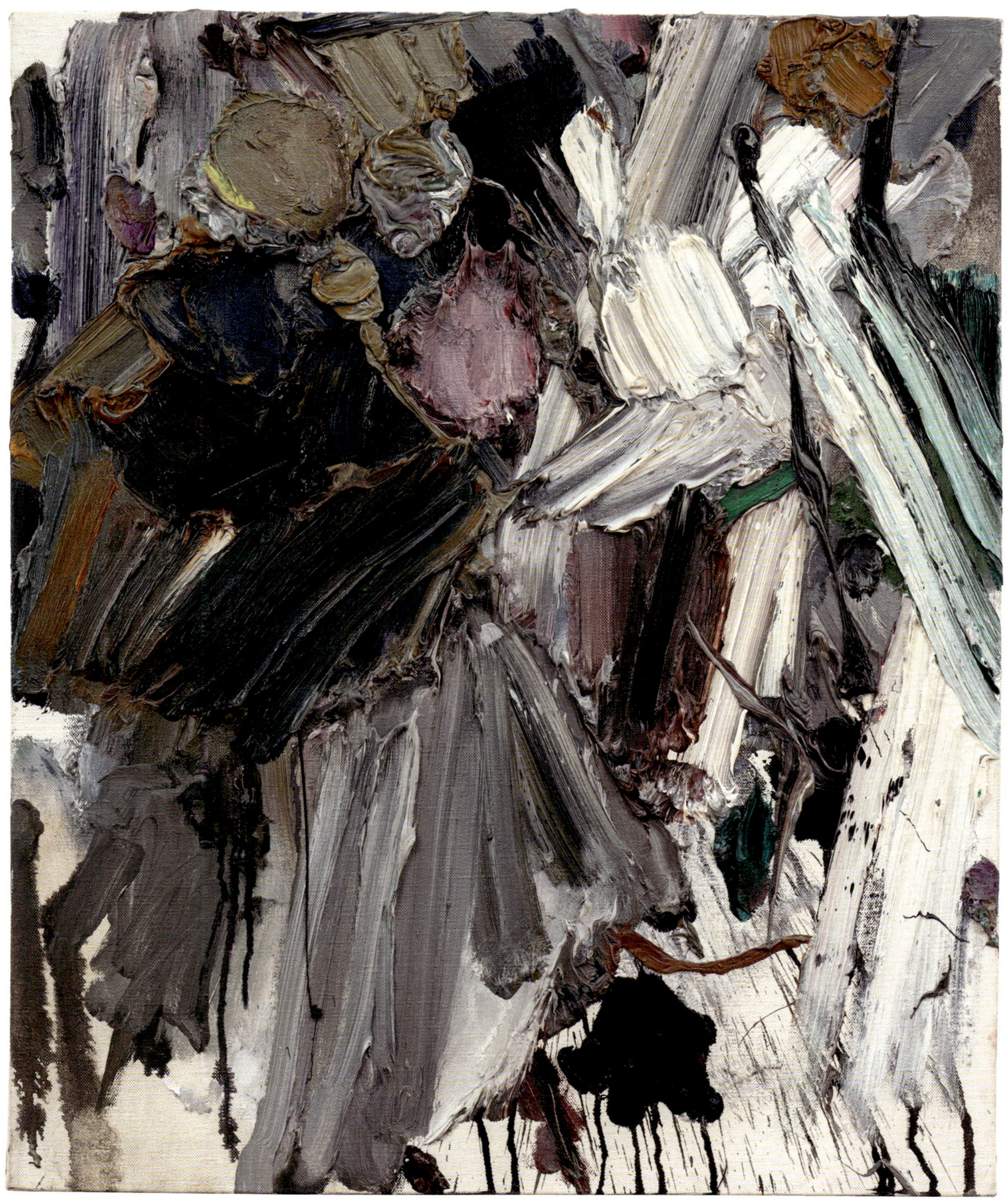

Untitled, 1958, oil on canvas, 21¾ × 19¾ inches (55.3 × 50.2 cm)

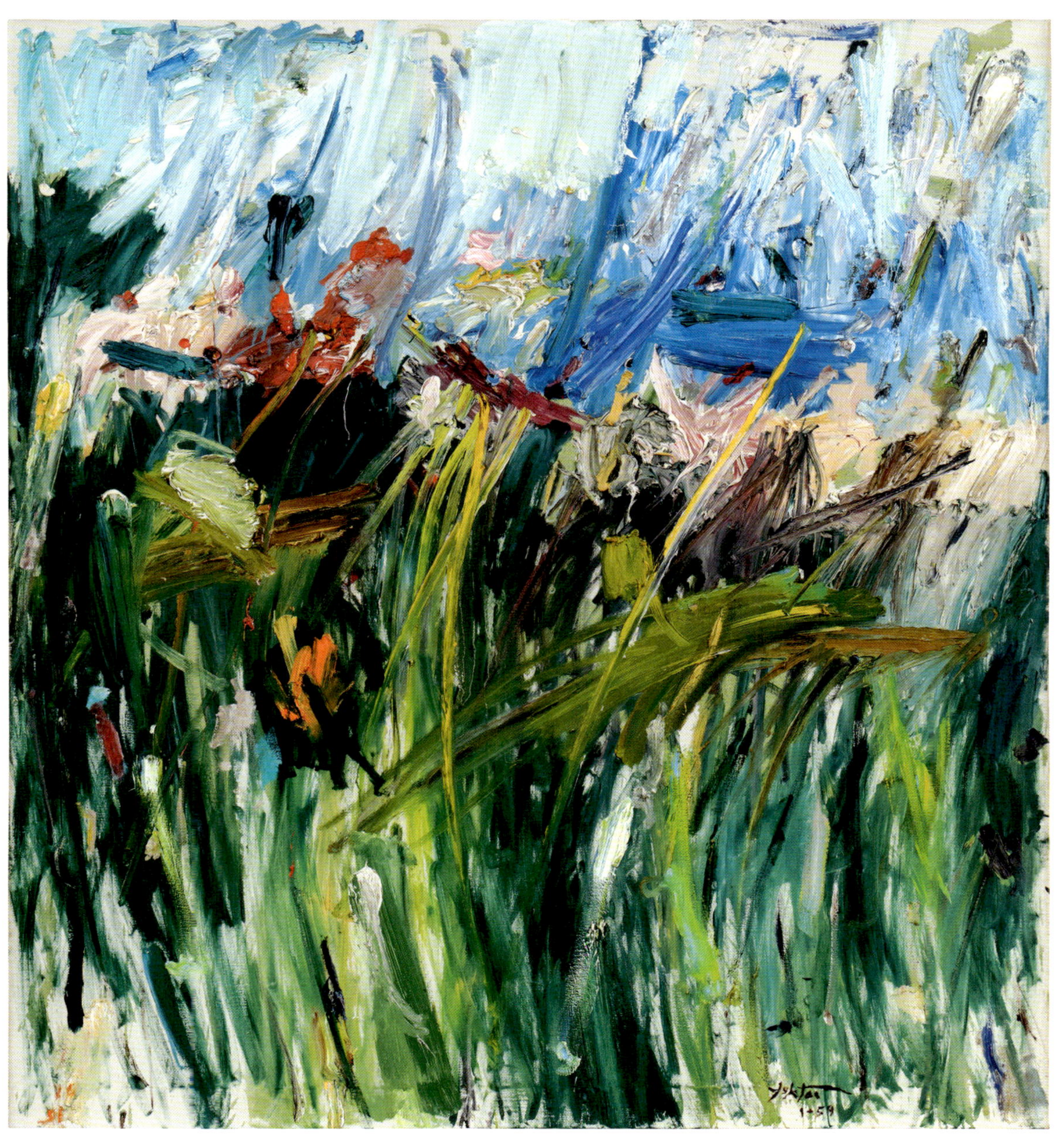

Landscape of Italy, 1959, oil on canvas, 75 × 68 inches (191 × 173 cm)

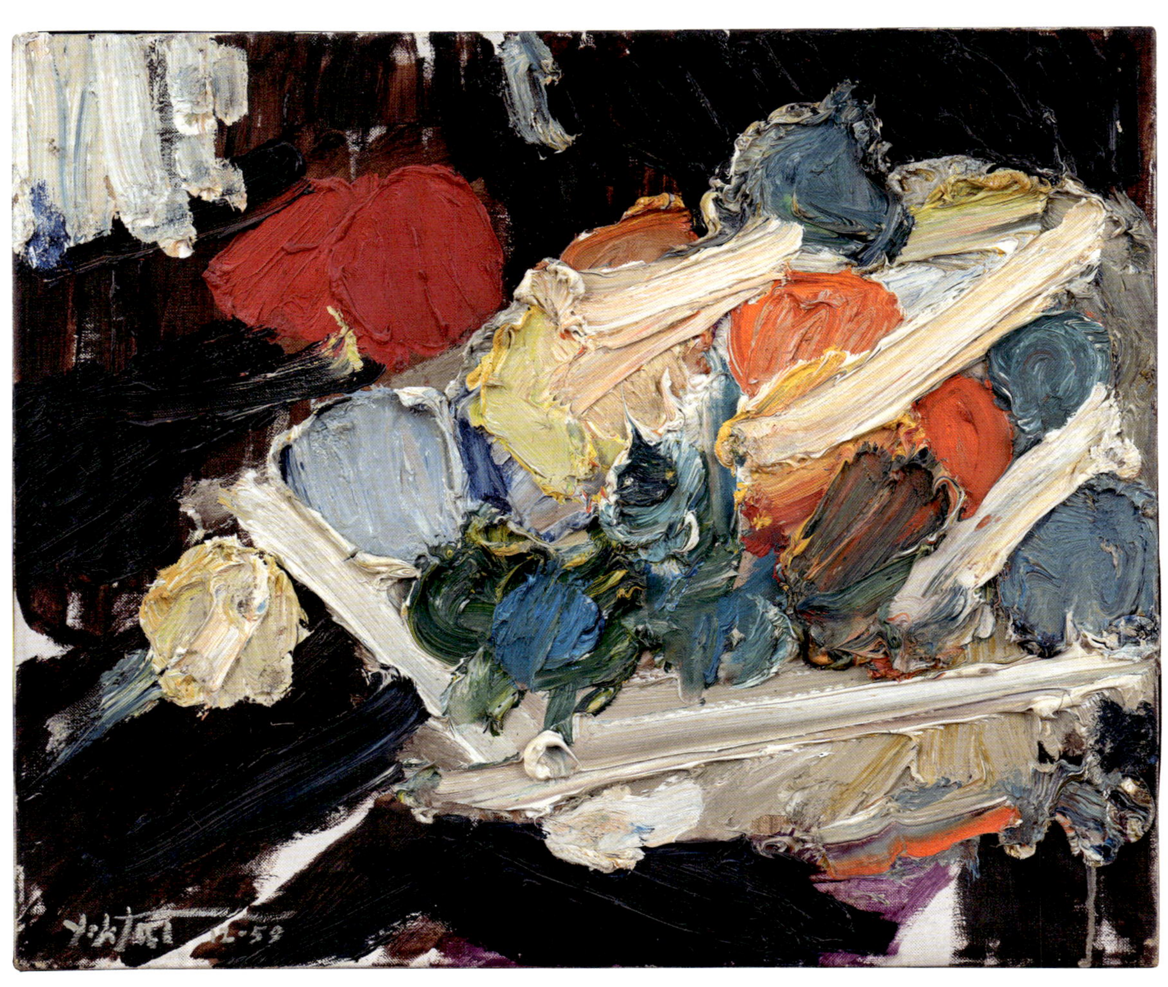

Untitled, 1959, oil on canvas, 32 × 42 inches (81.3 × 106.7 cm)

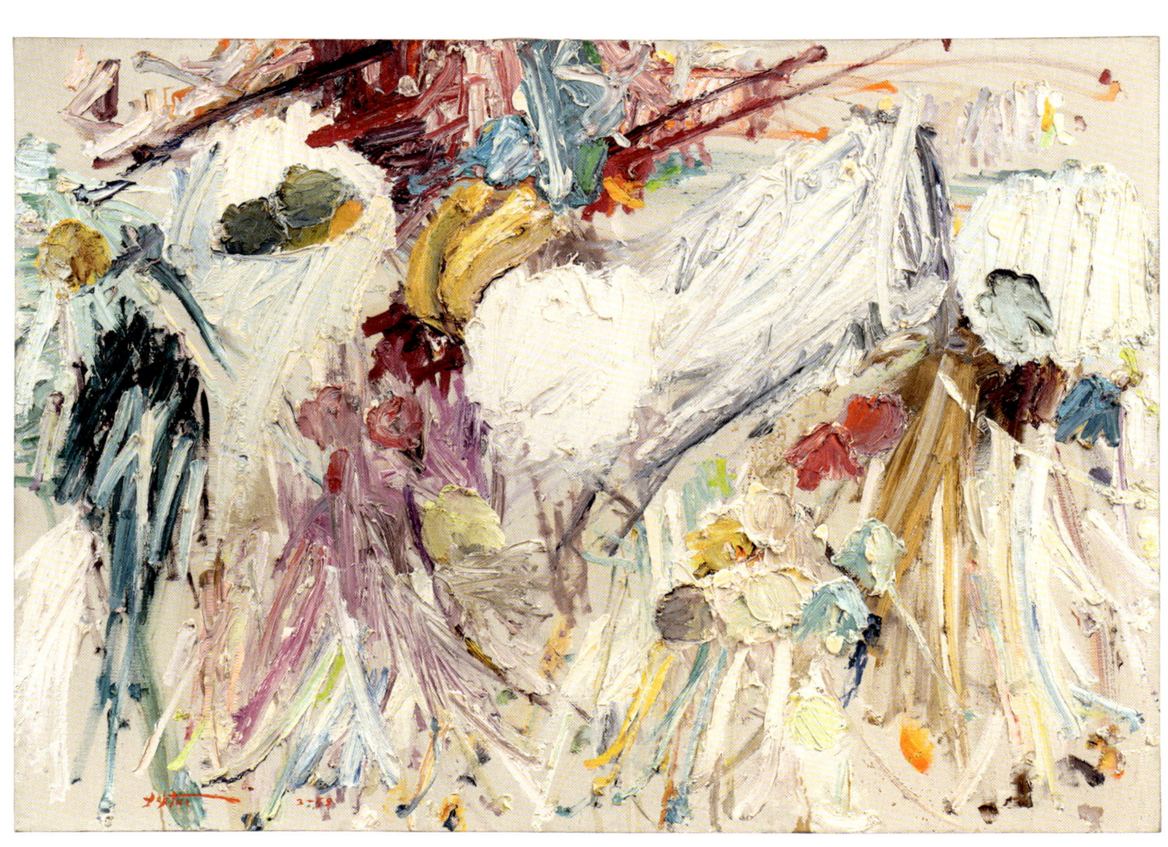

Still Life, 1959, oil on canvas, 48 × 68 inches (122 × 173 cm)

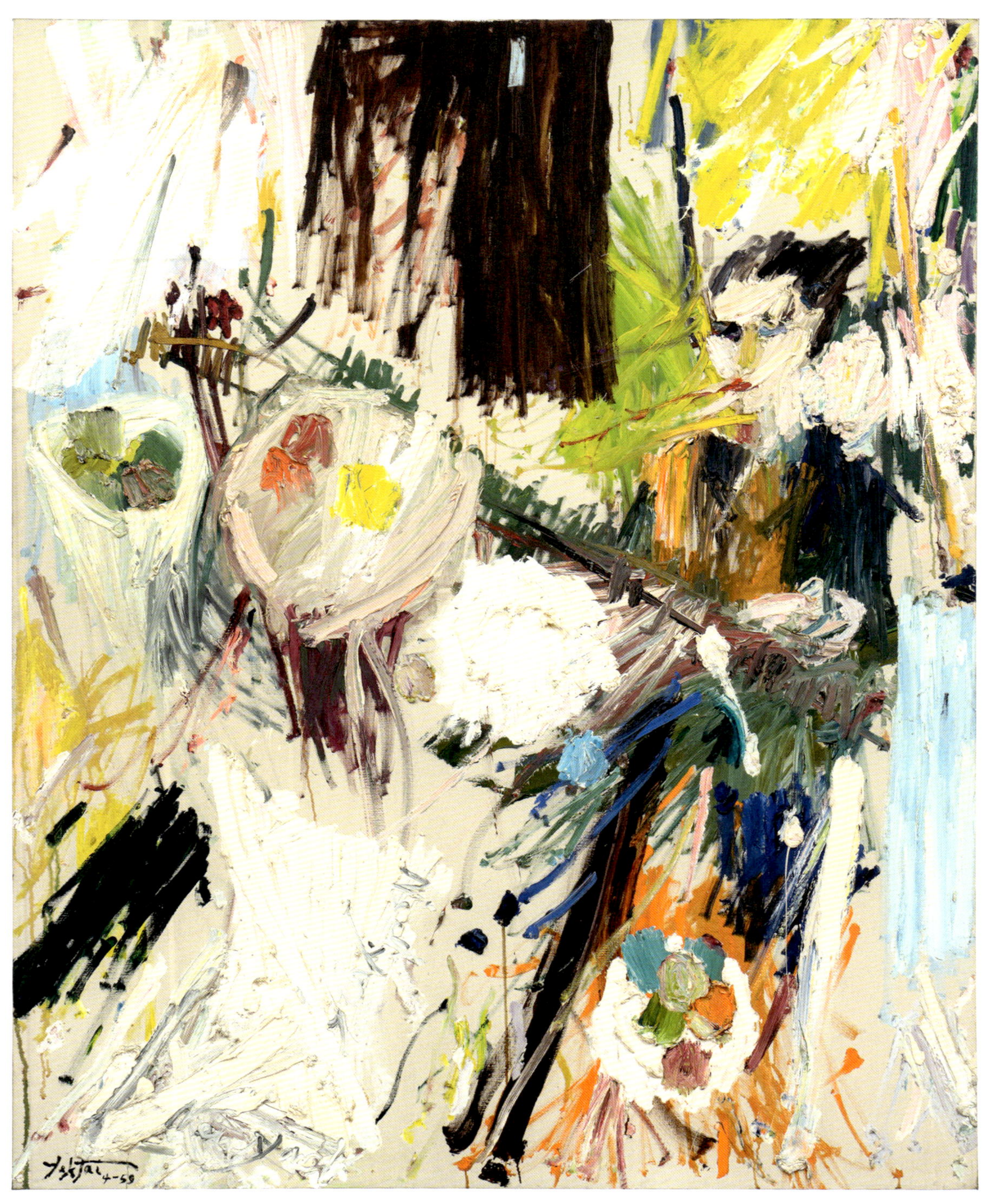

246 *Ilse with White Spoon*, 1959, oil on canvas, 83¾ × 67¾ inches (212.7 × 172.1 cm)

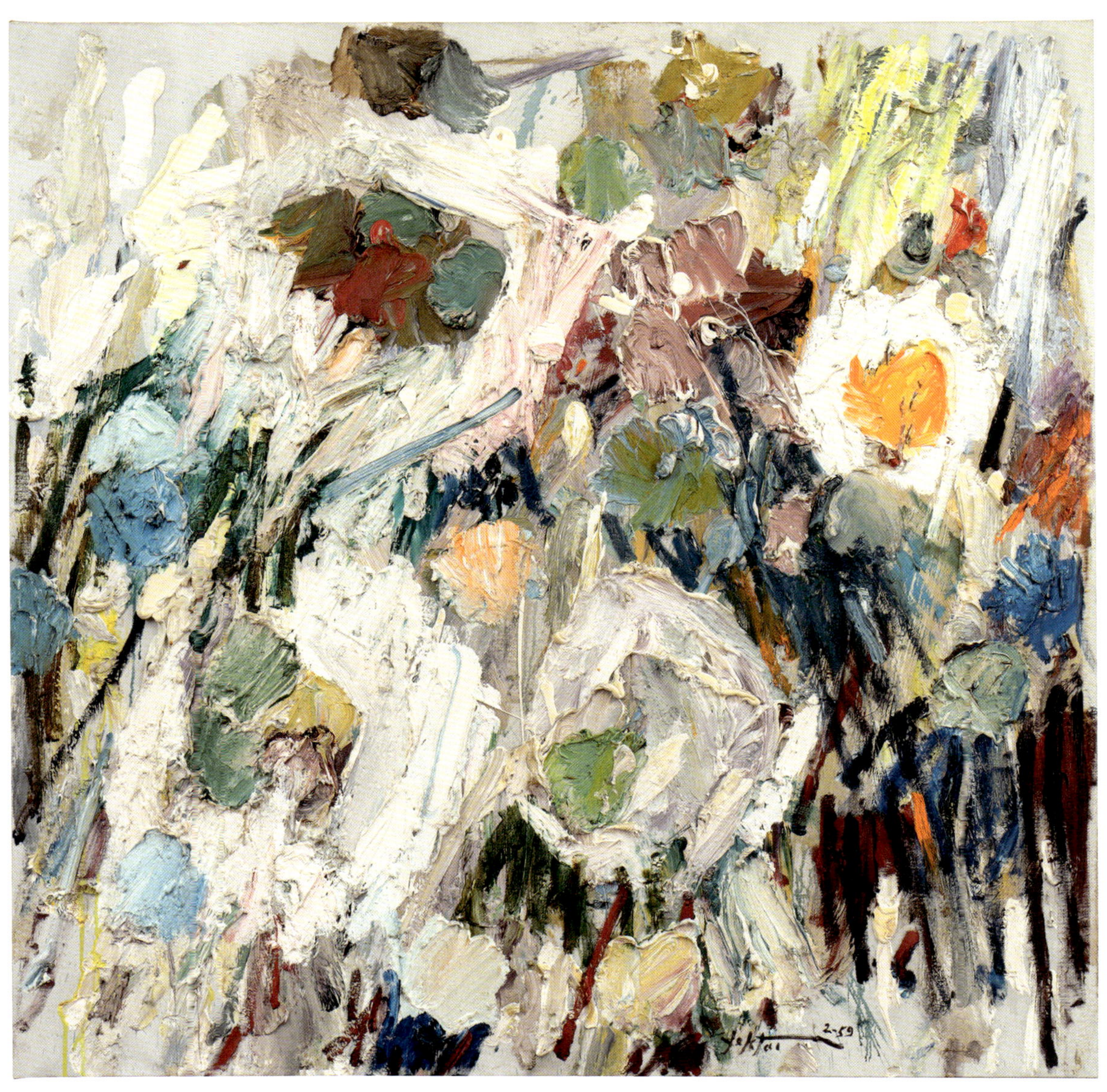

Untitled, 1959, oil on canvas, 44 × 44 inches (111.8 × 111.8 cm)

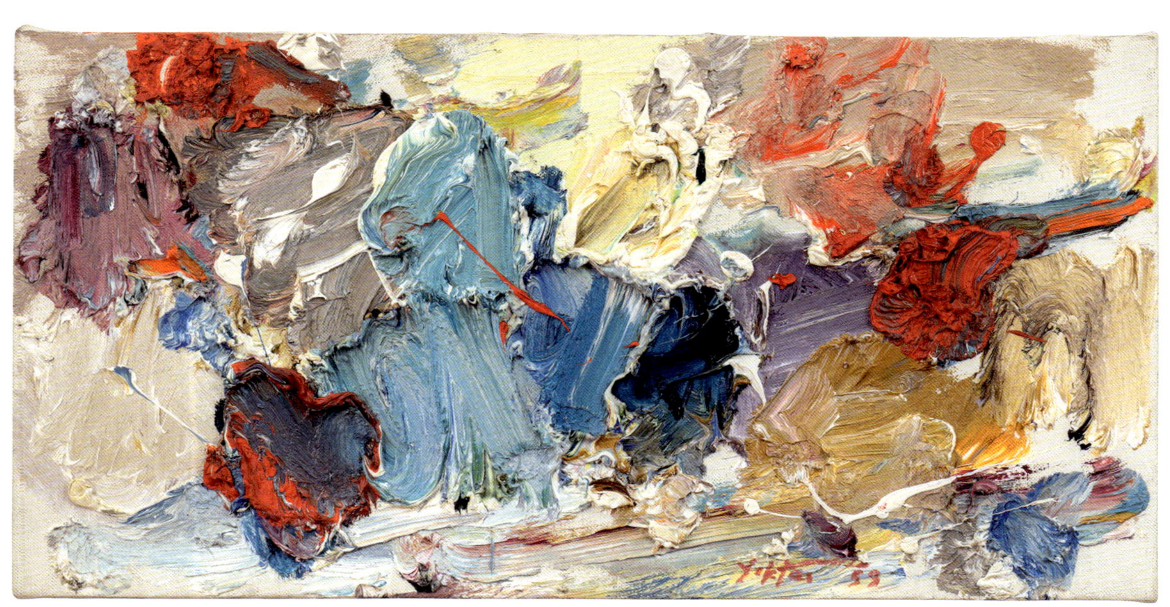

#21, 1959, oil on canvas, 11¾ × 24 inches (29.9 × 61 cm)

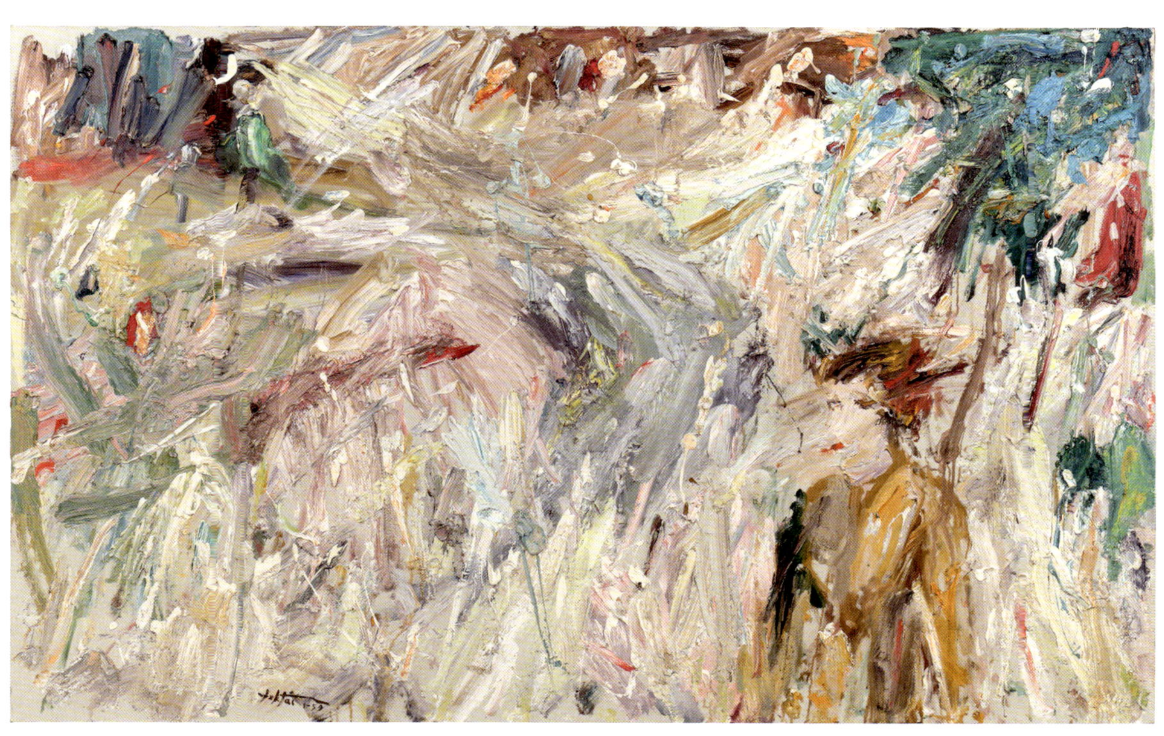

Untitled, 1959, oil on canvas, 60 × 96 inches (152.4 × 243.8 cm)

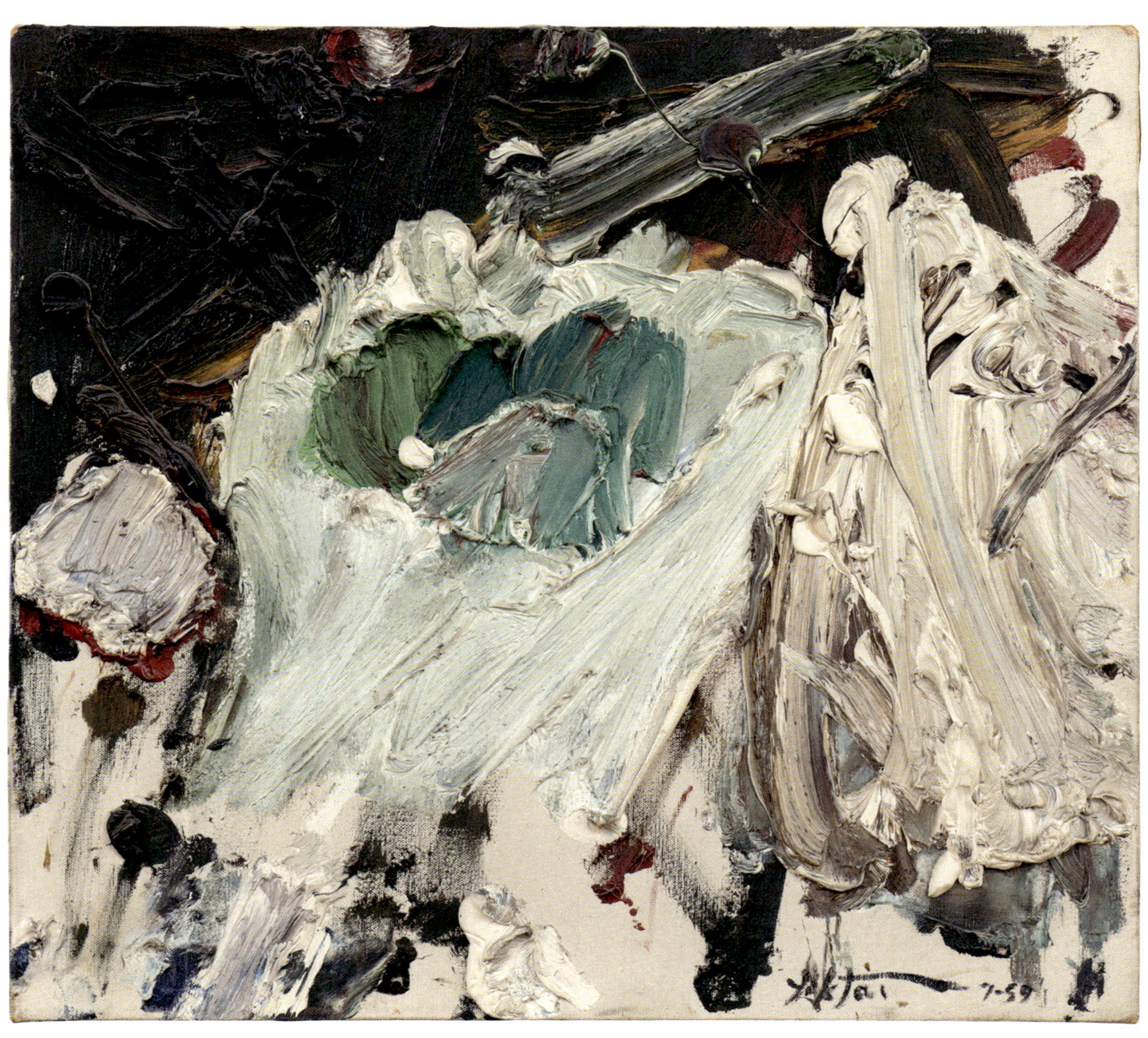

Still Life with Green Fruit, 1959, oil on canvas, 20 × 22 inches (50.8 × 55.9 cm)

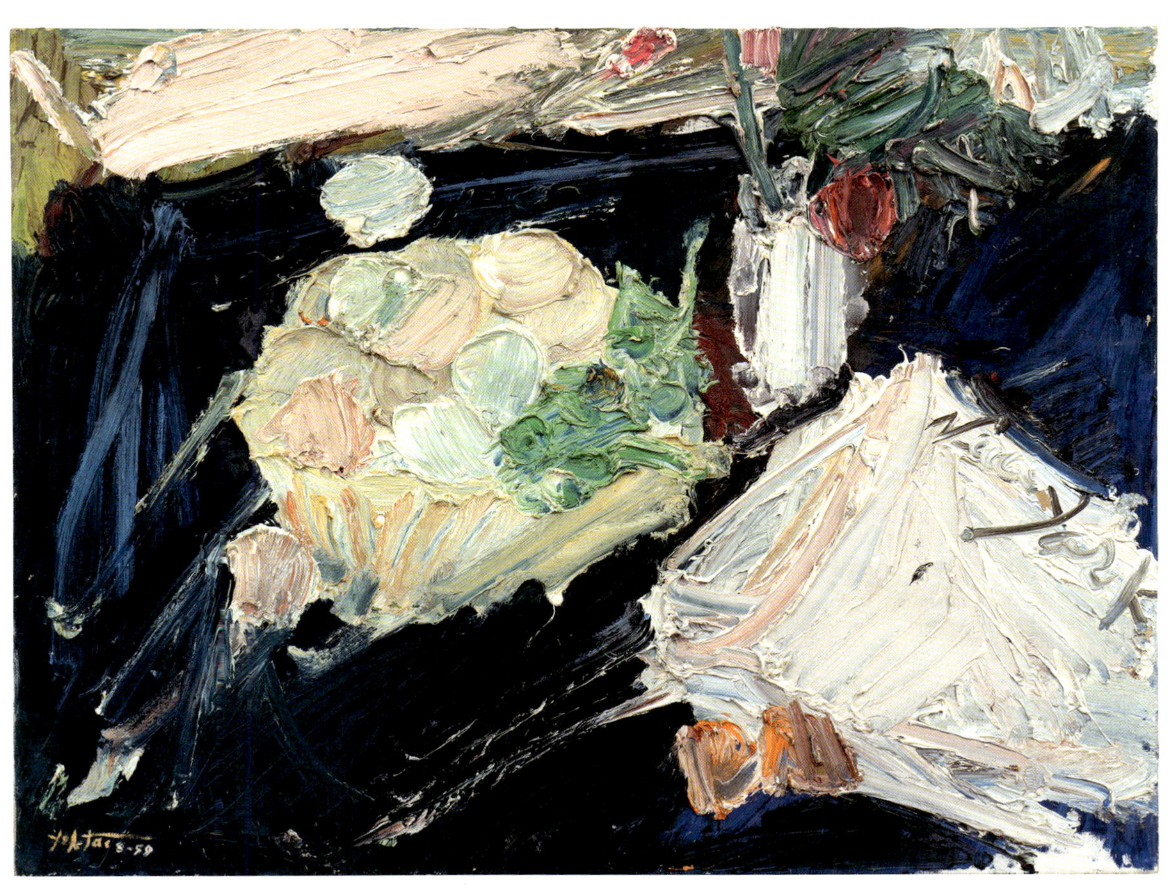

Dark Table, 1959, oil on canvas, 32 × 42 inches (81.3 × 106.7 cm)

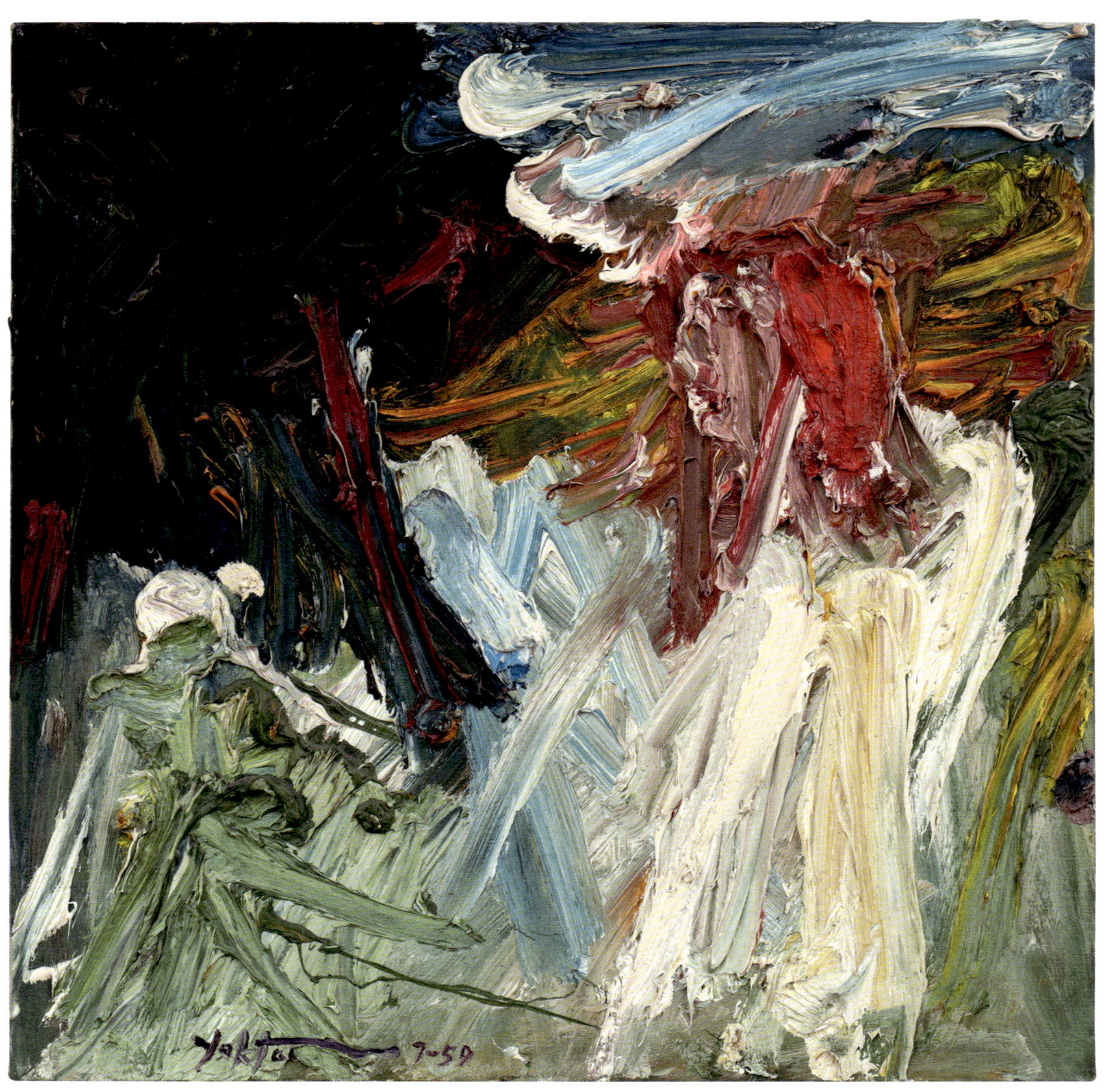

Red Tree, 1959, oil on canvas, 22 × 22 inches (55.9 × 55.9 cm)

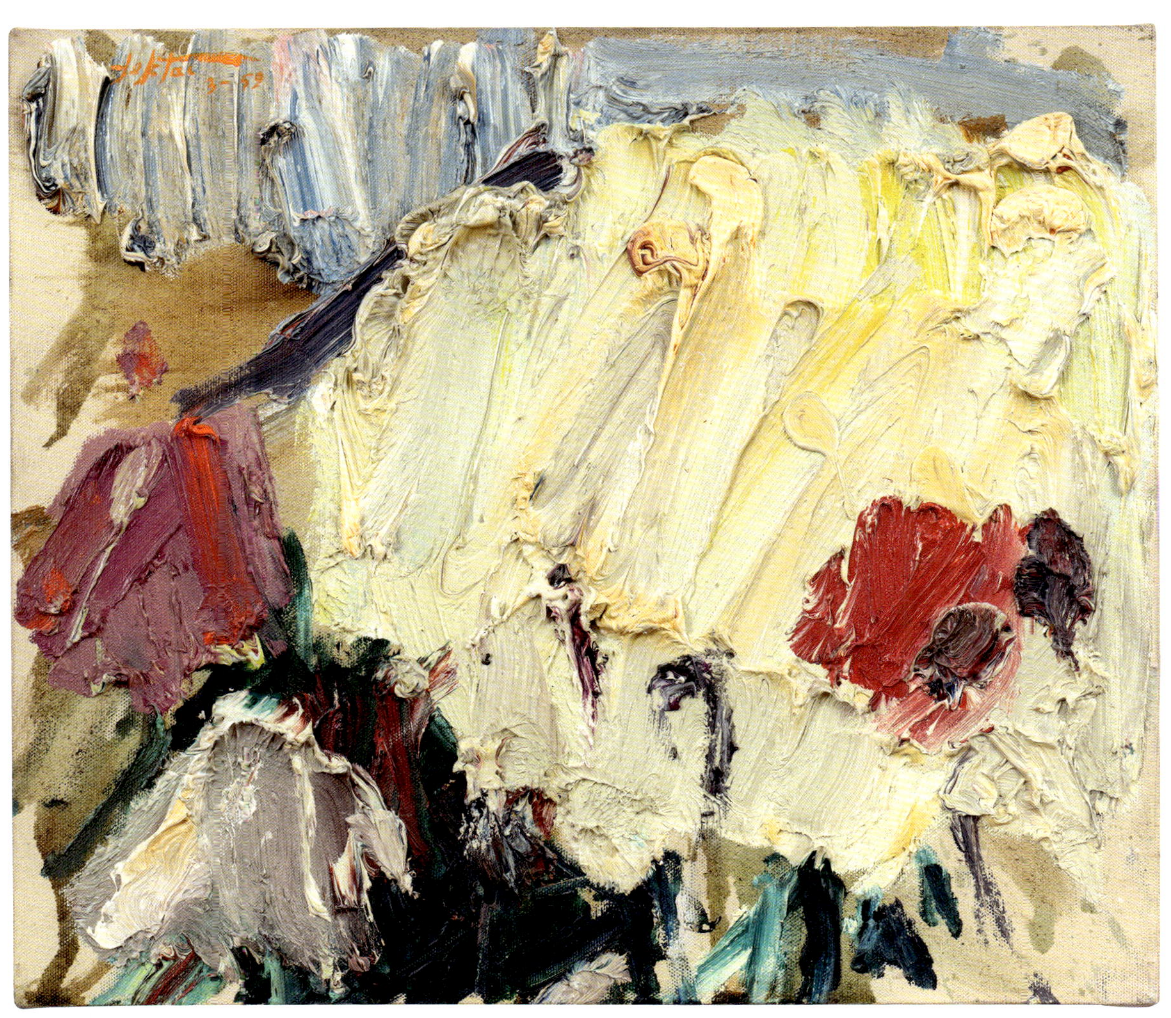

Yellow Plate, 1959, oil on canvas, 14 × 16 inches (35.6 × 40.6 cm)

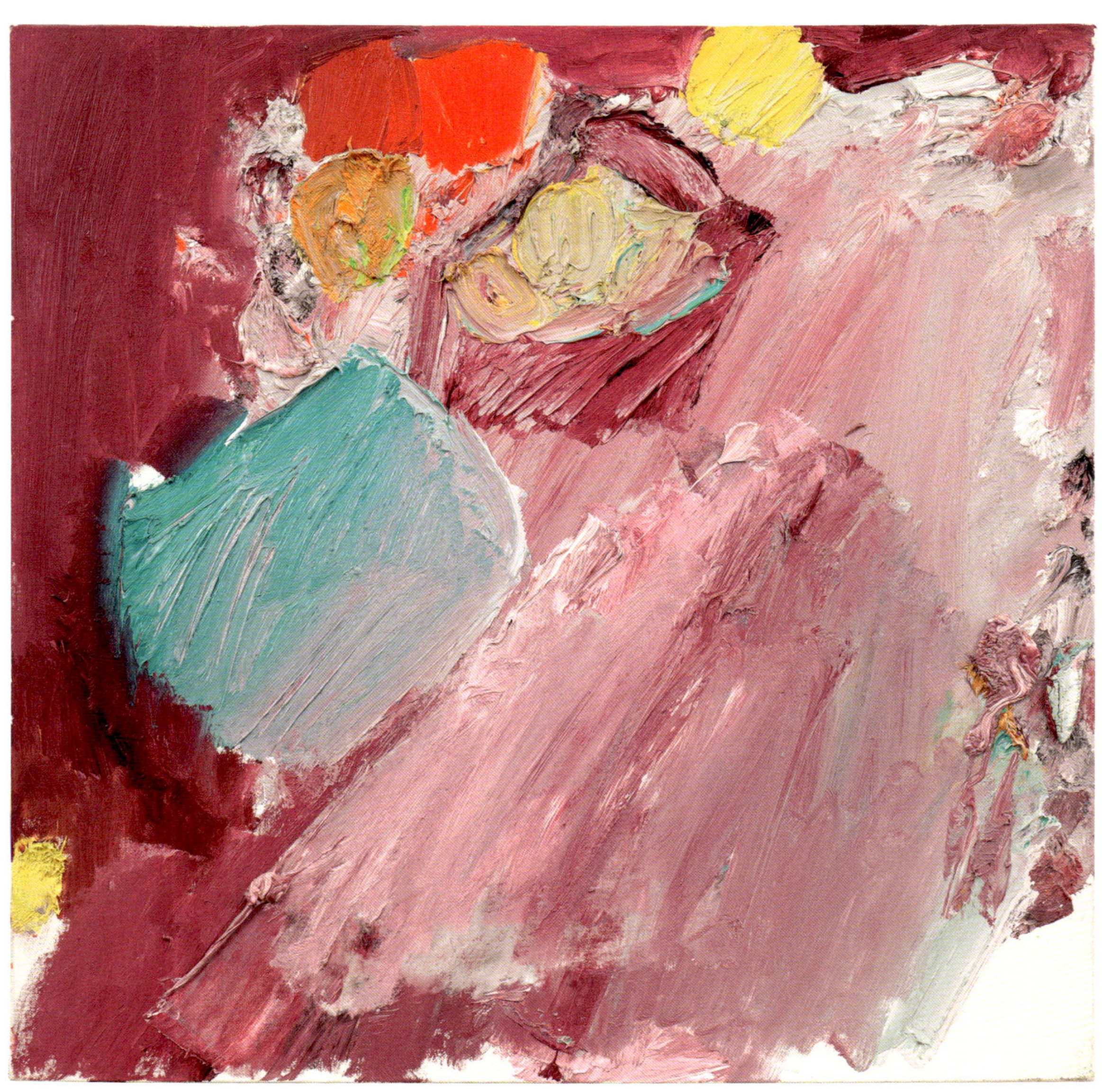

Untitled, 1959, oil on canvas, 31½ × 31½ inches (80 × 80 cm)

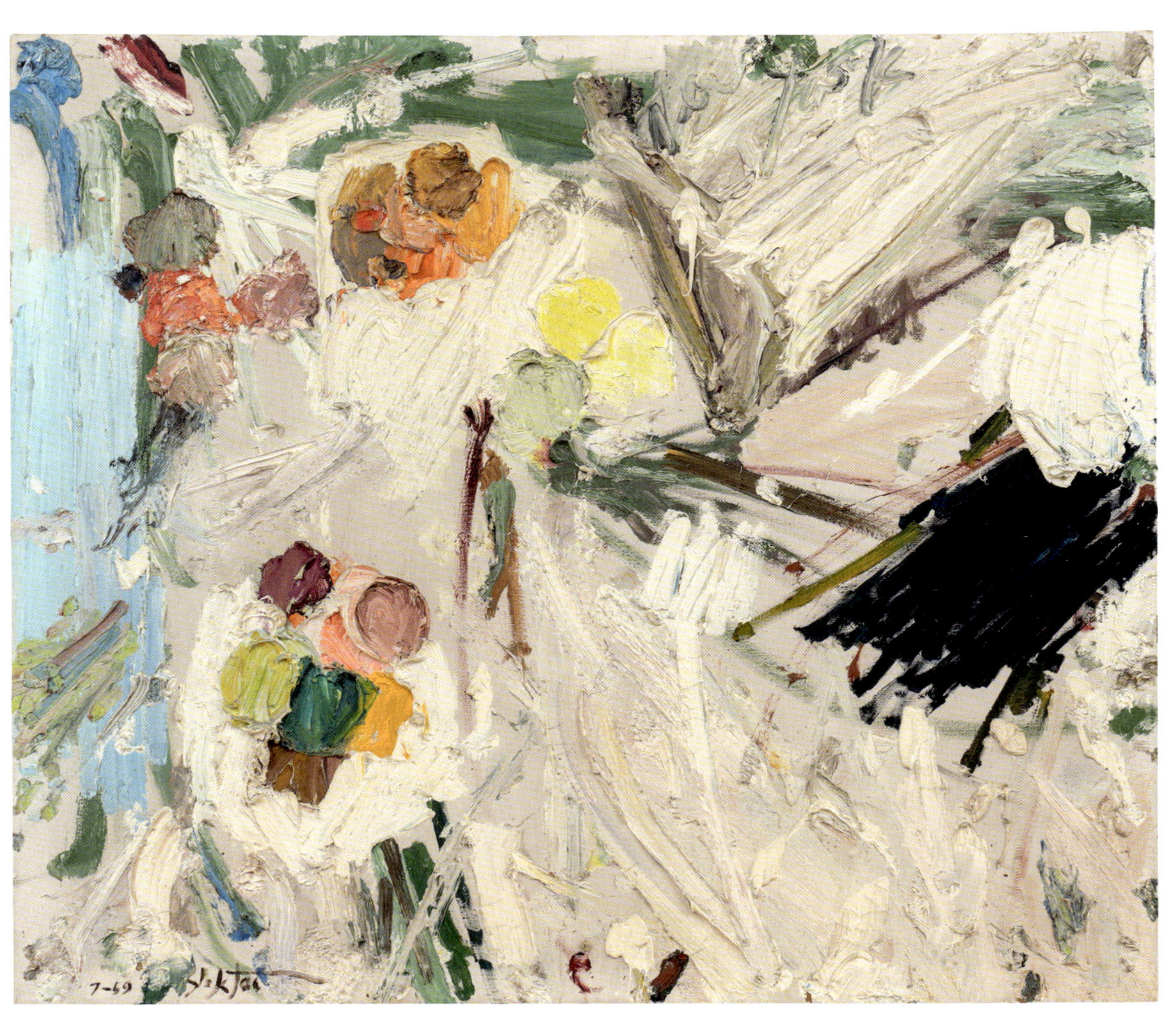

White Still Life, 1959, oil on canvas, 42 × 48 inches (106.7 × 121.9 cm)

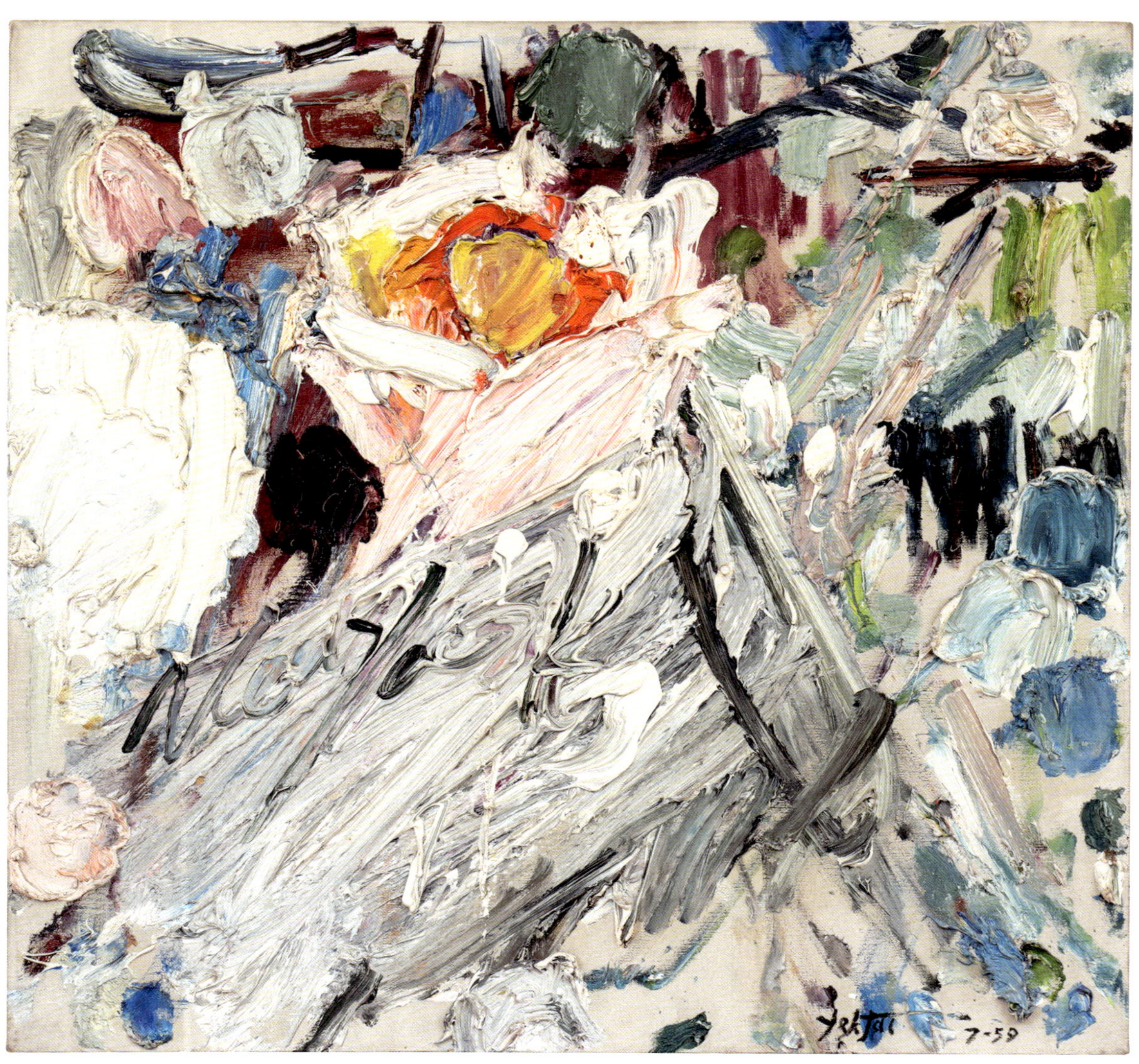

Fruit Bowl, 1959, oil on canvas, 30 × 32 inches (76.2 × 81.3 cm)

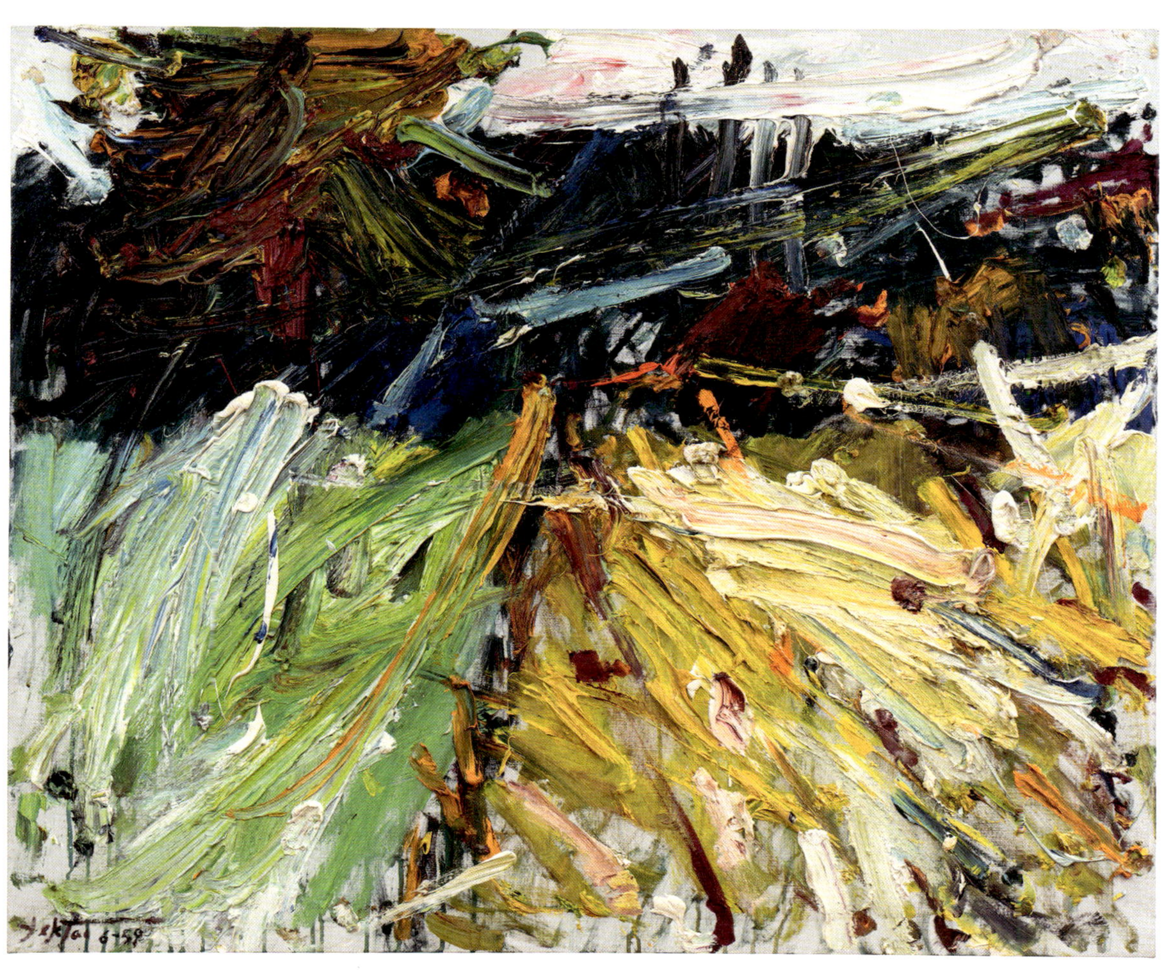

Untitled, 1959, oil on canvas, 35 × 42 inches (88.9 × 106.7 cm)

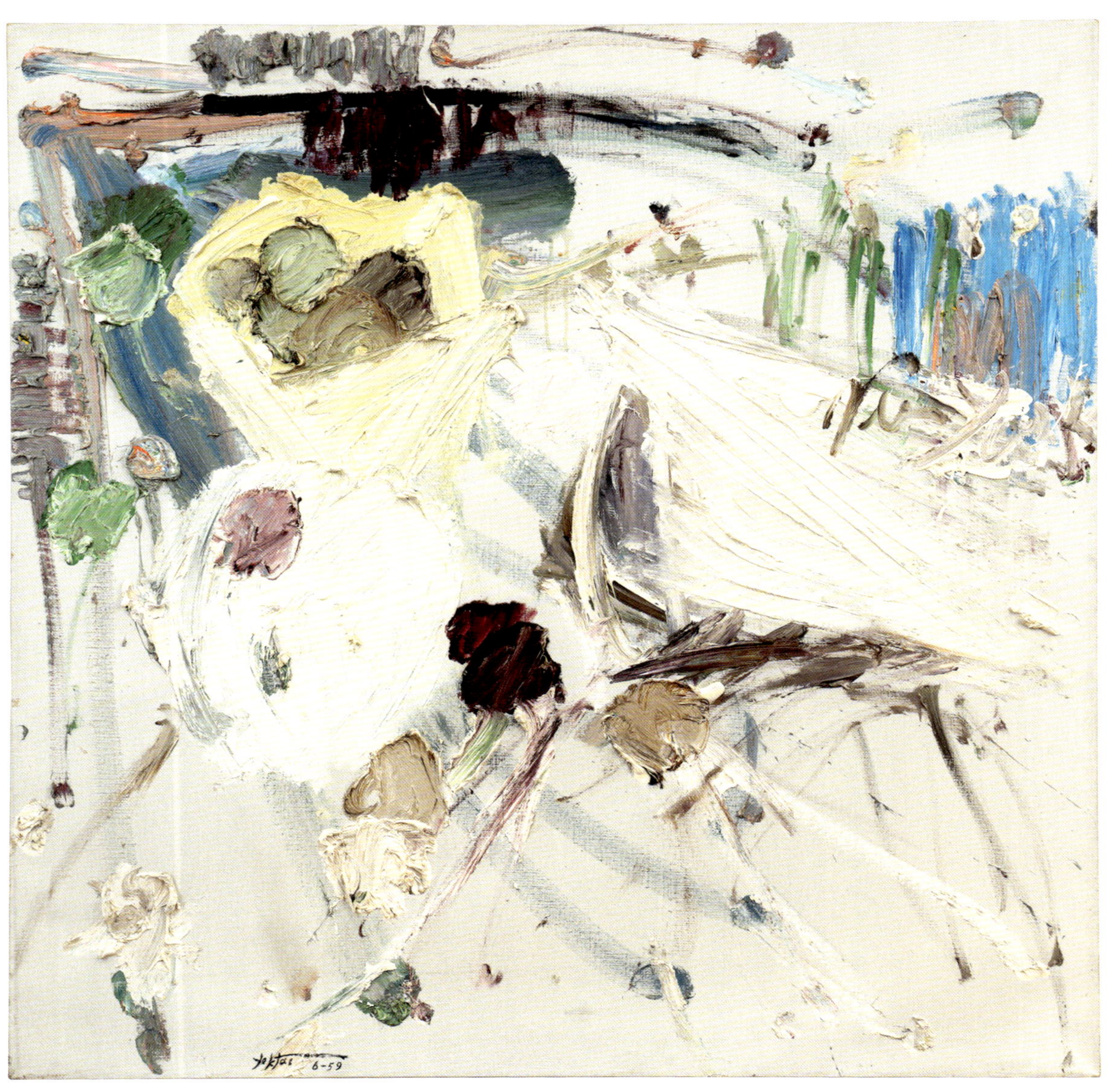

258 *Newspaper, Fruit Bowl, Plate*, 1959, oil on canvas, 42 × 42 inches (106.7 × 106.7 cm)

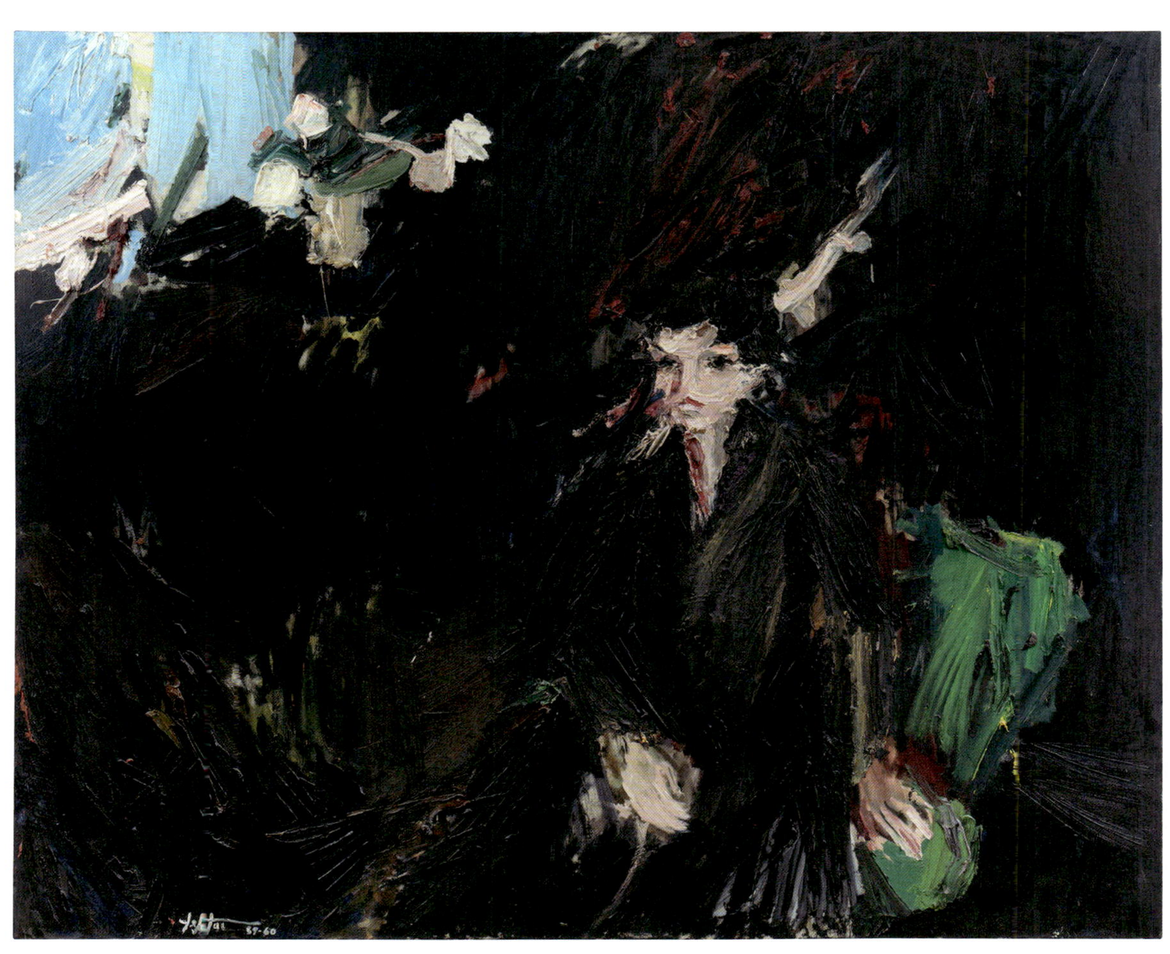

Untitled, 1959–60, oil on canvas, 68 × 84 inches (172.7 × 213.4 cm)

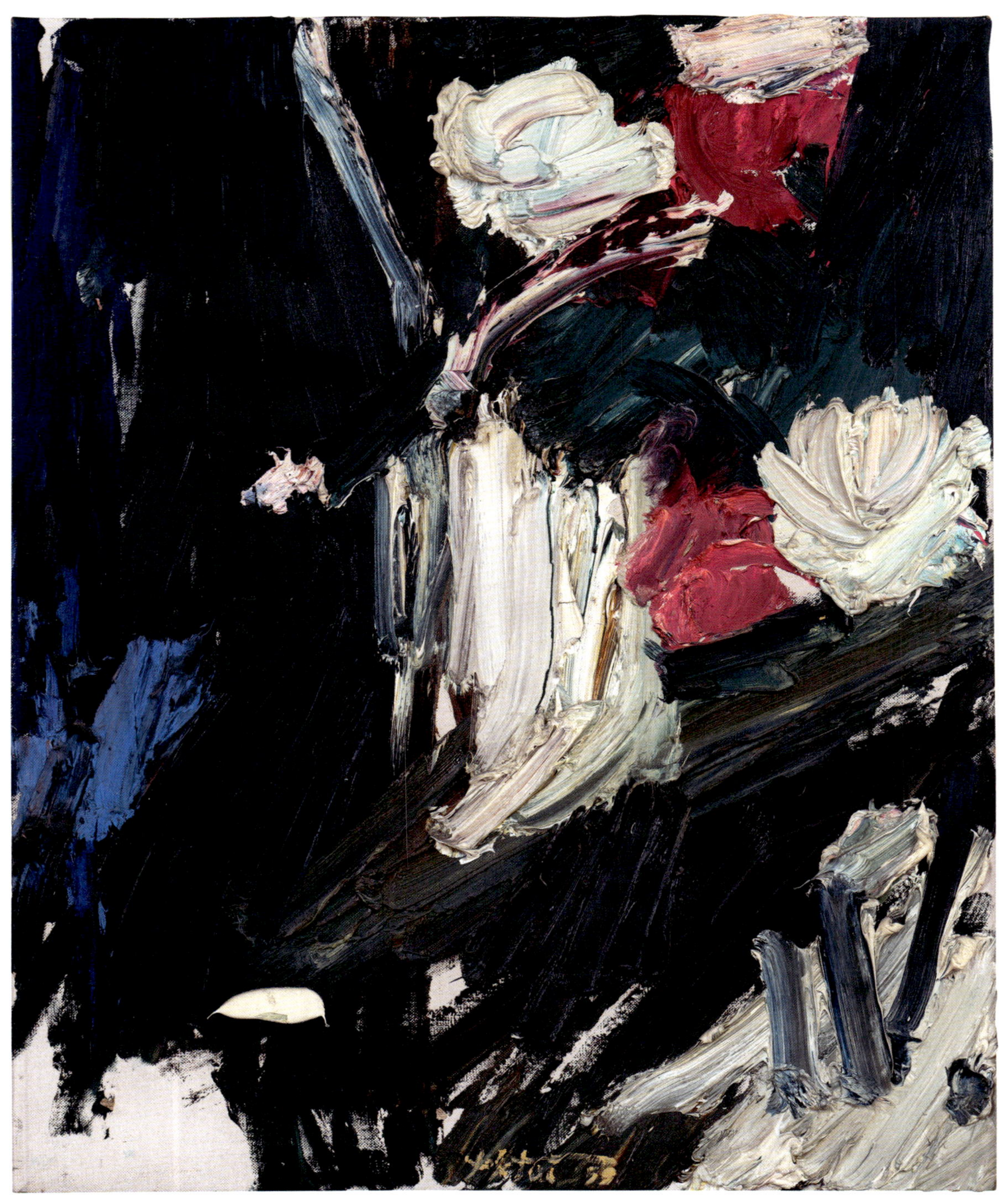

Untitled, 1959, oil on canvas, 22 × 18 inches (55.9 × 45.7 cm)

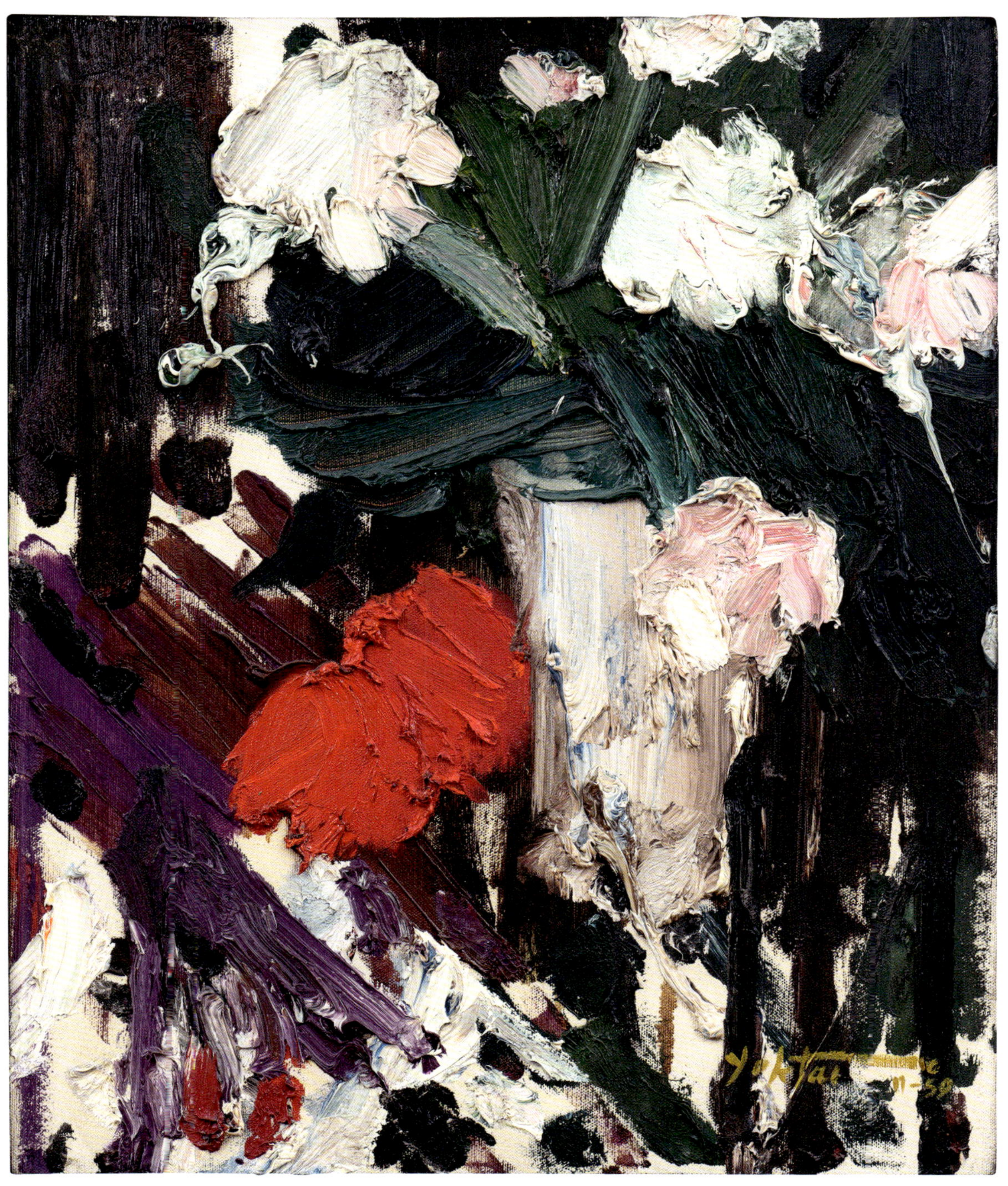

Untitled, 1959, oil on canvas, 19 × 19 inches (48 × 48 cm)

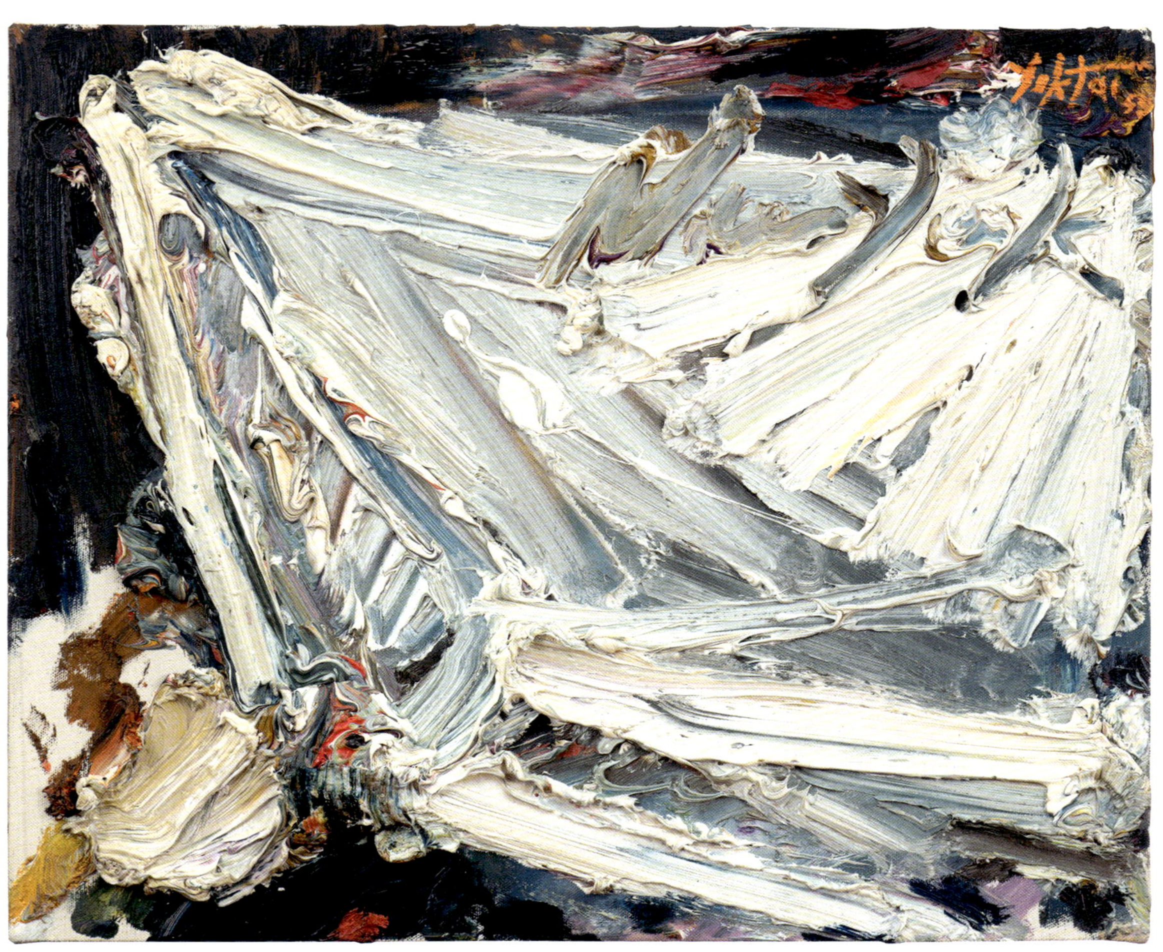

 Untitled, 1959, oil on canvas, 16 × 19½ inches (40.6 × 49.5 cm)

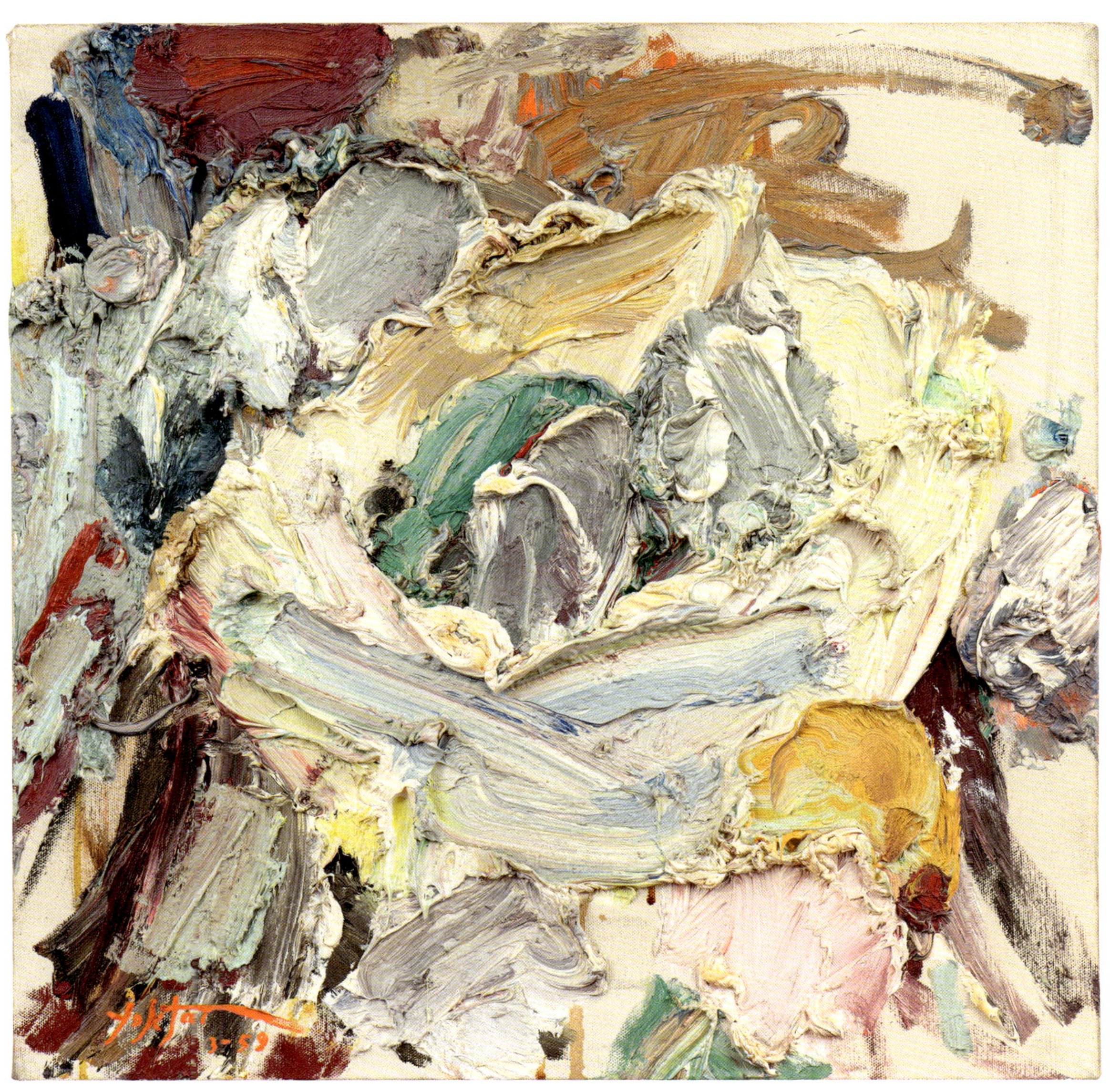

Untitled, 1959, oil on canvas, 18 × 18 inches (45.7 × 45.7 cm)

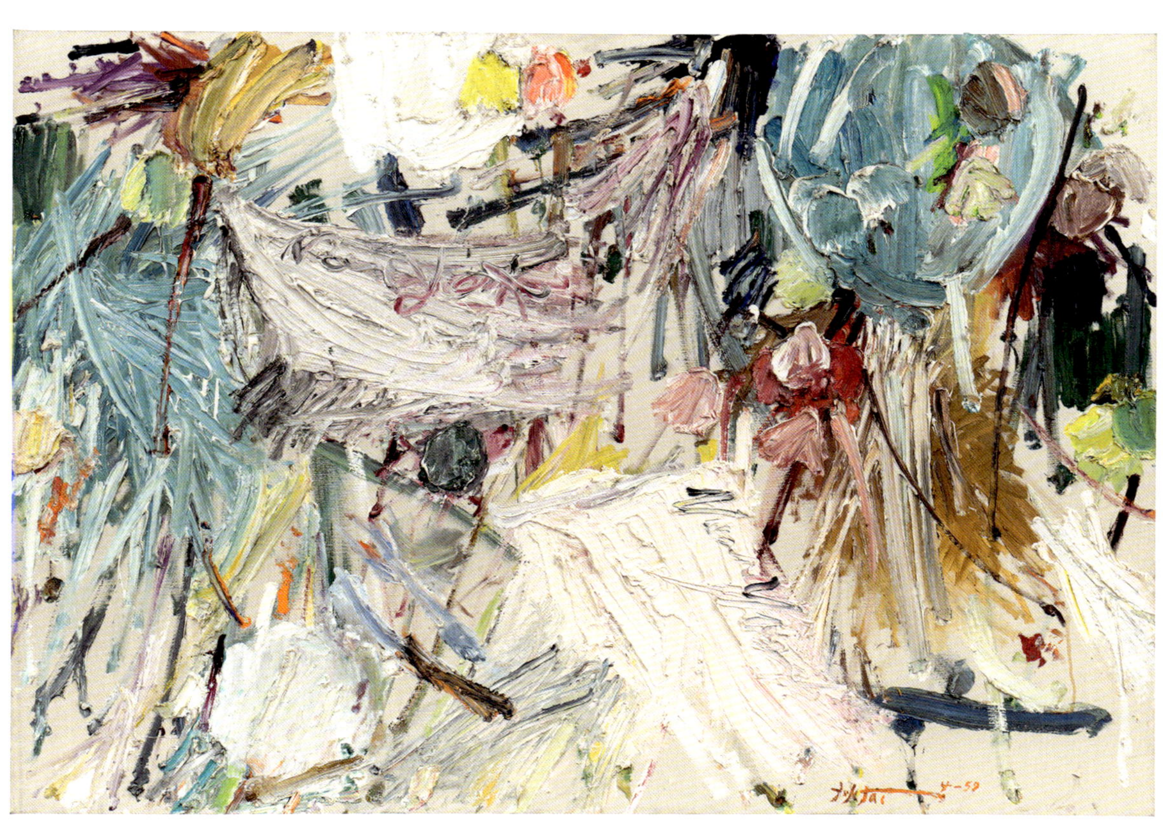

 Still Life with Bowl, 1959, oil on canvas, 48 × 68 inches (121.9 × 172.7 cm)

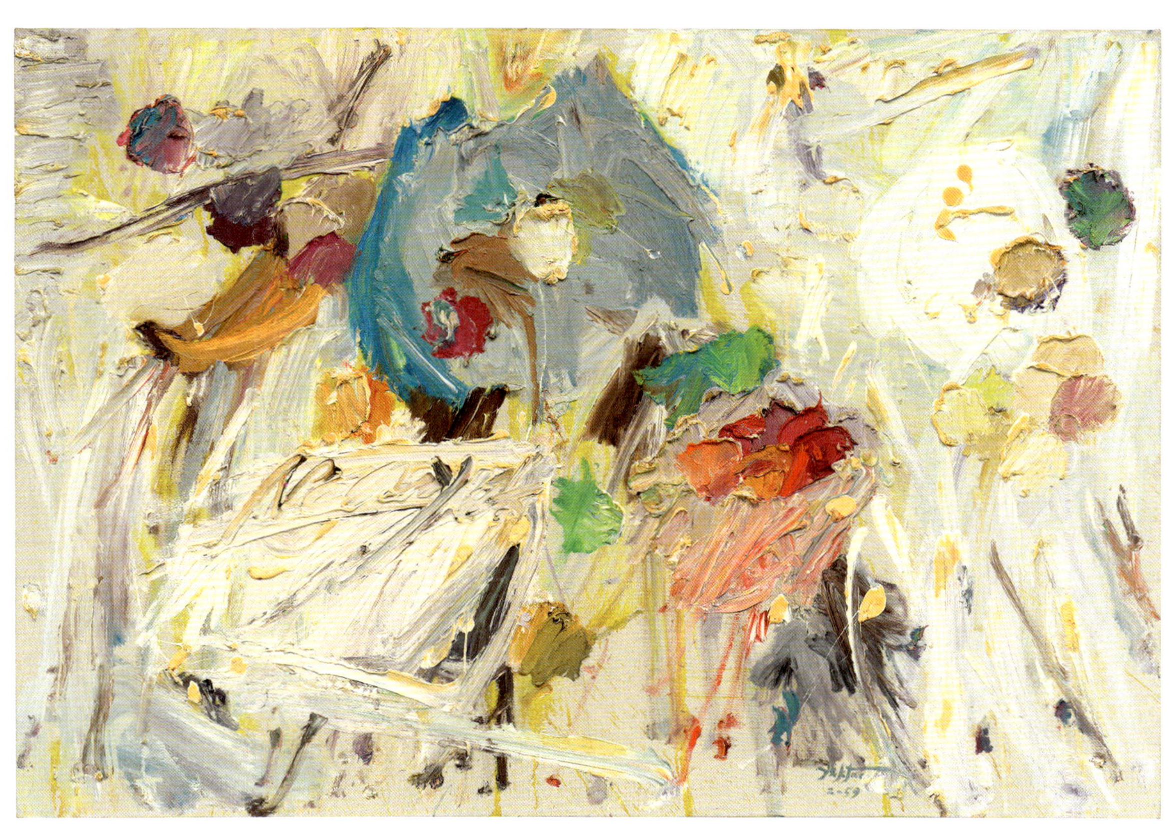

Still Life D, 1959, oil on canvas, 48¼ × 68 inches (122.3 × 172.8 cm)

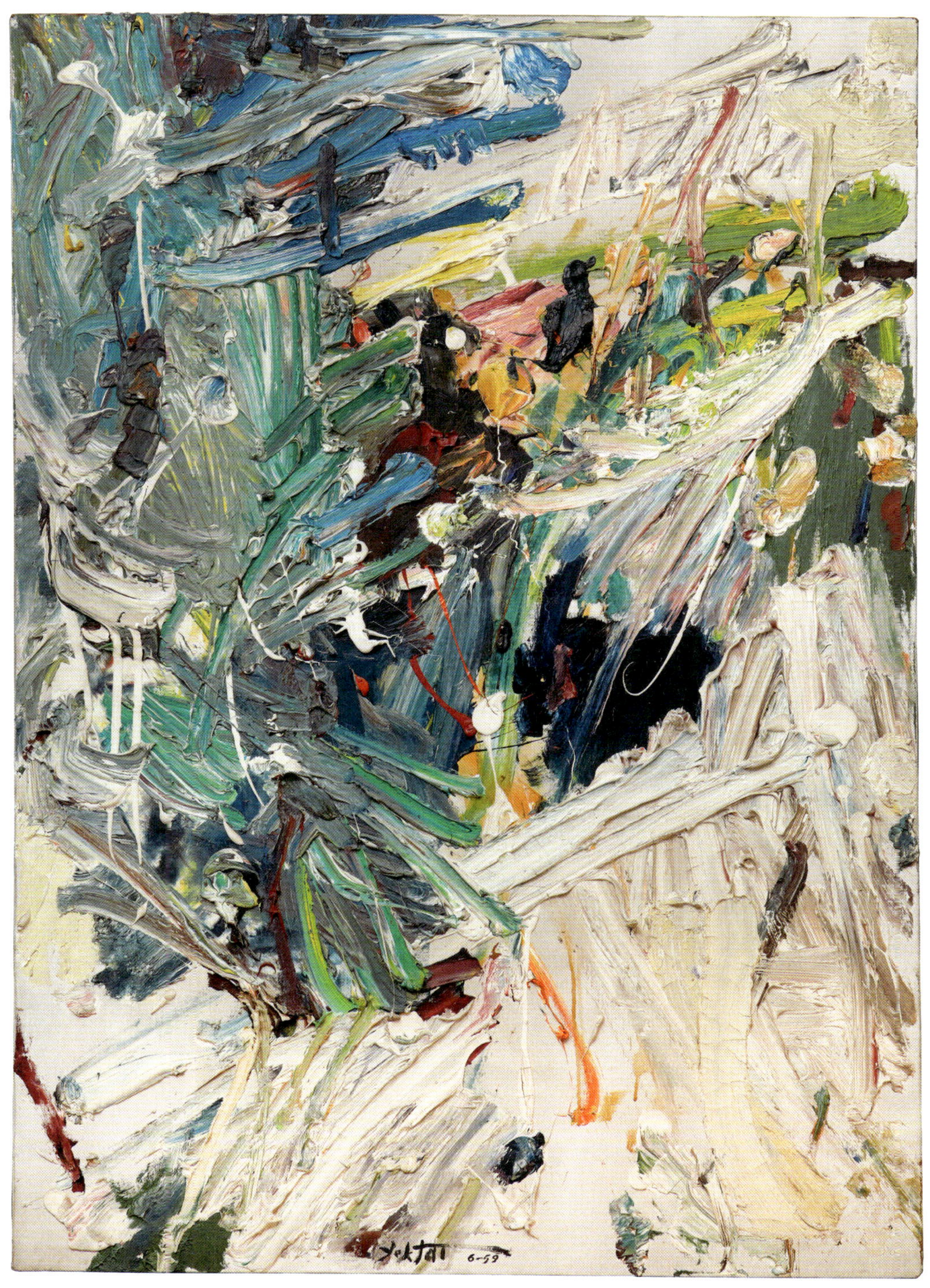

Untitled, 1959, oil on canvas, 48 × 38 inches (121.9 × 96.5 cm)

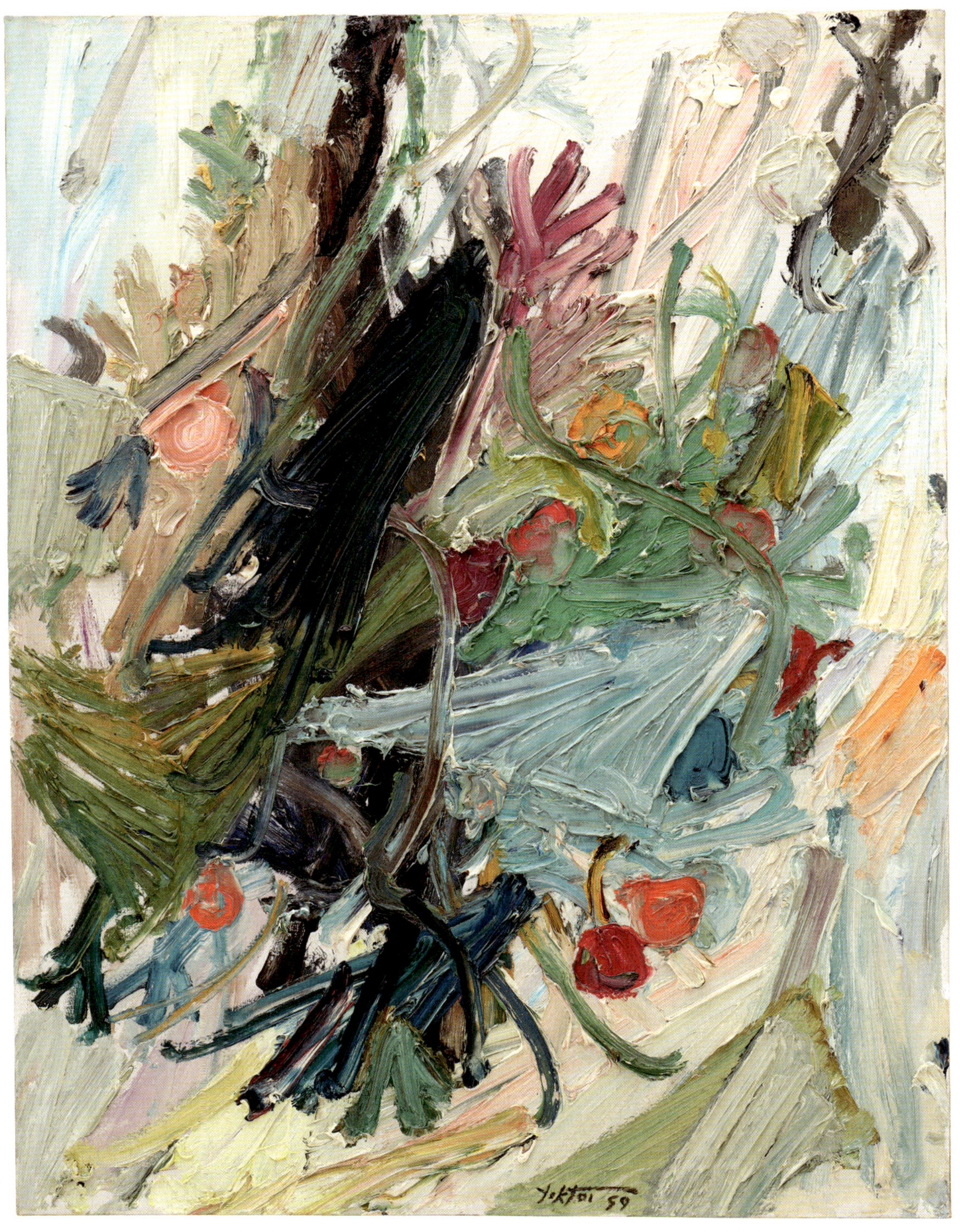

Tomato Plant, 1959, oil on canvas, 42 × 32 inches (106.68 × 81.28 cm)

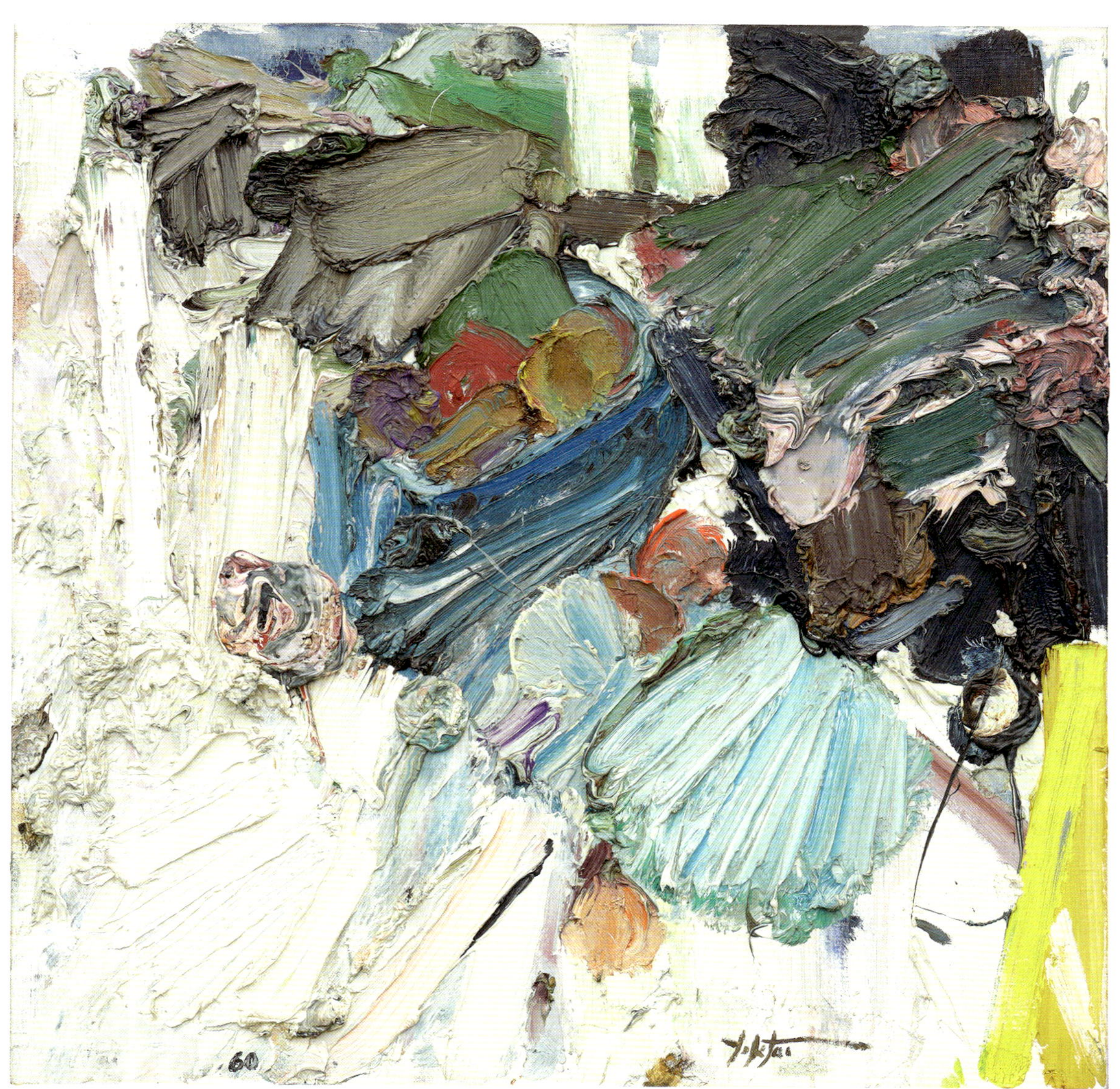

Untitled, 1960, oil on canvas, 31½ × 31½ inches (80 × 80 cm)

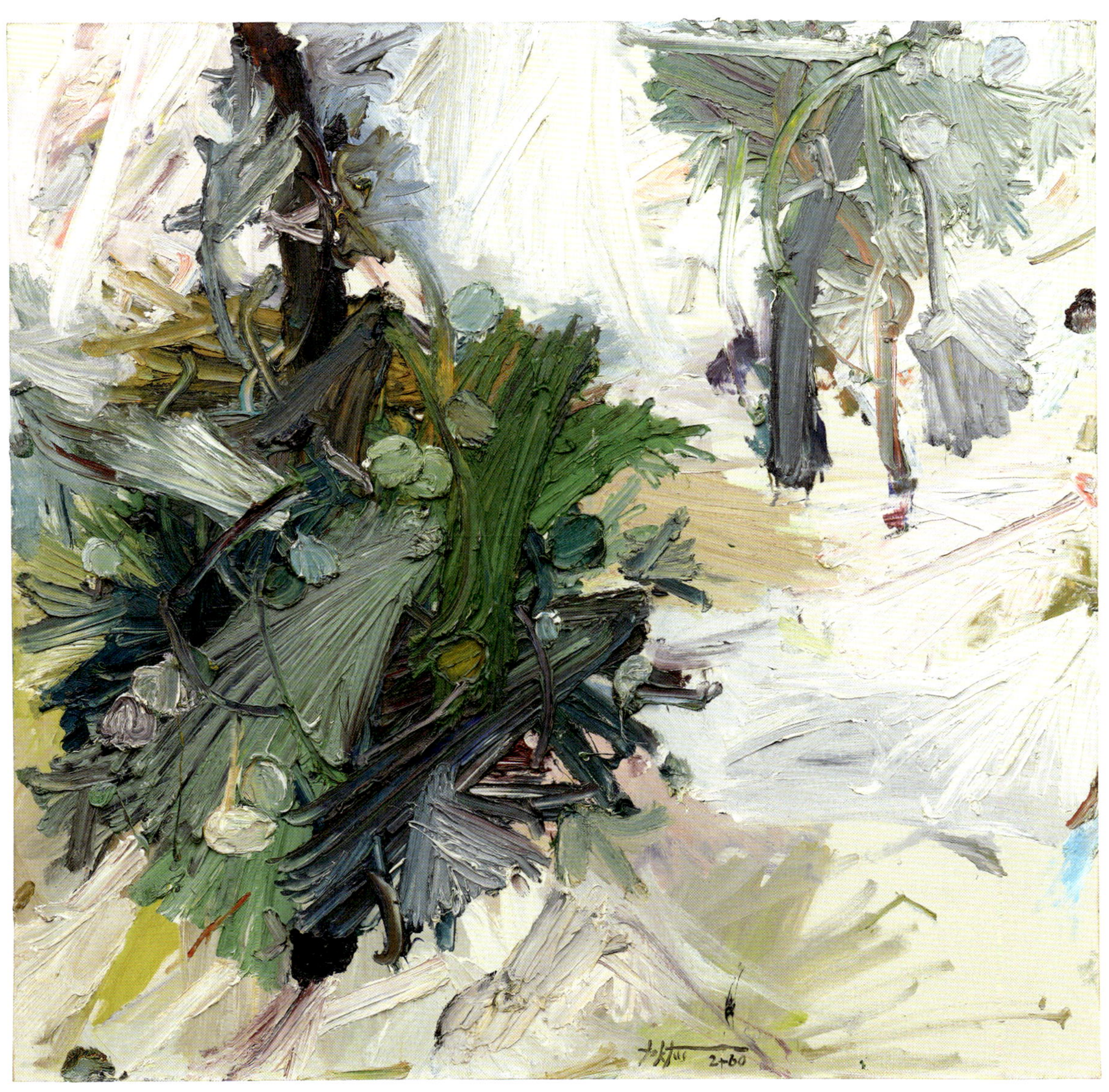

Three Tomato Plants, 1960, oil on canvas, 60 × 60 inches (152.4 × 152.4 cm)

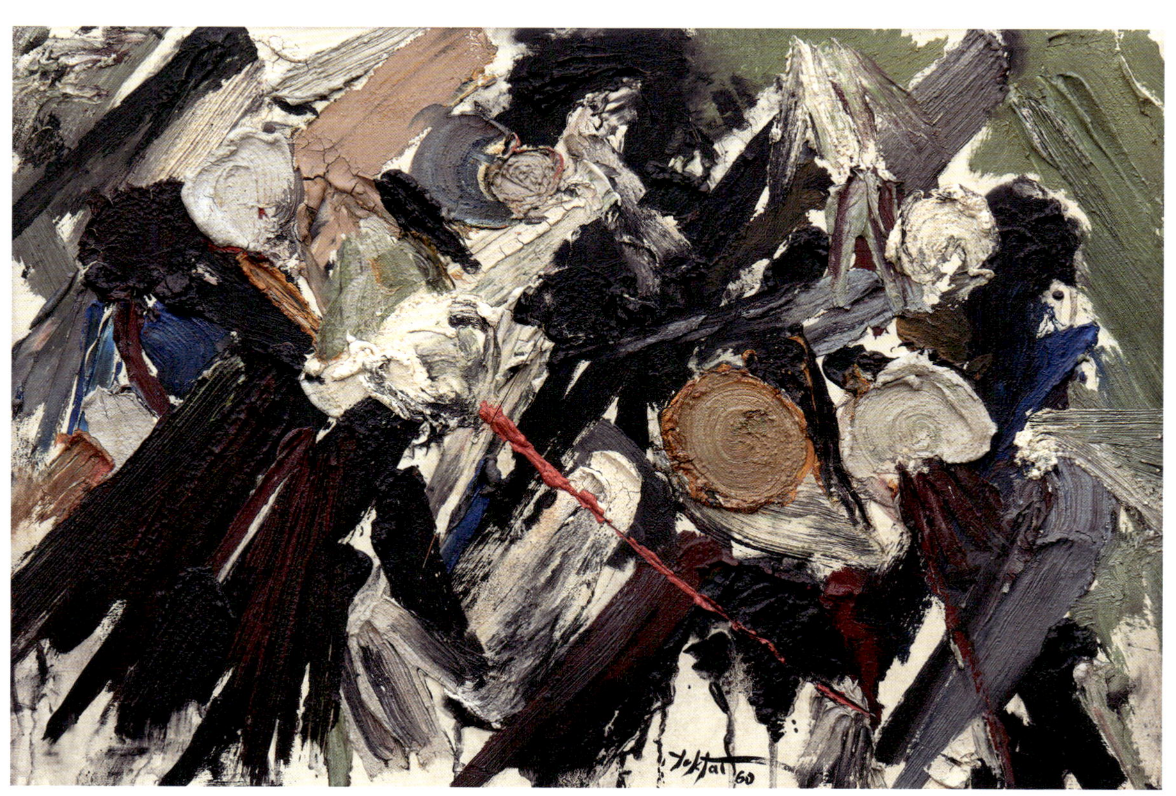

 Untitled, 1960, oil on canvas, 19¼ × 28⅜ inches (48.9 × 72.1 cm)

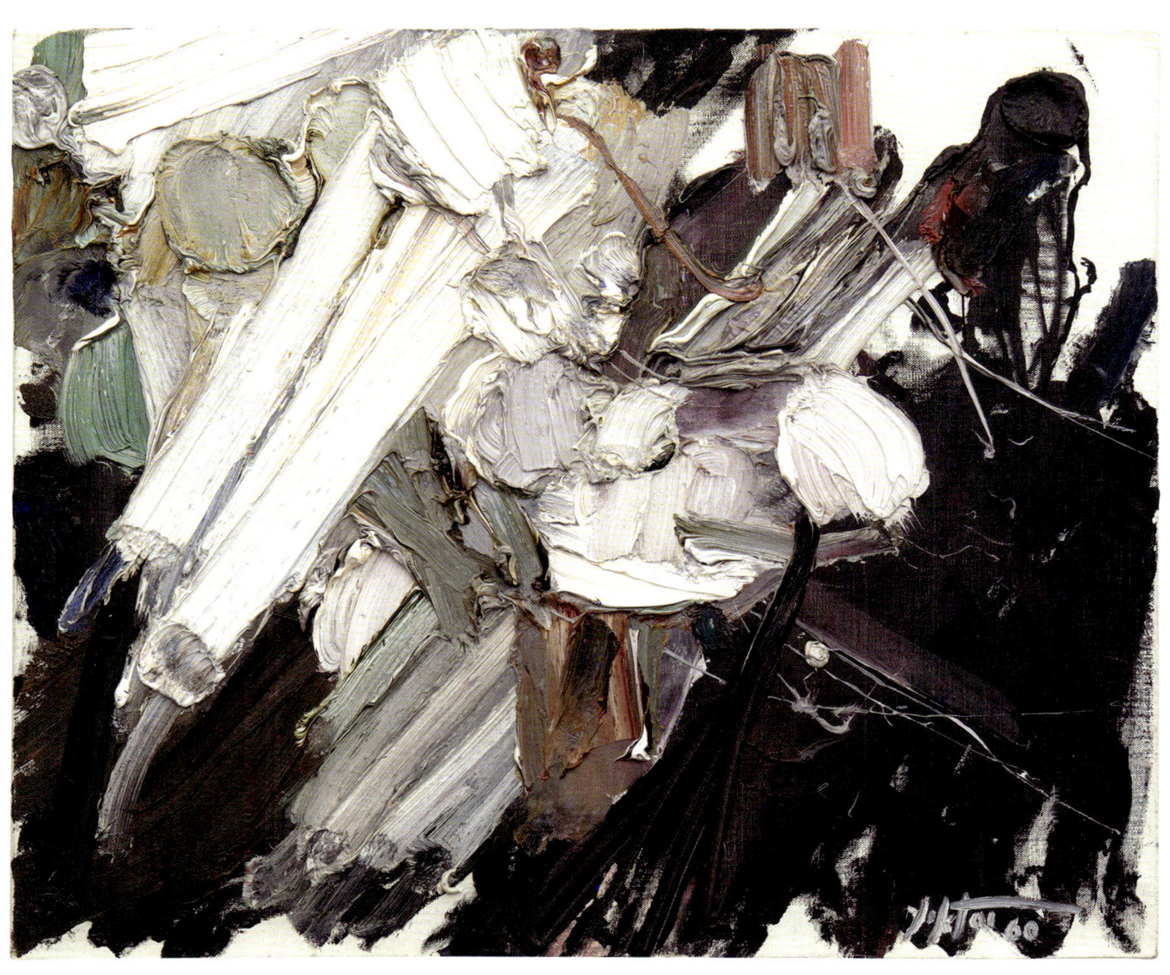

Nature Morte, 1960, oil on canvas, 21⅜ × 25⅝ inches (54.3 × 65.1 cm)

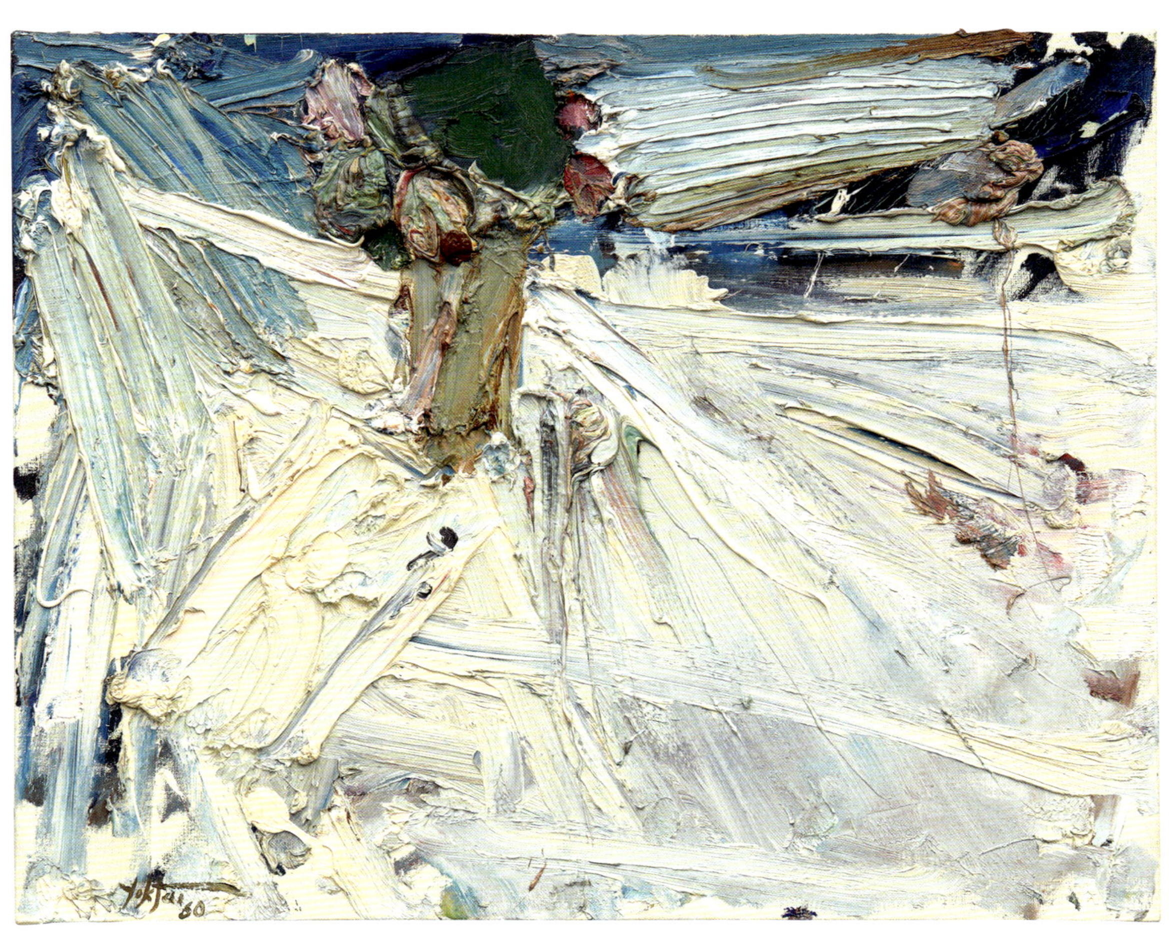

Untitled, 1960, oil on canvas, 25½ × 32 inches (64.8 × 81.3 cm)

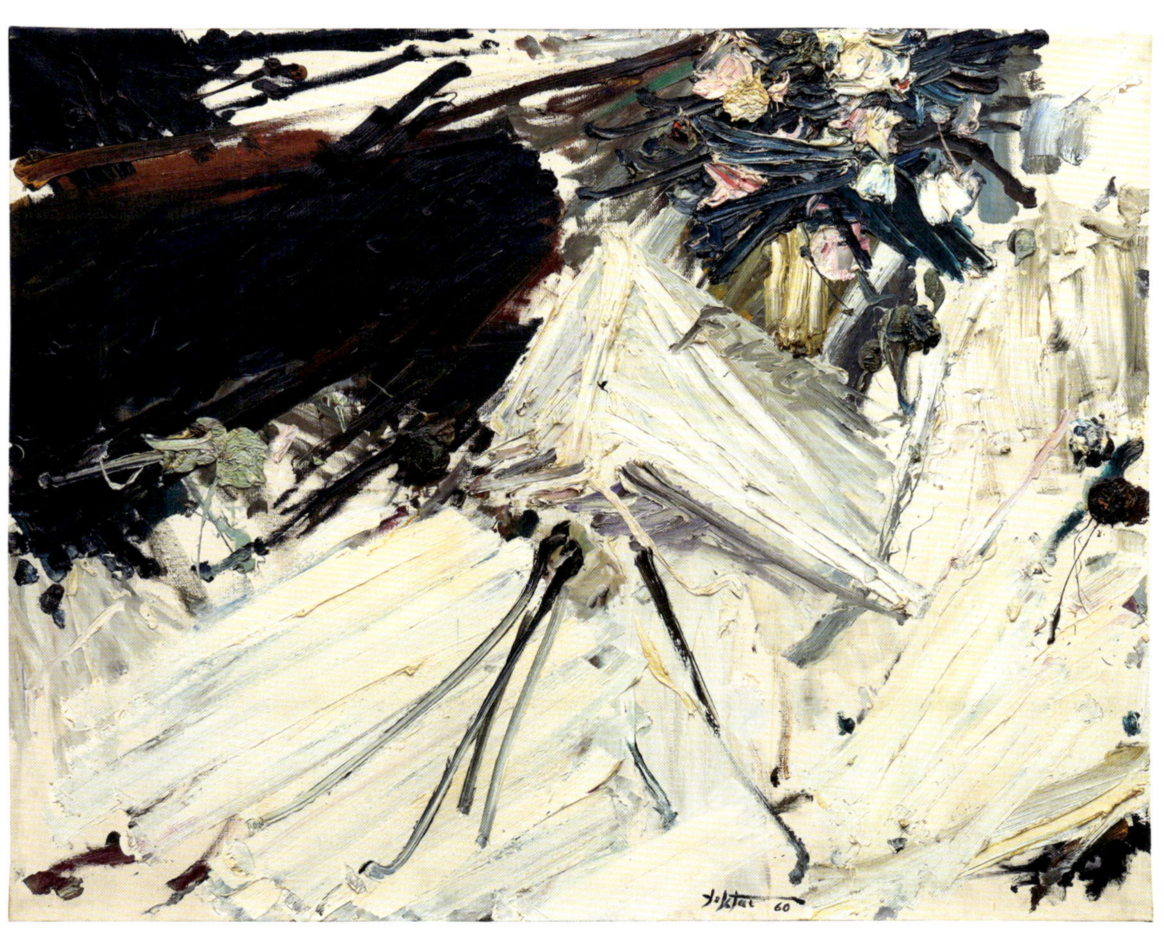

Untitled, 1960, oil on canvas, 51 × 63 inches (130 × 160 cm)

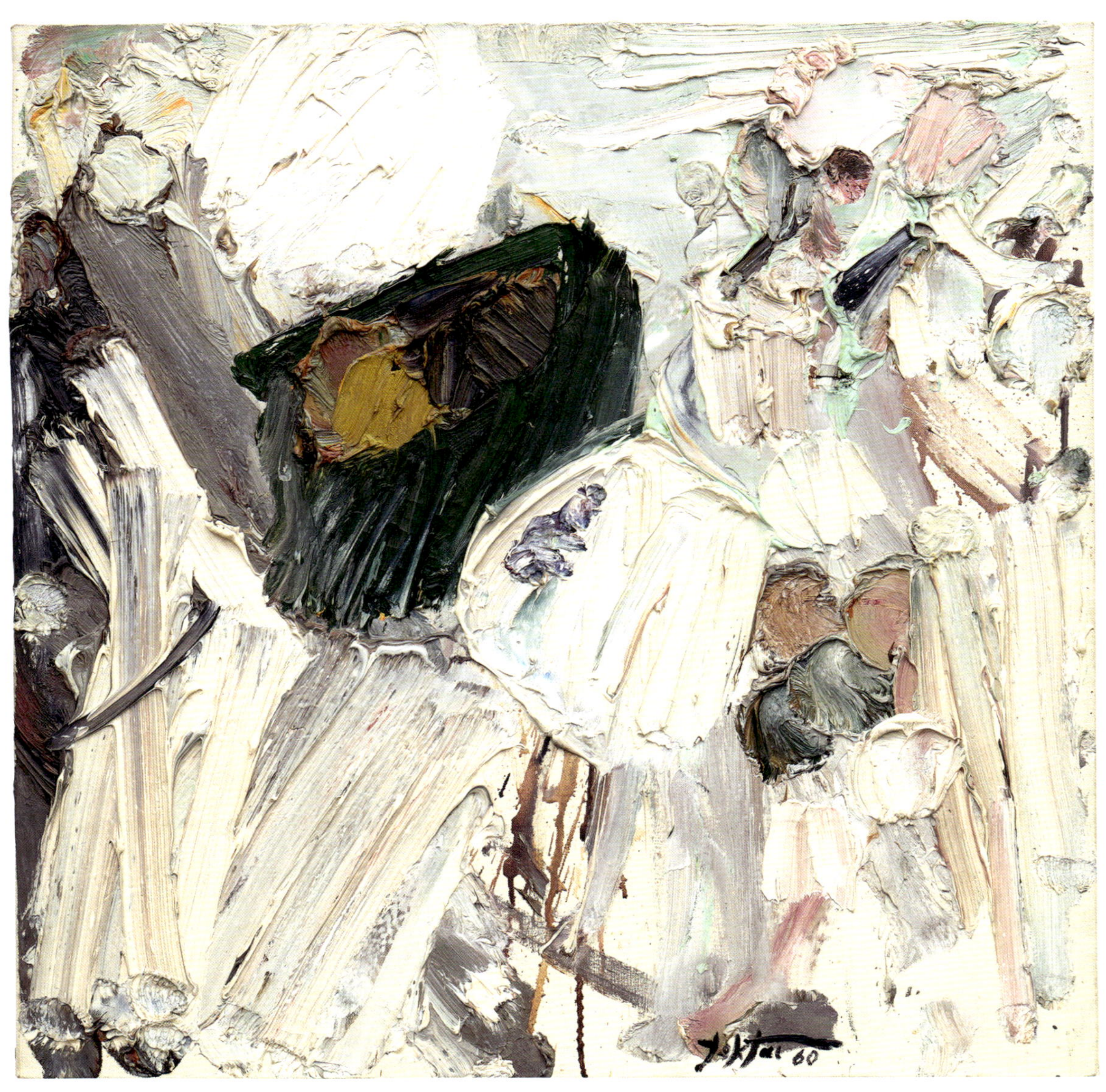

Untitled, 1960, oil on canvas, 31½ × 31½ inches (80 × 80 cm)

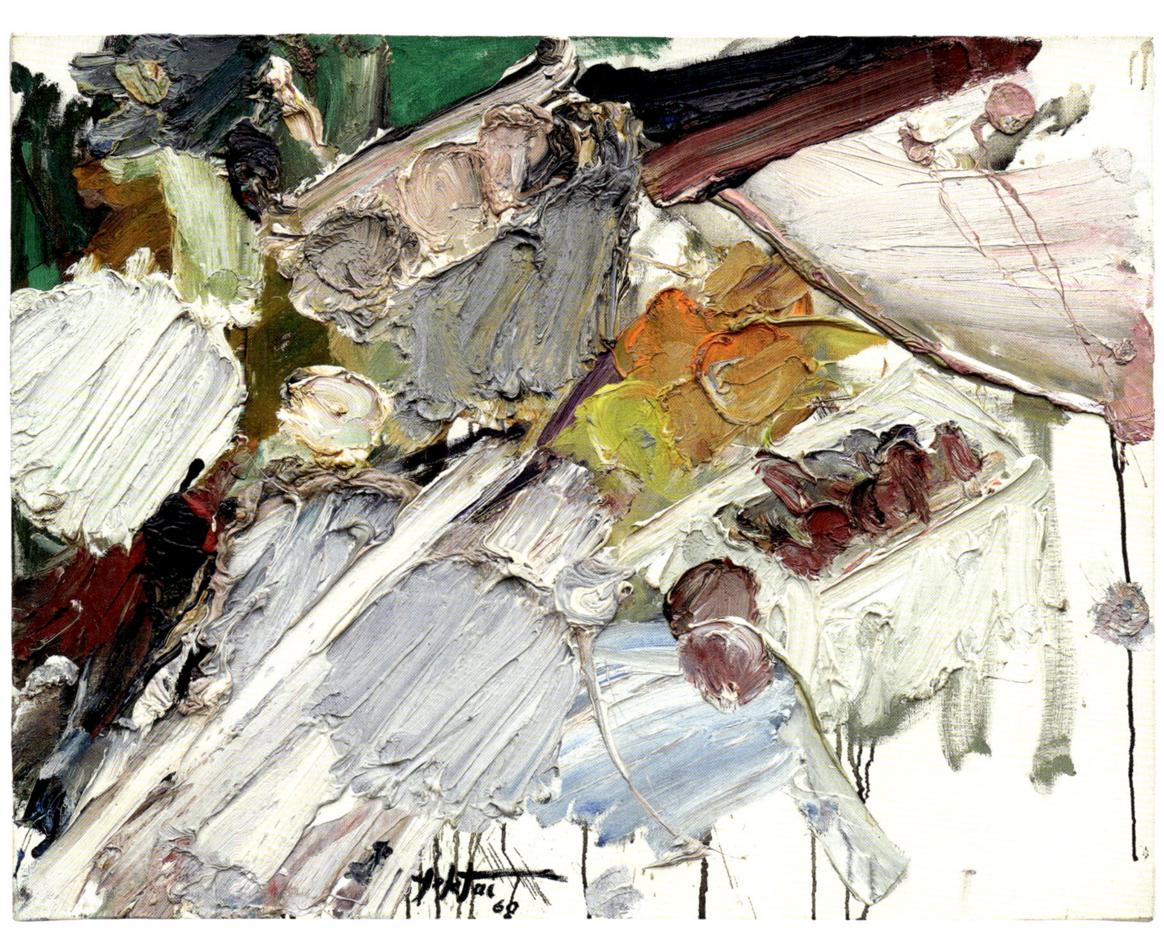

Untitled, 1960, oil on canvas, 28¾ × 36 inches (73 × 91.4 cm)

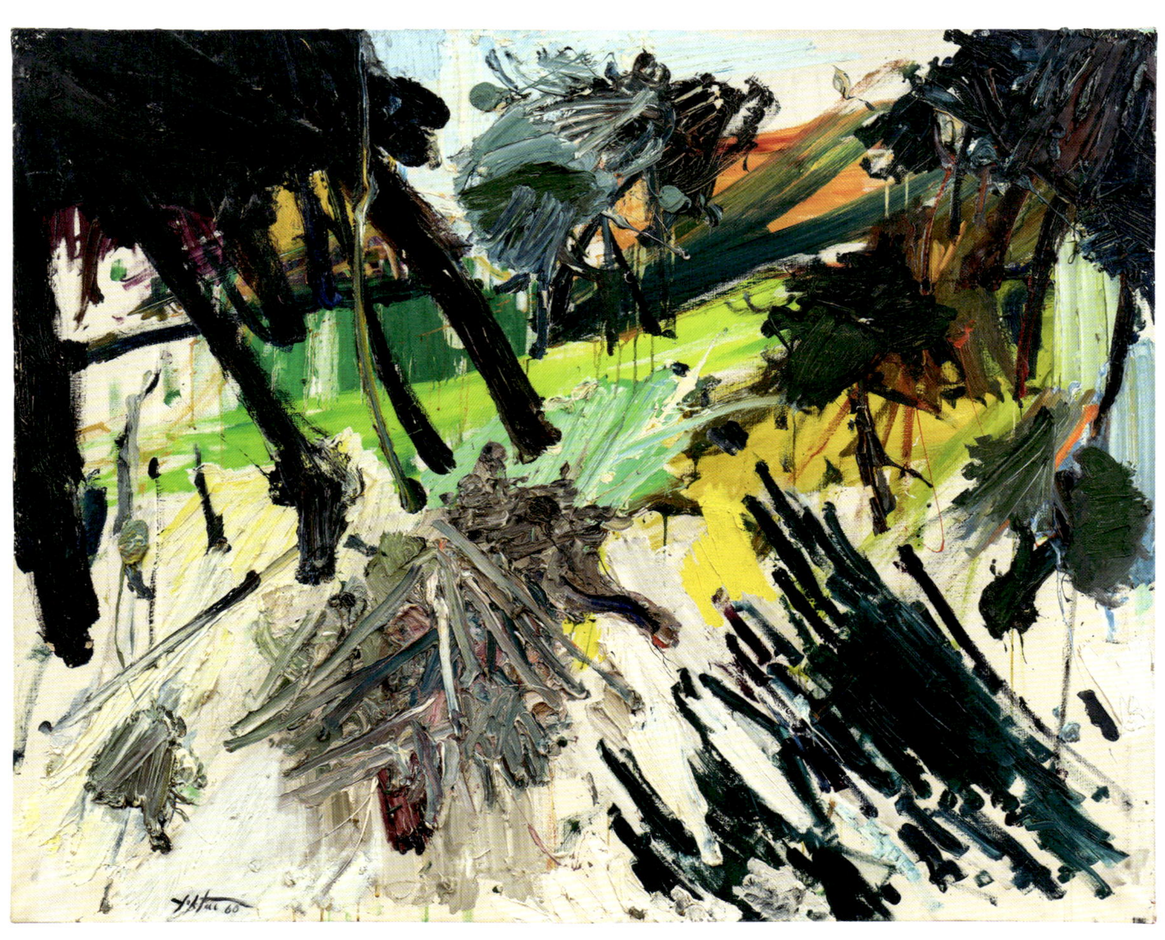

 Untitled, 1960, oil on canvas, 51 × 63½ inches (129.5 × 161.3 cm)

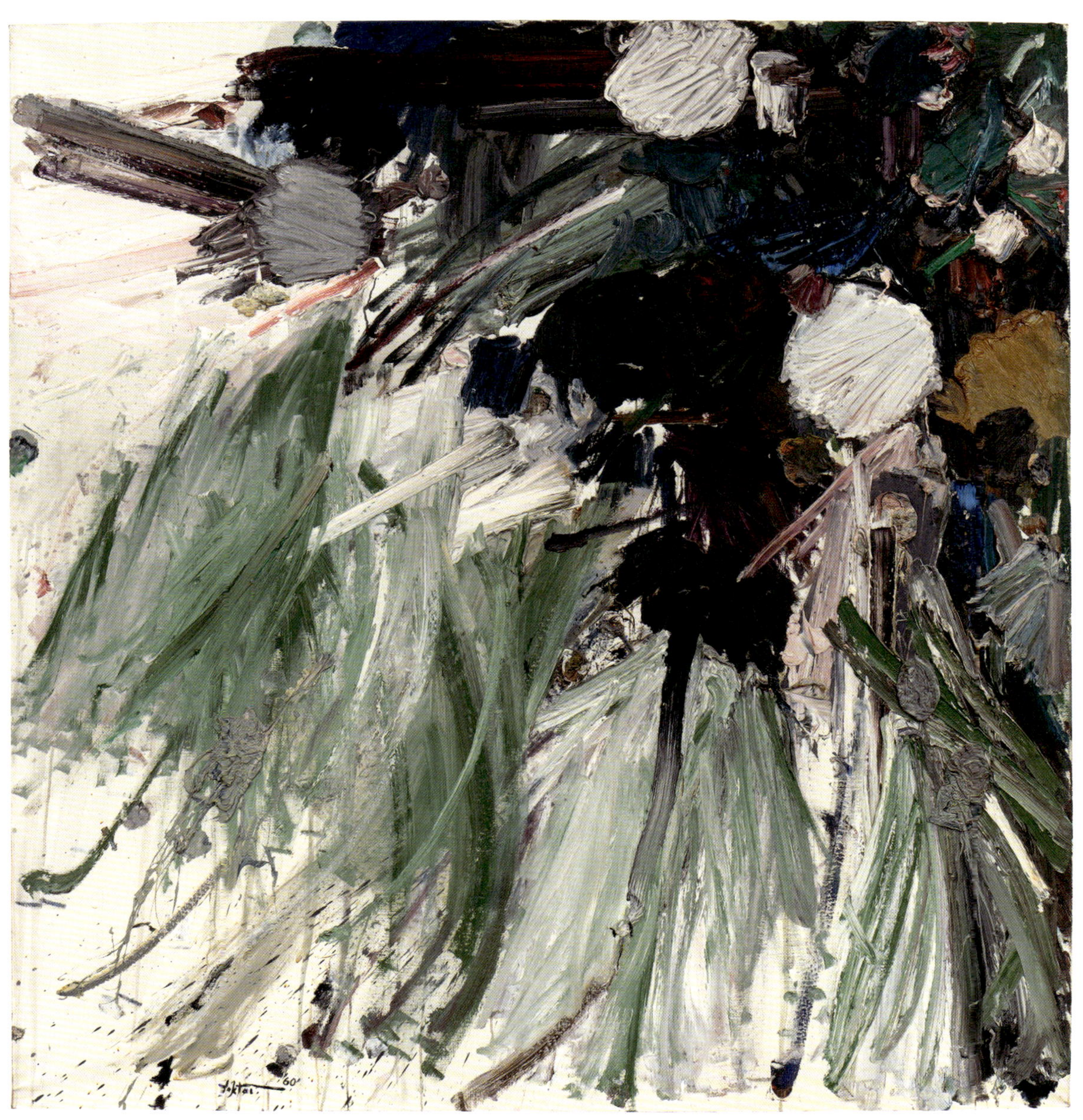

Untitled, 1960, oil on canvas, 74¾ × 70¾ inches (189.9 × 179.7 cm)

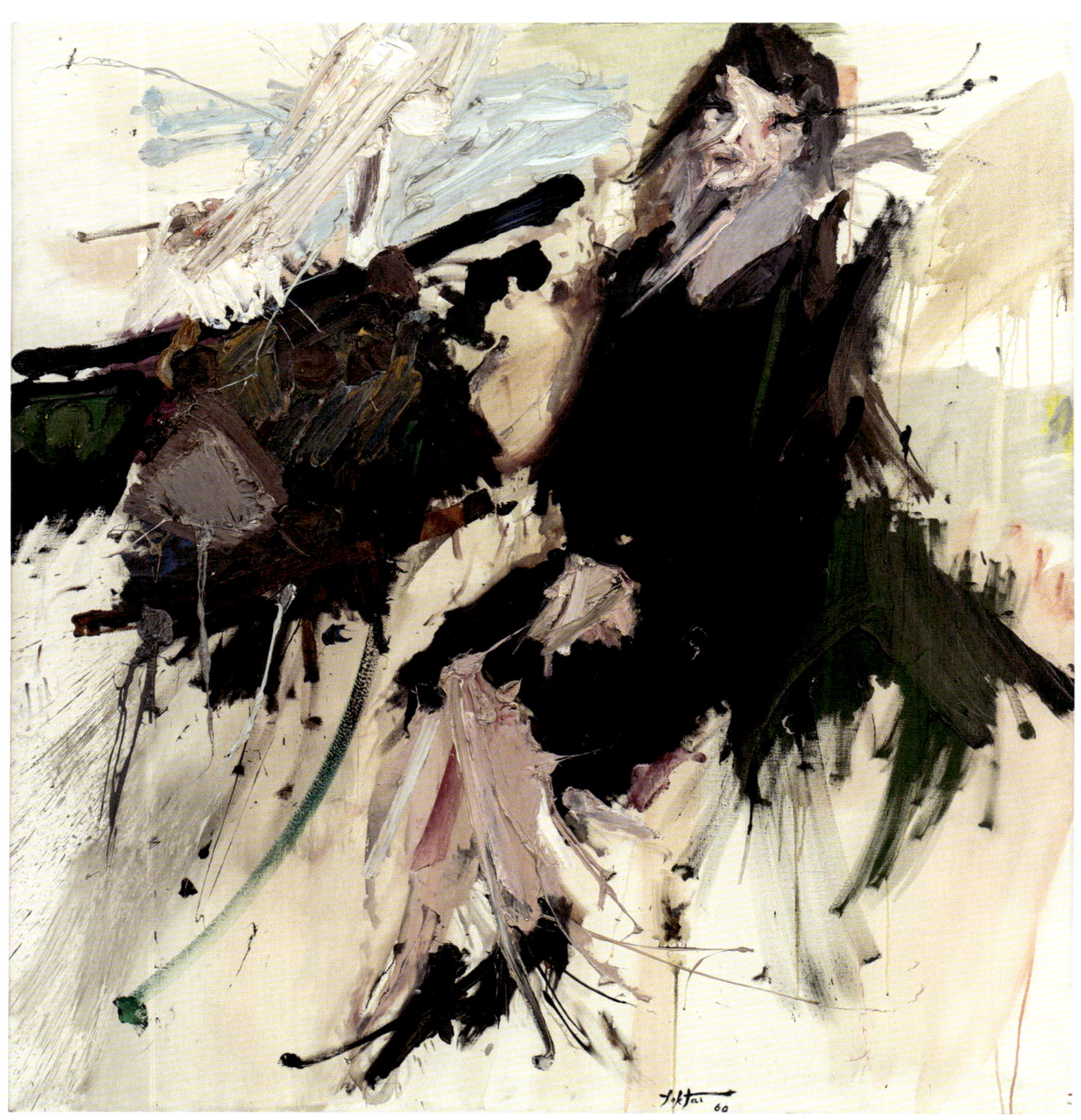

Concierge, 1960, oil on canvas, 75 × 70¼ inches (190.5 × 178.4 cm)

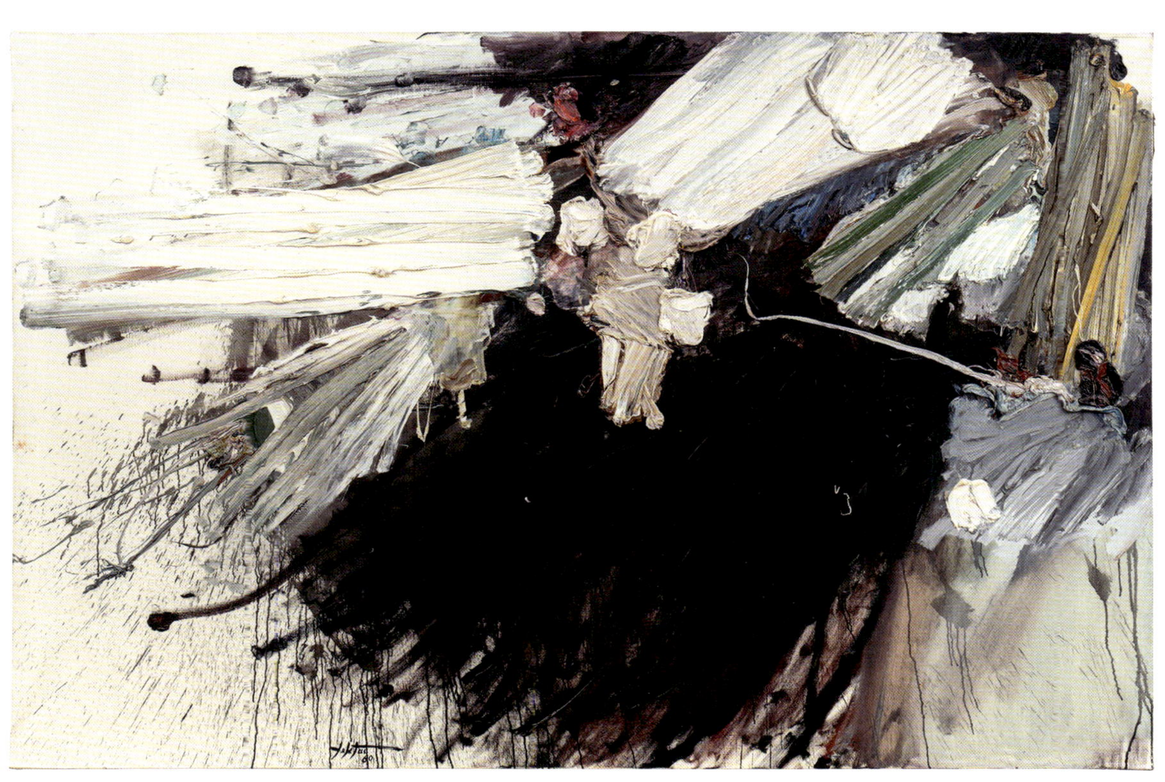

Untitled, 1960, oil on canvas, 51 × 76½ inches (129.5 × 194.3 cm)

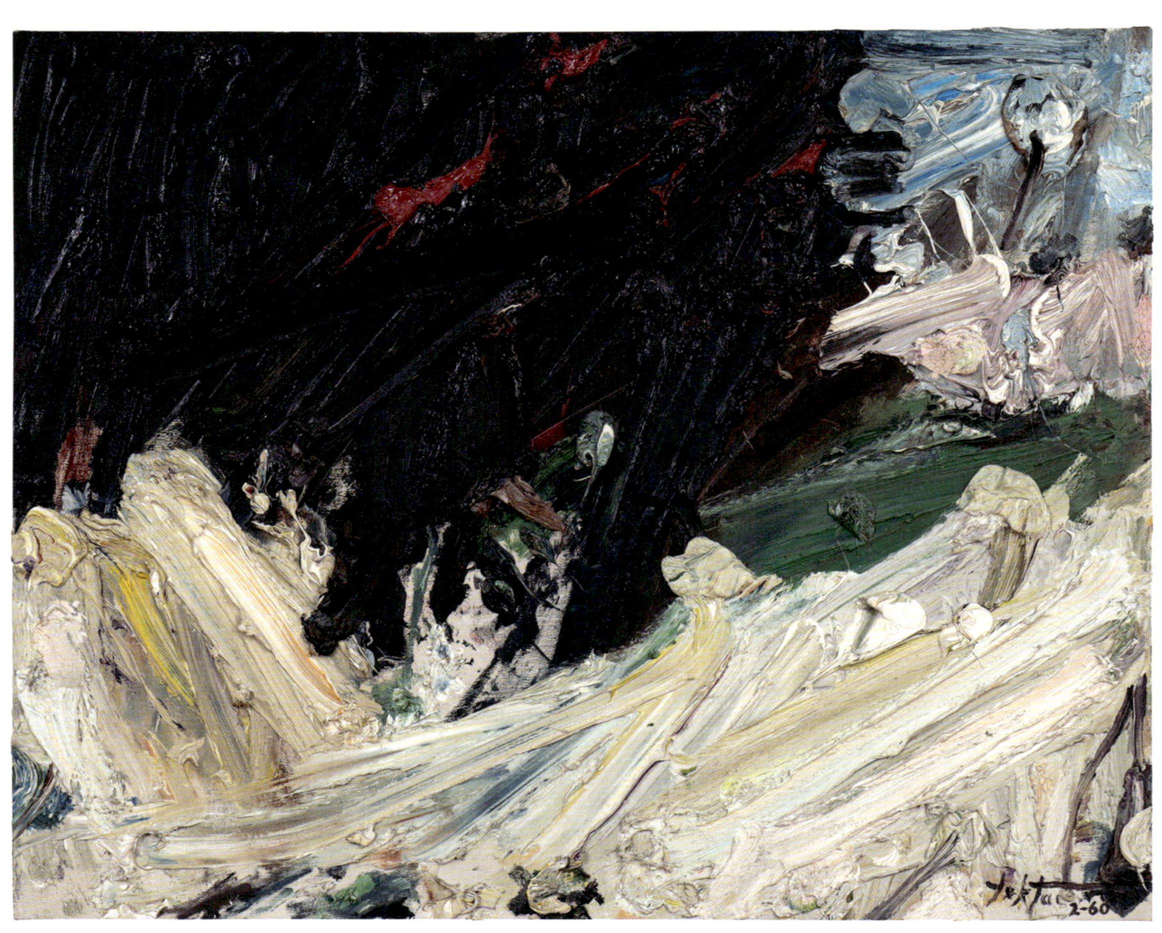

Untitled, 1960, oil on canvas, 24 × 30 inches (24 × 30 cm)

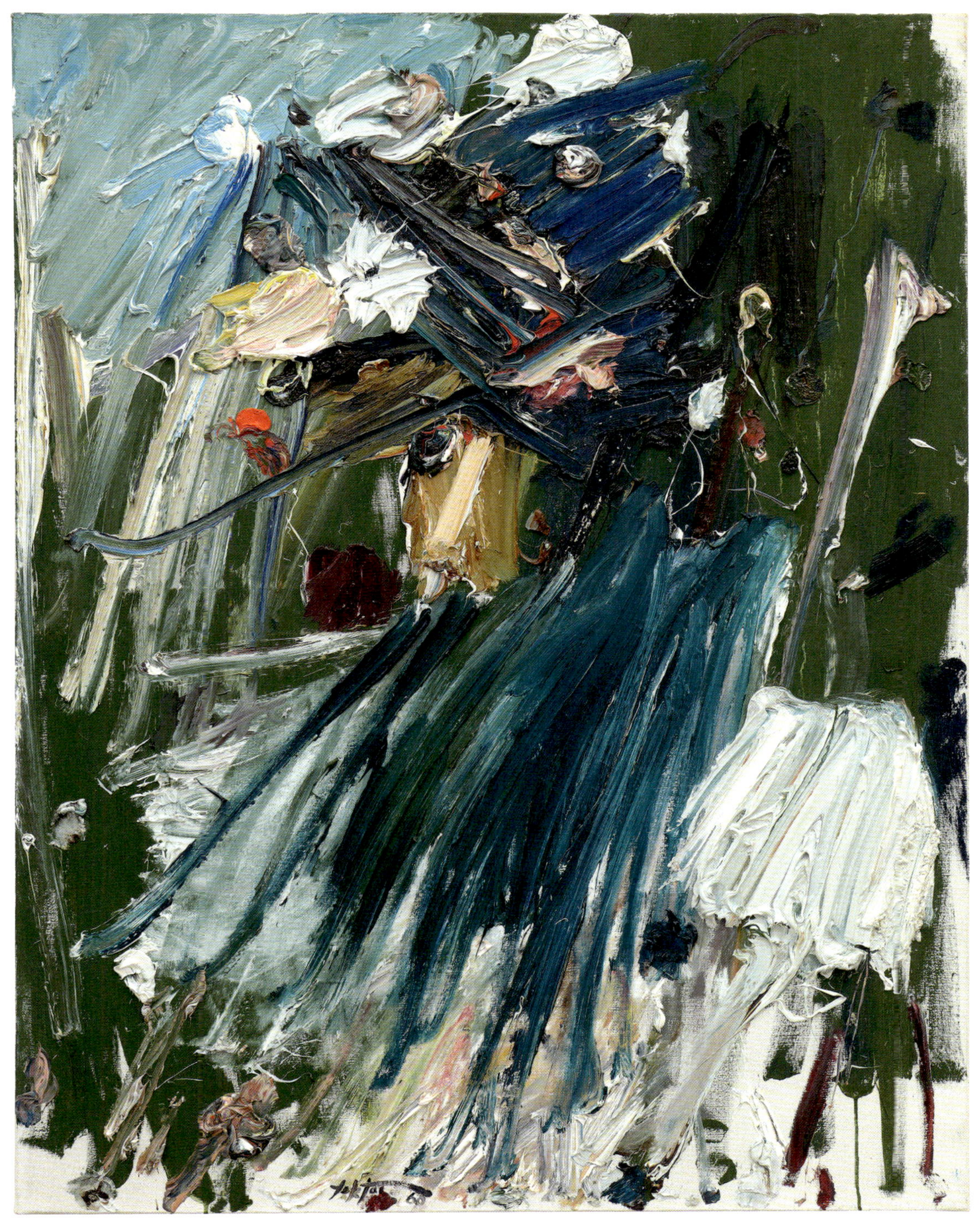

Untitled, 1960, oil on canvas, 45½ × 35 inches (115.6 × 88.9 cm)

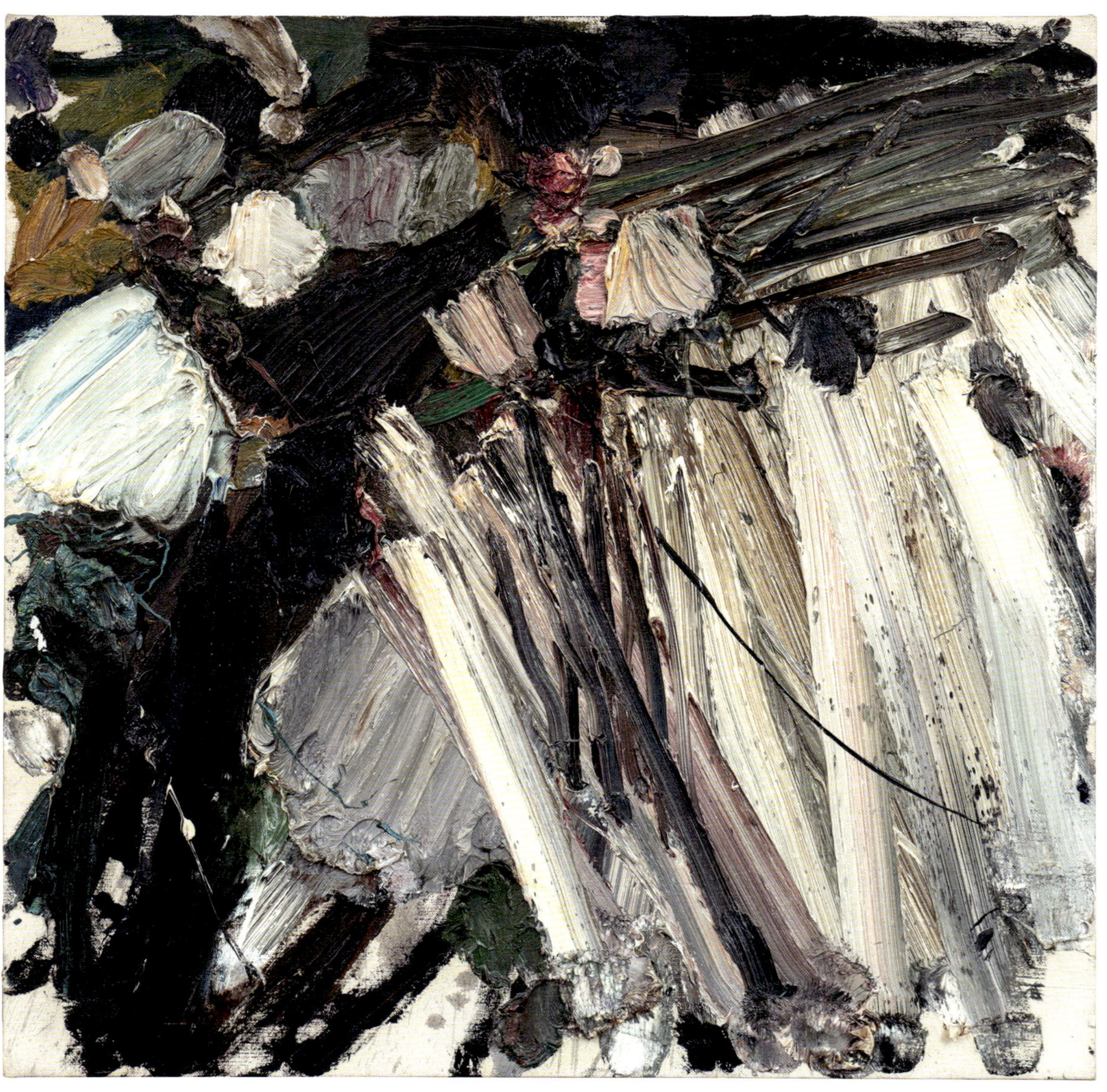

Untitled, 1960, oil on canvas, 32 × 32 inches (81.3 × 81.3 cm)

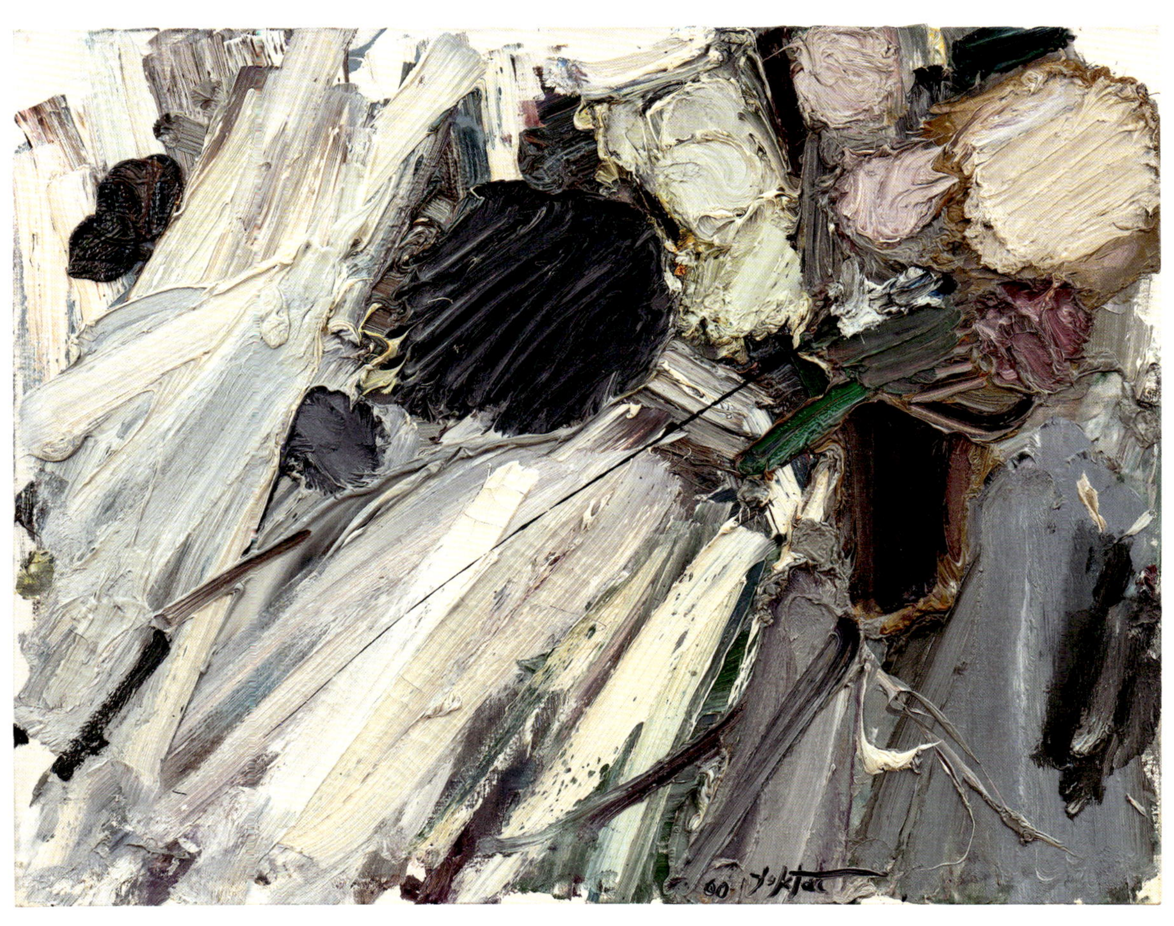

Untitled, 1960, oil on canvas, 28¾ × 36 inches (73 × 91.4 cm)

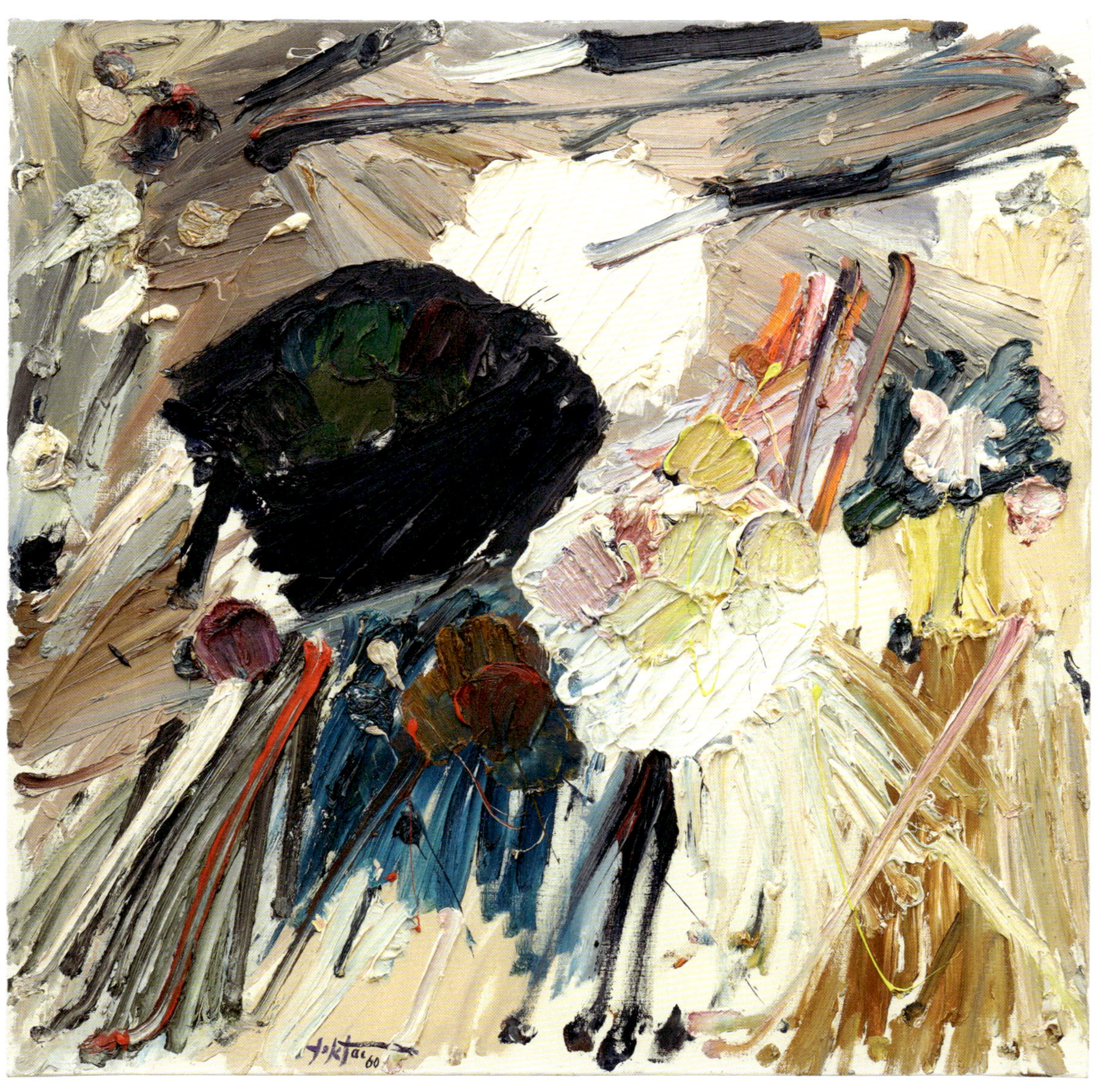

 Untitled, 1960, oil on canvas, 39¾ × 39¾ inches (100 × 100 cm)

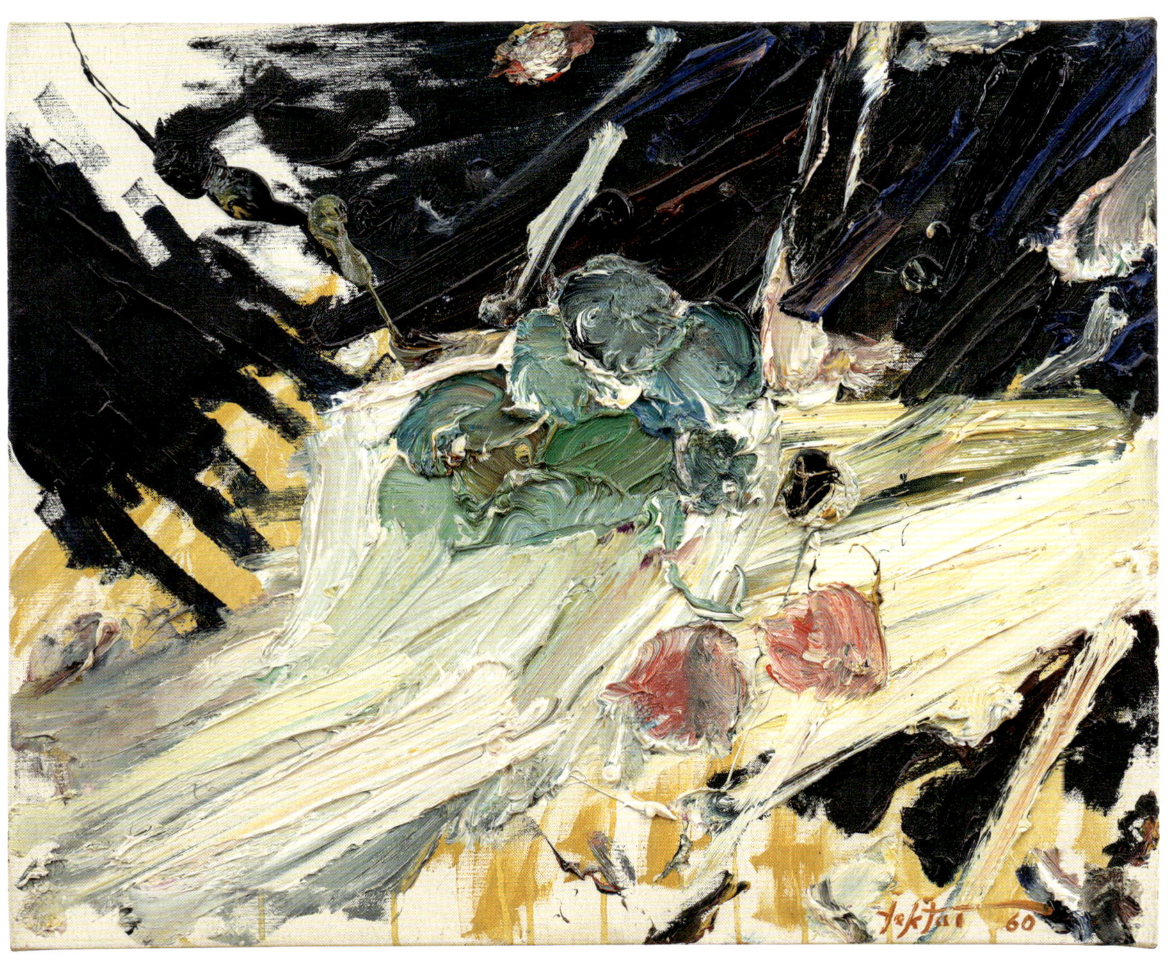

Untitled, 1960, oil on canvas, 21¼ × 25½ inches (54 × 64.8 cm)

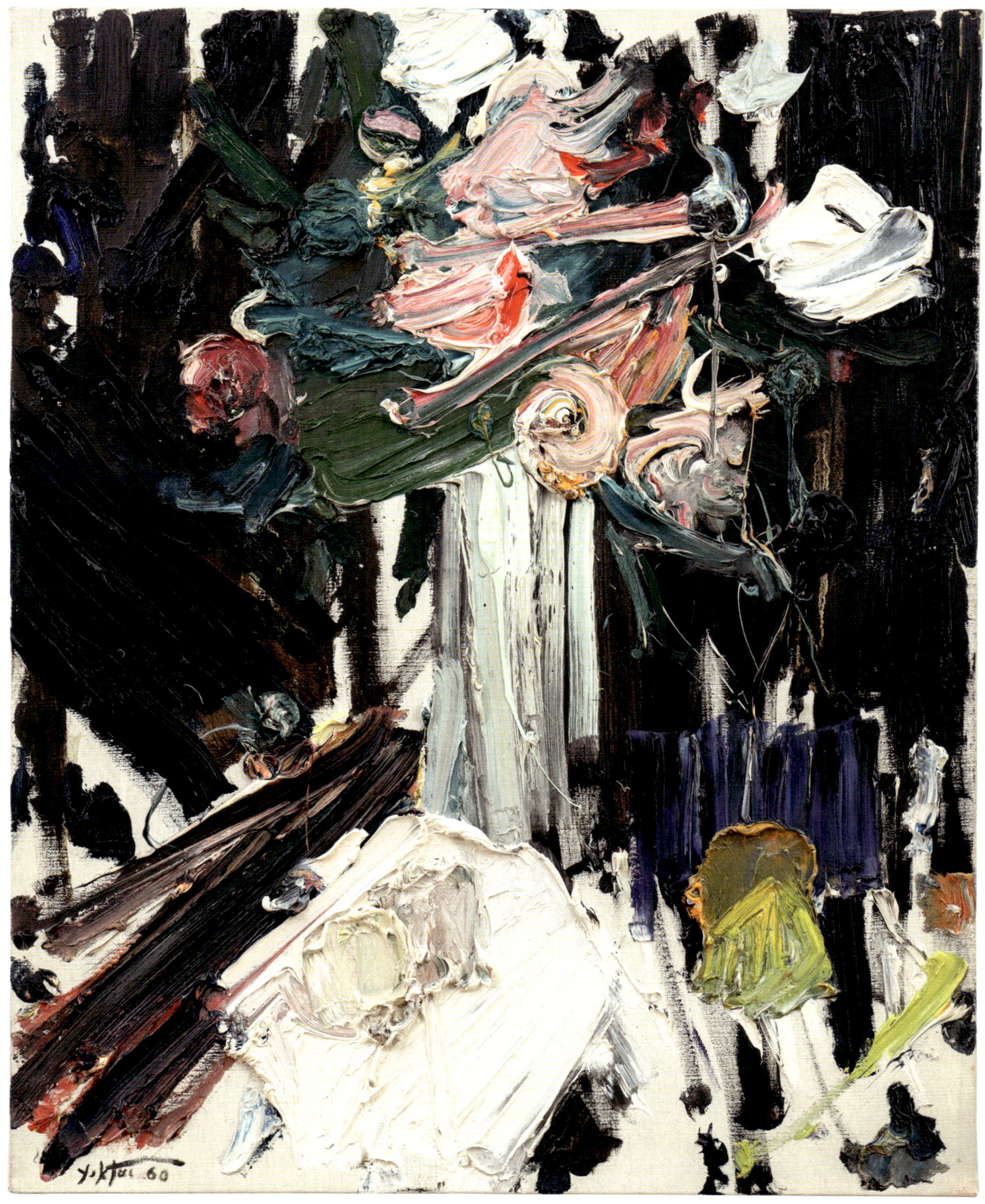

Untitled, 1960, oil on canvas, 32 × 25½ inches (81.3 × 64.8 cm)

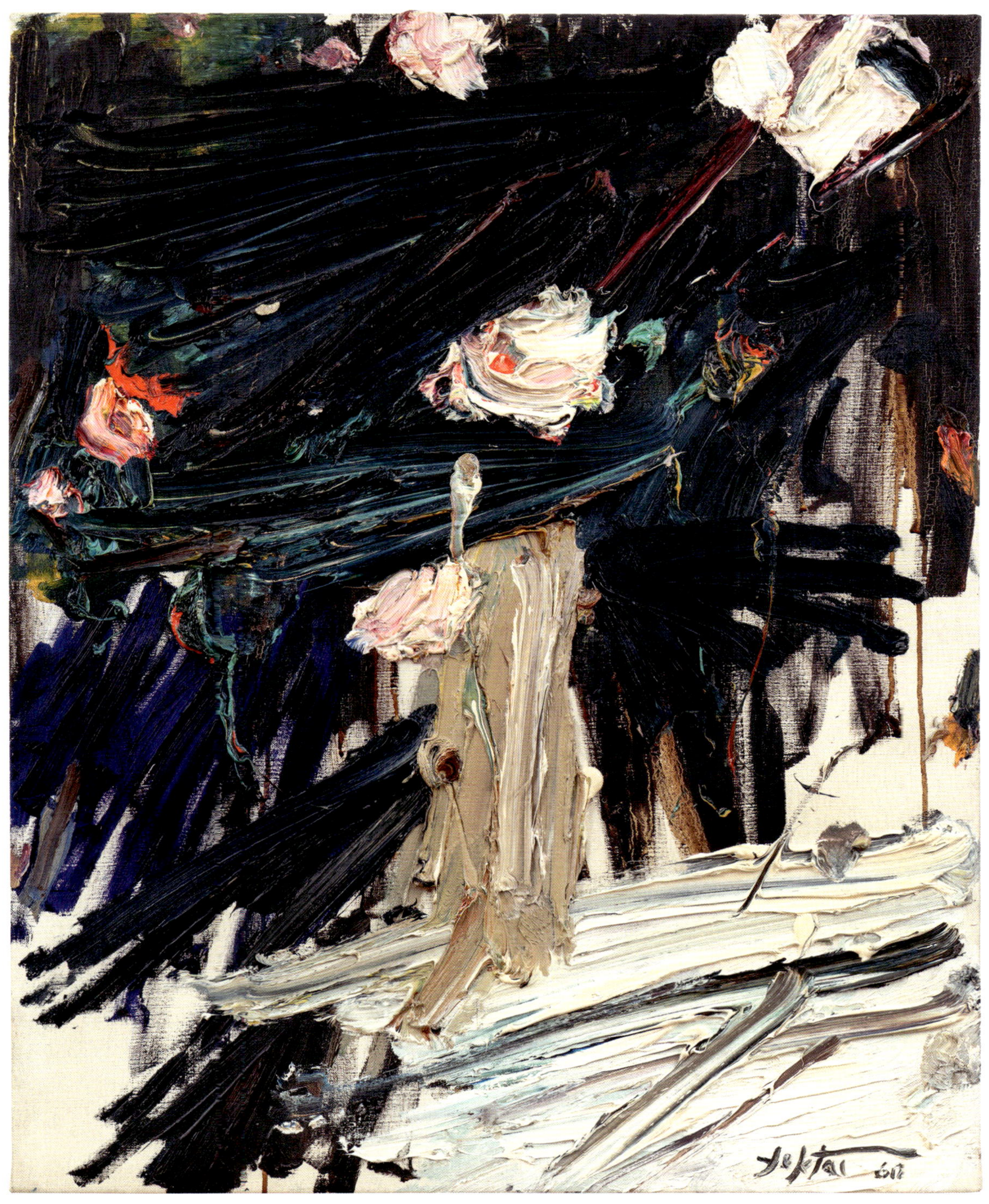

Pink Roses, 1960, oil on canvas, 32 × 25½ inches (81.3 × 64.8 cm)

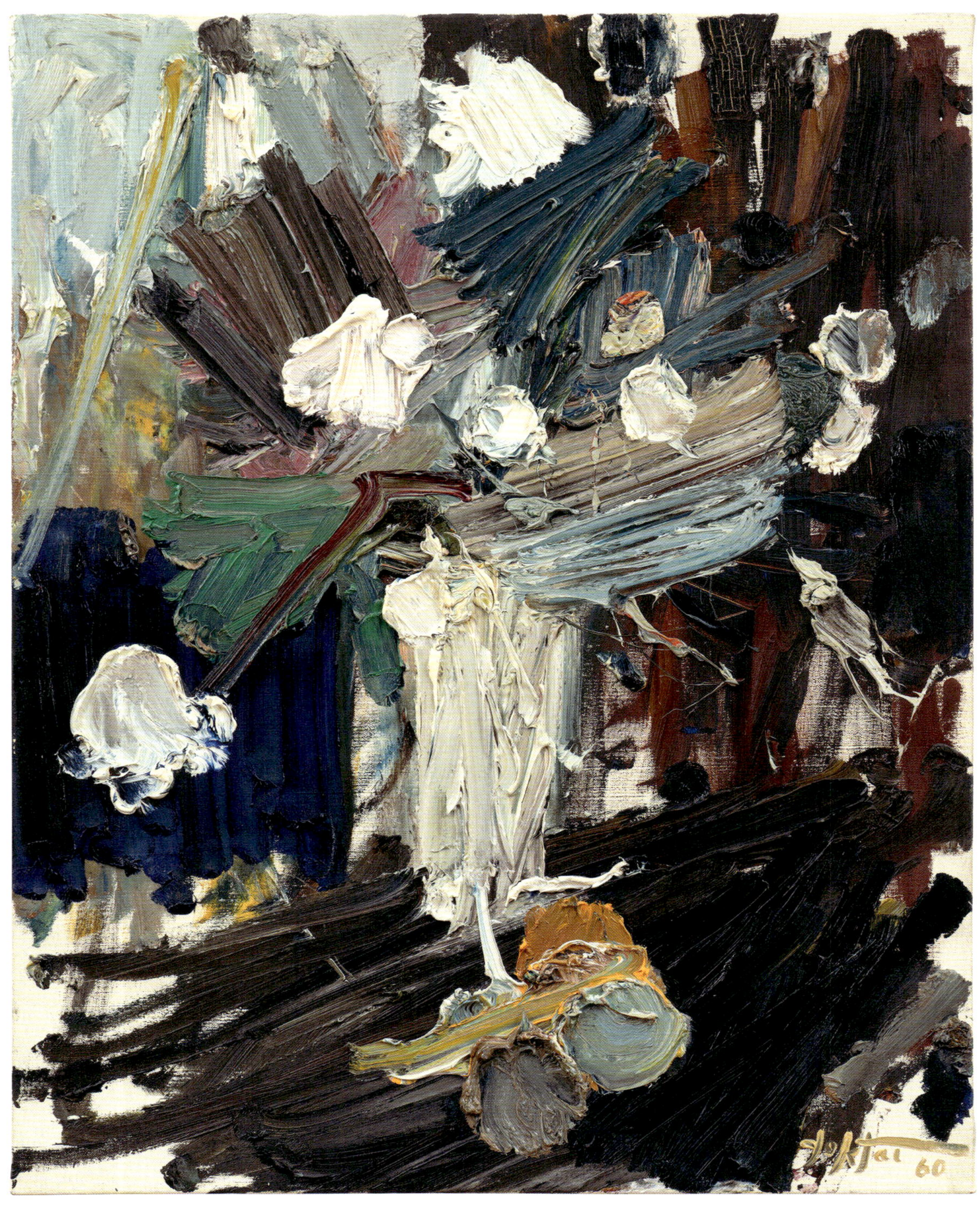

Untitled, 1960, oil on canvas, 32 × 25½ inches (81.3 × 64.8 cm)

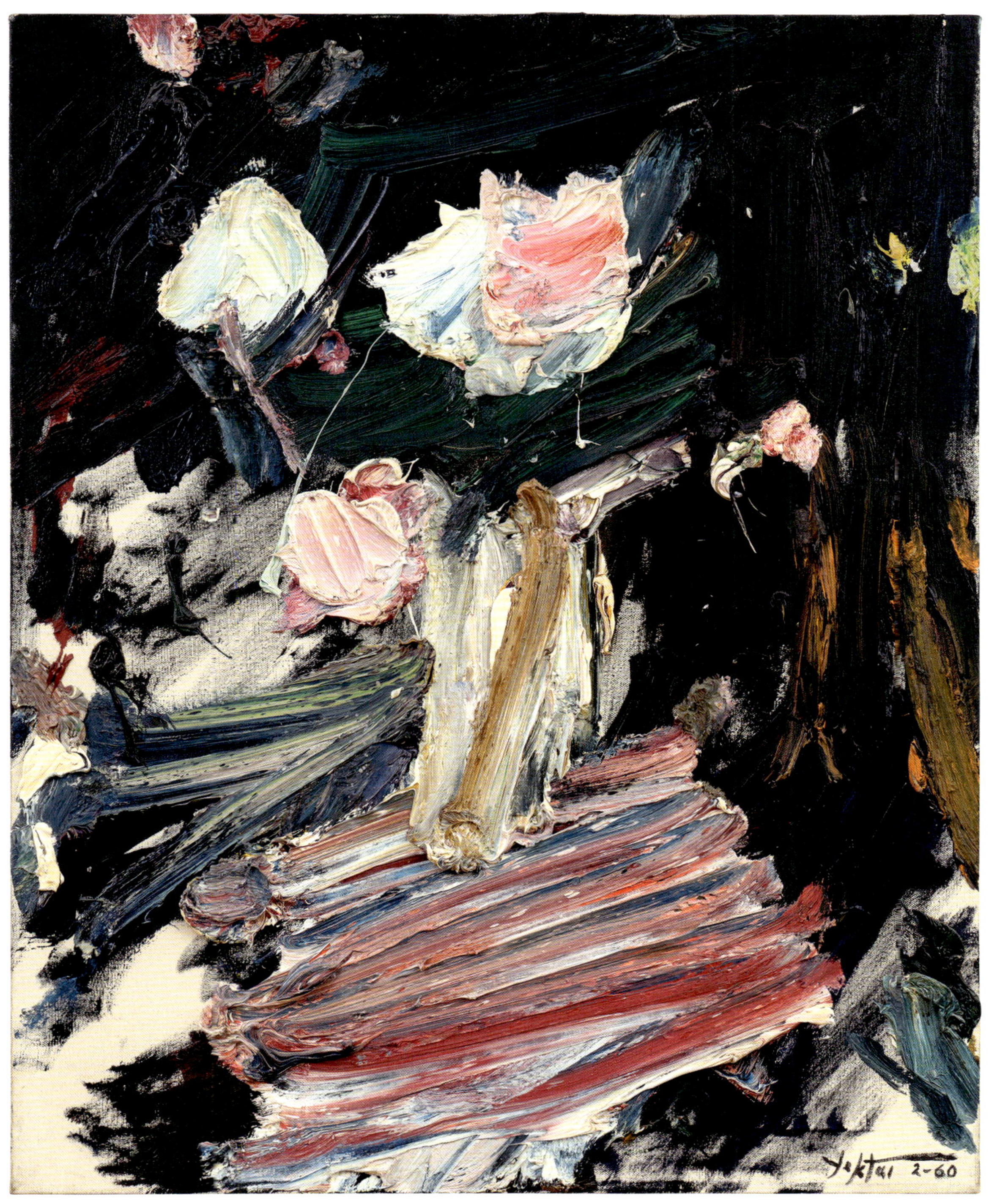

Untitled, 1960, oil on canvas, 30 × 24 inches (76.2 × 61 cm)

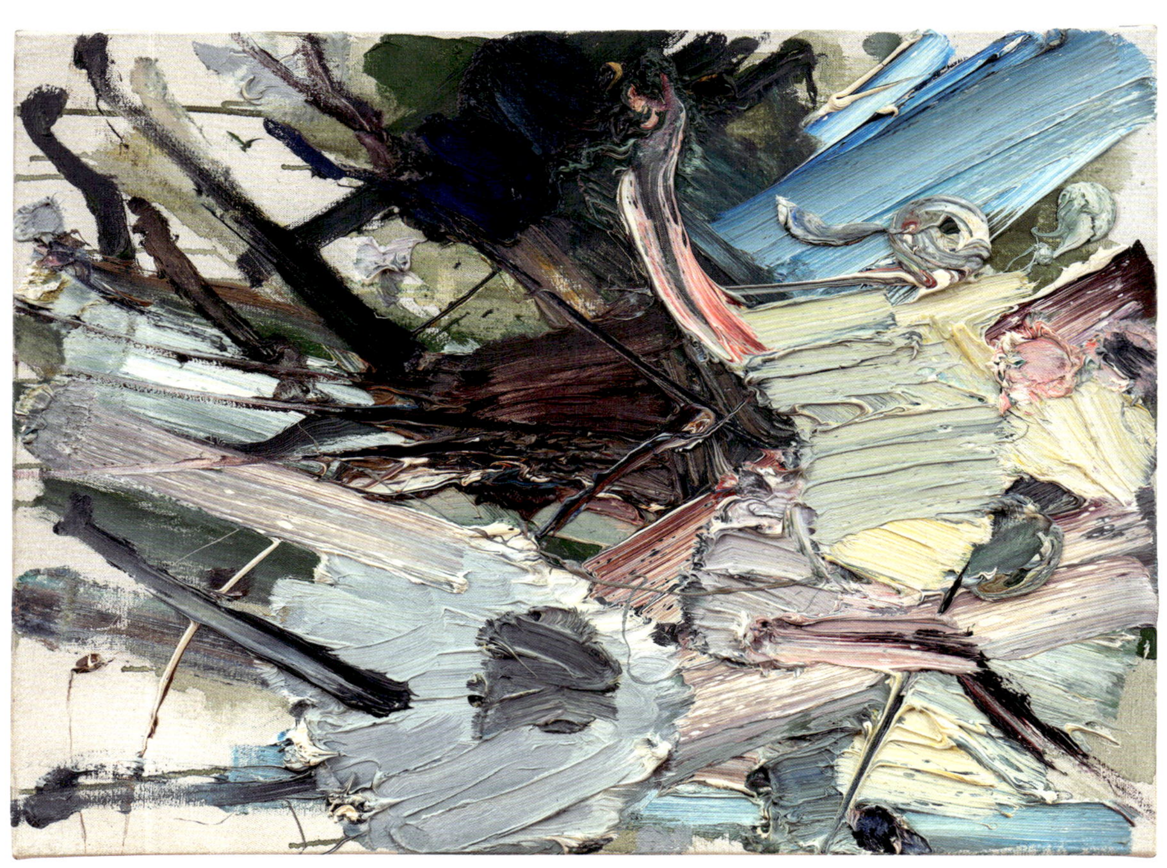

Untitled, 1960, oil on canvas, 24 × 18 inches (61 × 45.7 cm)

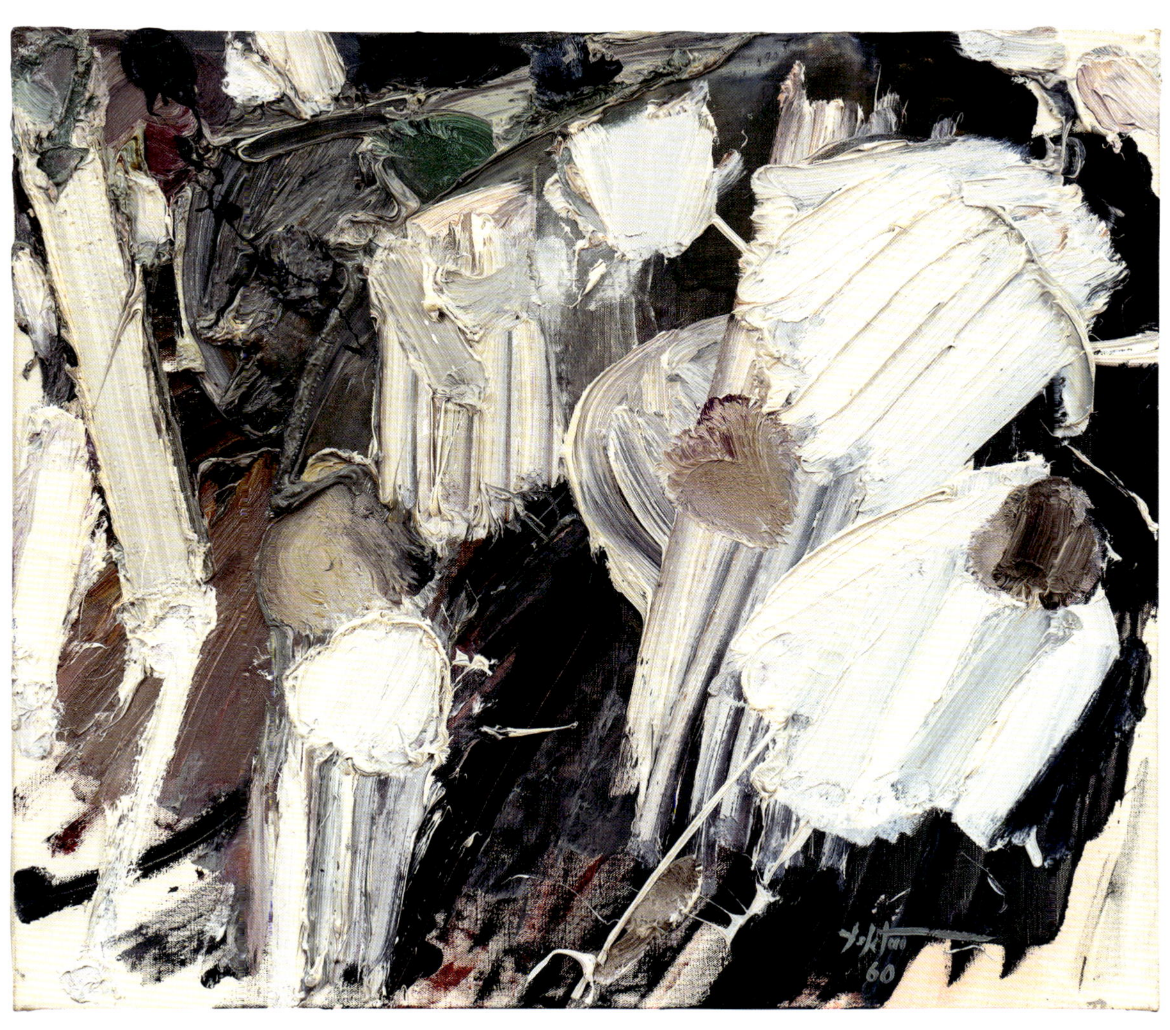

Untitled, 1960, oil on canvas, 22¾ × 26¼ inches (57.8 × 66.7 cm)

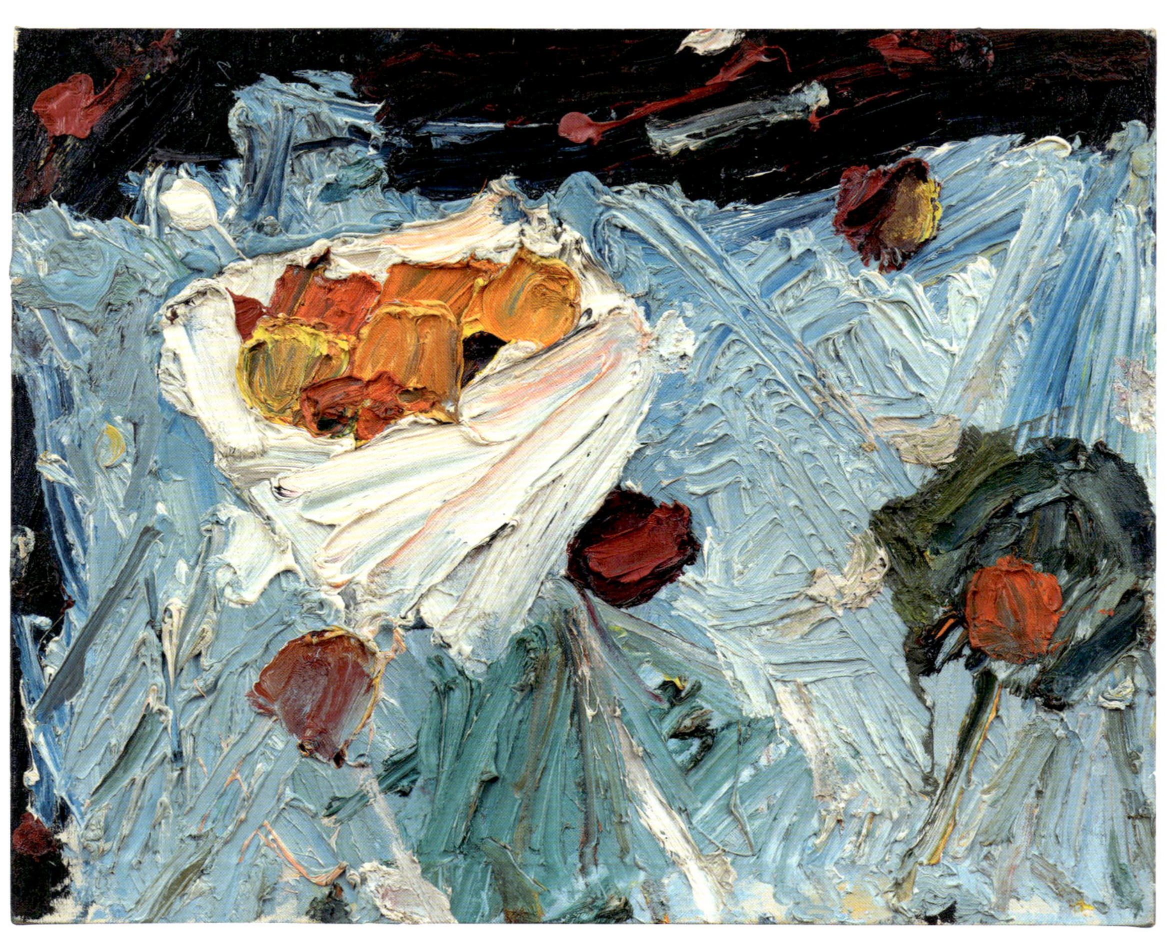

Blue Table, 1960, oil on canvas, 24 × 30 inches (61 × 76.2 cm)

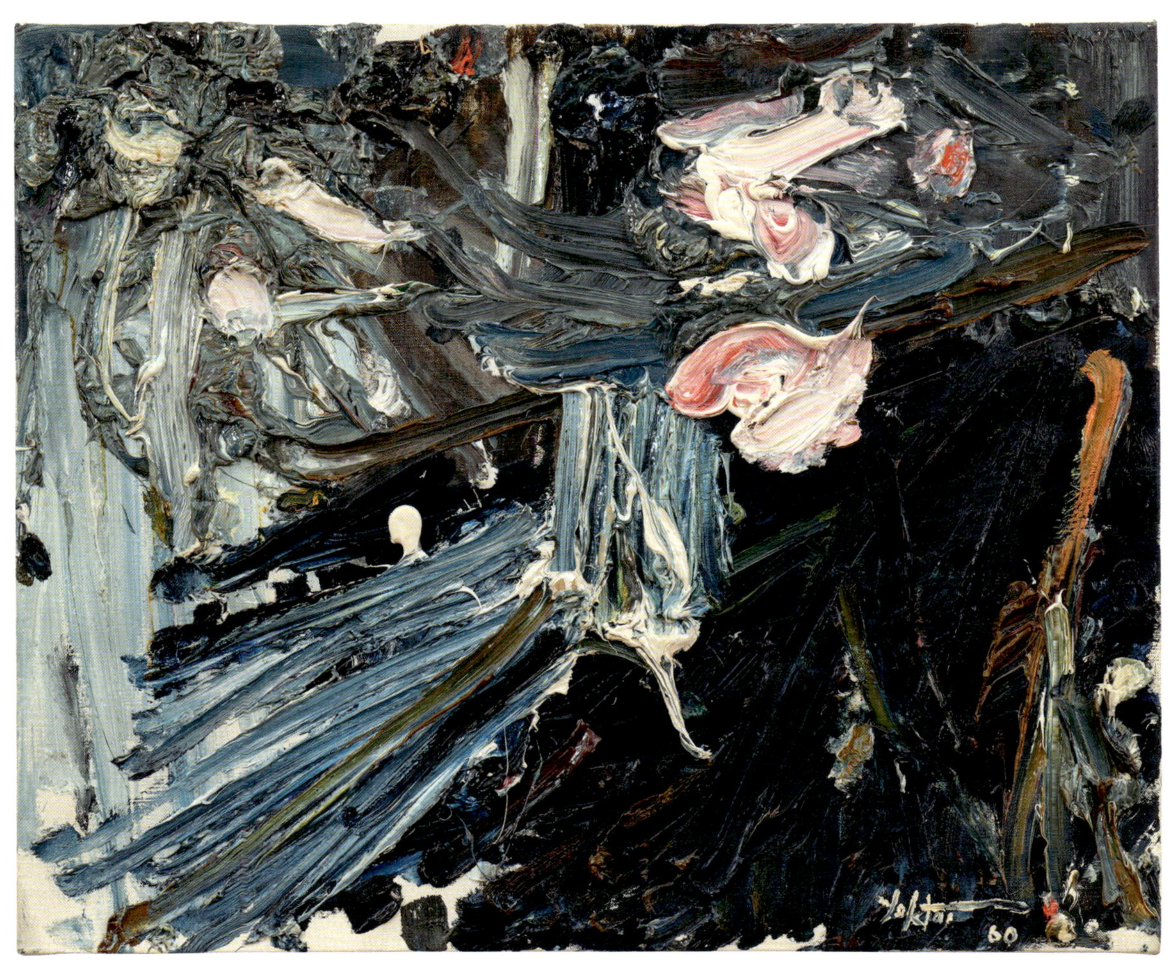

Untitled, 1960, oil on canvas, 21¼ × 25¾ inches (54 × 65.4 cm)

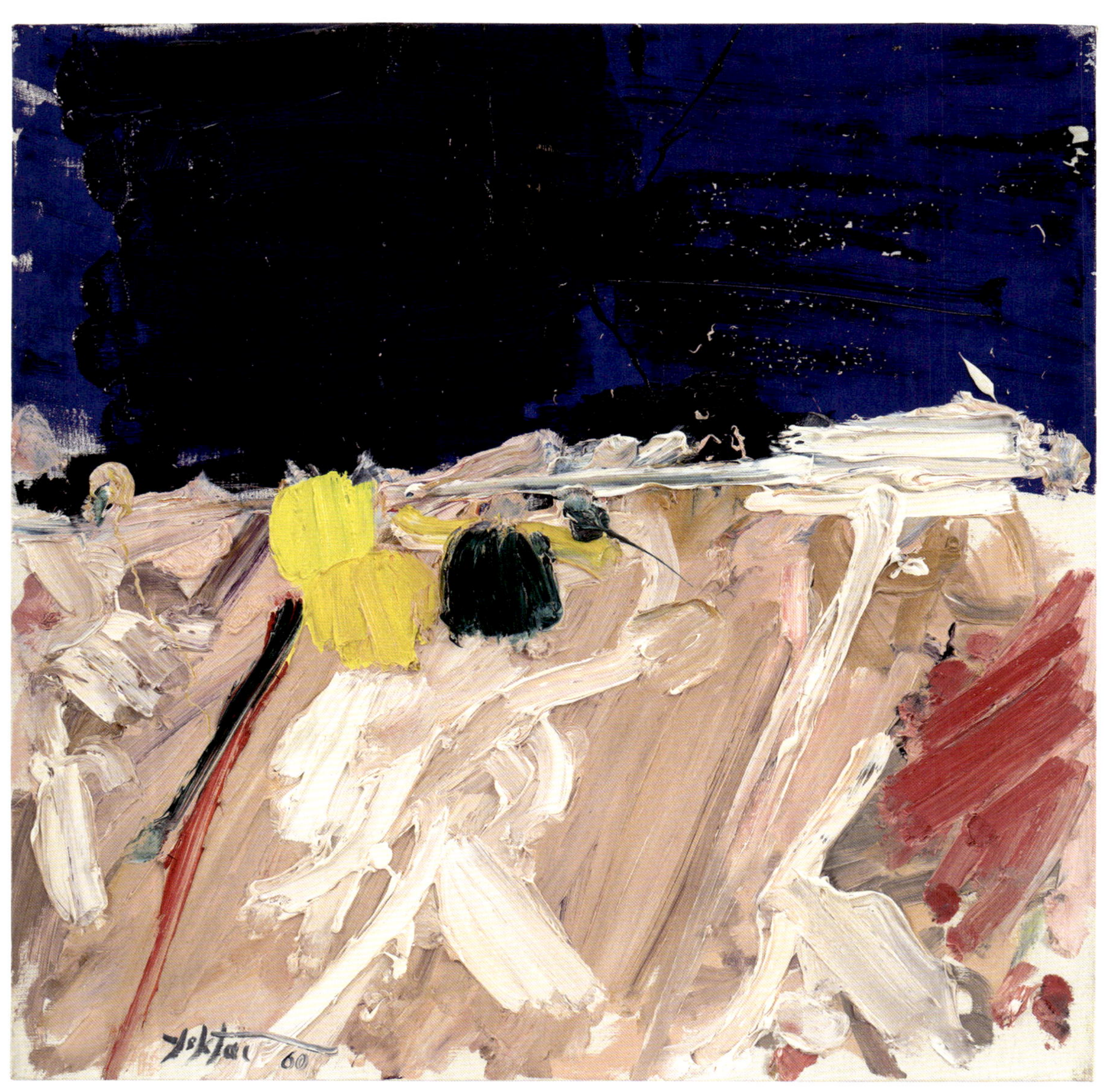

 Untitled, 1960, oil on canvas, 31½ × 31½ inches (80 × 80 cm)

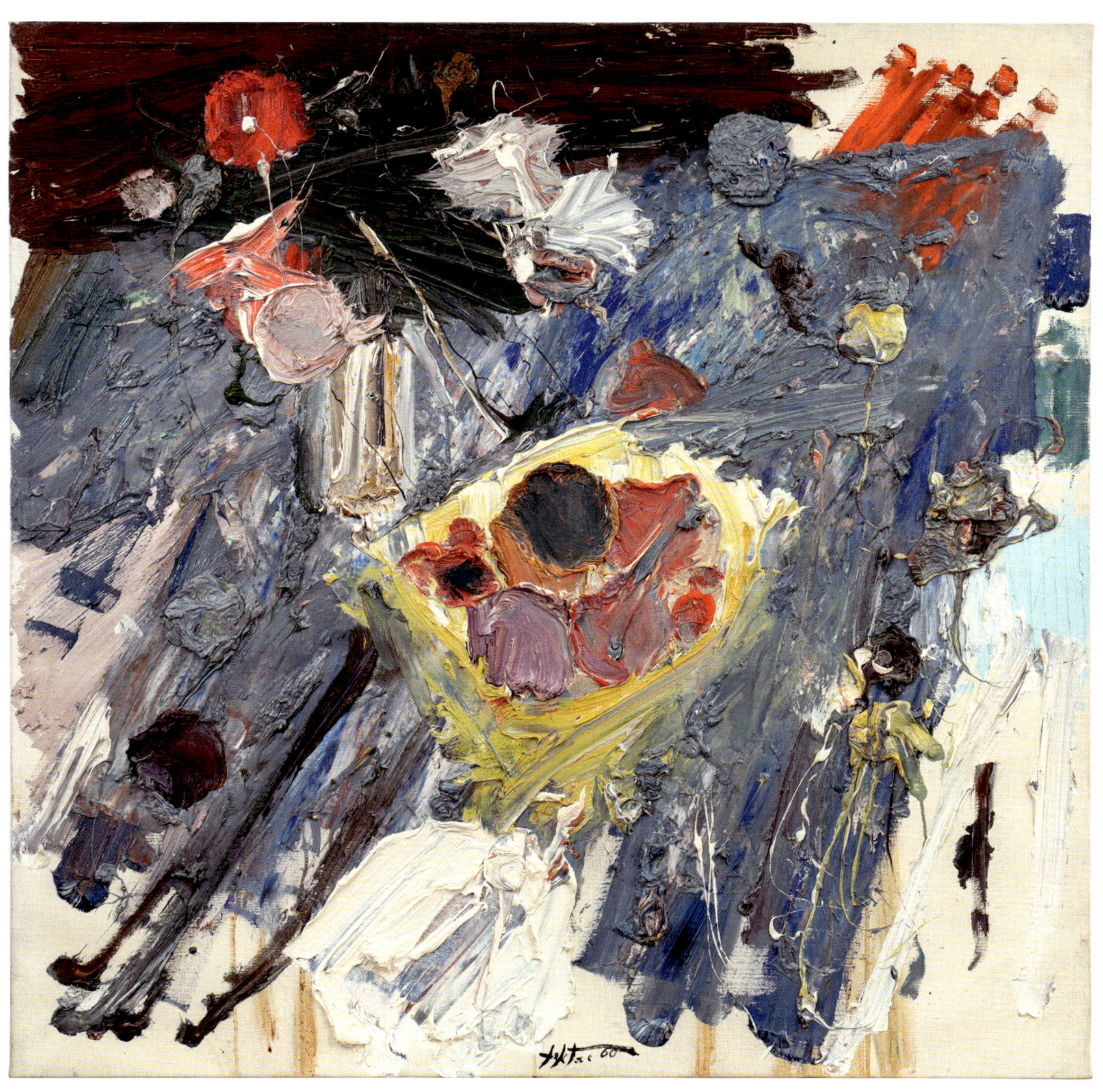

Untitled, 1960, oil on canvas, 39¼ × 39¼ inches (99.7 × 99.7 cm)

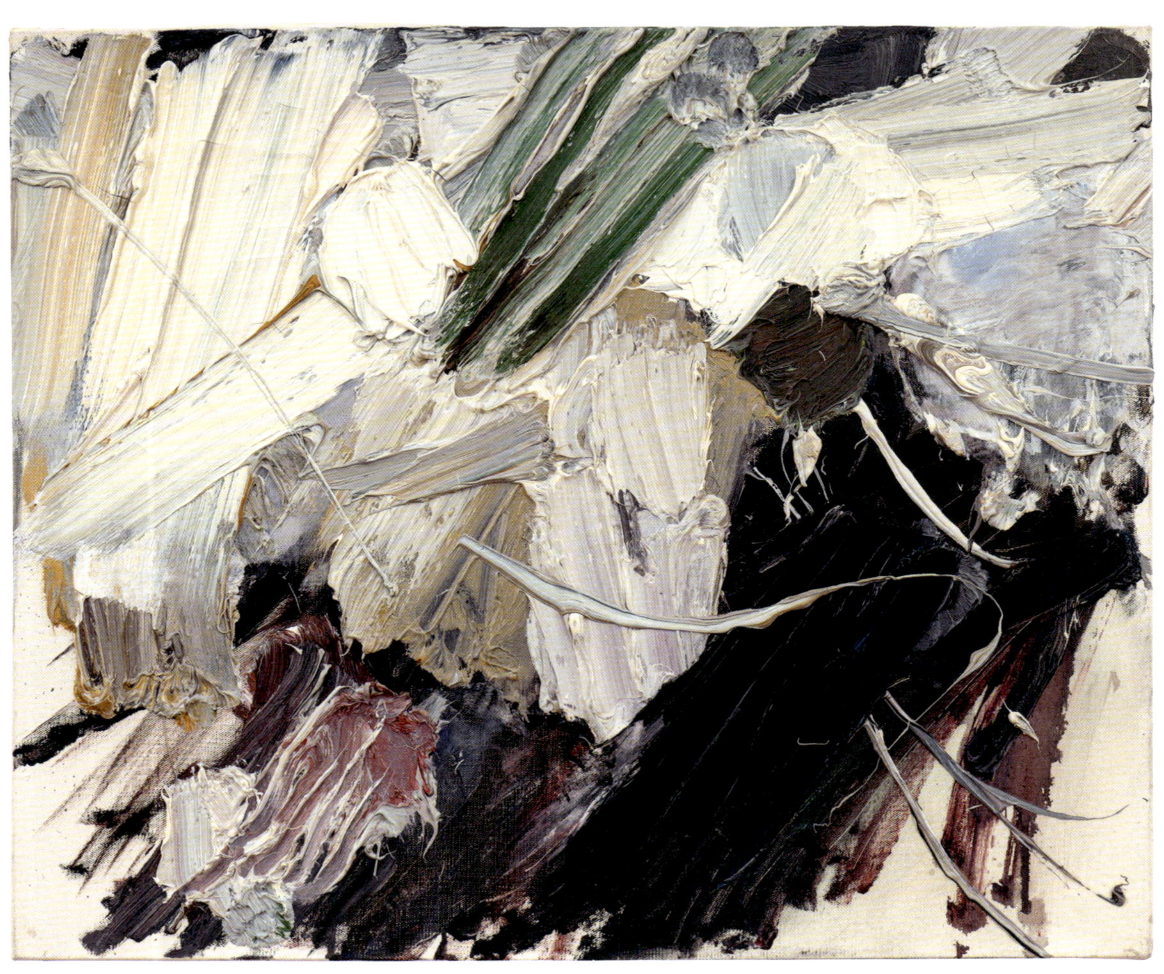

 Untitled, 1960, oil on canvas, 21¼ × 25¾ inches (54 × 65.4 cm)

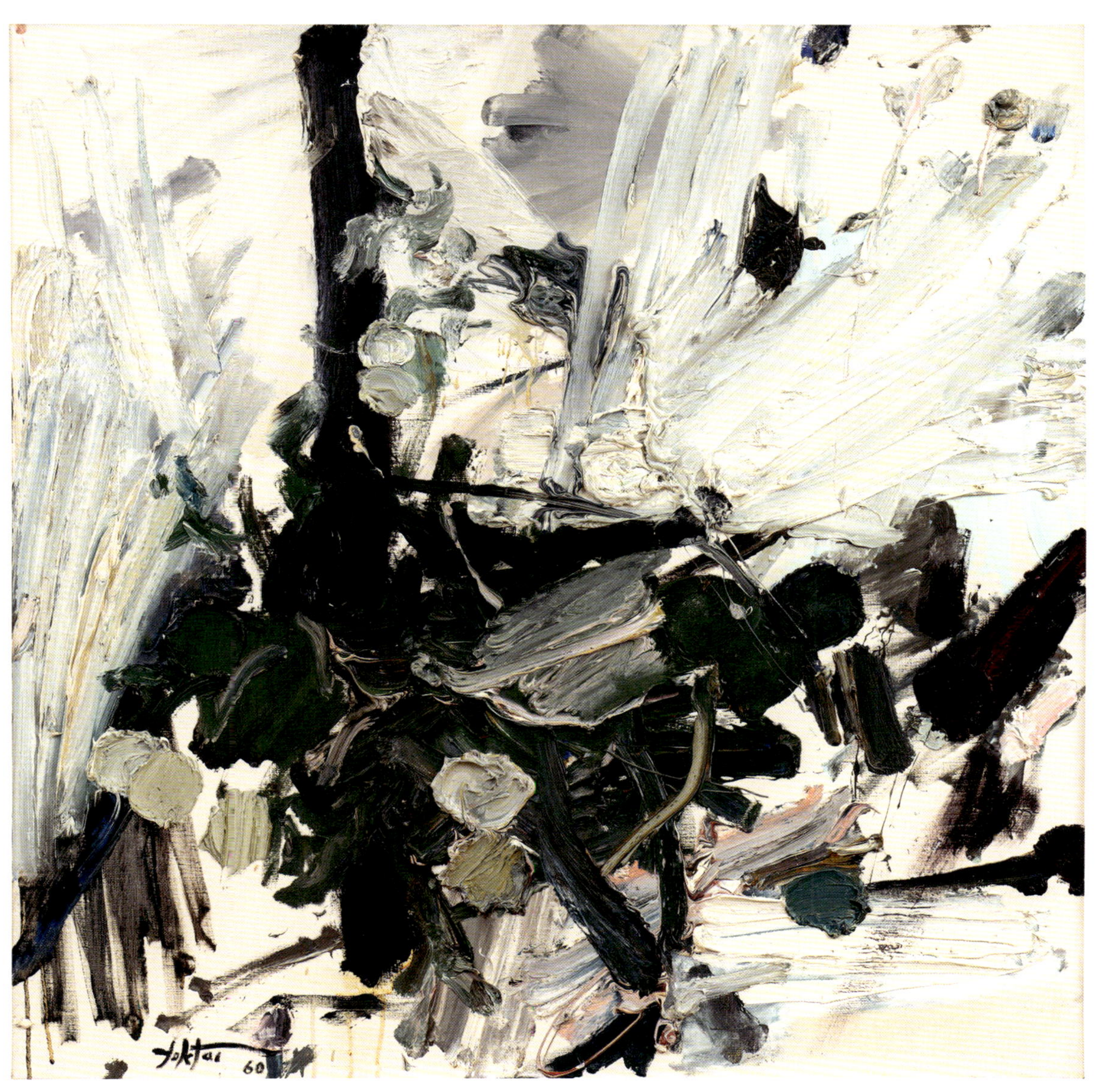

Untitled, 1960, oil on canvas, 39¼ × 39¼ inches (99.7 × 99.7 cm)

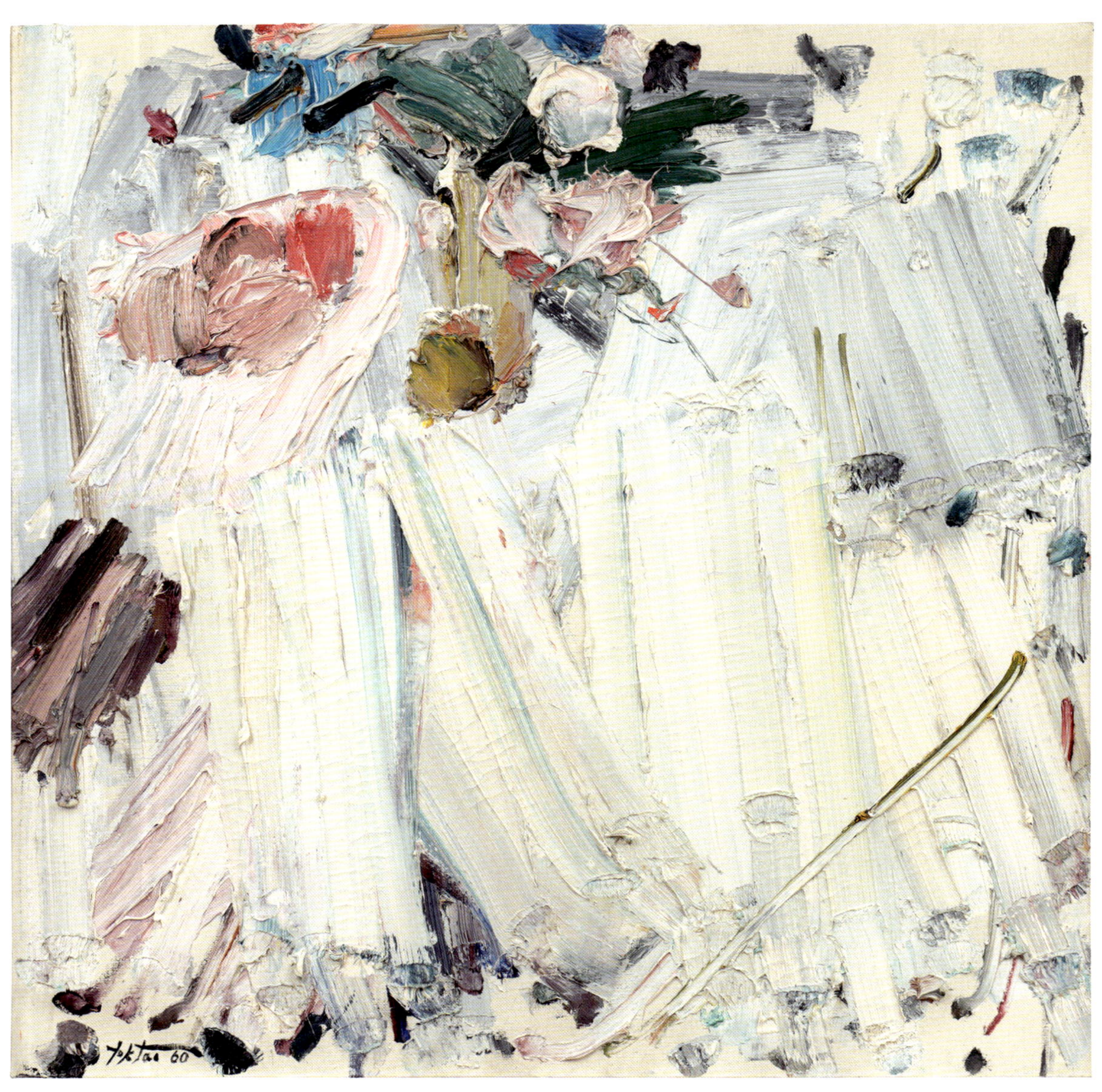

Nature Morte, 1960, oil on canvas, 39¼ × 39¼ inches (99.7 × 99.7 cm)

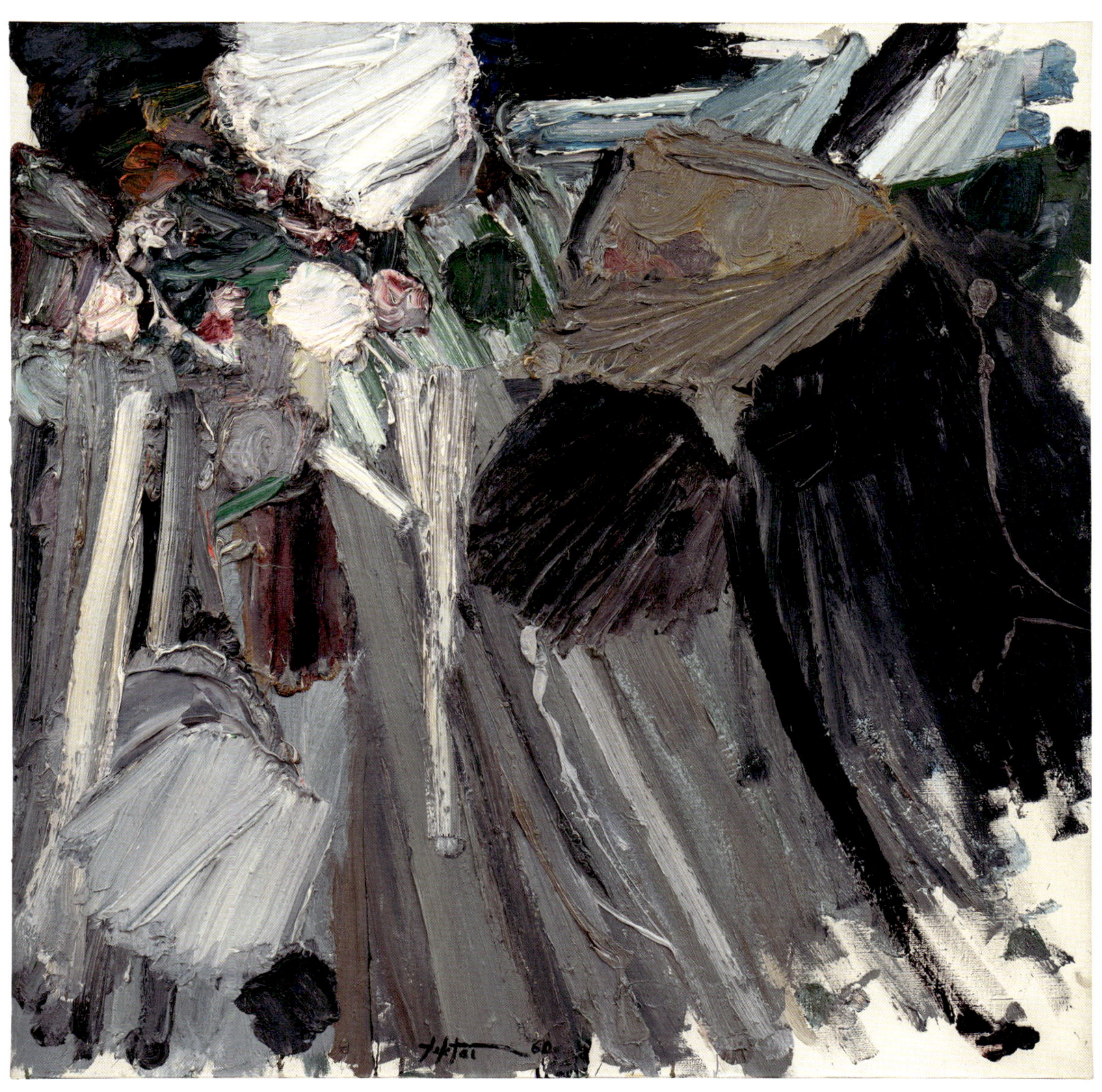

Nature Morte, 1960, oil on canvas, 39¼ × 39¼ inches (99.7 × 99.7 cm)

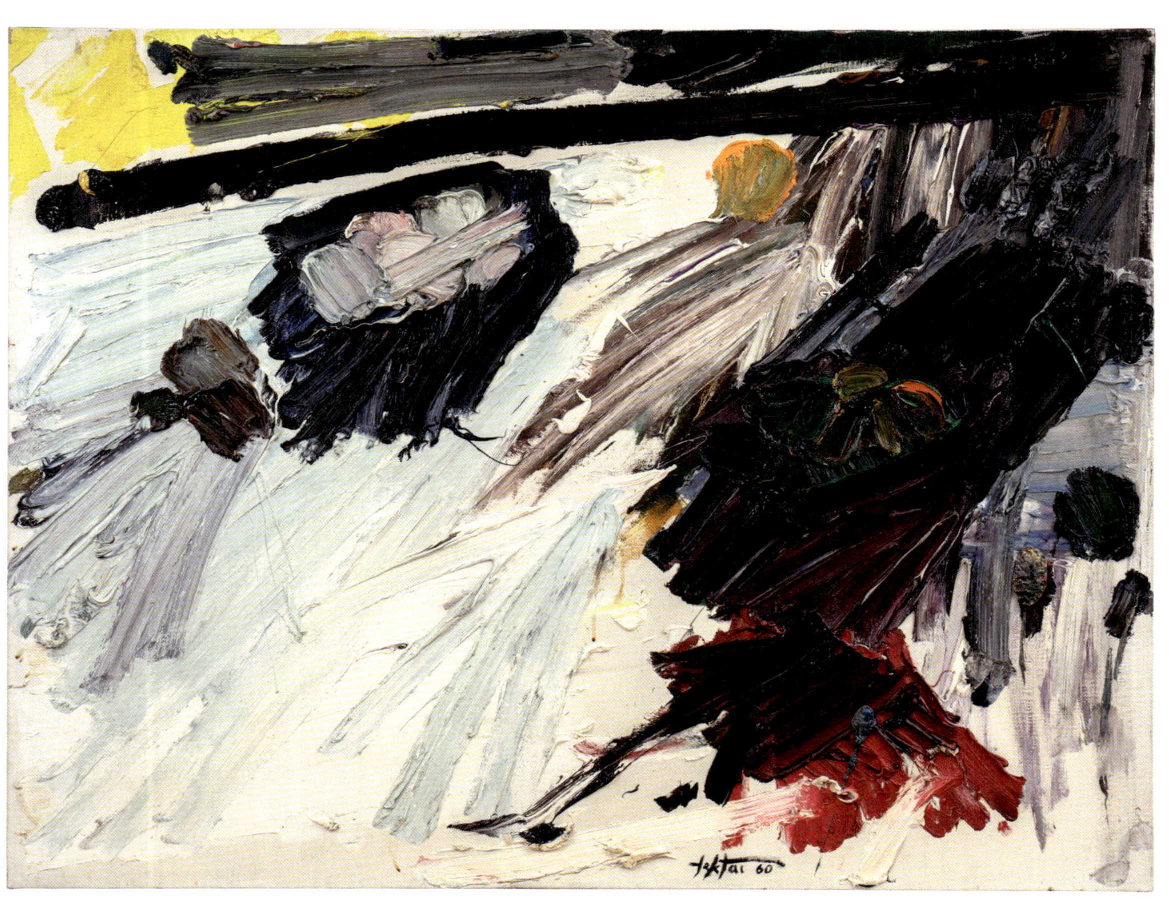

 Untitled, 1960, oil on canvas, 35 × 45½ inches (88.9 × 115.6 cm)

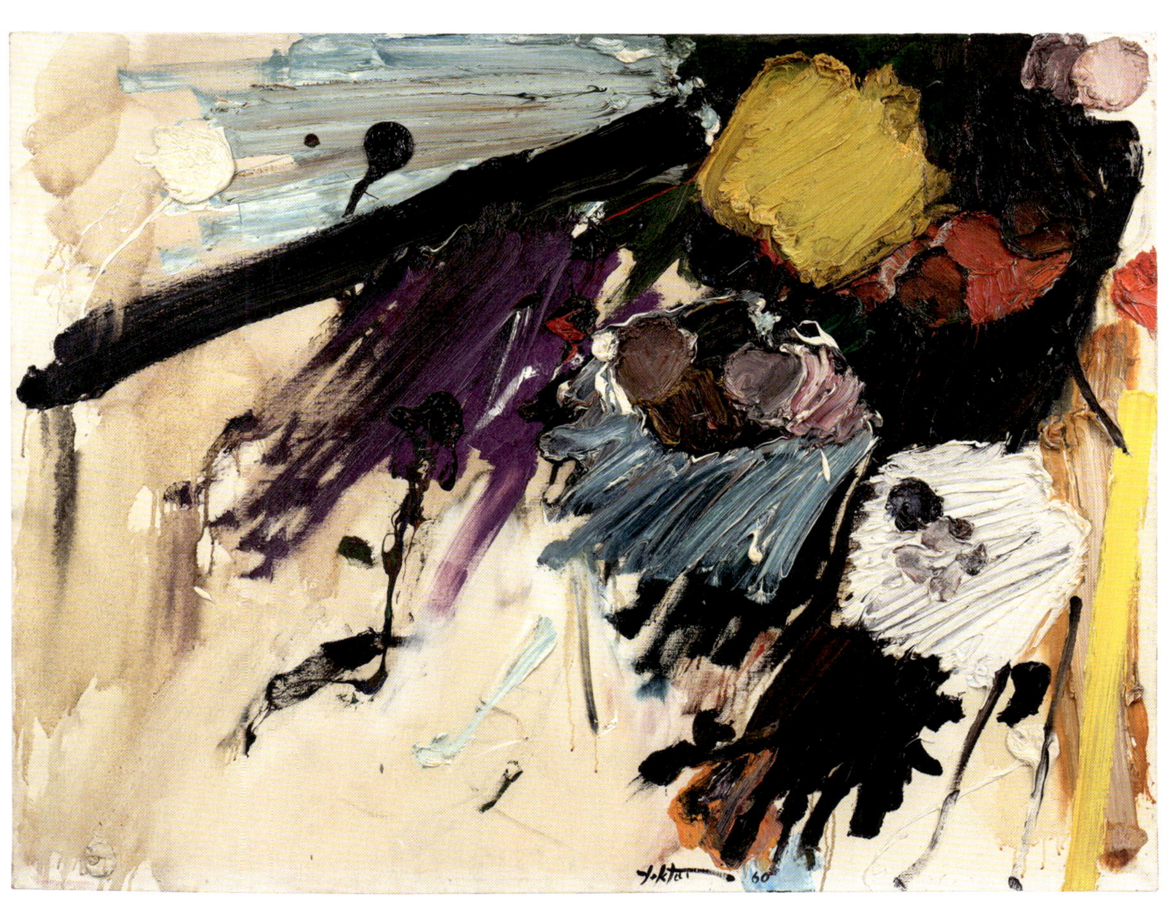

Untitled, 1960, oil on canvas, 35 × 45½ inches (88.9 × 115.6 cm)

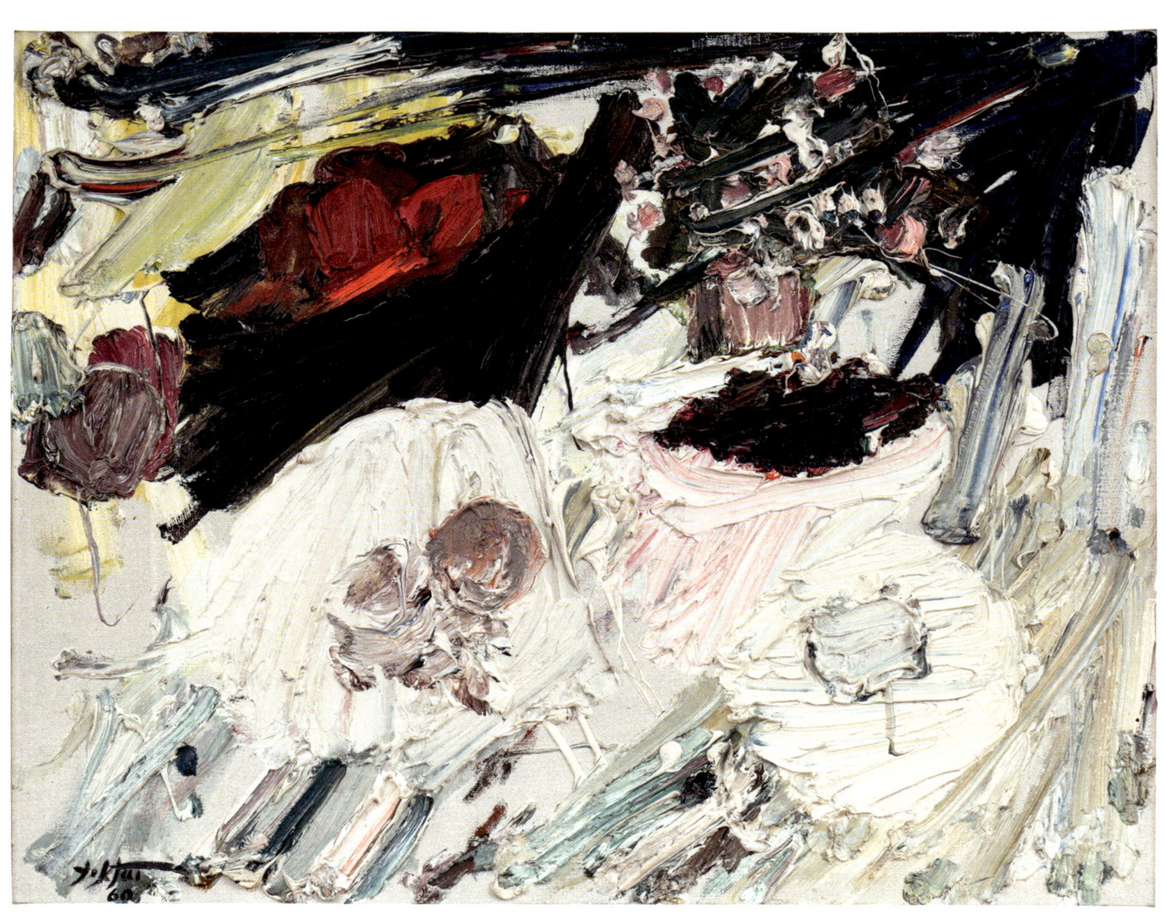

 Untitled, 1960, oil on canvas, 28 × 36 inches (71.1 × 91.4 cm)

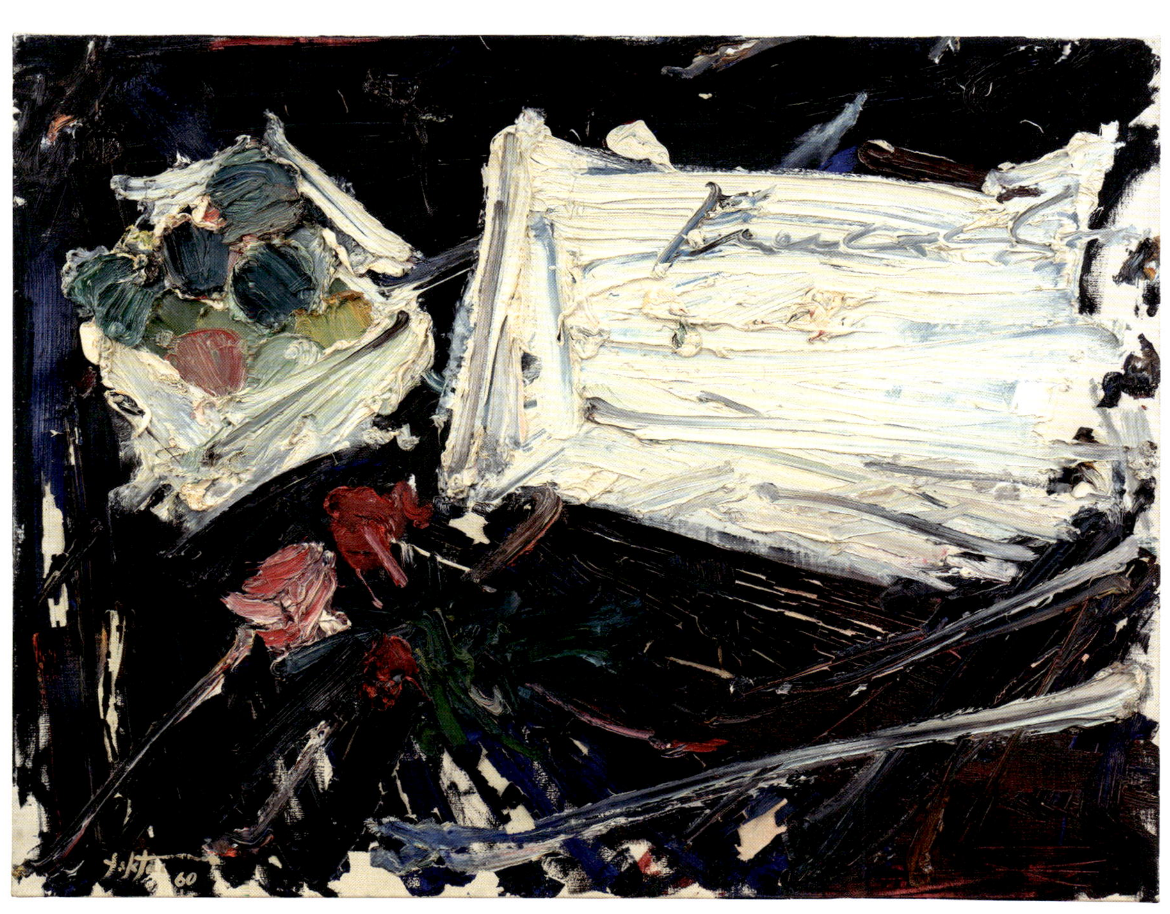

Untitled, 1960, oil on canvas, 35 × 45½ inches (88.9 × 115.6 cm)

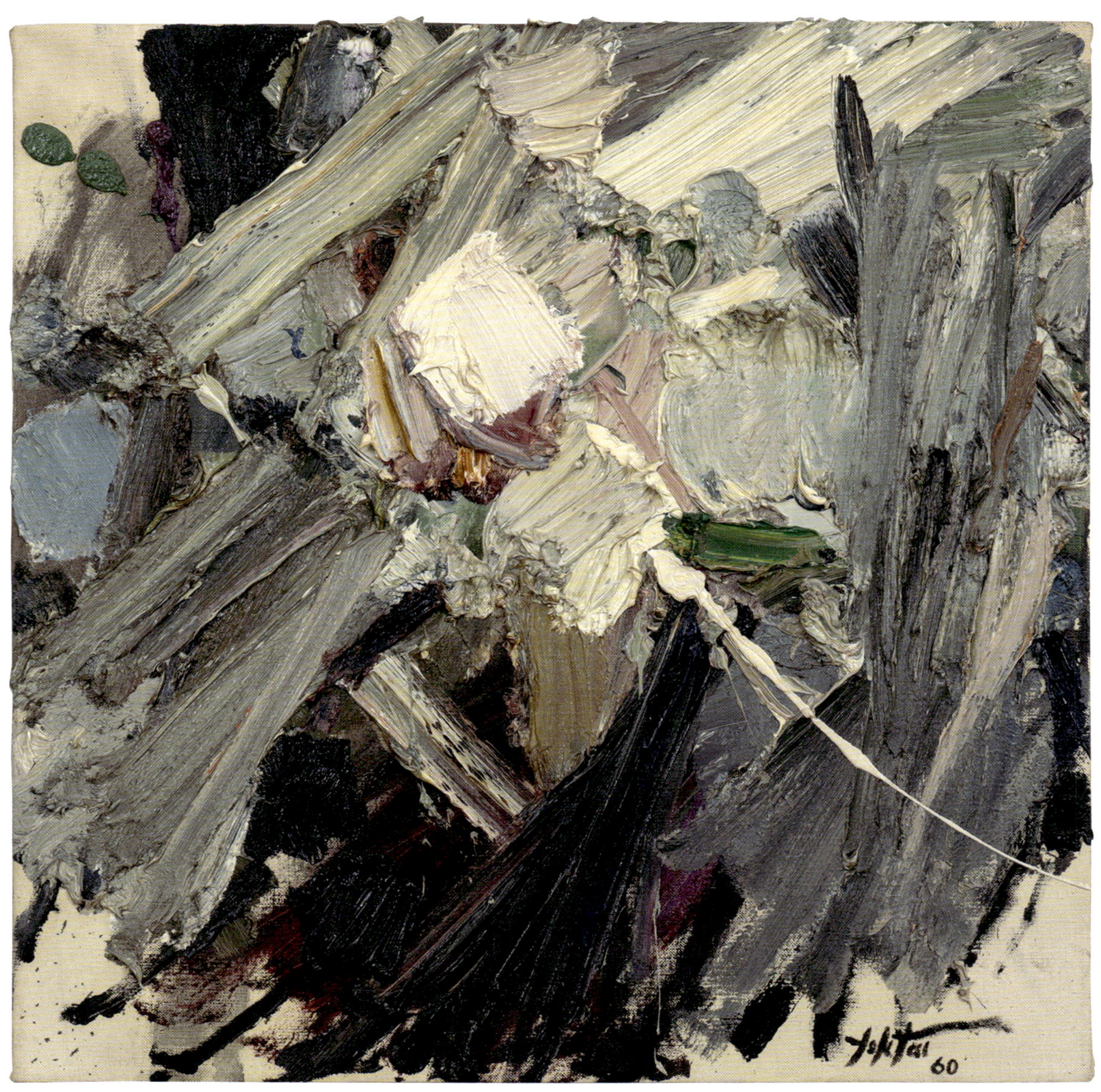

Untitled, 1960, oil on canvas, 24 × 24 inches (61 × 61 cm)

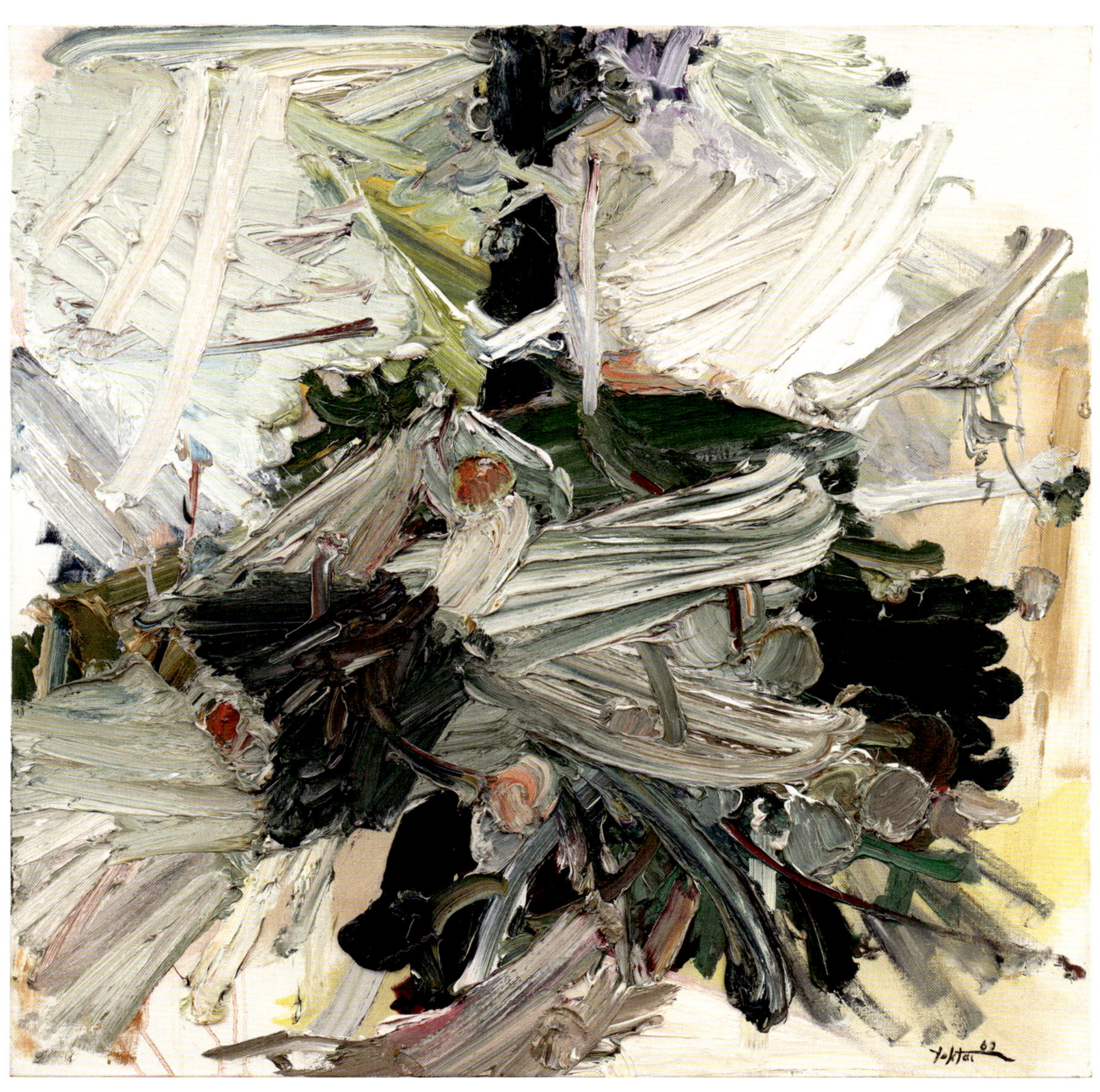

Untitled, 1960, oil on canvas, 39¼ × 39¼ inches (99.7 × 99.7 cm)

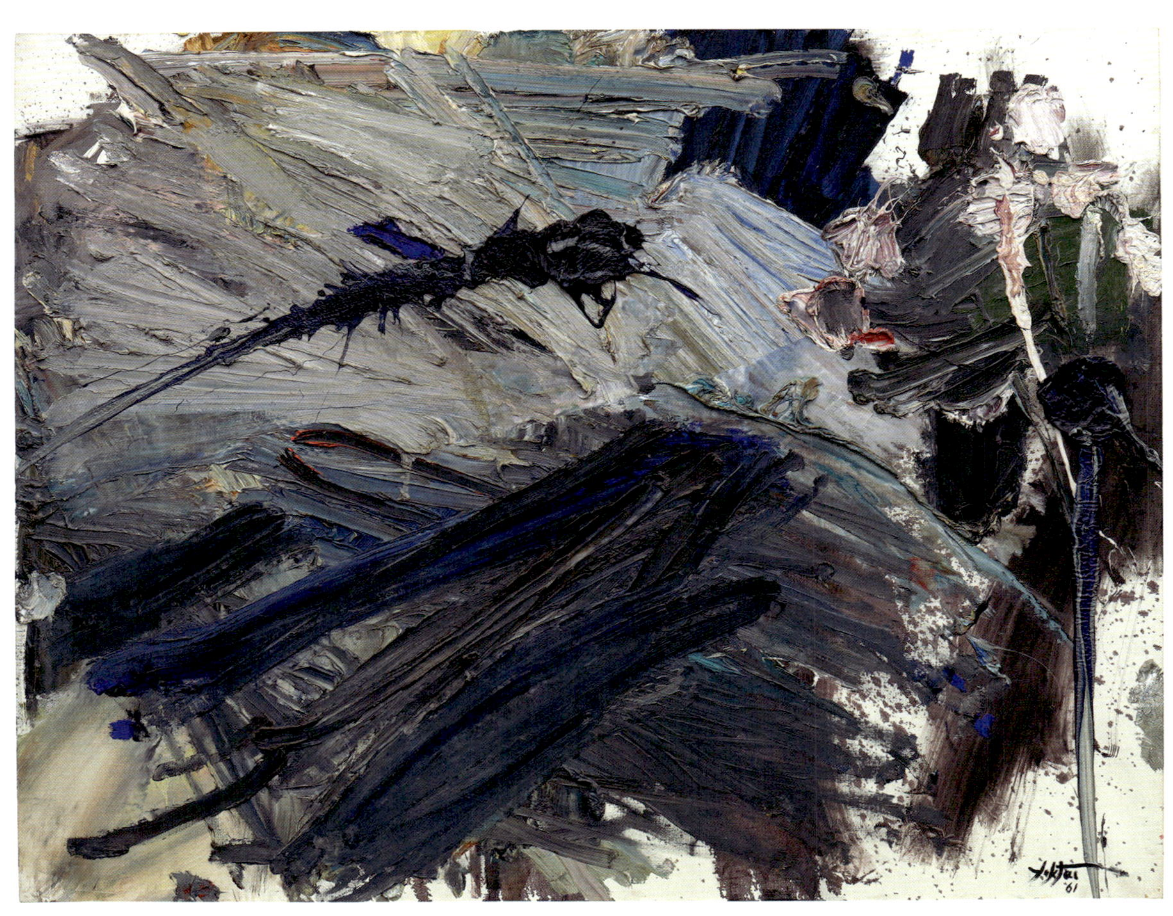

 Untitled, 1961, oil on canvas, 44½ × 57½ inches (113 × 146.1 cm)

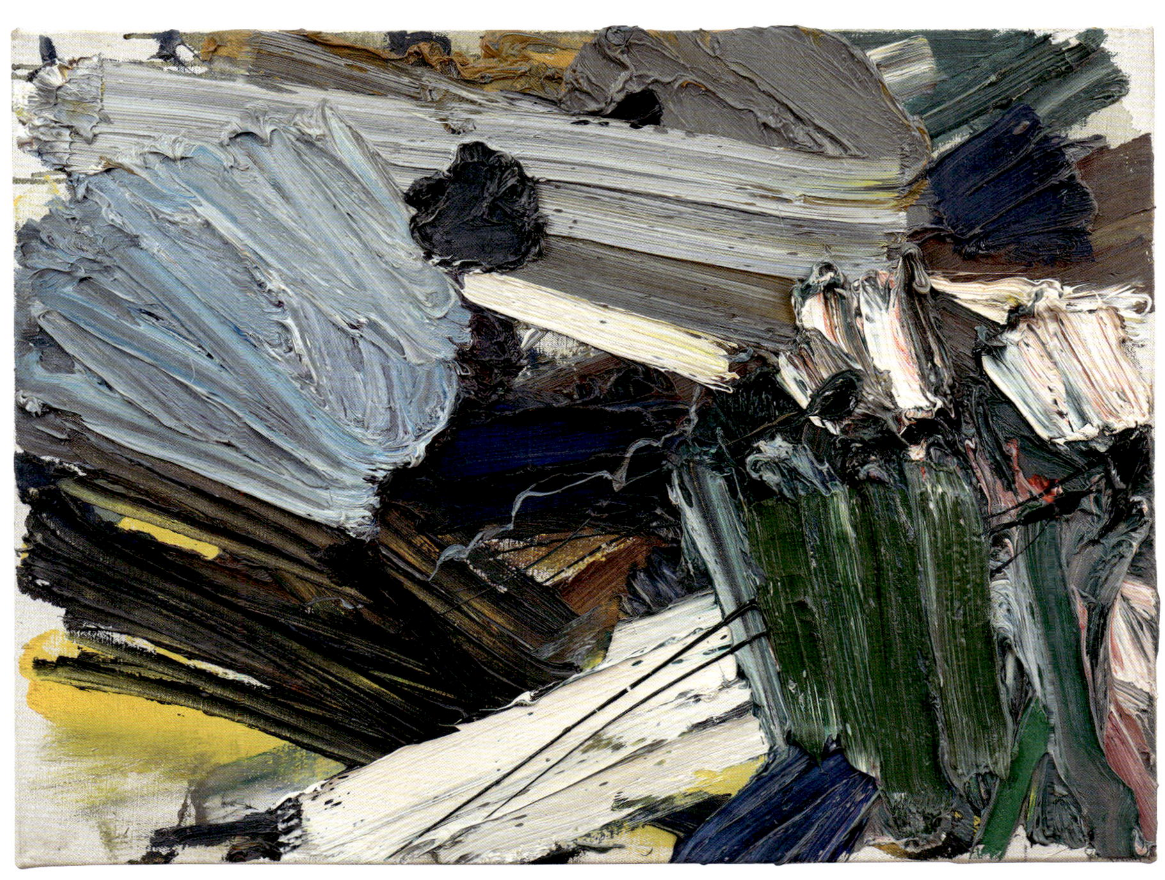

Untitled, ca. 1960, oil on canvas, 18 × 24 inches (45.7 × 61 cm)

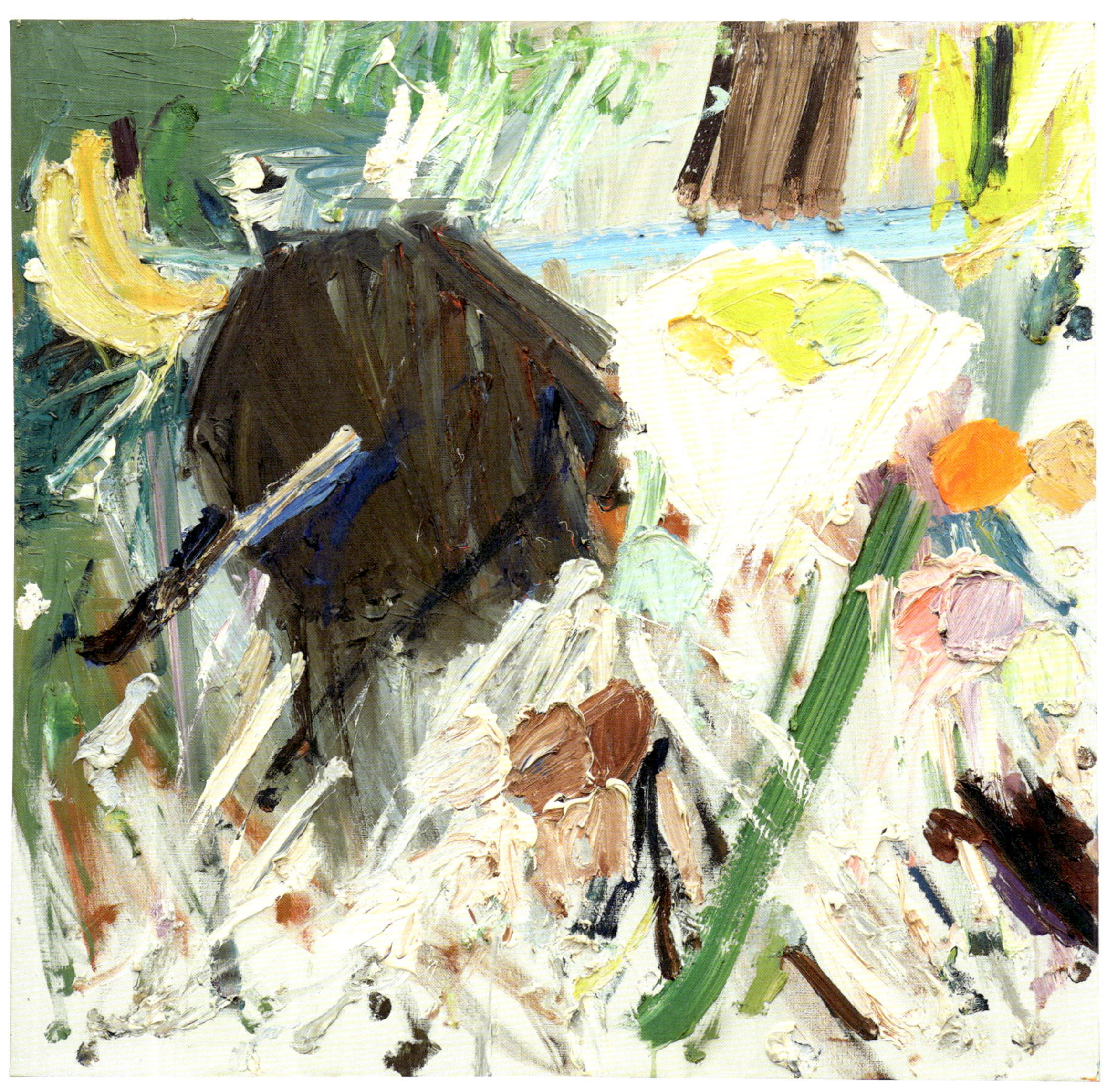

 Untitled, 1961, oil on canvas, 42 × 42 inches (107 × 107 cm)

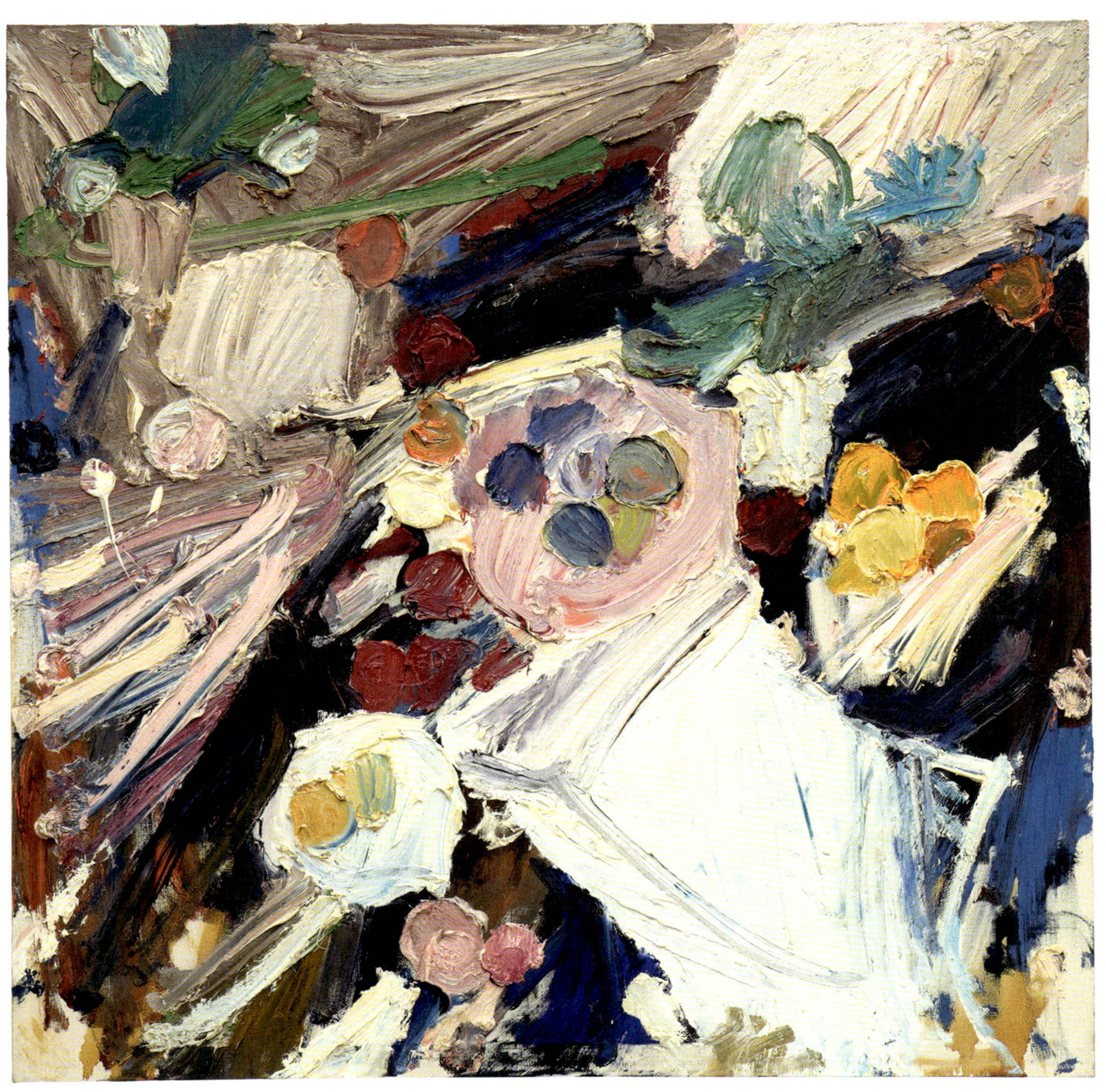

Untitled, 1961, oil on canvas, 48 × 48 inches (122 × 122 cm)

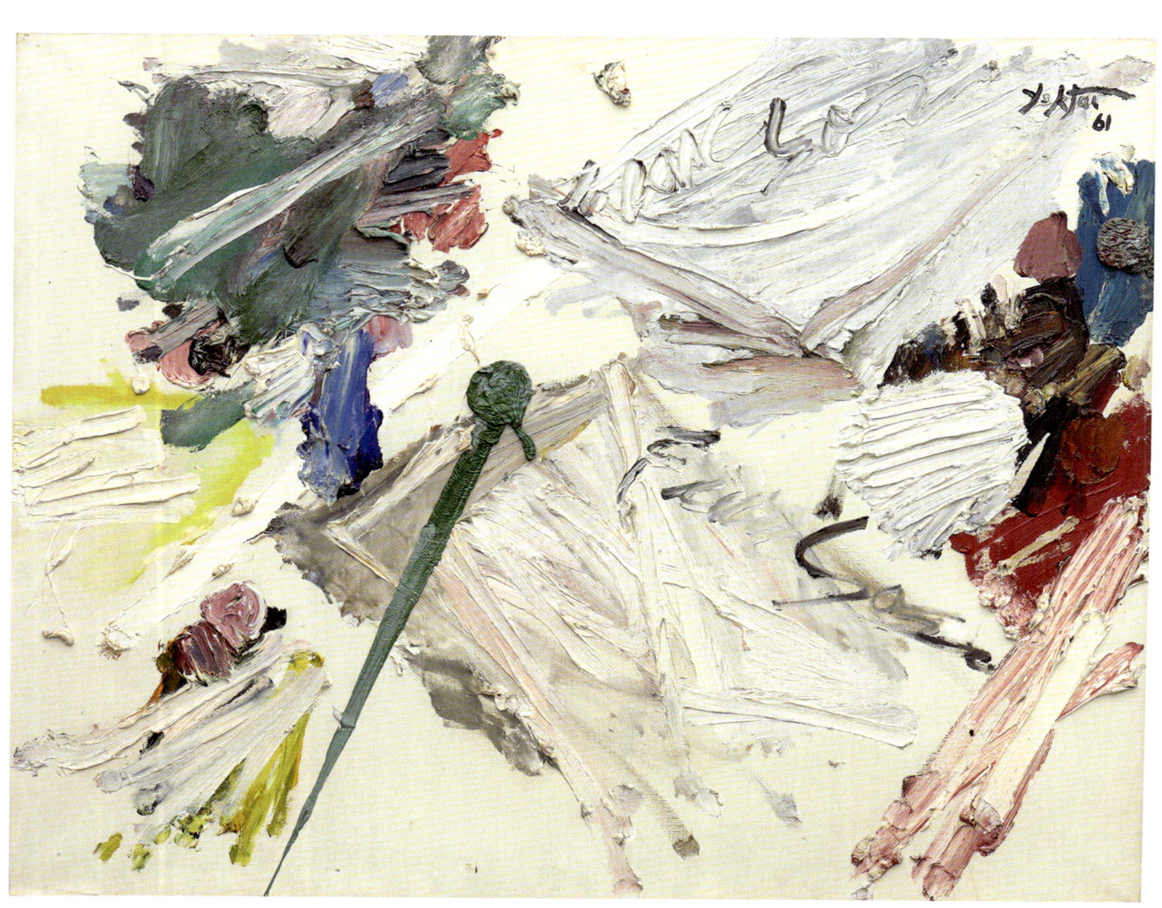

Untitled, 1961, oil on canvas, 45 × 57½ inches (114.3 × 146.1 cm)

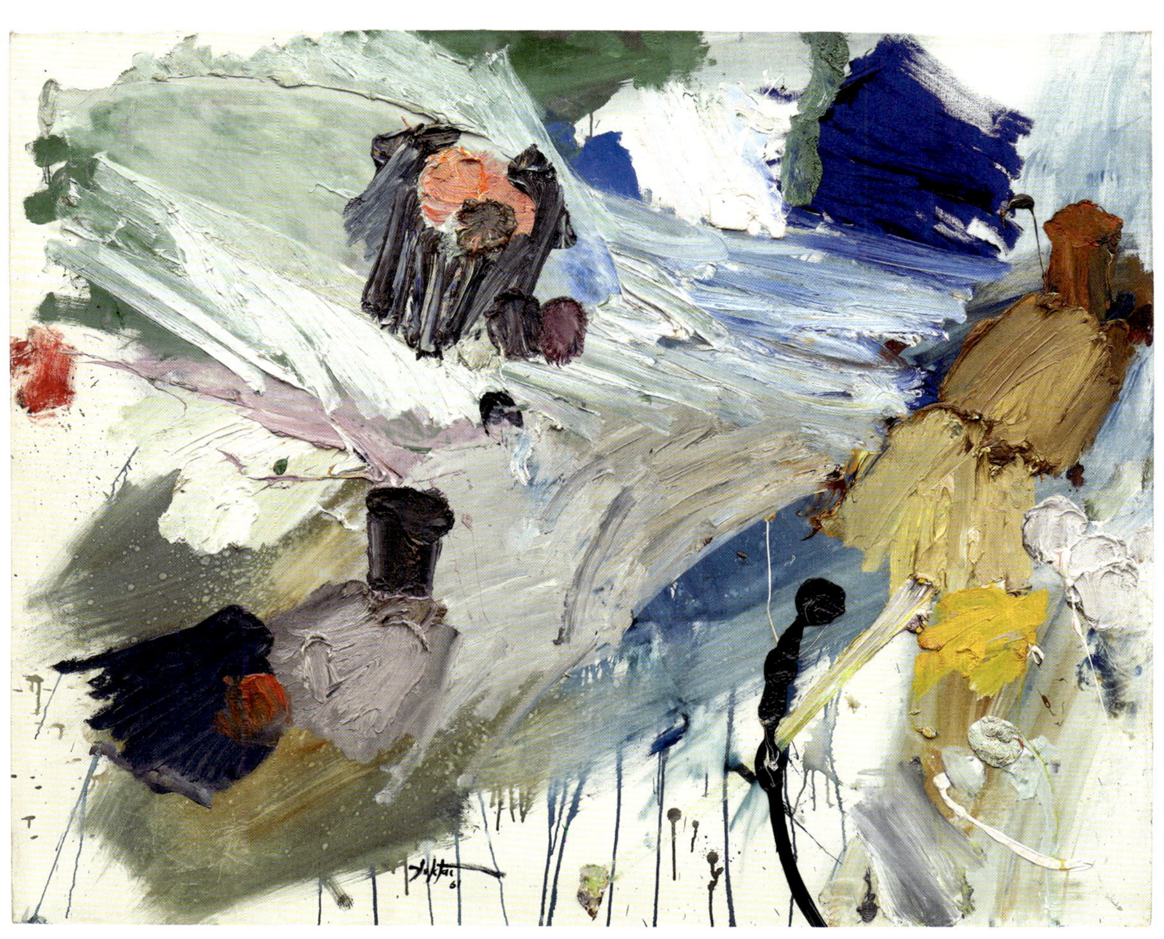

Untitled, 1961, oil on canvas, 51⅛ × 63¾ inches (130 × 162 cm)

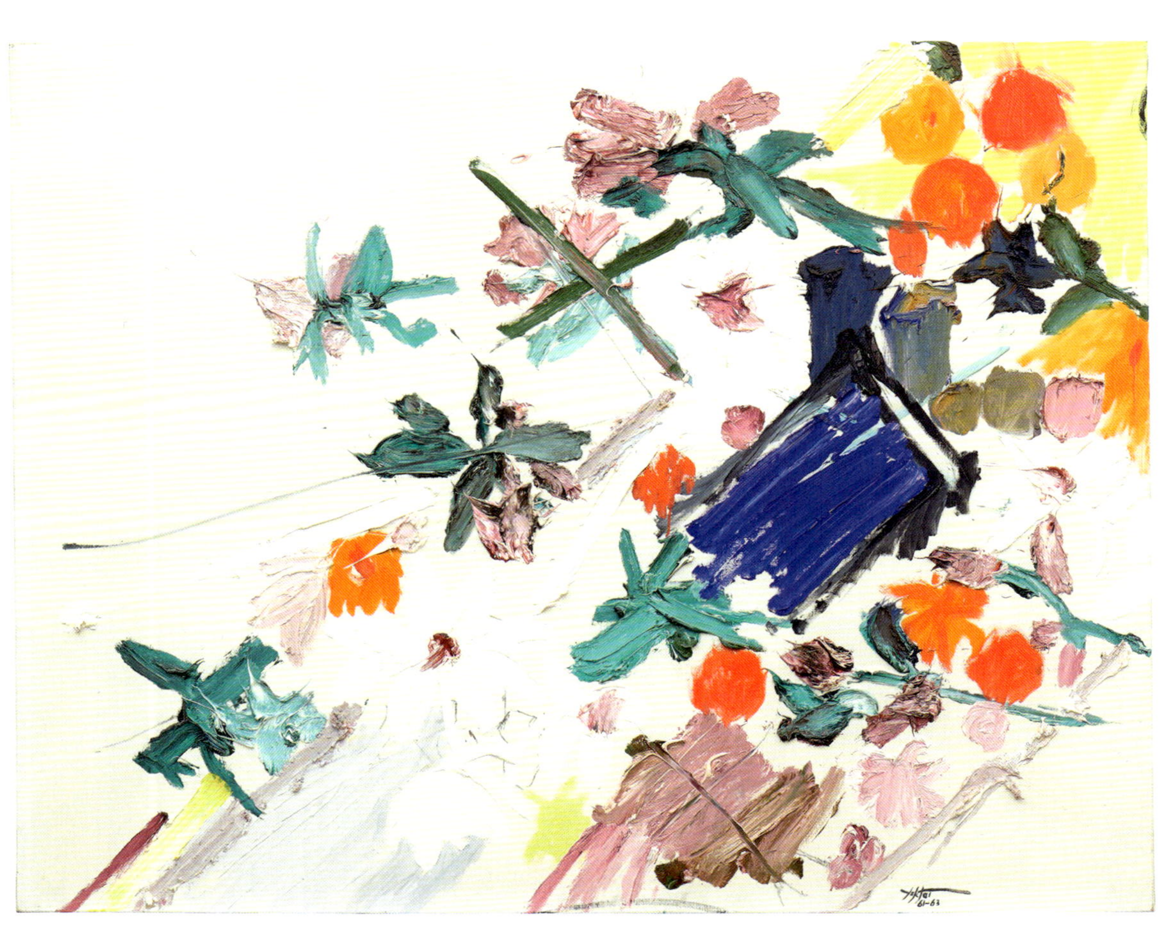

Untitled, 1961–63, oil on canvas, 45 × 57 inches (114 × 145 cm)

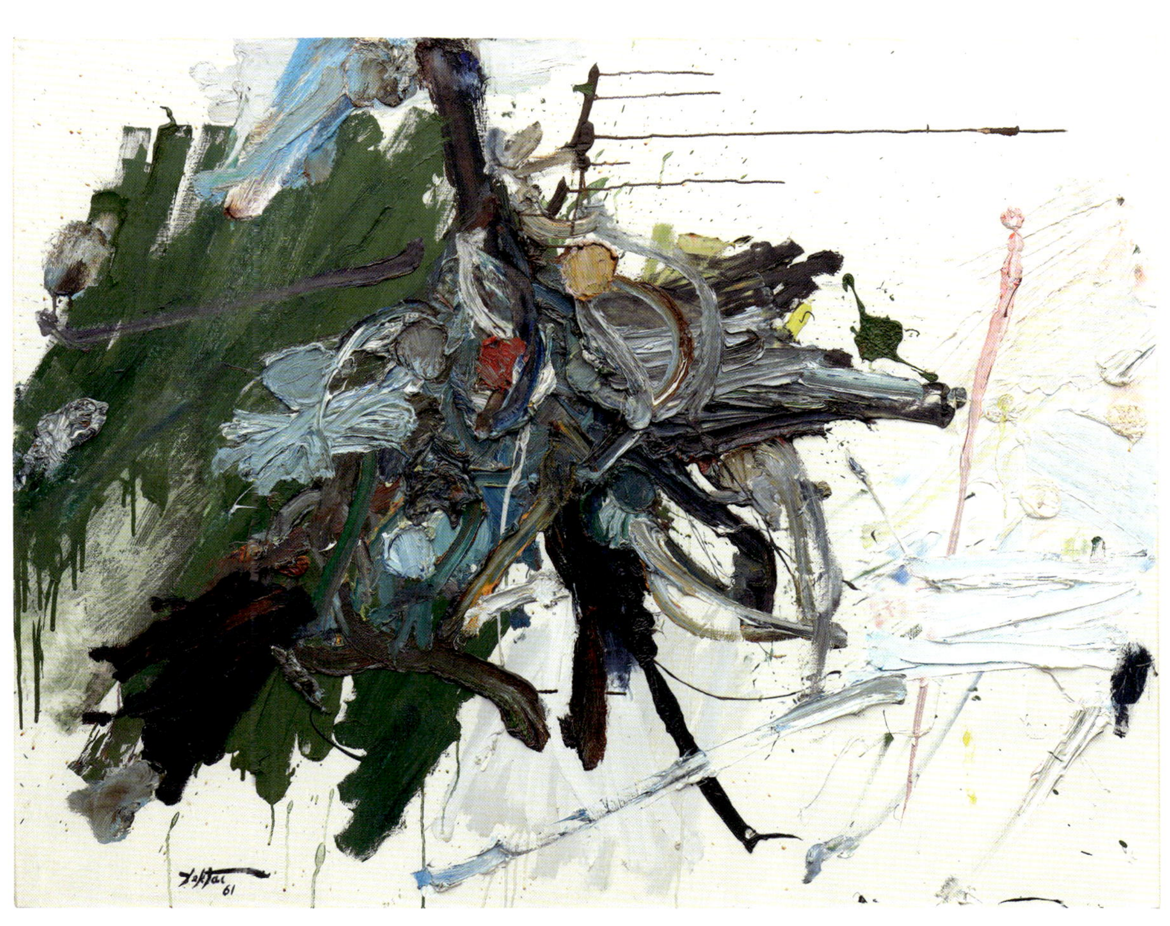

Untitled, 1961, oil on canvas, 44½ × 57 inches (113 × 144.8 cm)

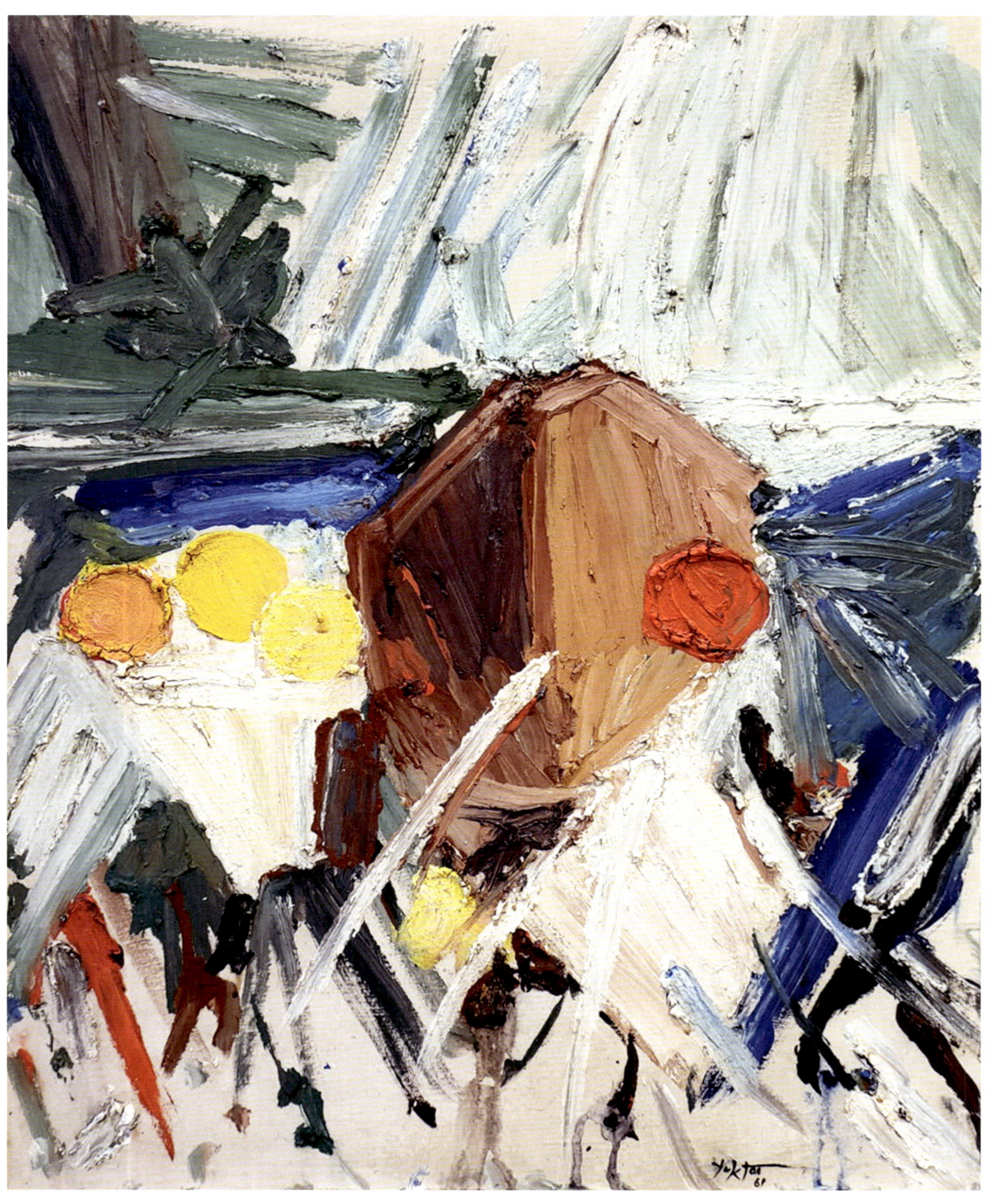

 Composition, 1961, oil on canvas, 31⅞ × 25⅝ inches (81 × 65.1 cm)

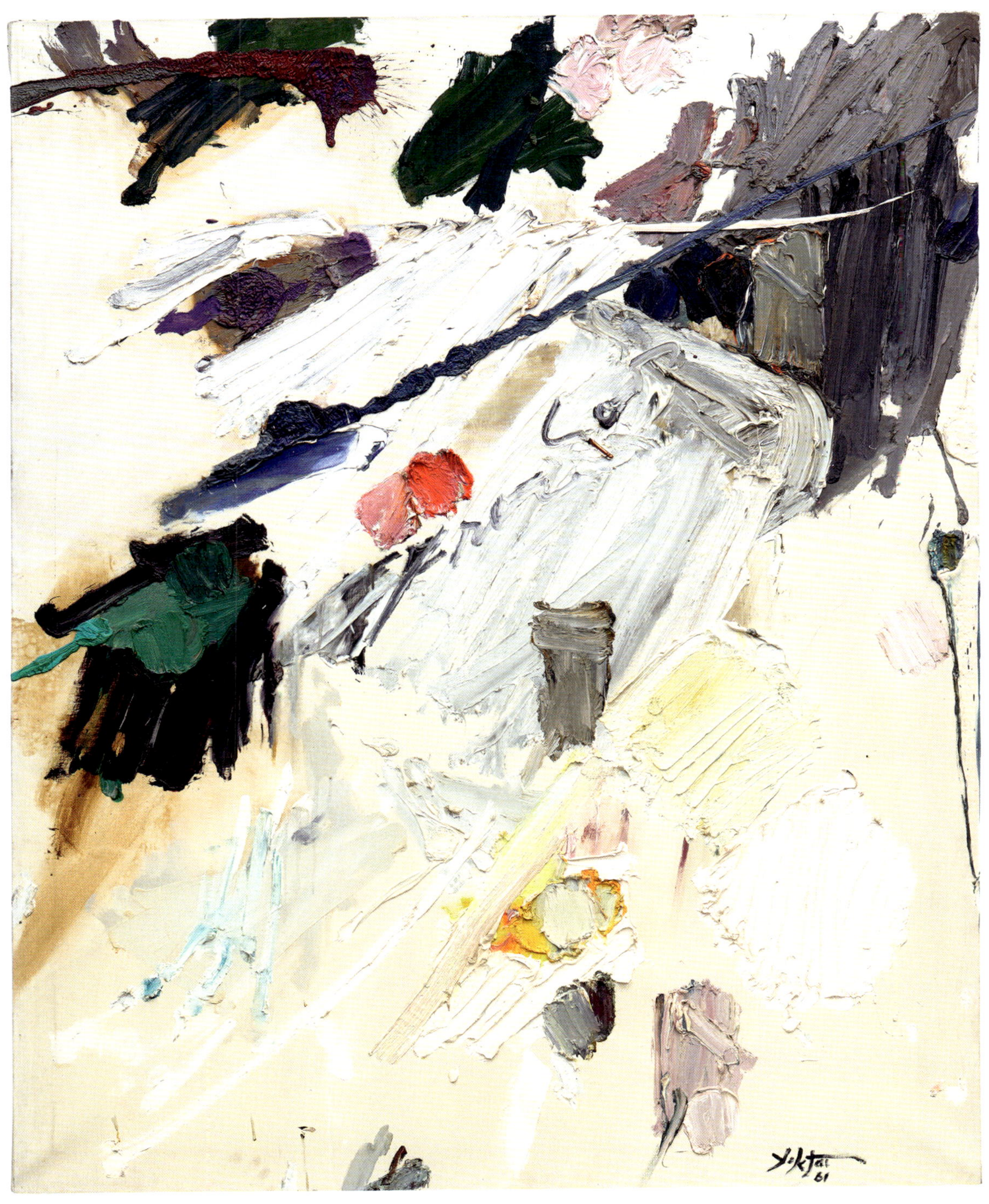

Untitled, 1961, oil on canvas, 63¾ × 51⅛ inches (162 × 130 cm)

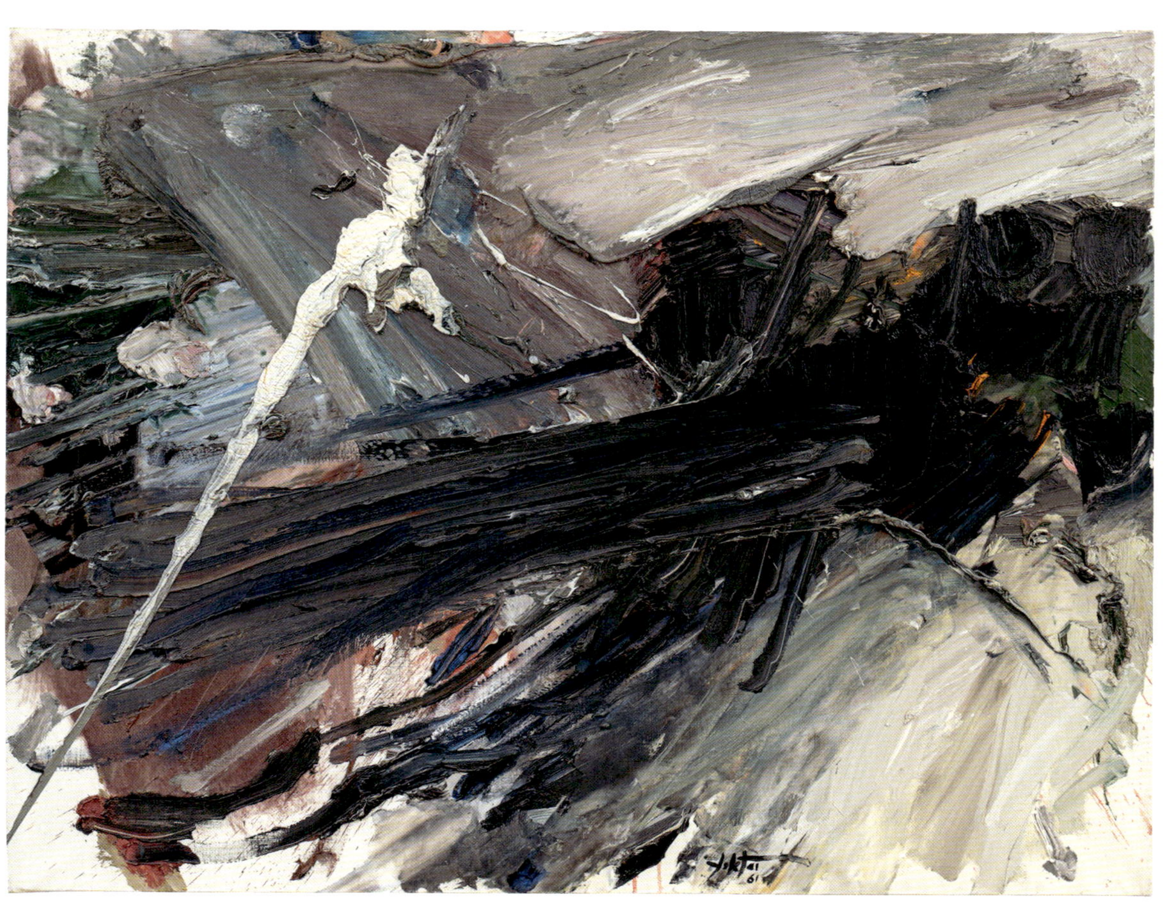

 Untitled, 1961, oil on canvas, 44½ × 57½ inches (113 × 146.1 cm)

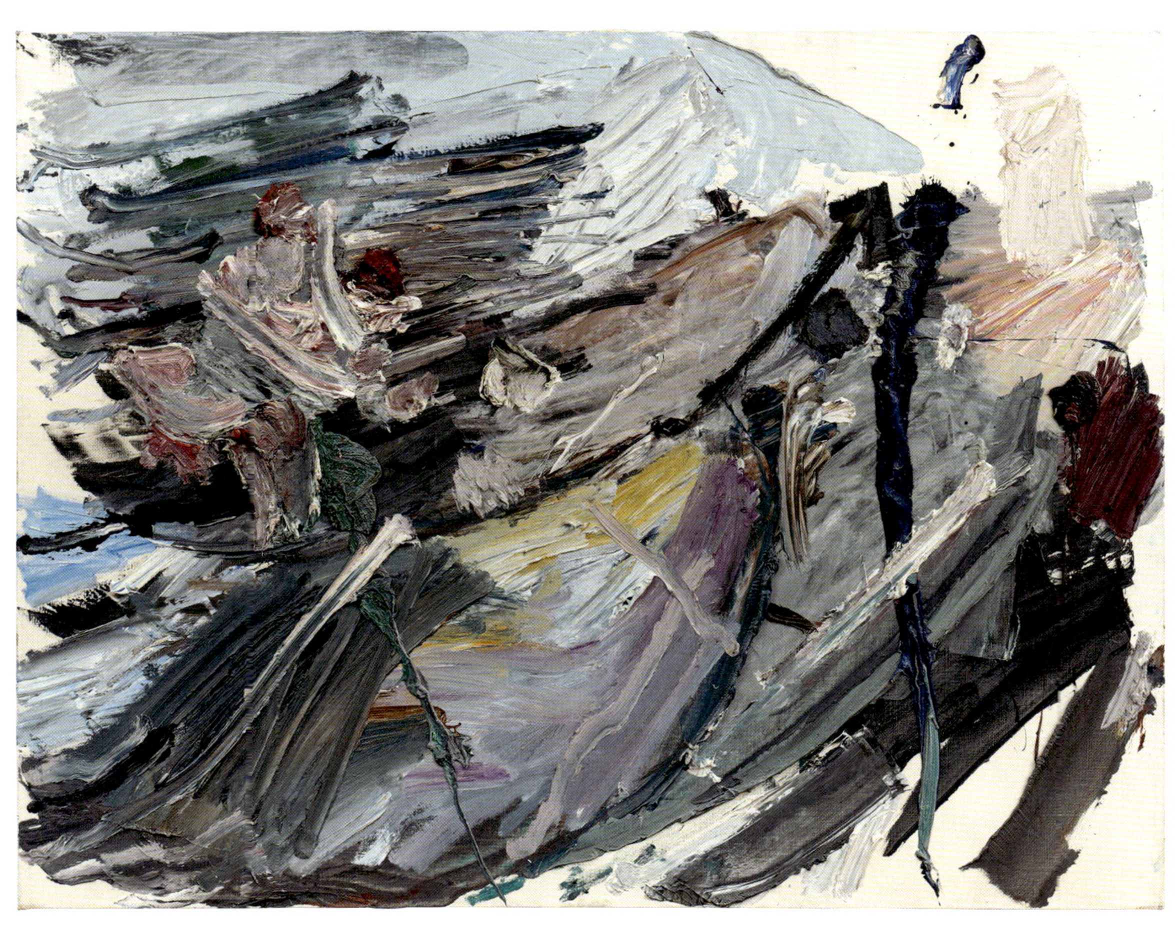

Untitled, 1961, oil on canvas, 44½ × 57¼ inches (114.3 × 145.4 cm)

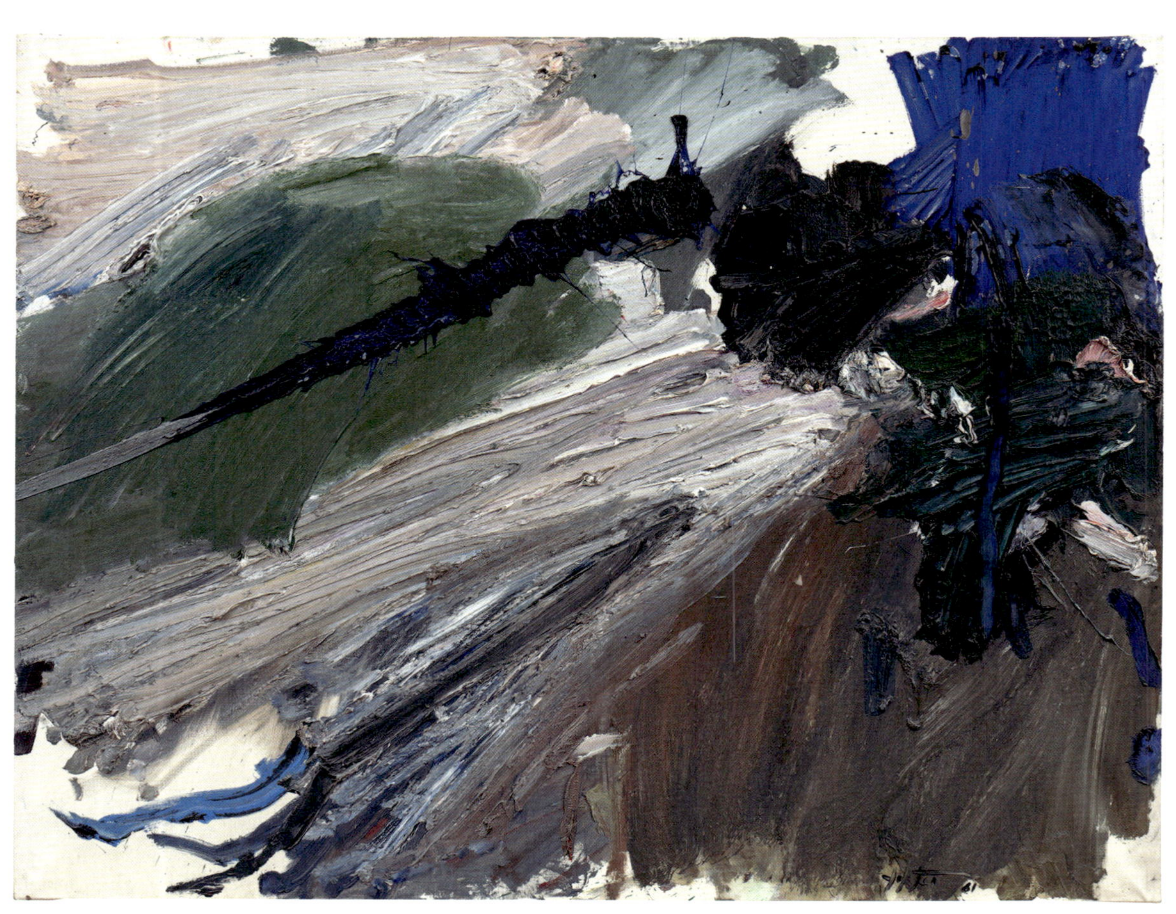

 Untitled, 1961, oil on canvas, 48 × 52 inches (121.9 × 132.1 cm)

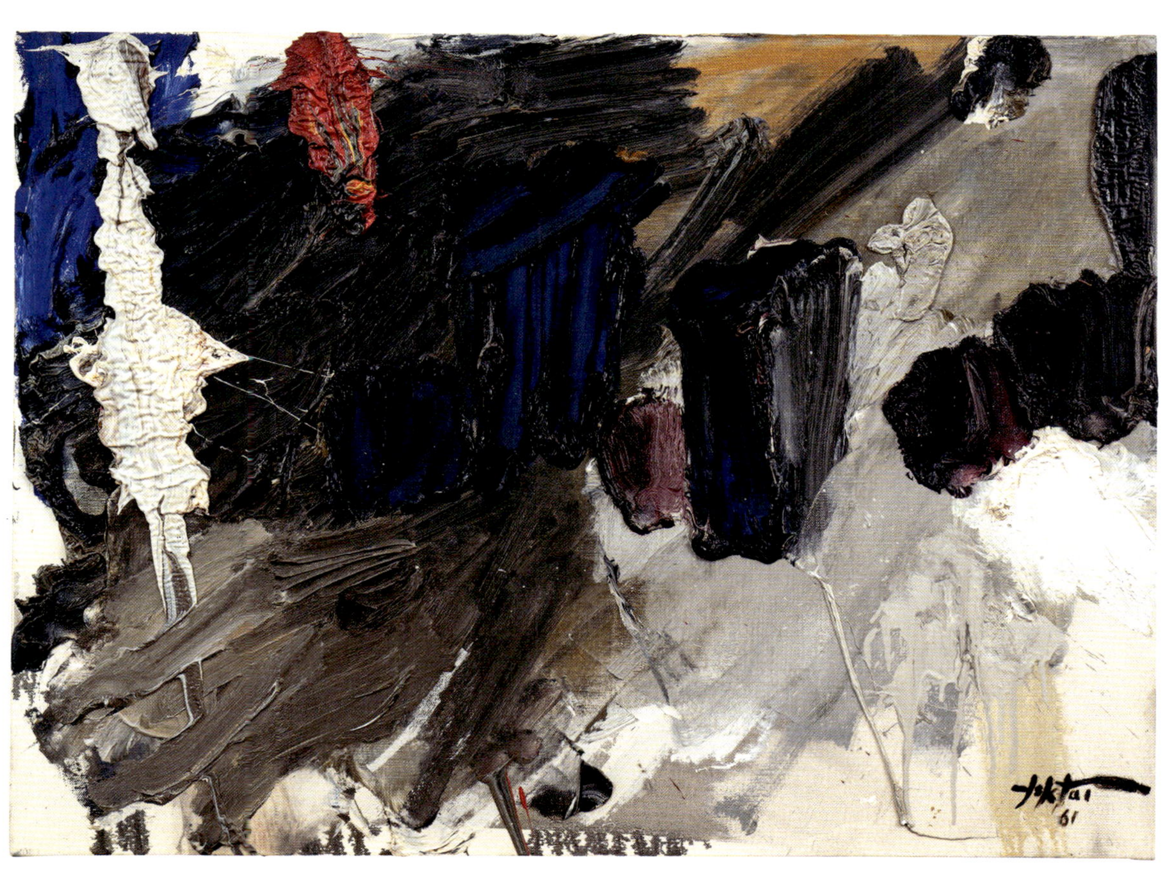

Untitled, 1961, oil on canvas, 21¼ × 28½ inches (54 × 72.4 cm)

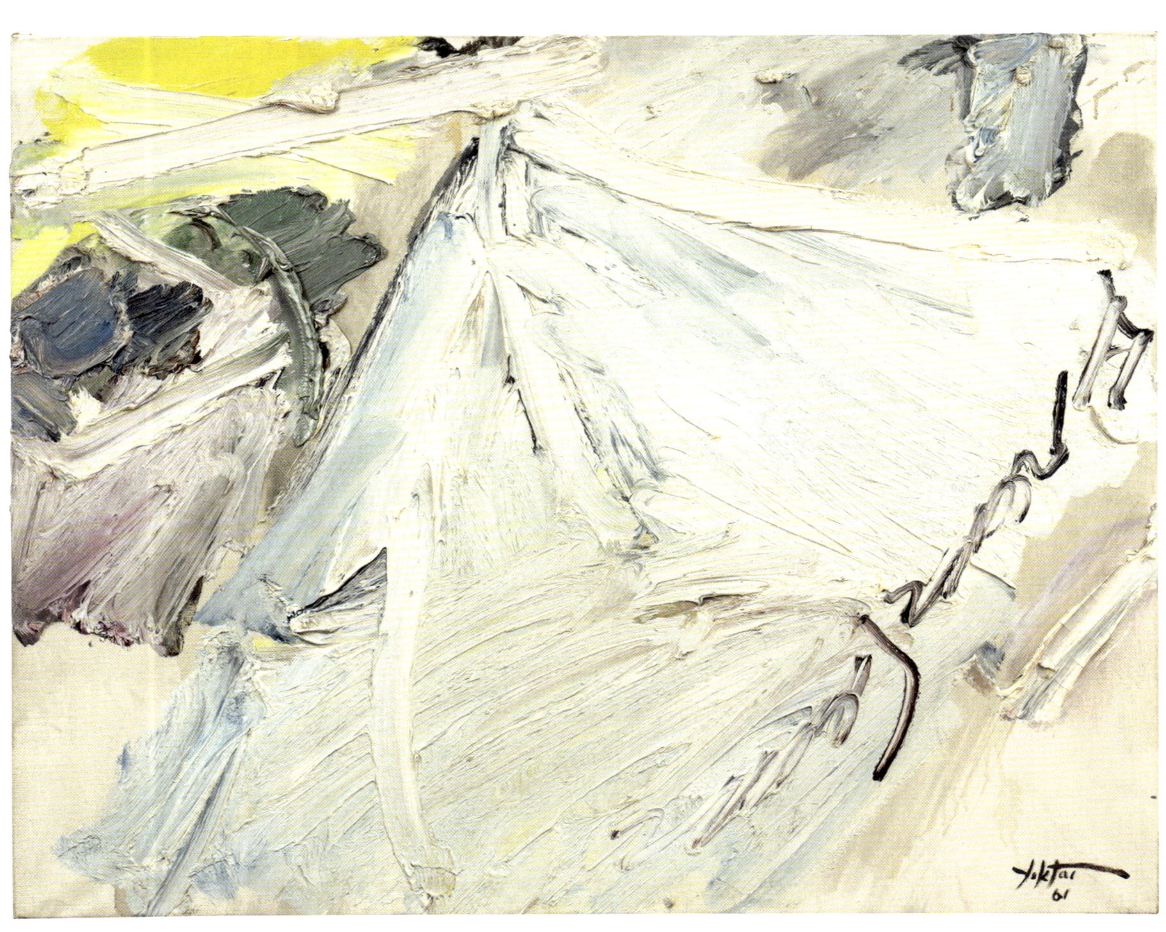

Untitled, 1961, oil on canvas, 20 × 24 inches (50.8 × 61 cm)

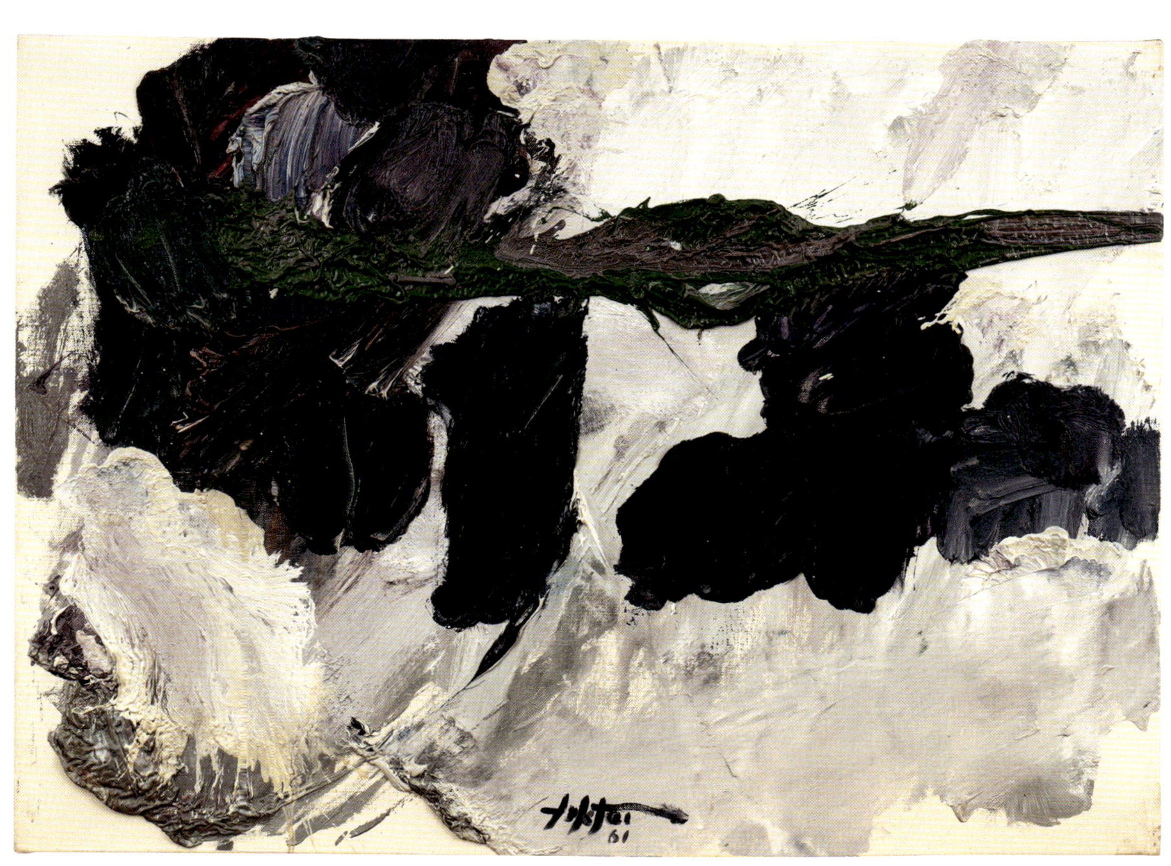

Untitled, 1961, oil on canvas, 21¼ × 28½ inches (54 × 72.4 cm)

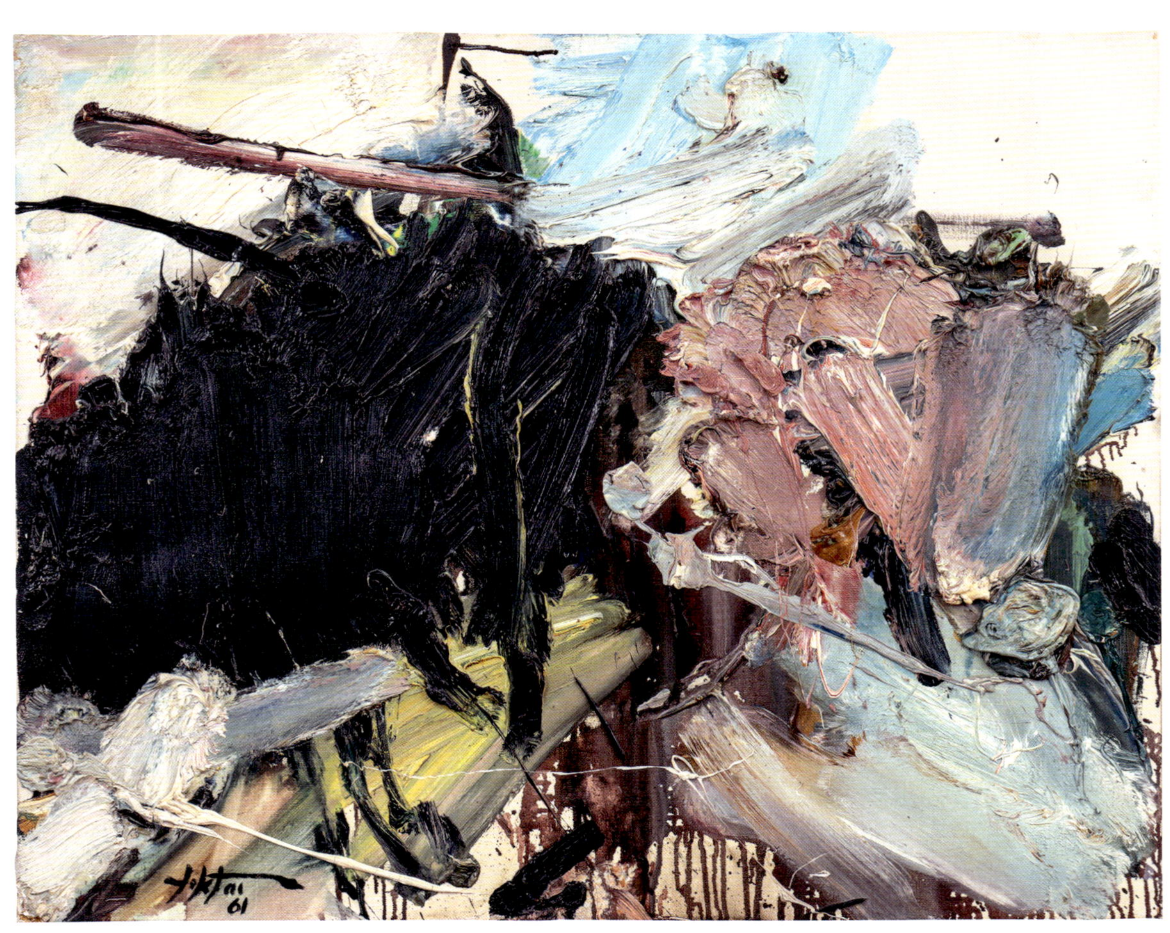

Untitled, 1961, oil on canvas, 11⅜ × 14⅛ inches (28.8 × 36 cm)

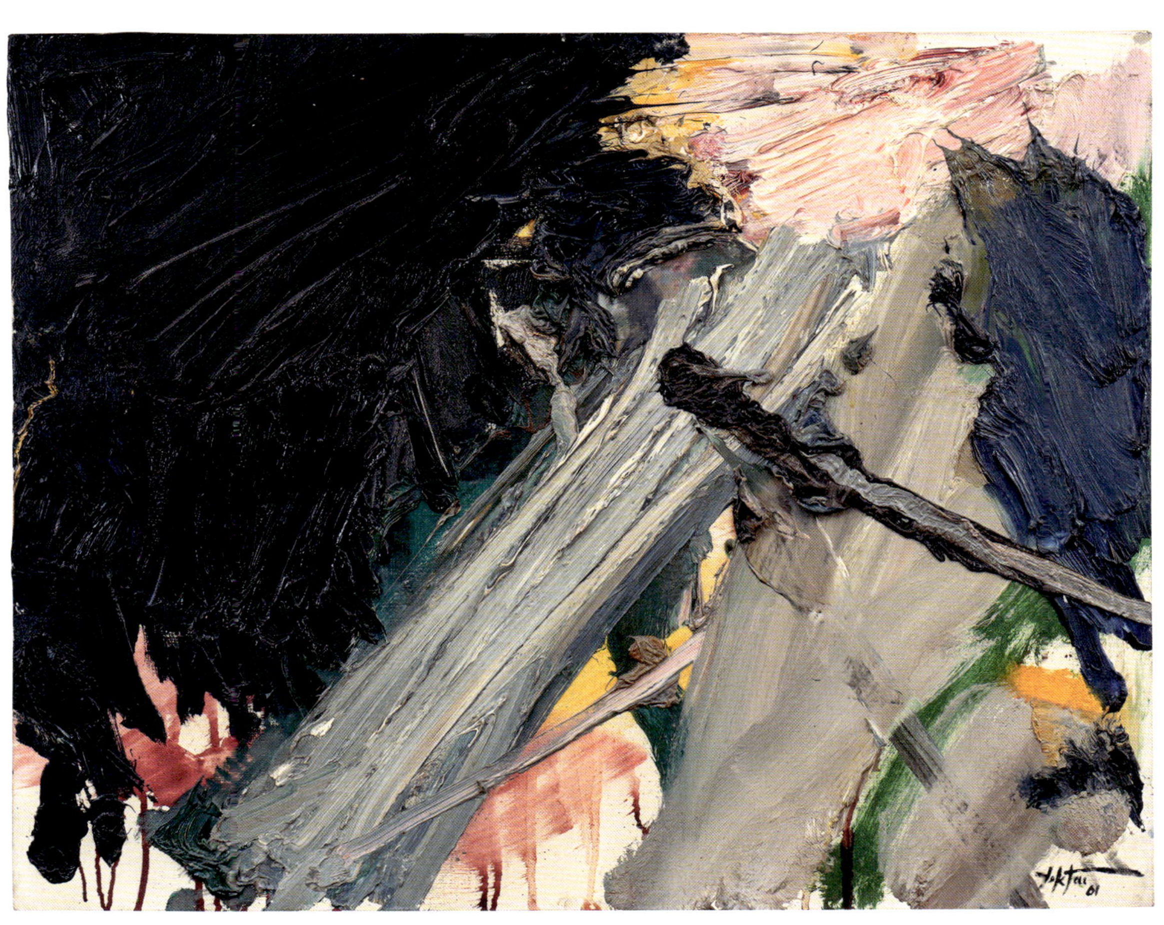

Untitled, 1961, oil on canvas, 28¾ × 36 inches (73 × 91.4 cm)

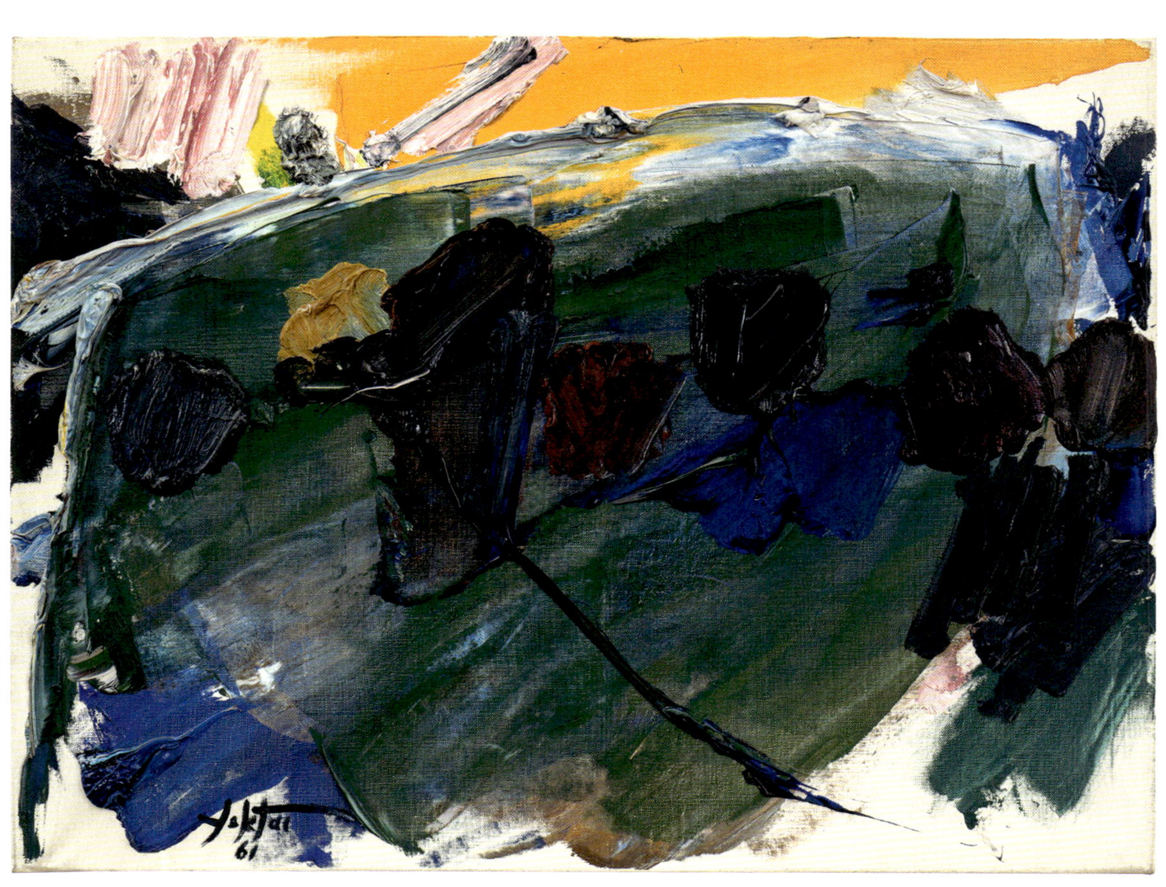

 Untitled, 1961, oil on canvas, 21¼ × 28¾ inches (54 × 73 cm)

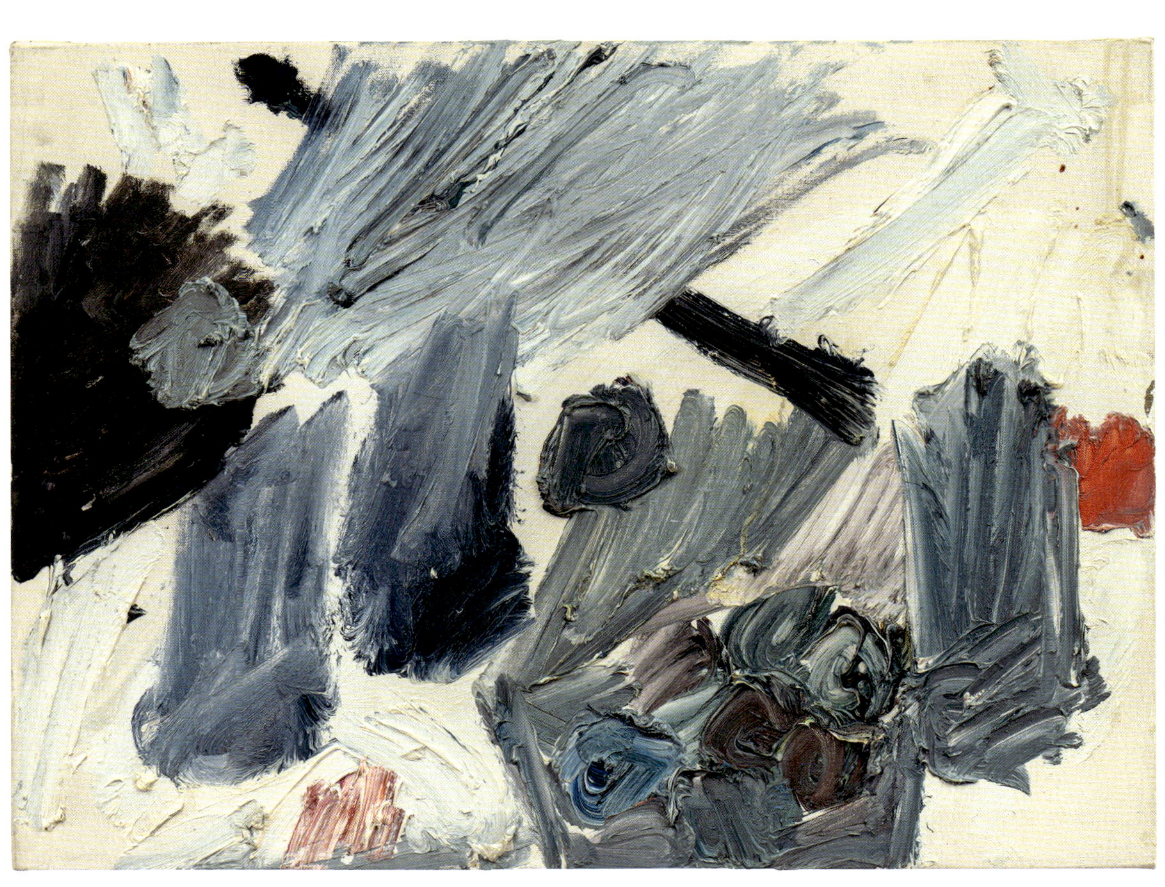

Untitled, 1961, oil on canvas, 21¼ × 28¾ inches (54 × 73 cm)

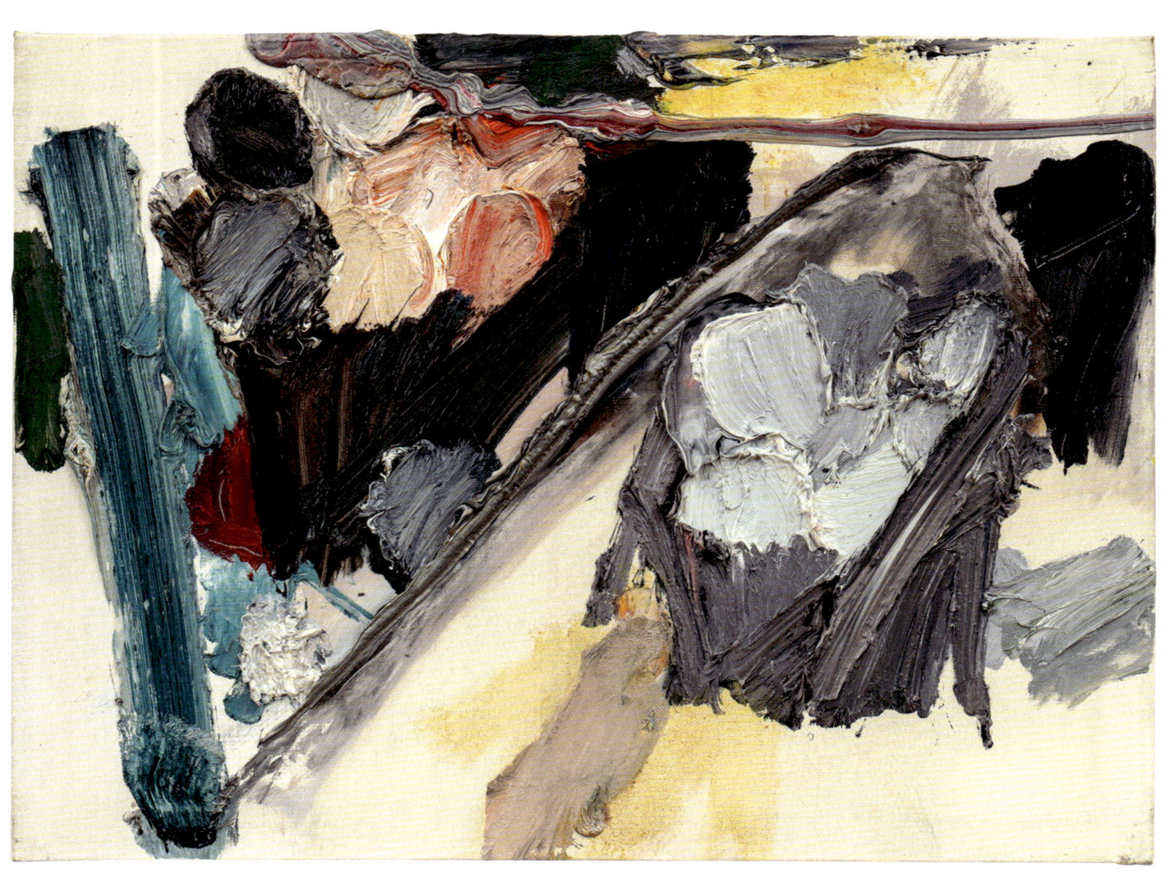

 Untitled, 1961, oil on canvas, 21¼ × 28¾ inches (54 × 73 cm)

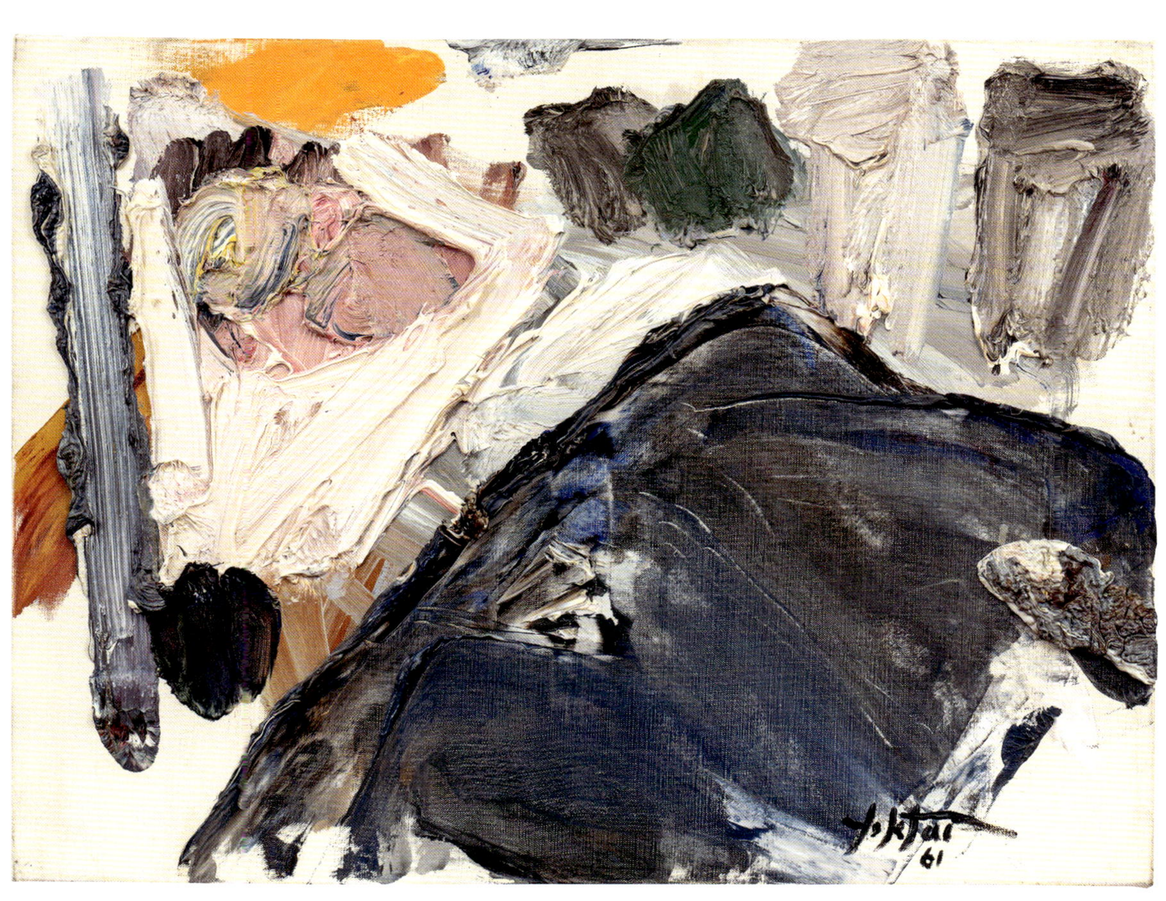

Untitled, 1961, oil on canvas, 21¼ × 28½ inches (54 × 72.4 cm)

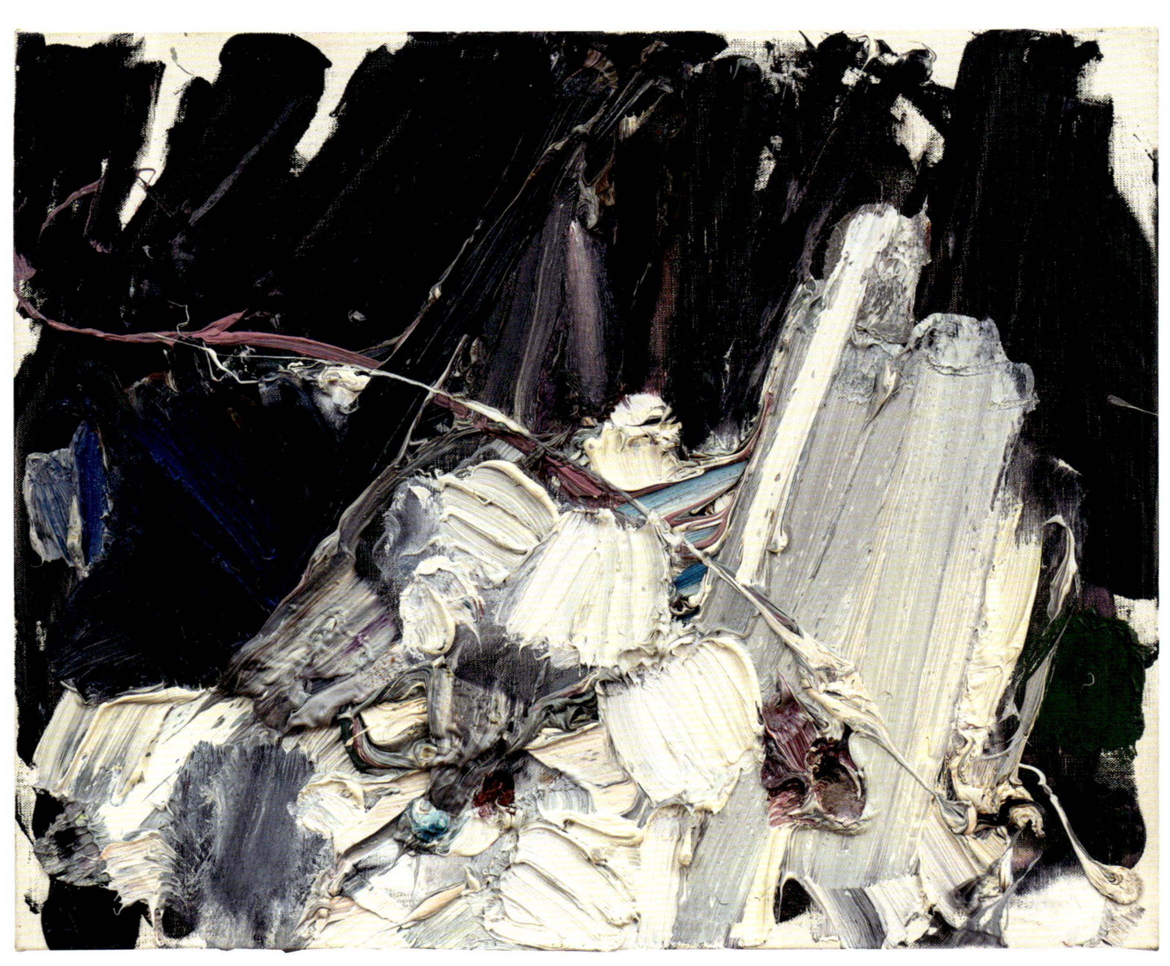

 Untitled, 1961, oil on canvas, 19¾ × 24 inches (50.2 × 61 cm)

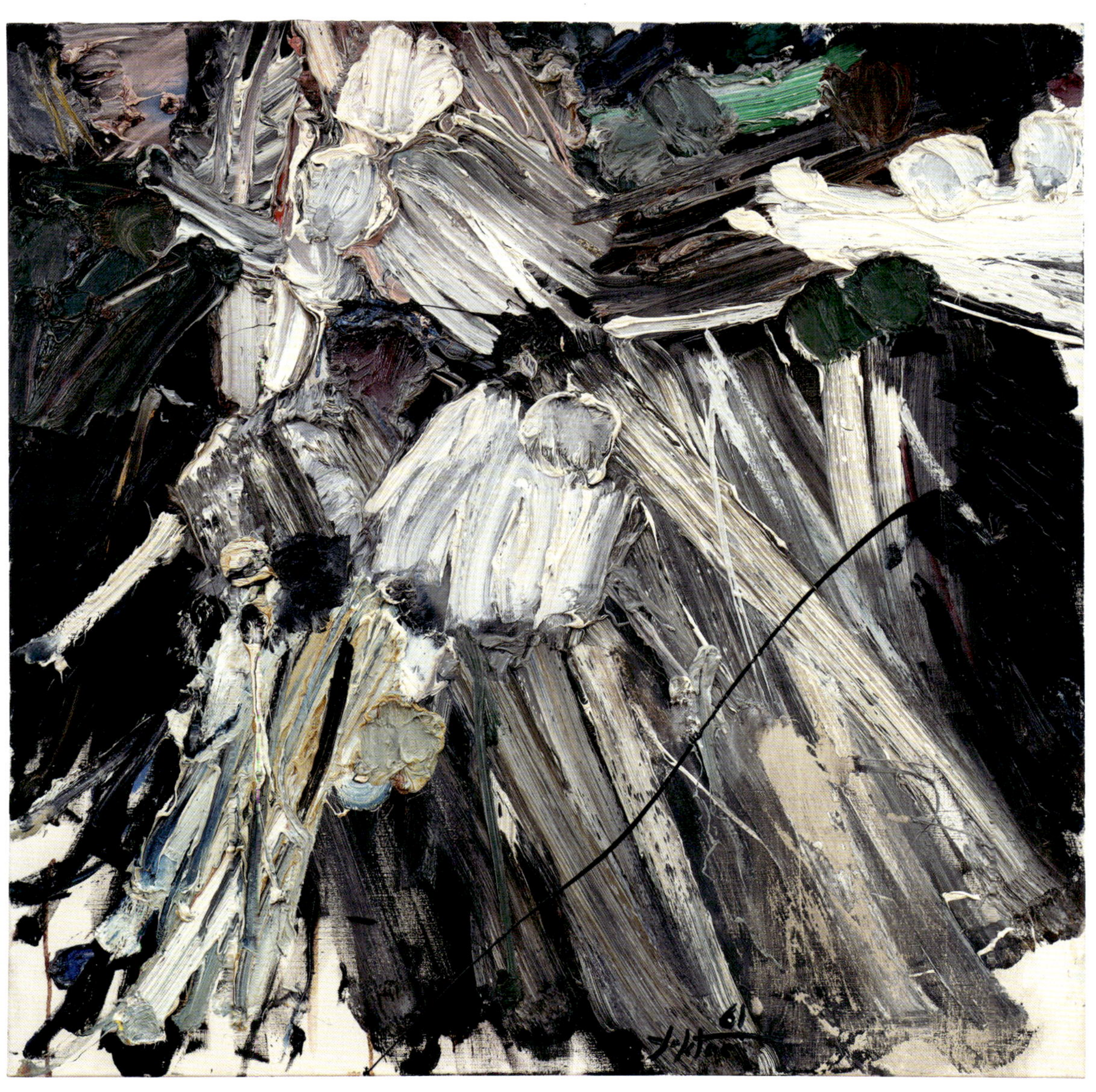

Untitled, 1961, oil on canvas, 39¼ × 39¼ inches (99.7 × 99.7 cm)

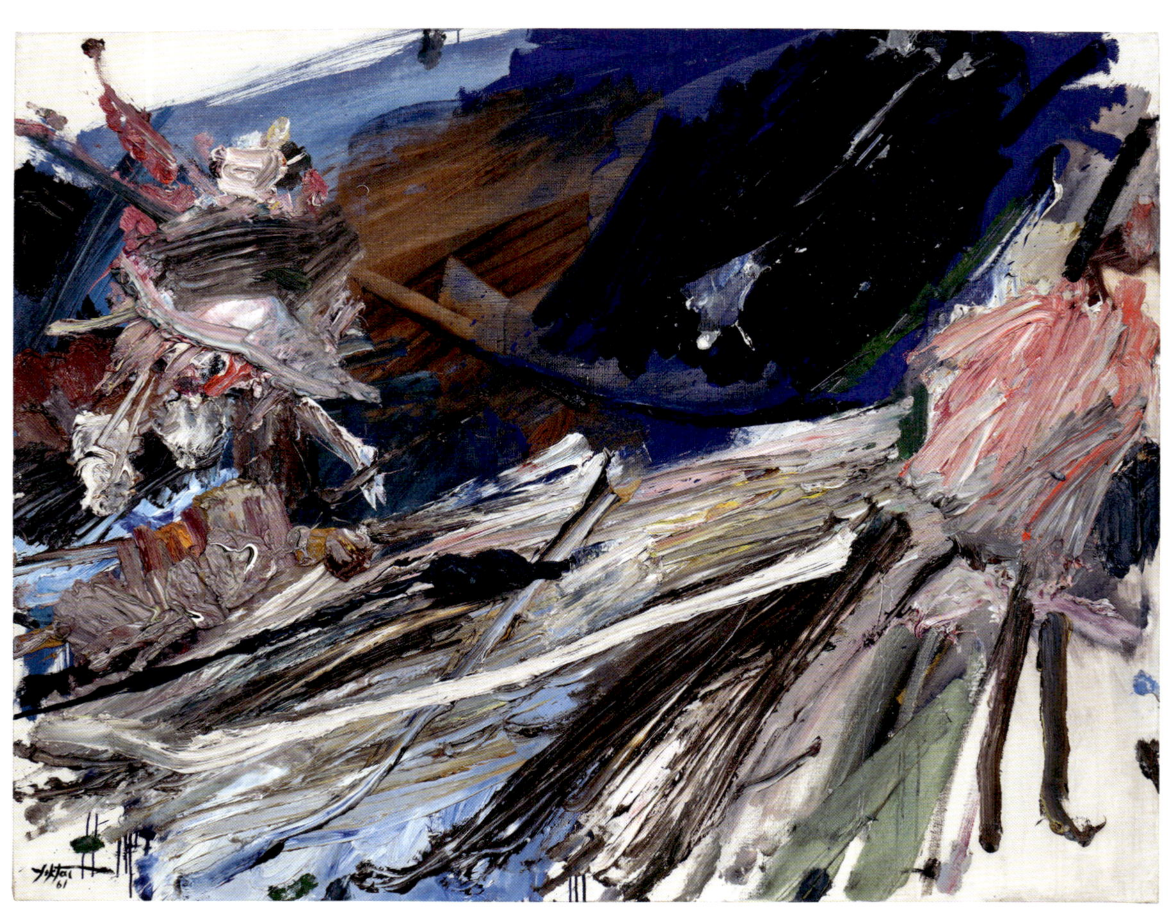

 Still Life, 1961, oil on canvas, 45 × 57 inches (114.3 × 144.8 cm)

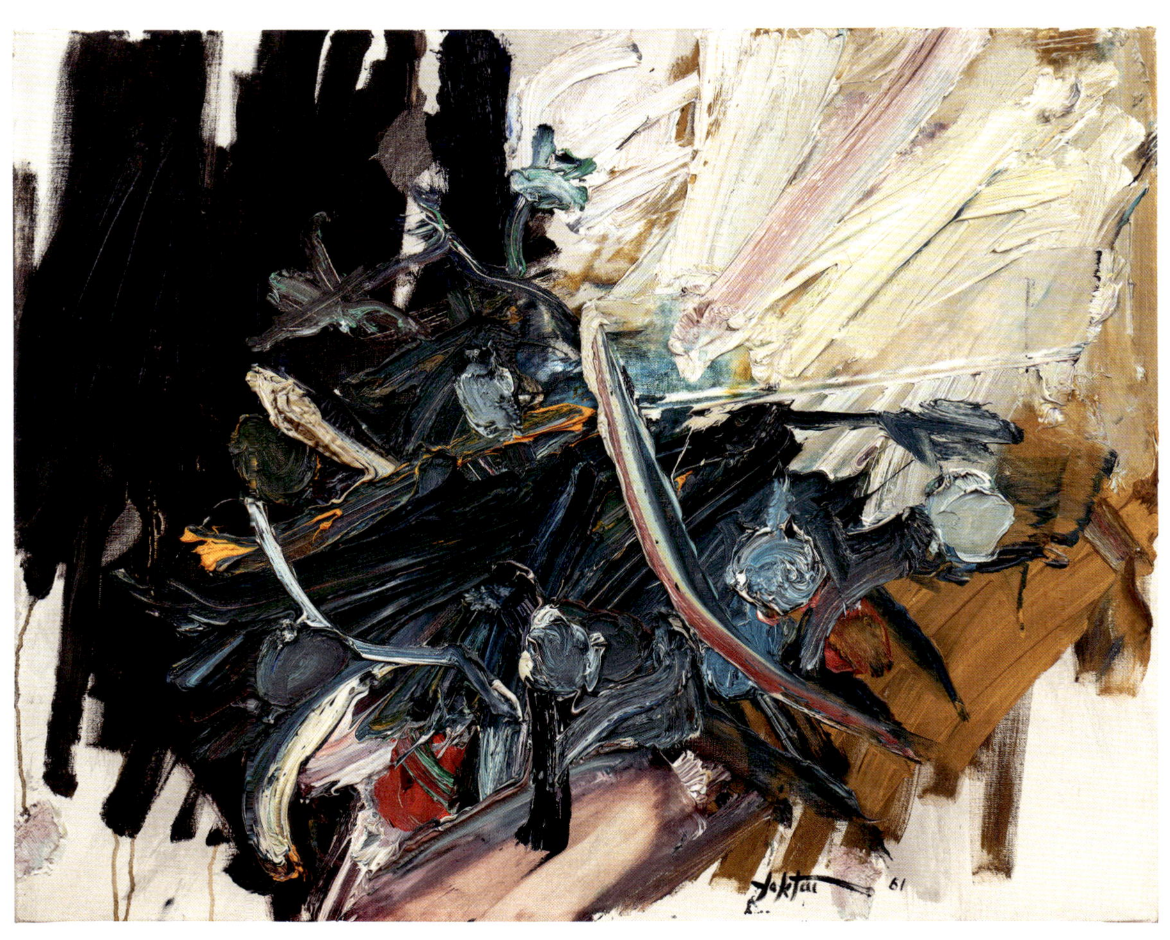

Untitled, 1961, oil on canvas, 28¾ × 36 inches (73 × 91.4 cm)

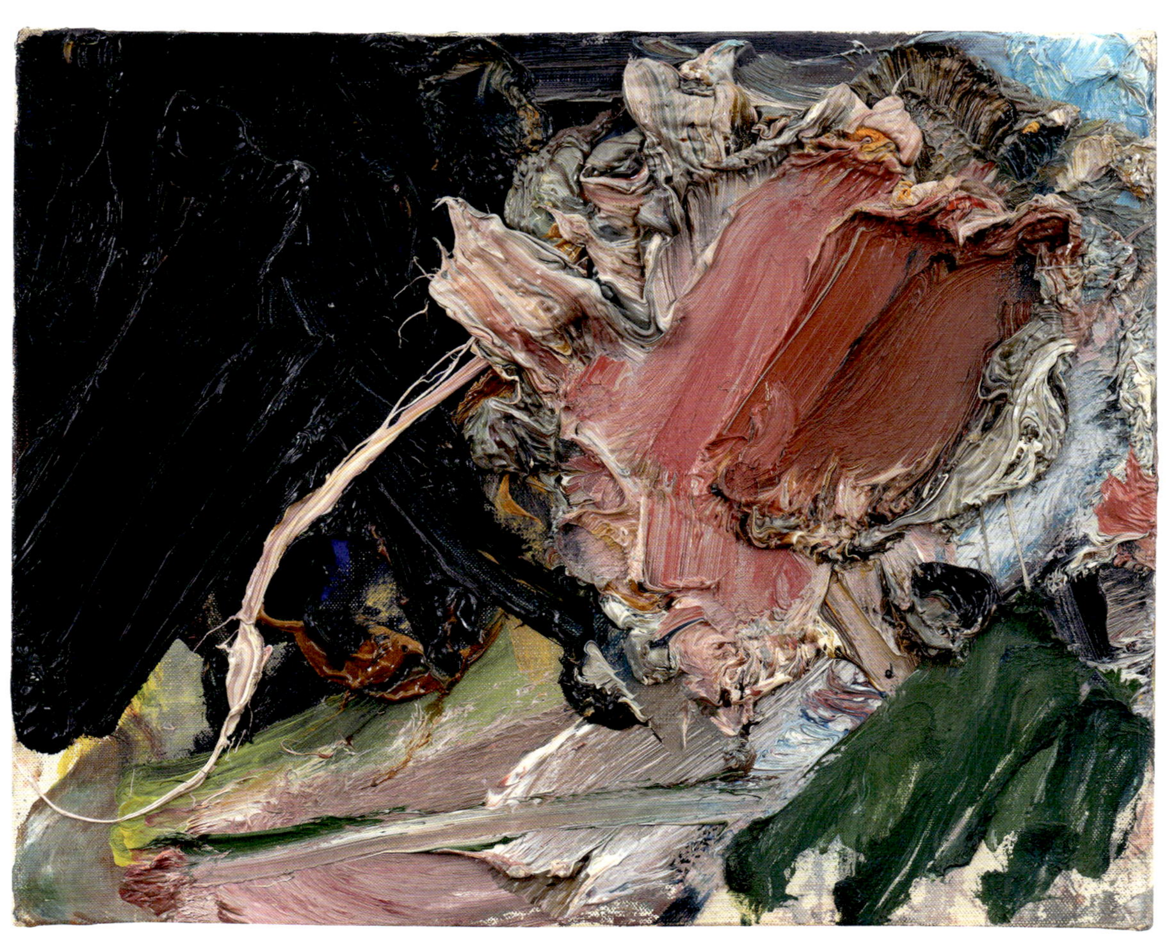

Untitled, 1961, oil on canvas, 13 × 16 inches (33 × 40.6 cm)

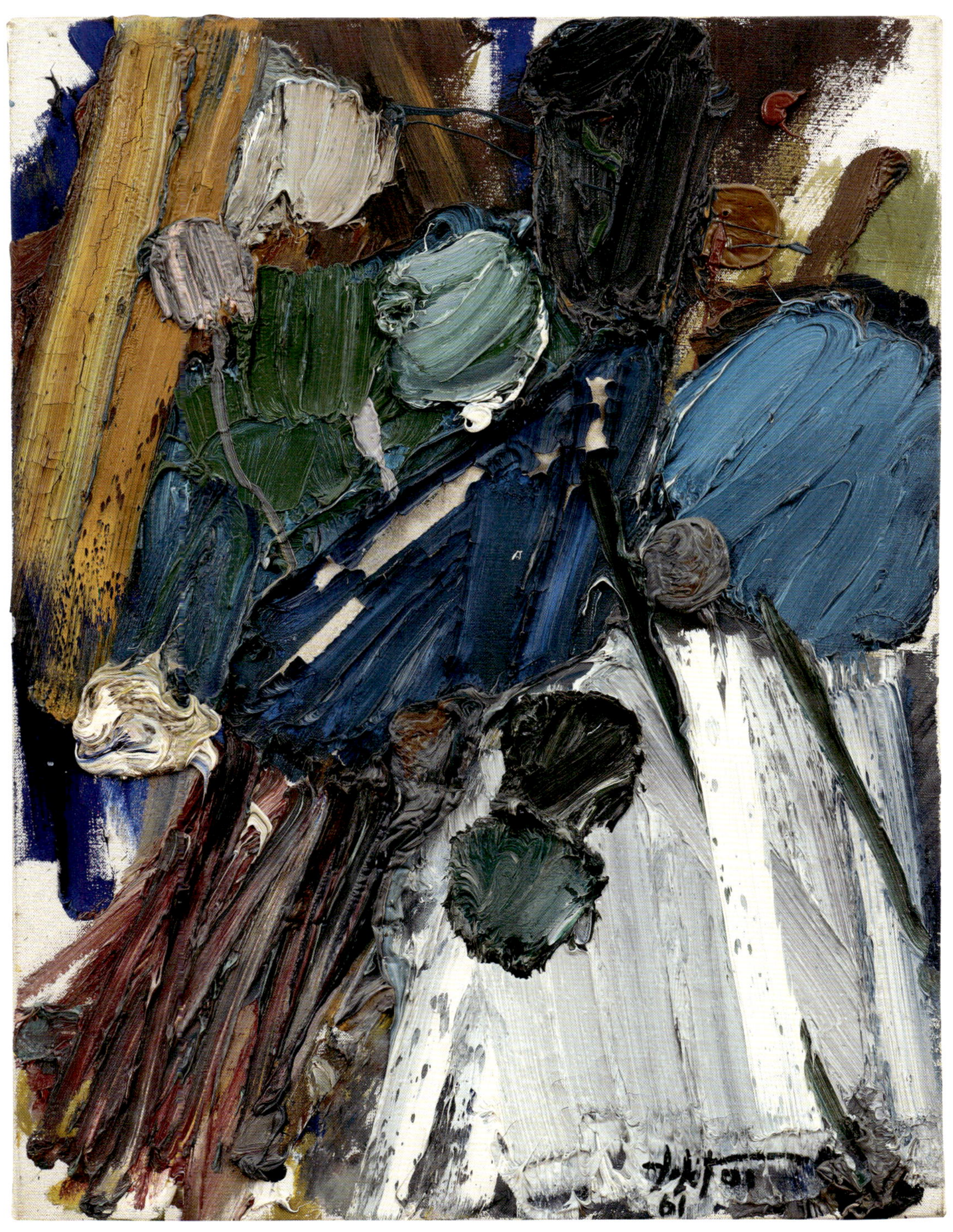

Untitled, 1961, oil on canvas, 24 × 18 inches (61 × 45.7 cm)

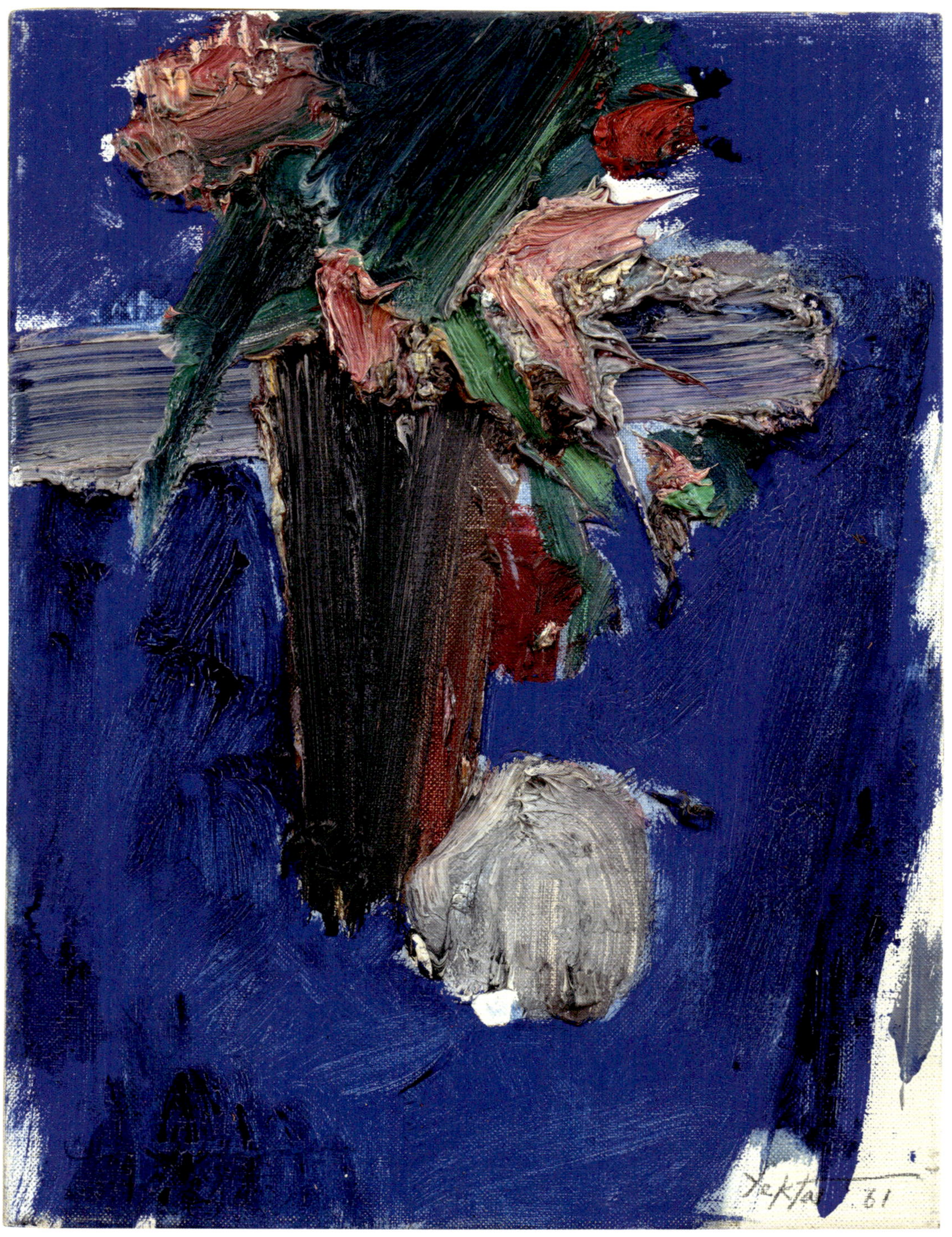

 Untitled, 1961, oil on canvas, 15¾ × 12 inches (40 × 30.5 cm)

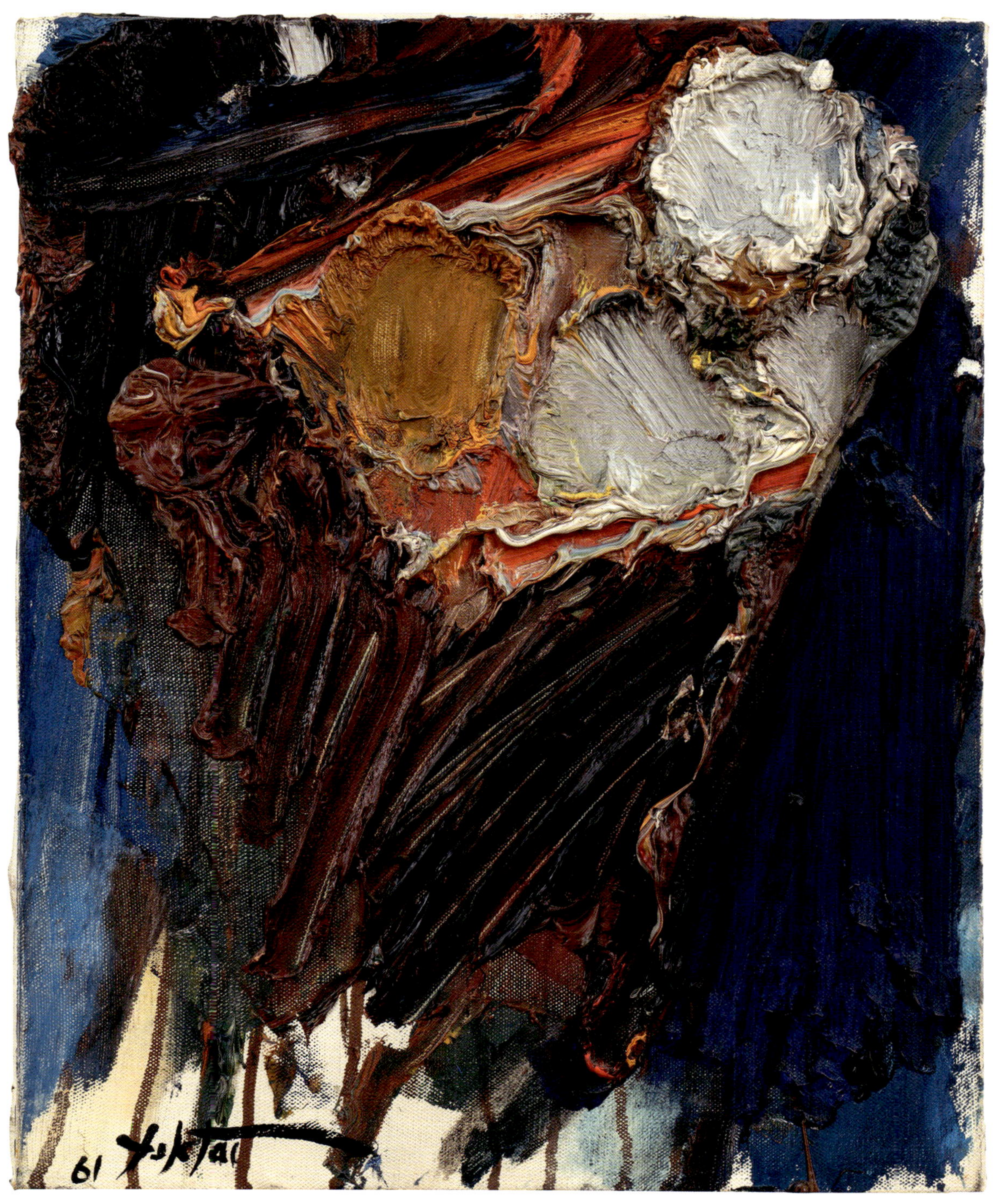

Untitled, 1961, oil on canvas, 16¼ × 13 inches (41.3 × 33 cm)

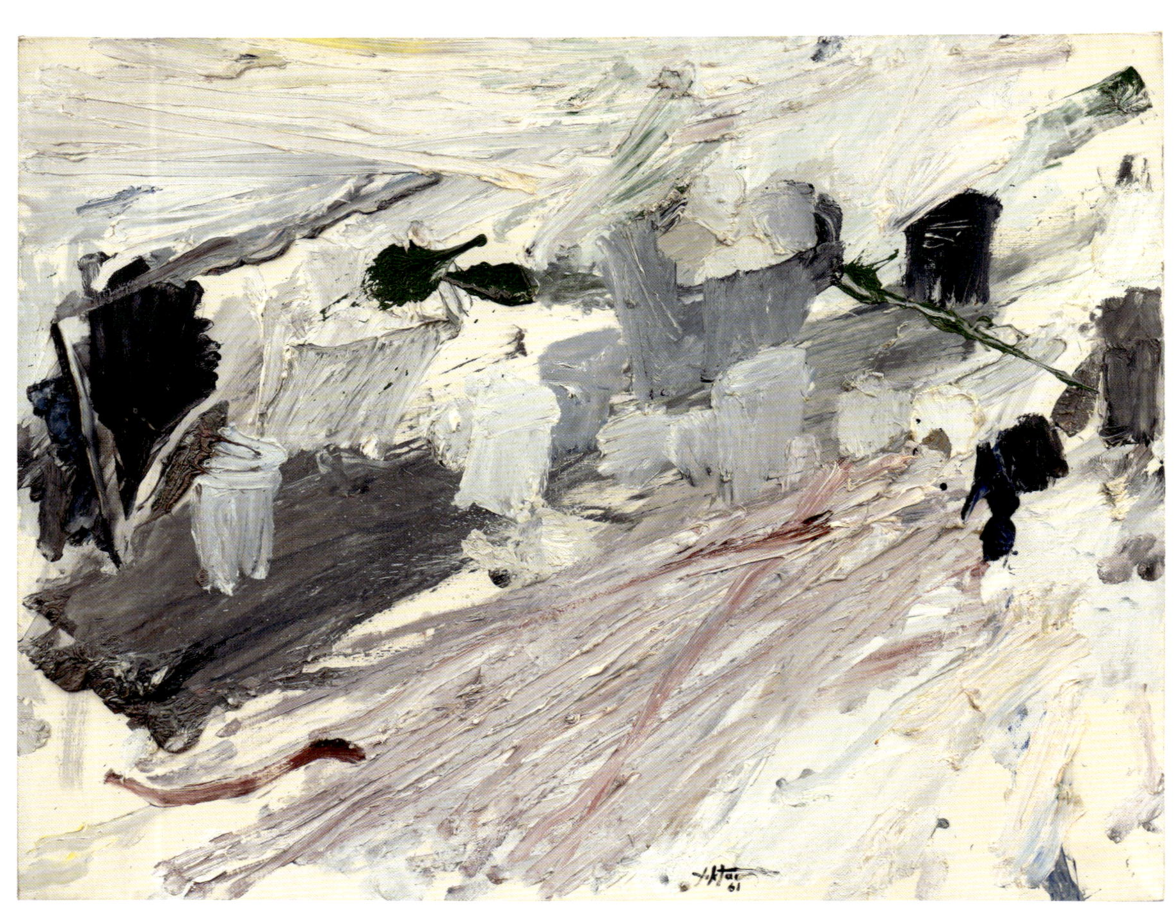

338 *Untitled*, 1961, oil on canvas, 44¾ × 57½ inches (113.7 × 146.1 cm)

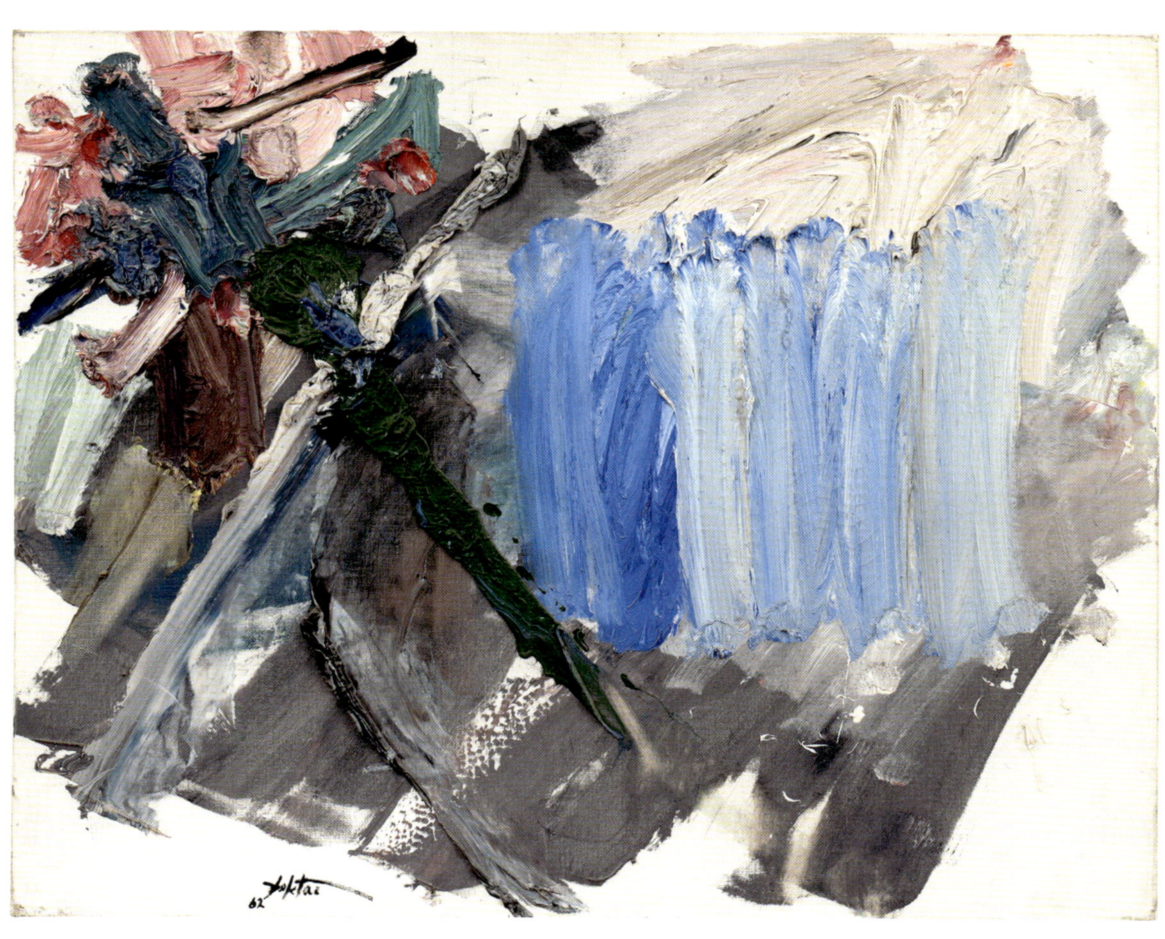

Untitled, 1962, oil on canvas, 28½ × 36 inches (72.4 × 91.4 cm)

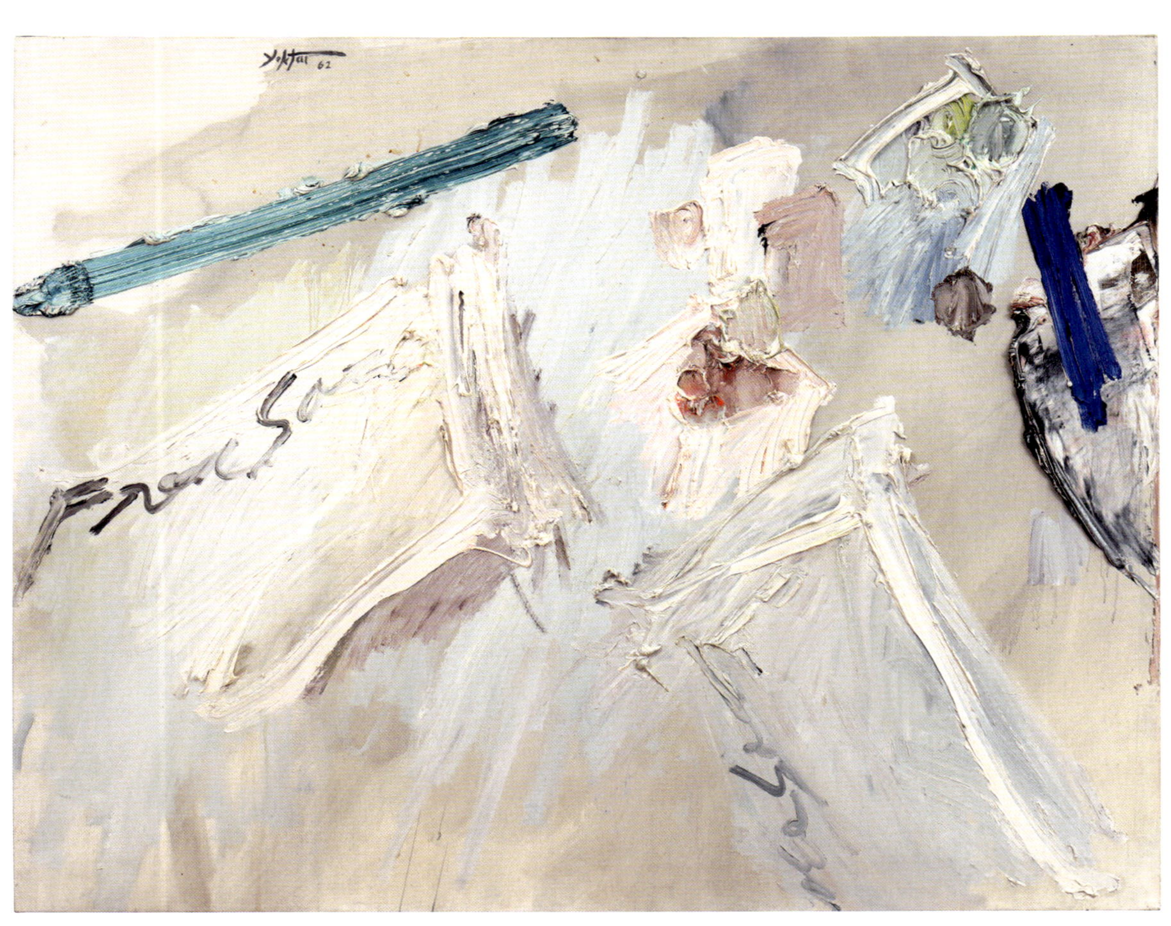

 Untitled, 1962, oil on canvas, 45 × 57½ inches (114.3 × 146.1 cm)

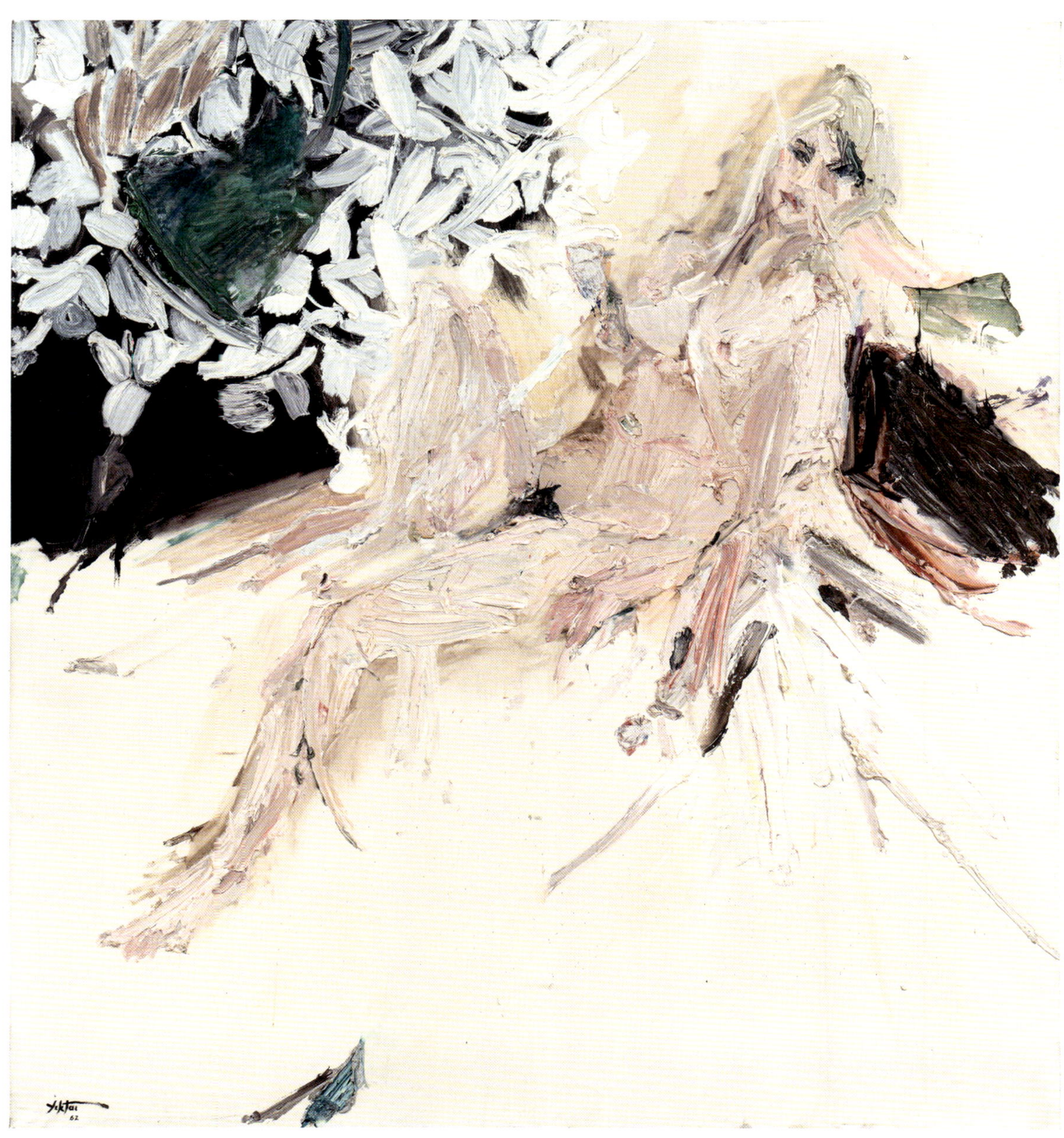

Untitled, 1962, oil on canvas, 82¾ × 76¾ inches (210.2 × 194.9 cm)

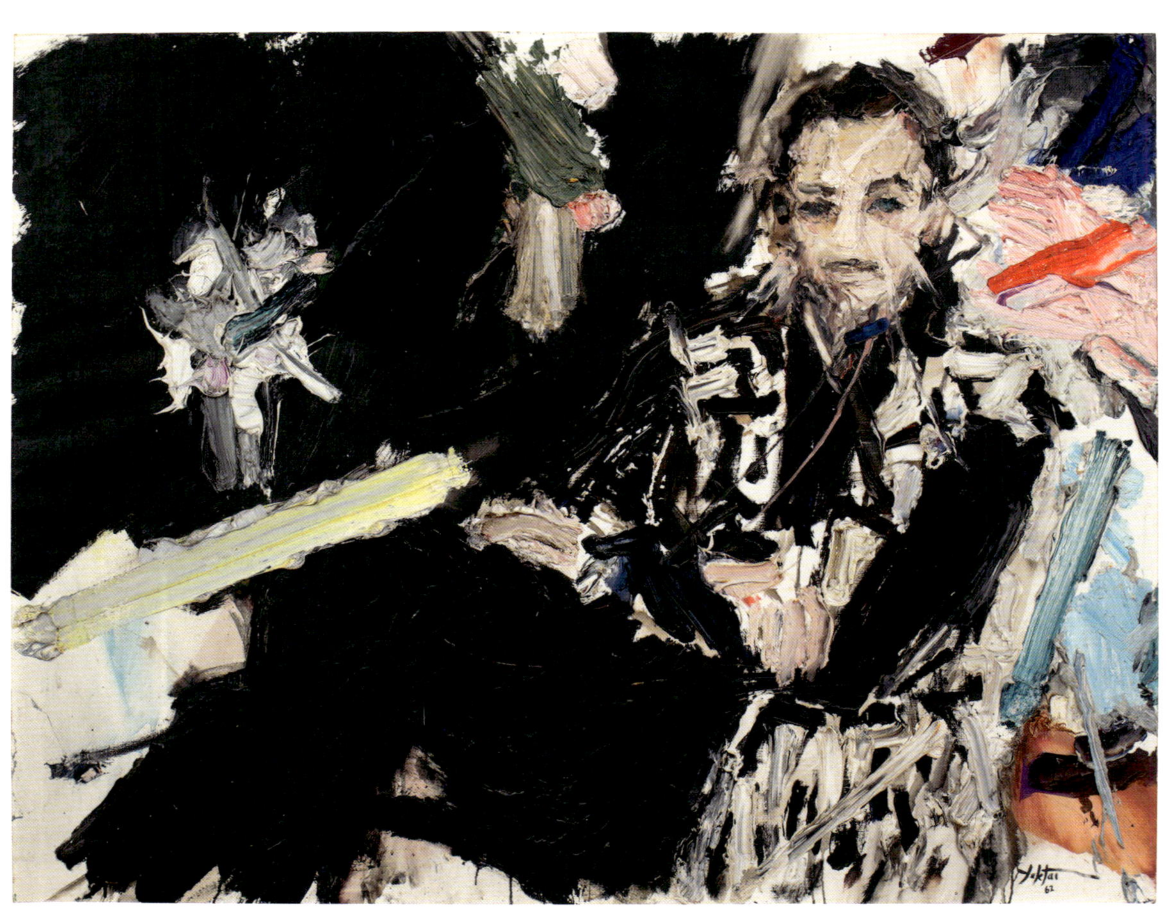

342 *Portrait de Romain Gary*, 1962, oil on canvas, 45 × 57½ inches (114.3 × 146.1 cm)

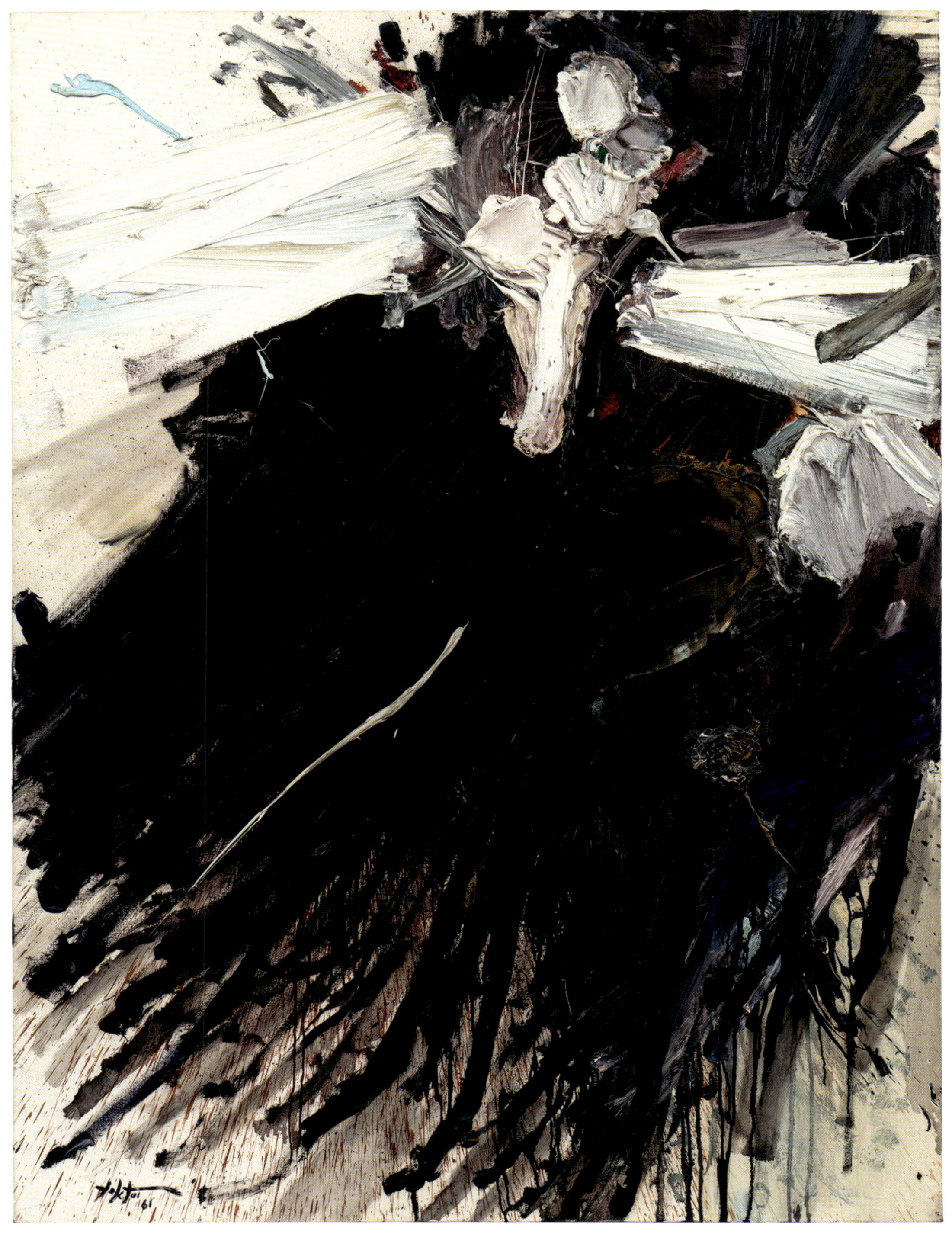

Untitled, 1961, oil on canvas, 63 × 47¼ inches (160 × 120 cm)

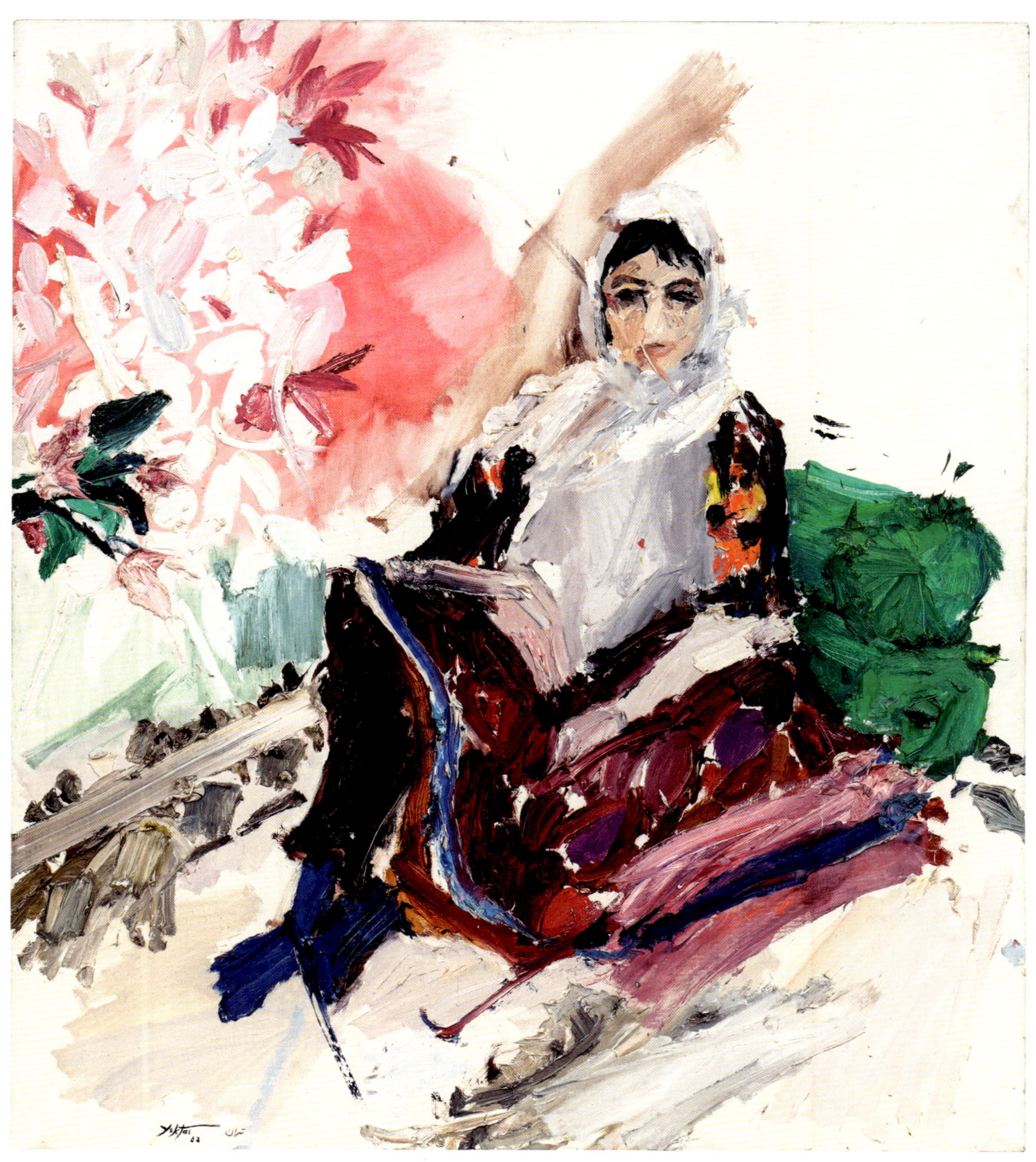

 Le Kurde, 1962, oil on canvas, 68½ × 60 inches (174 × 152.4 cm)

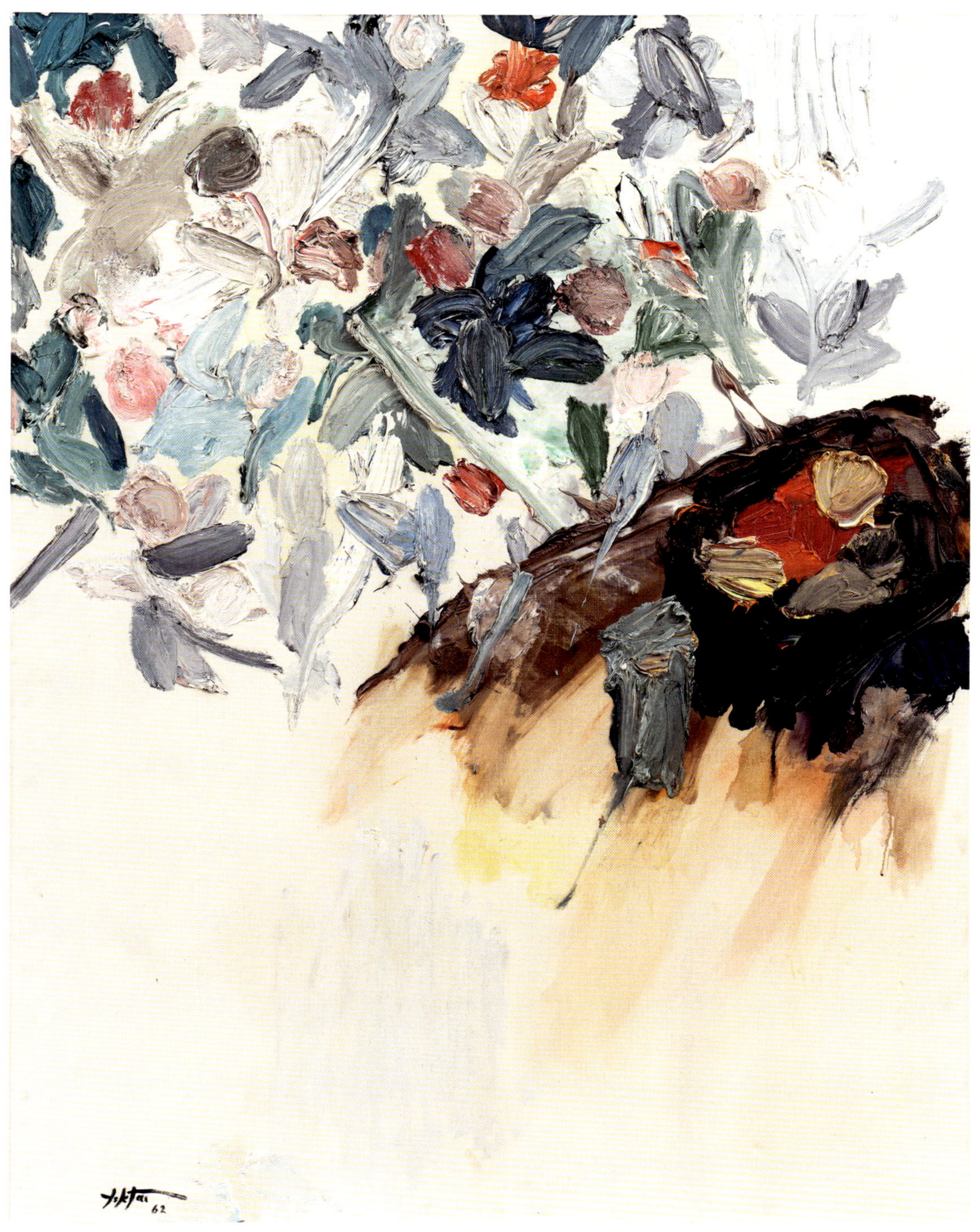

Fleurs sur Fond Blanc, 1962, oil on canvas, 57 × 44¼ inches (144.8 × 112.4 cm)

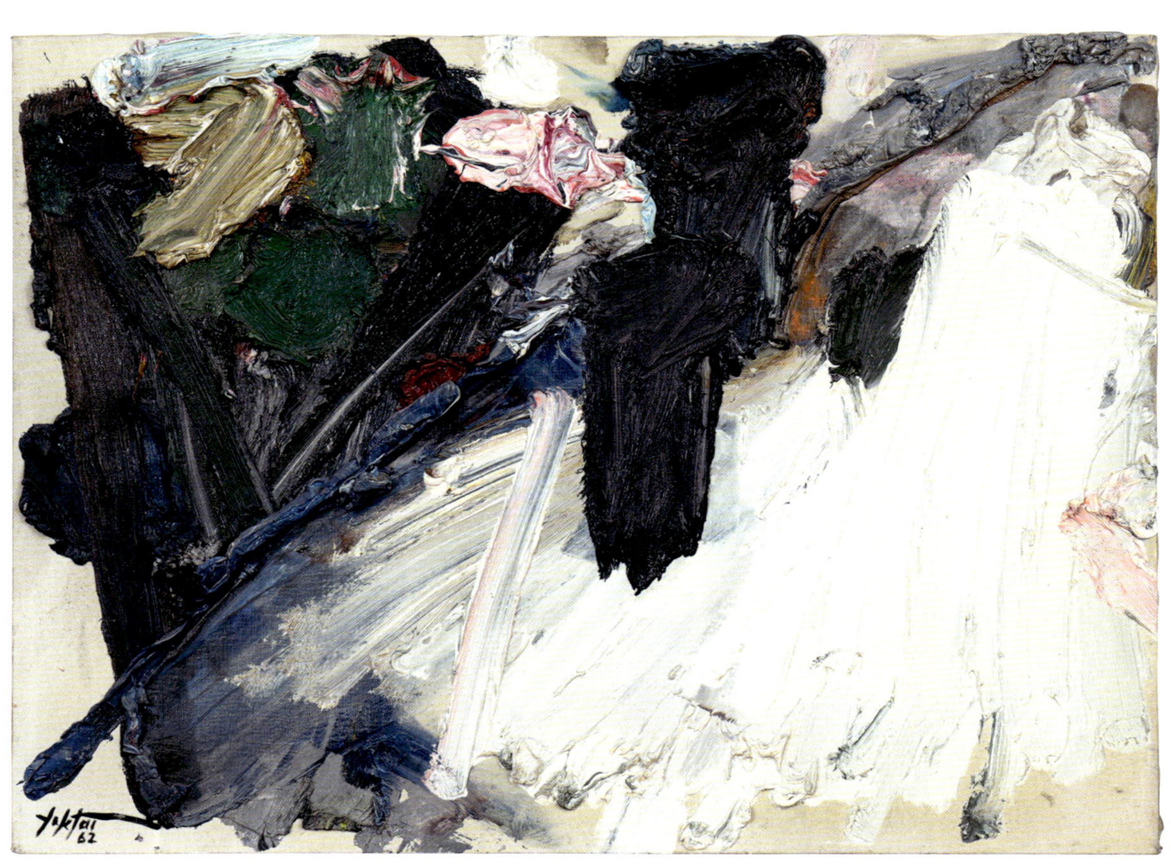

Untitled, 1962, oil on canvas, 22 × 30 inches (55.9 × 76.2 cm)

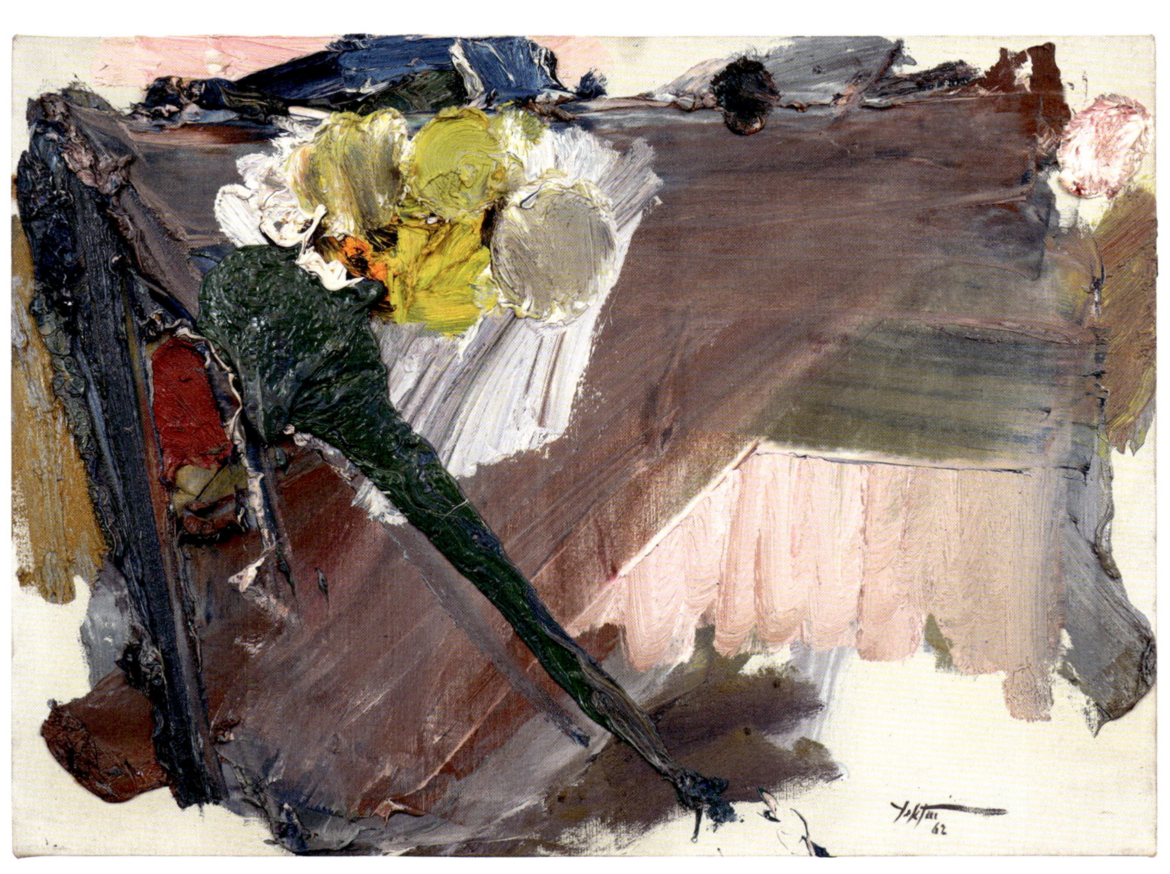

Untitled, 1962, oil on canvas, 22 × 30 inches (55.9 × 76.2 cm)

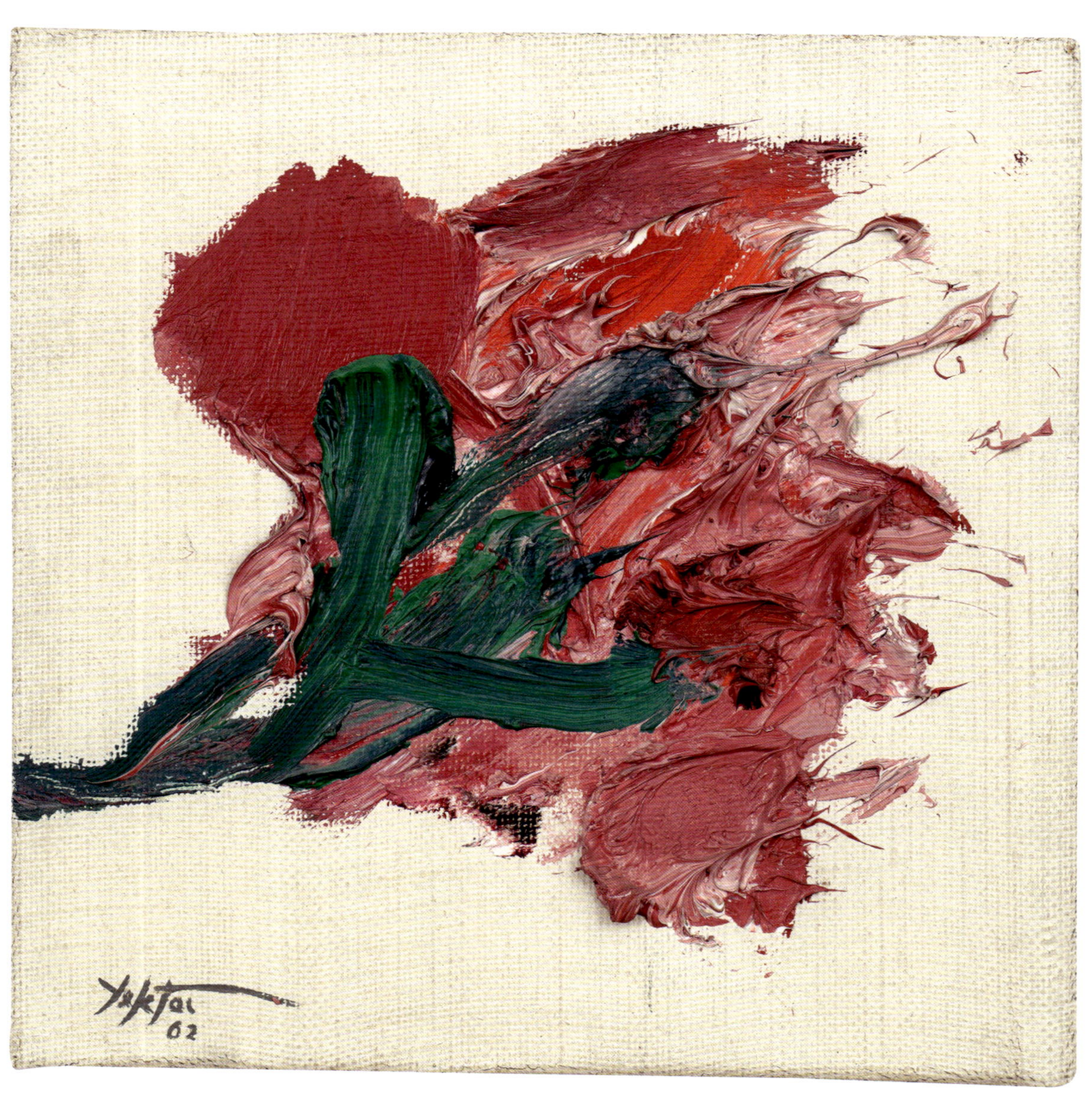

Untitled, 1962, oil on canvas, 12 × 12 inches (30.5 × 30.5 cm)

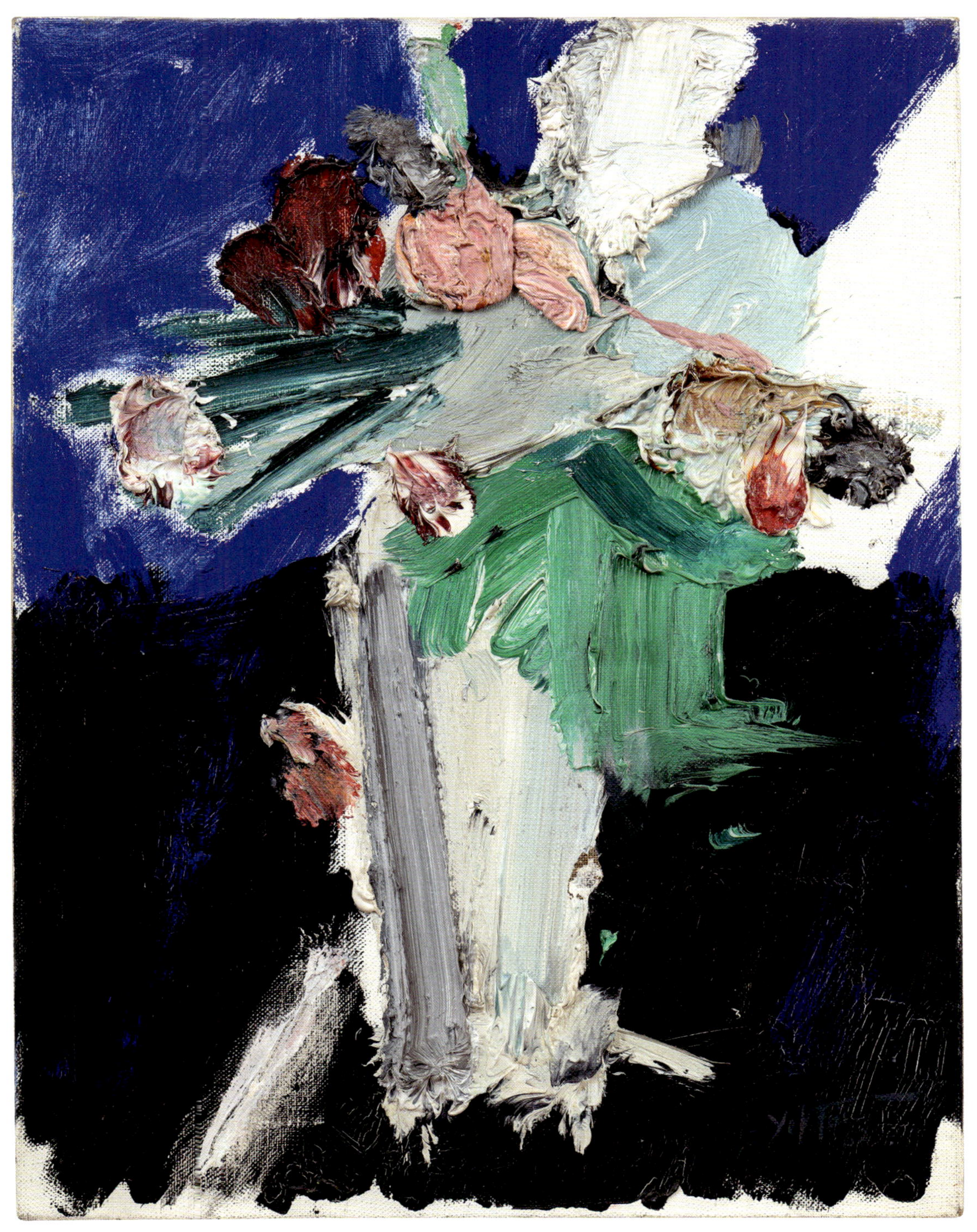

Untitled, 1962, oil on canvas, 17½ × 13½ inches (44.5 × 34.3 cm)

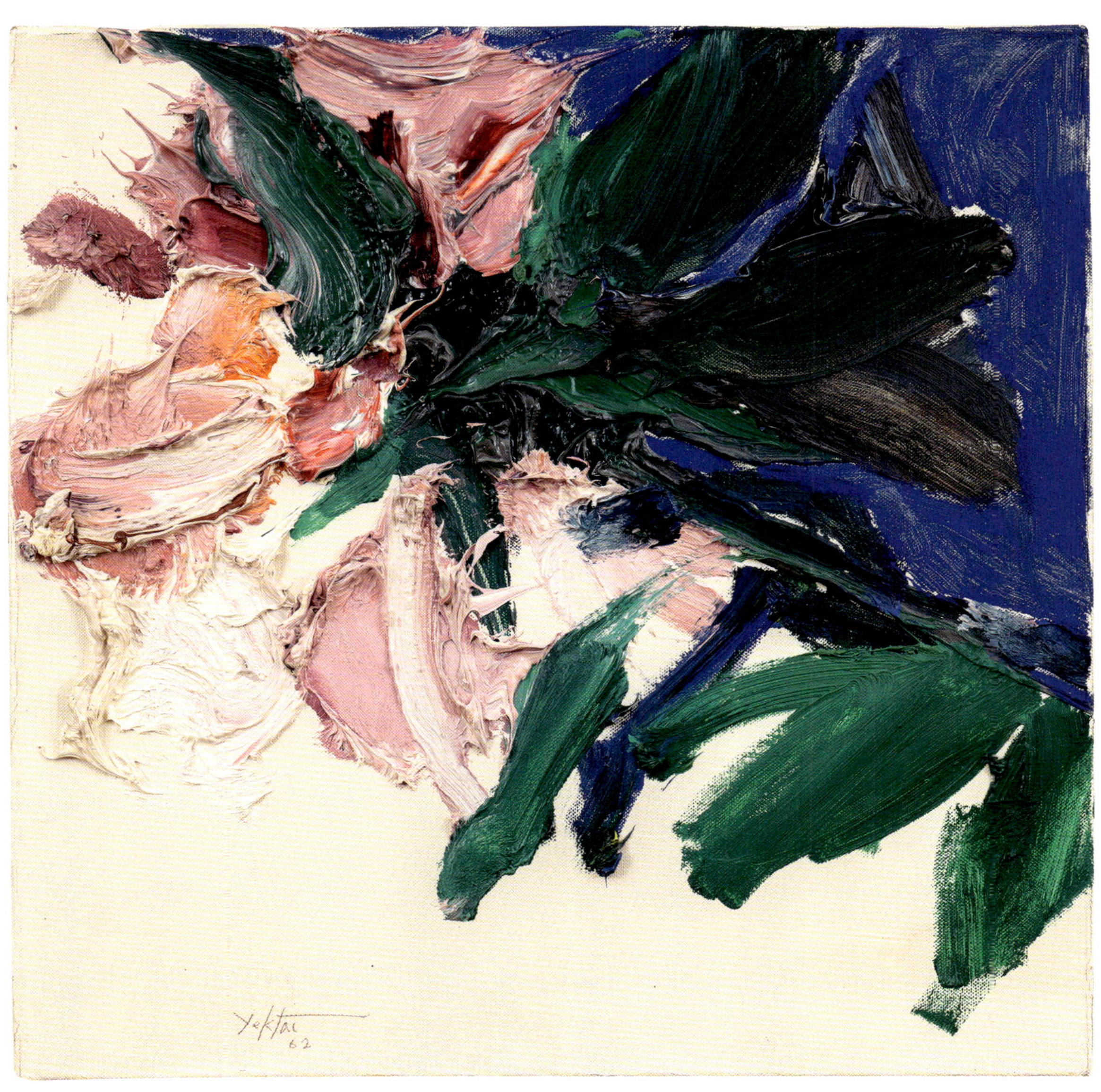

Untitled, 1962, oil on canvas, 15¾ × 15¾ inches (40 × 40 cm)

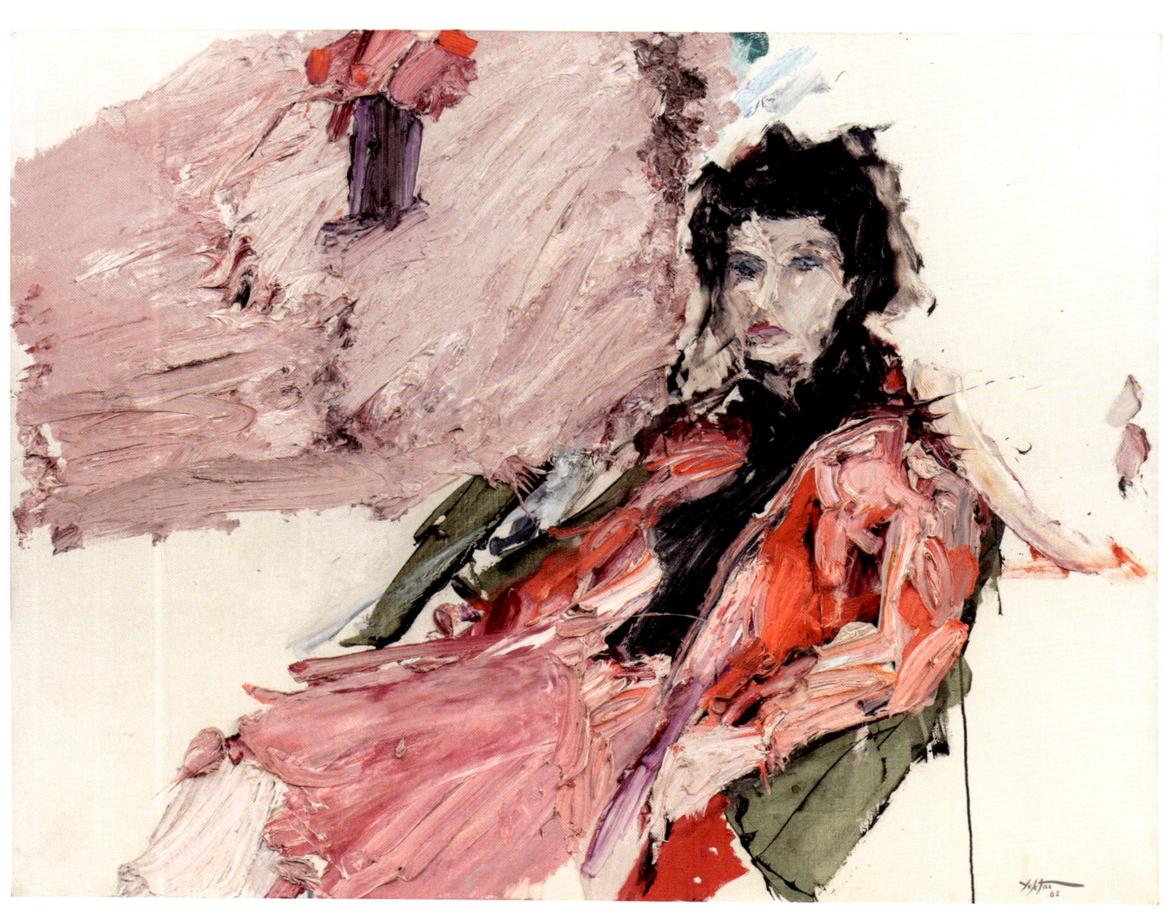

Ilse, 1962, oil on canvas, 45 × 57 inches (114.3 × 144.8 cm)

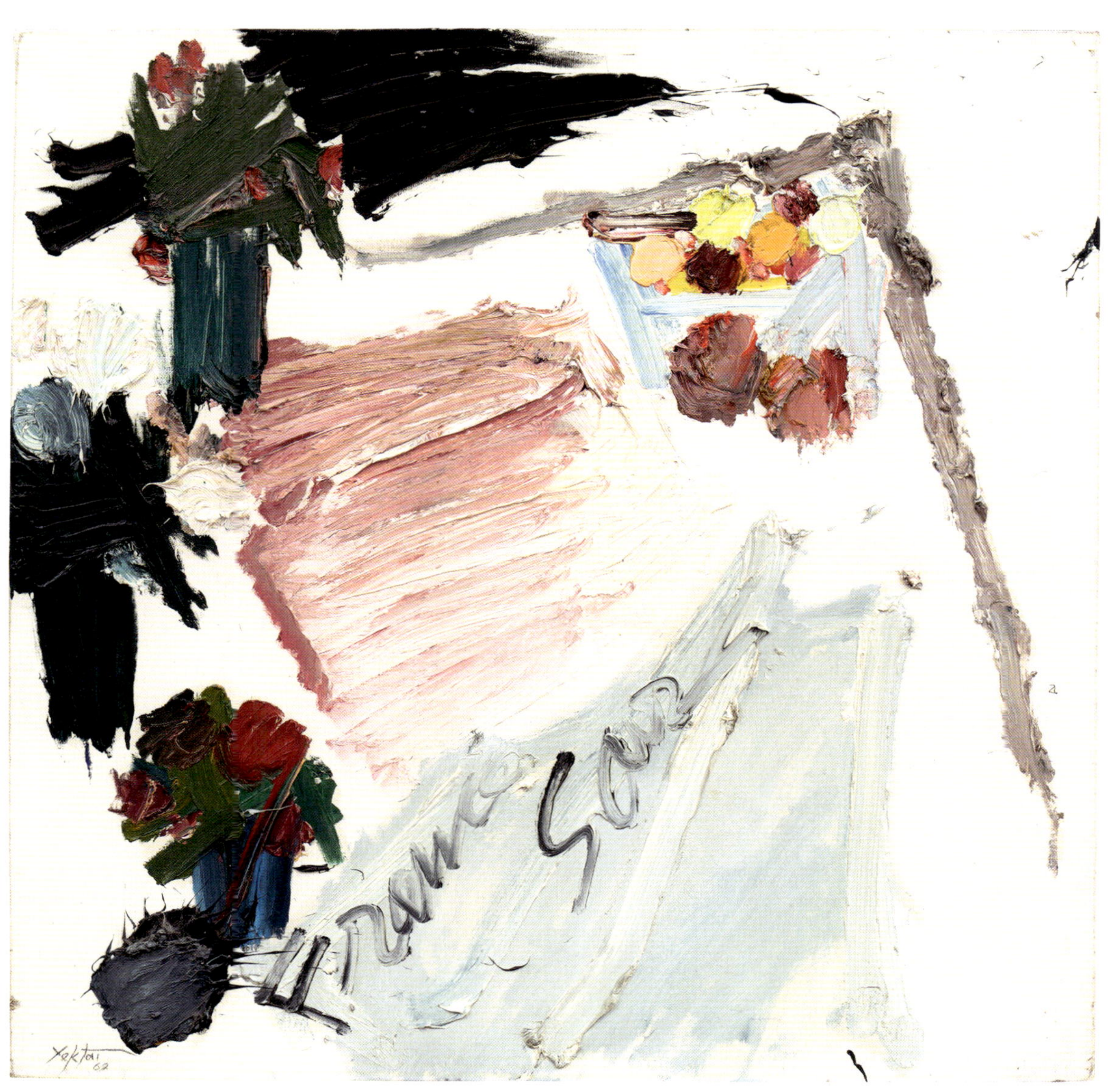

France-Soir with Flowers, 1962, oil on canvas, 39¼ × 39¼ inches (99.7 × 99.7 cm)

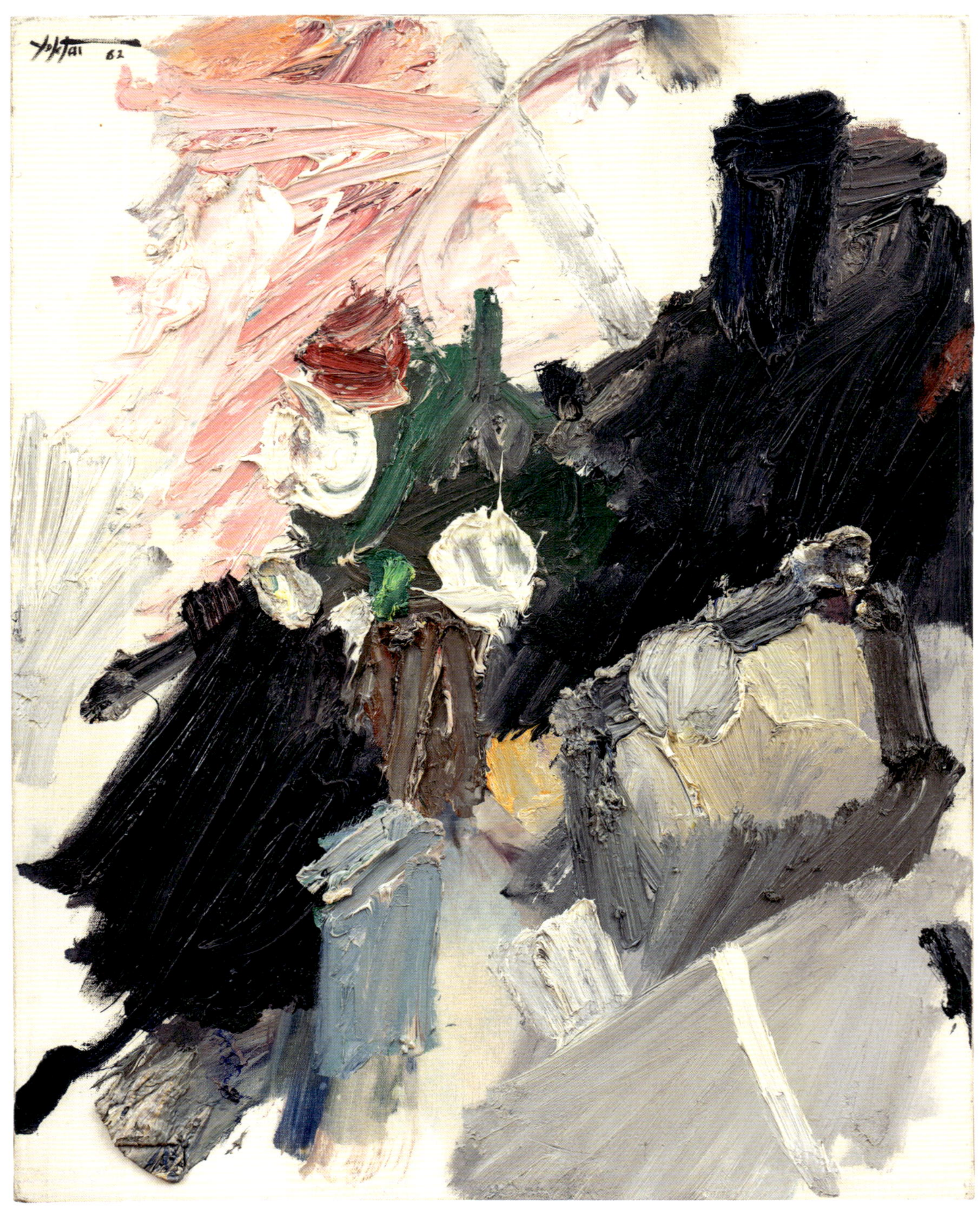

Still Life #12, 1962, oil on canvas, 36¼ × 29 inches (92.1 × 73.7 cm)

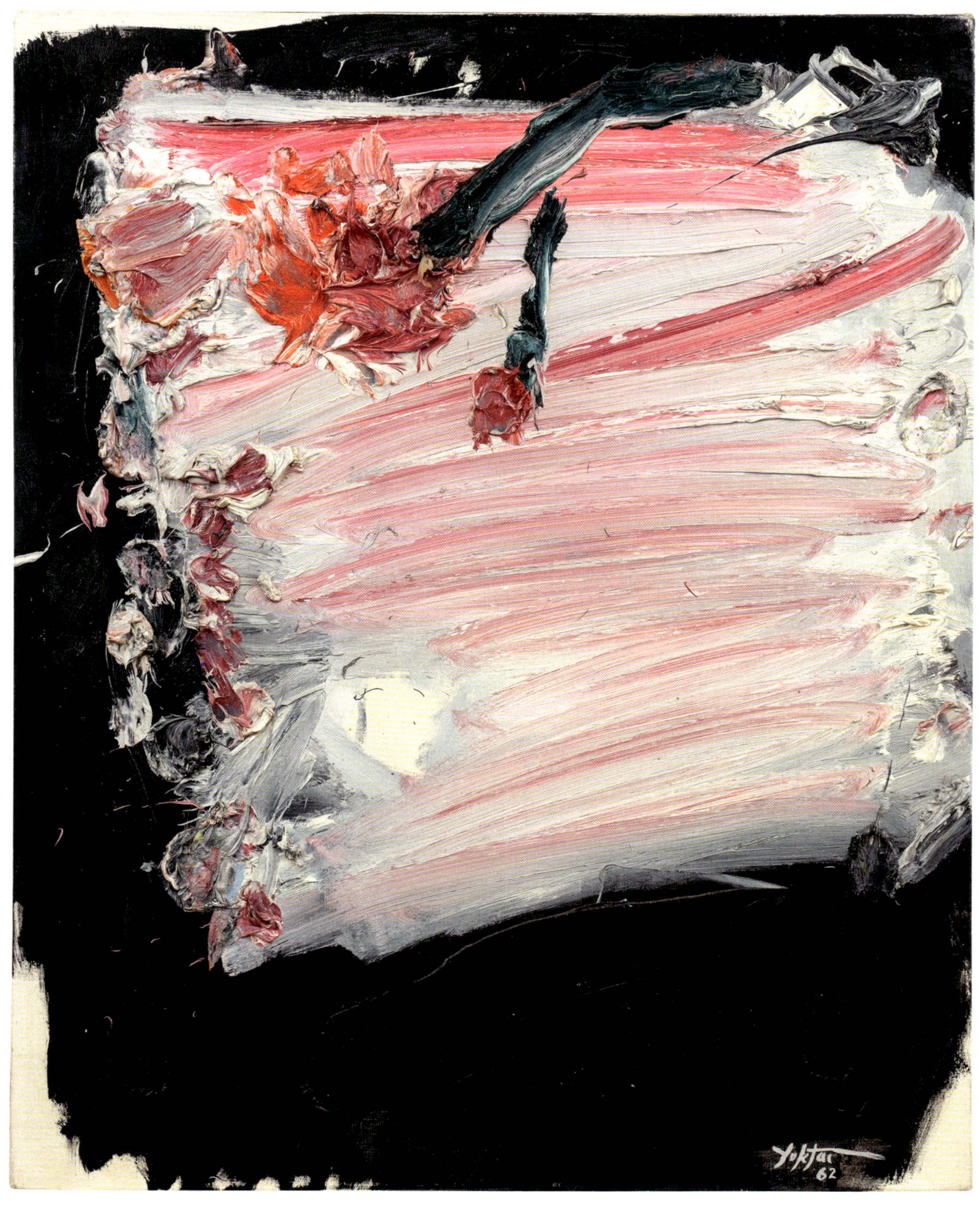

Untitled, 1962, oil on canvas, 36¼ × 28¾ inches (92.1 × 73 cm)

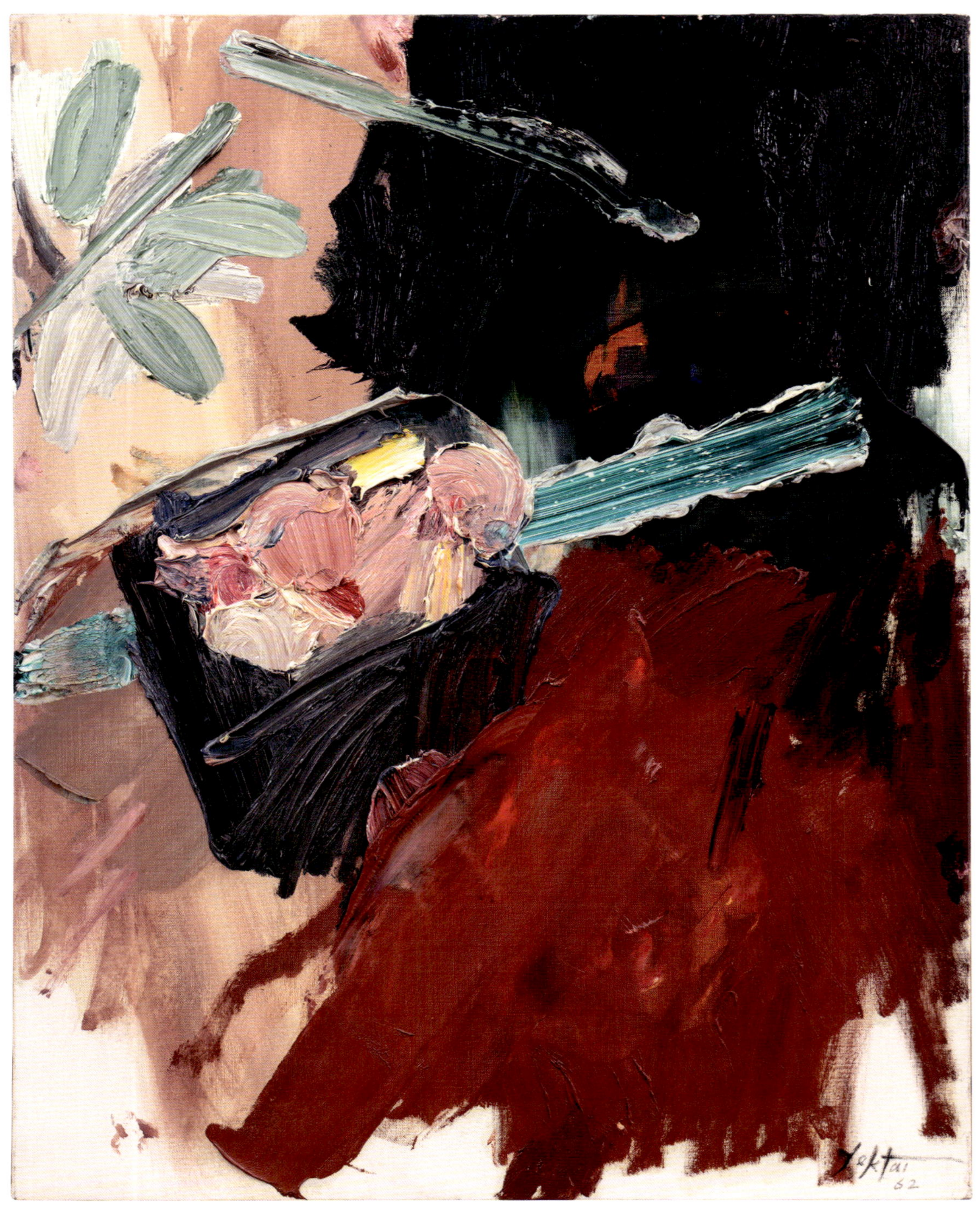

Untitled, 1962, oil on canvas, 36¼ × 28¾ inches (92.1 × 73 cm)

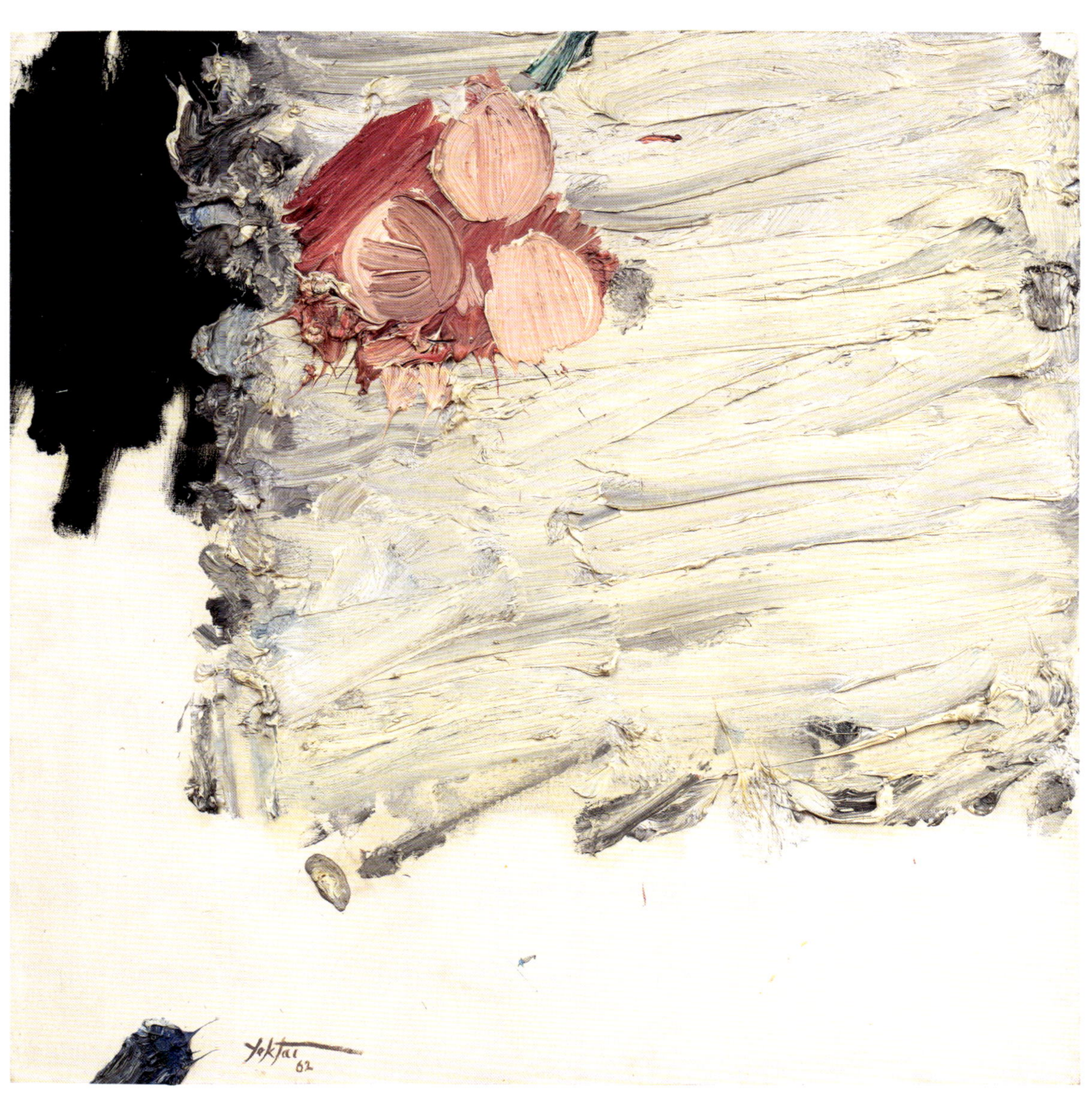

Untitled, 1962, oil on canvas, 31¼ × 31¼ inches (79.4 × 79.4 cm)

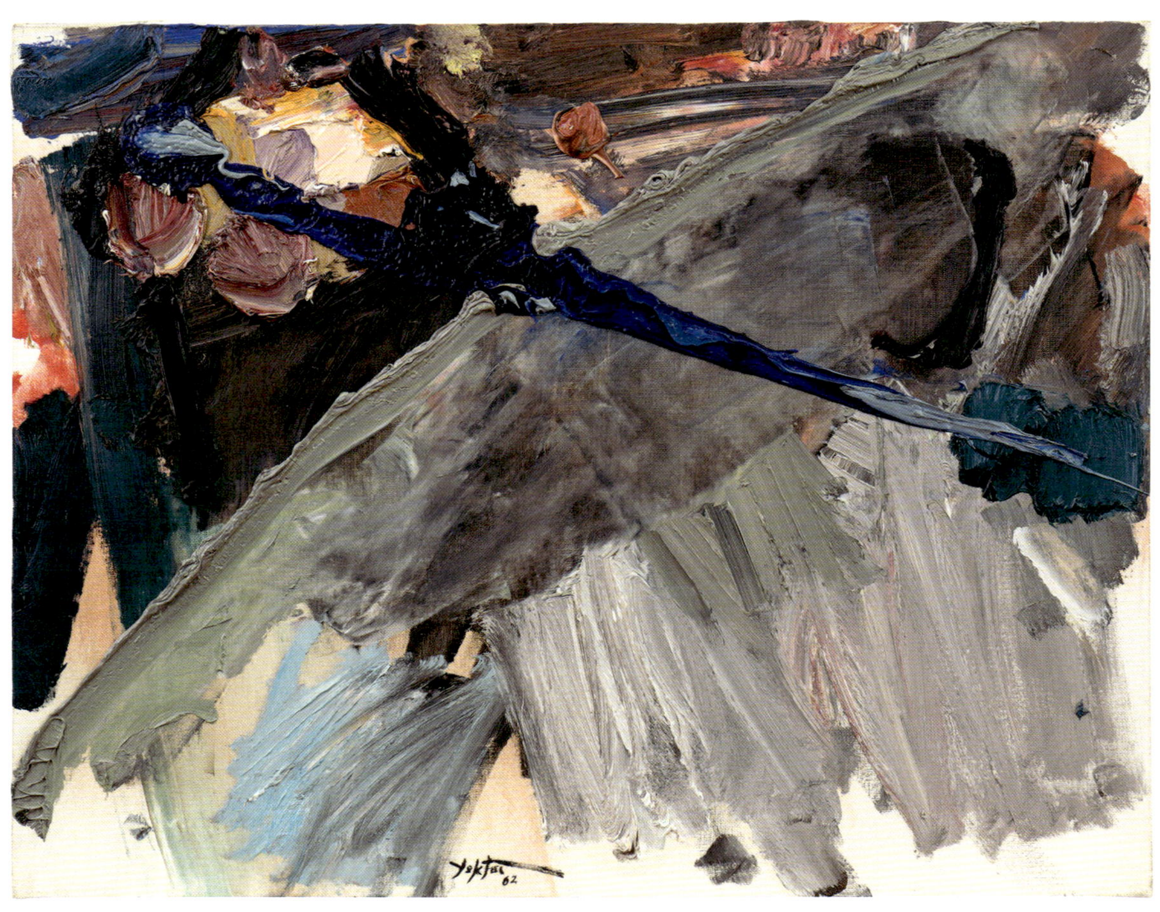

Untitled, 1962, oil on canvas, 28¼ × 36 inches (71.8 × 91.4 cm)

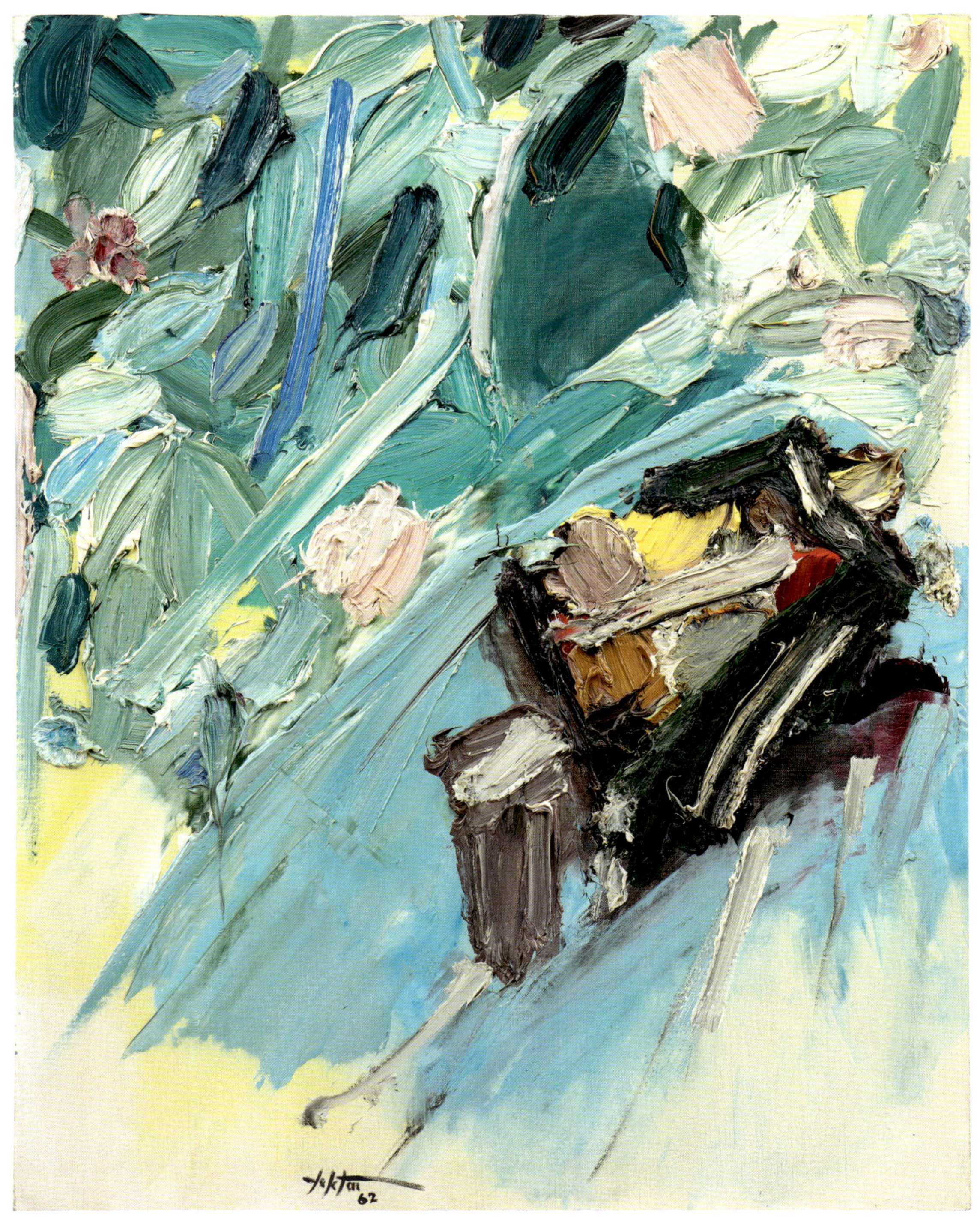

Untitled, 1962, oil on canvas, 36 × 28¾ inches (91.4 × 73 cm)

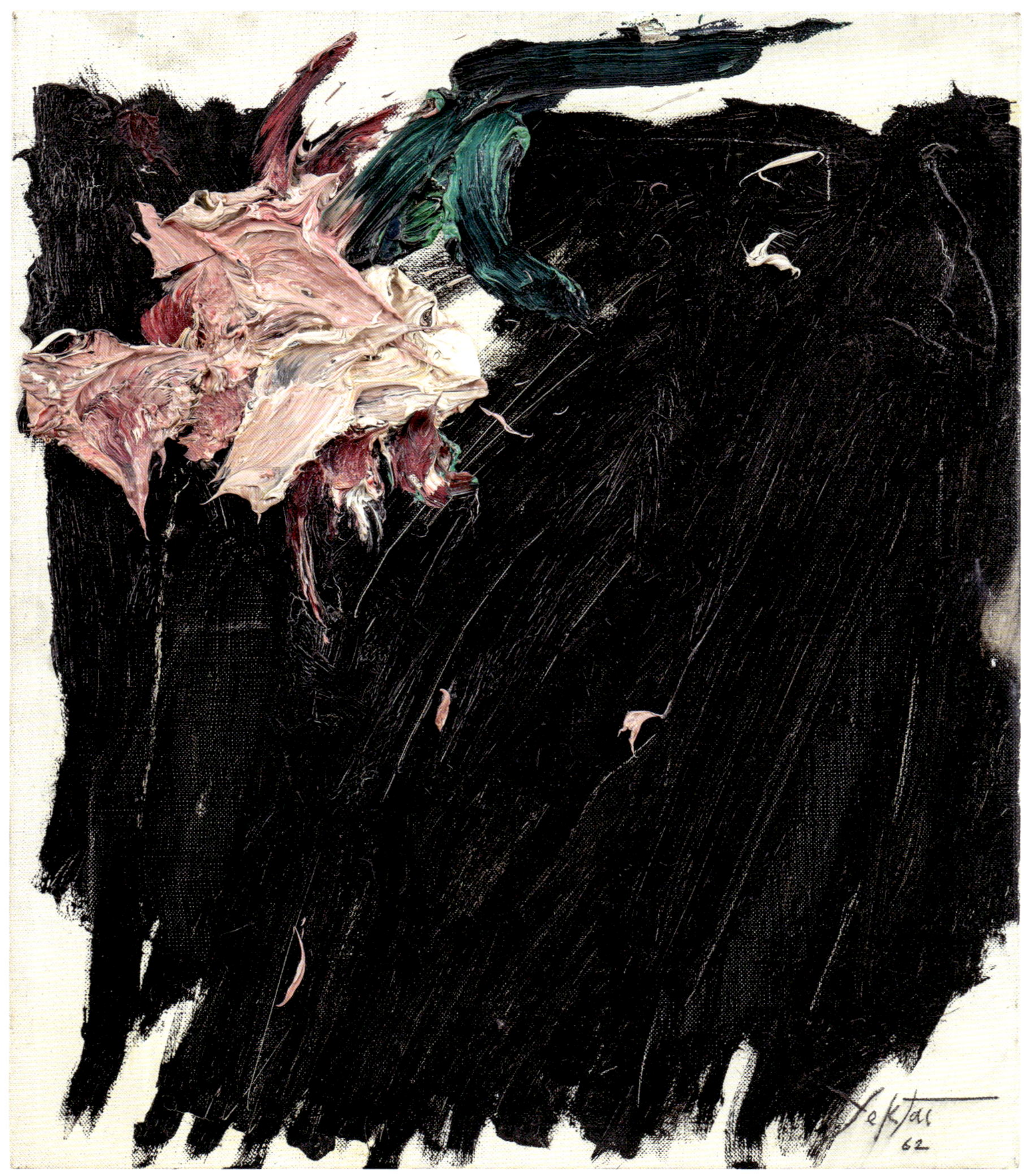

Untitled, 1962, oil on canvas, 20½ × 17½ inches (52.1 × 44.5 cm)

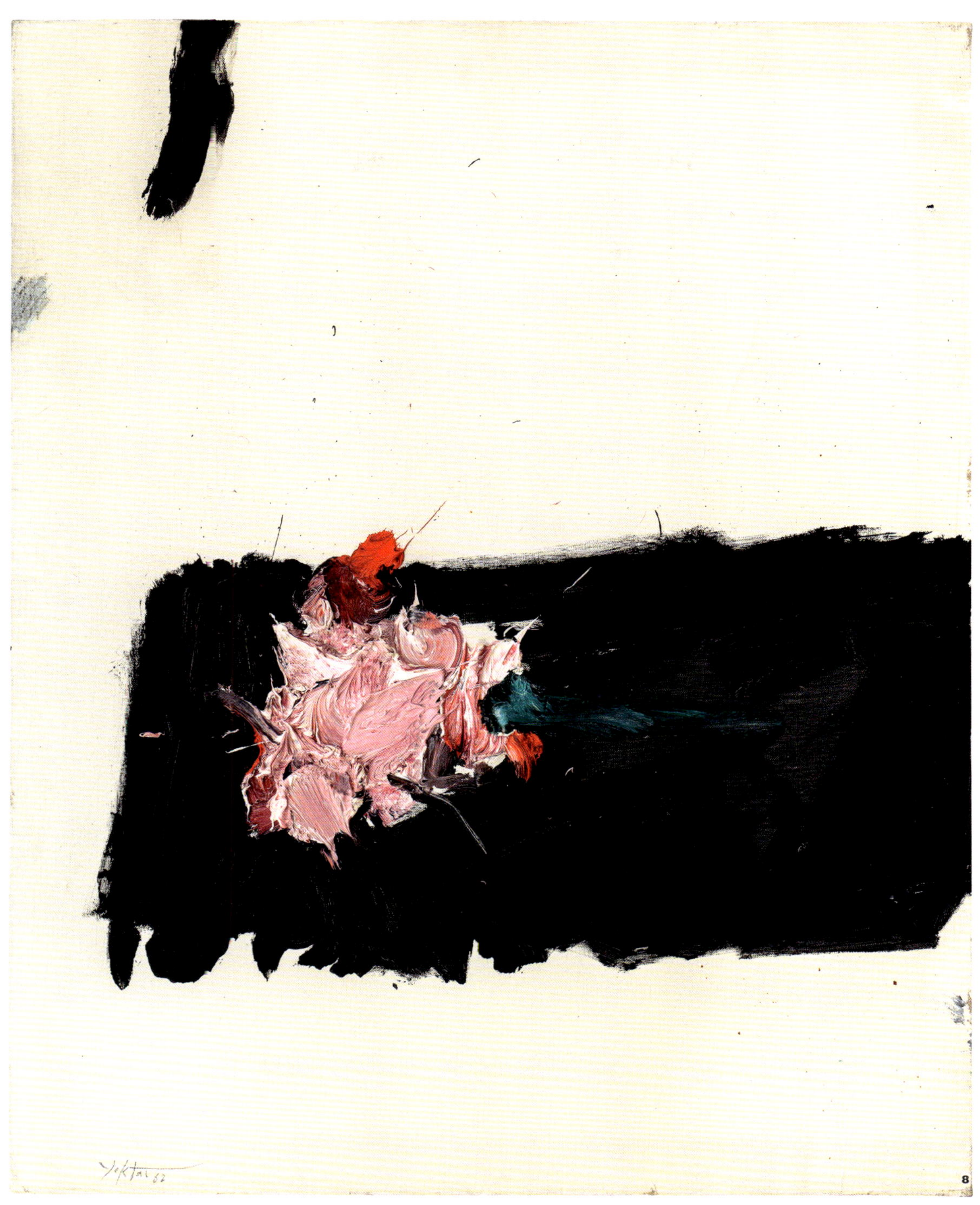

Untitled, 1962, oil on canvas, 36 × 28¾ inches (91.4 × 73 cm)

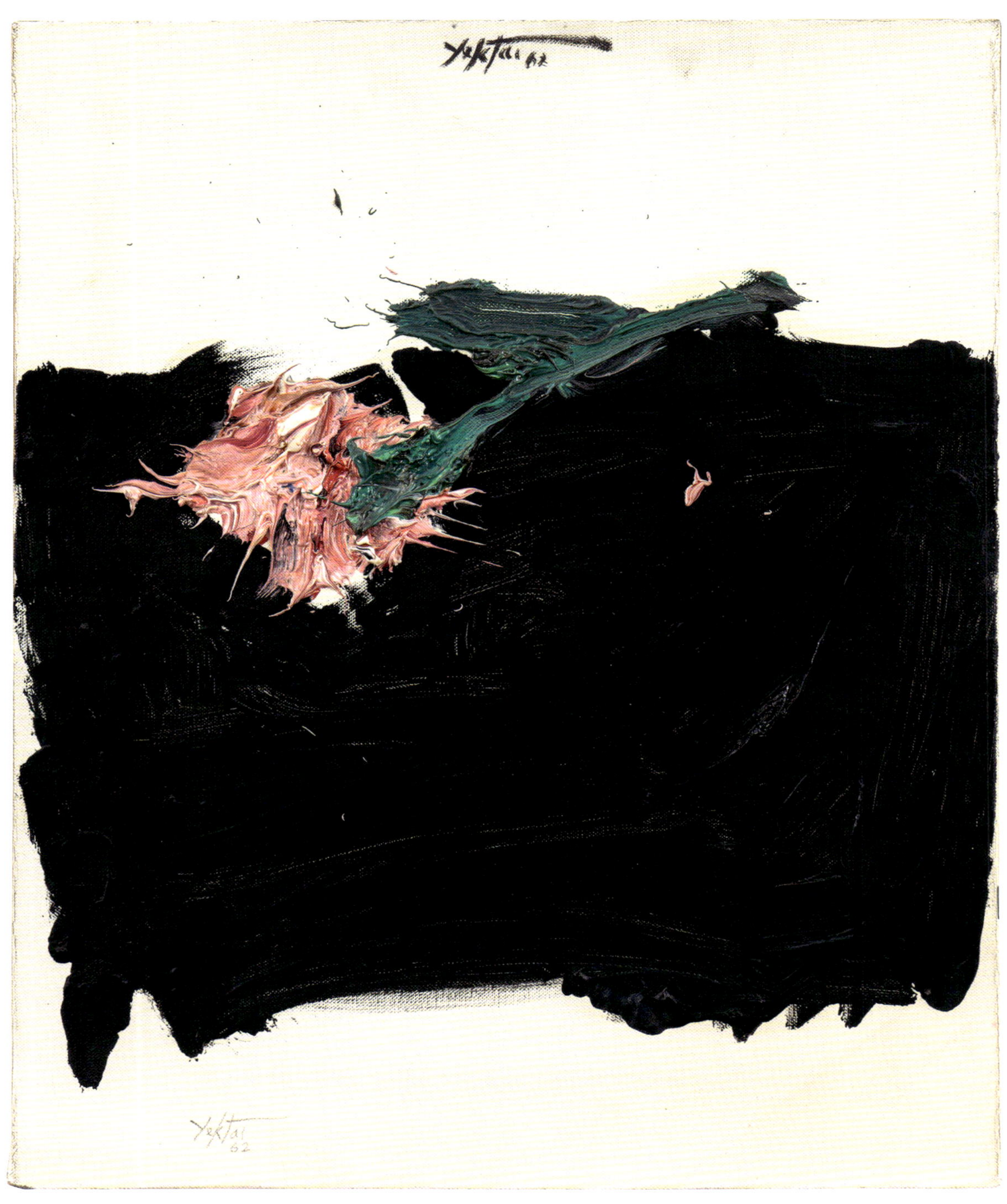

Flower, 1962, oil on canvas, 18⅛ × 14¾ inches (46 × 37.5 cm)

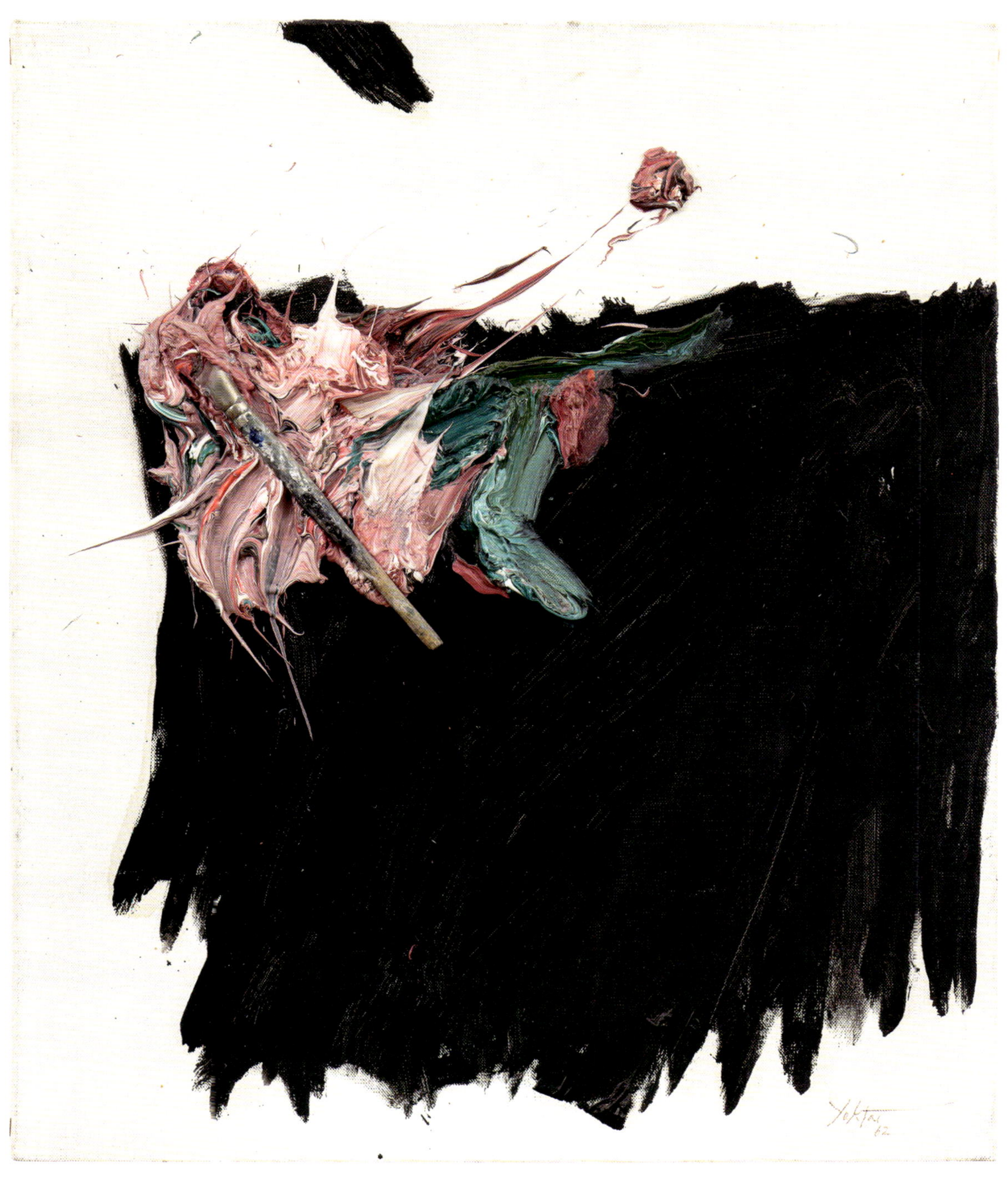

Untitled, 1962, oil on canvas, 21¾ × 18 inches (55.3 × 45.7 cm)

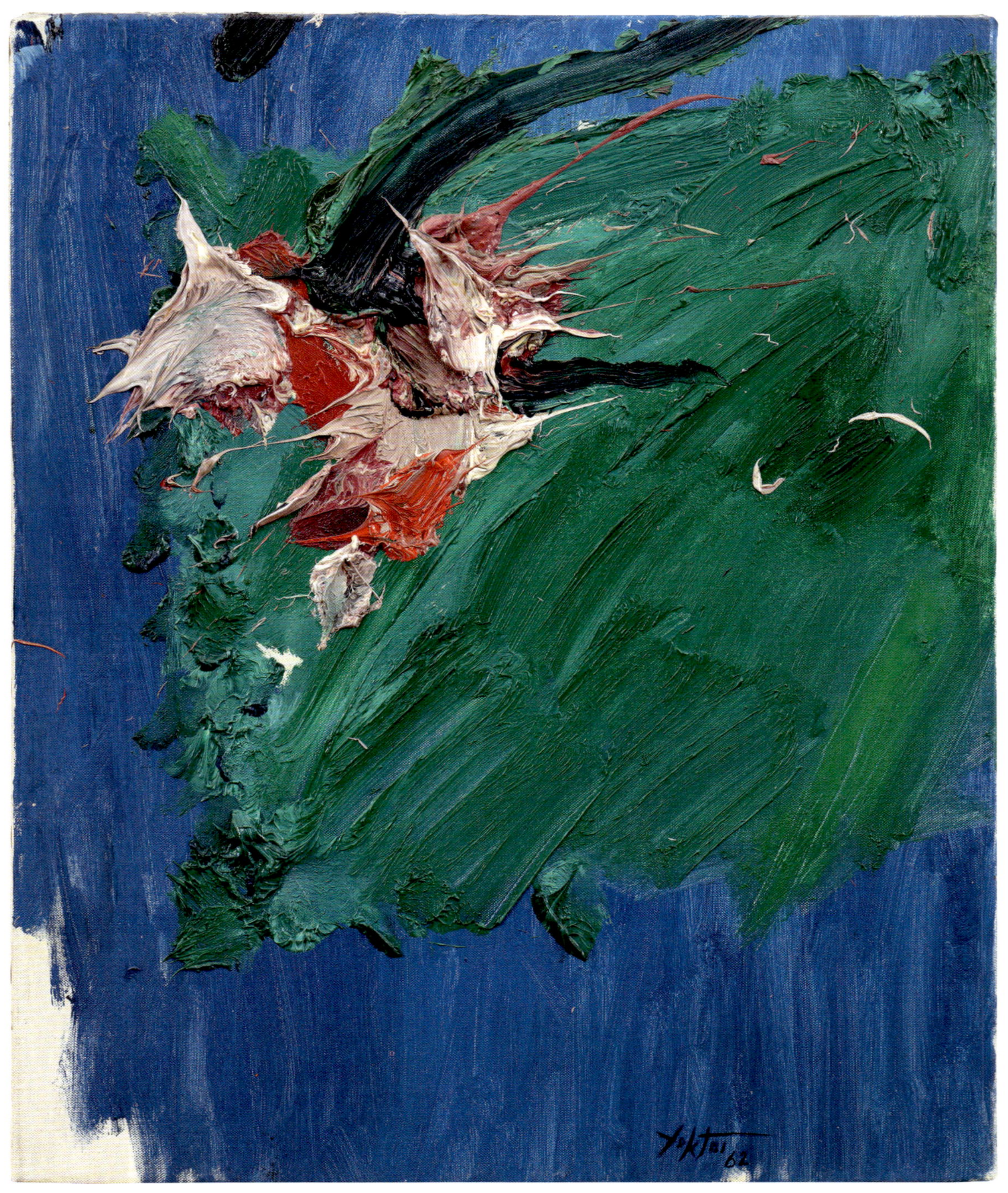

 Untitled, 1962, oil on canvas, 24 × 19¾ inches (61 × 50.2 cm)

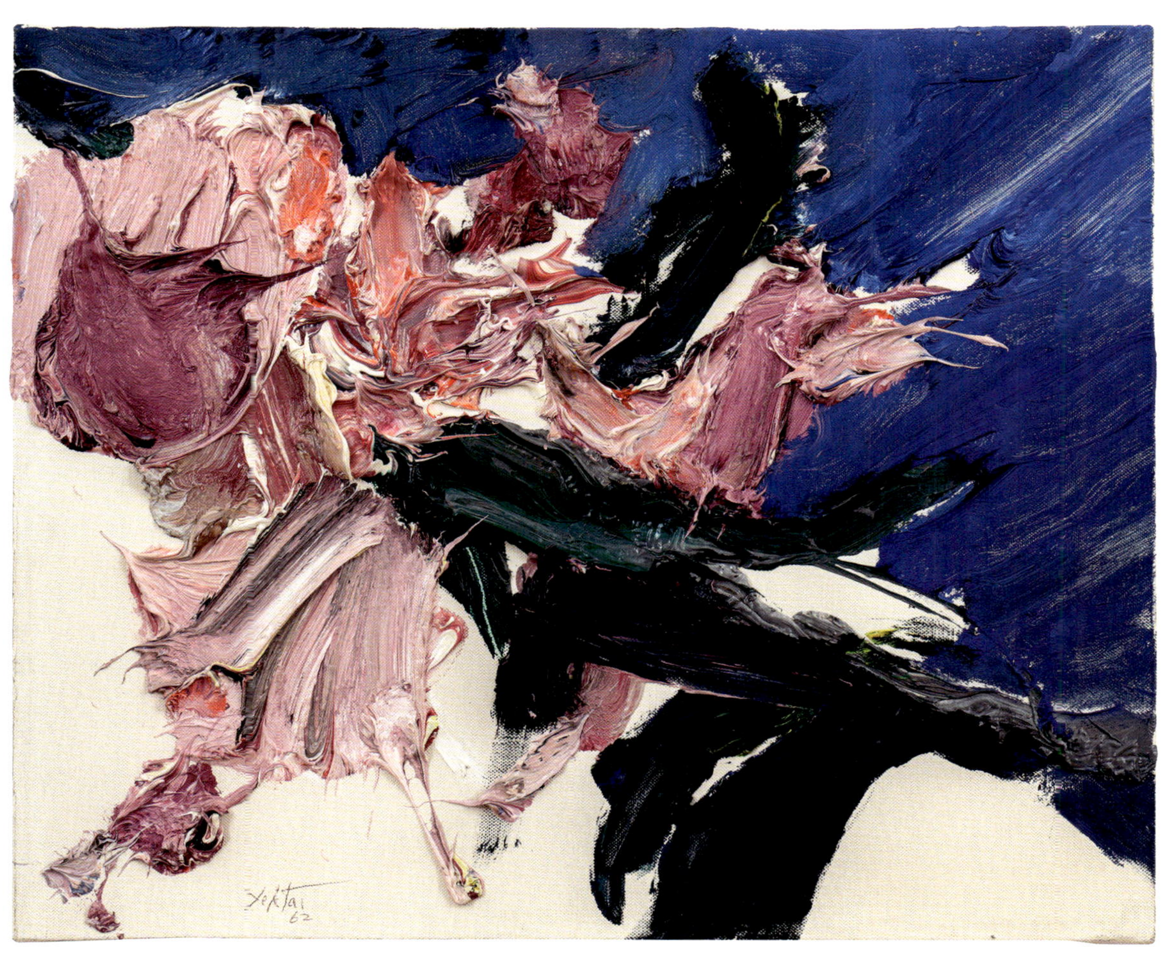

Untitled, 1962, oil on canvas, 15 × 18 inches (38.1 × 45.7 cm)

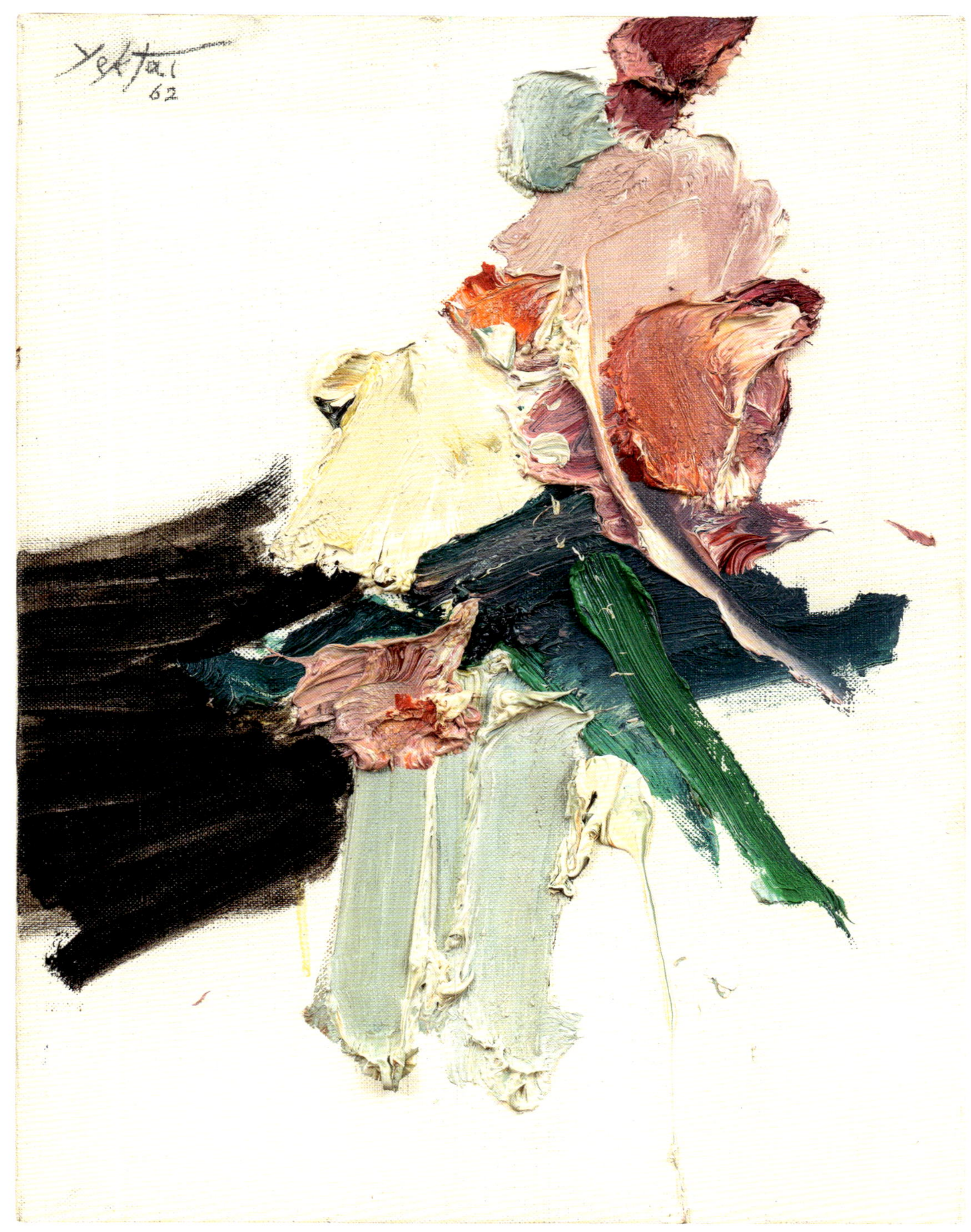

 Untitled, 1962, oil on canvas, 17½ × 13½ inches (44.5 × 34.3 cm)

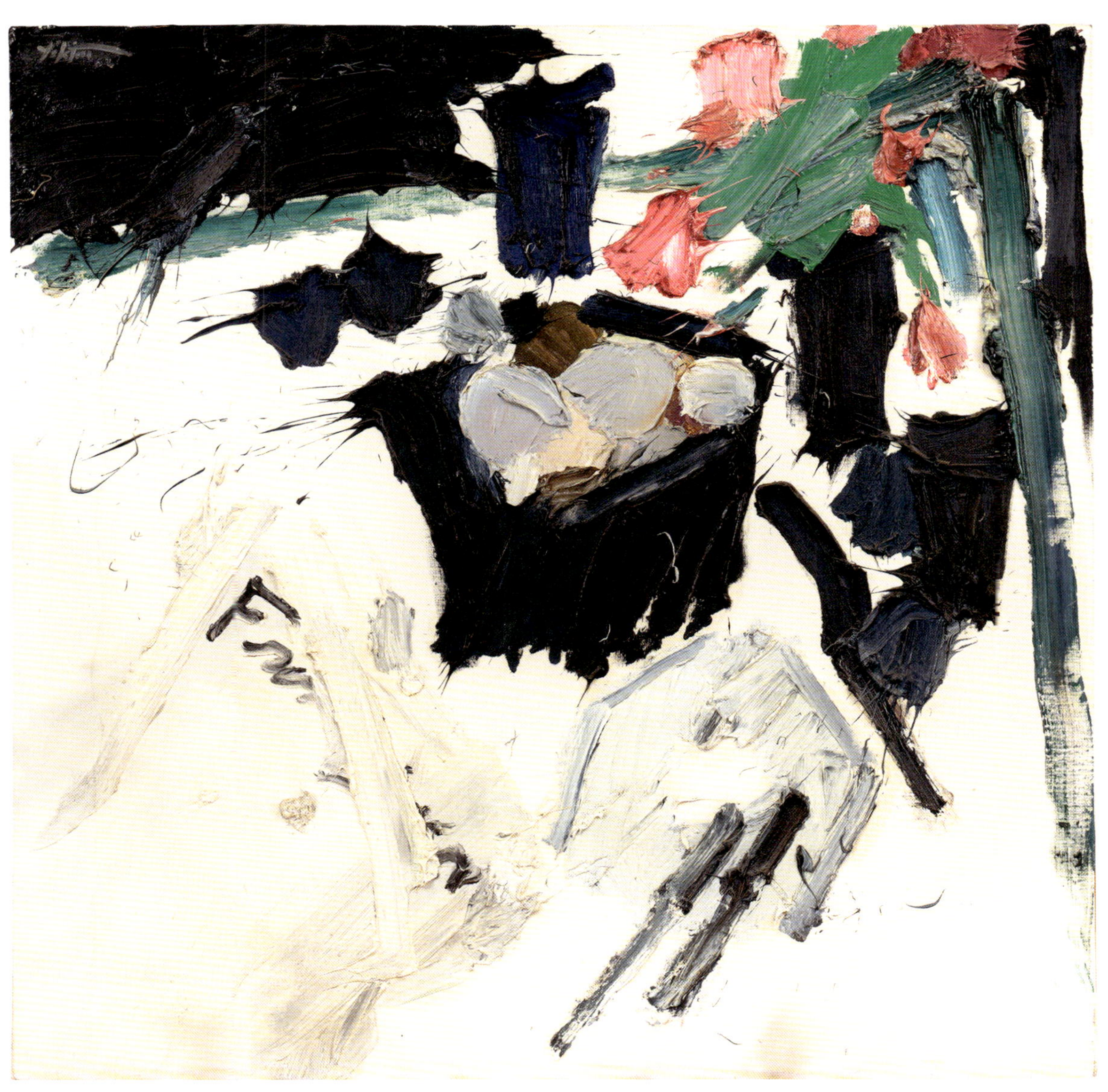

Untitled, 1962, oil on canvas, 39¼ × 39¼ inches (99.7 × 99.7 cm)

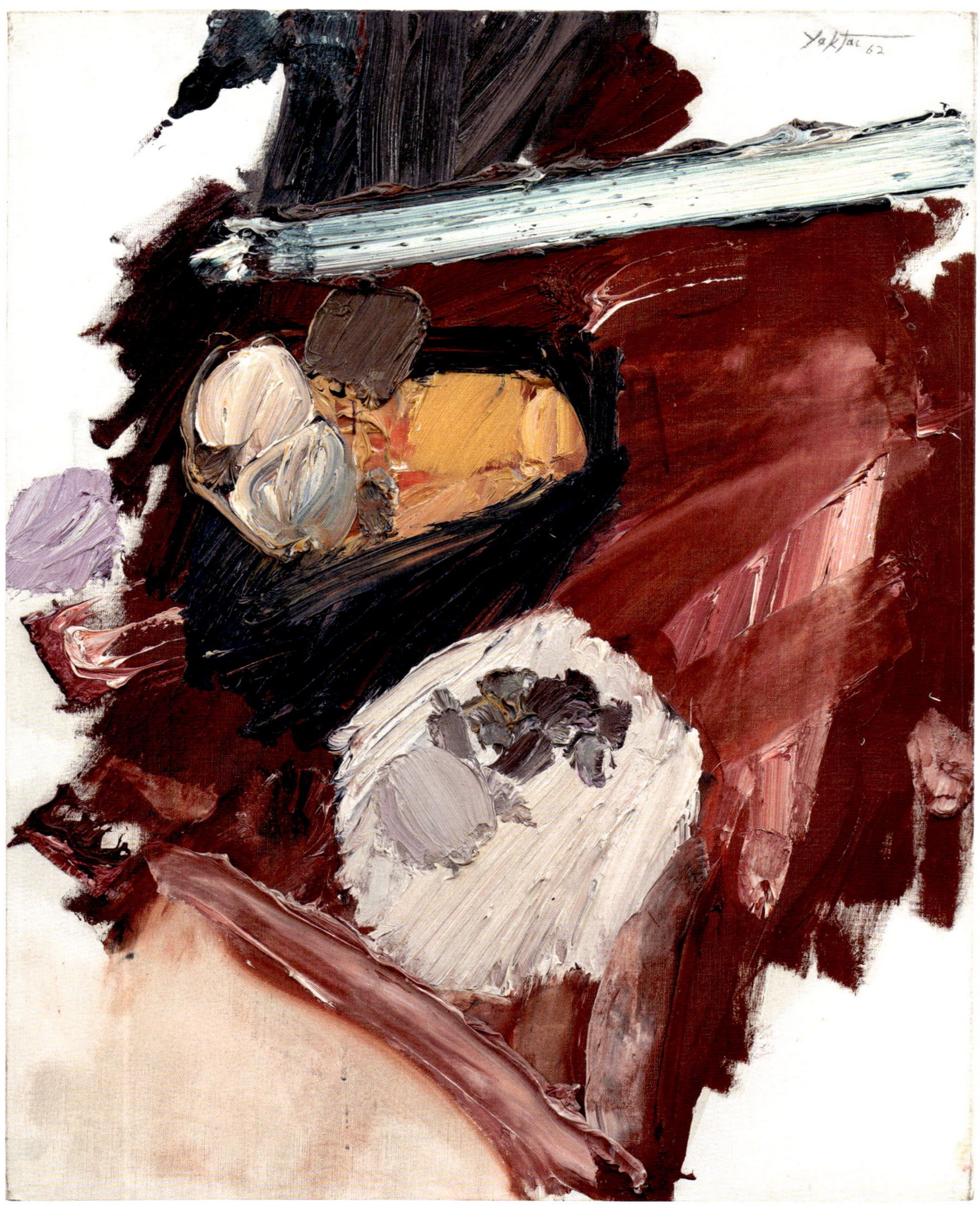

Untitled, 1962, oil on canvas, 36 × 29 inches (91.4 × 73.7 cm)

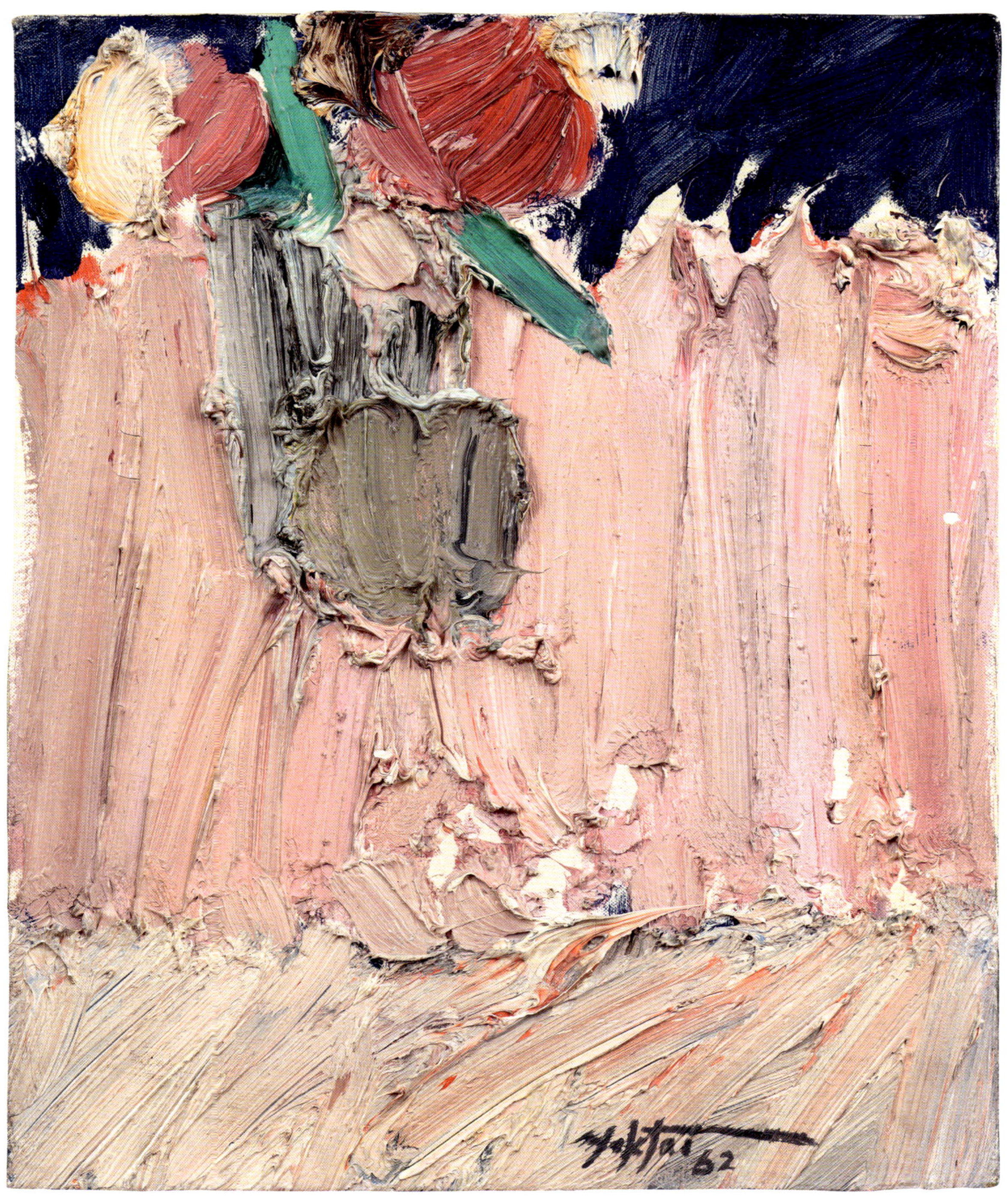

Untitled, 1962, oil on canvas, 18¼ × 14¾ inches (46.4 × 37.5 cm)

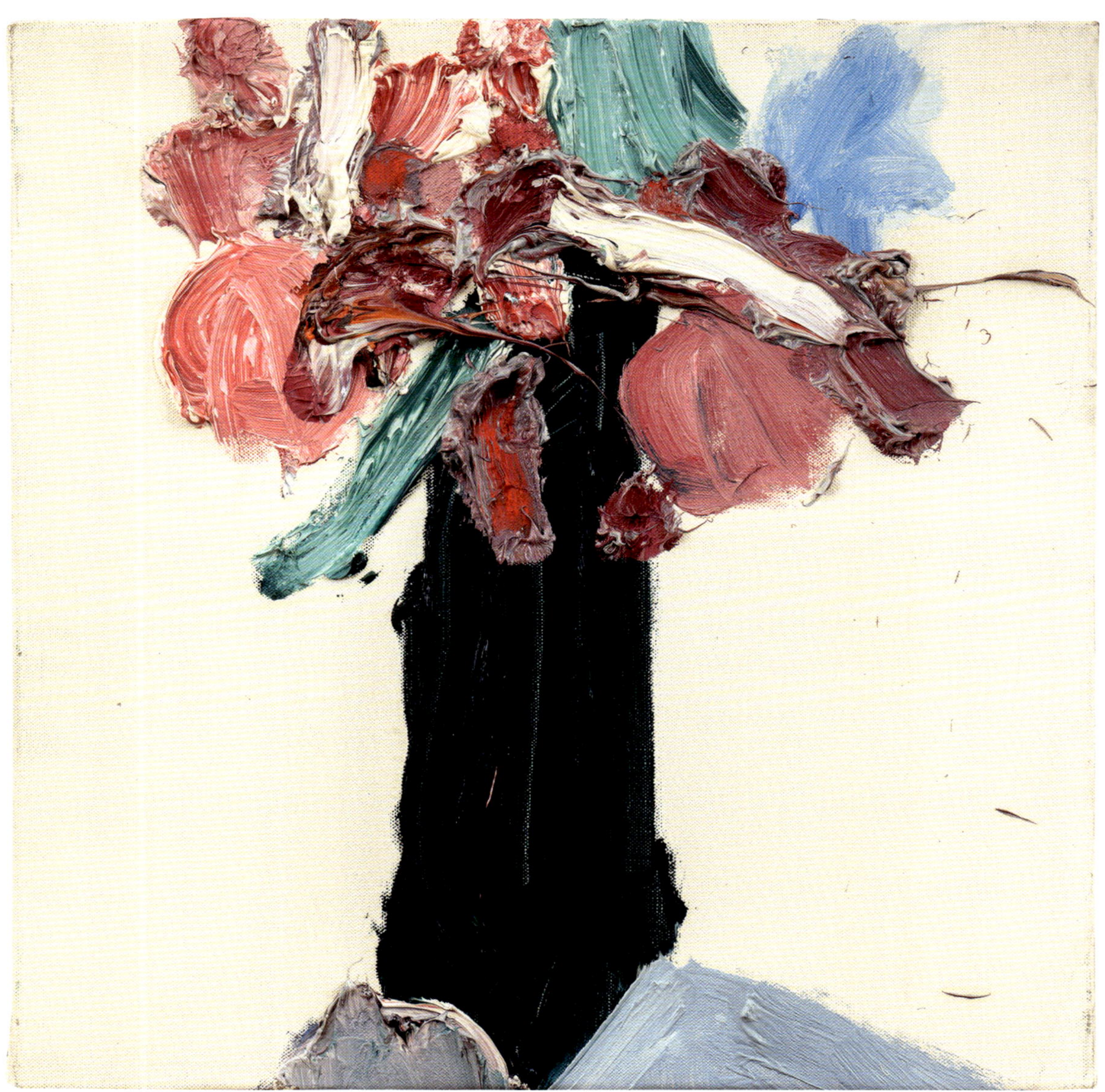

 Untitled, 1962, oil on canvas, 15⅝ × 15⅝ inches (39.7 × 39.7 cm)

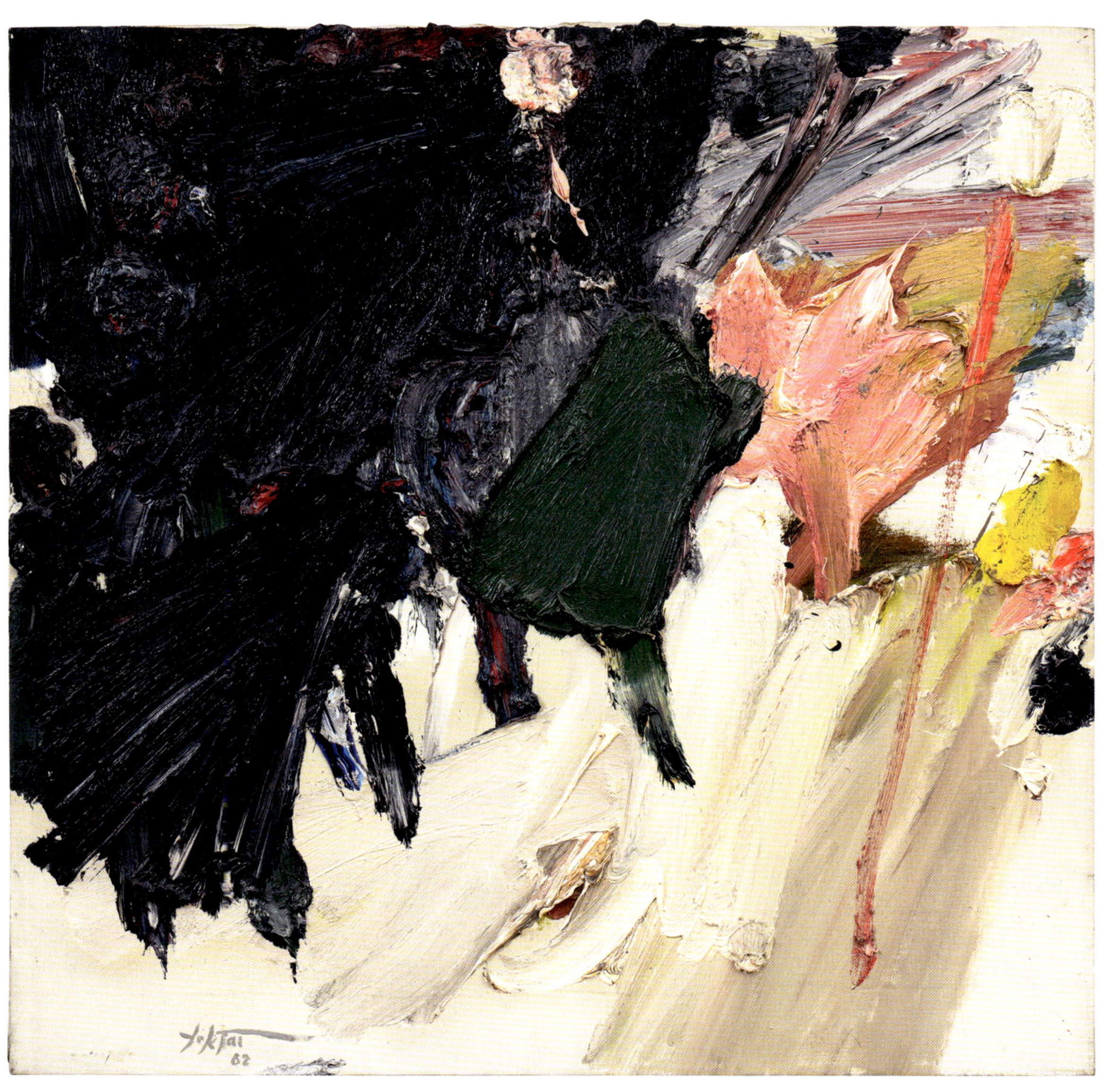

Untitled, 1962, oil on canvas, 32 × 32 inches (81.3 × 81.3 cm)

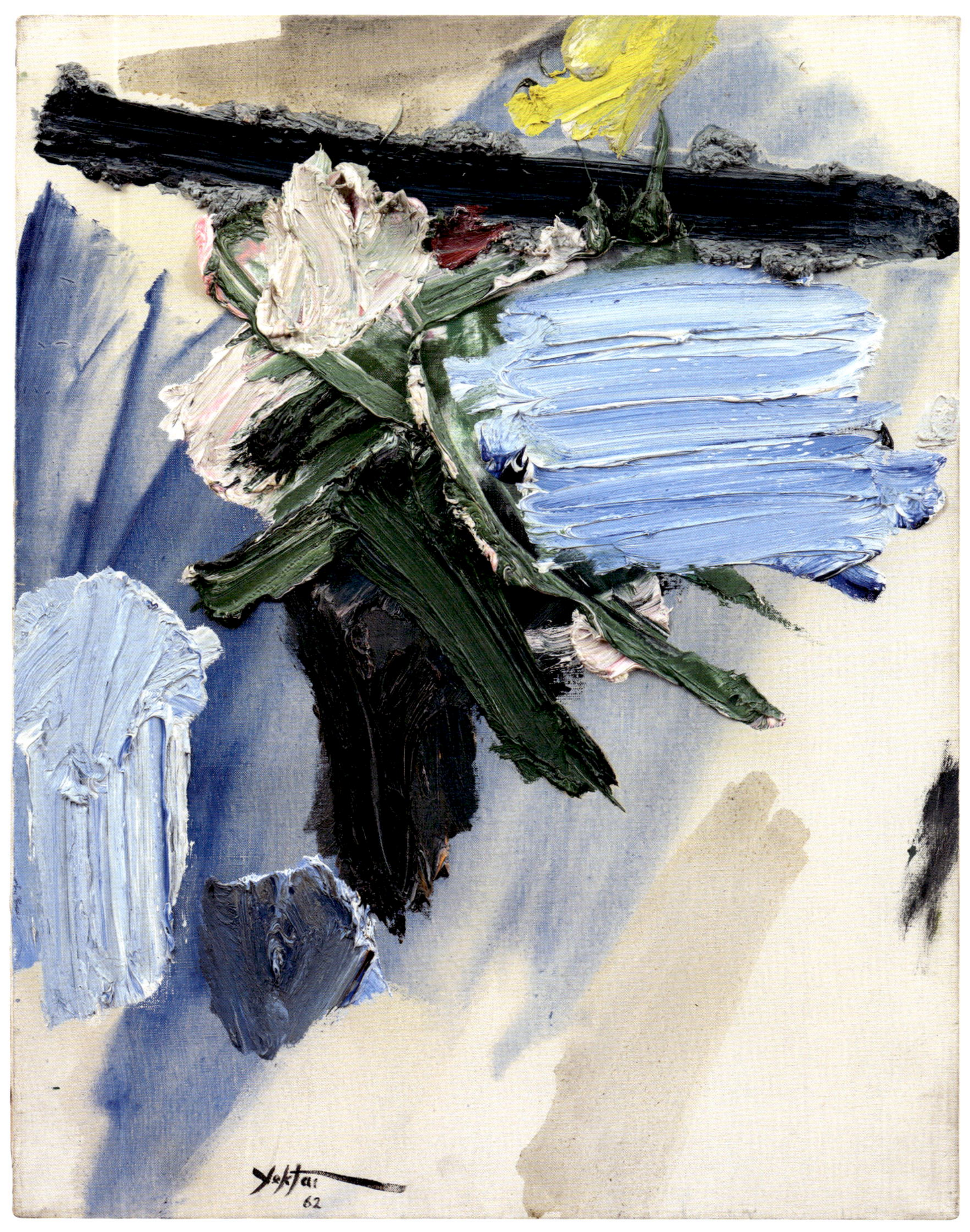

Untitled, 1962, oil on canvas, 28 × 20 inches (71.1 × 50.8 cm)

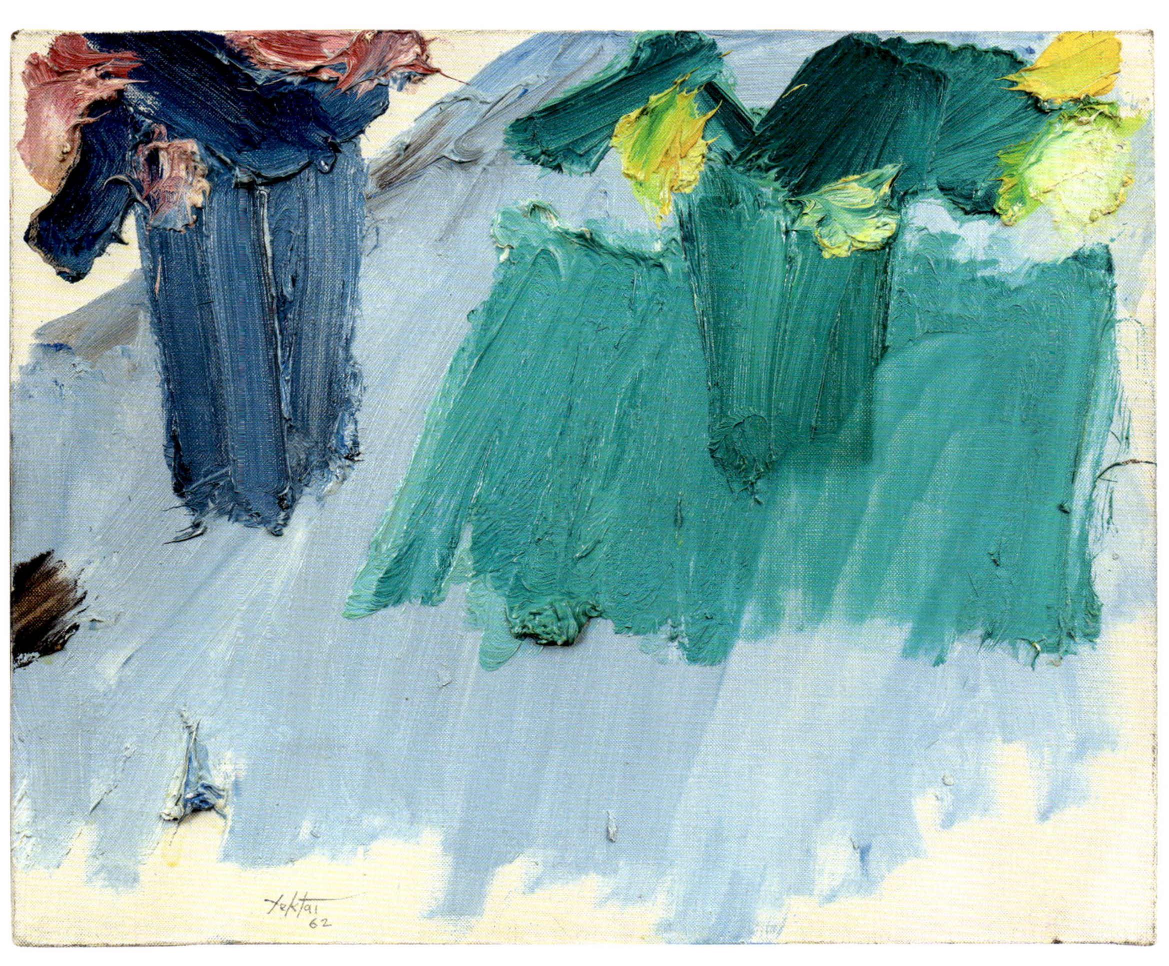

Blue Vase, 1962, oil on canvas, 15 × 18 inches (38.1 × 45.7 cm)

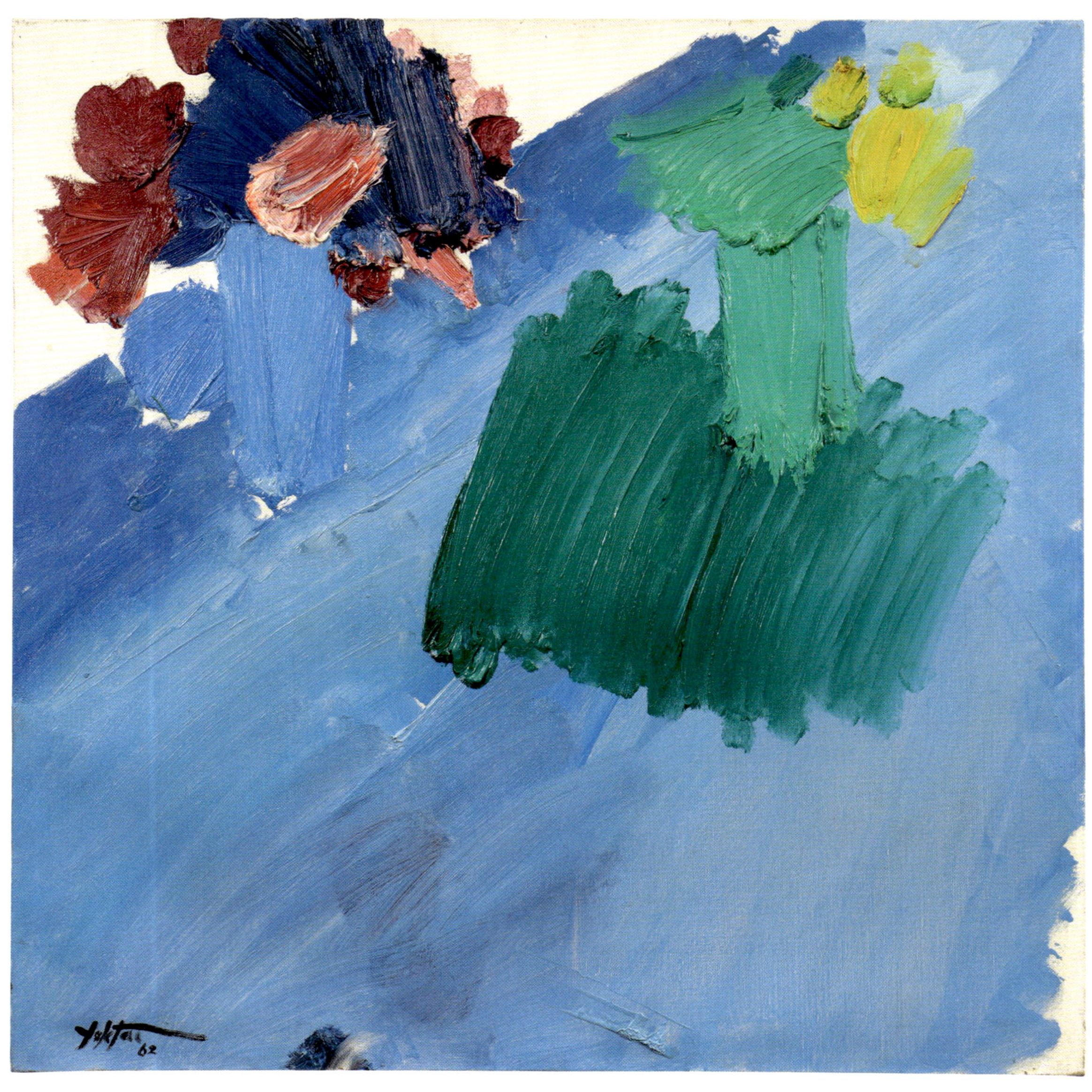

Untitled, 1962, oil on canvas, 31¼ × 31¼ inches (79.4 × 79.4 cm)

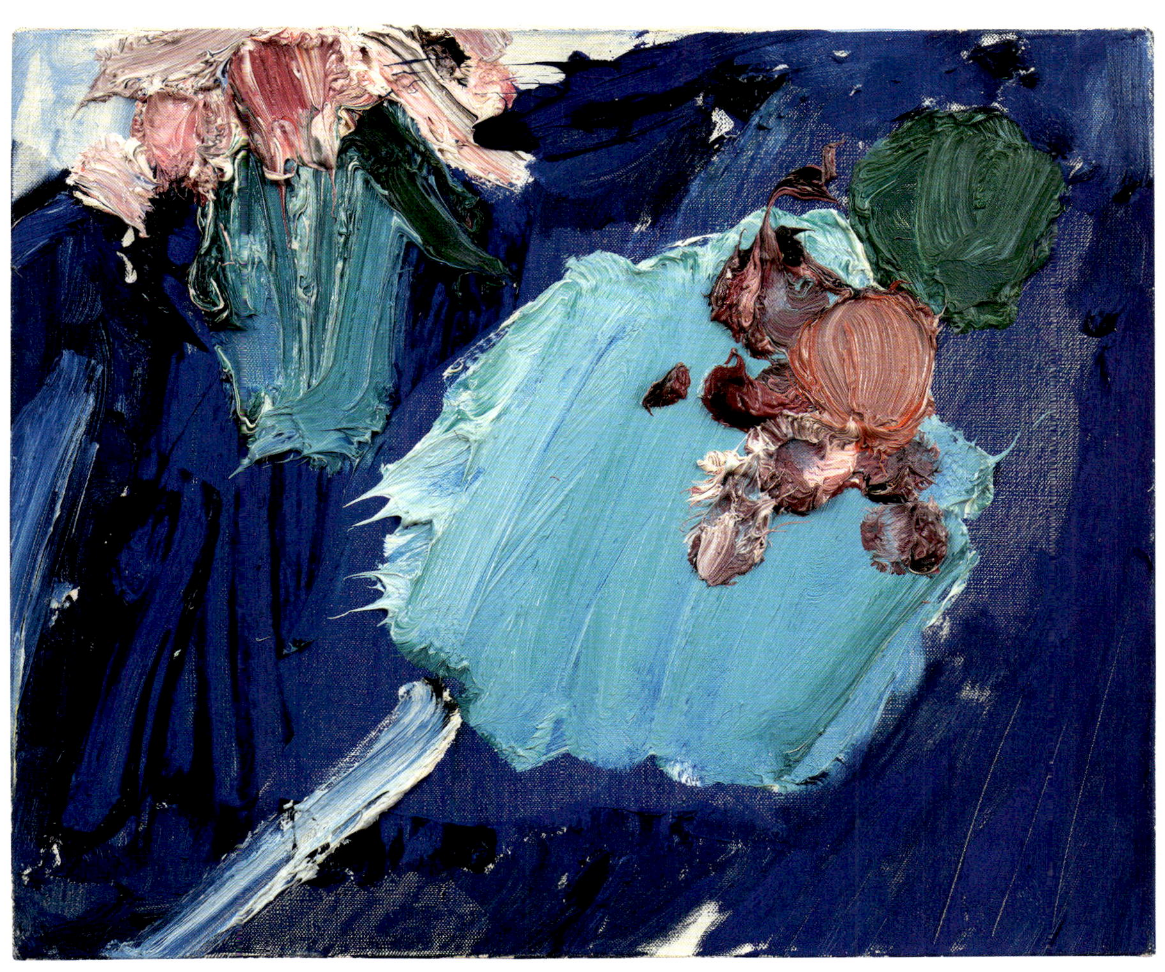

Untitled, 1962, oil on canvas, 15 × 18 inches (38.1 × 45.7 cm)

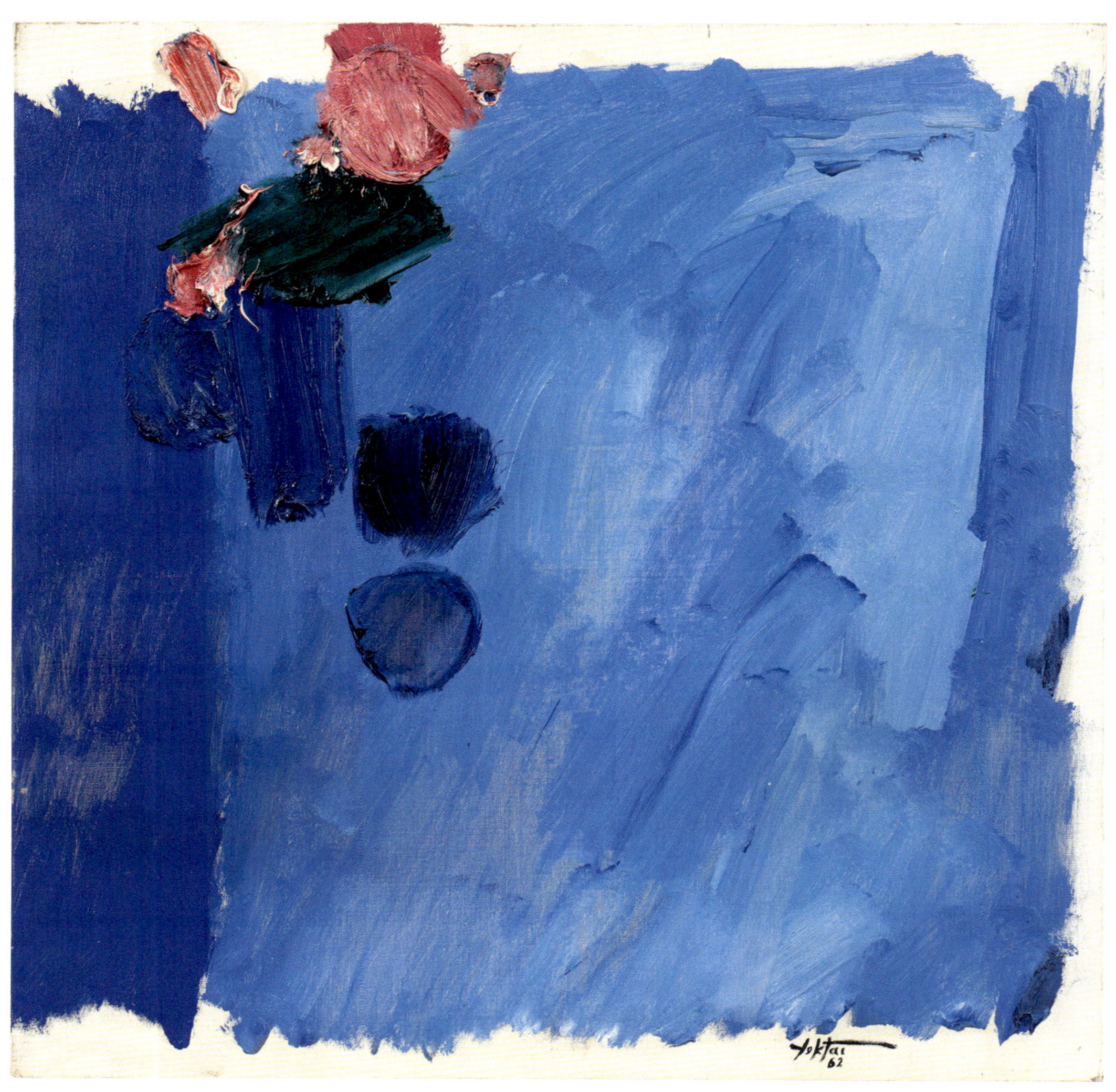

Untitled, 1962, oil on canvas, 31¼ × 31¼ inches (79.4 × 79.4 cm)

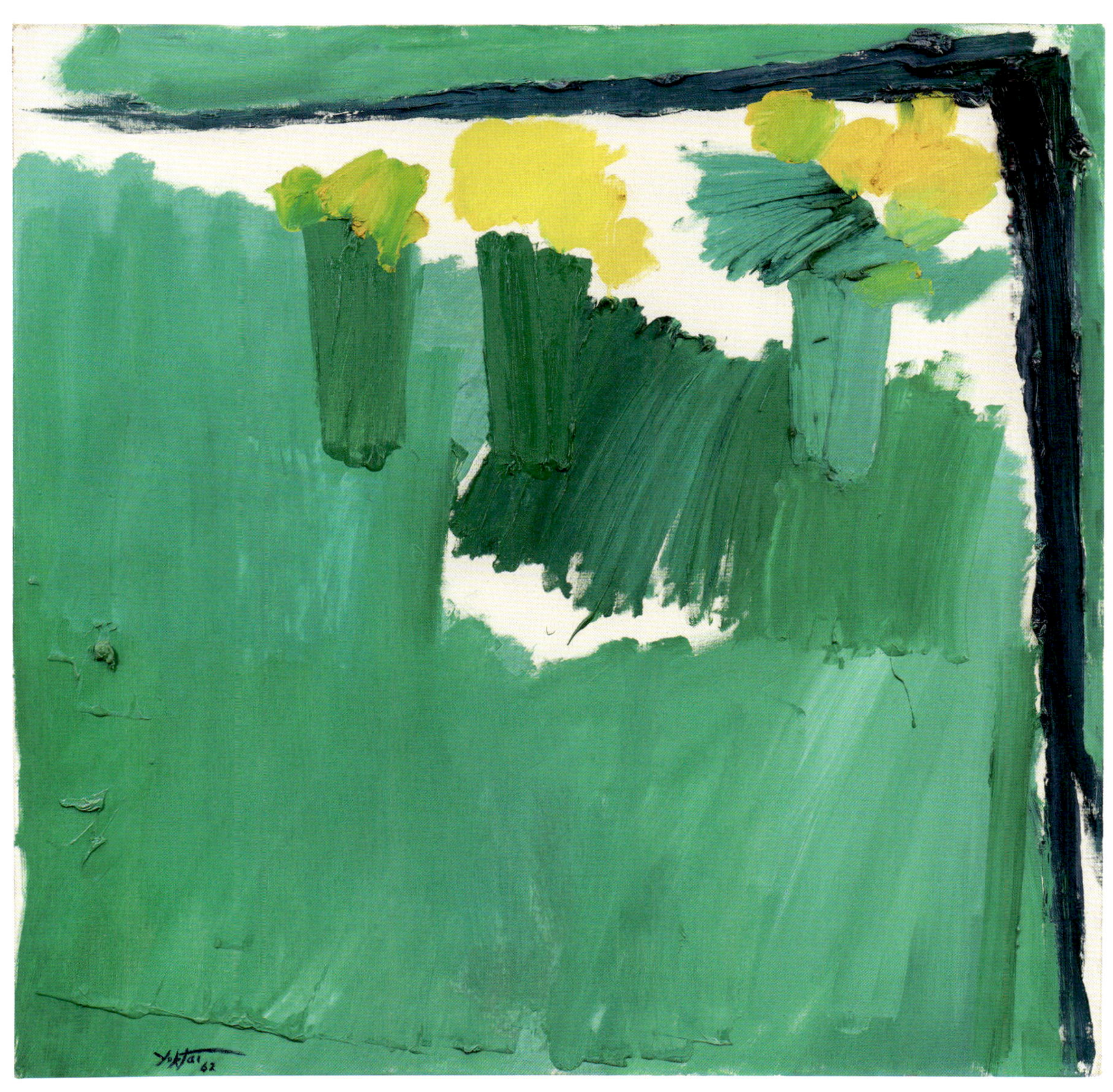

Untitled, 1962, oil on canvas, 39¼ × 39¼ inches (99.7 × 99.7 cm)

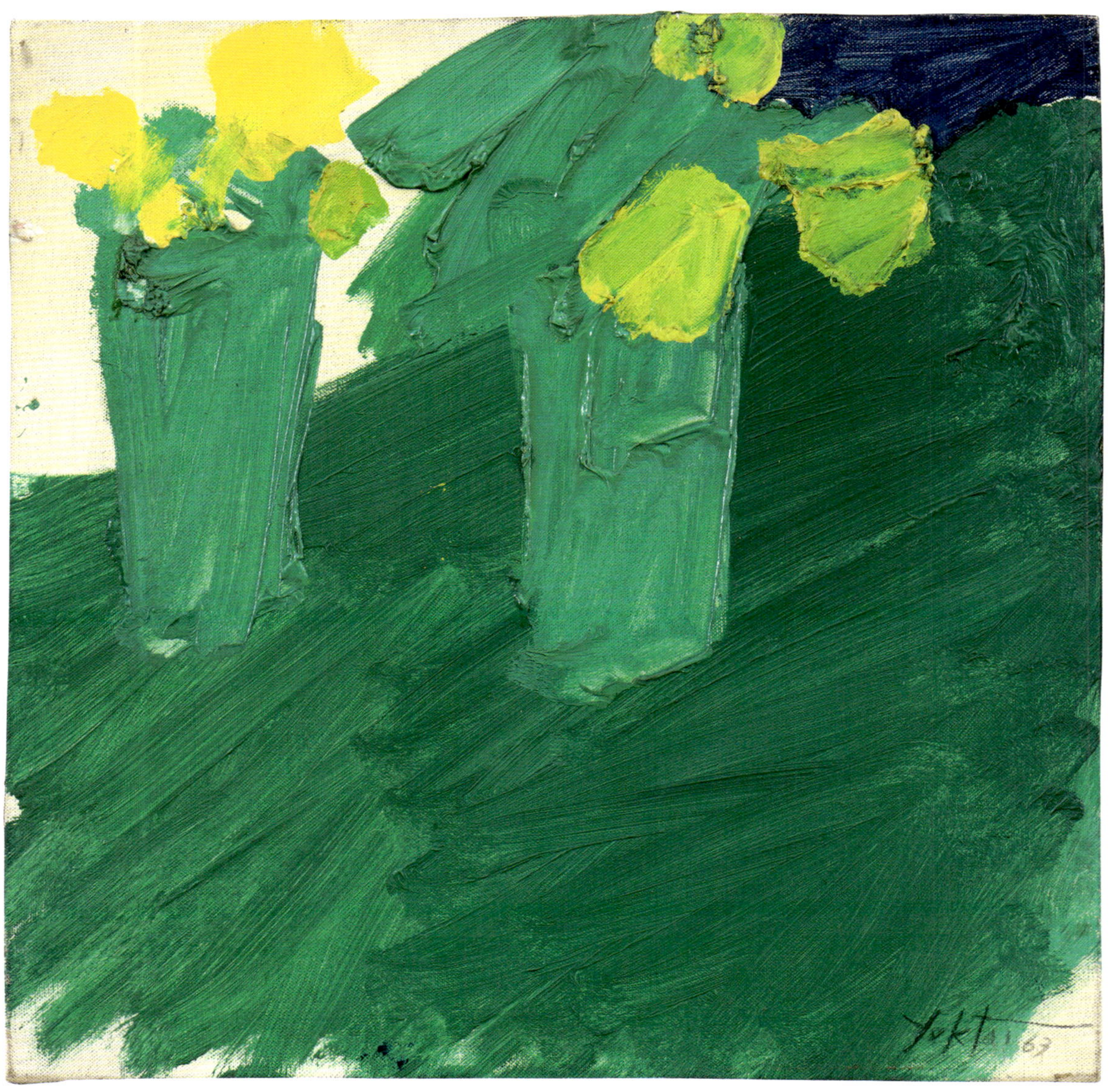

 Untitled, 1963, oil on canvas, 15⅝ × 15⅝ inches (39.7 × 39.7 cm)

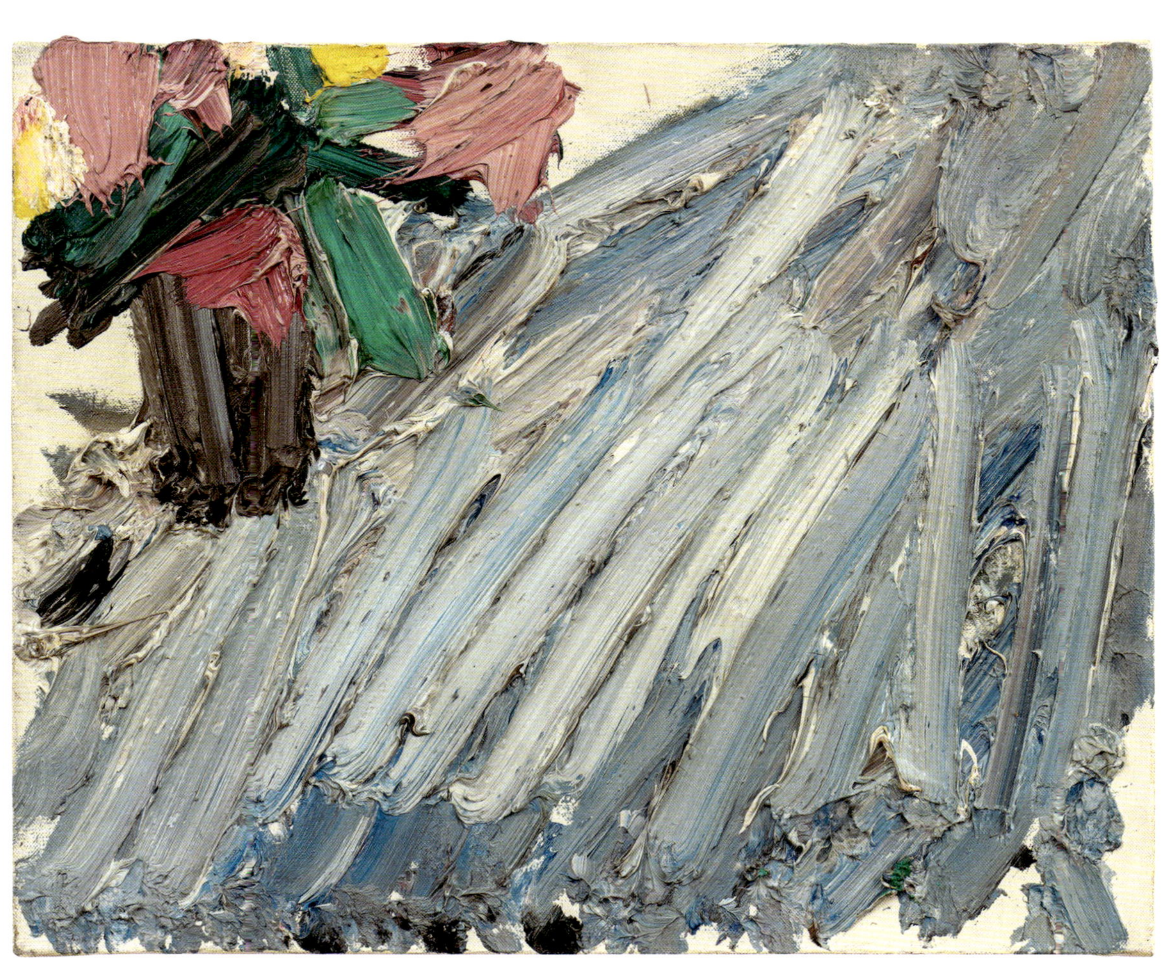

Untitled, 1963, oil on canvas, 15 × 18¼ inches (38.1 × 46.4 cm)

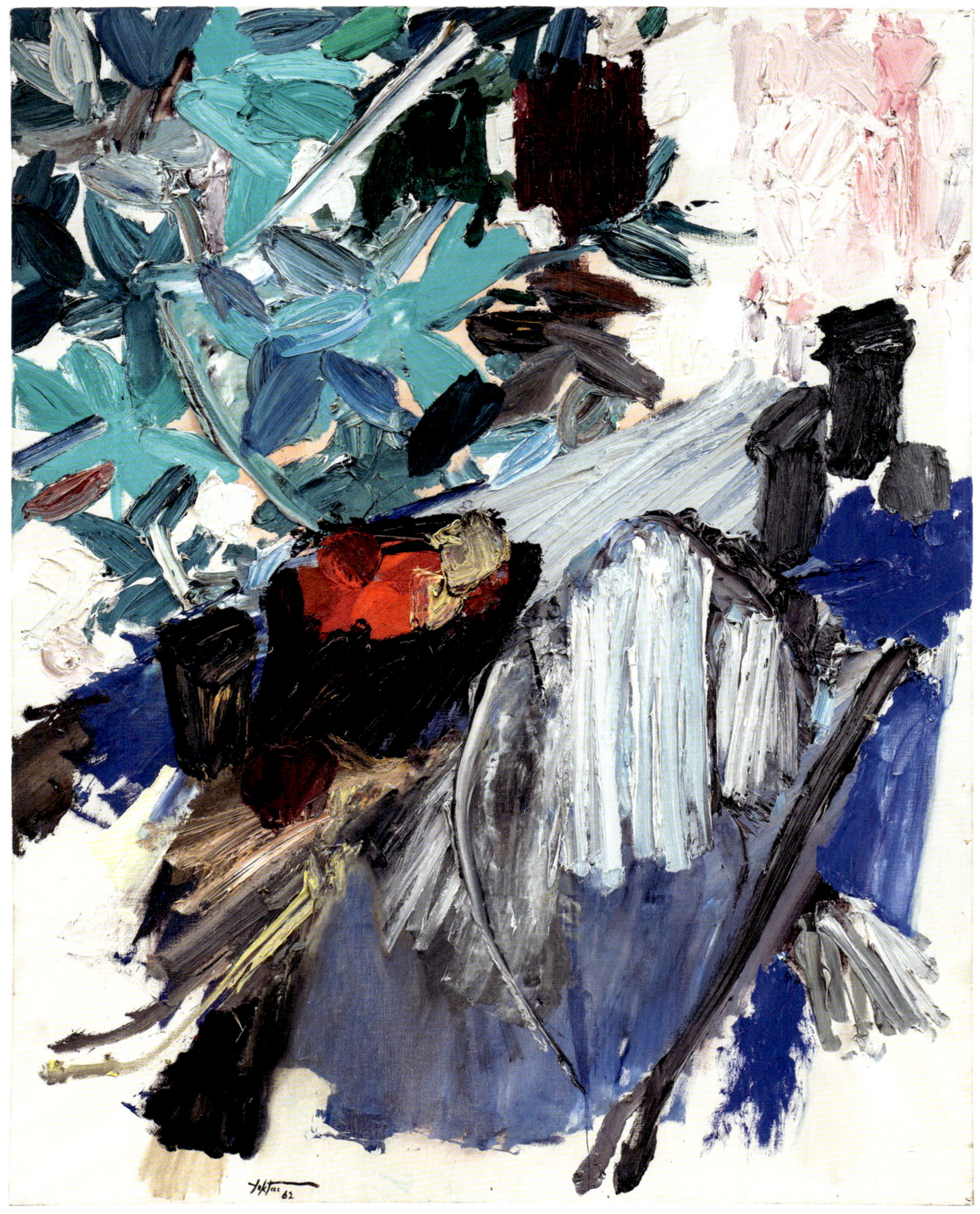

Untitled, 1962, oil on canvas, 53½ × 47¾ inches (135.9 × 121.3 cm)

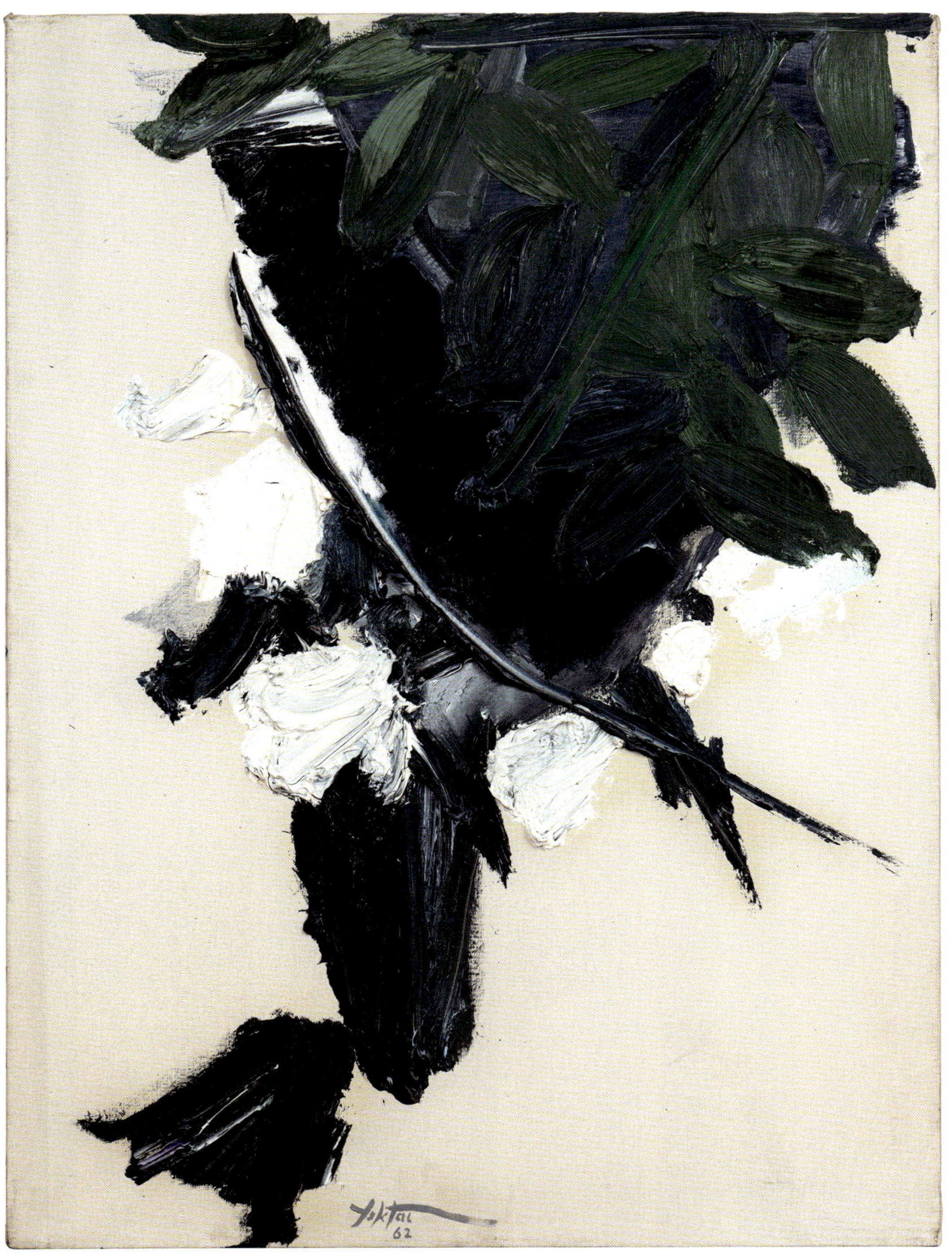

Untitled, 1962, oil on canvas, 23 × 27¼ inches (58.4 × 69.2 cm)

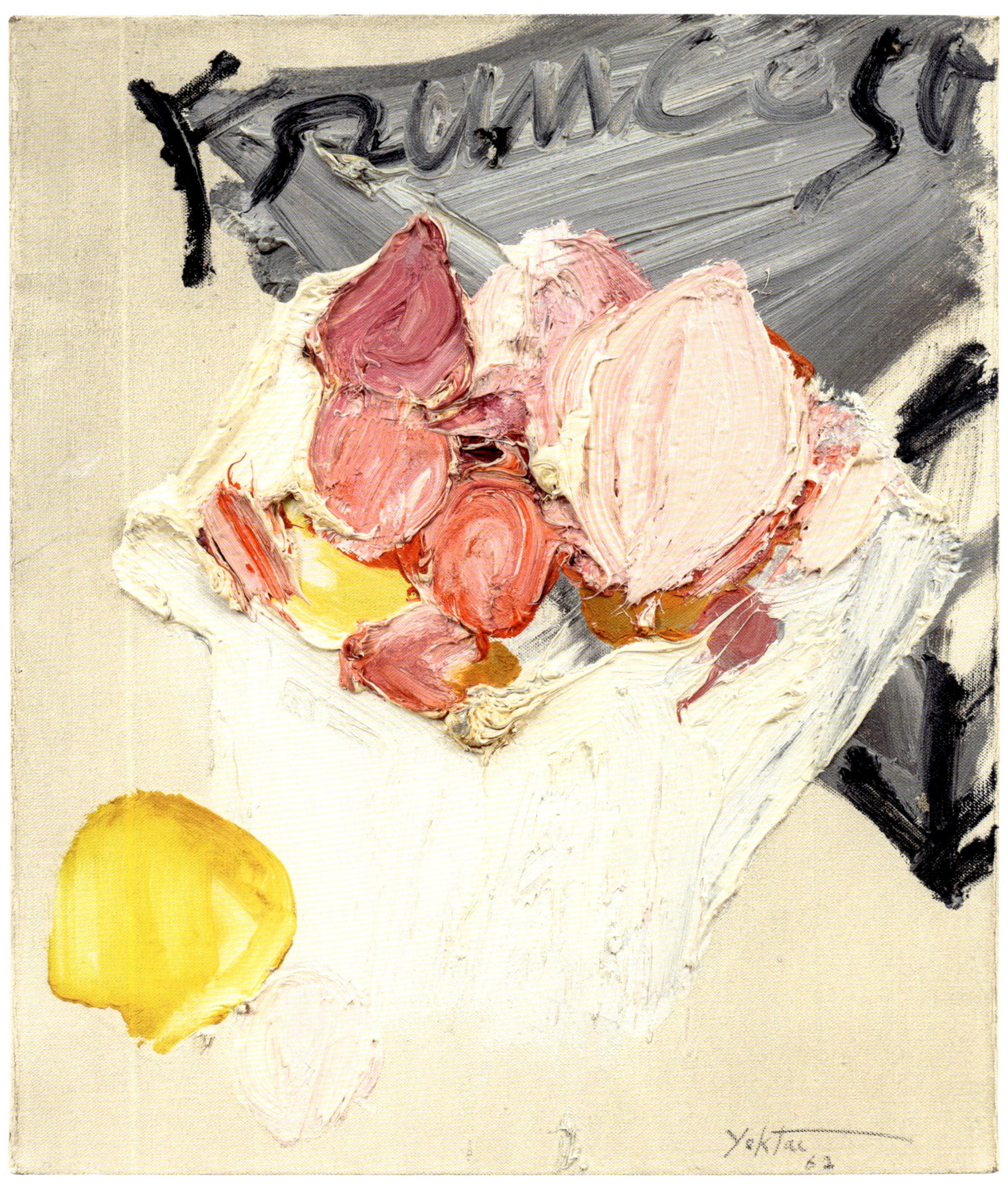

Untitled, 1962, oil on canvas, 18 × 15 inches (45.7 × 38.1 cm)

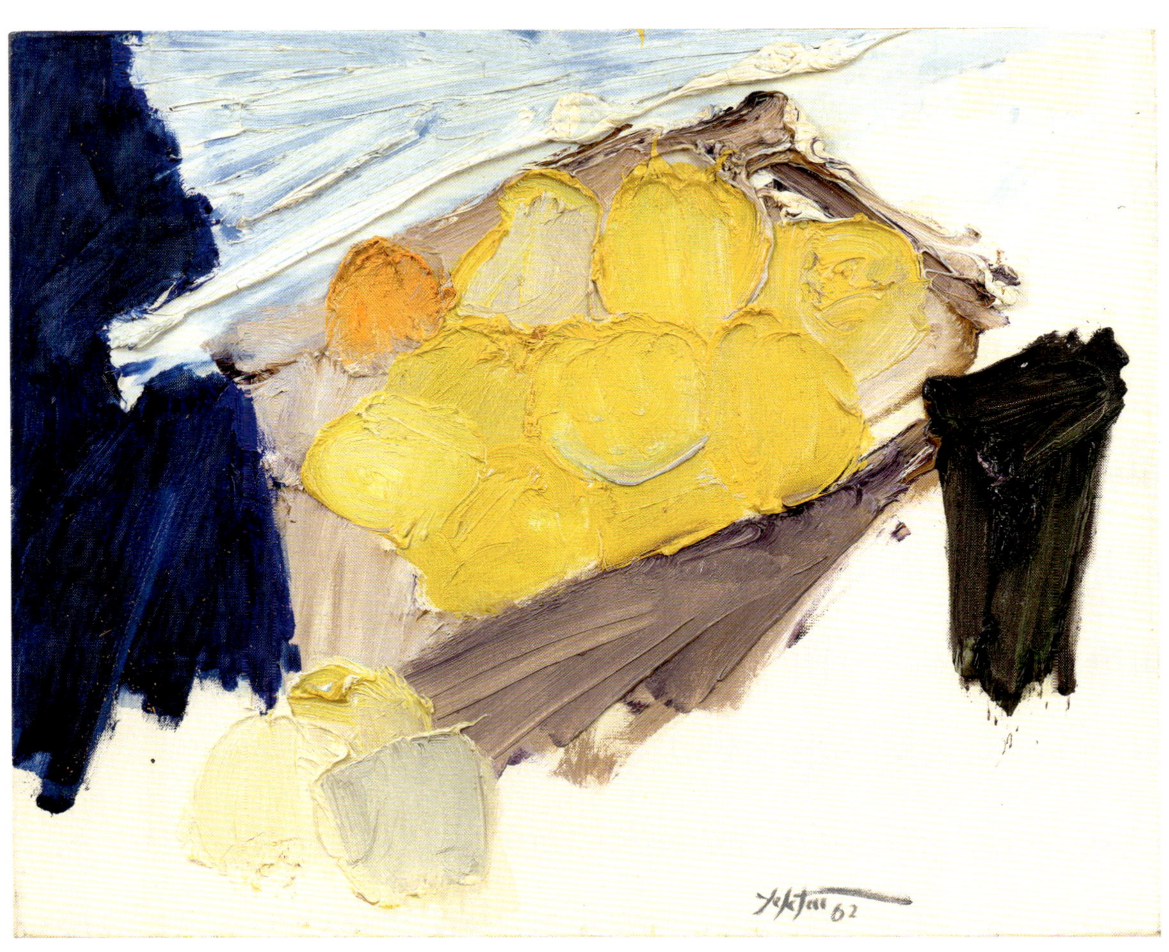

Untitled, 1962, oil on canvas, 19½ × 24 inches (49.5 × 61 cm)

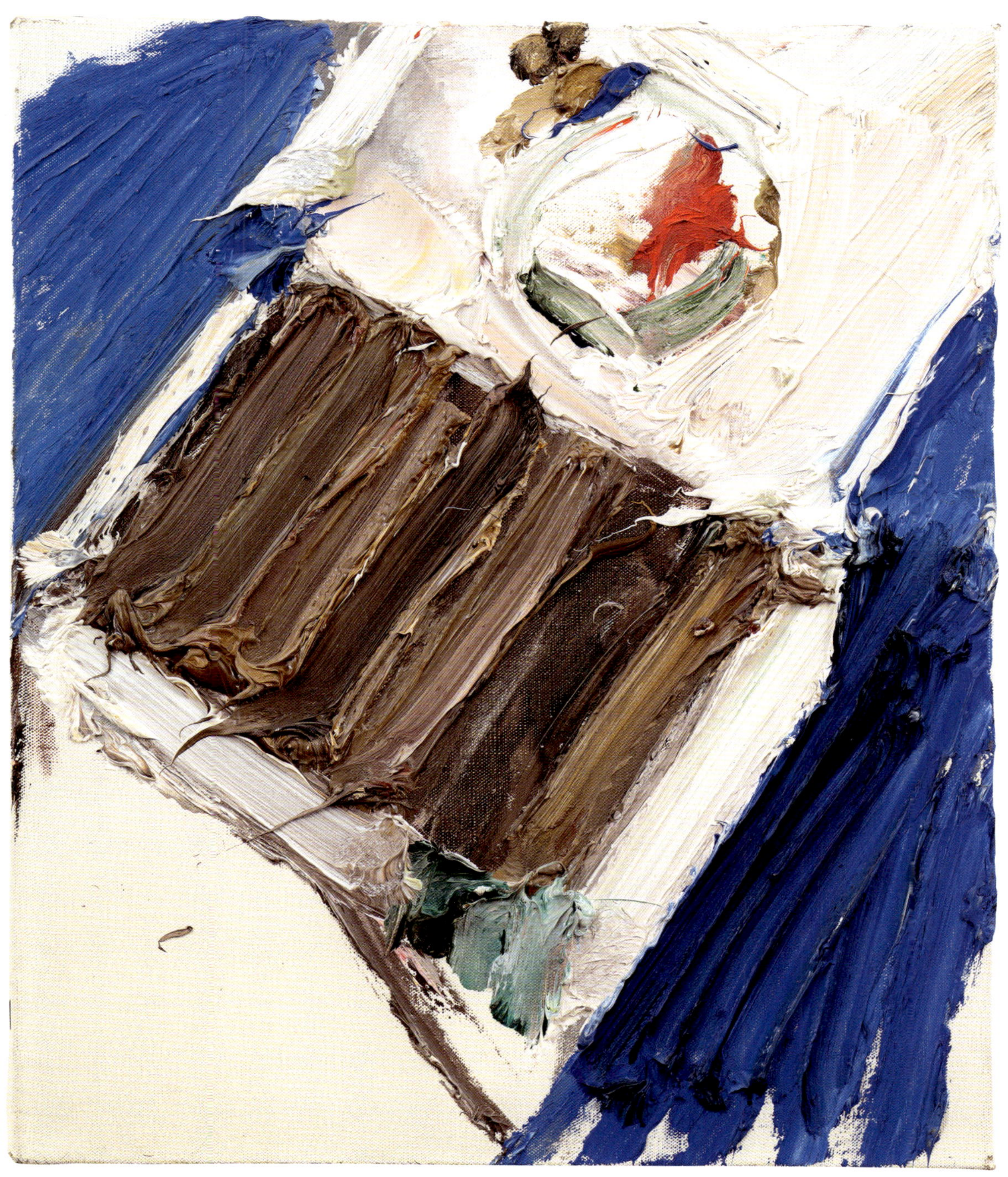

Box of Cigars, 1963, oil on canvas, 18 × 15 inches (45.7 × 38.1 cm)

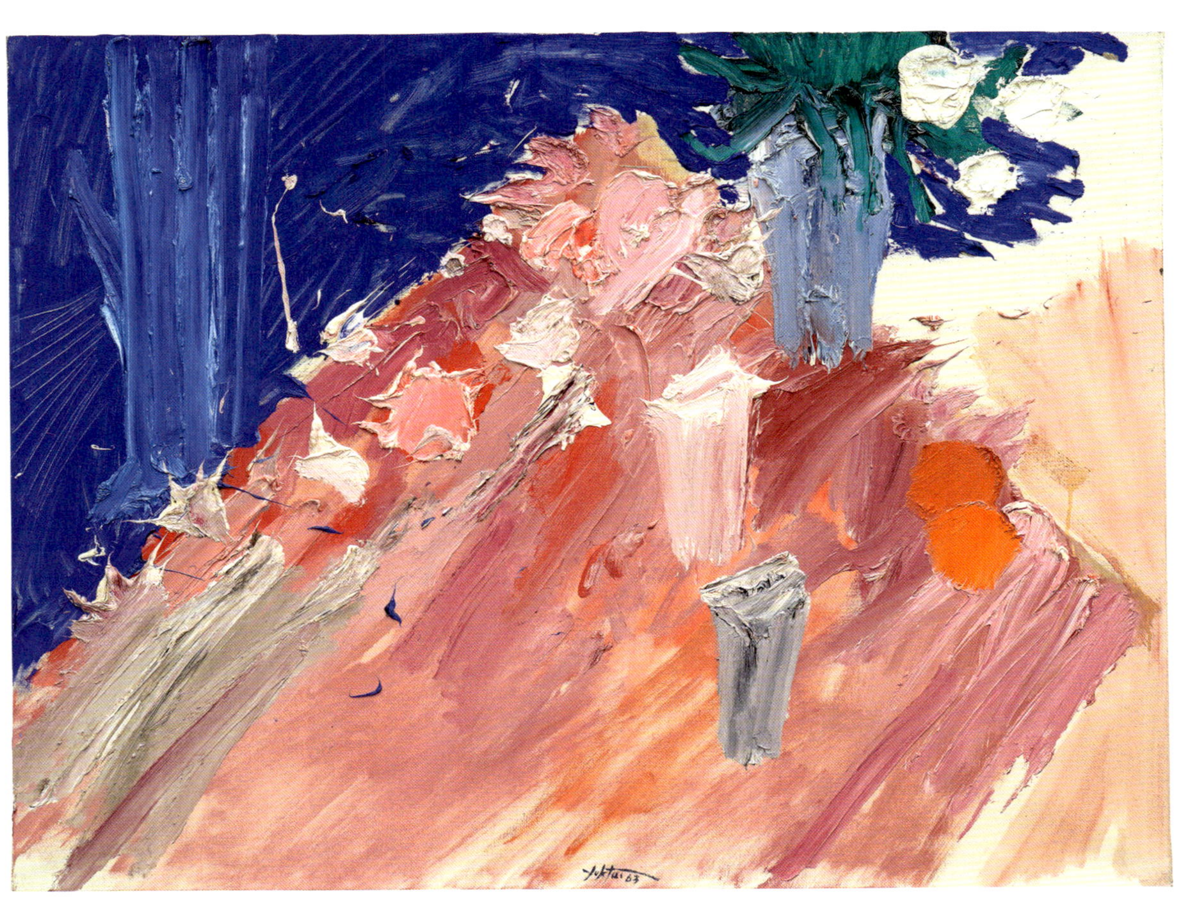

Untitled, 1963, oil on canvas, 34⅞ × 45⅝ inches (88.6 × 115.9 cm)

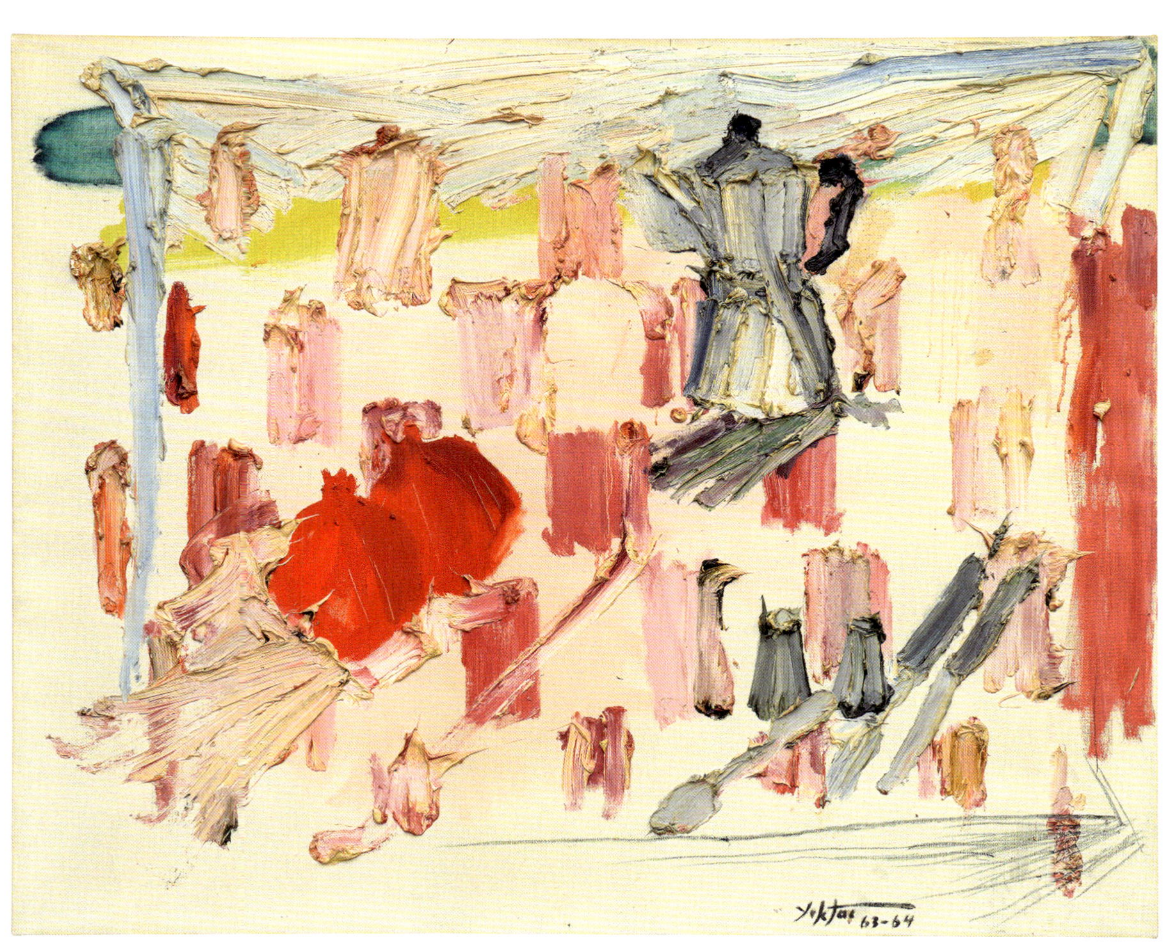

Untitled, 1963, oil on canvas, 34 × 42 inches (86.4 × 106.7 cm)

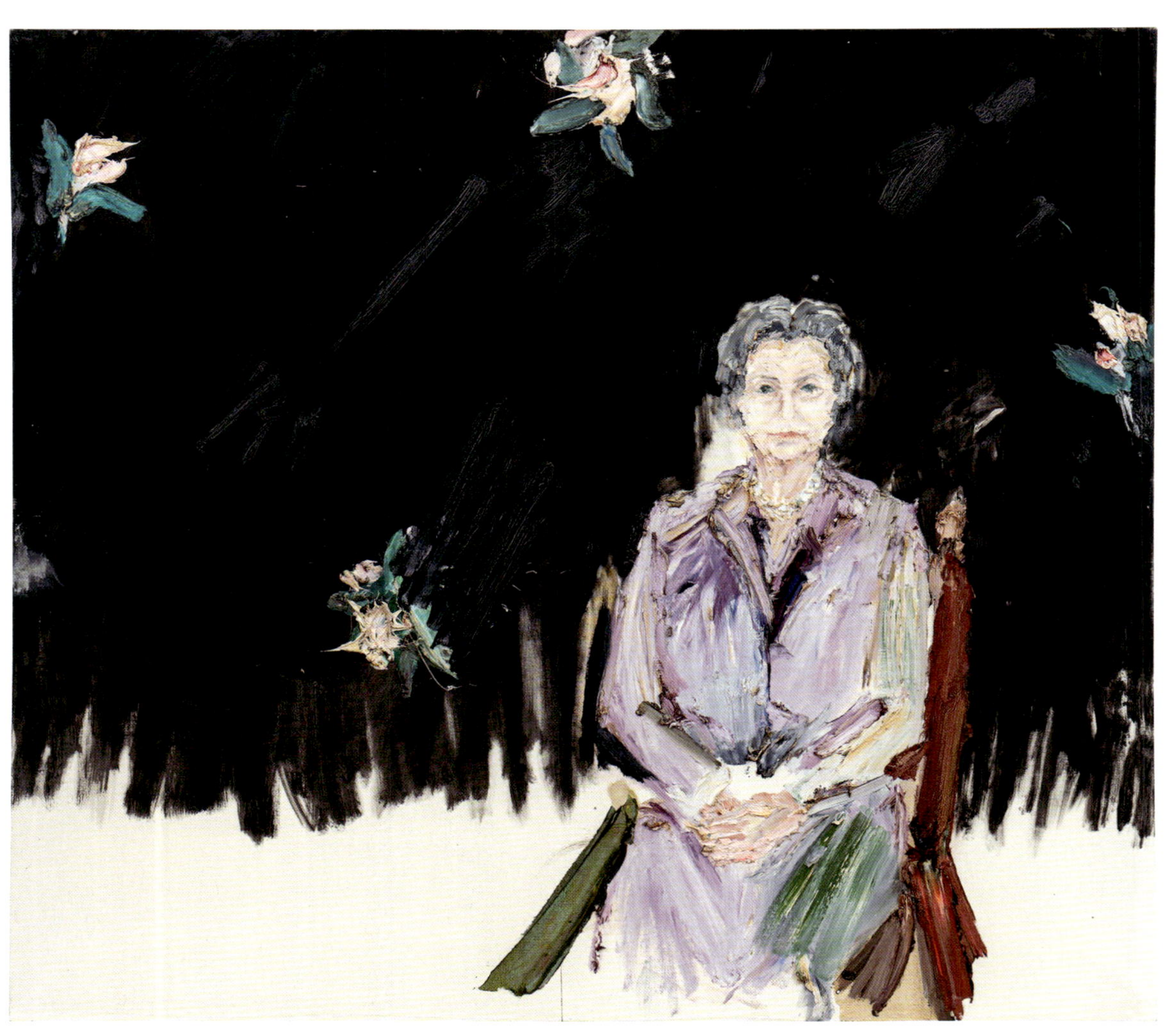

 Untitled, 1963, oil on canvas, 67 × 75¾ inches (170.2 × 192.4 cm)

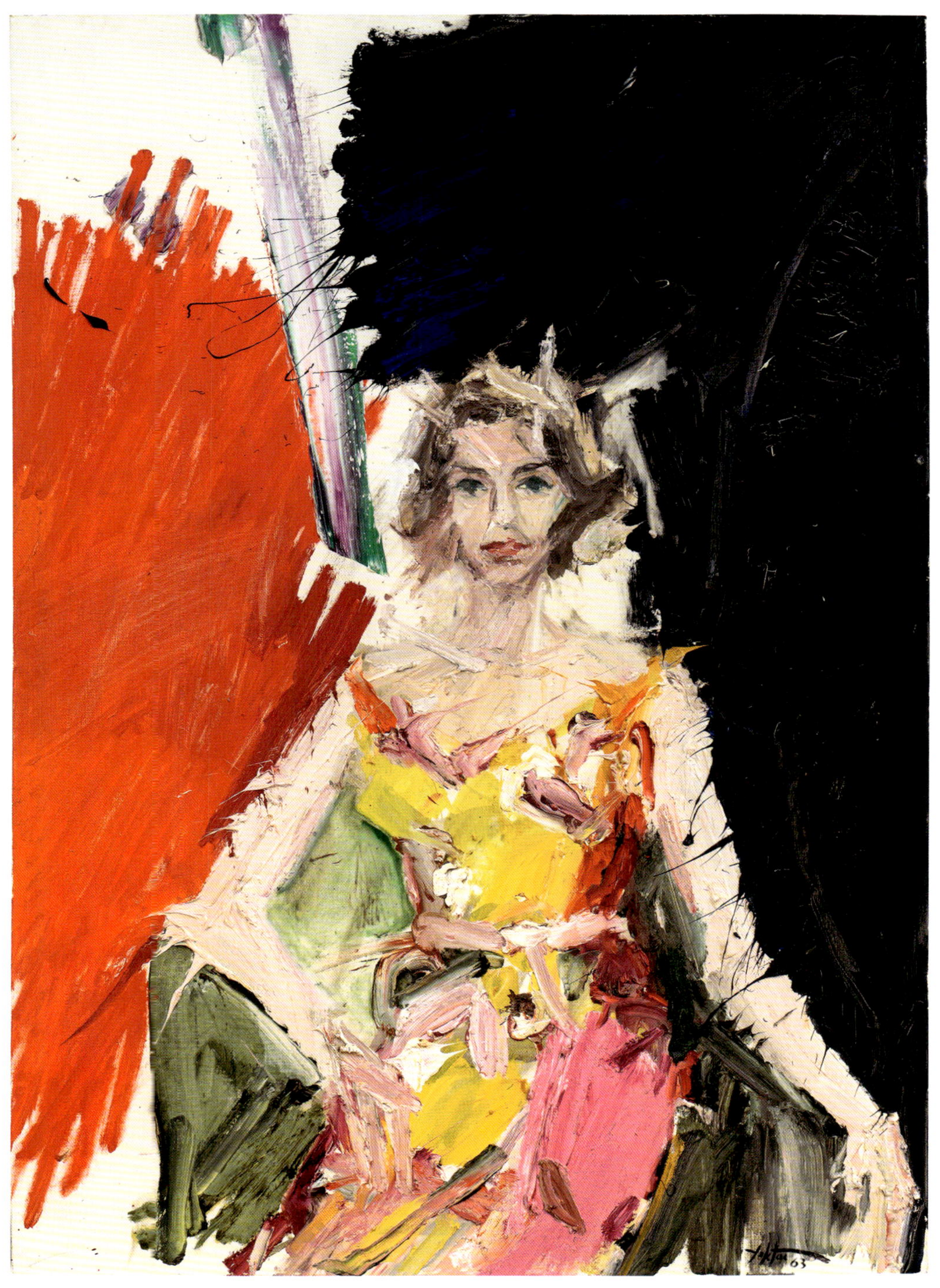

Portrait d'Eve, 1963, oil on canvas, 64½ × 45¼ inches (163.8 × 114.9 cm)

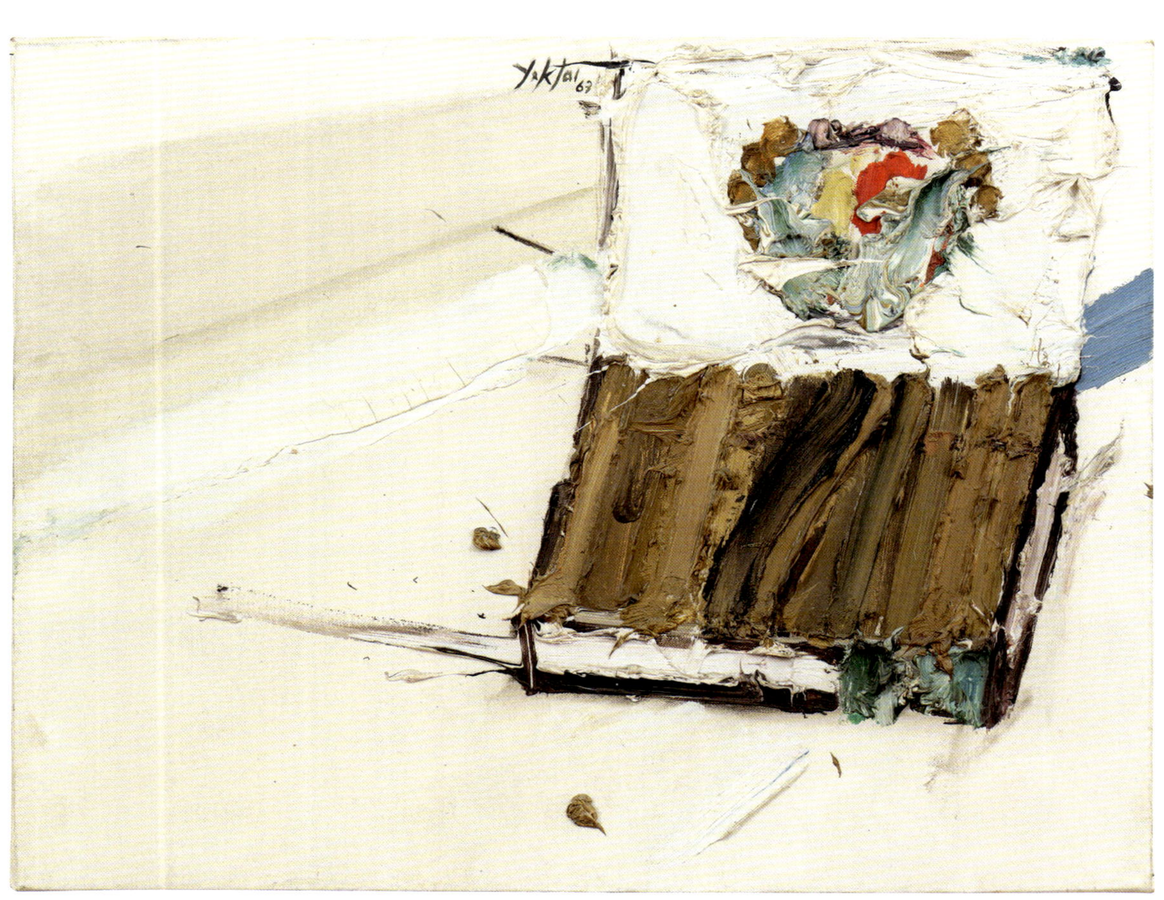

 Untitled, 1963, oil on canvas, 19¾ × 25½ inches (50.2 × 64.8 cm)

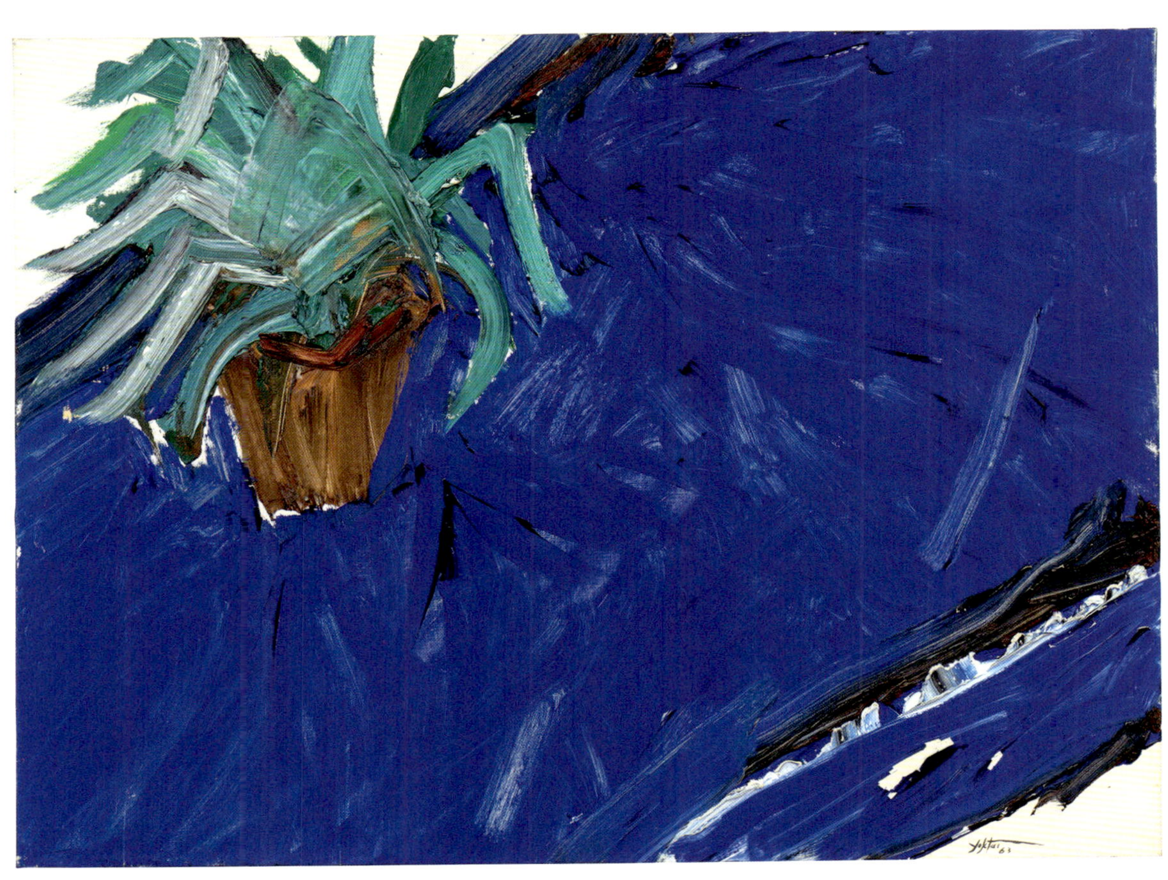

Untitled, 1963, oil on canvas, 38 × 51 inches (96.5 × 129.5 cm)

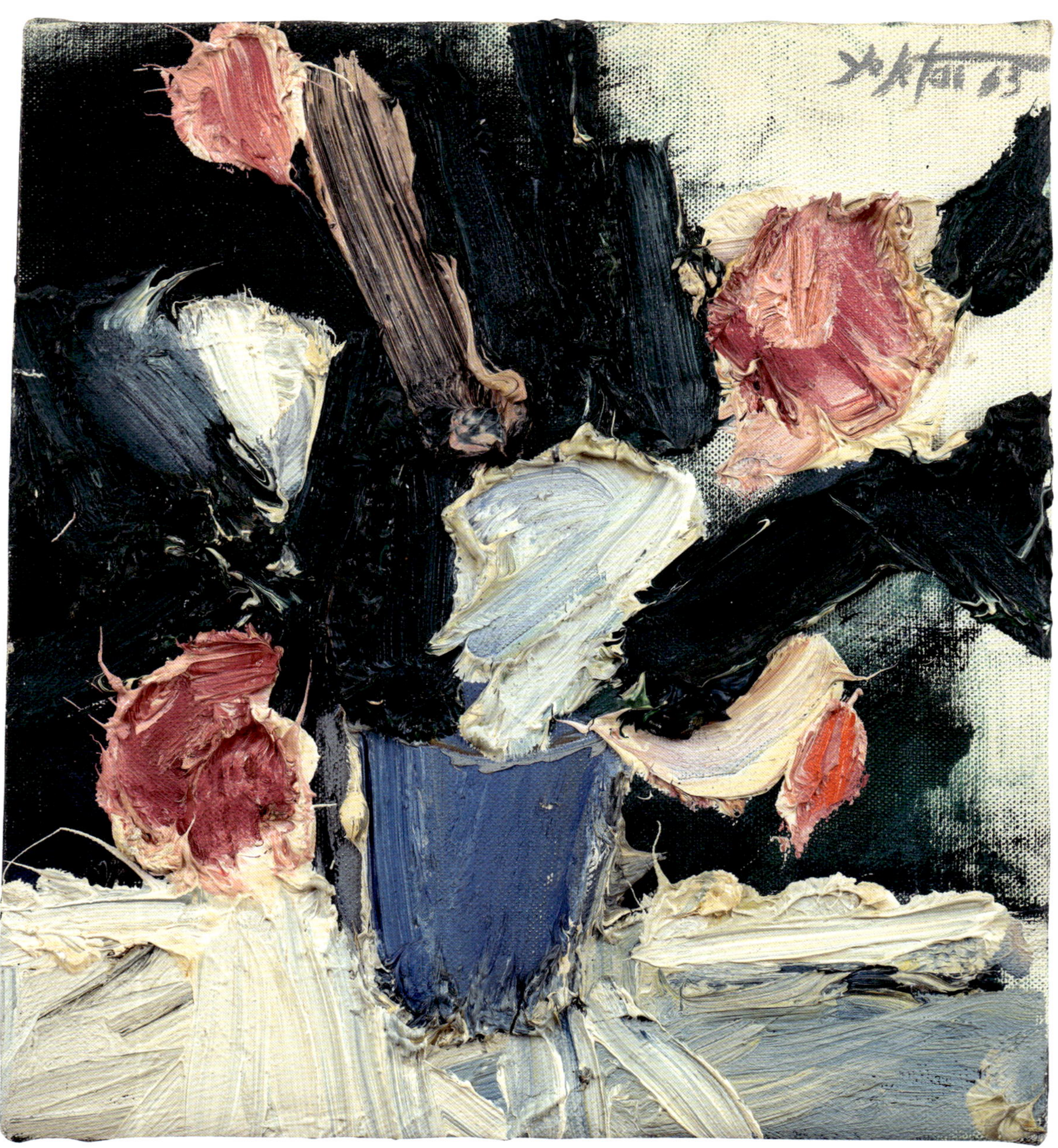

 Untitled, 1963, oil on canvas, 11¼ × 10 inches (28.6 × 25.4 cm)

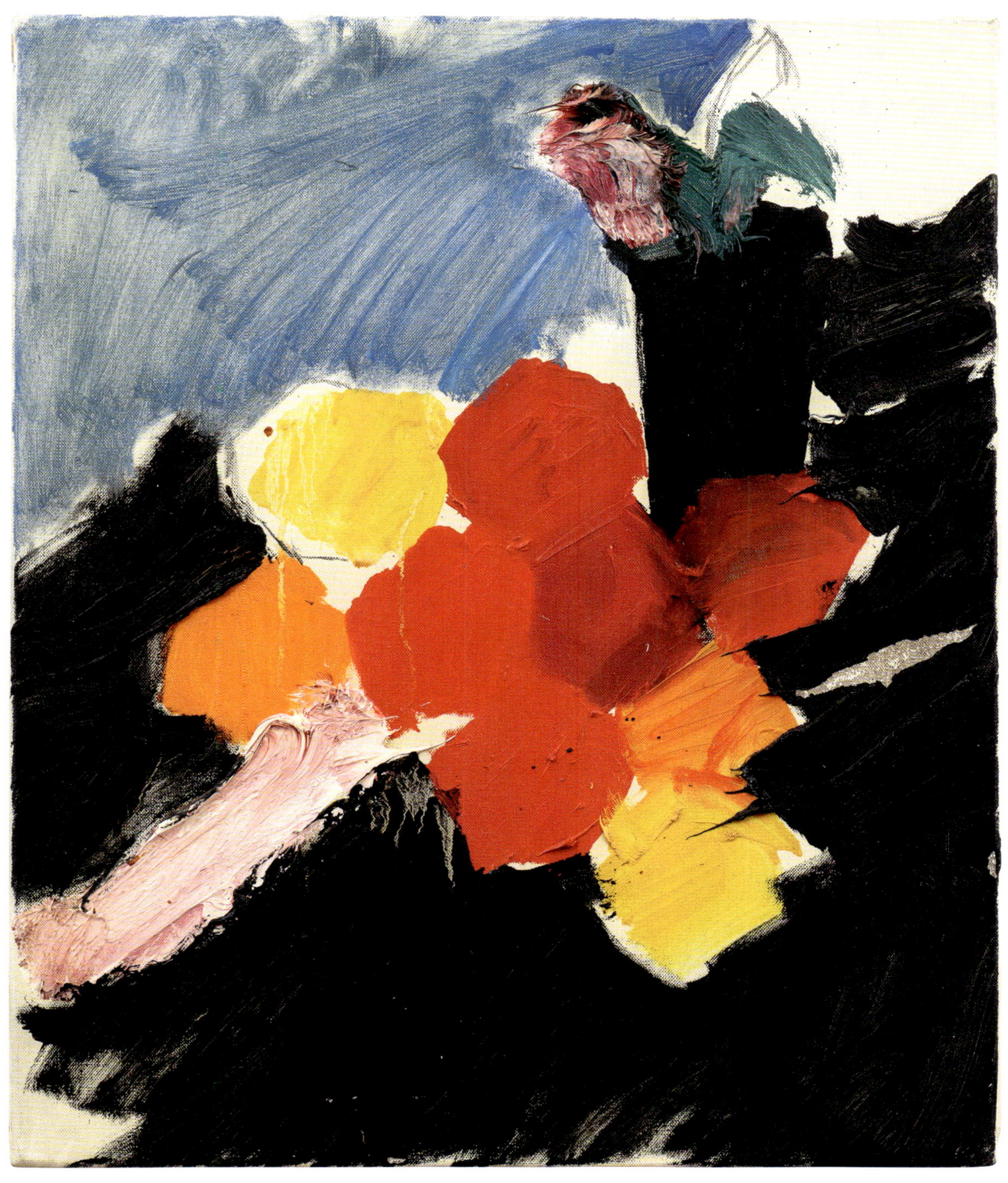

Untitled, 1963, oil on canvas, 21½ × 18 inches (54.6 × 45.7 cm)

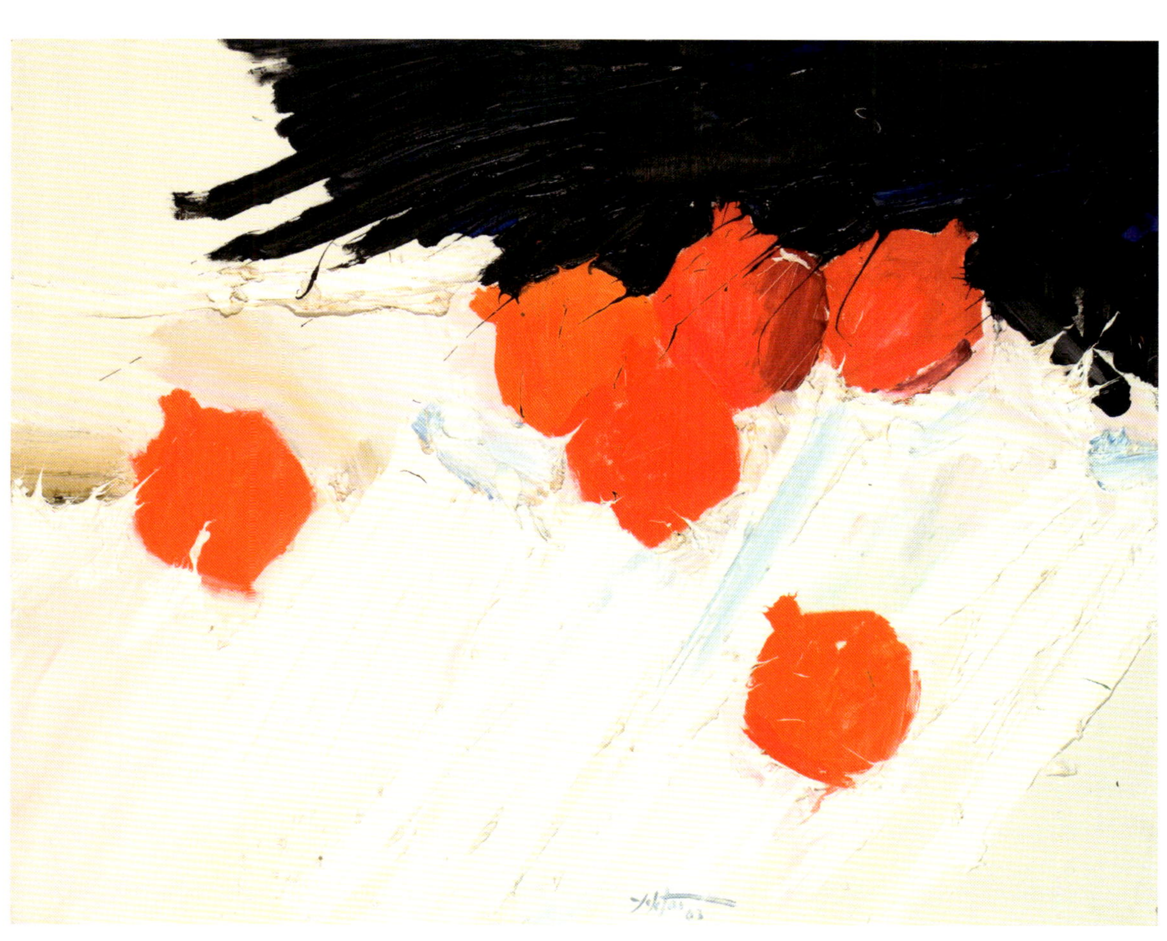

Nature Morte aux Granates, 1963, oil on canvas, 28¾ × 36¼ inches (73 × 92.1 cm)

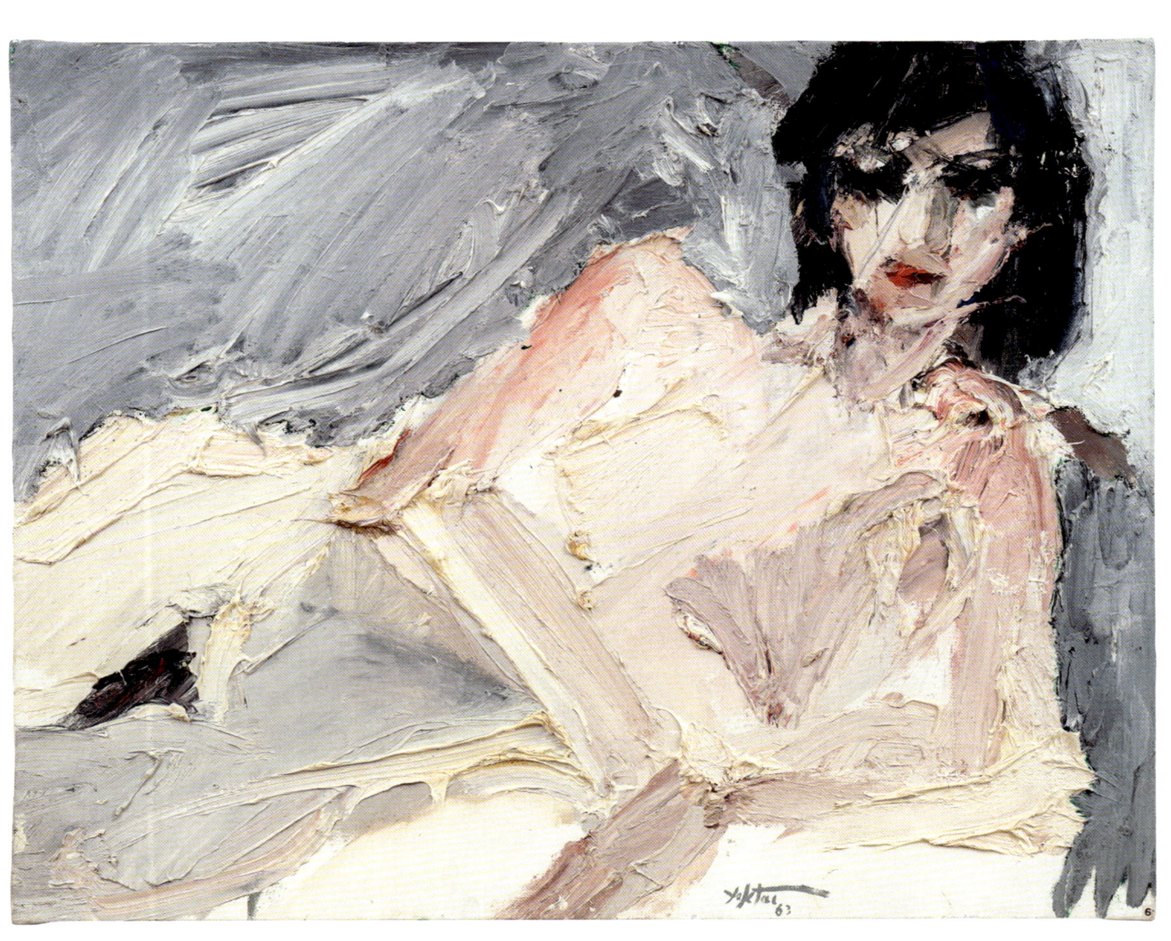

Untitled, 1963, oil on canvas, 28½ × 36 inches (72.4 × 91.4 cm)

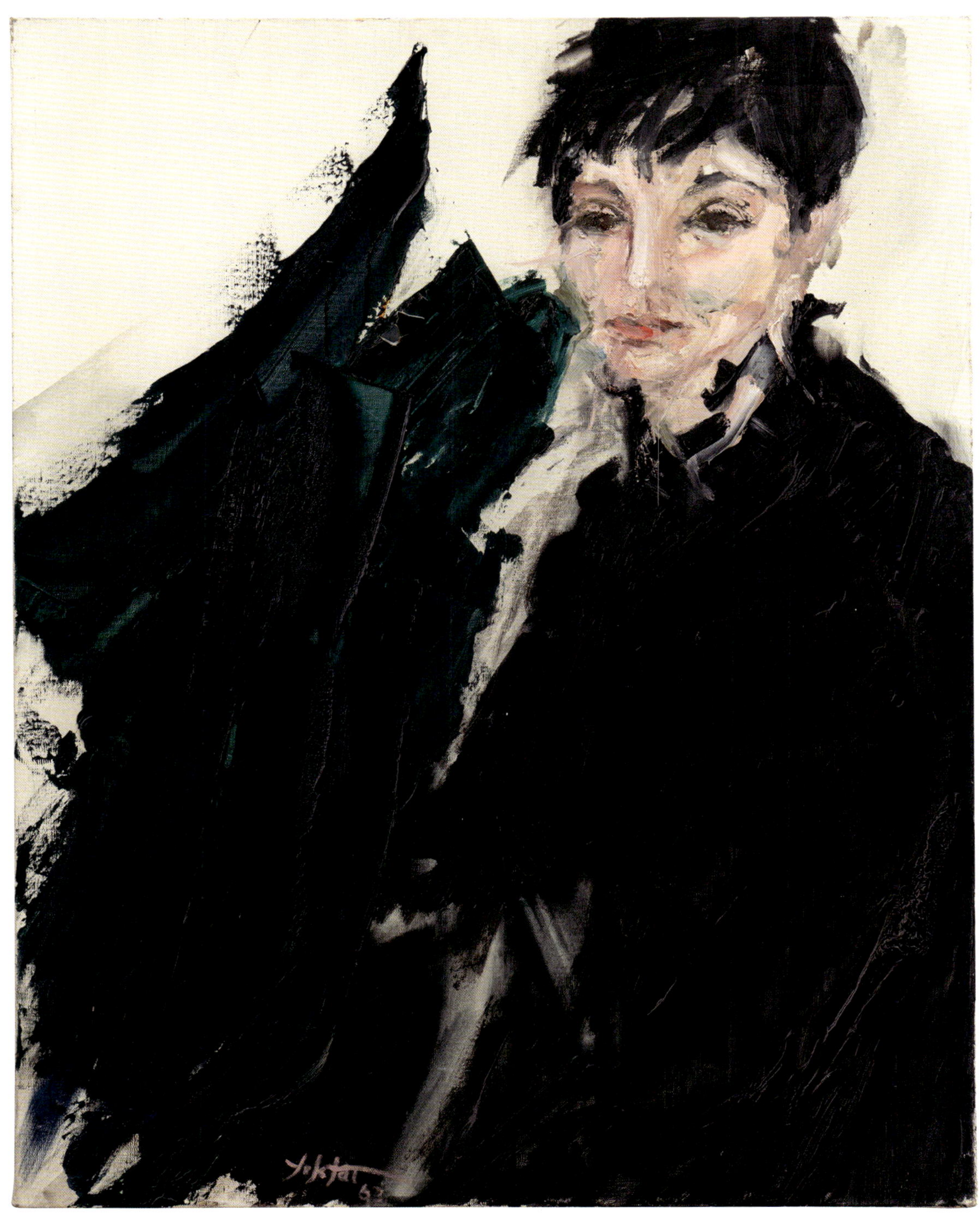

Portrait, 1963, oil on canvas, 36 × 28½ inches (91.4 × 72.4 cm)

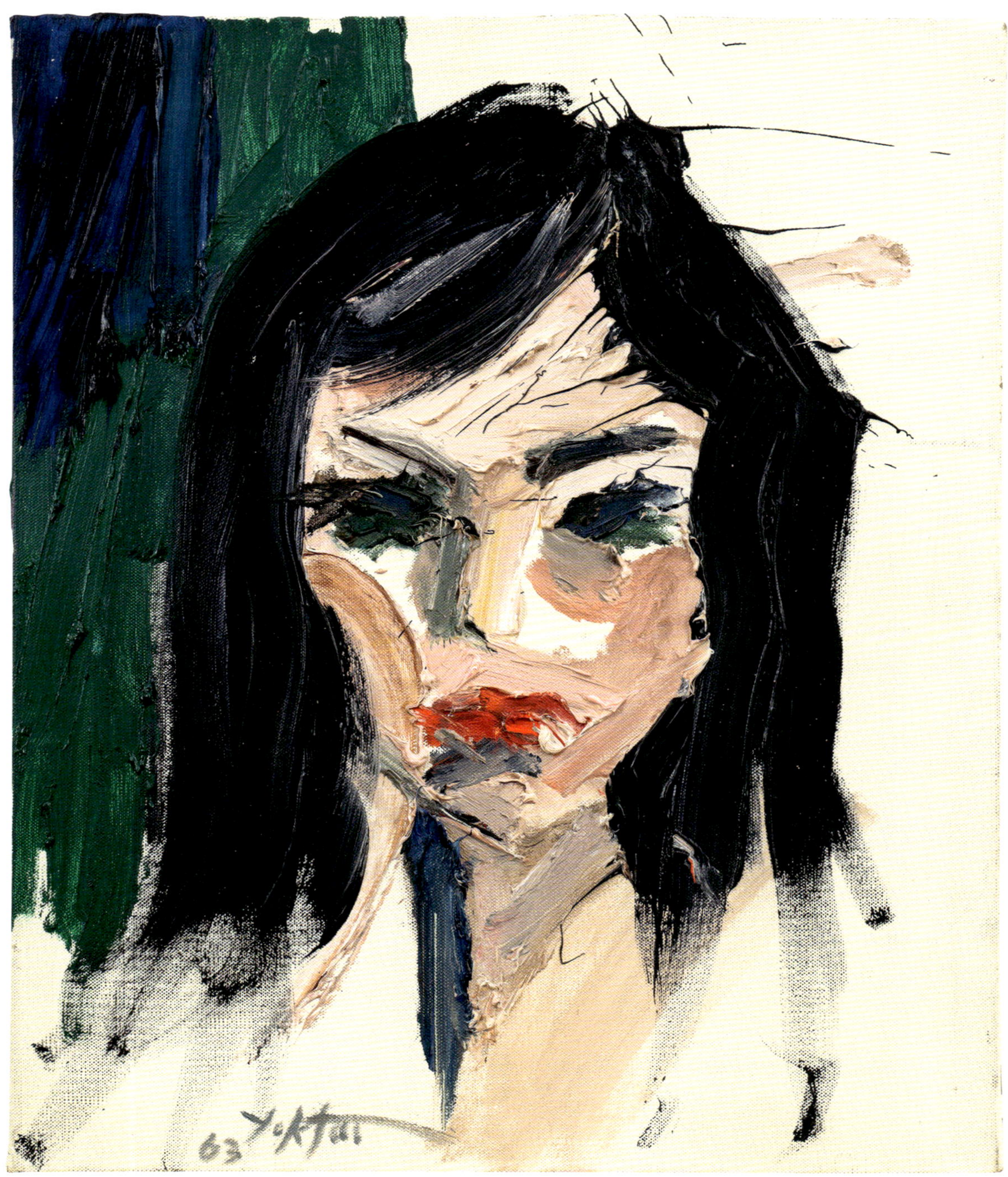

Untitled, 1963, oil on canvas, 18 × 15 inches (45.7 × 38.1 cm)

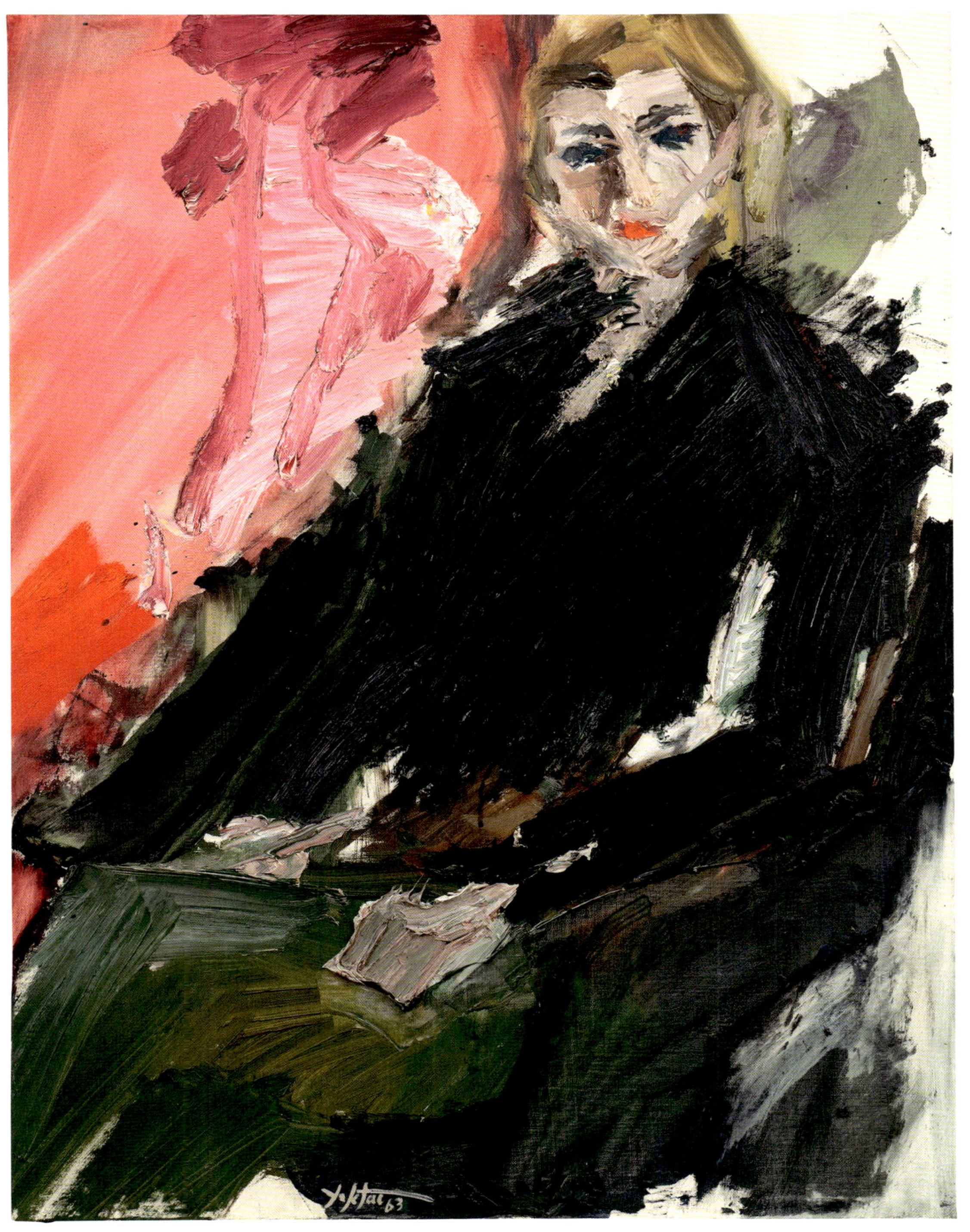

HC 13 Portrait, 1963, oil on canvas, 45½ × 34¾ inches (115.6 × 88.3 cm)

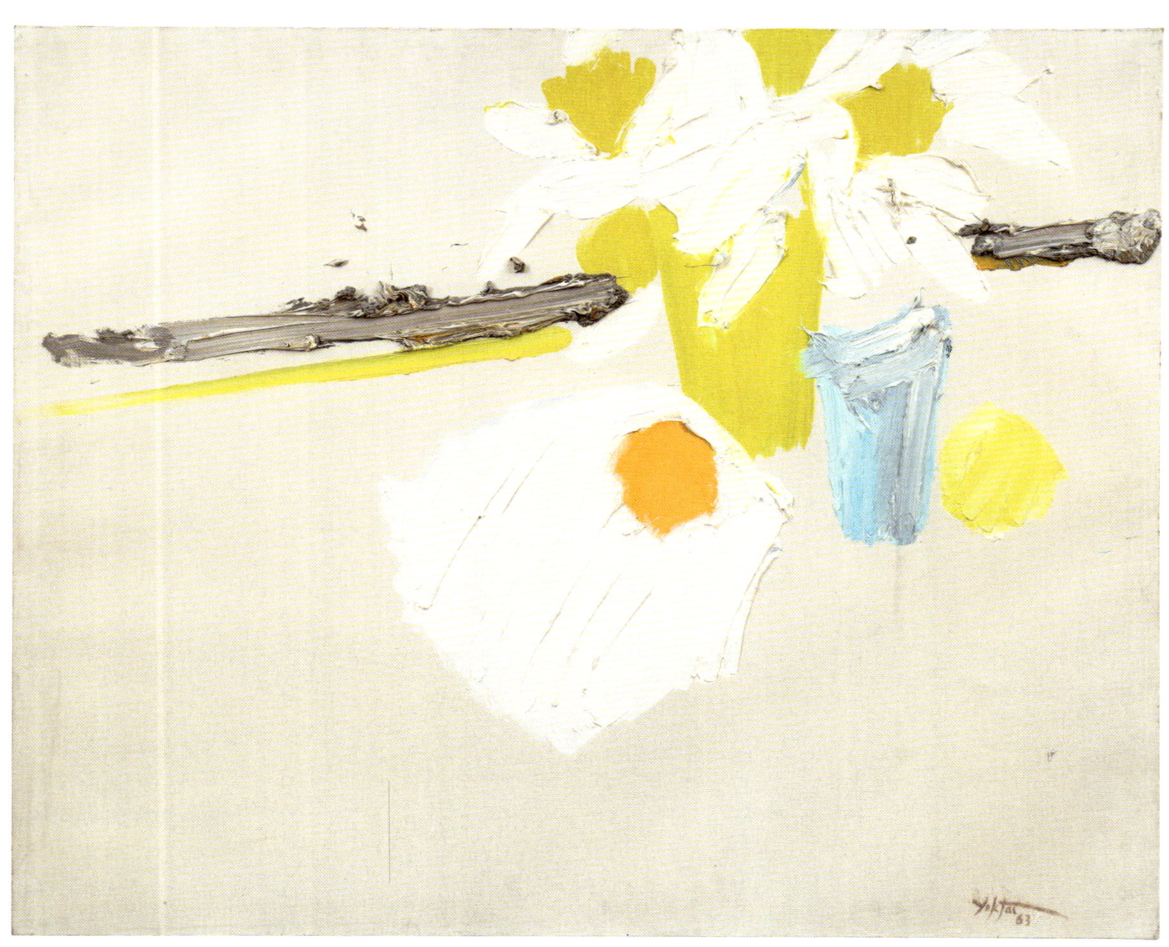

 Untitled, 1963, oil on canvas, 31¾ × 39¼ inches (80.7 × 80.7 cm)

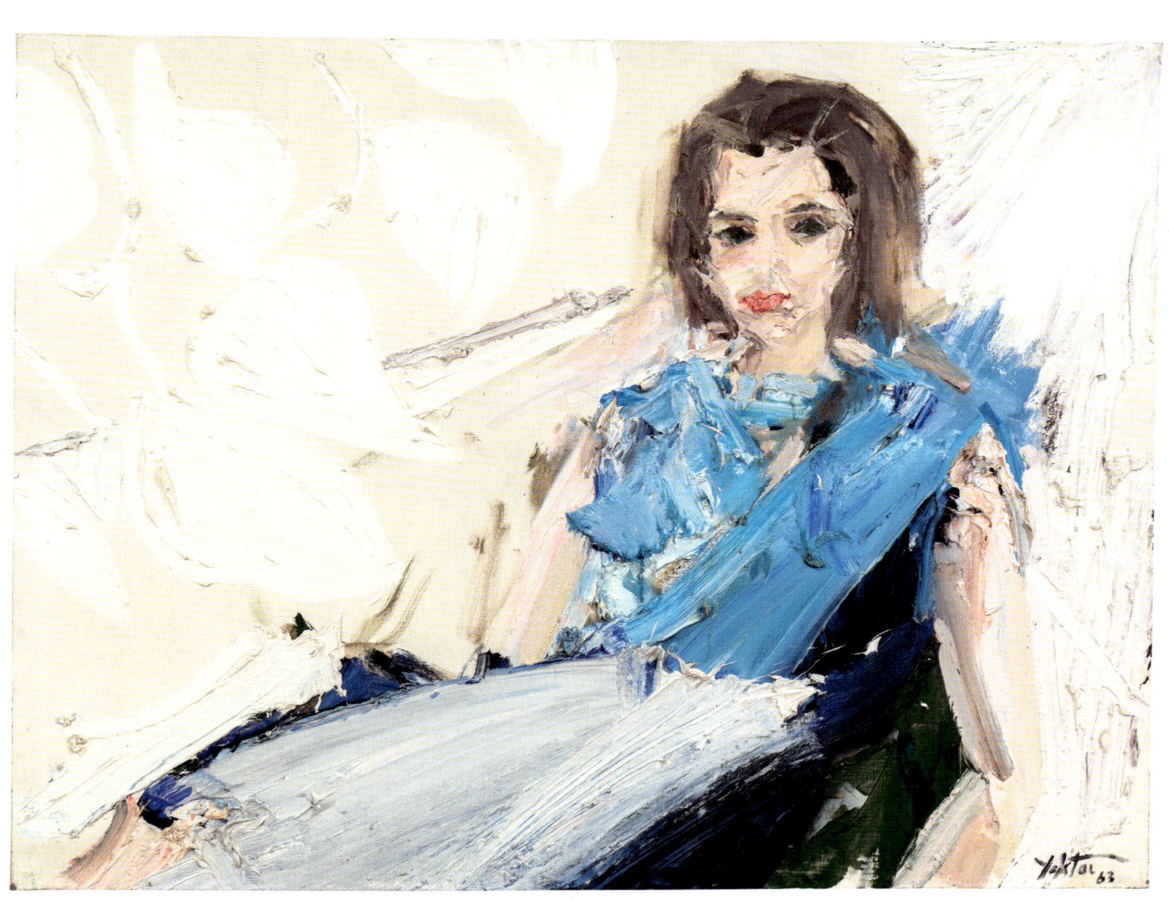

Nancy Schwartz, 1963, oil on canvas, 35 × 45½ inches (88.9 × 115.6 cm)

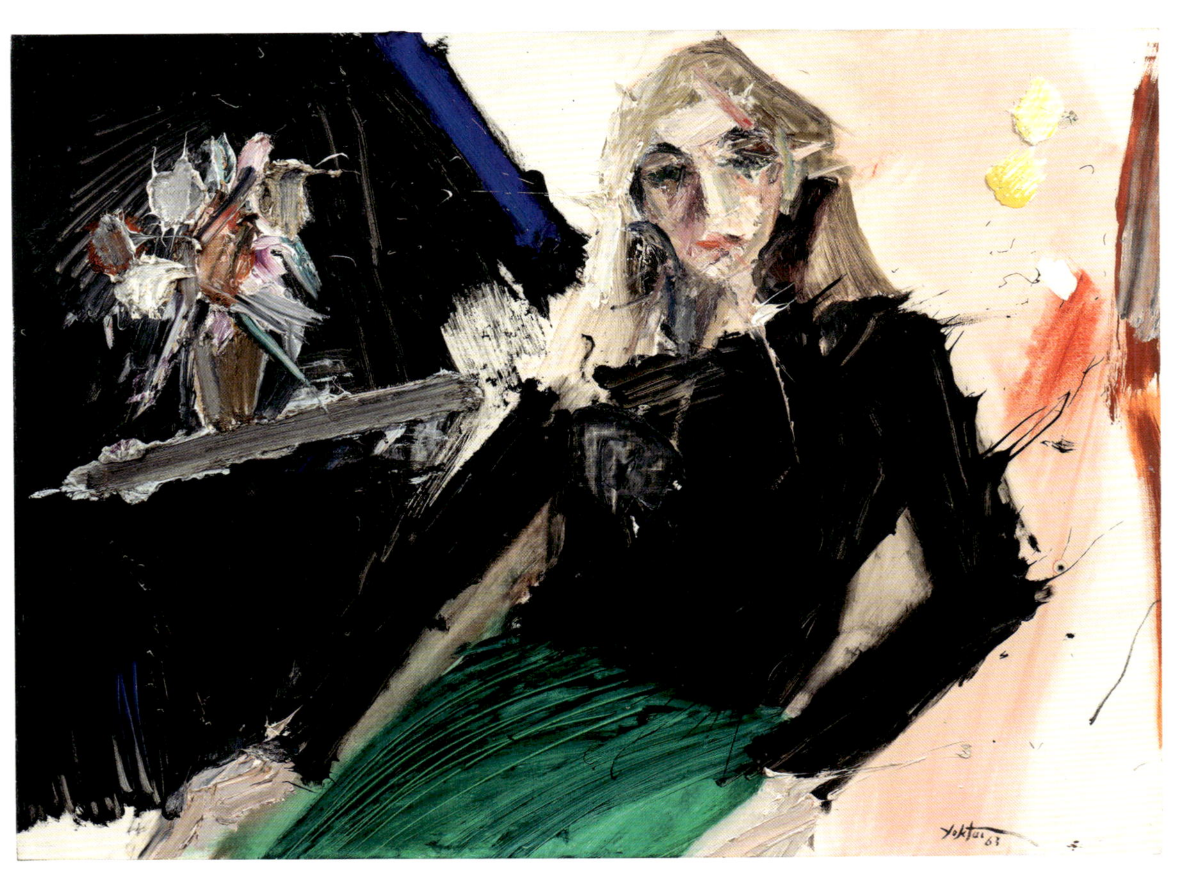

 Untitled, 1963, oil on canvas, 38 × 51 inches (96.5 × 129.5 cm)

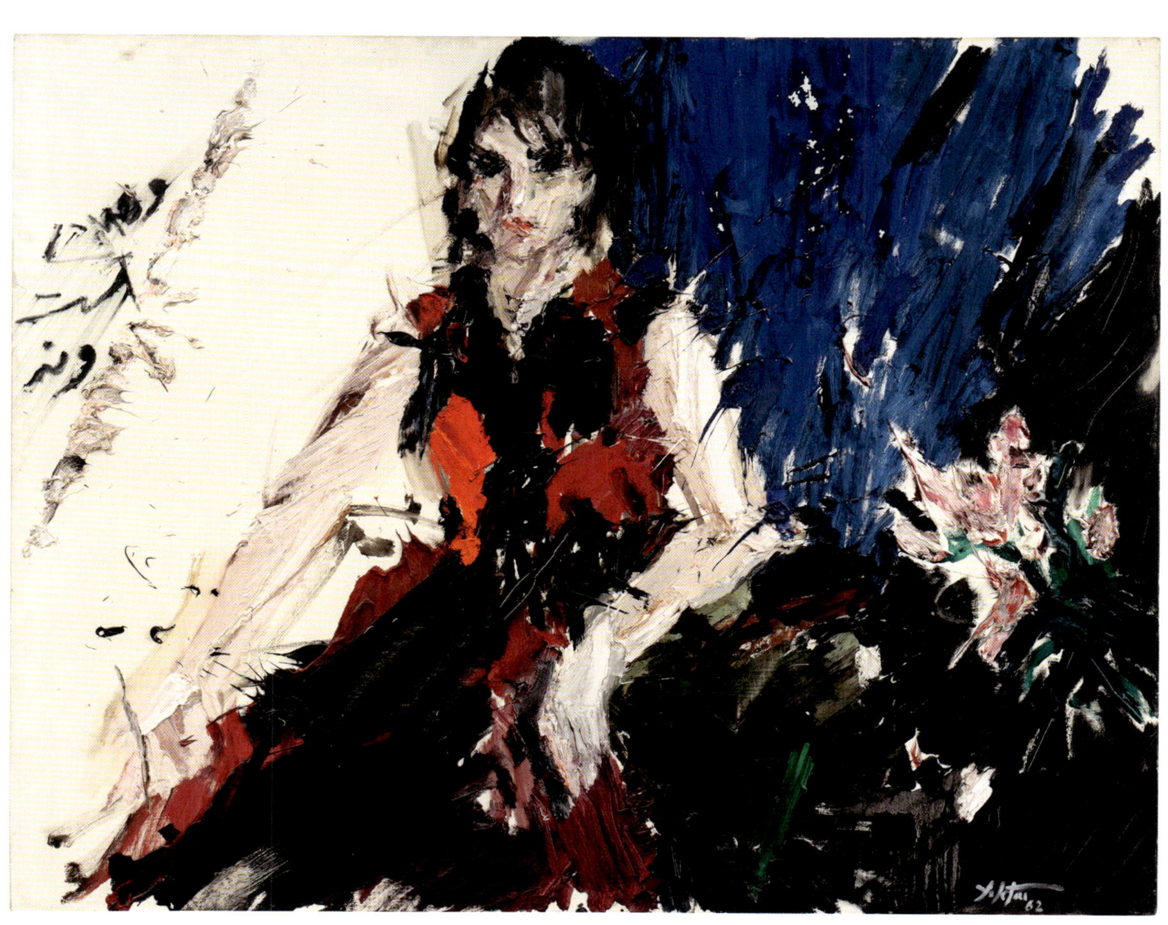

Untitled, 1963, oil on canvas, 44¾ × 57½ inches (113.7 × 146.1 cm)

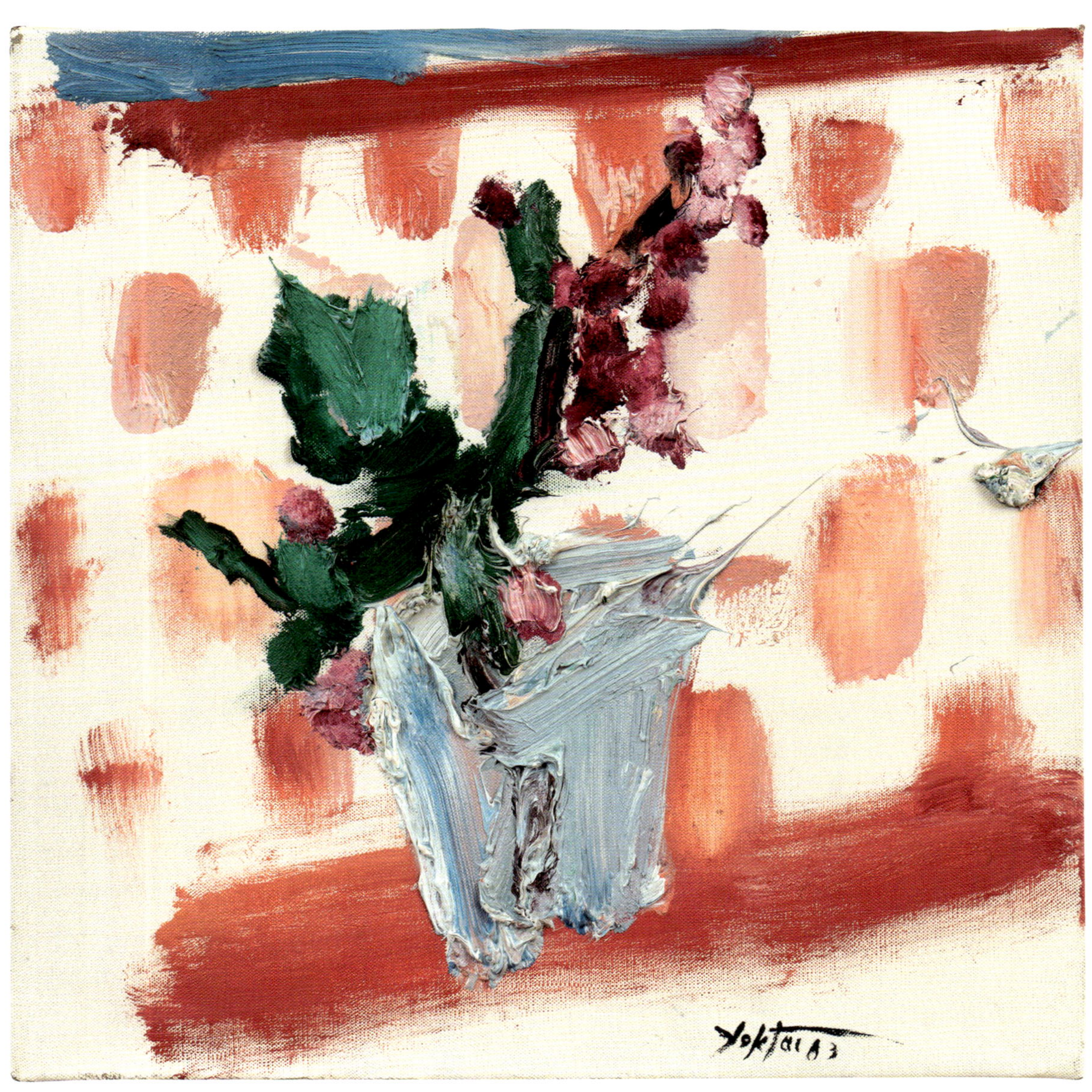

404 *Nappe à Carreaux*, 1963, oil on canvas, 15¾ × 15¾ inches (40 × 40 cm)

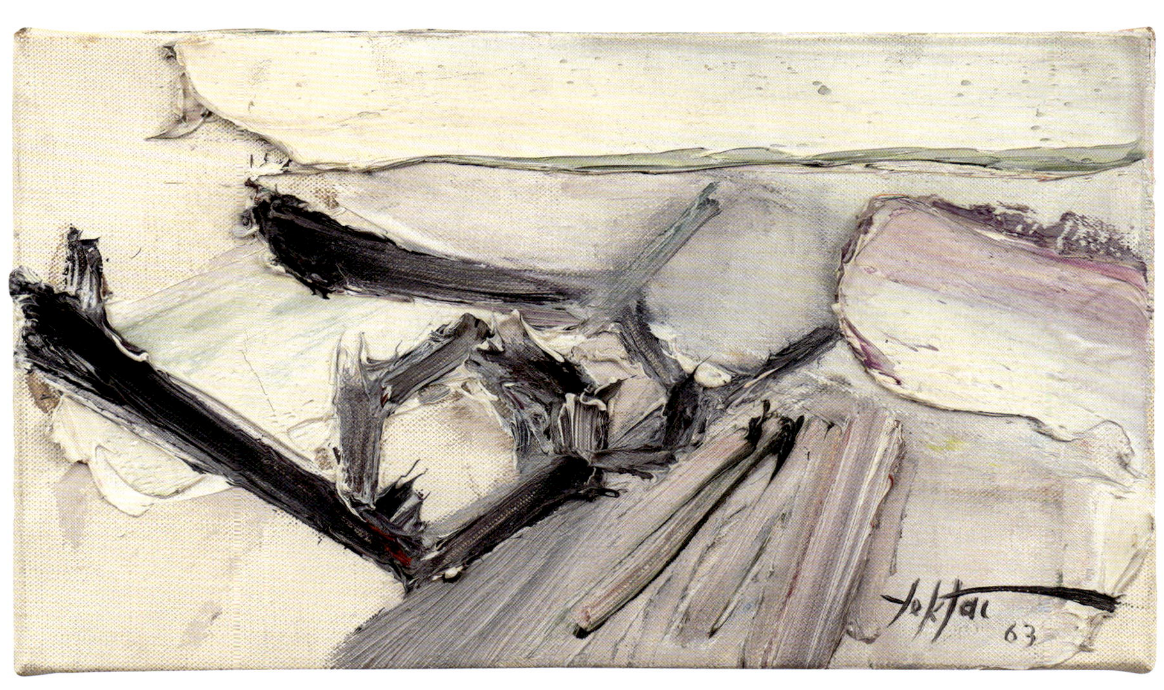

Eye Glasses, 1963, oil on canvas, 7¾ × 13 inches (19.7 × 33 cm)

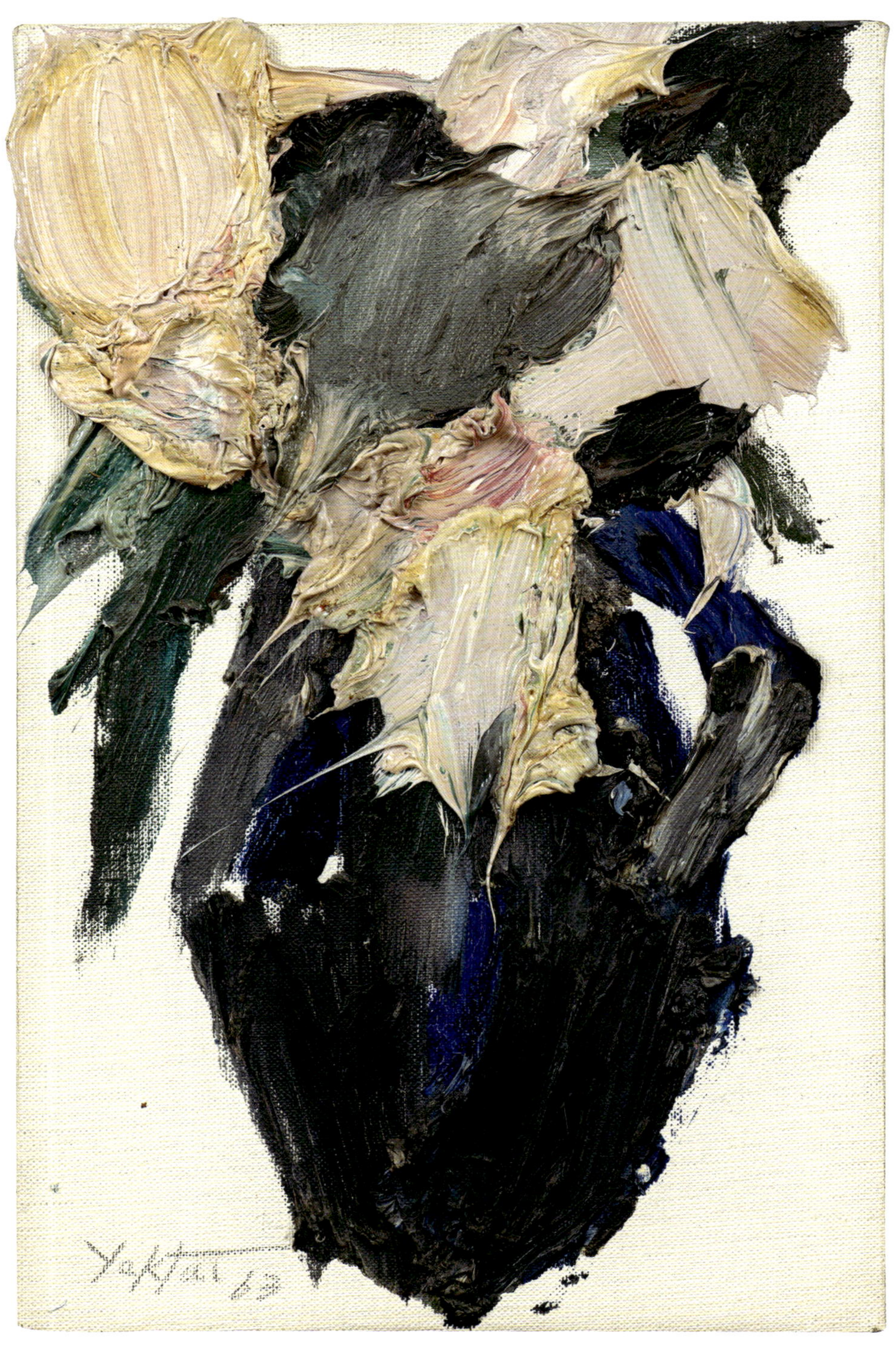

 Untitled, 1963, oil on canvas, 14 × 9 inches (35.6 × 22.9 cm)

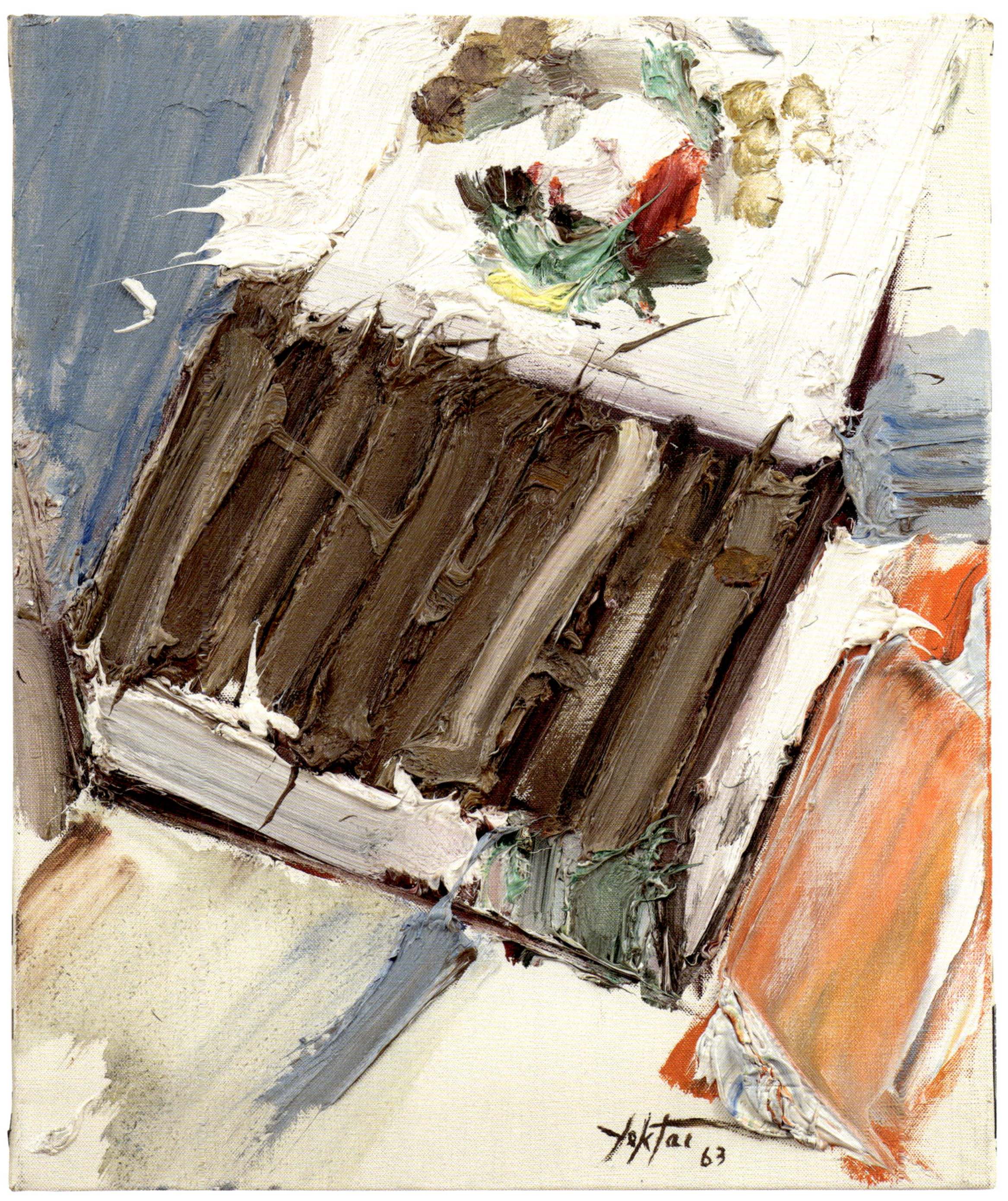

Boîte à Cigares, 1963, oil on canvas, 18 × 15 inches (45.7 × 38.1 cm)

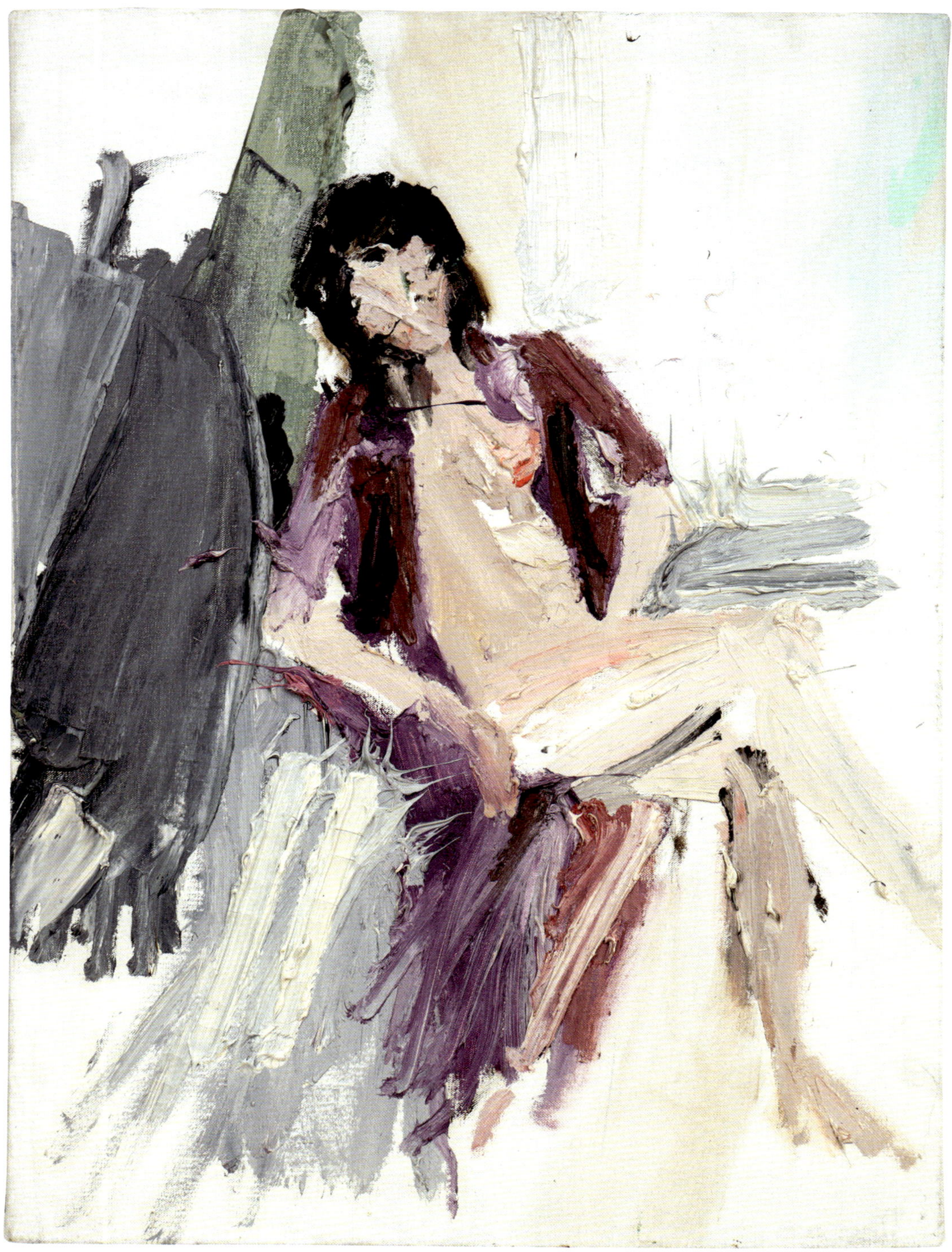

 Untitled, 1963, oil on canvas, 28¾ × 21¼ inches (73 × 54 cm)

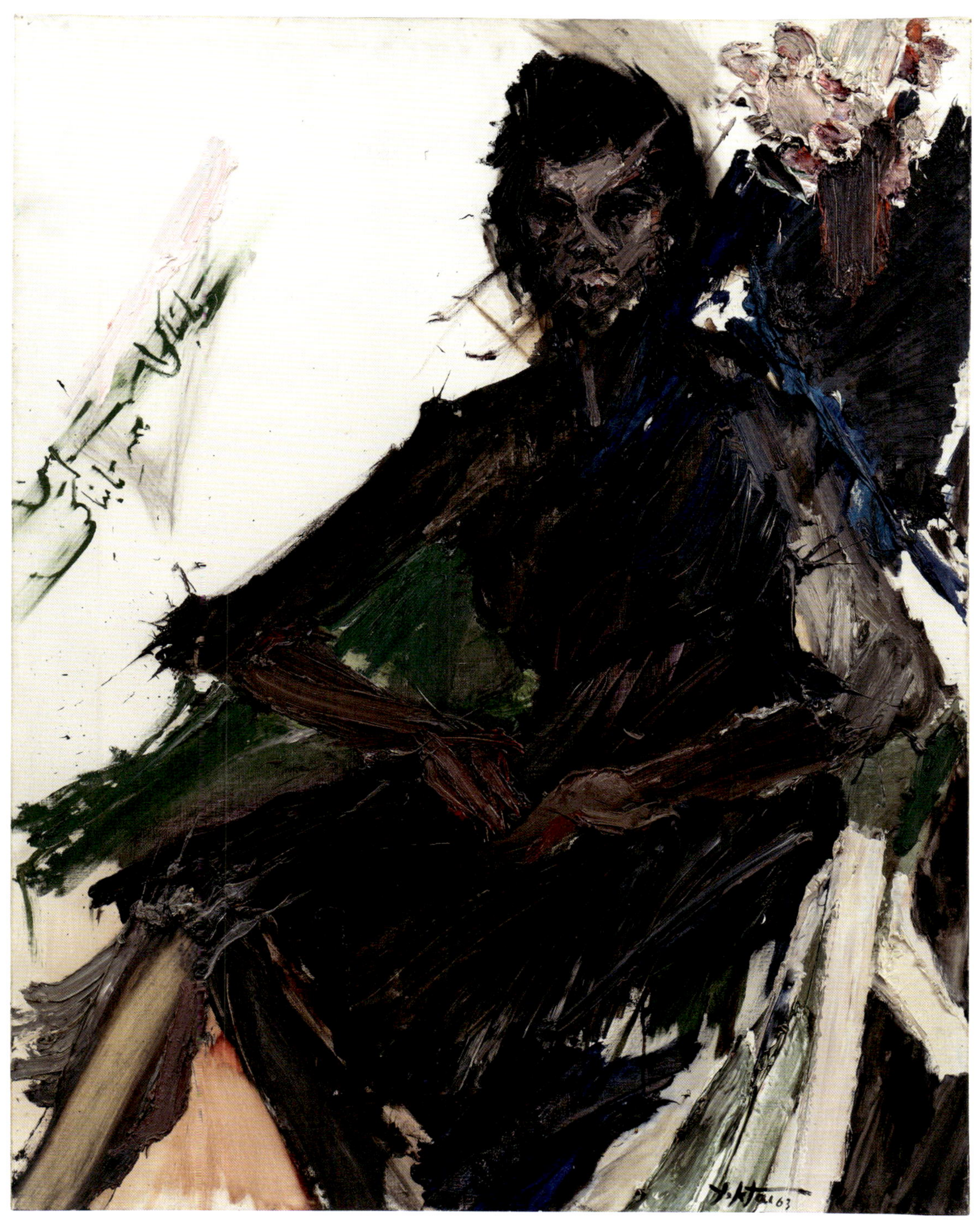

Portrait of Isa, 1963, oil on canvas, 57 × 44 inches (144.8 × 111.8 cm)

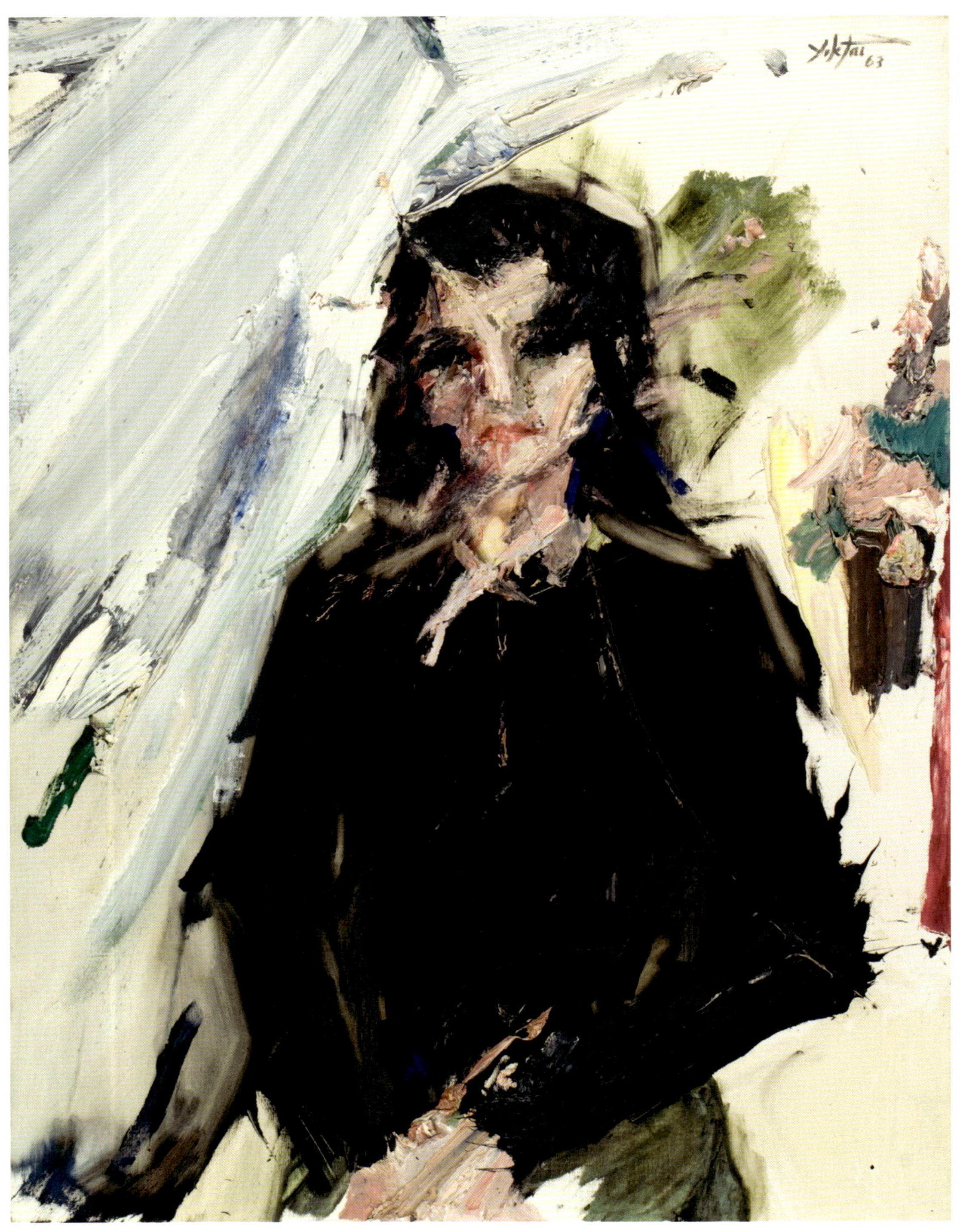

Figure, 1963, oil on canvas, 45⅝ × 35 inches (106 × 89 cm)

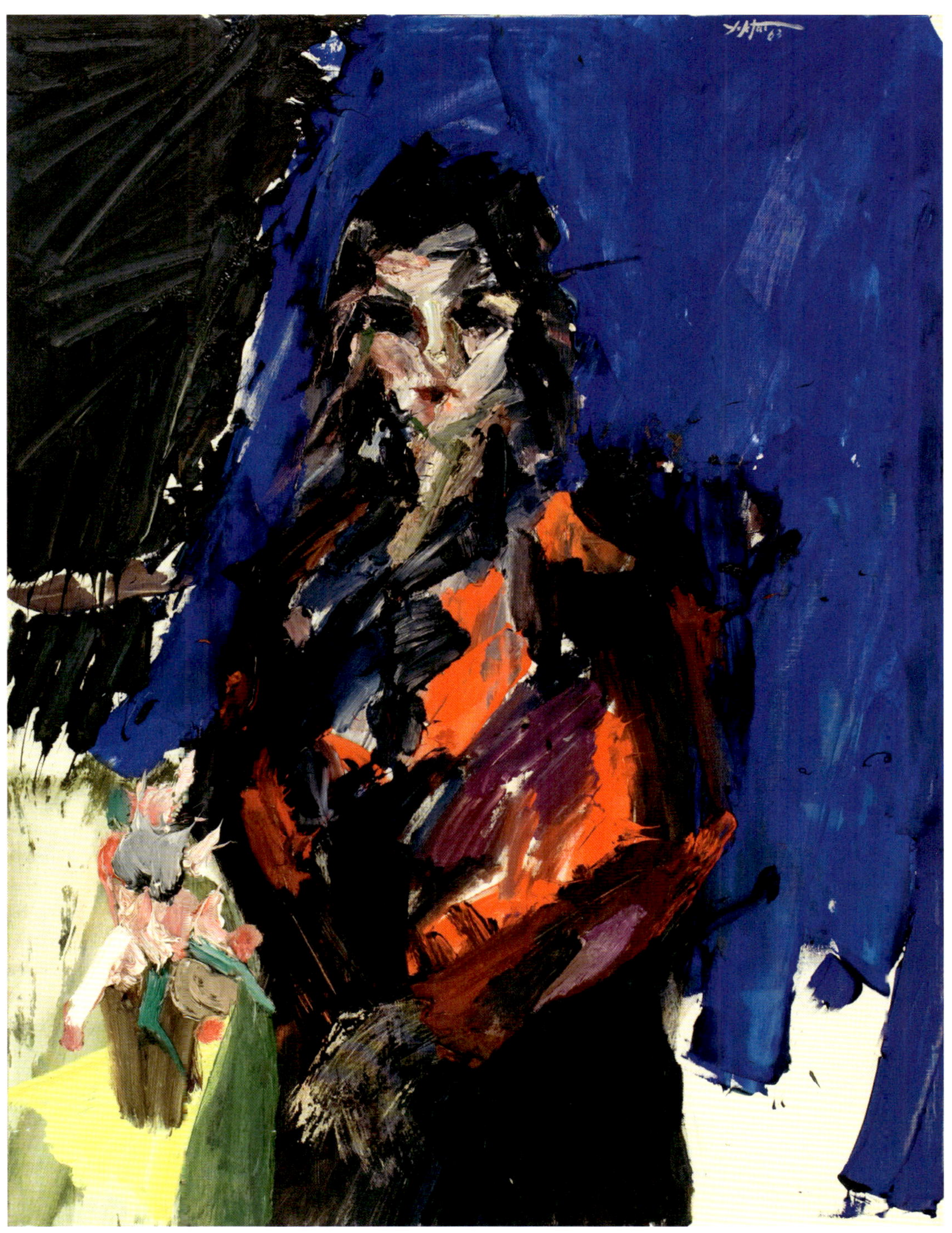

Femme aux Mains Egratignees, 1963, oil on canvas, 51¼ × 38⅛ inches (130 × 96.9 cm)

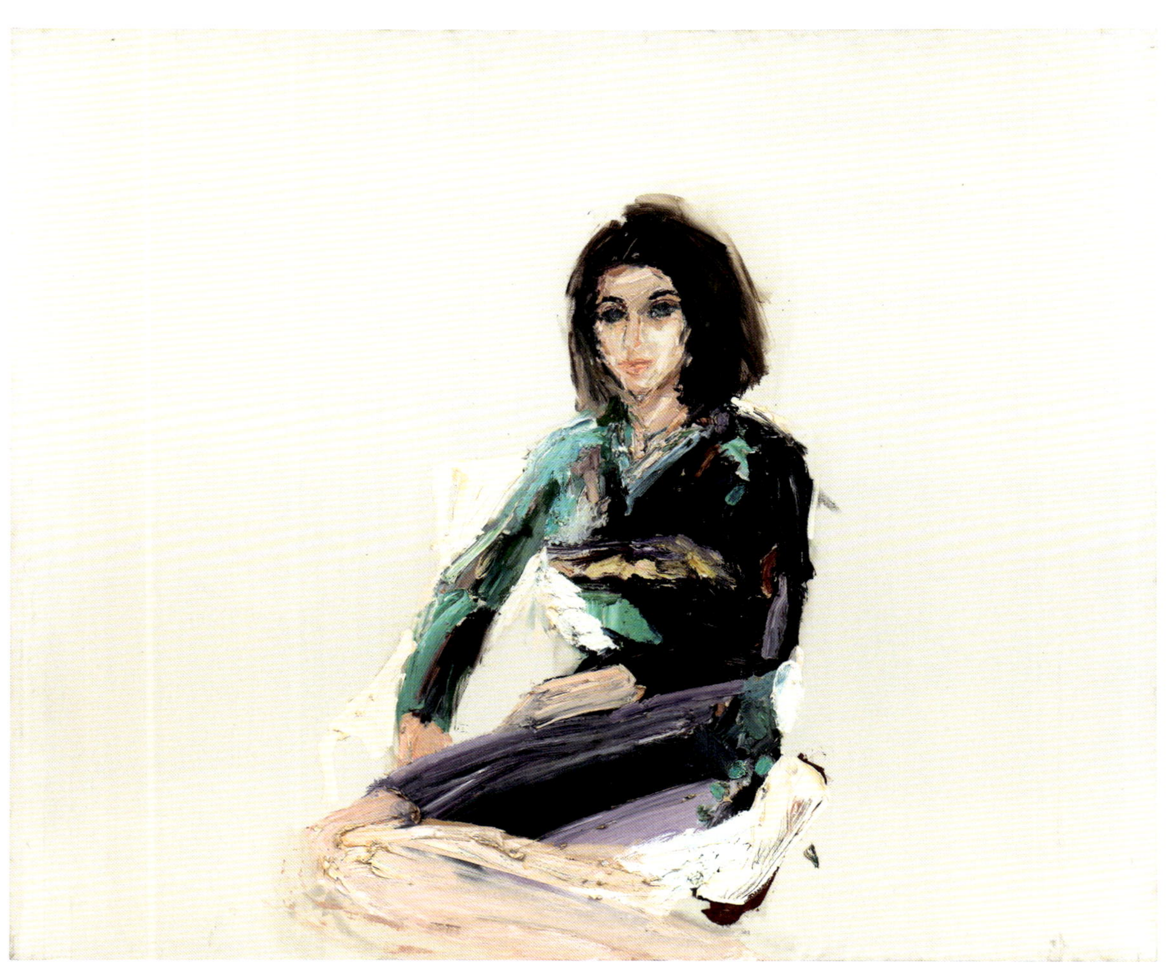

 Betsy Langman, 1964, oil on canvas, 50 × 60 inches (127 × 152.4 cm)

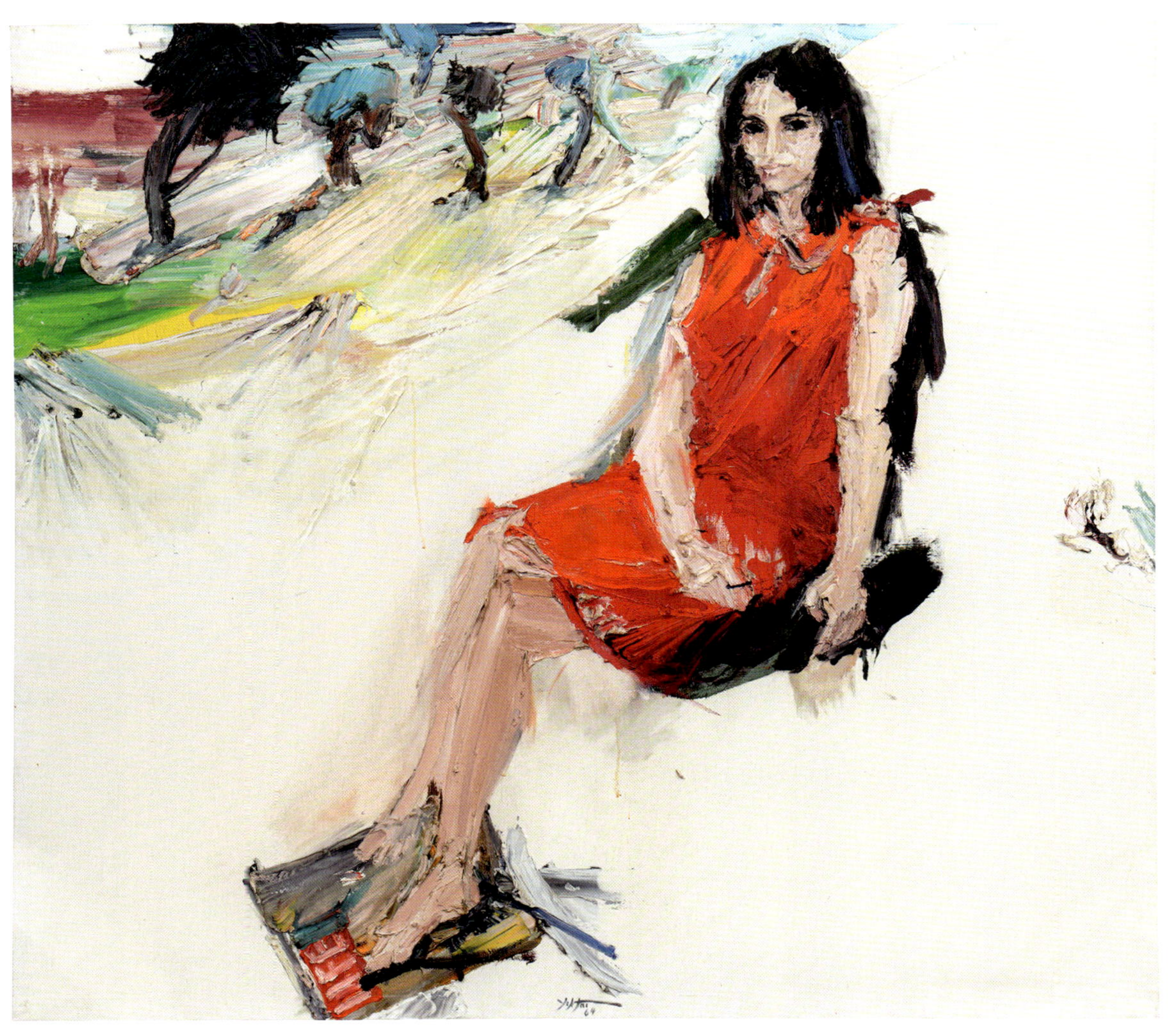

Eleni II, 1964, oil on canvas, 67 × 74 inches (170.2 × 188 cm)

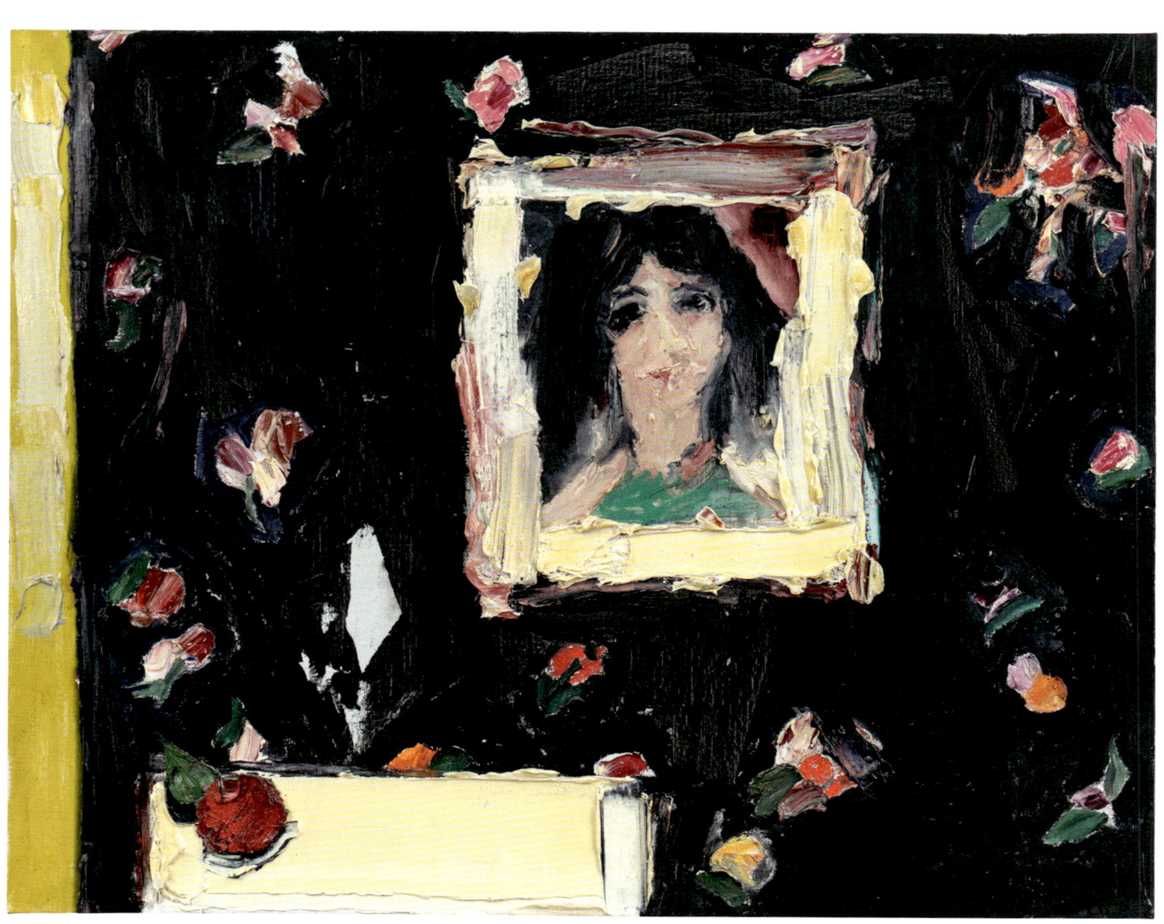

Untitled, 1964, oil on canvas, 46 × 58 inches (117 × 147 cm)

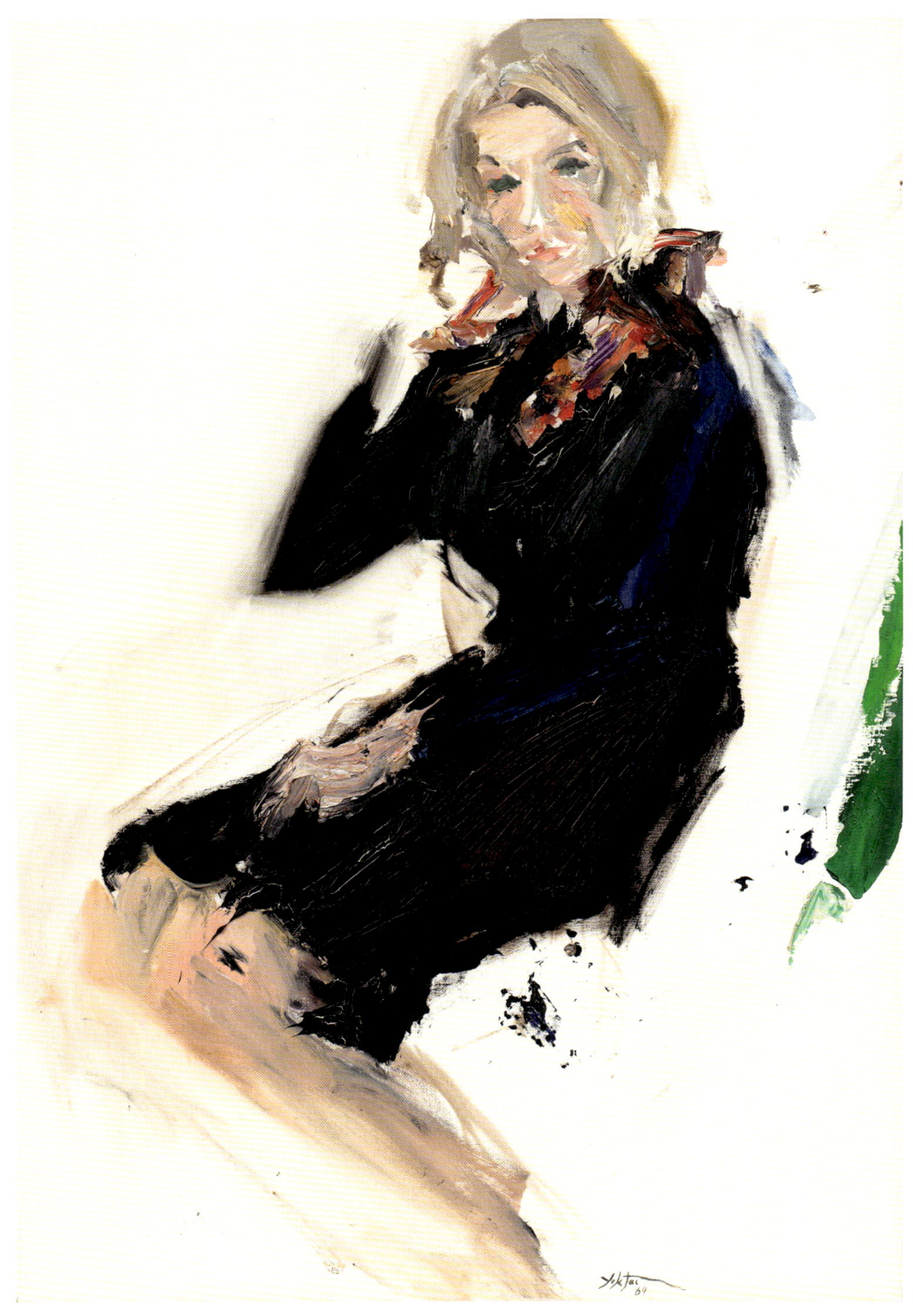

Dotsy, 1964, oil on canvas, 56 × 38 inches (142.2 × 96.5 cm)

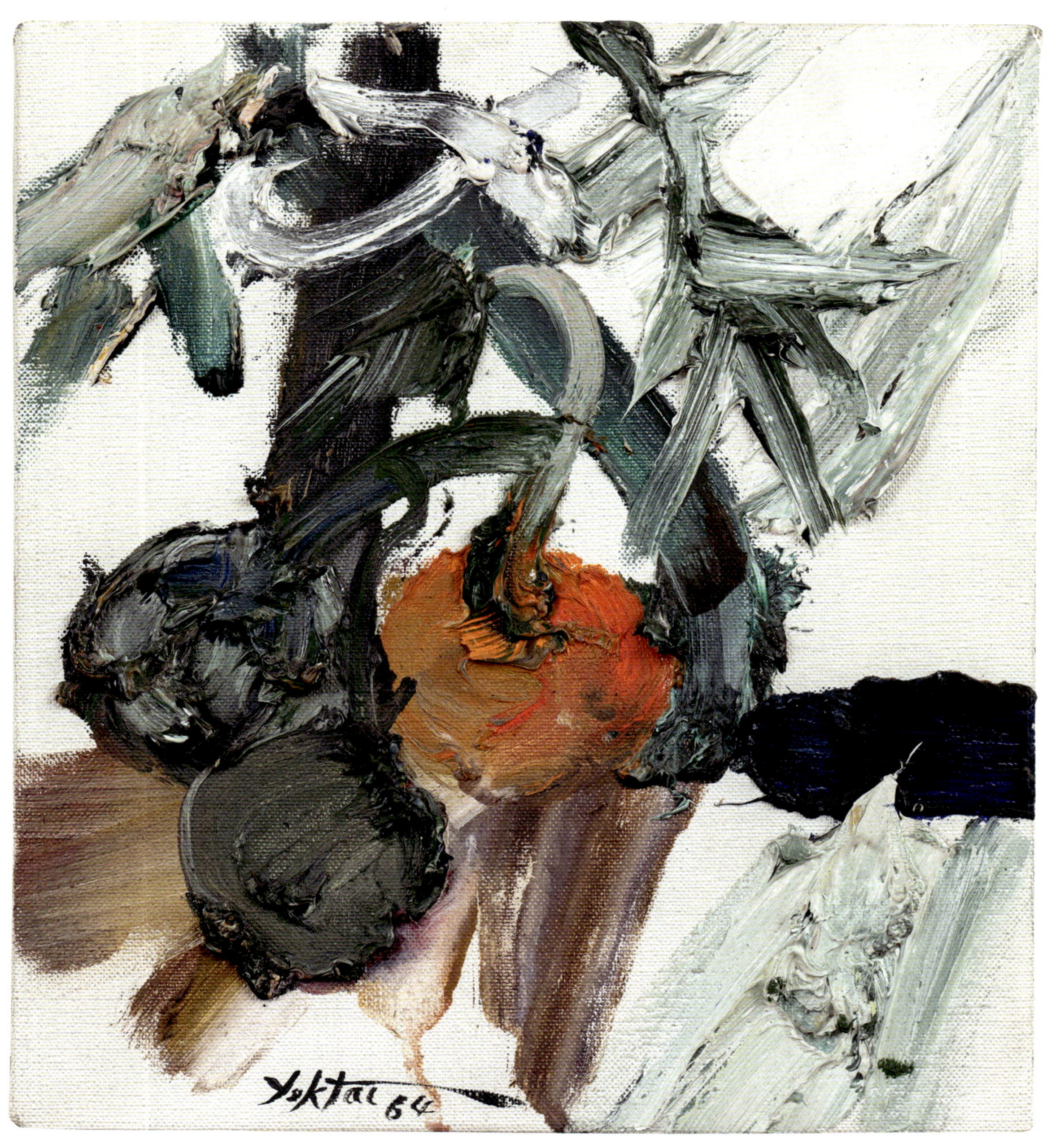

 Tomato Plant, 1964, oil on canvas, 11 × 10 inches (27.9 × 25.4 cm)

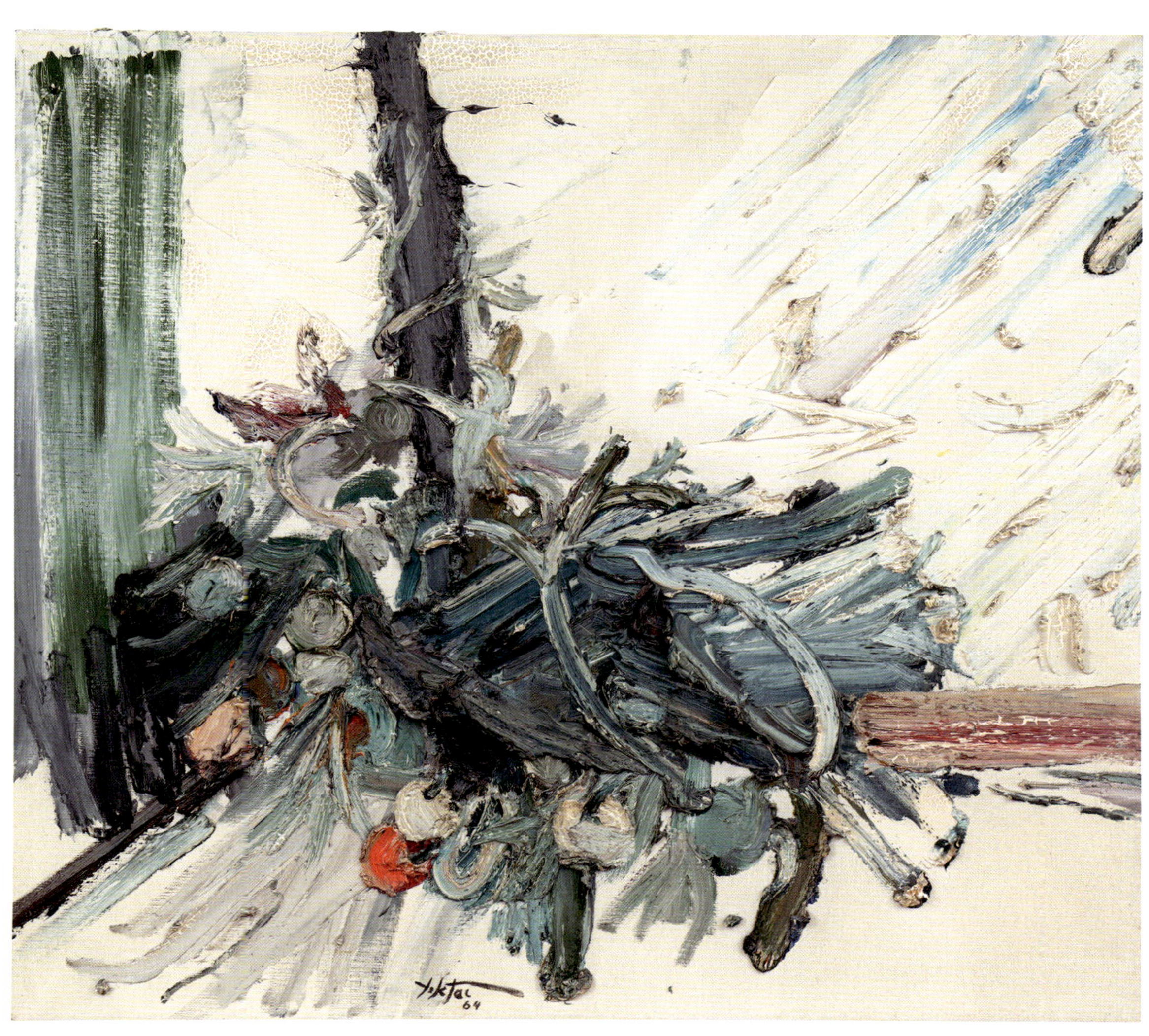

Untitled, 1964, oil on canvas, 36 × 40 inches (36 × 40 cm)

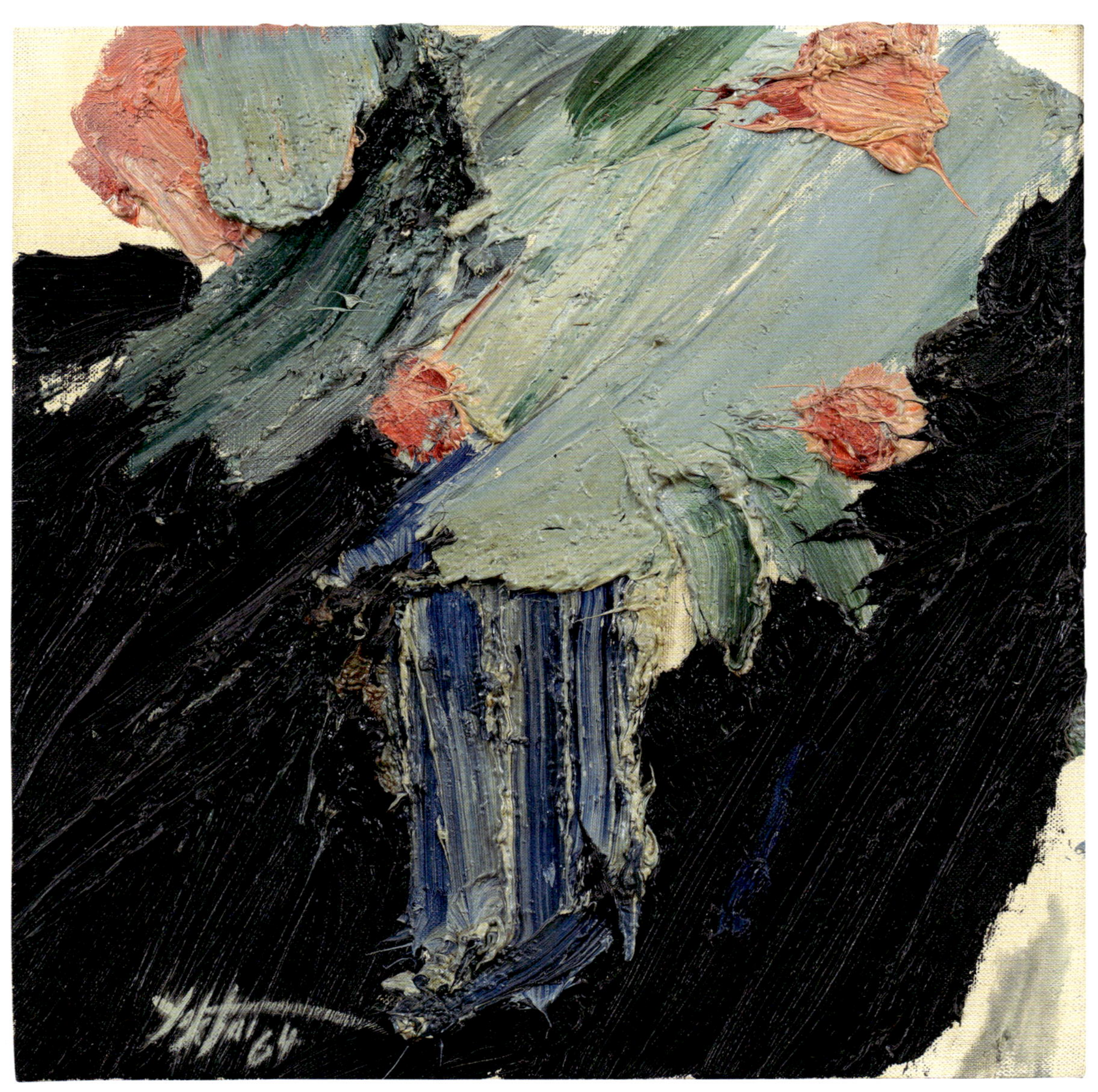

Untitled, 1964, oil on canvas, 14 × 14 inches (35.6 × 35.6 cm)

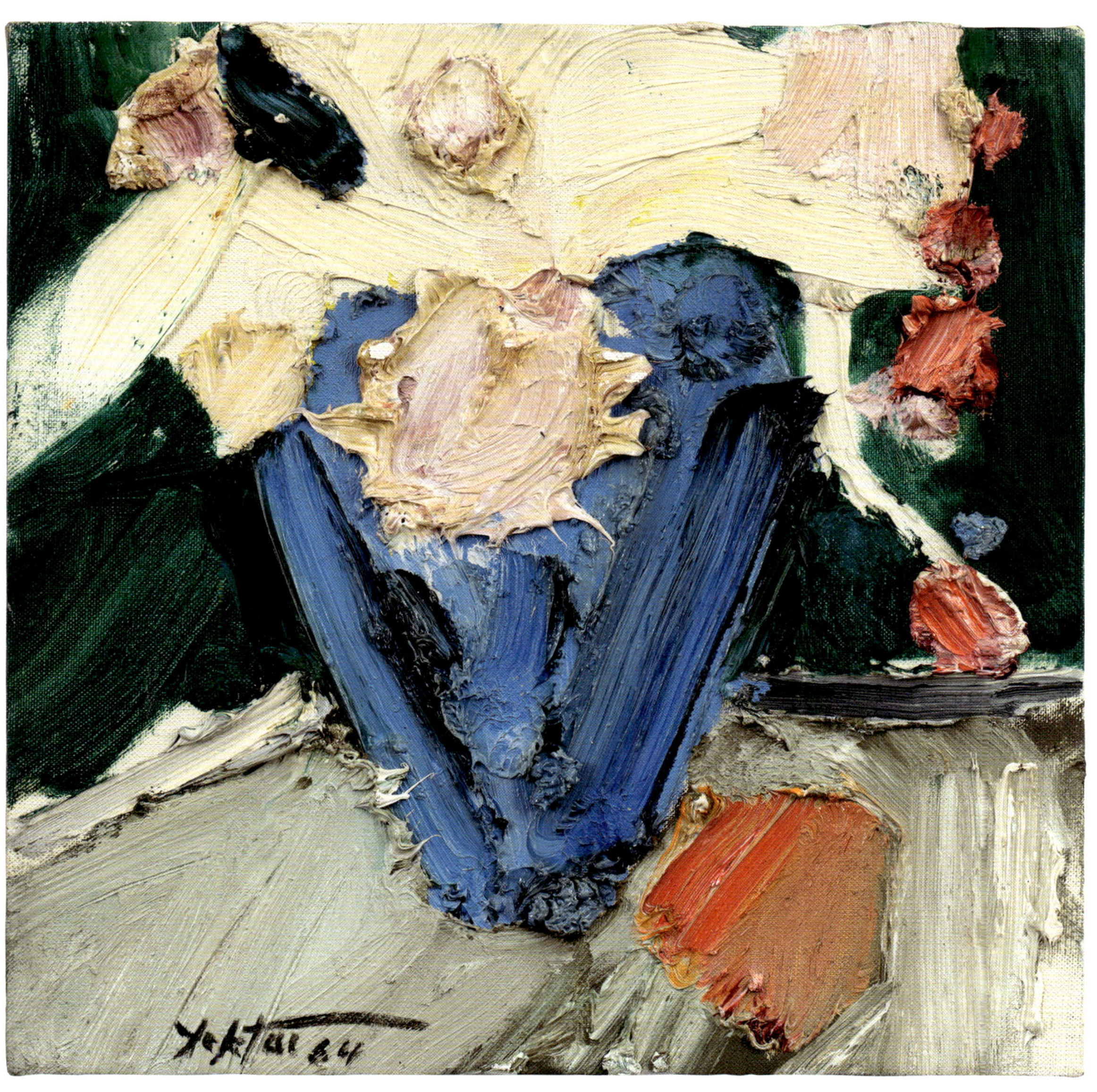

Flowers in Blue Vase, 1964, oil on canvas, 14 × 14 inches (35.6 × 35.6 cm)

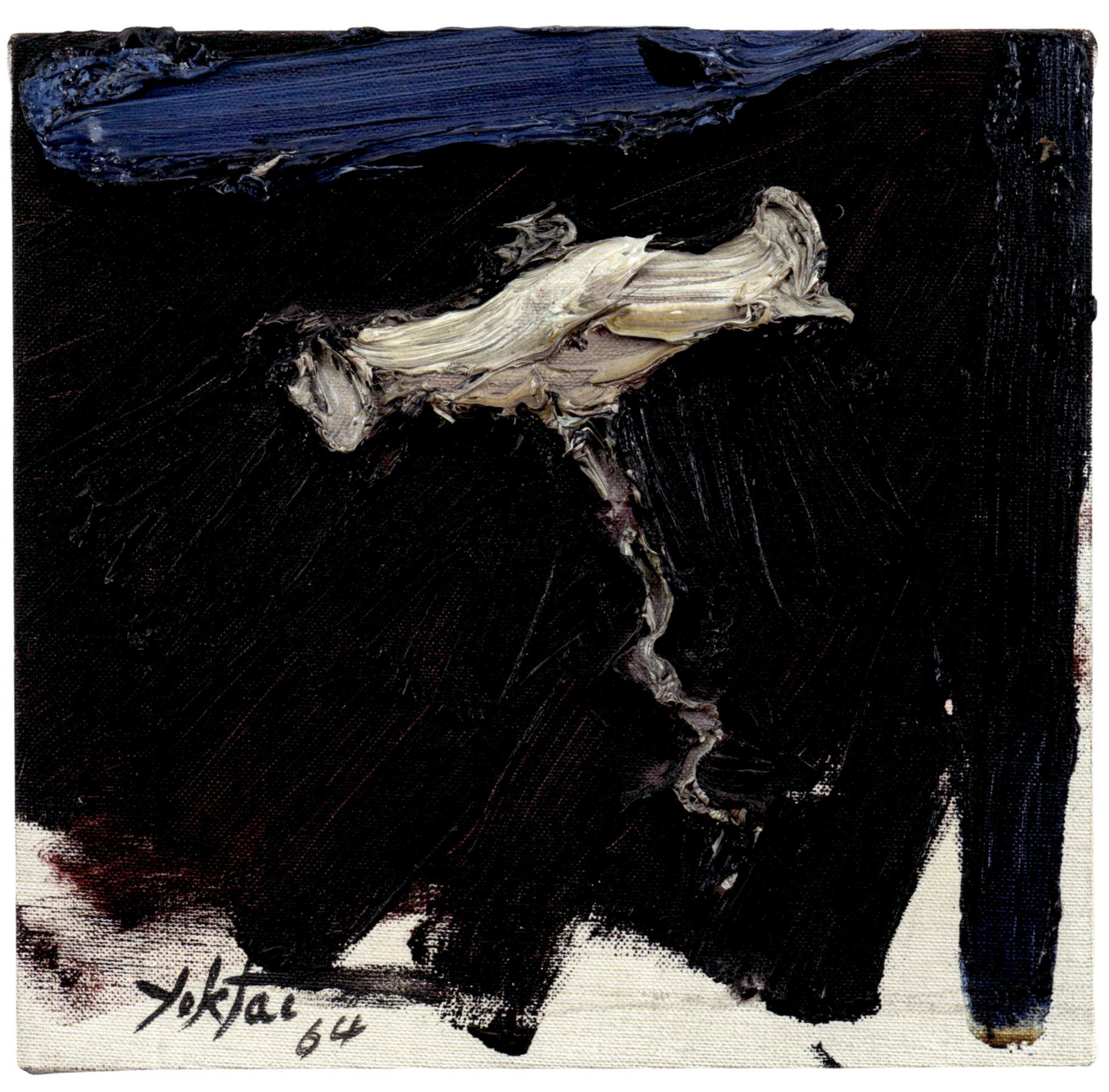

Untitled, 1964, oil on canvas, 10 × 10 inches (25.4 × 25.4 cm)

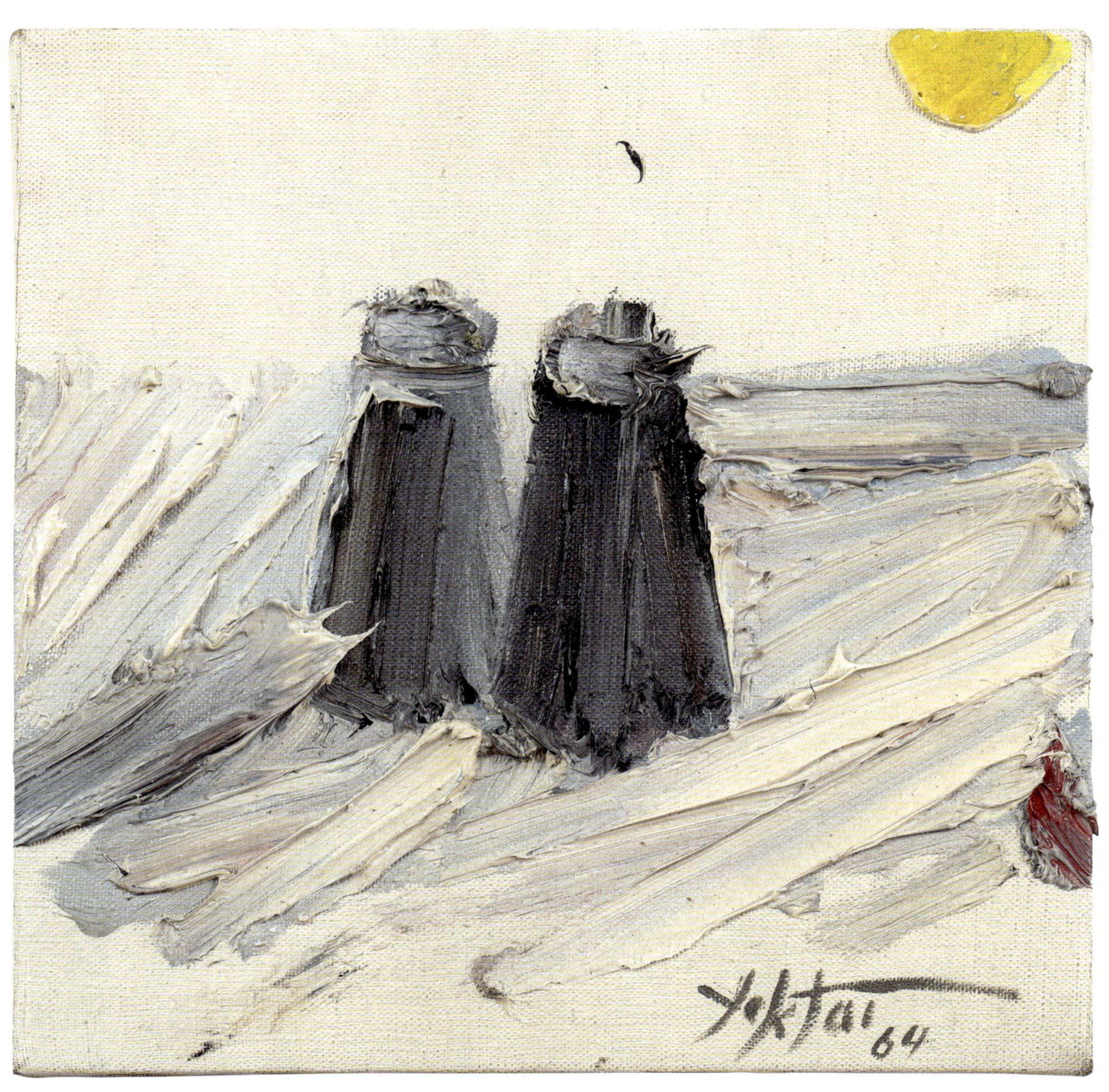

Untitled, 1964, oil on canvas, 10 × 10 inches (25.4 × 25.4 cm)

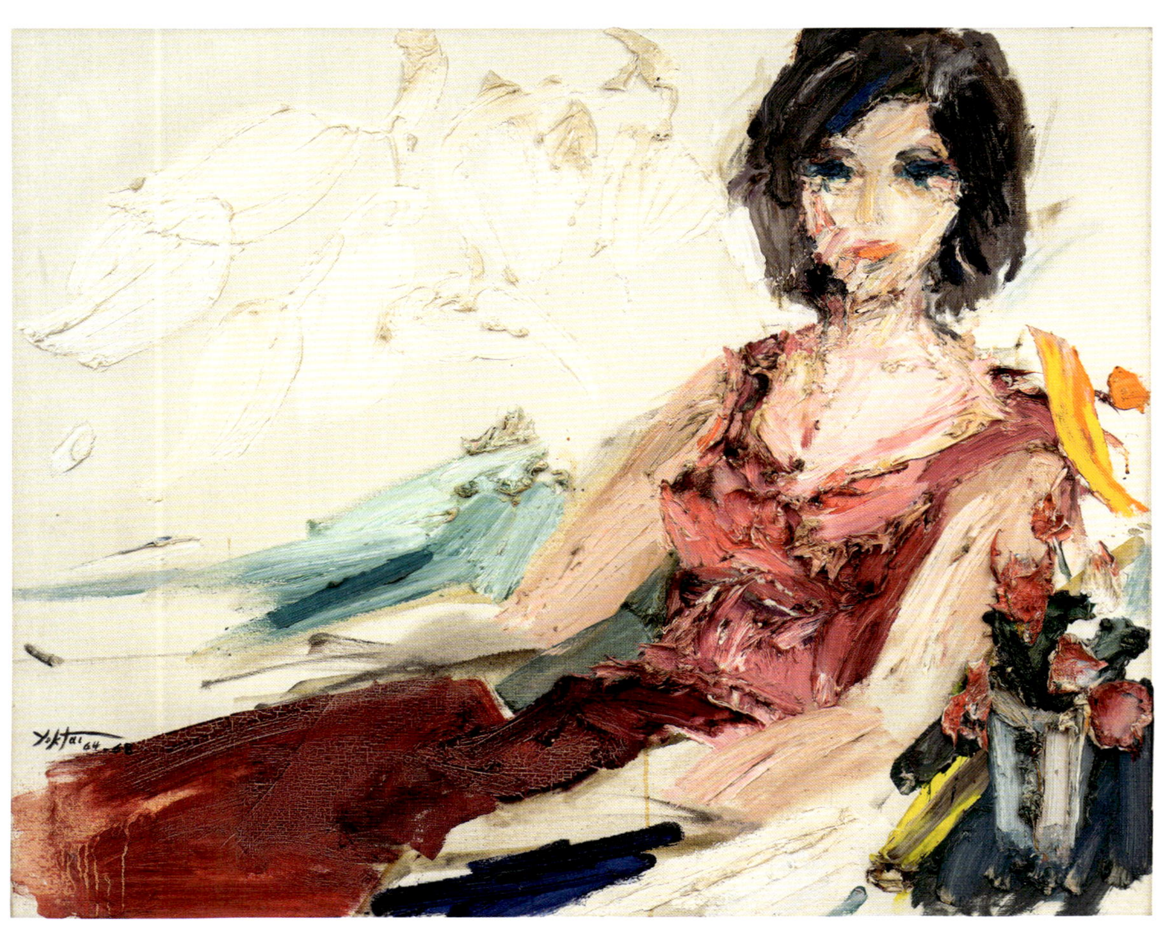

 Untitled, 1964, oil on canvas, 32 × 40 inches (81.3 × 101.6 cm)

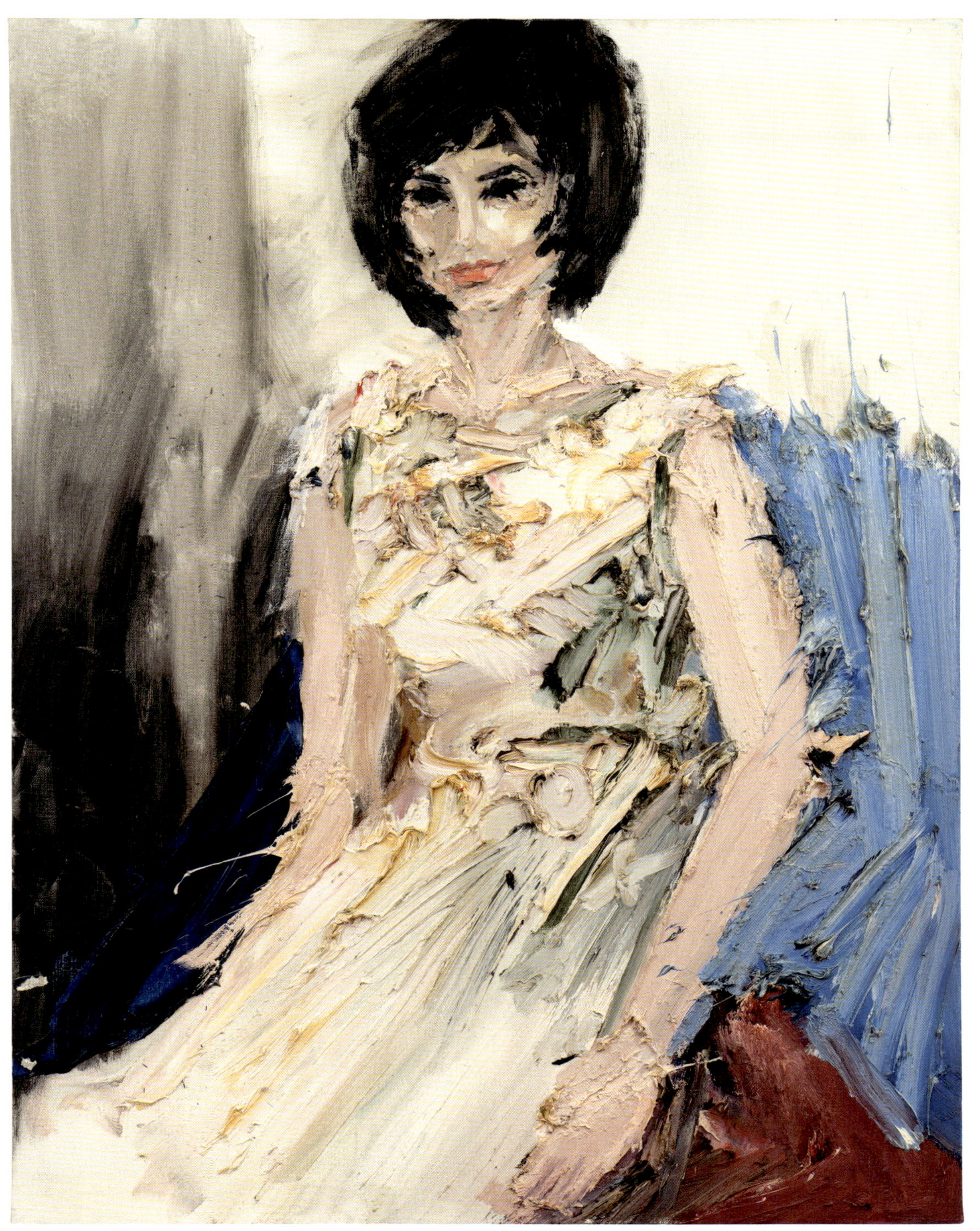

Untitled, 1964, oil on canvas, 44 × 34 inches (111.8 × 86.4 cm)

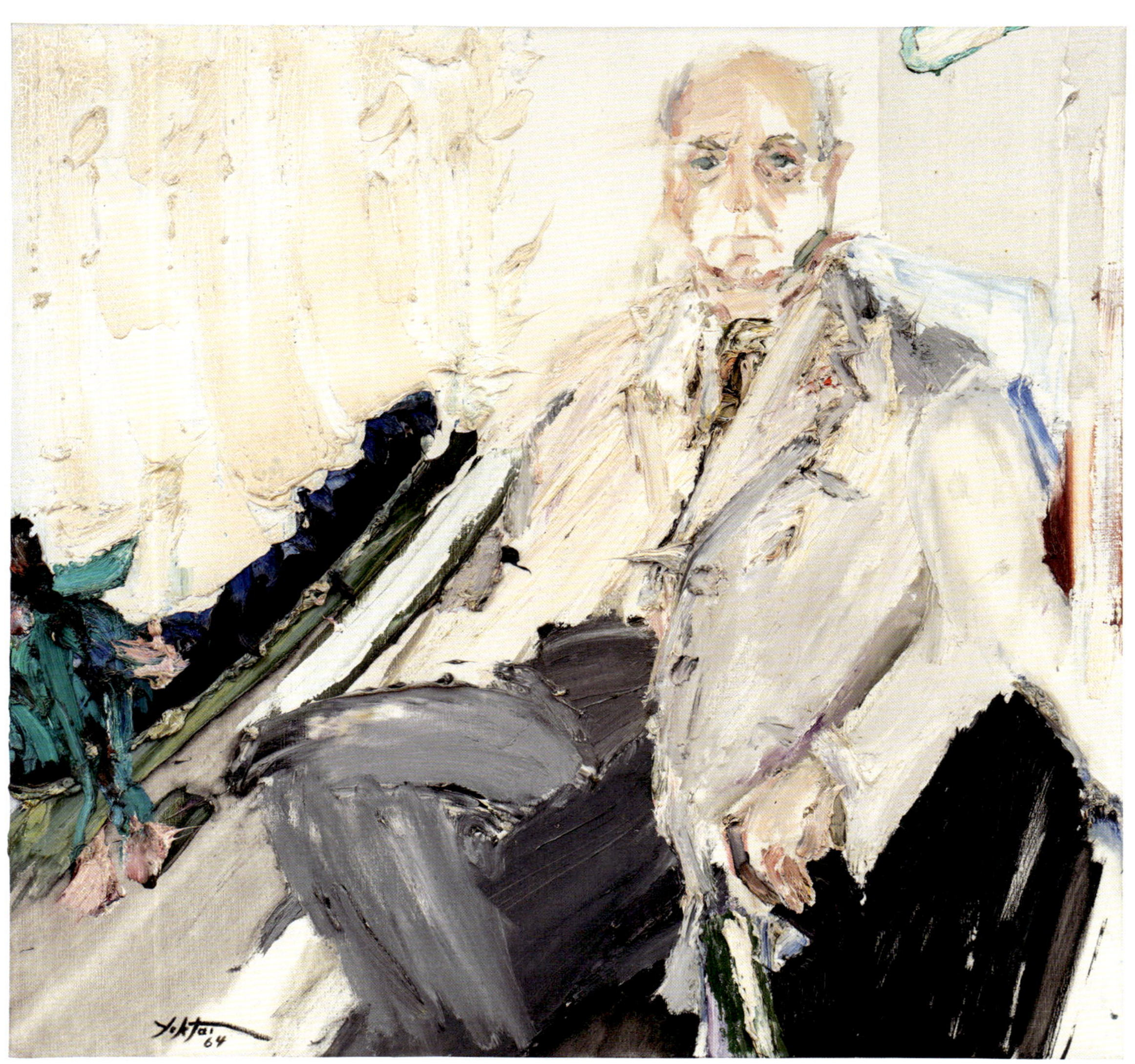

424 *Virgil Thompson*, 1964, oil on canvas, 42 × 44 inches (106.7 × 111.8 cm)

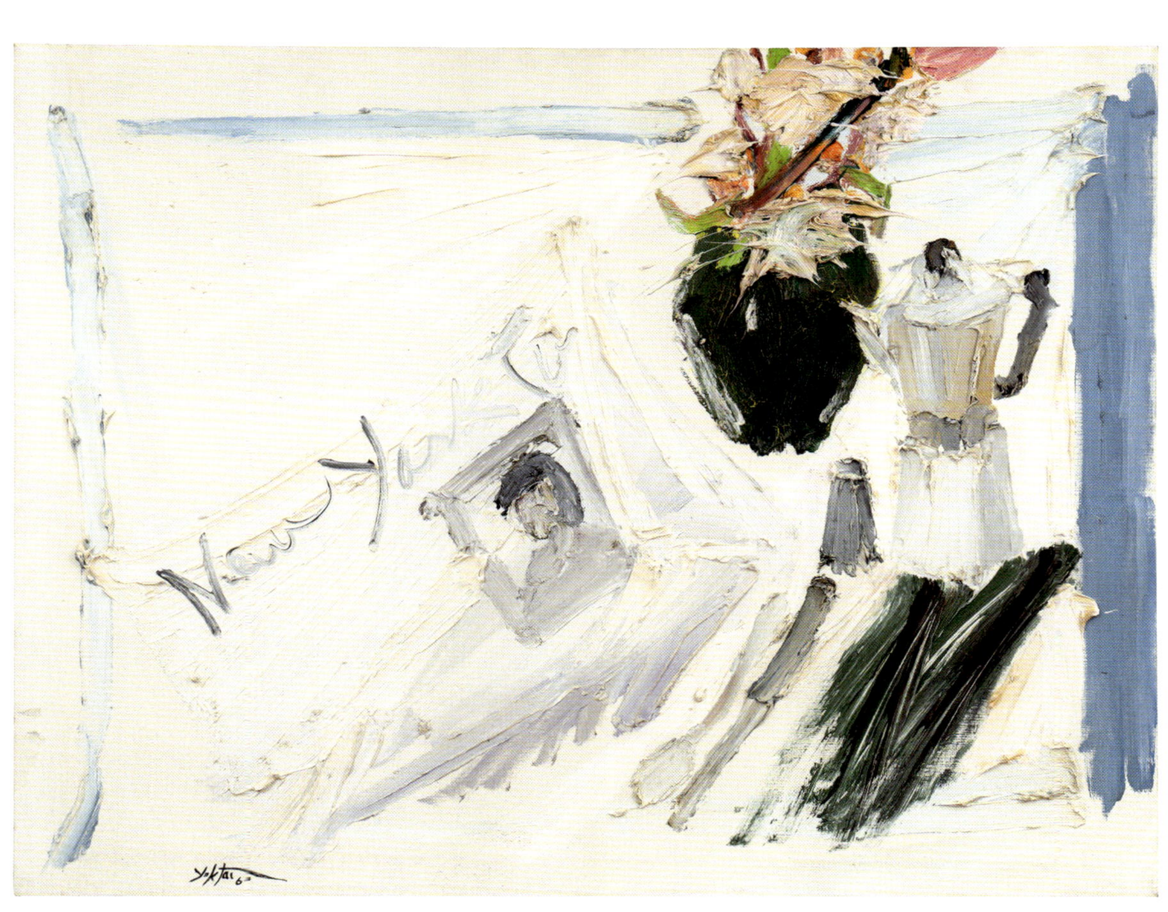

Still Life with Coffee Pot, 1964, oil on canvas, 32 × 42 inches (81.3 × 106.7 cm)

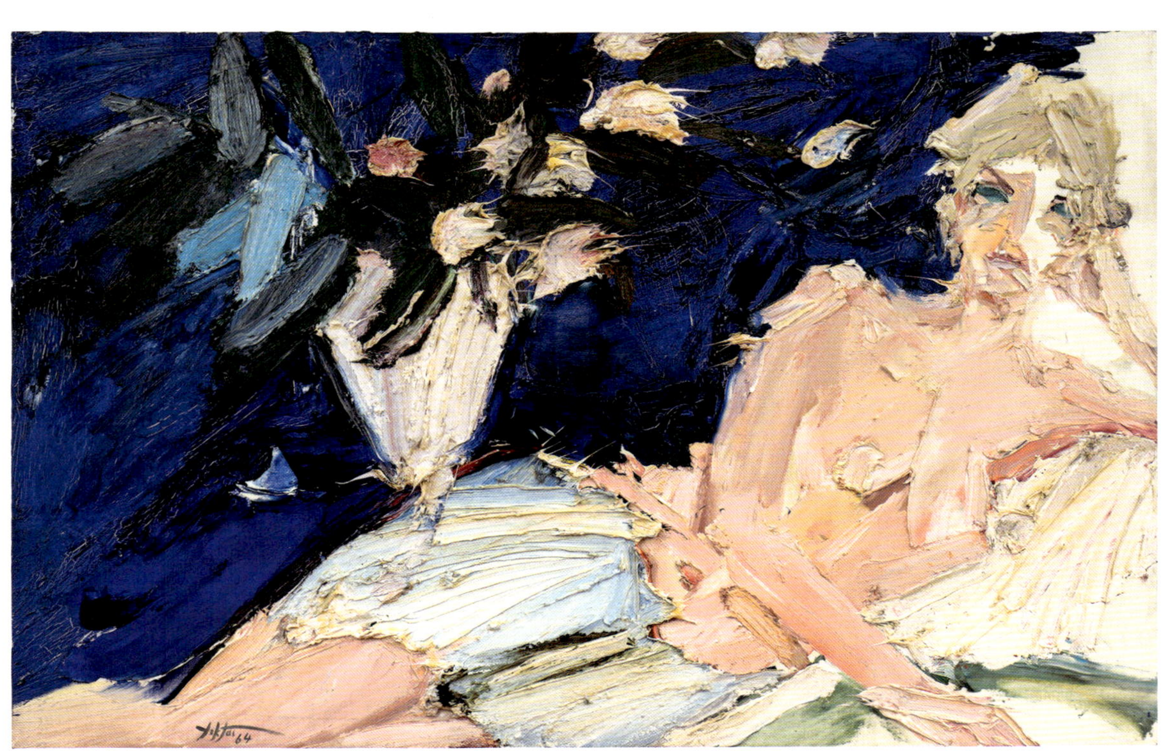

 Untitled, 1964, oil on canvas, 14⅛ × 22 inches (36 × 56 cm)

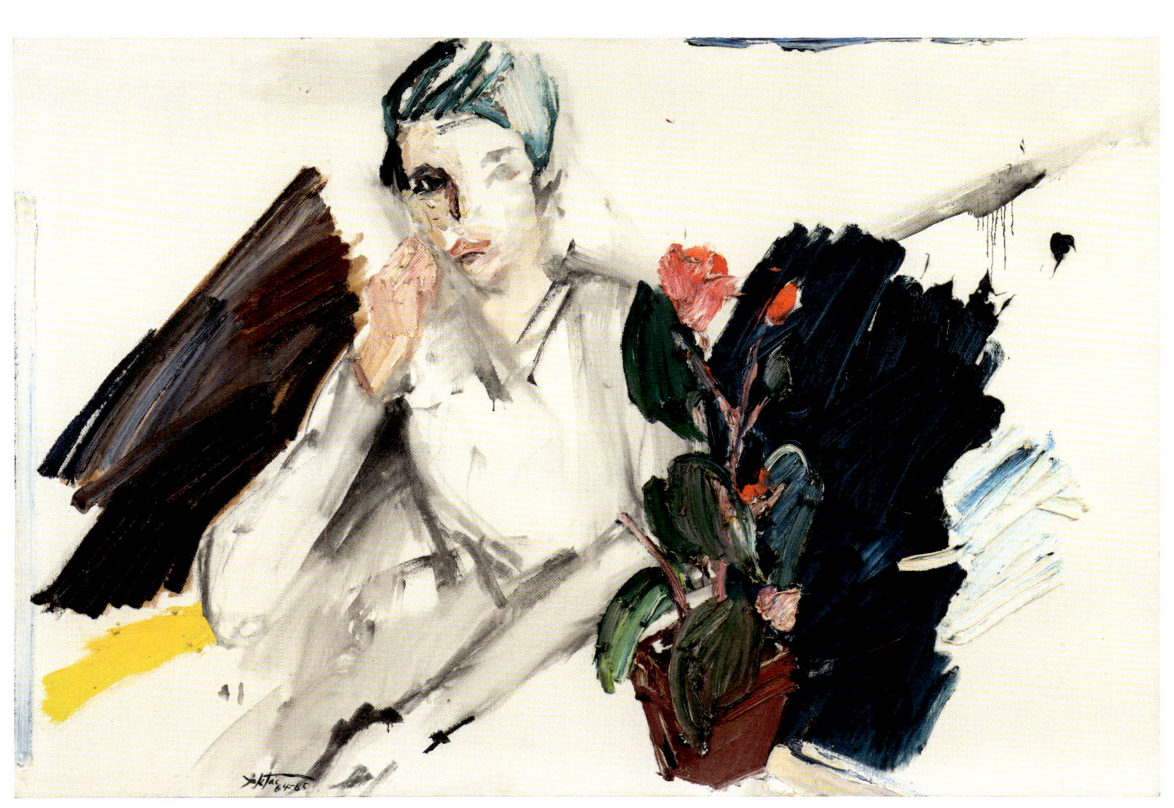

Untitled, 1964, oil on canvas, 38 × 56 inches (96.5 × 142.2 cm)

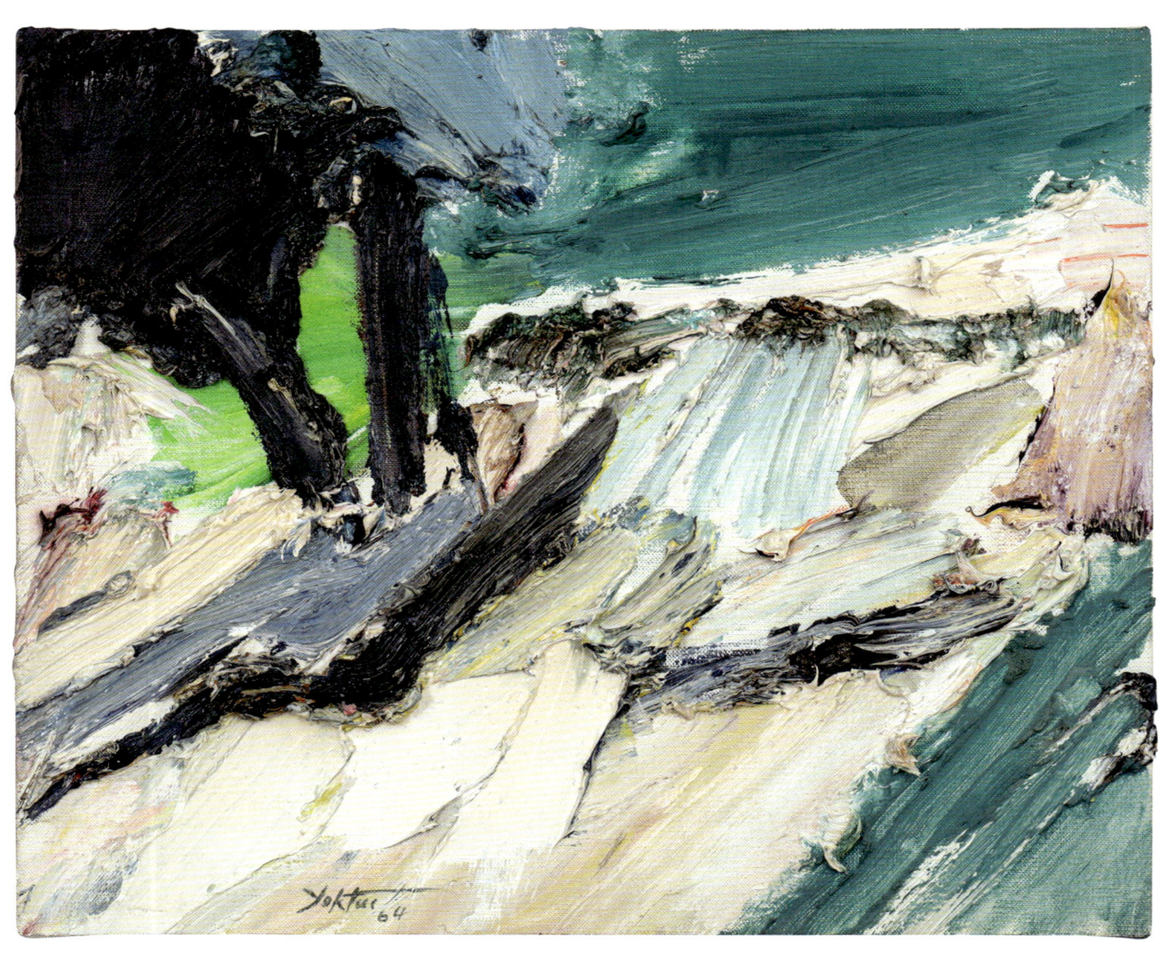

Untitled, 1964, oil on canvas, 13¾ × 17 inches (34.9 × 43.2 cm)

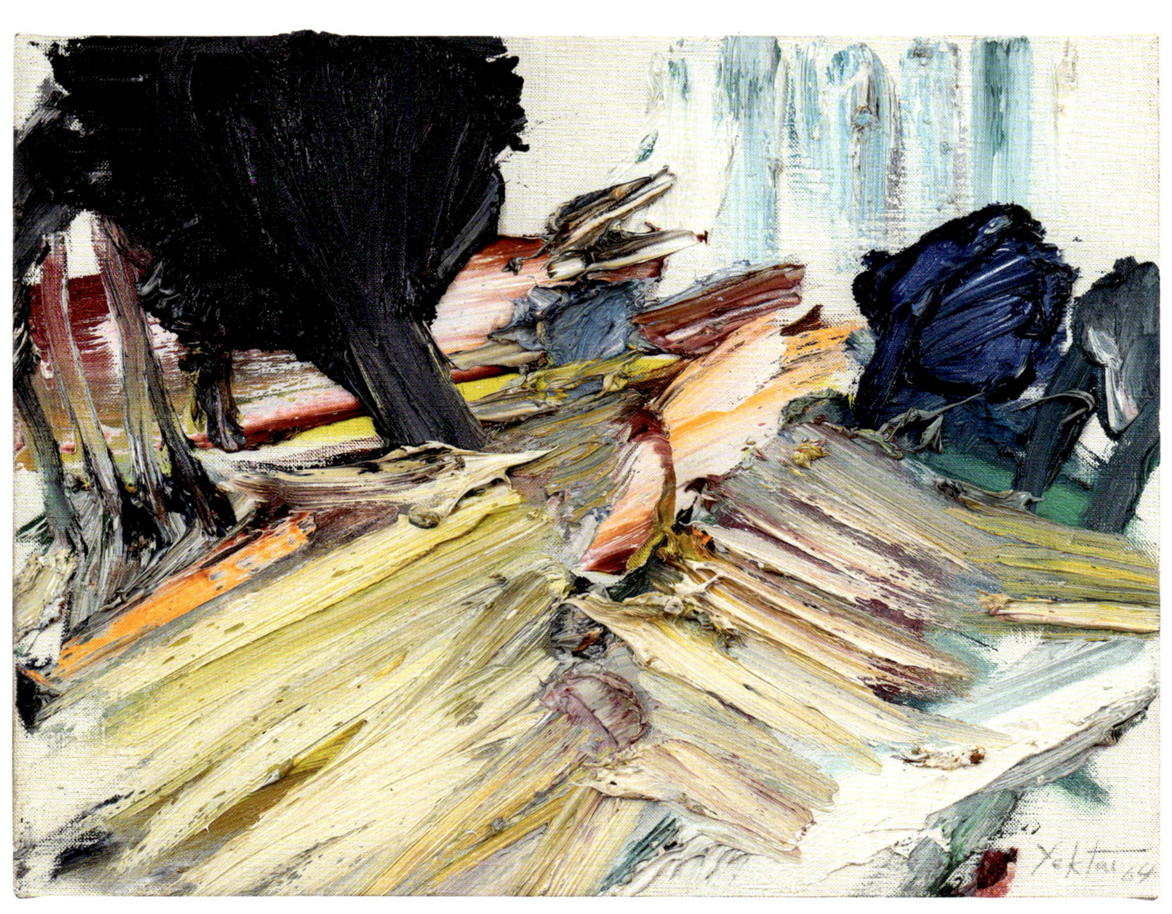

Untitled, 1964, oil on canvas, 14 × 18¼ inches (35.6 × 46.4 cm)

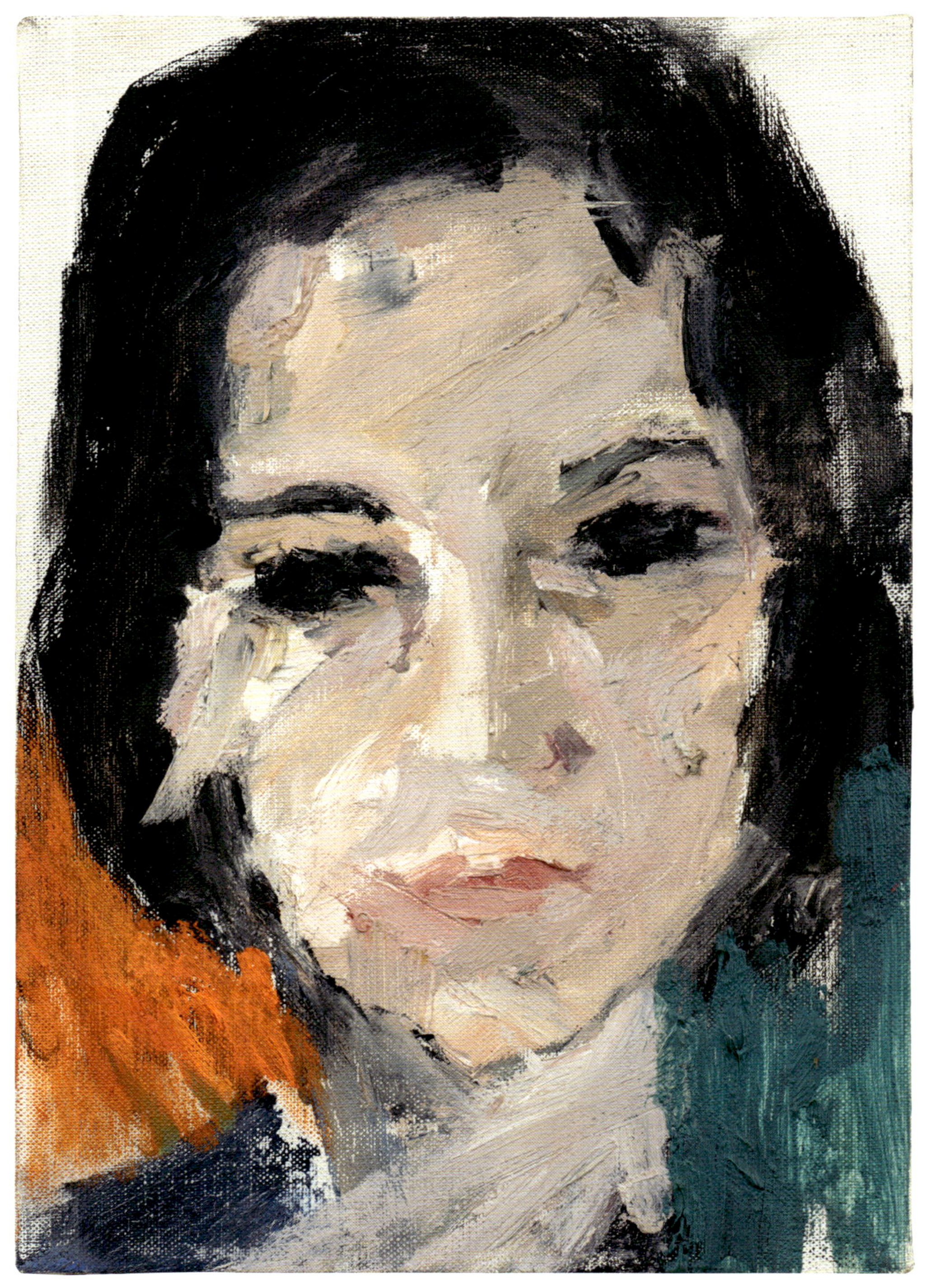

Gloria, 1964, oil on canvas, 13 × 9 inches (33 × 22.9 cm)

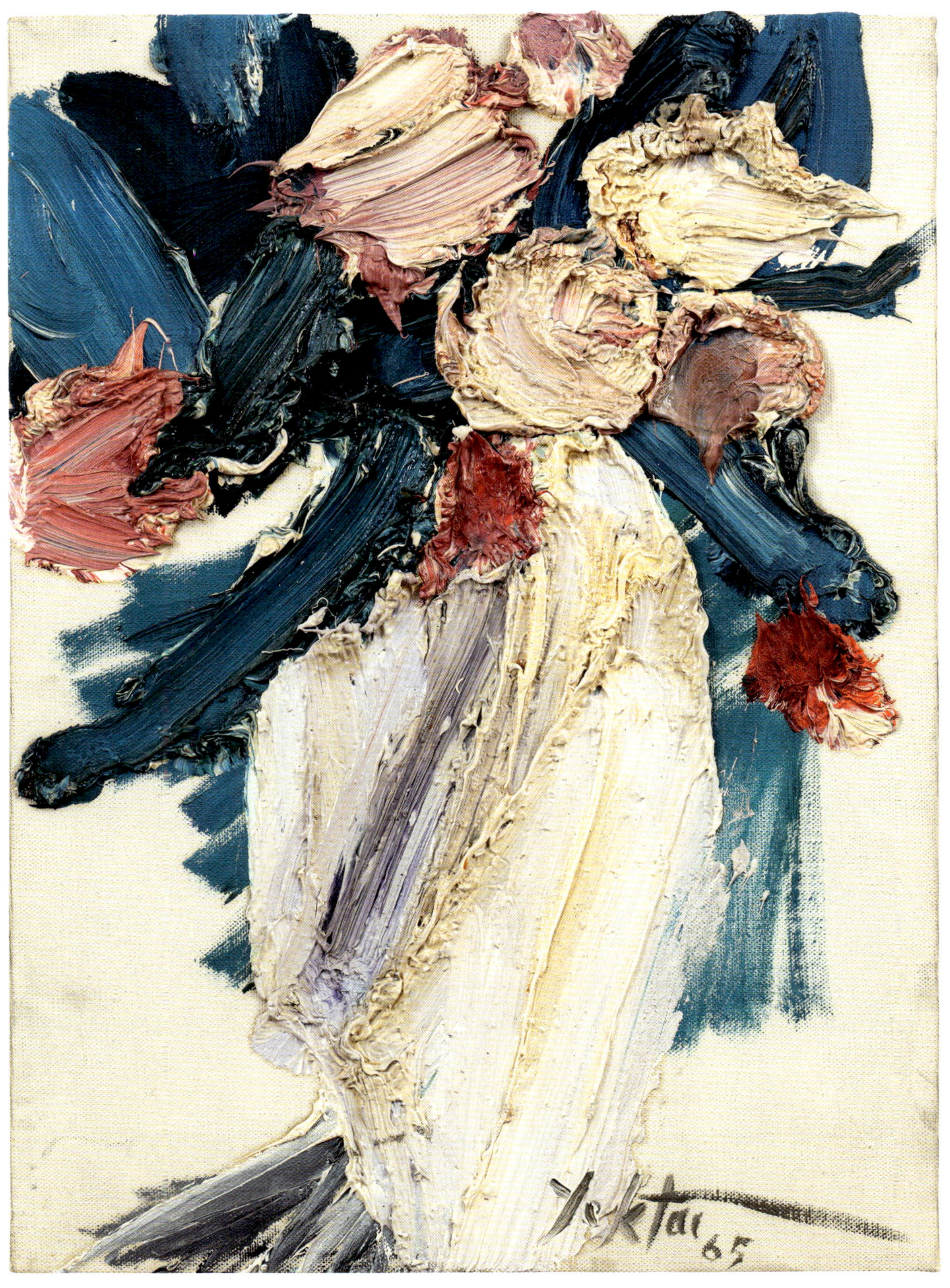

Untitled, 1965, oil on canvas, 14 × 10 inches (35.6 × 25.4 cm)

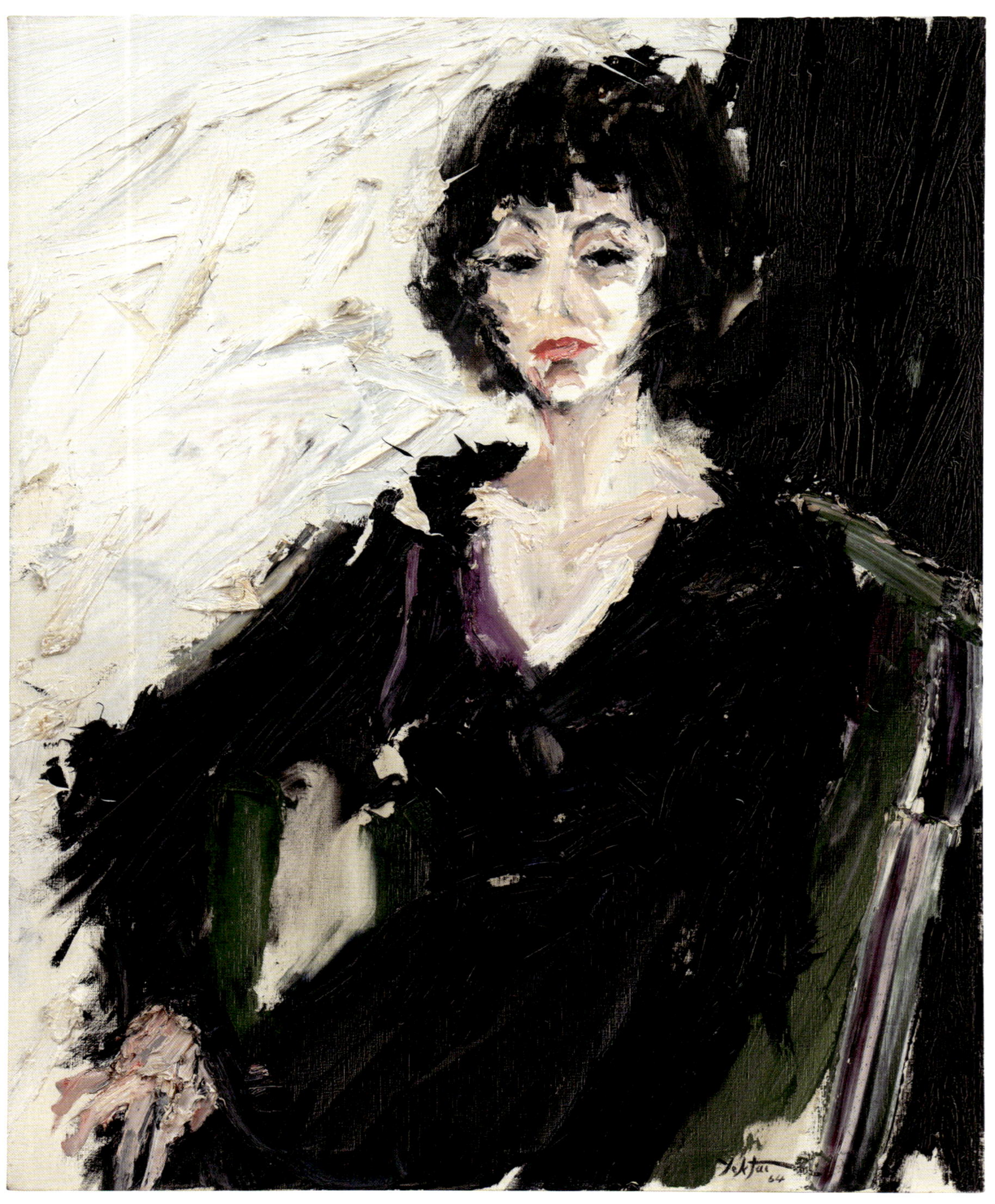

432 *Portrait of Hortense Calisher*, 1964, oil on canvas, 44 × 36 inches (111.8 × 91.4 cm)

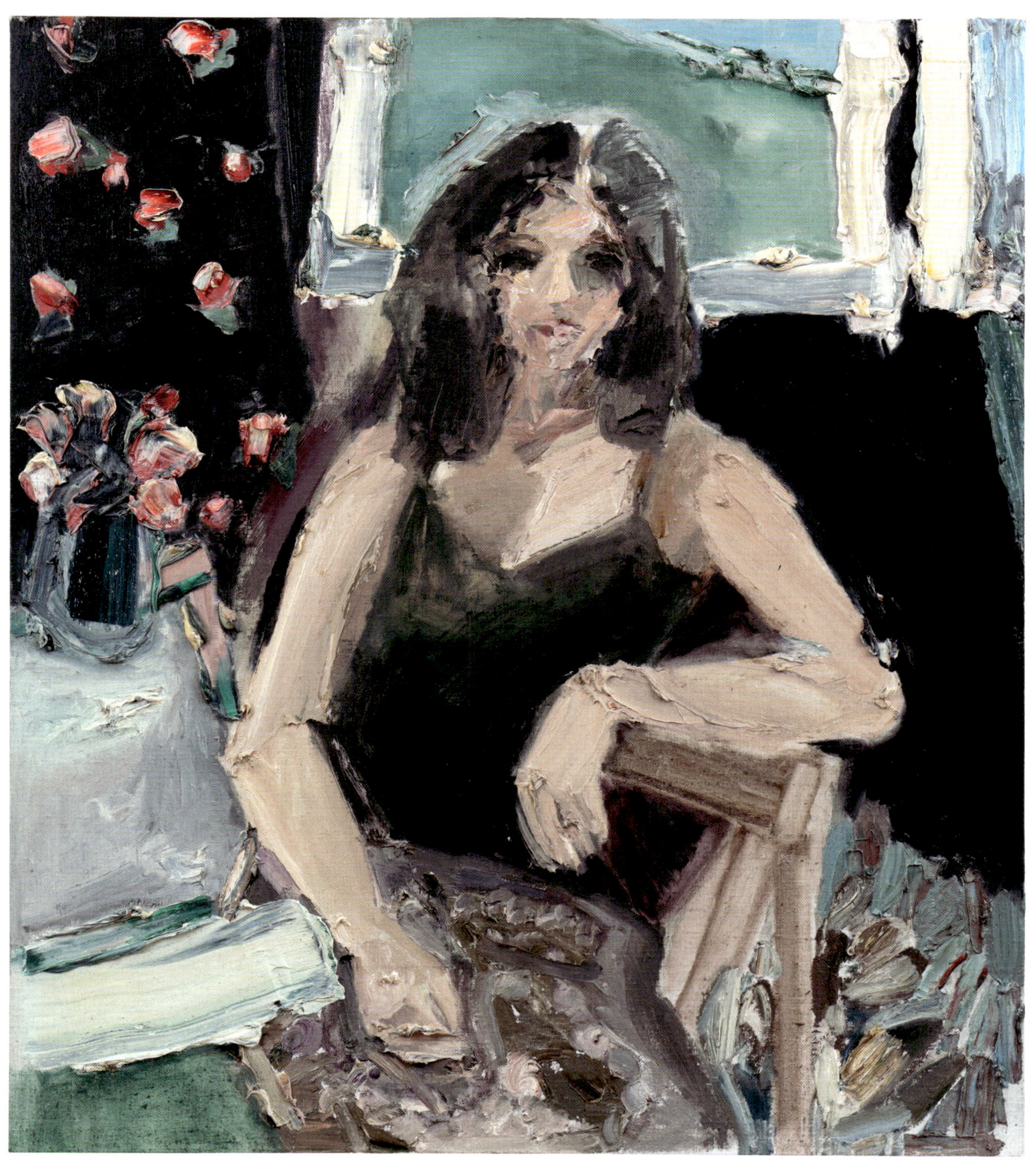

Untitled, 1965, oil on canvas, 48 × 42 inches (121.9 × 106.7 cm)

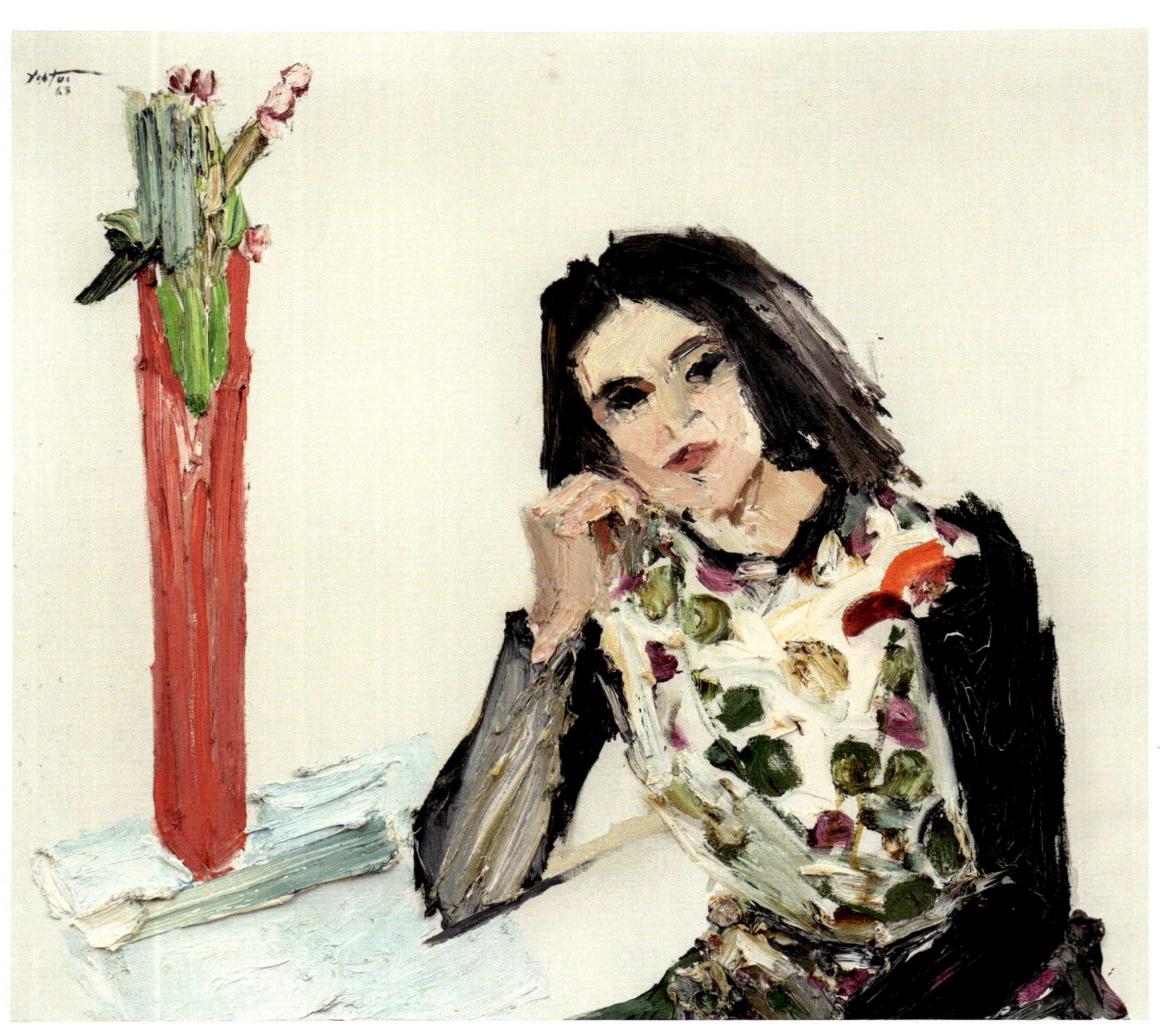

Untitled, 1968, oil on canvas, 35¾ × 39¾ inches (90.8 × 101 cm)

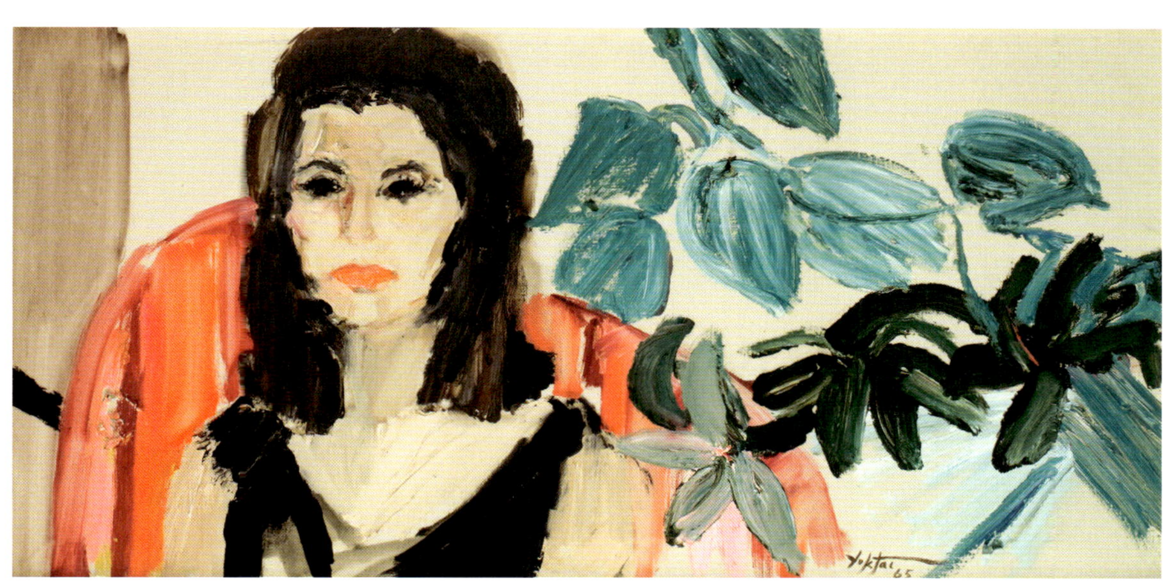

Portrait of S.H., 1965, oil on canvas, 20⅛ × 40⅛ inches (51.1 × 101.8 cm)

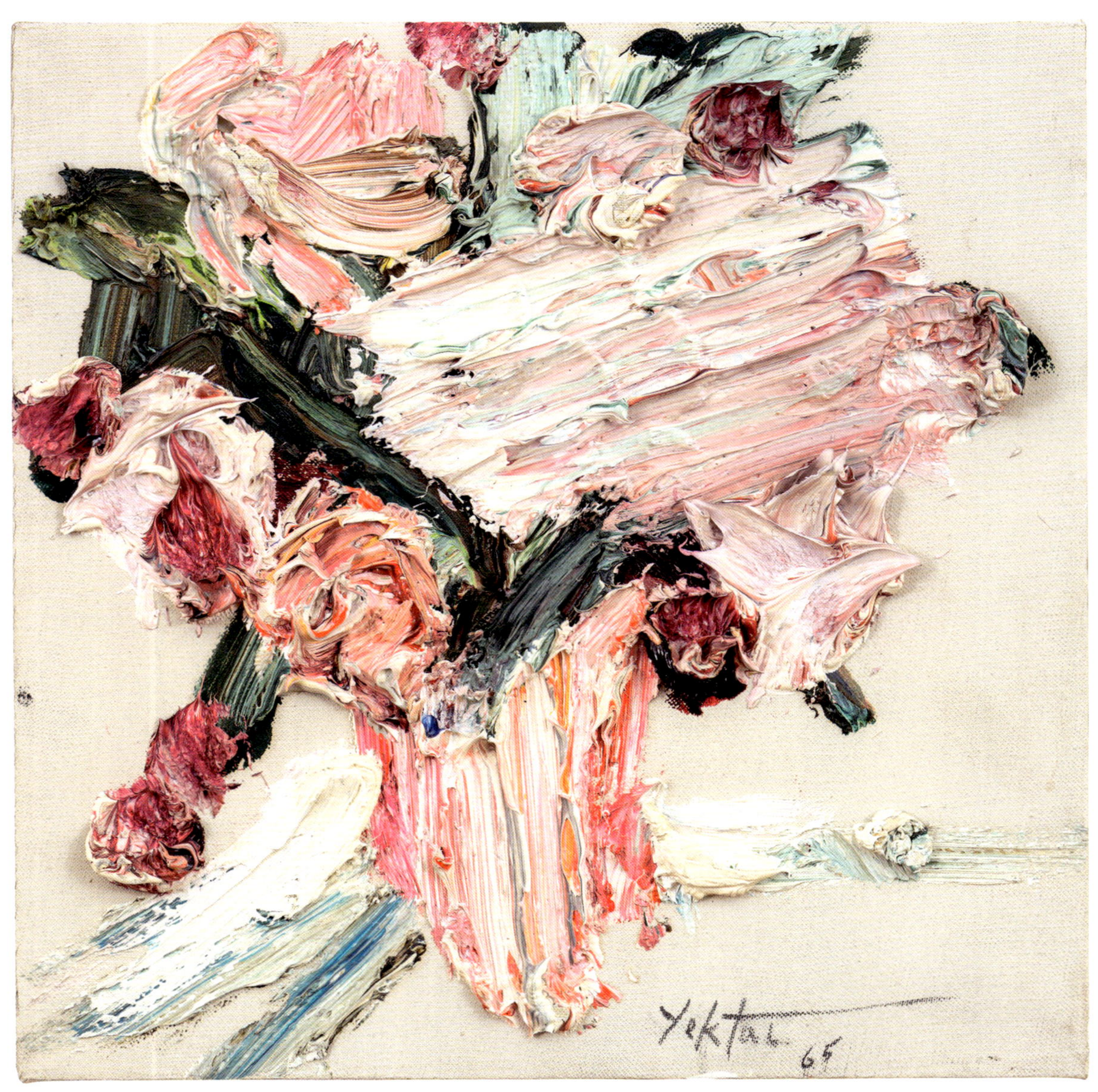

Untitled, 1965, oil on canvas, 13⅜ × 12¾ inches (34 × 32.4 cm)

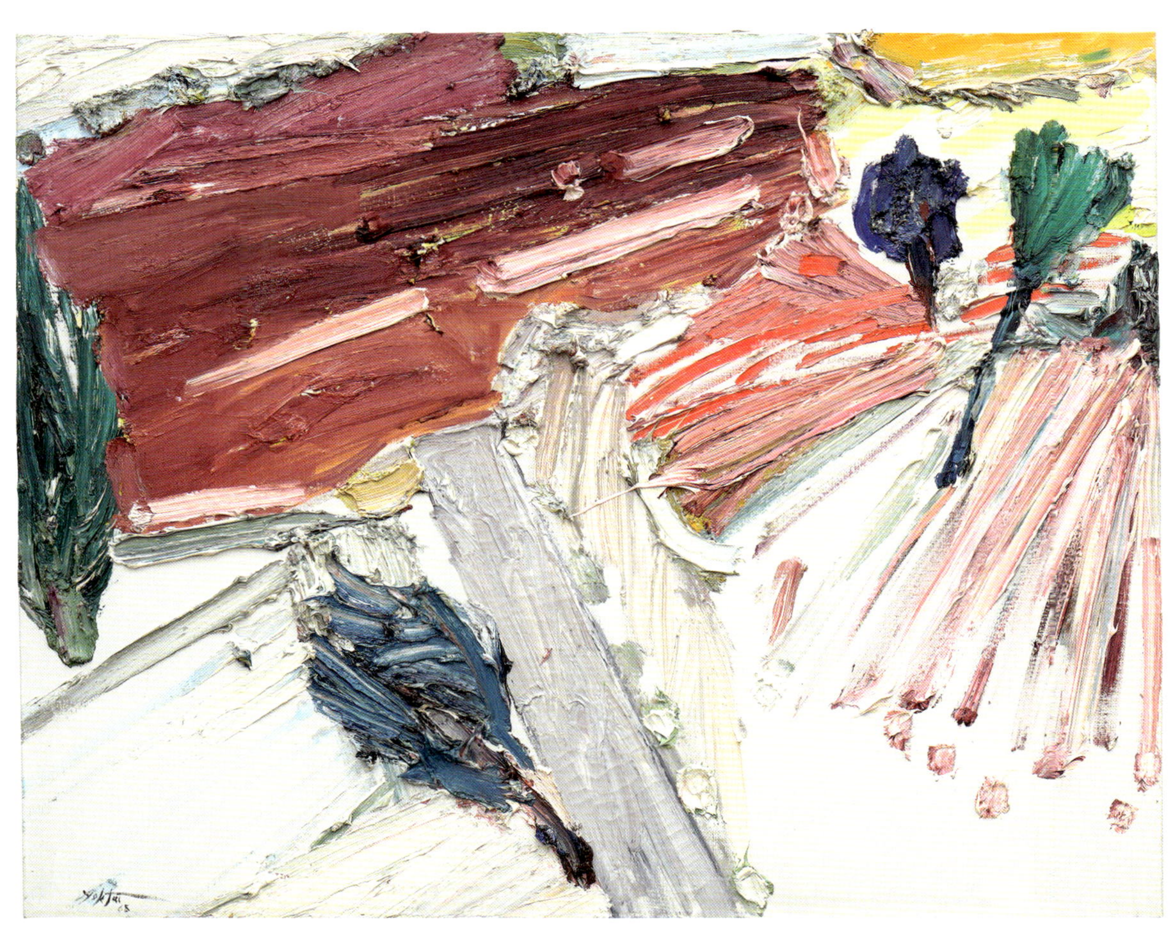

Road, 1965, oil on canvas, 36 × 45 inches (91 × 114 cm)

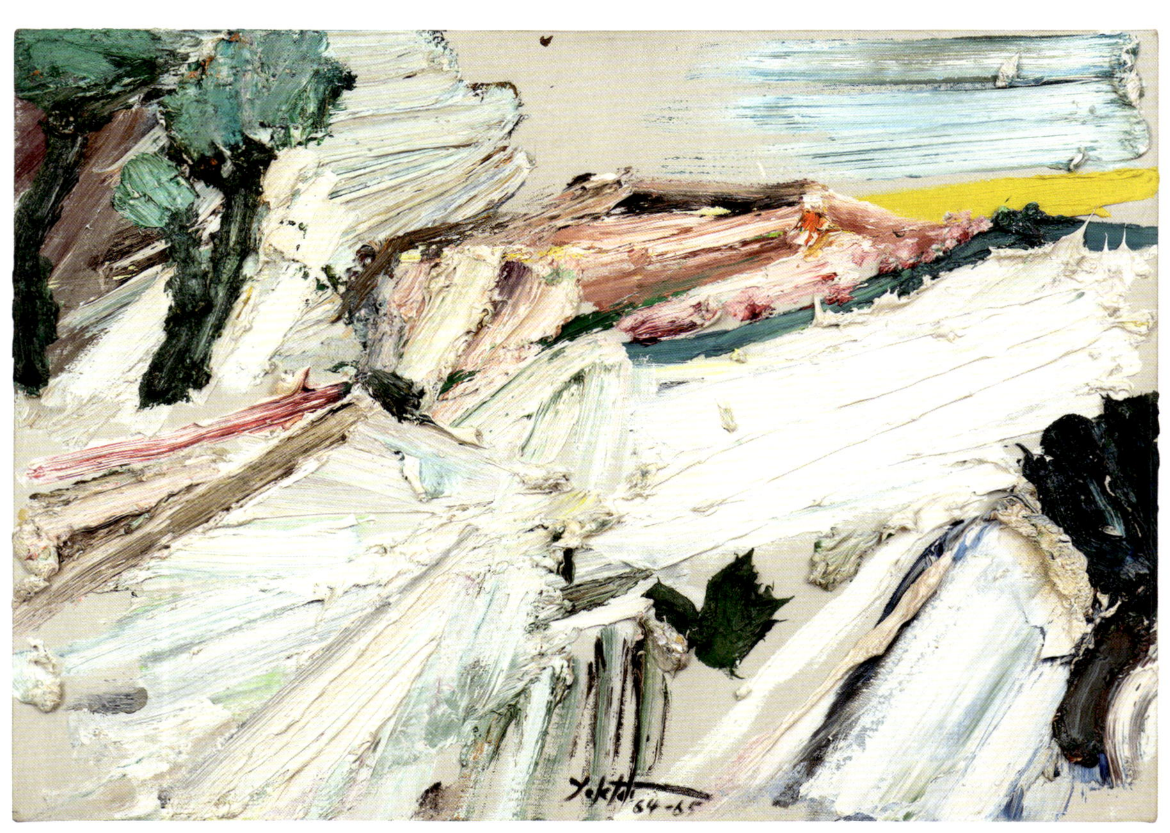

Landscape with Tree, 1964–65, oil on canvas, 20 × 28 inches (50.8 × 71.1 cm)

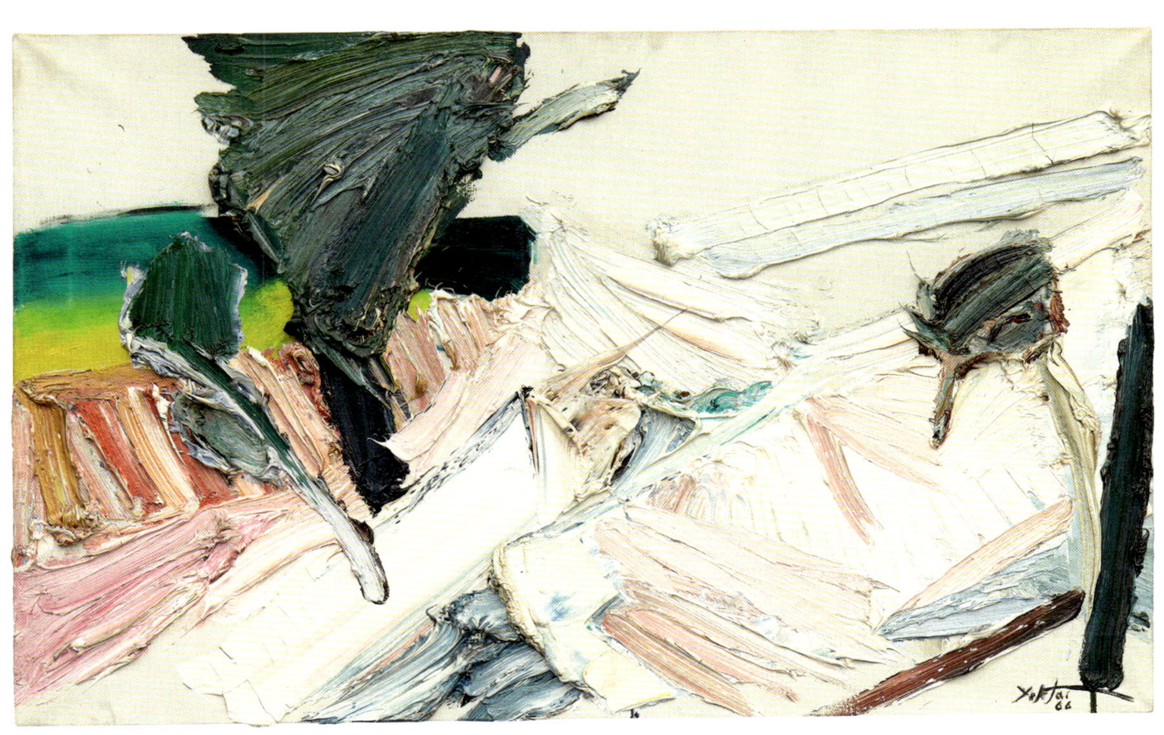

Untitled, 1966, oil on canvas, 20 × 32 inches (51 × 81 cm)

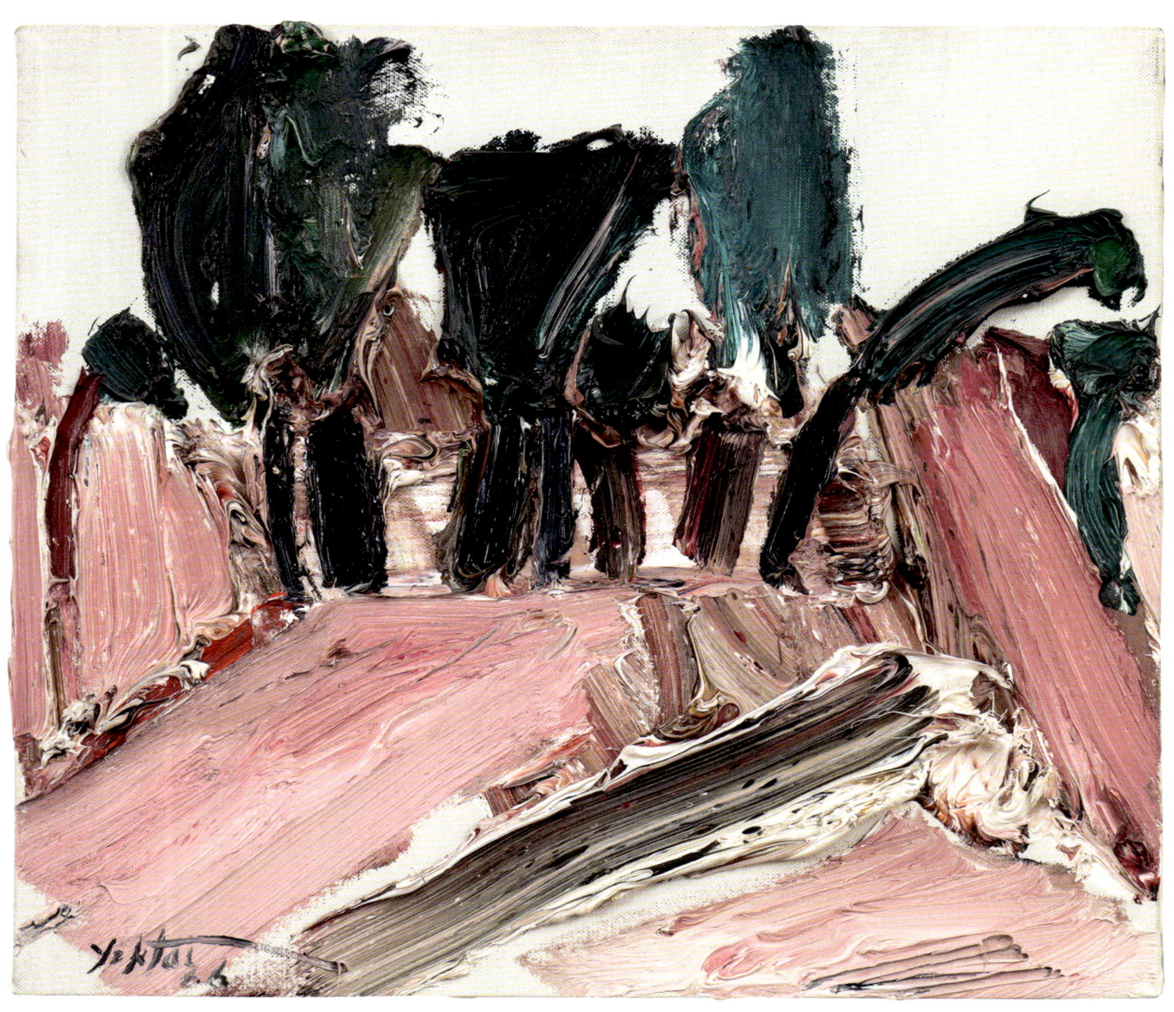

Untitled, 1966, oil on canvas, 12 × 14 inches (30.5 × 35.6 cm)

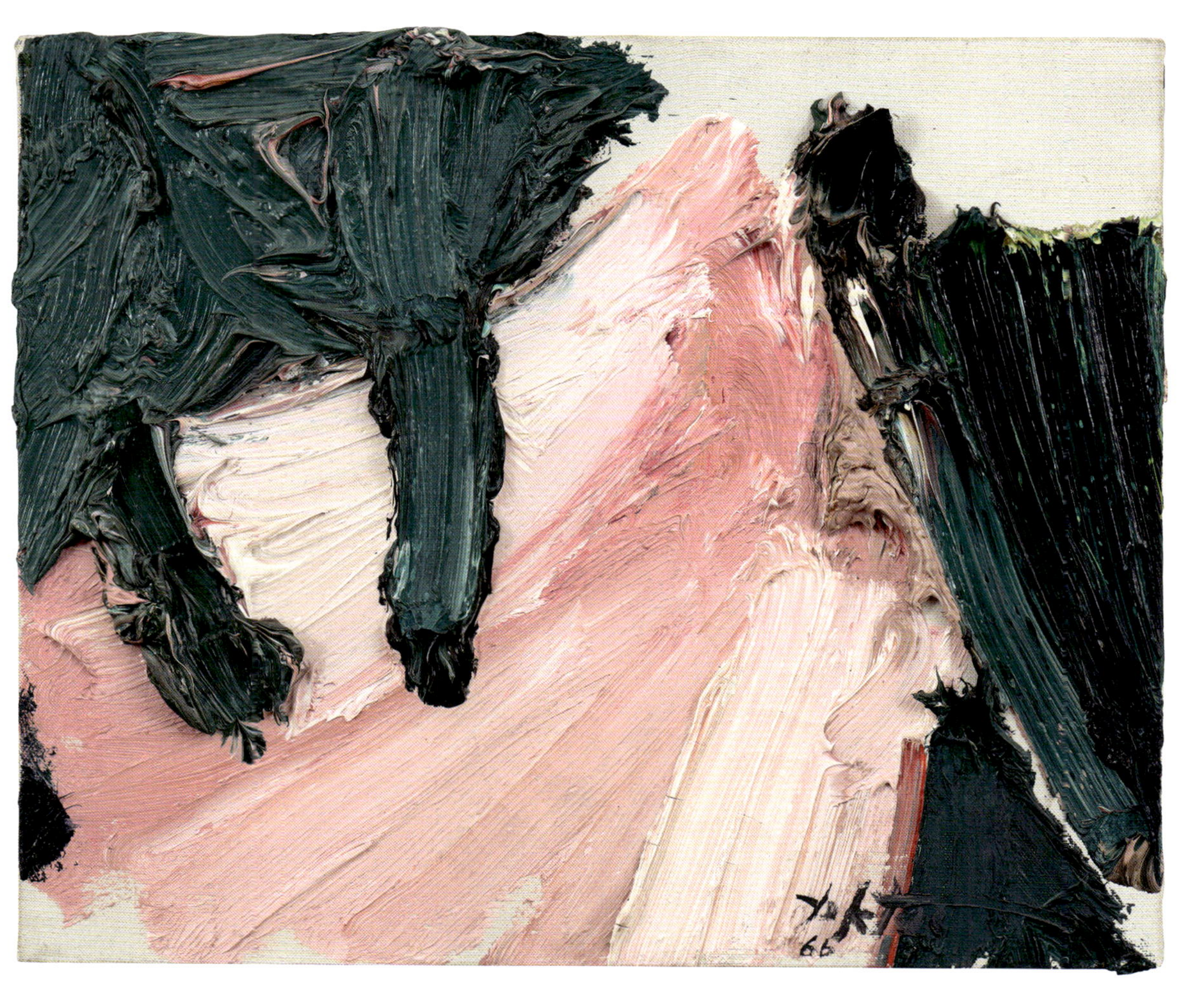

Untitled, 1966, oil on canvas, 11 × 13 inches (27.9 × 33 cm)

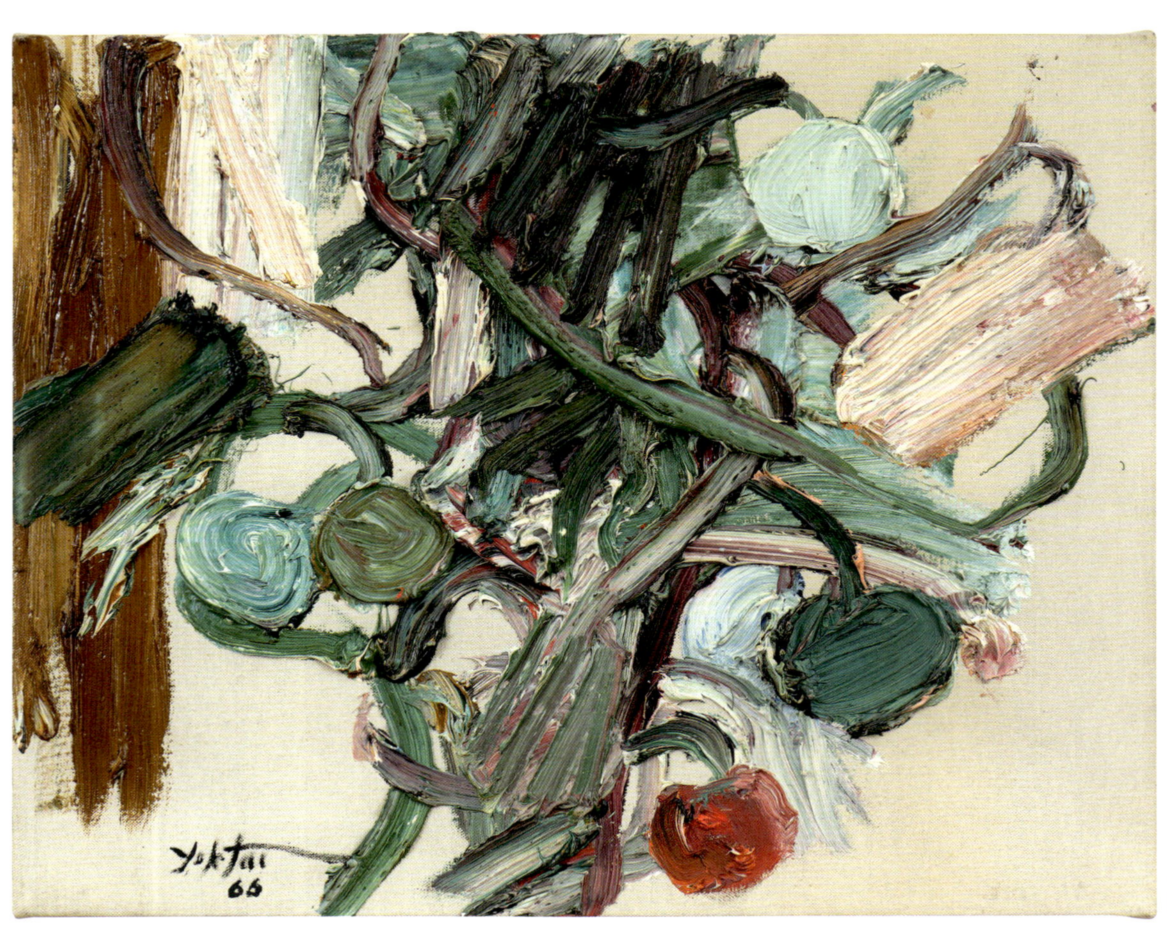

Untitled, 1966, oil on canvas, 16 × 20¼ inches (91.4 × 101.6 cm)

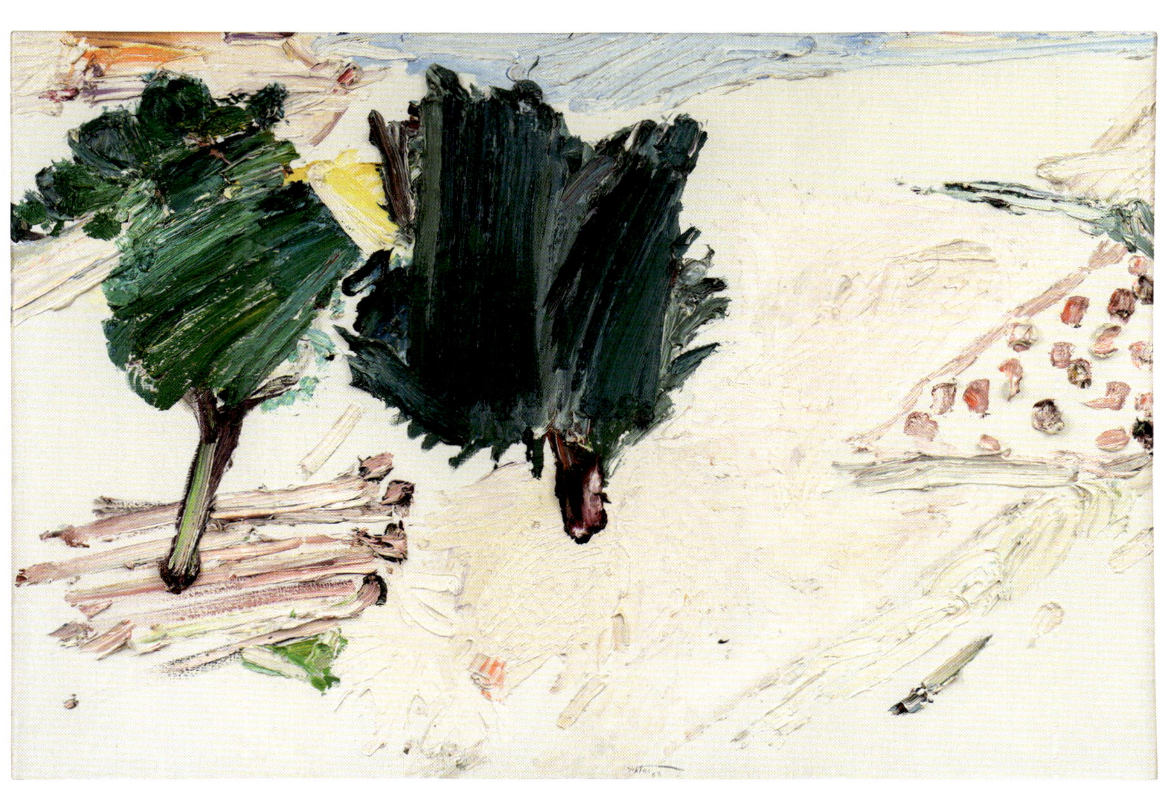

Untitled, 1968, oil on canvas, 40 × 59½ inches (101.6 × 151.1 cm)

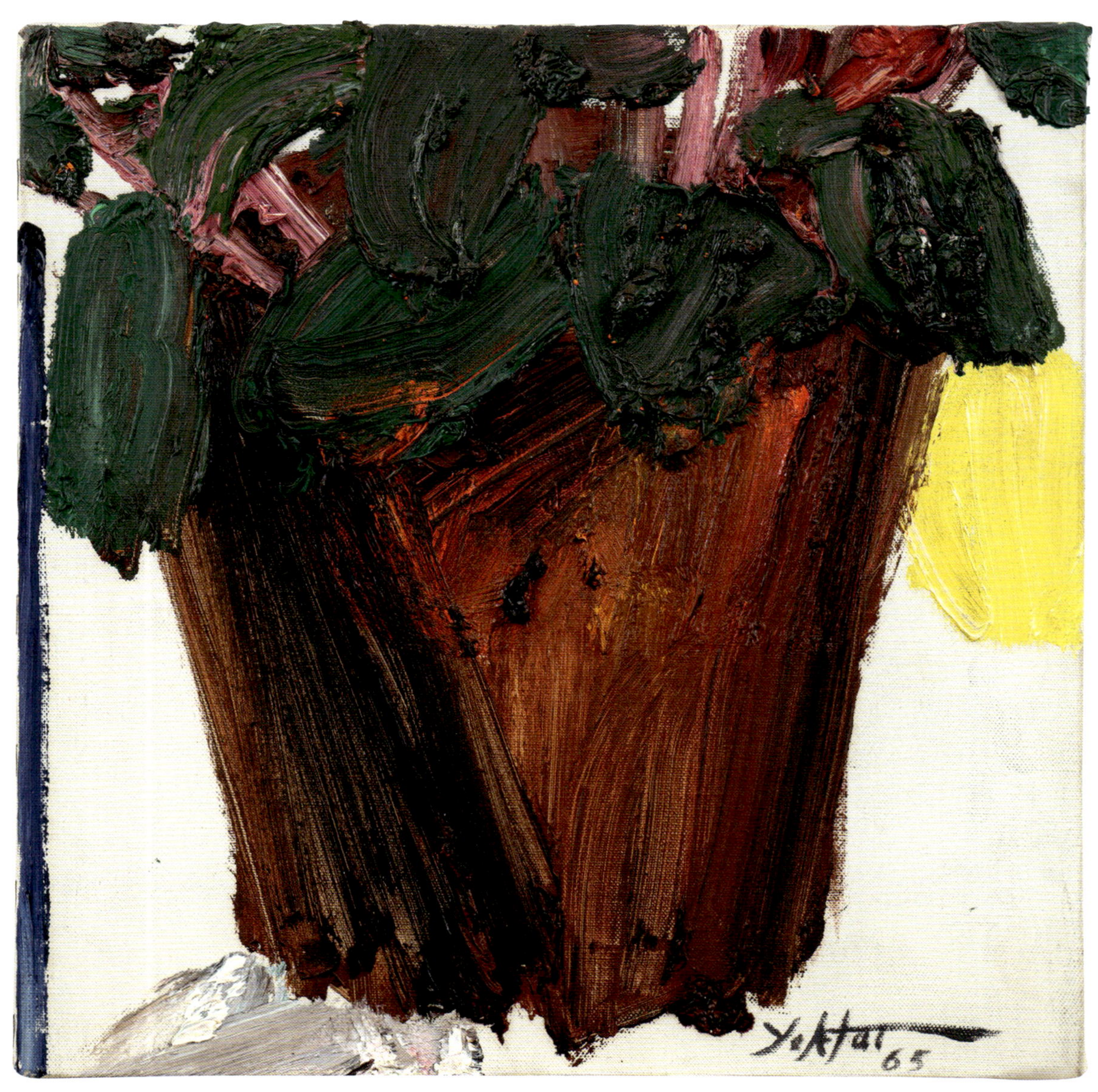

Untitled, 1965, oil on canvas, 12 × 12 inches (30.5 × 30.5 cm)

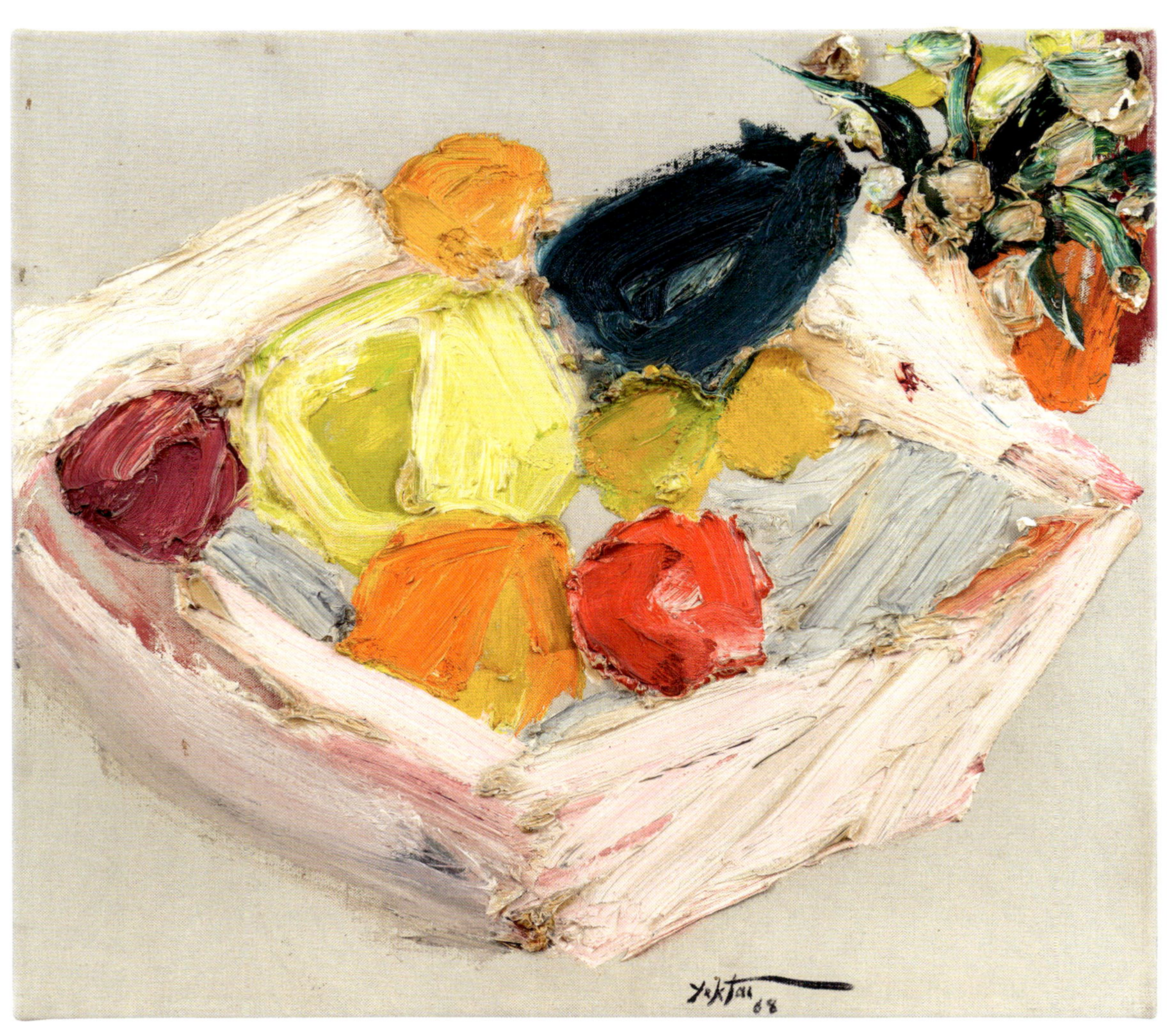

Untitled, 1968, oil on canvas, 18 × 20¼ inches (45.7 × 51.4 cm)

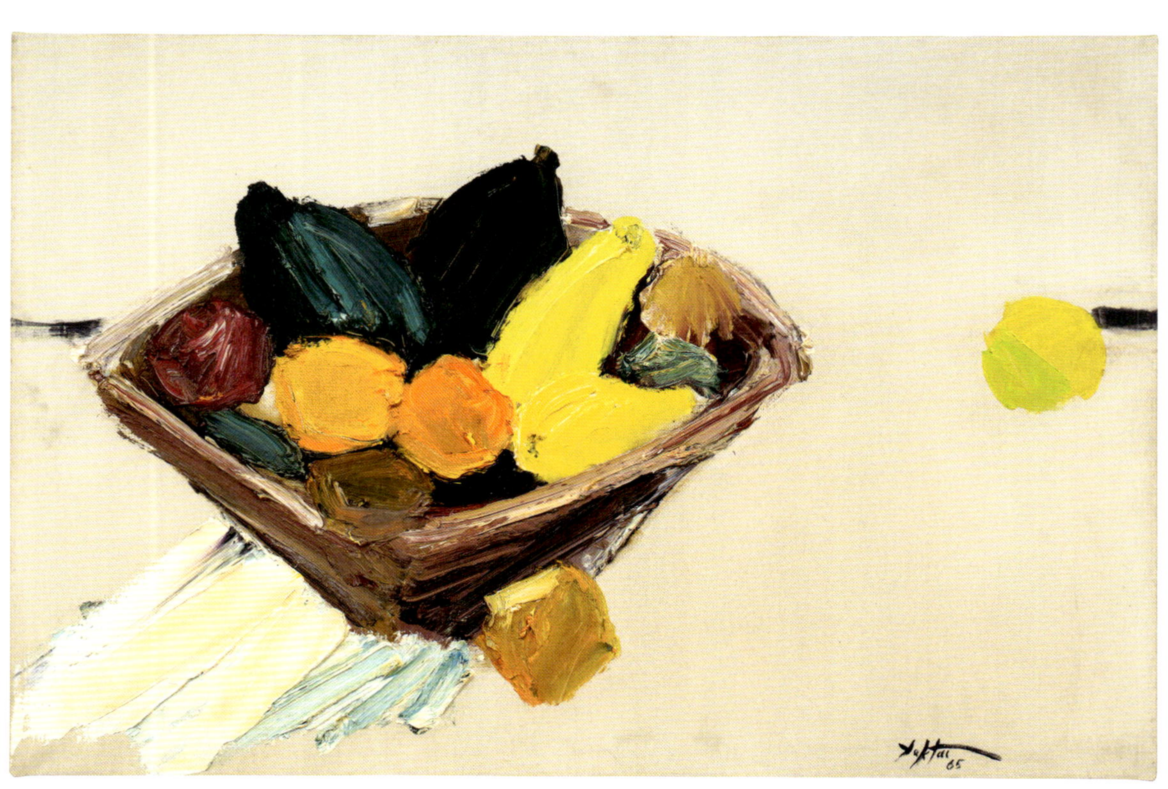

Untitled, 1965, oil on canvas, 24 × 36 inches (61 × 91.4 cm)

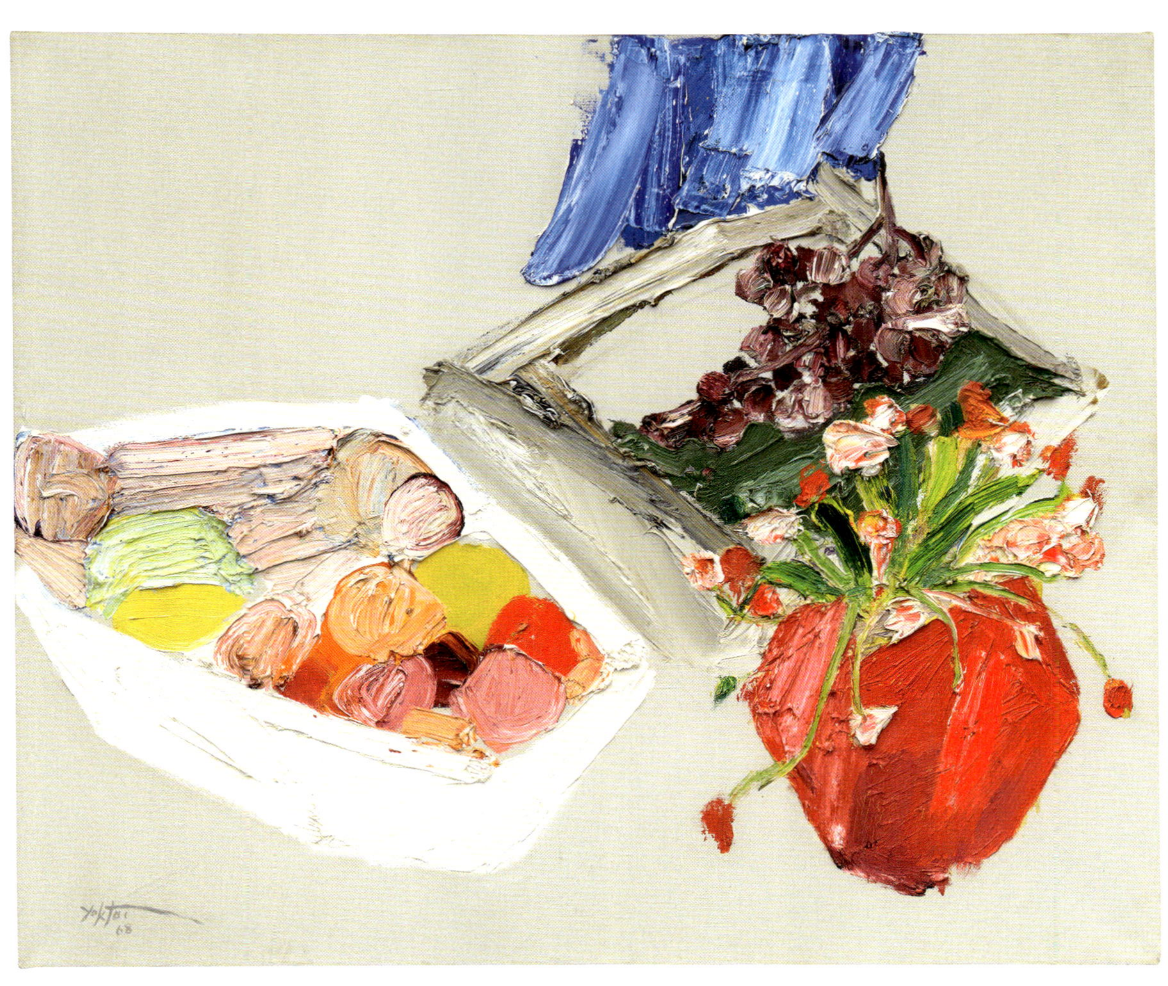

Untitled, 1968, oil on canvas, 30¼ × 36 inches (76.8 × 91.4 cm)

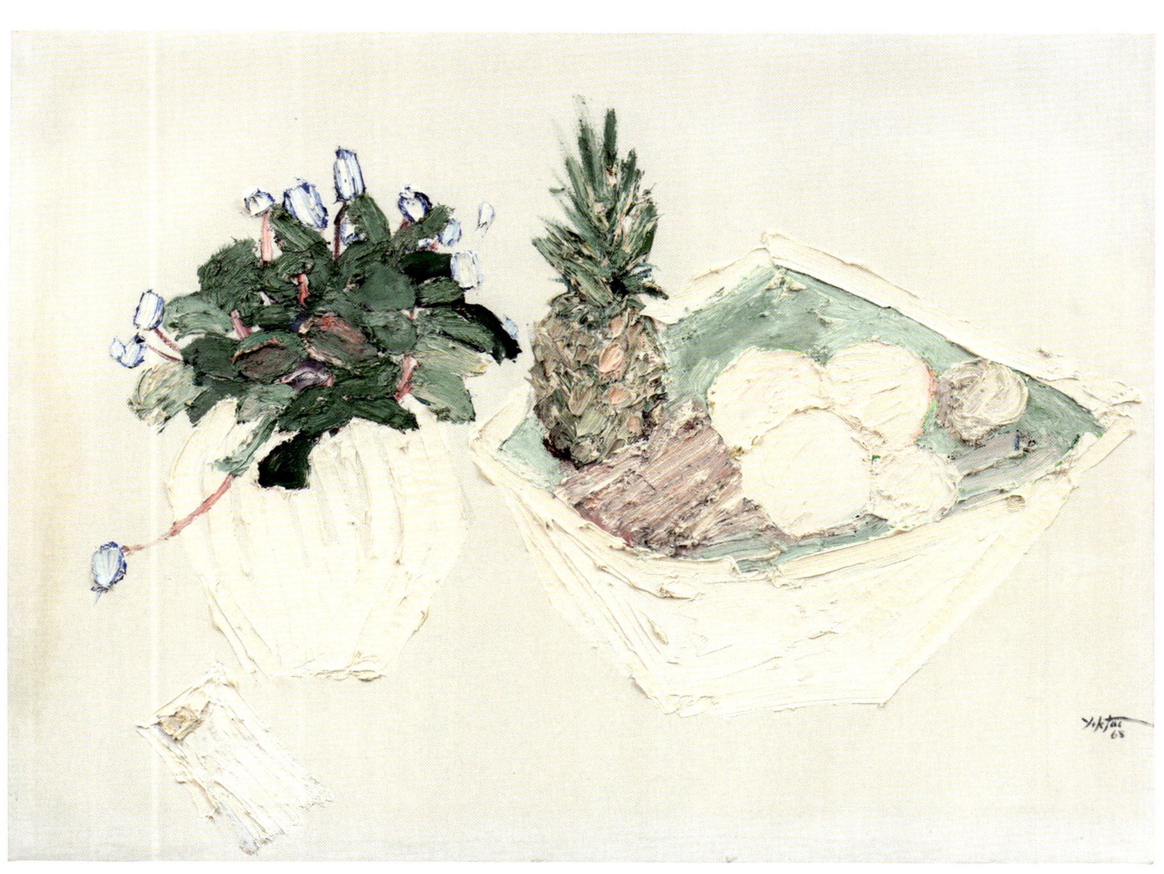

Untitled, 1968, oil on canvas, 36 × 48 inches (91.4 × 121.9 cm)

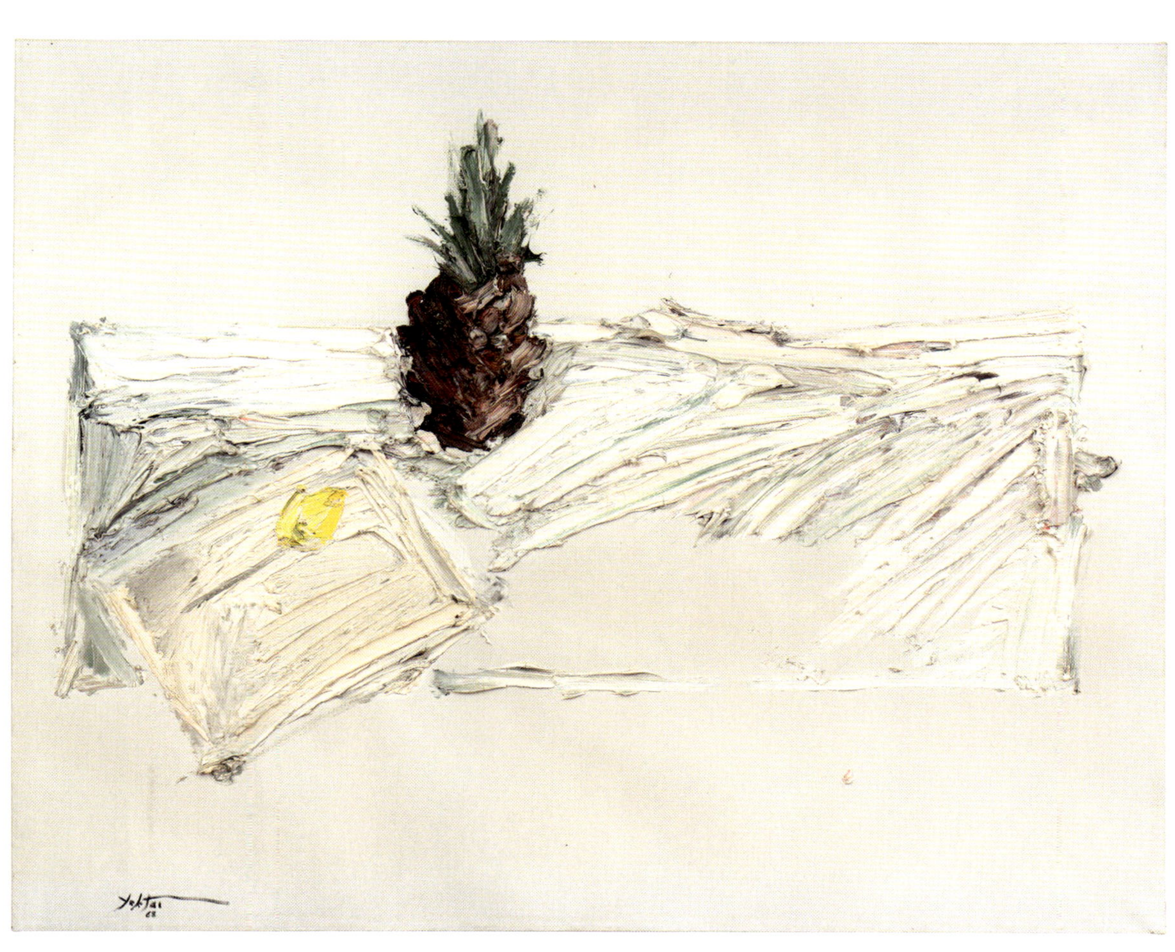

Untitled, 1968, oil on canvas, 40 × 50 inches (101.6 × 127 cm)

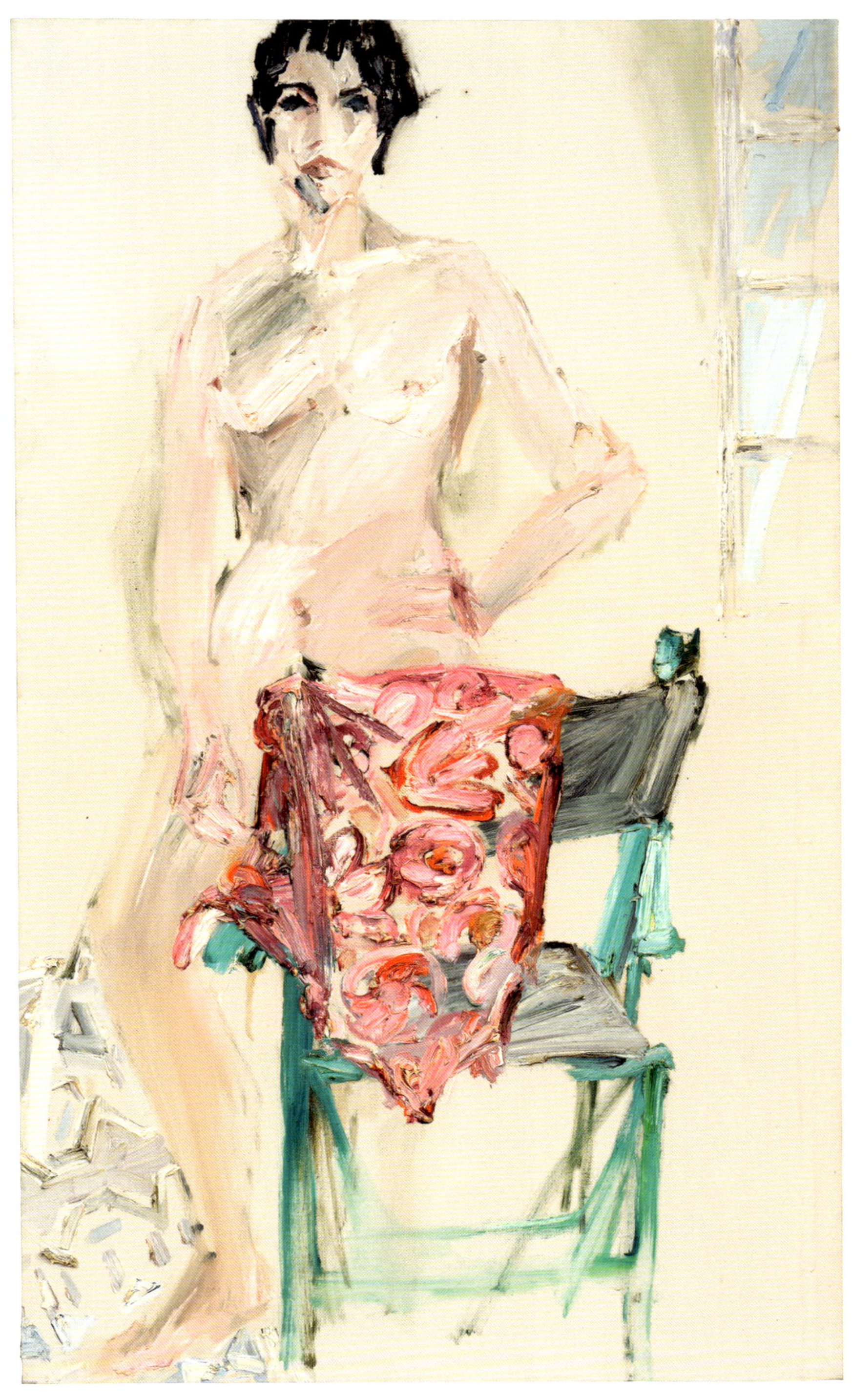

 Untitled, 1969, oil on canvas, 68 × 40 inches (172.7 × 101.6 cm)

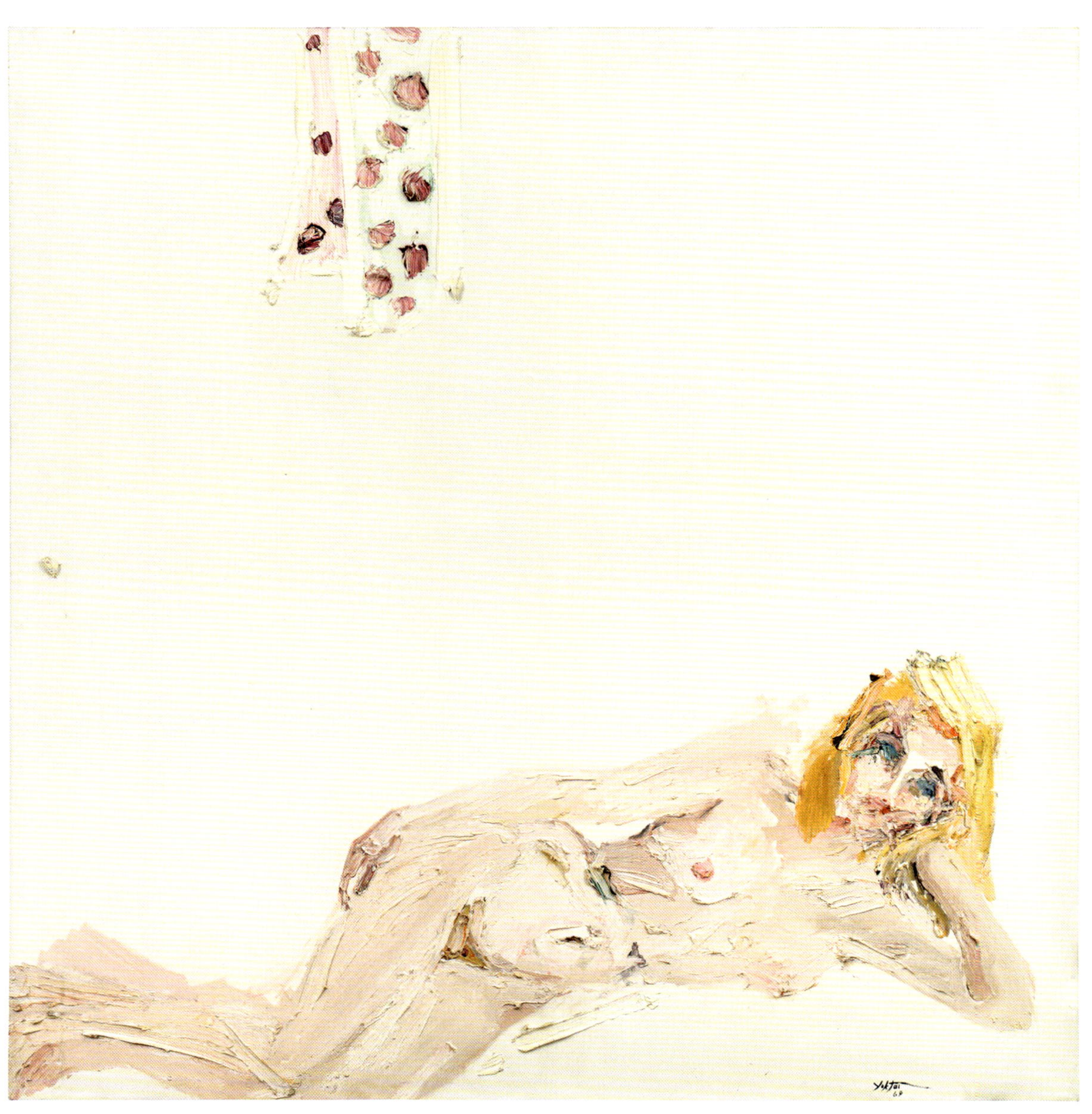

Untitled, 1969, oil on canvas, 72 × 70 inches (182.9 × 177.8 cm)

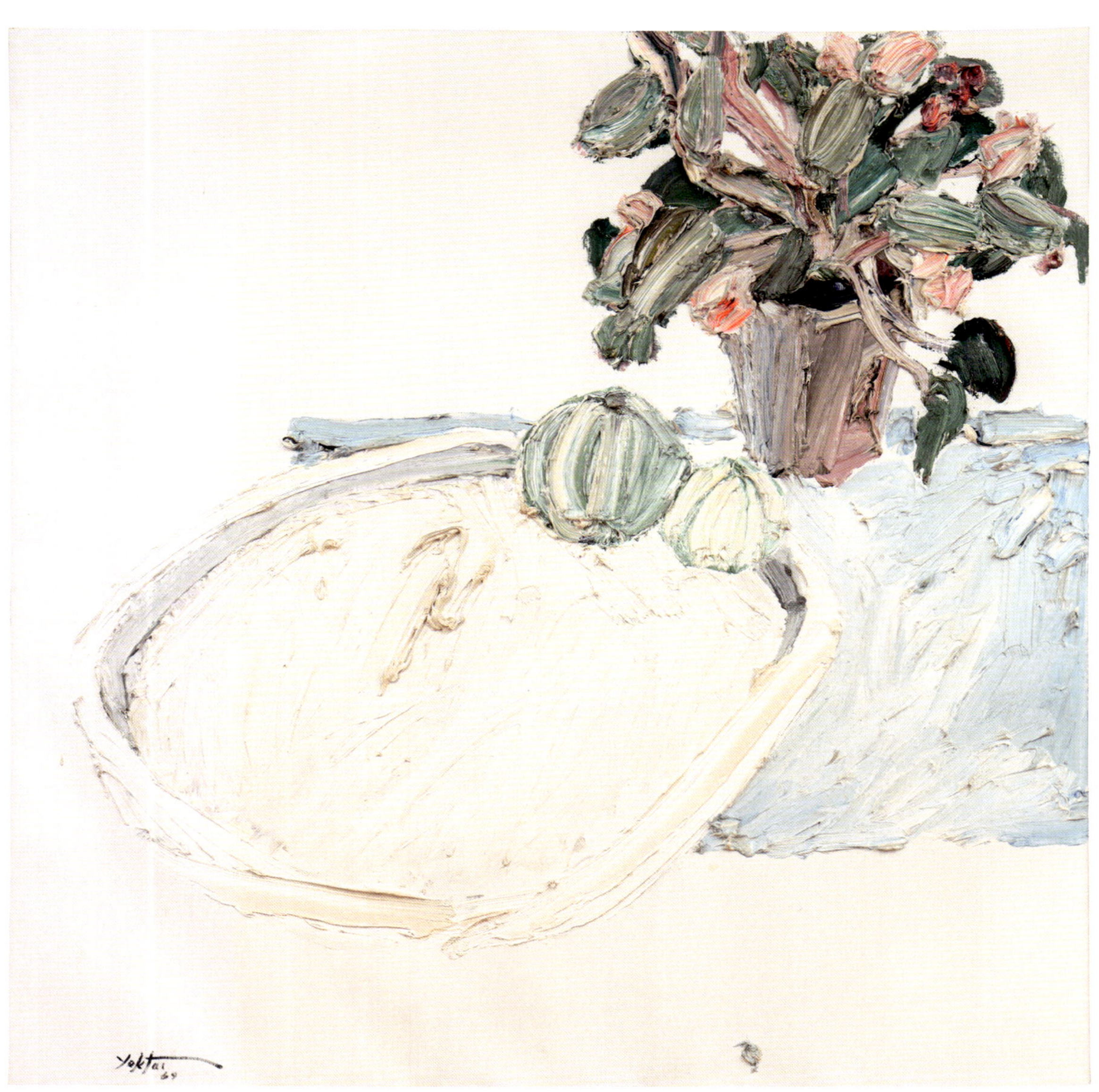

 Untitled, 1969, oil on canvas, 43 × 43 inches (109.2 × 109.2 cm)

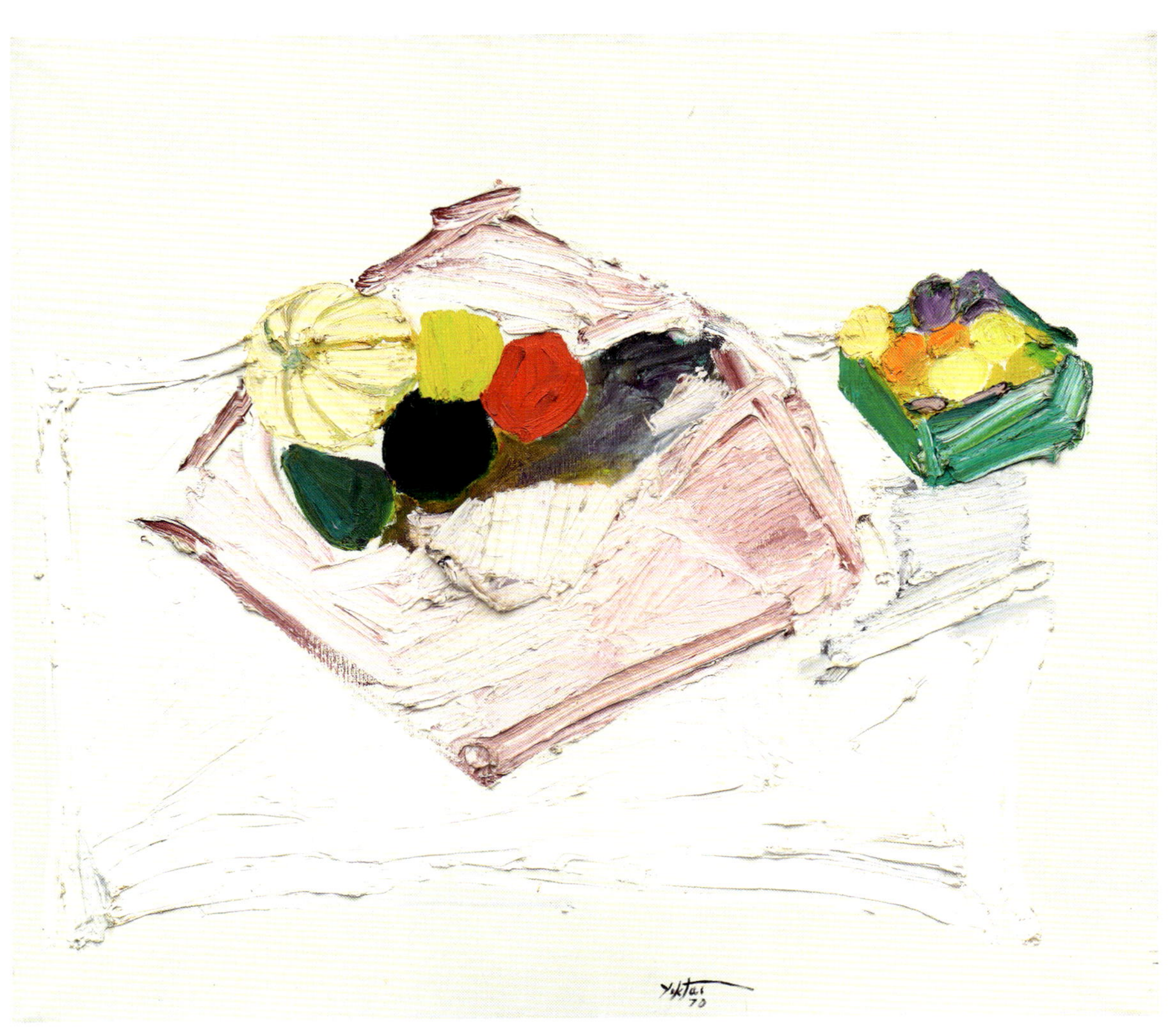

Untitled, 1970, oil on canvas, 44 × 50 inches (112 × 127 cm)

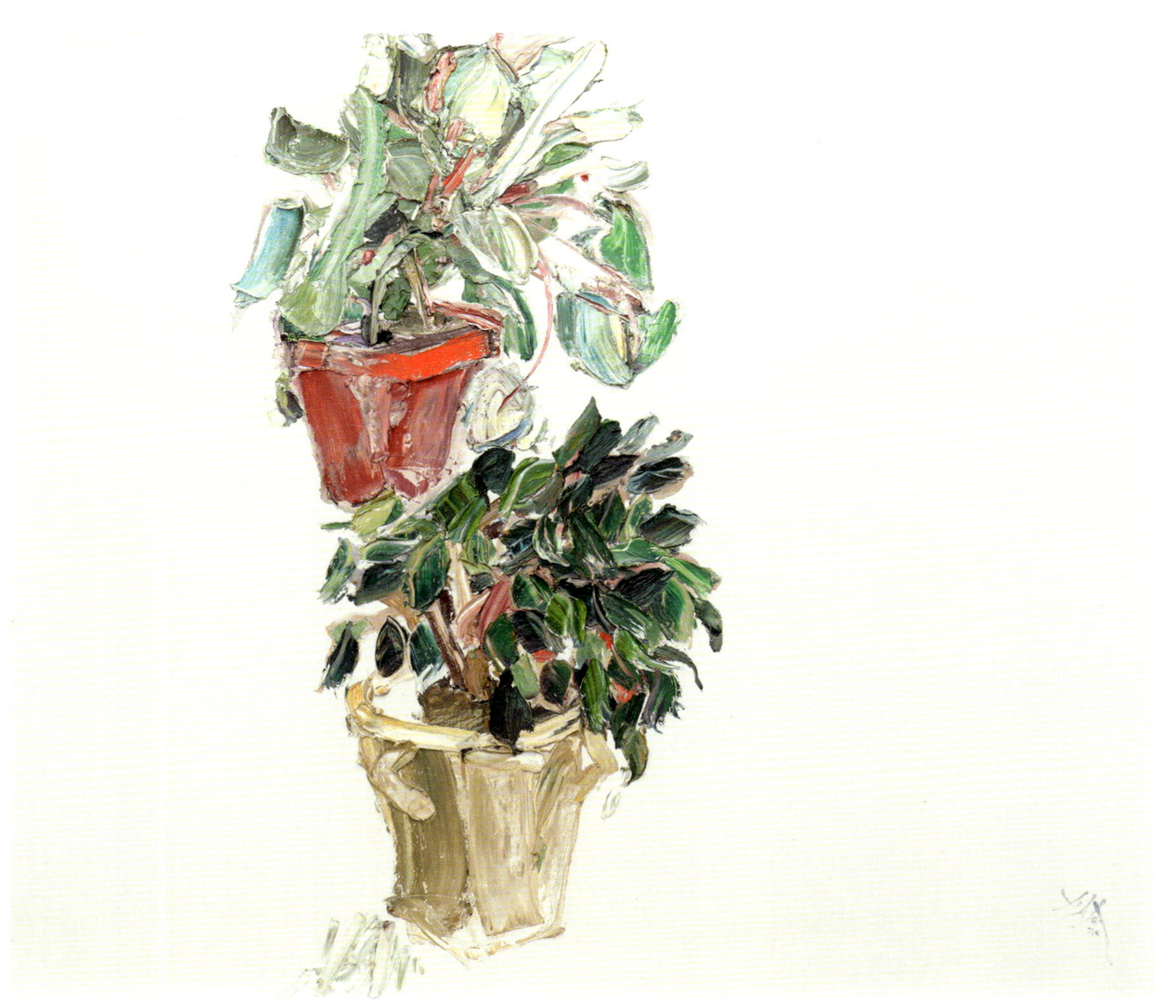

 Untitled, 1970, oil on canvas, 78 × 90 inches (198.1 × 228.6 cm)

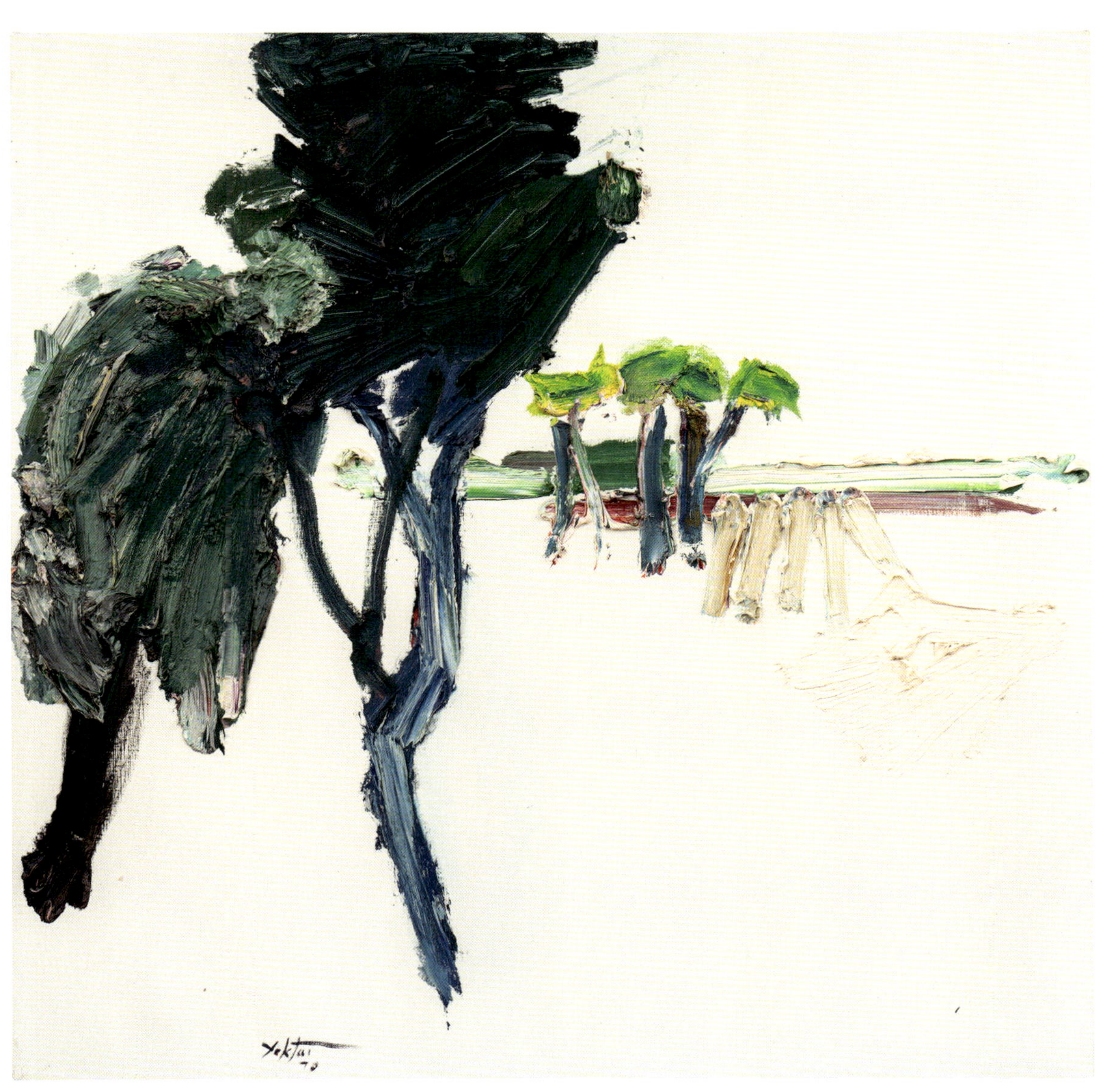

Untitled, 1970, oil on canvas, 36 × 36 inches (91.4 × 91.4 cm)

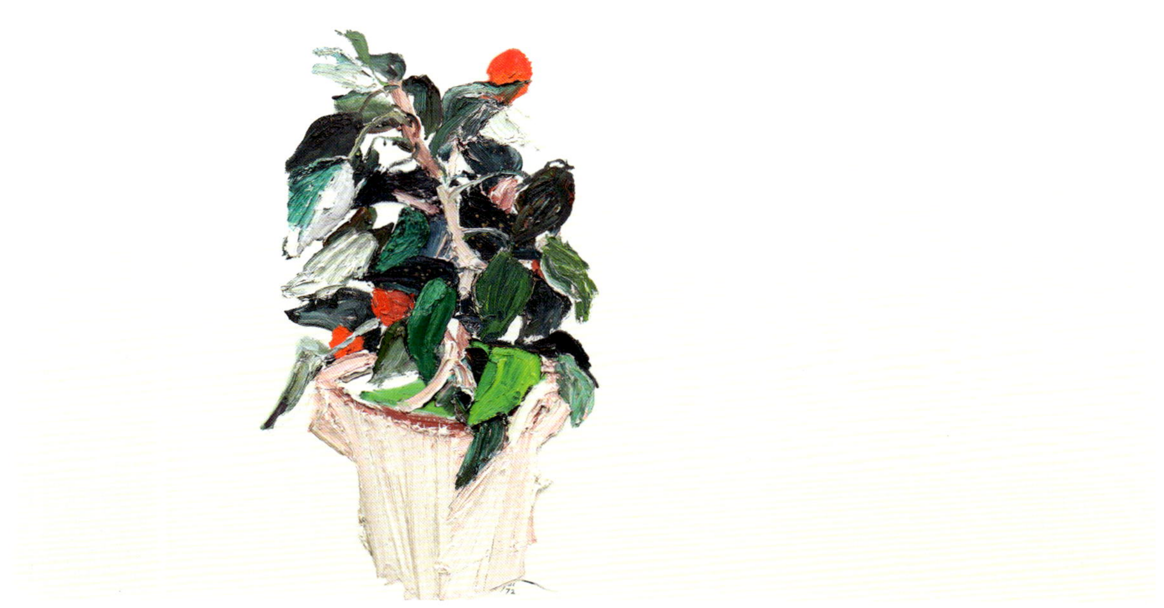

Untitled, 1972, oil on canvas, 42 × 80 inches (106.7 × 203.2 cm)

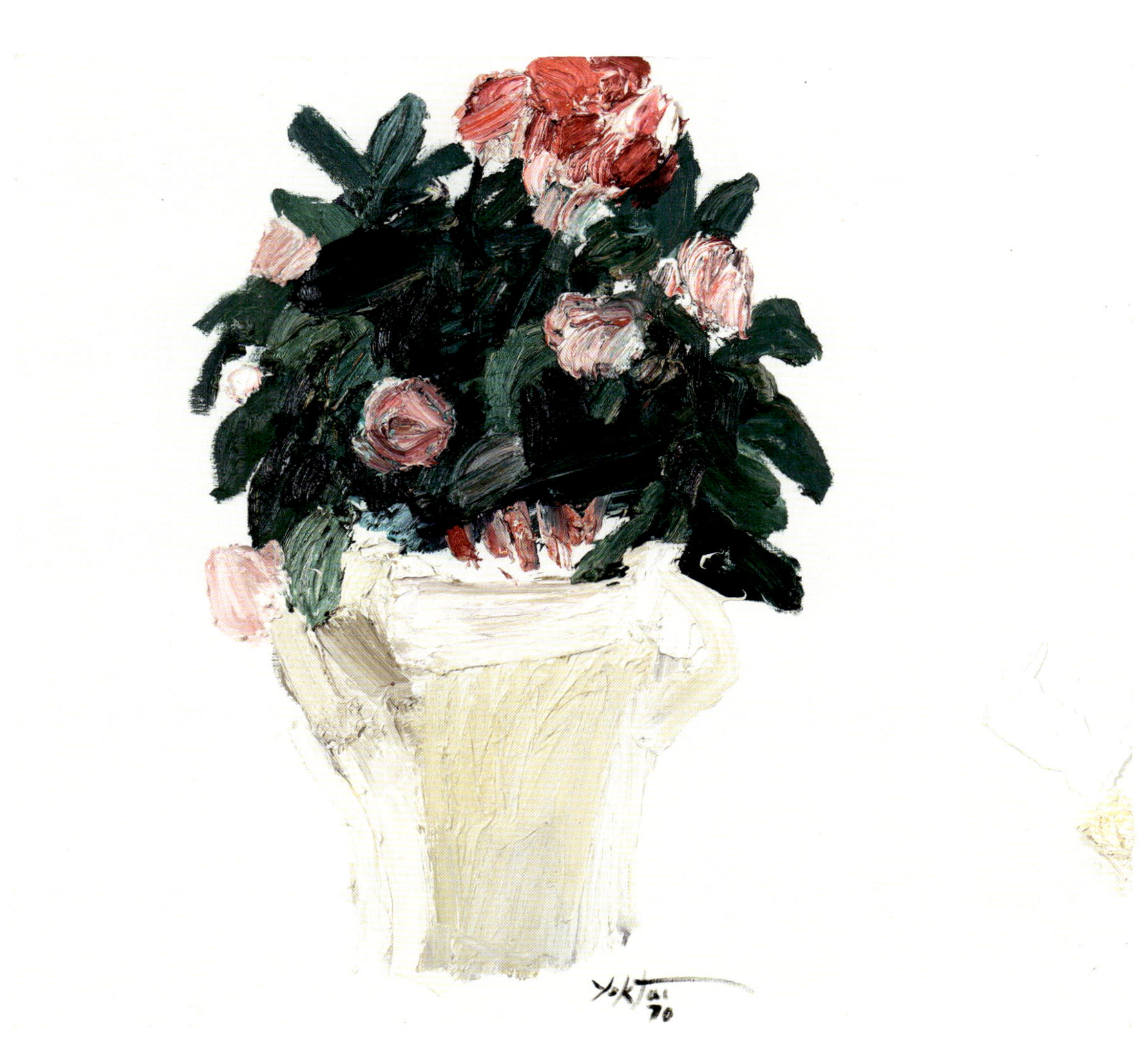

Untitled, 1970, oil on canvas, 32 × 36 inches (81.3 × 91.4 cm)

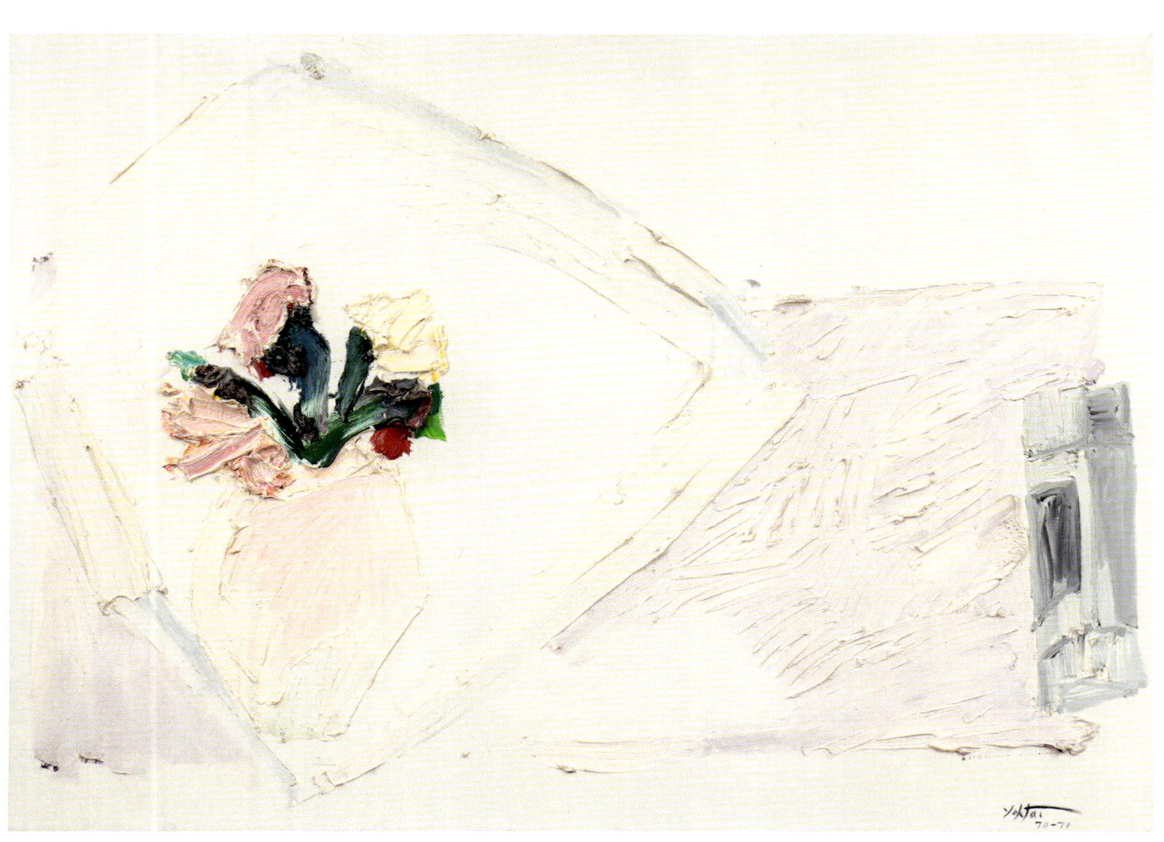

Untitled, 1970–71, oil on canvas, 36 × 50 inches (91.4 × 127 cm)

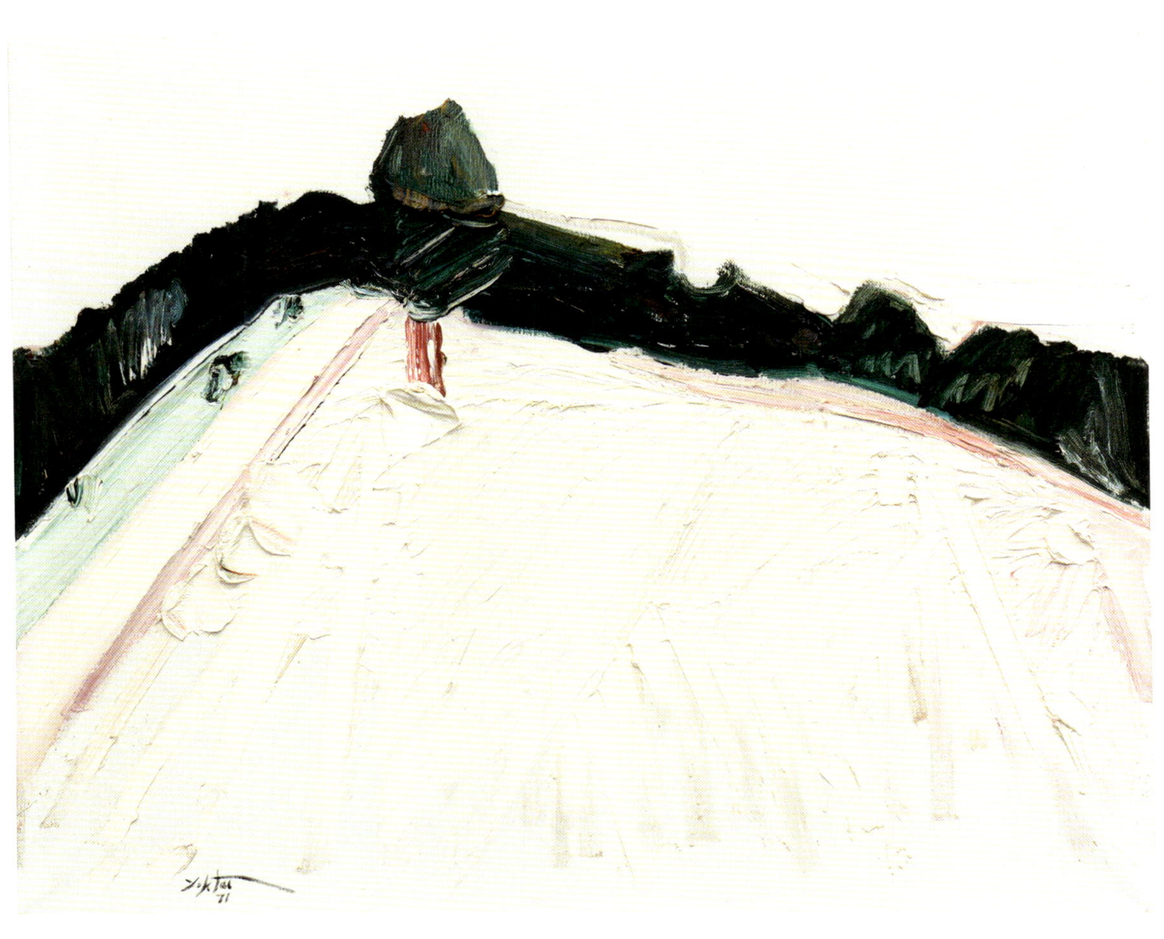

Untitled, 1971, oil on canvas, 40 × 50 inches (101.6 × 127 cm)

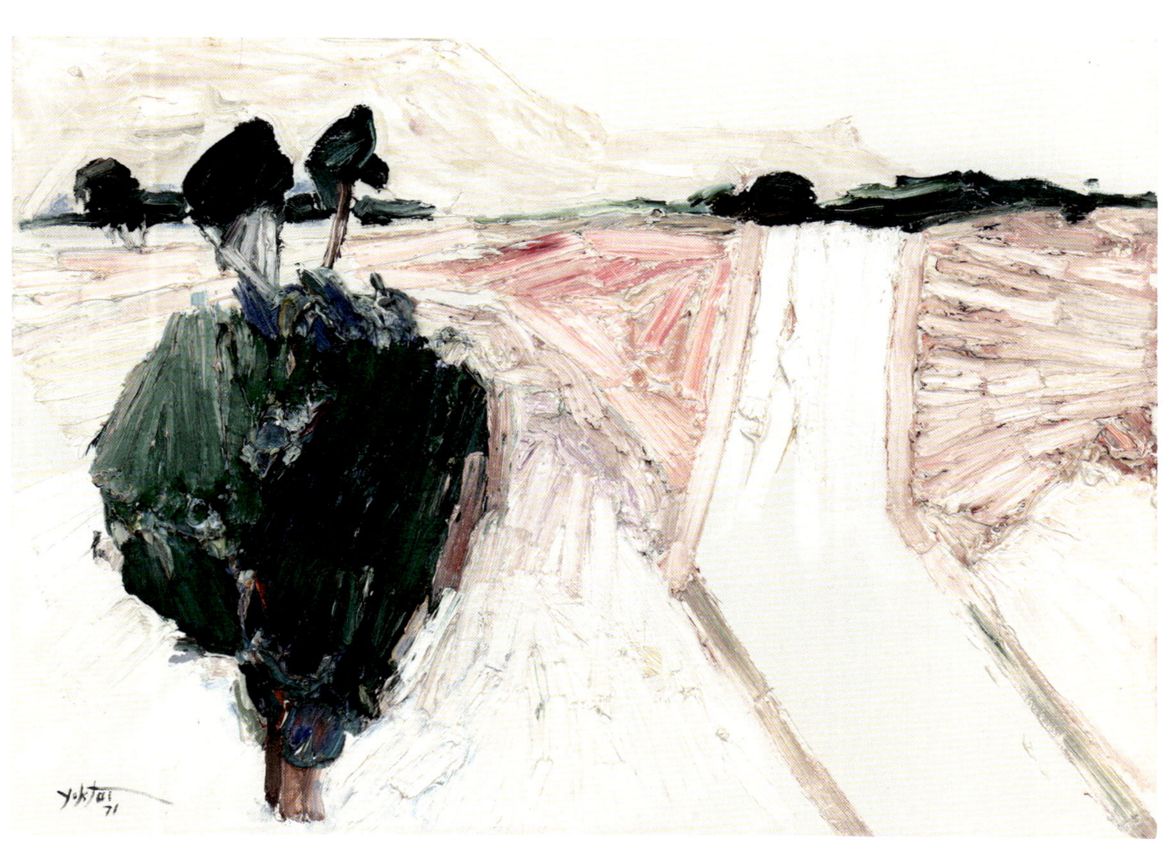

Untitled, 1971, oil on canvas, 36 × 50 inches (91.4 × 127 cm)

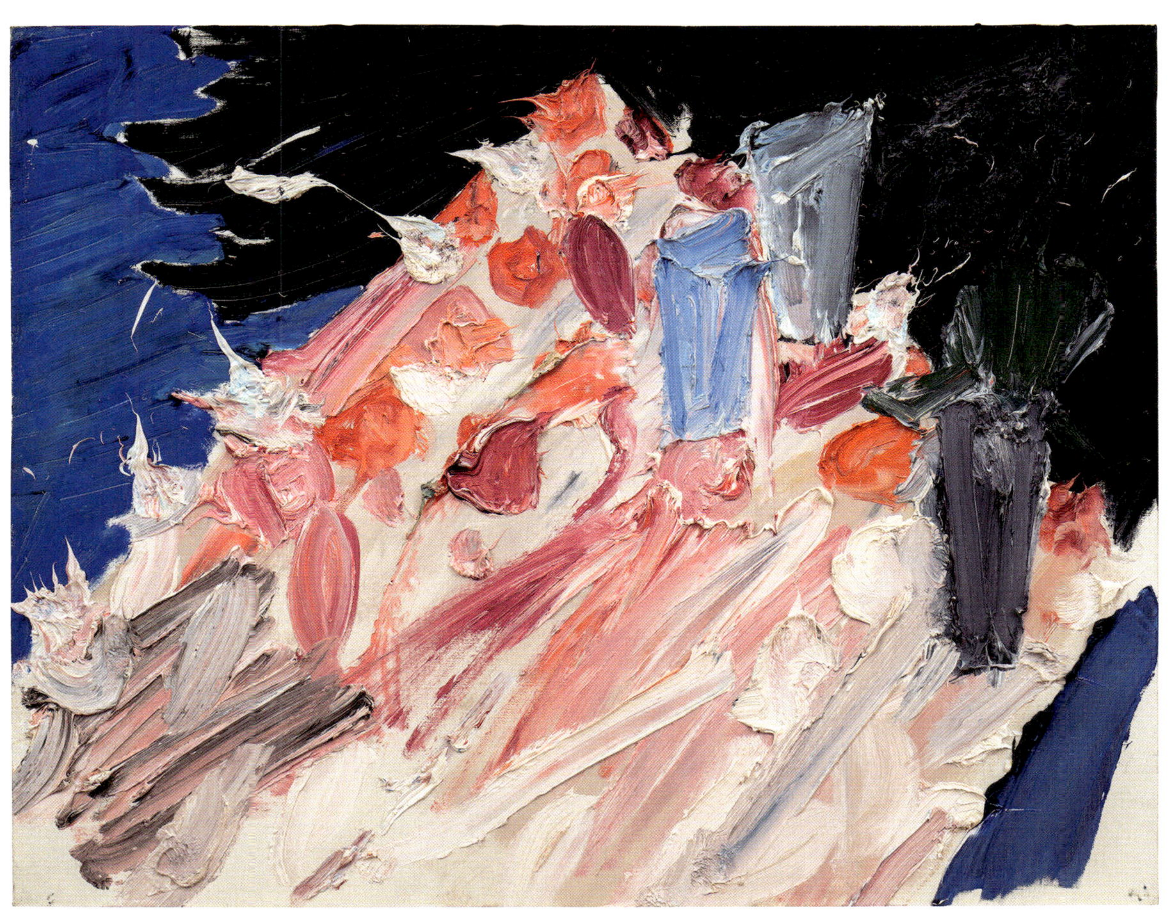

Untitled, 1972, oil on canvas, 28½ × 36 inches (72.4 × 91.4 cm)

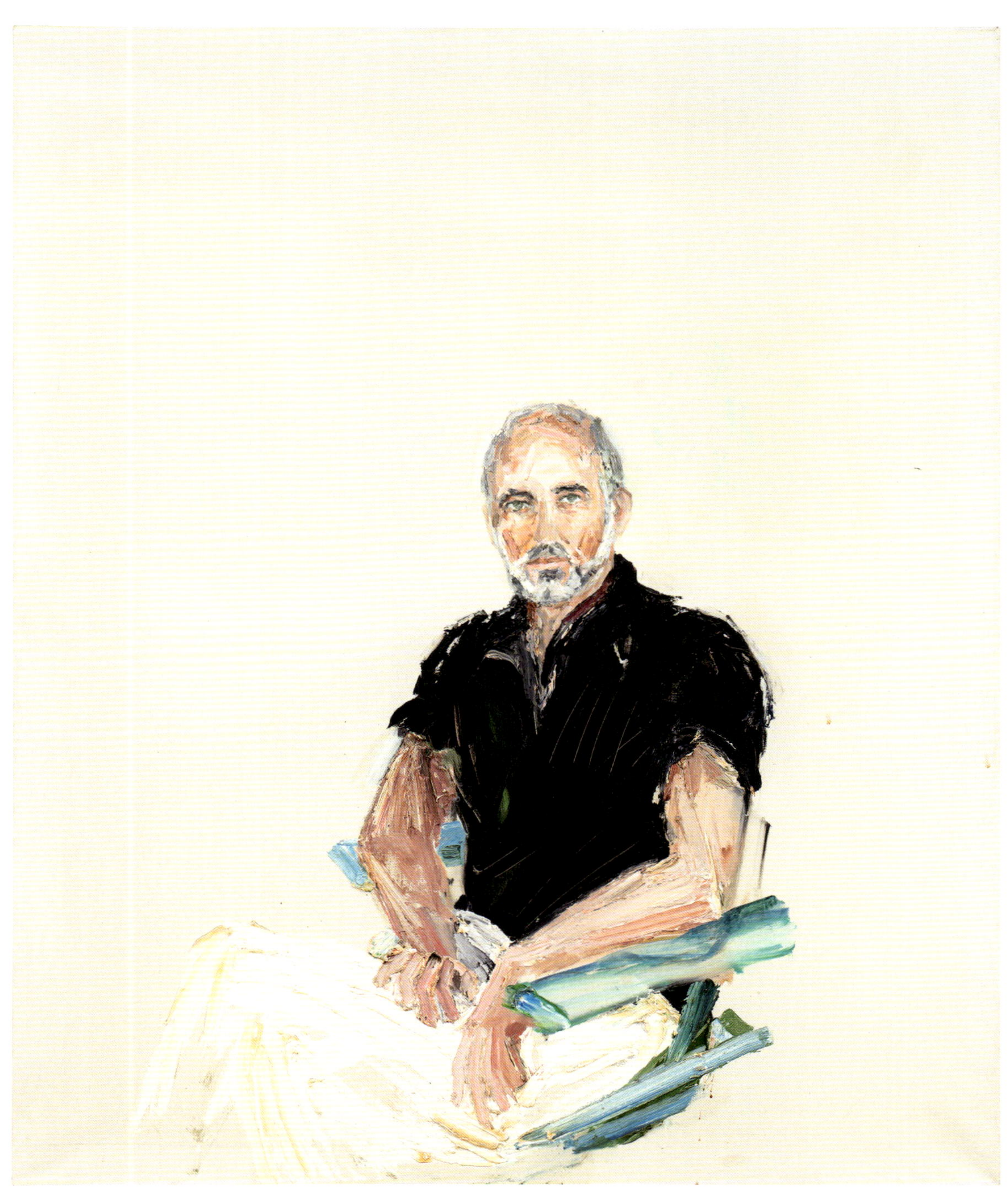

Jerome Robbins, 1972, oil on canvas, 60 × 50 inches (152 × 127 cm)

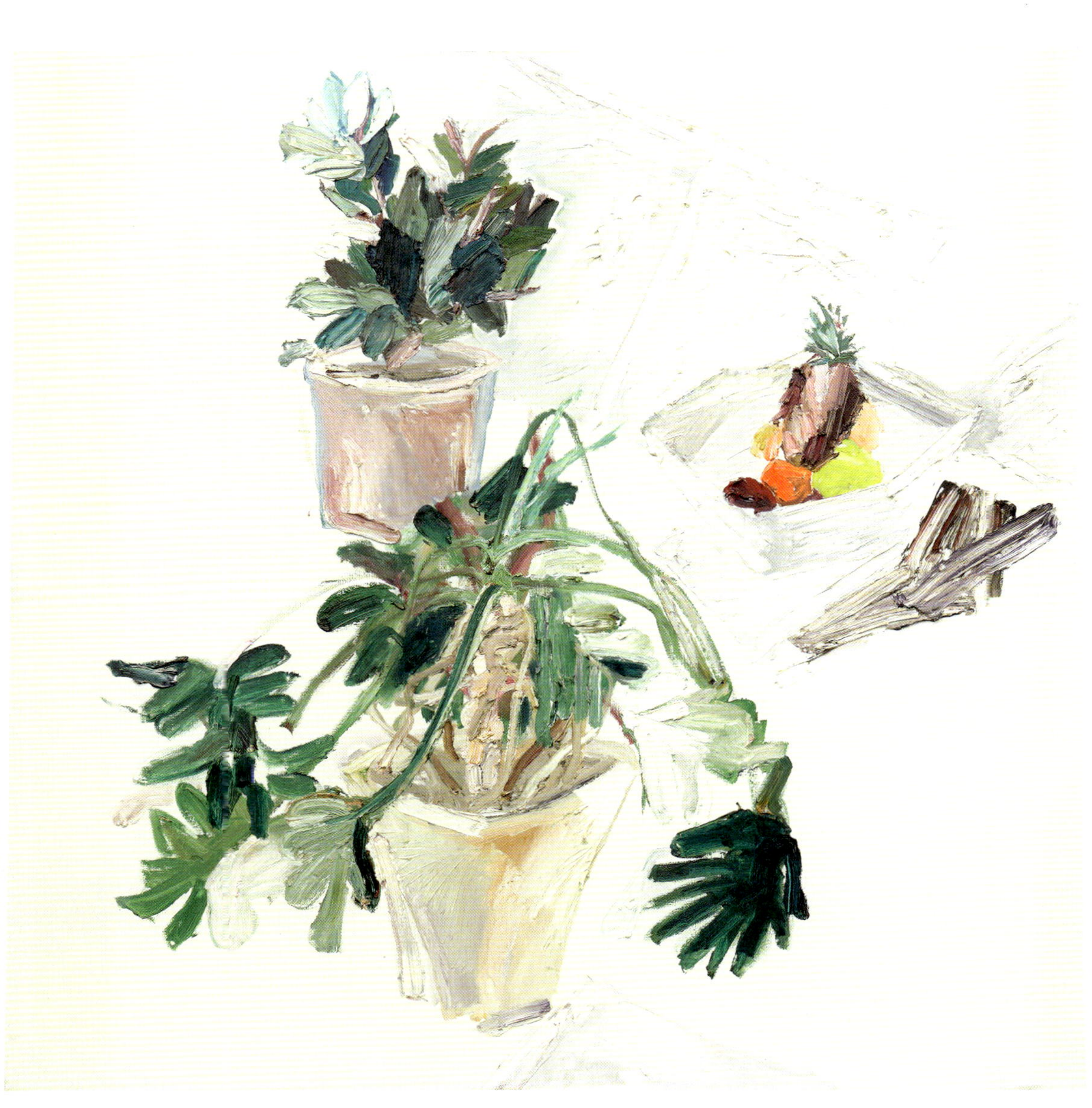

Untitled, 1973, oil on canvas, 72 × 72 inches (182.9 × 182.9 cm)

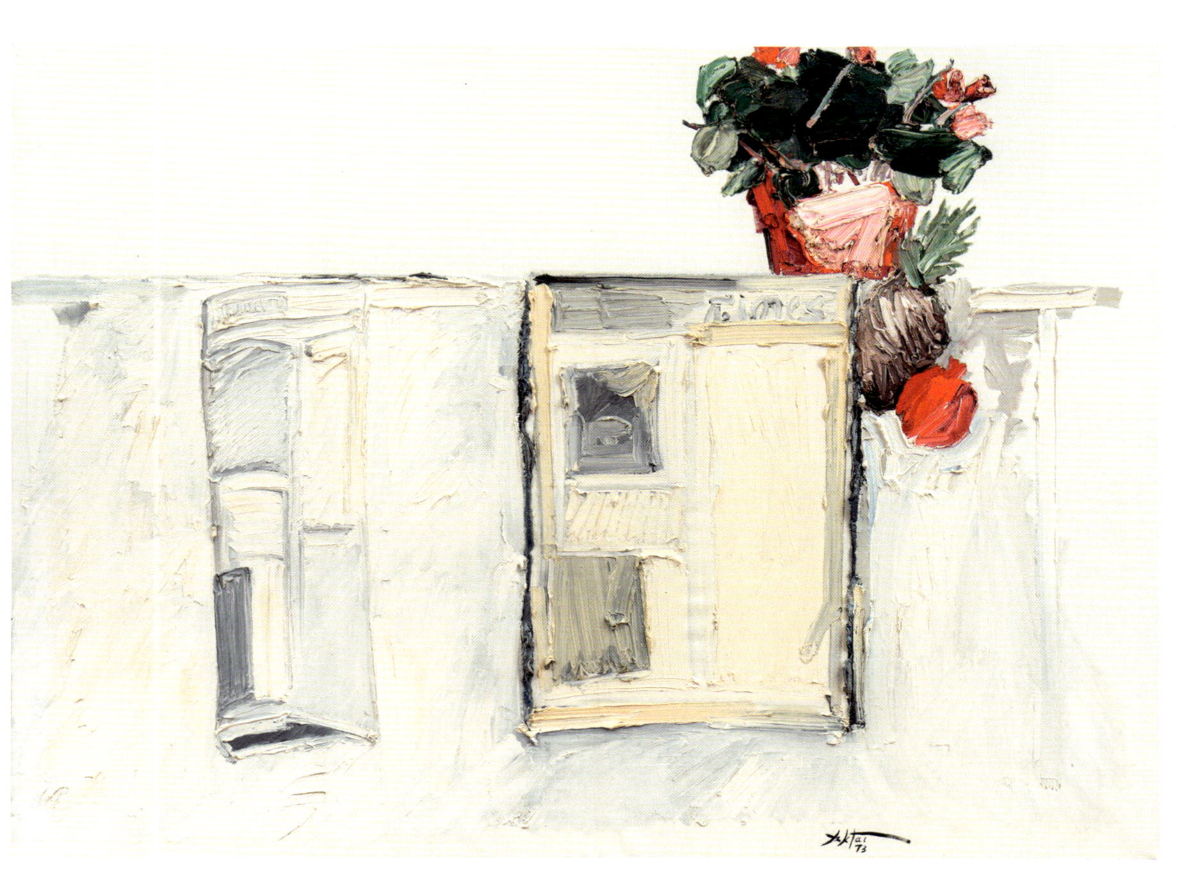

 Untitled, 1973, oil on canvas, 47½ × 66 inches (120.7 × 167.6 cm)

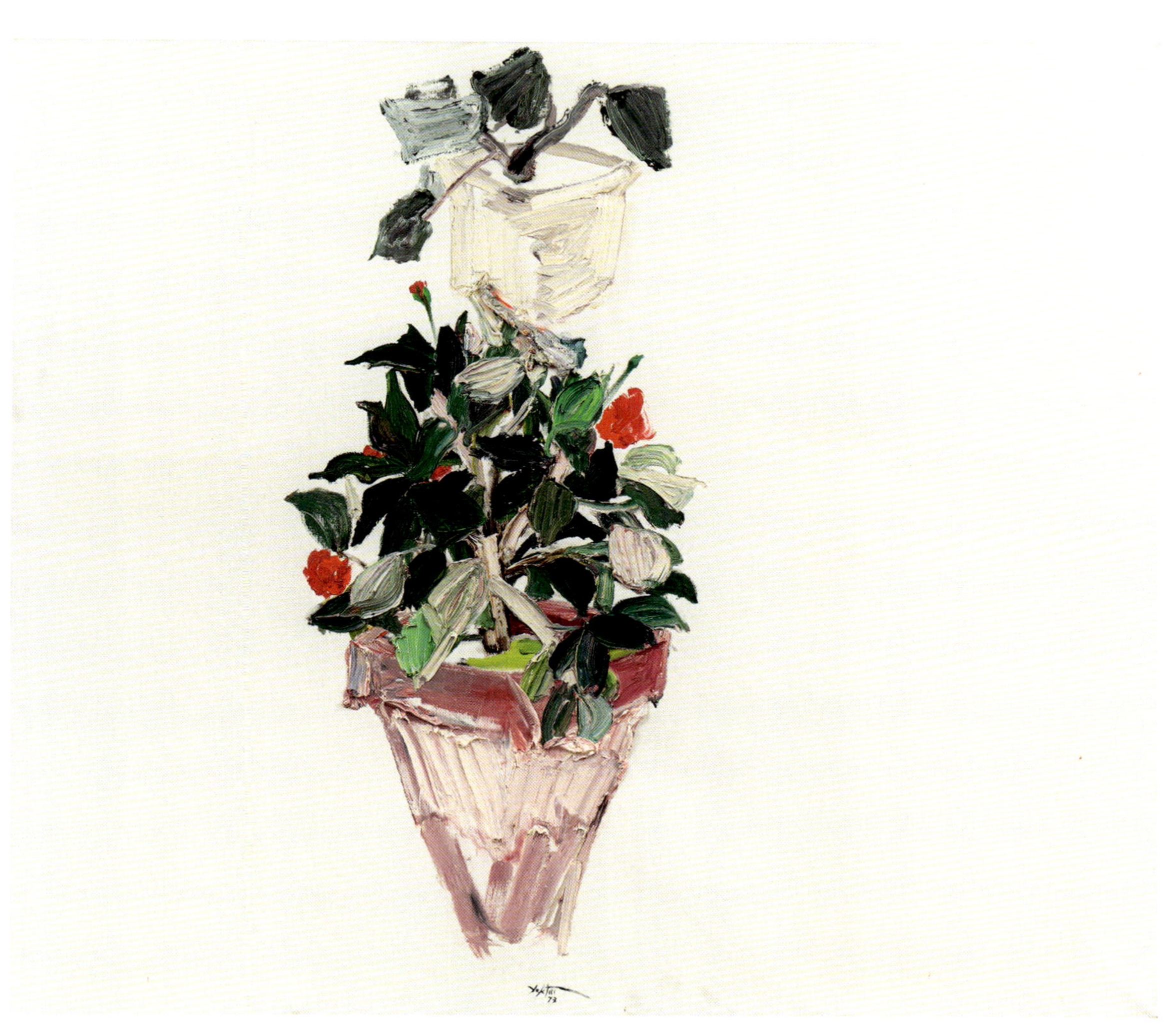

Untitled, 1973, oil on canvas, 56 × 64 inches (142.2 × 162.6 cm)

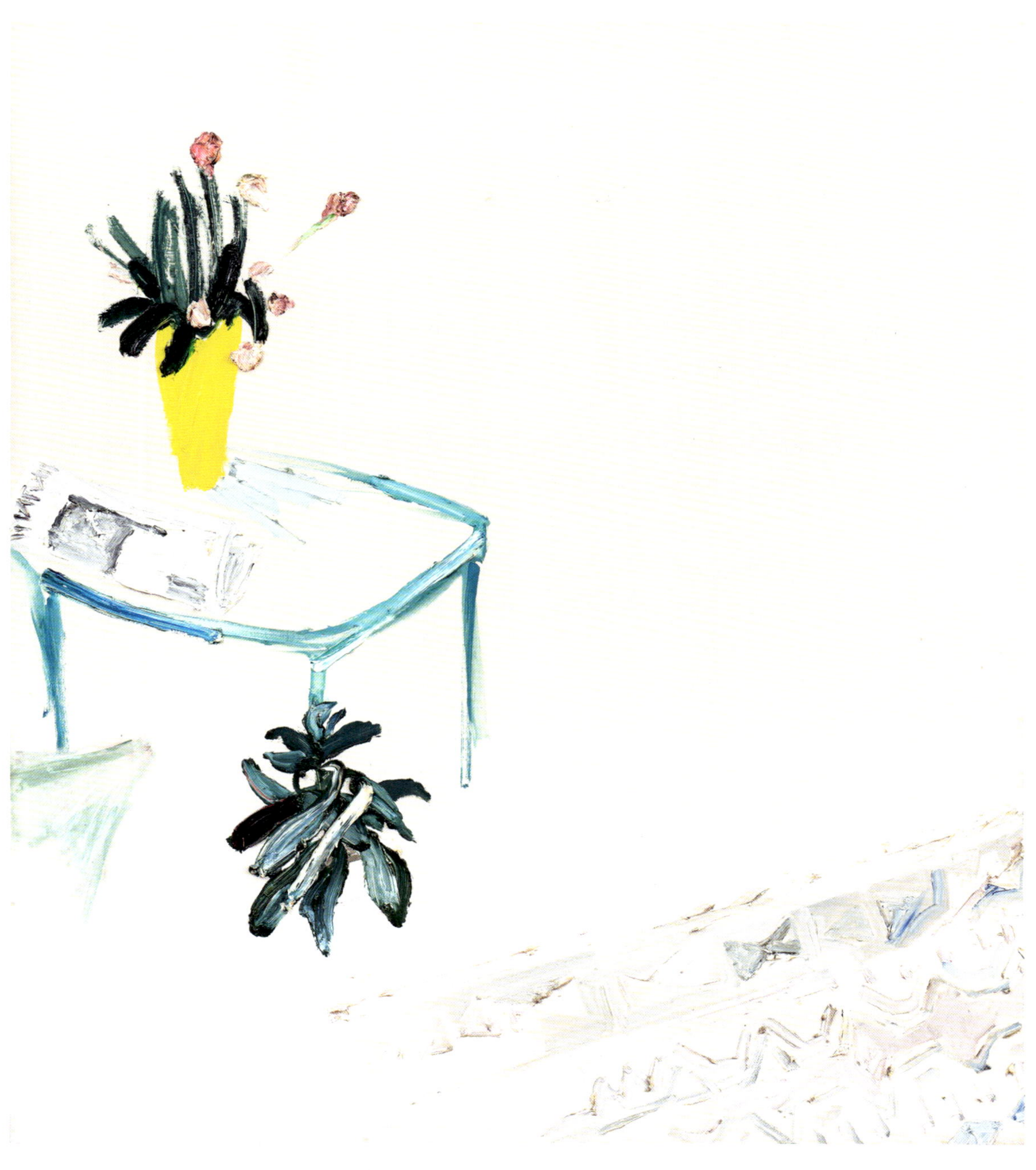

Untitled, ca. 1972, oil on canvas, 68 × 60 inches (172.7 × 152.4 cm)

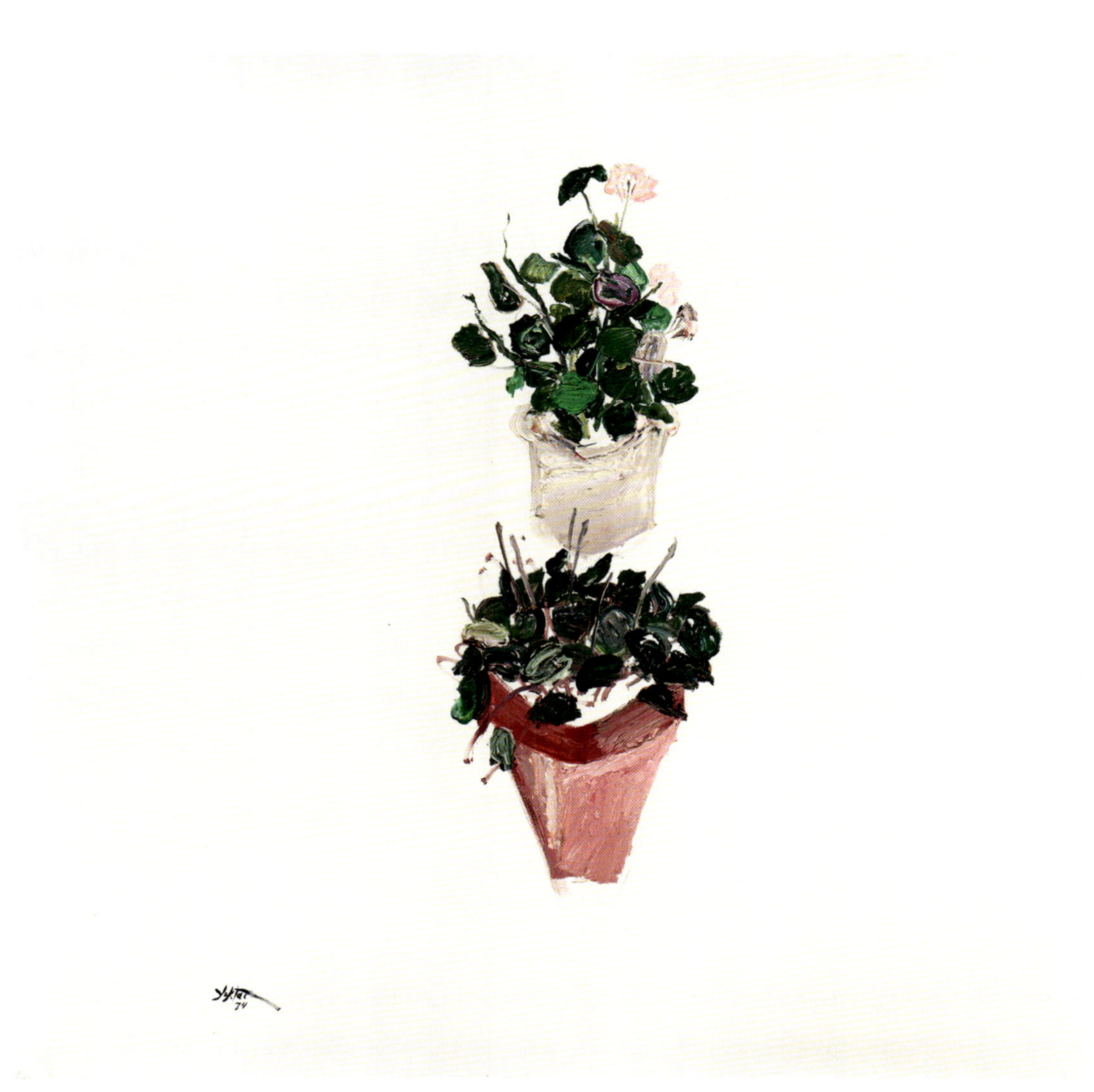

Untitled, 1974, oil on canvas, 72 × 78 inches (182.9 × 198.1 cm)

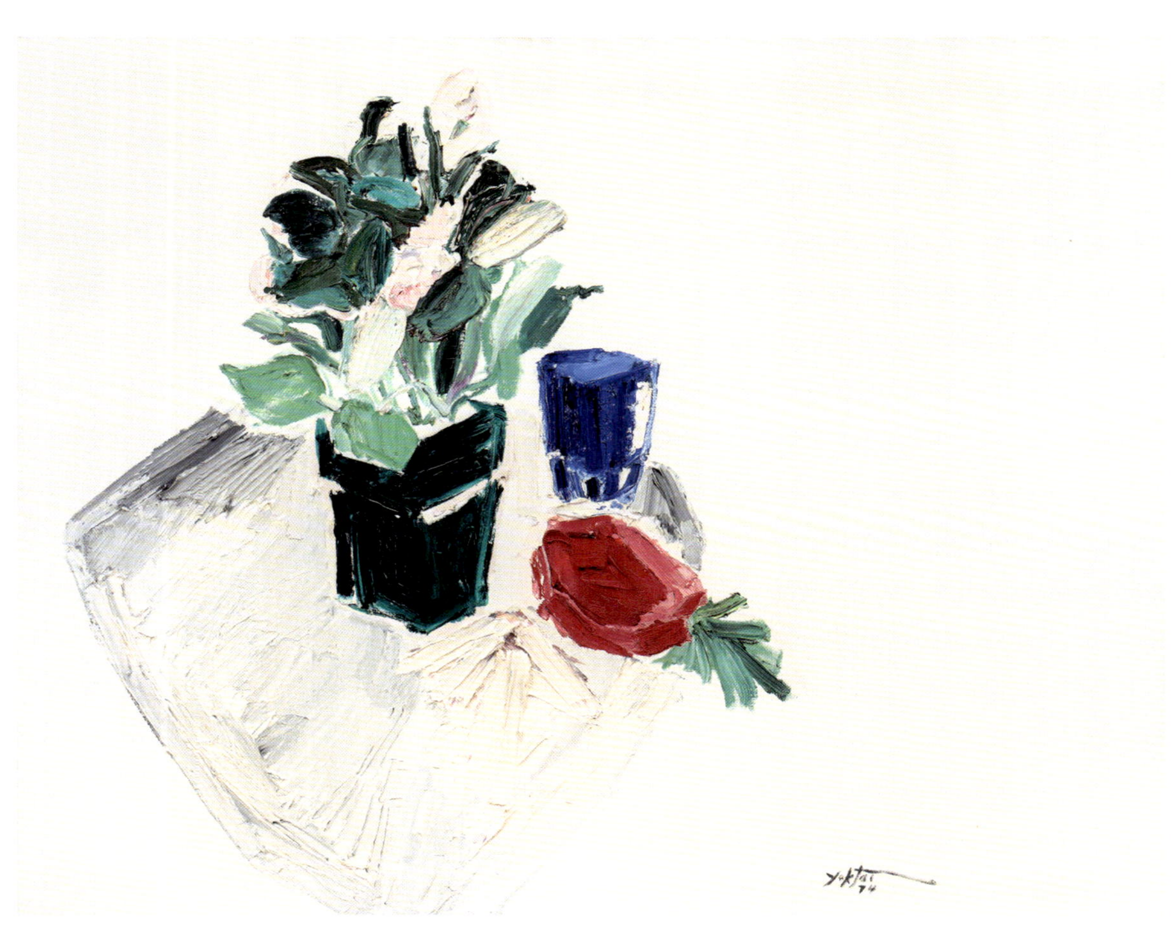

Untitled, 1974, oil on canvas, 36 × 46 inches (91.4 × 116.8 cm)

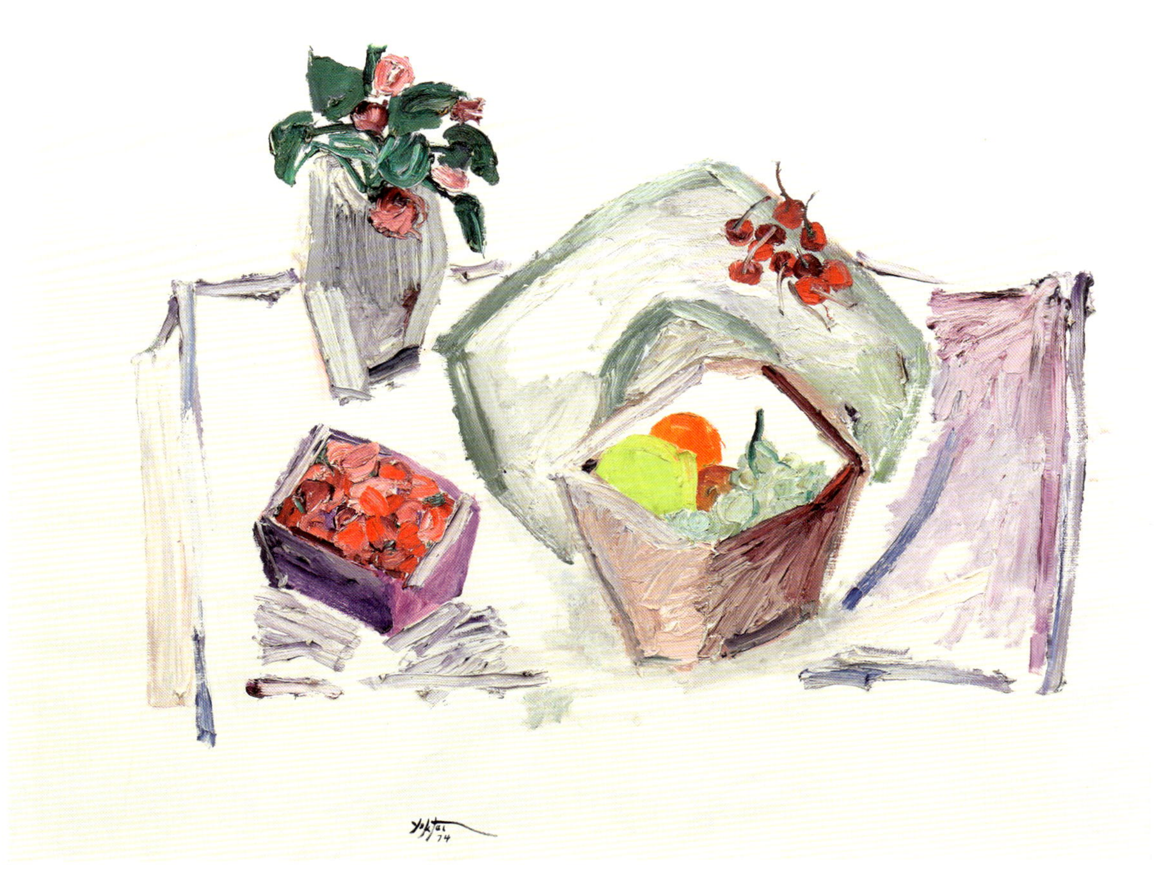

Untitled, 1974, oil on canvas, 52 × 56 inches (132 × 142 cm)

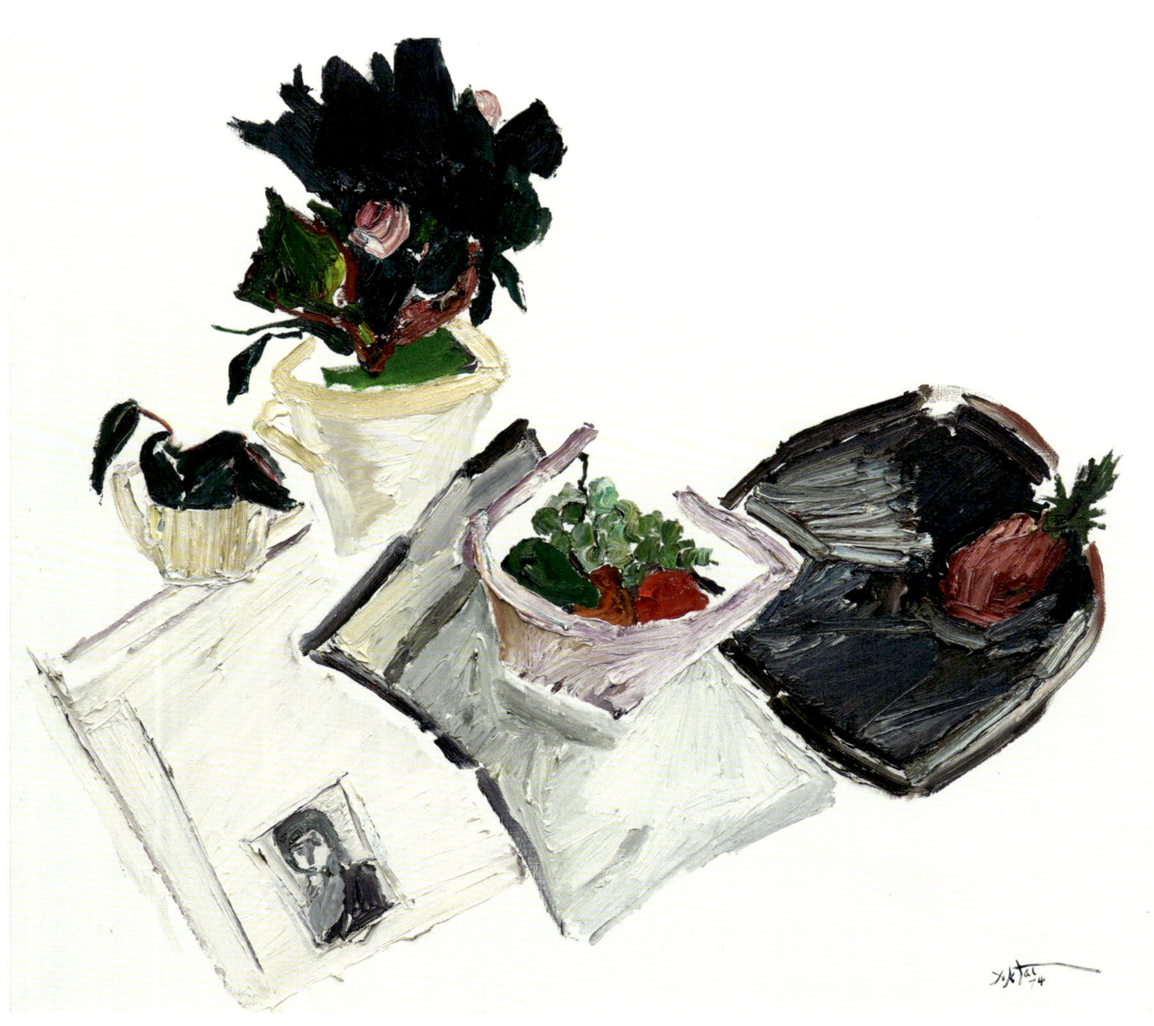

Untitled, 1974, oil on canvas, 56 × 64 inches (142.2 × 162.6 cm)

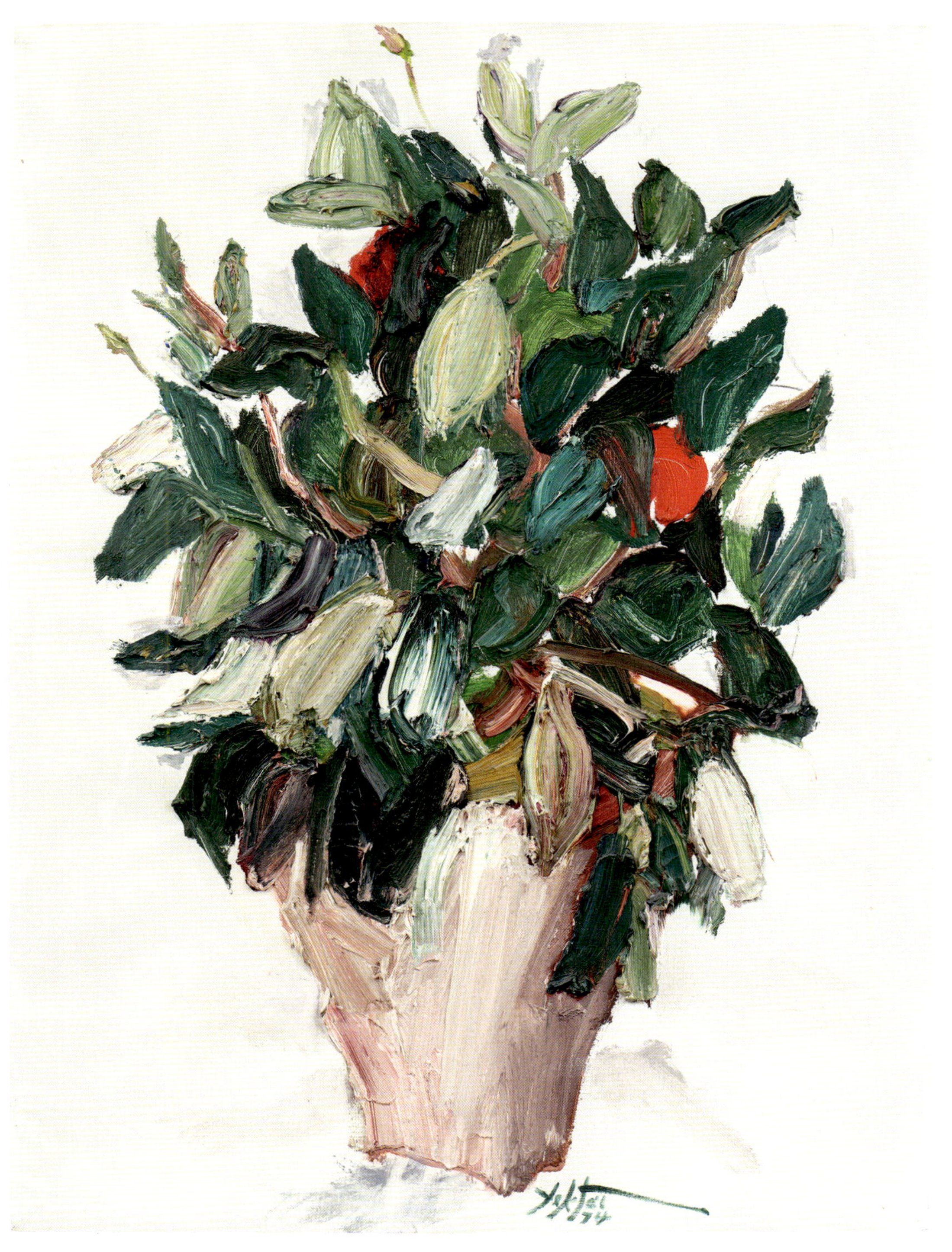

Untitled, 1974, oil on canvas, 40 × 30 inches (101.6 × 76.2 cm)

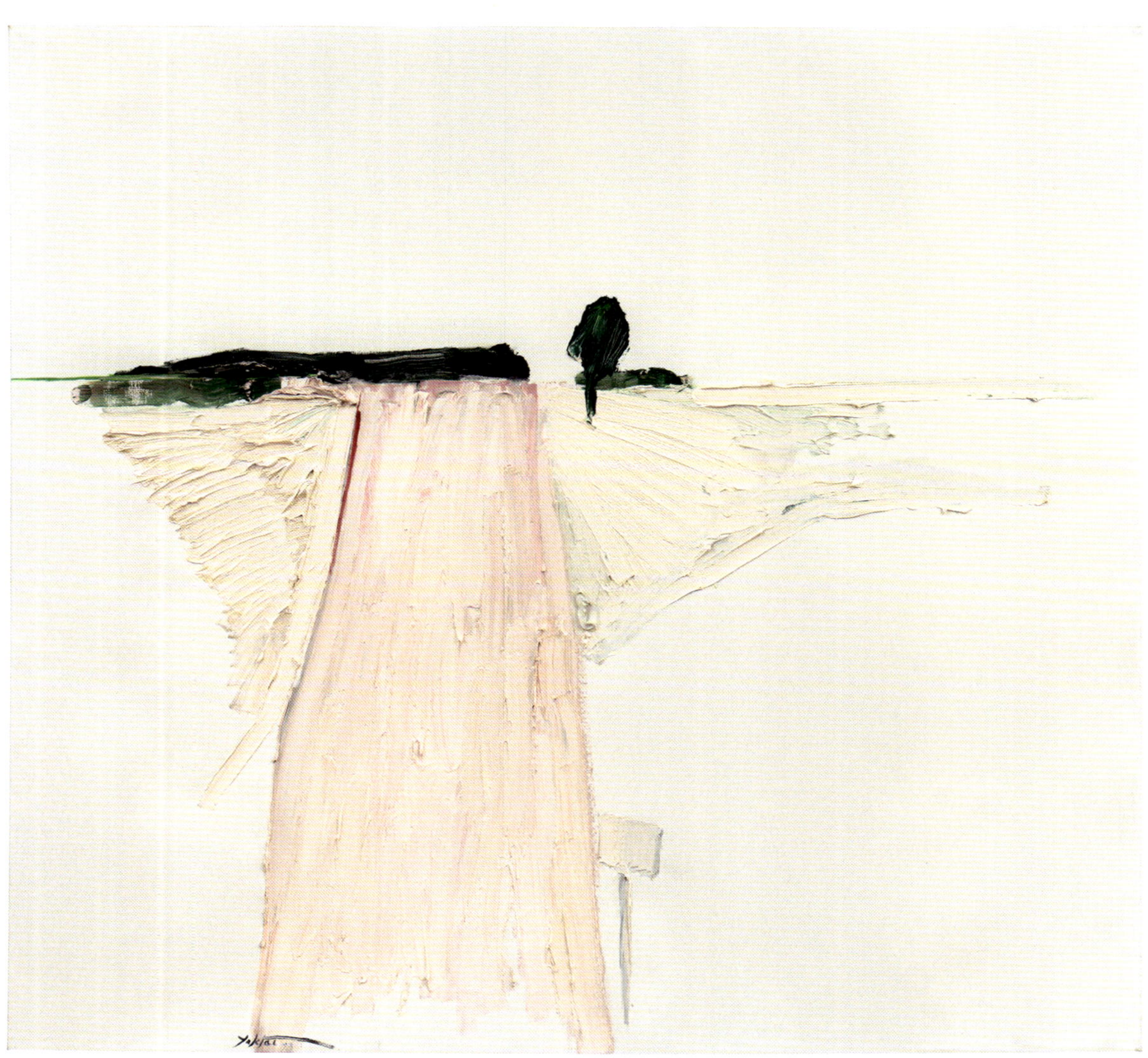

Untitled, 1973, oil on canvas, 52 × 58 inches (132.1 × 147.3 cm)

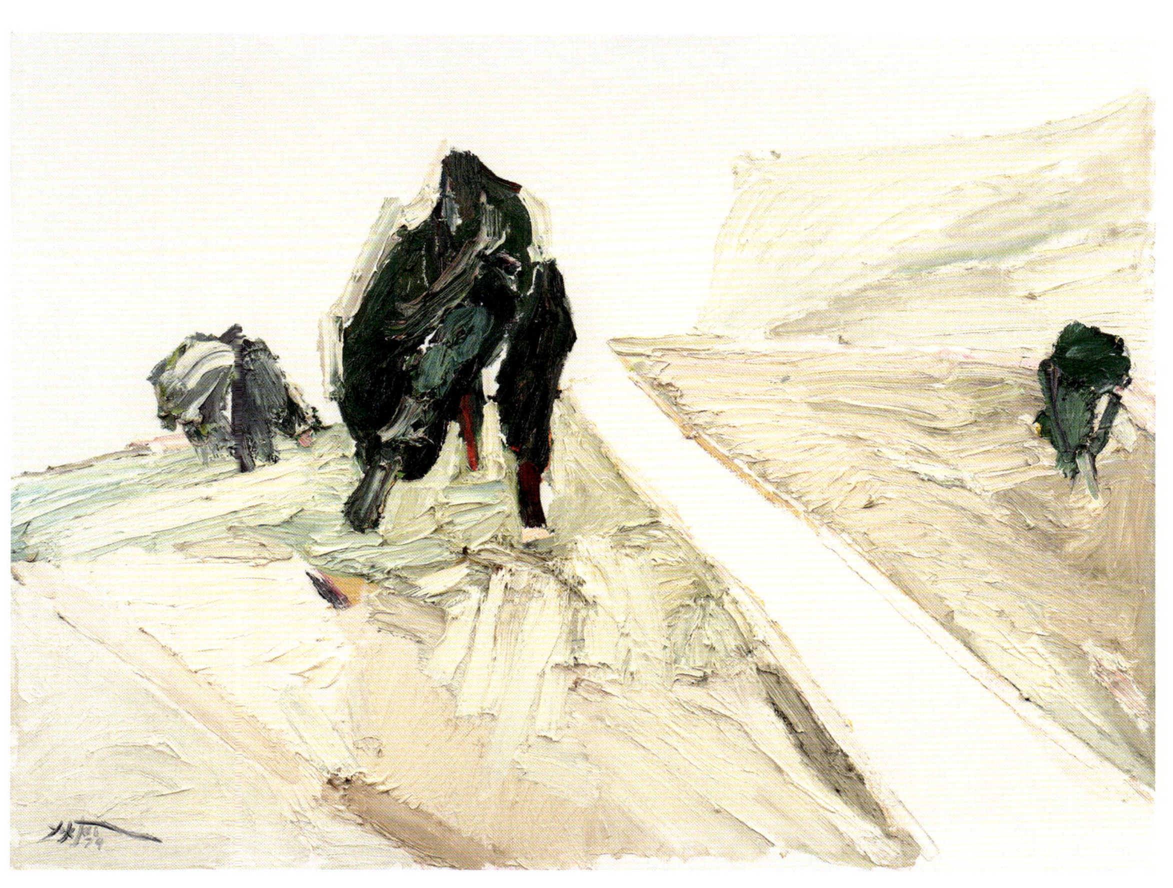

Untitled, 1974, oil on canvas, 34 × 48 inches (86.4 × 121.9 cm)

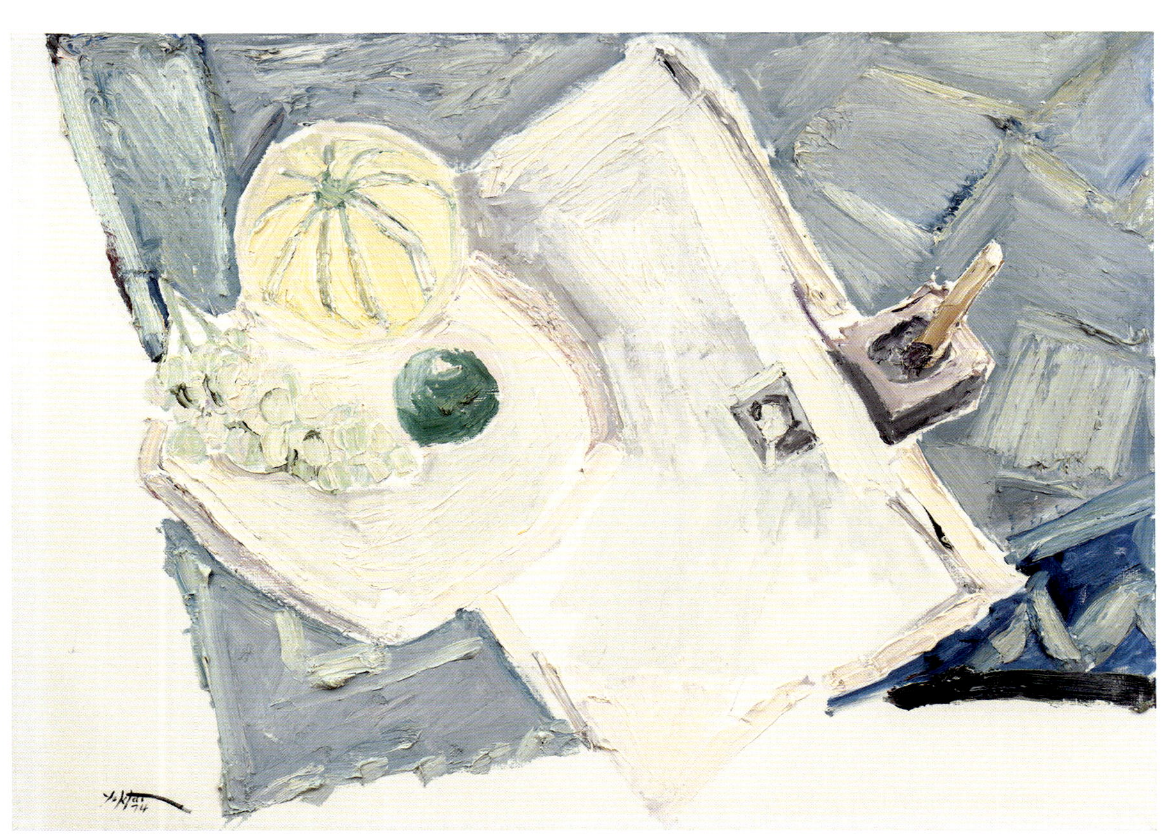

 Untitled, 1974, oil on canvas, 34 × 48 inches (86.4 × 121.9 cm)

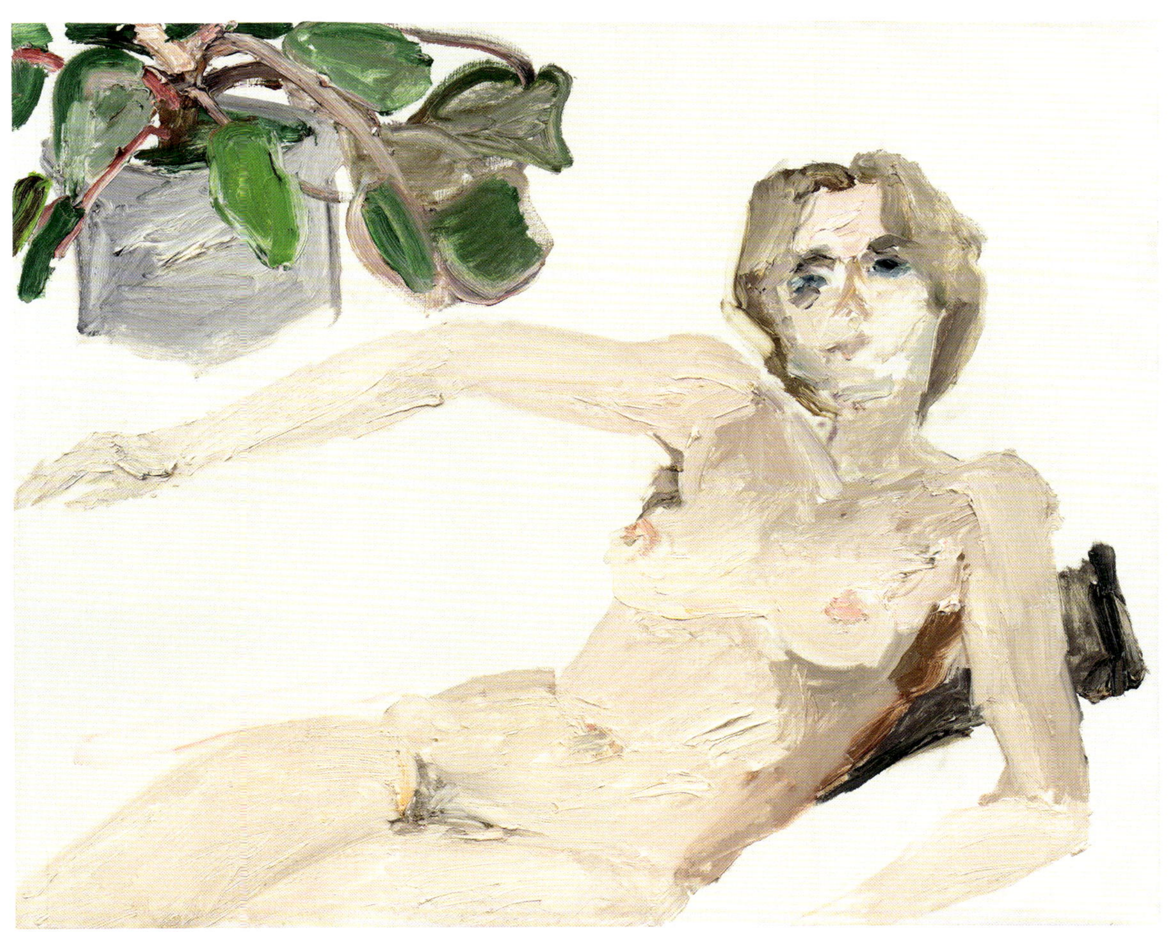

Untitled, 1974, oil on canvas, 36 × 44 inches (91.4 × 111.8 cm)

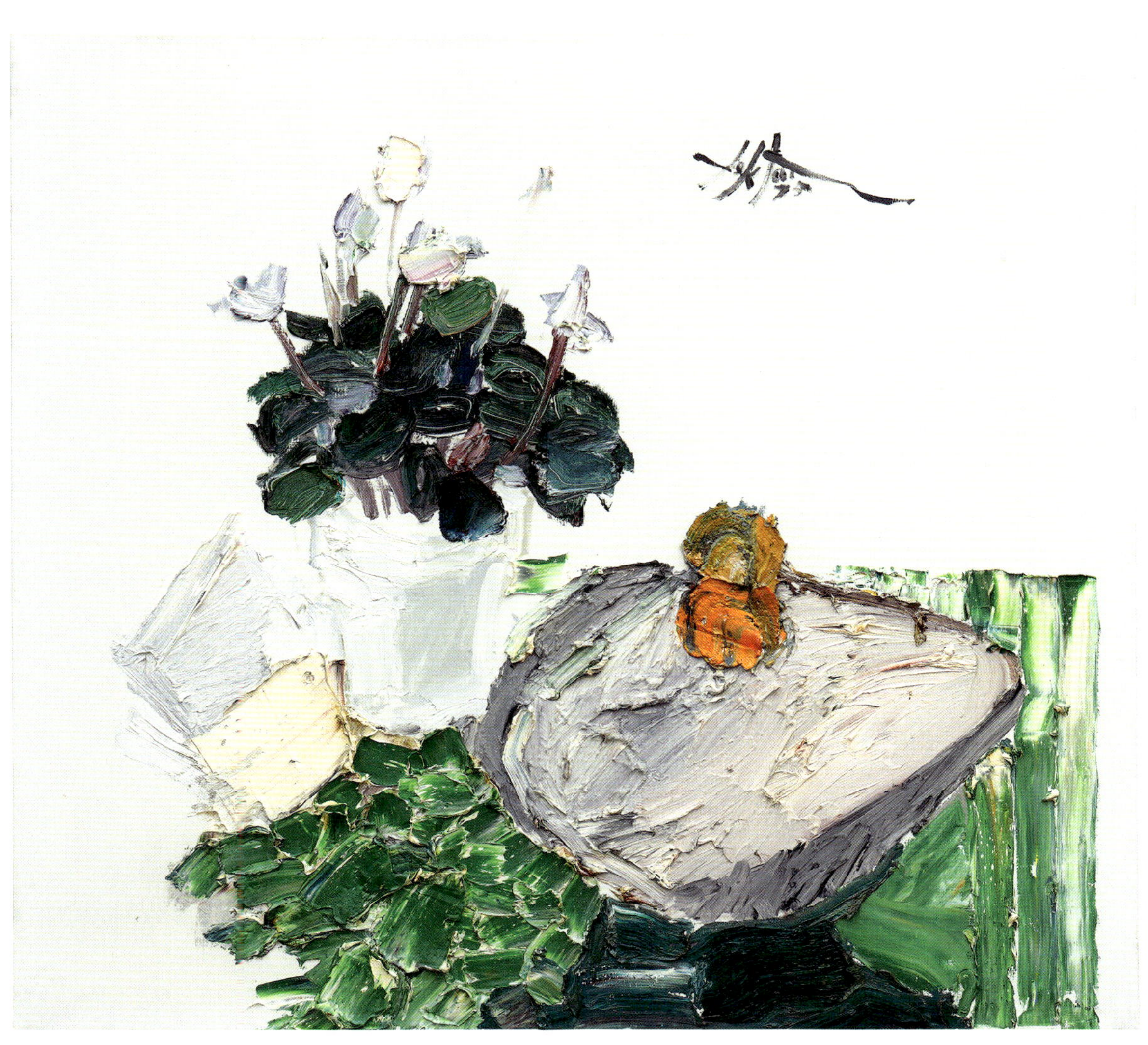

Untitled, 1975, oil on canvas, 40 × 44 inches (101.6 × 111.8 cm)

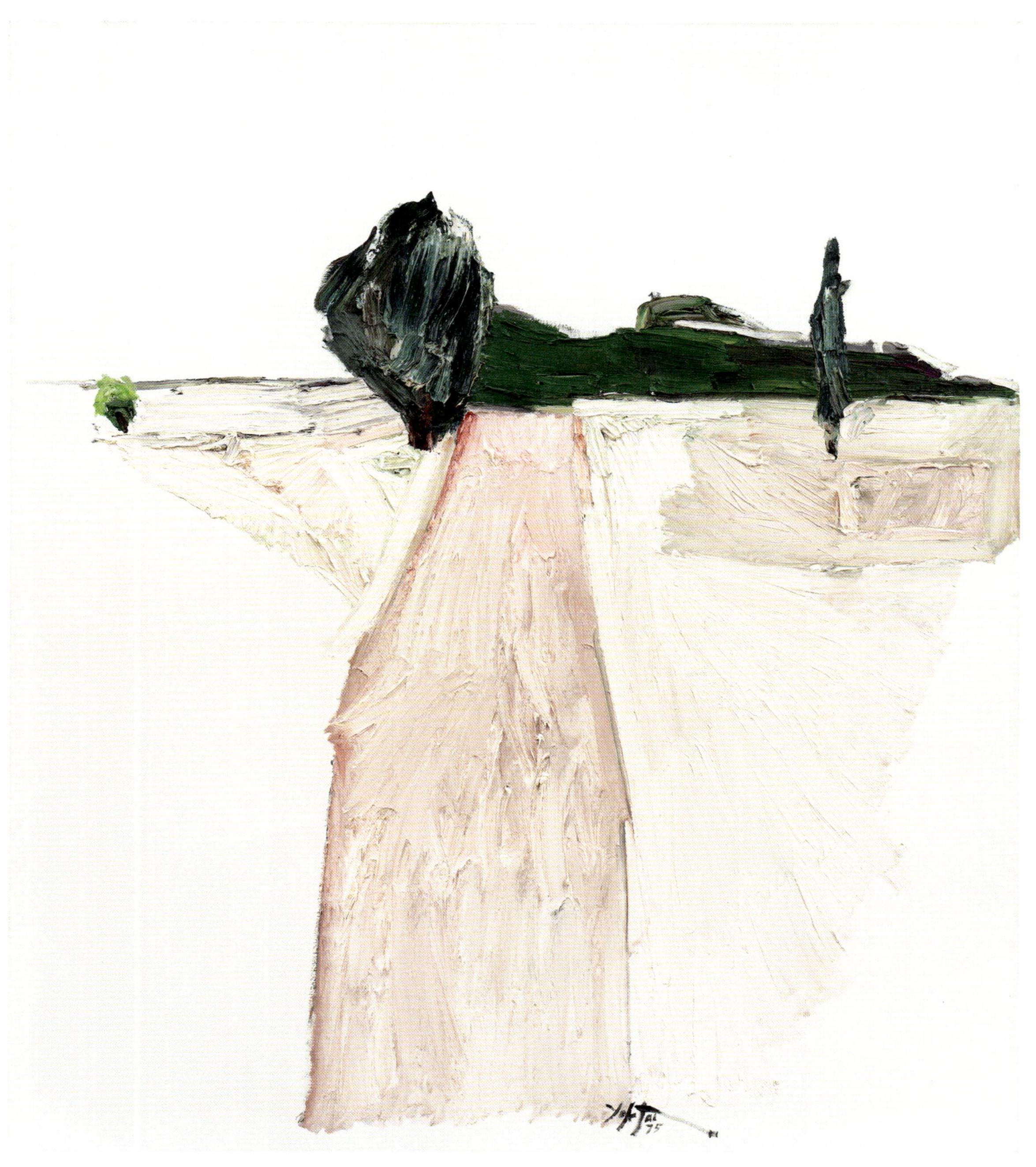

Untitled, 1975, oil on canvas, 64 × 56 inches (162.6 × 142.2 cm)

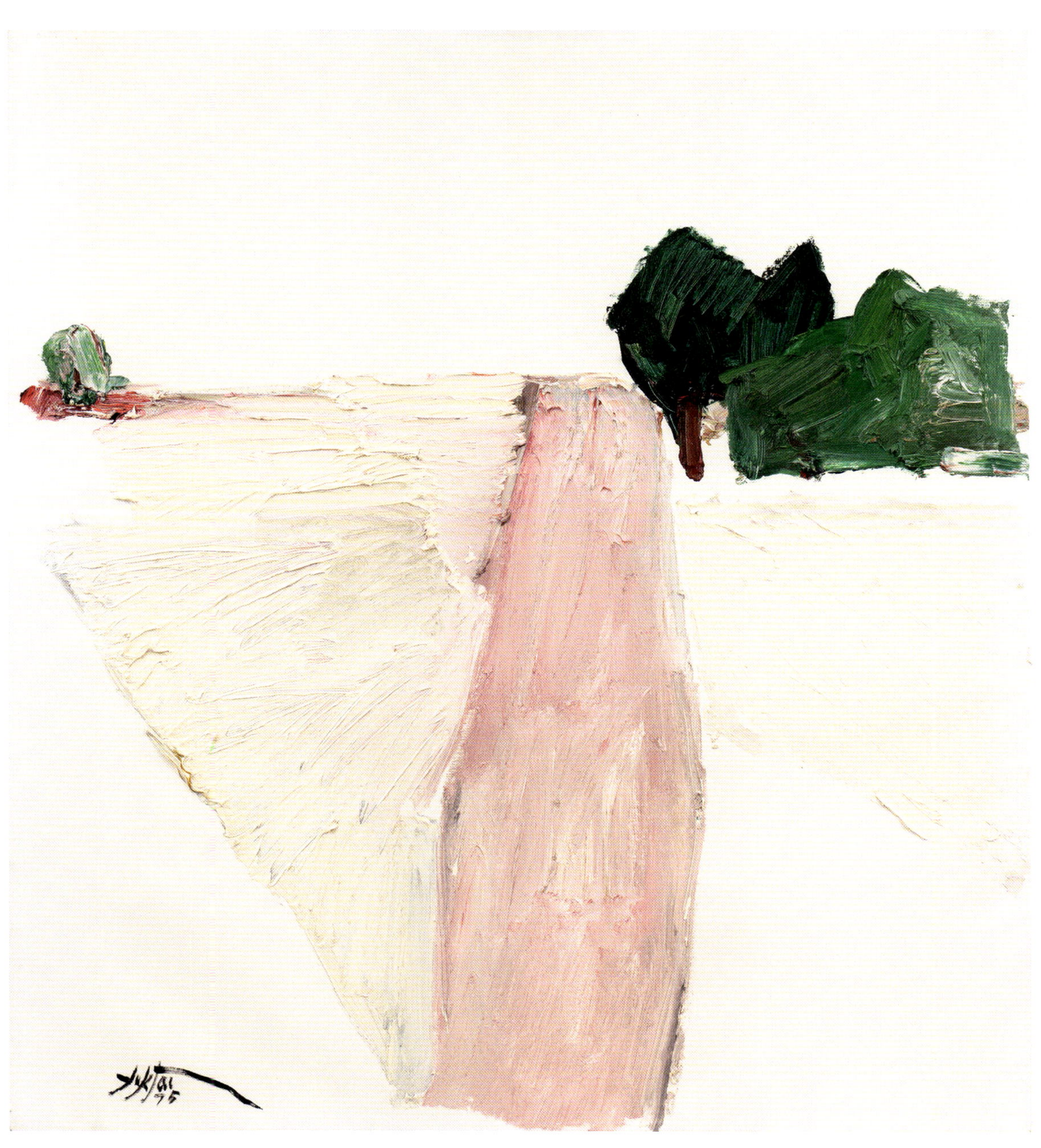

Untitled, 1975, oil on canvas, 40 × 36 inches (101.6 × 91.4 cm)

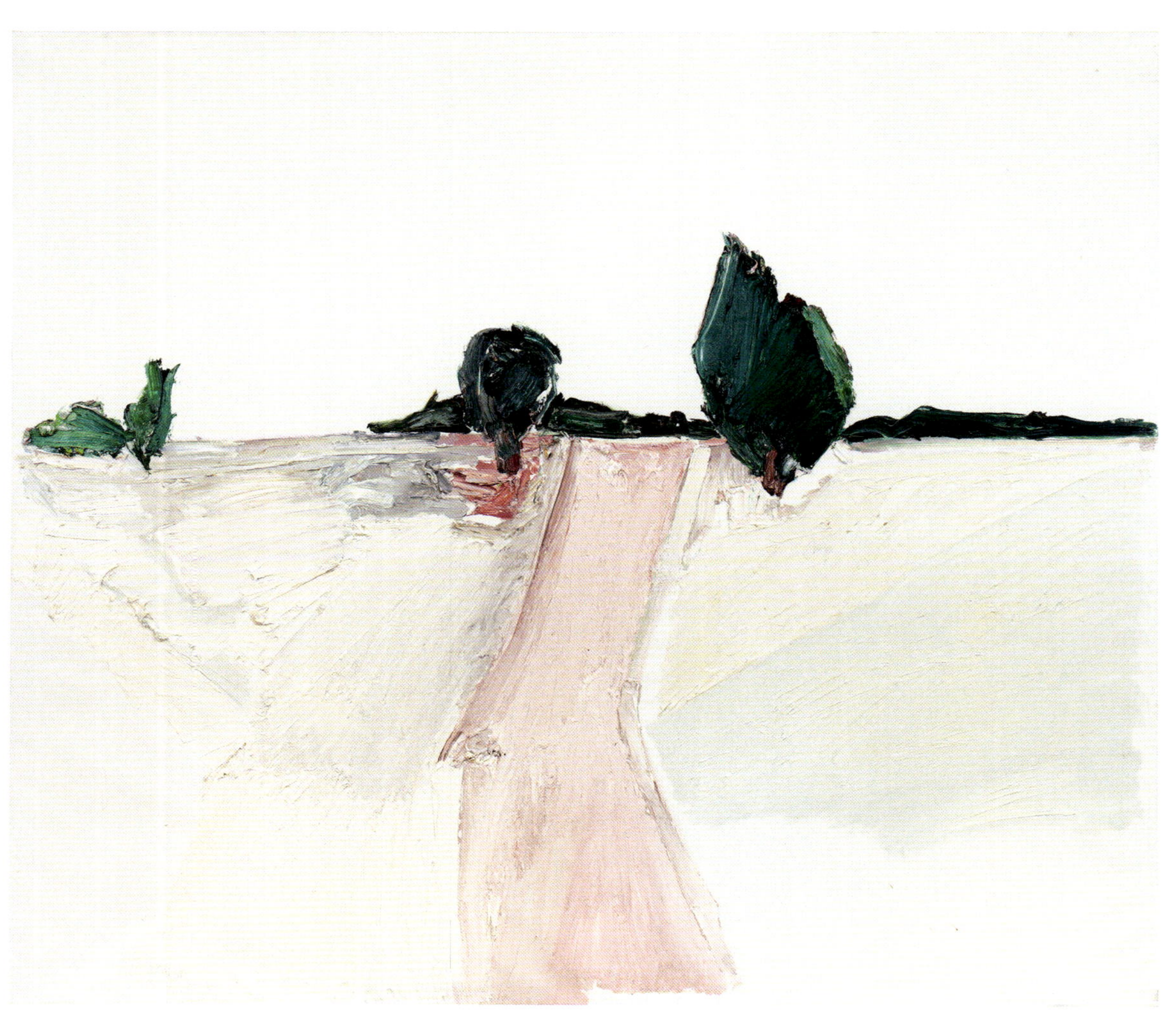

Untitled, 1975, oil on canvas, 56 × 64 inches (142 × 163 cm)

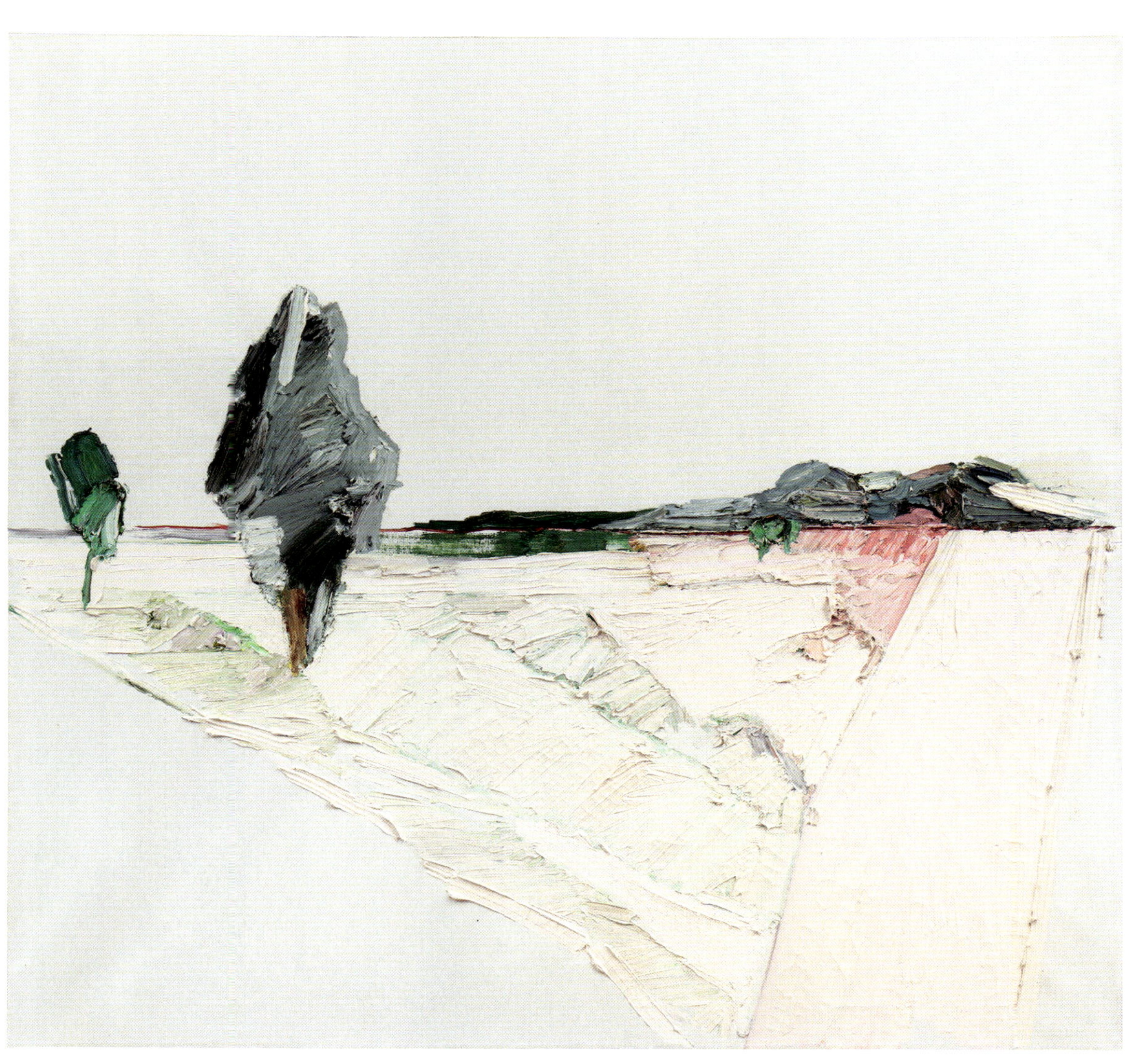

Untitled, 1975, oil on canvas, 52 × 56 inches (132.1 × 142.2 cm)

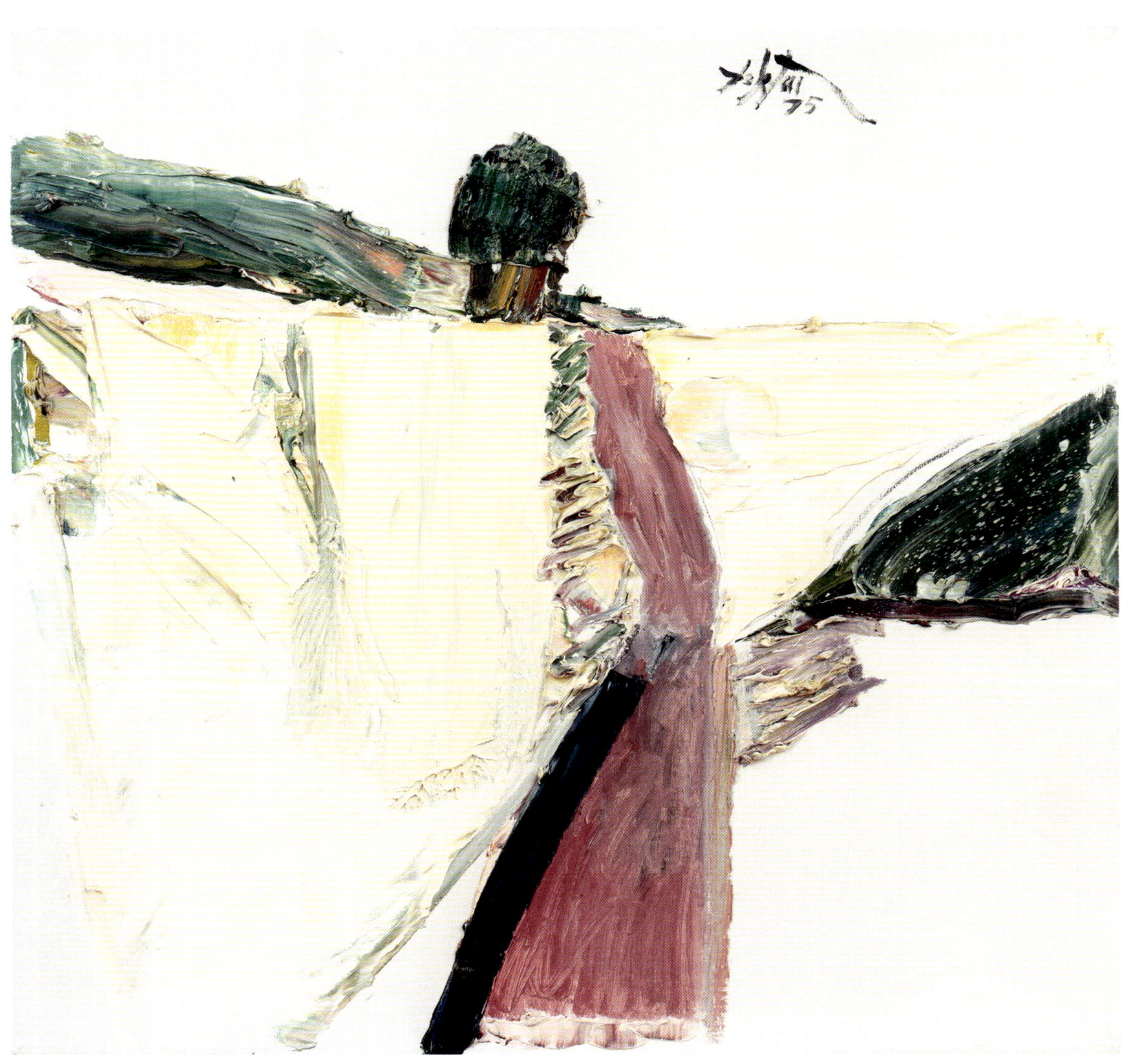

 Untitled, 1975, oil on canvas, 38 × 40 inches (96.5 × 101.6 cm)

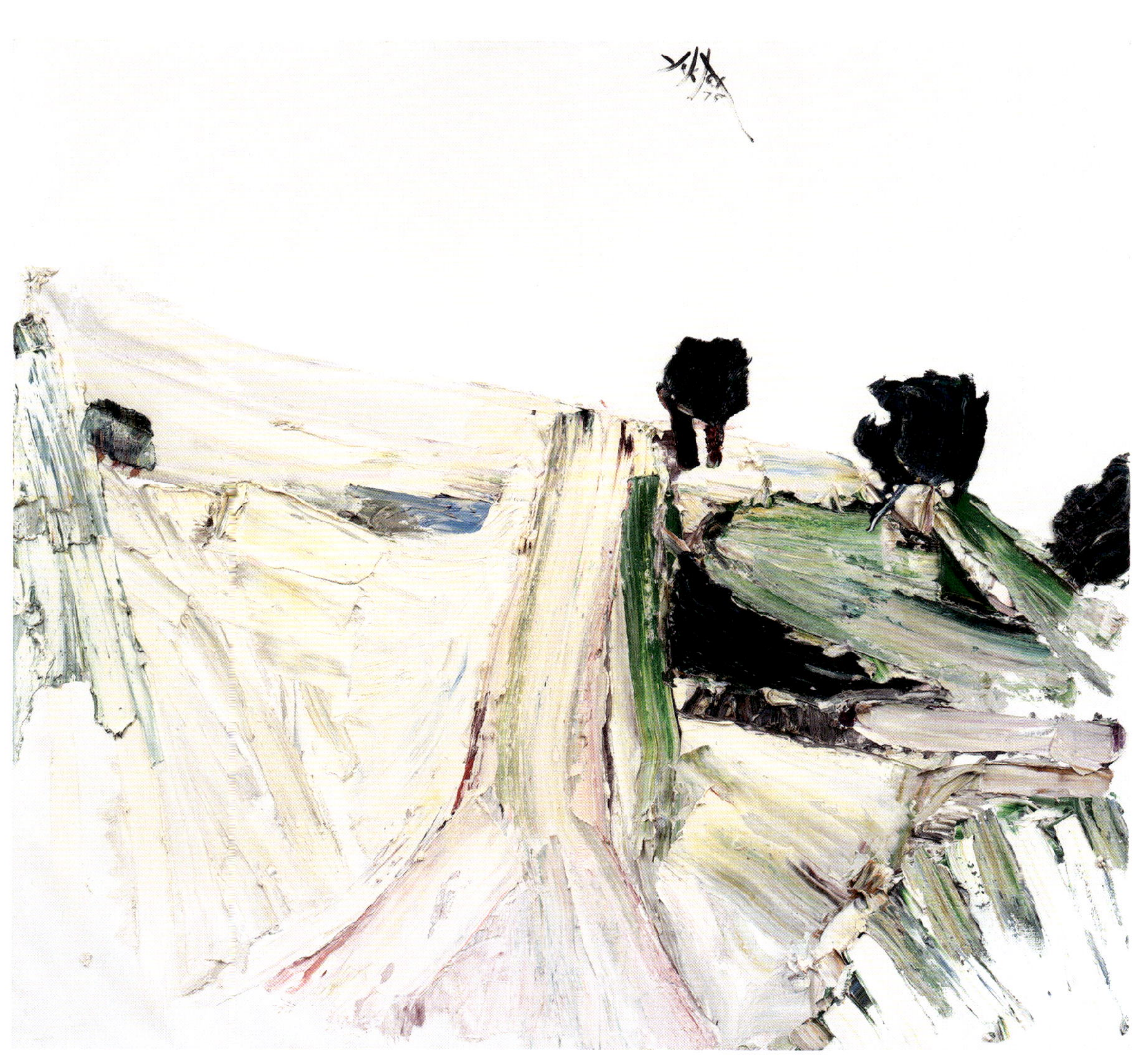

Untitled, 1975, oil on canvas, 52 × 56 inches (132.1 × 142.2 cm)

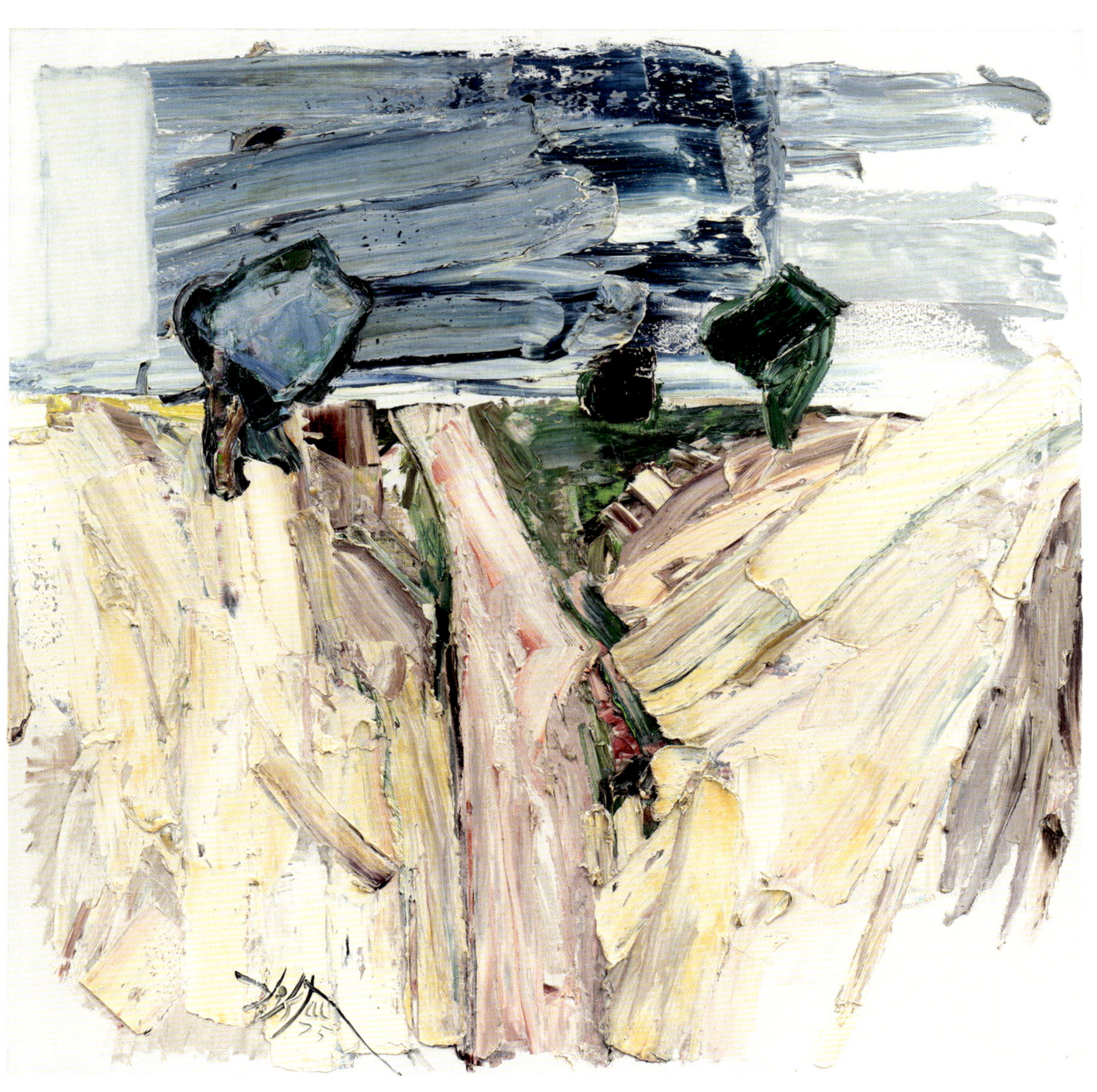

Untitled, 1975, oil on canvas, 60 × 60 inches (152.4 × 152.4 cm)

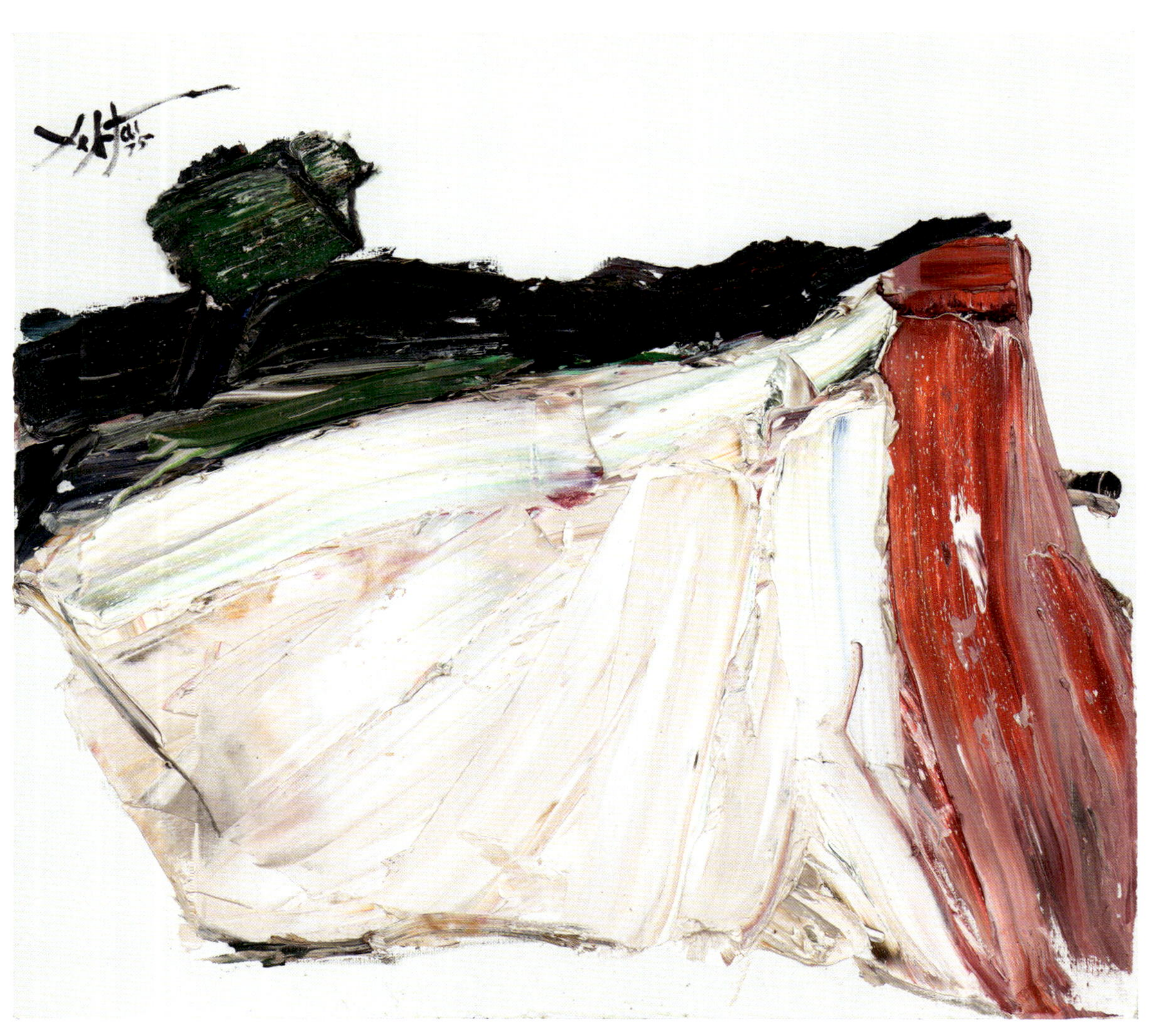

Untitled, 1975, oil on canvas, 36 × 40 inches (91.4 × 101.6 cm)

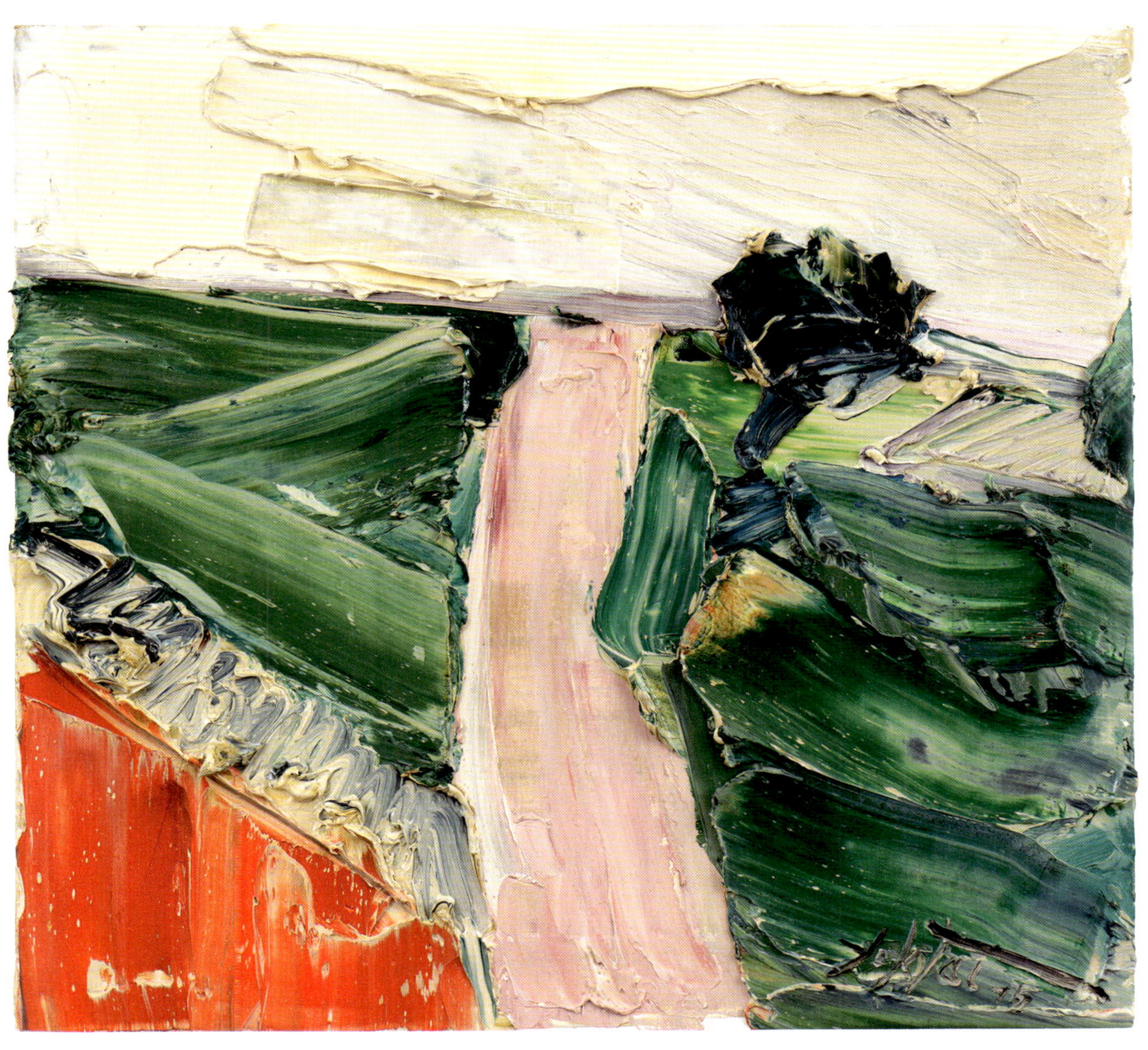

Untitled, 1975, oil on canvas, 22 × 24 inches (55.9 × 61 cm)

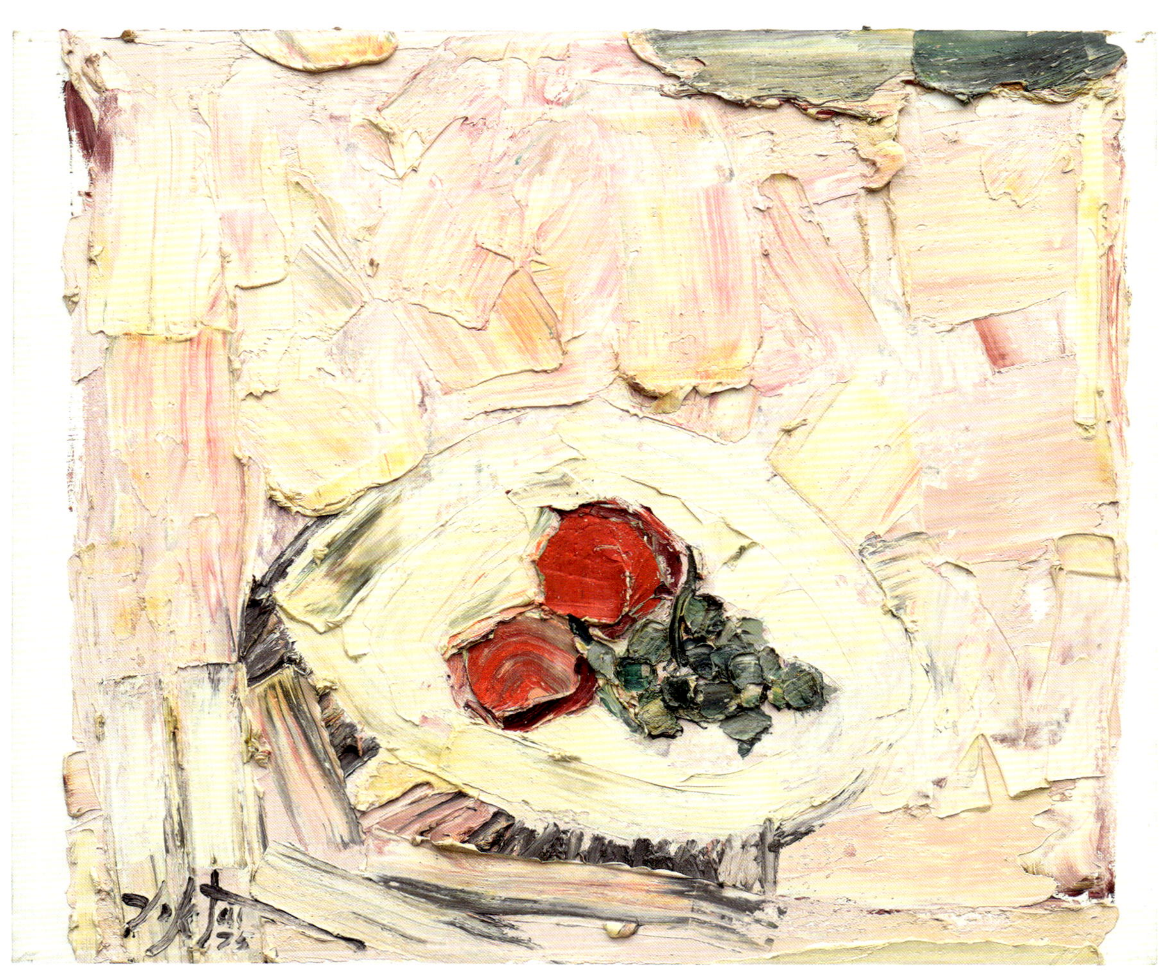

Untitled, 1975, oil on canvas, 32 × 38 inches (81 × 97 cm)

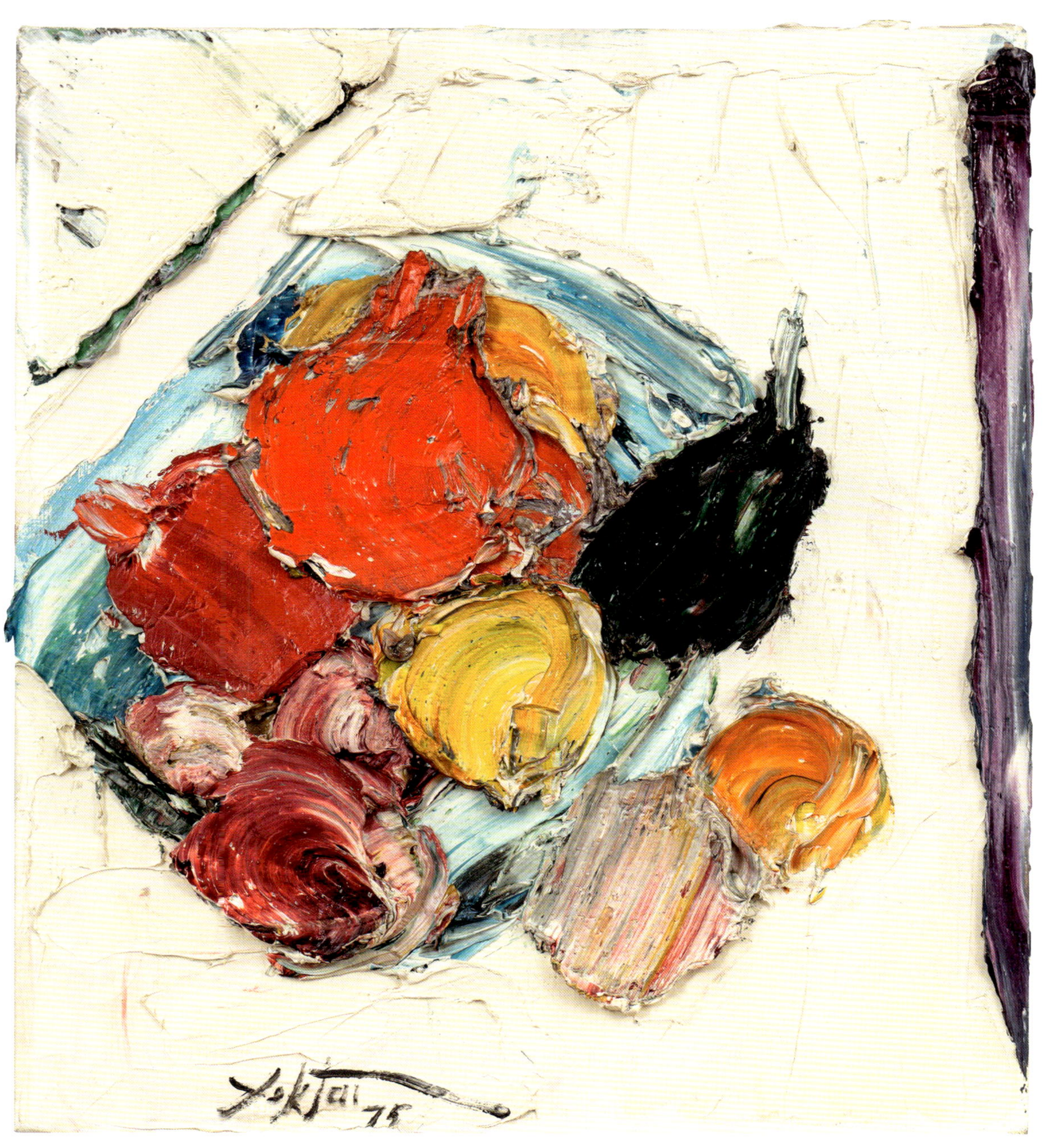

Untitled, 1975, oil on canvas, 20 × 18¼ inches (50.8 × 46.4 cm)

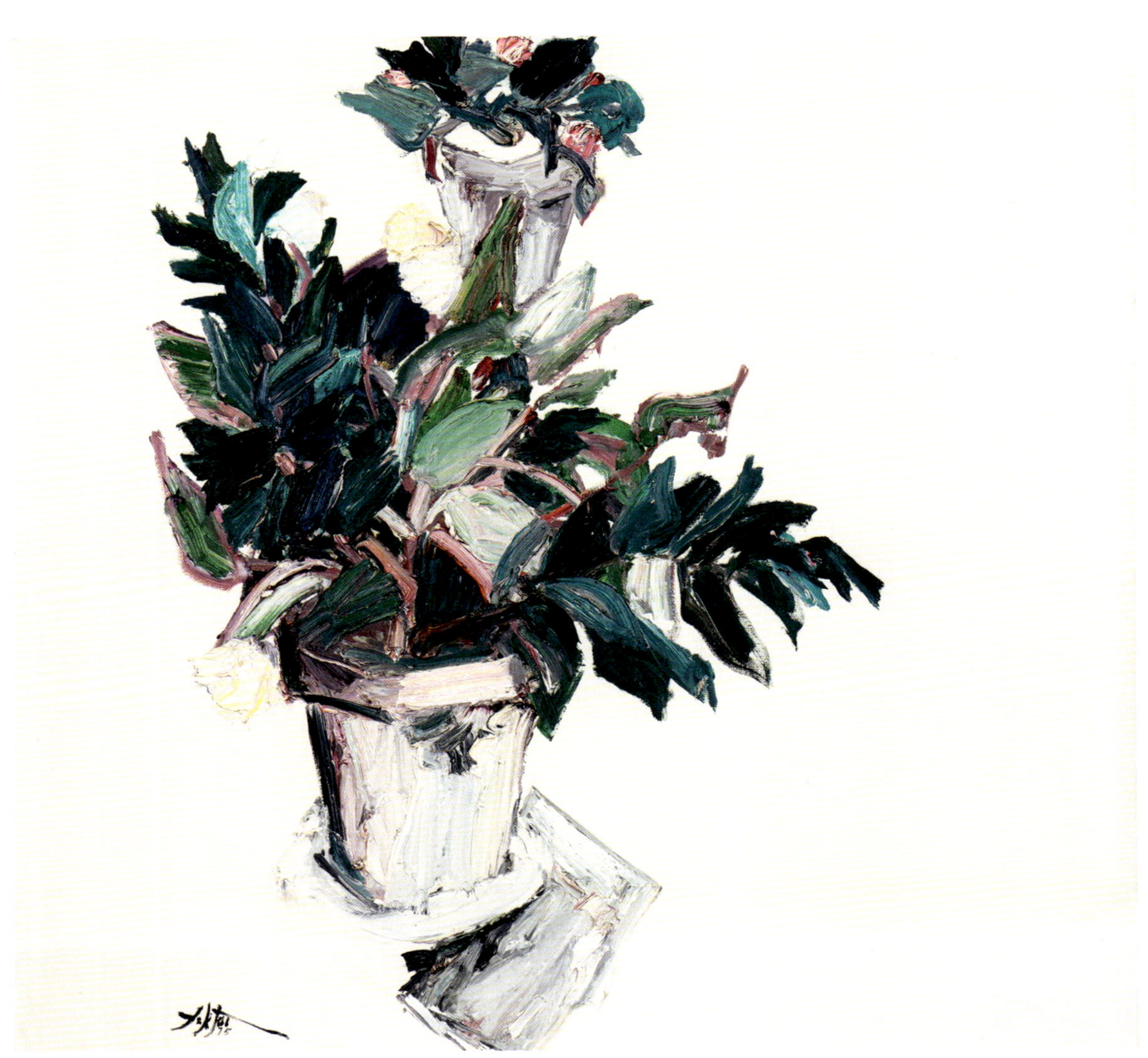

Untitled, 1975, oil on canvas, 52 × 56 inches (132 × 142 cm)

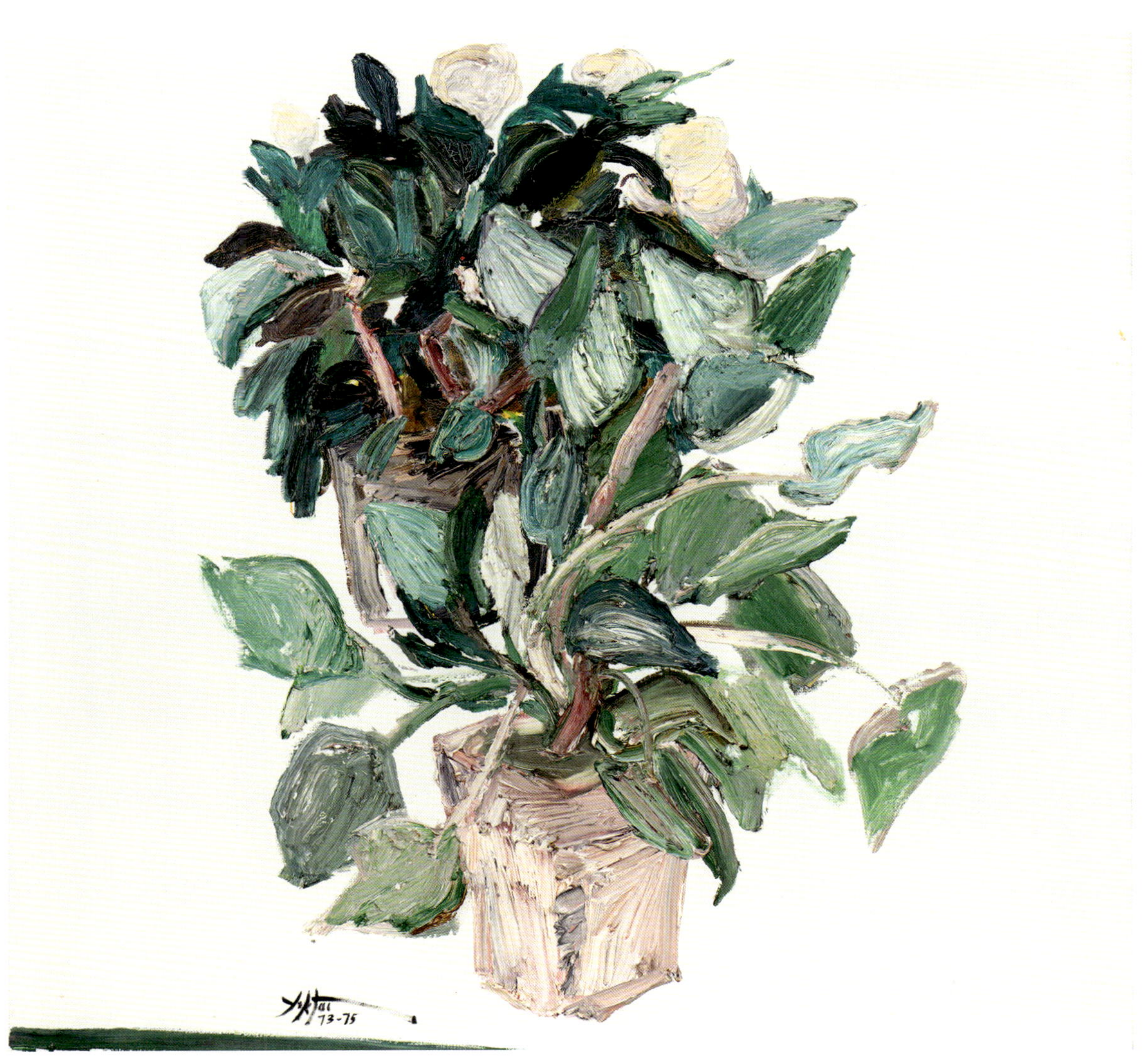

Untitled, 1973–75, oil on canvas, 52 × 56 inches (132 × 142 cm)

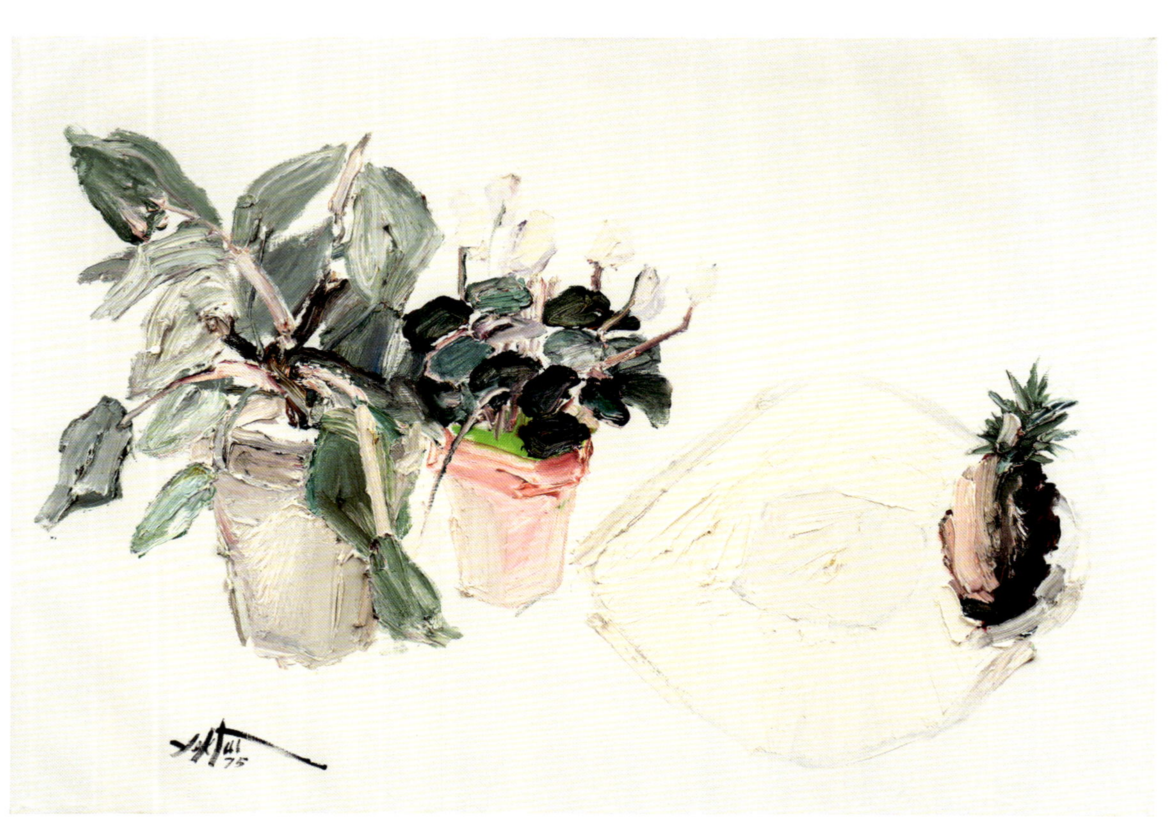

 Untitled, 1975, oil on canvas, 34 × 48 inches (86.4 × 121.9 cm)

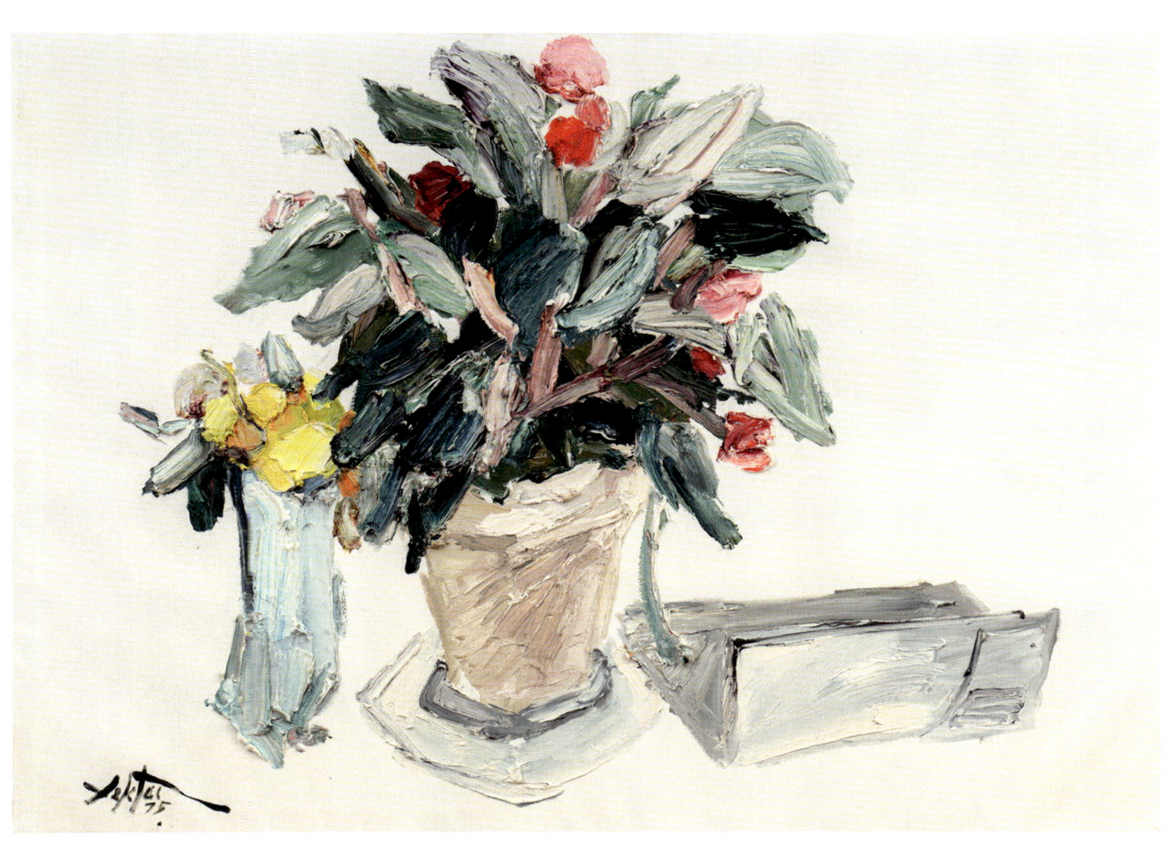

Untitled, 1975, oil on canvas, 34 × 48 inches (86.4 × 121.9 cm)

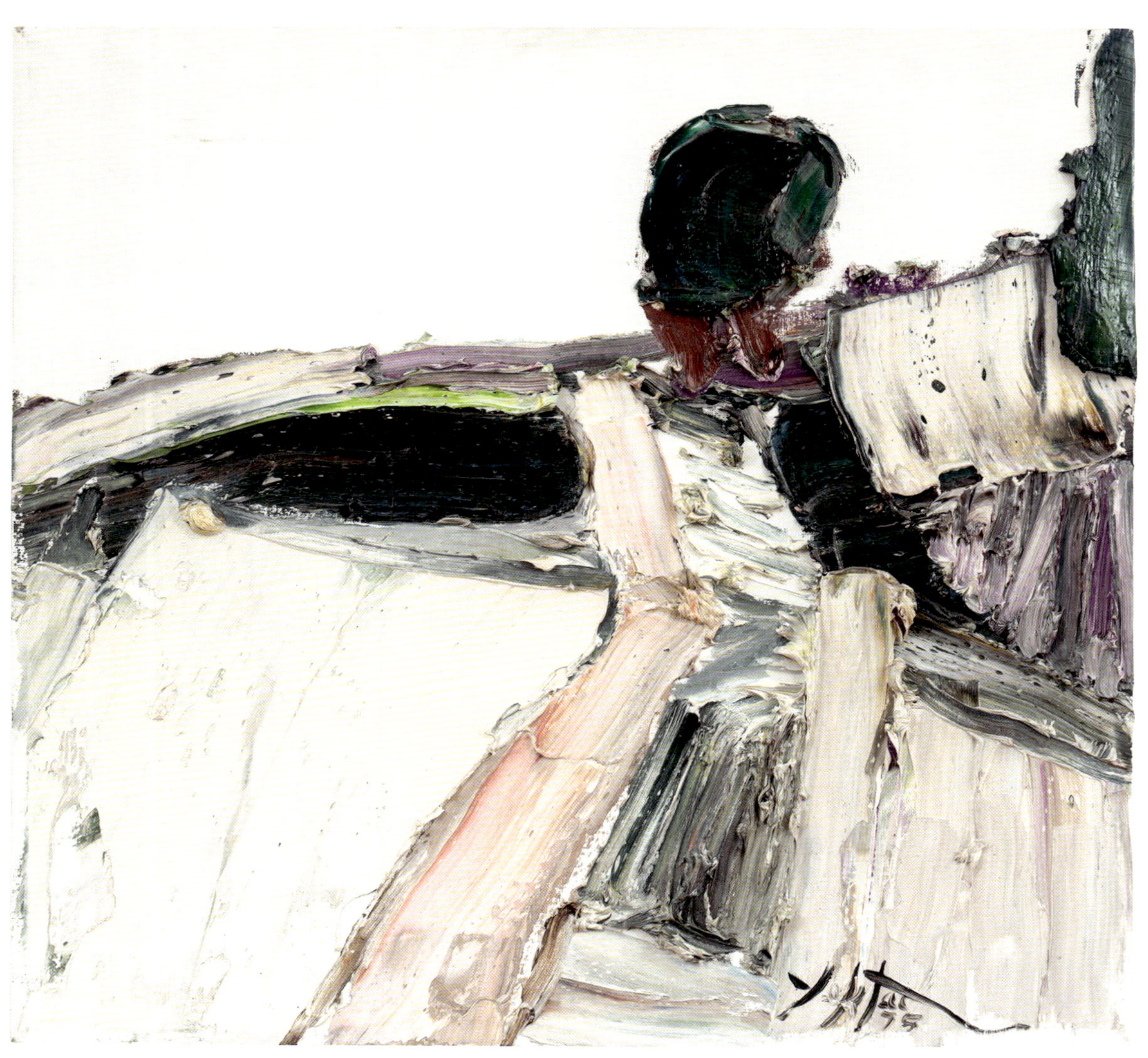

 Untitled, 1975, oil on canvas, 22 × 24 inches (55.9 × 61 cm)

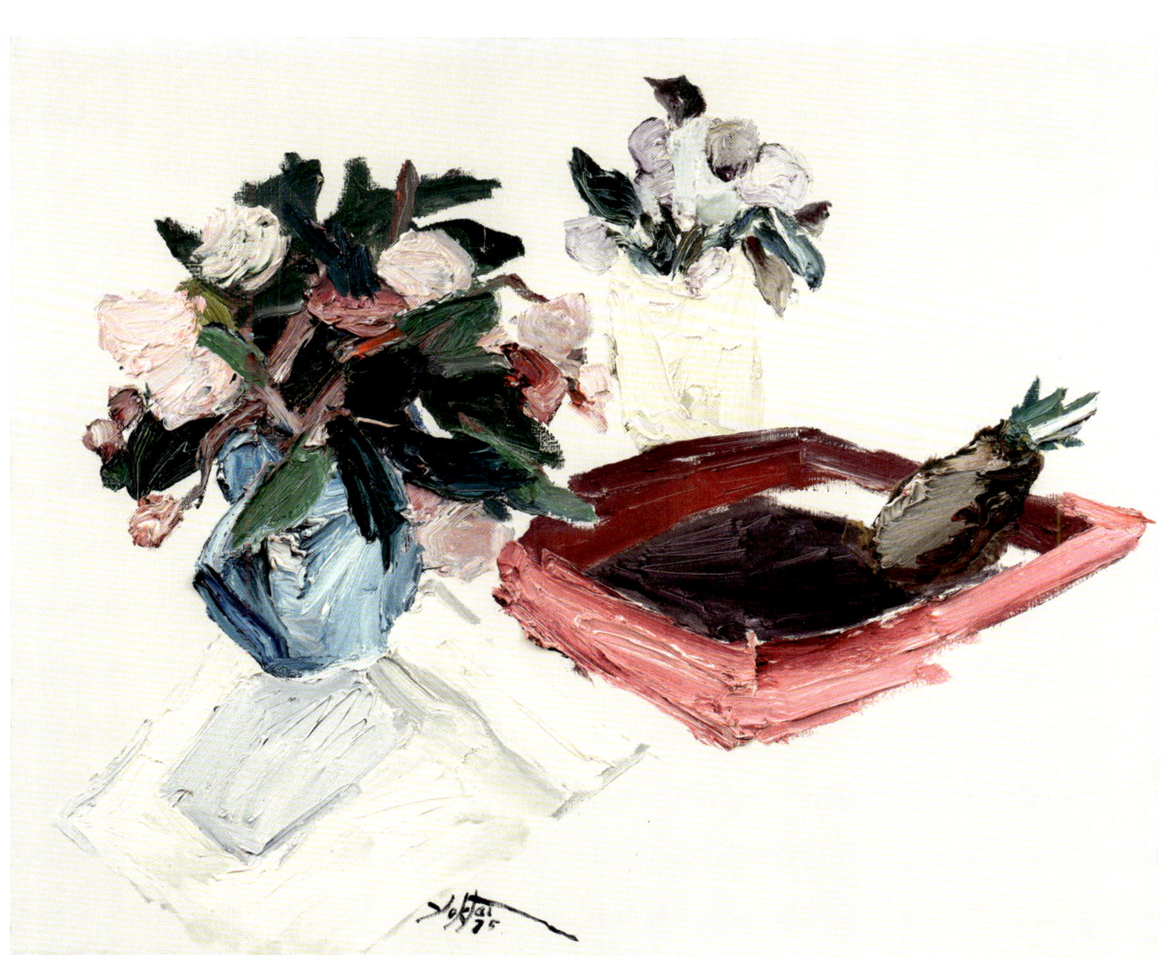

Untitled, 1975, oil on canvas, 36 × 44 inches (91.4 × 111.8 cm)

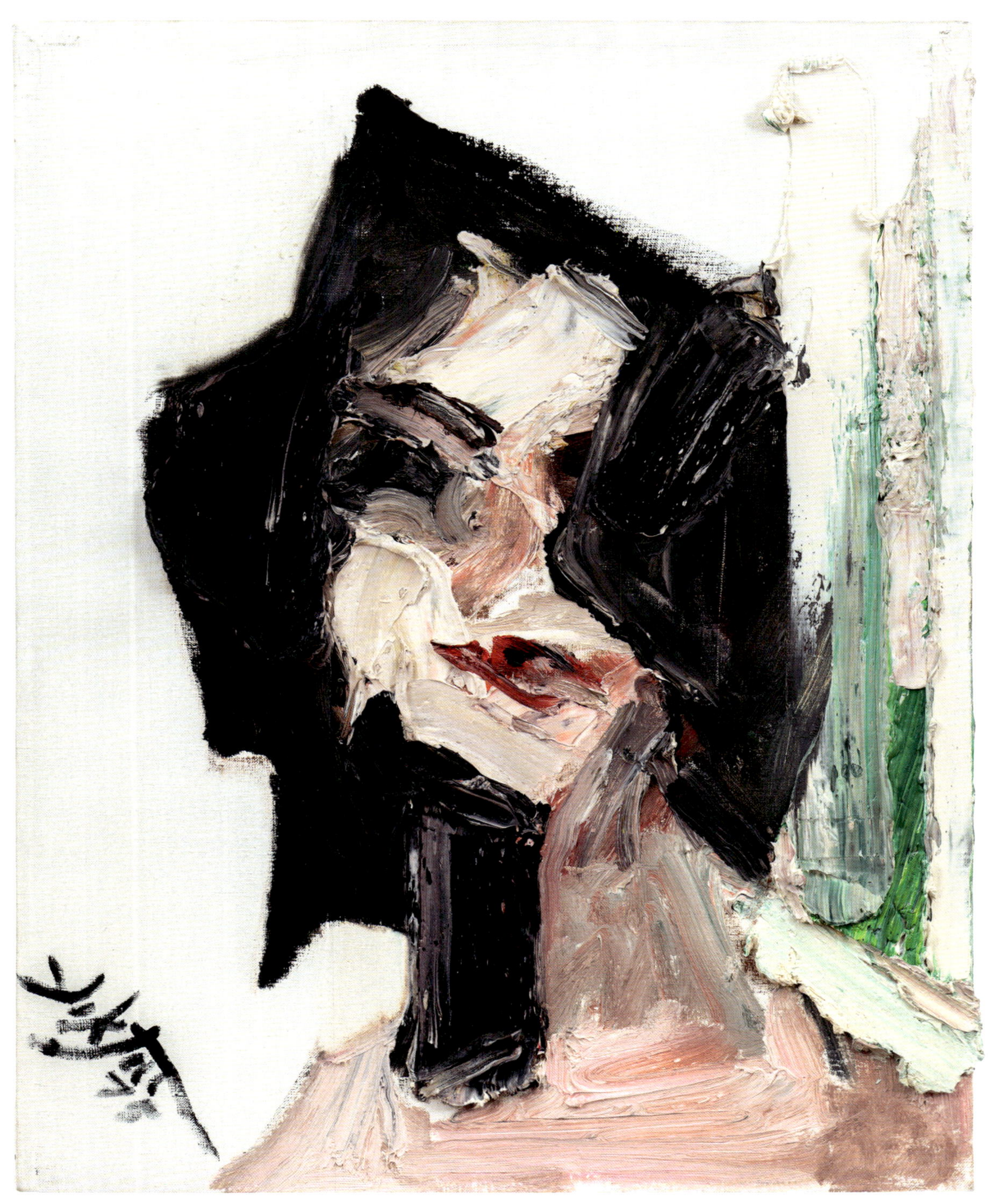

Untitled, 1975, oil on canvas, 20 × 16 inches (50.8 × 40.6 cm)

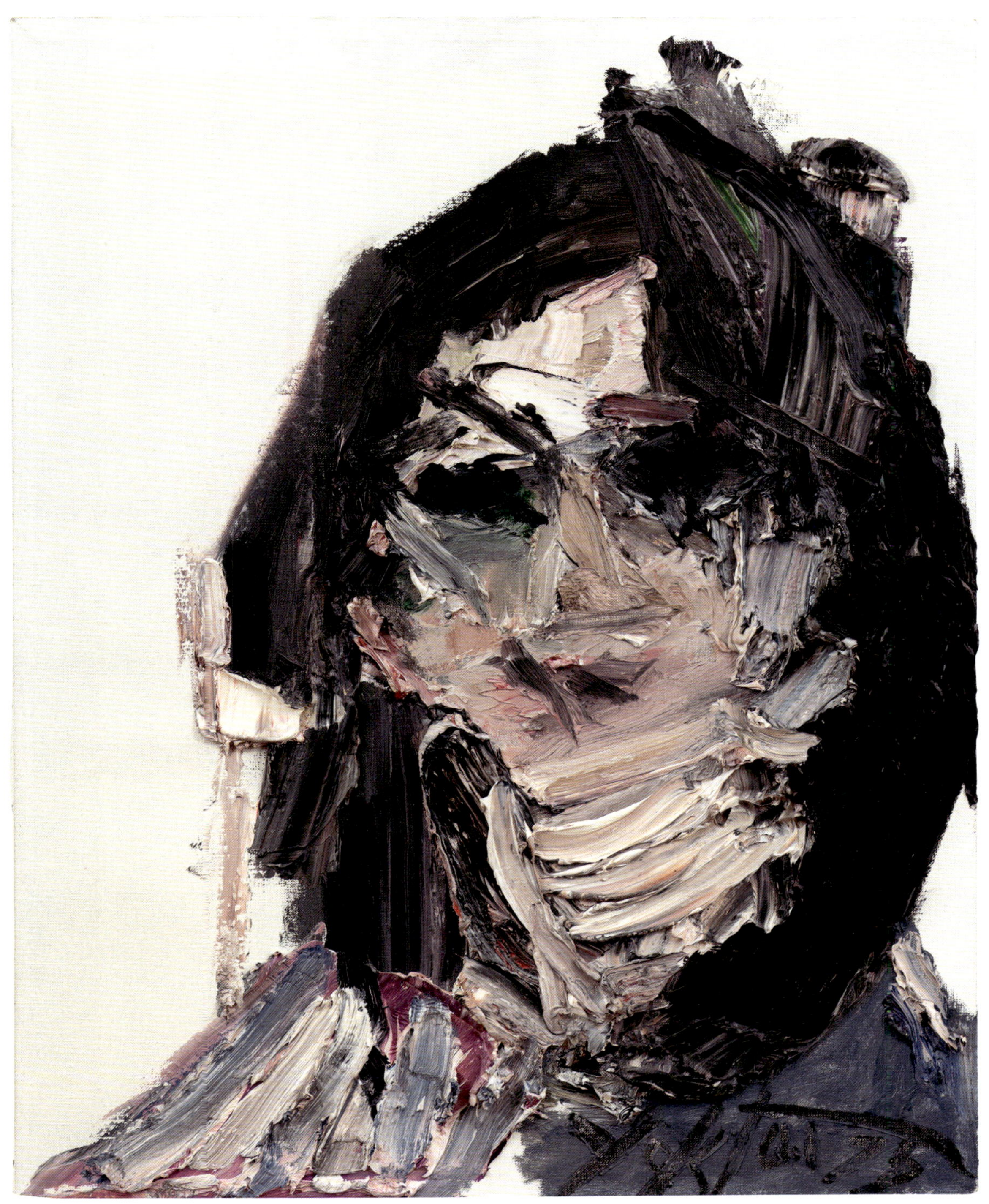

Untitled, 1975, oil on canvas, 20 × 16 inches (50.8 × 40.6 cm)

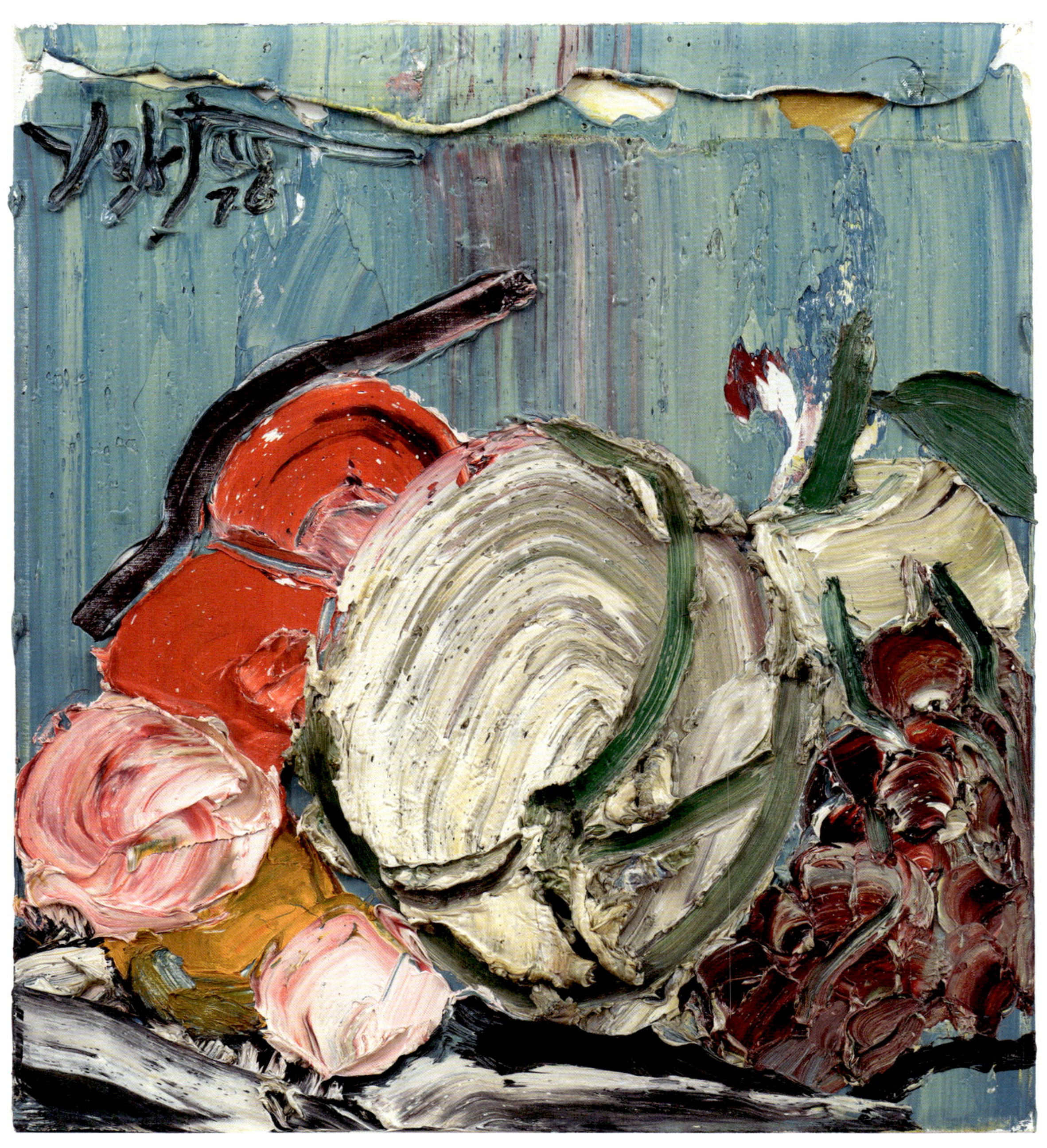

 Untitled, 1975, oil on canvas, 20 × 18 inches (50.8 × 45.7 cm)

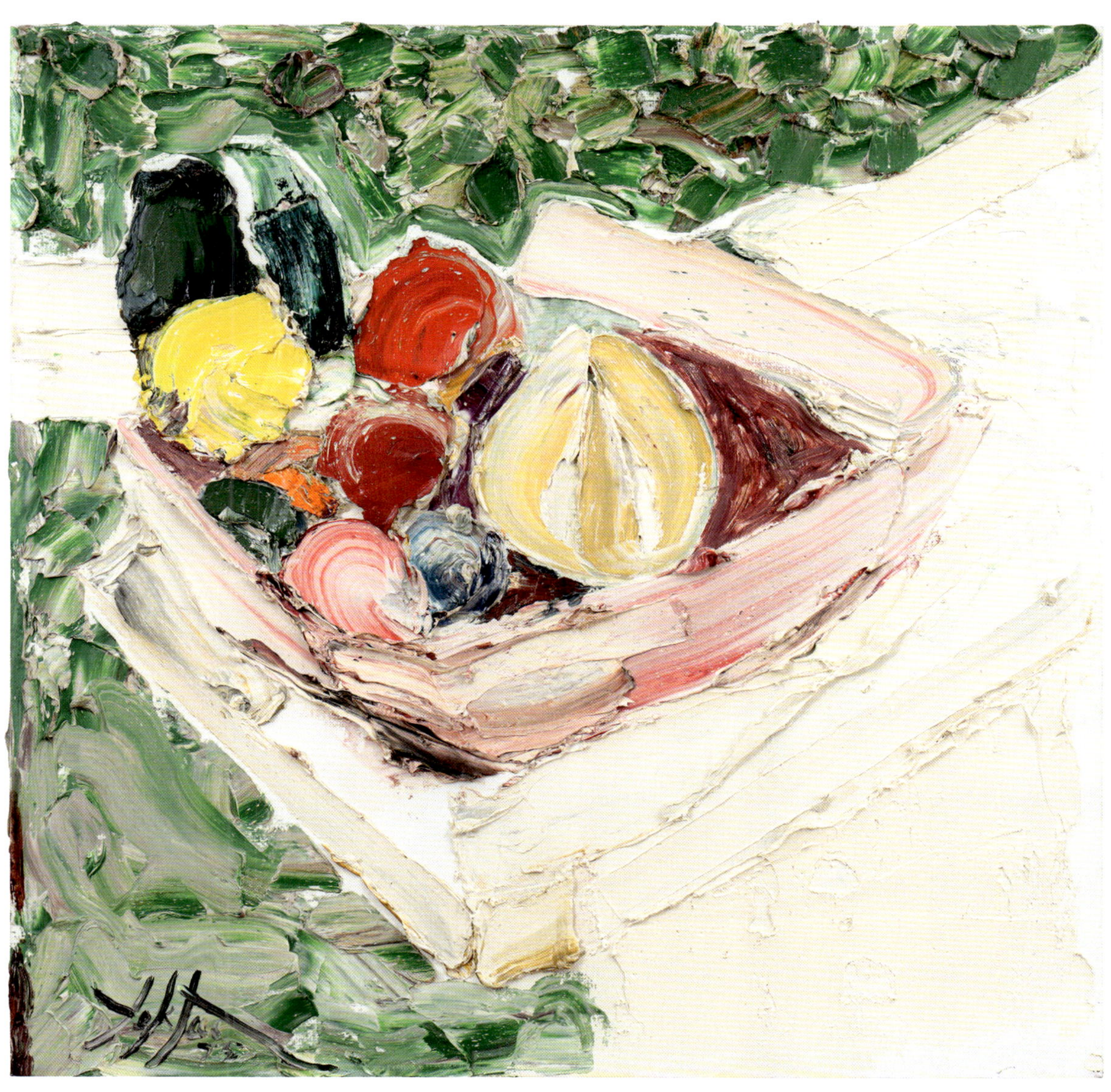

Untitled, 1975, oil on canvas, 32 × 32 inches (81.3 × 81.3 cm)

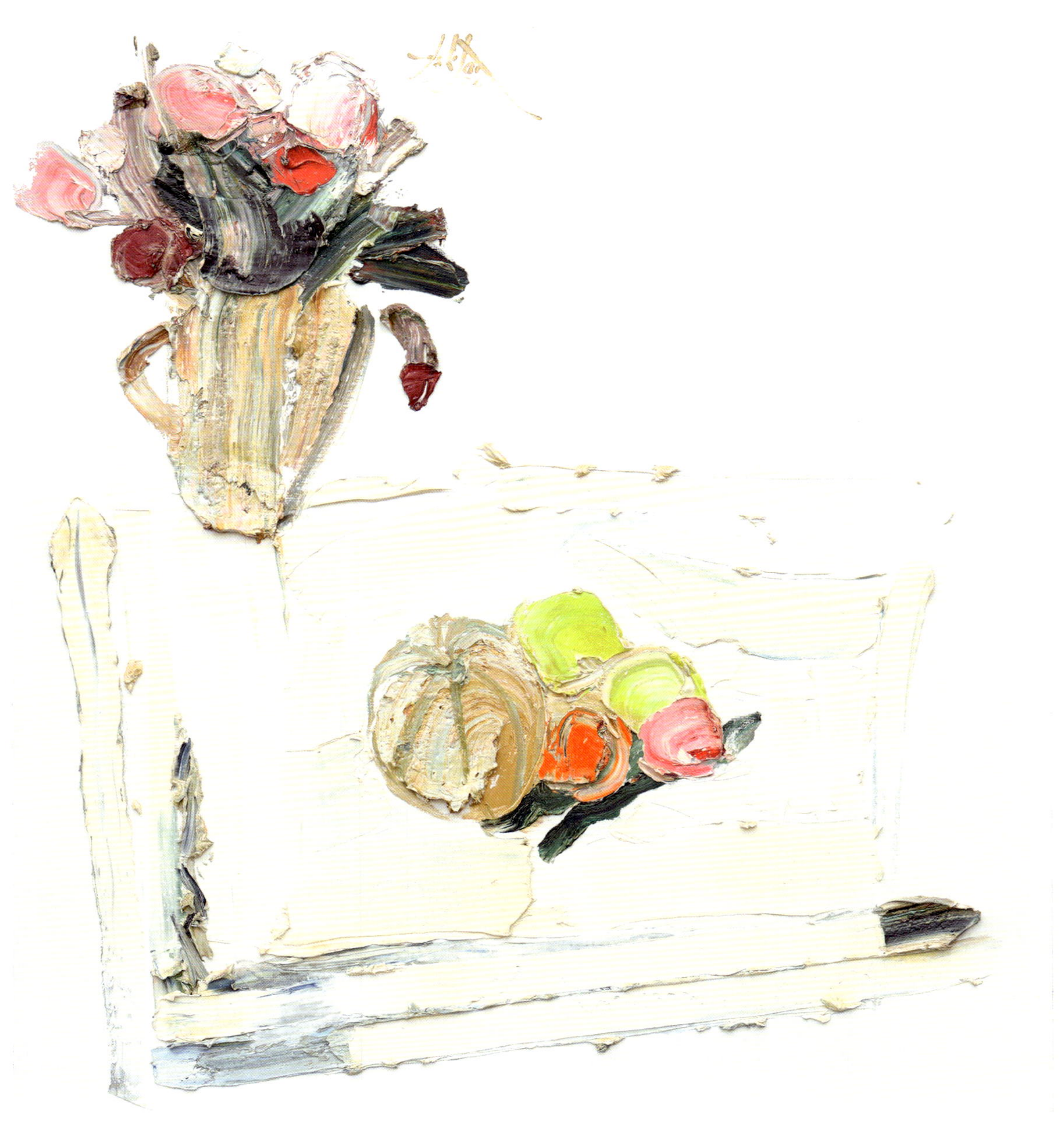

Untitled, 1976, oil on canvas, 72 × 78 inches (182.9 × 198.1 cm)

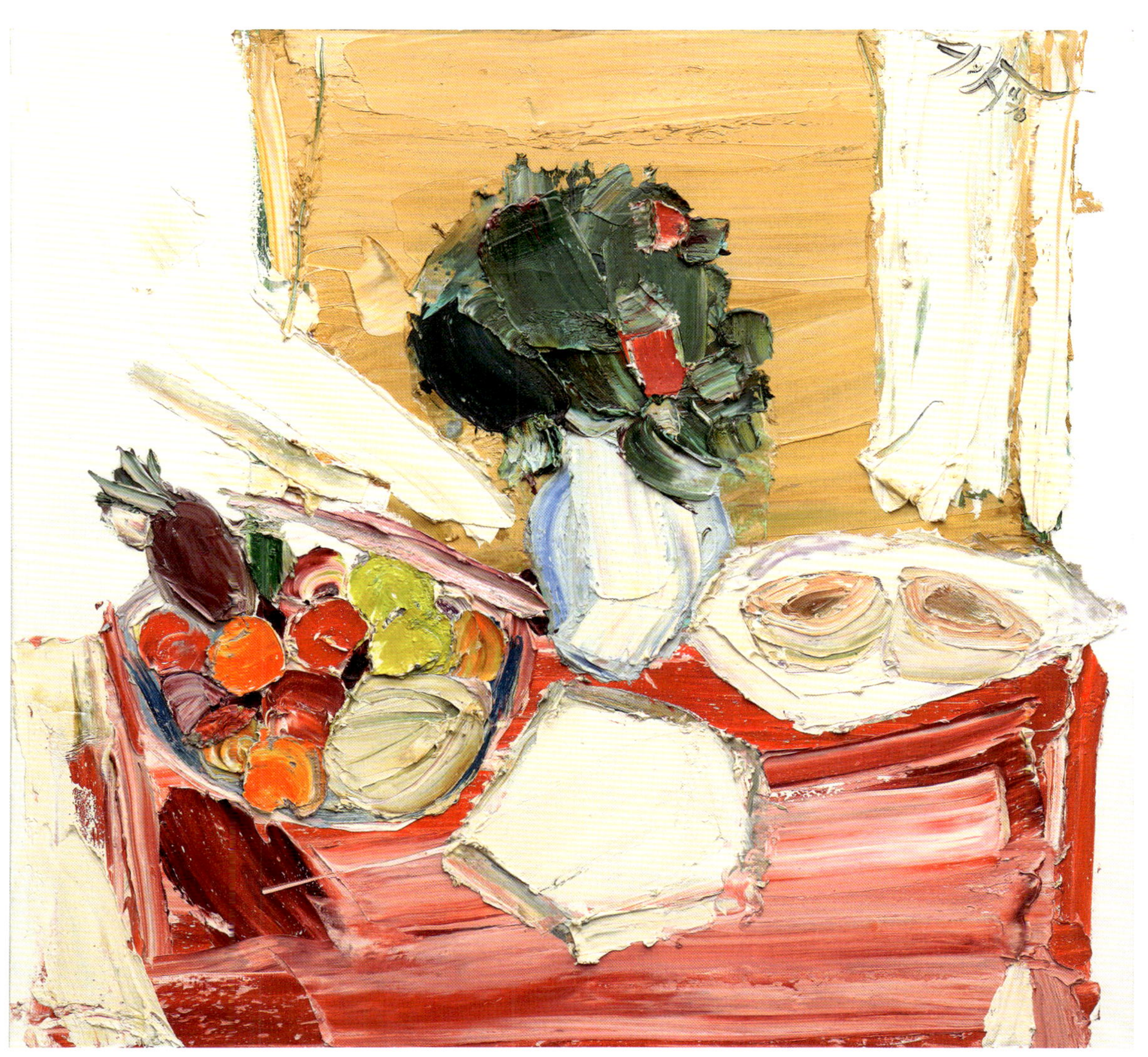

Still Life with Cantaloupe, 1976, oil on canvas, 52 × 56 inches (132 × 142 cm)

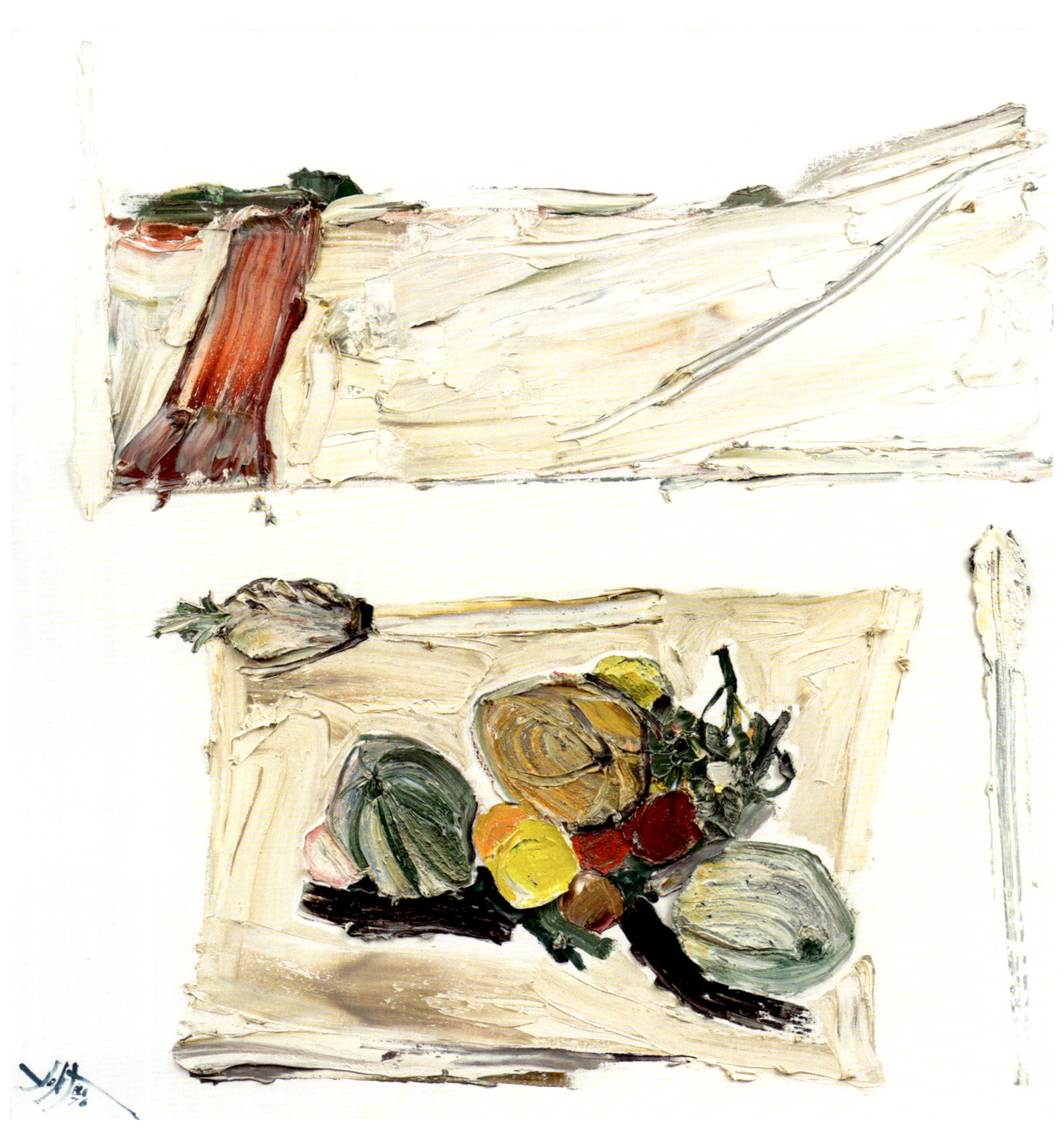

 Untitled, 1976, oil on canvas, 64 × 60 inches (162.6 × 152.4 cm)

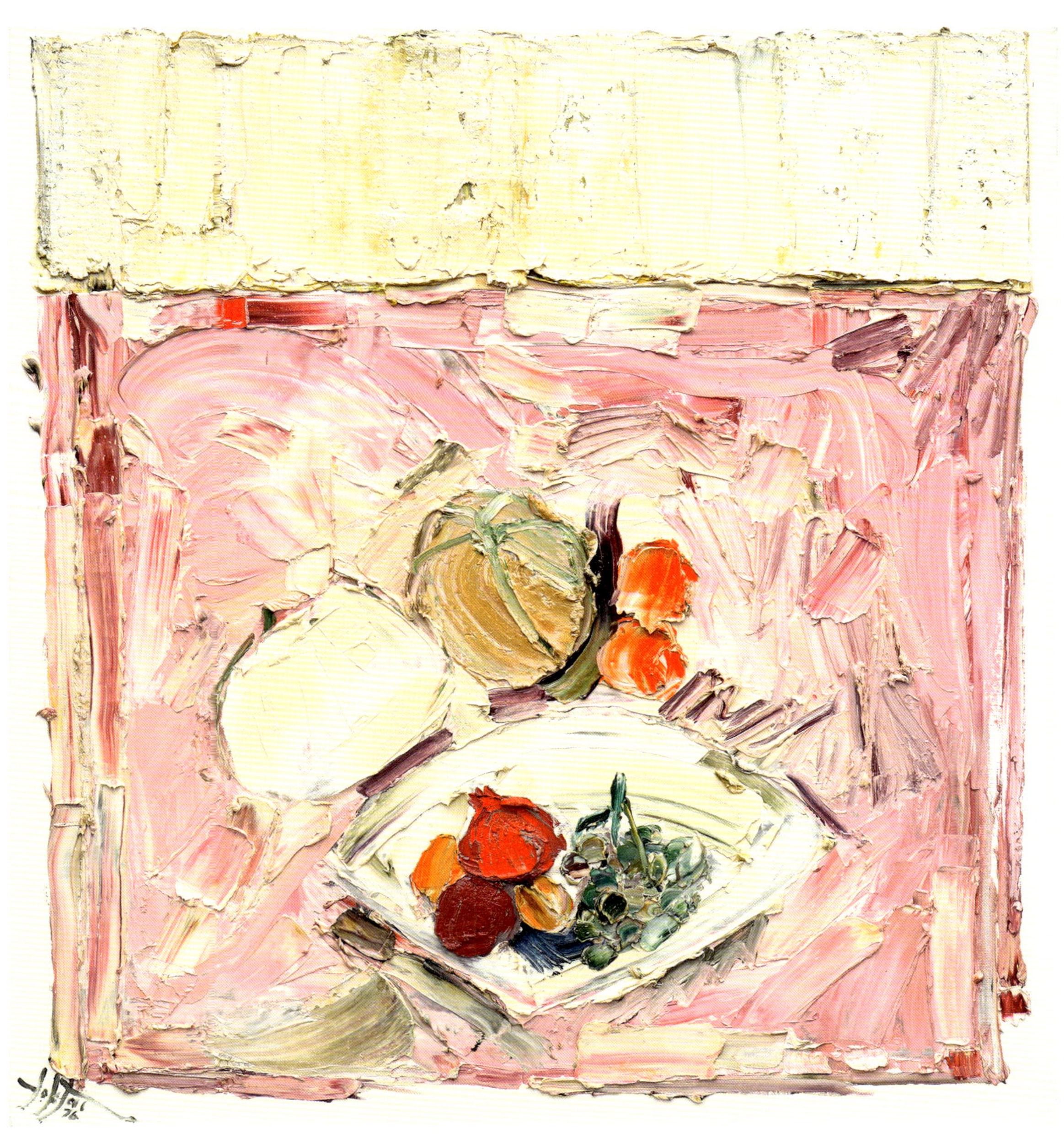

Pink Table, 1976, oil on canvas, 56 × 52 inches (142.2 × 132.1 cm)

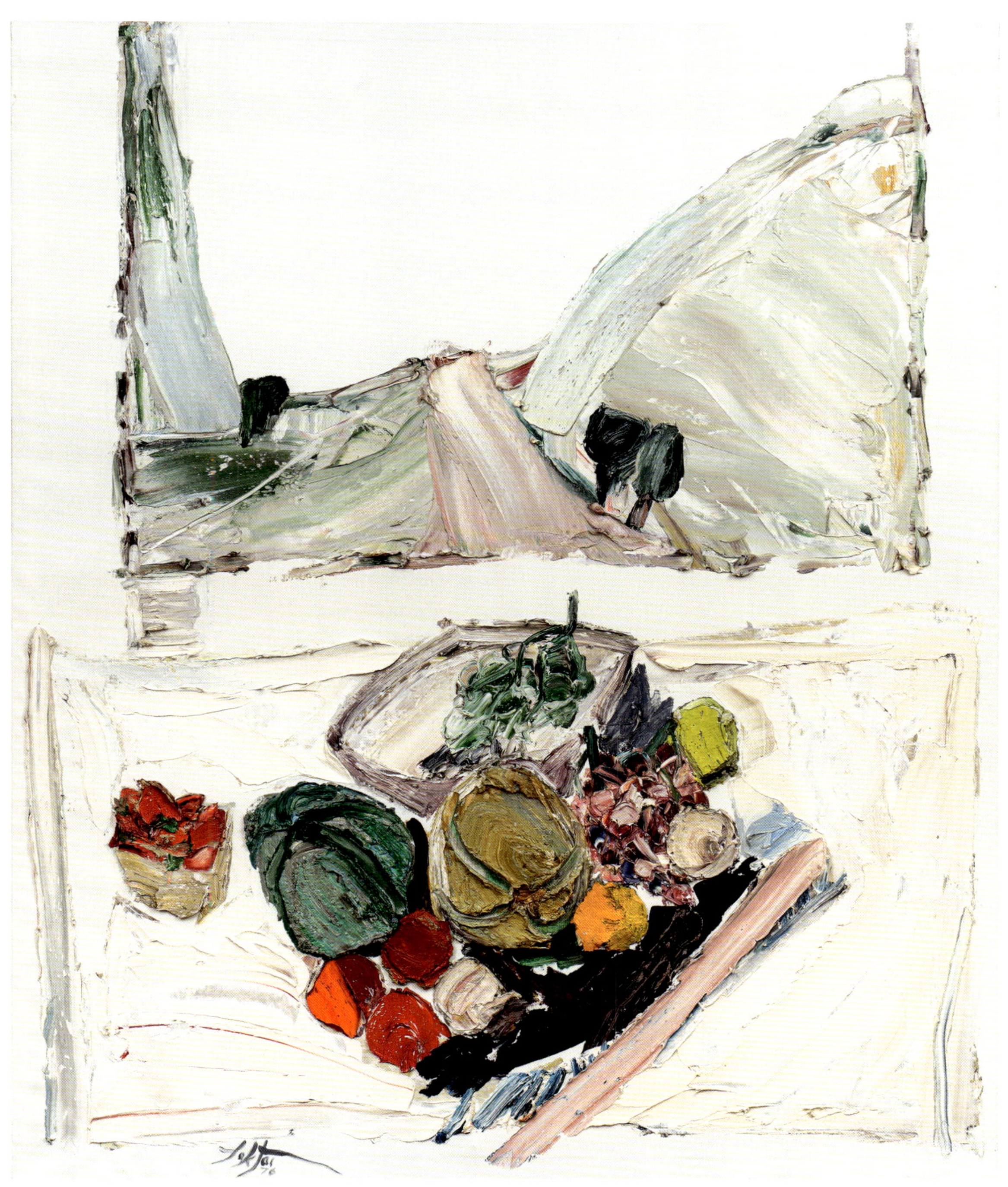

Untitled, 1976, oil on canvas, 72 × 60 inches (182.9 × 152.4 cm)

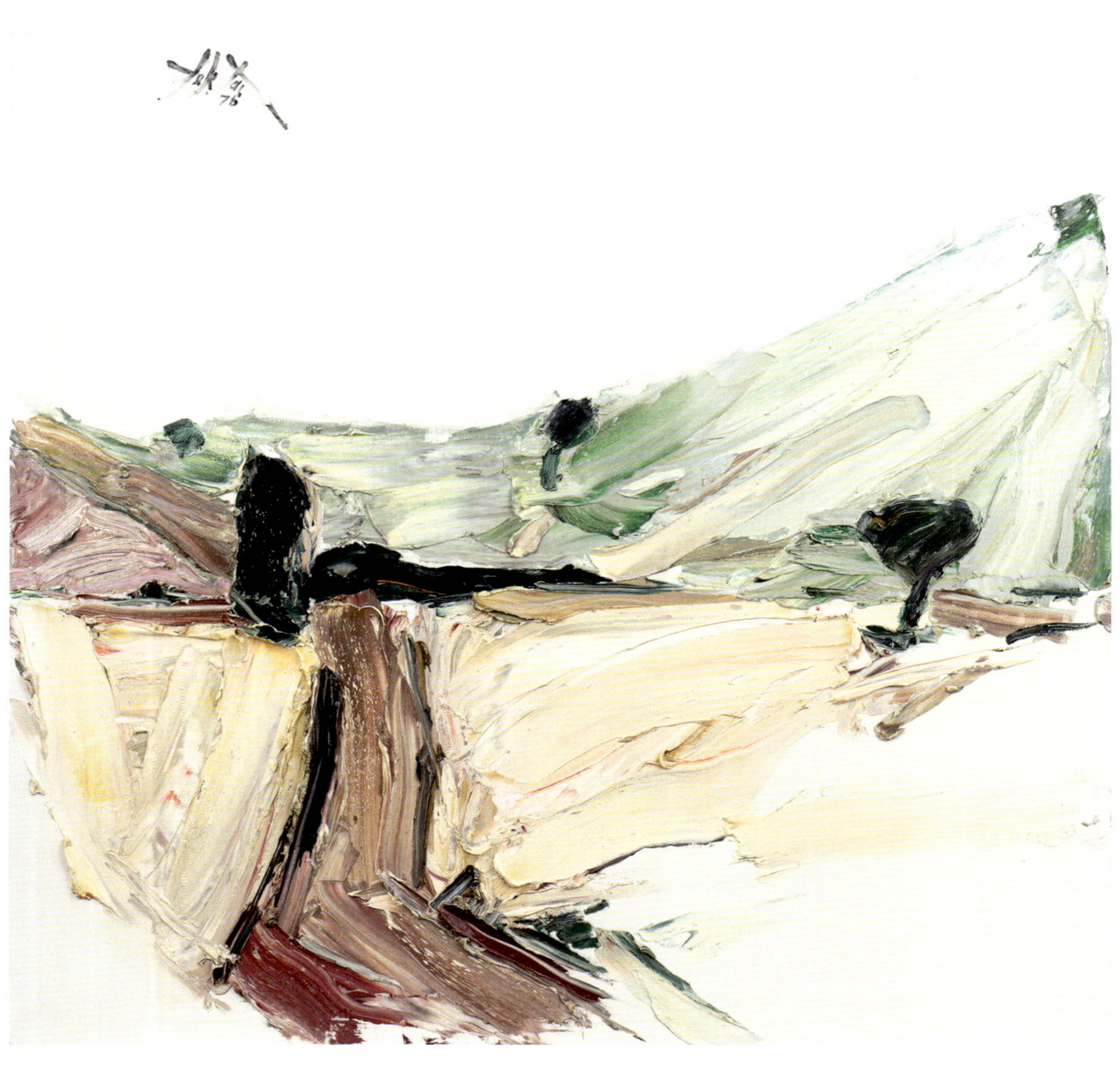

Untitled, 1976, oil on canvas, 60 × 64 inches (152.4 × 162.6 cm)

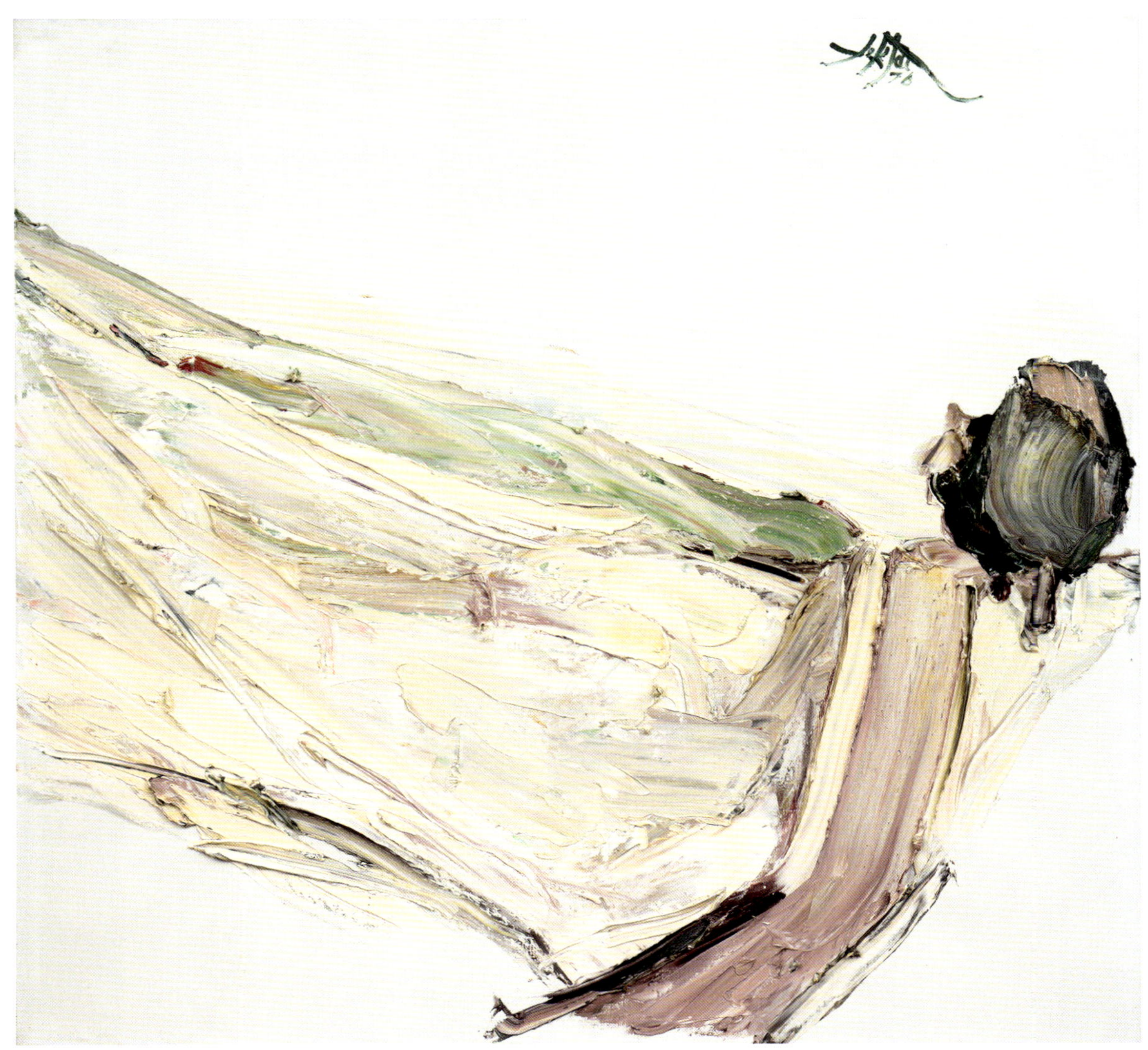

Untitled, 1976, oil on canvas, 60 × 64 inches (152.4 × 162.6 cm)

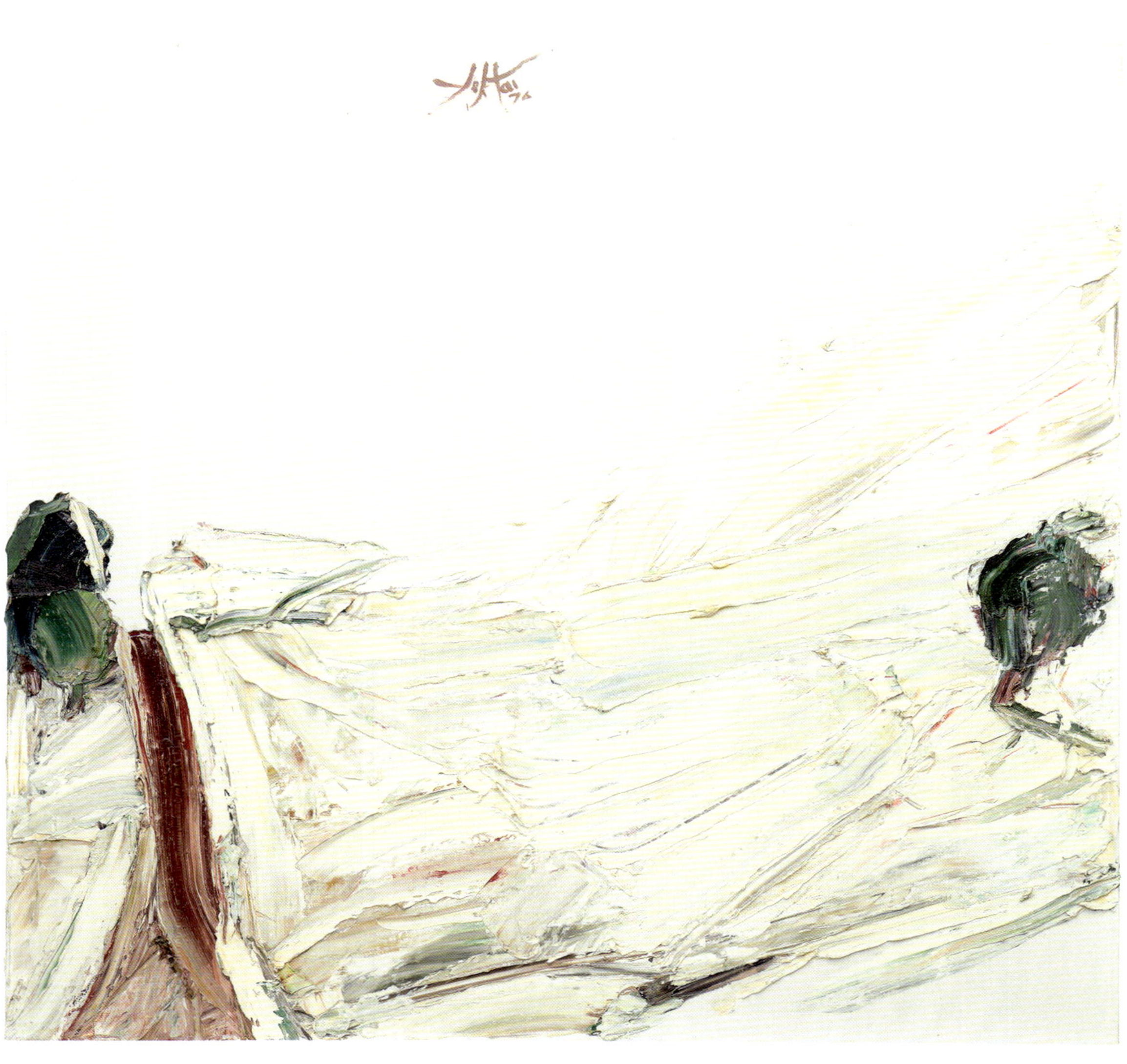

 Untitled, 1976, oil on canvas, 72 × 78 inches (182.9 × 198.1 cm)

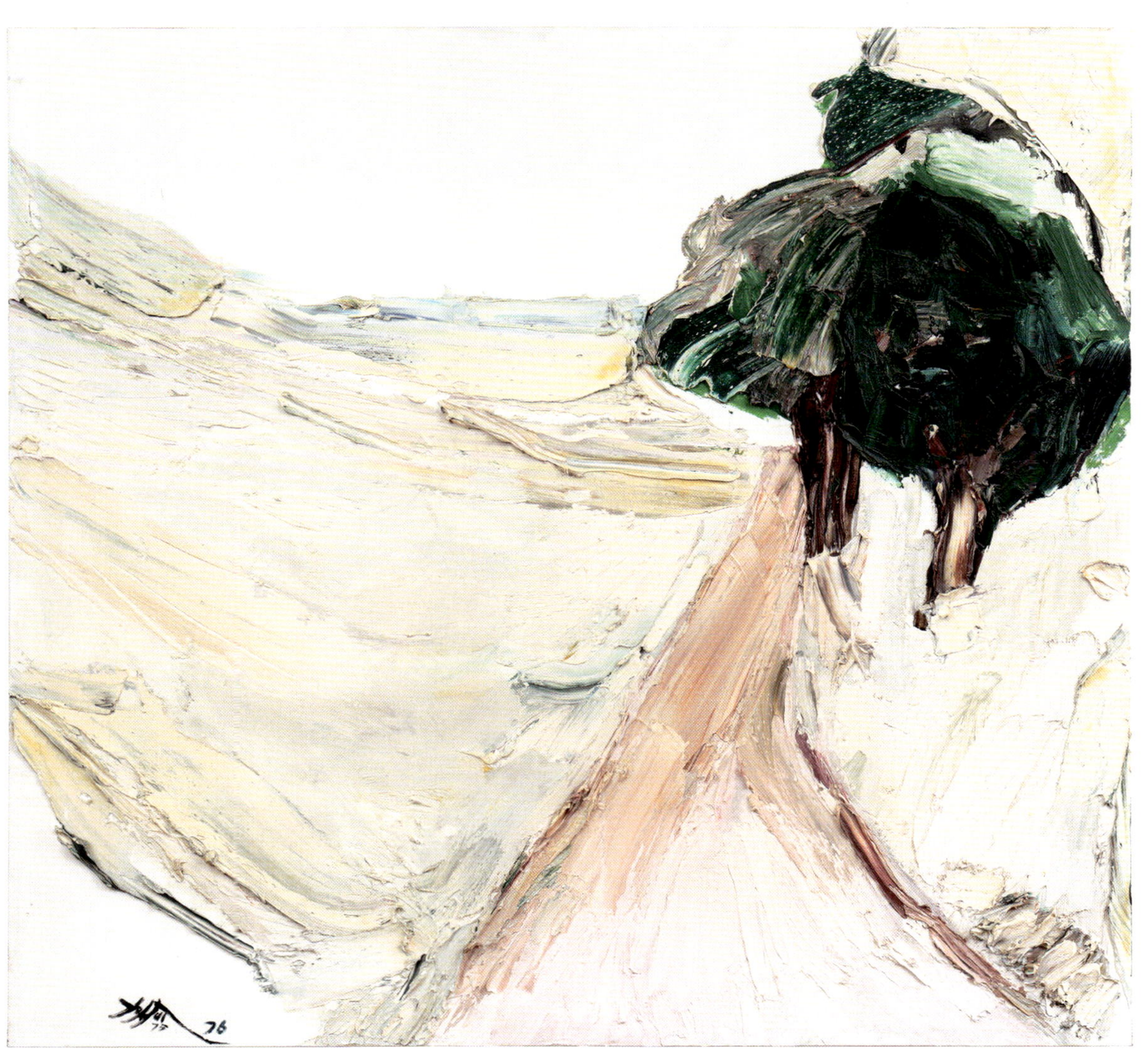

Untitled, 1976, oil on canvas, 52 × 56 inches (132.1 × 142.2 cm)

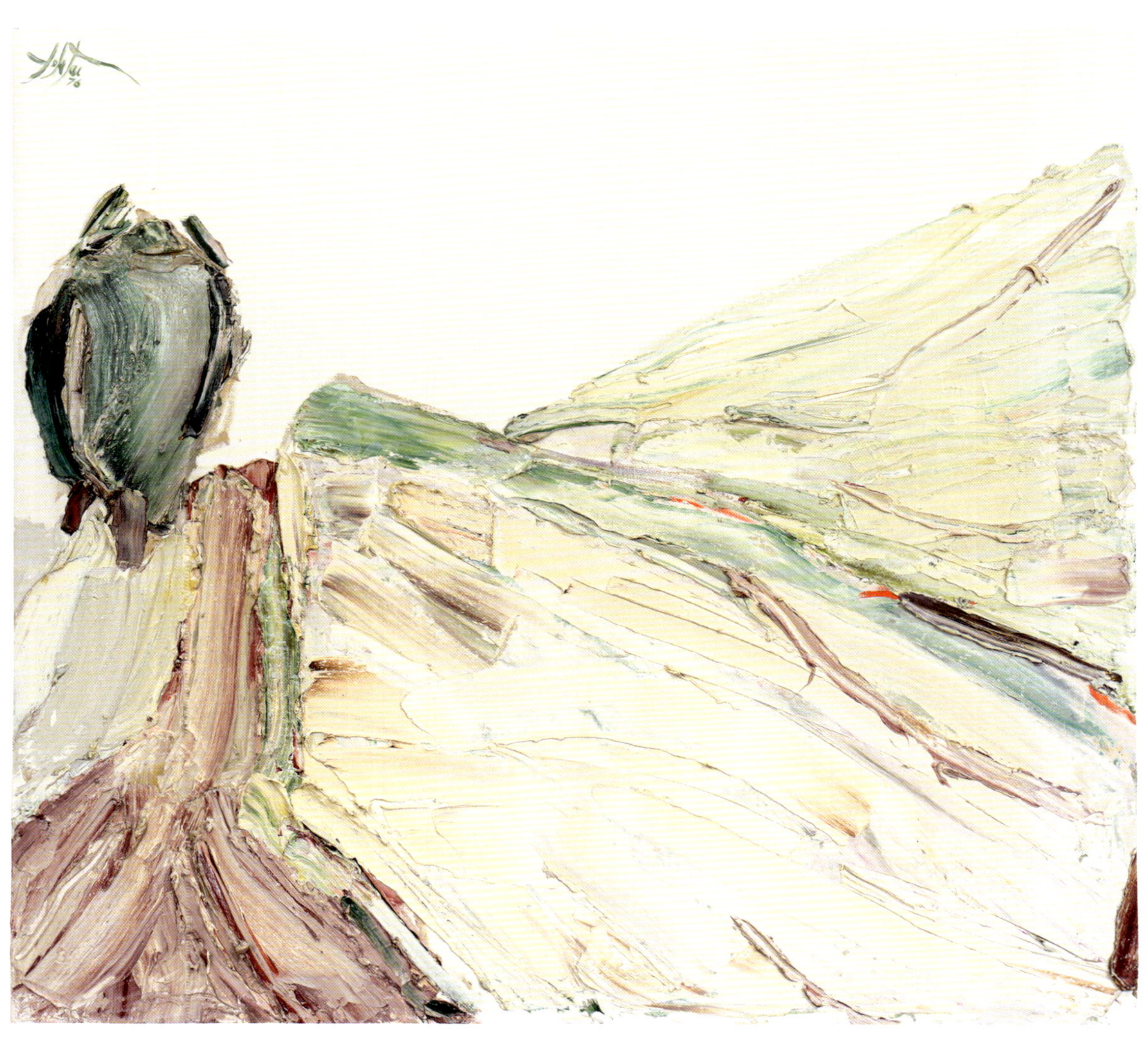

Untitled, 1976, oil on canvas, 60 × 66 inches (152.4 × 167.6 cm)

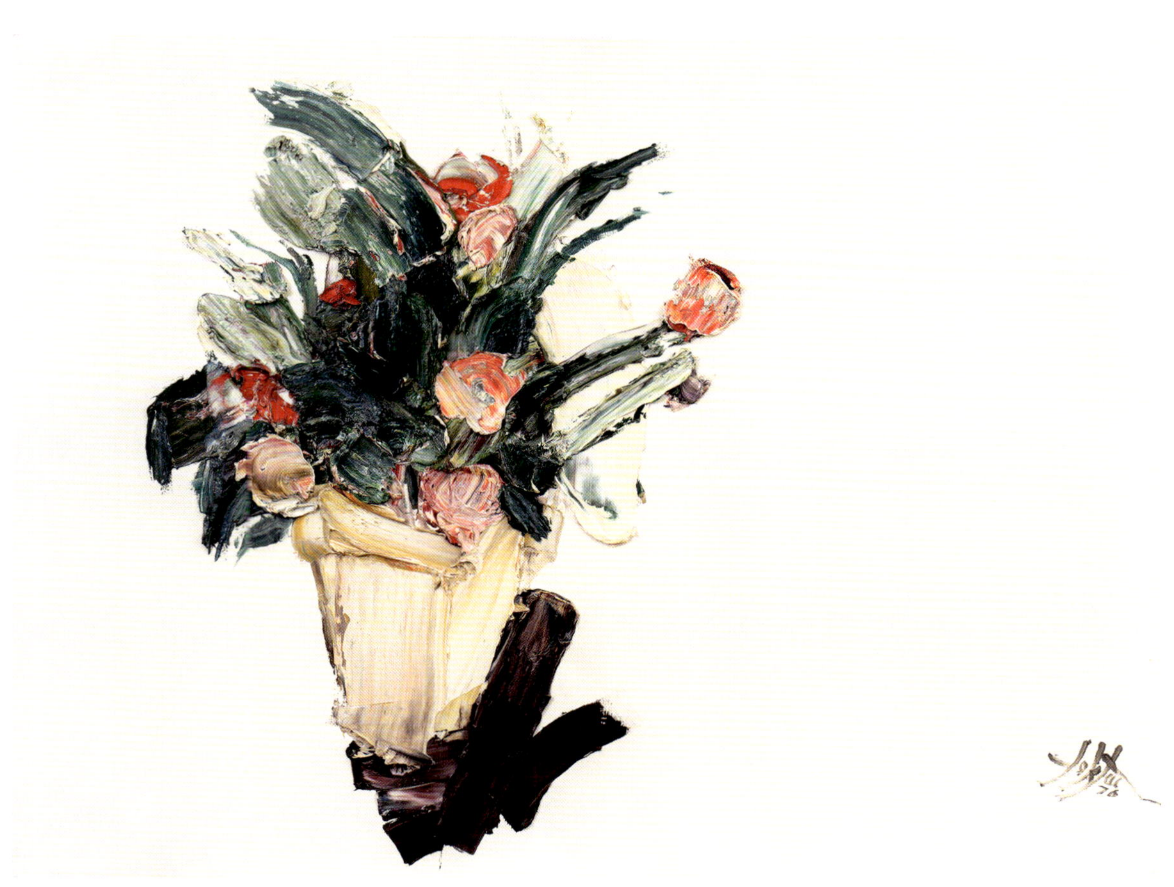

Untitled, 1976, oil on canvas, 38 × 50 inches (96.5 × 127 cm)

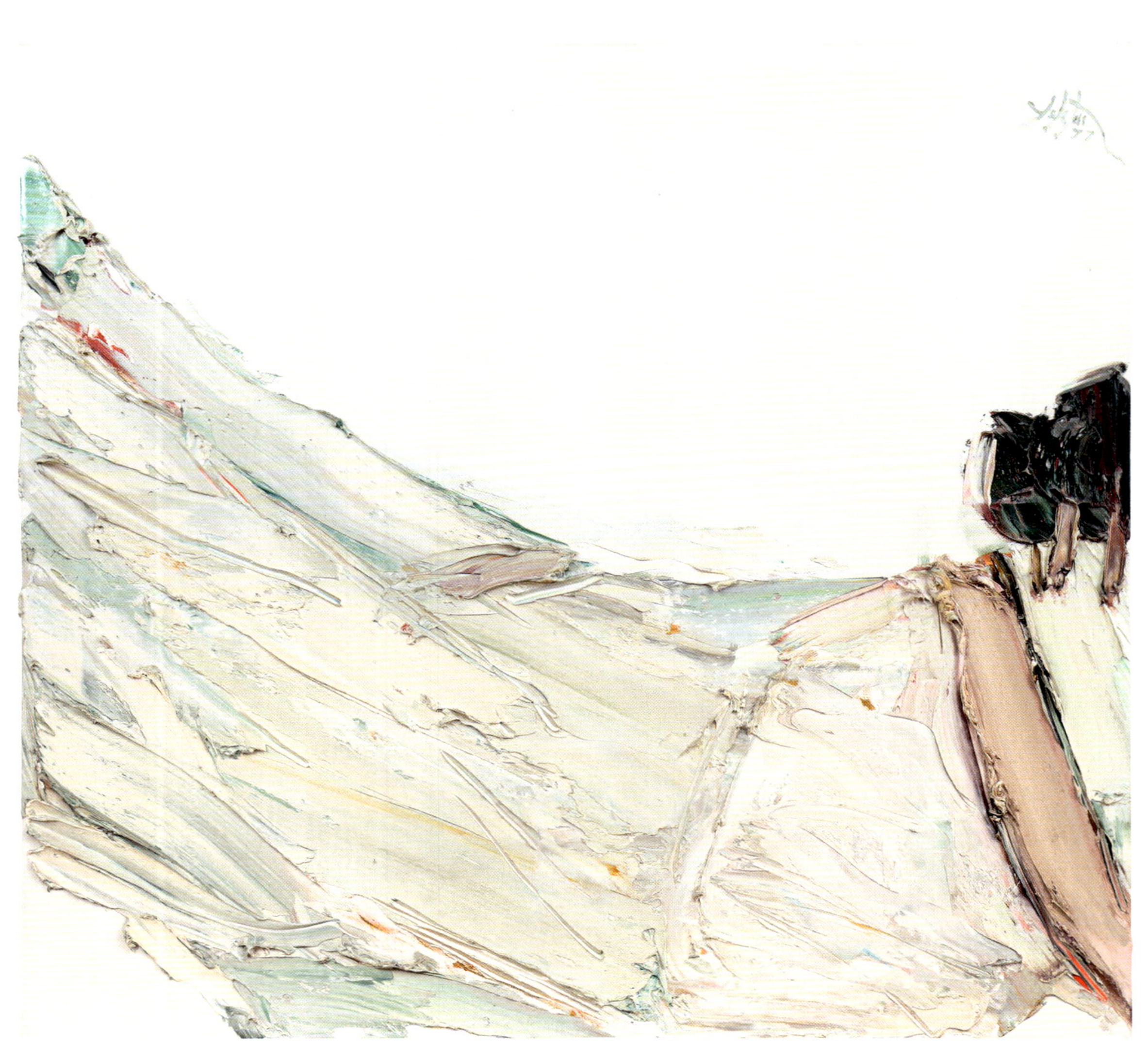

 Untitled, 1977, oil on canvas, 48 × 52 inches (121.9 × 132.1 cm)

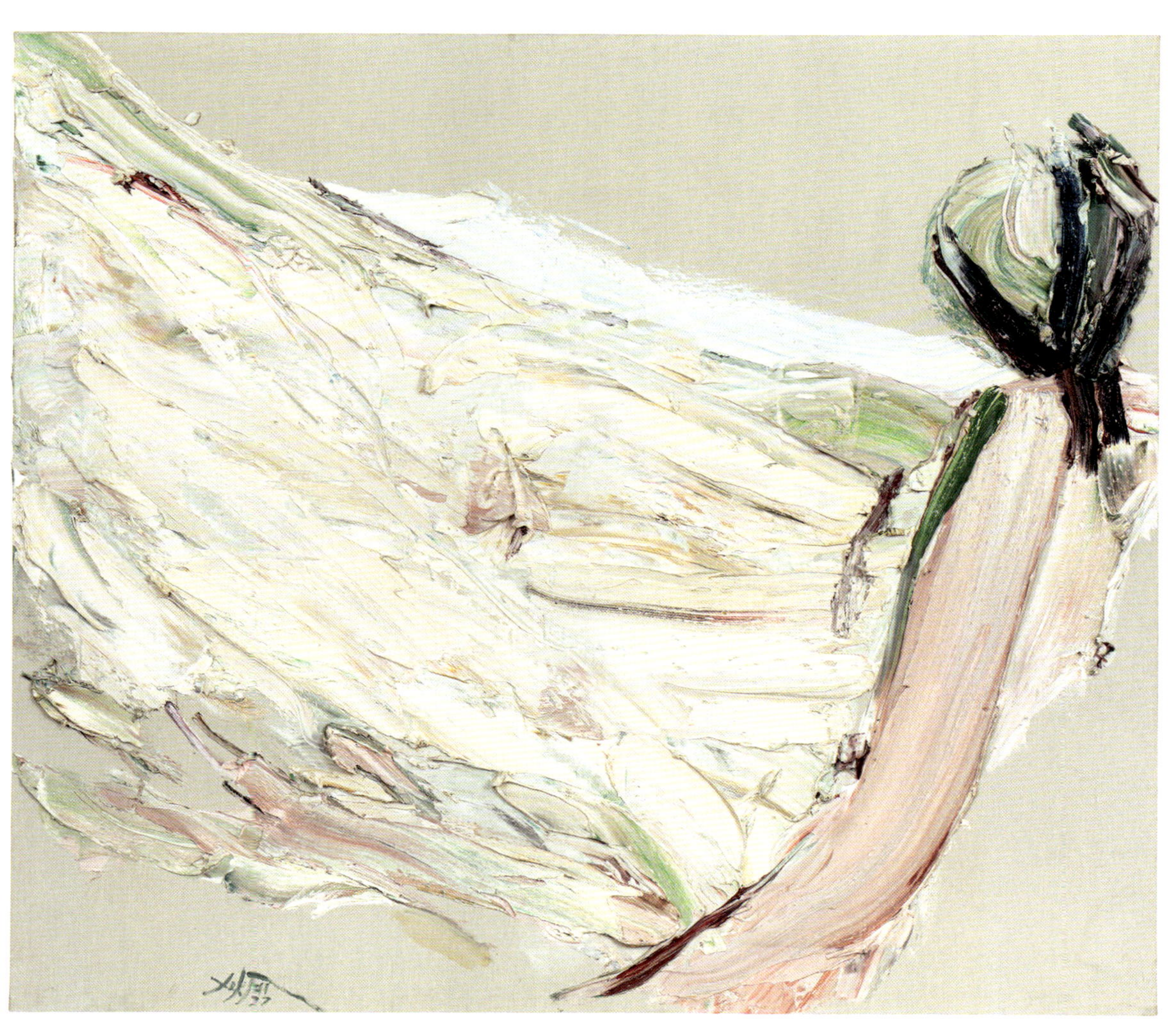

Untitled, 1977, oil on canvas, 42 × 48 inches (106.7 × 121.9 cm)

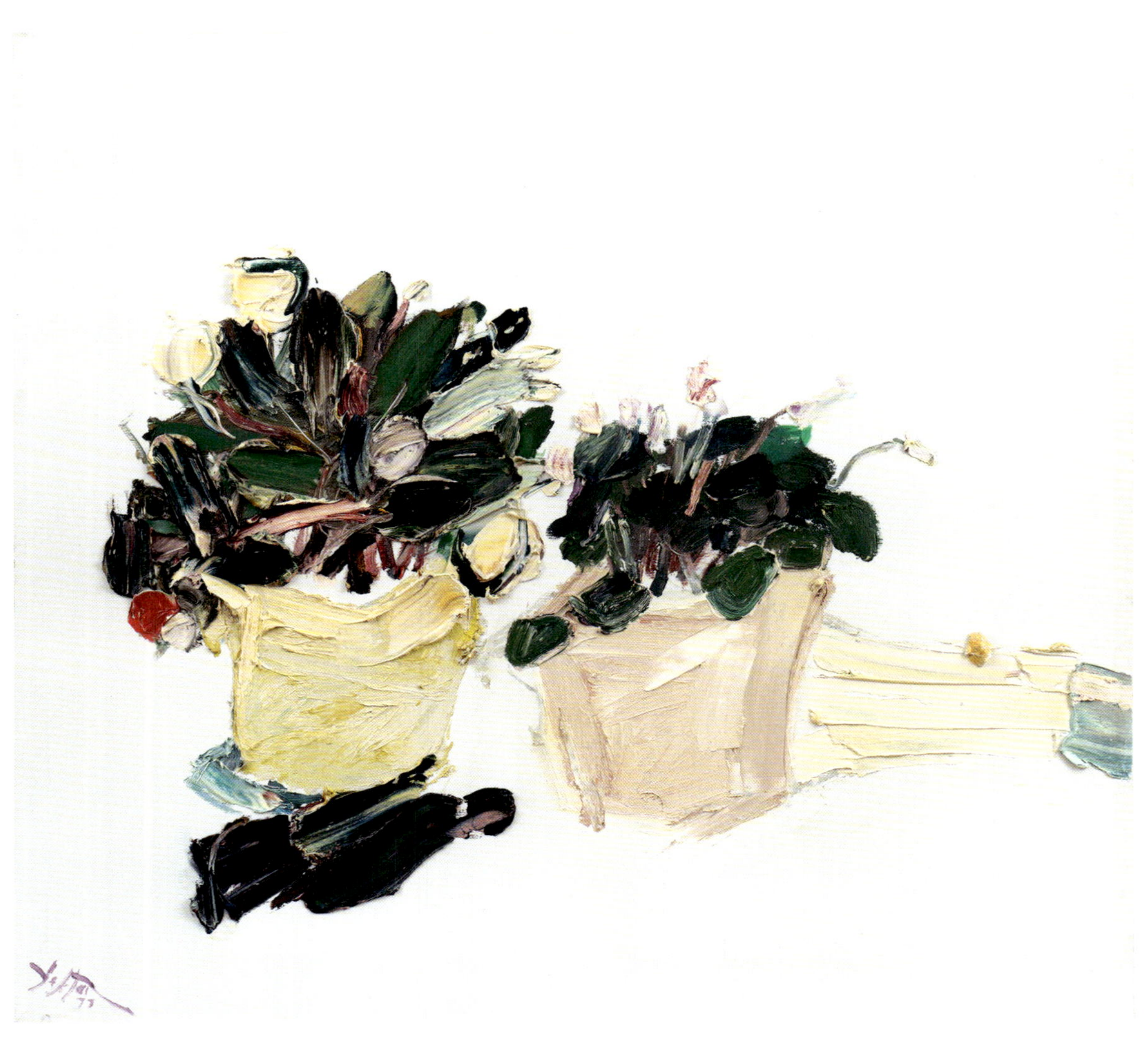

Untitled, 1977, oil on canvas, 48 × 52 inches (121.9 × 132.1 cm)

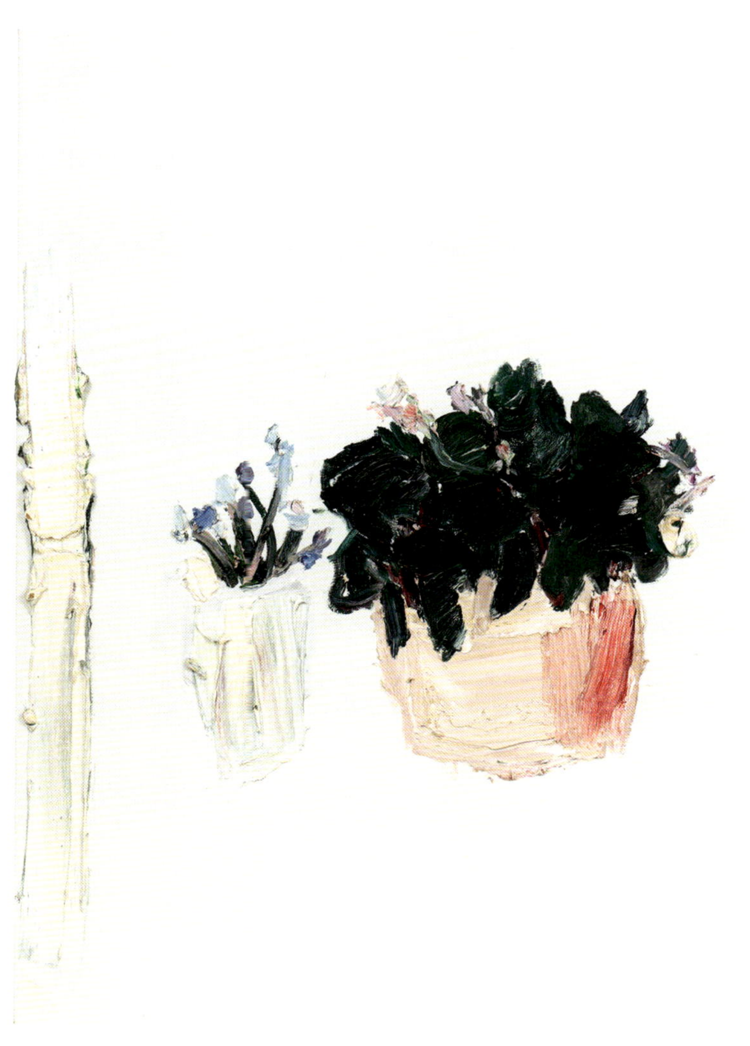

Untitled, 1977, oil on canvas, 48 × 54 inches (121.9 × 137.2 cm)

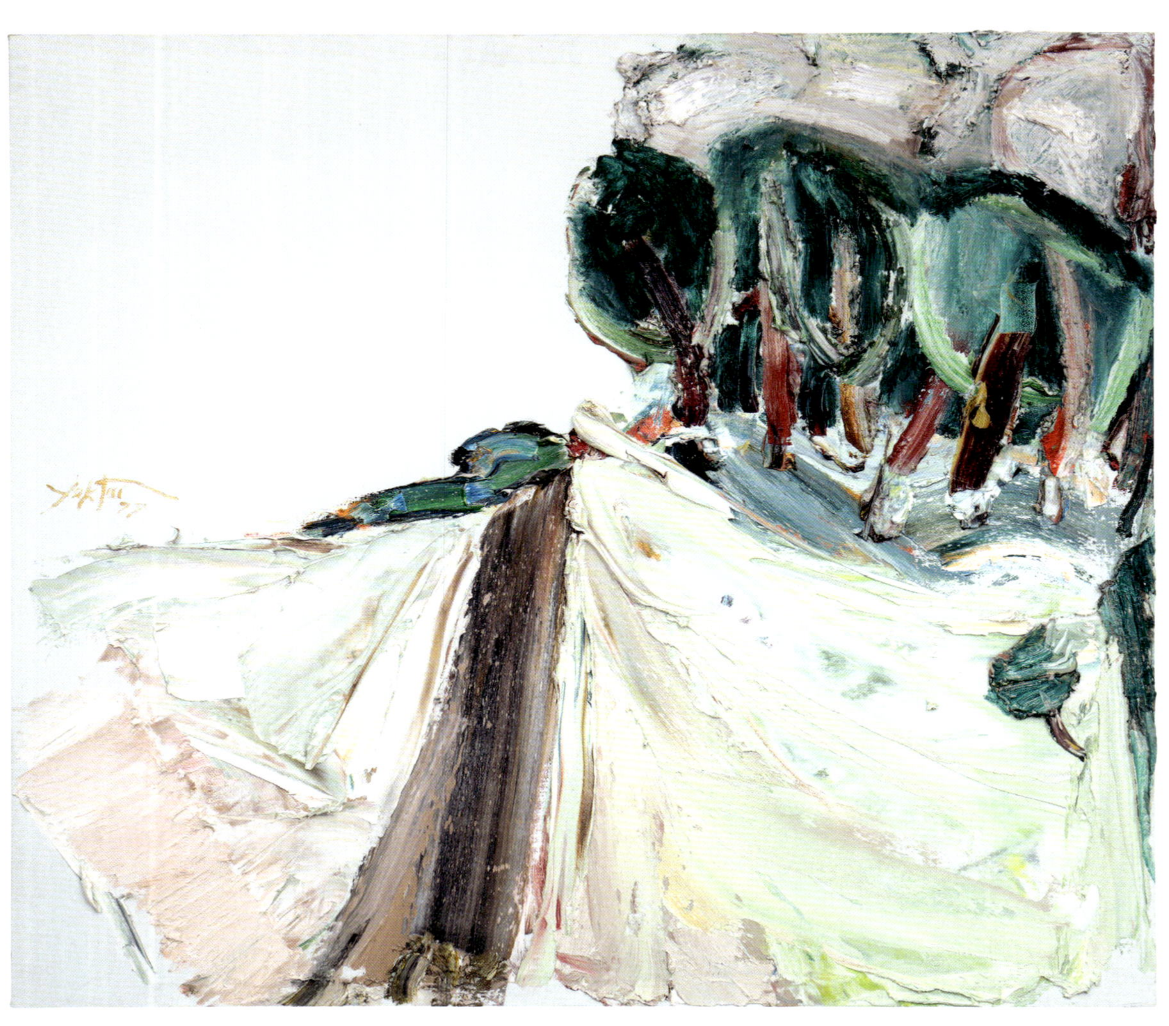

 Untitled, 1977, oil on canvas, 42 × 48 inches (106.7 × 121.9 cm)

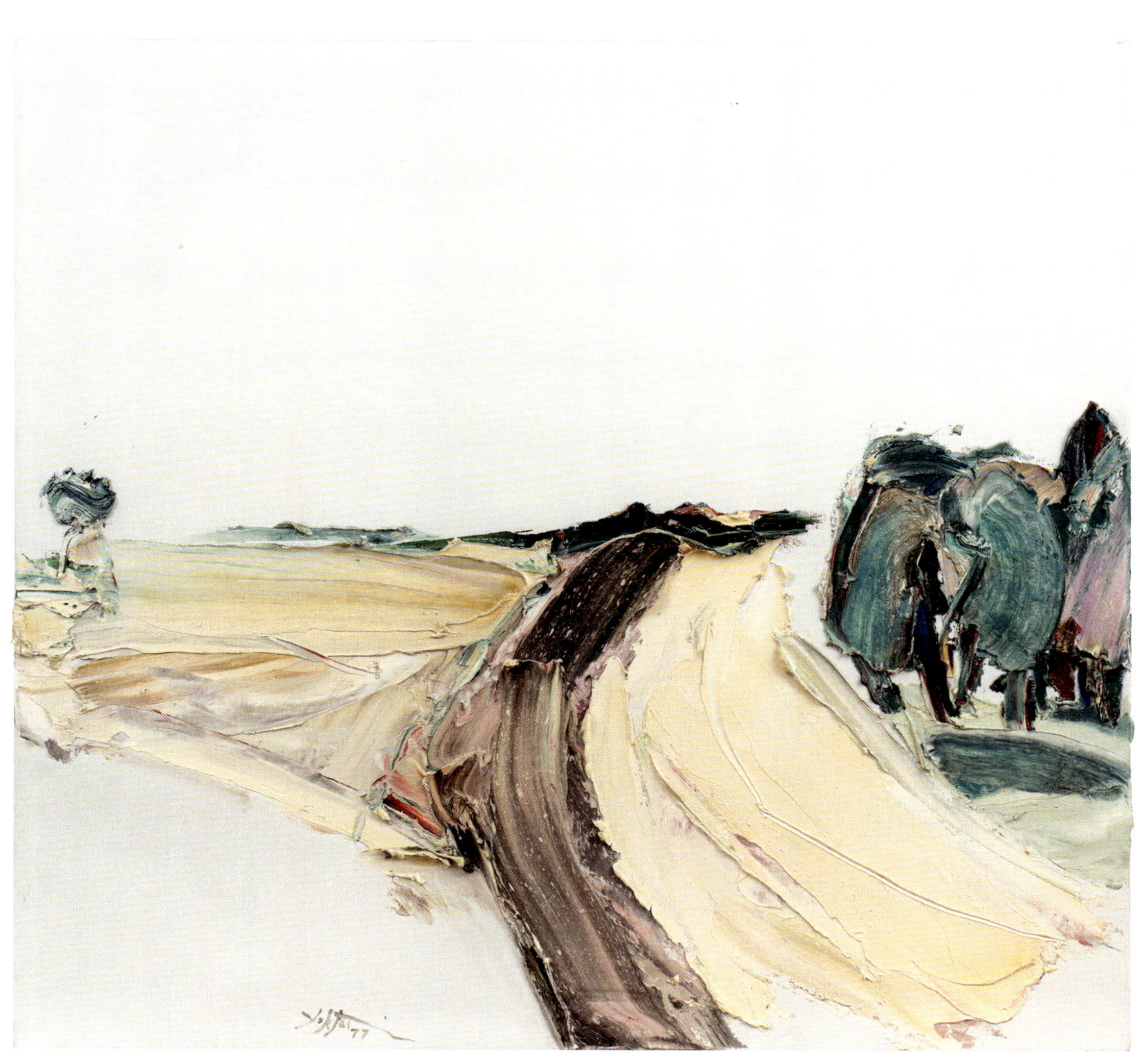

Corner of Forest, 1977, oil on canvas, 52 × 56 inches (132.1 × 142.2 cm)

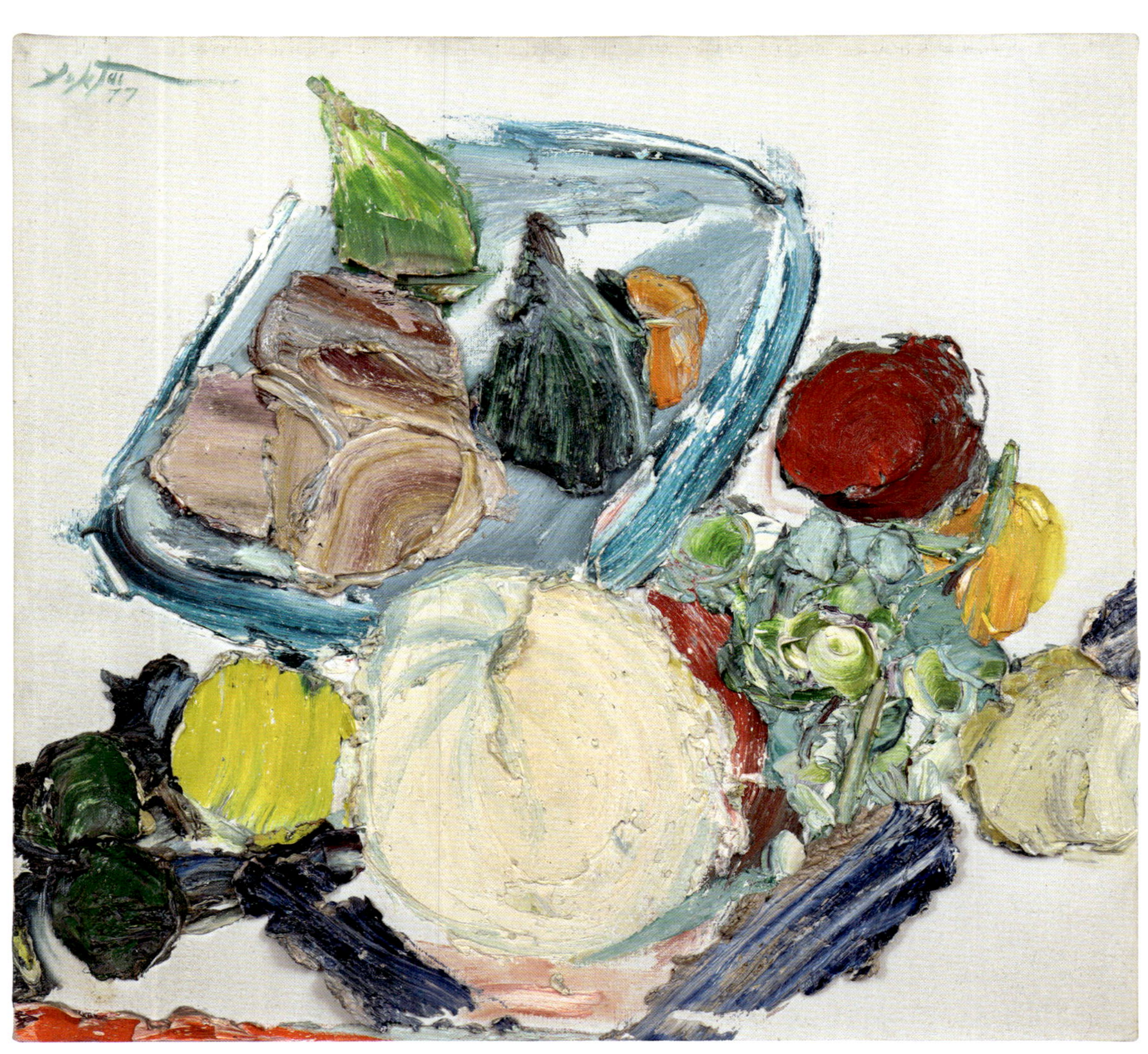

Untitled, 1977, oil on canvas, 24 × 26 inches (61 × 66 cm)

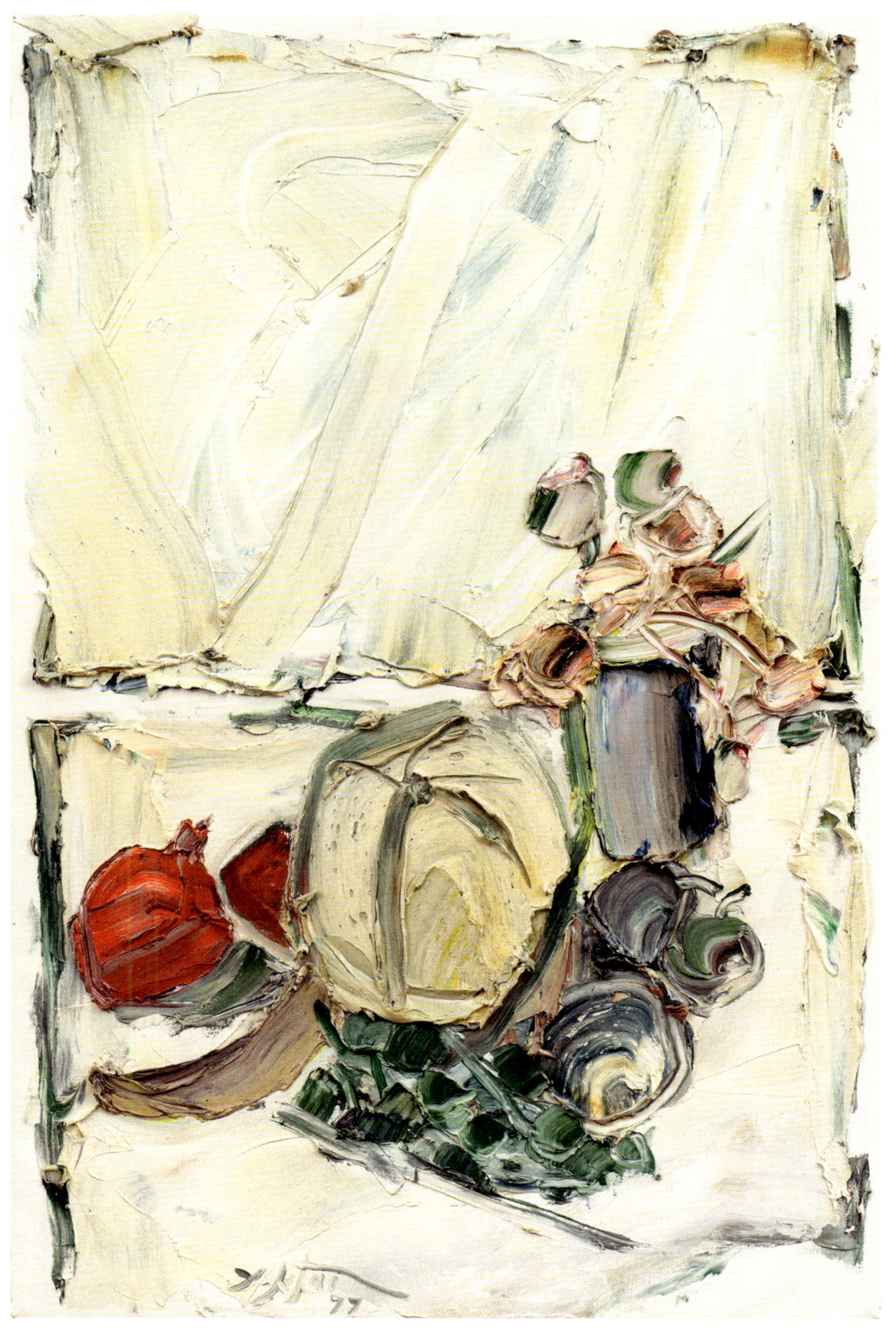

Untitled, 1977, oil on canvas, 40 × 26 inches (101.6 × 66 cm)

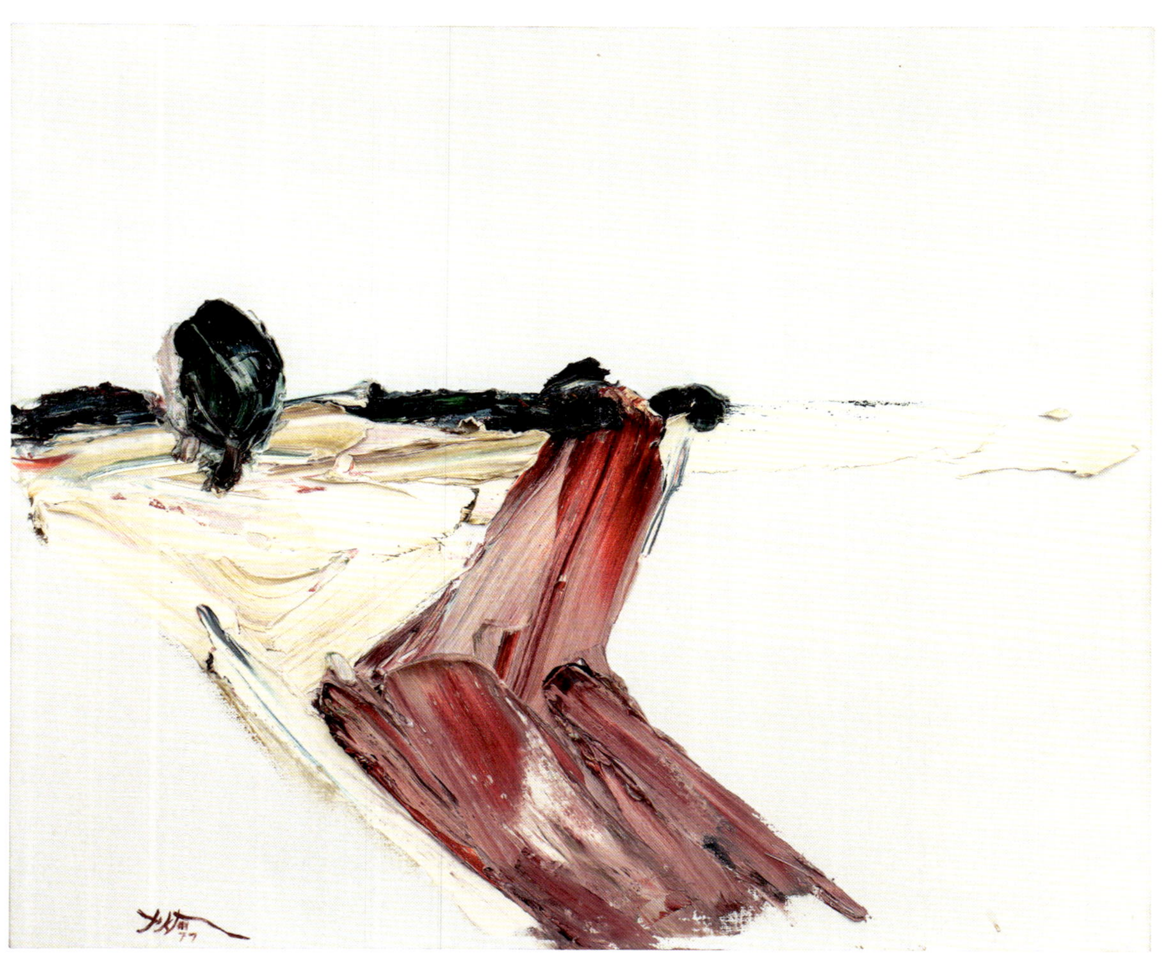

Untitled, 1977, oil on canvas, 46 × 50 inches (115.8 × 127 cm)

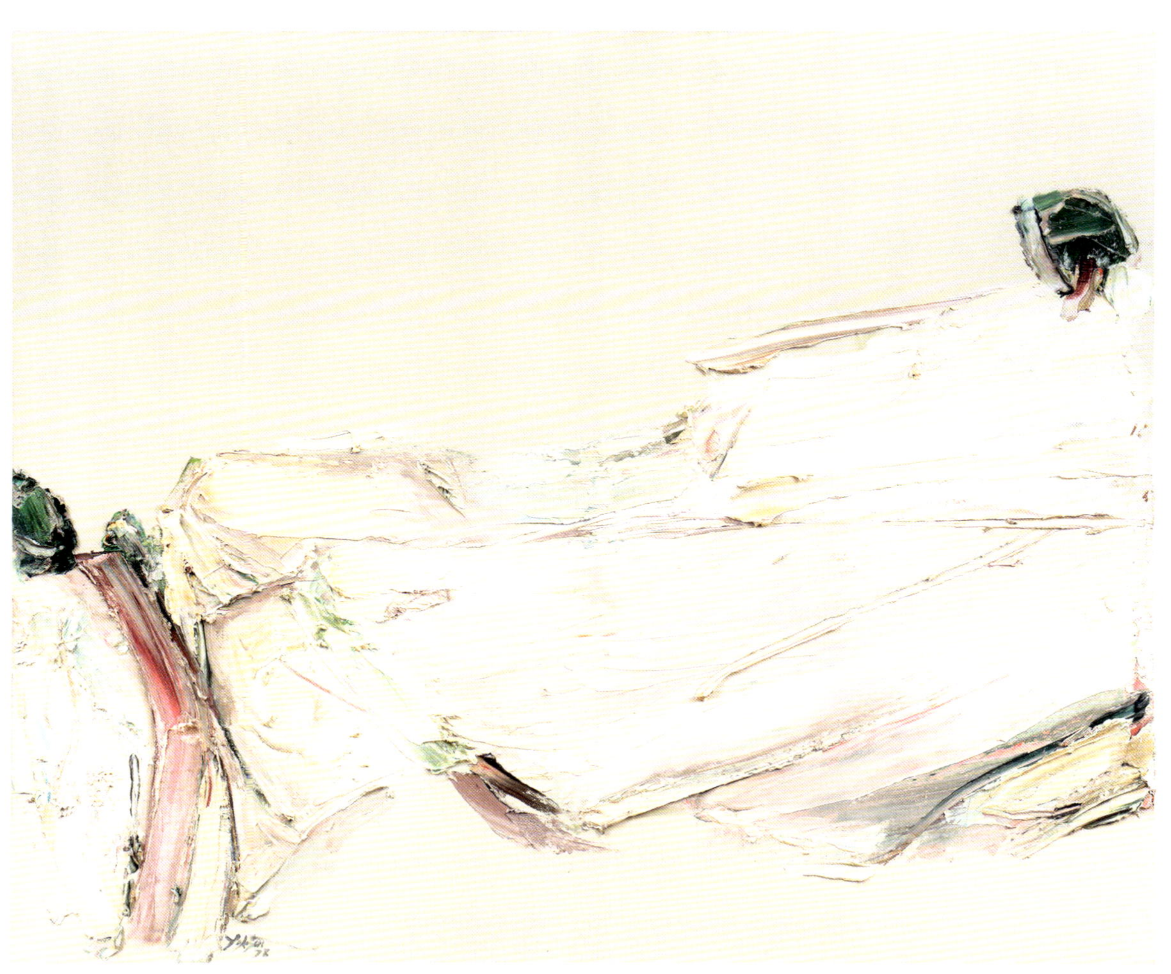

Road Landscape, 1978, oil on canvas, 60 × 72 inches (152.4 × 182.9 cm)

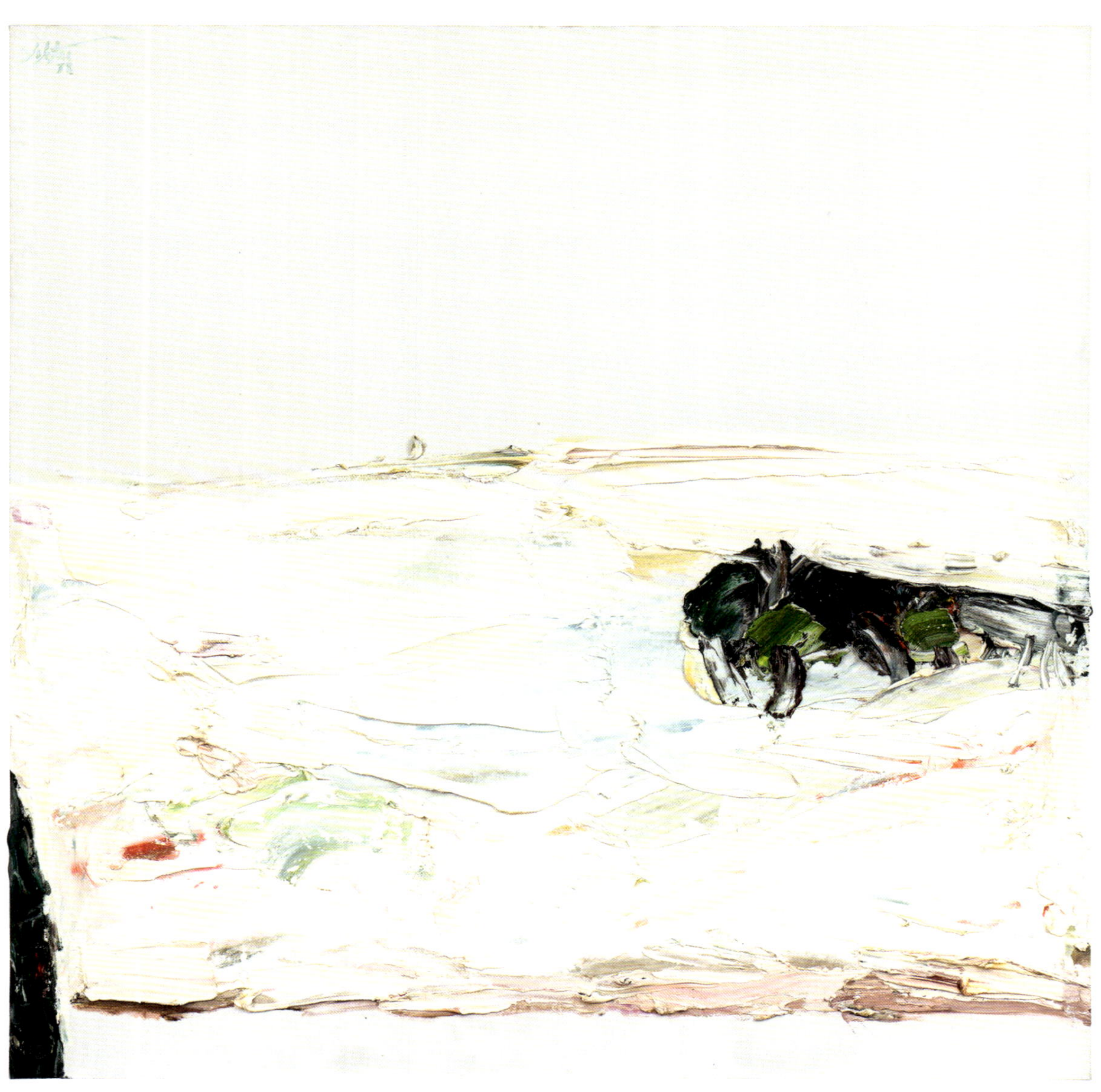

 Untitled, 1978, oil on canvas, 60 × 60 inches (152.4 × 152.4 cm)

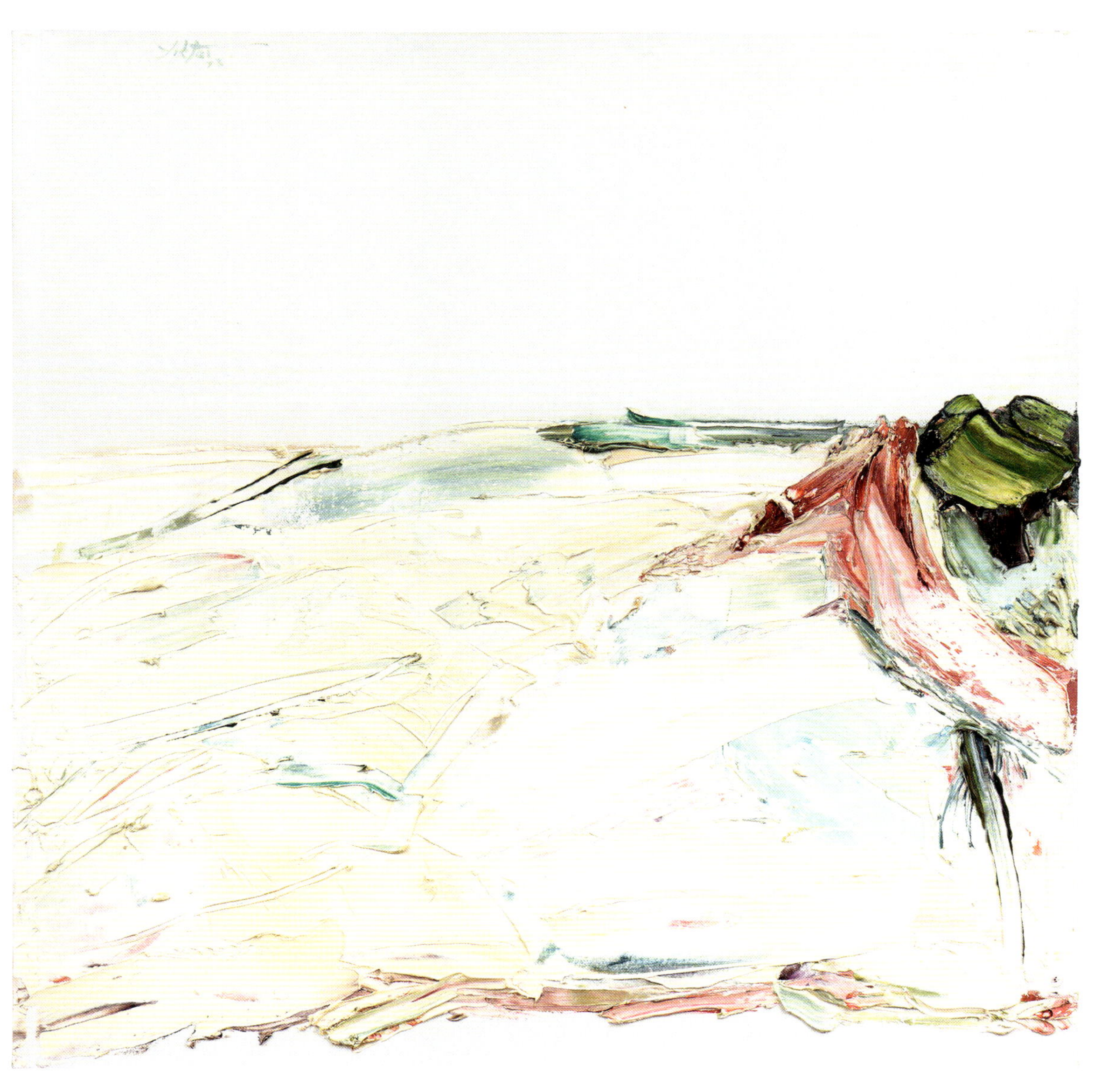

Ur titled, 1978, oil on canvas, 60 × 60 inches (152.4 × 152.4 cm)

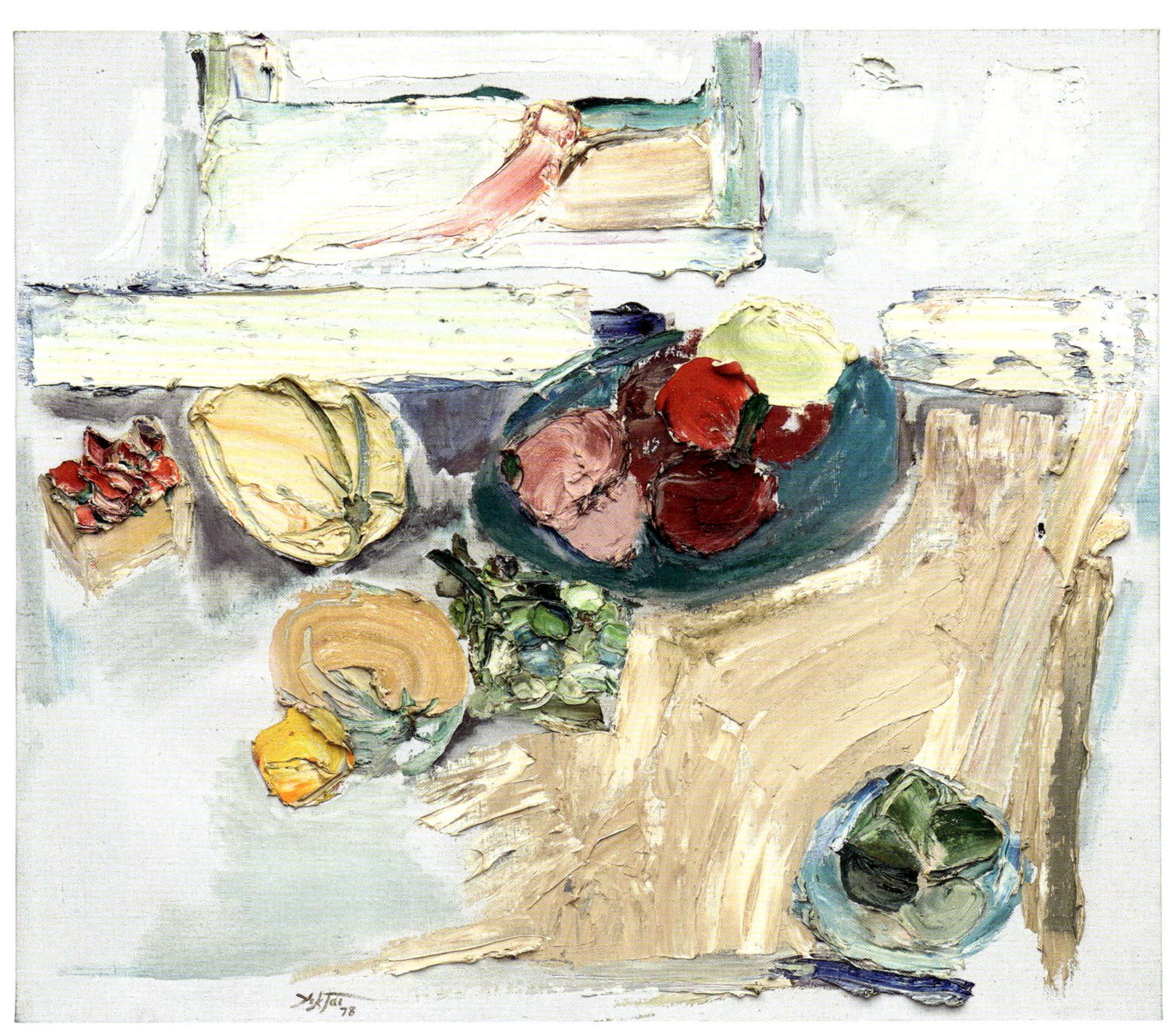

Untitled, 1978, oil on canvas, 48 × 54 inches (121.9 × 137.2 cm)

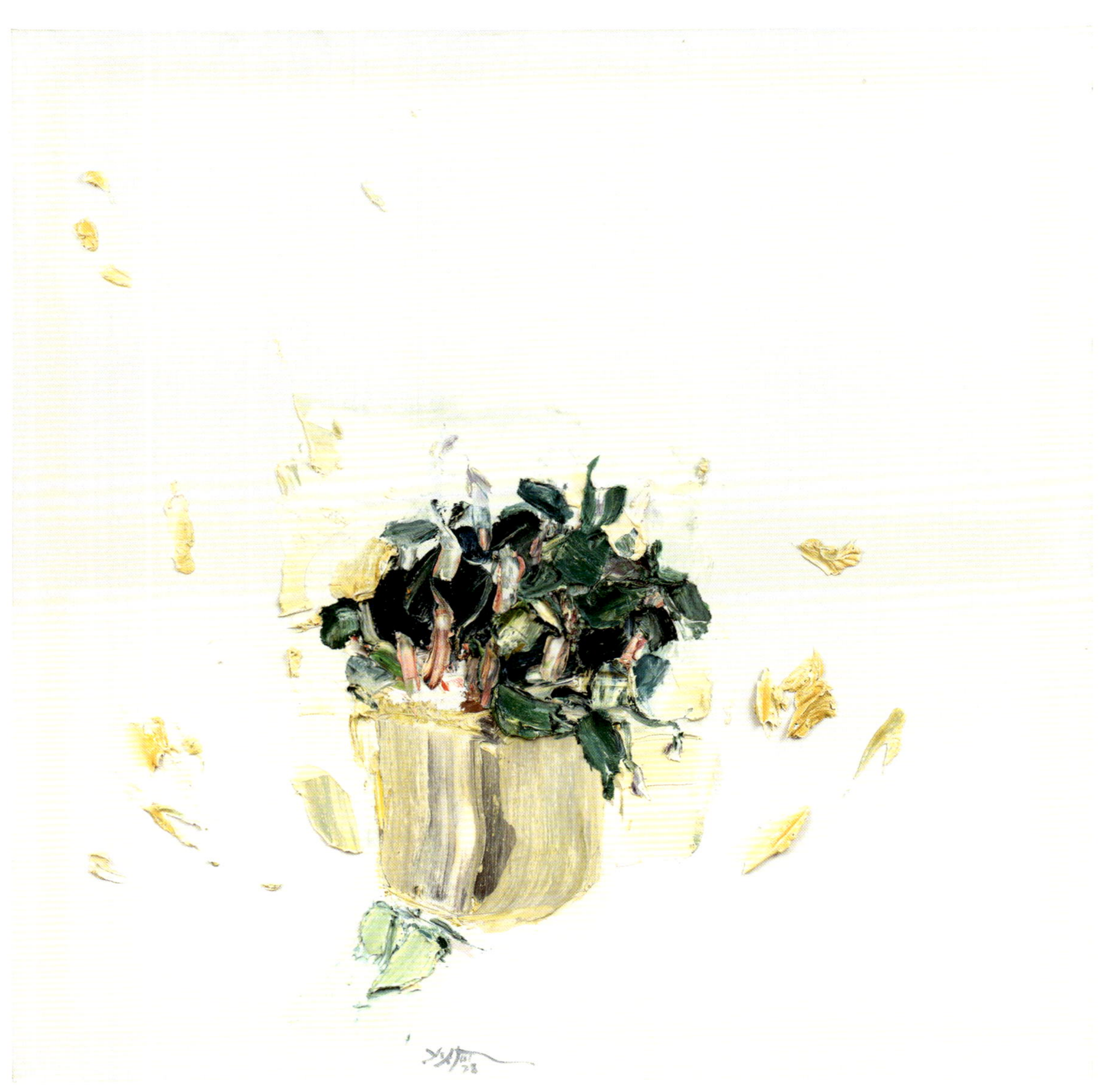

Untitled, 1978, oil on canvas, 60 × 60 inches (152.4 × 152.4 cm)

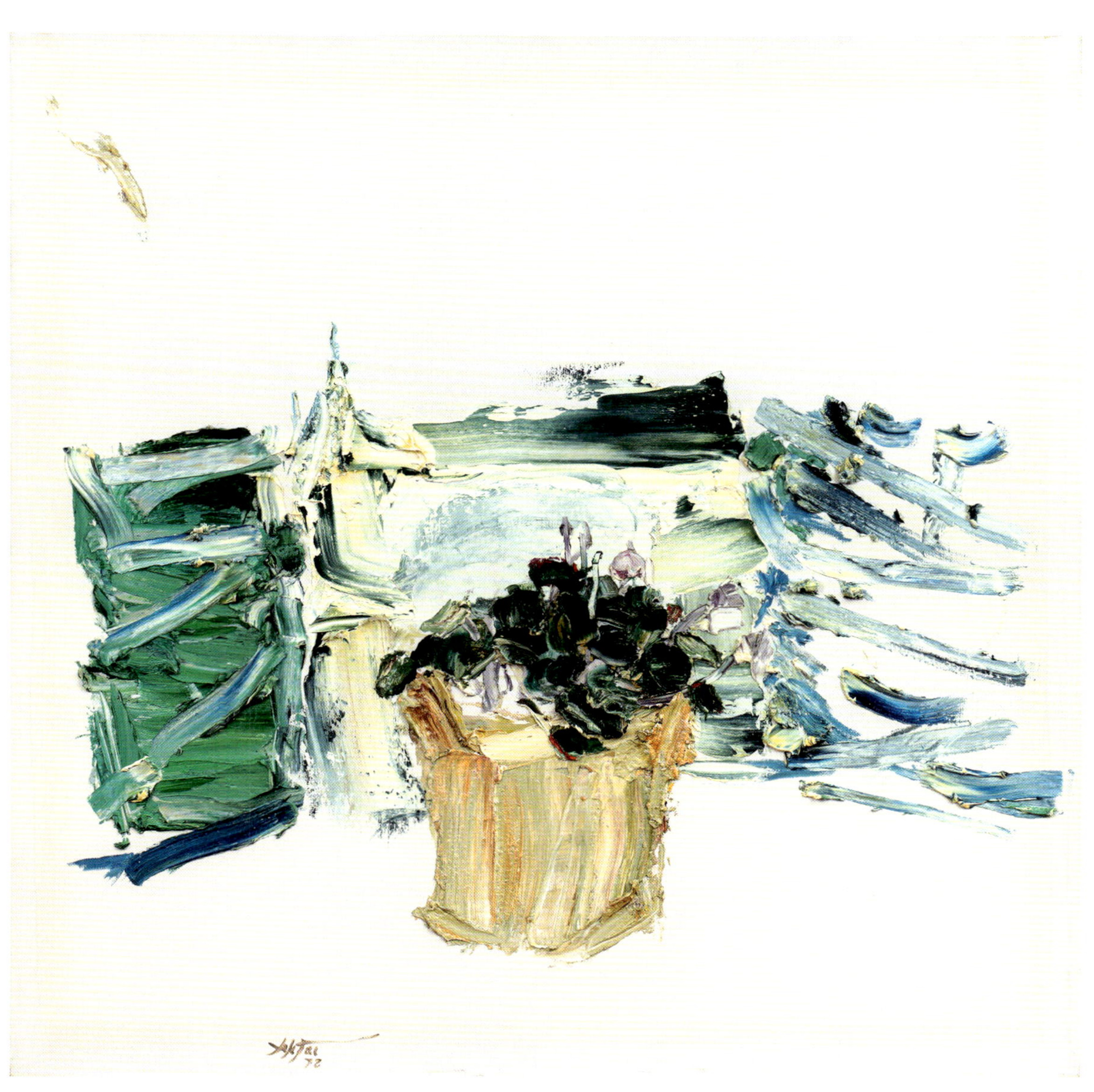

Untitled, 1978, oil on canvas, 60 × 60 inches (152.4 × 152.4 cm)

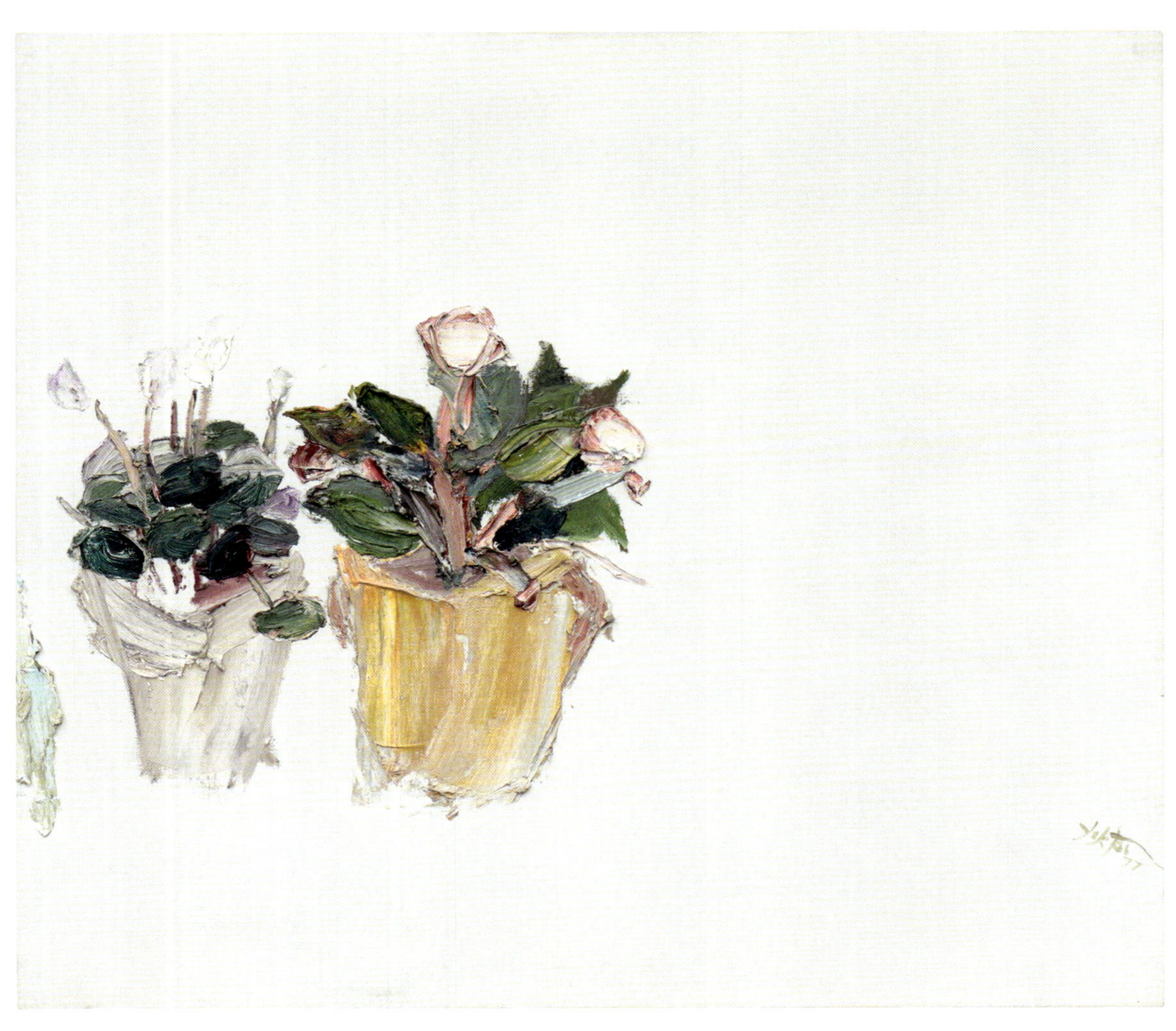

 Untitled, 1978, oil on canvas, 42 × 48 inches (106.7 × 121.9 cm)

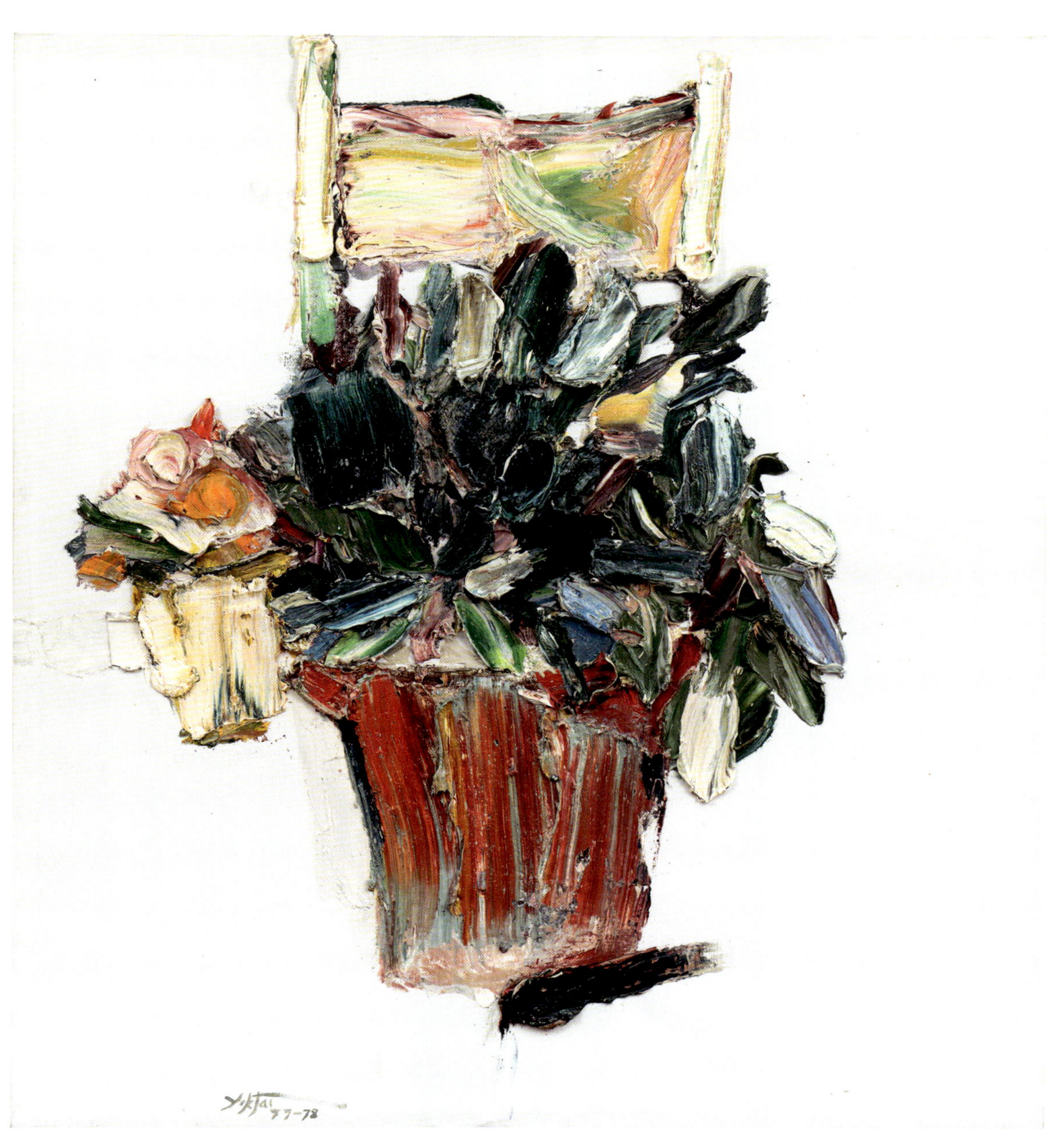

Untitled, 1978, oil on canvas, 52 × 48 inches (132.1 × 121.9 cm)

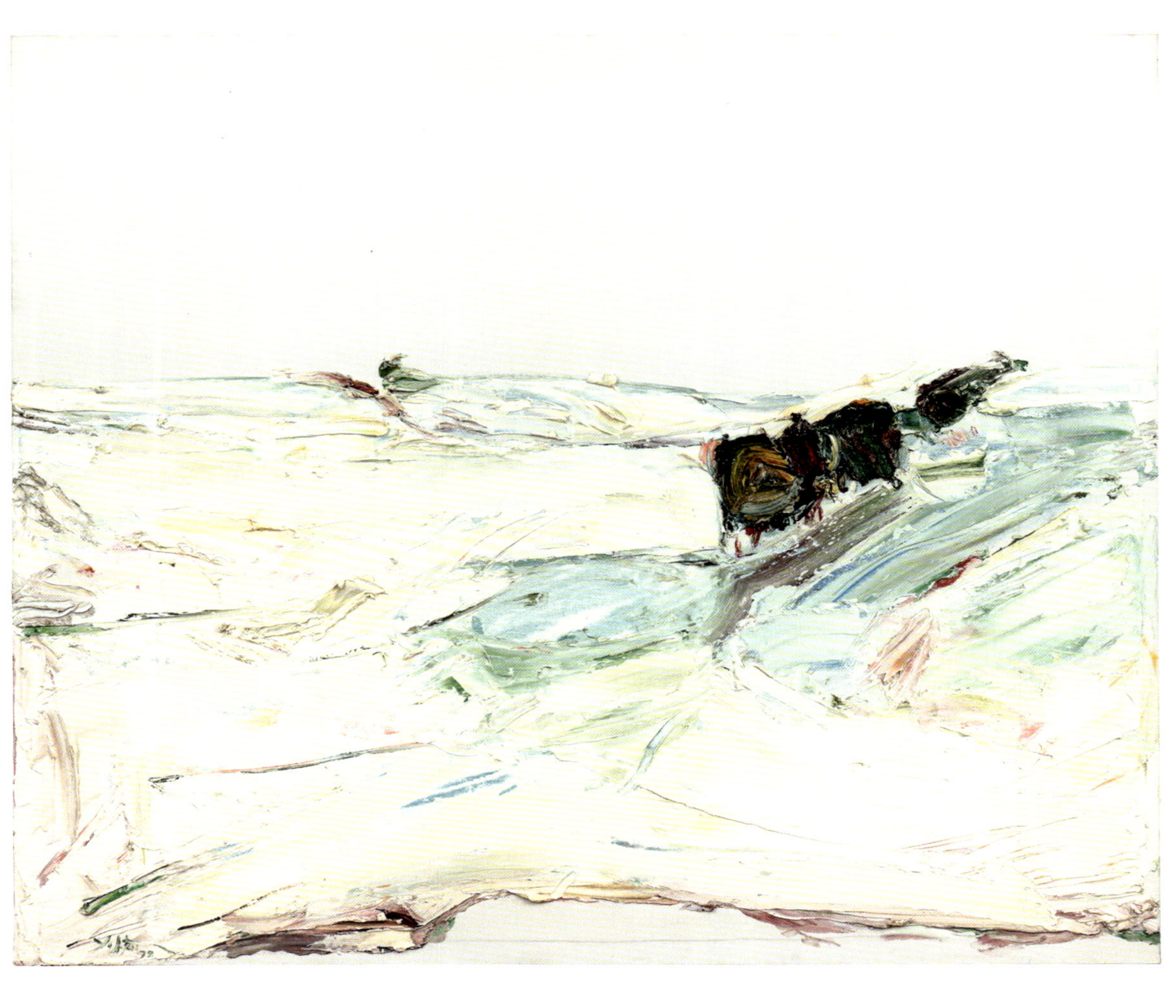

 Untitled, 1978, oil on canvas, 60 × 72 inches (152.4 × 182.9 cm)

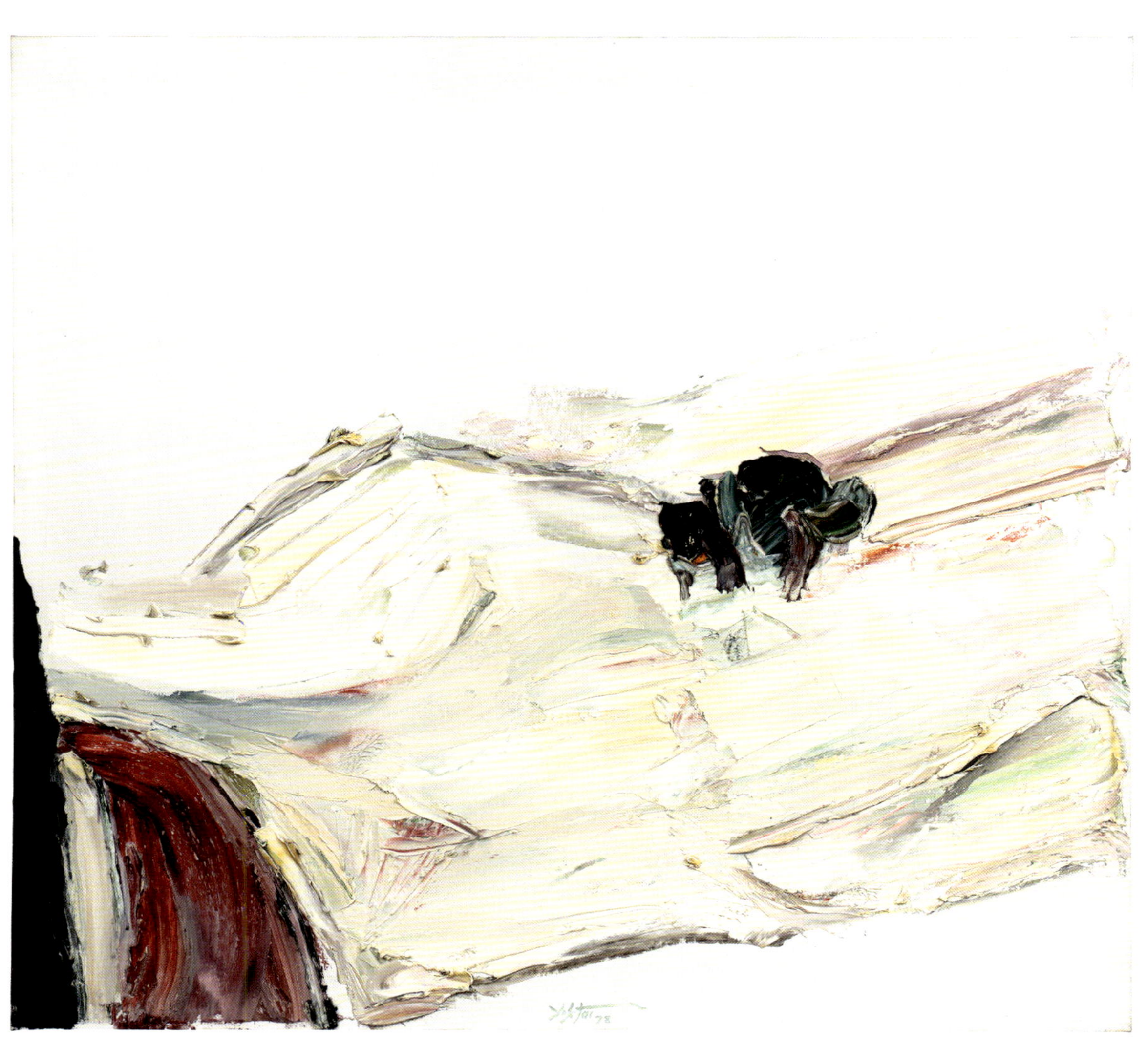

Untitled, 1978, oil on canvas, 60 × 60¾ inches (152.4 × 154.3 cm)

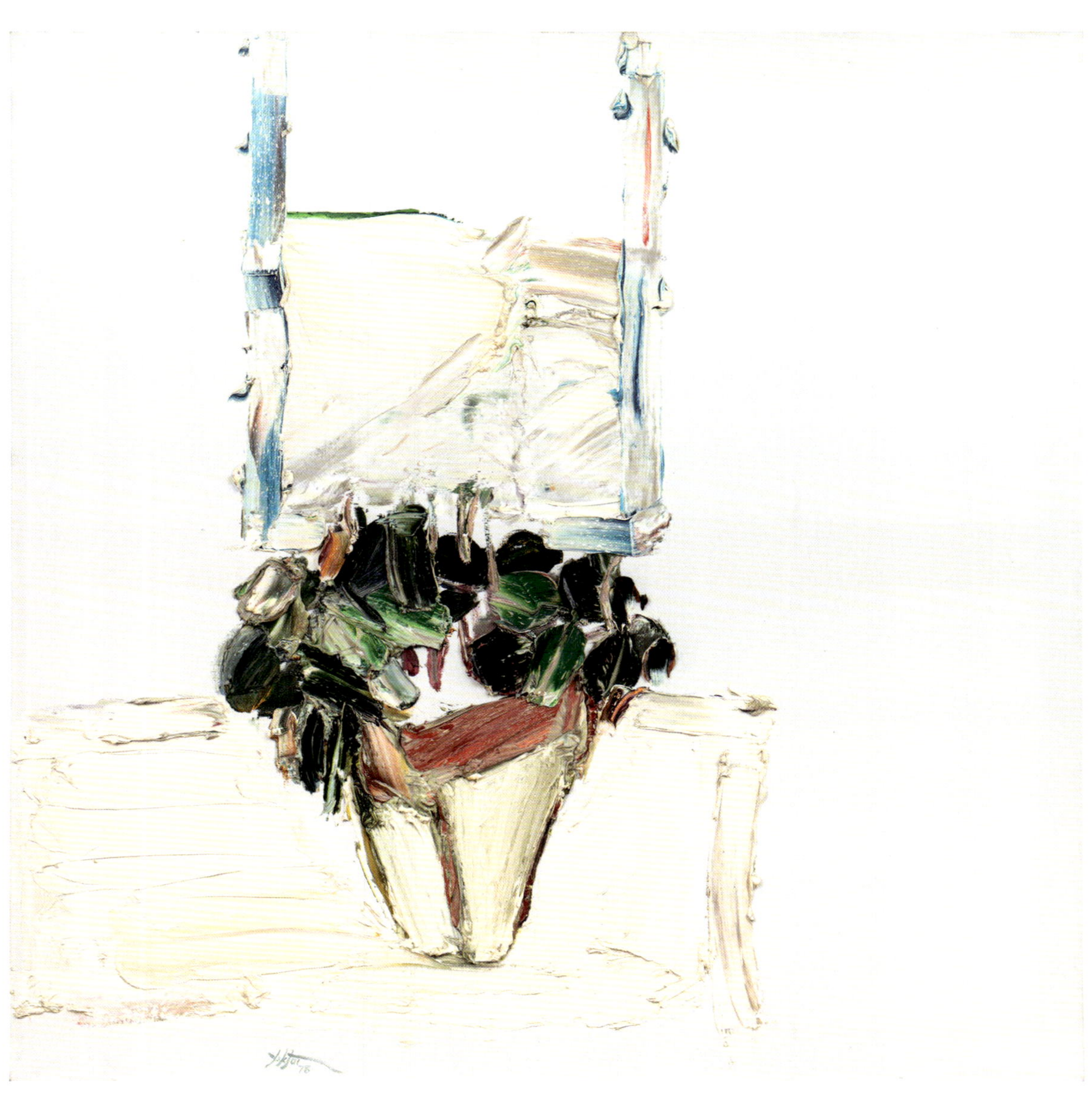

 Untitled, 1978, oil on canvas, 60 × 60 inches (152.4 × 152.4 cm)

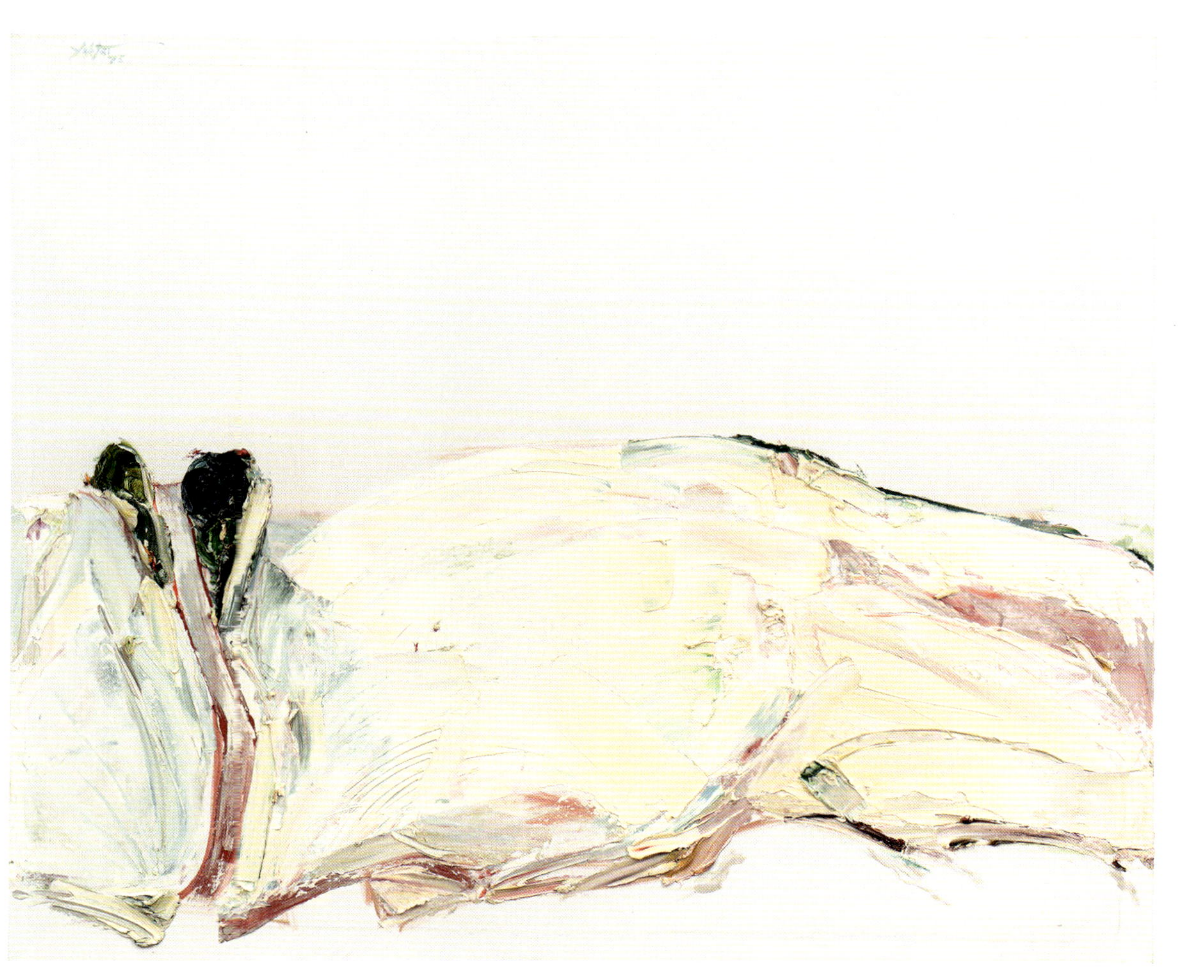

Body of Landscape, 1978, oil on canvas, 60 × 72 inches (152.4 × 182.9 cm)

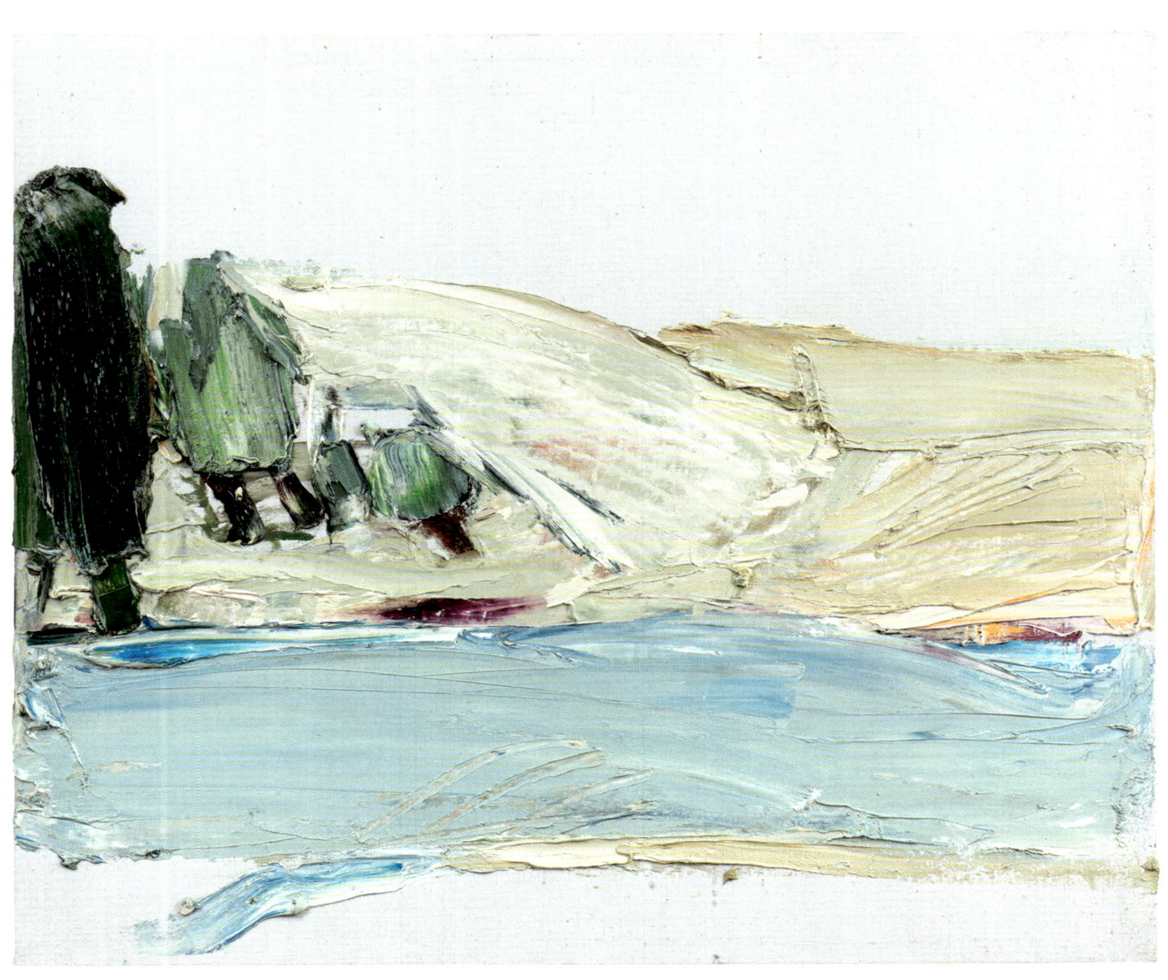

 Untitled, 1978, oil on canvas, 42 × 50 inches (106.7 × 127 cm)

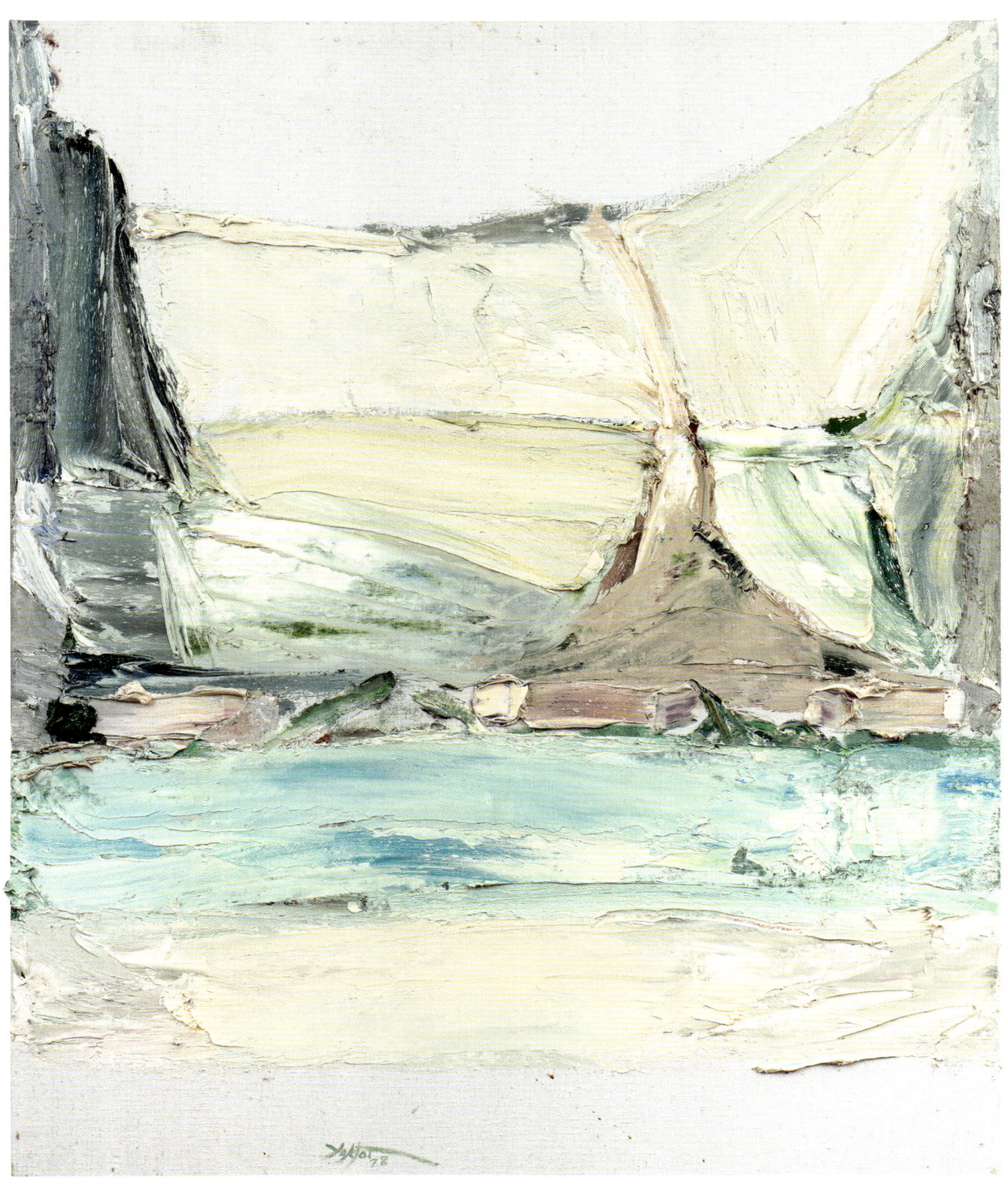

Untitled, 1978, oil on canvas, 50 × 42 inches (127 × 106.7 cm)

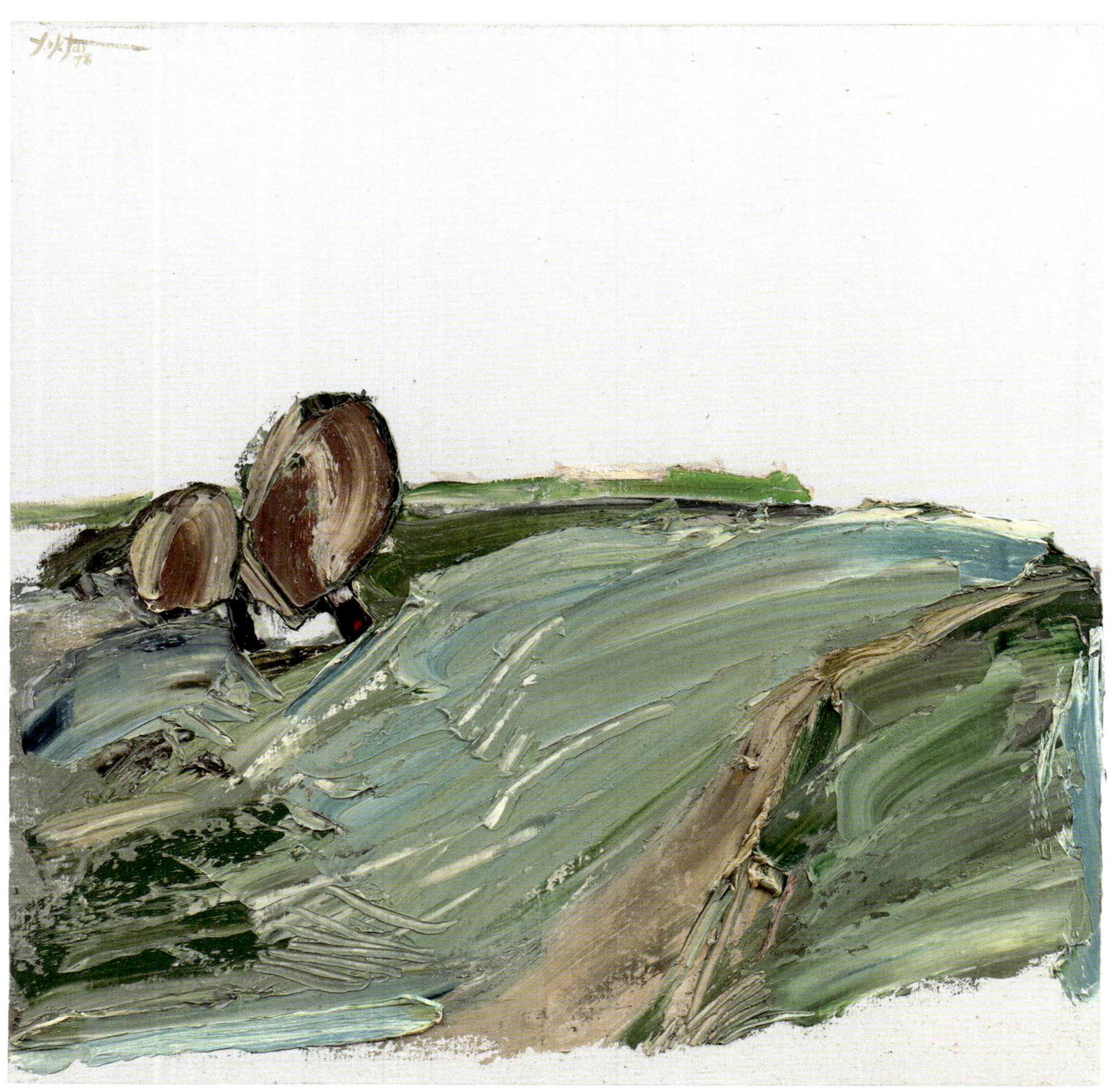

Untitled, 1978, oil on canvas, 48 × 48 inches (121.9 × 121.9 cm)

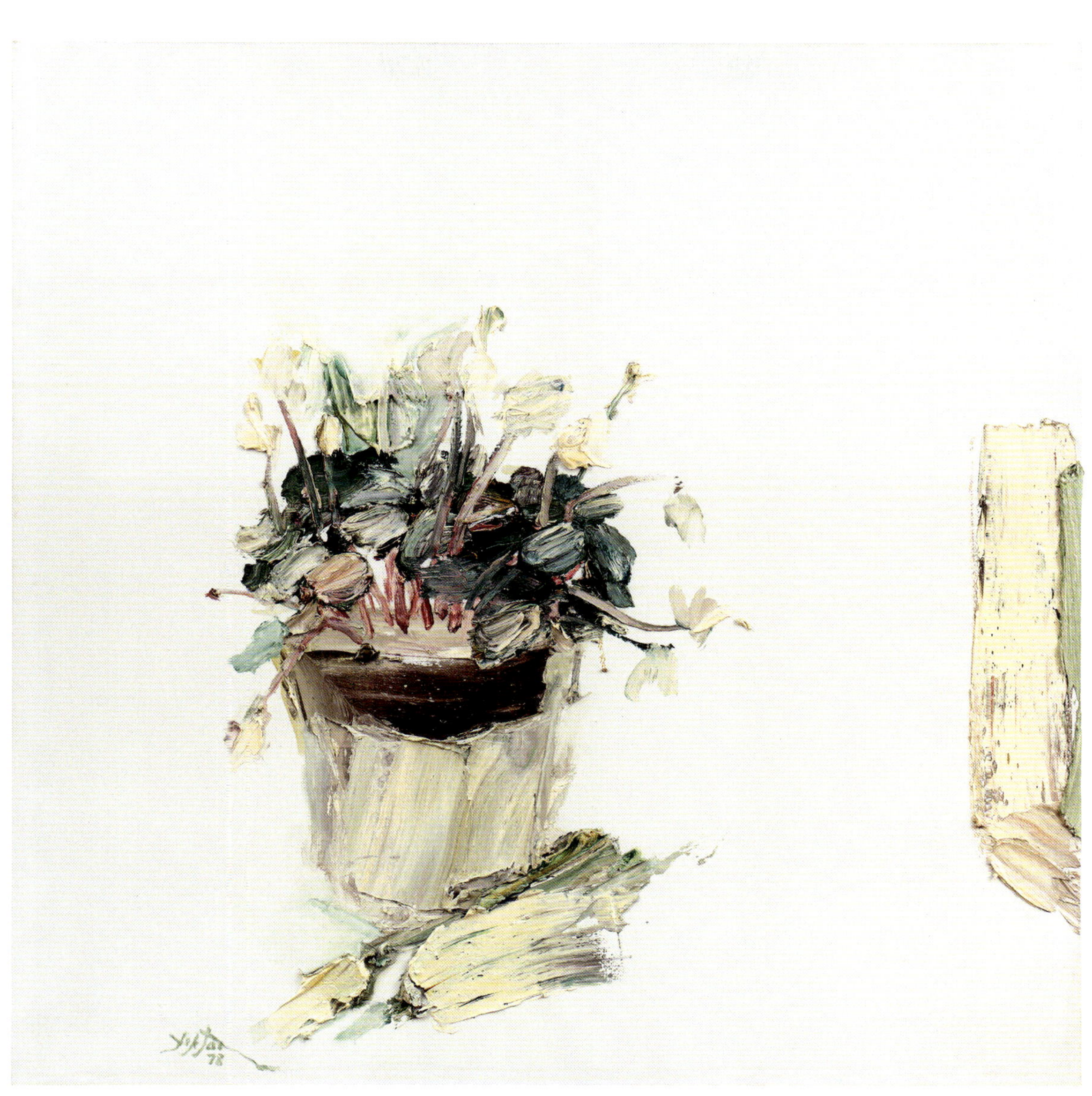

Untitled, 1978, oil on canvas, 48 × 52 inches (121.9 × 132.1 cm)

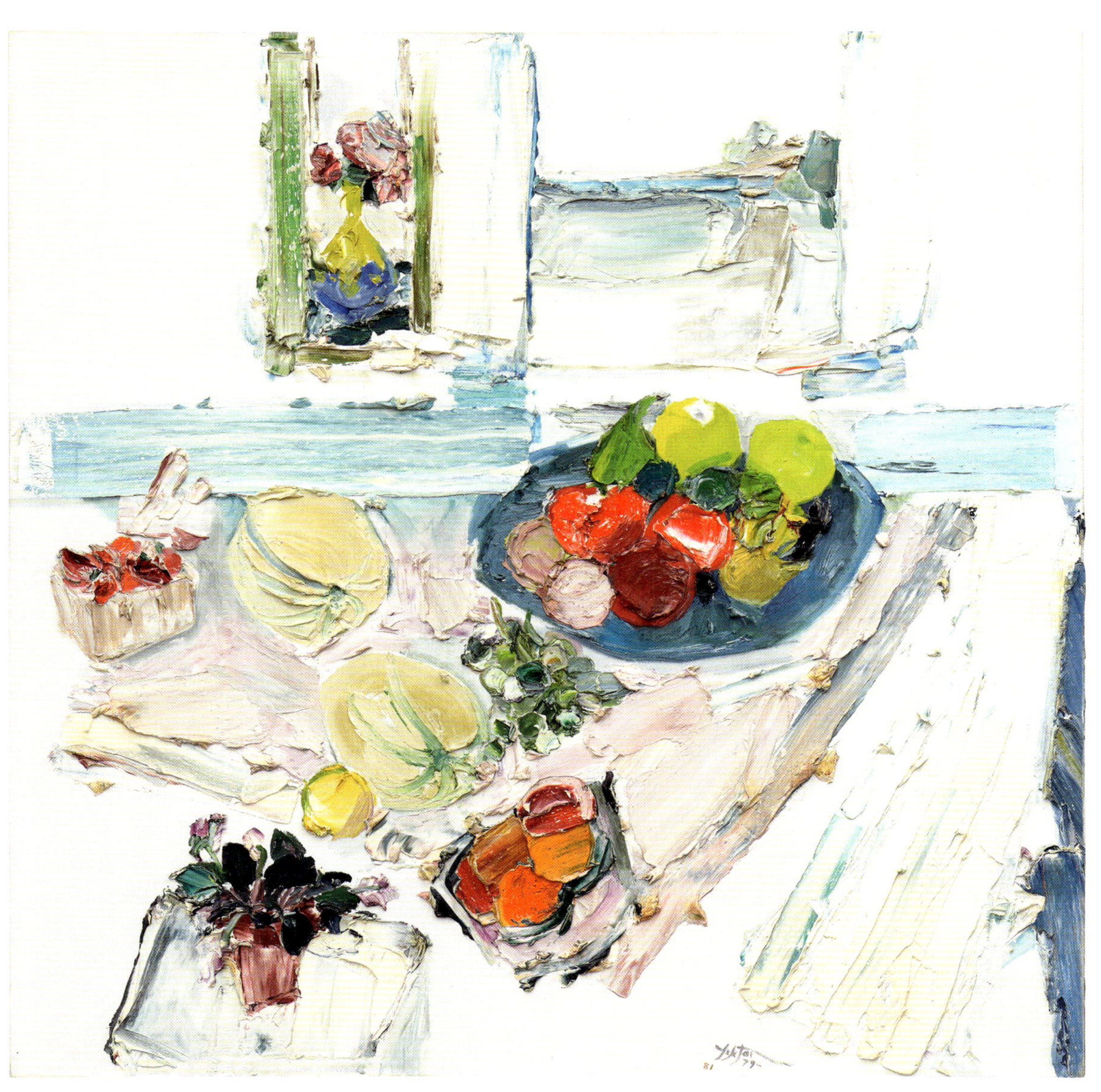

Interior with Two Tables, 1979–81, oil on canvas, 60 × 60 inches (152.4 × 152.4 cm)

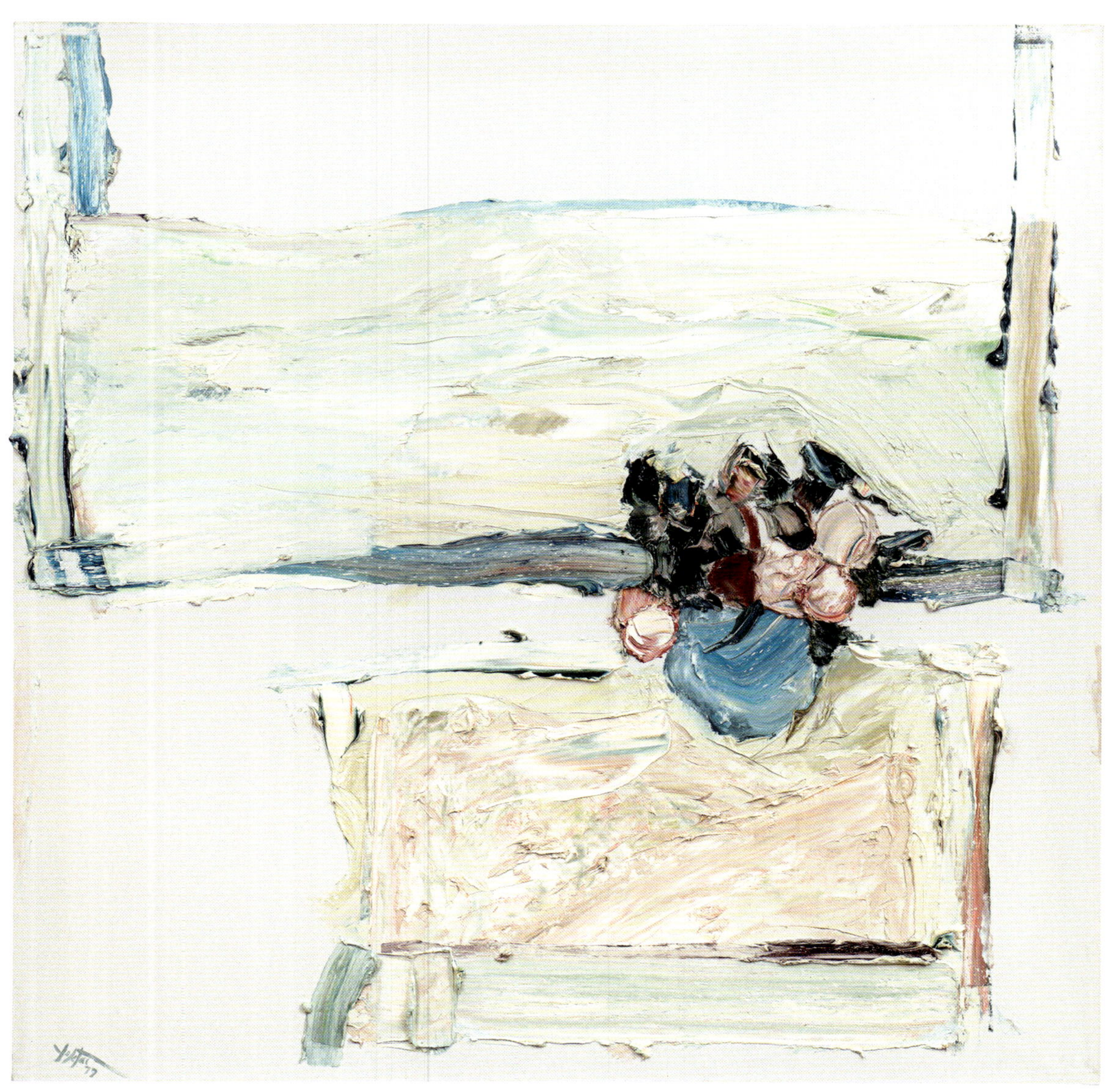

 Untitled, 1979, oil on canvas, 60 × 60 inches (152.4 × 152.4 cm)

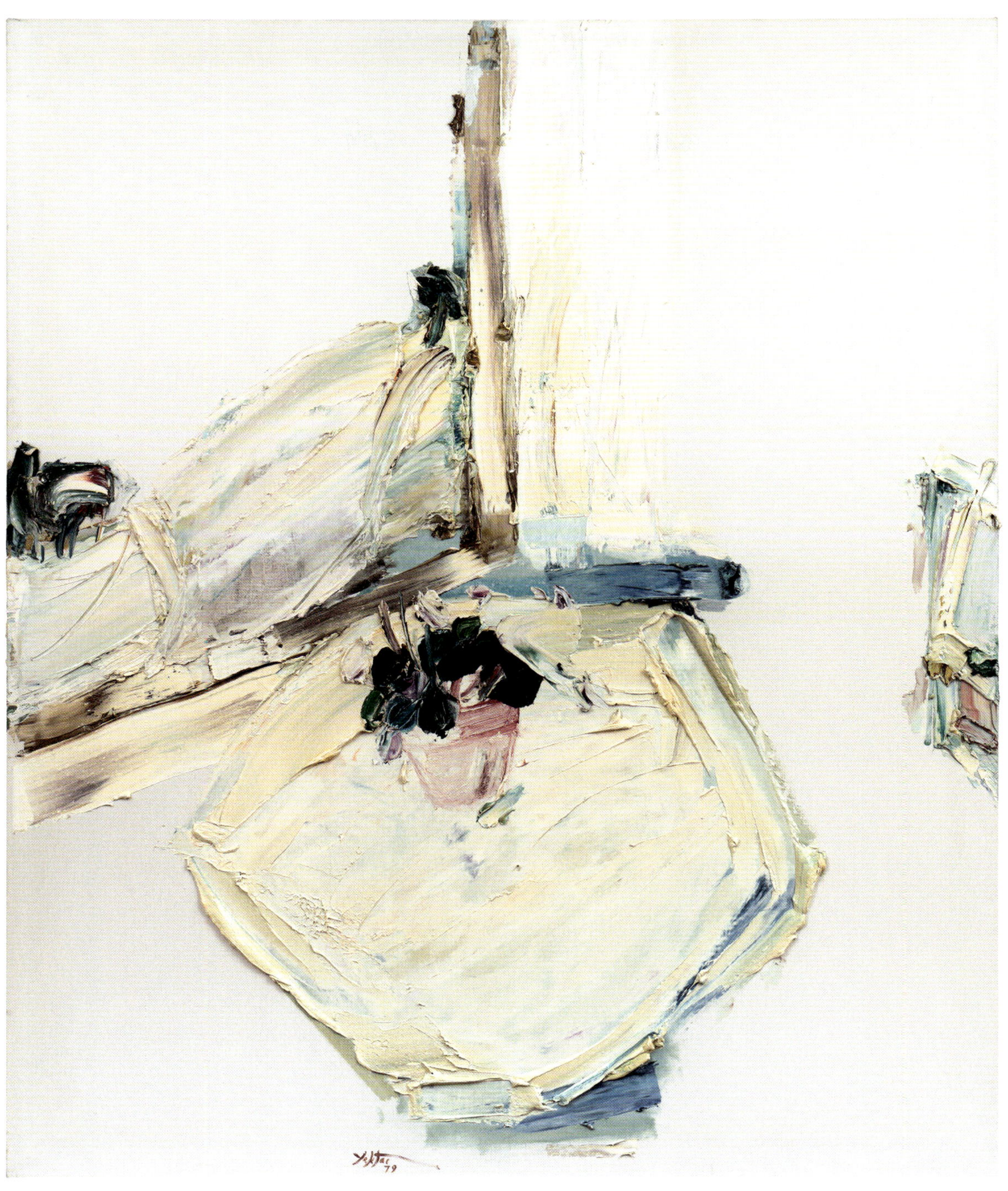

Untitled, 1979, oil on canvas, 72 × 60 inches (182.9 × 152.4 cm)

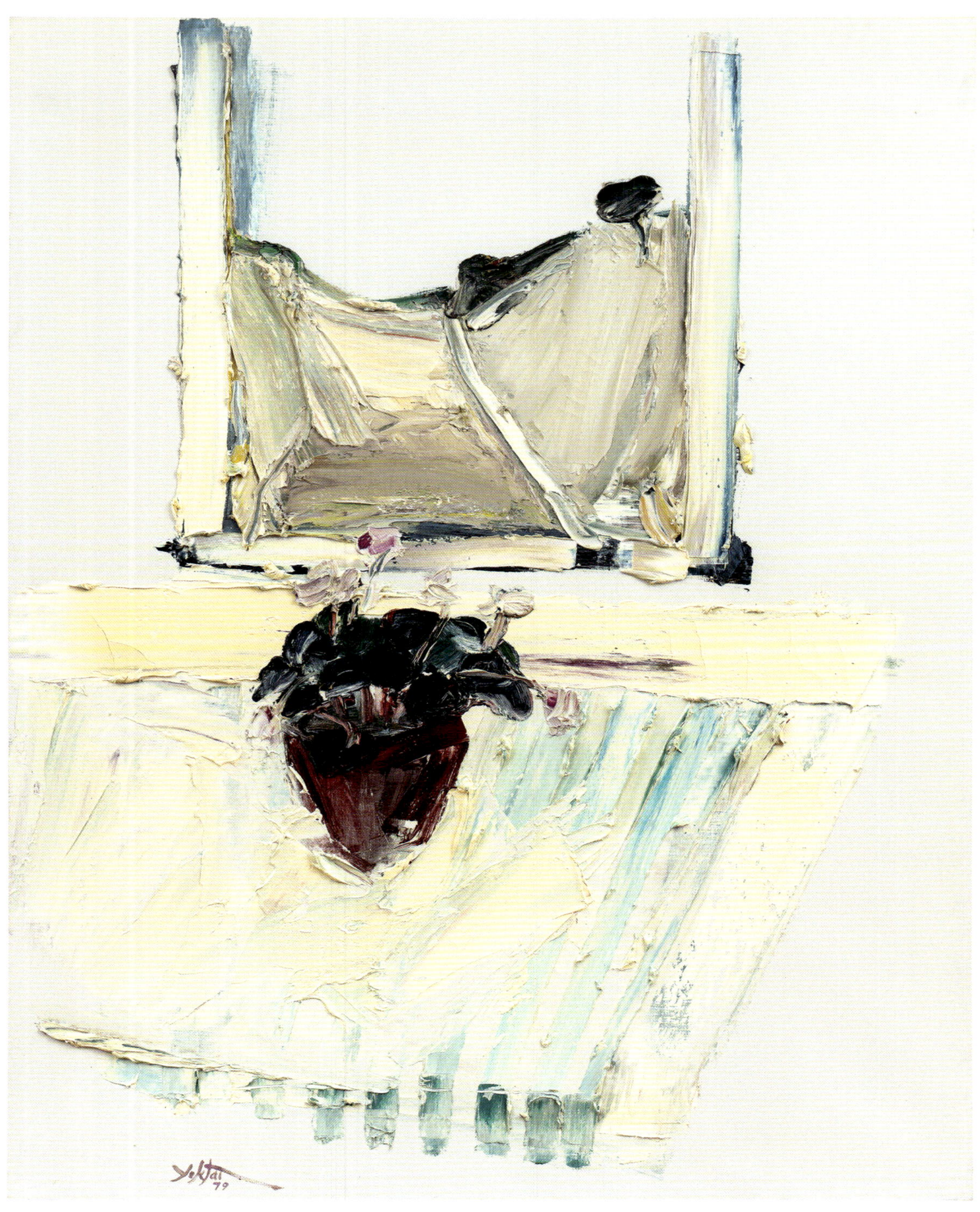

Untitled, 1979, oil on canvas, 58 × 46 inches (147.3 × 116.8 cm)

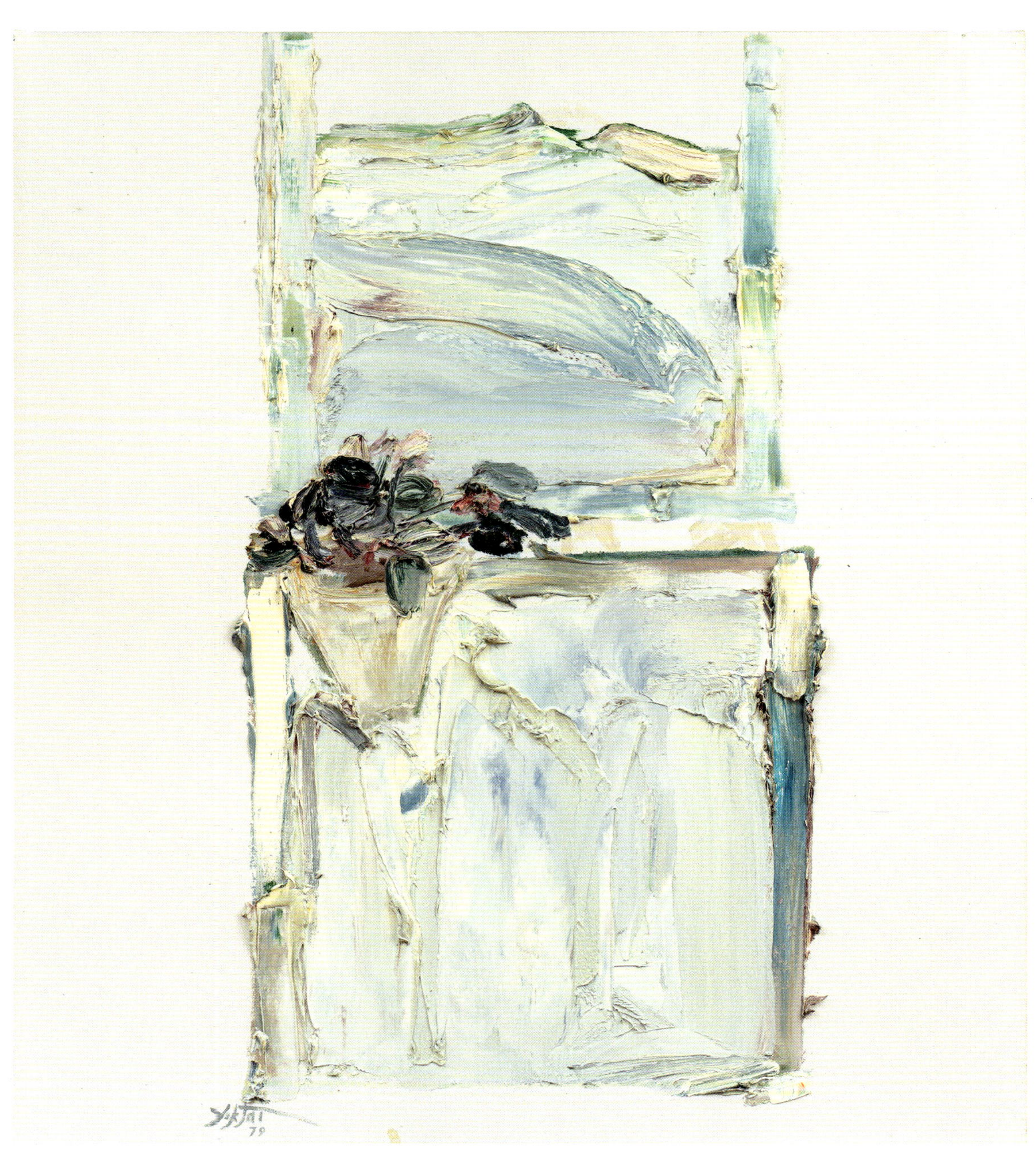

Untitled, 1979, oil on canvas, 54 × 48 inches (137.2 × 121.9 cm)

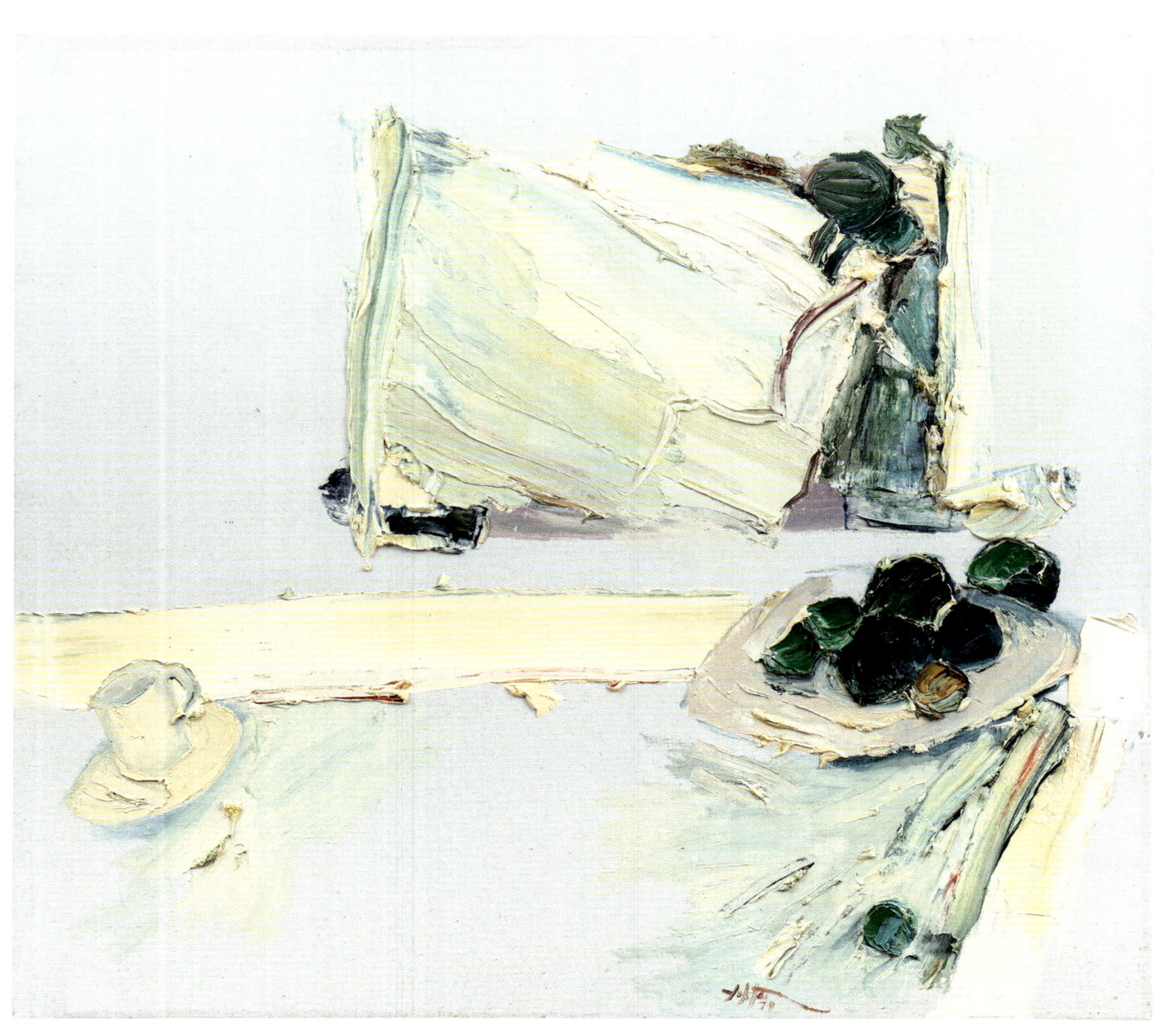

 Untitled, 1979, oil on canvas, 48 × 54 inches (121.9 × 137.2 cm)

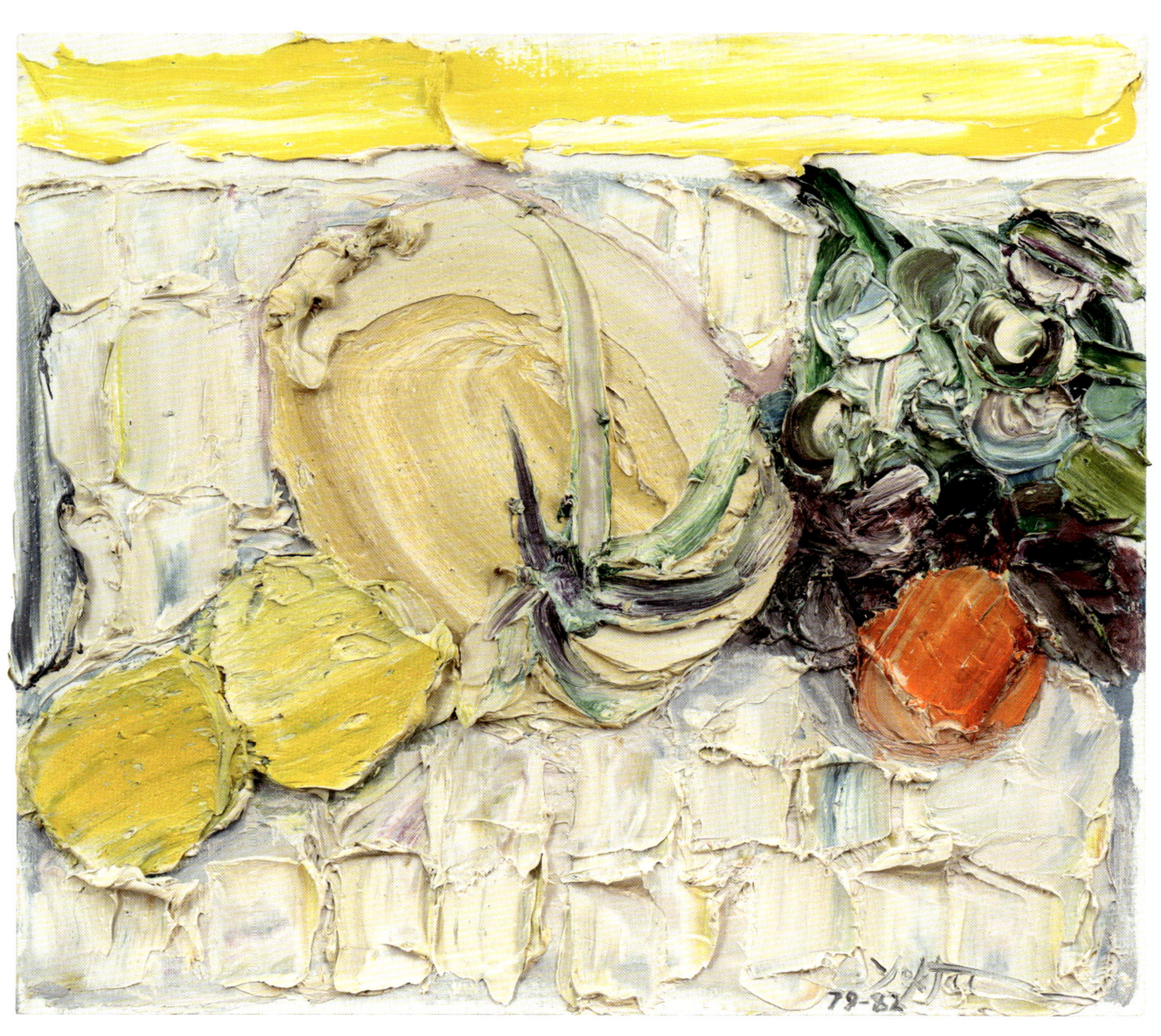

Untitled, 1979, oil on canvas, 18 × 20 inches (45.7 × 50.8 cm)

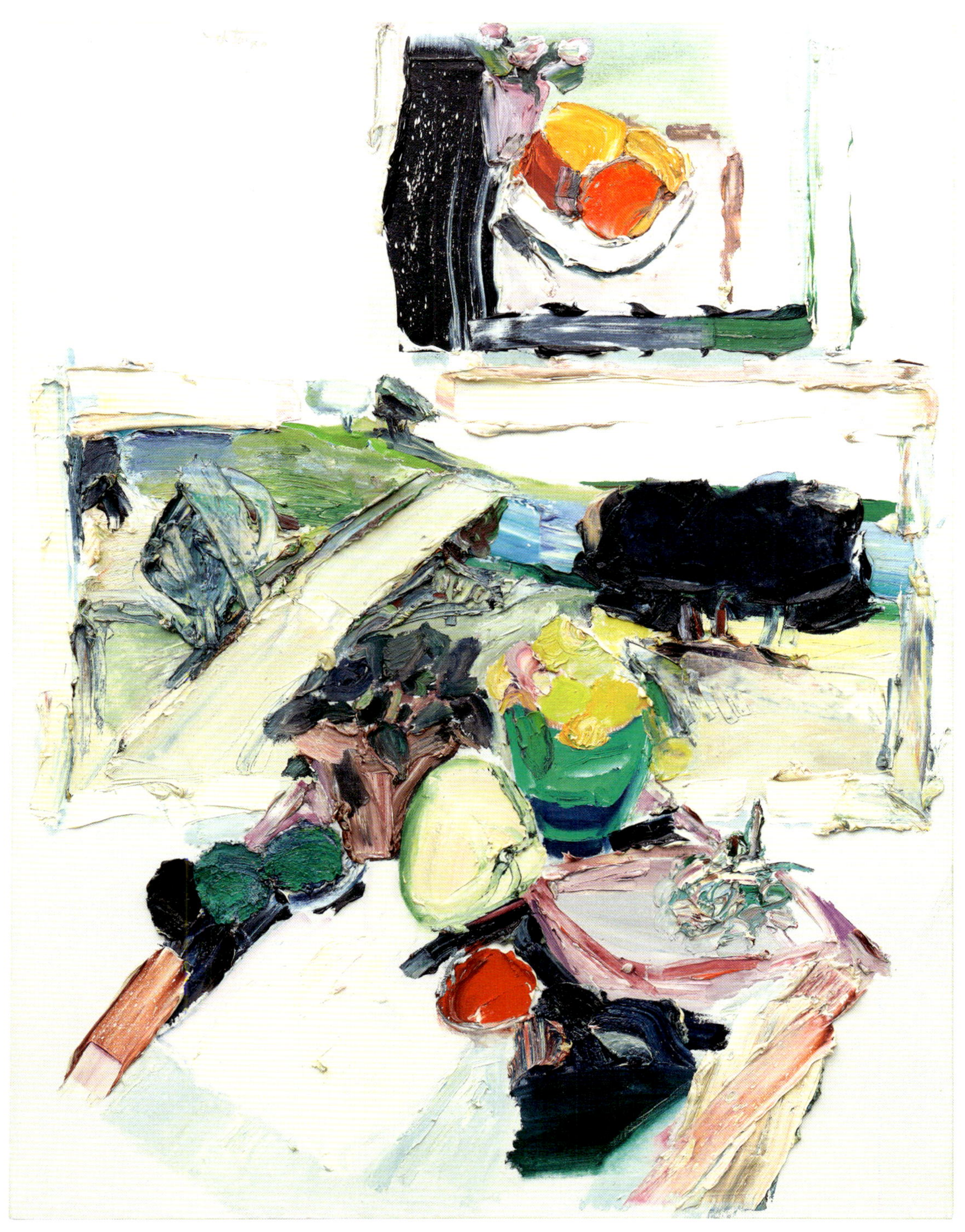

Untitled, 1980, oil on canvas, 60 × 46⅛ inches (152.4 × 117.2 cm)

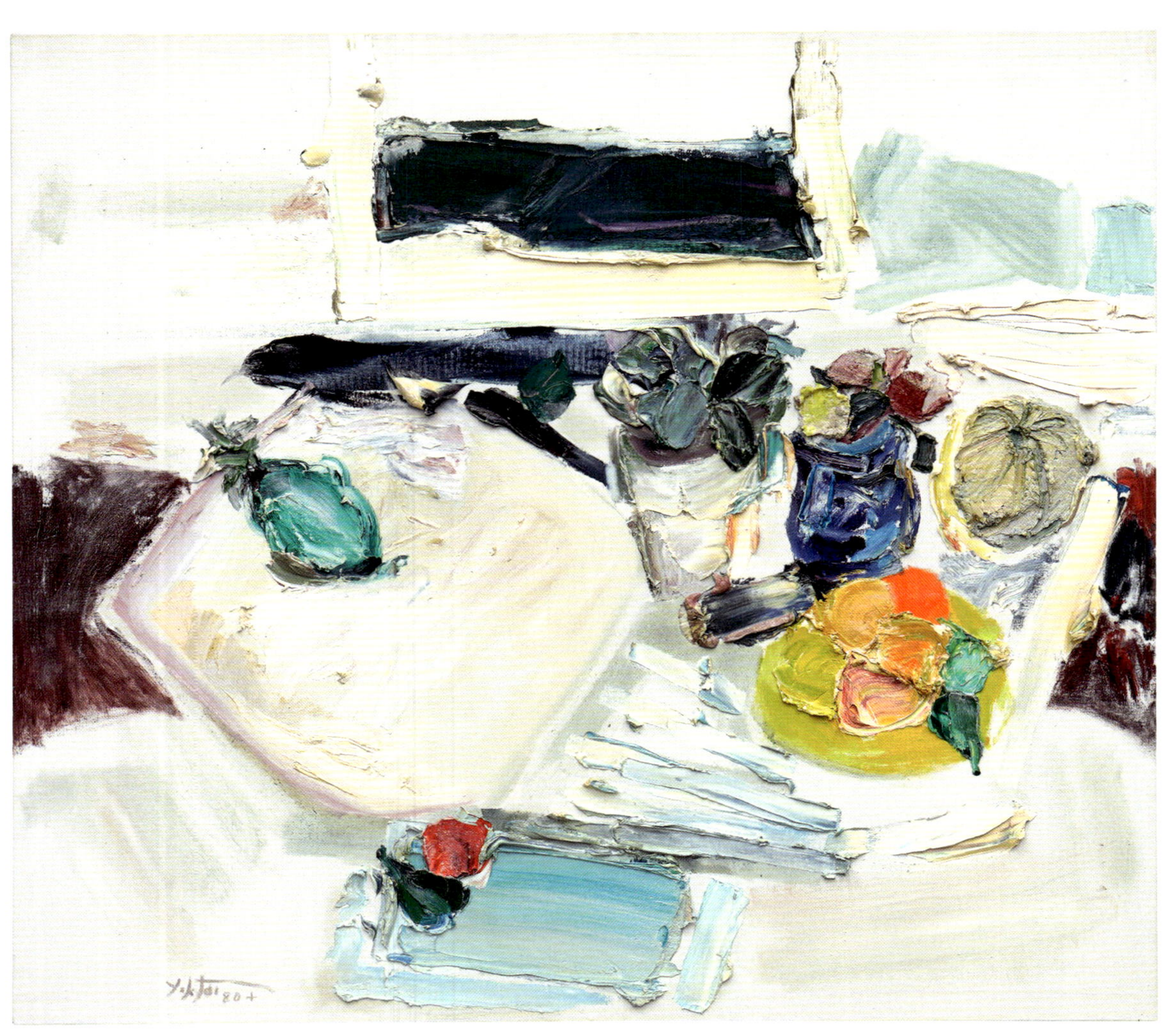

 Untitled, 1980, oil on canvas, 48 × 54 inches (121.9 × 137.2 cm)

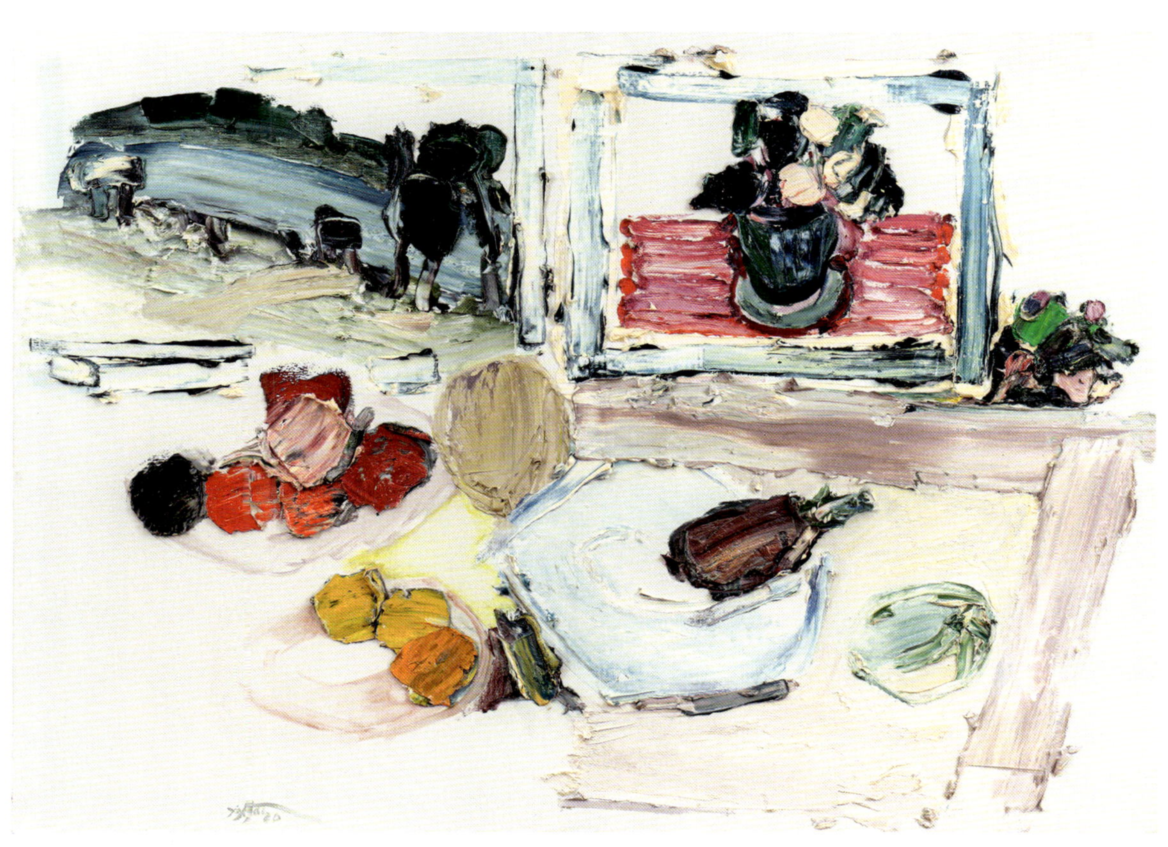

Untitled, 1980, oil on canvas, 46 × 64 inches (116.8 × 162.6 cm)

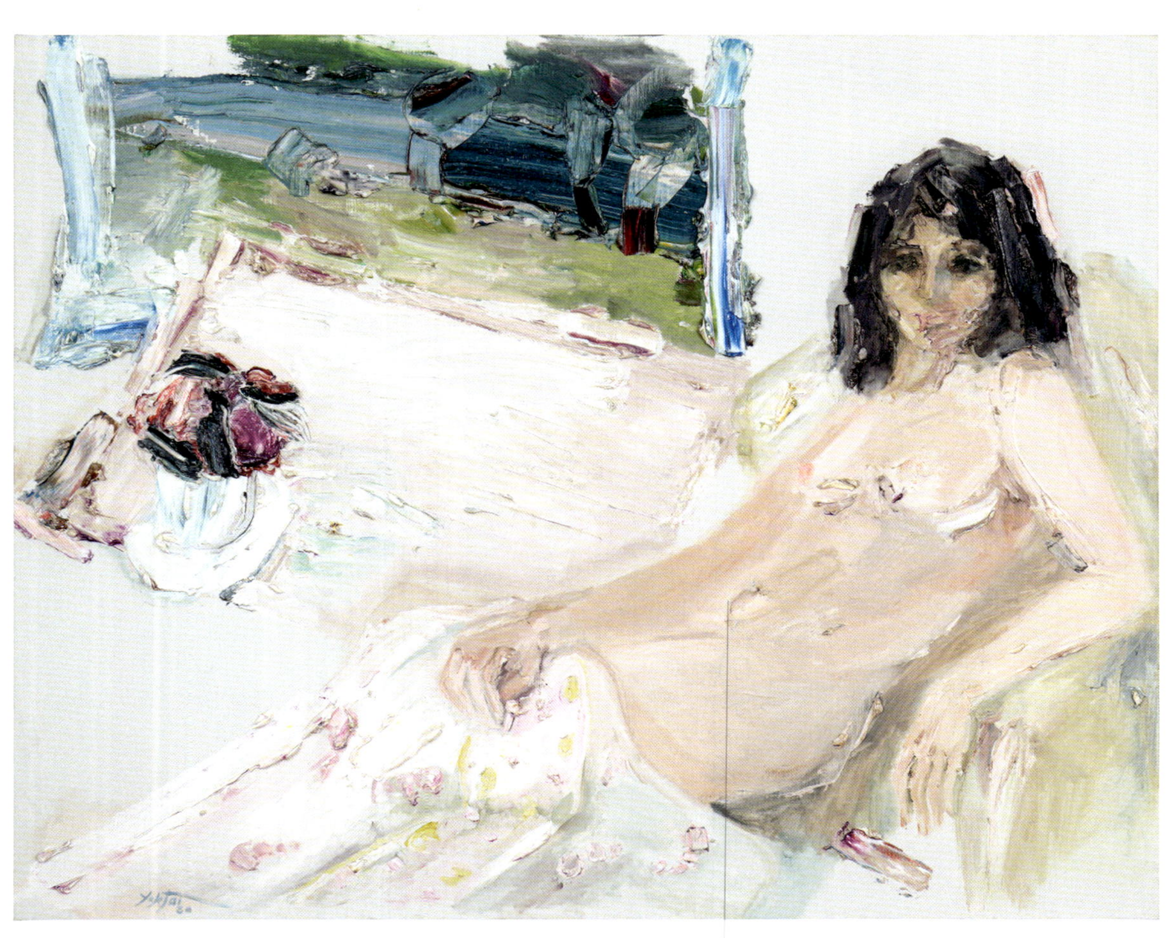

Portrait of Nikki, 1980, oil on canvas, 46 × 58 inches (116.8 × 147.3 cm)

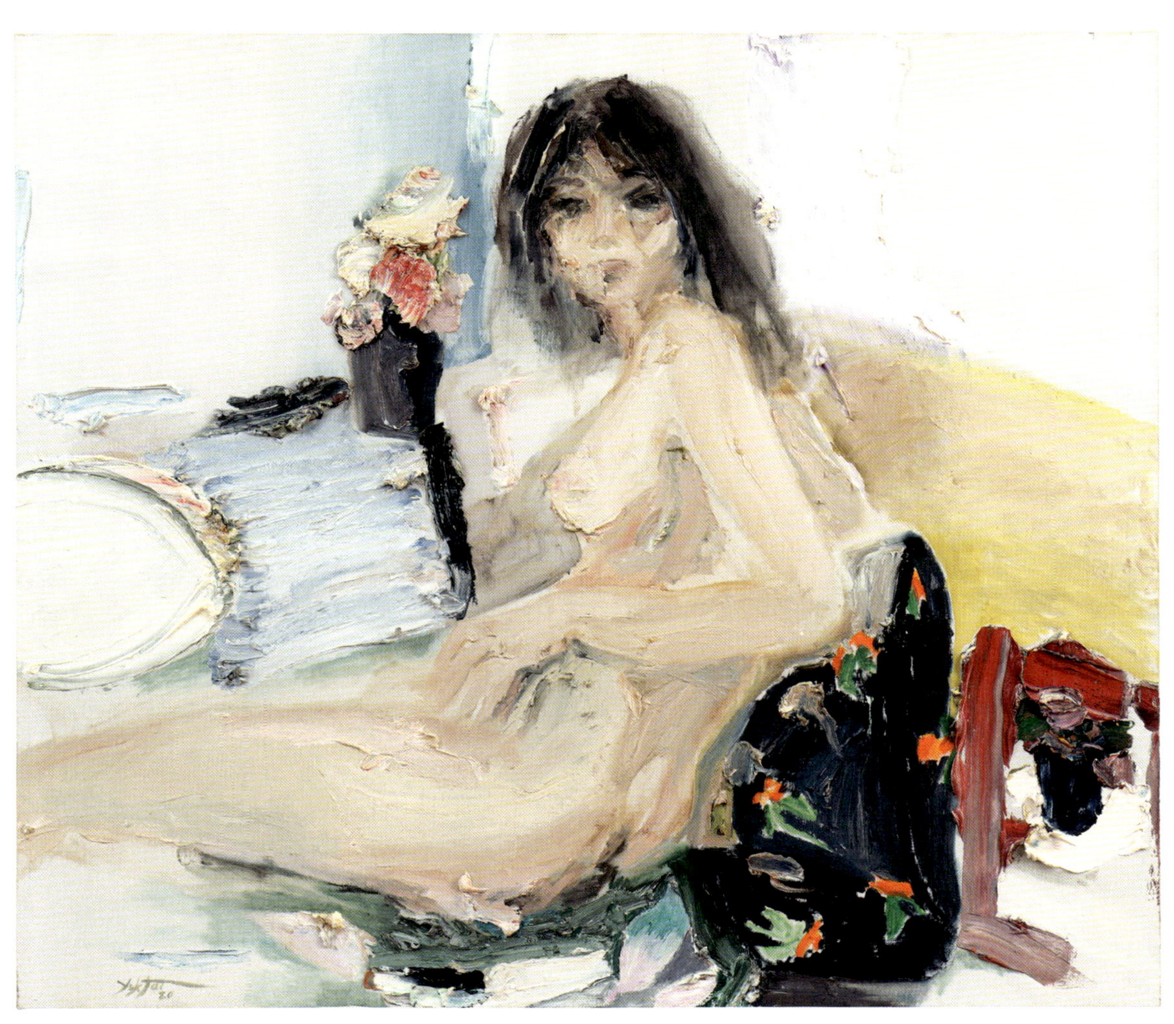

Nude, 1980, oil on canvas, 42 × 48 inches (106.7 × 121.9 cm)

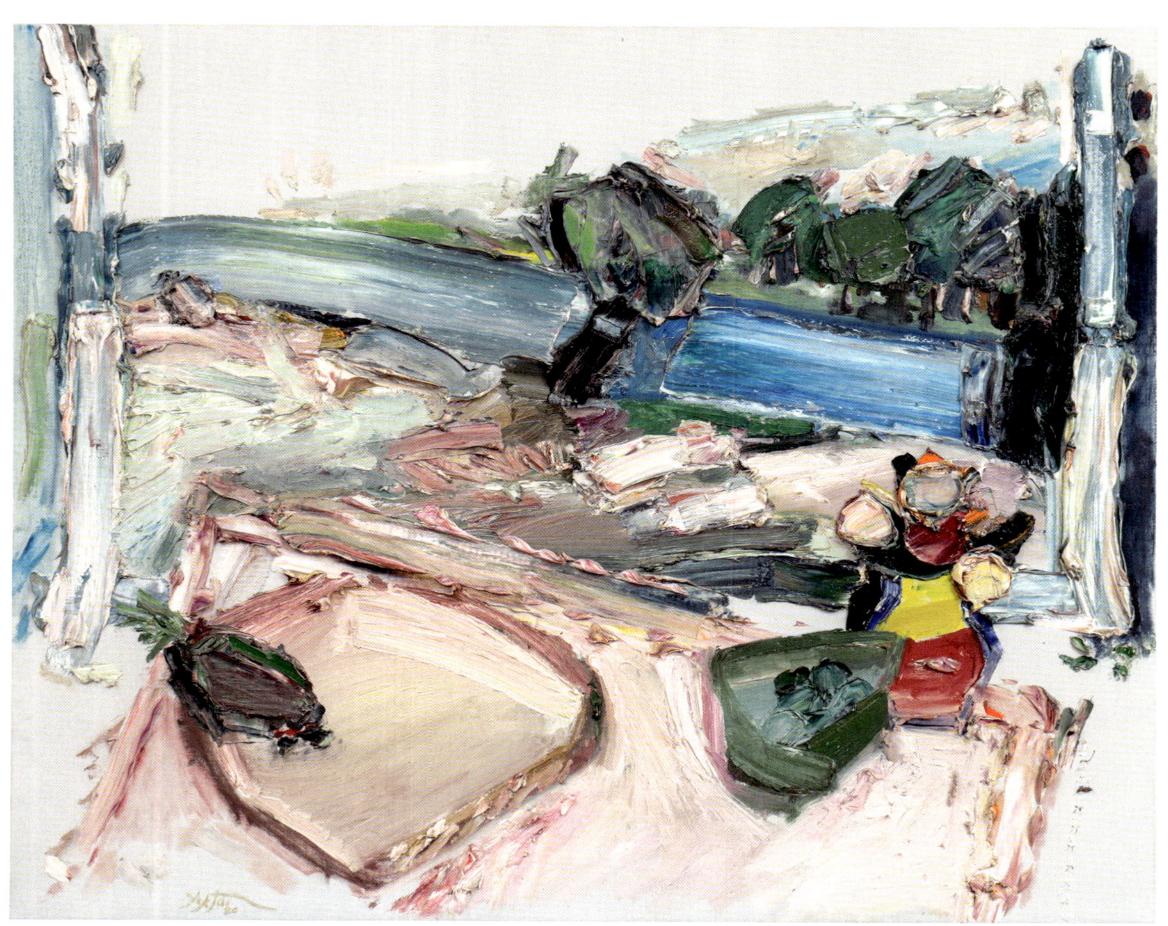

 Untitled, 1980, oil on canvas, 46 × 58 inches (116.8 × 146.3 cm)

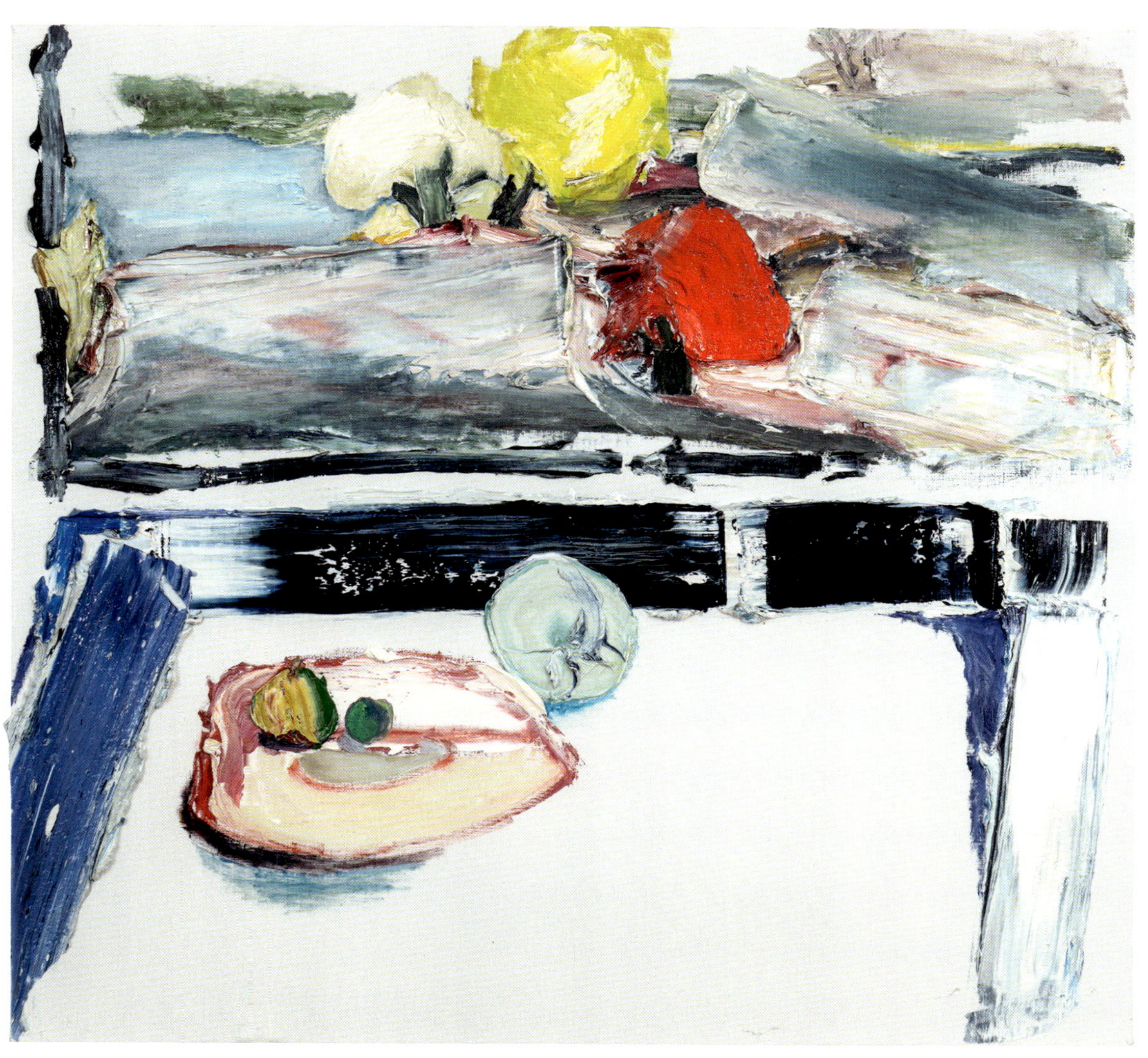

Untitled, 1980, oil on canvas, 48 × 52 inches (121.9 × 132.1 cm)

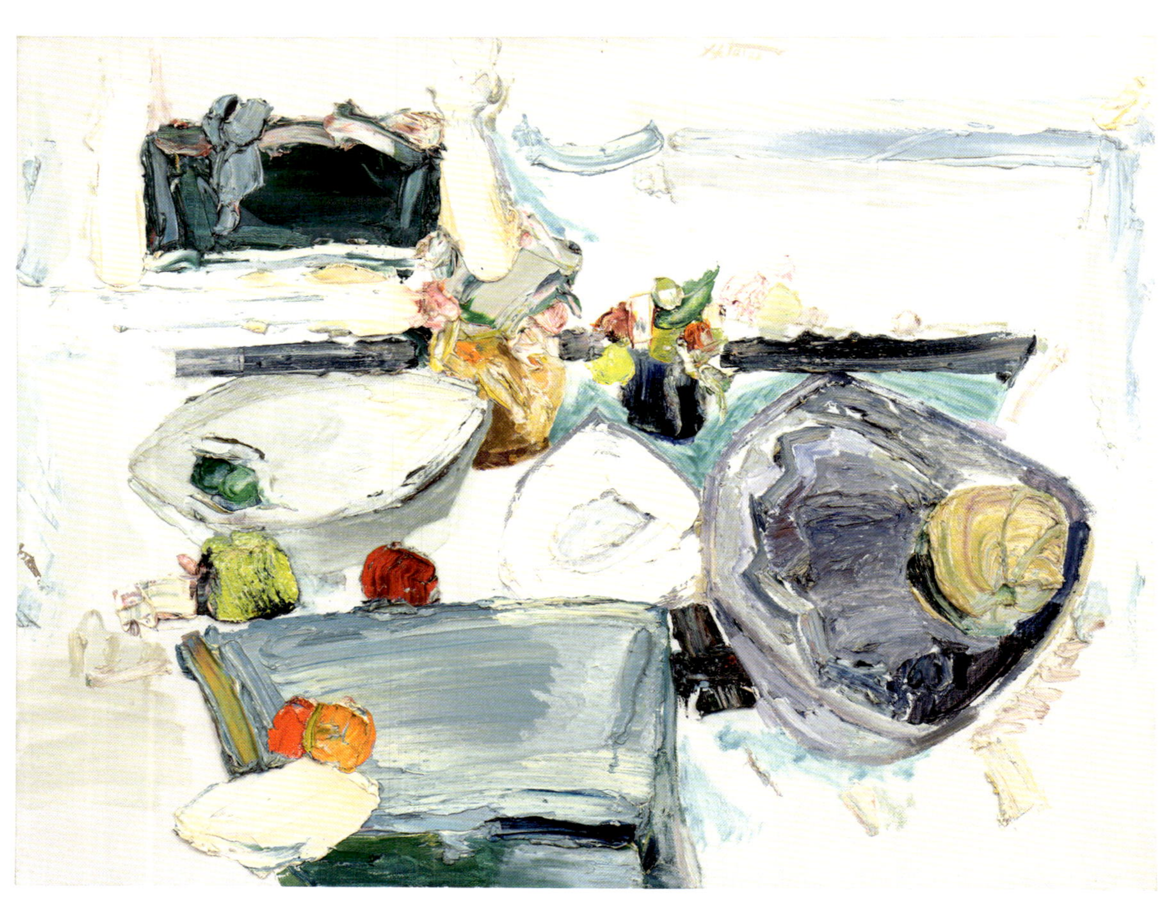

 Wall Still Life, 1980, oil on canvas, 46 × 60 inches (116.8 × 152.4 cm)

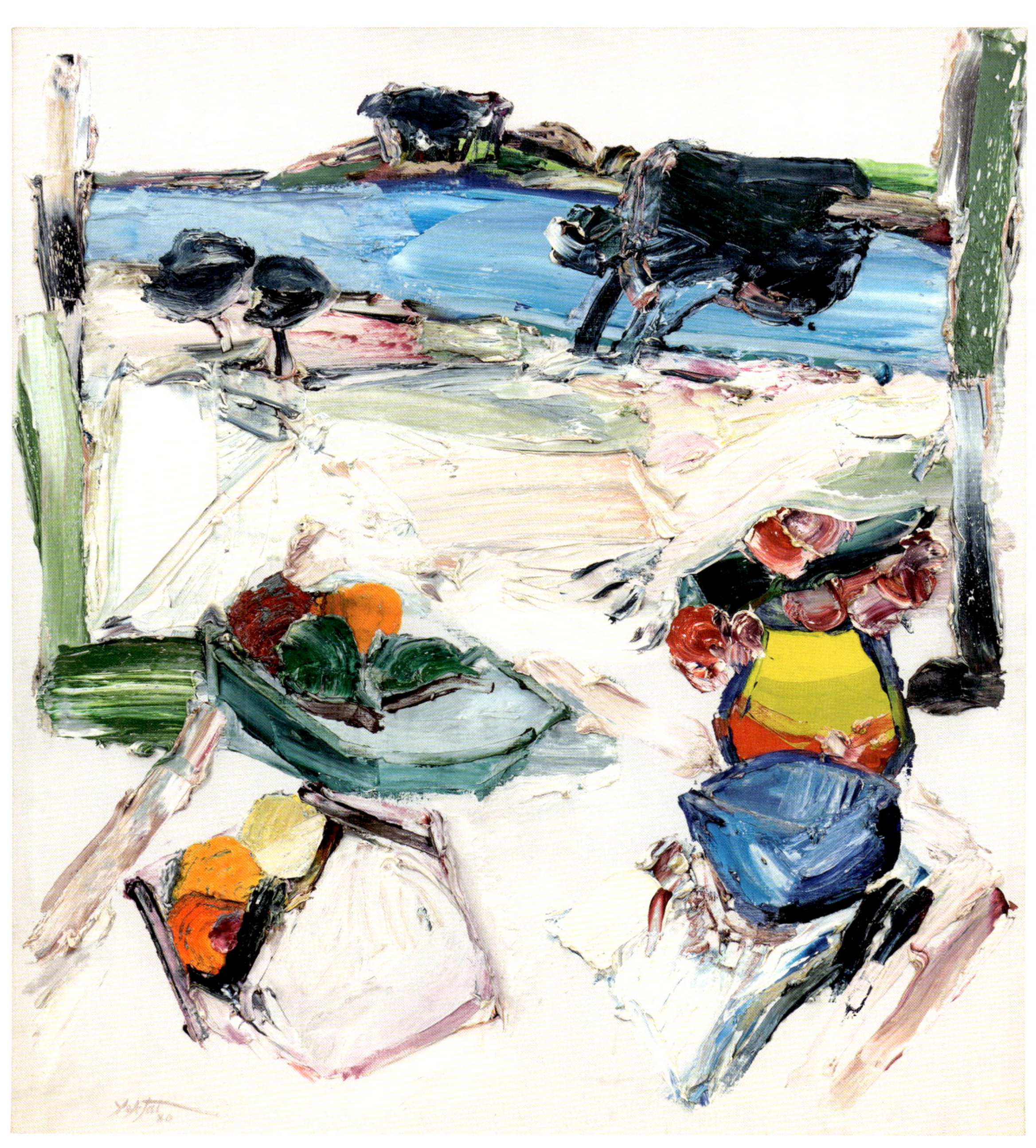

Interior, 1980, oil on canvas, 54 × 48 inches (137.2 × 121.9 cm)

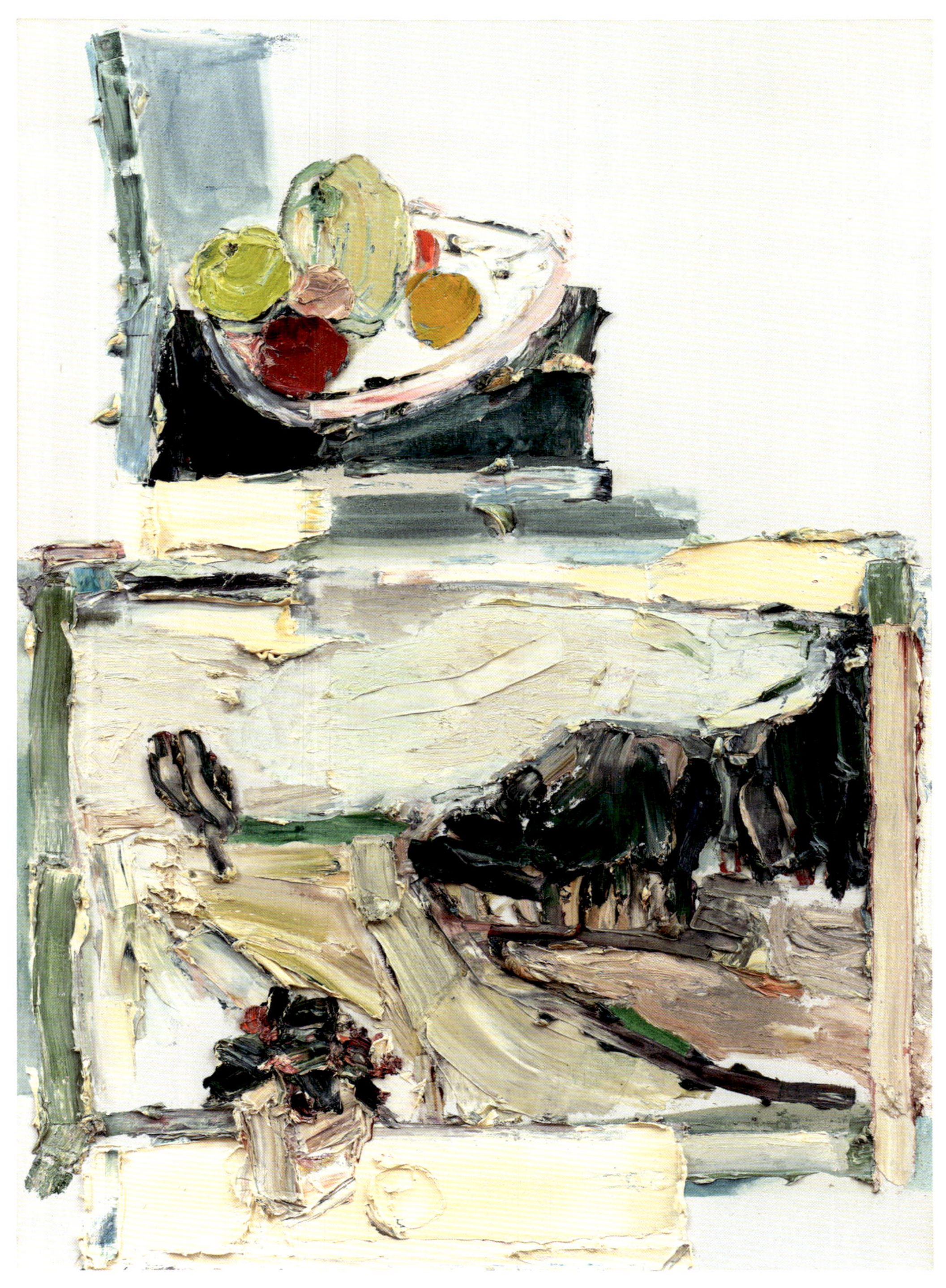

 Wall Still Life II, 1980, oil on canvas, 64 × 46 inches (162.6 × 116.8 cm)

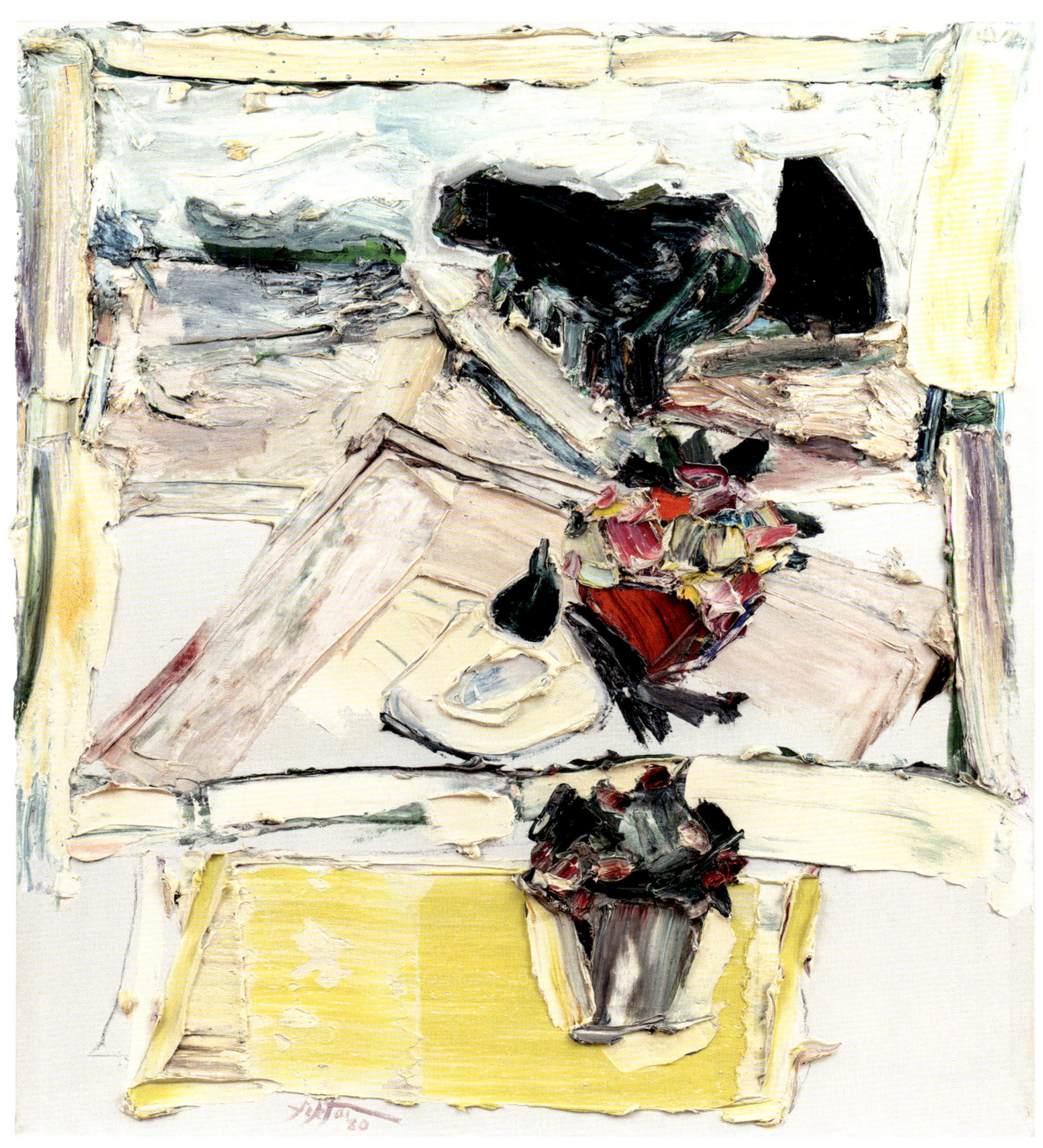

Untitled, 1980, oil on canvas, 54 × 48 inches (137.2 × 121.9 cm)

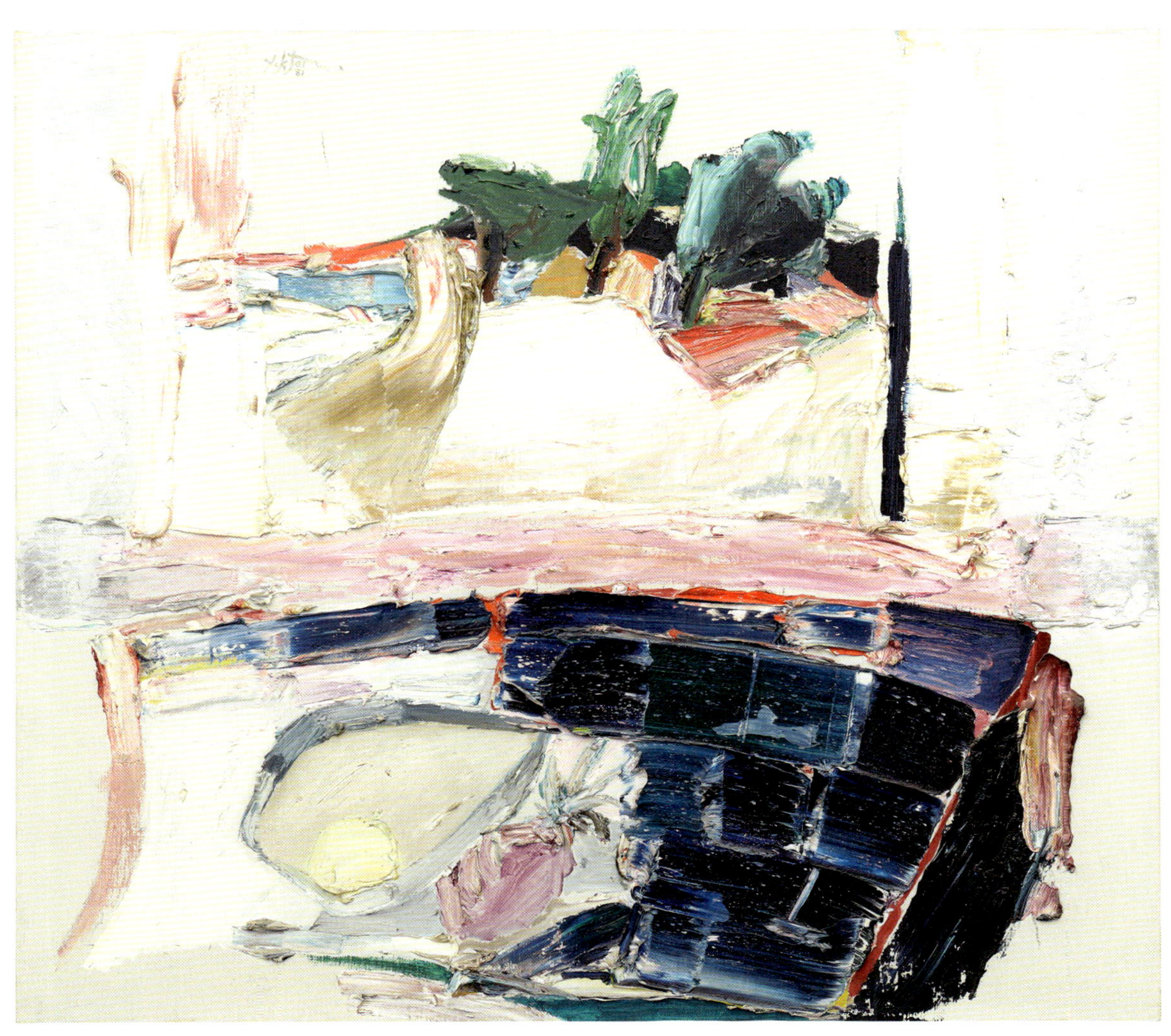

Blue Checkered Tablecloth, 1981, oil on canvas, 48 × 54 inches (121.9 × 137.2 cm)

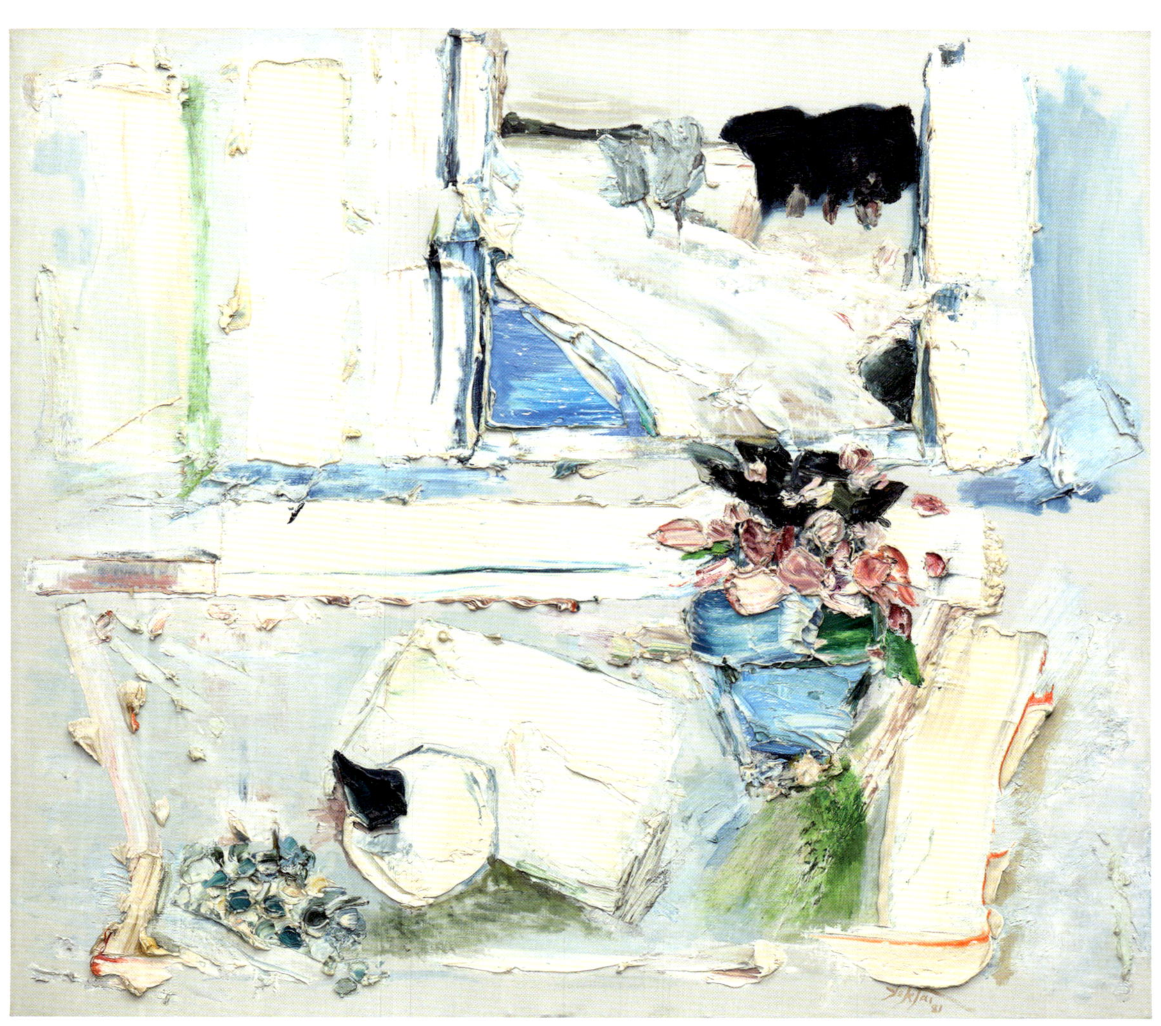

 Untitled, 1981, oil on canvas, 48 × 54 inches (121.9 × 137.2 cm)

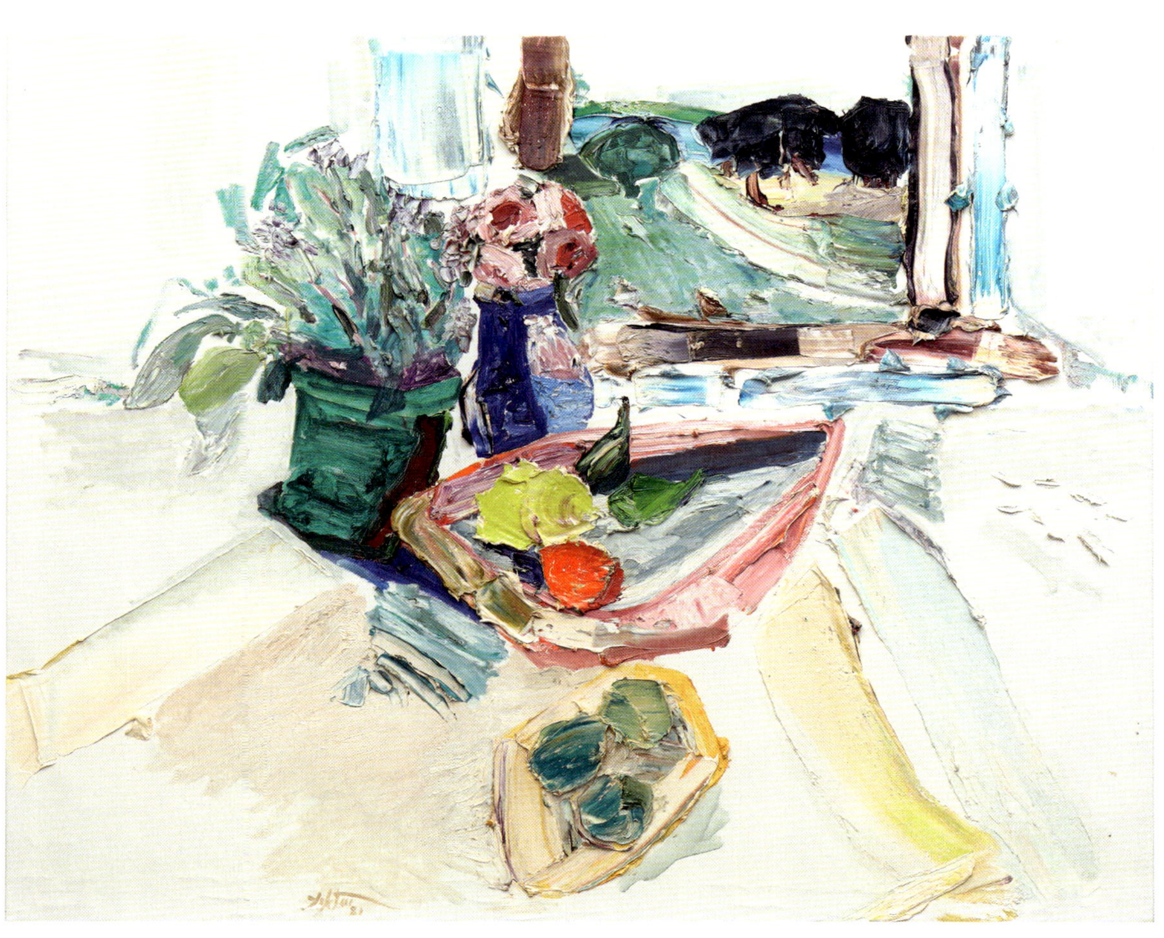

Untitled, 1981, oil on canvas, 46 × 58 inches (117 × 147 cm)

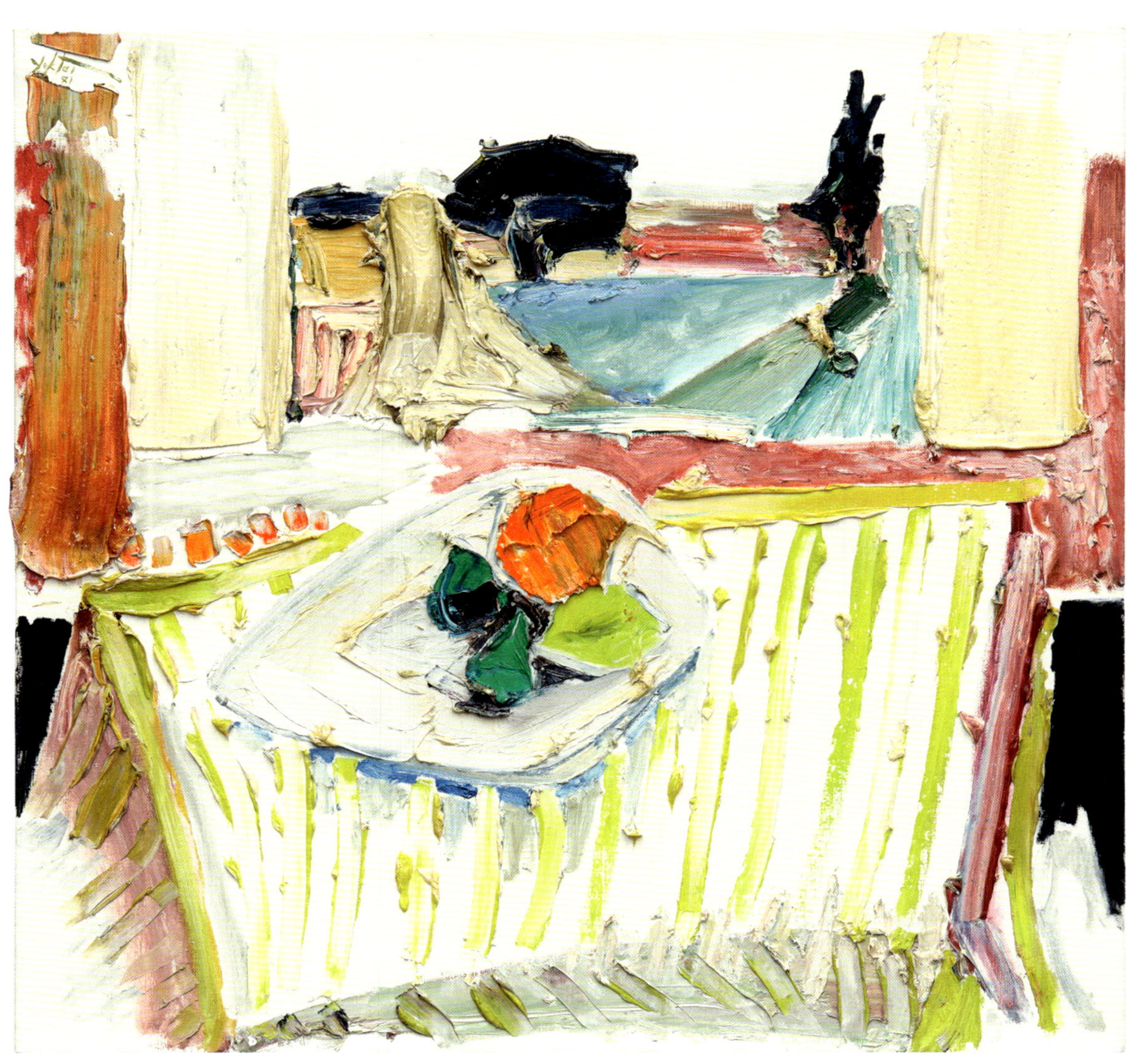

 Untitled, 1981, oil on canvas, 36 × 38 inches (91.4 × 96.5 cm)

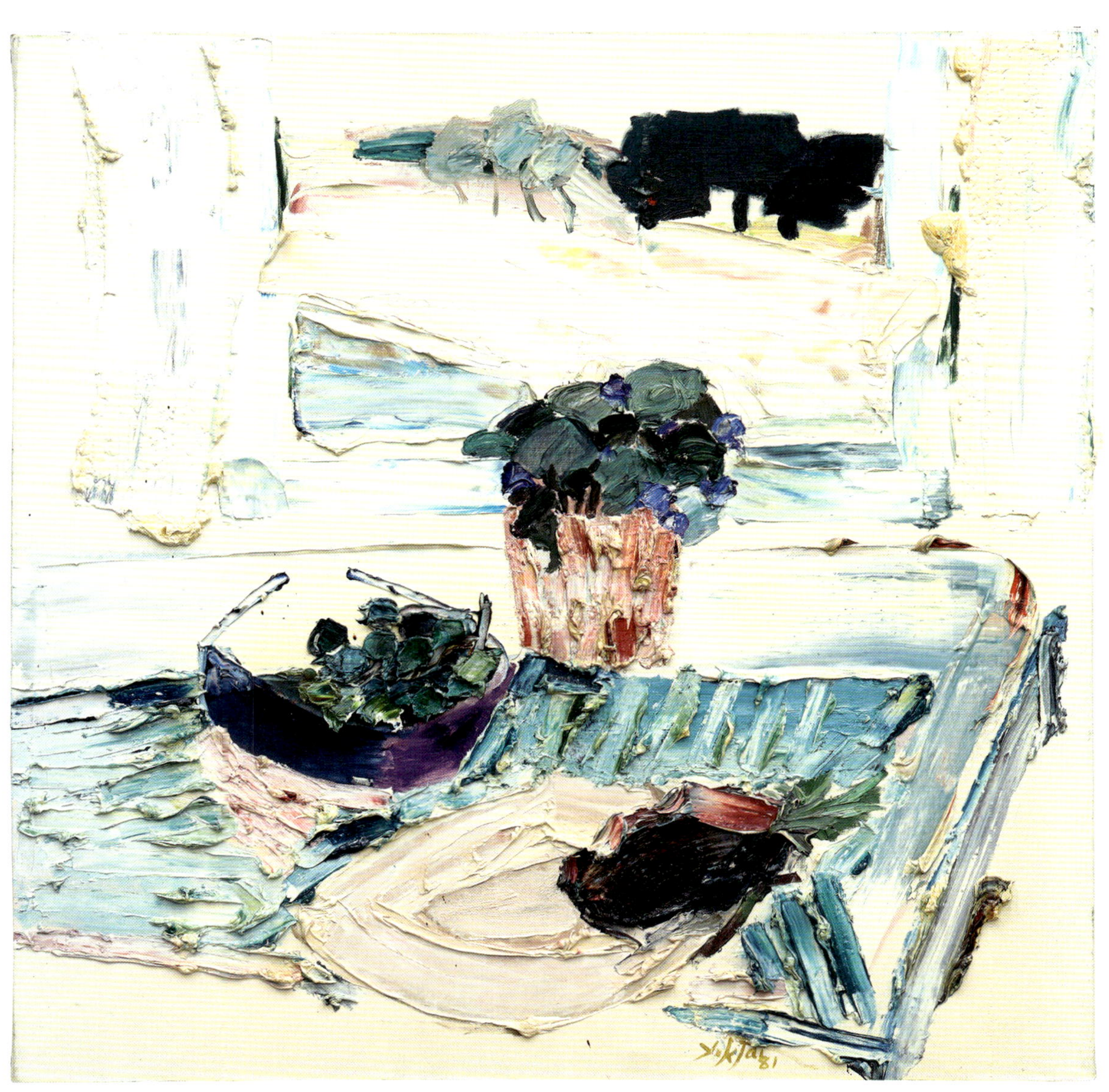

Untitled, 1981, oil on canvas, 39¼ × 39¼ inches (99.7 × 99.7 cm)

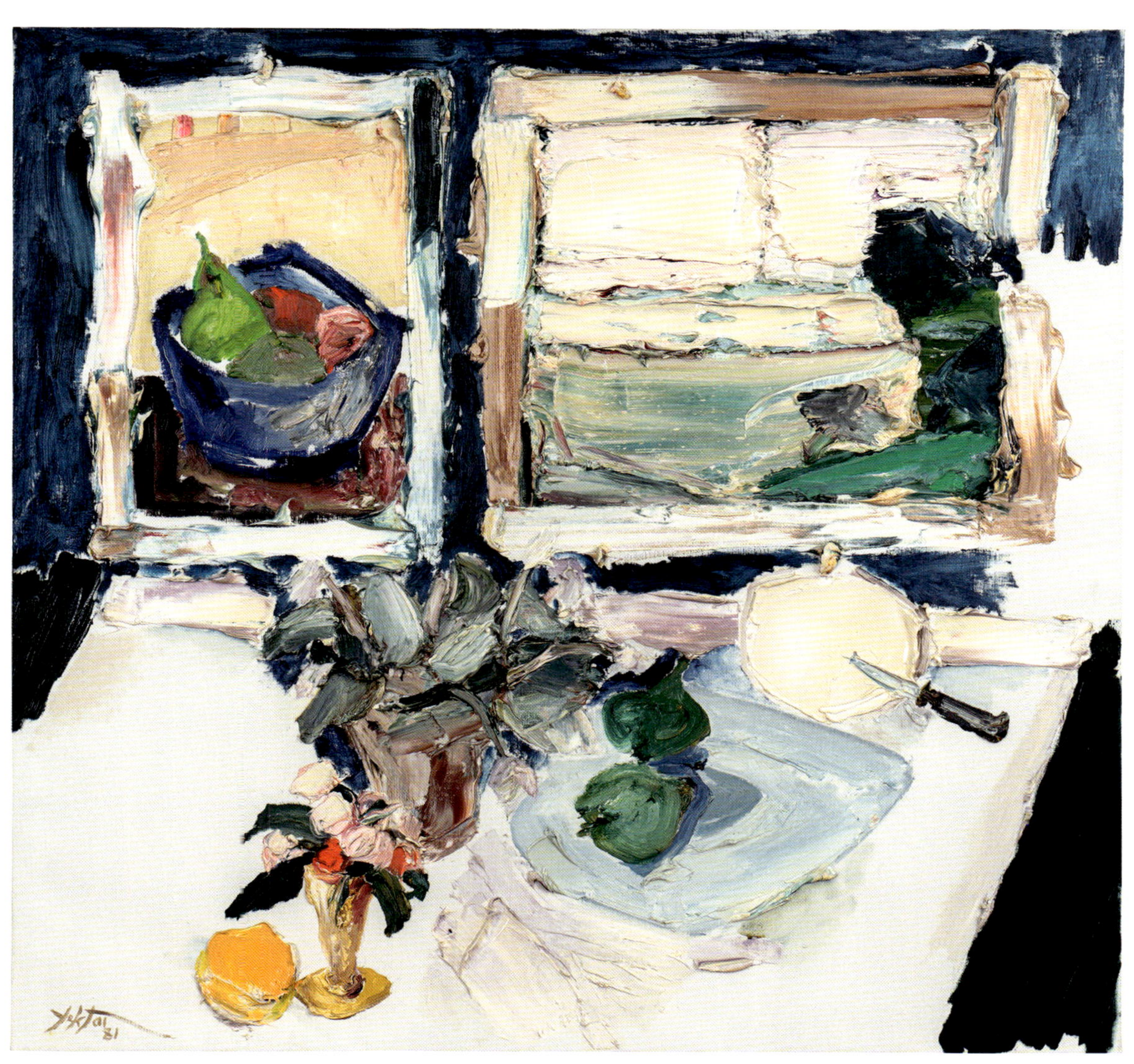

Untitled, 1981, oil on canvas, 36 × 38 inches (91.4 × 96.5 cm)

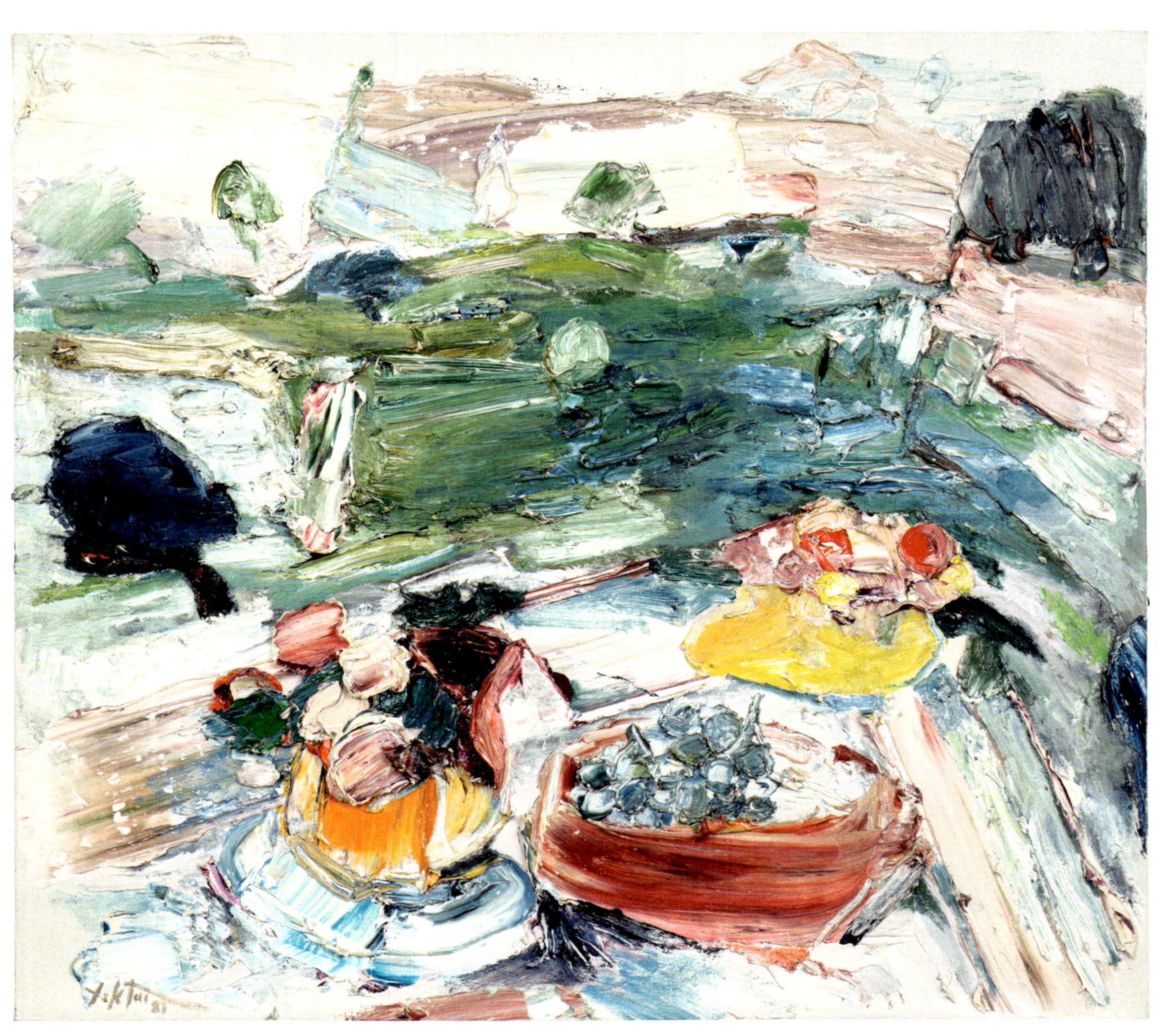

 Untitled, 1981, oil on canvas, 36 × 40 inches (91.4 × 101.6 cm)

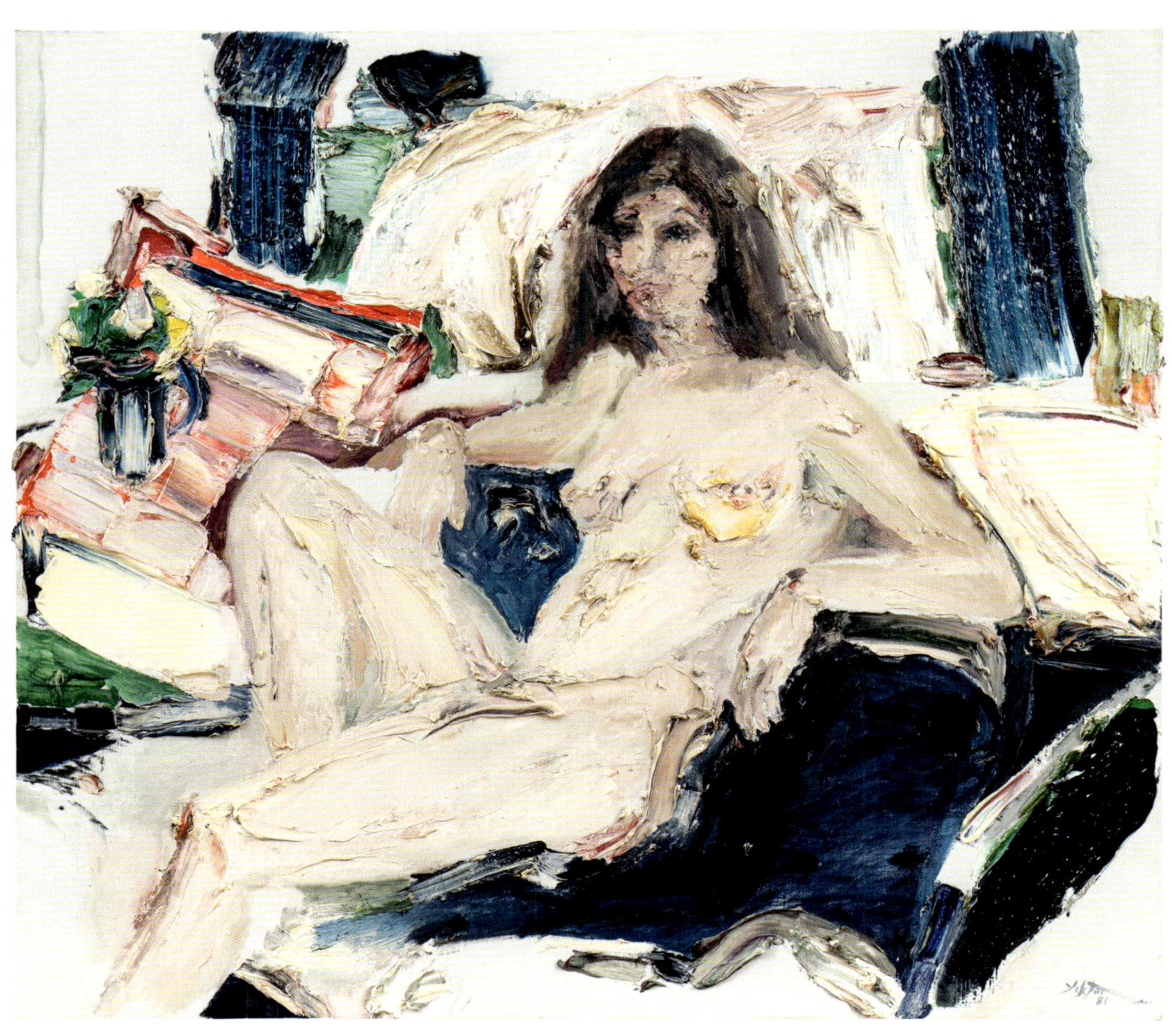

Untitled, 1981, oil on canvas, 48 × 54 inches (121.9 × 137.2 cm)

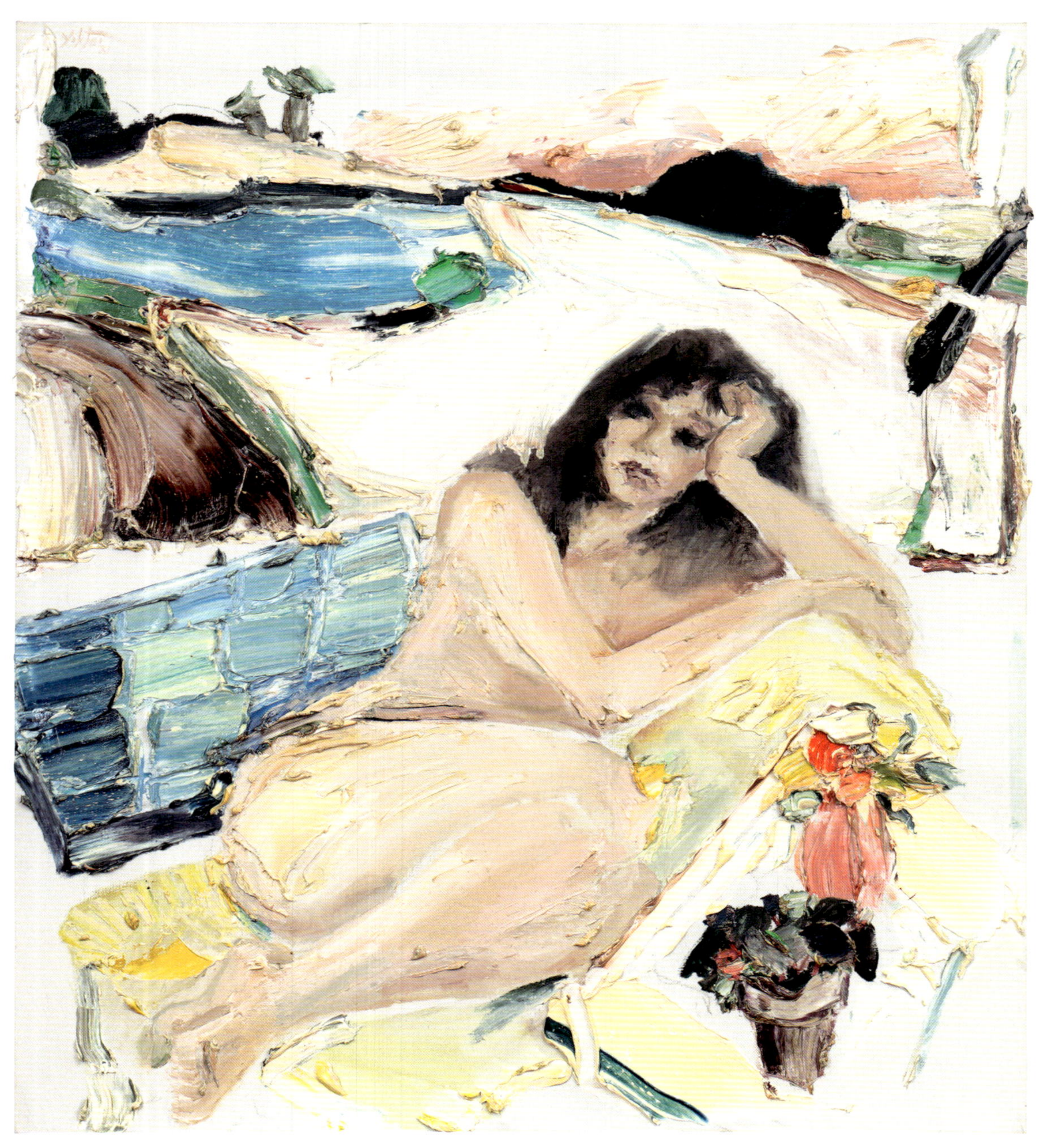

Untitled, 1981, oil on canvas, 54 × 48 inches (137.2 × 121.9 cm)

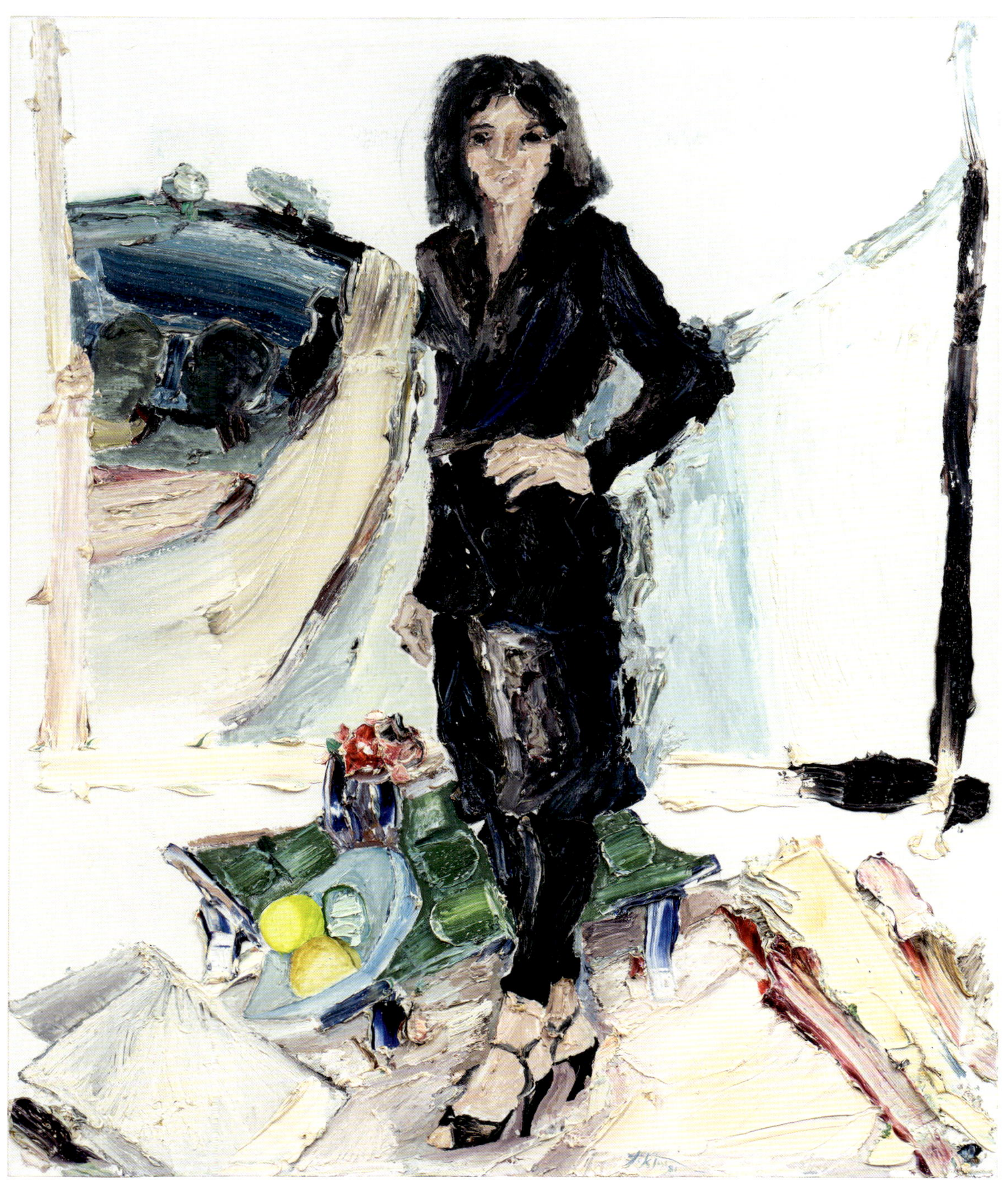

Standing Figure, 1981, oil on canvas, 60 × 72 inches (152 × 183 cm)

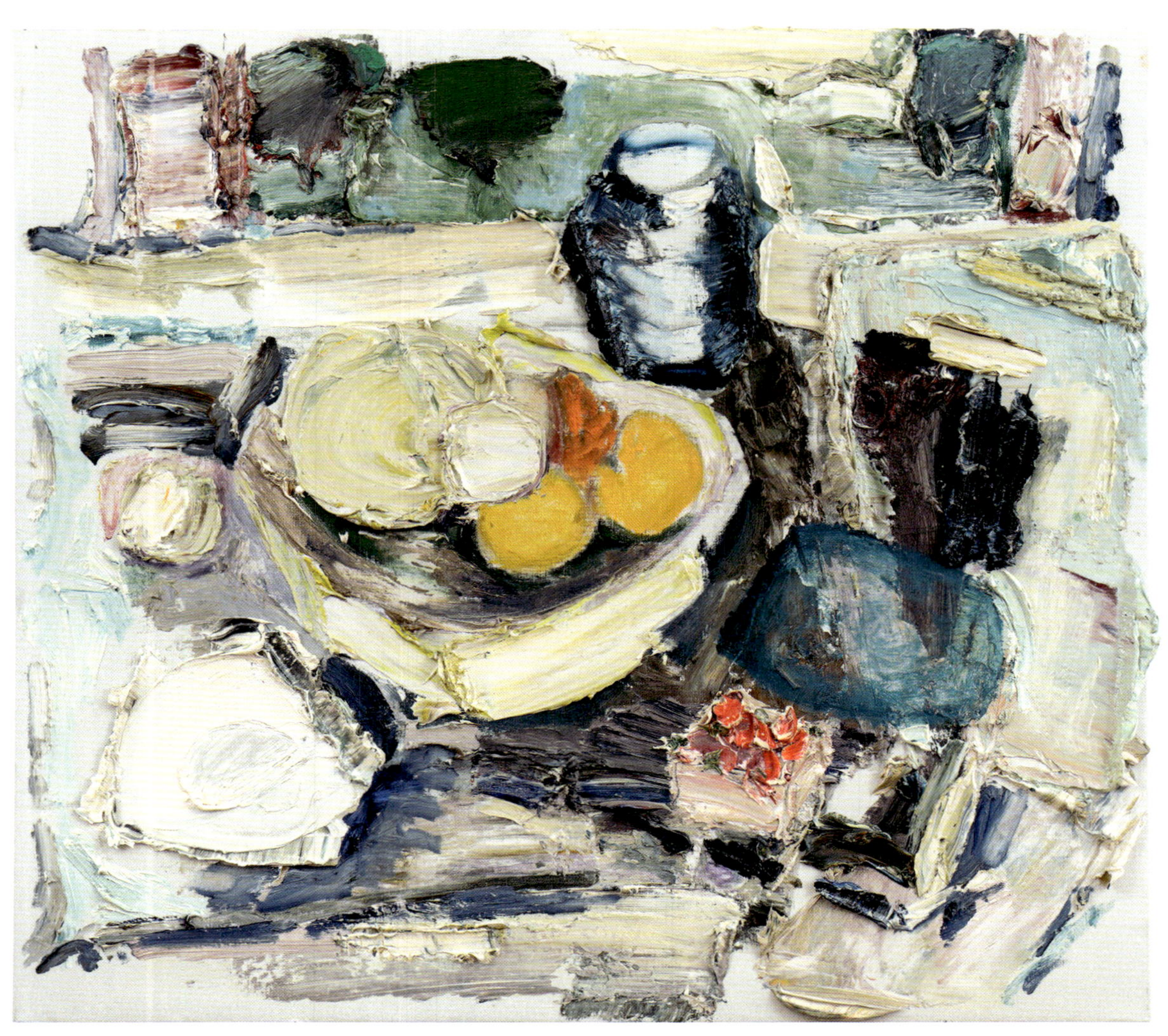

 Untitled, 1981, oil on canvas, 36 × 40 inches (91.4 × 101.6 cm)

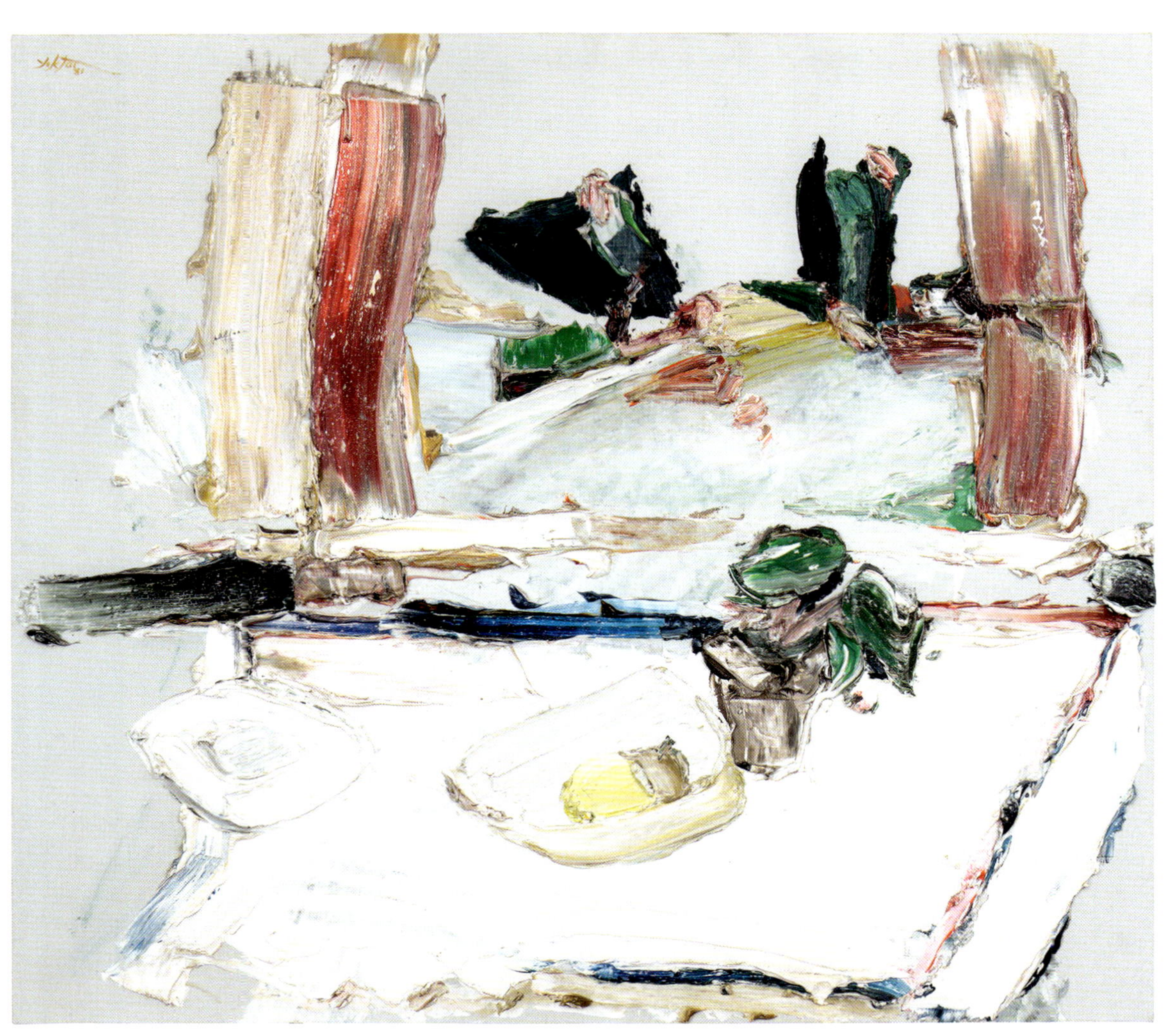

White Table, 1981, oil on canvas, 48 × 54 inches (121.9 × 137.2 cm)

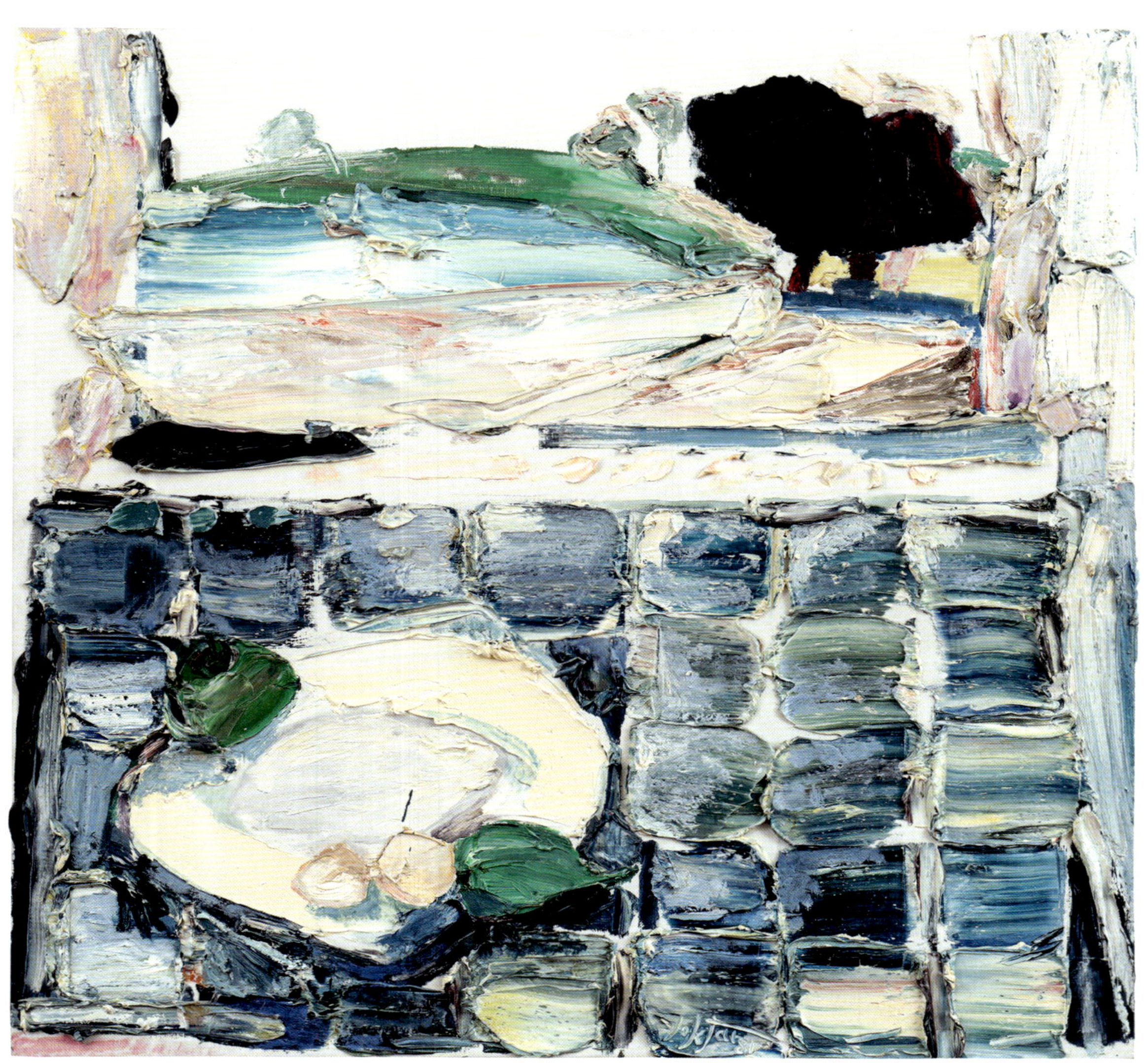

 Untitled, 1981, oil on canvas, 36 × 38 inches (91.4 × 96.5 cm)

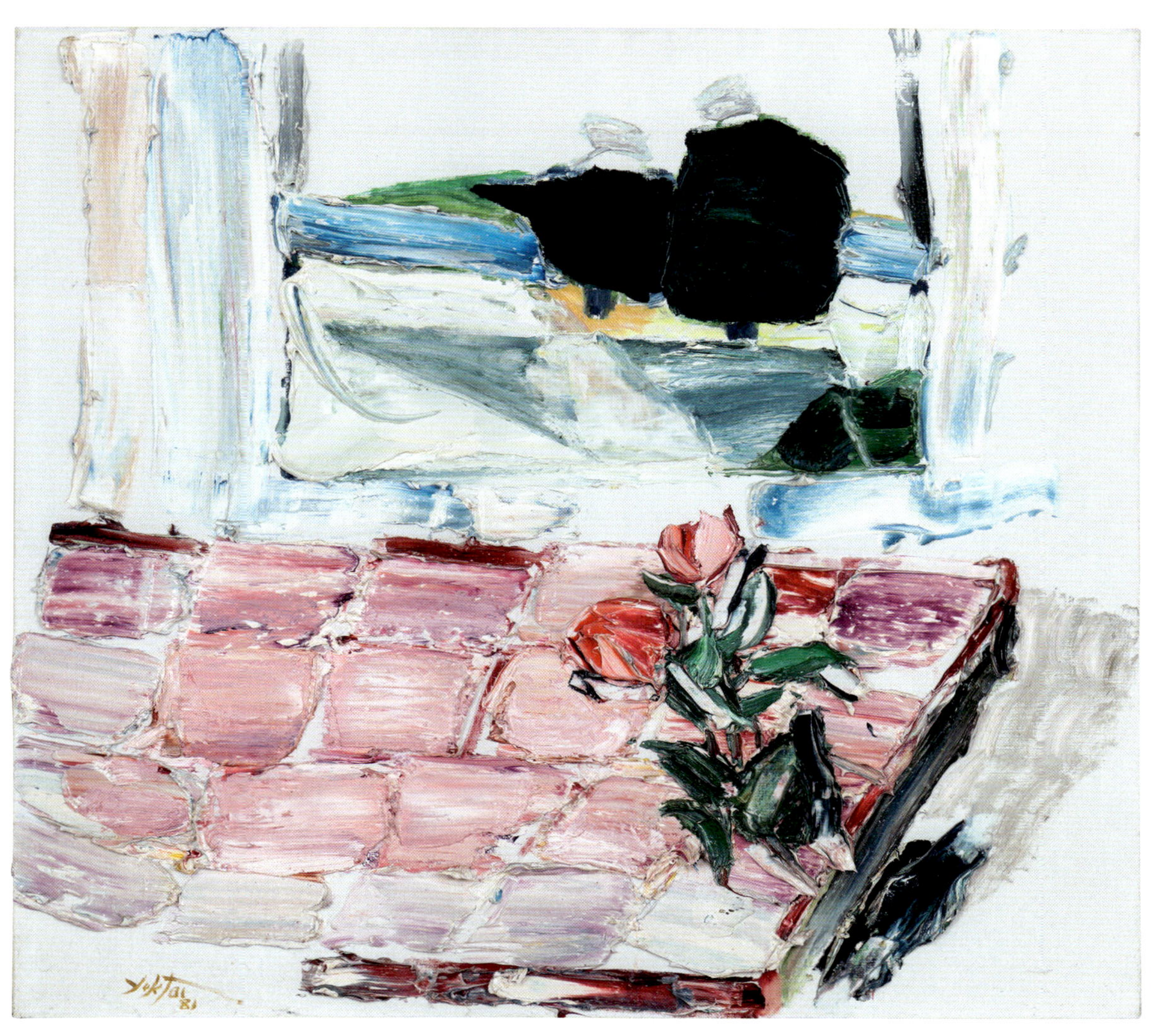

Roses, 1981, oil on canvas, 36 × 40 inches (91.4 × 101.6 cm)

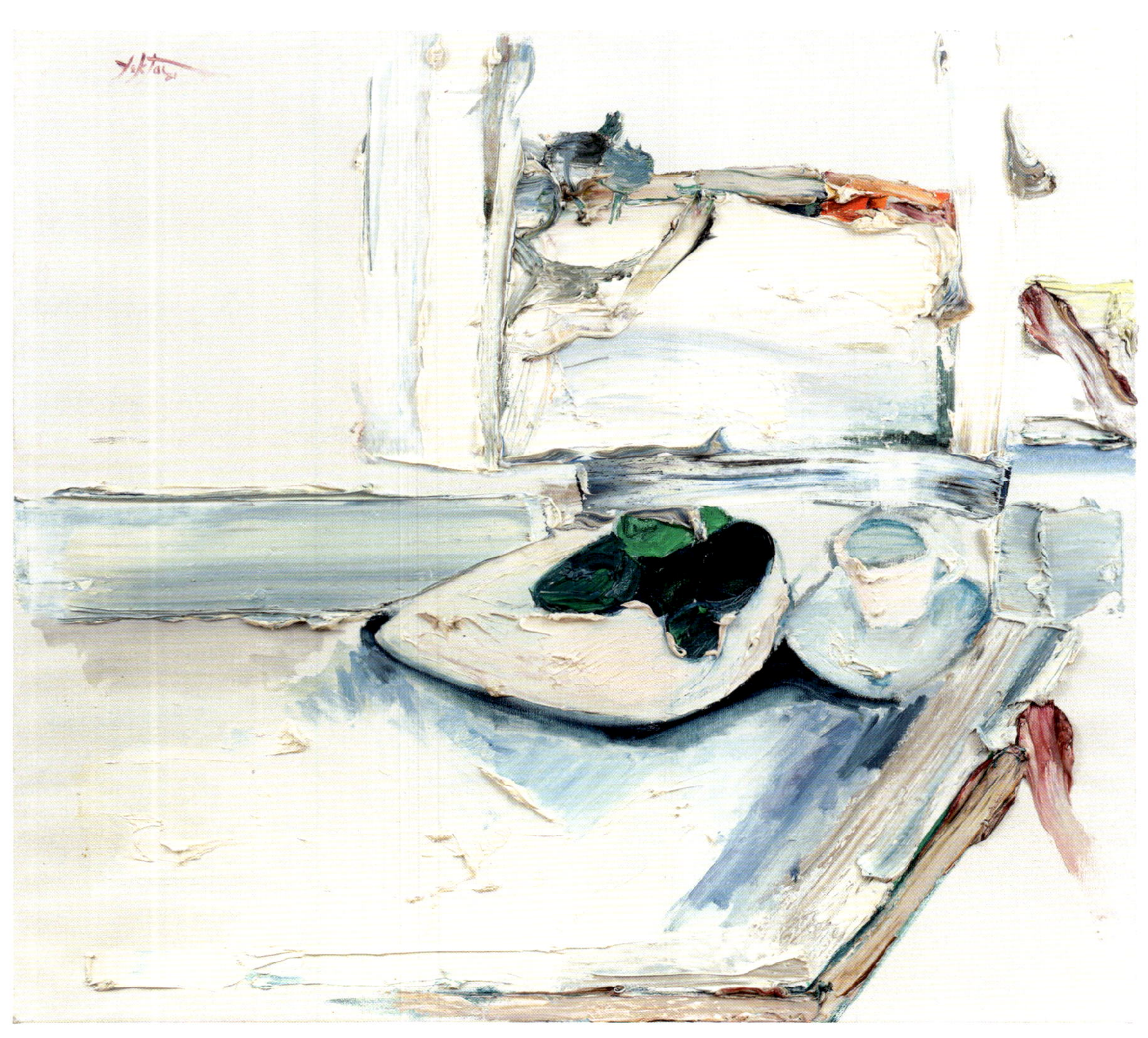

Untitled, 1981, oil on canvas, 40 × 44 inches (101.6 × 111.8 cm)

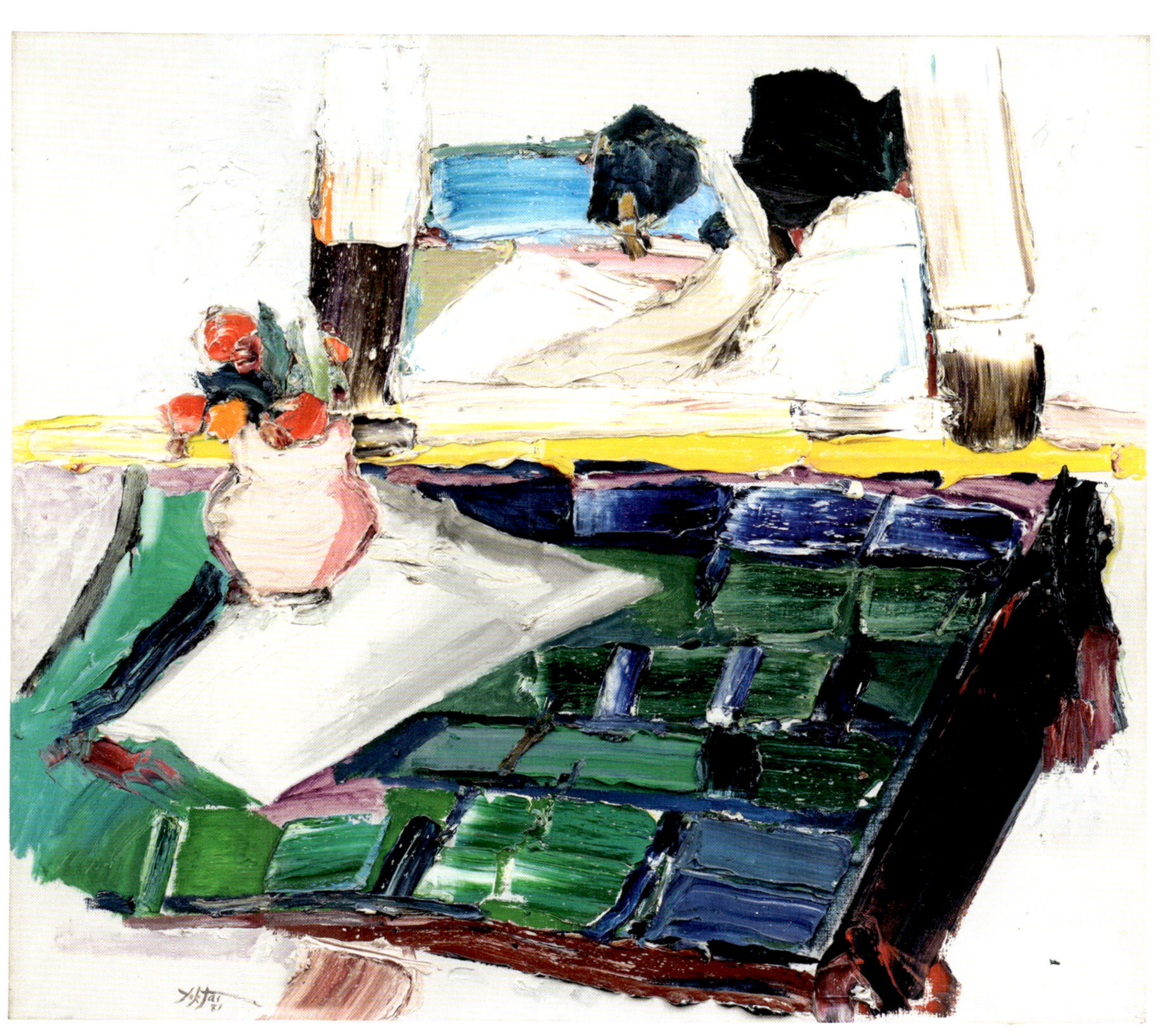

Green Table, 1981, oil on canvas, 48 × 51 inches (121.9 × 129.5 cm)

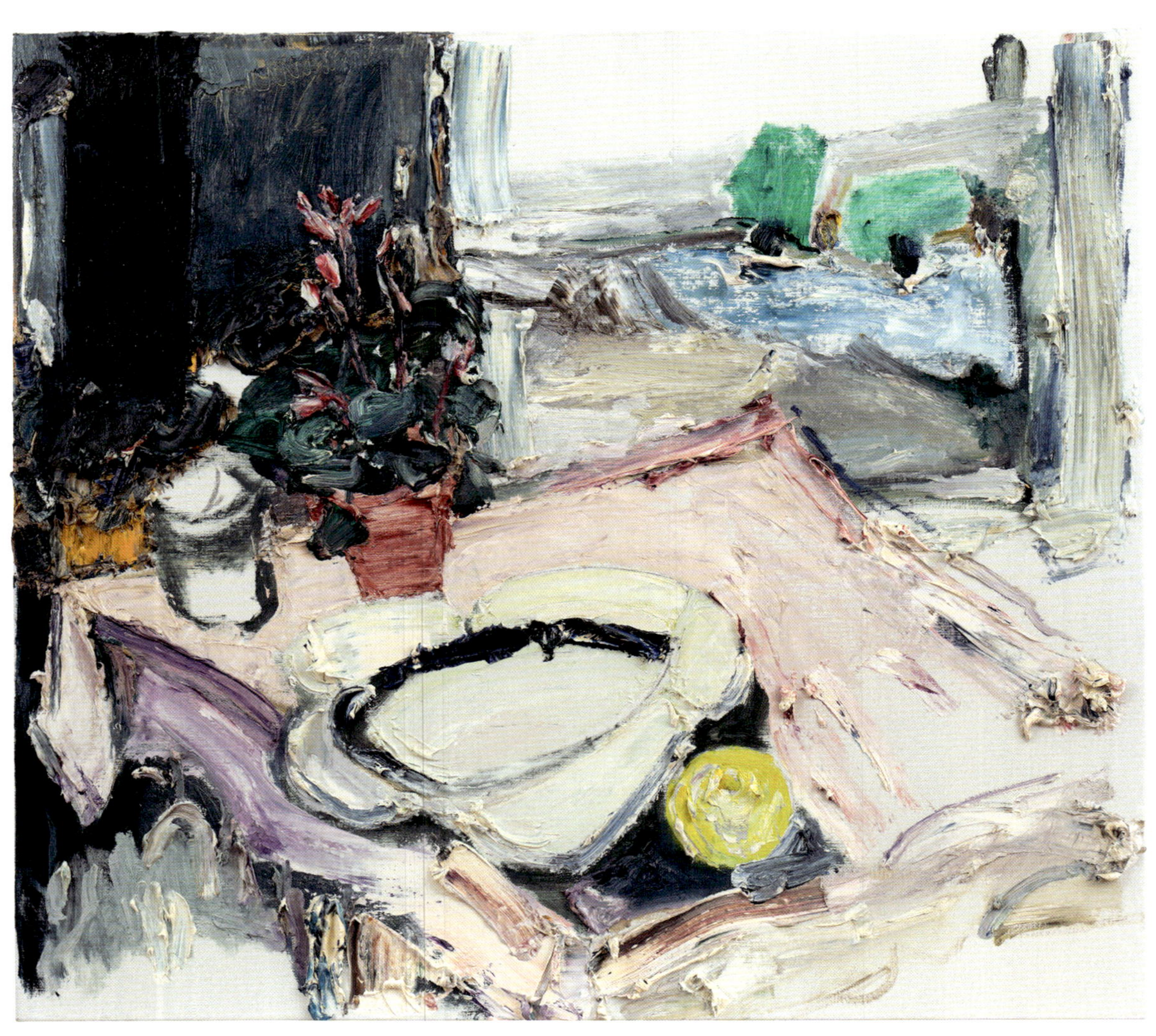

 Untitled, ca. 1982, oil on canvas, 36 × 40 inches (91.4 × 101.6 cm)

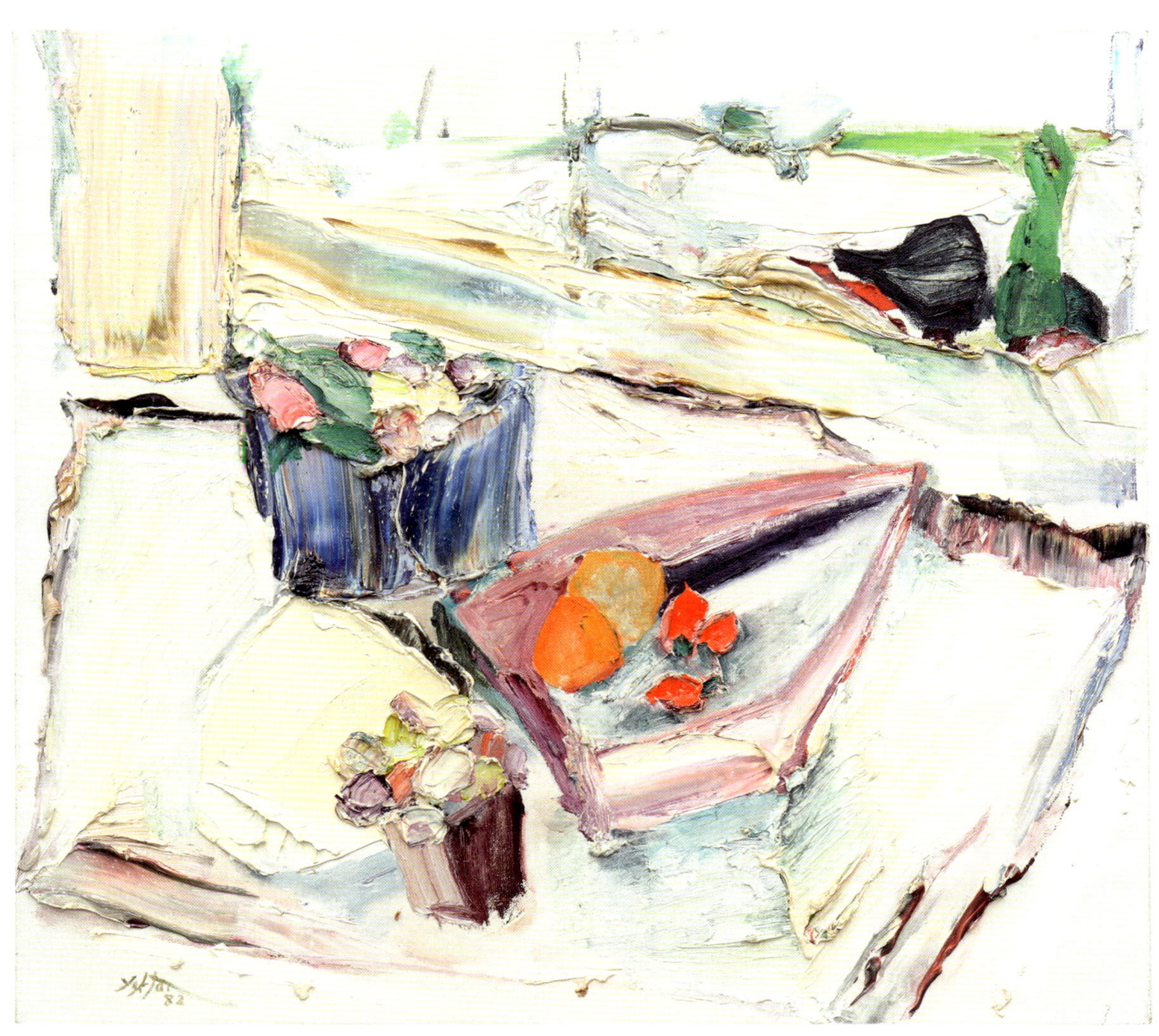

Roses, 1982, oil on canvas, 36 × 40 inches (91.4 × 101.6 cm)

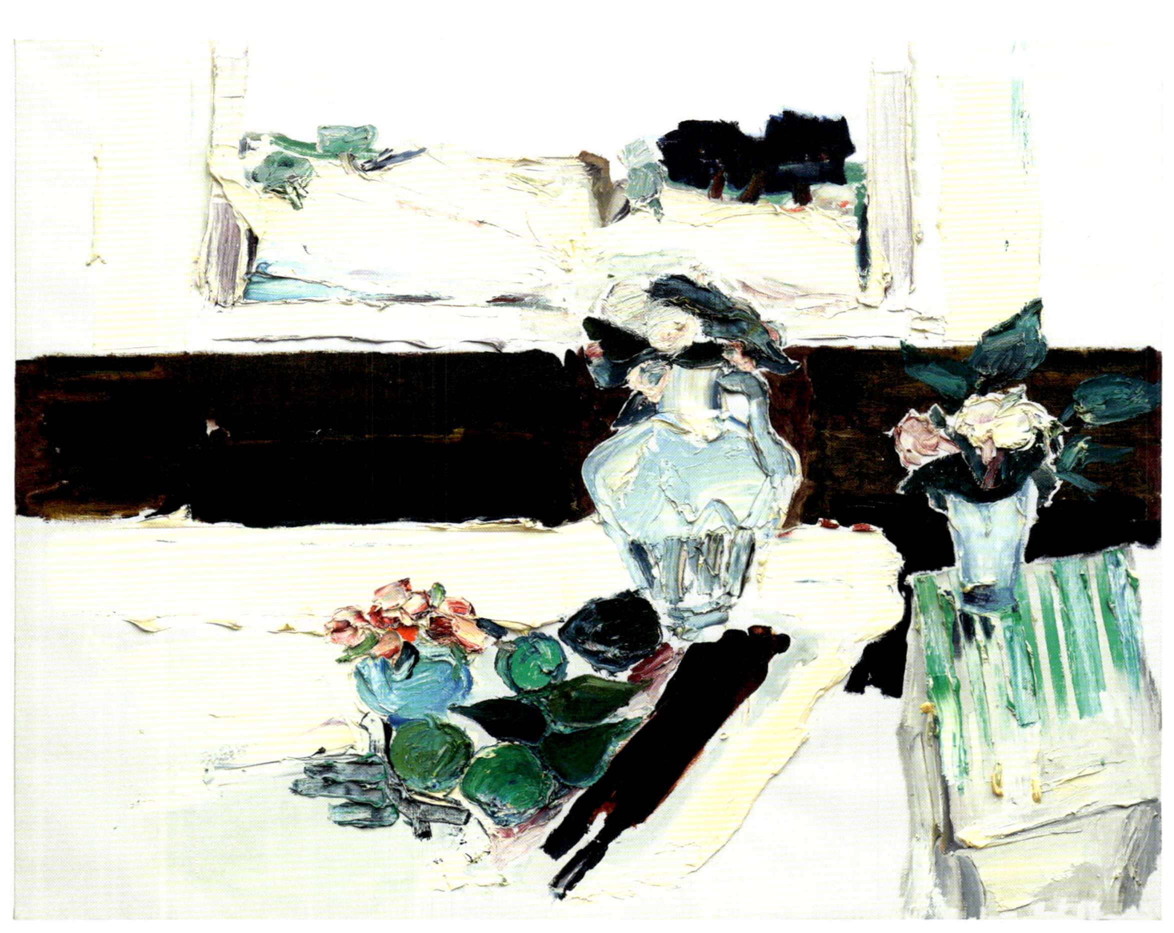

Untitled, 1982, oil on canvas, 46 × 58 inches (116.8 × 147.3 cm)

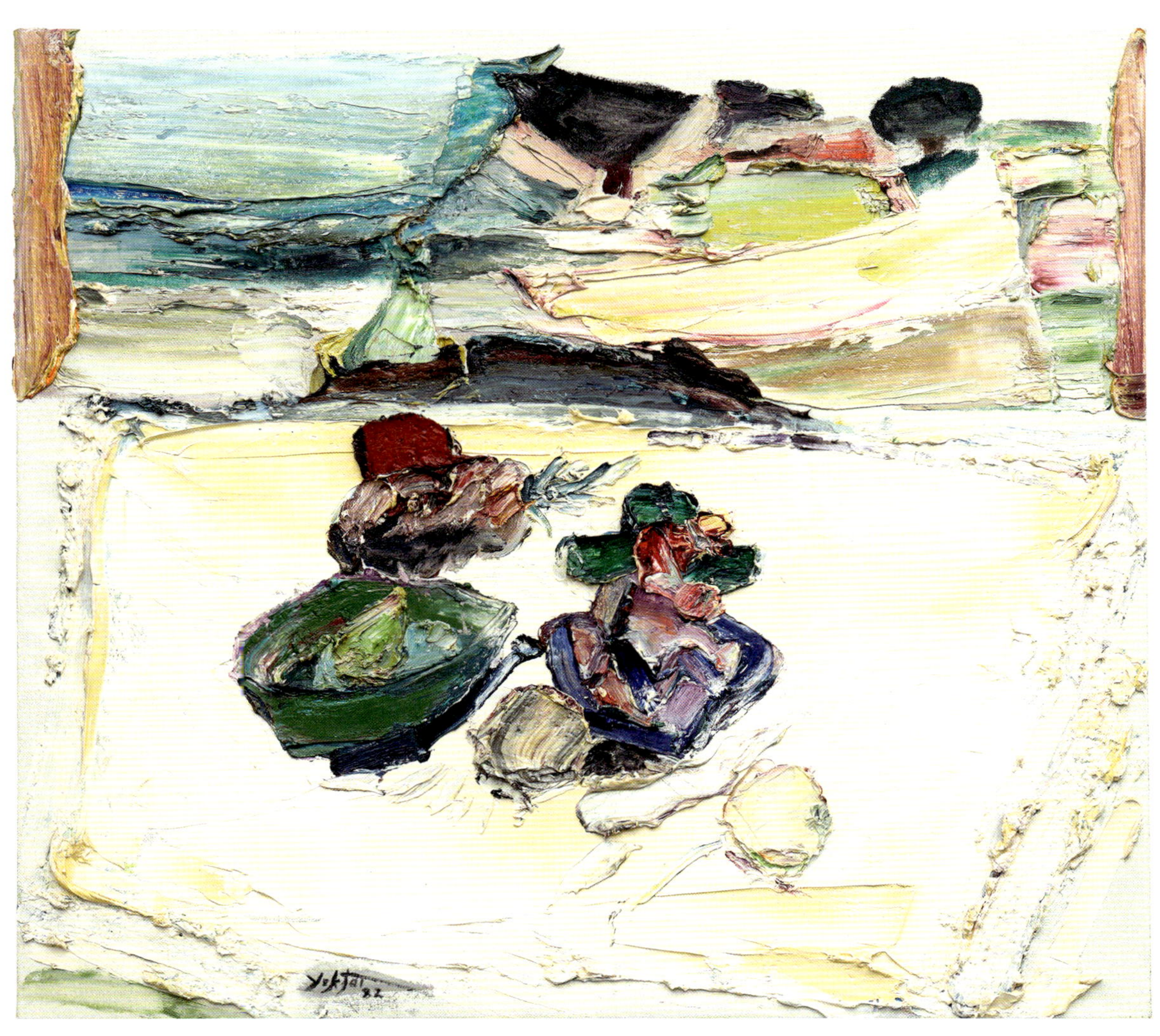

Untitled, 1982, oil on canvas, 36 × 40 inches (91.4 × 101.6 cm)

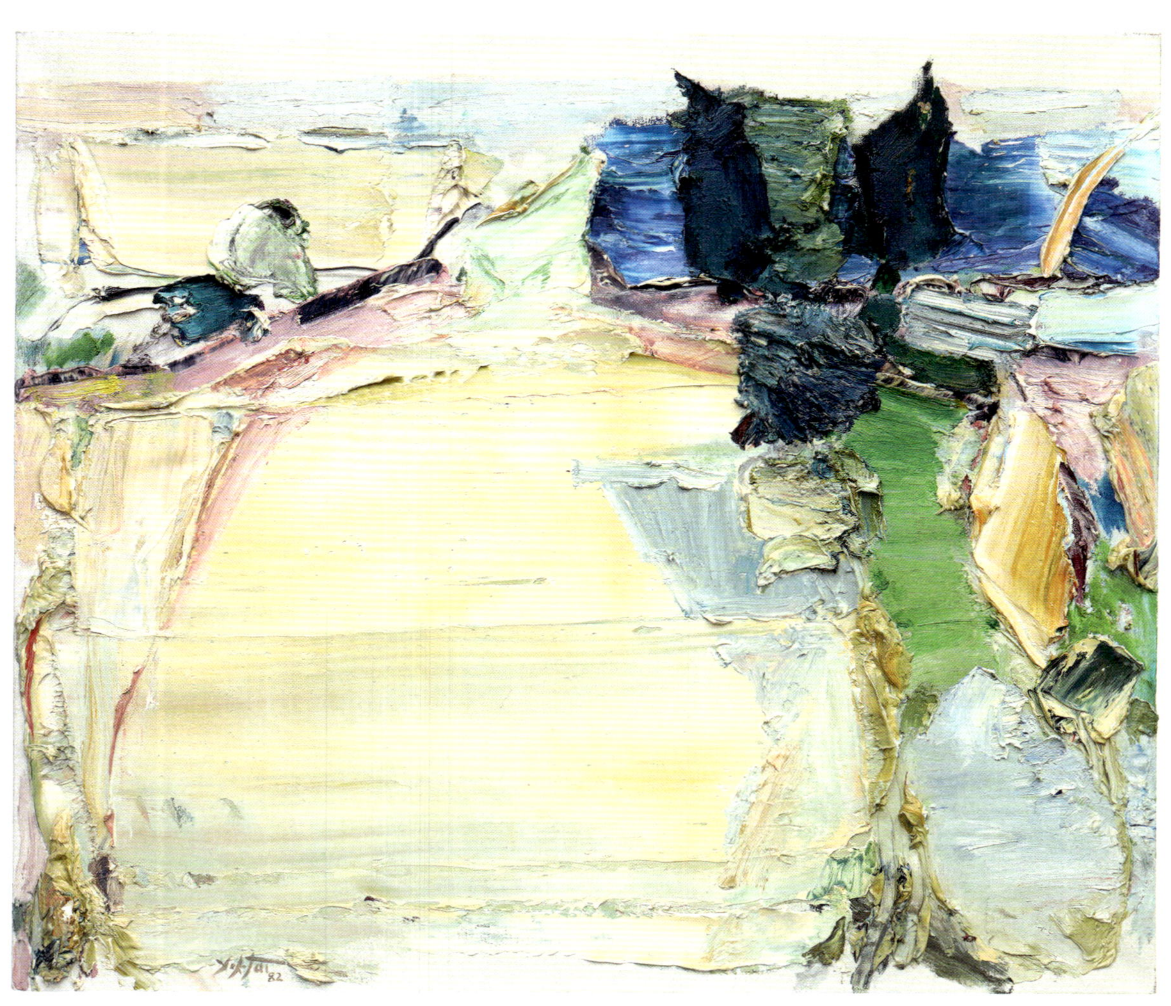

 Untitled, 1982, oil on canvas, 38 × 44 inches (96.5 × 111.8 cm)

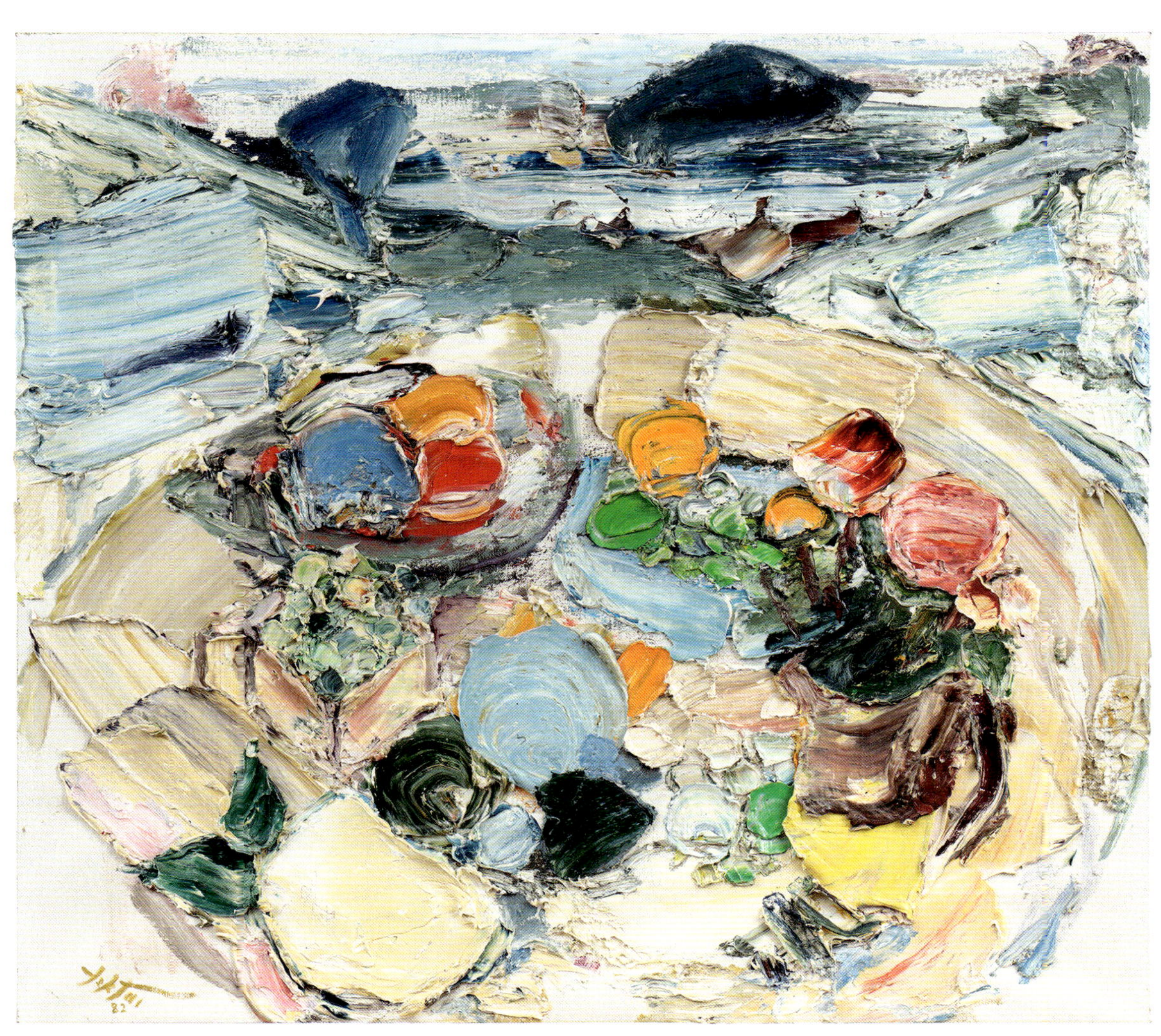

The Round Table, 1982, oil on canvas, 36 × 40 inches (91.4 × 101.6 cm)

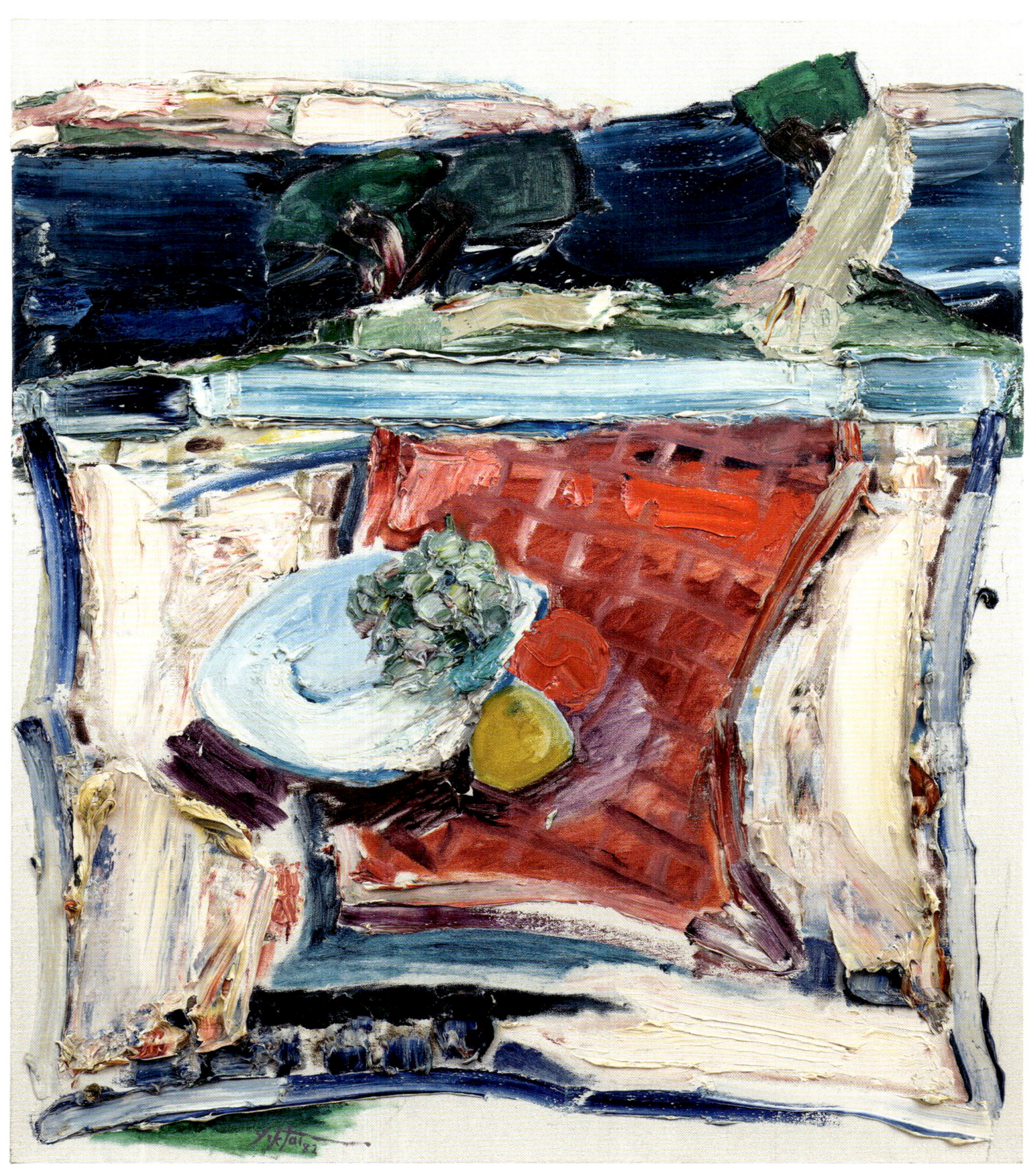

Untitled, 1982, oil on canvas, 44 × 38 inches (111.8 × 96.5 cm)

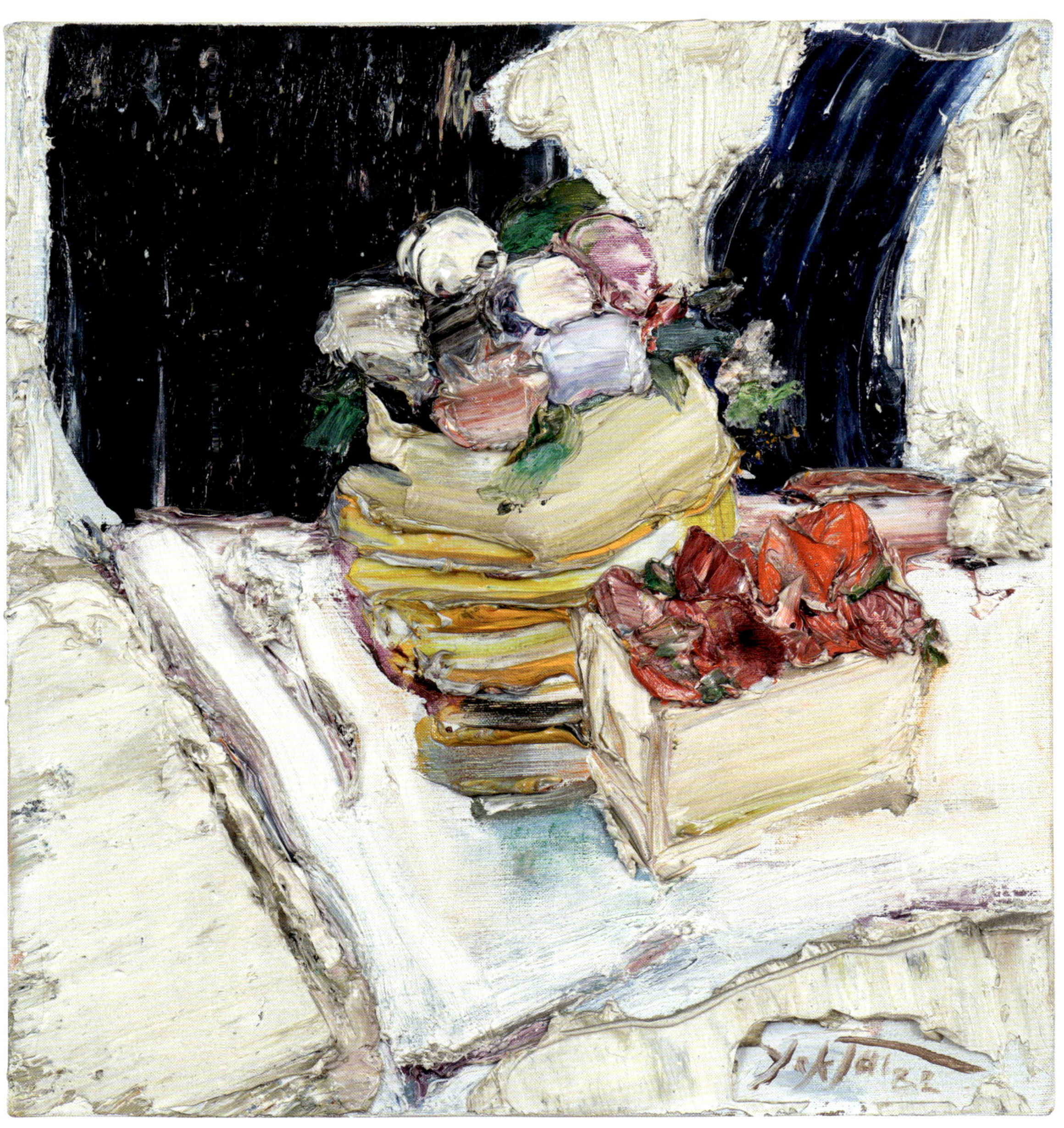

Strawberries, 1982, oil on canvas, 15 × 14 inches (38.1 × 35.6 cm)

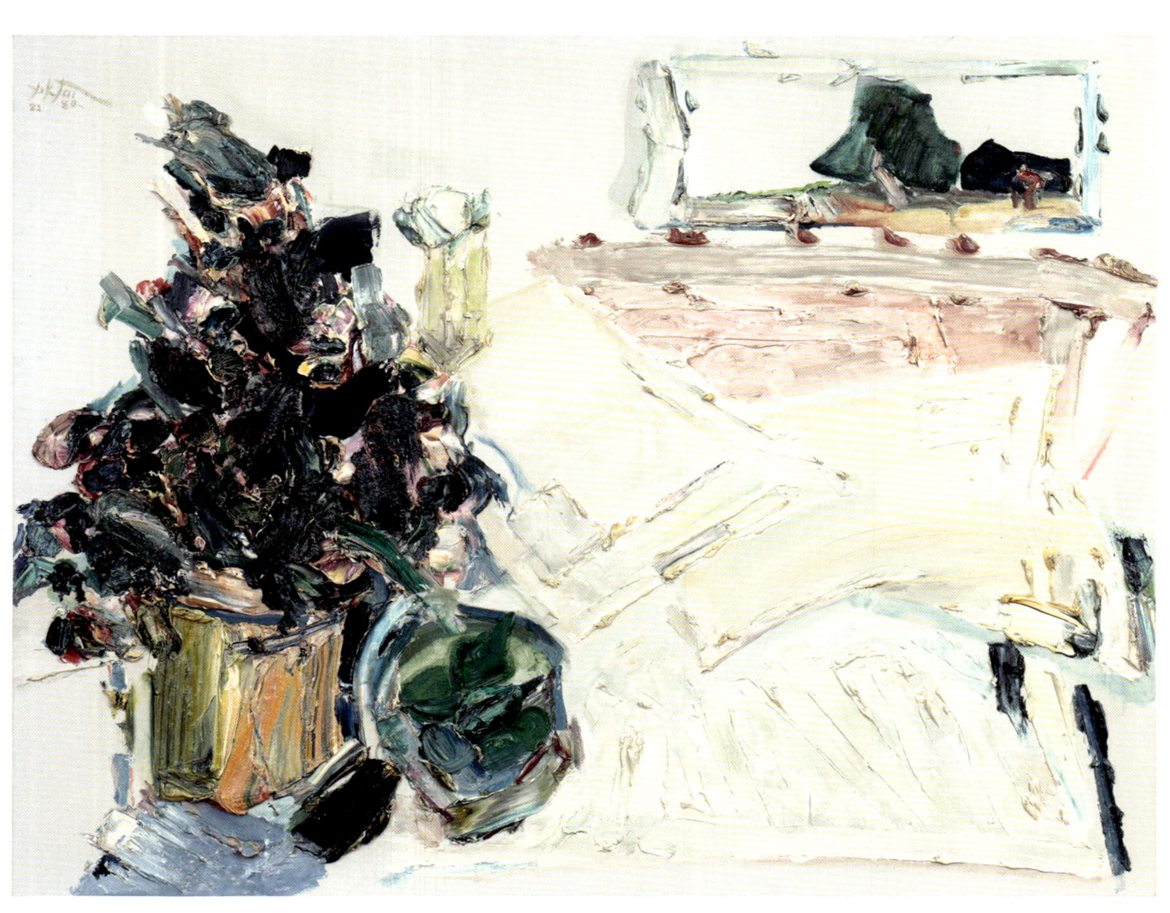

 Untitled, 1980–82, oil on canvas, 46 × 60 inches (116.8 × 152.4 cm)

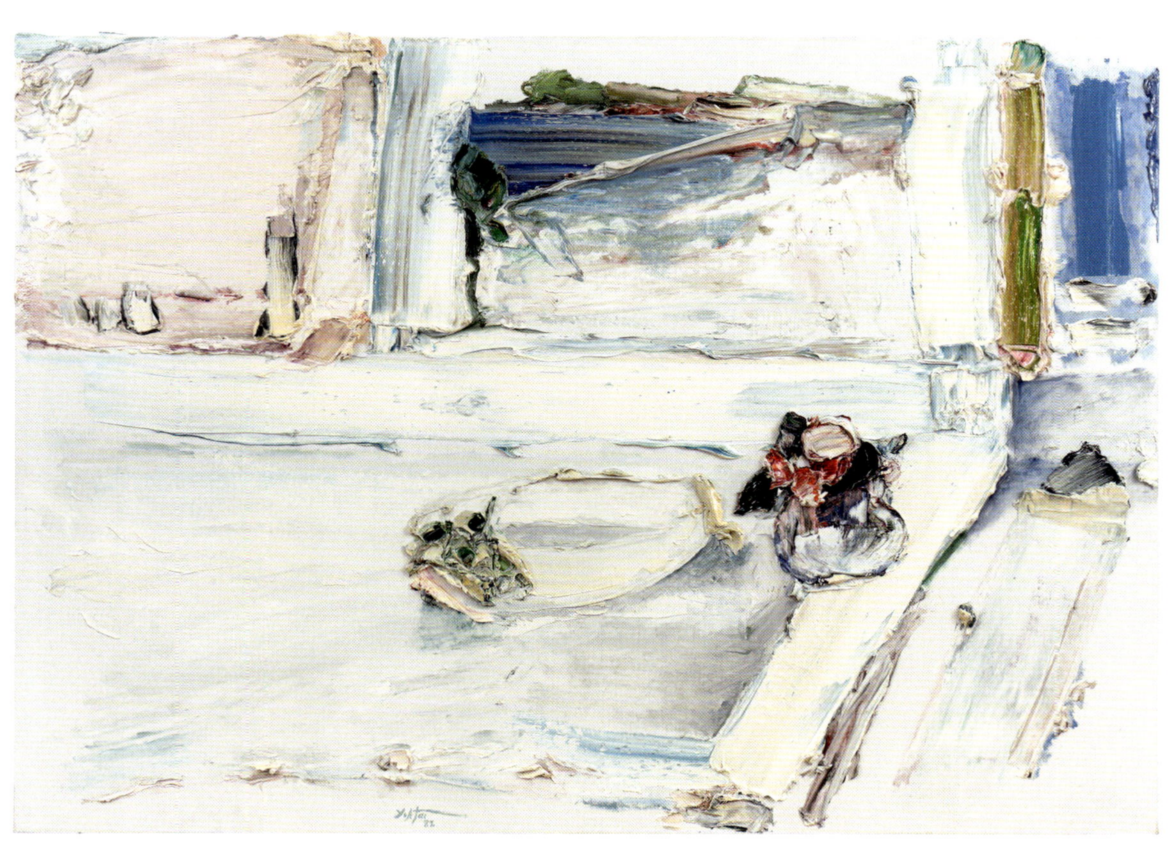

Blue Sea Blue Wall, 1982, oil on canvas, 46 × 64 inches (116.8 × 162.6 cm)

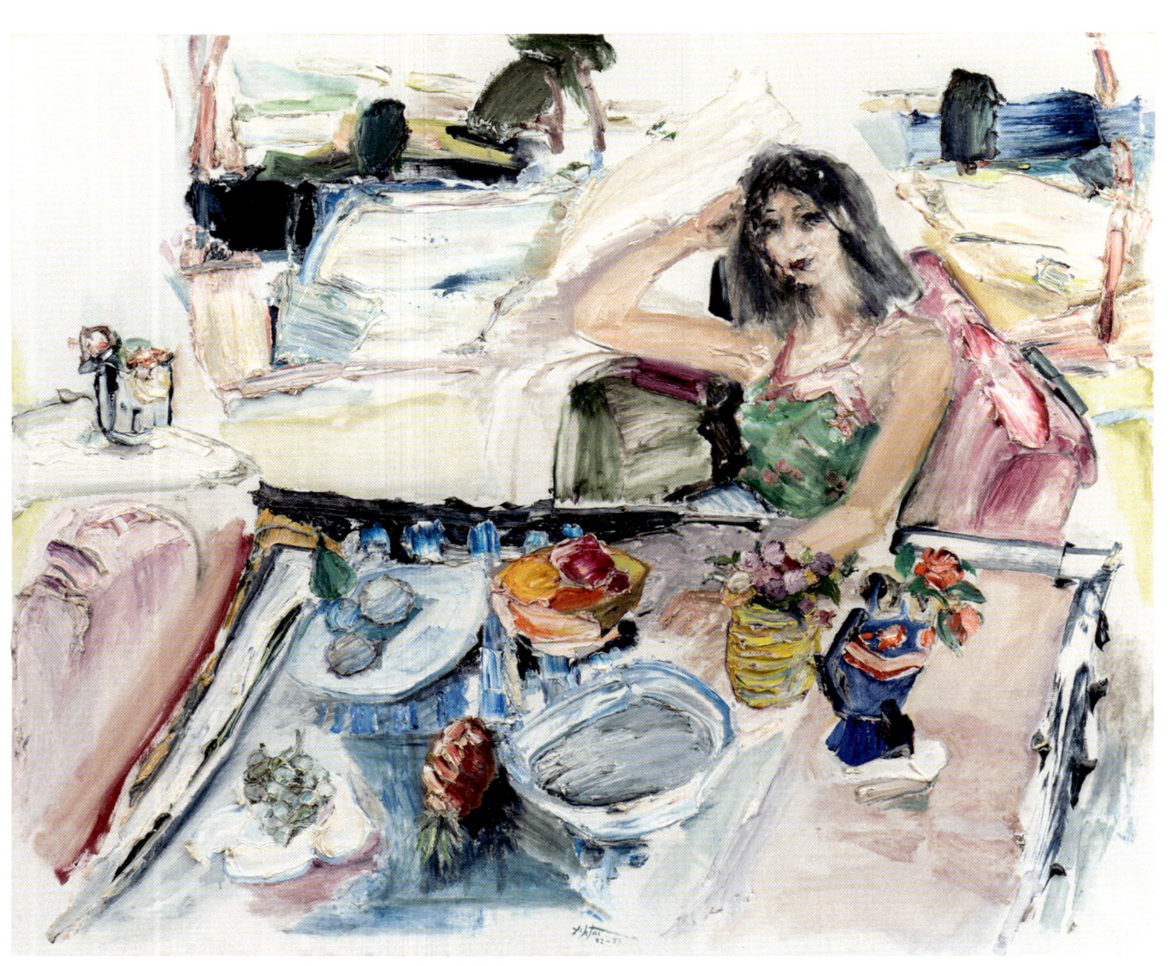

 Green Dress, 1982–83, oil on canvas, 60 × 72 inches (152.4 × 182.9 cm)

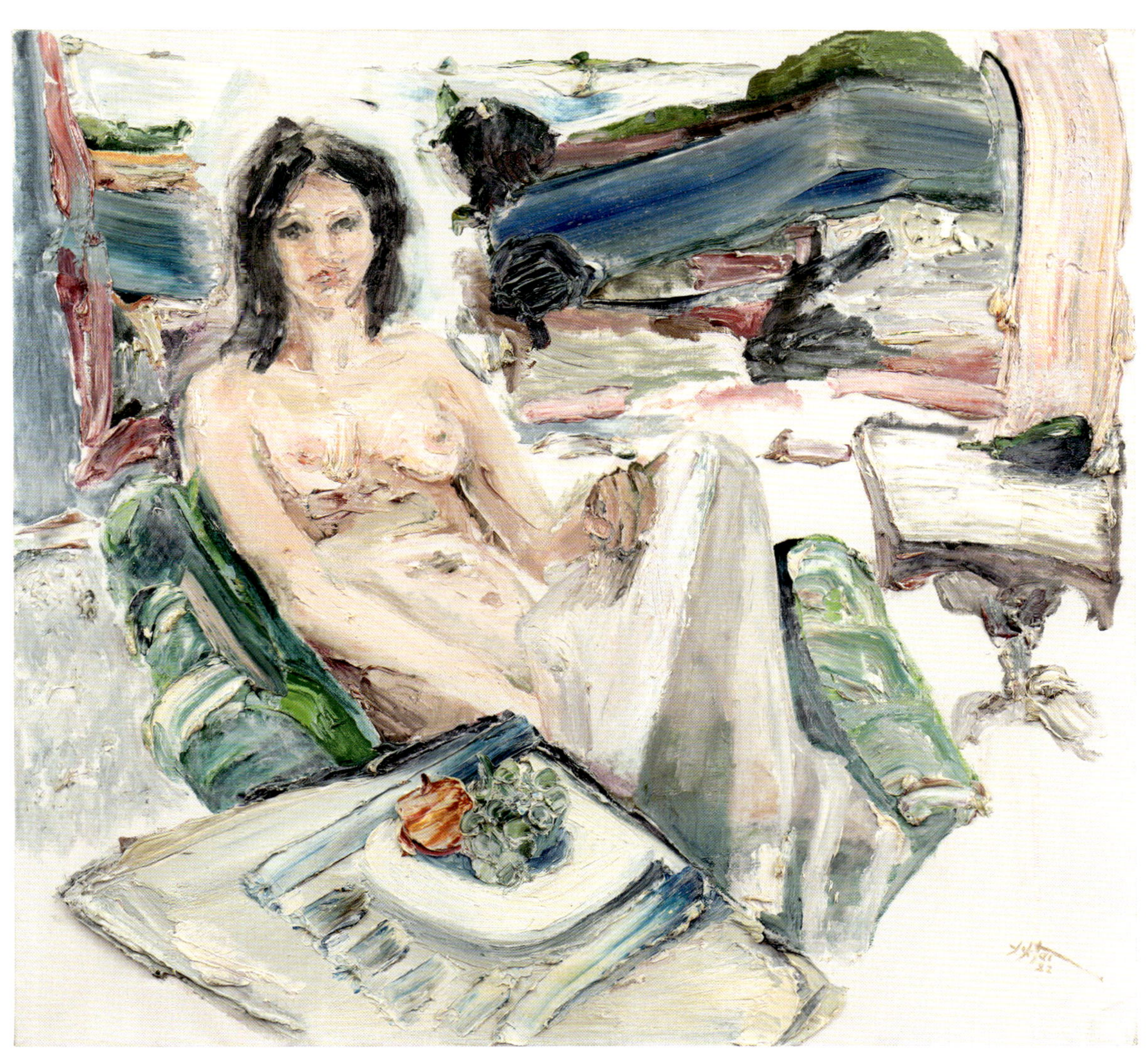

Green Couch, 1982, oil on canvas, 48 × 52 inches (121.9 × 132.1 cm)

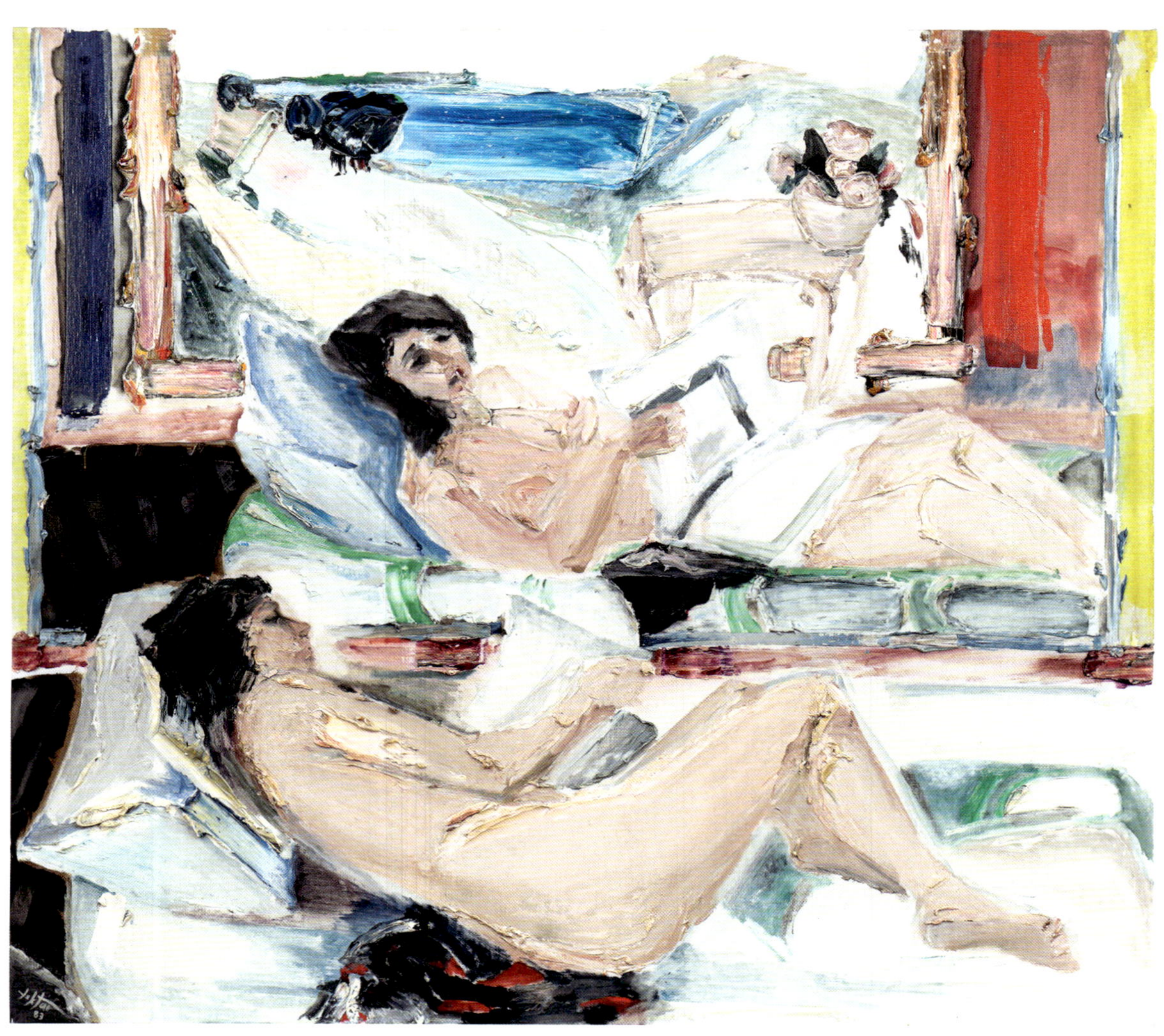

 Reflections, 1983, oil on canvas, 64 × 72 inches (162.6 × 182.9 cm)

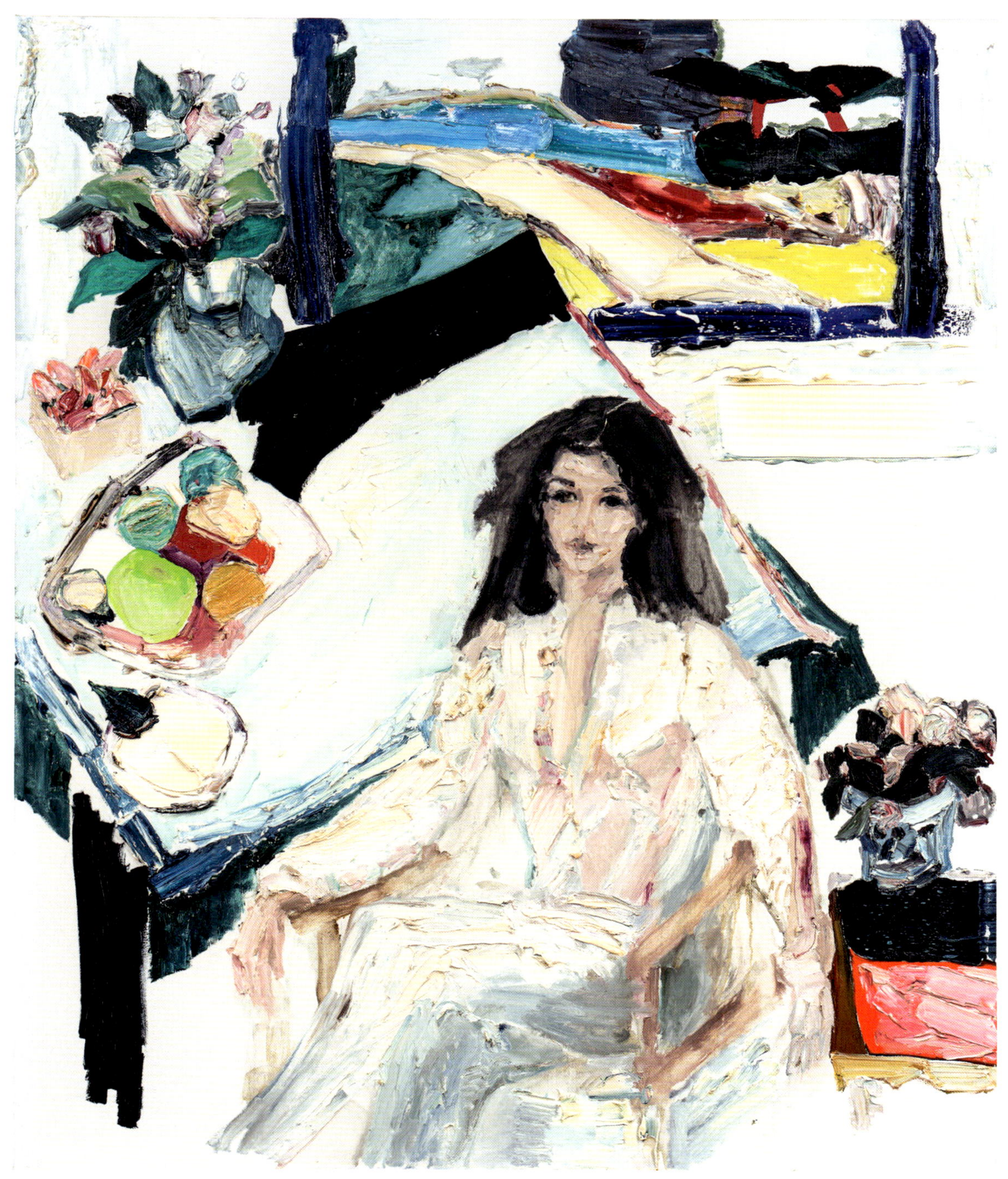

Untitled, 1983, oil on canvas, 72 × 60 inches (183 × 152 cm)

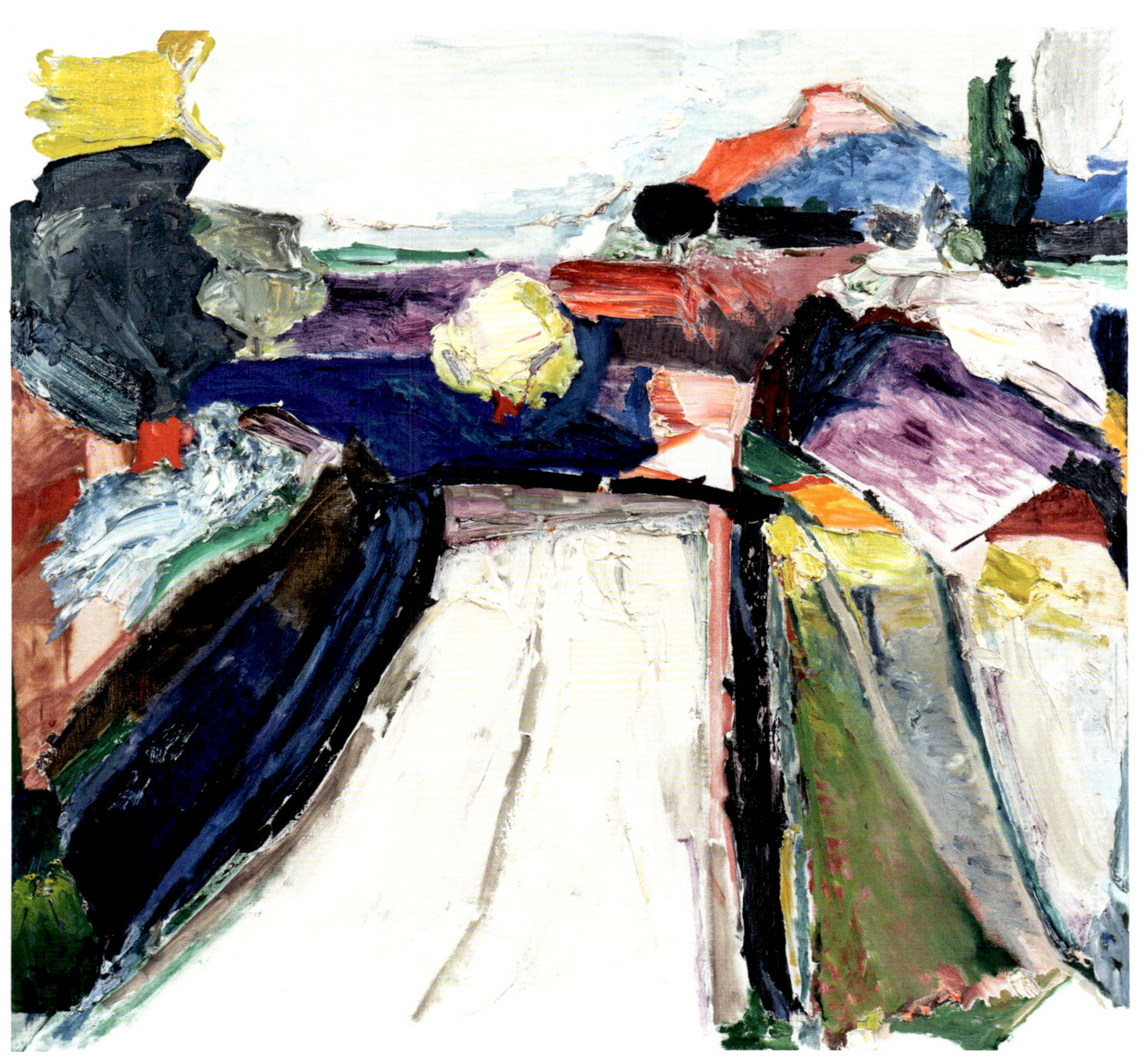

 Untitled, 1983, oil on canvas, 64 × 68 inches (162.6 × 172.7 cm)

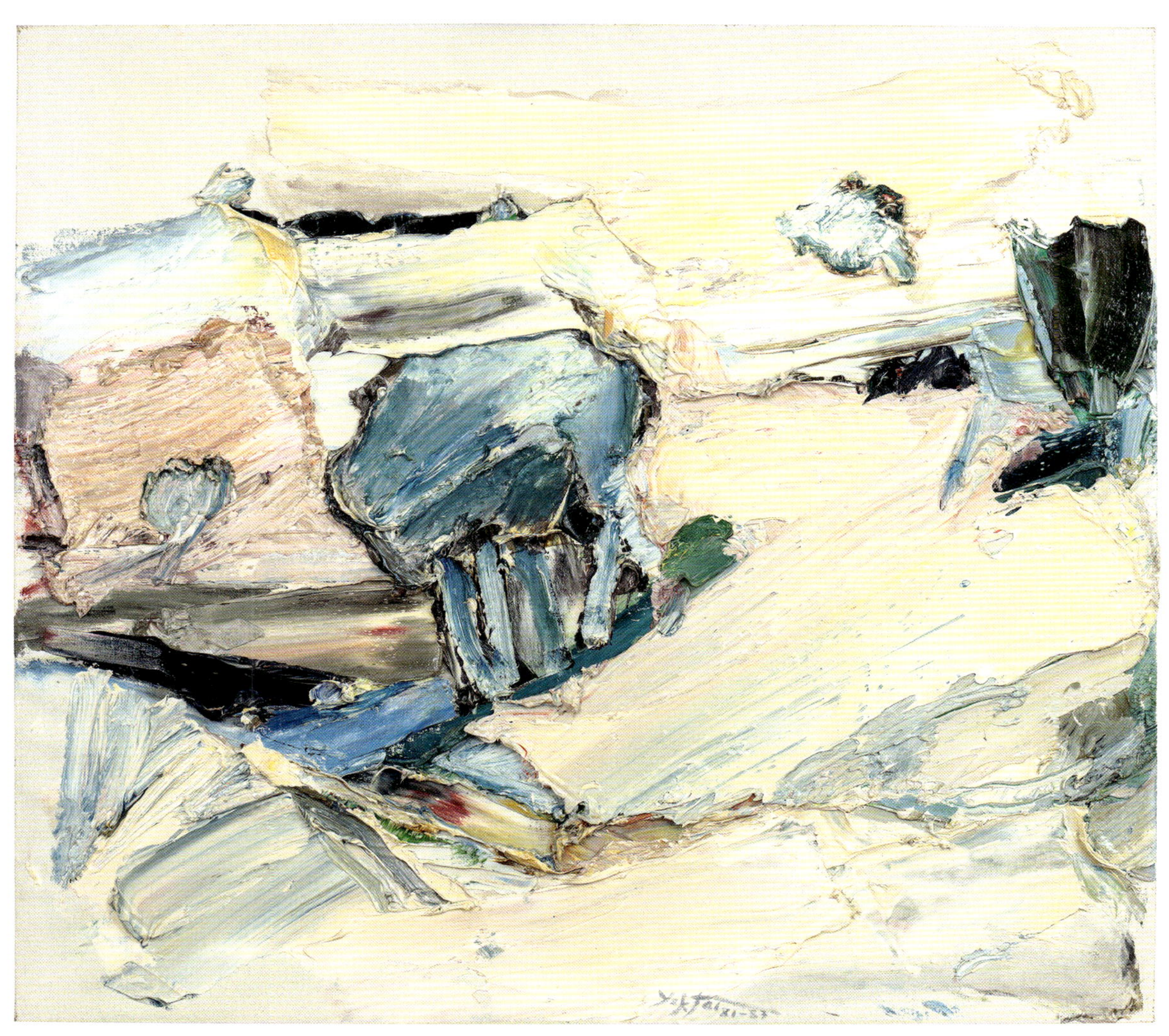

Small Pond, 1983, oil on canvas, 36 × 40 inches (91.4 × 101.6 cm)

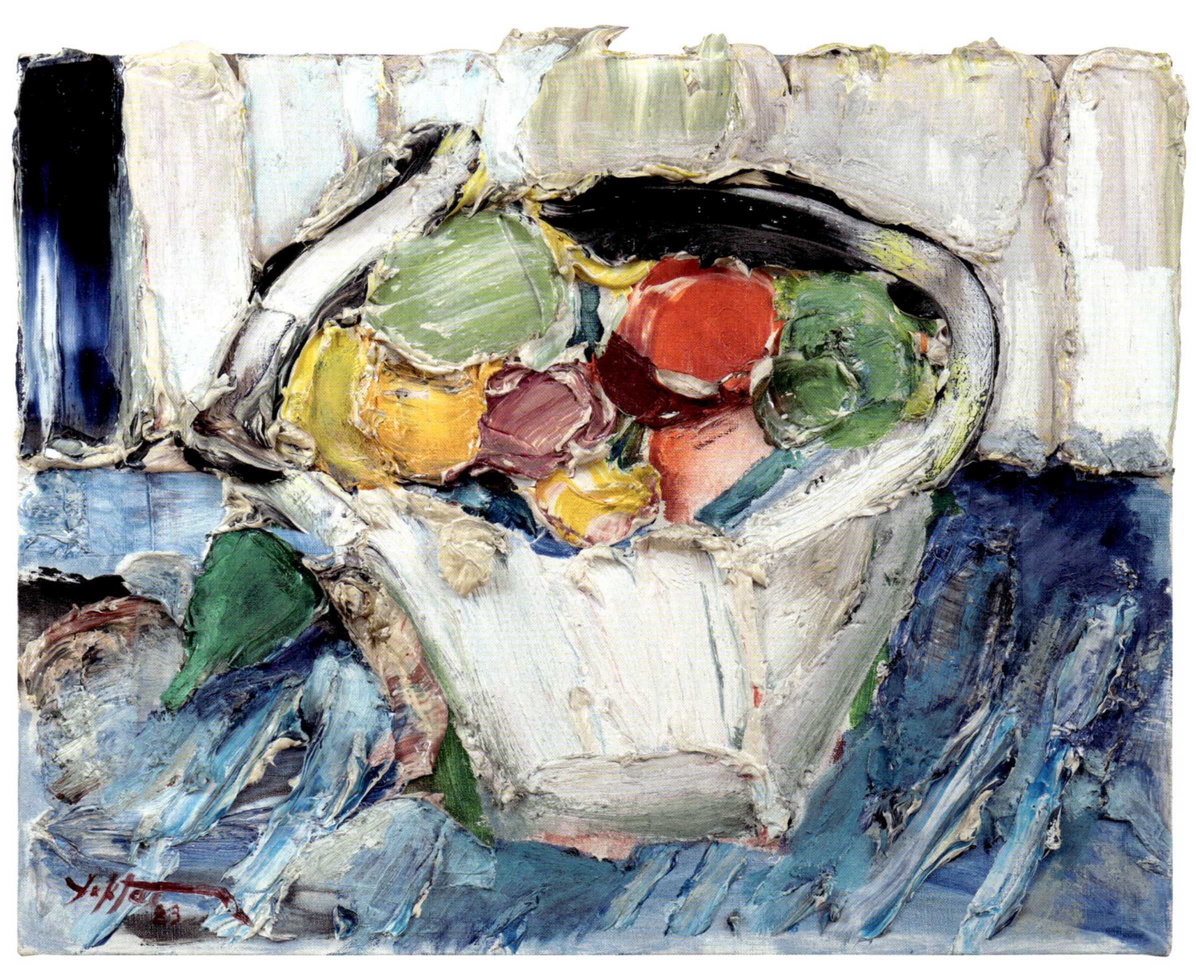

 Untitled, 1983, oil on canvas, 16 × 18 inches (40.6 × 45.7 cm)

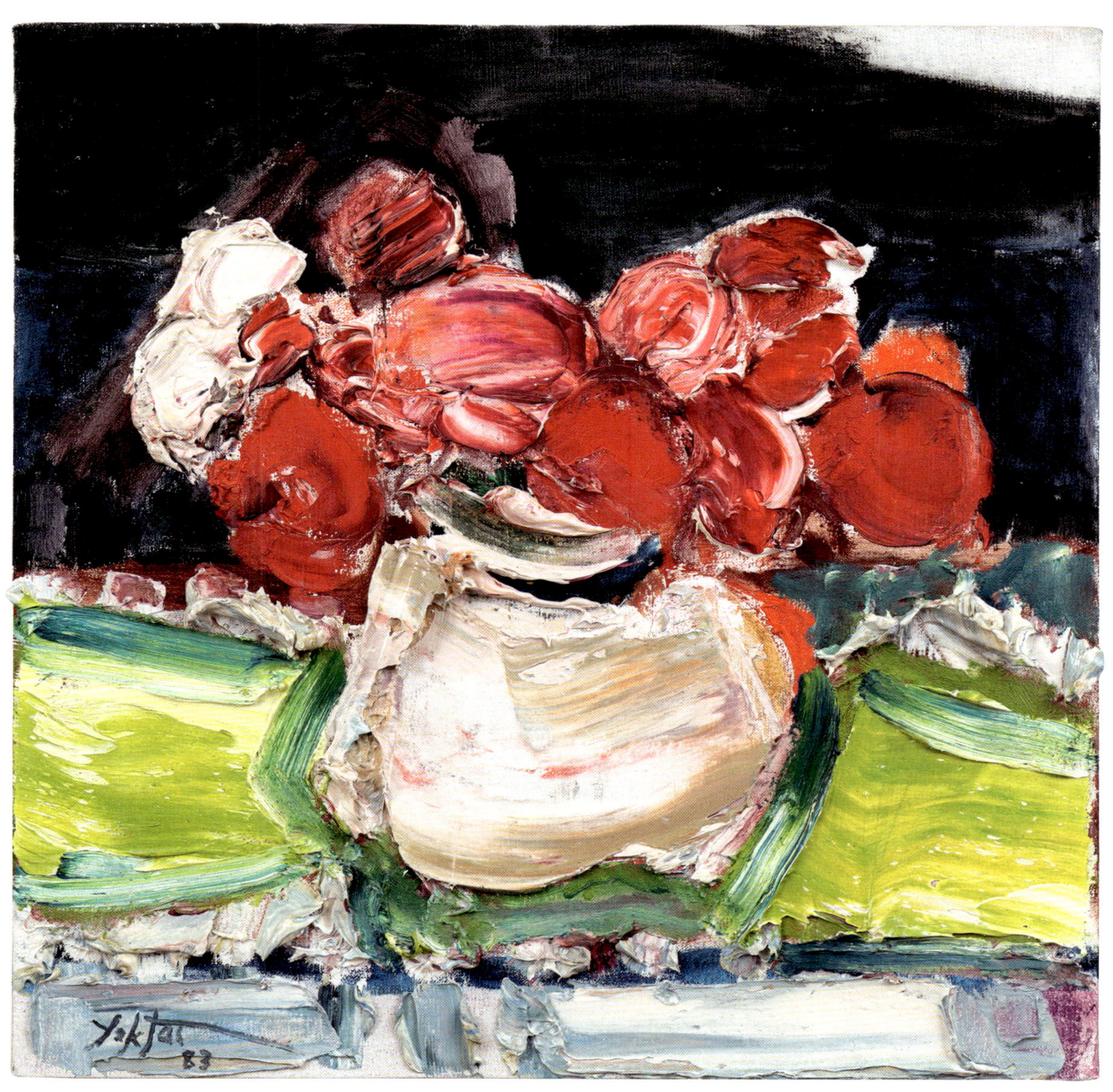

Untitled, 1983, oil on canvas, 18 × 18 inches (45.7 × 45.7 cm)

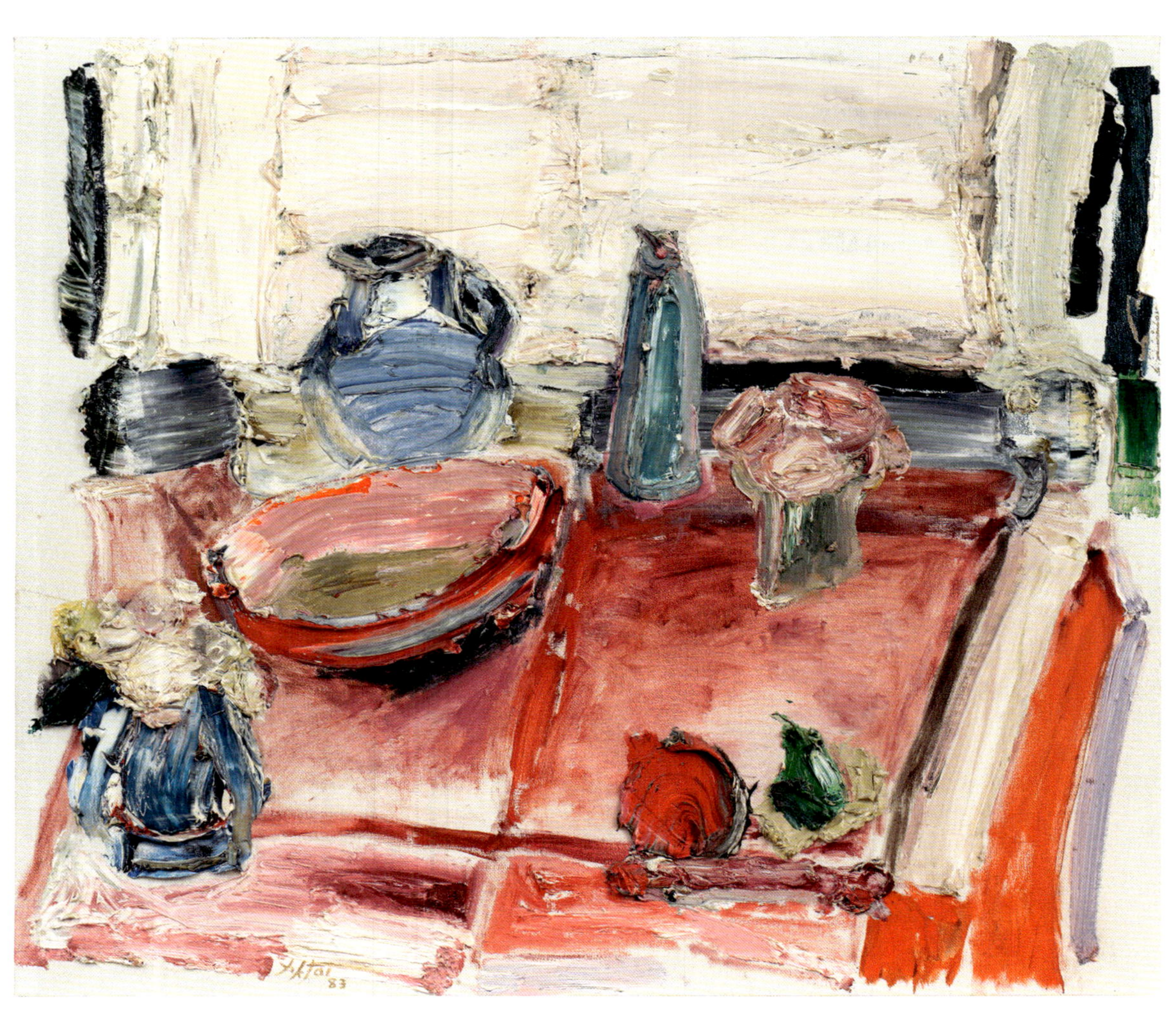

 Untitled, 1983, oil on canvas, 38 × 44 inches (96.5 × 111.8 cm)

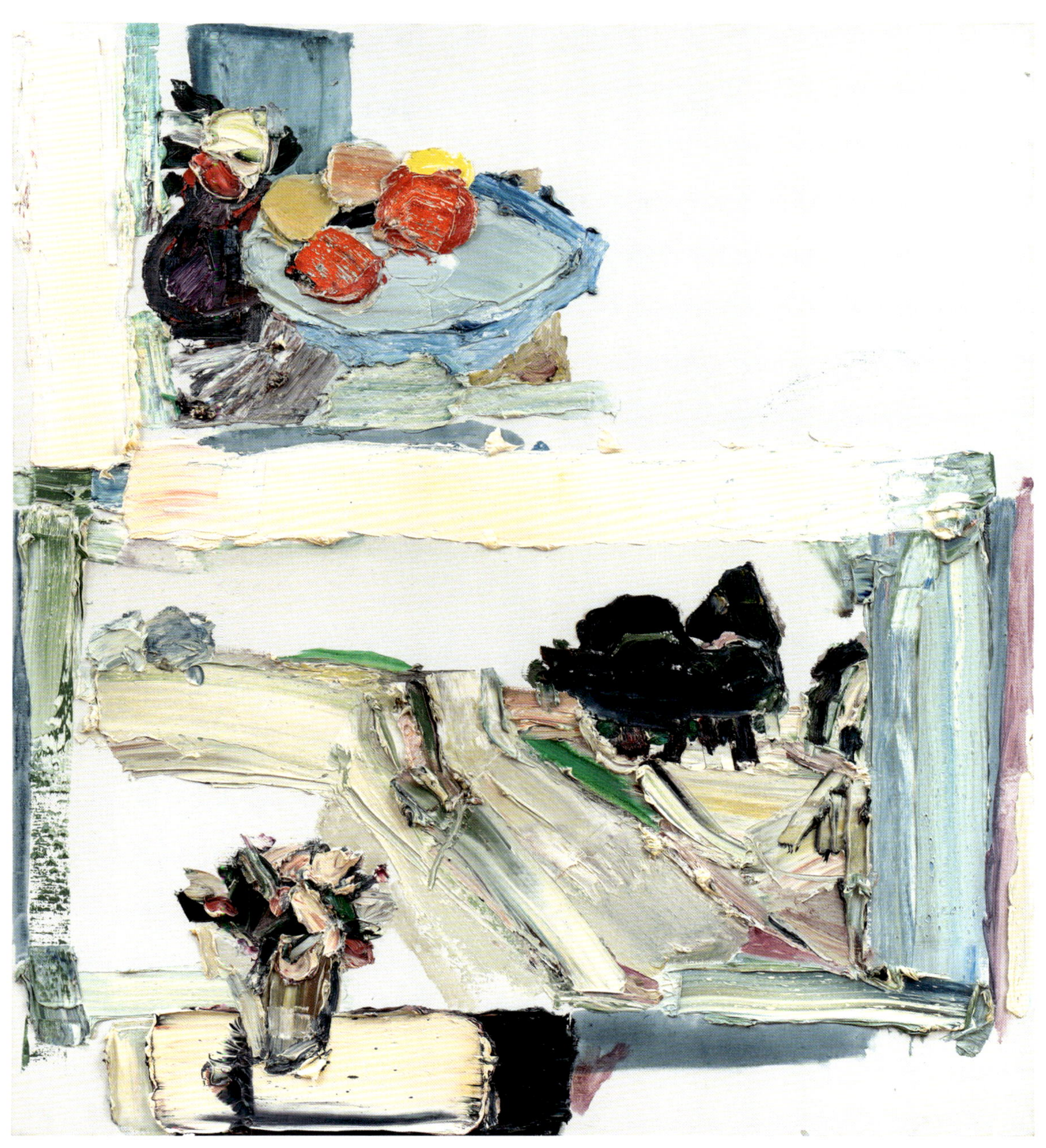

Untitled, 1983, oil on canvas, 54 × 48 inches (137.2 × 121.9 cm)

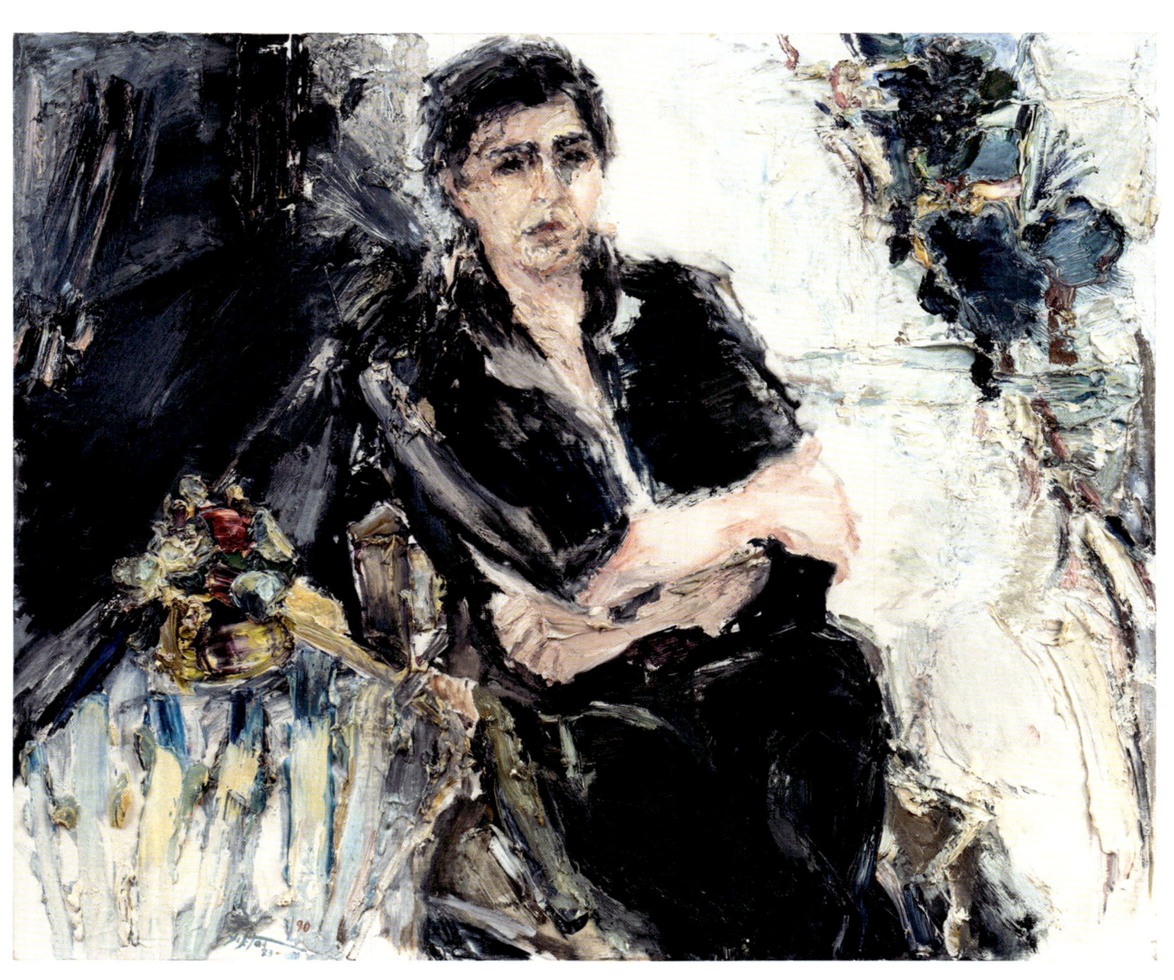

 Ali Molina, 1983, oil on canvas, 42 × 58 inches (106.7 × 147.3 cm)

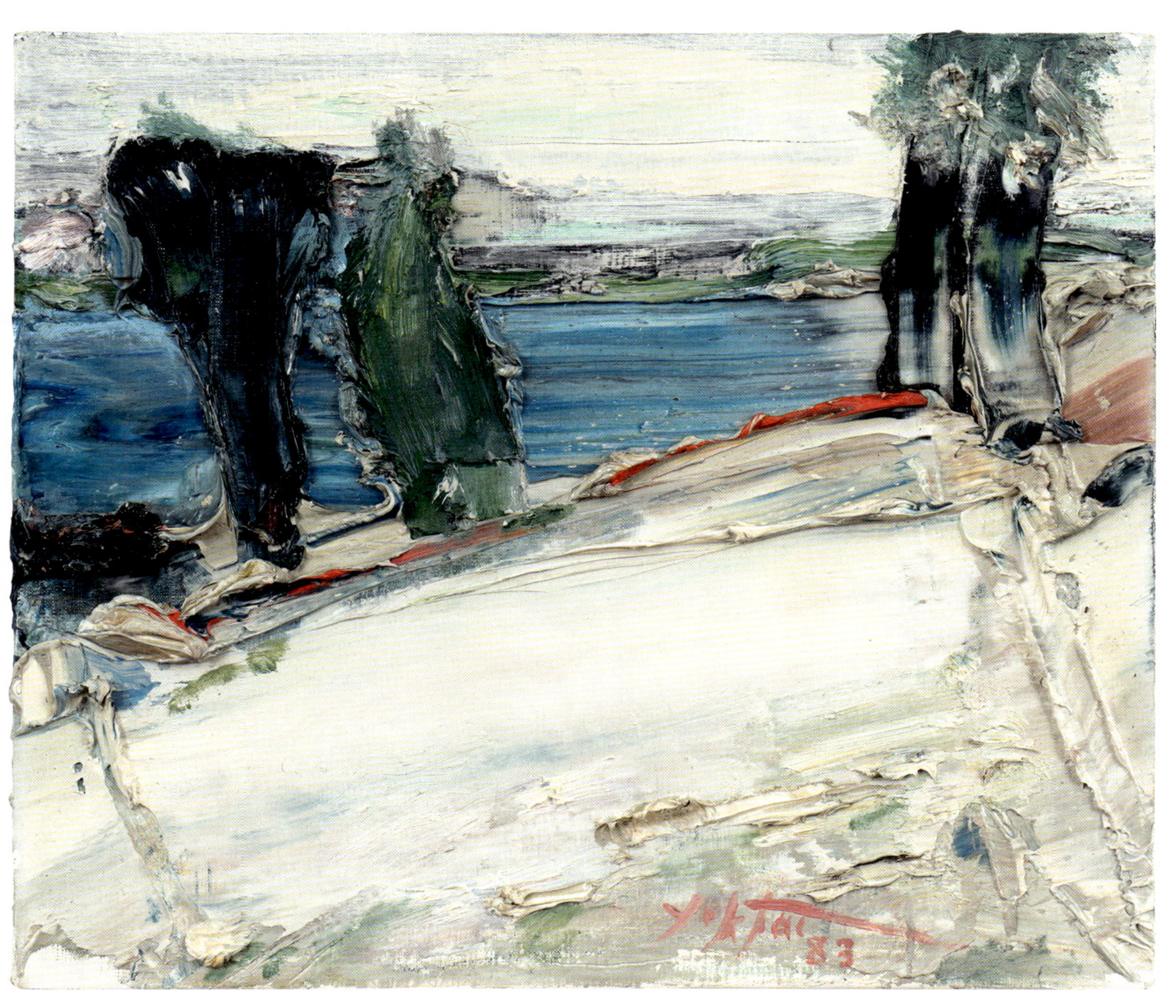

Untitled, 1983, oil on canvas, 13¾ × 16¼ inches (34.9 × 41.3 cm)

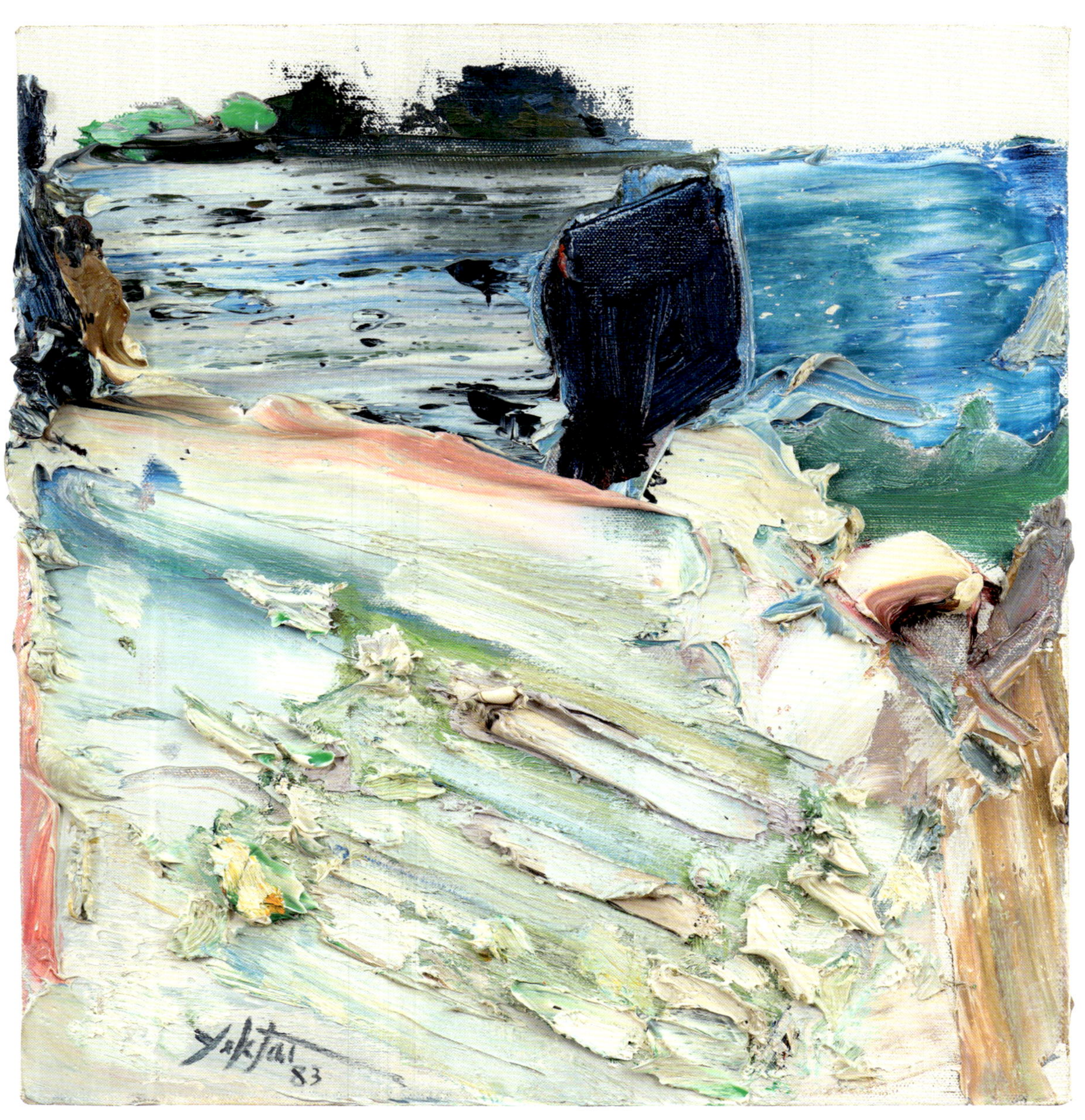

 Untitled, 1983, oil on canvas, 16 × 15¼ inches (40.6 × 38.7 cm)

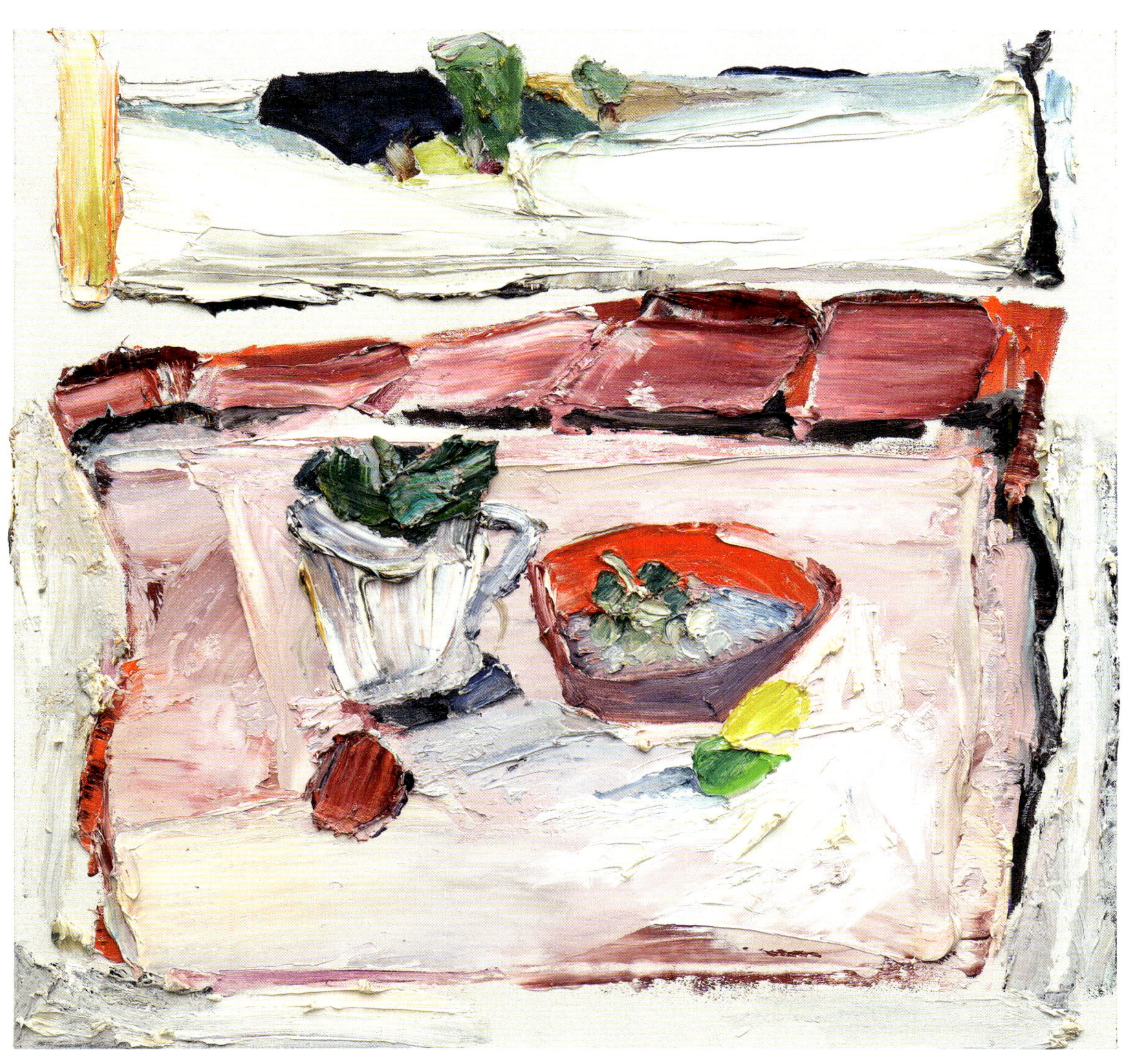

Still Life Landscape, 1984, oil on canvas, 36 × 38 inches (91.4 × 96.5 cm)

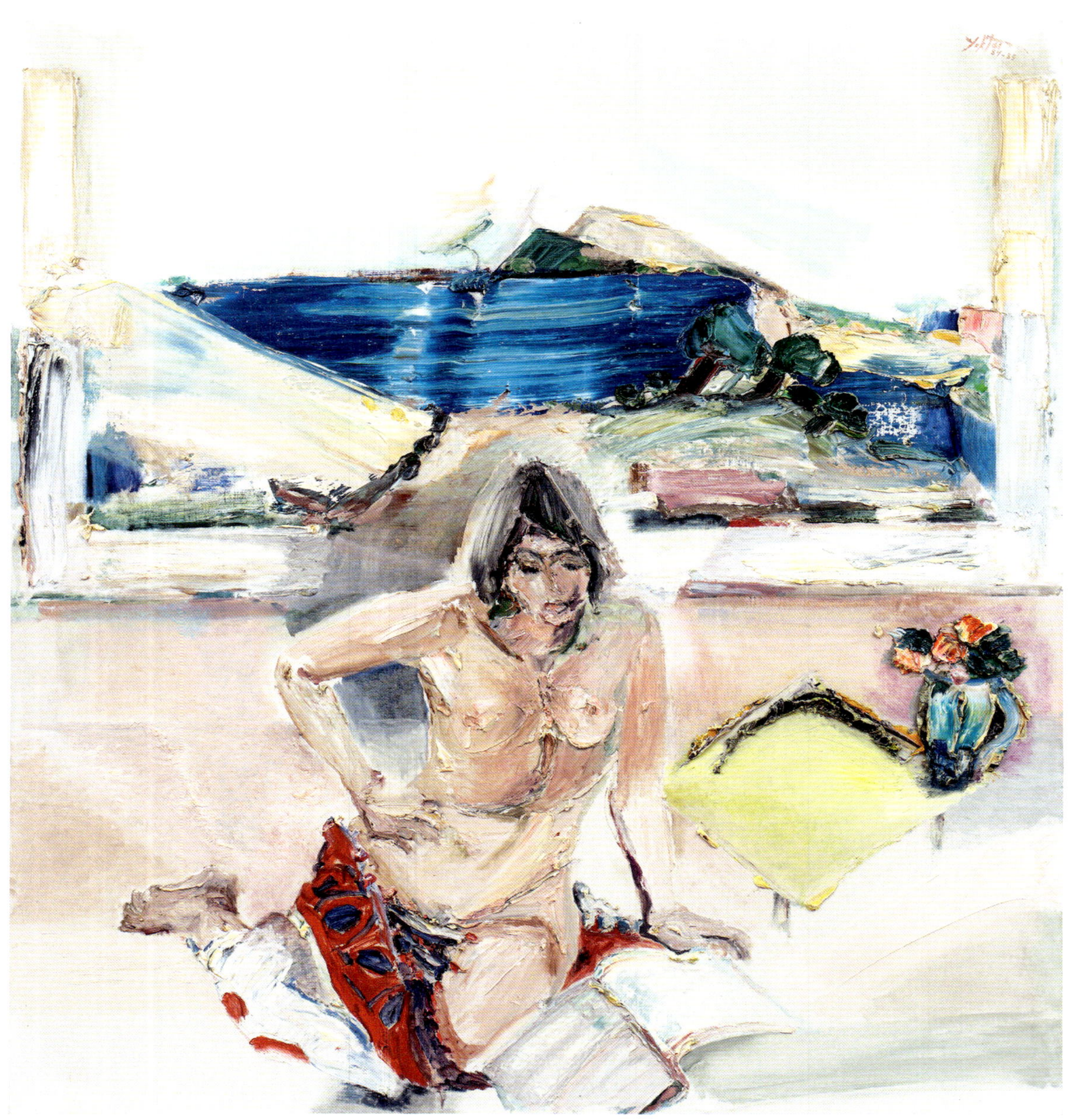

600 *Seated Nude*, 1984–85, oil on canvas, 68 × 64 inches (172.7 × 162.6 cm)

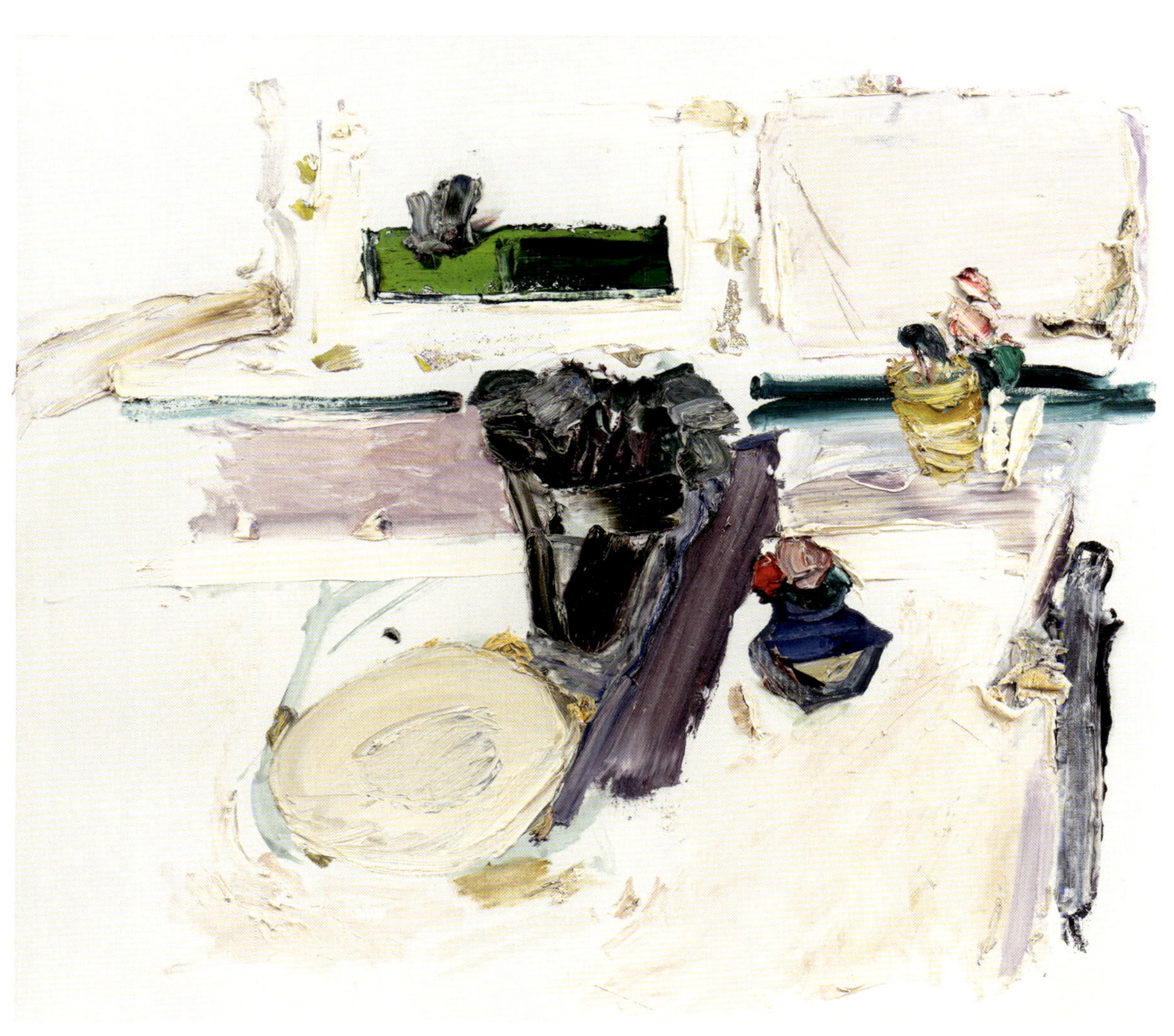

Untitled, 1985, oil on canvas, 48 × 54 inches (121.9 × 137.2 cm)

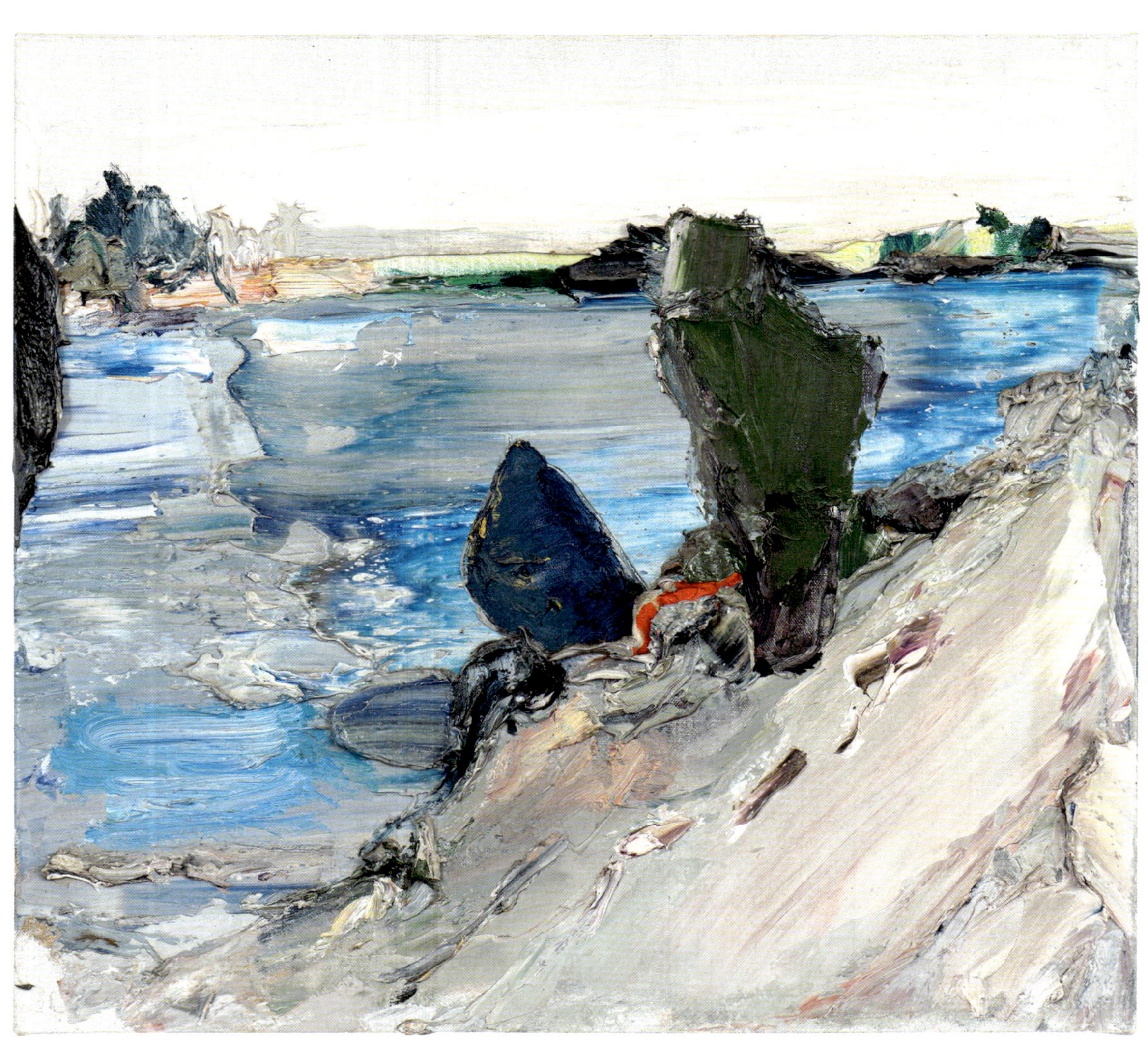

 Untitled, 1985, oil on canvas, 22 × 24 inches (55.9 × 61 cm)

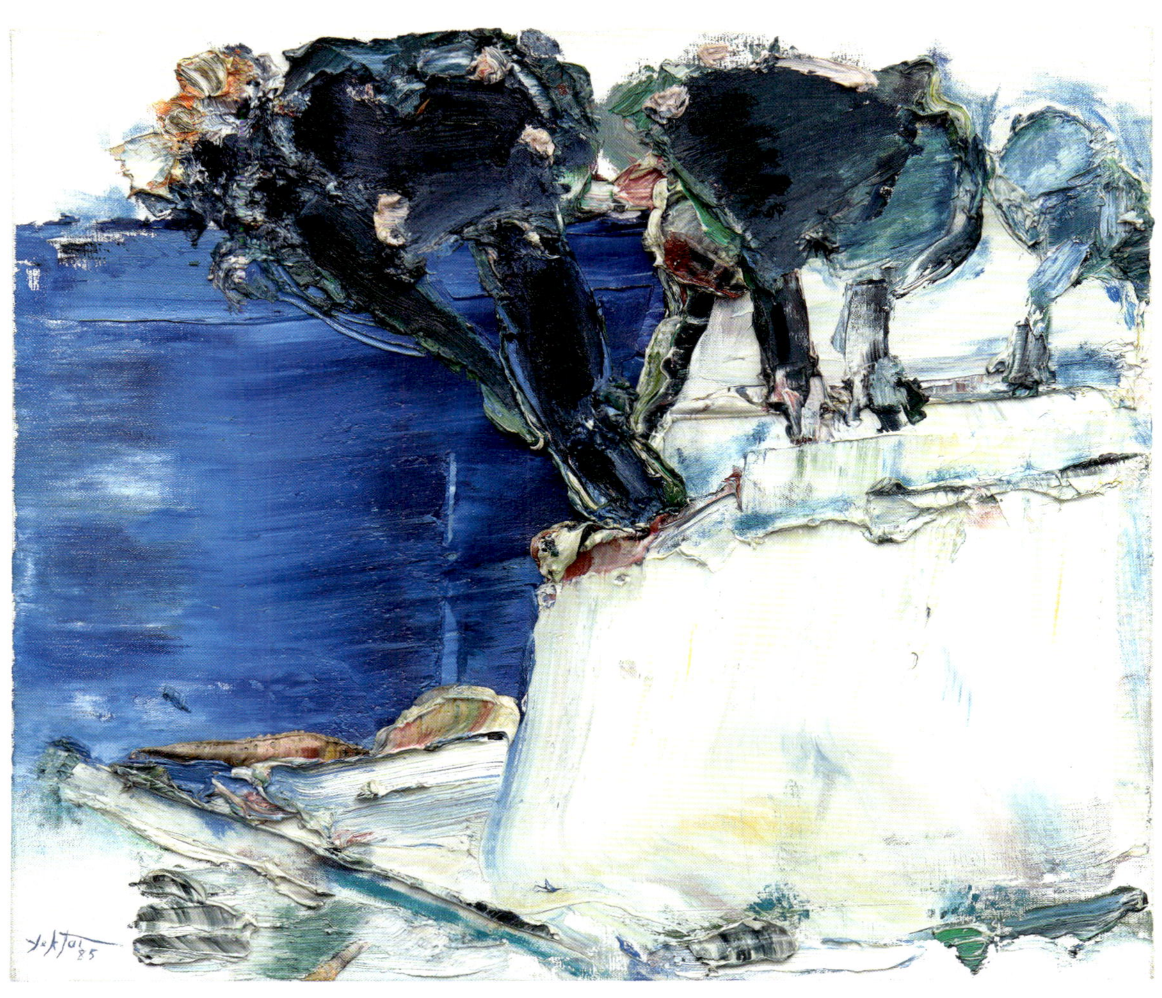

Untitled, 1985, oil on canvas, 24 × 28 inches (61 × 71.1 cm)

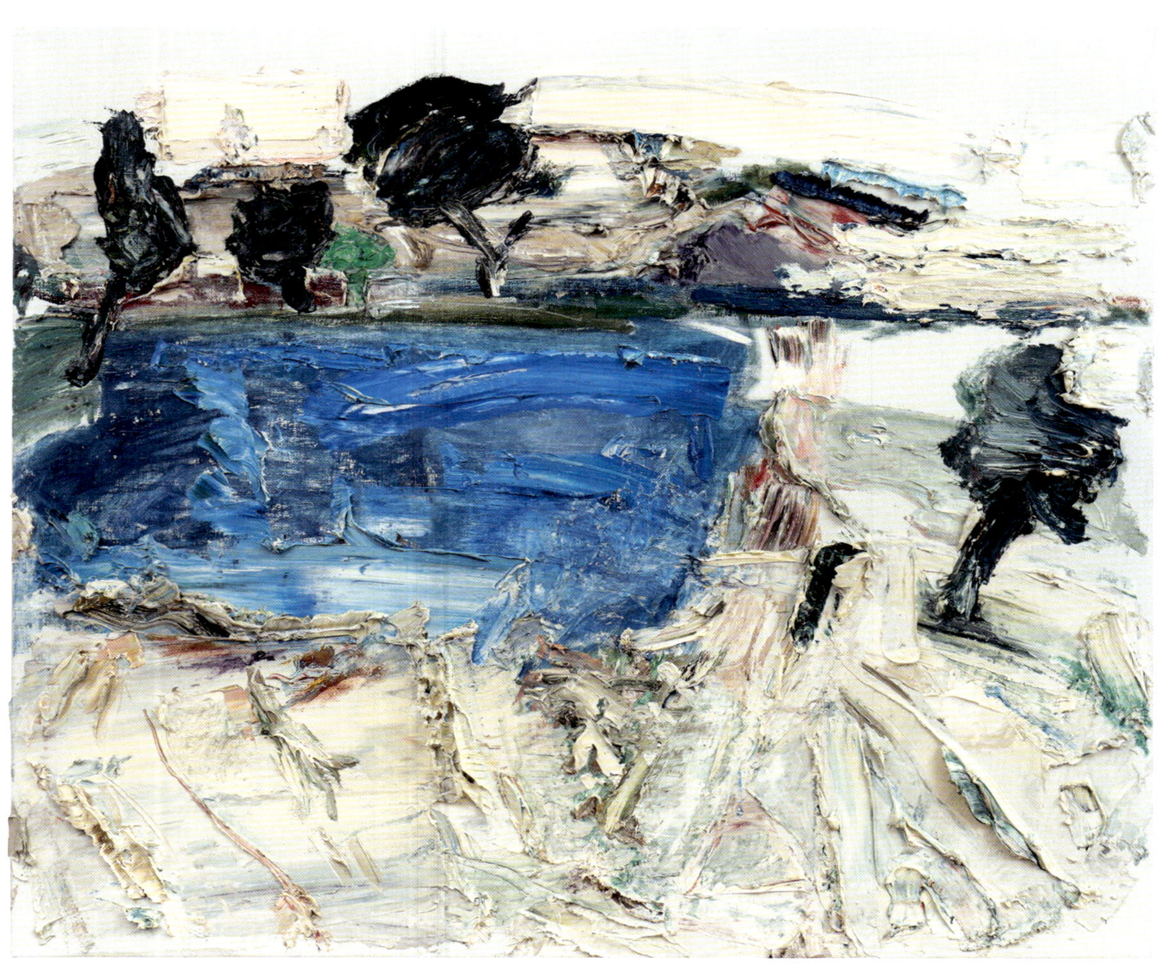

 Untitled, 1985, oil on canvas, 42 × 50 inches (106.7 × 127 cm)

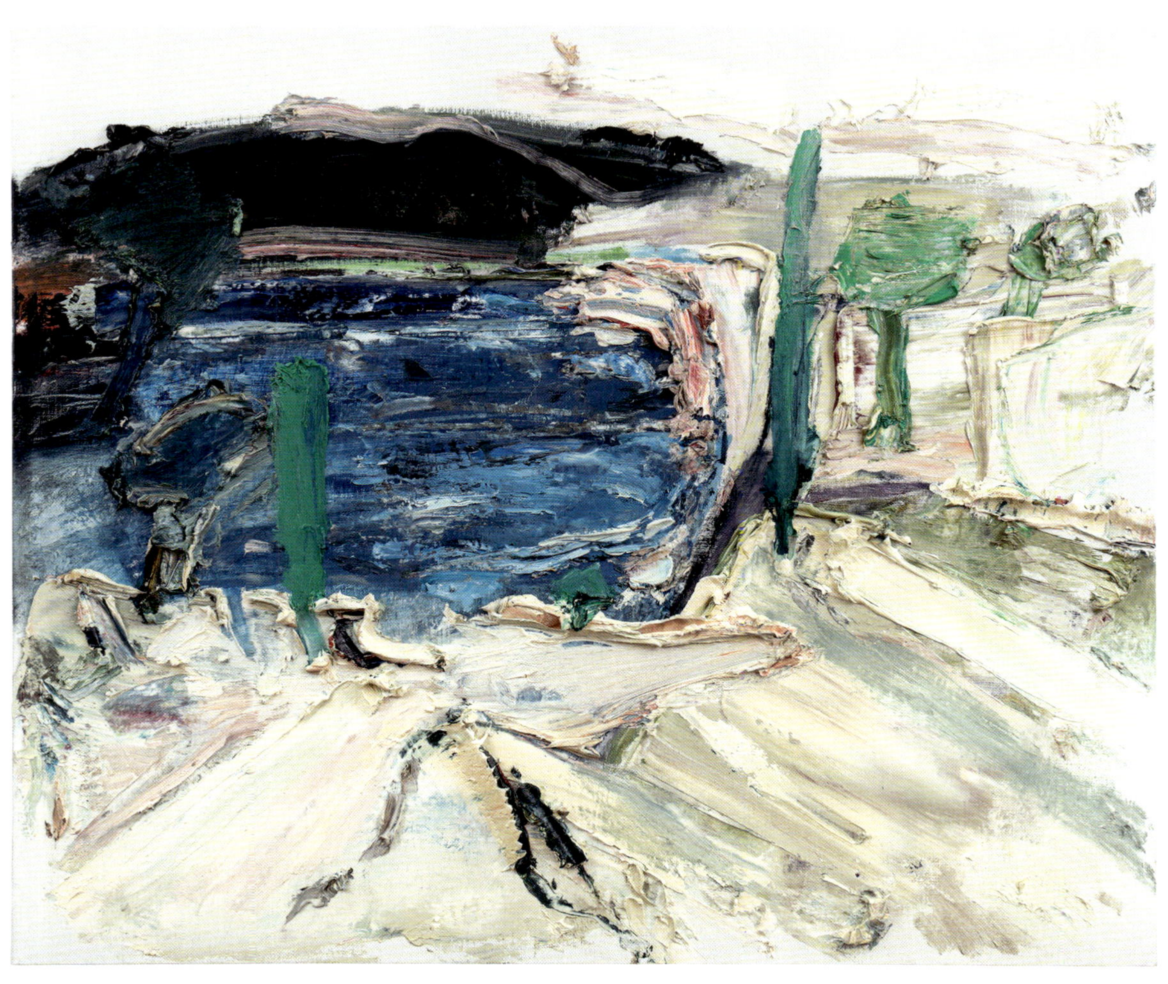

Untitled, 1985, oil on canvas, 42 × 50 inches (106.7 × 127 cm)

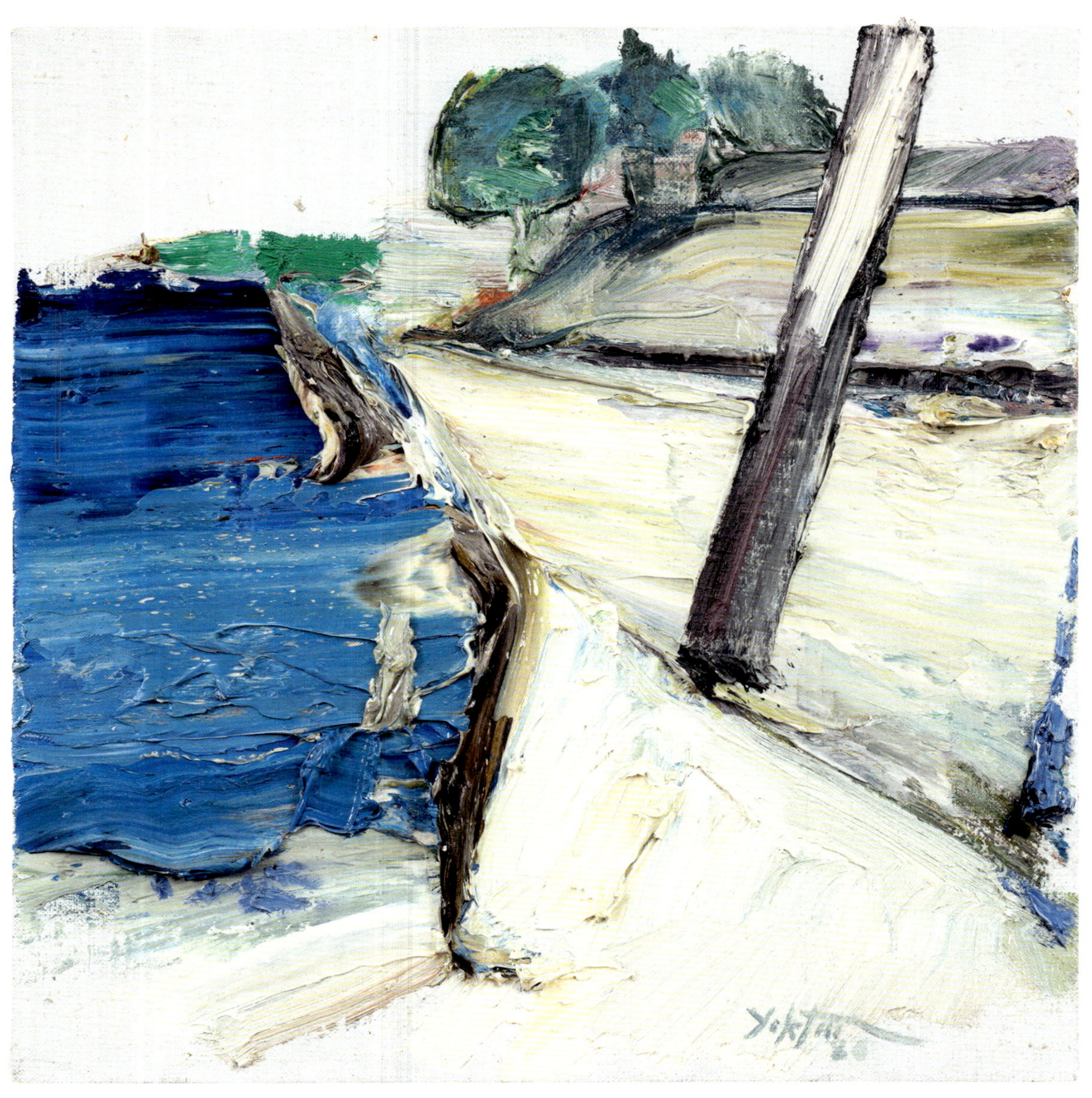

Untitled, 1986, oil on canvas, 16¼ × 16 inches (41.3 × 40.6 cm)

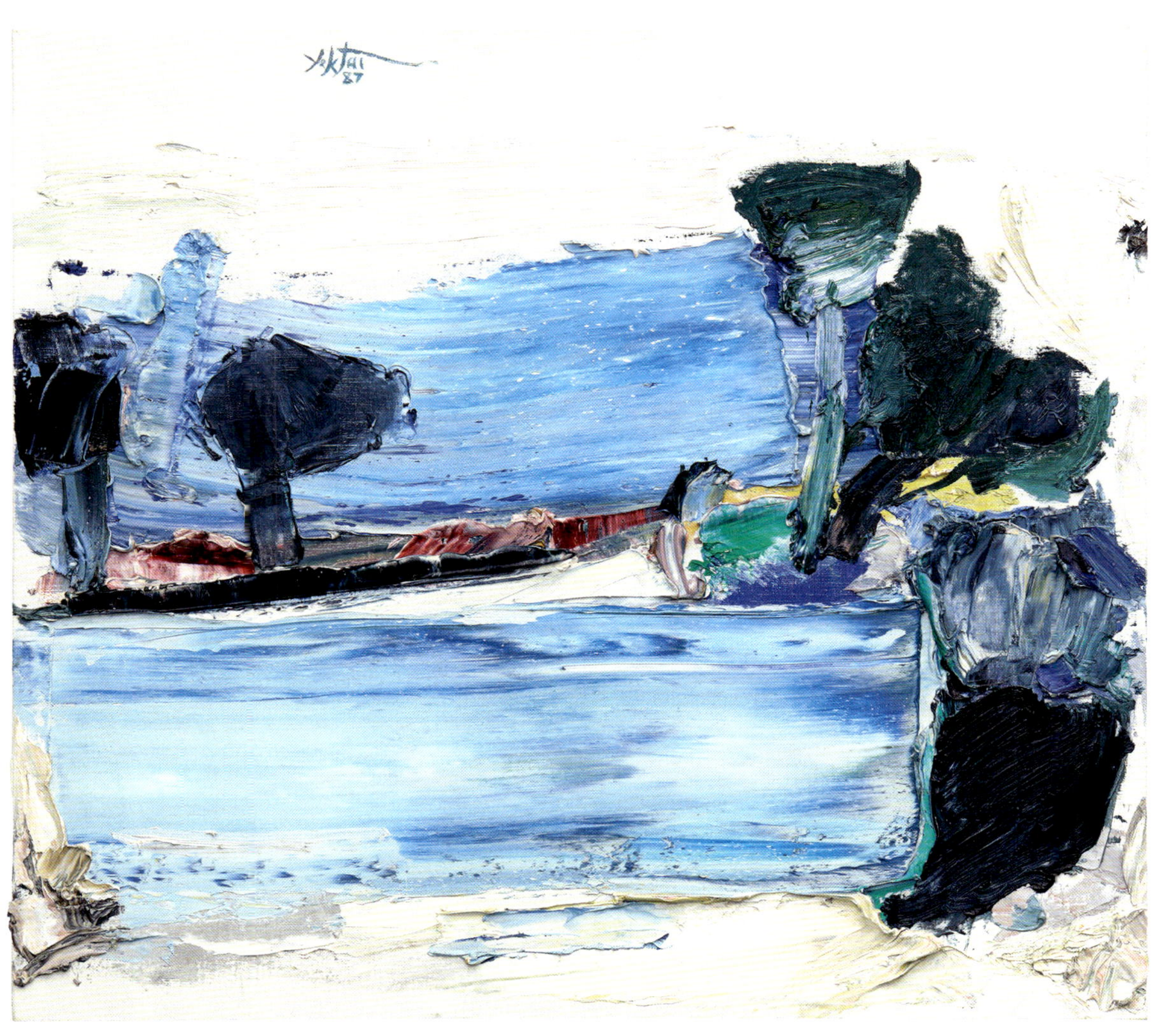

Untitled, 1987, oil on canvas, 36 × 40 inches (91.4 × 101.6 cm)

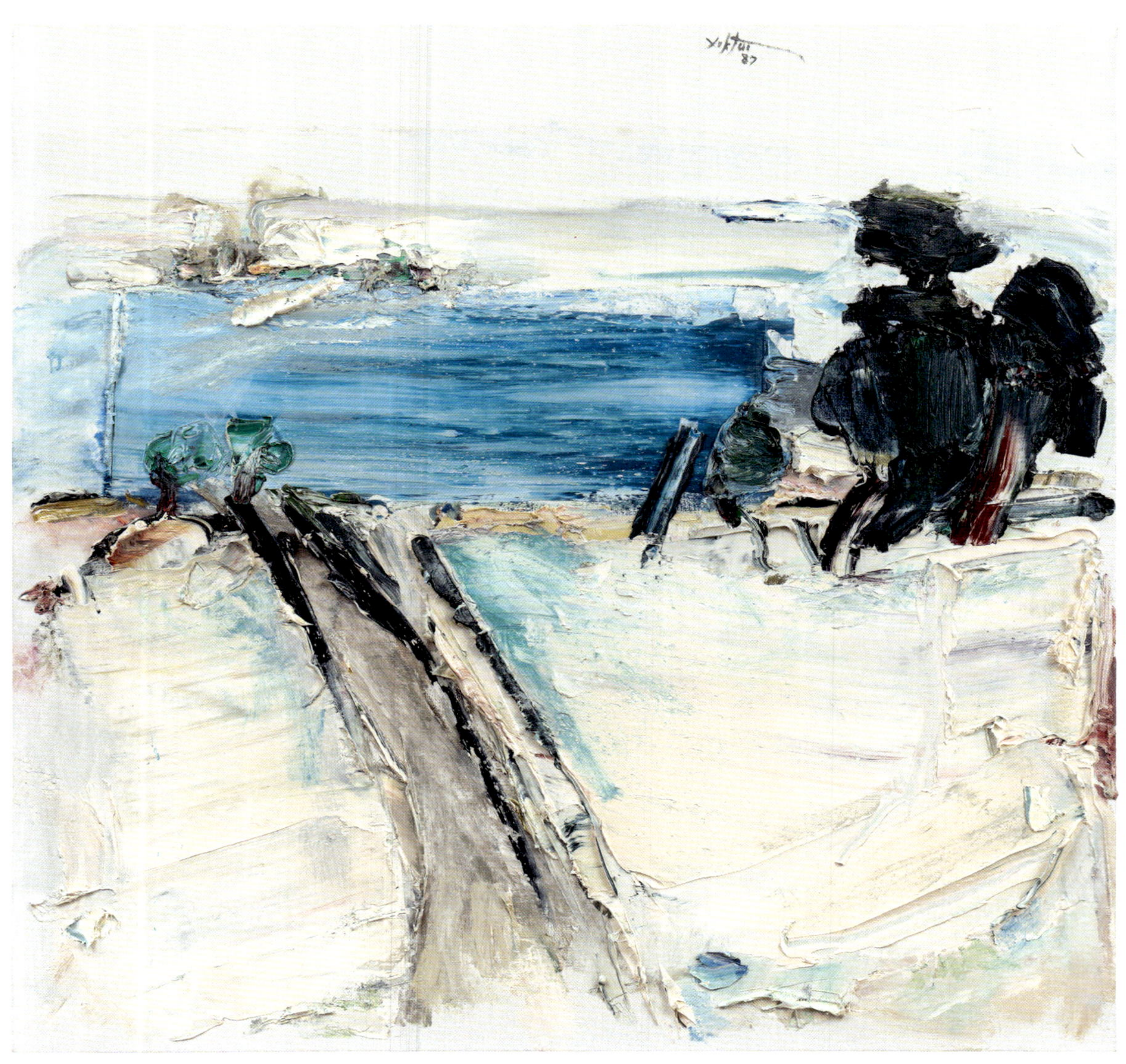

 Untitled, 1987, oil on canvas, 48 × 50 inches (121.9 × 127 cm)

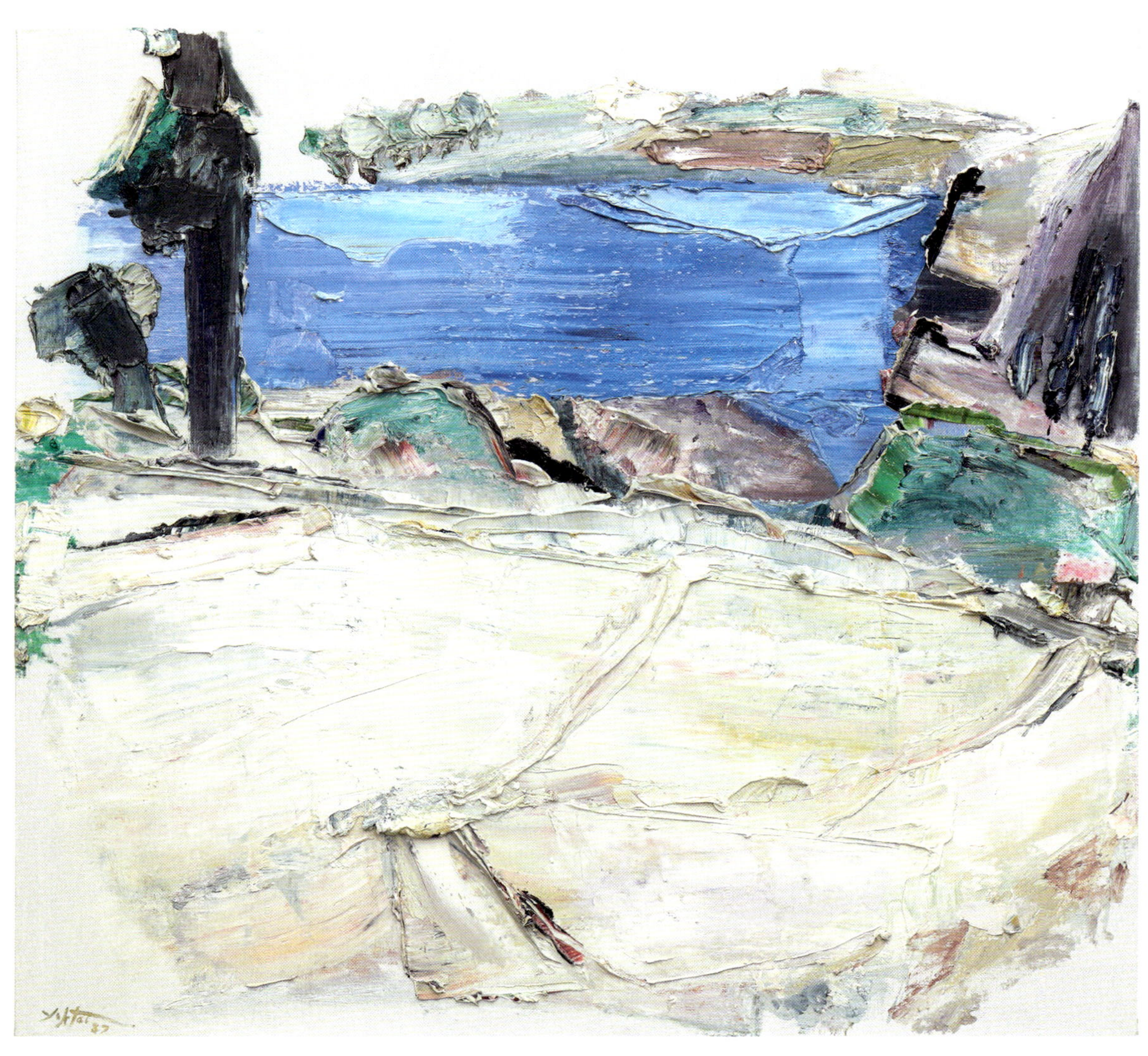

Untitled, 1987, oil on canvas, 48 × 52 inches (121.9 × 132.1 cm)

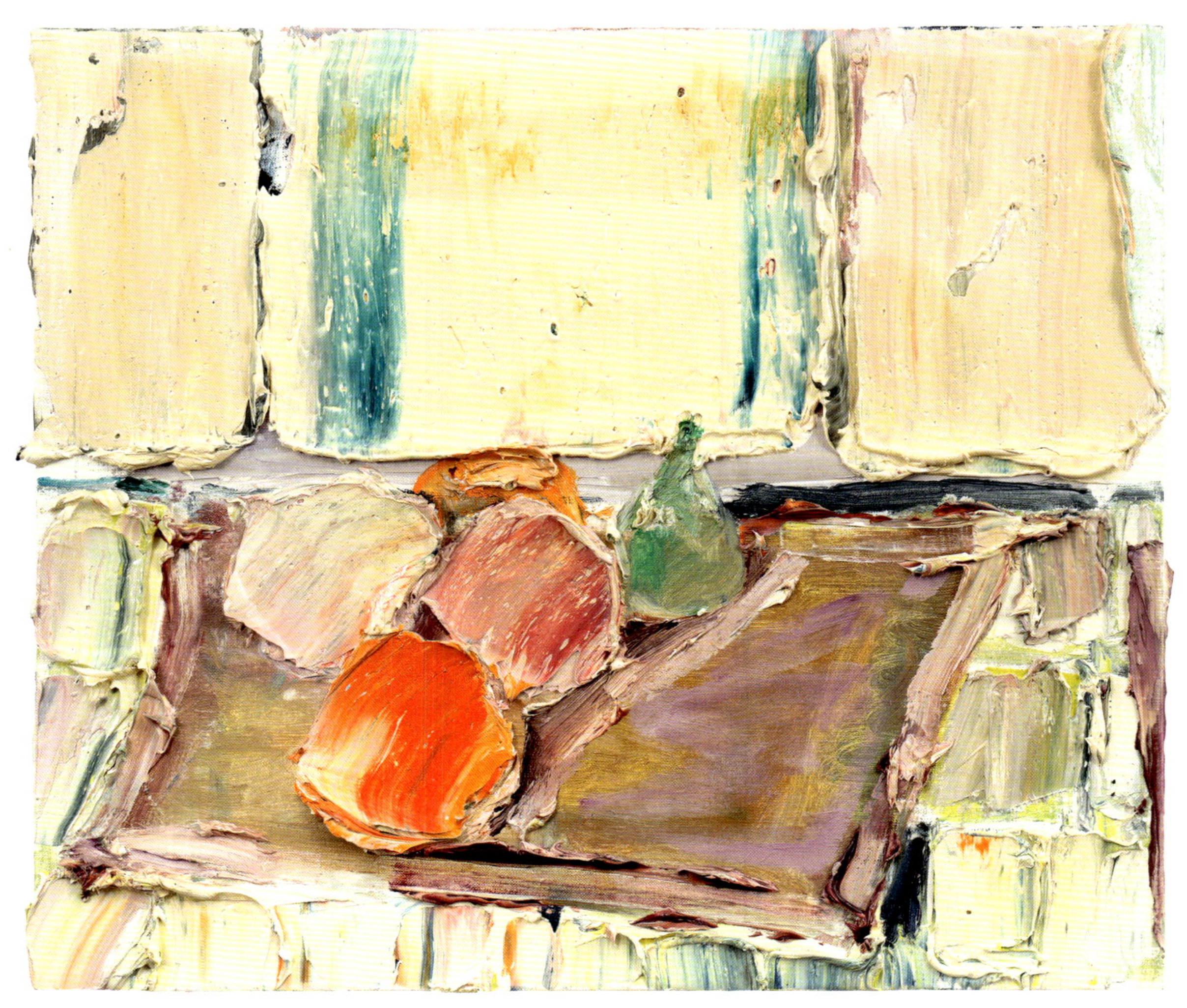

 Untitled, 1986, oil on canvas, 16 × 18½ inches (40.6 × 47 cm)

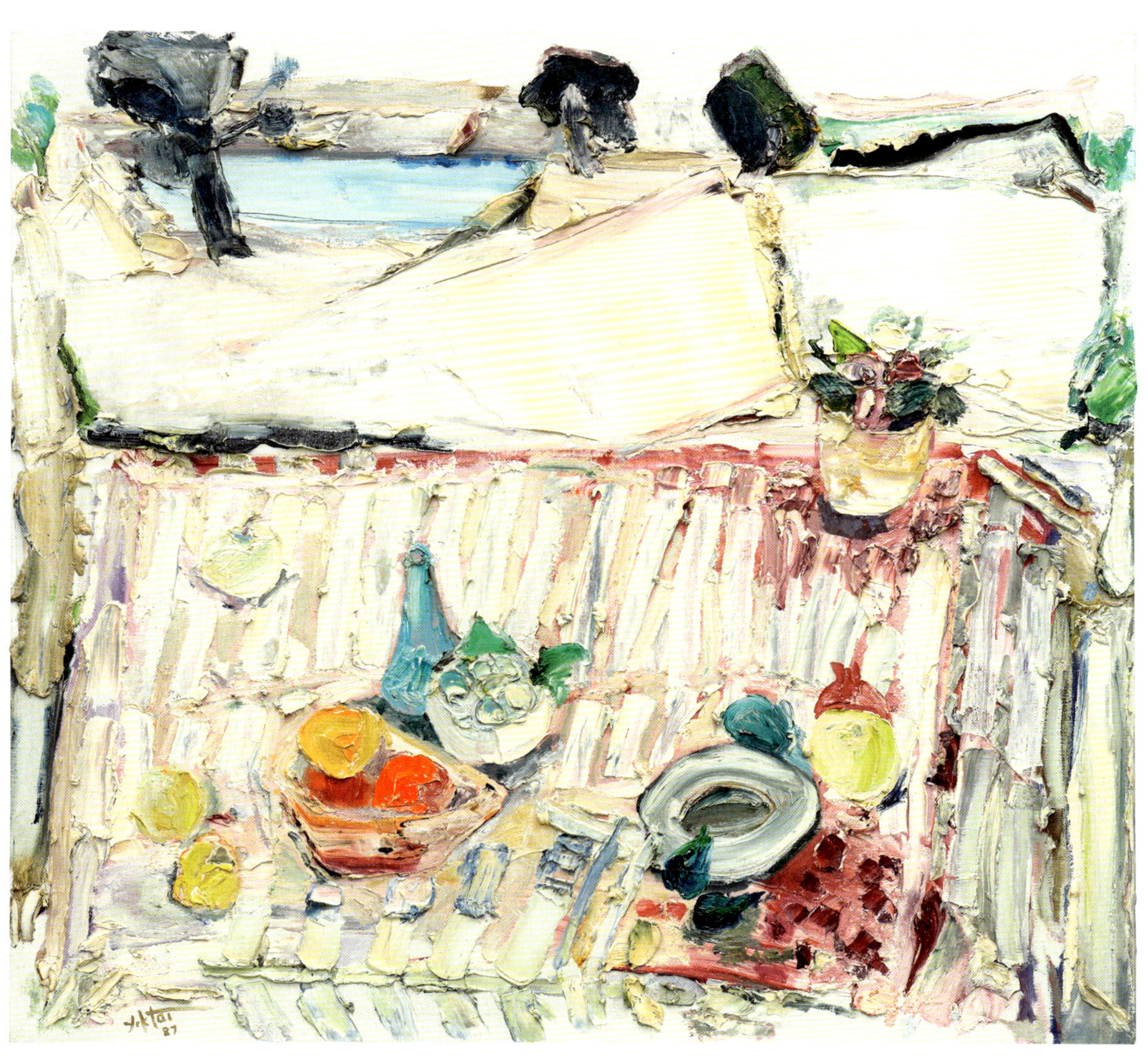

Untitled, 1987, oil on canvas, 48 × 52 inches (121.9 × 132.1 cm)

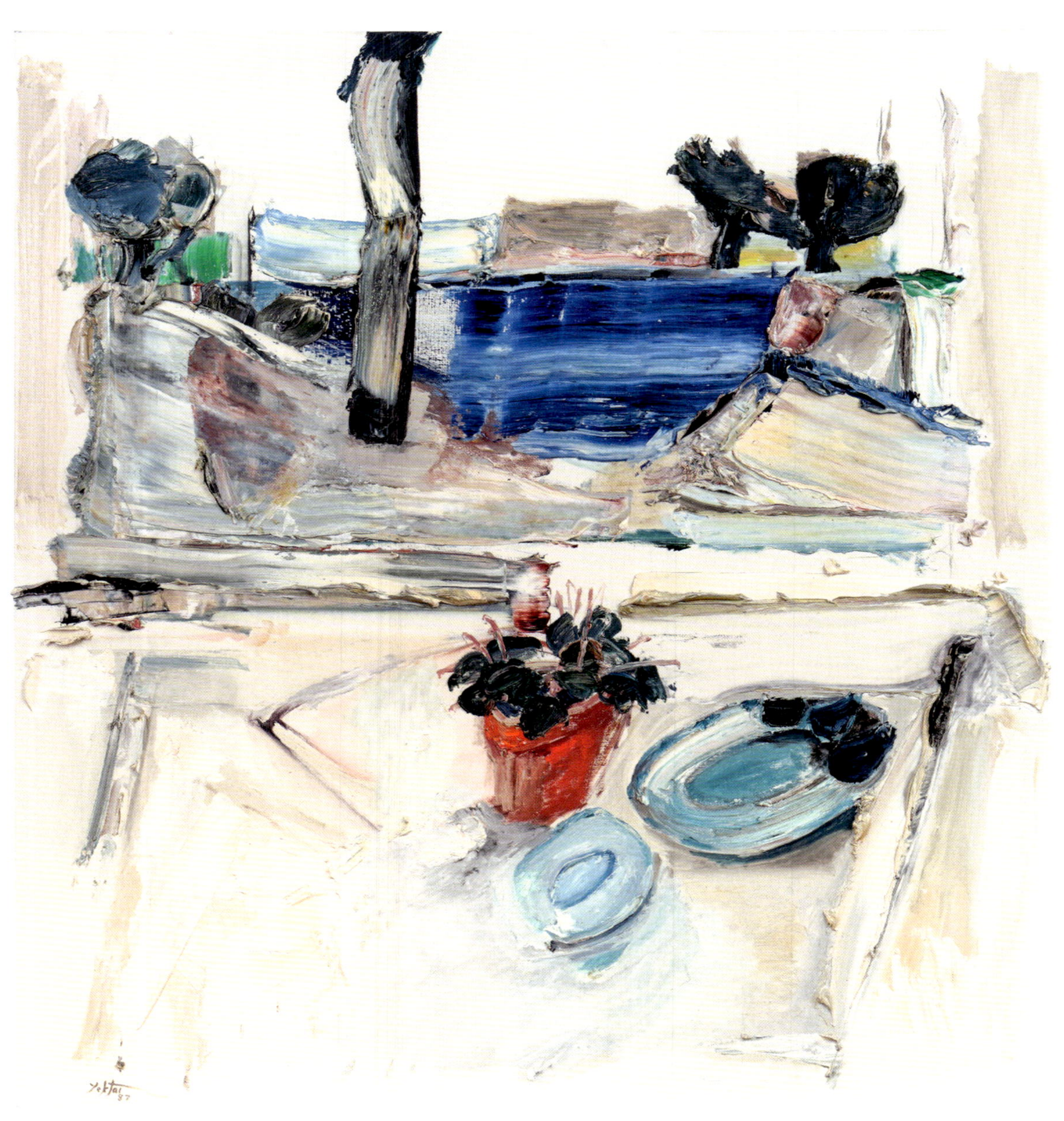

 Untitled, 1987, oil on canvas, 26¾ × 25¼ inches (68 × 64 cm)

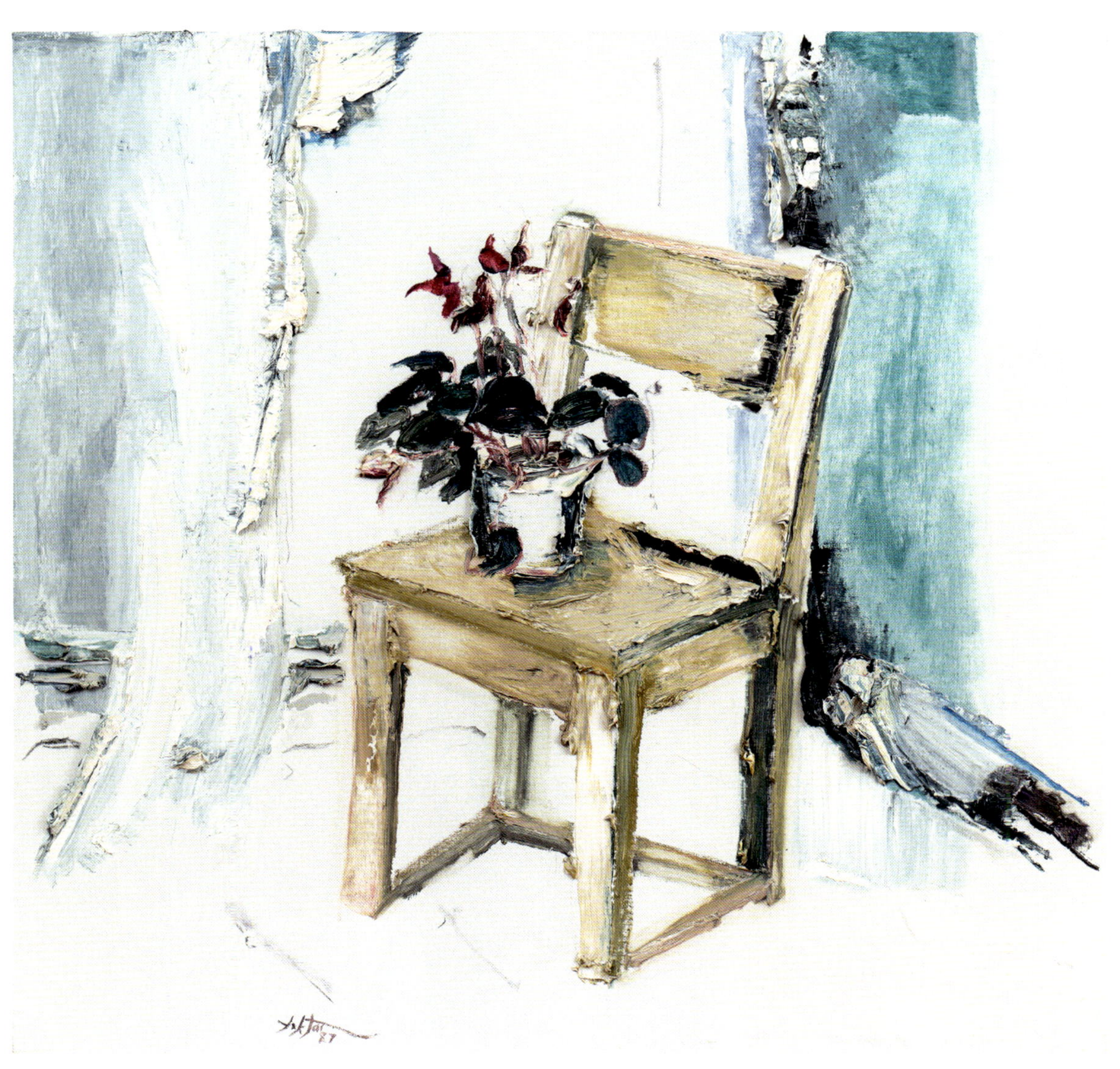

Cyclamen on Chair, 1987, oil on canvas, 48 × 50 inches (121.9 × 127 cm)

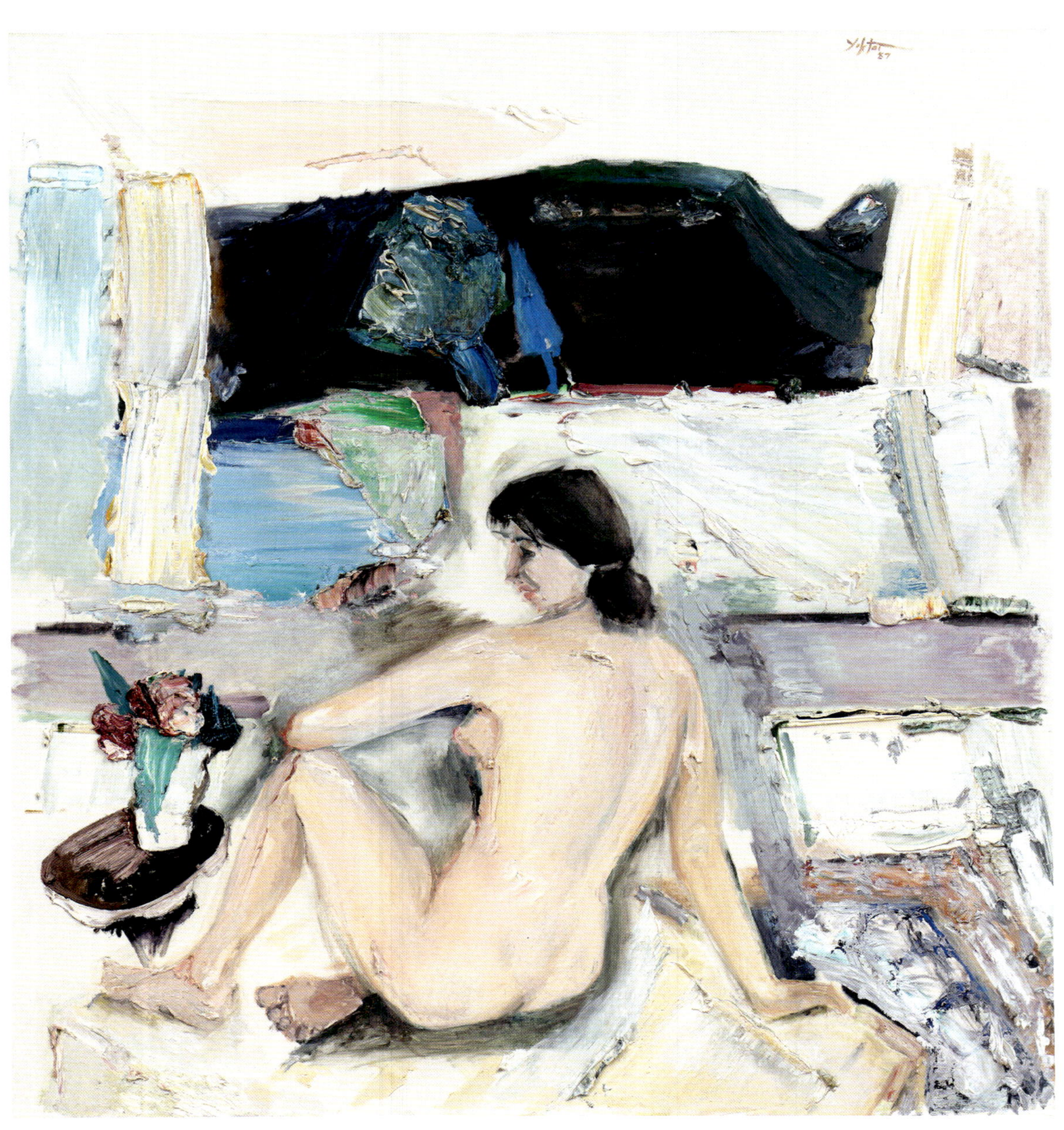

 Untitled, 1987, oil on canvas, 68 × 64 inches (172.7 × 162.6 cm)

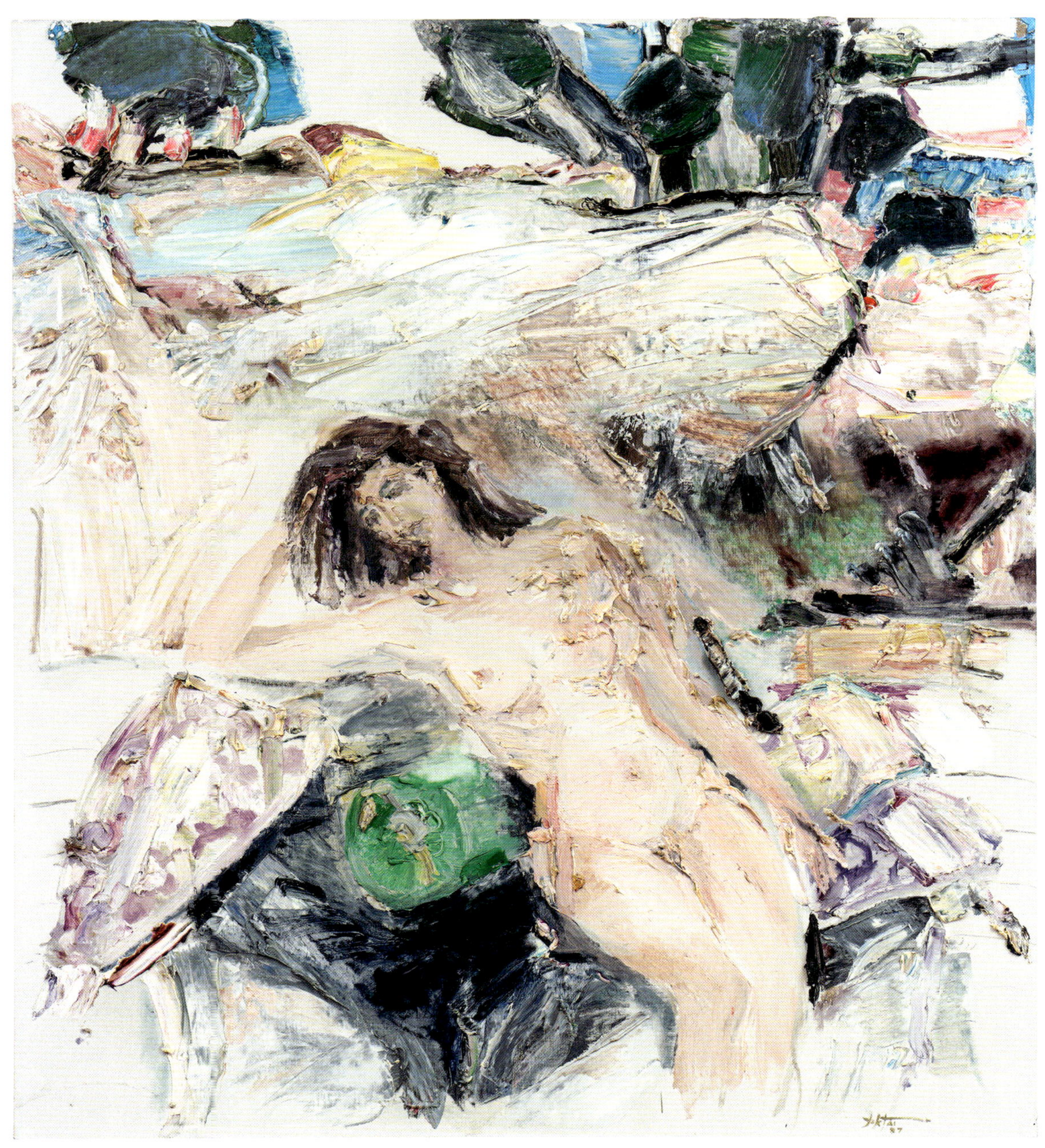

Untitled, 1987, oil on canvas, 72 × 64 inches (182.9 × 162.6 cm)

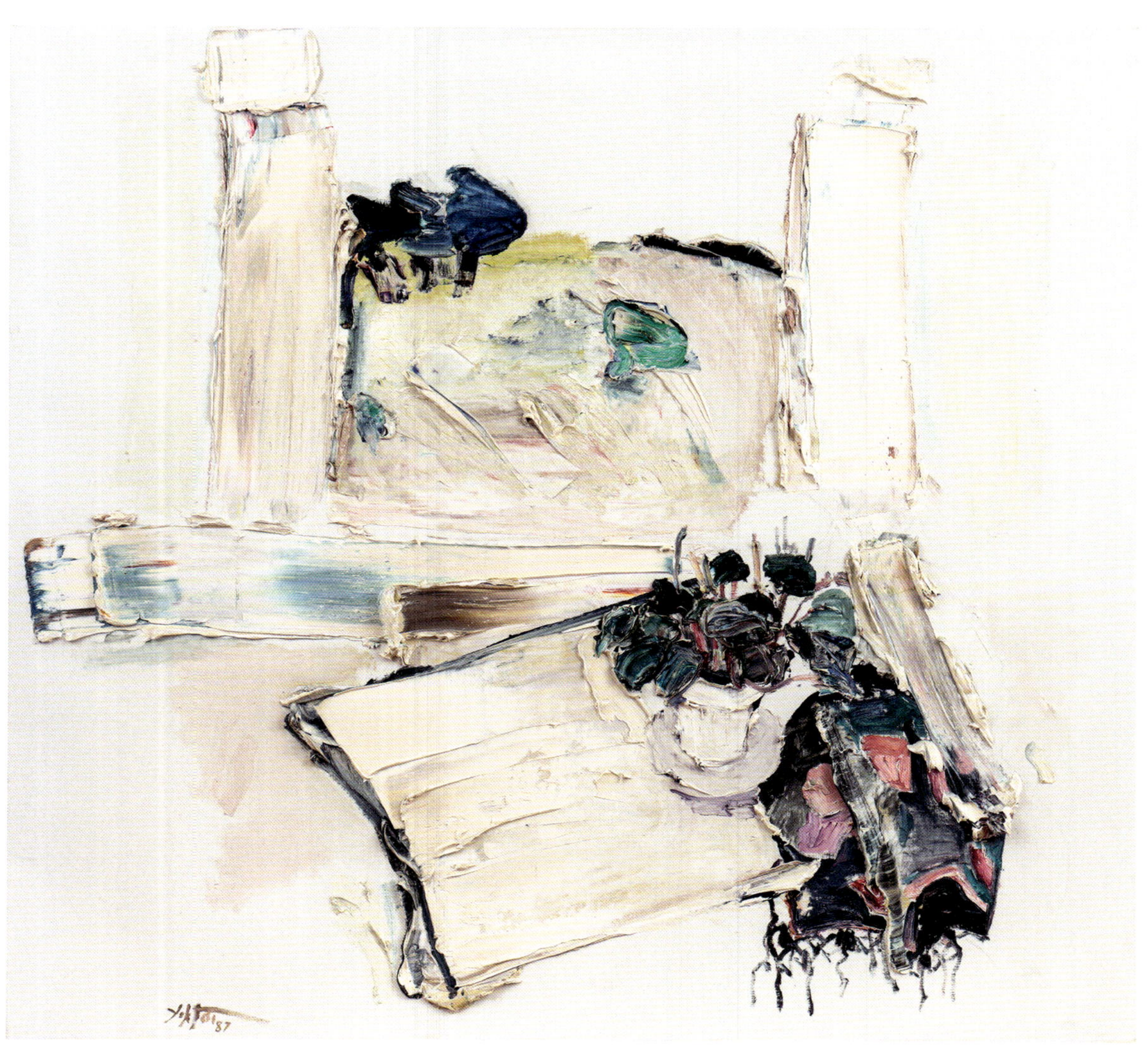

 Untitled, 1987, oil on canvas, 48 × 52 inches (121.9 × 132.1 cm)

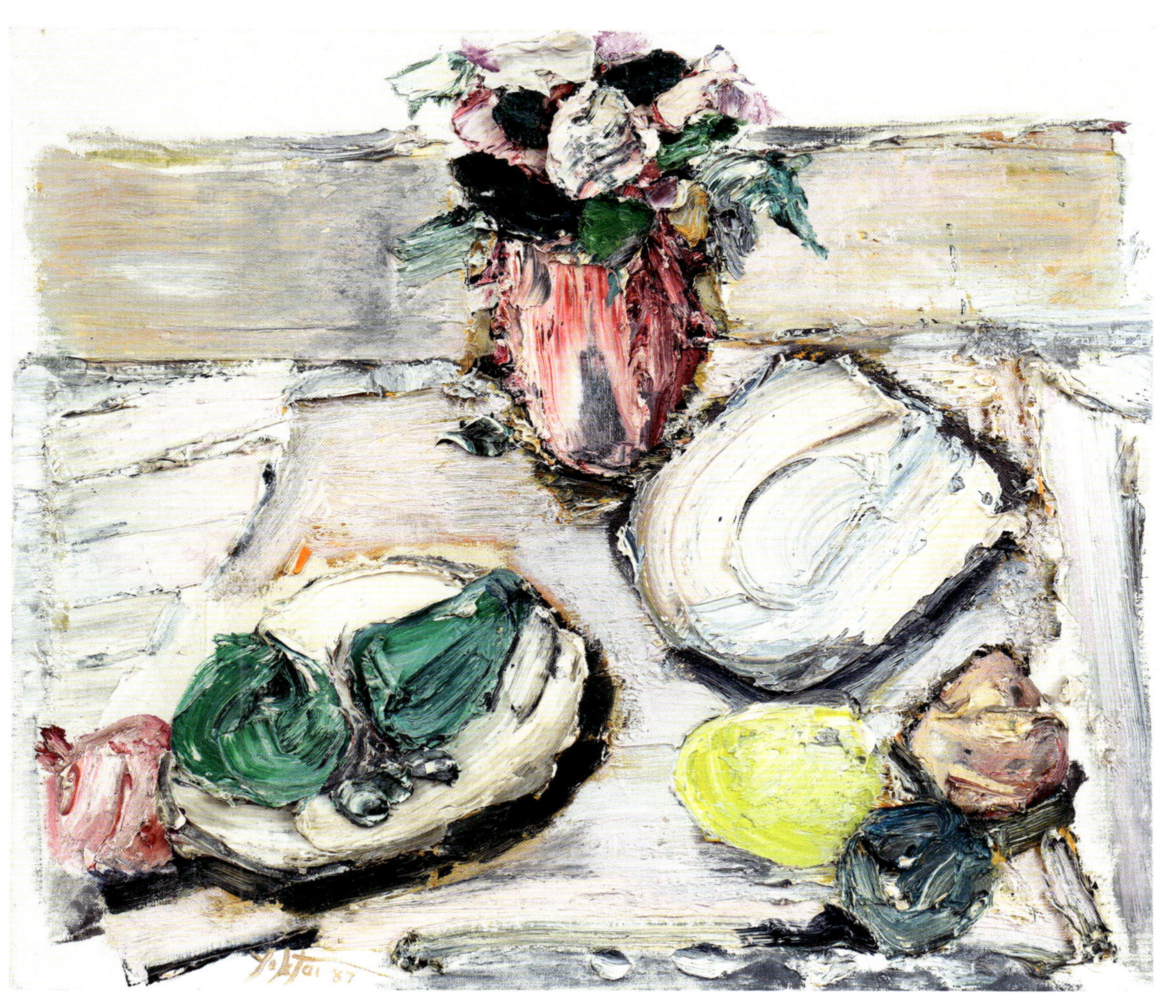

Untitled, 1987, oil on canvas, 48 × 50 inches (121.9 × 127 cm)

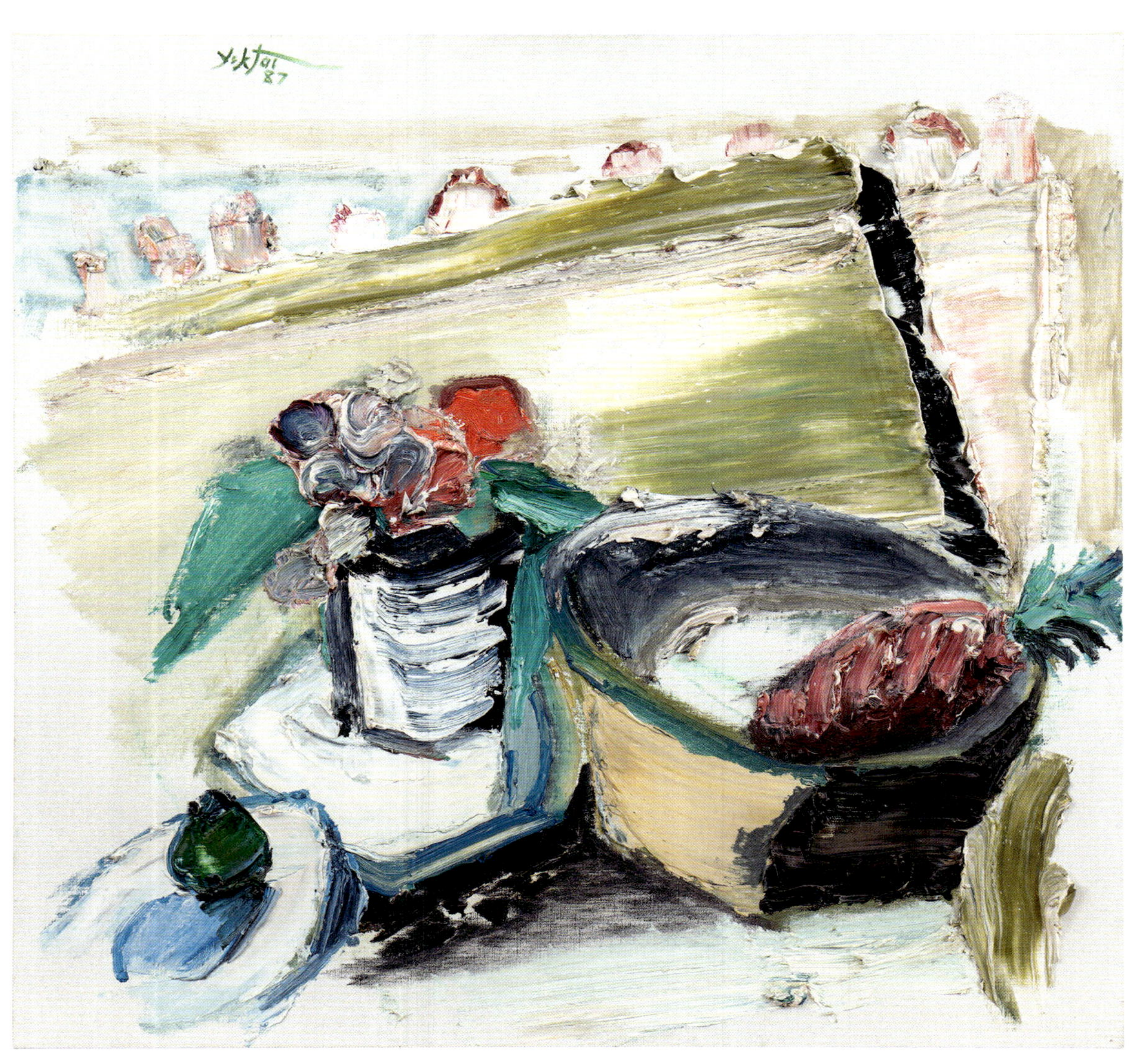

 Untitled, 1987, oil on canvas, 30 × 32 inches (76.2 × 81.3 cm)

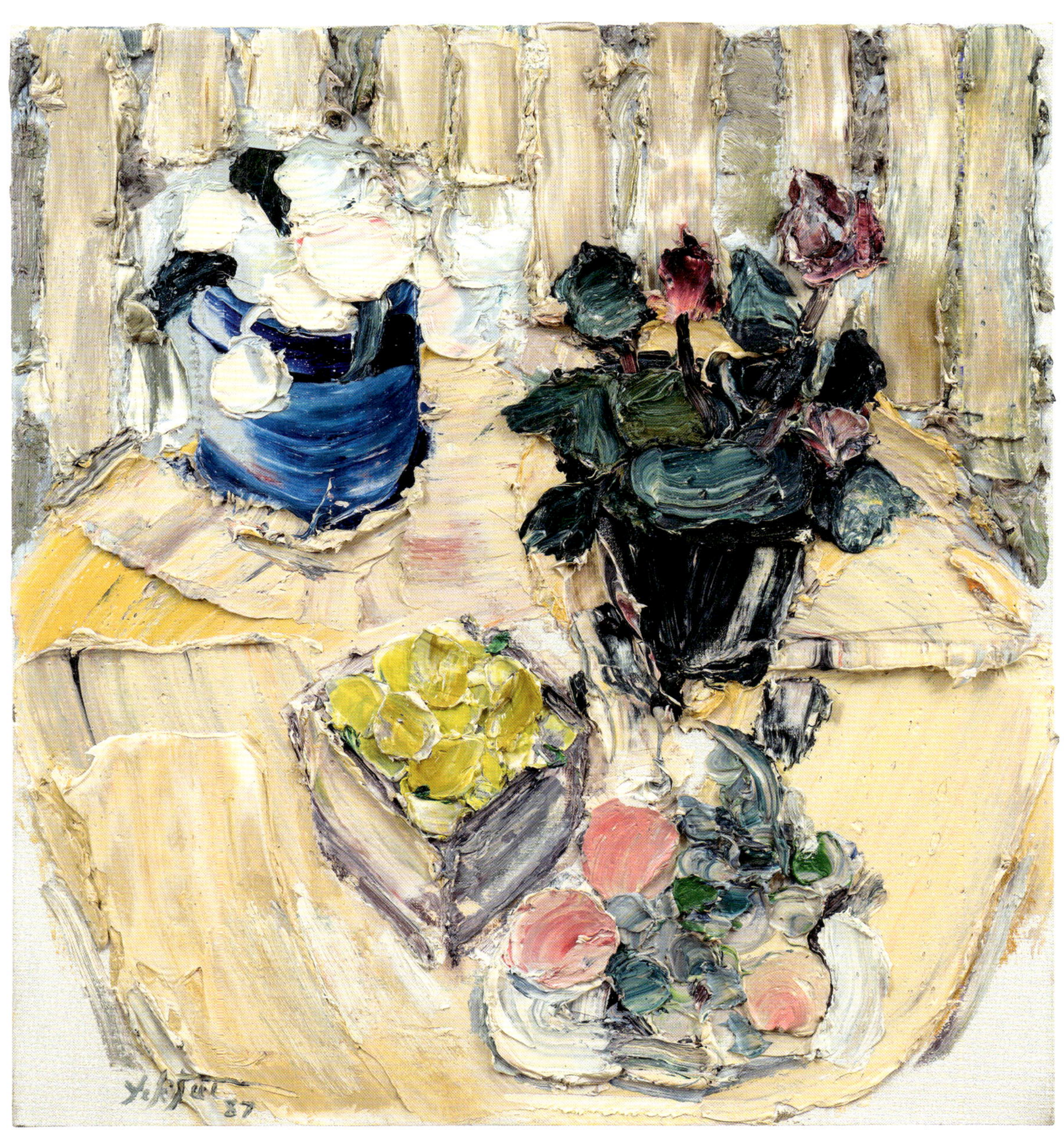

Untitled, 1987, oil on canvas, 26 × 24 inches (66 × 61 cm)

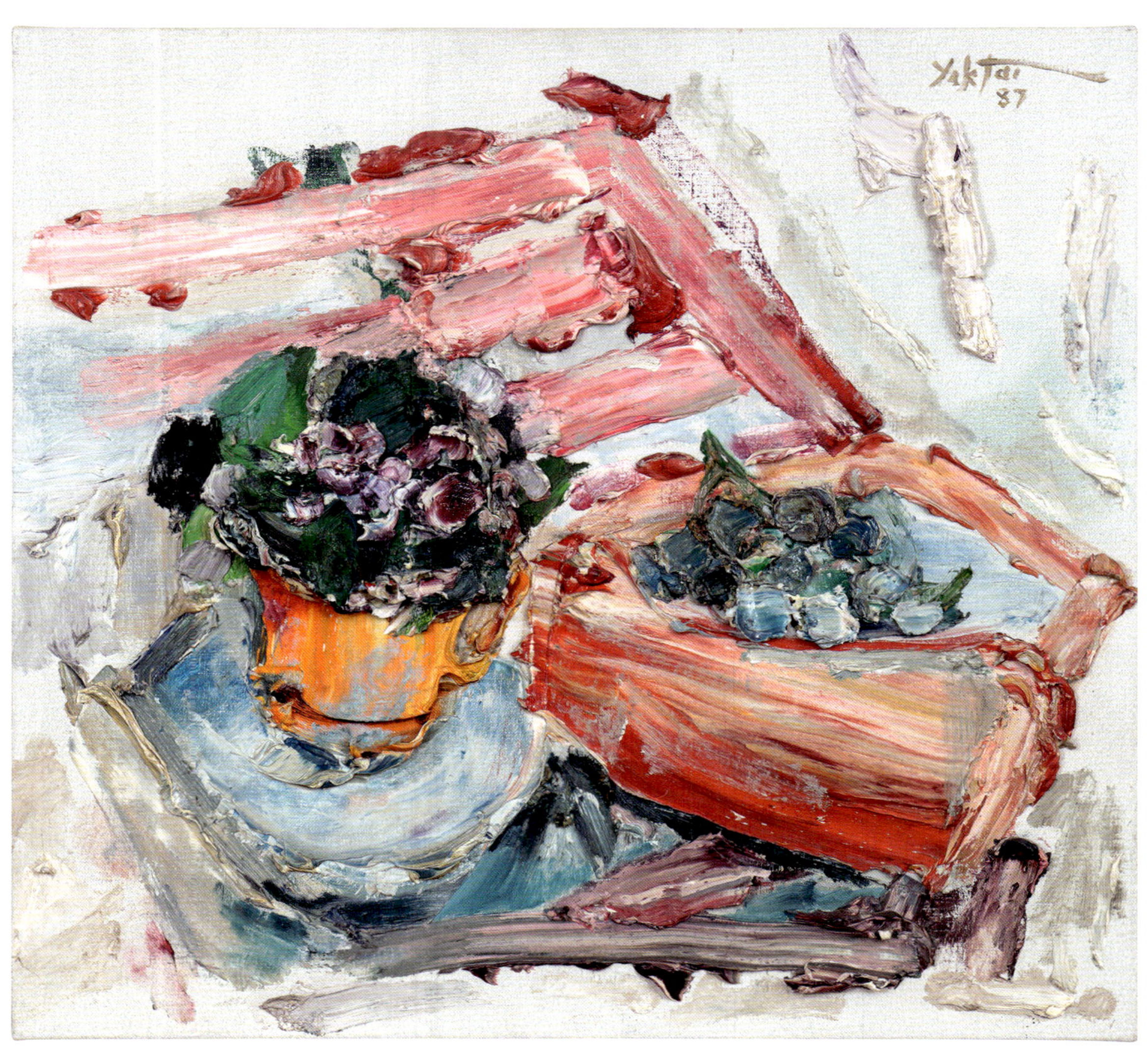

Untitled, 1987, oil on canvas, 24 × 26 inches (61 × 66 cm)

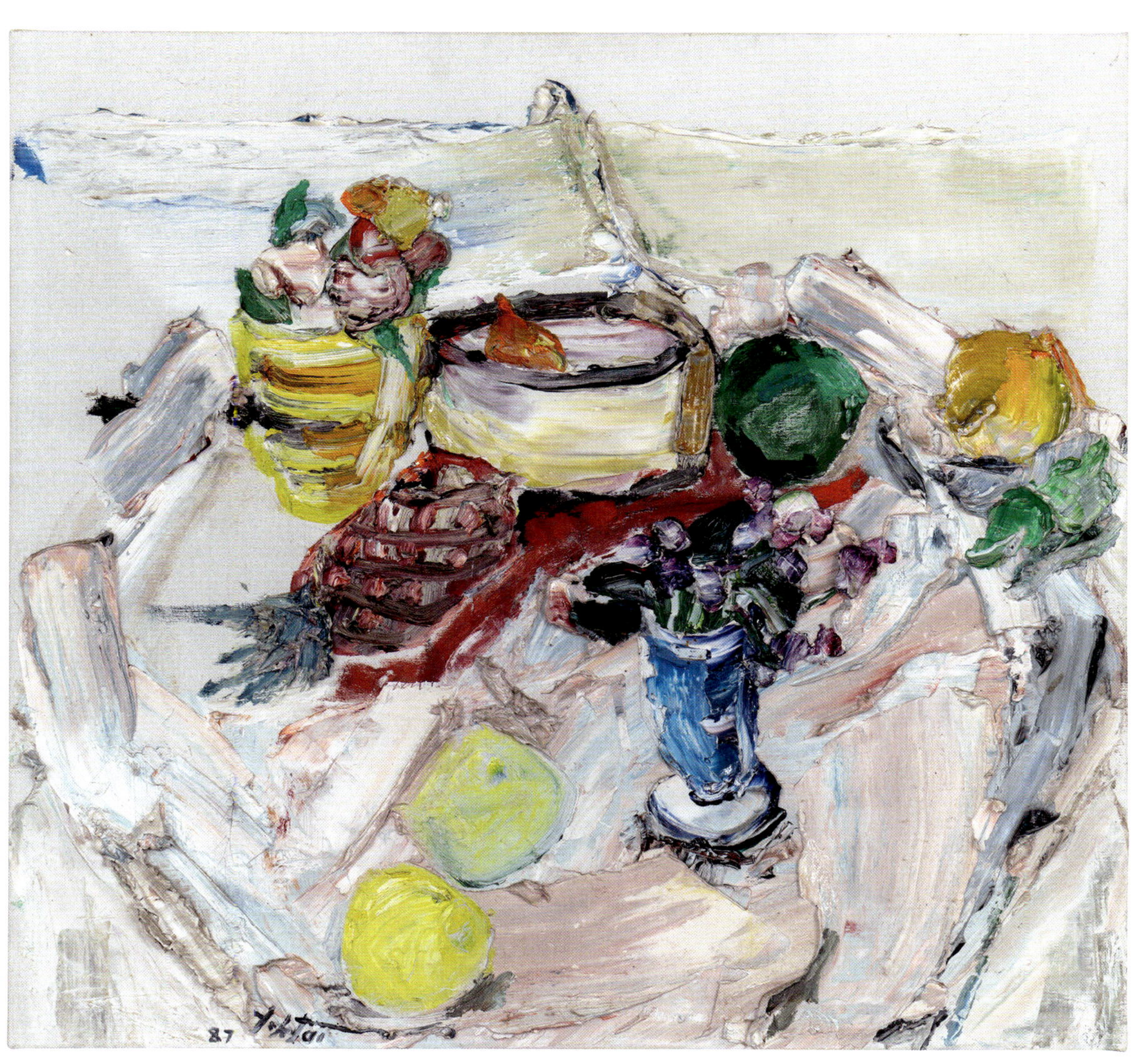

Untitled, 1987, oil on canvas, 30 × 32 inches (76.2 × 81.3 cm)

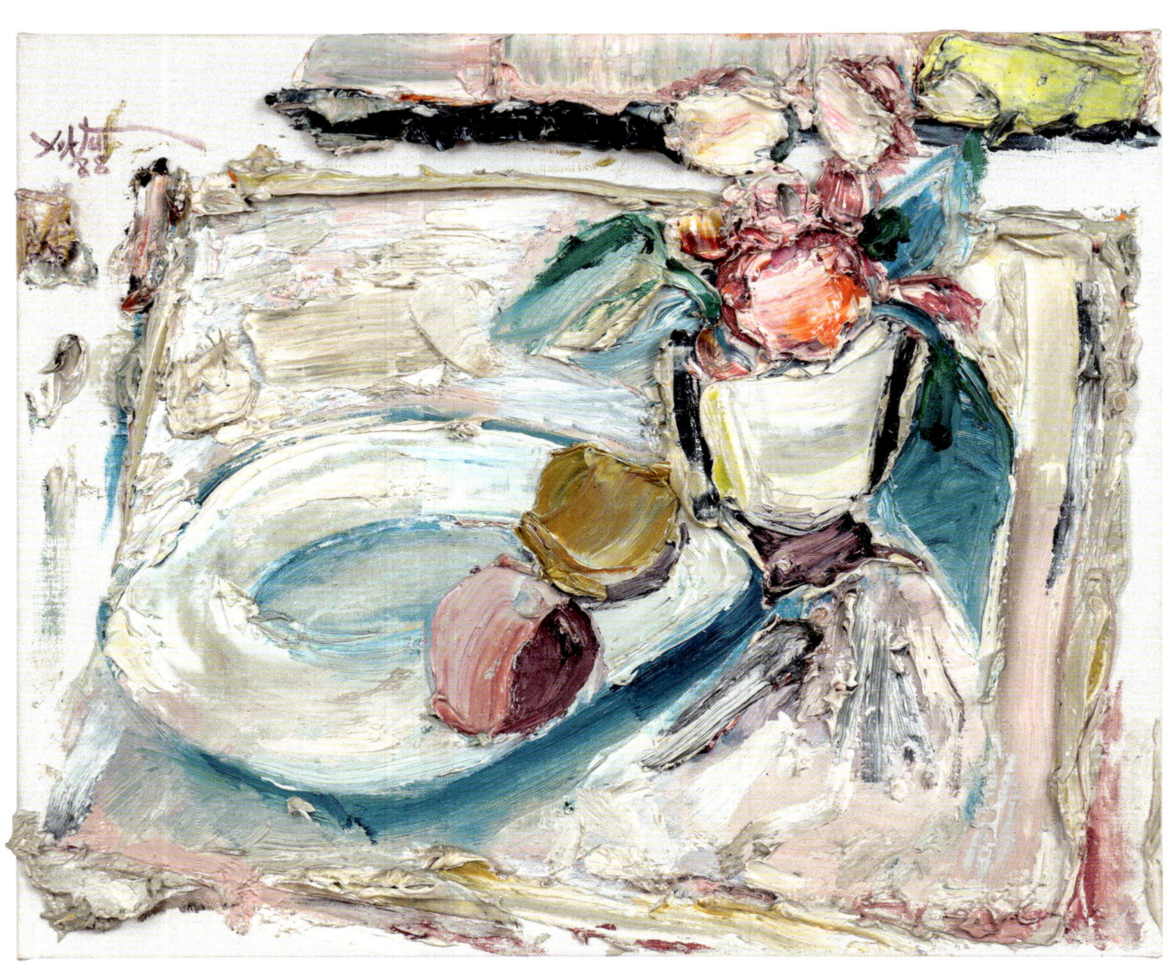

 Untitled, 1988, oil on canvas, 20 × 24 inches (50.8 × 61 cm)

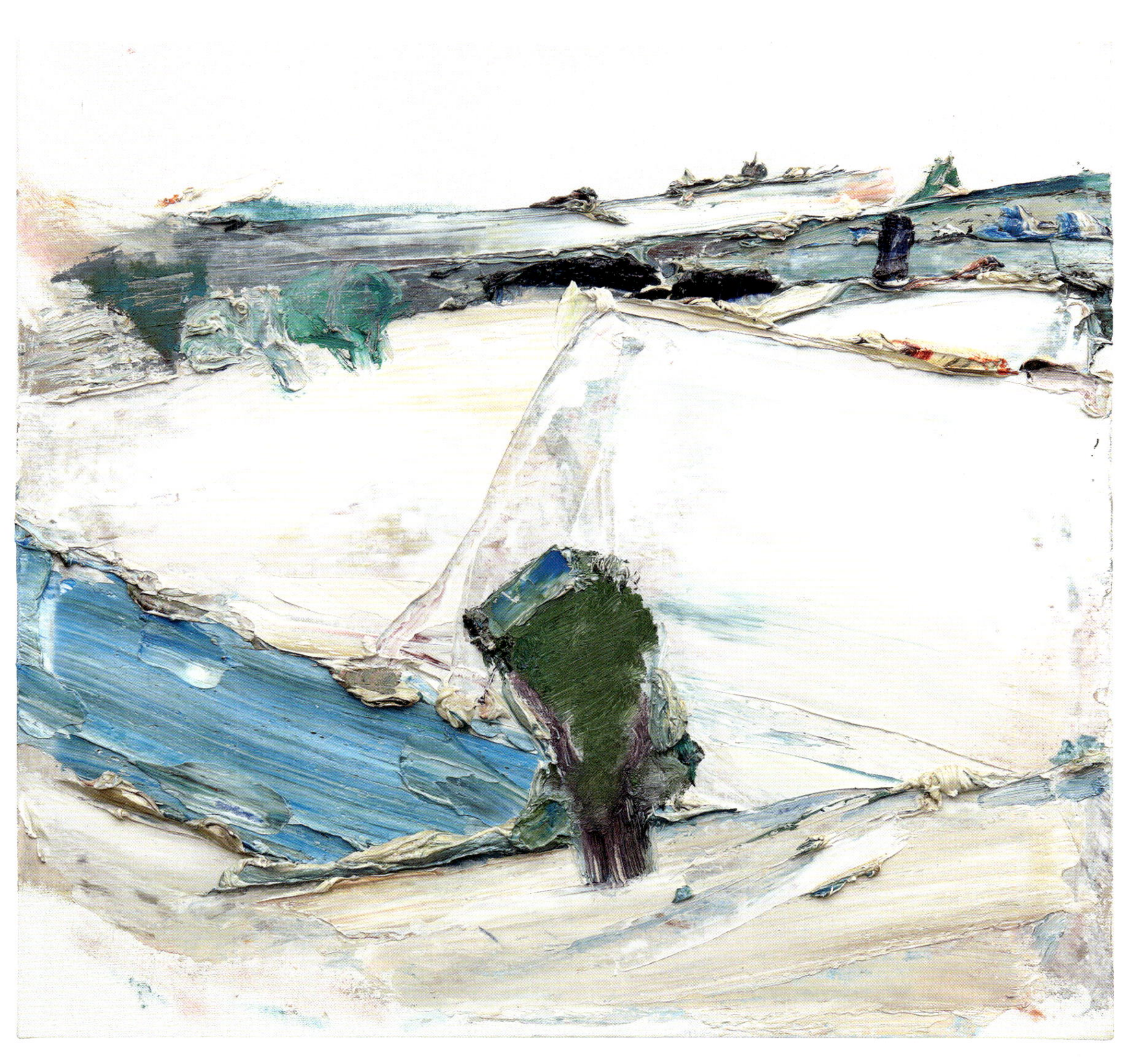

Untitled, 1988, oil on canvas, 30 × 32 inches (76.2 × 81.3 cm)

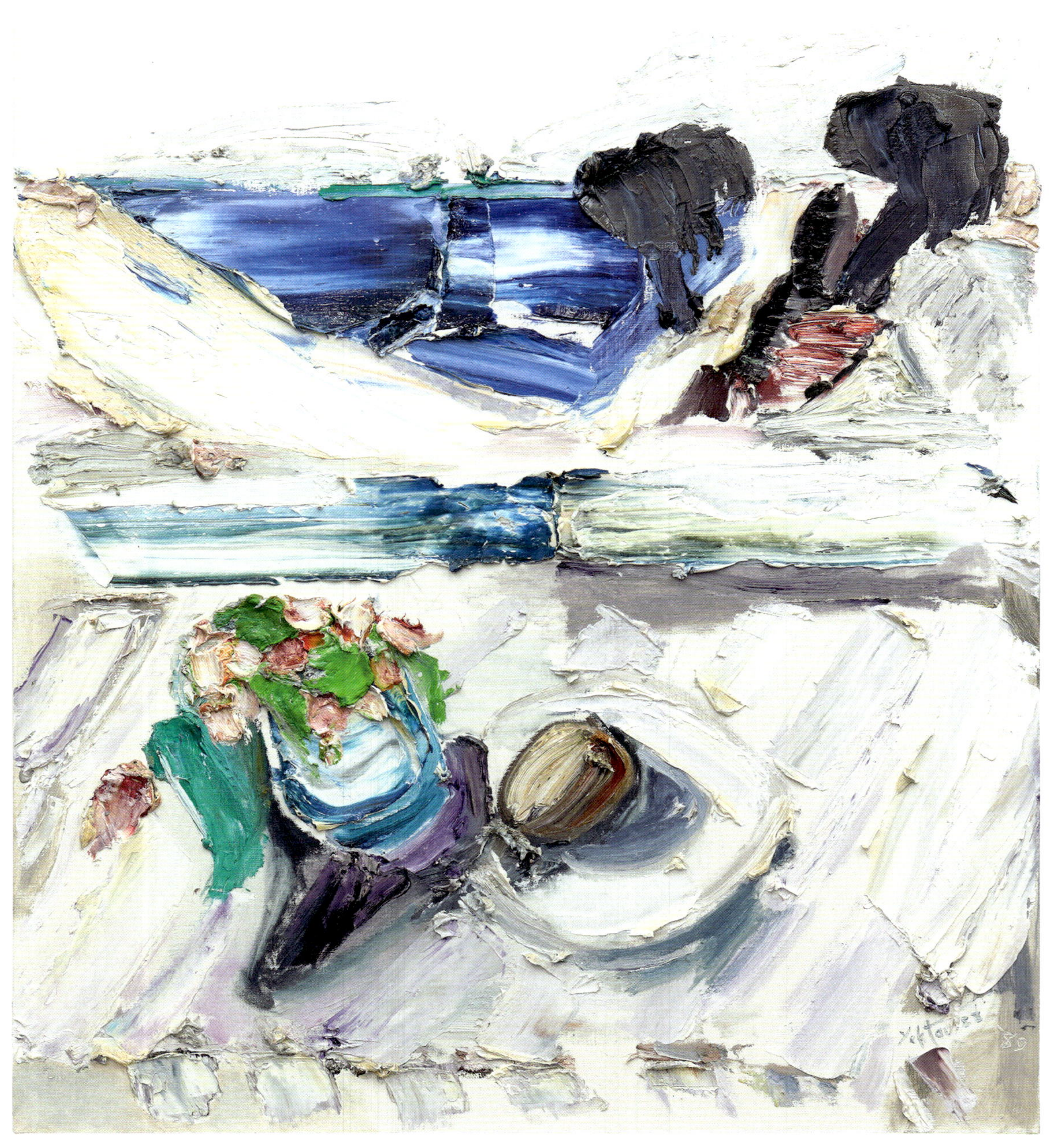

Untitled, 1988–89, oil on canvas, 40 × 36 inches (101.6 × 91.4 cm)

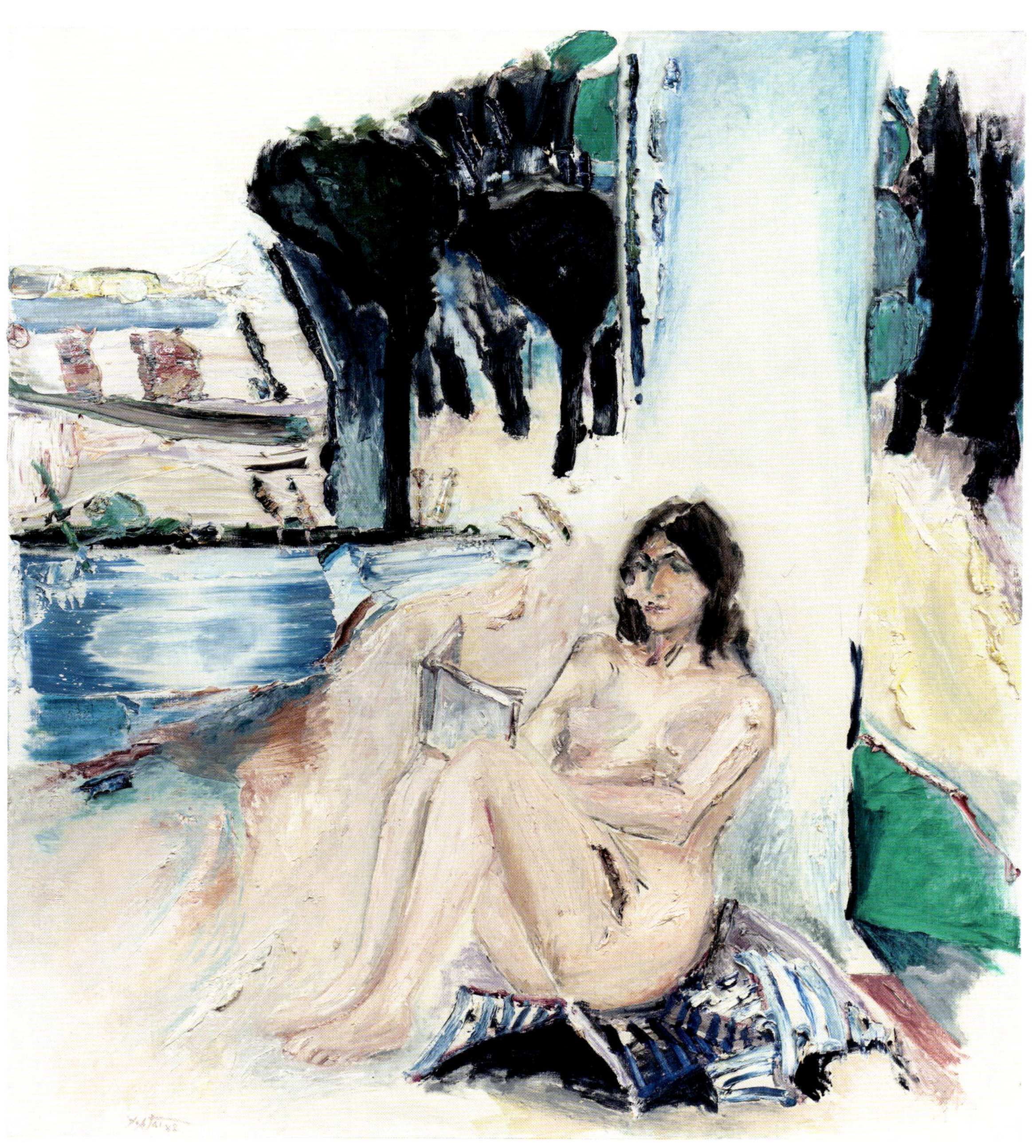

Untitled, 1988, oil on canvas, 72 × 64 inches (182.9 × 162.6 cm)

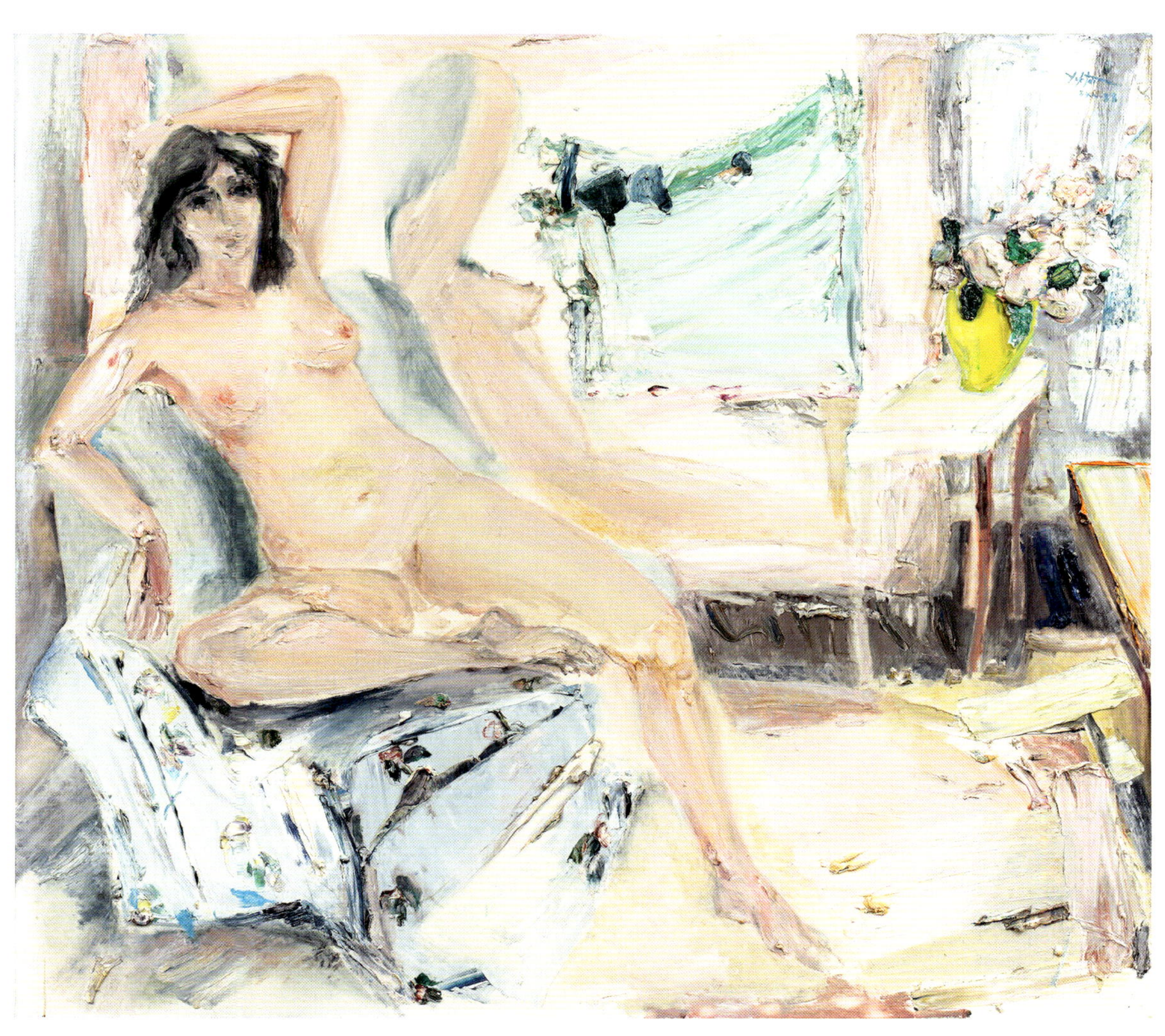

Untitled, 1984–88, oil on canvas, 64 × 72 inches (162.6 × 182.9 cm)

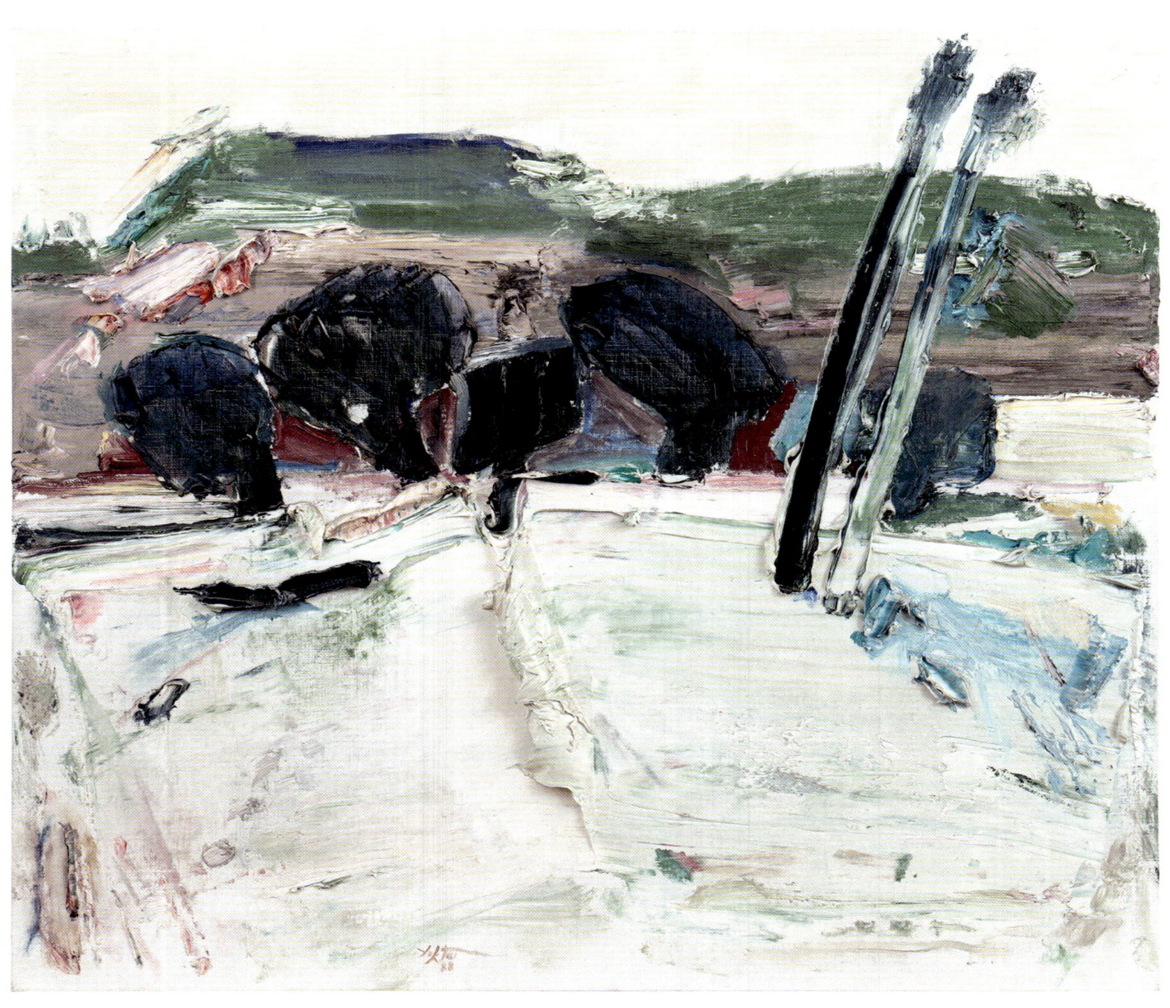

Untitled, 1988, oil on canvas, 38 × 44 inches (96.5 × 111.8 cm)

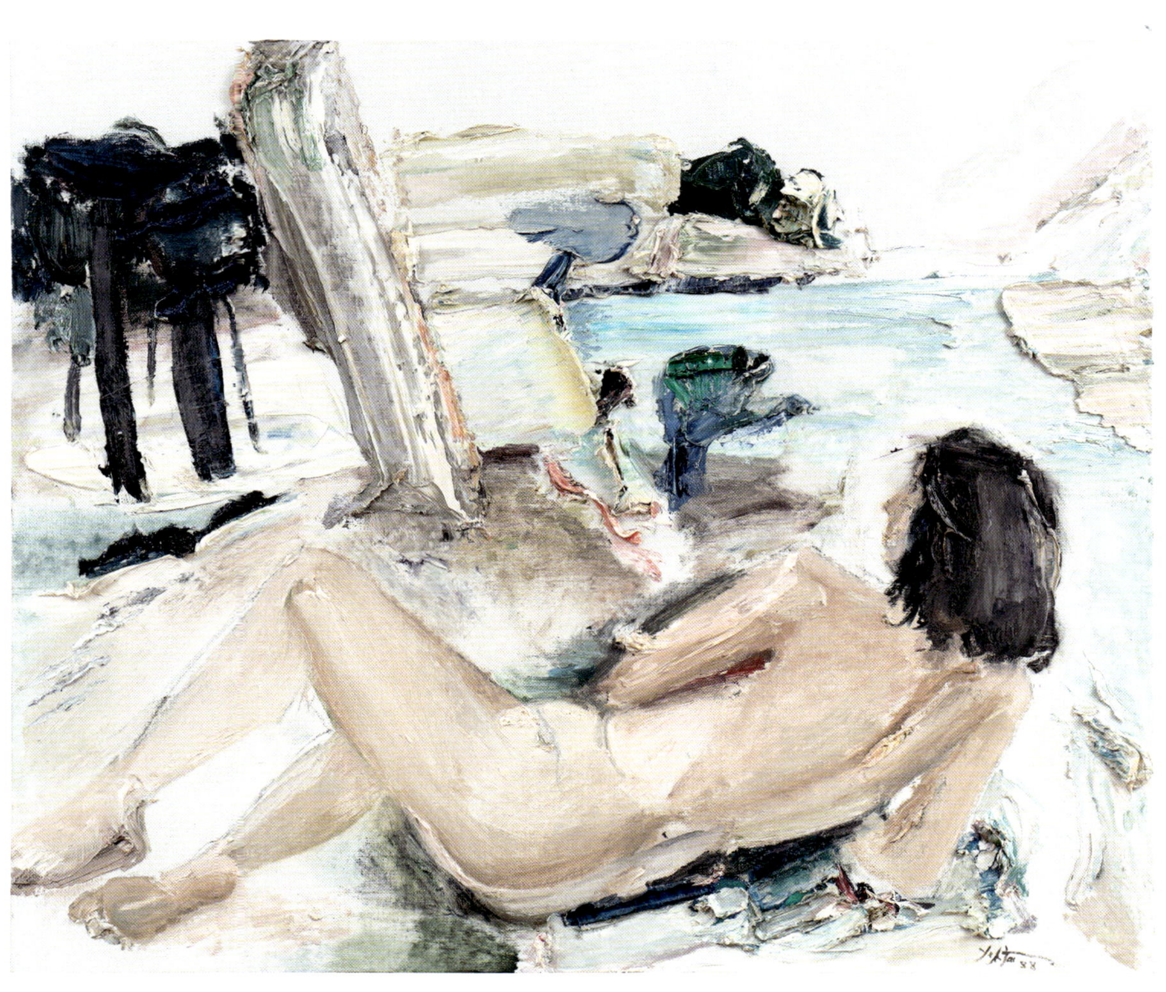

Untitled, 1988, oil on canvas, 42 × 50 inches (106.7 × 127 cm)

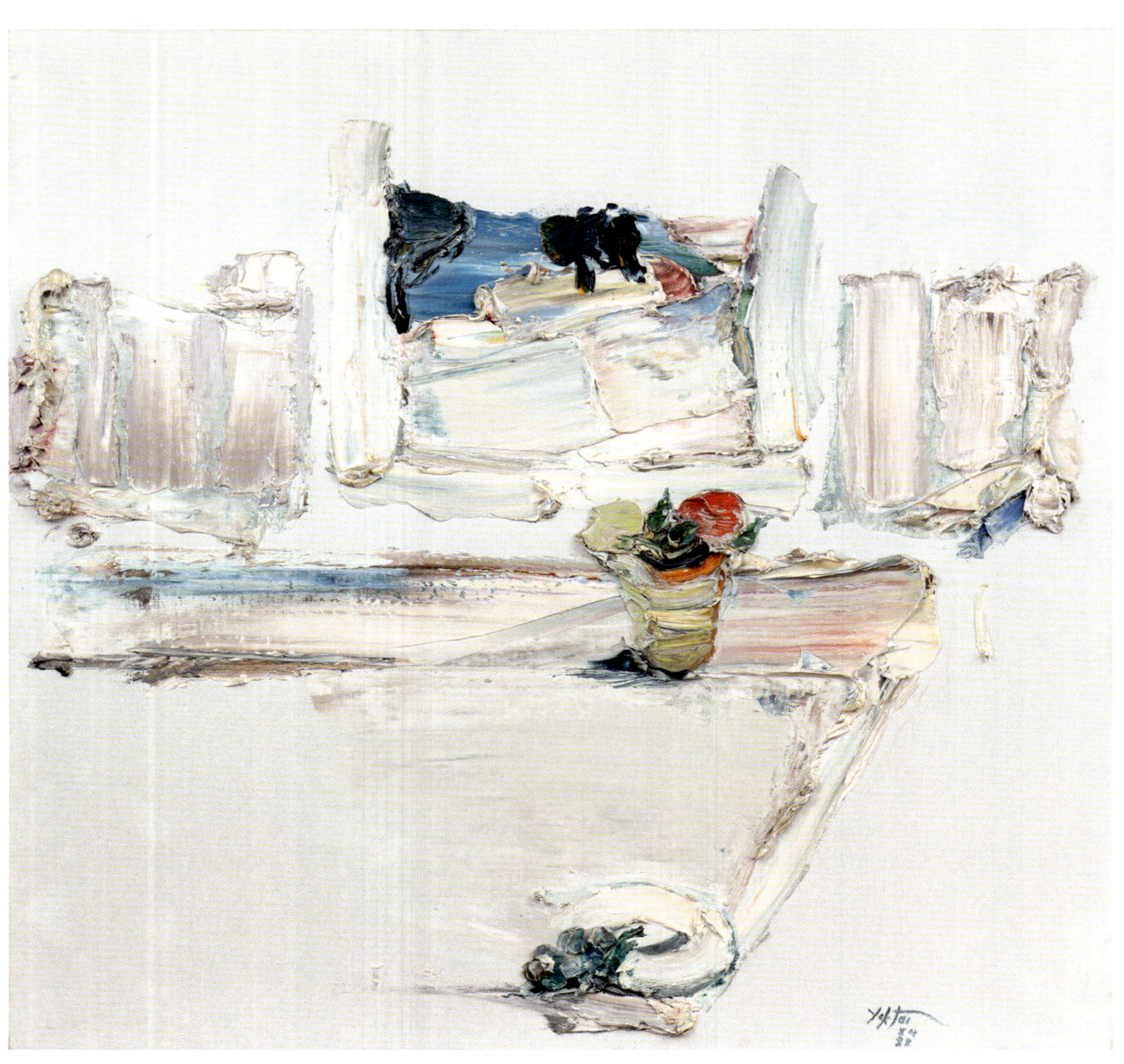

Untitled, 1984–88, oil on canvas, 48 × 50 inches (121.9 × 127 cm)

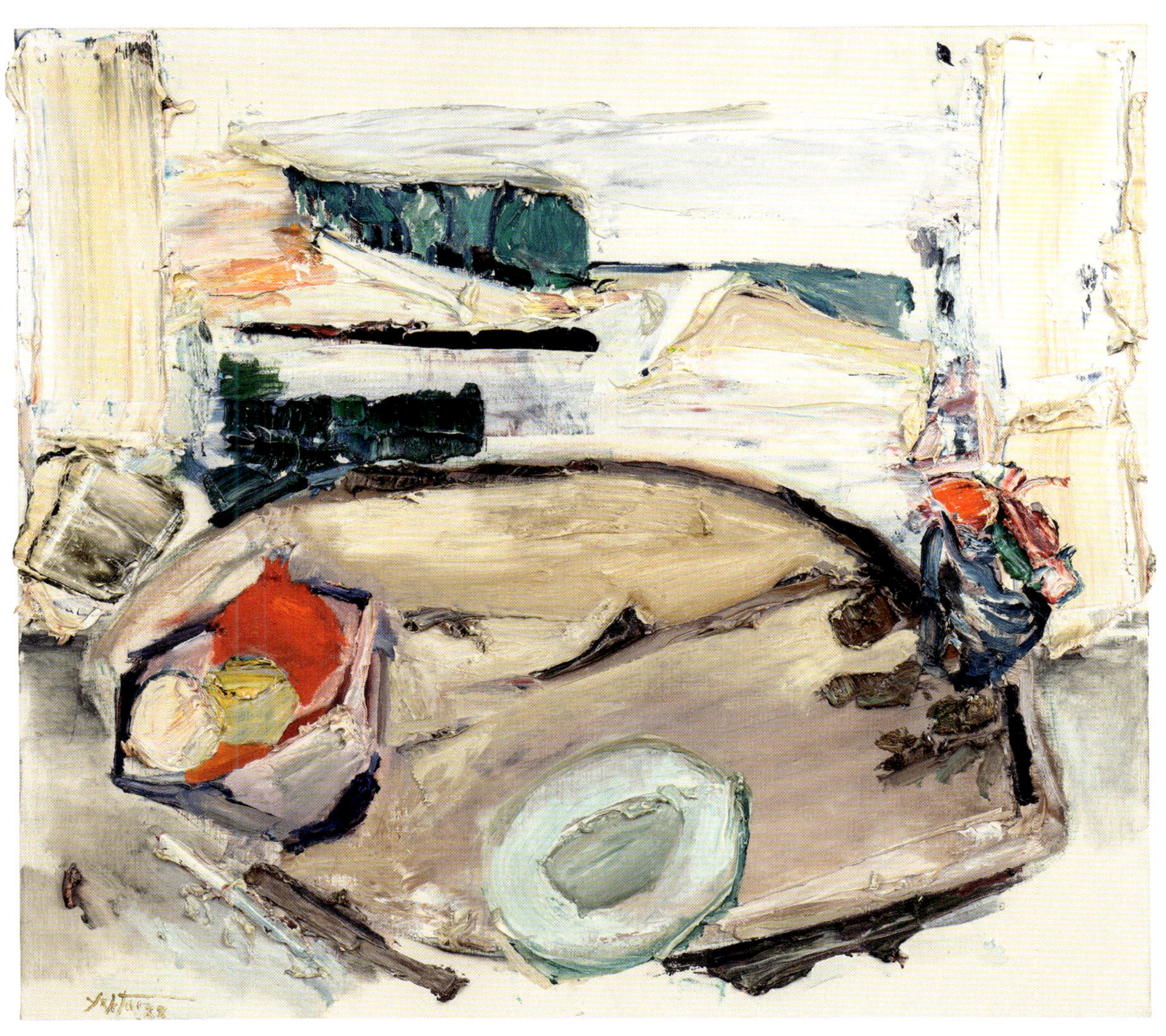

Untitled, 1988, oil on canvas, 36 × 40 inches (91.4 × 101.6 cm)

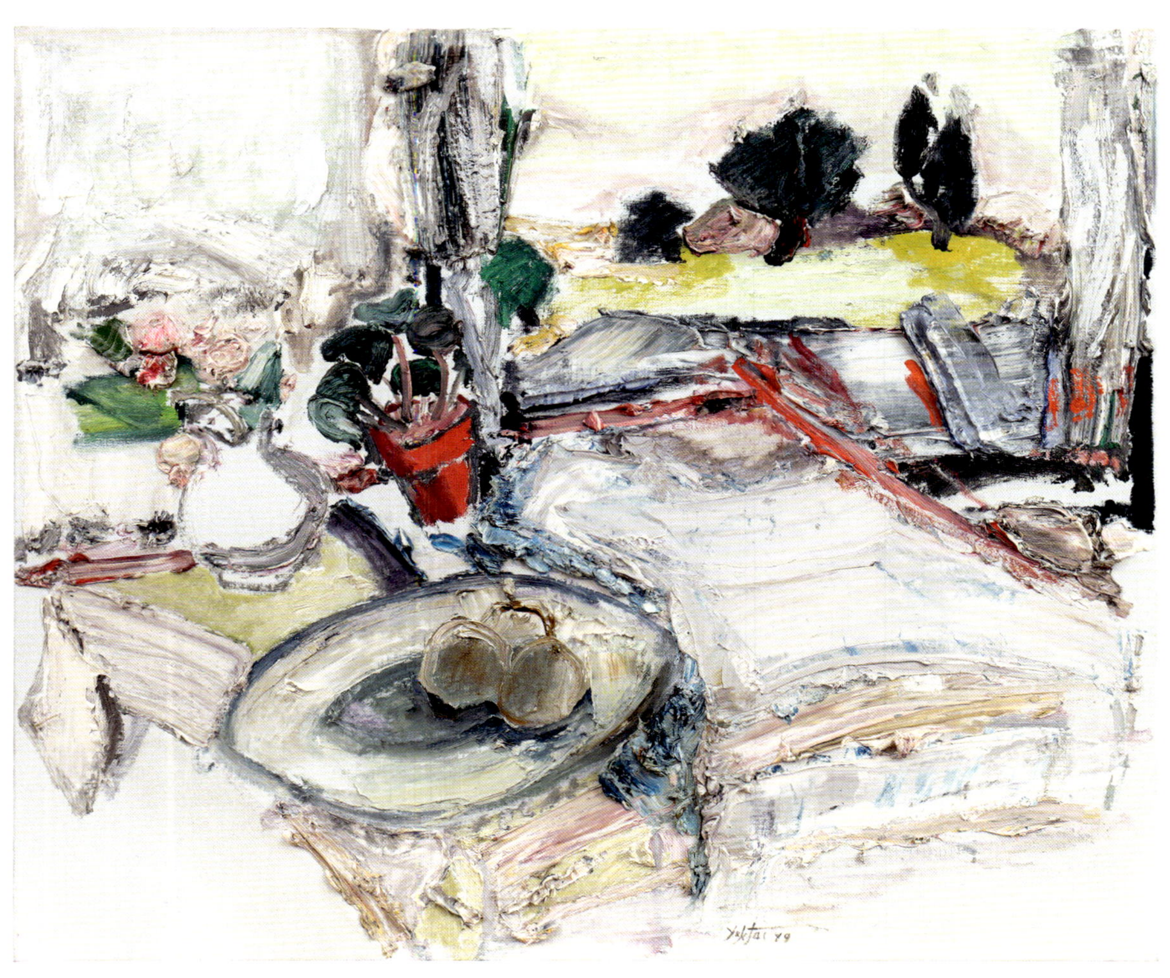

 Untitled, 1989, oil on canvas, 42 × 50 inches (106.7 × 127 cm)

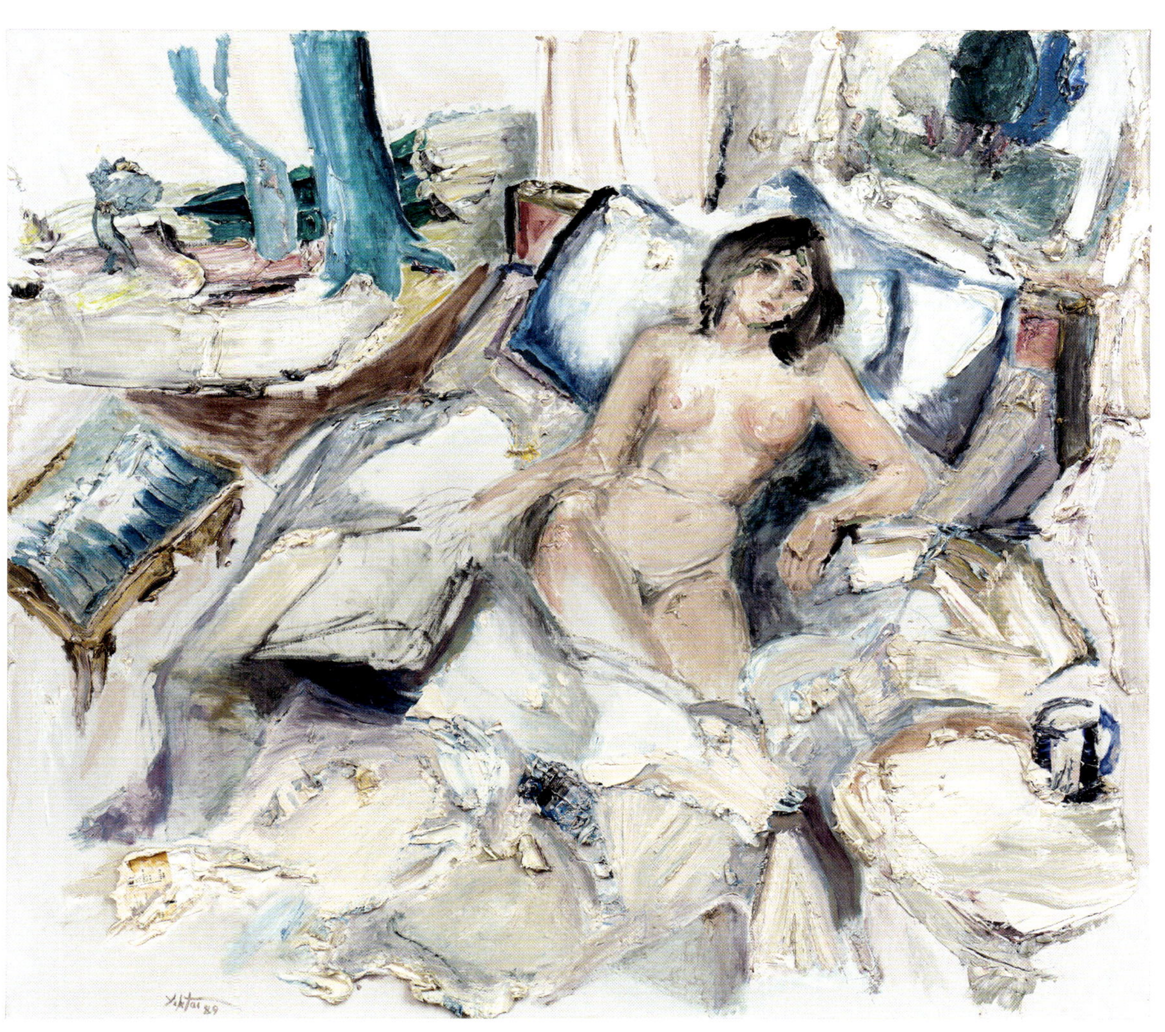

Untitled, 1989, oil on canvas, 68 × 76 inches (172.7 × 193 cm)

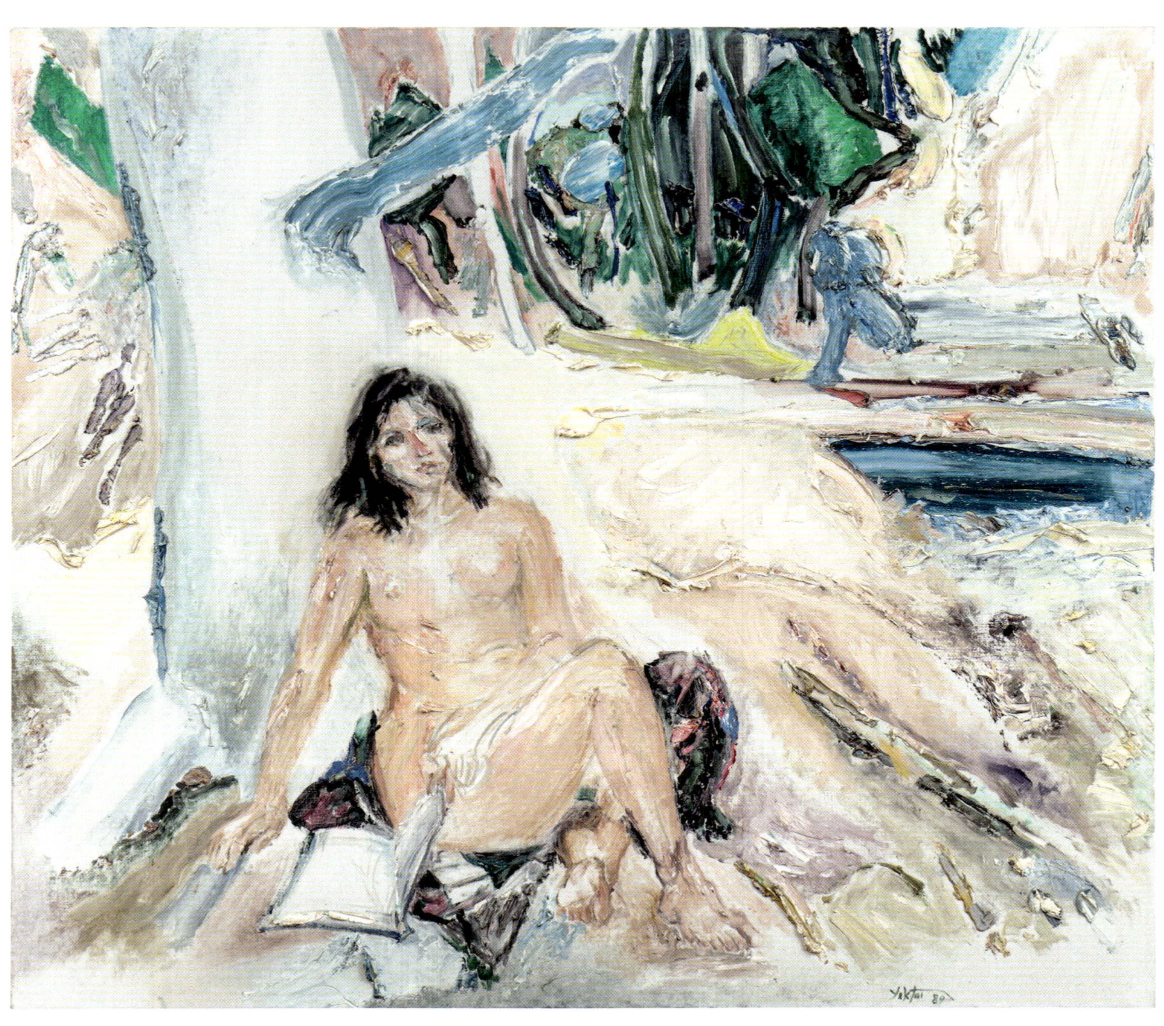

Untitled, 1989, oil on canvas, 64 × 72 inches (162.6 × 182.9 cm)

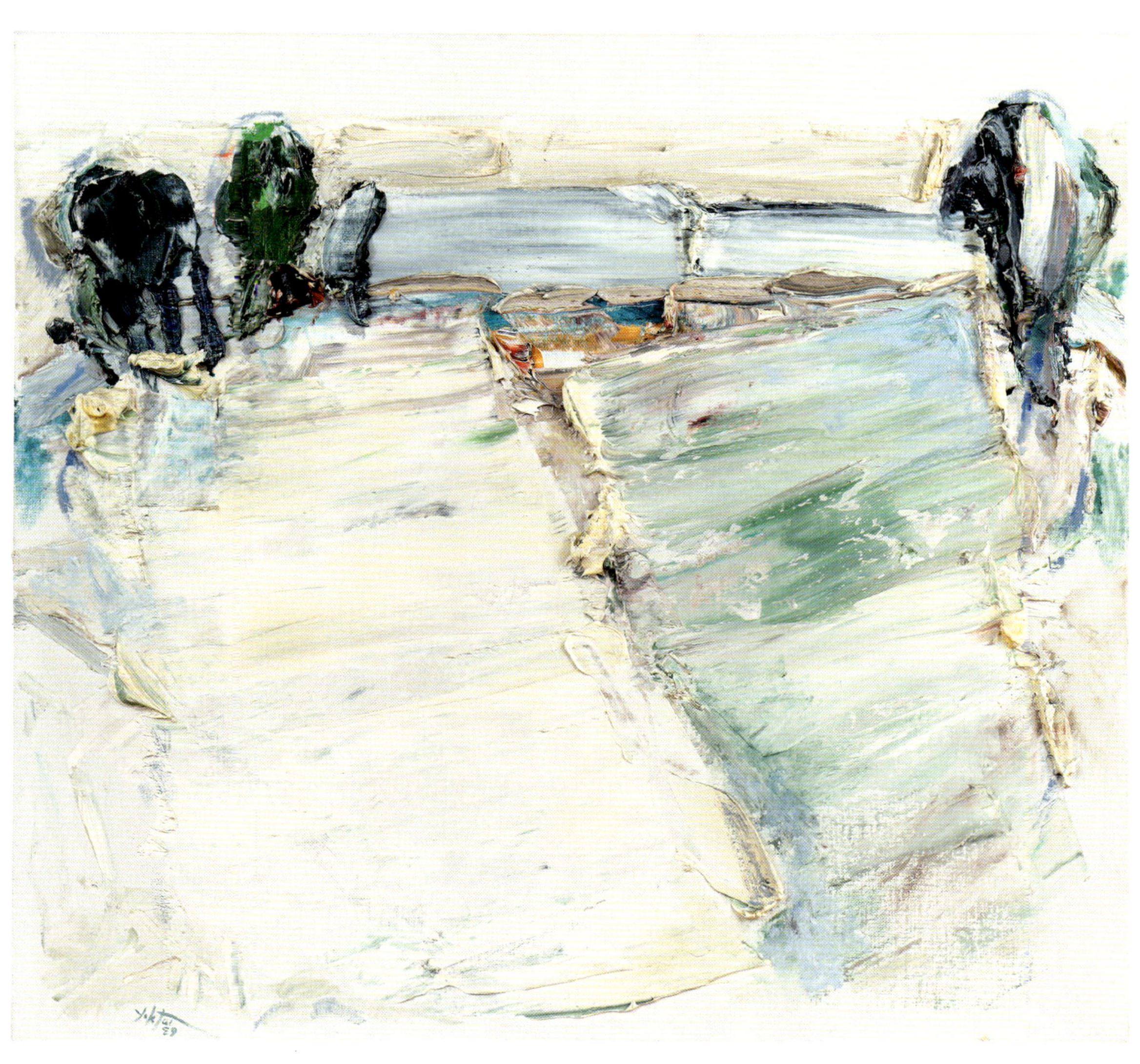

Untitled, 1989, oil on canvas, 48 × 52 inches (121.9 × 132.1 cm)

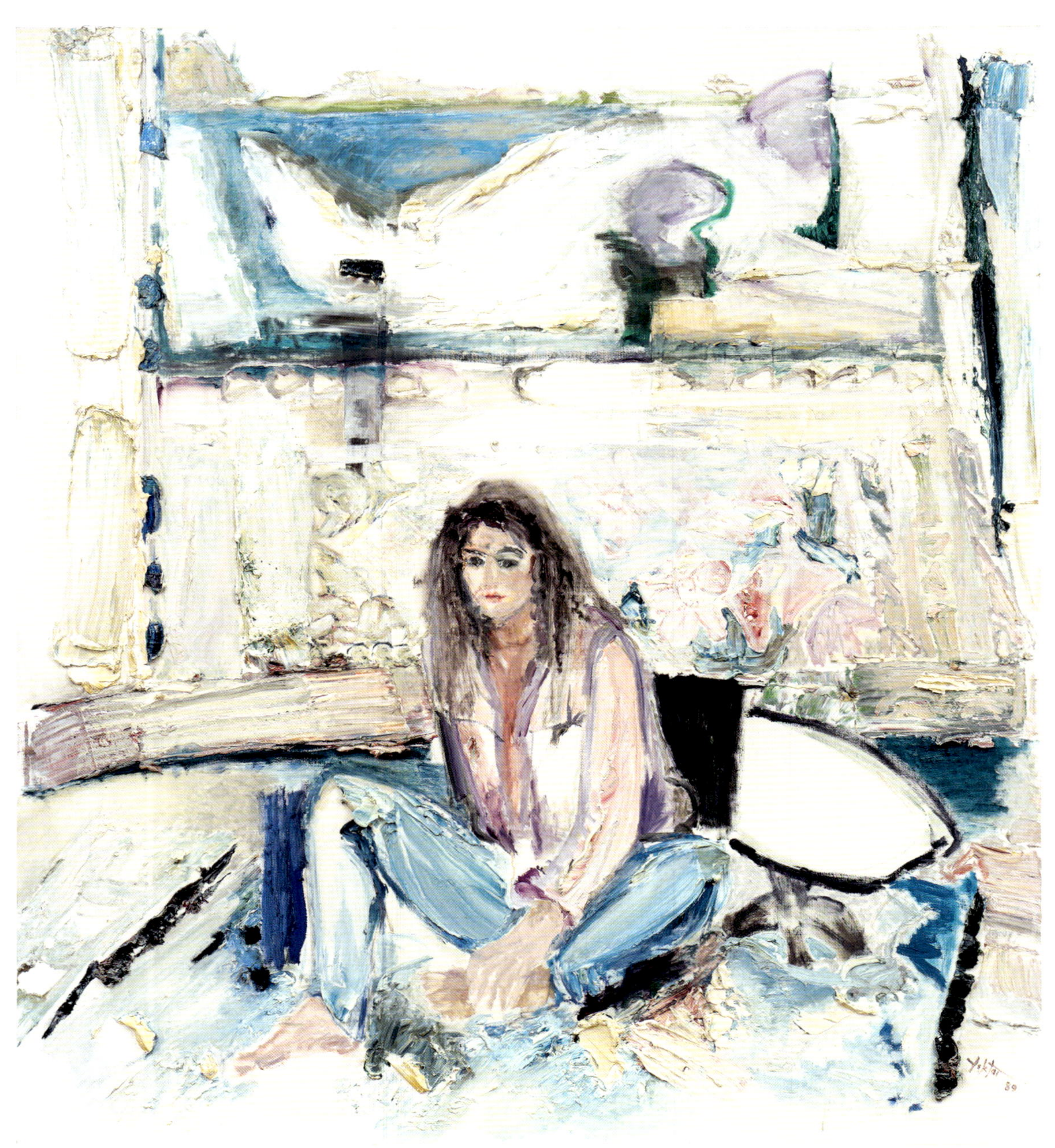

Mahan, 1989, oil on canvas, 72 × 64 inches (182.9 × 162.6 cm)

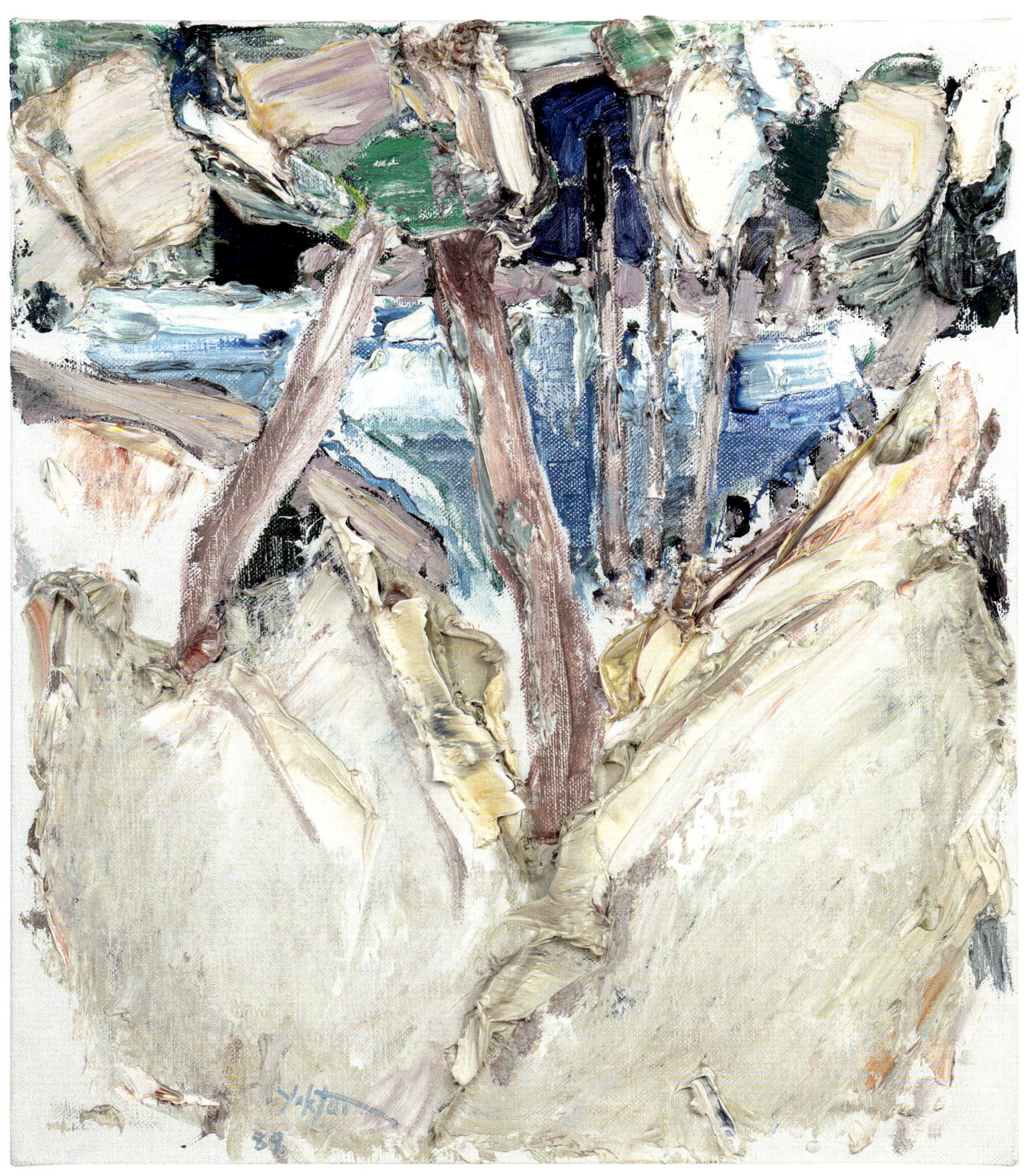

Untitled, 1989, oil on canvas, 28 × 24 inches (71.1 × 61 cm)

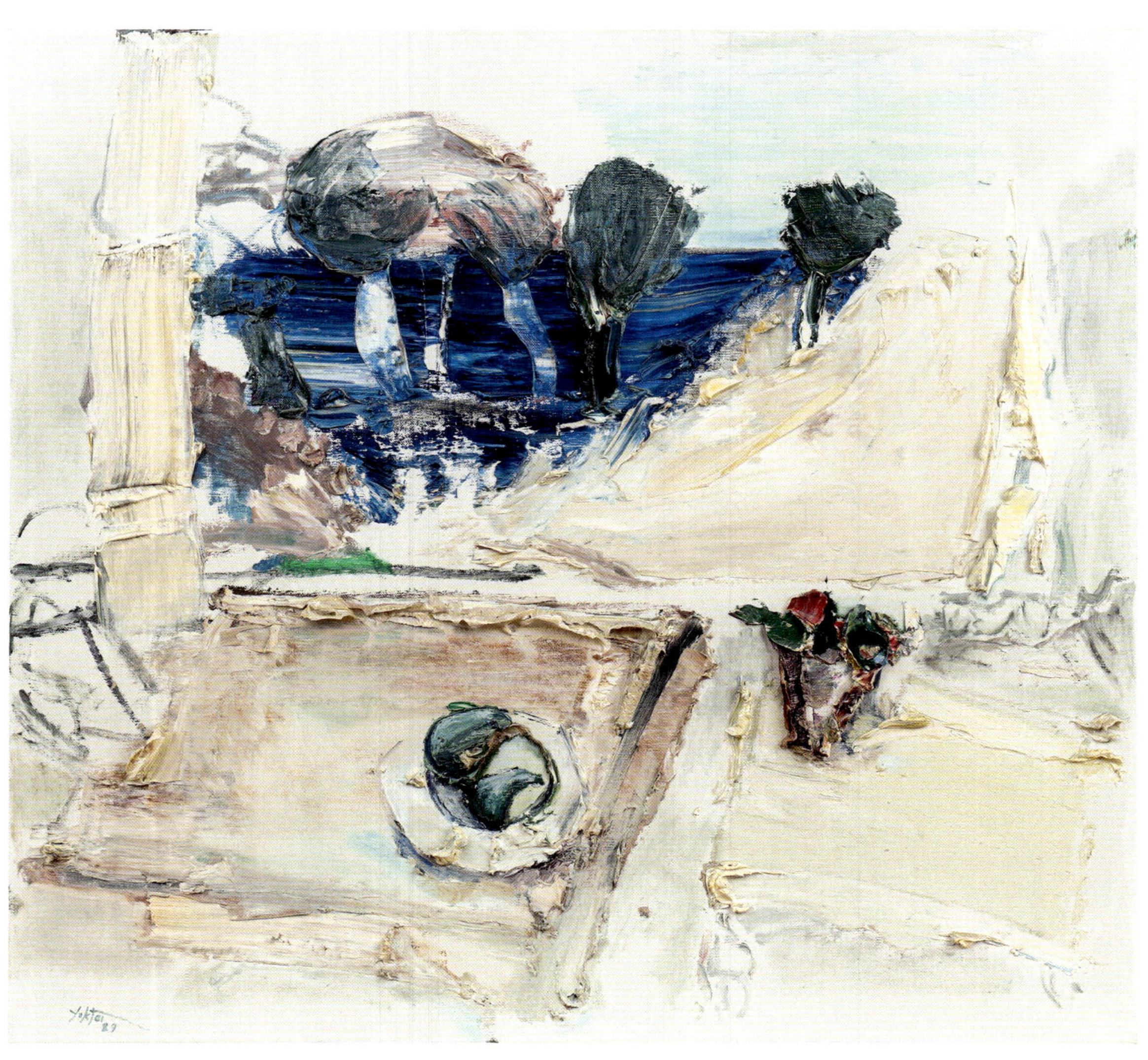

 Untitled, 1989, oil on canvas, 48 × 52 inches (121.9 × 132.1 cm)

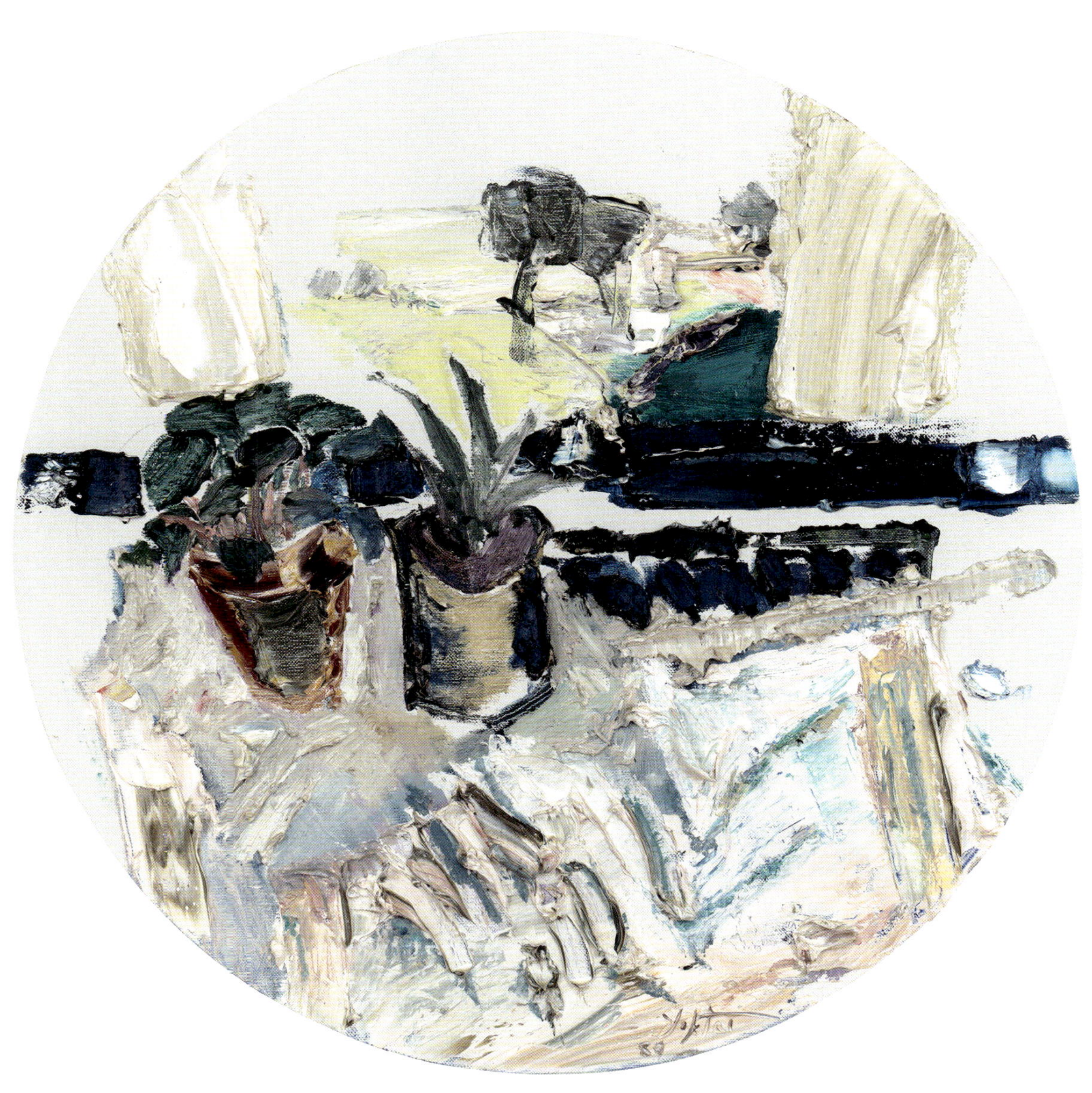

Untitled, 1989, oil on canvas, 48 × 52 inches (121.9 × 132.1 cm)

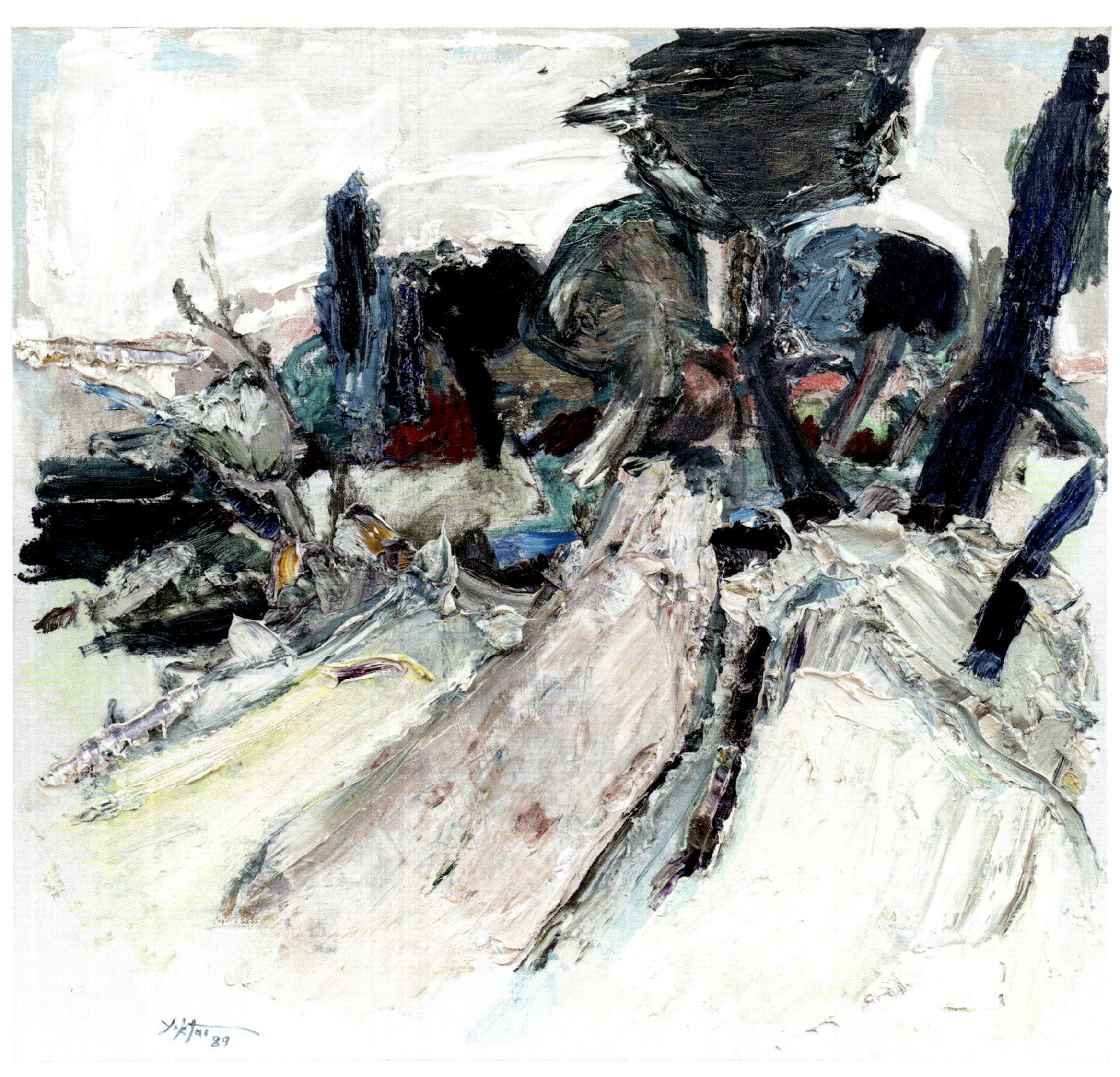

 Untitled, 1989, oil on canvas, 48 × 50 inches (121.9 × 127 cm)

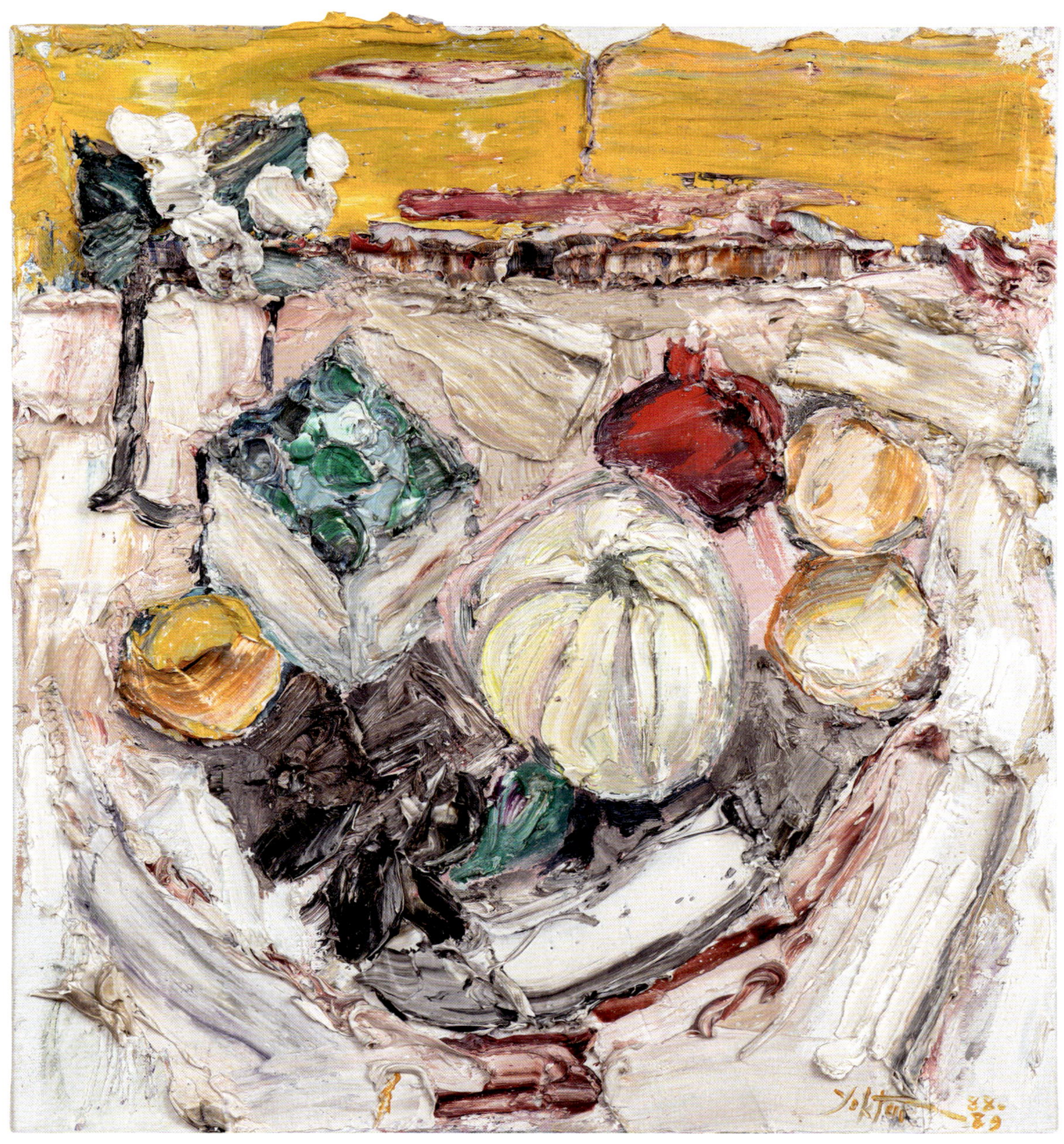

Untitled, 1989, oil on canvas, 26 × 24 inches (66 × 61 cm)

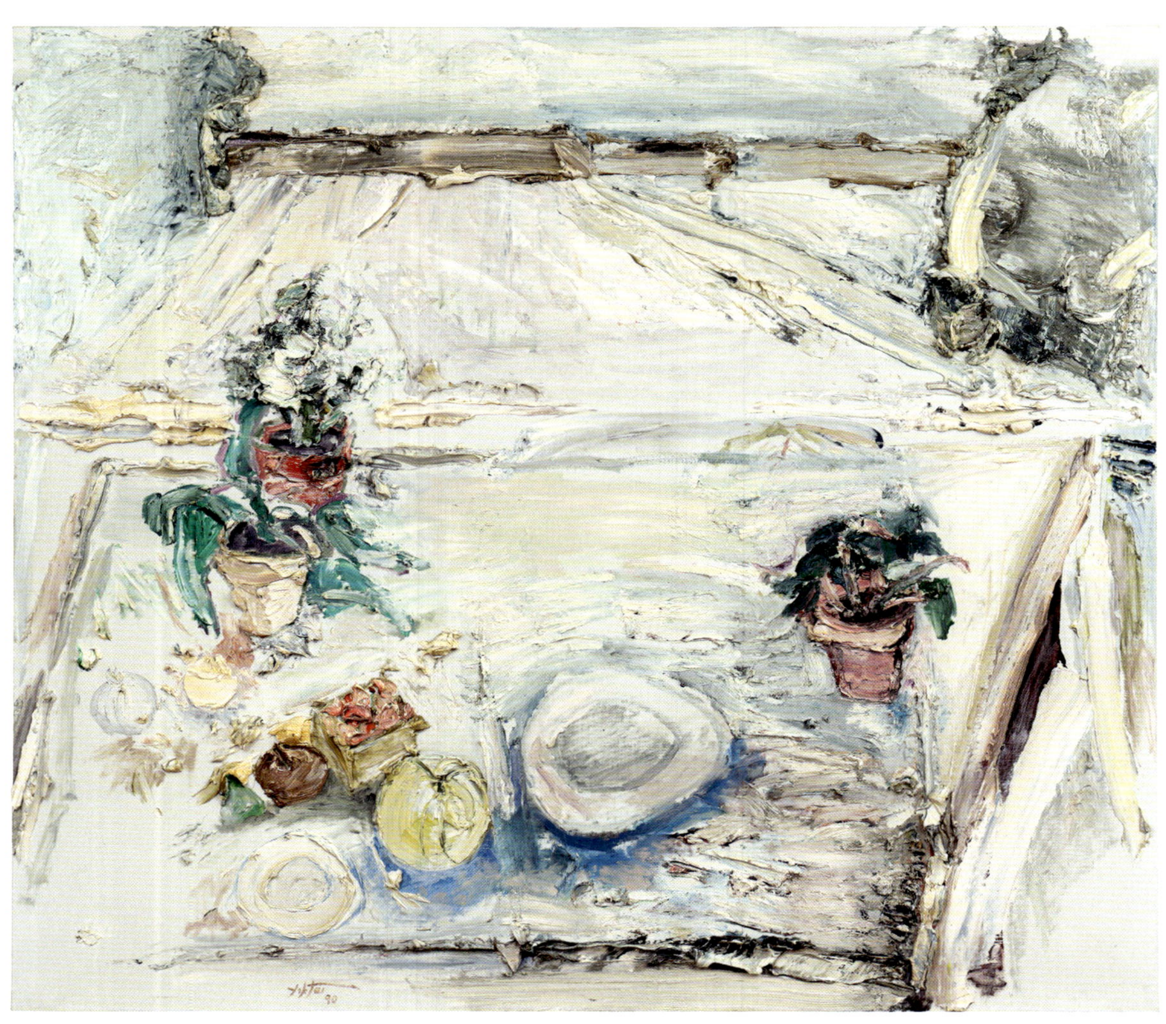

Untitled, 1990, oil on canvas, 64 × 72 inches (162.6 × 182.9 cm)

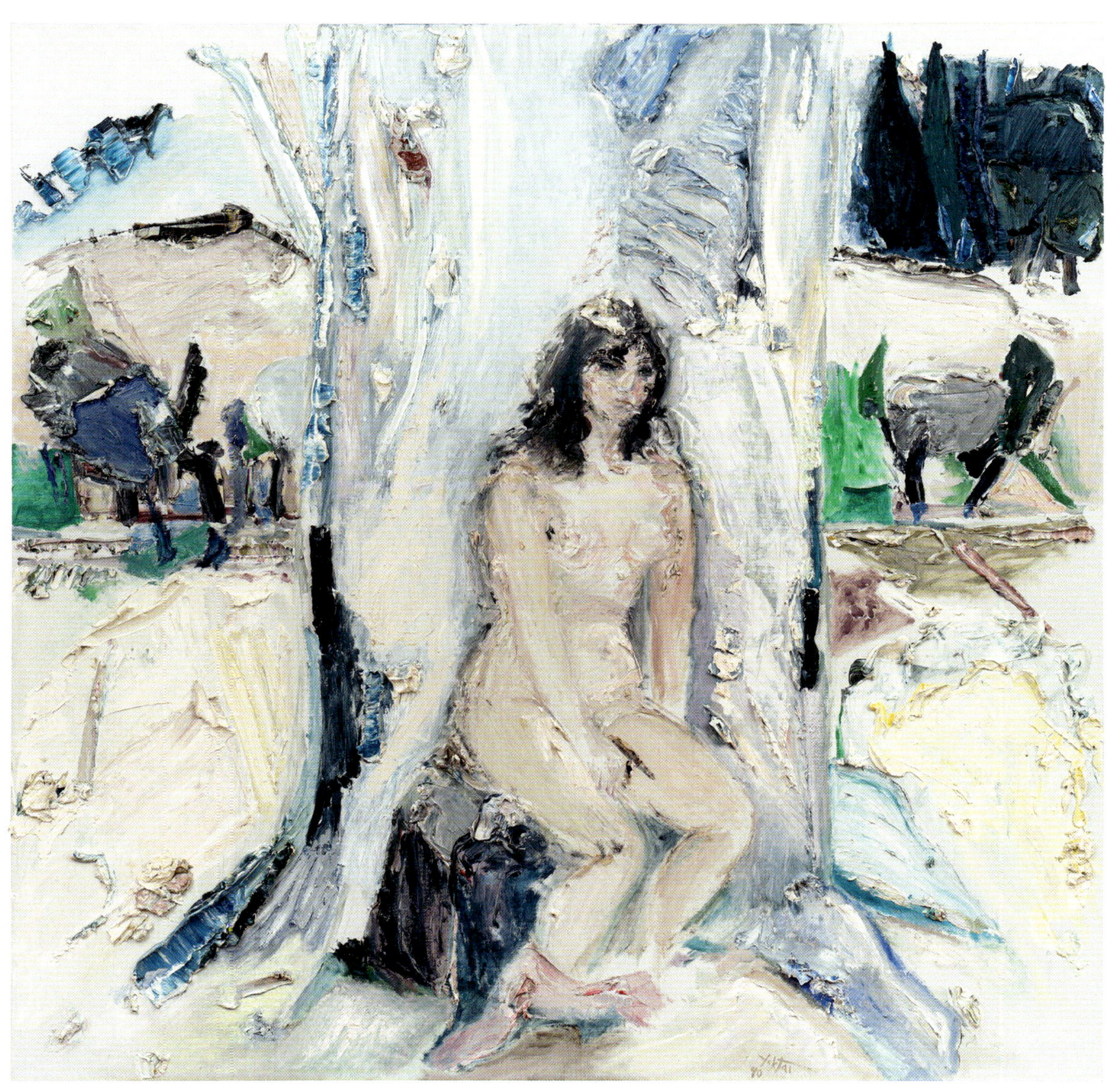

Untitled, 1990, oil on canvas, 72 × 72 inches (182.9 × 182.9 cm)

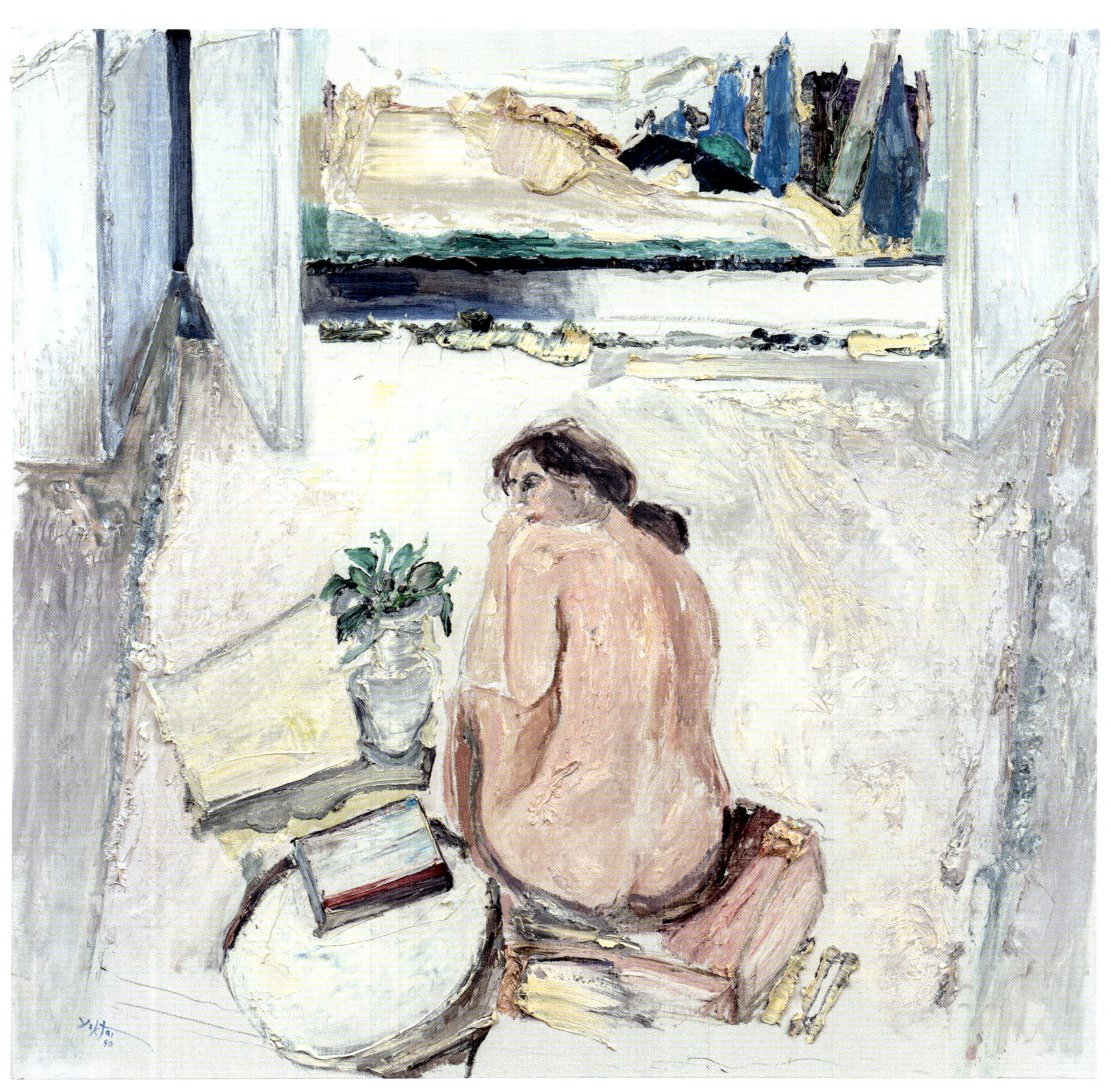

644 *In Front of the Window*, 1990, oil on canvas, 72 × 72 inches (182.9 × 182.9 cm)

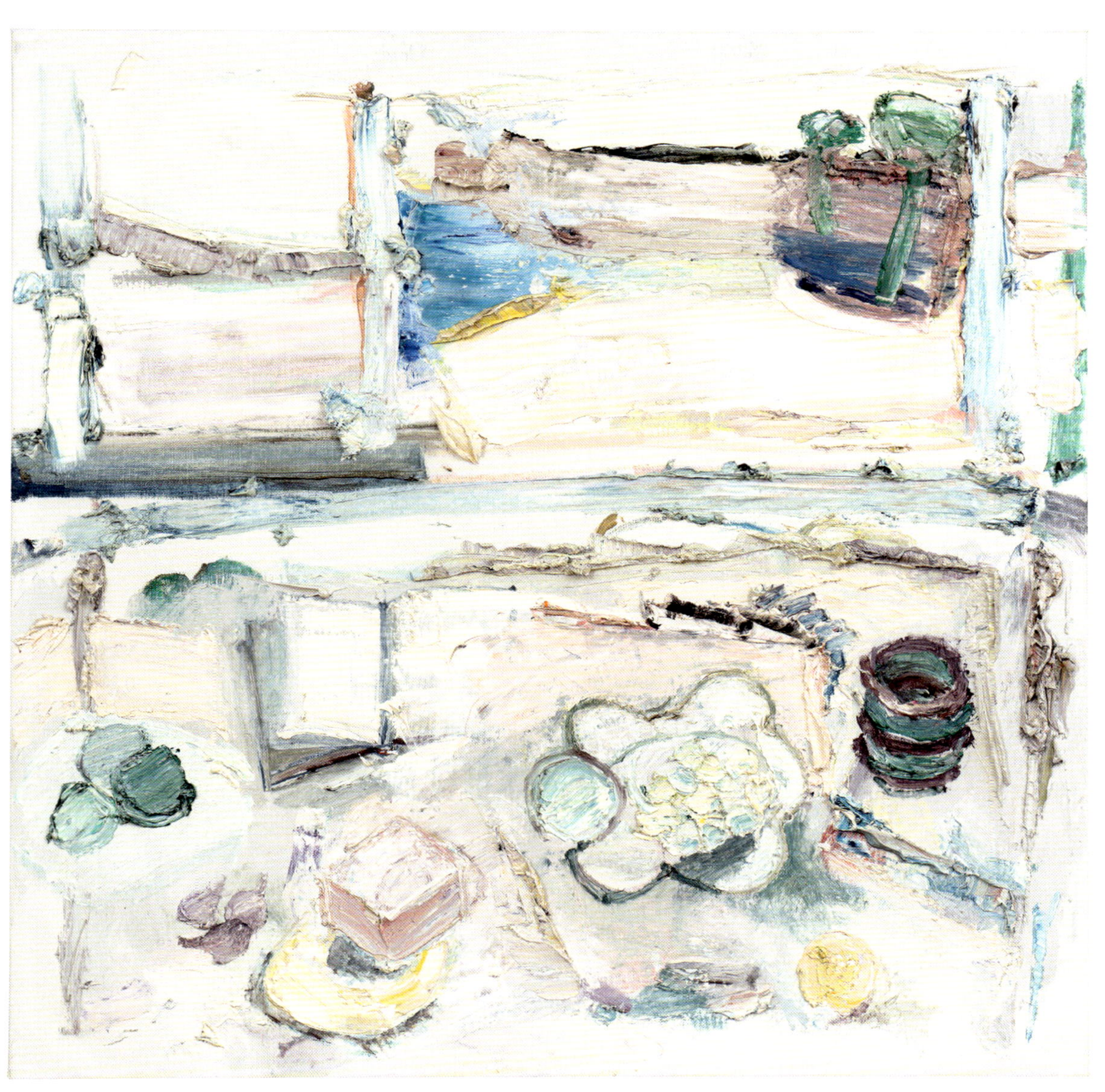

Untitled, 1990, oil on canvas, 52 × 52 inches (132.1 × 132.1 cm)

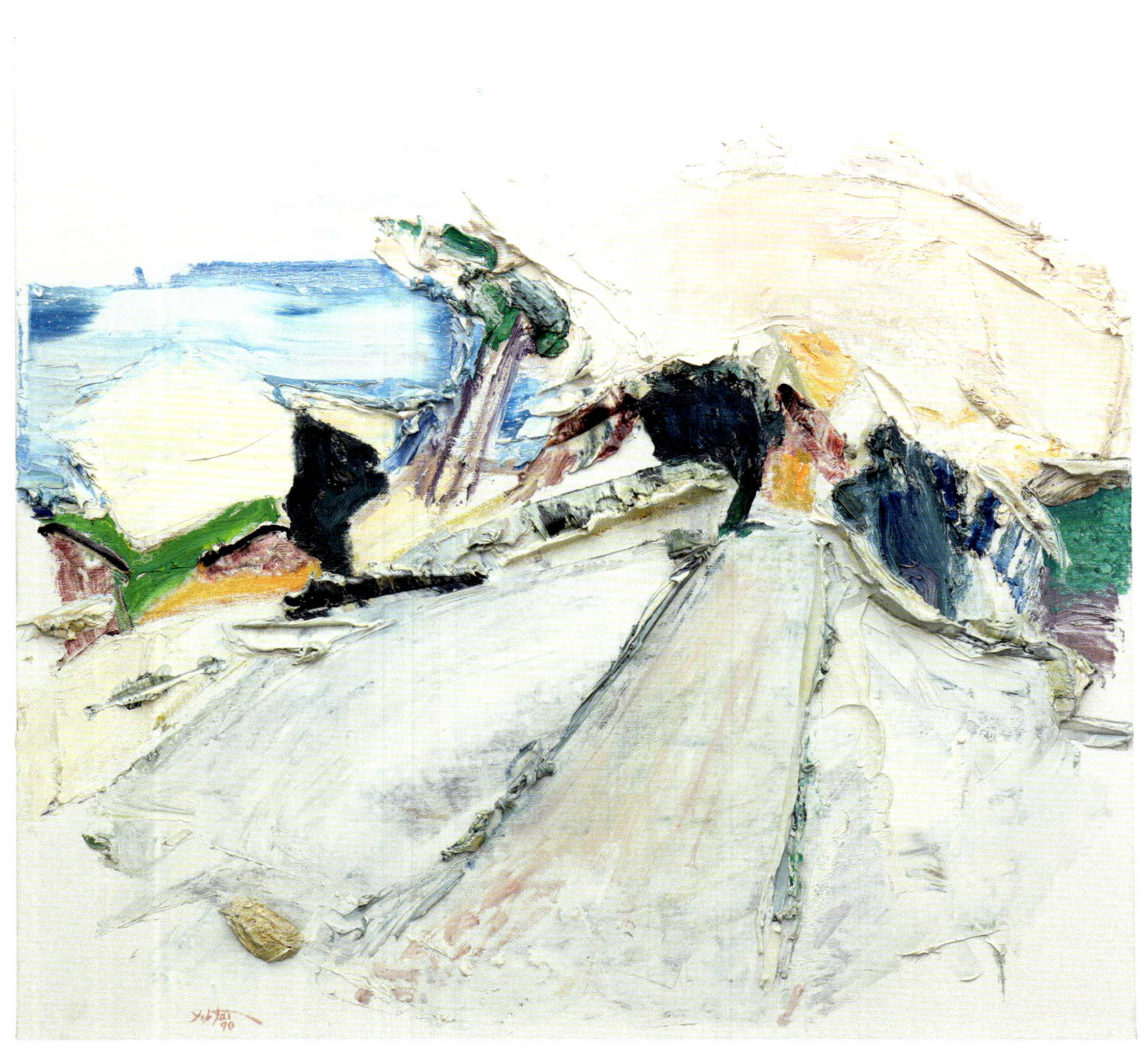

 Untitled, 1990, oil on canvas, 48 × 52 inches (121.9 × 132.1 cm)

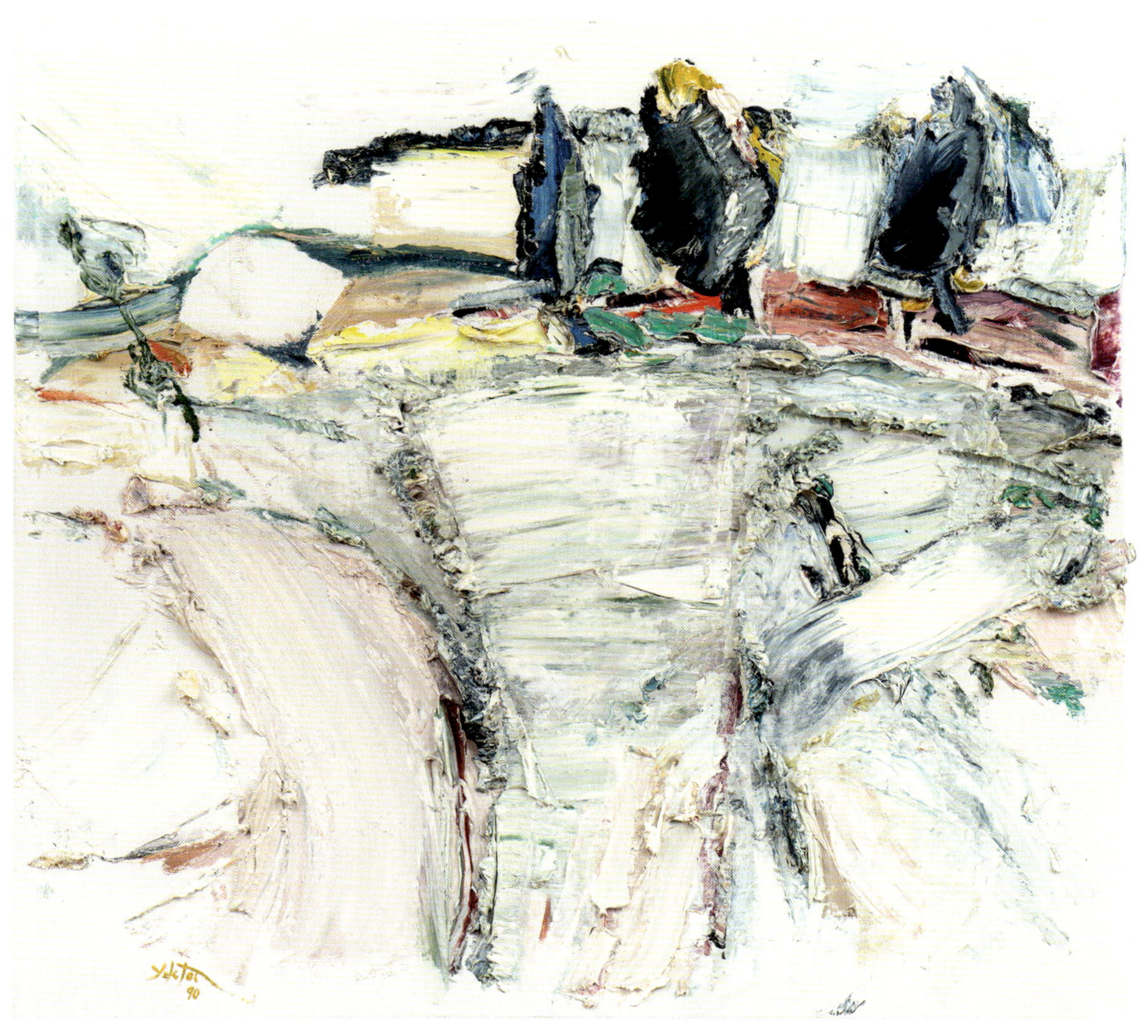

Untitled, 1990, oil on canvas, 48 × 52 inches (121.9 × 132.1 cm)

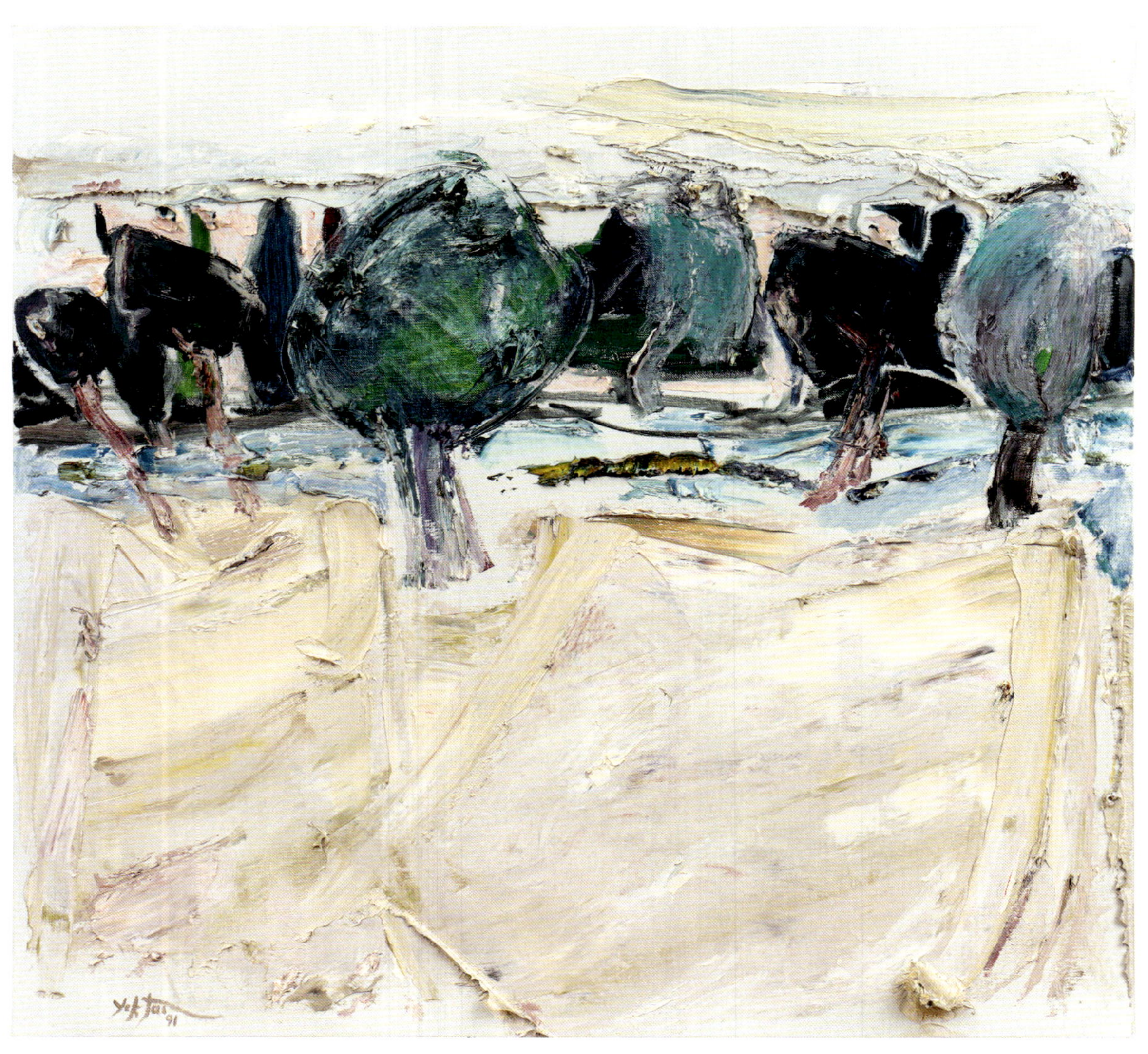

 Untitled, 1991, oil on canvas, 48 × 52 inches (121.9 × 132.1 cm)

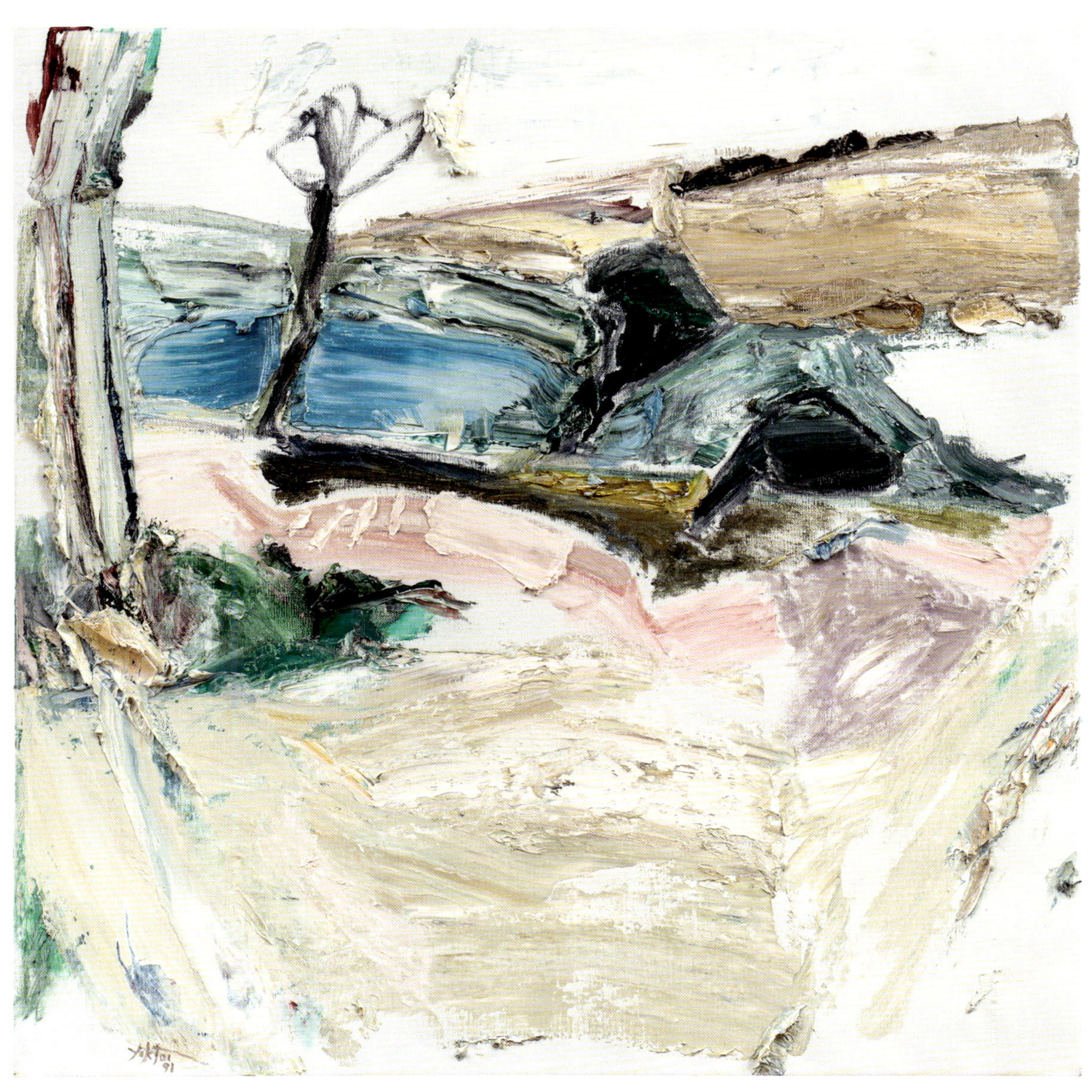

Untitled, 1991, oil on canvas, 52 × 52 inches (132.1 × 132.1 cm)

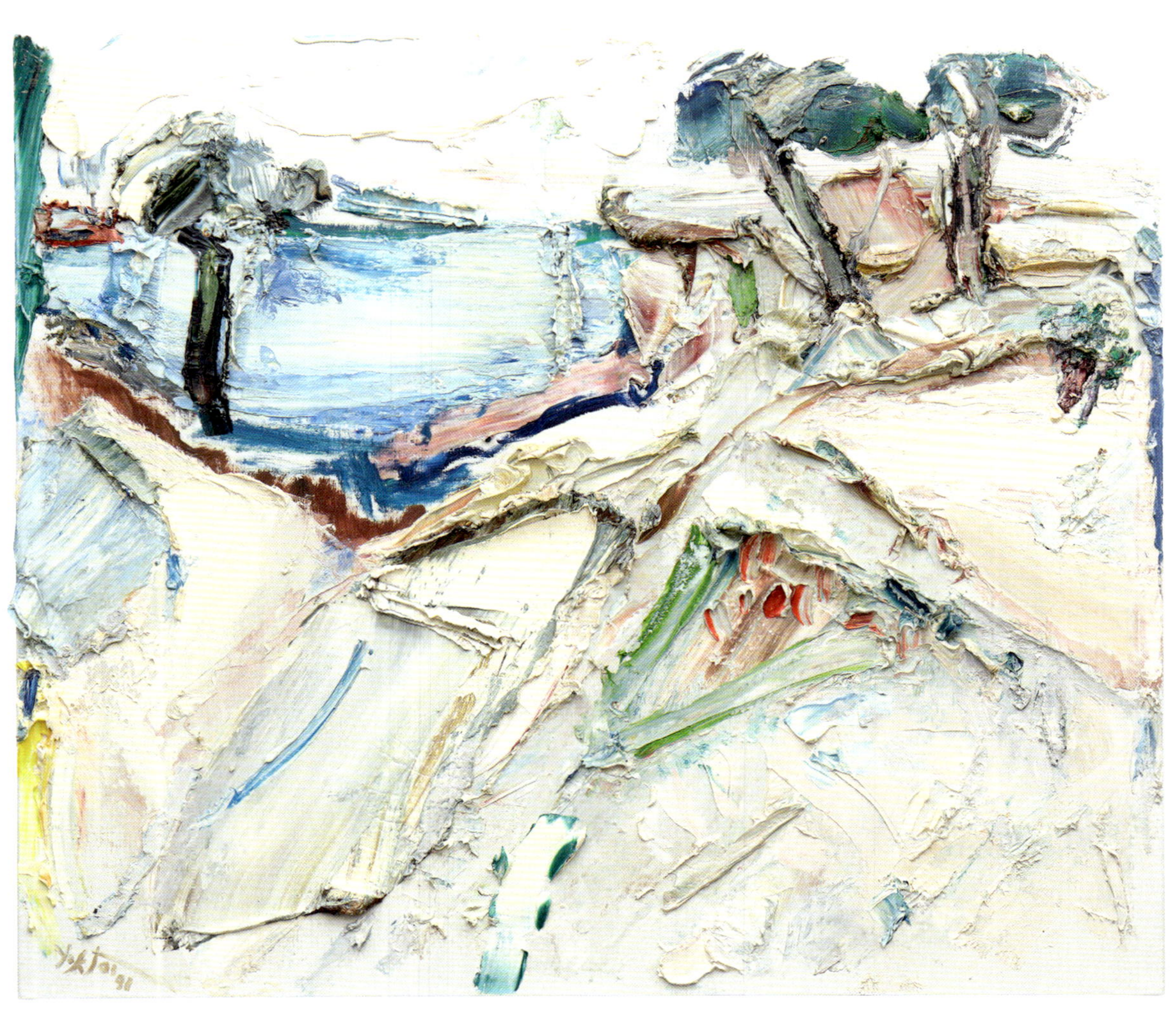

 Untitled, 1991, oil on canvas, 38 × 44 inches (96.5 × 111.8 cm)

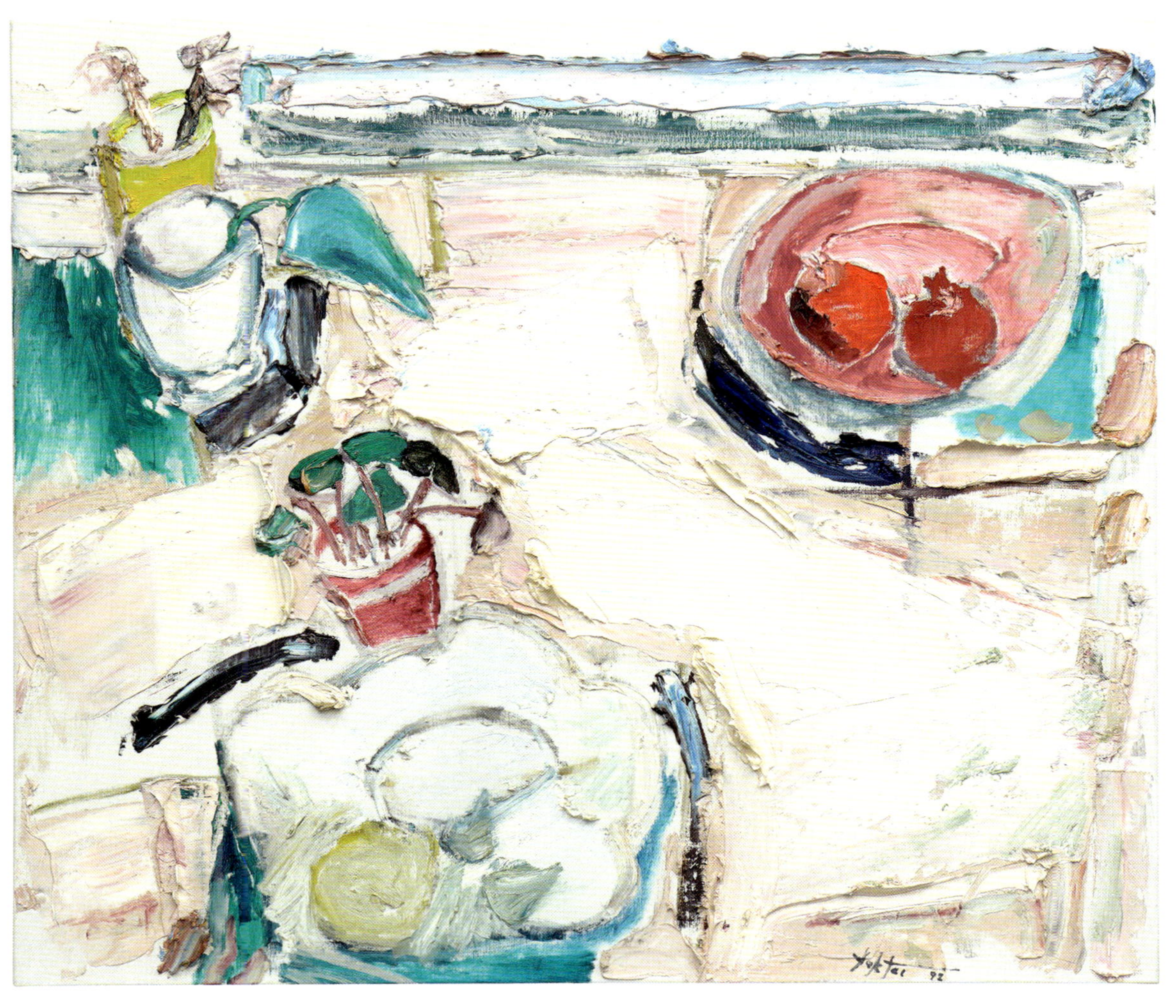

Untitled, 1992, oil on canvas, 38 × 44 inches (96.5 × 111.8 cm)

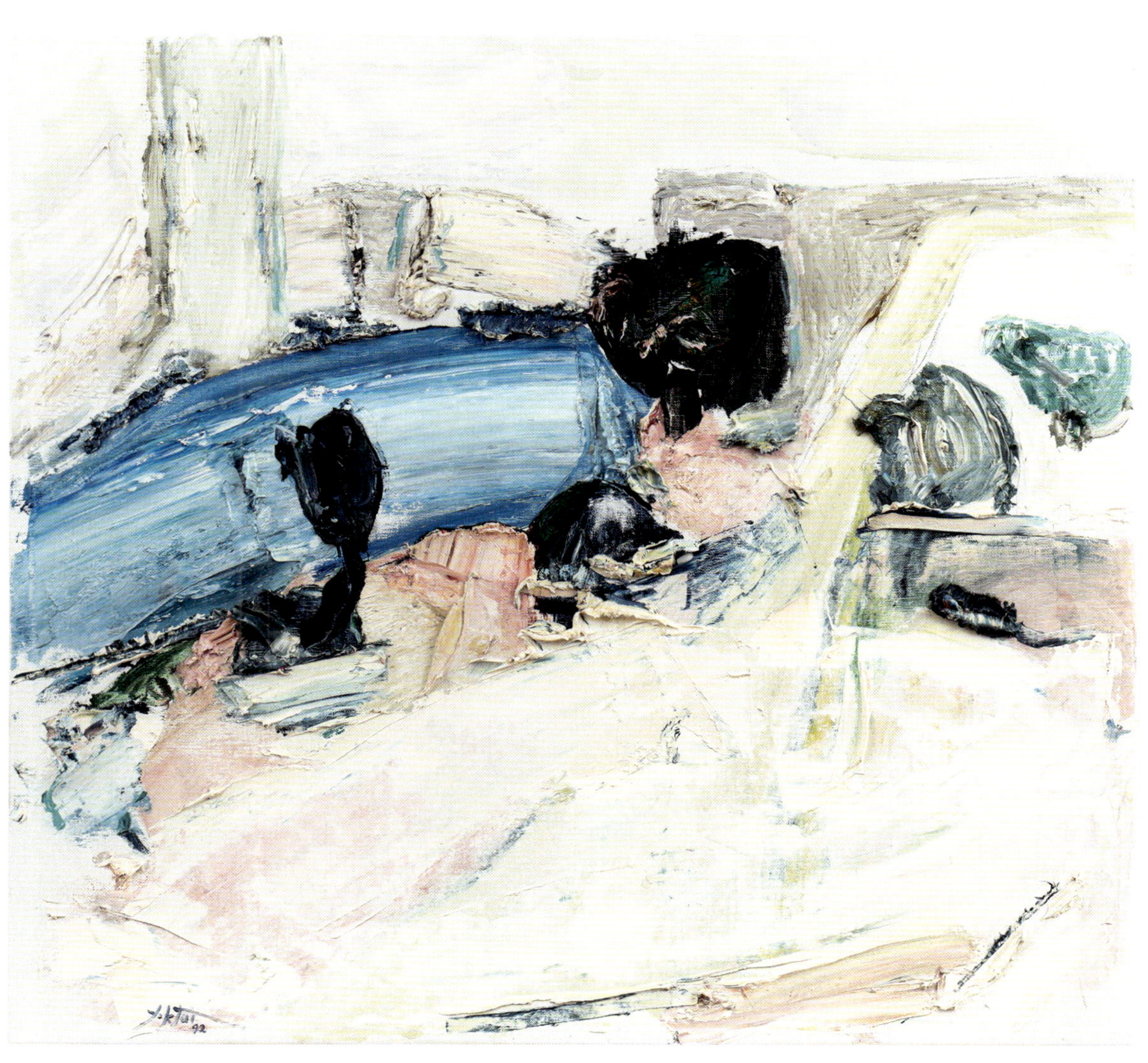

Untitled, 1992, oil on canvas, 48 × 52 inches (121.9 × 132.1 cm)

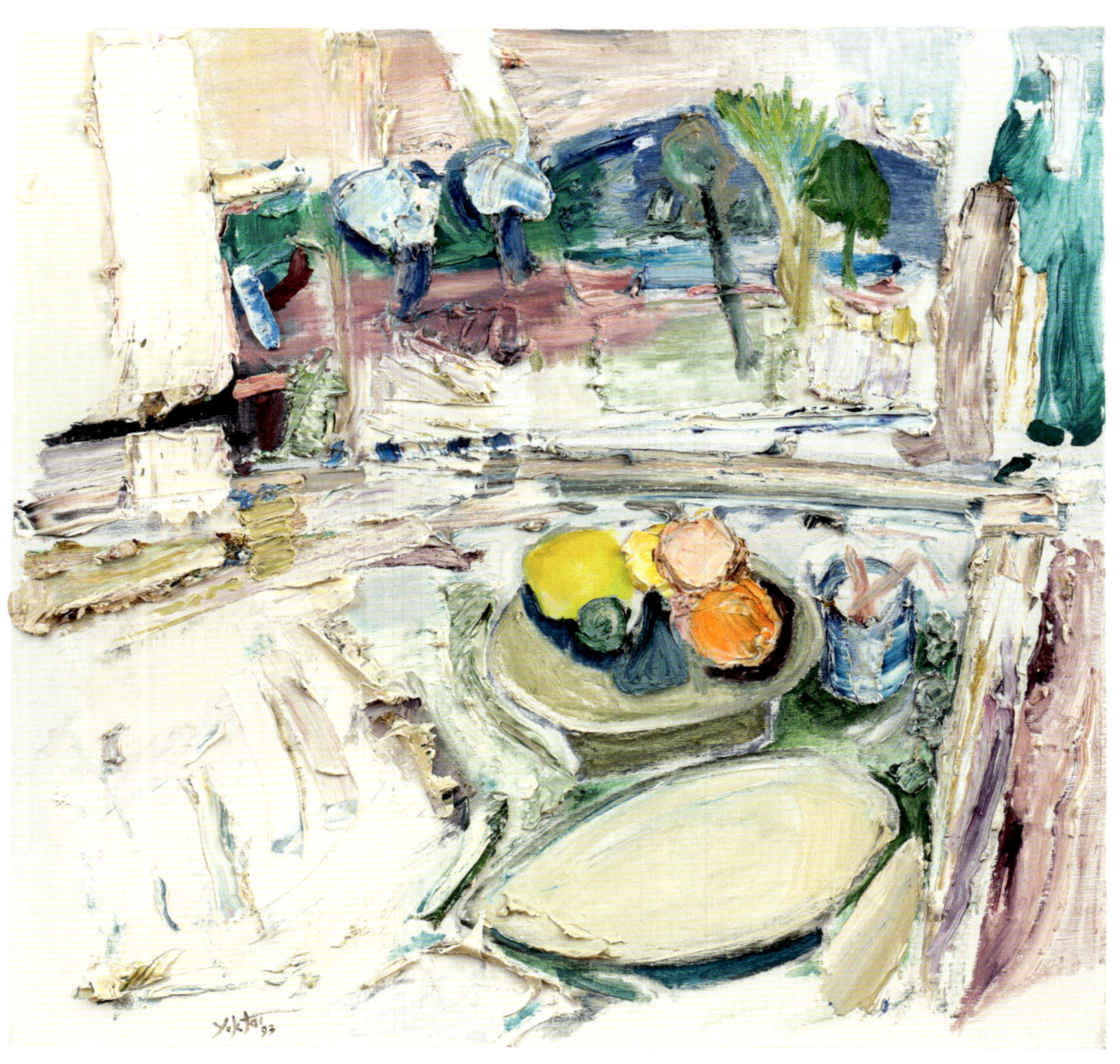

654 *Untitled*, 1993, oil on canvas, 48 × 50 inches (121.9 × 127 cm)

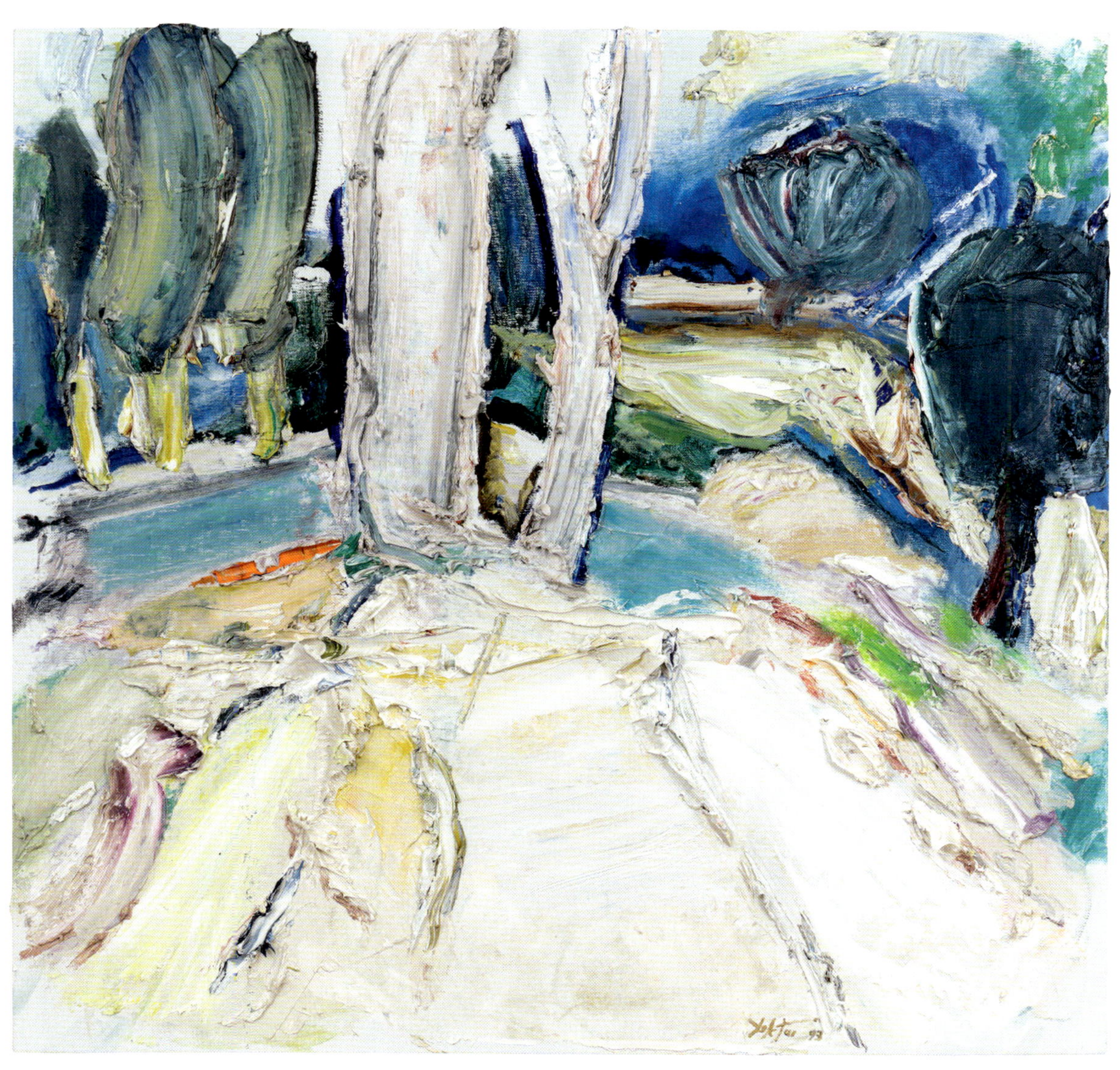

Untitled, 1993, oil on canvas, 48 × 50 inches (121.9 × 127 cm)

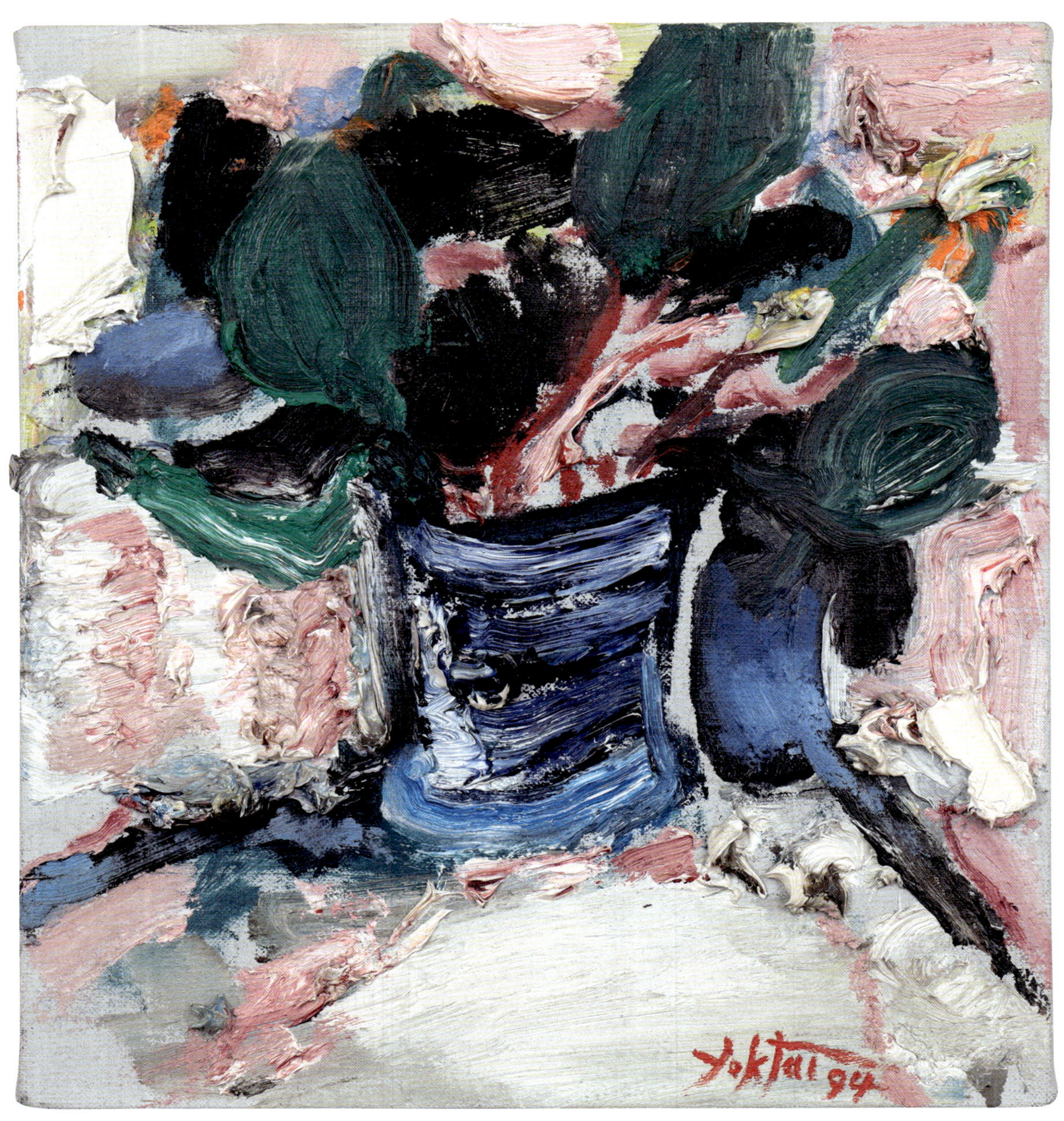

Untitled, 1994, oil on canvas, 15 × 14 inches (38.1 × 35.6 cm)

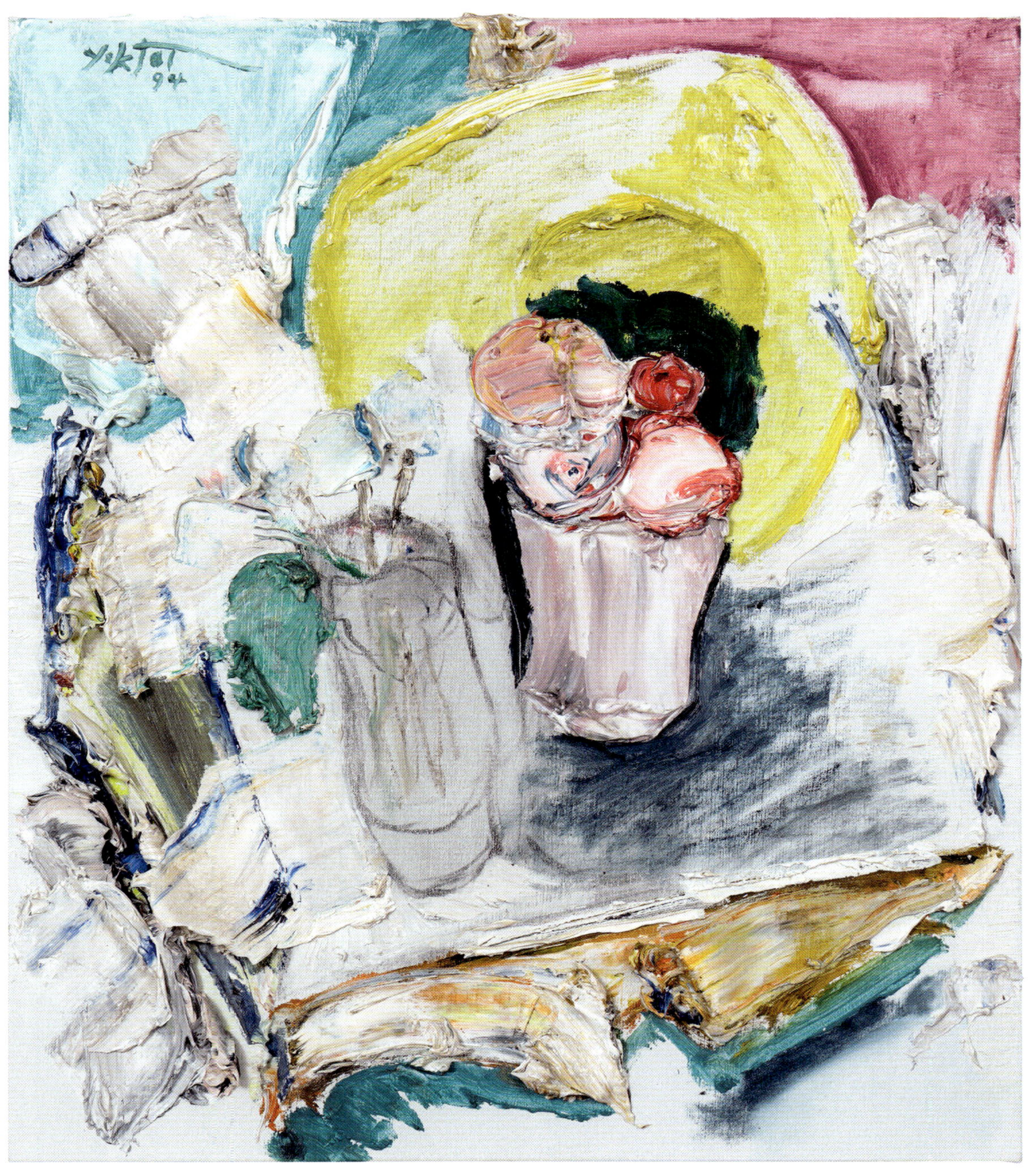

Untitled, 1994, oil on canvas, 28 × 24 inches (71.1 × 61 cm)

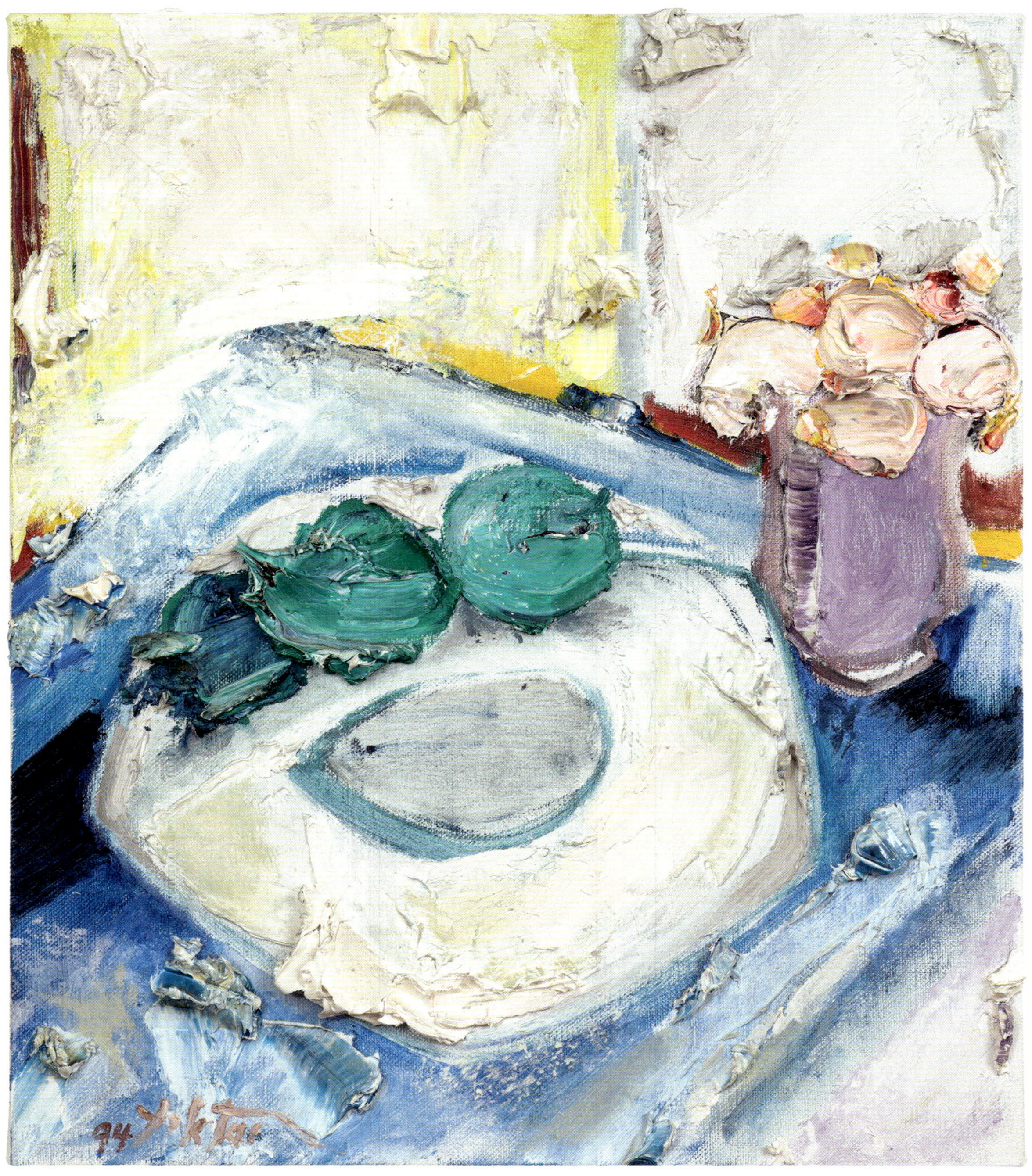

Untitled, 1994, oil on canvas, 28 × 24 inches (71.1 × 61 cm)

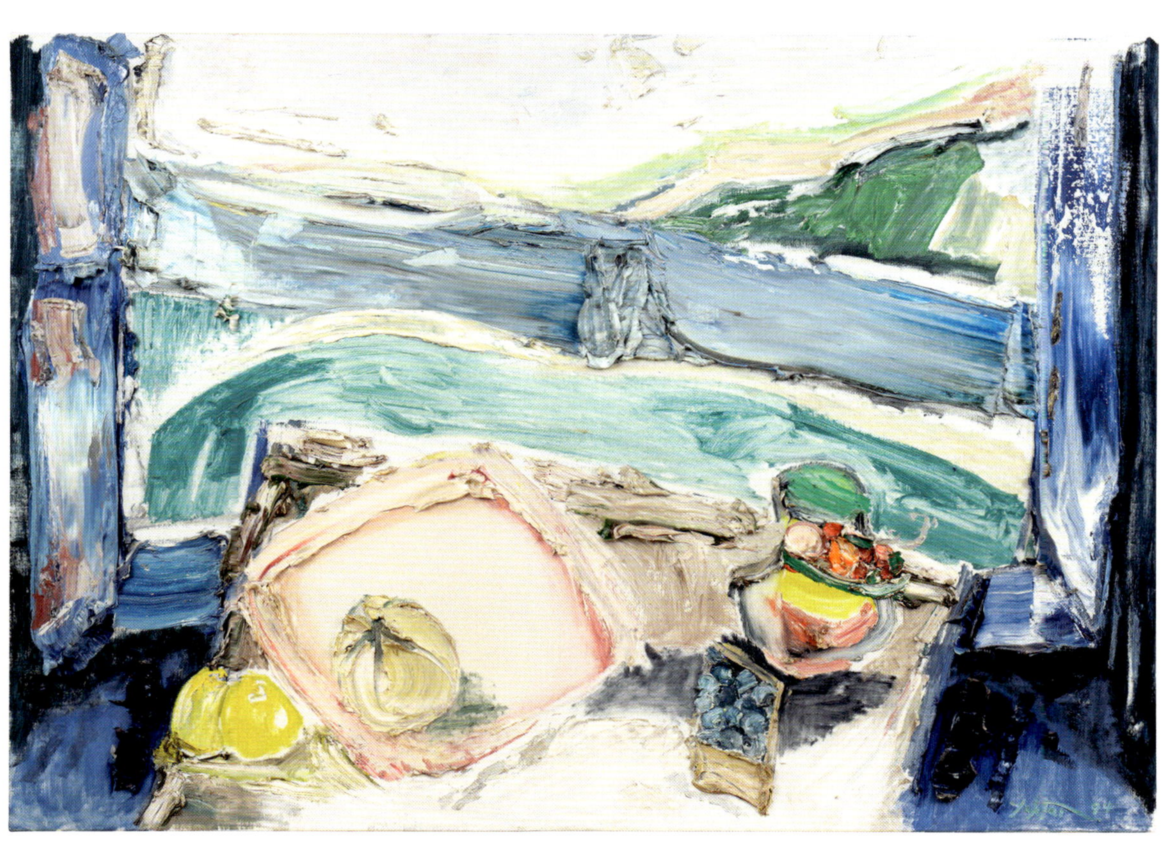

Untitled, 1994, oil on canvas, 46 × 64 inches (116.8 × 162.6 cm)

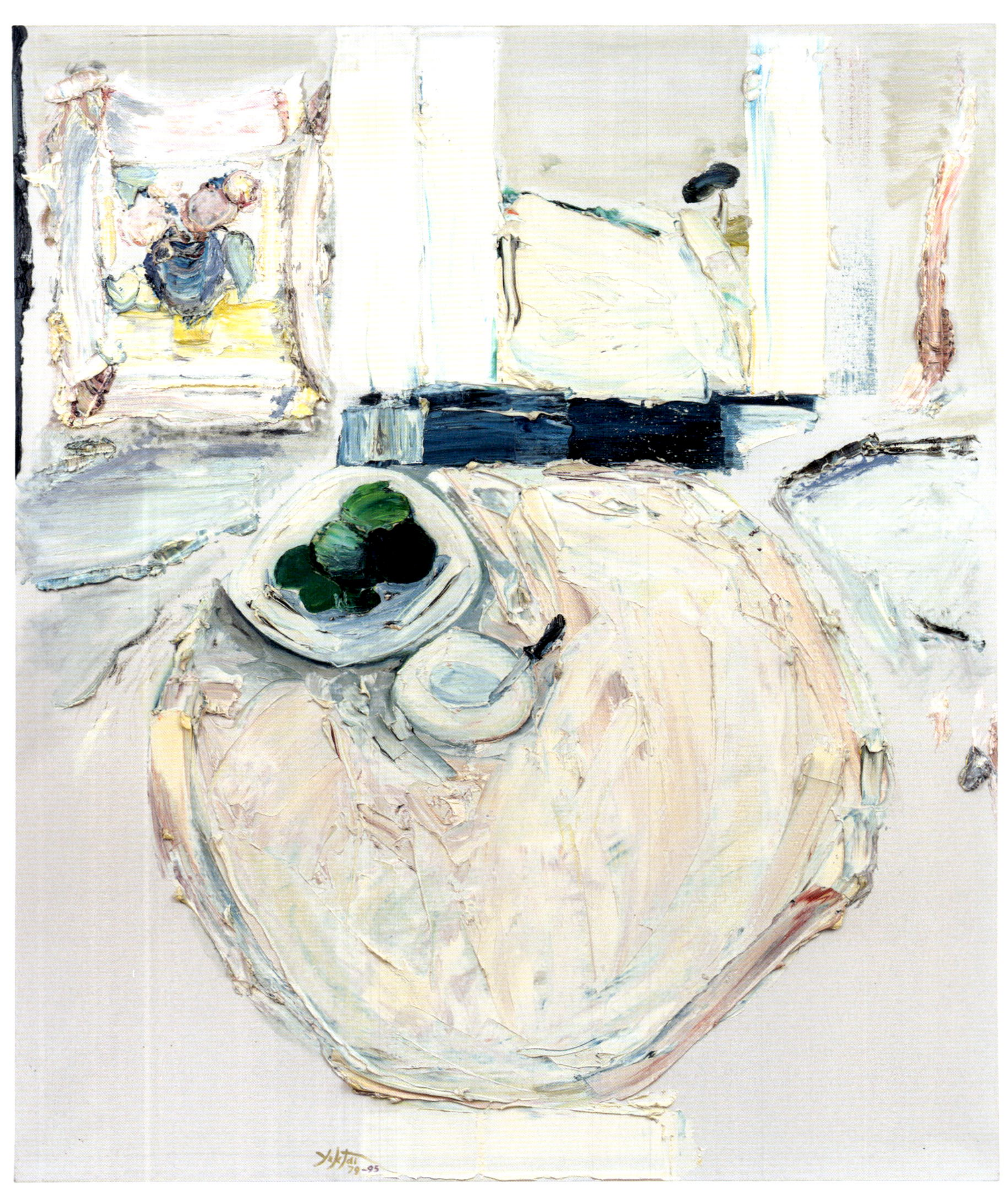

Two Paintings and Two Plates, 1979–95,
oil on canvas, 72 × 60 inches (182.9 × 152.4 cm)

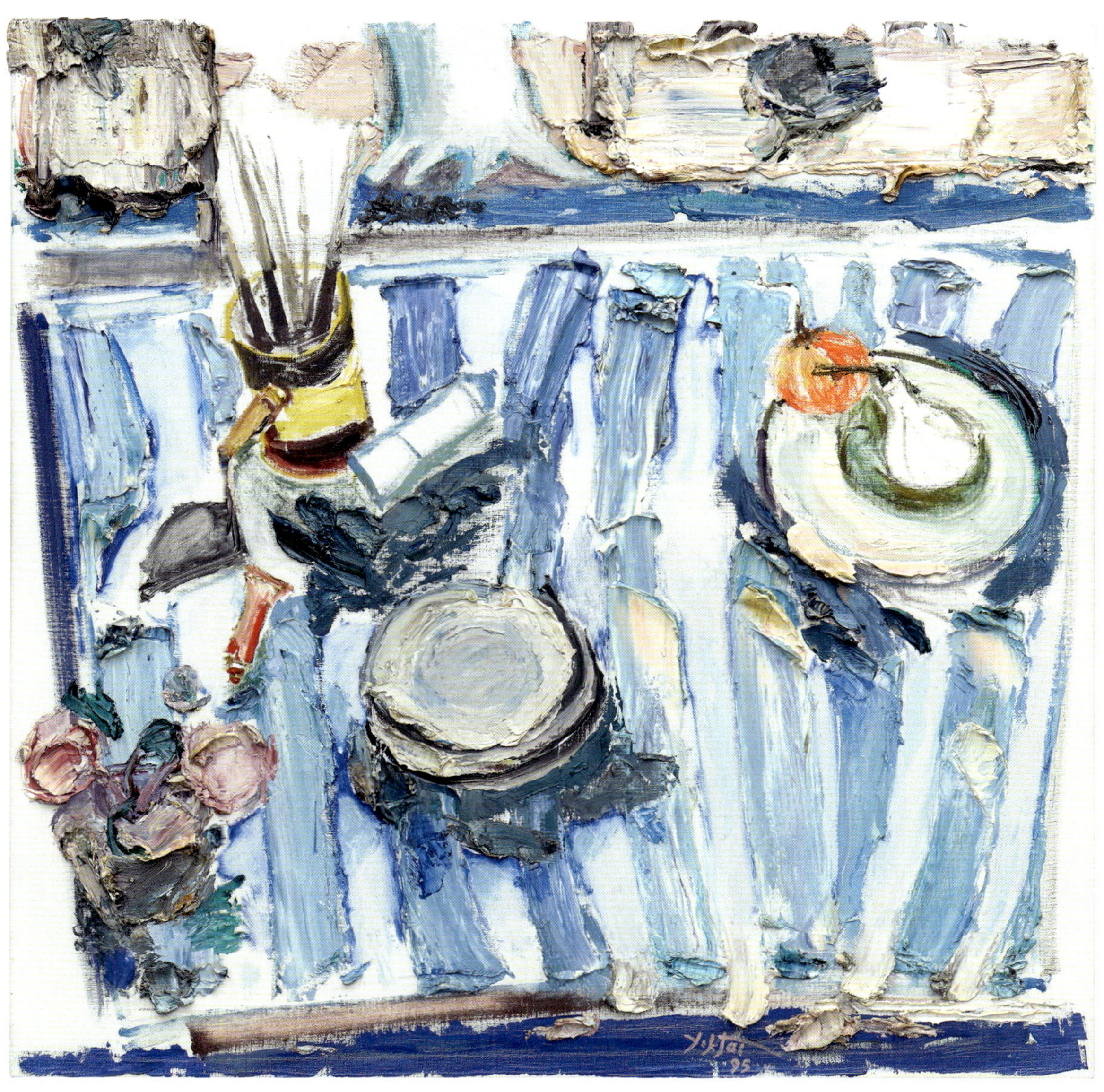

Striped Table, 1995, oil on canvas, 48 × 48 inches (121.9 × 121.9 cm)

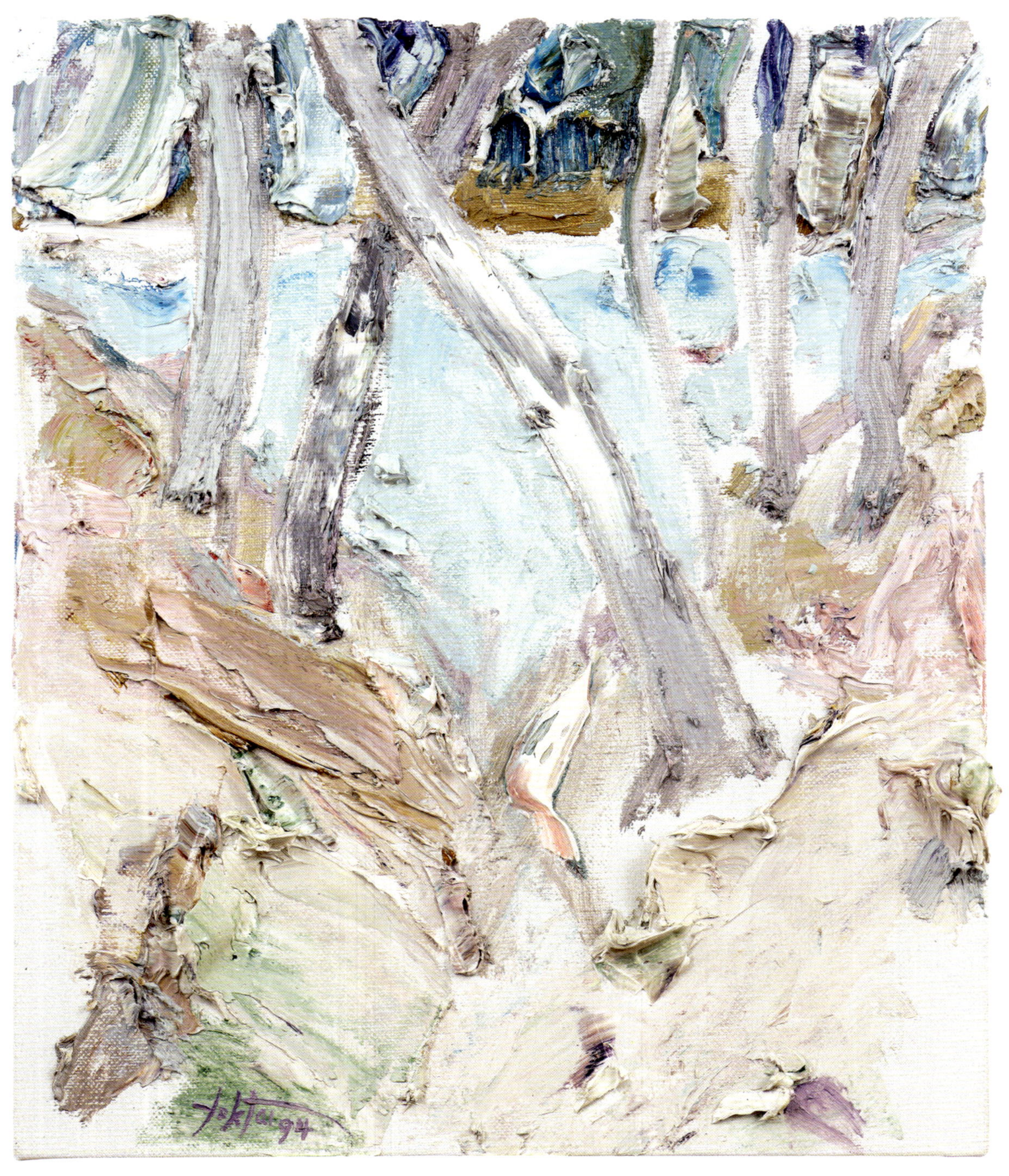

 Untitled, 1994, oil on canvas, 24 × 20 inches (61 × 50.8 cm)

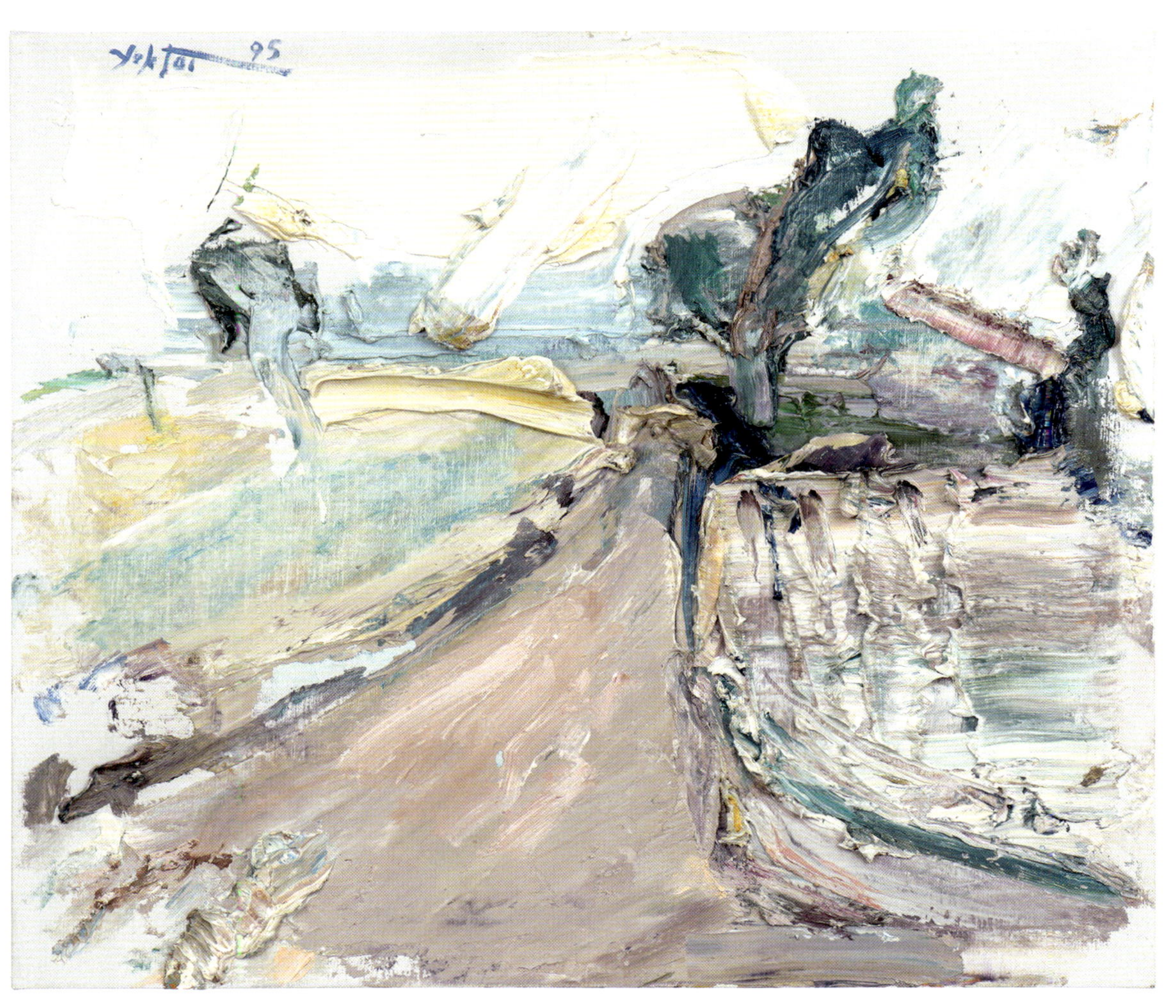

Untitled, 1995, oil on canvas, 24 × 28 inches (61 × 71.1 cm)

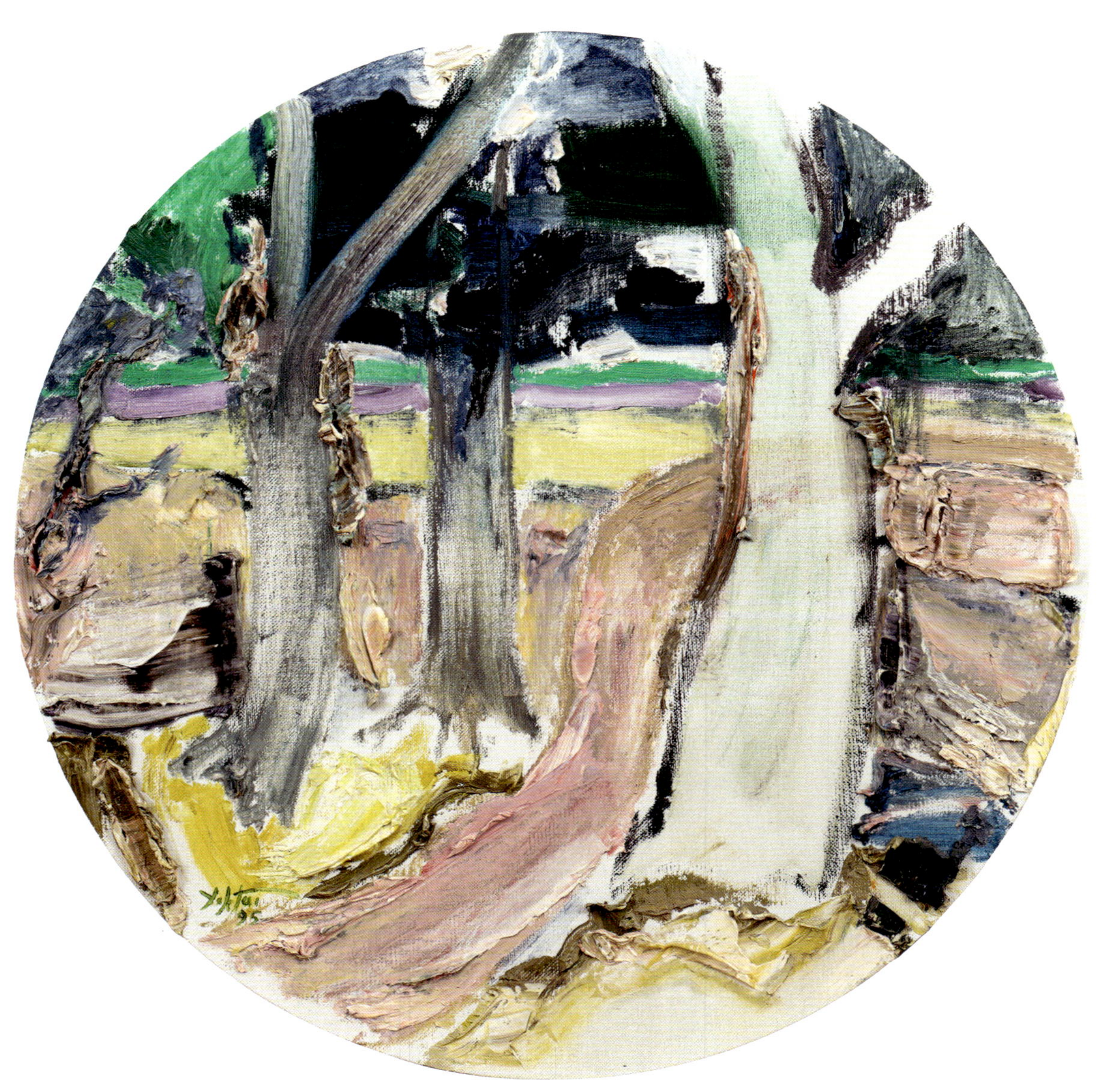

 Untitled, 1995, oil on canvas, 24 × 20 inches (61 × 50.8 cm)

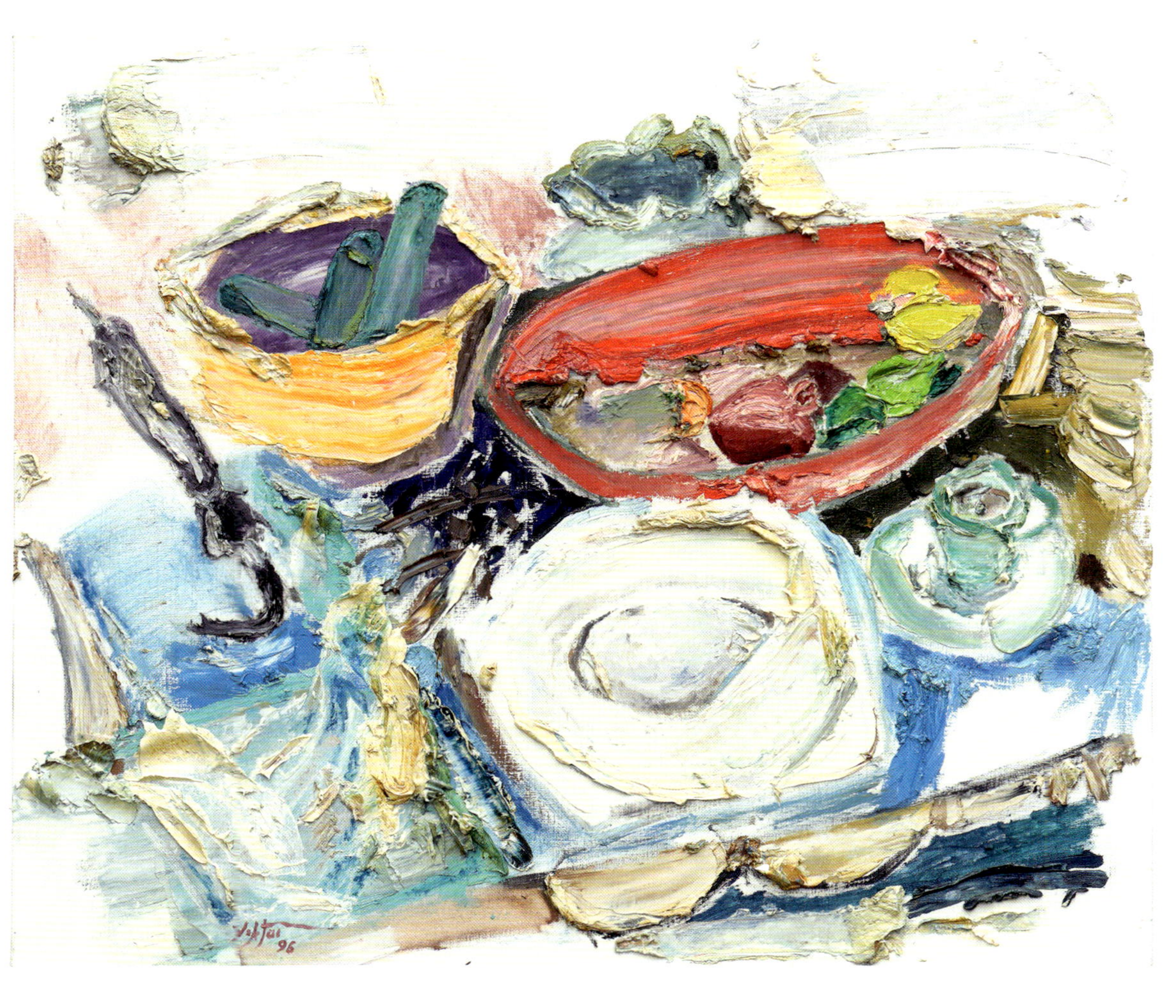

Untitled, 1996, oil on canvas, 42 × 50 inches (106.7 × 127 cm)

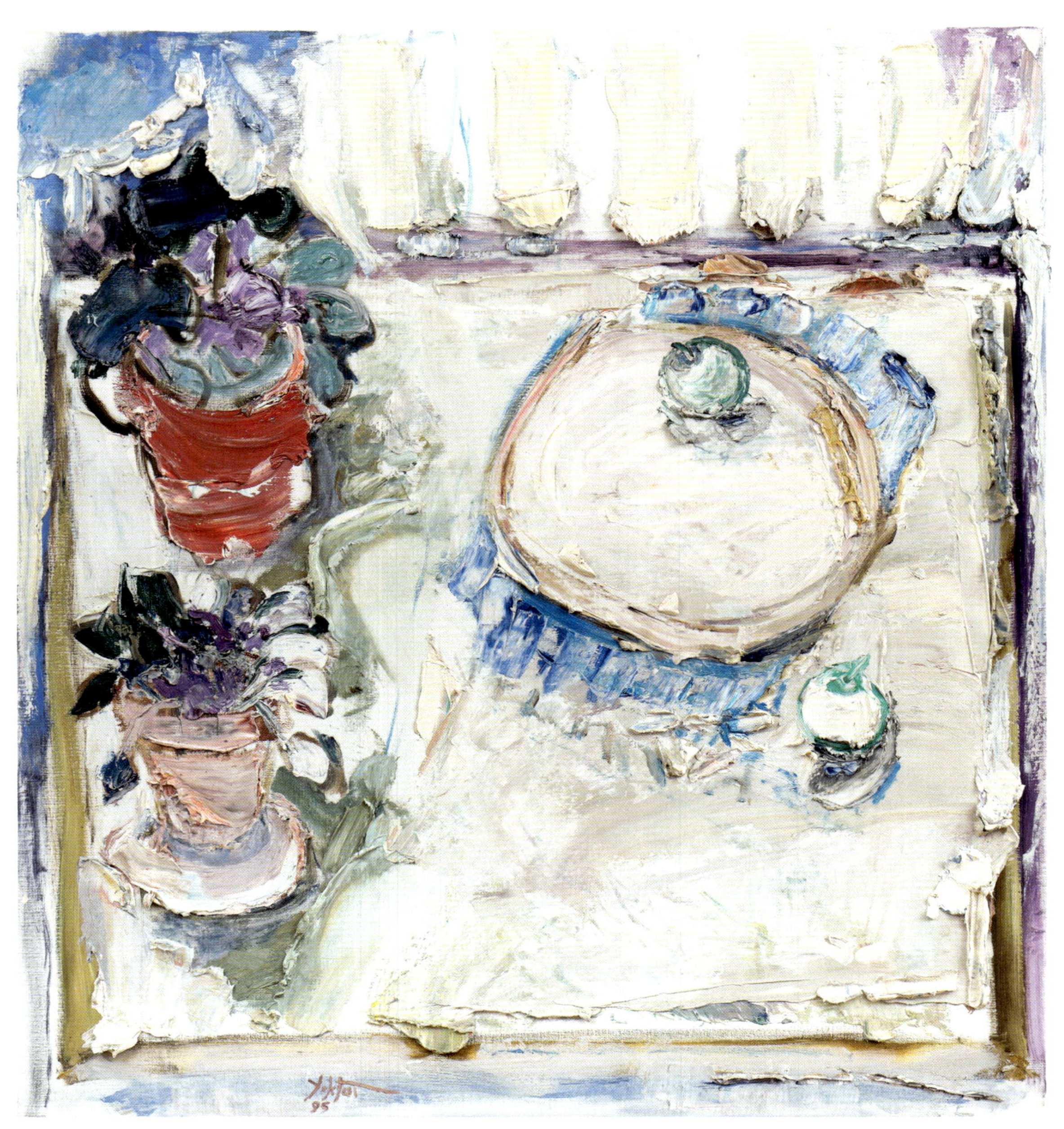

666 *Untitled*, 1995, oil on canvas, 52 × 48 inches (132.1 × 121.9 cm)

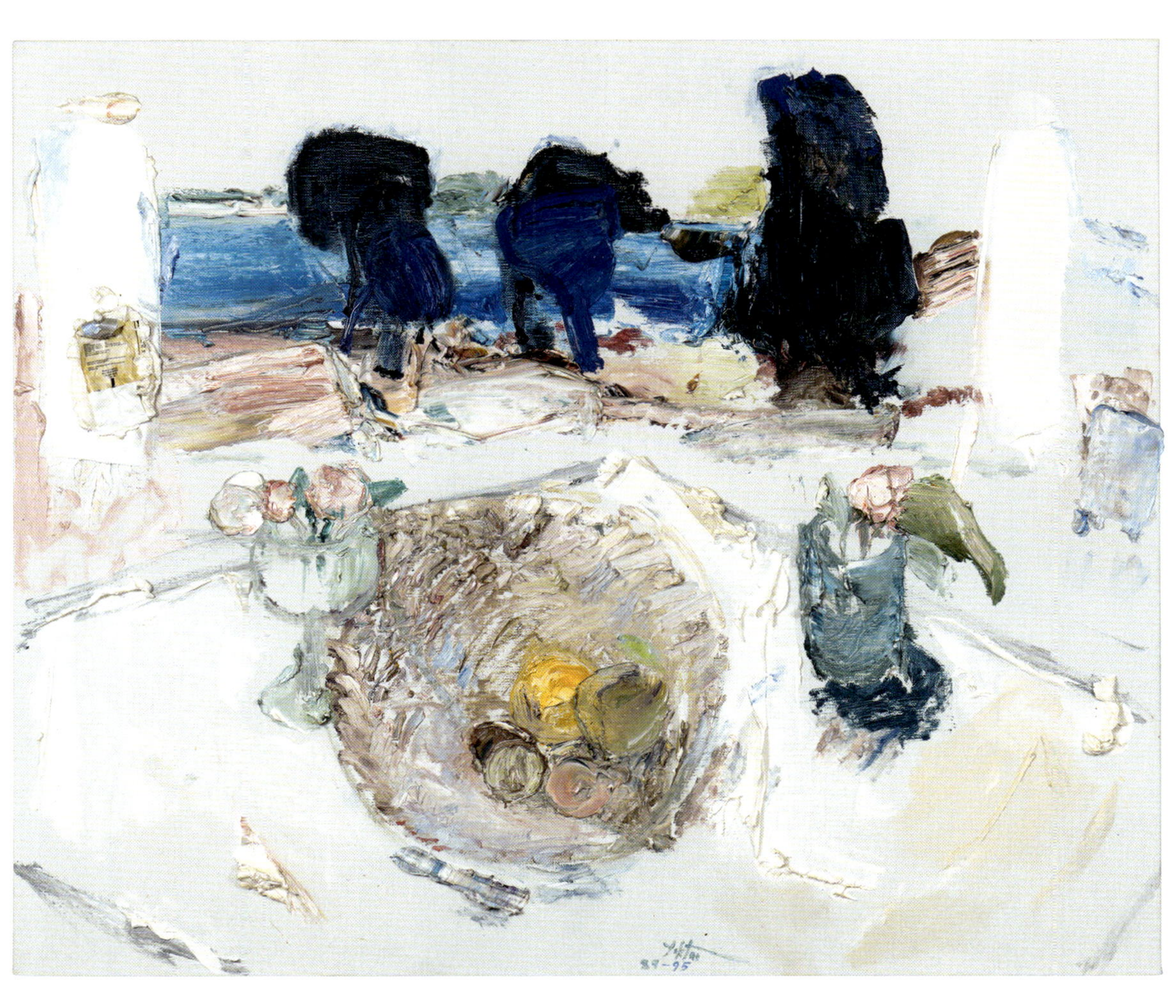

Untitled, 1989–95, oil on canvas, 42 × 50 inches (106.7 × 127 cm)

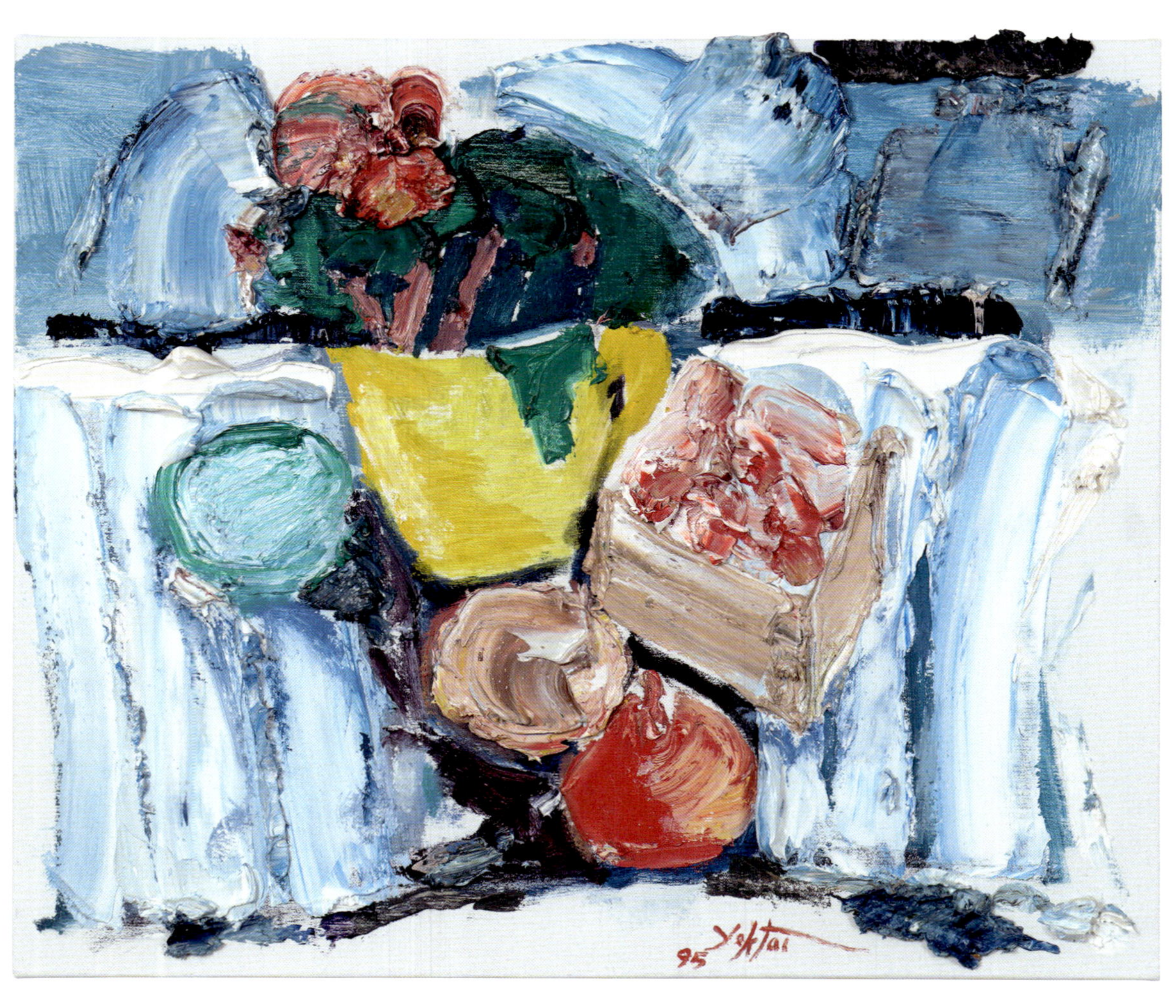

 Untitled, 1995, oil on canvas, 20 × 24 inches (50.8 × 61 cm)

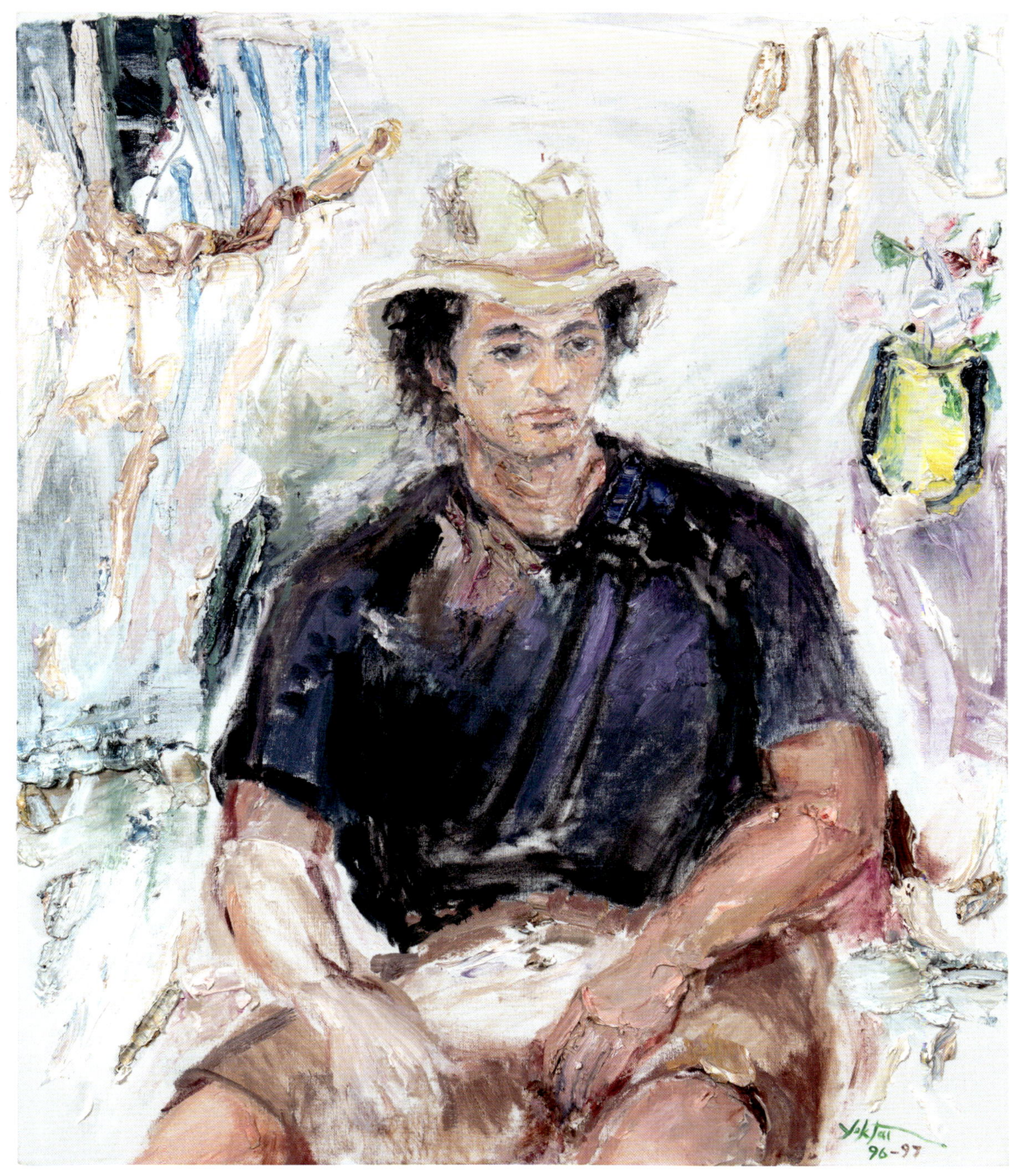

Nico, 1996–97, oil on canvas, 50 × 42 inches (127 × 106.7 cm)

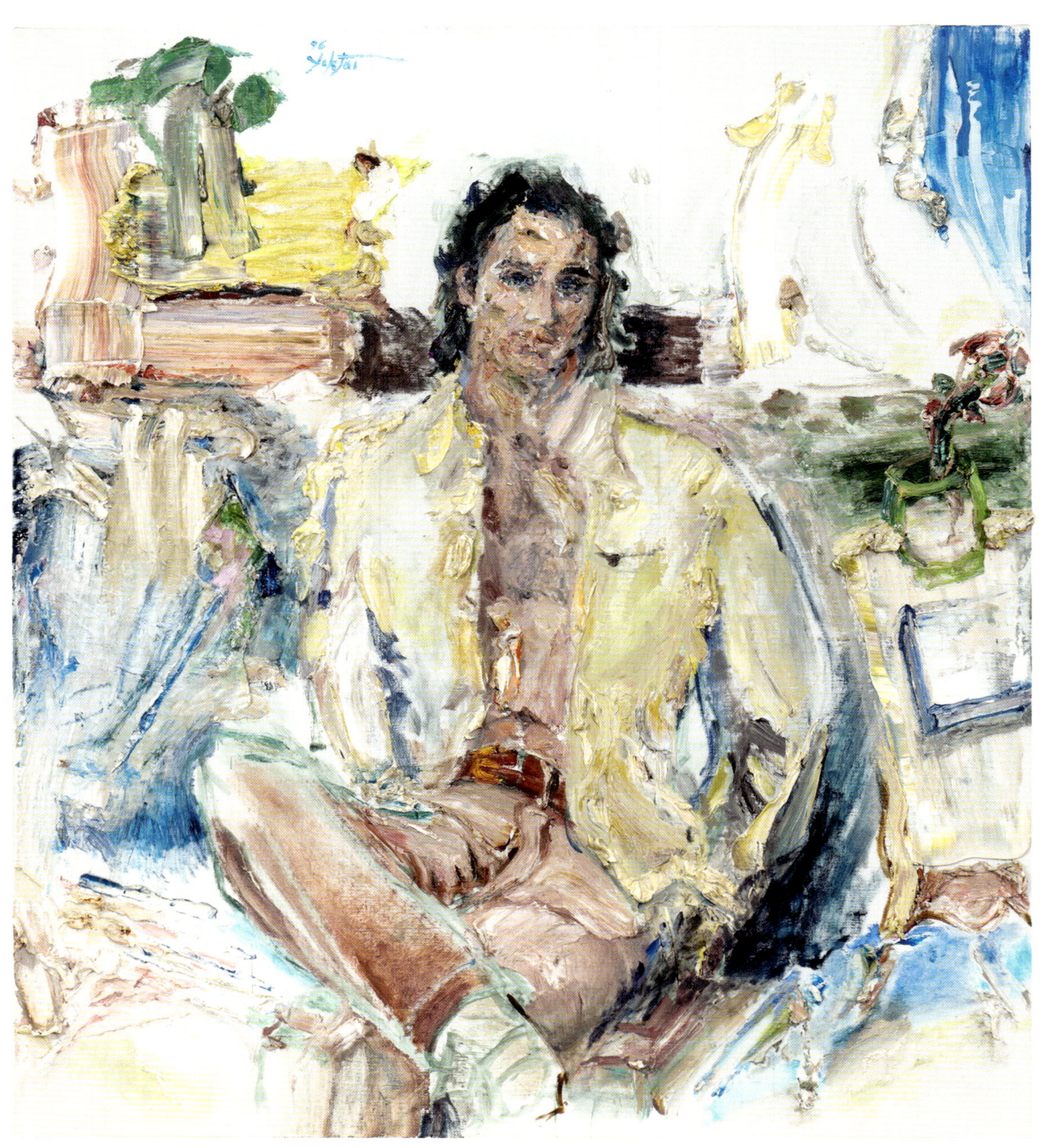

670 *Portrait of Darius Yektai*, 1996, oil on canvas, 54 × 48 inches (137.2 × 121.9 cm)

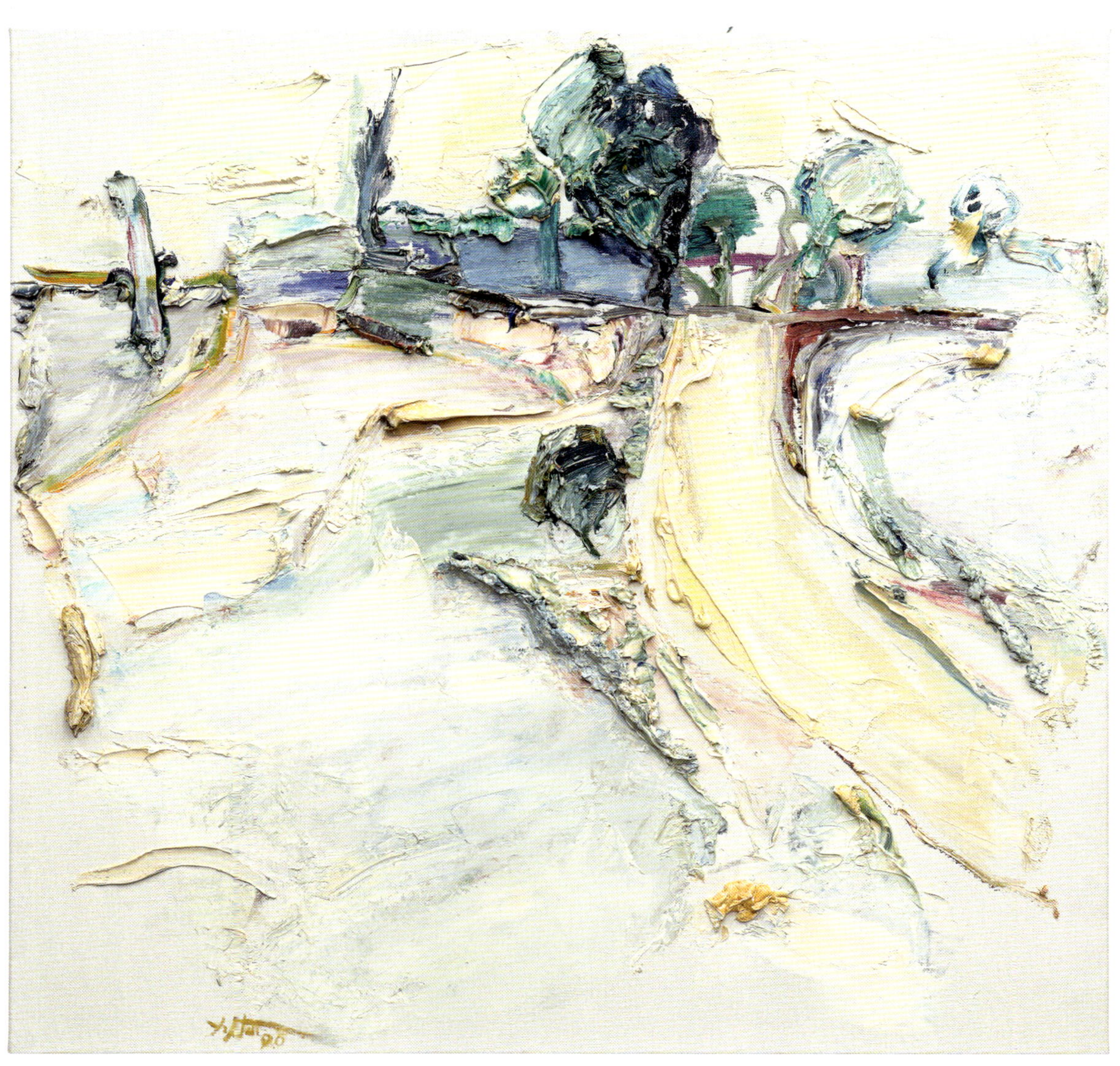

Untitled, 1996, oil on canvas, 48 × 50 inches (121.9 × 127 cm)

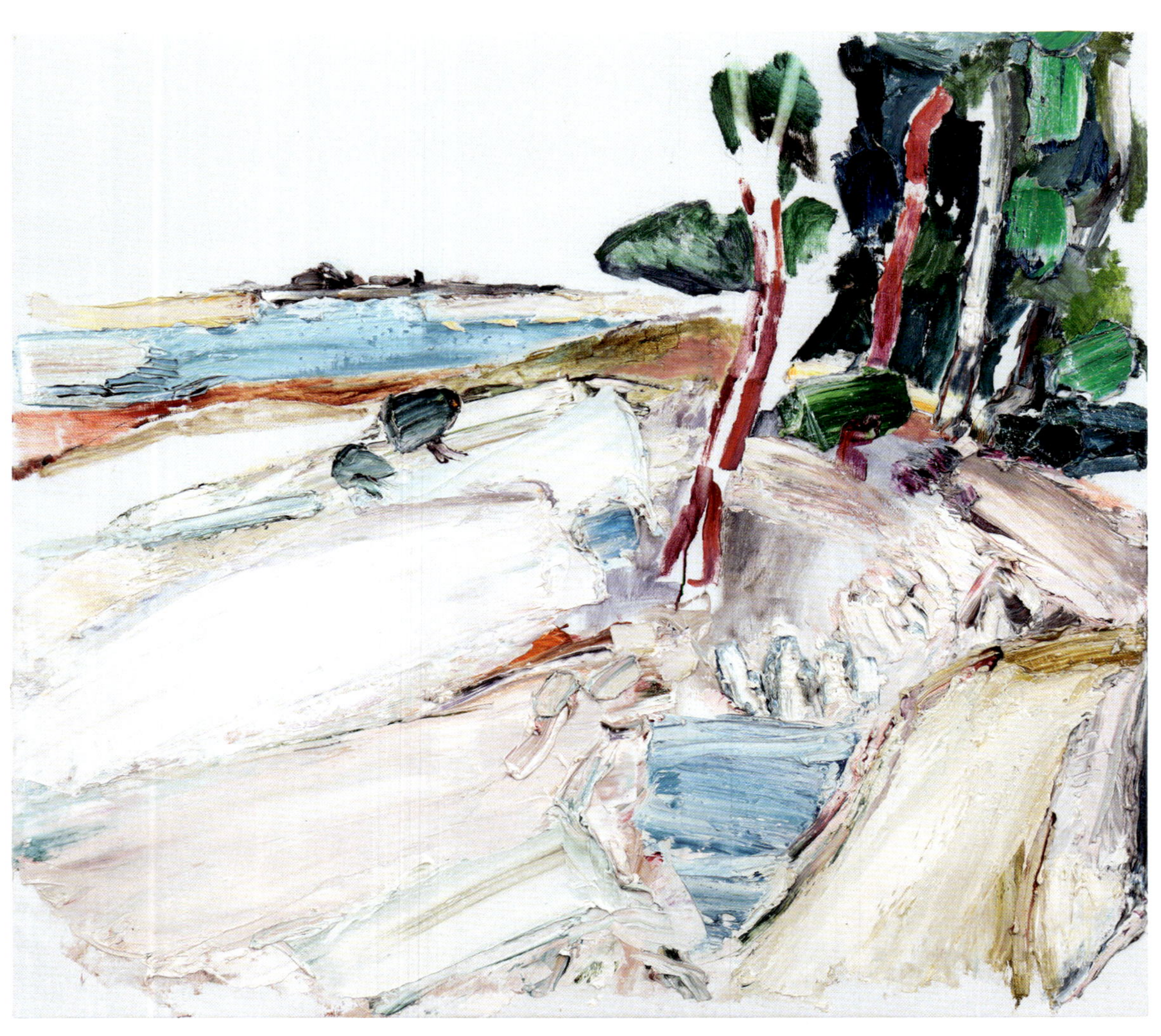

 Untitled, 1997, oil on canvas, 48 × 54 inches (121.9 × 137.2 cm)

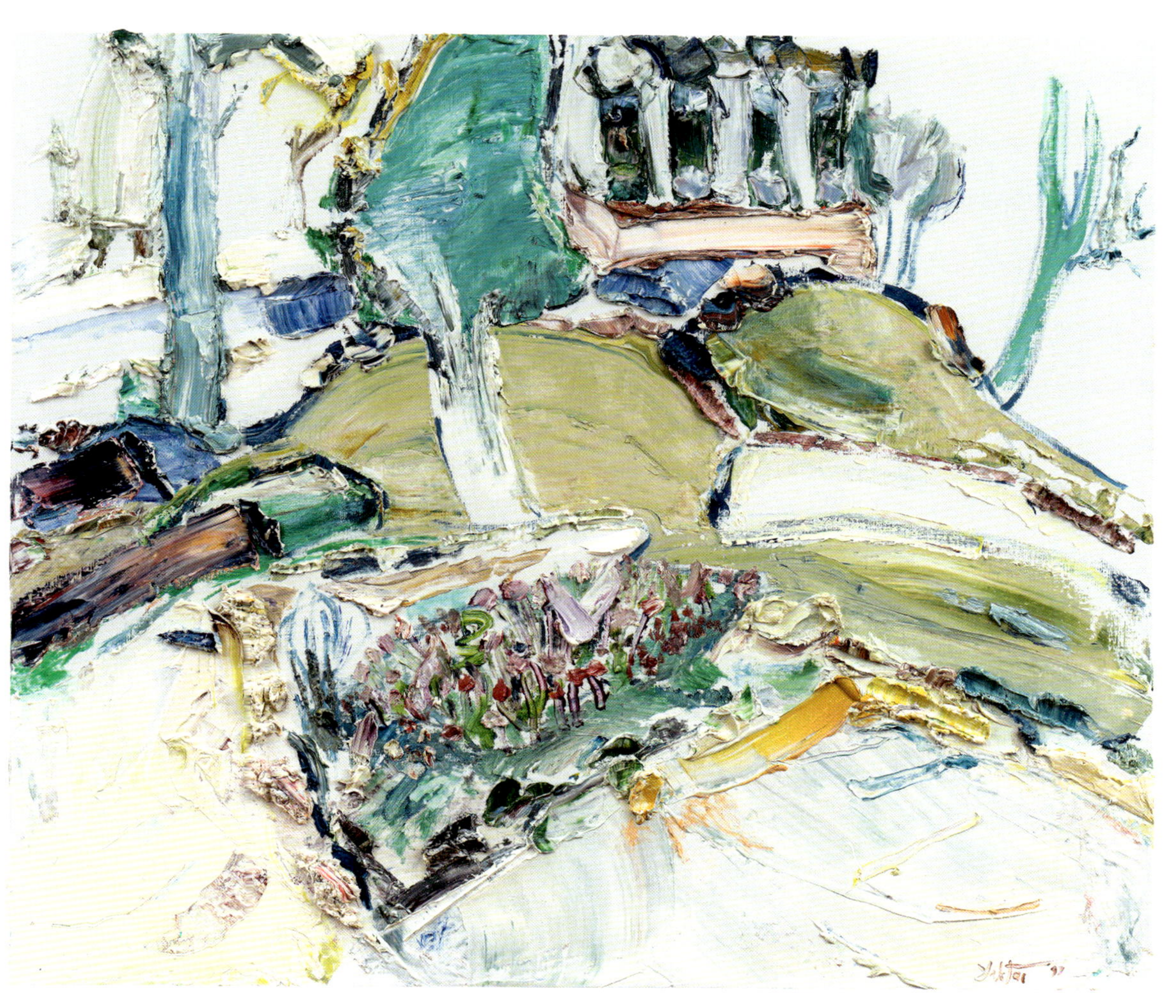

Flower Garden, 1997, oil on canvas, 48 × 56 inches (121.9 × 142.2 cm)

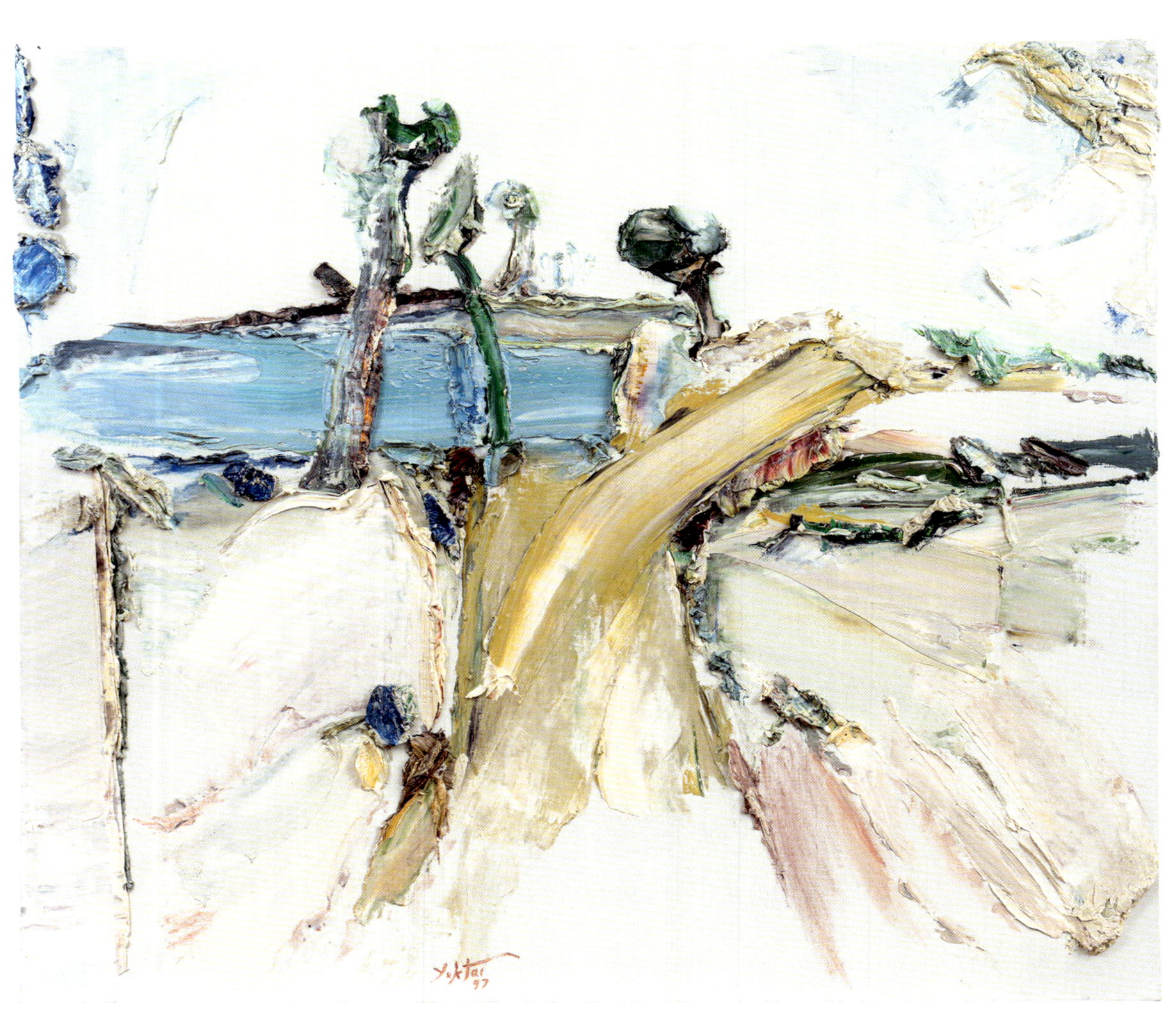

 Untitled, 1997, oil on canvas, 48 × 56 inches (121.9 × 142.2 cm)

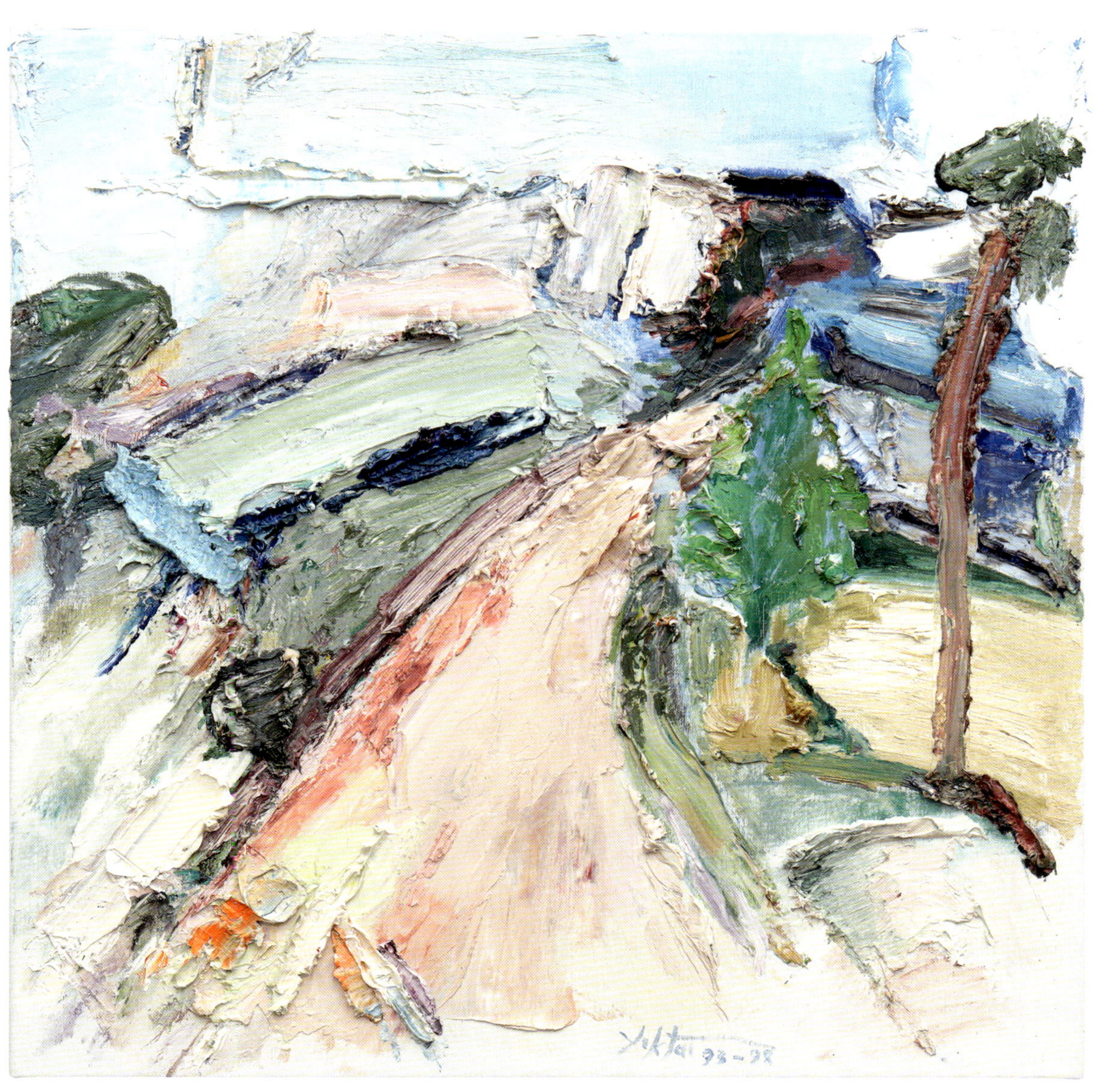

Untitled, 1993–98, oil on canvas, 30 × 30 inches (76.2 × 76.2 cm)

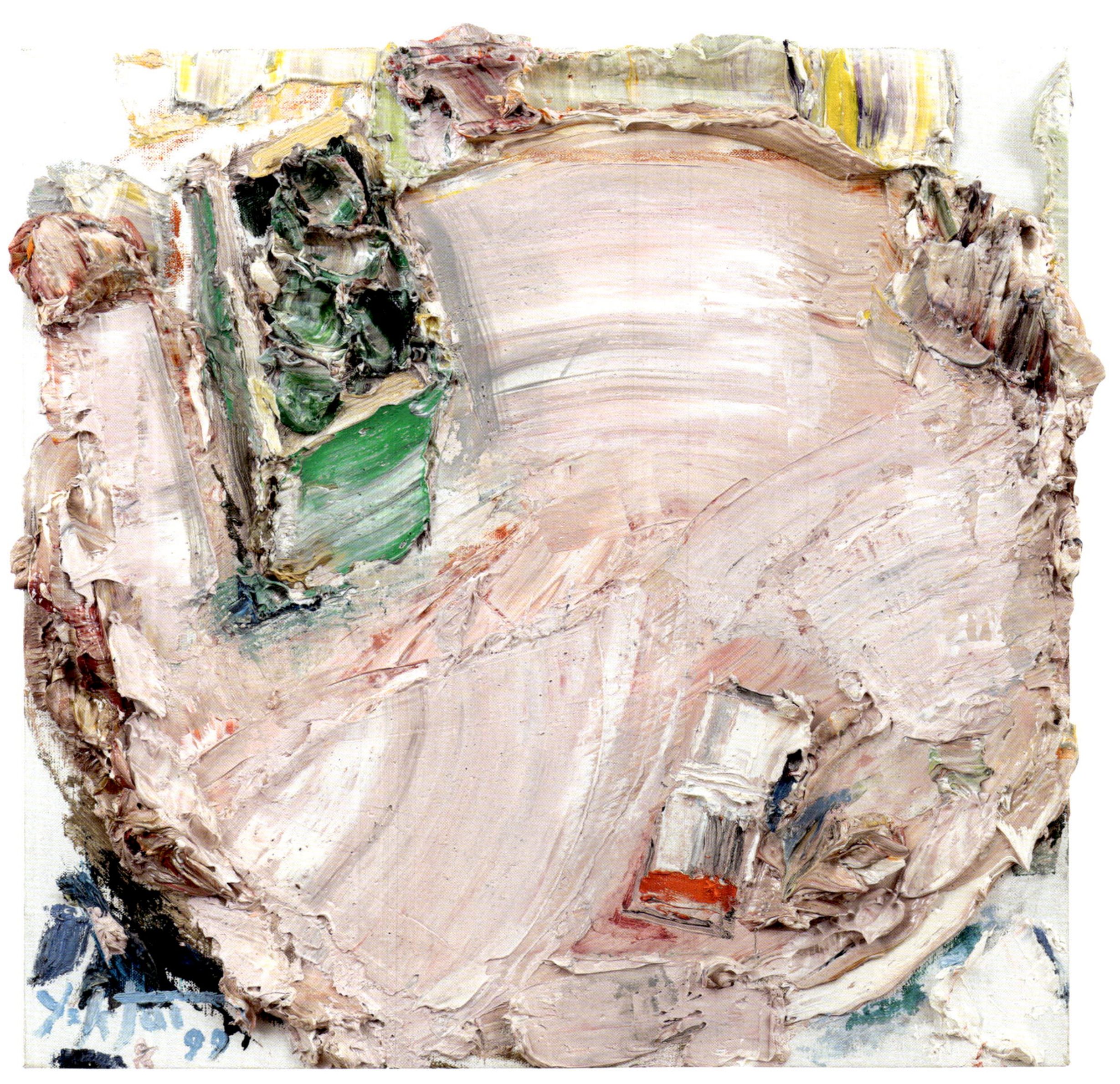

Untitled, 1999, oil on canvas, 18 × 18 inches (45.7 × 45.7 cm)

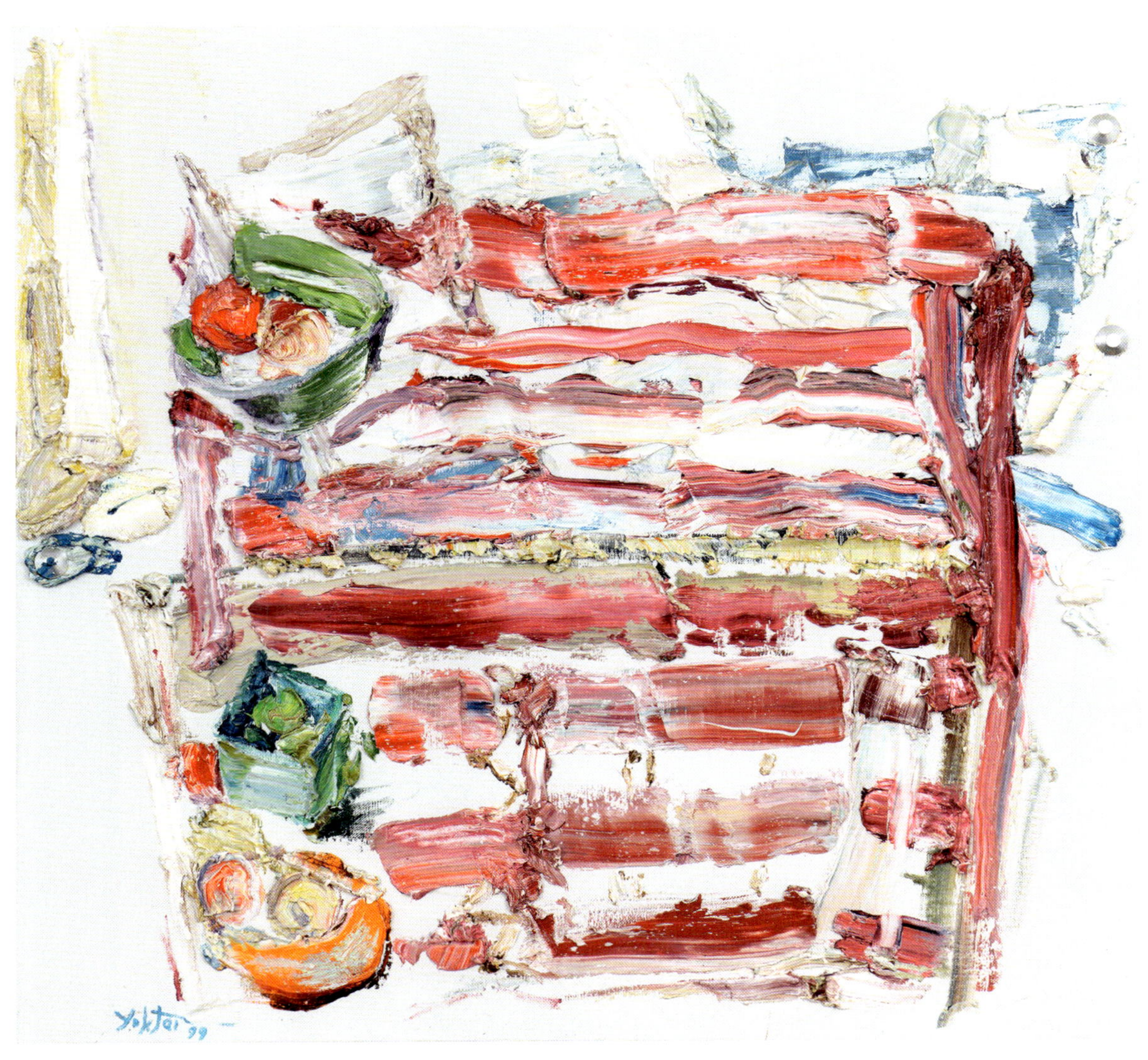

Striped Tablecloth, 1999, oil on canvas, 48 × 52 inches (121.9 × 132.1 cm)

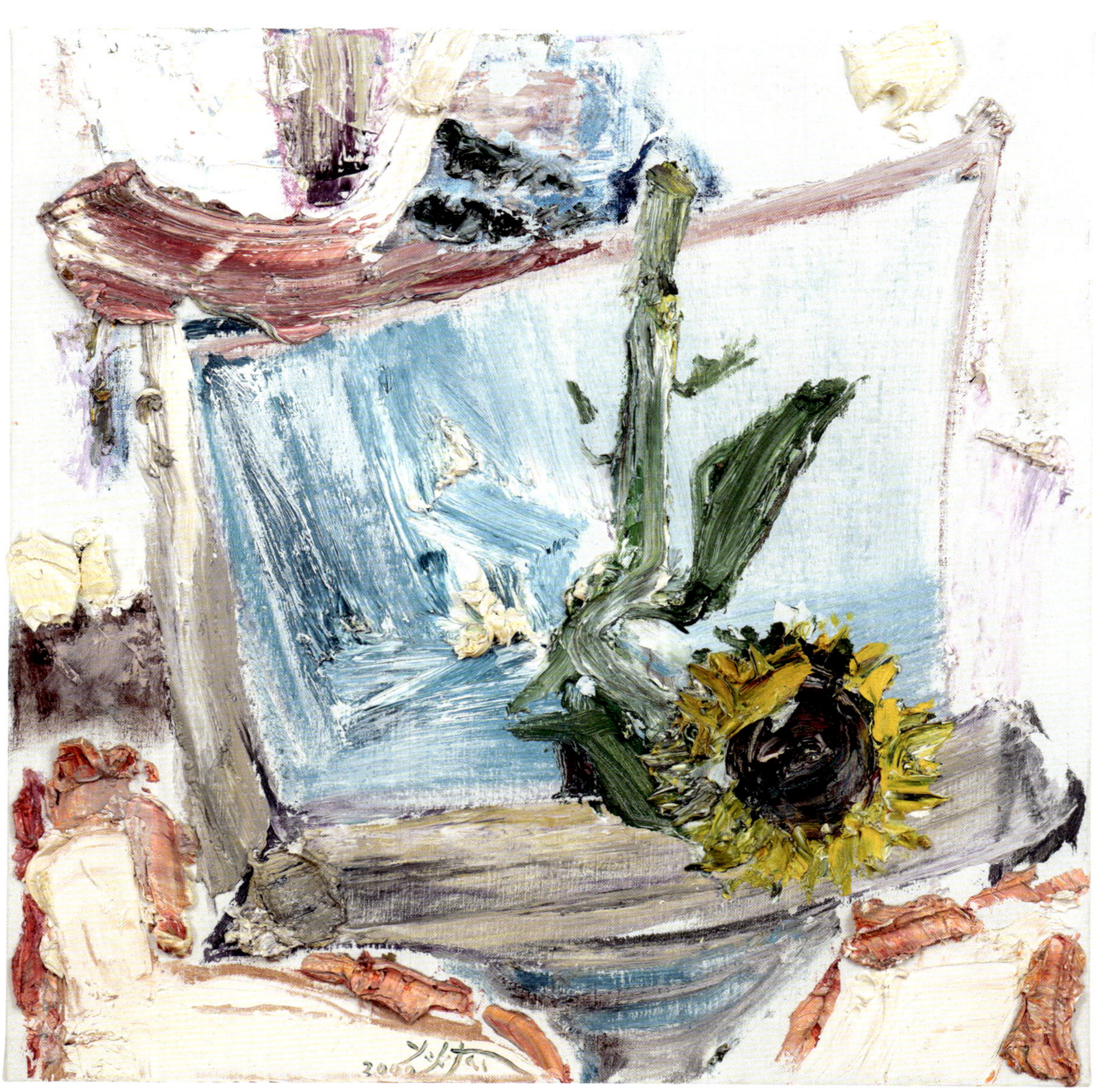

 Untitled, 2000, oil on canvas, 24 × 24 inches (61 × 61 cm)

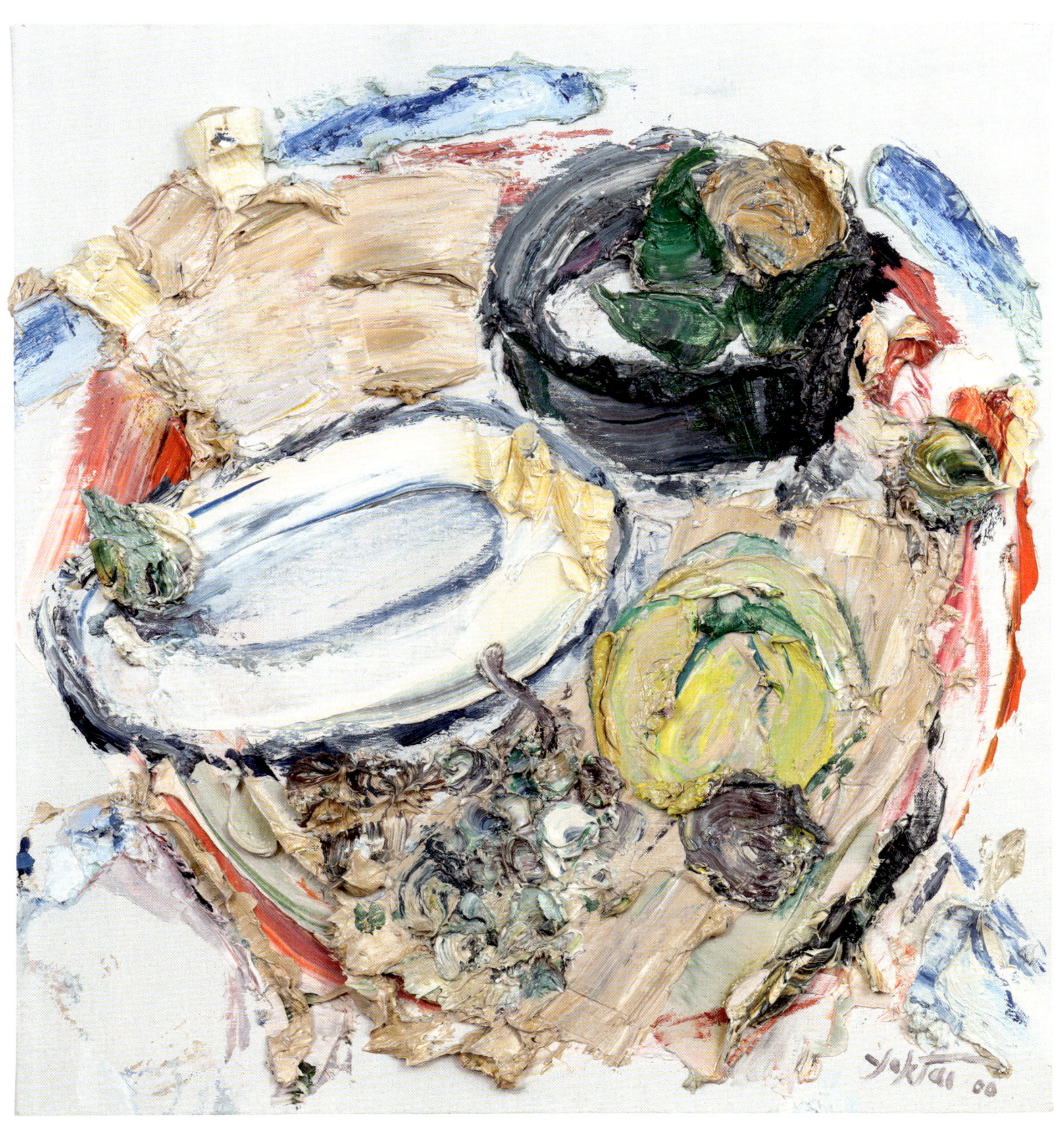

Untitled, 2000, oil on canvas, 26 × 24 inches (66 × 61 cm)

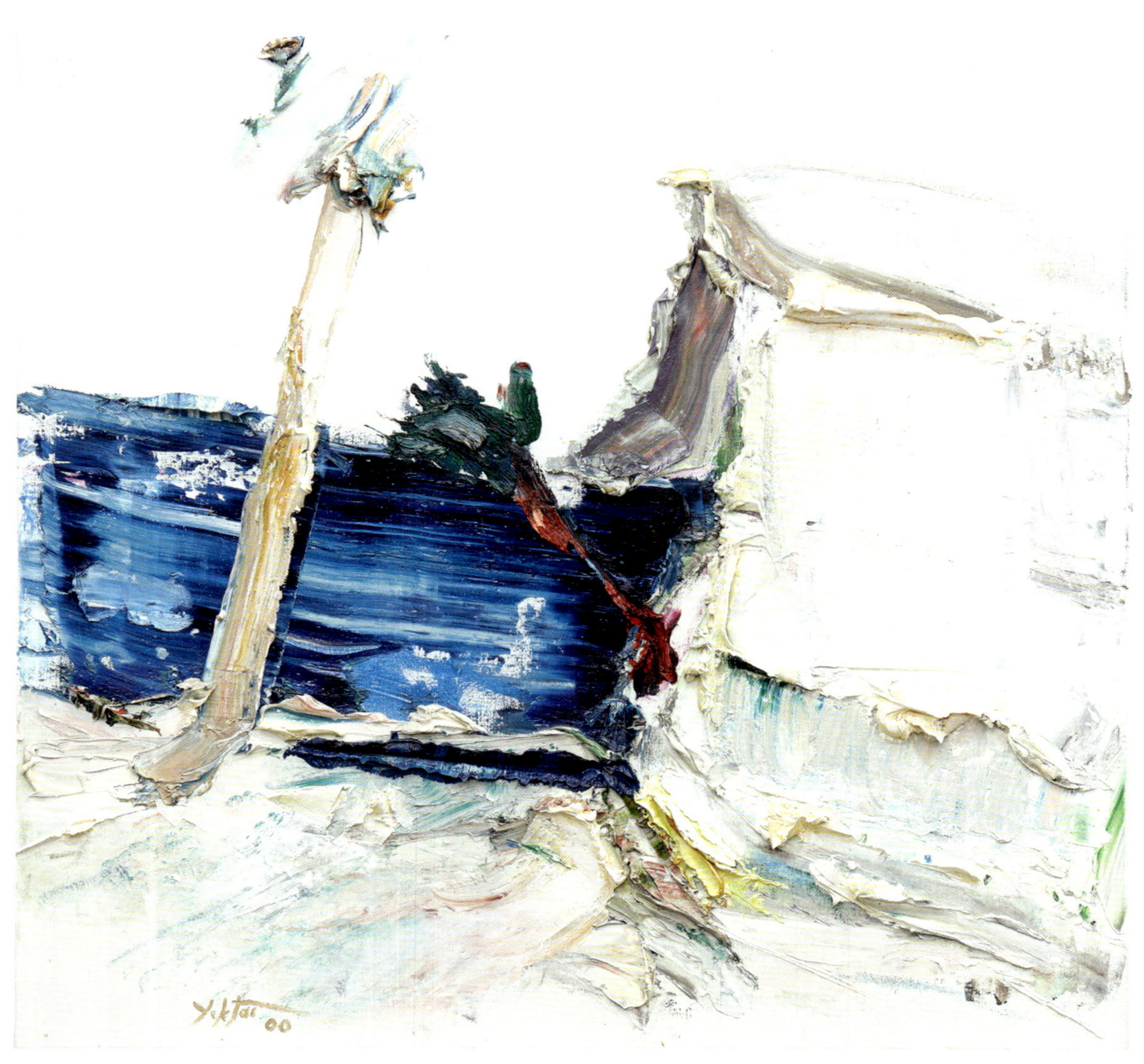

Untitled, 2000, oil on canvas, 30 × 32 inches (76.2 × 81.3 cm)

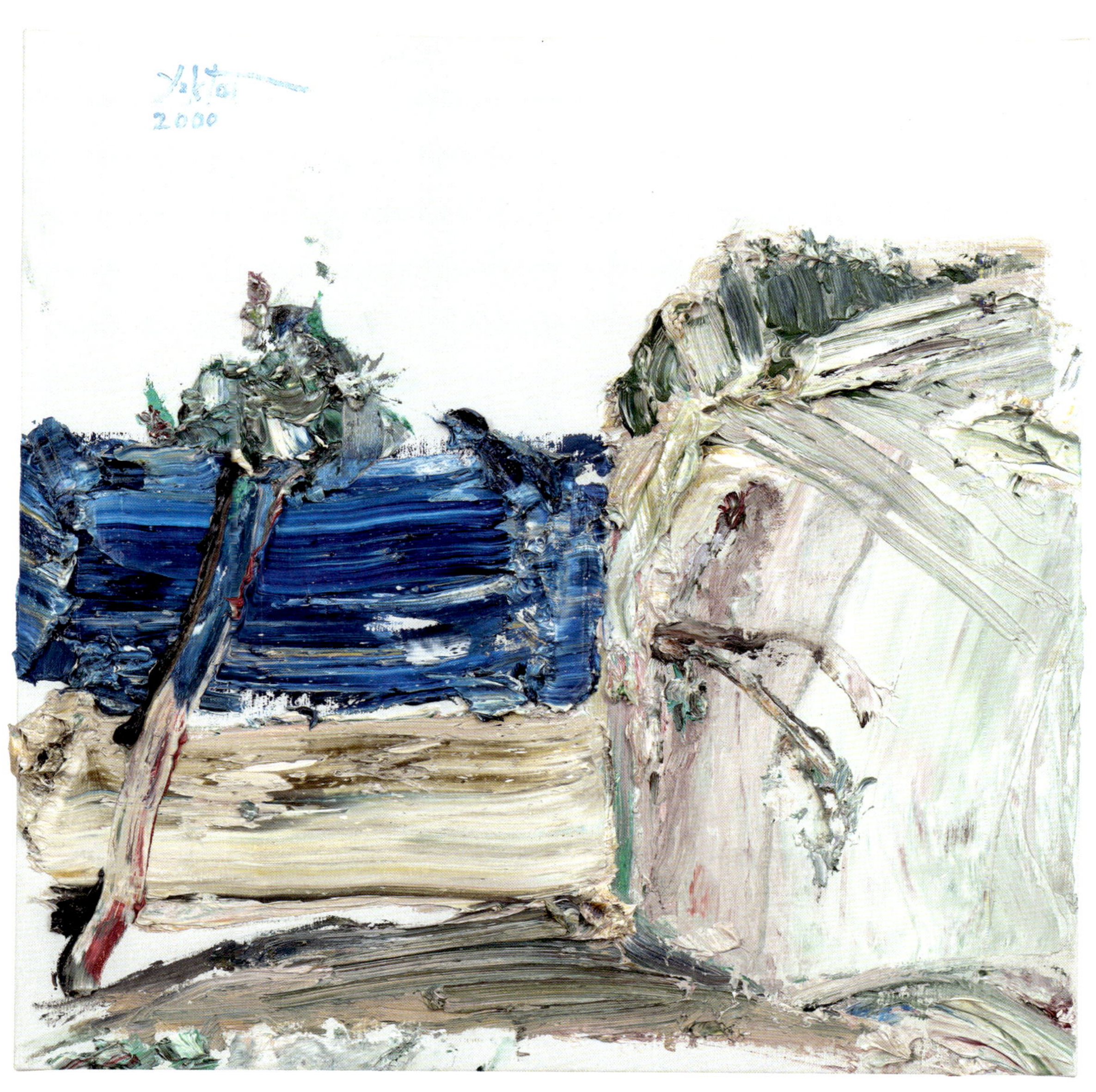

Untitled, 2000, oil on canvas, 24 × 24 inches (61 × 61 cm)

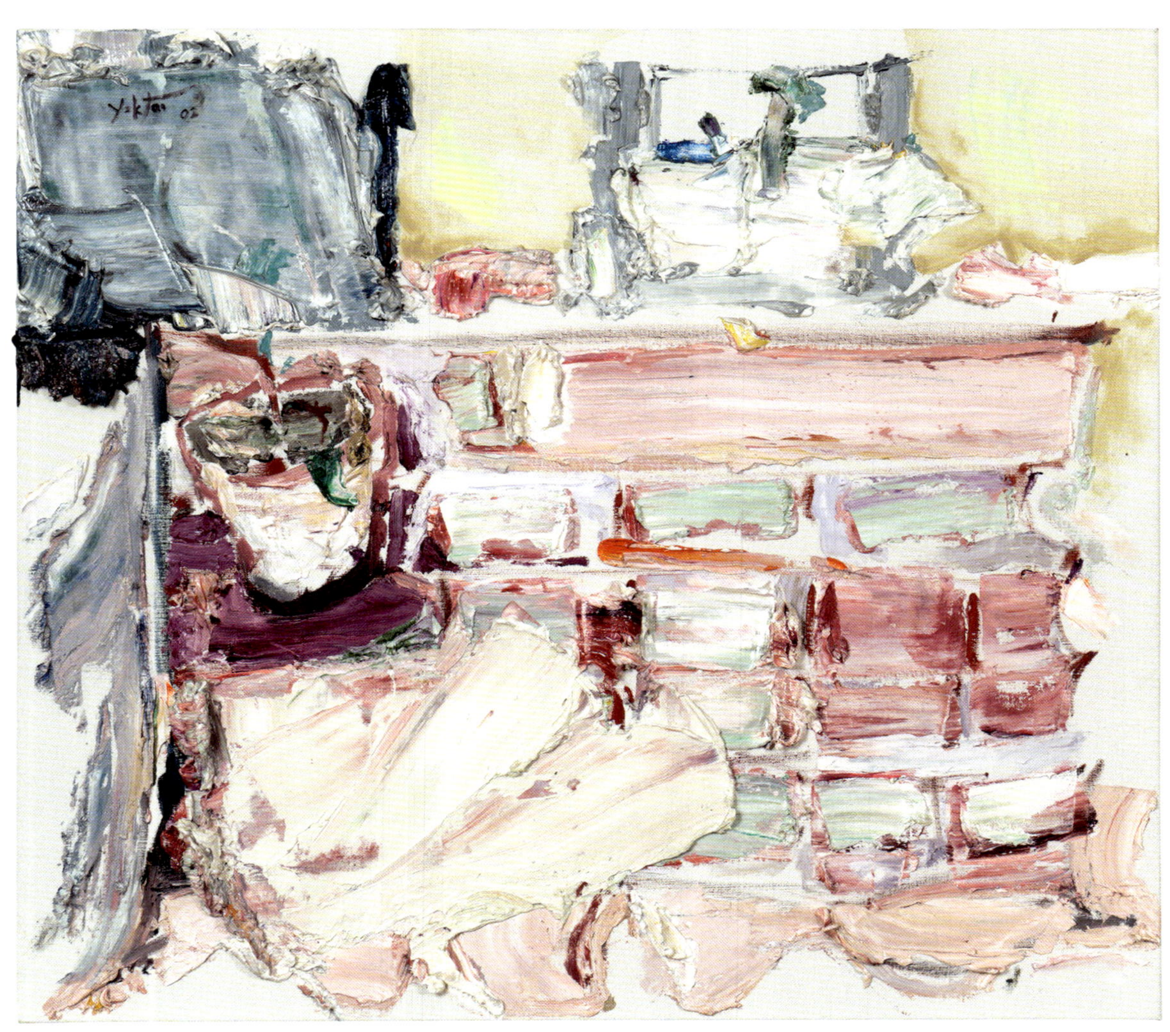

 Untitled, 2002, oil on canvas, 34 × 38 inches (86.4 × 96.5 cm)

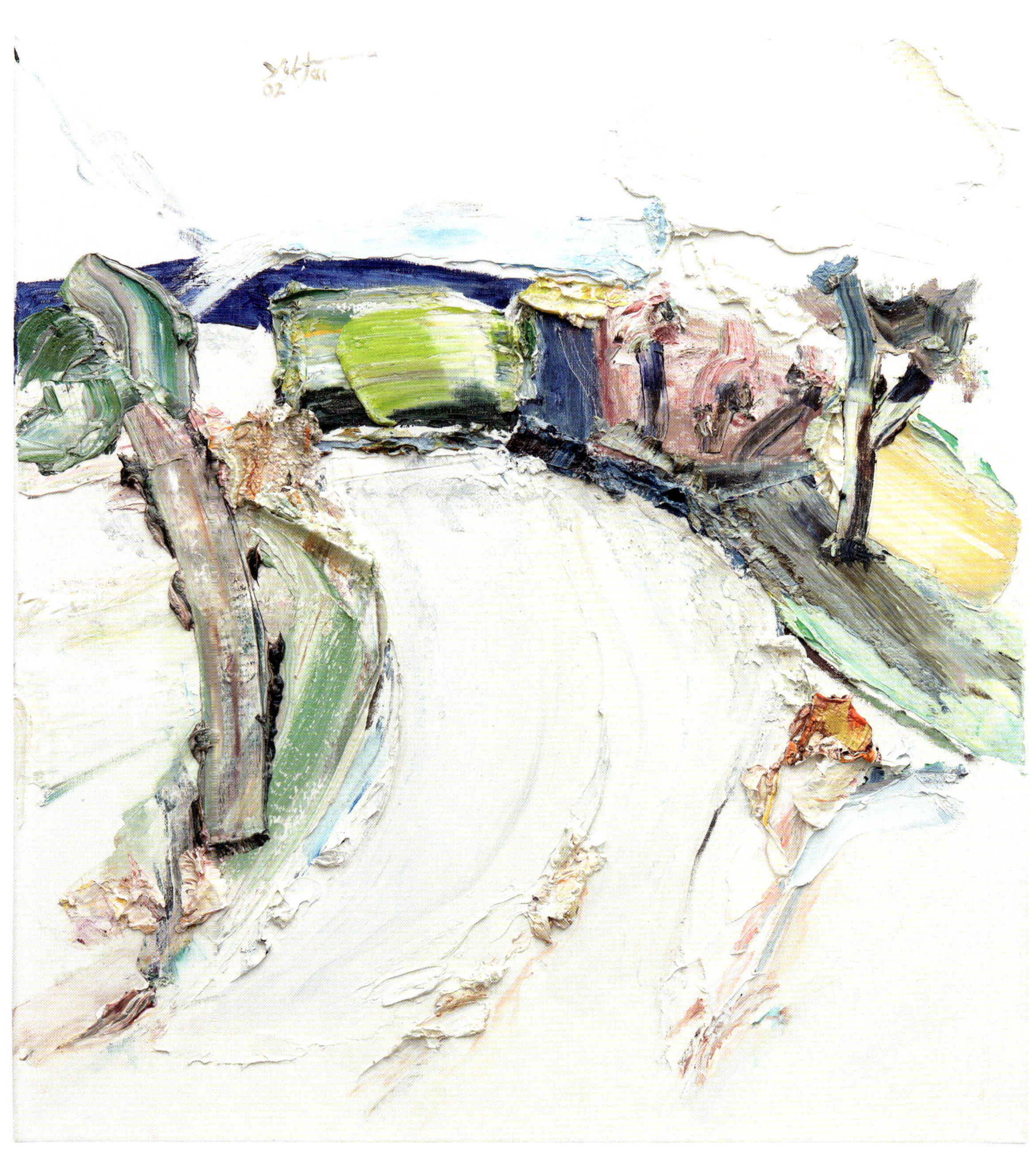

Untitled, 2002, oil on canvas, 38 × 34 inches (96.5 × 86.4 cm)

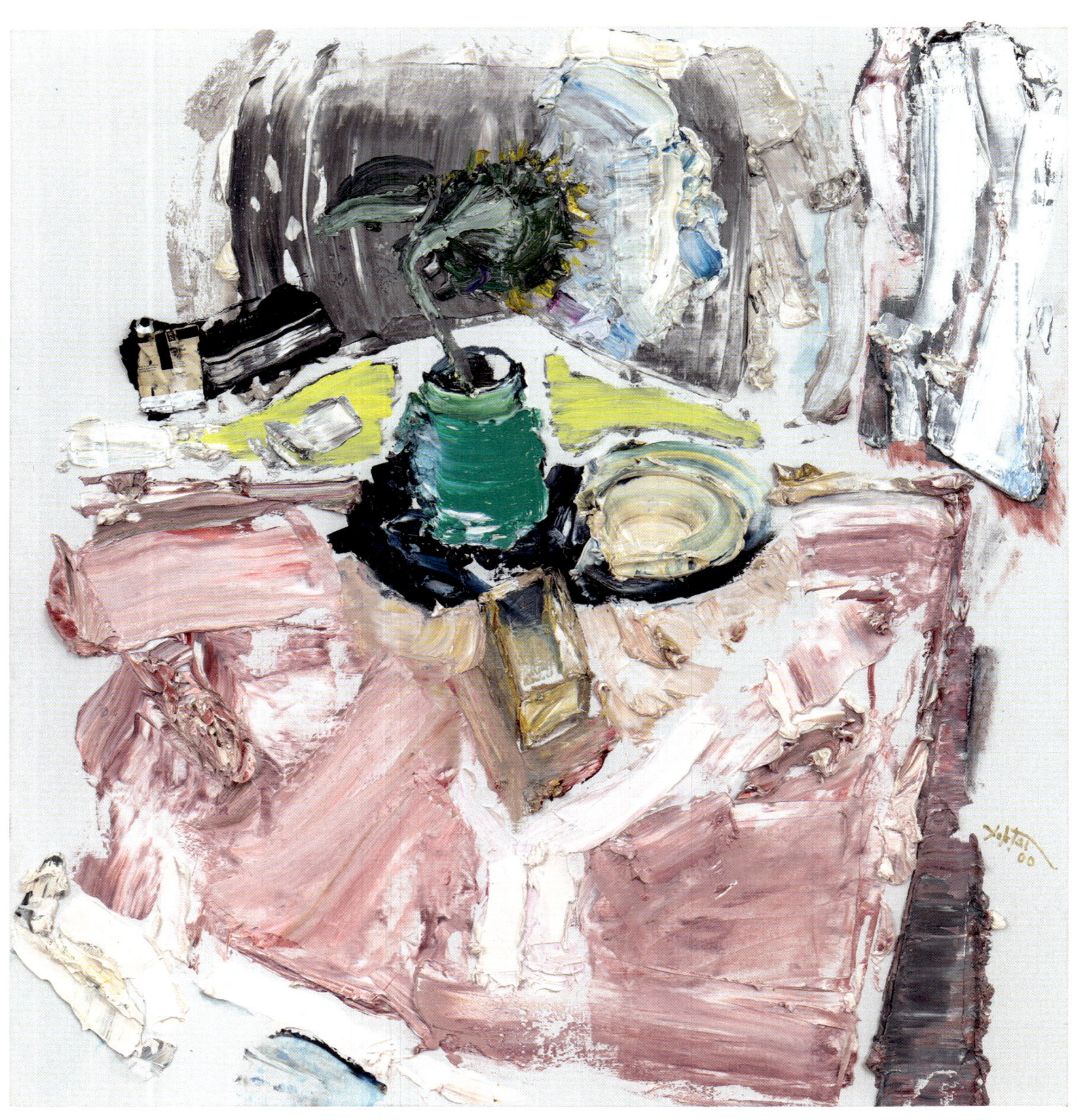

 Back of Sunflower, 2000, oil on canvas, 50 × 48 inches (127 × 121.9 cm)

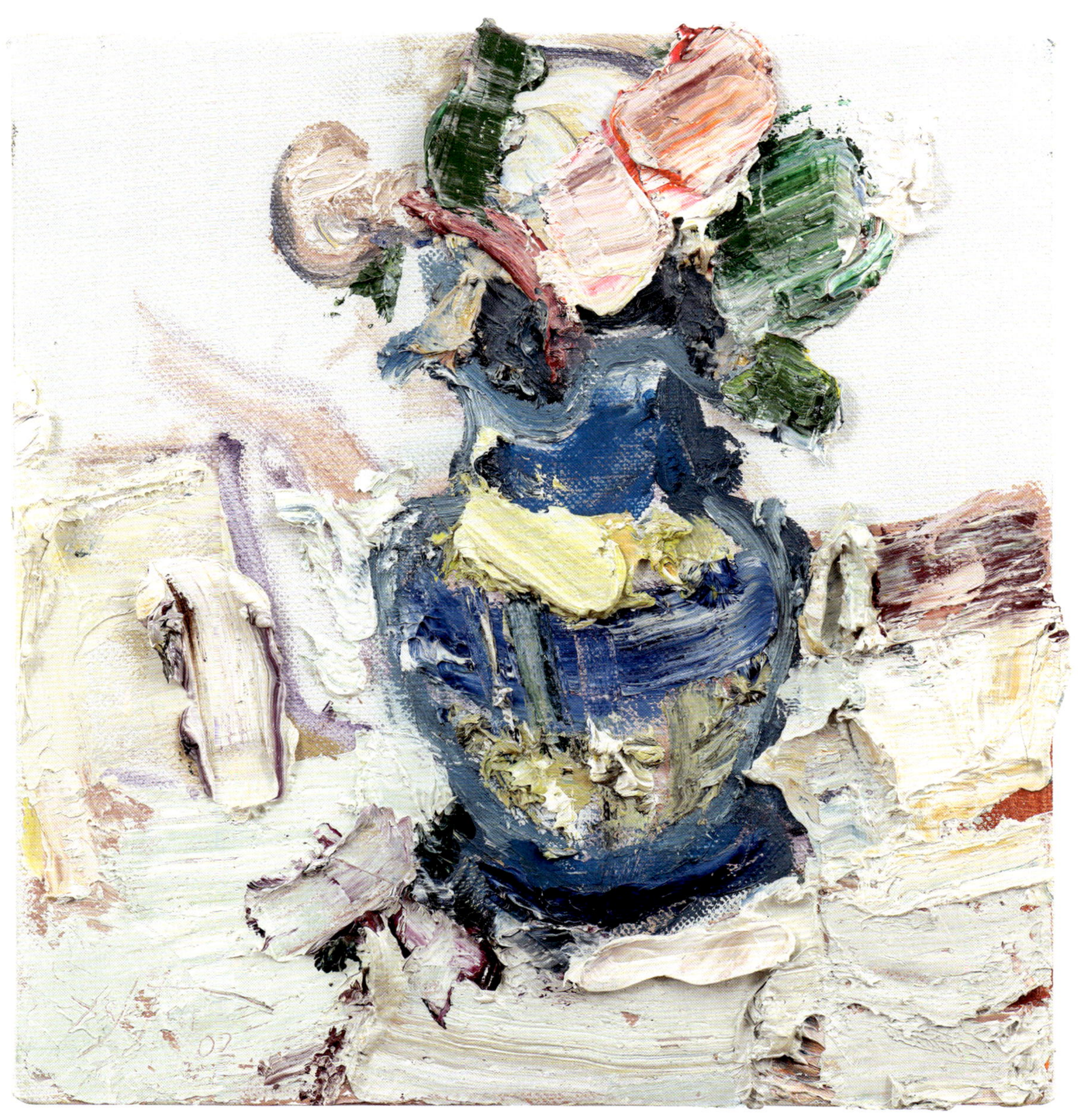

Striped Vase, 2002, oil on canvas, 16 × 15 inches (40.6 × 38.1 cm)

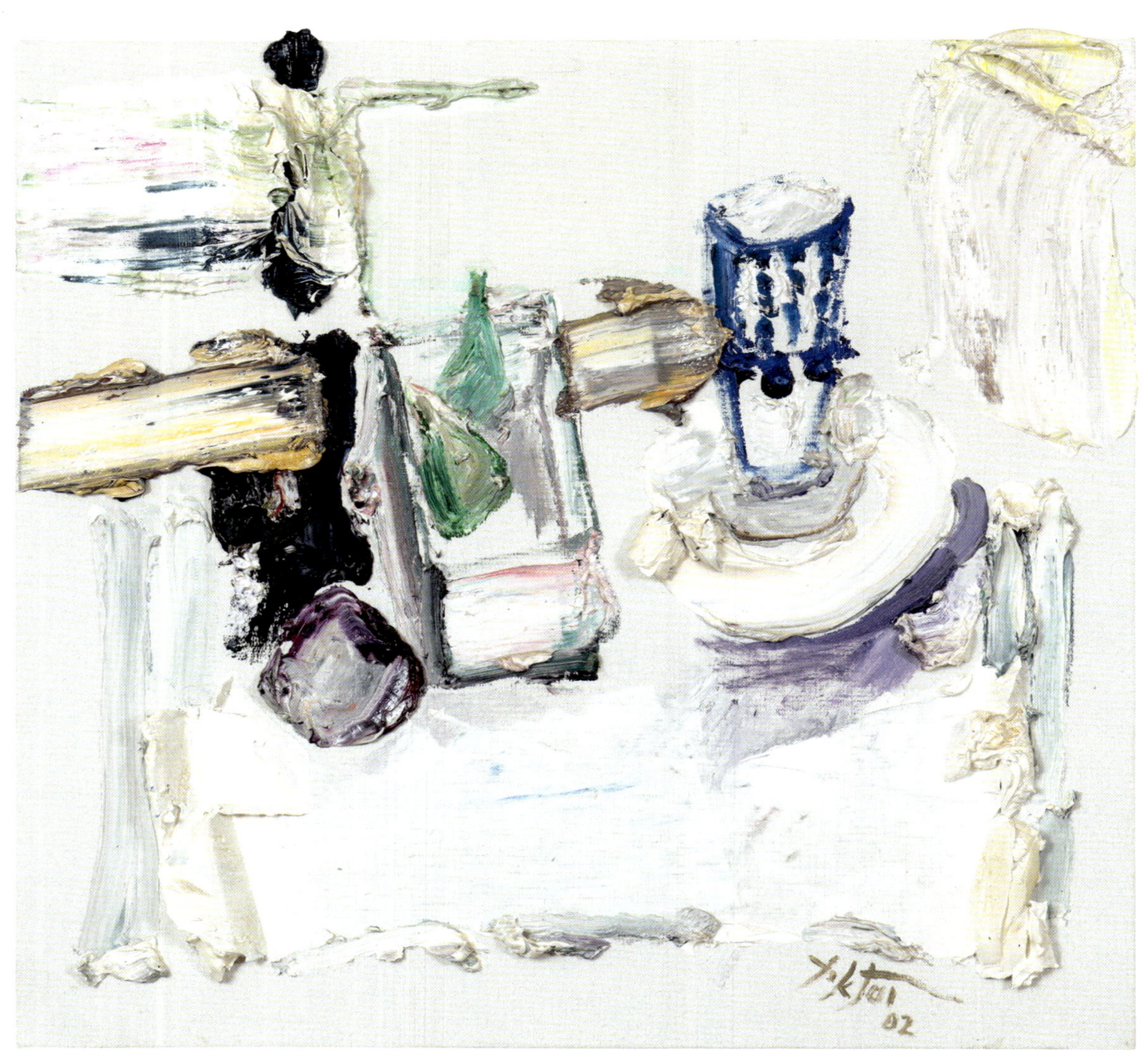

 Untitled, 2002, oil on canvas, 24 × 26 inches (61 × 66 cm)

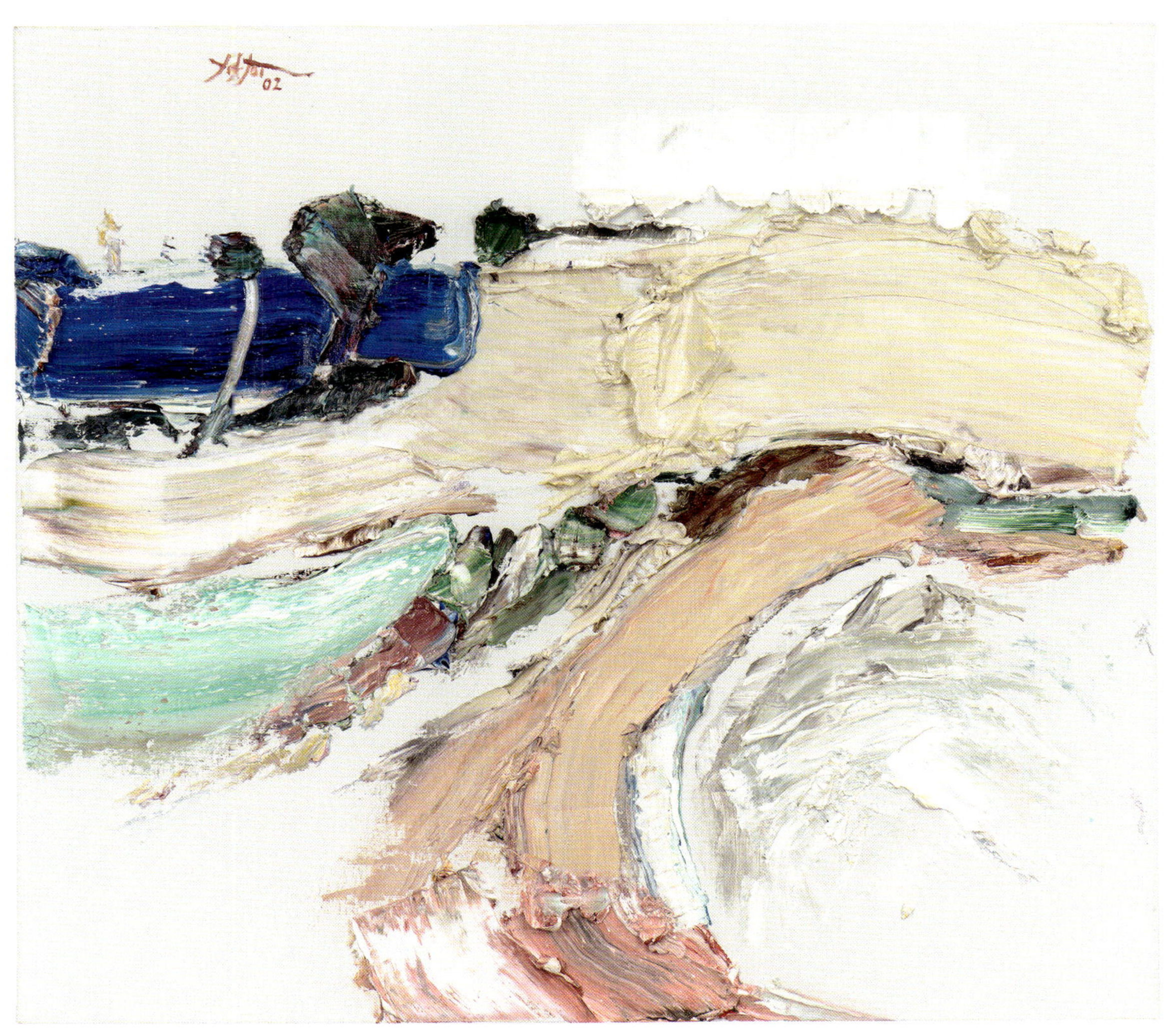

Untitled, 2002, oil on canvas, 34 × 38 inches (86.4 × 96.5 cm)

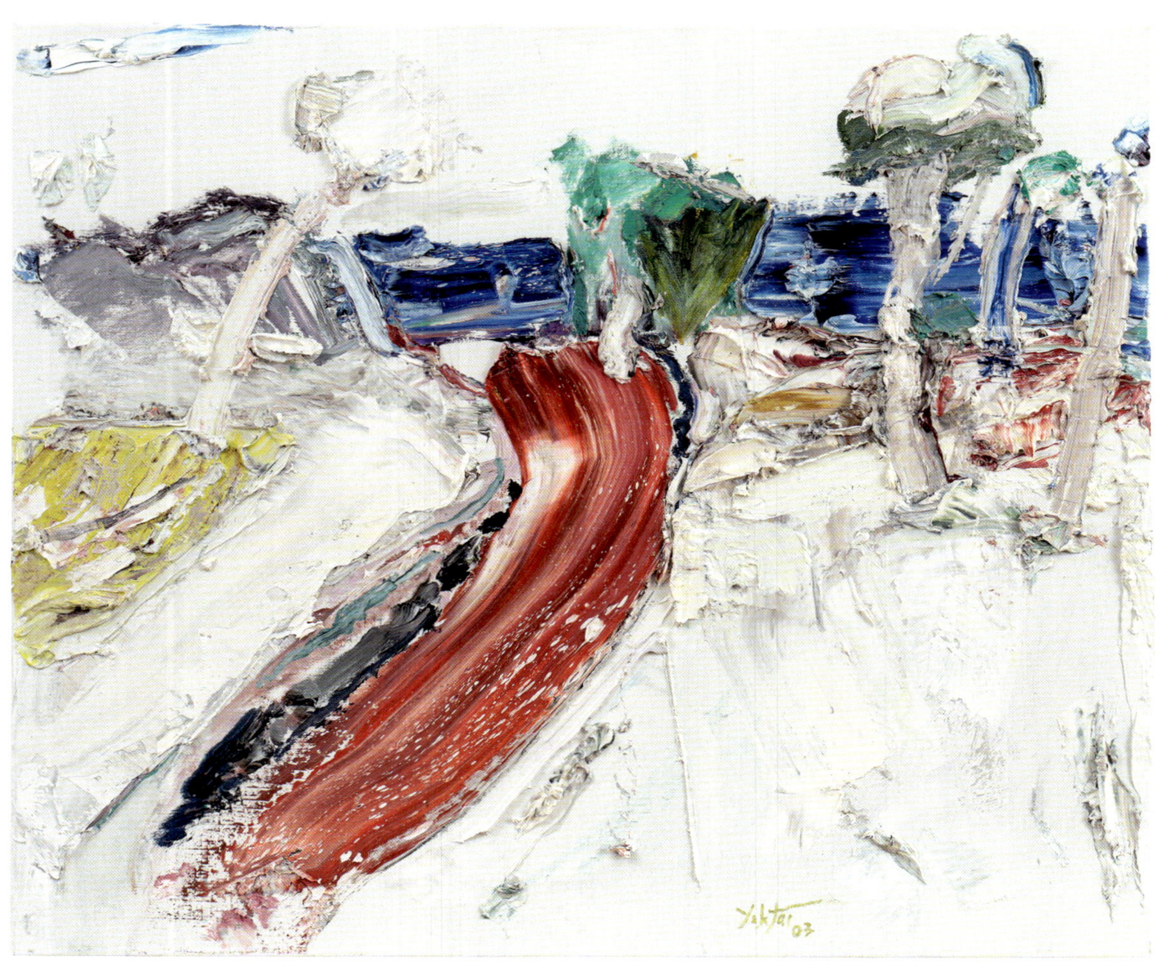

Untitled, 2003, oil on canvas, 32 × 38 inches (81.3 × 96.5 cm)

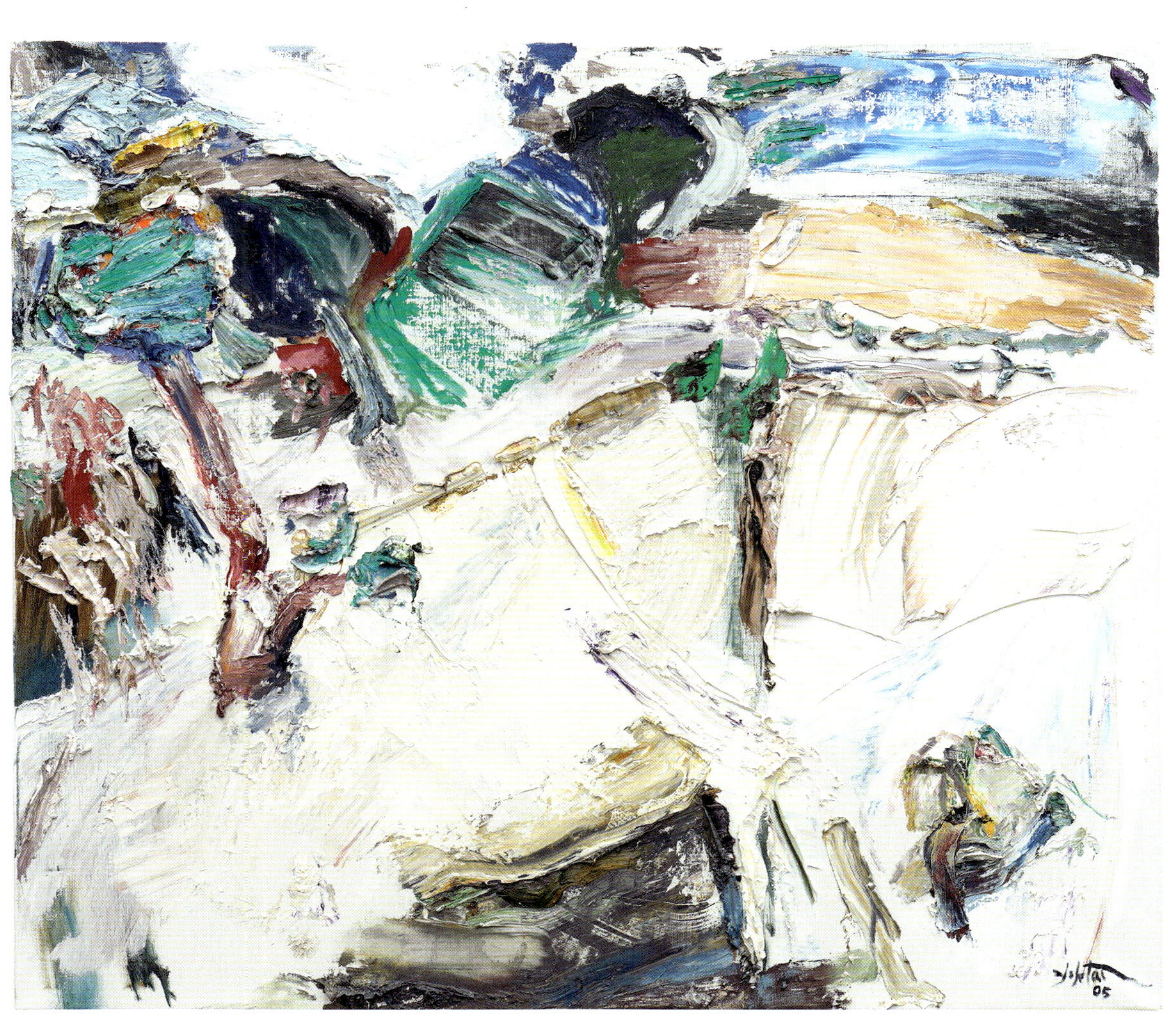

Untitled, 2005, oil on canvas, 38 × 44 inches (96.5 × 111.8 cm)

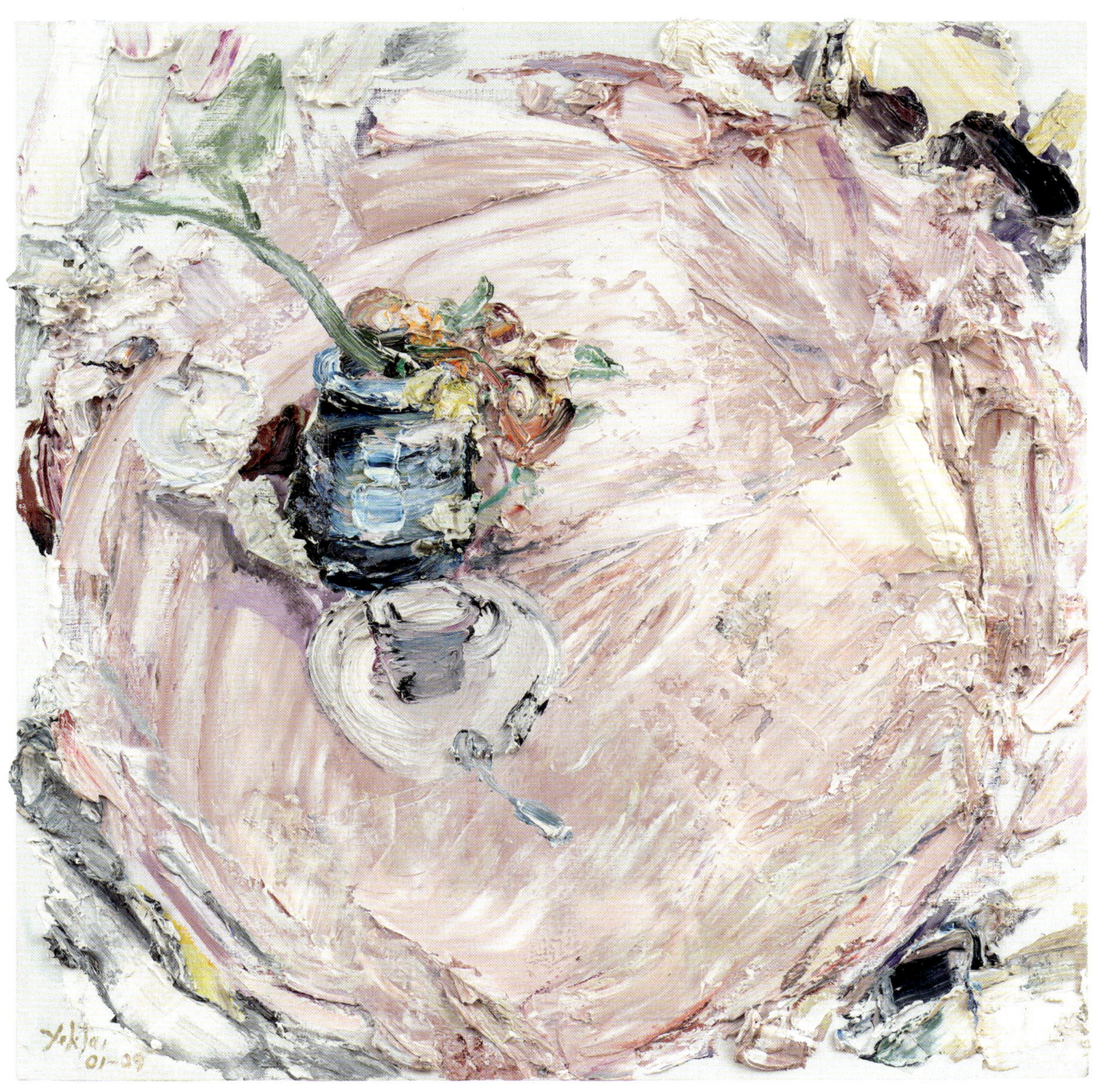

Untitled, 2001–9, oil on canvas, 32 × 32 inches (81.3 × 81.3 cm)

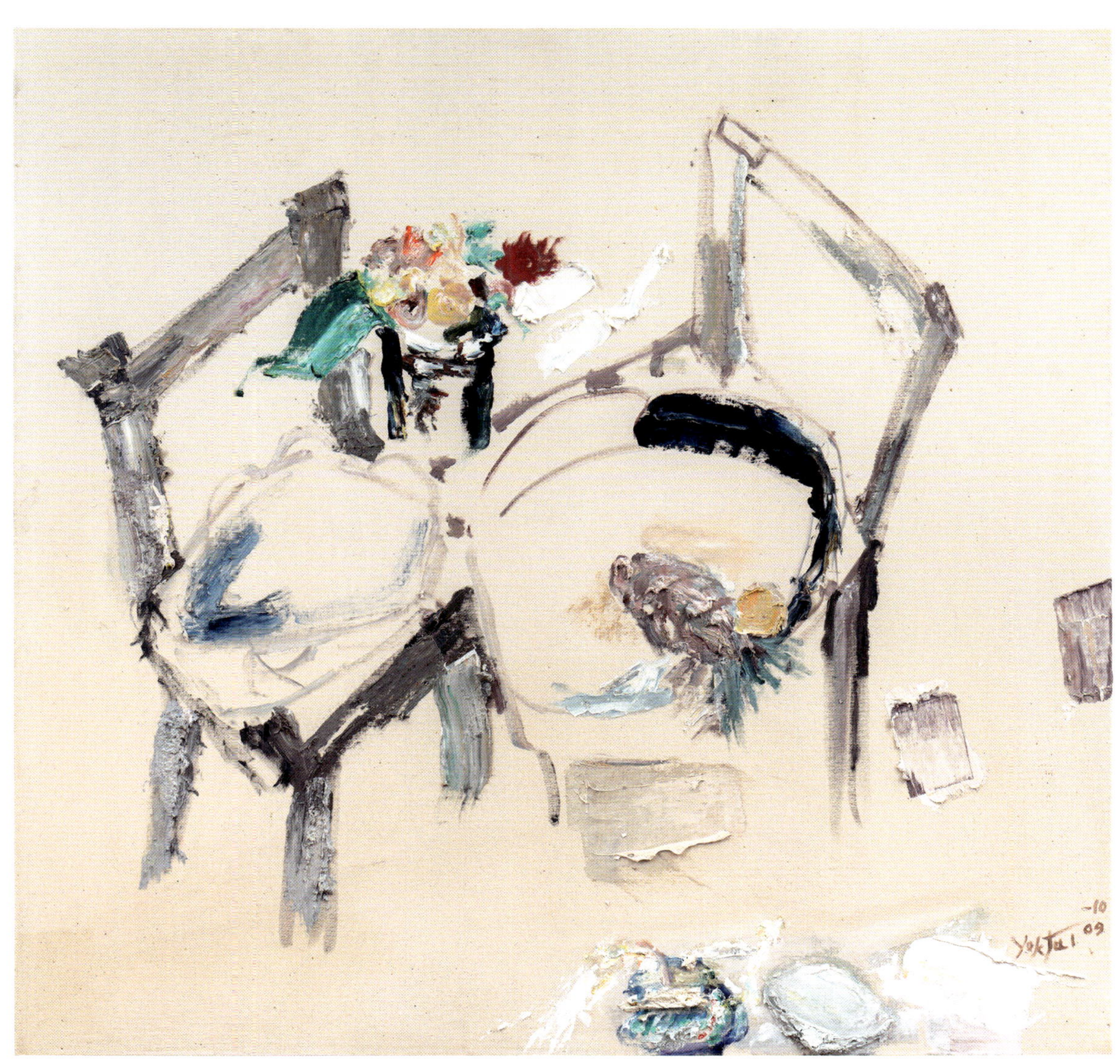

Untitled, 2009, oil on canvas, 48 × 50 inches (121.9 × 127 cm)

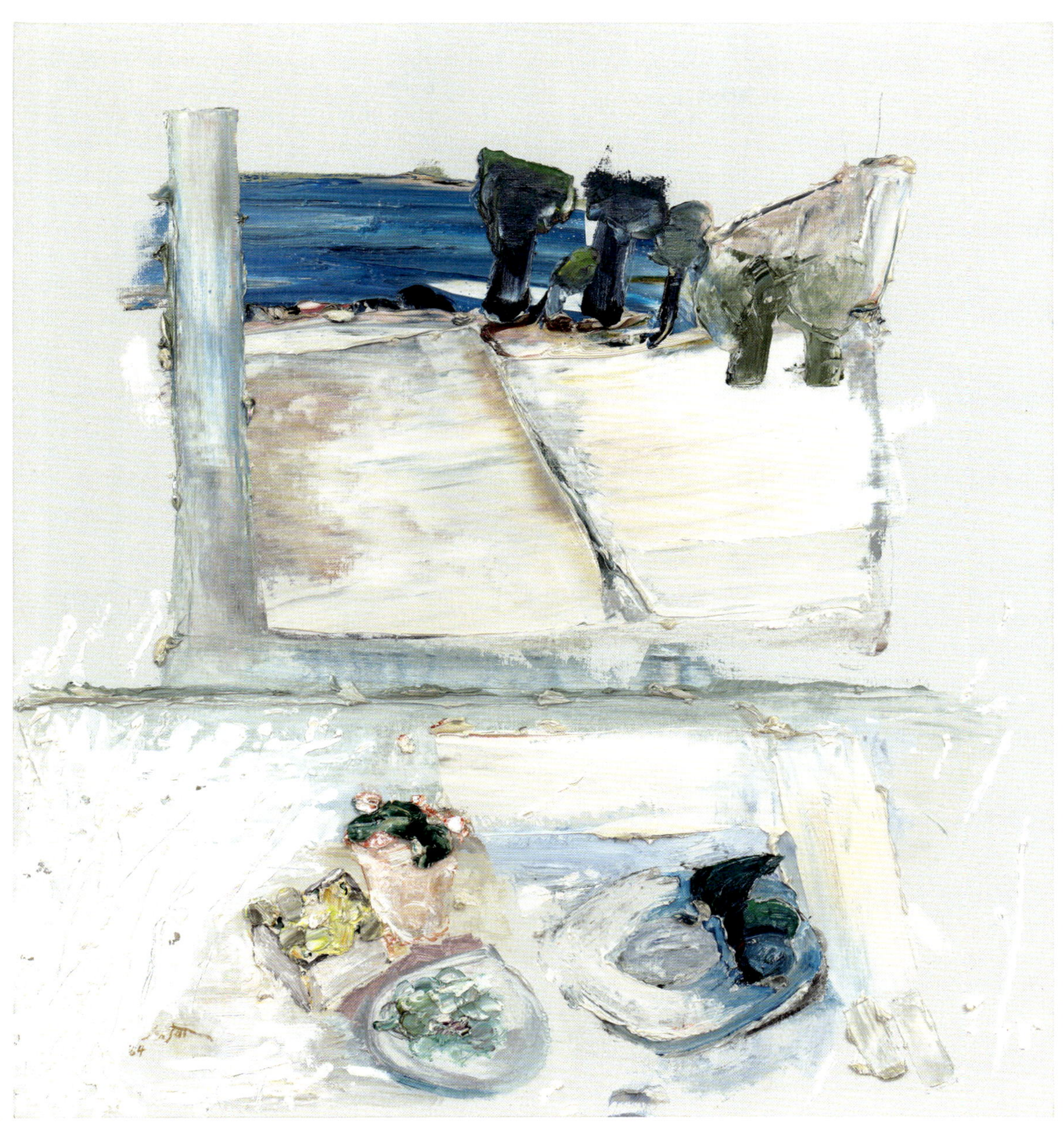

Untitled, 1984–2019, oil on canvas, 52 × 48 inches (132.1 × 121.9 cm)

Published on the occasion of

Manoucher Yektai
September 30–November 13, 2021

Karma
188 East 2nd Street
172 East 2nd Street
New York, NY 10009

Published by
Karma Books, New York

Edition of 1,500

ISBN 978-1-949172-68-3

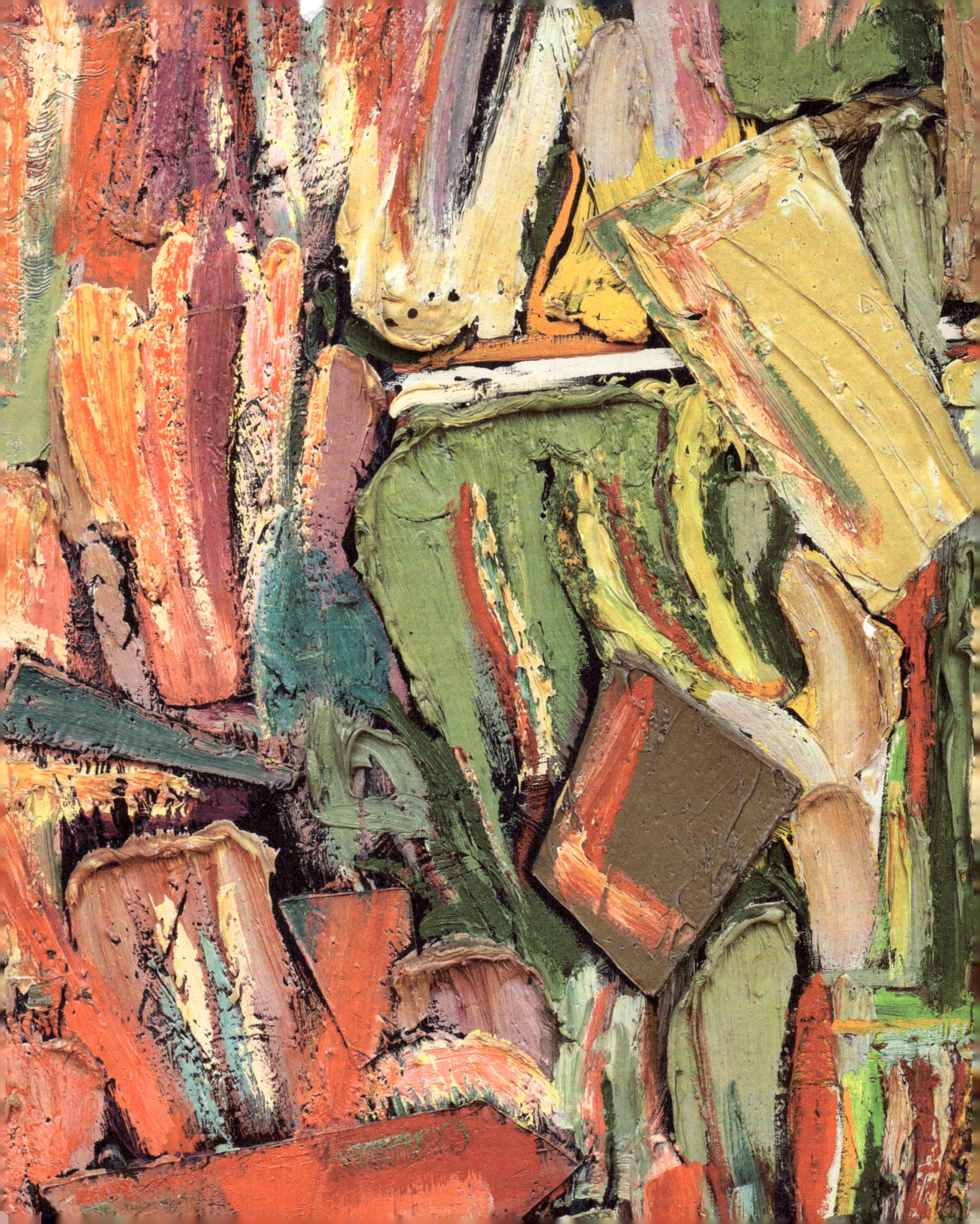